Swithland: Church and Estate

THE STORY OF A LEICESTERSHIRE VILLAGE

Dedication

This book is dedicated to Bob Osborne who began Swithland's 'definitive history' and spent four years researching and writing it, but died before the project was completed. A true 'public servant' and Christian gentleman, he loved our village and church, serving both faithfully and affectionately over many years.

Fear God and keep his commandments,
for this is the whole duty of man.

Swithland: Church and Estate

THE STORY OF A LEICESTERSHIRE VILLAGE

Bob Osborne   *Anne Horton*

© R. Anne Horton 2011

All Rights Reserved. Except as permitted under current legislation
no part of this work may be photocopied, stored in a retrieval system,
published, performed in public, adapted, broadcast,
transmitted, recorded or reproduced in any form or by any means,
without the prior permission of the copyright owner

The rights of Anne Horton and Bob Osborne to be identified as
the authors of this work have been asserted in accordance with
sections 77 and 78 of the Copyright, Designs and Patents Act 1998

First published 2011
Swithland Parish Press

ISBN-13-978095693240

The publisher has no responsibility for the continued existence or accuracy of URLs for external or third-party internet websites referred to in this book, and does not guarantee that any content on such websites is, or will remain, accurate or appropriate.

A CIP catalogue record for this book is available
from the British Library

Papers used in the production of this book are natural, recyclable products
made from wood grown in sustainable forests

Book production by Boydell & Brewer Ltd
PO Box 9, Woodbridge, Suffolk IP12 3DF, UK
website: www.boydellandbrewer.com

Designed and typeset by Tina Ranft, Woodbridge, Suffolk
Printed in Great Britain by
CPI Antony Rowe, Chippenham and Eastbourne

Contents

Dedication		ii
List of Illustrations		vi
Acknowledgements		xiii
Subscribers to Swithland: Church and Estate, first edition		xv
Introduction		xix
1	A Considerable Lordship	1
2	Groby Peculiar	42
3	Local Government	49
4	The Parish Church	71
5	The Clergy	112
6	Civil War	143
7	Dissent	159
8	The Story of the Land	185
9	Woodland	217
10	Swithland Slate	228
11	Reservoirs and Railways	248
12	Village Buildings and Families	258
13	Education	328
14	Family Connections	347
15	Myths and Legends	368
16	Rothley Plain	379
17	The Old Order	422
18	Transition	448
19	A Mile Worth a Million Pounds	485
Appendix A	Wills	553
Appendix B	Incumbents and Other Ministers	581
Appendix C	Swithland School Admissions 1865–1980	589
Appendix D	Parish Registers	599
Appendix E	Danvers, Butler and Bunney Family Trees	679
Glossary		685
Bibliography		690
Index		695

List of Illustrations

CHAPTER ONE
Fig 1.1   Swithland 1777, John Prior's Map of Leicestershire
Fig 1.2   Royal Charter, 1316
Fig 1.3   No.6 Cheyne Walk, 1940. *Courtesy Country Life*
Fig 1.4   Portrait of an Unknown Man, Bartholomew Dandridge, 1750
Fig 1.5   Hatchment for Sir Joseph Danvers, St Leonard's Church
Fig 1.6   Swithland Hall, 1790, John Throsby
Fig 1.7   Lantern Cross, Swithland Hall Park
Fig 1.8   Butter Market, Mountsorrel
Fig 1.9   John Flower engraving, Swithland Hall c. 1826 (Lantern Cross in foreground)
Fig 1.10   George John Danvers Butler Danvers, fifth Earl
Fig 1.11   Frederica Emma, fifth Countess
Fig 1.12   John Vansittart Danvers Butler, sixth Earl, 1879
Fig 1.13   The sixth Earl, funeral cortege, 1905, Dale Walk
Fig 1.14   Charles John Brinsley Butler, seventh Earl, with his mother and brothers, Henry Cavendish, Francis Almeric, Brian
Fig 1.15   Funeral Cortege for the seventh Earl, 1929, passing the Danvers Chapel
Fig 1.16   Henry Cavendish Butler, eighth Earl
Fig 1.17   The eighth Earl and his Countess, in fancy dress
Fig 1.18   Denis, Lord Newtown Butler, with Yeomanry colleagues
Fig 1.19   The ninth Earl entertaining Yvonne de Carlo
Fig 1:20   The ninth Earl at Kegworth with John Leatherland
Fig 1:21   The Lanesborough tombs, Swithland churchyard

CHAPTER 3
Fig 3.1   Gweneth Gimson, Bernard Durham, Wardens, at the installation of the Revd Anne Horton as priest-in-charge, May 1994
Fig 3.2   Gweneth Gimson MBE, Buckingham Palace, 2009
Fig 3.3   'Old Jack' Tomlin, roadsweeper, outside The Griffin, c. 1920

CHAPTER 4
Fig 4.1   St Leonard's Church, Swithland, 1995, by Tony Danvers
Fig 4.2   Chancel Boss in St Leonard's Church, 1925, showing loosed padlock and chains symbolising St Leonard
Fig 4.3   The ruins of St Evroult Abbey, 2009
Fig 4.4   John Nichols' sketch of the monumental brass to Agnes Scot, 1455

List of Illustrations vii

Fig 4.5   St Leonard's Church, 1790, by Nichols, showing the new south aisle
Fig 4.6   Swithland's mediaeval font
Fig 4.7   Christ's Resurrection, east window, 1867
Fig 4.8   A sketch of the interior c. 1920 indicating layout of seating and nave burials
Fig 4.9   Interior of St Leonard's Church, c.1900, facing east
Fig 4.10 Interior of St Leonard's Church, c. 1900, facing west
Fig 4.11 Exterior of St Leonard's Church from the south c. 1900
Fig 4.12 Exterior of St Leonard's Church from the south-east c. 1900
Fig 4.13 Exterior of St Leonard's Church from the north c. 1900
Fig 4.14 Interior of church showing new chancel arrangements, 1927
Fig 4.15 Memorial Stone to John Prier, May 1673
Fig 4.16 St Leonard's Church, north side, before 1918
Fig 4.17 The Lych Gate, 1929

CHAPTER 5
Fig 5.1   Dean Henry Erskine, Princeton University Library
Fig 5.2   The old rectory next to the church
Fig 5.3   James Murray Dixon in the Old Rectory garden
Fig 5.4   The Revd. James Murray Dixon
Fig 5.5   James and Etheldreda Murray-Dixons' Diamond Wedding Anniversary, 1942 with Charles Edward Dixon, Helen Dixon, Rosamund Dixon, Patrick Hamilton, Cynthia Hamilton, John Underhill-Faithorne, Barbara Nicholson, Kate (Kitty) Dixon, James, Etheldreda, Amy Knott (bridesmaid)
Fig 5.6   Canon Raymond Walters
Fig 5.7   Canon Anne Horton
Fig 5.8   The Rectory, 157 Main Street

CHAPTER 6
Fig 6.1   Prescott Manor in 1998
Fig 6.2   Sir John Danvers' shield in the panelled room at Prescott Manor

CHAPTER 7
Fig 7.1   The Matthews' family graves at the nave crossing of St Leonard's Church, as discovered during restoration work in the 1920s
Fig 7.2   Sherriffhales Academy, the house in 1999
Fig 7.3   Bardon Meeting House, John Throsby, 1790
Fig 7.4   Swithland Wesleyan Methodist Chapel
Fig 7.5   Interior of Swithland Wesleyan Methodist Chapel, Easter 1924

CHAPTER 8
Fig 8.1   Swithland fields and field names
Fig 8.2   Swithland Enclosure Award Map, 1799
Fig 8.3   Mary Ann Cuffling (née Dakin), widow of William Cuffling, c. 1880
Fig 8.4   Fanny Cuffling, William Henry Cuffling and Mary Ann Milner (née Cuffling)
Fig 8.5   The farmyard at Forest End
Fig 8.6   Jack Leatherland of Pit Close Farm with his son John

Fig 8.7 Invitation to the 1945 Michaelmas Annual Audit
Fig 8.8 Swithland Estate Tenants 1945 at the Griffin Inn

CHAPTER 9
Fig 9.1 Buddon and Swithland woodlands, 1777, John Prior's map of Leicestershire
Fig 9.2 'Button Wood view', John Throsby, 1790
Fig 9.3 The old woods within Swithland Woods
Fig 9.4 Benjamin Hemsley snr., Benjamin Hemsley jnr. and Joe Bunney working in Swithland Woods, c. 1900
Fig 9.5 Swithland Woods in the early twentieth century
Fig 9.6 The Great Slate Quarry, Swithland Woods
Fig 9.7 The Bluebell Service, 1998
Fig 9.8 Swithland Wood Camp Farm, c. 1920
Fig 9.9 Fairey family members outside their Swithland Camp chalet, c. 1940

CHAPTER 10
Fig 10.1 Millennium Commemoration Slate – Mrs May Musgrove, Mrs Sarah May, Miss Beatrice Bunney, Canon Anne Horton
Fig 10.2 The Hinds table tombs
Fig 10.3 The Hind sisters' tomb
Fig 10.4 Sir Joseph Danvers' tomb, 1745, with slate carvings showing detail of a ship and horse
Fig 10.5 Detail of 1794 carving, The Doom, W. Hunt tombstone, Rothley
Fig 10.6 Swithland Church Millennium Extension plaque 2000
Fig 10.7 Memorial Stone for Robert Brian Osborne, d. 1999

CHAPTER 11
Fig 11.1 Land required for Swithland Reservoir and works, 1891
Fig 11.2 Water works, engine house and pumping station
Fig 11.3 The formal gardens around the filter beds of Swithland Reservoir
Fig 11.4 Olive Allen, daughter of the outdoor foreman at the water works, relaxing by the reservoir with her fiancé Eric North, c. 1920
Fig 11.5 Olive Allen and friends
Fig 11.6 Railway viaduct across Swithland Reservoir, 1925
Fig 11.7 Rail bridge at Swithland under construction, 1897
Fig 11.8 Steps up to the proposed Swithland Station, now bricked up
Fig 11.9 View across Swithland Reservoir to railway viaduct in the distance, 1928
Fig 11.10 Aerial view of the Reservoir, 2010

CHAPTER 12
Fig 12.1 Kinchley Hill Farmhouse, c. 1950
Fig 12.2 Swithland Water Works, the foreman's house on the right
Fig 12.3 Proposed road diversion to the north of Swithland (Old) Hall, 1821
Fig 12.4 Swithland Hall, front view, c. 1900
Fig 12.5 Swithland Hall, rear view, c. 1900
Fig 12.6 North Lodge to Swithland Hall
Fig 12.7 The Cuffling family outside Hall Farm

List of Illustrations

Fig 12.8   Hall Farm dairy cart
Fig 12.9   Hall Farm workers
Fig 12.10   Ambrose Copson with his grand-daughter Rosemarie
Fig 12.11   The Gazebo near Hall farm
Fig 12.12   Hall Gardens house before demolition c. 1990
Fig 12.13   The Old Rectory, late nineteenth century photograph
Fig 12.14   Postcard view of Keeper's Cottage, c. 1910
Fig 12.15   Keeper's Cottage 1950s
Fig 12.16   Percy Lloyd, Phyllis with Rodney, Dorothy and Harold Sharpe with Paul, VE Day 1945
Fig 12.17   Jim Carpenter, keeper, with son David
Fig 12.18   Village pump outside Keeper's Cottage
Fig 12.19   Swithland School and School House, c. 1910
Fig 12.20   The Griffin Inn, early twentieth century
Fig 12.21   Samuel Briers, arresting police officer, with Emmeline Pankhurst
Fig 12.22   Rose Cottage, c. 1900
Fig 12.23   Otto Murray Dixon outside the 1898 Rectory, c. 1910
Fig 12.24   Thatched Cottage (No. 144) and the Laundry (No. 146), a laundress in the doorway
Fig 12.25   Samuel Bunney outside Thatched Cottage with his horse, Polly
Fig 12.26   Samuel Bunney and his son Alwyn with their sheep, c. 1890
Fig 12.27   Nos. 142–130 Main Street, and, opposite, No. 137
Fig 12.28   No. 137 Main Street, garden view from footpath, 1990s
Fig 12.29   Pit Close Cottage, early twentieth century, offering 'tea and hot water'
Fig 12.30   Memorial Hall
Fig 12.31   War Memorial
Fig 12.32   Post Office Cottage and Lanesborough Cottage
Fig 12.33   Another view of Post Office Cottage
Fig 12.34   Sarah Jane 'Granny' Hodges with a friend
Fig 12.35   Joe Bunney (1870–1960), Swithland's town crier
Fig 12.36   Outside No. 120 Main Street, early 1930s – Renée Hemstock, Ada Leatherland, Dolly Hemstock (holding Mary), Mrs Mitchell (and daughter)
Fig 12.37   Dolly Pratt of Long Close, c. 1900
Fig 12.38   Longlands Farm 1935, with Pit Close Farm in the distance
Fig 12.39   Benjamin and Eliza Hemsley, c. 1900
Fig 12.40   John (Jack) and Ada Leatherland, Pit Close Farm
Fig 12.41   Pit Close Farmhouse, c. 1951
Fig 12.42   John and Joan Leatherland, 1996
Fig 12.43   Holly Croft
Fig 12.44   Jack Copson
Fig 12.45   The White House, from the front, 1947
Fig 12.46   The slate staircase in The White House, 2005, Mrs E.P.D. Brook-Lawson
Fig 12.47   William Hayward Gamble of Cherry Tree Cottage
Fig 12.48   Wedding group, Emily Adams of Penny Cottage to Charles Sherman, 1896
Fig 12.49   Cherry Tree Cottage
Fig 12.50   William James Bates, tenant farmer at Forest End Farm 1871–96

Fig 12.51 Approach to Swithland from Woodhouse Eaves, Pollard House in the distance
Fig 12.52 Joseph Matts, tailor and draper, living at Pollard House in 1871
Fig 12.53 Pollard House, Forest End Cottages, Methodist Chapel
Fig 12.54 Beatrice Bunney and her mother Ethel May Bunney outside No. 46
Fig 12.55 Nos. 50 and 48 Main Street (No. 50 now demolished)
Fig 12.56 Sough Mouth Spring, 1999
Fig 12.57 Wood Lane End Cottage, postcard sent by Olive Ellis, 1911,
Fig 12.58 Wood Lane End, during Moore's tenancy, showing exterior stair case
Fig 12.59 The Cottage, c. 1977
Fig 12.60 Gladys Turner, 1917
Fig 12.61 The marriage of Lois Turner to Lindesay (Frederick) Godfrey, 1932

CHAPTER 13
Fig 13.1 Swithland School c. 1900, headmistress, Mrs Blackwell
Fig 13.2 Swithland School, teacher's house and school, 1920s
Fig 13.3 Olive Allen from Kinchley Hill Farm, at school in Mountsorrel, 1920s
Fig 13.4 Swithland scholars at the wedding of Margaret Dixon and Henry James Walsh, 27th June 1923
Fig 13.5 Swithland School 1929
Fig 13.6 Swithland School 1939
Fig 13.7 Mrs Millicent Nettleton, headmistress 1911–40, watching a game of cricket at Swithland
Fig 13.8 Miss Winifred Dixon and pupils c. 1959
Fig 13.9 Swithland School 1977

CHAPTER 14
Fig 14.1 Sir John Danvers, Regicide. National Portrait Gallery collection, reproduced with permission
Fig 14.2 Charles II Grant to Grace Danvers, 4 July 1662
Fig 14.3 Dedication page of Prior's Map of Leicestershire, 1777
Fig 14.4 Otto Murray Dixon, 4th Battalion Seaforth Highlanders, 1915
Fig 14.5 Fox and Rabbit by Otto Murray Dixon
Fig 14.6 Woodcock and Wren by Otto Murray Dixon, 1915
Fig 14.7 Hooded Crows on a French cornstack by Otto Murray Dixon, 1916
Fig 14.8 Louie Burrows, a family portrait

CHAPTER 16
Fig 16.1 Rothley Plain, 1777, John Prior's Map of Leicestershire
Fig 16.2 Enclosure Map, Rothley Plain, 1829
Fig 16.3 The Rothley Temple Estate, 1892, from sale details
Fig 16.4 Railway Cottages, built 1897, from a 1933 postcard
Fig 16.5 Site of Roman villa, Rothley, sketch plan of excavated remains, 1901
Fig 16.6 The Oak, 'New Road' (The Ridgeway), looking towards The Ridings, 1911
Fig 16.7 'New Road' from The Ridings, Holly Lodge on the right, 1911
Fig 16.8 The Spinneys, 2000

Fig 16.9   William Henry Lead of Holly Lodge, with son William and grandson David
Fig 16.10   Holly Lodge, 2000
Fig 16.11   Rothley Garden Suburb, 1909 plan
Fig 16.12   Rothley Garden Suburb, 1910 plan
Fig 16.13   Architect's drawing of Red Walls, from the 1909 brochure
Fig 16.14   Charnwood Preparatory School, garden view
Fig 16.15   Charnwood Preparatory School classroom
Fig 16.16   Newlands, 2000
Fig 16.17   Fairview, 3 Swithland Lane, sketch by G.E. Clare
Fig 16.18   The Shrubbery, from a 1913 sale catalogue
Fig 16.19   The Gables in 1916, with Albert Herbert's son in the foreground
Fig 16.20   Nos. 61, 59 and 57 Swithland Lane
Fig 16.21   The Homestead
Fig 16.22   Miss Gweneth Kilby in Maplecote's back garden
Fig 16.23   Maplecote, Ben and Gweneth Gimson after their wedding, 22 March 1947
Fig 16.24   Sir Cyril and Lady Osborne, with daughters Jill and Hazel, West Acre

CHAPTER 17
Fig 17.1   Forest End Farm, harvesting team, c. 1900
Fig 17.2   Swithland village cricket team c. 1880
Fig 17.3   Swithland village cricket team, c. 1930, outside Keeper's Cottage
Fig 17.4   Cyclists visiting Swithland Woods c. 1912
Fig 17.5   Swithland Pavilion: Croquet and tennis lawns, 1904
Fig 17.6   A navvy family settlement outside Swithland, 1897
Fig 17.7   Swithland navvies 1897
Fig 17.8   Swithland Camp, c. 1920
Fig 17.9   Leicestershire Caravan Mission visiting Swithland, c. 1920

CHAPTER 18
Fig 18.1   Francis Almeric Butler with Fred Copson, c. 1922
Fig 18.2   Shooting Party: the seventh Earl and his second Countess, c. 1922, Charles Copson leading the horses
Fig 18.3   The eighth Earl with his daughter Freda, Wedding in 1931
Fig 18.4   Swithland men at work on the Rectory garden c. 1925
Fig 18.5   Swithland men relaxing, 1920s
Fig 18.6   Swithland men outside the Post Office, 1920s
Fig 18.7   Walter, Mary and Gweneth Kilby
Fig 18.8   Fritz Appel, after the war, with his family
Fig 18.9   Home Guard Jim Carpenter
Fig 18.10   Cedric Kilby, killed in action, 1944

CHAPTER 19
Fig 19.1   Swithland Estate, sale by auction, 22 July 1954
Fig 19.2   The Cook children and friends, with the new council houses in the background
Fig 19.3   From the Cradle to the Grave, 1955, Confirmation

Fig 19.4   From the Cradle to the Grave, 1955, Wedding,
Fig 19.5   Sunday School Pageant
Fig 19.6   Sally, Cynthia and Rosemarie Copson, Sunday School Festival
Fig 19.7   Elmleah, 153 Main Street, built for John Woolley
Fig 19.8   Outing to the Wedgewood factories, Swithland ladies 1962
Fig 19.9   Swithland Revels at The Cottage in the 1950s
Fig 19.10   Tug of War, Swithland Revels
Fig 19.11   Cycling for Swithland, September 1998
Fig 19.12   Swithland bellringers, 2000
Fig 19.13   The Rectory, 157 Main Street
Fig 19.14   The Woodyard, 188 Main Street
Fig 19.15   Bob Osborne, 1944–1999
Fig 19.16   The Osborne Memorial Window
Fig 19.17   Dedication of the Millennium Extension, June 25th 2000

COLOUR PRINTS
Plate 1   Approximate Location of Swithland Open Fields at Enclosure, 1799
Plate 2   Swithland Land Ownership after Enclosure, 1799
Plate 3   Swithland Land Ownership, 1834
Plate 4   Swithland Hall Estate Tenant Farmers, 1903
Plate 5   Land Tax Survey of Swithland Hall Estate, 1909
Plate 6   Survey of Swithland Hall Estate Tenant Farmers, 1921
Plate 7   Swithland Hall Estate Farms, 1954
Plate 8   Swithland WWII Sixty Year Celebration Party, 16th July 2005

Acknowledgements

Bob Osborne, Swithland resident and Parochial Church Council Secretary, started this book; Anne Horton, Rector of Swithland, finished it. The research began in 1995 when we agreed that a 'definitive history' of Swithland would be an enjoyable and worthwhile project, nothing as extended as that having been attempted before. From the beginning we had the encouragement and support of Swithland villagers and parishioners, all enthused by the knowledge that 'their' story would be written down for posterity. That encouragement ensured that this book at last reached publication, despite the tragedy of Bob Osborne's sudden death in 1999.

My own indebtedness to Bob is great. He introduced me to the world and discipline of local historical research and, before he died, had done much of the necessary research and written a good part of the book. Mine has been the privilege and joy of bringing the project to completion.

Many people have contributed to the writing of this book, but I would like to pay particular tribute to Joan Leatherland, who 'married into' Swithland village in 1954 and has spent many years building up a treasure trove of records from the last two centuries, most especially photographs. Joan's support and interest has been consistently generous and unstinting. Many of her photographs illustrate this history and many have been the e-mails between us; I was for ever asking questions to which she had virtually all the answers. I have also been really grateful for the encouragement and support of Bob's sister and brother, Hazel Byford and Peter Osborne, and for their sharing of their local knowledge, particularly in relation to life on Rothley Plain.

Bob and I enjoyed being the recipients of many Swithland stories from parishioners past and present. Among those who have loaned photographs and books and provided invaluable information are Sally Allen, Beatrice Bunney, Maurice Bunney, Jean Bowley, Janet and Brian Beeby, Trish Brook-Lawson, Dick Burrows, Anne Carpenter, members of the Copson family, Willoughby Garton, Gweneth Gimson, Paschal Griffin, Janet Hunt, Jean Ironside, John Lane, John Leatherland, Rodney Lloyd, Sarah May, May Musgrove, David North, Adam and Alice Page, Hilda and Neville Price. I am grateful for permission to use family photos from Grahame Briers (12.21), Lilian Harrison (12.25, 12.26), David Stanley (8.6, 8.7) and Noel Wakeling (8.5, 12.50, 17.1). We also received informative support from many beyond Swithland's immediate parishioners, not least from those who had been researching their family histories, some of whom we met in the Leicestershire Records Office. I am indebted to Tony (Shepshed) Danvers for allowing me to include his pen and ink drawings of St Leonard's Church (frontispiece, 4.1) and the Mountsorrel Butter Cross (1.8). Christopher Hamilton and members of his family have shared stories of their ancestors James and Etheldreda Murray-Dixon and Otto Murray Dixon and have allowed me to reproduce several examples of Otto's paintings (14.4, 14.5, 14.6, 14.7). Bruce Graham sent the photograph of William Haywood Gamble (12.48). The late Mrs Anne Crossman graciously welcomed us into her home at Prescott Manor, allowing us to take photographs (6.1, 6.2). Brian Cooper and Brian Axon generously allowed me to copy photographs from their impressive post card collections. Research into the chapter on Dissent was assisted by church members of Quorn and Woodhouse Eaves Baptist Churches, Woodhouse Eaves Methodist Church and the Great Meeting, Leicester. Richard Norburn of Bardon Park Chapel and Maureen Piper of Longdon in Staffordshire helped with information on our Presbyterian links. Kelcey Wilson-Lee asked for our support when she was preparing her thesis on 'a fifteenth century brass at Swithland' in 2009, and was generous in sharing the information in her lecture notes.

Several images (1.2, 8.2, 11.1, 11.6, 11.7, 11.8, 11.9, 12.3, 14.2, 16.2, 17.6, 17.7) are reproduced by permission of the Record Office for Leicestershire, Leicester and Rutland. Bob and I benefitted hugely from the assistance and advice of the staff at the Records Office who shared our interest and enthusiasm for the project from its inception. The photograph of Dean Henry Erskine (5.1) is used with permission from Princeton University Library, those of Sir John Danvers (14.1) and the fifth Earl and Countess of Lanesborough (1.10, 1.11) with permission from the National Portrait Gallery and that of 6 Cheyne Walk (1.3) with permission from Country Life. The cover photographs and other images (1.5, 4.2, 4.15, 1.4, 10.6, 12.11) were kindly taken by Steve Godley, who, with the assistance of his daughter Saskia, spent hours in a cold churchyard trying to find the perfect picture for the front cover, and achieved it! Terry Sheppard contributed the photograph of the Rothley 'Doom' headstone (10.5).

There are five other local people whose support I would like to acknowledge by name: my assistants Pat Sharpe and Ruth Page in the benefice office, who, out of hours, have given me great practical help, David Joyce of Rothley, who did an initial proof-reading of the book and Gill and Michael Kelly of Woodhouse Eaves who assisted with the second. I have much appreciated the professional support of Peter Clifford and Mike Webb from The Boydell Press, of Tina Ranft, who has designed and typeset this publication and of Angela Hall who has indexed it. I want to express my affection and appreciation for the patient understanding and support of my own family members and friends, as well as of all my parishioners, those of Woodhouse and Woodhouse Eaves as well as those of Swithland. They have watched me struggle to find the time to complete this book over the last eleven years and are more than ready to rejoice in its publication and possibly even to buy a copy! Thanks are also due to those who have generously subscribed to the publication of this book, even before they were able to see a copy for themselves. Last, but not least, I acknowledge that I am not, and never can be, a 'Swithlander', but it has been a tremendous joy and privilege for me to have been received so affectionately into the village's extended family during my time as Rector and I thank each one for their friendship and many kindnesses.

Subscribers to Swithland: Church and Estate, first edition

The Rt Revd Tim Stevens
The Rt Revd Christopher J. Boyle
Sally E Allen
Keith Andrews
Christopher Aspinall
Liz & Mike Atkins
David & Eileen Atkinson
Bill Avery
Hedley Bailey
Pat Bailey
Patricia Baker
Roger Barber
Mrs J Bartholomew
Miss Helen L Bartlett
Biddy Baxter
Brian & Janet Beeby
Audrey Benson
Mrs J.M.F Bentley
Doreen Bevan
Gillian Bocock
Jean Bowley
Professor Patrick Boylan
Mrs Janet Brewin
Grahame Briers
Trish Brook-Lawson
Joan & Cedric Brown
David & Janet Bruce
Dick & Kate Burrows
Stephen Burrows
Derek & Ann Buswell
Hazel & Barrie Byford
Laura & Toby Byford
Miss M.Z Byford
John & Valerie Capewell
Alan & Norma Carpenter
Anne Carpenter
Jayne Carter
Paul Cavill
Steve Churton

Margaret Clarke (née Rudkin)
Annette Rowntree Clifford
John R Clifford
John Cooledge
Brian Cooper
Judith Copson
Pat Copson
J.A.E & S.D Cranage
Penny Craven
Jim Crookes
Jean Curd
The Revd Richard Curtis
Norman & Pam Cutler
Dawn E Daly
Gary Danvers
Jim Danvers
Richard Danvers
Tony & Carol Danvers
Mrs P.M Davies
Roy & Nesta Davies
Richard Dimblebee
Andrew & Susan Dixon
Betty & Bernard Durham
David Edwards
Jane Egglestone
Susan Ellway
Marcel Larraz-Lacosta
Peter Finch
Jane Fisher (née Orton)
Mr & Mrs P.W Freer
Derek & Ruth Freestone
Andrew Furlong
David & Barbara Gardner
Mrs Jo Garton
Gweneth Gimson
Steve & Philippa Godley
John & Pat Gourlay
Bruce W Graham
Dr P.R Granger

Helen Green
Mr & Mrs Peter Green
Martin & Corinne Greenwood
Peggy Gregory
Dr Susan Gripper (née Barrett)
Rebecca Grace Hackett
Stephen Wilson Hales
William Danvers Hales
Christopher Hamilton
Jane Hamilton
Mrs Mary R Hancock
Miss Margaret Hands
Margaret Hardwicke
Emma Harniman
Mrs Olga Harris
Jeff & Valerie Harrison
Derek Hemsley
Hayley Hemsley
Barbara Hercock
Clive R Hilton
Peter Hodson
Brenda & Ken Holloway
Tony & Stasia Holmes
Pam & Bill Howlett
Amanda Hubbard
Janet Hunt
Cal Hurst
Mr & Mrs Arnold Hutchins
Mrs Grace Ingham
Richard Ingram
Ann Irving
Derrick Jackson
Fiona John (née Brook-Lawson)
Celia Joice
Hazel Jones (née Rudkin)
Father Tony Jordan
Valerie & David Joyce
Angela Keates
Gillian Kellie
Alastair Kelly
Michael & Gill Kelly
Jeff Kindleysides
The Revd Clare King
Dr Roberta S Klein
Trish Laurence
Martin & Julia Leake
Ann Leatherland
Joan & John Leatherland
Gary & Janet Lee
Paul & Lynne Leeming
William Leeson
Leicestershire Archaeological and
    Historical Society
Mr & Mrs David Lindley
Jo Ling
Rodney Lloyd
Barry Lynch
Geraldine Mason
Geoffrey & Sarah May
Ian D McChrystal
Linzi & Michael McGunnigle
Dennis R Minkley
F.W & P Morris
Alan & Jane Mortimore
Dorothy Mugleston
Mrs M Musgrove
Laura Nesbitt
The Ven. David Newman,
    Archdeacon of Loughborough
Andrew J.P Newton
Mr H.H Newton
David North
Josephine Northam
Kathy Oliver
Peter & Catherine Osborne
Felicity & Peter Padley
Mr & Mrs Adam Page
Ruth Page
Liz Paling
C.J.S Palmer
Jennifer Parrott
David Partridge
Lucy Pavesi
Bernard Payne
David Perry
Amanda Pellicier
Mrs Mary Pollard
Carole Priestley
Mrs E.M Quillan
John Radford
in memory of Jack & Dorothy
    Radford
Emma Ray (née Lloyd)
John & Louise Reynolds

John & Janet Roberts
Mrs Rosemary F Roberts
Joan Rowbottom
Mrs Eve Rowland
Christopher Saul
Julia Saul & Guy Watts
Liz Saul
Samantha Saul, Scott Flower, Matilda Saul-Flower
Graham K Sharp
Patricia & Kate-Zillah Sharpe
Terry Sheppard
The Revd Peter & Mrs Hilda Sheridan
Mrs Betty C Smith
Donald Smith
Sandra Smith
David Snarrt
Edmund A Stacey
Frank Stimpson
Colin Stinchcombe
Mr J.A Stone
John Sugden
St Leonard's School, Swithland
Rachel Sykes
Nick & Jenny Tarratt
Peter Tatham
Barbara Taylor
Louise, Rupert & Claudia Taylor
Sue Templeman
John Trost
Ginnie Turnbull
Julie Turner
Peter Turner
Robert & Diana Turner
Peter J Tyrrell
Marion Vincent
Michael Waggett
Marcus Wainwright
Alison Wakeling
Noël S Wakeling
Dorothy Walters (née Rudkin)
The Revd Canon & Mrs FR Walters
Gillian Walters
Mrs Judy Warrilow
Mrs Judith A Watts
Roger Watts
Geoff White
The Revd John Whittaker
Anna Whowell
Mrs Raynor Wilson
Richard Wollaston
Paul Worth
Mrs Susan Wren
Bill Wright
Jeff, Ali & Beth Wright

Introduction

This is the story of Swithland, a small village that lies on the edge of Charnwood Forest in Leicestershire and that became, for a short while in its long history, a home base for the two people who committed themselves to writing its story. It is a story that springs from love – love of the place and love of the people whose lives have been caught up in the life of this place. It is a story that celebrates friendship, roots, community and the significance of place in our lives.

In his play King Richard II, William Shakespeare dramatically described our country as 'this blessed plot, this earth, this realm, this England' – but in the extended speech of which this is only one phrase, he appears to see this England as a fortress to be 'defended against the envy of less happier lands'. Now, as then, in Western society, 'place' is seen as an impoverished second cousin of 'time' and 'space'. Distances in time and space seem to shrink ever faster, however, and we in our turn can pine for the settled nature of the past. There are unhelpful ways to value place, though, that can lead to an overly homogenous community that is suspicious of outsiders. We see how easy it is to succumb to the attractiveness of that temptation in the 'little England' reaction of some in our country to national integration and political evolution. It is not thus, however, that we should value the small place that is Swithland.

A balance is necessary and it may be that in contemporary Swithland, where tradition and modernity are alike valued, we, who have freely chosen to live here, can discover the value of common experience and common effort on our common ground. Places have their own way of claiming people, but we are all free to choose whether to embrace a fortress mentality or to rejoice in being part of a network of inter-related meanings and open the doors to neighbourliness. At the beginning of this third millennium, the community of Swithland is home to a new diversity of inhabitants. Is it unrealistic to hope that we can inhabit this village today in such a way that we eschew the temptations of 'little England' and together nurture the civic virtues of trust, honesty, justice, tolerance, co-operation, hope and remembrance?

History shows successes and failures in the ways the people of Swithland have inhabited our common space. Its future story, however, is still to be written, and some of the people who read this book will be among its writers. This history has been written in the hope that we will be able to rejoice as much in the future of this village as we have rejoiced to tell the story of its past.

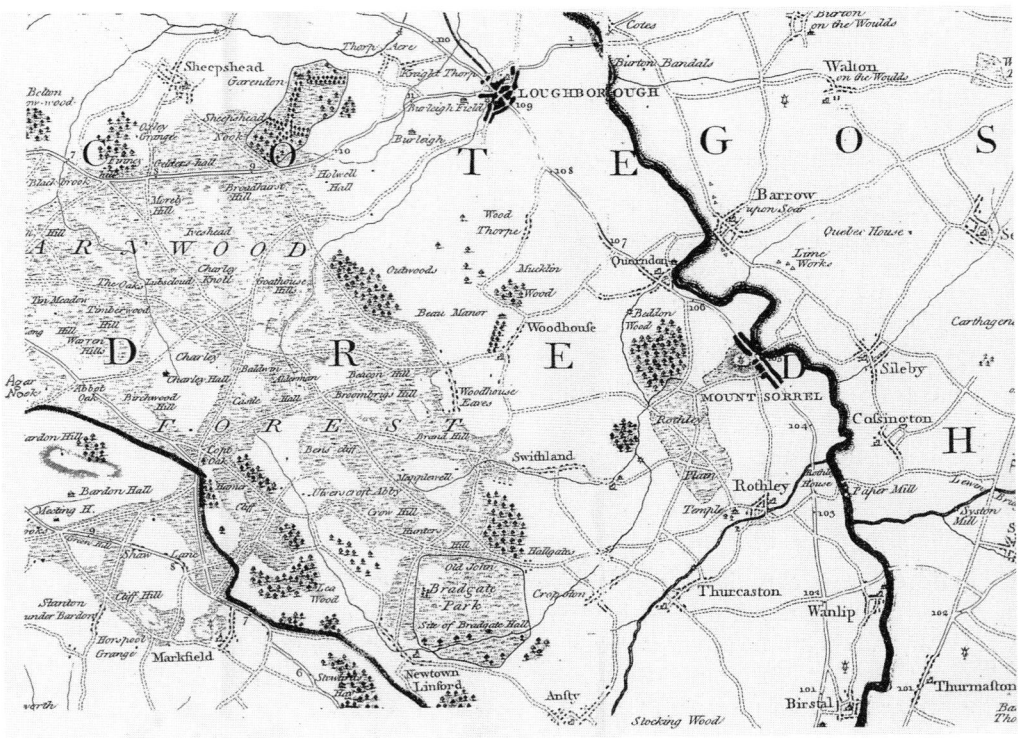

Fig 1.1 Swithland 1777, John Prior's Map of Leicestershire.

– CHAPTER 1 –

A Considerable Lordship

'At the Westerley corner of the Forest', says Mr Wyrley, 'is seated Swithland, by a little brook, that runneth toward Rodley.'[1] Swithland – a considerable lordship, containing about 1080 acres, two miles from Mountsorrel, five from Loughborough, and six from Leicester, is bounded on the North by Woodhouse; on the East by a detached part of Newtown Linford,[2] i.e. the South-east end of Rothley Plain; on the South by Thurcaston and Cropston; and on the West by Charnwood Forest; and, in the ecclesiastical division of the county, is within the deanery of Akeley.'[3]

The 'considerable lordship' of Swithland was established over eight hundred years ago. For almost all that time one family, or rather a succession of related families, has owned its lands; for when one family failed to produce male heirs, the estate passed by marriage to another branch. This 'closed' estate village, therefore, has been powerfully influenced and shaped by the fortunes and misfortunes of successive lords of the manor.

A settlement at Swithland had been established some time before 1189, since a 1204 Inquisition Post Mortem into the lands held by Robert Fitzparnel, fourth Earl of Leicester, recorded the value of Swithland in 1189 at the time of the death of the previous earl. Furthermore, an ecclesiastical document of 1206[4] indicates that there was already a chaplain in Swithland in 1206.

The name Swithland is said to be of Scandinavian origin and to mean 'a grove cleared by burning'.[5] It was not unknown for peasants of marginal settlements to add to their holdings by grubbing up adjacent woodland or by enclosing common pasture, but the Beaumont Earls of Leicester had positively encouraged the settlement of land in Swithland in the middle of the twelfth century by ordering the clearing of its wood and scrub. Early thirteenth century documents mention Swithland in connection with assarting – the process of bringing portions of waste into a more formal regime of land management.

If there was a settlement in Swithland before 1066, it would have been governed by the Saxon theign Ulf as he held the manor of Groby and its sister manor of Ratby. With the coming of the Conqueror, however, the old Saxon regime was swept away. The new 'Norman' world brought significant change to the administration of the whole English countryside, not just in Leicestershire. After the Conquest, when William claimed the whole of England as his, he dispossessed all but a handful of the Saxon theigns and gave large areas of land to his own men, to be held from him by feudal tenure. Hugh de Grandmesnil was among these men.

Hugh de Grandmesnil (c. 1032–1094)

The young Hugh de Grandmesnil had inherited extensive estates in the Calvados area of Normandy in 1040 of which Duke William was the overlord. In 1050, he and his younger brother Robert restored the abbey of Saint-Evroul (St Evroult) in the Charontonne valley, of which abbey Robert became a member, eventually prior, and then in 1059 abbot.[6] Hugh continued his connection with the abbey through his lifetime; his wife Adeliza was buried there as was he. Between 1058 and 1063 Hugh was banished from William's court, but was back in favour by 1066, and accompanied William on his expedition to England, fighting with him at the Battle of Hastings. In about 1068, as a reward for services rendered, William gave Hugh significant estates in Leicestershire and elsewhere. He also appointed him Sheriff of Leicestershire and Constable of Leicester Castle. Hugh's Leicestershire estates included the manor of Groby, of which the land of Swithland parish was part. Several sources indicate that the name 'Swithellund' appears in Domesday, but not as a specific village entry.[7]

Under the feudal system, when a man put himself under the protection of someone more rich and powerful, he became his vassal or liege man. As such, he had an obligation to render his lord aid and counsel. Aid essentially meant military service. In return for such service, the vassal was granted a benefit, consisting of an office or position, or land – a fief. When William the Conqueror took over the two thousand or so cultivated estates in England he converted them into about two hundred major fiefs, granting them to those of his vassals who had helped him. In their turn, they granted portions of their fiefs to lower vassals.

Service and homage to William did not necessarily mean fealty to his successor. In 1088, Hugh de Grandmesnil and his son Ivo supported Bishop Odo of Bayeux in a rebellion against William (Rufus) II. The rebellion failed, but the Grandmesnils appear to have been forgiven, for the family retained their English estates.

With land in both France and England, Hugh divided his attention between the two parts of his manor; there were times, for example, when Hugh had to return to France to defend his Normandy estates against rebellion or attack. His heart and real home, however, was in Normandy. During his last illness, in Leicester, Hugh was received as a monk at Leicester Abbey and, when he died a few days later in February 1094[8] his corpse was packed in salt, sewn into an ox-hide and sent to Normandy, to be buried at the Abbey of St Evroult next to his wife.

Ivo de Grandmesnil (d. 1102)

Hugh's estates passed to his son, Ivo de Grandmesnil. In 1100 when William II died, Ivo, like his father before him, backed the losing side in another dispute over the succession to the English throne, this time between Robert of Normandy and Henry I. Henry imposed a heavy fine on Ivo, who sought to mitigate the damage by enlisting the help of Robert Beaumont, Count of Meulan. Beaumont's price included a mortgage of Ivo's lands, so, when Ivo died on crusade in 1102, Beaumont, with the connivance of the king who had raised him to the Earldom of Leicester, appropriated the de Grandmesnil estates.

The Earls of Leicester

For the next hundred years the de Grandmesnil estates, including the parish of Swithland, passed in succession from one earl of Leicester to the next. The first Earl, Robert Beaumont, was succeeded in 1118 by his son, Robert 'le Bossu' (hunchback). Bossu was succeeded in 1169 by his son, Robert 'Blanchmains' (white hands) who was married to Petronella de Grandmesnil. In 1173, Blanchmains joined the Baron's War against Henry II. The barons were defeated and Blanchmains and his wife were briefly exiled to Normandy. They were later released and their property and position restored. Blanchmains died in Greece in 1190 on his way back from a pilgrimage to Palestine and was succeeded by Robert Fitzparnel, the fourth Earl, who died without issue in 1204. His lands were divided between his two sisters, Margaret, wife of Saer de Quincy, and Amicia, wife of Simon de Montfort.[9] The manor of Groby, including Swithland, passed to Margaret, and therefore to her husband Saer de Quincy.

There was a dispute in 1231, leading to legal action, in which Swithland is named.[10] Godfrey de Quatremars and his wife Lucy brought an action against Margaret de Quincy disputing the ownership of eight virgates of land in Swithland. They claimed that, on their marriage in 1204, Petronella, Margaret's mother, had given them the land. Margaret, however, claimed that the land was not Petronella's to give, since she had previously divested herself of all her English land and given it to her son, Margaret's brother, the fourth Earl. Judgement was awarded to Margaret, but a fine was levied on her in the following year by which she had to give Godfrey and Lucy, for the term of Lucy's life, 24 shillings rent in Swithland, Syston and Bradgate.

Saer de Quincy, created Earl of Winchester by King John in 1207, was among the barons who rebelled against King John in 1215, when they won the concessions of Magna Carta.[11] Saer garrisoned Mountsorrel Castle during this rebellion on behalf of Prince Louis, Dauphin of France. He eventually submitted to Henry III, but died in 1219 while on the Fifth Crusade and was buried in Acre. His heart, however, was brought back and interred at Garendon Abbey, a house endowed by his wife's family. He was succeeded by his second son, Roger de Quincy. Roger, having no male heir, was succeeded in 1264 by his three daughters: Margaret, wife of William Ferrers, Earl of Derby; Elena, wife of Alan Zouche, baron of Ashby; and

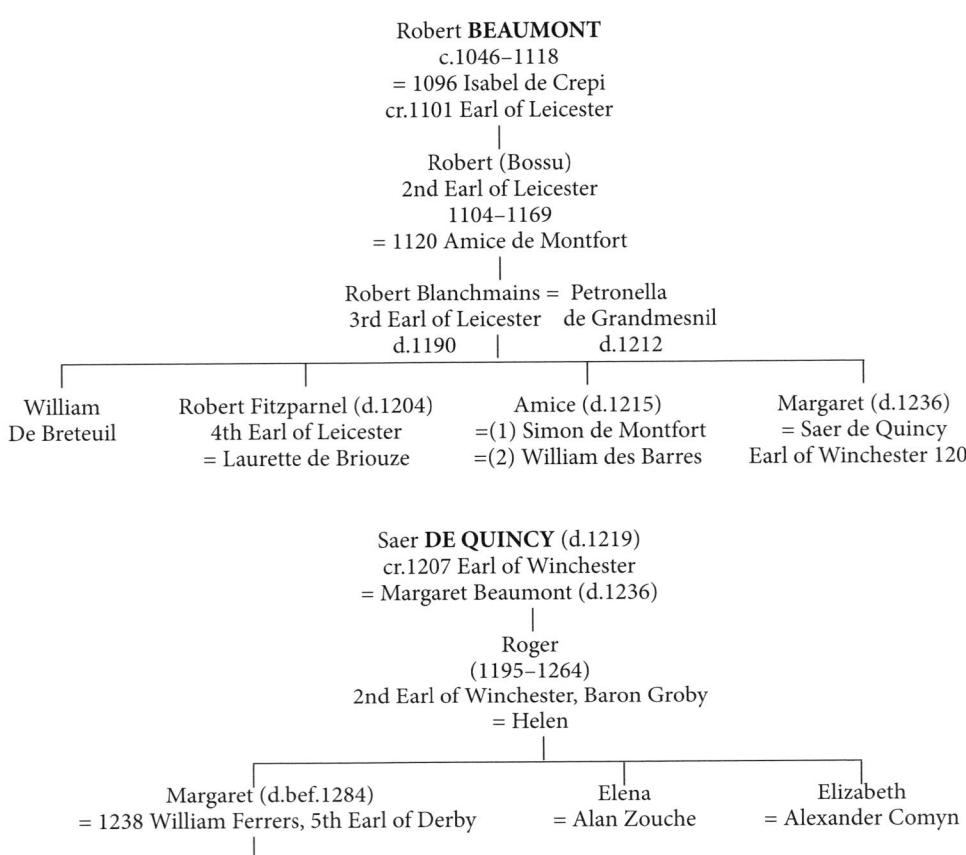

Elizabeth, wife of Alexander Comyn, Earl of Buchan. His earldom of Winchester reverted to the Crown. Margaret Ferrers received the manor of Groby as part of her share, gifting it in 1273 to her second son, William Ferrers. Groby remained with the Ferrers family until 1445, when it passed by marriage to the Greys.

Manorial Rights

In 1255, Robert le Waleys had acquired manorial rights in Swithland from Roger de Quincy for a yearly rent of £22 4s. 8d.[12] An Inquisition Post Mortem on the estates of Roger de Quincy, Earl of Winchester (died 1264), records that Robert le Waleys held twenty-seven virgates of land in Swithland for a twentieth part of a knight's fee. Ultimate ownership of land in England was, as it is in theory now, in the Crown. A lord, as 'landowner', merely held an 'estate' or 'interest' in the land, directly or indirectly, from the sovereign. A person holding an estate from the Crown could, in turn, grant all or part of it to another, but the land remained part of the estate of

A Considerable Lordship

the grantor, and ultimate ownership still remained in the Crown. The grant to Robert le Waleys allowed him to establish a manor court at Swithland, but as part of the manor of Groby and not separate from it.

A deed of 1277 refers to a 'Record of a Chapel' built by Robert Waleys, Lord of the Manor of Swithland, 'by which the Abbot and Convent of St Ebrulph (Evroult), patrons of the Mother Church', gave leave that 'by Licence from the Bishop of Lincoln he might have a Chaplain at his own proper charges in the Chapel lately built in his Court of Swithland ... the Mother Church, in their patronage, being secured in all things and indemnified'.[13]

In a 1260 suit Robert le Waleys' name appeared in connection with his calling William de Shefeud and Margaret his wife to warrant to Robert two virgates of land in Bradgate, which Robert held from them by charter. 'This led to a fine levied between the parties at Michaelmas 1268 by which William and Margaret acknowledged the land which they held between Holegate (probably Hallgates) and Bybrok (the stream which runs by Swithland) to be the right of Robert le Waleys at a yearly rent of a halfpenny at Christmas. For which acknowledgement Robert have of them five silver marks'.[14]

The le Waleys, who were significant local landholders, came into conflict with their monarch when, in the Barons' War (1258–65) against Henry III led by Simon de Montfort, Robert le Waleys took the losing side. He was, however, 're-admitted to the king's peace' in 1268, and pardoned 'for his trespasses in the time of the disturbance'.

```
                    Robert WALEYS = Isabella
                    (d.1298)      |
                         Nicholas = Margaret de Meynell
                    (d.vita patris) |    of Old Dalby
                              Oliver = Beatrice
                            (d.1331) |
                                John = Elizabeth
                             (d.1363) |
         ┌─────────────────────────────────────┐
    Elizabeth (d.1427)                       Agnes
    =(1) John de Walcote (d.c.1400)    = John Fitzjohn Mareschal
    =(2) William Byspham
    =(3) John Mapilton (d.1424)
```

Nicholas le Waleys, Robert's son who predeceased his father, had married Margaret de Meynell and through her had acquired the manor of Dalby-on-the-Wolds (Old Dalby), Leicestershire. Their relationship, however, was unhappy. In 1299, shortly after her husband's death, Margaret brought an action against her father-in-law, William de Ferrers, Lord of the Manor of Groby and guardian of her son Oliver during his minority. She claimed ten marks of rent, asserting that Nicholas had promised her the sum as dowry before they married. William de Ferrers said that she was entitled to nothing, since whilst Nicholas was still alive she had deserted him, 'and lived in adultery with a certain Walter Basset at Essheby, Dalby, and elsewhere in the county, and never in the lifetime of Nicholas was reconciled to him'.[15]

Robert le Waleys was succeeded by his grandson, Oliver, who was named in the earliest surviving royal charter relating to the manor of Swithland. In 1316, Edward II granted him free warren in all his lands in Old Dalby and Swithland.[16]

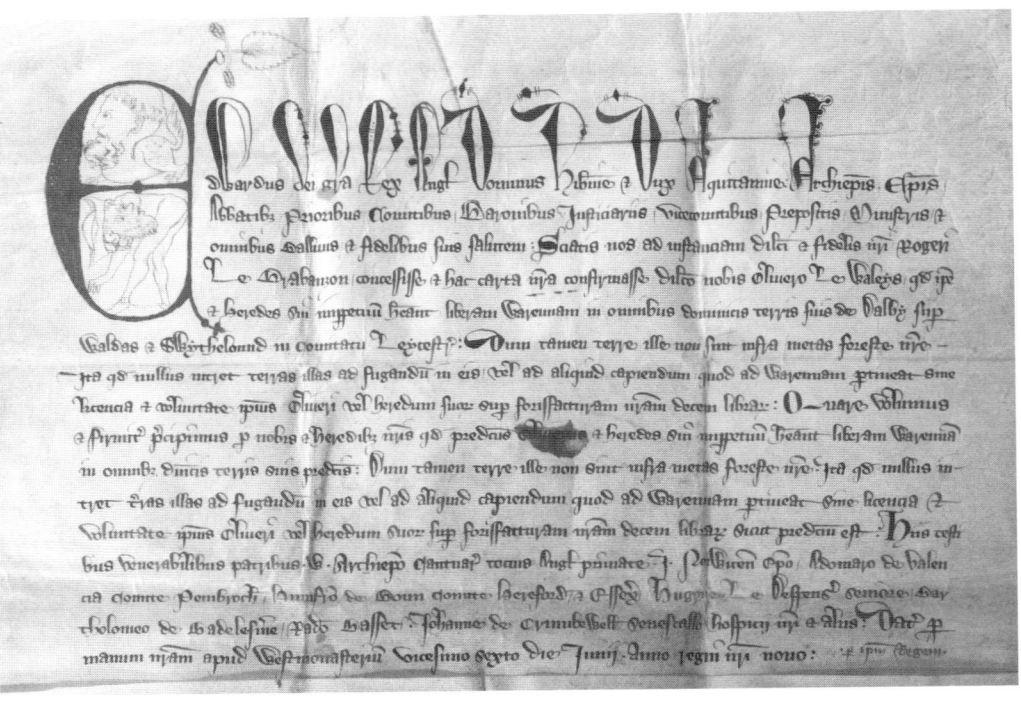

Fig 1.2 Royal Charter, 1316.

Royal Charter translation:
Edward by the grace of God King of England, Lord of Ireland and Duke of Aquitaine, to Archbishops, Bishops, Abbots, Priors, Earls, Barons, Justices, Sheriffs, Reeves, Sergeants, Bailiffs and all his faithful [people], greeting. Know that we at the instance of our beloved and faithful Roger Le Brabanzon have given and by this our charter confirmed to our beloved Oliver Le Waleys that he and his heirs shall have free warren in all his demesne lands of Dalby super Waldas and Swythelonnd in the county of Leicester for ever, provided however that those lands are not within the bounds of our forest; so that no-one shall enter those lands to hunt therein or to take anything which belongs to the warren without the licence and will of the same Oliver or his heirs on pain of our penalty of ten pounds. Wherefore we will and firmly order for ourselves and our heirs that the same Oliver and his heirs shall have free warren in all his demesne lands aforesaid for ever, provided however that those lands are not within the bounds of our forest; so that no-one shall enter those lands to hunt therein or to take anything which belongs to the warren without the licence and will of the same

Oliver and his heirs on pain of our penalty of ten pounds as aforesaid. These being witnesses: the venerable father W[alter] Archbishop of Canterbury primate of all England, J[ohn] Bishop of Norwich, Aymer de Valence Earl of Pembroke, Humphrey de Boun Earl of Hereford and Essex, Hugh Le Despenser senior, Bartholomew de Badelesmere, Ralph Basset, John de Crumbewell steward of our household, and others. Given by our hand at Westminster the twenty sixth day of June in the ninth year of our reign. By the King himself.

Oliver le Waleys was appointed Leicester's coroner at some time before 1317. In that year, however, as well as in 1320 and 1322, the king asked the Sheriff of Leicestershire to replace him. Oliver had claimed to be unable to attend to his duties because he was in the retinue of John de Seagrave, and so bound by deed to set out with him in the king's service. He allowed himself to be caught up in rebellion against Edward II when, in 1322, he joined the Duke of Lancaster's rising. A warrant was issued for his arrest, and his lands were seized. On le Waleys finding suitable sureties, however, the writ was rescinded and his property restored.[17] Despite his history, he was appointed Sheriff of Leicestershire in 1326.

In 1331, Oliver le Waleys fell out with his bailiff, William Pullhare of Old Dalby. Pullhare brought an action against Beatrice, wife of Oliver de Waleys, and others. He alleged that Beatrice, together with Thomas de Outheby, parson of East Bridgeford, and Robert, son of Oliver le Waleys, had seized him at Swithland and imprisoned him for one month. In addition, they had carried off three heifers, three oxen, seven cows, twelve sheep and three pigs, which belonged to him. The issue went to a jury, but the matter had still not been resolved a year later, by which time Oliver was dead.

John le Waleys succeeded his father in 1331. He was appointed Sheriff of Leicestershire in 1343, Escheater in 1344, and Commissioner of Array in 1346. He too had problems with his bailiff, Hugh Scot. In 1339, Waleys started an action against Scot in a plea of accounts, but the outcome is unknown. In 1352 John exchanged the manor of Old Dalby for the manor of Thrumpton in Nottinghamshire, becoming escheater for Nottinghamshire in 1353 and sheriff in 1355. He was created a knight and, in 1361, went to Ireland with Ralph de Ferrers to fight for Edward III.

Sir John Waleys had two daughters, Elizabeth and Agnes. Agnes Waleys married John Mareschal, and in about 1365 Elizabeth Waleys married John Walcote of Walcote. On Sir John Waleys' death in 1363, the estate passed to John and Elizabeth Walcote, though not without dispute. In 1372, John Mareschal claimed that he had been unjustly deprived of the manor of Swithland[18] and in 1380 a jury found that he had indeed been disseized.[19] But in 1382 John Walcote recovered seizin and nothing more is heard of John Mareschal. This suggests that, in the meantime, Agnes, Mareschal's wife, had died without issue. An Inquisition Post Mortem of 1387 records that John Walcote held of Sir Henry de Ferrers all of the twenty-seven virgates of land in Swithland which the Waleys had previously held.[20]

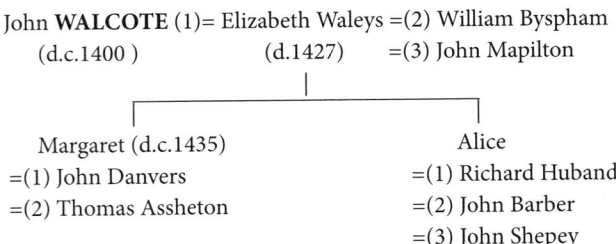

Elizabeth bore John Walcote two daughters, Alice and Margaret, before he died in about 1400. By 1405 Elizabeth had married William Byspham,[21] a Burgess in Parliament in 1399 and a Bailiff of the Duchy of Lancaster. This marriage did not last long before Byspham died and Elizabeth went on to marry for a third time – to John Mapilton.

In 1413, Elizabeth's relations with her third husband were extremely poor. So bad, indeed, that she left him. In the process, she moved a large collection of belongings from Swithland to the home of her daughter, Alice, who was married to John de Shepey. Among the possessions removed were some twelve beds, twenty pairs of sheets, ten basons with covers, sixty-eight brass and copper pots and pans, together with kettles, spoons and brewing vessels. Elizabeth complained that John Mapilton had severely ill-treated her – not only by beating her, but by almost starving her, so that she despaired of her life. John Mapilton, however, successfully brought an action against John and Alice Shepey for the abduction of his wife, for the value of the goods that he did not get back and for his expenses in bringing the case. How he settled with Elizabeth is not recorded.[22] Ten years later, however, John Mapilton came to an untimely end. According to the subsequent inquest, he was ambushed and murdered in Swithland on Friday 15th January 1424. At 4.00pm, Stephen Farnham of Quorn gent, John Prychet of Quorn and William Saunder of Barrow husbandman, had lain in wait in a close in Swithland called 'Le Carre'. (A close next to Hall Farm, subsequently called Carr Close, might have been the site of the ambush.) There they made an assault on Mapilton, beating, wounding and murdering him; although it was alleged that it was Peter Carter of Waltham-on-the-Wolds who actually killed him. Elizabeth herself survived another three years until 1427. On her death the manor of Swithland passed to Margaret and Alice, her two daughters by John Walcote.[23] In 1429 they agreed that the manor be divided between them.

Some time earlier, and before 1412, Elizabeth's older daughter, Margaret Walcote, had married John Danvers of Shakerstone (died c. 1425) by whom she had a son, John. Although Margaret married again in 1427, to Thomas Assheton, her half share of the manor of Swithland passed on her death to her son John Danvers, and to his heirs.[24]

Alice Walcote, Margaret's sister, married Richard Huband, then, after his death, John Barber. It is thought that during their marriage John Barber leased his half of the manor of Swithland to his brother-in-law, John Danvers. On John Barber's death, however, Alice married John Shepey of Smisby in Derbyshire so that when she died, her half share of Swithland passed to their son, also named John Shepey. The two halves of Swithland manor remained separated for nearly two hundred years.

The Danvers Moiety

The moiety or share of the manor of Swithland inherited by John Danvers from his mother remained with the Danvers family, and for the next hundred and fifty years succeeding generations of the Danvers family seem to have lived quietly in Swithland, barring occasional legal actions over land. None of them held important government positions, but they did marry well.

John Danvers' grandson, Thomas, married Alice Venables, daughter of Baron Kinderton.[25] Their son John married Anne Shirley, sister of Ralph Shirley of Staunton Harold, and their eldest son Francis, who died relatively young, married local heiress, Margaret Kingston of Rothley.[26] Francis and Margaret Danvers' only son John married Isabel, daughter of Richard Coke of Trusley in Derbyshire. Their marriage connected the Danvers family with Sir John Coke, famed common law lawyer and Secretary of State to King Charles I.

It is this John Danvers (1530–1598) who is thought to have rebuilt the mansion house at Swithland in the late 1550s, but he would appear to have lived for some time at Rothley. In 1481 Ralph Kingston had bought a house in Rothley, called 'The Hall'.[27] John Danvers purchased 'The Hall' and remnants of the estate from Edmund Kingston in 1570. When he died in 1598, John was living in the former Kingston house in Rothley, rather than at Swithland, which was home to Francis, his eldest son.

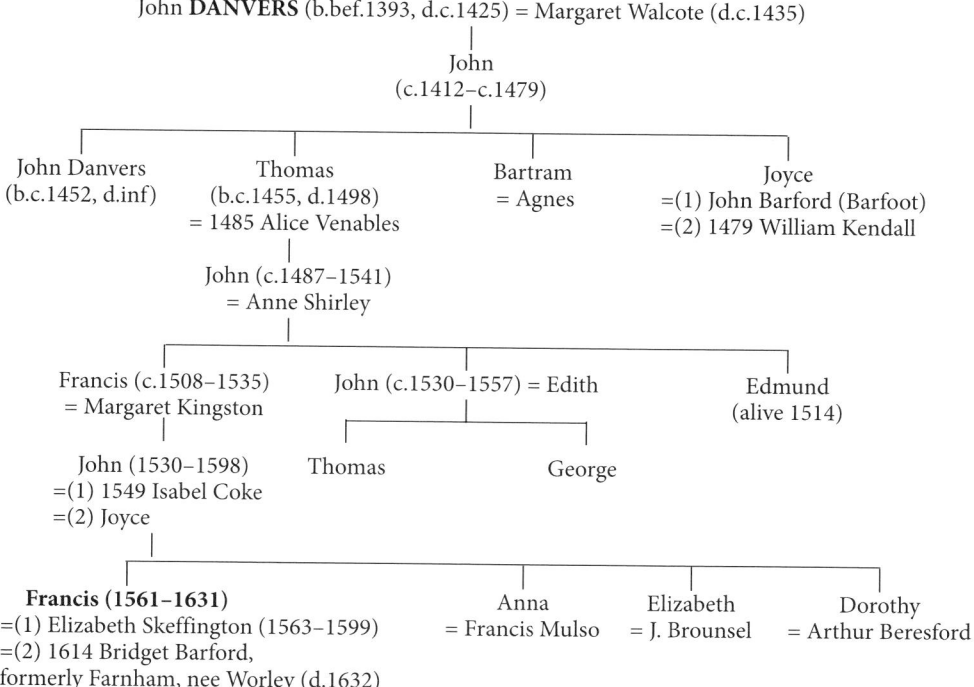

The Shepey Moiety

Alice Shepey's son John, who owned the other half share of the manor in Swithland, also lived in Swithland, though it is not known where. When John Shepey died his moiety passed to his son Edmund, who at his death in 1509 was recorded as owning lands in Smisby,[28] Lutterworth and Frolesworth, as well as in Swithland.

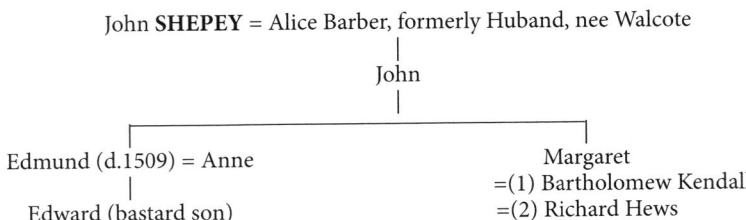

Edmund Shepey's heir was his sister, Margaret Kendall, wife of Bartholomew Kendall of Twycross, by whom she had three sons. She was about sixty years old when her brother died. In his will, Edmund bequeathed his moiety in Swithland to his widow, Anne, for life. After her death, the land was to be sold to provide for his bastard son, Edward Shepey, for his life, with remainders to Edmund's legitimate heirs. Edward Shepey must, however, have predeceased his mother, for the land was not sold. Margaret Kendall went on to marry Richard Hews of Swithland, yeoman, but her half share of Swithland passed to the Kendall family.

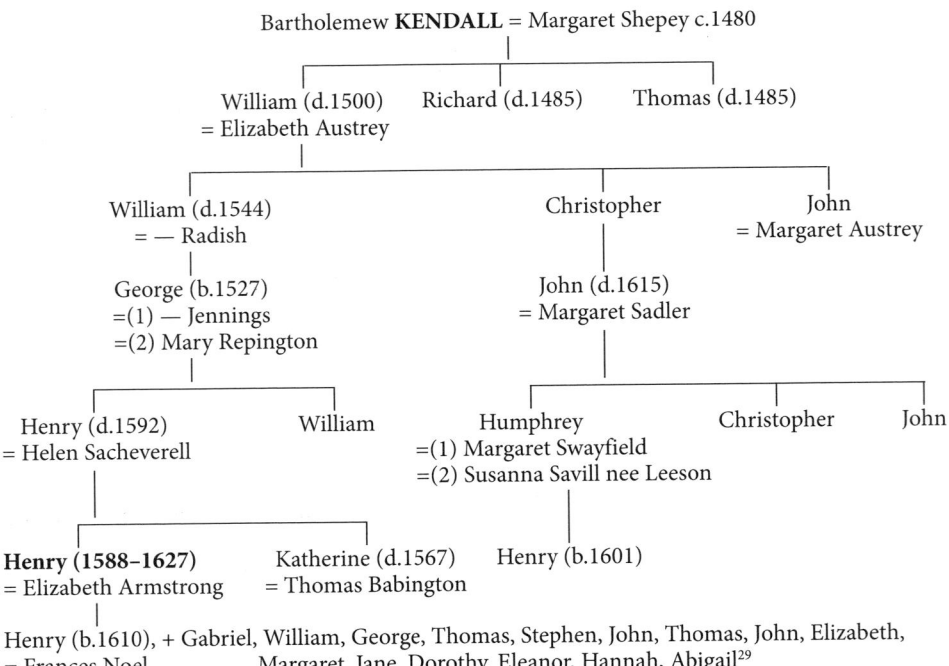

A Considerable Lordship

The Kendalls were already related by marriage to the Danvers. In 1479 Joyce Barford, widow, the daughter of John Danvers (c. 1412–c. 1479), had married a William Kendall. And in 1618 William Danvers (1591–1656) married Elizabeth Babington (1595–1676), the daughter of Thomas Babington of Rothley Temple whose wife Katherine was the eldest daughter of Henry Kendall of Smisby (d. 1592).

The Kendalls were landowners of some substance. When William Kendall died an Inquisition Post Mortem (1549) showed that he owned land in Leicestershire at Sheepy Parva and Lutterworth, as well as at Swithland. Henry Kendall of Smisby (1588–1627) inherited the half share in Swithland. We do not know whether Henry actually lived in Swithland, but it would appear that another Kendall, Humphrey, William's great-nephew, did. He lived in Swithland between 1608 and 1619.

In the five years before he died, Henry Kendall started to sell off his Leicestershire interests. In 1622, he sold part of his Swithland moiety; not, however, to Francis Danvers who held the other half share, but to a number of local yeomen and tradesmen.[30] In 1629, however, the remainder of the Shepey/Kendall share of Swithland was bought up by Francis Danvers, and the two halves of the manor were again united.

Francis Danvers (1561–1631)

Francis Danvers married first Elizabeth Skeffington (d. 1599) and secondly, in 1614, the twice-widowed Bridget Worley.[31] He lived to see his family beginning to play a more prominent public role: John Danvers, his son, was elected Member of Parliament for Oxford in 1621.

His second wife's Barford relatives, however, brought him into dispute with Sir William Herrick from nearby Beaumanor.[32] They accused Herrick's son, William Herrick junior, of acting dishonourably towards the daughter of Robert Barford. On Thursday 5th September 1622, it was alleged that Francis Danvers attacked Sir William and Lady Herrick and their son in Loughborough, and was disarmed by Herrick's family and servants. The matter came to the notice of the fifth Earl of Huntingdon, who summoned Sir William Herrick to Donington in order to settle the issue without resort to duelling. The dispute must have caused considerable ill-feeling, because, on 17th September, Herrick was still resisting the settlement urged by Huntingdon and insisting on additional clauses to clear his son's reputation and to suppress slanderous statements concerning his wife. He continued to refuse to admit that any wrong had been done by his son, but indicated that he was prepared to accept arbitration and to make such reparations as the arbitrators might agree. The case was heard before three deputy lieutenants of the county and forty other worthy gentlemen in the great chamber of the Angel Inn in Leicester on 26th September, and agreement reached both between Danvers and Herrick and between Barford and Herrick.

Another side of Francis' character, a touching concern for his wife, is shown in his will.

> Item, for my wyff, she being an olde woman and not fit to keep
> house free from debts and hath as good as five or six score pounds
> a year to live on, notwithstanding all this, I give her all the
> household stuff that she brought from Shakerston, except that
> which I have given to my son John. I give her more her gray mare,
> four kyne, her sheepe and would give her more but I must
> consider them that have more need and pay my own debts.[33]

Francis was, in fact, a man of reasonable substance. He had been willing in 1626 to join with forty other Leicestershire subscribers 'content to lend to His Majesty such sums of money as they were assessed at the last Parliament'.[34] At his death in 1631 he owned land at Shakerstone, Swithland and Barrow-on-Soar, the holding including 40 acres of arable land, 40 of meadow, 200 of pasture, 200 of wood, and 60 of furze and heath in Swithland and Barrow-on-Soar. The land at Barrow probably consisted of part of Buddon Wood. Certainly the fortunes of the family were sufficient after his death for his son William to purchase in 1633 some further 80 acres of Buddon Wood from Henry Kendall for £60. They were also sufficient for William to erect a substantial monument to his father in the south aisle of Swithland church.[35] Today only the brass memorial plate remains, fixed to the south wall of the church.[36]

> True faith in God, to man firme faithfulness
> Honour of vertue, succour of distres
> Just holiness, prudent simplitye.
> With Danvers liv'd, and yet in this grave do lie,
> With Danvers Dead, and yet not so, for they
> immortal are and make him live for aye.

William Danvers (1591–1656)

William Danvers married Elizabeth Babington of Rothley Temple in 1618; they had sixteen children. For most of his life William lived at Swithland, though, as the Civil War approached, he spent more time in London. The family took the parliamentary side during the Civil War and William Danvers was a captain in the parliamentary forces. He sat on the County Committee for Leicestershire and loaned money to Parliament for arms and ammunition.[37] After the war, William returned to Swithland and served as a Justice of the Peace during the Commonwealth. His name appears in many parish record books.[38] He had a kind heart; he protected[39] his eccentric and 'royalist' rector for as long as he was able and he made sensible provision for his children. In 1656, just before he died, he and his wife made a legal settlement on their own younger children, William, Charles, Margaret, Elizabeth, Anne and Diana, 'provided they all marry with the consent of their parents and the trustees'.[40]

Their daughter, Elizabeth Danvers (1639–1669), made a short and sadly childless marriage in 1660 with William Palmer, son of Archdale Palmer, Lord of the Manor of Wanlip. A collection of recipes belonging to Archdale

Palmer[41] includes some given to him by the 'D'Anvers' family of 'Sweathland' in 1662 and 1664. She, or another member of her family, gave him in 1662 a recipe for 'a purge for Melancholy or waterish humours'.

> Take 1 oz. Seena ½ pound Raysons of ye sun stoned ¼ pound prunes putt them in 2 Quarts runninge water & boyle them till halfe be consumed, then putt them into a Bole and stampe them, then putt them into a quart white wine & sett them on ye fier againe, and boyle them but a very little more, then straine them well & putt ye liquor in a bottle for y^r use. Take about 6 spoonefulls in ye Morninge fasting & 6 spoonefulls at night when you goe to bed until all bee taken.

Elizabeth's younger sister Anne and her brother William also contributed recipes to Palmer's collection. These were for ailments such as spleene or wind, agues, feavers or mother fits and a surfett. Cousin William's contribution in 1664 was a recipe to 'keepe from Gallinge in ridinge or a bile'.

> Beate the yolk of an egg to an oile, & mixe therewith a little flower & honey, till it come to a Salve, then spread it upon the fleshy side of a fine Sheepe leather apply it to yor sitting place.[42]

Henry Danvers (1622–1687)

Henry Danvers, William's son and heir, was more dramatically involved than his father in the religious and political dissent of the time.[43] In 1642, at the outbreak of the Civil War, Henry was on the parliamentary side and was made a colonel in the Roundhead army. In 1644 he married Ann Sacheverell,[44] née Coke, the third daughter of Sir John Coke of Melbourne in Derbyshire, also a Parliamentarian. In 1653 Henry was elected Member of Parliament to the Barebones Parliament. He differed with Cromwell, however, and was arrested and briefly imprisoned in 1657, suspected of plotting to overthrow him.[45]

After the Restoration of Charles II in 1660, Henry Danvers spent the remaining twenty-seven years of his life in repeated conspiracies to overthrow the Stuart monarchy by renewed revolution. He was fortunate to escape arrest for treason and for holding illegal conventicles. He spent some time as a fugitive from government justice and died in exile in Holland in 1687. Charles II attempted to confiscate the Danvers family estates because of Henry's treasonous activities, but failed. Confiscation was avoided in part because Henry had placed his estates in the hands of trustees,[46] and because of his self-imposed exile. When Henry was not on the run from warrants for his arrest, he lived mostly in Stoke Newington and only very rarely at the house at Swithland, which was managed by his mother.

Ann, his wife, was an intelligent and courageous woman. She supported her husband during the difficult and dangerous post-Restoration years. Her grandson, Sir Joseph, from the 'other side' of government, proudly paid tribute to her learning in the Hebrew and Greek scriptures.[47]

Samuel Danvers (d. 1693)

Little is known of Henry's son, Samuel Danvers, who died at a relatively young age in 1693. In 1683 Samuel married Elizabeth, the daughter of Joseph Morewood, a London merchant. They too lived at Stoke Newington and not at Swithland. On Samuel's death, Elizabeth remarried. Her second husband was John Danvers, whose father, Sir John Danvers of Oxford, was one of the fifty-nine signatories of the death warrant of Charles I, and whose estates had been forfeited at the Restoration. John Danvers held the manor of Prescott in Oxfordshire, which manor house he substantially rebuilt, but he and Elizabeth appear to have lived for most of the time in Chelsea.

In 1719, Elizabeth's son, Joseph, wrote:

> My mother was seized with an apoplectic fit about 9 at night and she died about 8 the next night, being the 11th December at Chelsea near London...
> I set out from Great Chelsea towards Swithland with my brother and my mother's two servants to accompany my mother's corpse to be interred in Leicestershire. We had with us a coach and hearse and two sets of horses and four horsemen. She was buried in the chapel at Swithland after the morning sermon on Sunday 20th December, and we returned to Chelsea on the 25th.[48]

Her husband, Sir John Danvers, outlived her by two years, dying in 1721. He is buried in the church at Cropredy, the parish church of Prescott Manor. A magnificent wall memorial was erected in his memory.

Joseph Danvers (1686–1753)

Joseph Danvers restored his family's reputation and fortune. He accomplished this in no uncertain terms, for, as far as increasing the family's landed interests went, he was the most successful of all the Lords of the Manor of Swithland. As the third son of Samuel Danvers, Joseph may not have expected to succeed to the estates, but his two elder brothers both died before their mother, aged eighteen and twenty-three. Joseph was educated at Lincoln's Inn in 1709 and in 1721 married a local girl, Frances, daughter of Thomas Babington of Rothley Temple.

There is every indication that Joseph Danvers acquired his substantial wealth through commerce and trade. In 1718, at the age of thirty-two, he was evidently prosperous enough to have a house built for himself at No. 6 Cheyne Walk, Chelsea.[49] Danvers' house was built within the great garden of Henry VIII's Manor House. (In 1712 Sir Hans Sloan had purchased the manor from Lord Cheyne and sold the building leases.) The house was built of warm-coloured brickwork and its fine cornice-mouldings and string-courses still impress. The original main entrance to the house was from the garden side. The Danvers arms can still be seen on the two lead rainwater heads on this entrance front, and, impaled with those of Babington, on a wrought-iron grille inside the house.

Fig 1.3 No. 6 Cheyne Walk, 1940.

On Joseph Danvers' tomb, which he had built in Swithland churchyard some years before he died, this couplet is engraved:

> When young, I sailed to India east and west.
> But aged in this port must lye at rest.⁵⁰

From 1729–30, Joseph was an assistant of the Royal Africa Company, which was incorporated by royal charter in 1672, in succession to the failed Merchant Adventurers Company, to trade with Africa. It was re-constructed between 1712–13, but had failed to prosper. Between 1725–29 only five hundred and sixty-three slaves, one of its principal activities, were delivered to the colonies. The company effectively ceased as a trading corporation in 1730, only continuing thereafter thanks to a government subsidy from 1730 to 1746. After 1746, the subsidy was withheld and the company dissolved in 1752. Joseph Danvers' interest in the company would seem to have been a misplaced investment.

Other investments must have been more successful, however, for Joseph Danvers considerably extended his Leicestershire estates into neighbouring parishes. In 1727 he purchased a cottage and 18 acres of land, Albaster Hay near Hallgates, Newtown Linford. He acquired the lordship of the manor of Mountsorrel in 1732, gaining both land and a considerable number of dwelling-houses in the process. These he let, mostly to sitting tenants, in a series of 99-year leases. In 1735 he bought the lordship of the manor of Thurcaston from George Wright. He also bought up parcels of land in Rothley, Mountsorrel and Newtown Linford, and, in 1751, Thornton's Farm (now Cropston Leys Farm), Cropston. In 1752 he purchased the 100 acres of Buddon Wood, of which he had been the tenant, from Judith Letitia Bury of Headon, Notts. For the next two hundred years, the manors of Swithland, Thurcaston and Mountsorrel, together with Buddon Wood, remained the core of the family landholding. Joseph also came into possession of estates outside Leicestershire: in 1721, on the death of his step-father, John Danvers of Prescott, he inherited the manor of Prescott in Cropredy, Oxon, and the manor of Basmey, Eaton Soken, Bedfordshire.

Joseph Danvers spent much of his life in public service. In 1721 he became Sheriff of Leicestershire and in 1722 started a long parliamentary career. He represented Boroughbridge from 1722–27, Bramber from 1727–34, and Totnes from 1734–47. It was alleged that he was first brought into Parliament by the Duke of Newcastle, at the request of Lord Sunderland who had been asked by the Duke of Rutland to find Danvers a seat – apparently in return for his standing down at an election in favour of Rutland's brother, Lord William Manners. Joseph was a frequent speaker in parliamentary debate, belonging to a group of independent members who normally supported Walpole, but sometimes went against him. In 1737 he was described as a 'dull joker'. More recently he has been described as uttering 'the most inapt statement of the political mood',[51] when he said at some point before the 1734 election, that he had 'never heard any man reproach the ministry; on the contrary they all seemed to think that the only dispute among us here was who should be minister; and as this is a dispute which the generality of the people of England are by no means concerned in, gentlemen are much mistaken if they imagine that the people of England trouble their heads about it'.[52]

At the opening of Parliament in 1741 Horace Walpole described Danvers as 'a rough, rude beast, but now and then mouths out some humour'.[53] Of one debate that year, Danvers memorably described Robert Walpole and Pulteney as 'two old bawds debauching younger members'.[54] Danvers, possibly for political reasons, gave Walpole the portrait of the Earl of Danby by Van Dyck that he had inherited from his step-father. The painting was subsequently among the pictures acquired from Walpole in 1779 by Catherine the Great for the Hermitage in St Petersburg, and is still part of the Hermitage collection.[55] When he retired from Parliament in 1746, Joseph Danvers was created a baronet and served as a Deputy Lieutenant of Leicestershire as well as an acting Justice of the Peace in the county.

There is no confirmed portrait of Sir Joseph Danvers, but a 'portrait of an unknown man' aged sixty-three, painted by Bartholomew Dandridge in 1750, hung in Swithland Hall until the contents sale in 1978.[56] The date of the painting – Sir Joseph would also have been sixty-three in 1750 – as well as the Danvers baronetcy arms and the rolled 'act of parliament', encourages speculation that this might be a portrait of Sir Joseph.

Despite spending much of his time at his house at Great Chelsea, Joseph Danvers was responsible for major structural changes to Swithland church. In 1727 he rebuilt the south aisle, which included his family 'chapel', almost doubling its size. By then, he clearly felt confident enough of the family's position to erect a monument in the new Danvers 'chapel' commemorating not only his father, Samuel, but also his parliamentarian ancestors – his grandfather Henry, who had died abroad in exile, and his great-grandfather William Danvers, whose tomb he may well have levelled in order to create his new 'chapel'.

Sir Joseph was assisted in running his Swithland estate by his steward, Joseph Prior, with whom he corresponded regularly from his London home at Great Chelsea. Danvers made generous provision for Prior in his will, as he did also for his servant Thomas Brookhouse.

In 1742 Sir Joseph established a school for poor boys from Mountsorrel and Swithland in Mountsorrel.[57]

> This English School
> for poor boys out of
> Mountsorrel and Swithland
> given by Joseph Danvers Esq
> 1742[58]

In a 1753 codicil to his will,[59] Sir Joseph bequeathed one hundred pounds to his wife and the overseers of the poor with the request that they build a school on the Upper Green at Swithland. As far as we know, however, it was never built.

Sir Joseph Danvers died in 1753 at the age of sixty-seven. He was buried in the fine vault and tomb that he had previously built in 1745, which lies across the east wall of Swithland churchyard. Sir Joseph, in his will, asked that his housekeeper and servants be paid for six months after his death. He left his son John five pounds, requesting that it be paid to poor people in Swithland and made similar provisions for the poor of Thurcaston, Mountsorrel and Rothley. He directed that his tenants be paid ten shillings and that every tenant and his wife who lived in Swithland should be given a pair of black gloves each and should walk at his funeral.

As Sir Joseph must have wished, his aggrandizement of the south aisle of Swithland church is his lasting memorial, with its builder's mark still proud in proclamation. Underneath it now, high up on the east wall of his 'private' chapel, and moved from their original situation on the now demolished west wall, are the funeral armorial bearings of his baronetcy – helmet and gauntlets, sword and shield of arms – and below them, the door leading to his churchyard tomb. The funeral hatchments to his wife and himself, which would have been carried to the church in their funeral processions, hang on the north wall of the south aisle.

*Fig 1.4
Portrait of an Unknown Man, Bartholomew Dandridge, 1750.*

*Fig 1.5
Hatchment for Sir Joseph Danvers, St Leonard's Church.*

John Danvers (1723–1796)

Sir Joseph was succeeded by his son, the flamboyant Sir John Danvers. Sir John sold the house at Chelsea in 1764, but he added significantly to the other estates that his father had built up, becoming a large landowner with estates in Northamptonshire, Bedfordshire, Oxfordshire and Middlesex, as well as in Leicestershire. Sir John was High Sheriff of Leicestershire in 1755.

A near contemporary, William Gardiner of Leicester (1770–1853) described Sir John as:

> …a man of sound common sense, though in some things highly eccentric. He was remarkably fond, like the Chinese, of painting everything red: so much that every door, window, shutter and gatepost in the towns of Swithland and Mountsorrel was so decorated.
>
> He did not stop here; he adopted it in his own dress. But the effect of red was tempered with a mixture of black. If I remember right, his coat was of dull scarlet, with black buttons, black waistcoat and small clothes, red buttons and red stockings. Being a thick, broadset man, his appearance was like that of the knave of spades…[60]

And John Throsby (1740–1803)

> Whenever he appeared abroad, it was in a sort of stage coach richly emblazoned with his arms, and when at home a flag was kept flying from the highest turret.[61]

Throsby noted somewhat waspishly that 'the streamer seen on Sir John's house is set up on those days he is in the country. He now spends much of his time in Lon.'[62]

One of John Throsby's 'Excursions' in 1790 saw him visiting the church in Swithland, where he noted the memorial that the still living Sir John had erected to himself in anticipation of his death. He also remarked on the support that Sir John, according to his memorial tablet, had given to 'the assertors of Revolution principles', commenting 'for which I once saw him rewarded, after a Revolution feast dinner in Leicester. Being steward of the feast, he was dragged around the market place by a shouting drunken mob, in his carriage, in the Wilkes and liberty style – 'Huzza! Sir John for ever!' – But this Sir John could not with-

Fig 1.6 Swithland Hall, 1790, John Throsby.

stand; mobs are unruly, they sometimes govern the state ... Mark, Reader, Sir John was not thrown, though in danger'.[63]

John Danvers had many singularities, one of which was that no coal should be used in his house; but in every corner of the mansion were piled up short billets cut from the neighbouring woods.[64] It was reported of Sir John that, although he owned a good library, he claimed that a gentleman's library was complete if it consisted of four books only: the Bible, the Book of Common Prayer, Don Quixote, and the Court Circular.

Sir John was a philanthropist and Swithland church was a significant beneficiary of his largesse; he donated the organ, the bells, the church silver and at some point he rebuilt the rectory.[65] He was also generous in his giving to the local communities in his lordship, Mountsorrel as well as Swithland. In 1759 he purchased a cottage with an orchard attached from Richard Fowkes of Rothley[66] and, 'out of regard for the welfare and convenience of the inhabitants of Mountsorrel', he made a free gift of the orchard as a burial ground for the townsfolk. As the relevant conveyance recites; 'there is no burying ground belonging to the said town of Mountsorrel which is a very great inconvenience to the inhabitants thereof who are obliged to carry their dead to be buried in the adjacent towns with great trouble and expense'.[67] (At the time, the north end of Mountsorrel lay in the ecclesiastical parish of Barrow, and the south end of Mountsorrel in the ecclesiastical parish of Rothley).[68] In 1778, he leased land to the Mountsorrel Granite Company for the construction of a private or village hospital.[69] Sir John was responsible for moving the fifteenth century market cross, known as the Lantern Cross, from Mountsorrel to Swithland Hall park,[70] replacing it in 1793 with the Butter Market that still stands there.

Fig 1.7 Lantern Cross, Swithland Hall park.

Sir John owned the granite quarries (and the associated mineral rights) in Mountsorrel, as well as having other interests in that village. The development of the Mountsorrel quarries began in earnest during Sir John's lifetime, with the stone being used for road building and surfacing. In 1758, Sir John gave £200, spread over four years, to the Turnpike Trustees on condition that they laid 'a granite causeway' eighteen feet wide through Mountsorrel village.[71] This stone was broken with 30lb hammers into roughly squared blocks and laid in rows, with the smoothest face upwards.[72]

*Fig 1.8
Butter Market,
Mountsorrel.*

Between 1754–60, Sir John purchased small pockets of land in Barrow, Quorn, Mountsorrel, Rothley and Woodhouse, including Quorn water mill. In 1770 he bought the last 144 acres of Buddon Wood from Jane Symes, a descendant of the Chaveneys. In Swithland, he not only continued the process of buying up land and property but was probably responsible for rebuilding some of the farmsteads.

Joseph Prior continued to serve as Danvers' steward until his death in 1767. Thomas Thomas acted as Sir John's servant and butler for many years; in his will[73] Sir John left £150 per annum to 'my trusty servant and butler Thomas Thomas for his many years care and fidelity towards me'. John Vernum served as his coachman.

Nichols mentions another of Sir John's servants:

> Among the other domestics of Sir John Danvers was an old stout porter, a famous walker, who has not unfrequently been dispatched as a pedestrian, distinguished by a sort of ancient constable's staff, as a badge of office, from Swithland to London and then occasionally to Bath.[74]

Another story, which may or may not be true, has been linked to Sir John and his maintenance of the traditional manor court practices.

> The court of East Goscote was originally held at Mowde Bush Hill in Syston Parish. When the Hundred of Goscote was divided into East and West, the court of East Goscote was transferred to Mountsorrel, where what was still called the Mowde Bush Court was held within the present century by Sir John Danvers. In order that the court might be properly constituted, a turf was duly cut on Mowde Bush Hill and carried to Mountsorrel whenever a sitting was held.[75]

After a long illness, Sir John died in Bath on 21st September 1796. After lying in state at the Crown Inn, Leicester, 'surmounted by a magnificent plumage, decorated with escutcheons, and all the paraphernalia of funeral pomp',[76] he was interred in the Danvers chapel at Swithland under the memorial plaque that he had erected some years previously.

> Died on Wednesday se'nnight, after a long illness, at his lodgings on the South Parade, Bath. Sir John Danvers, Bart. of Swithland, in this county, age 75. His estates, real and personal, have devolved by will to his daughter, the Hon Mrs Butler Danvers; at her decease to her husband, the Hon Augustus Butler Danvers, second son of the Countess of Lanesborough, and in remainder to their only son, now an infant. The real estates in this and other counties amount in old rents to near £10,000 per annum, in which the property of timber is immense. The personal estate consists of near £200,000. By a former Will the family of the male branches of the Danvers were made sole heirs but (this) was lately revoked soon after the birth of his daughter's son.[77]

The sale of Sir John's effects is reported to have lasted fifteen days. Furniture, prints, books, paintings and one hundred and fifty cases of wine were sold. Among the paintings, Nichols lists a portrait of the Earl of Danby by Sir Anthony van Dyck (more reliable sources suggest that this portrait had been presented by Sir Joseph Danvers to Sir Robert Walpole some years previously), a picture of Sir John and Lady Danvers with two of their children by Edward Penny and one of Sir Joseph Danvers and his family.

Mary Danvers (1753–1802)

Mary Danvers was the only one of Sir John Danvers' six children to survive into adulthood, and he was clearly anxious that his family name should not die out with his daughter. He therefore arranged a marriage for her, when she was thirty-nine years old, with the sixteen-year-old Augustus Richard Butler, second son of the second Earl of Lanesborough. The marriage took place in March 1792.

On the death of Sir John Danvers, therefore, the Swithland estate passed by marriage to the Butler family of Ireland. Sir John's choice for a marriage partner for his daughter was, however, unfortunate. Augustus Richard's stewardship of his inheritance was a near unmitigated disaster.

The Butlers originated in Waresley, Huntingdonshire, but settled in Ireland in the reign of James I. Sir Stephen Butler of Belturbet, Co. Cavan, was one of the 'undertakers' in the plantation of Ulster – for which he received a grant of 2,000 acres called Clonose in Co. Cavan. Succeeding generations of the family were involved in government service, particularly in Ireland.

Sir Stephen Butler's second son, Francis Butler of Belturbet, espoused the Royalist cause during the Civil War. He and his brother Stephen represented Belturbet in the first Parliament after the Restoration of Charles II: Francis in 1662 and from 1692–99, Stephen from 1661–62.

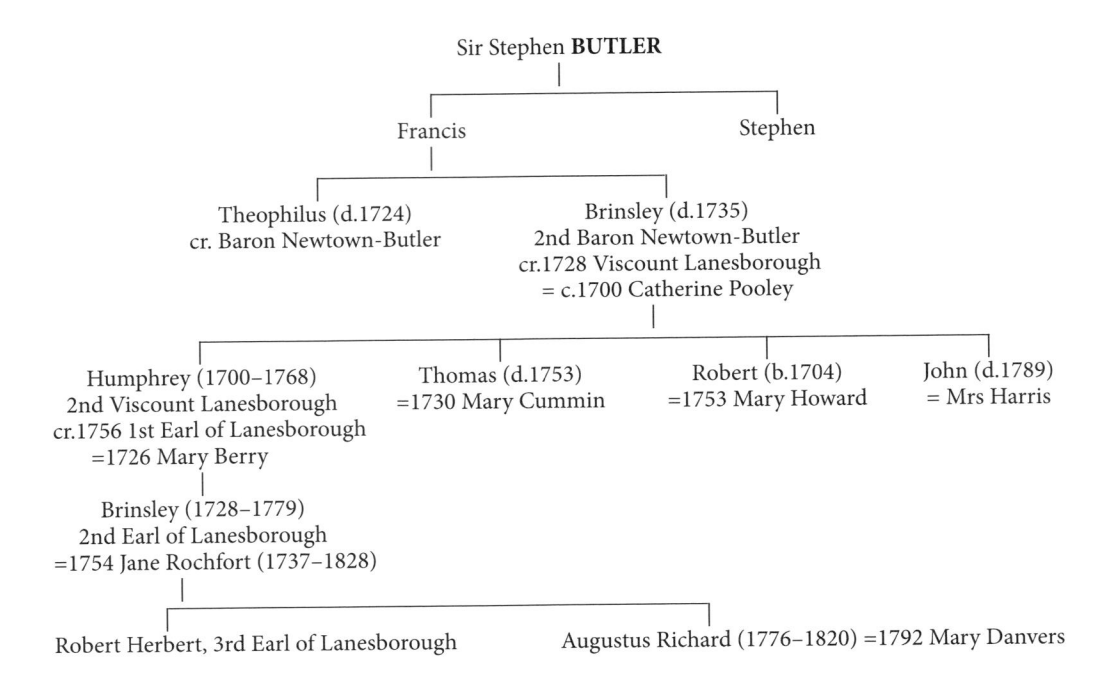

```
                          Sir Stephen BUTLER
                    ┌───────────┴───────────┐
                 Francis                 Stephen
           ┌────────┴────────┐
   Theophilus (d.1724)      Brinsley (d.1735)
   cr. Baron Newtown-Butler  2nd Baron Newtown-Butler
                             cr.1728 Viscount Lanesborough
                             = c.1700 Catherine Pooley
```

Humphrey (1700–1768)	Thomas (d.1753)	Robert (b.1704)	John (d.1789)
2nd Viscount Lanesborough	=1730 Mary Cummin	=1753 Mary Howard	= Mrs Harris
cr.1756 1st Earl of Lanesborough			
=1726 Mary Berry			

Brinsley (1728–1779)
2nd Earl of Lanesborough
=1754 Jane Rochfort (1737–1828)

Robert Herbert, 3rd Earl of Lanesborough   Augustus Richard (1776–1820) =1792 Mary Danvers

Francis Butler, however, fell out with James II; he was involved in the Act of Attainder in 1689 and his estates were sequestrated. His son Theophilus, Member of Parliament for Belturbet and Privy Councillor, was created Baron of Newtown Butler, but died without heir. Under a special provision in the creation of the barony, therefore, he was succeeded by his brother, Brinsley, as Lord Newtown, second Baron of Newtown Butler in 1724. Brinsley had entered Trinity College, Dublin, in 1686, and married Catherine Pooley in about 1700 with whom he had twenty-three children. Sometime Colonel of the Irish Battle-Axe Guards, Brinsley served as MP for Kells 1703–13 and Belturbet 1713–24 and became an Irish Privy Councillor in 1726. He was created a Viscount in the Irish peerage in 1728, taking the lately extinct title of Viscount Lanesborough of Co. Longford.

Brinsley's son, Humphrey Butler, the second Viscount Lanesborough, followed his father's career of public service. Sometime Captain of the Battle-Axe Guards, he served as MP for Belturbet 1725–35 in succession to his father. He was Sheriff of Co. Cavan in 1727 and of Co. Westmeath in 1728. After succeeding to the title as second Viscount Lanesborough in 1736, he was appointed a privy councillor for Ireland in 1749 and served as Governor of Co. Cavan. In 1756 he was created Earl of Lanesborough in the Irish peerage. Humphrey's only son, Brinsley Butler, the second Earl, was educated at Trinity College, Dublin, from 1745–50. He was appointed Sheriff of Co. Cavan in 1755 and of Co. Westmeath 1763, and served as MP for Co. Cavan from 1751 to 1768, when he succeeded to the title. In 1765 he was appointed a member of the Privy Council for Ireland, but then was removed from office in 1770 for voting against the Government. He was re-sworn in

1774, and served until his death in 1779. Brinsley had two sons, Robert Herbert (who succeeded to the title as third Earl) and Augustus Richard, who married Mary Danvers in March 1792.

Augustus Richard Butler Danvers (1776–1820)

Augustus Richard did at least fulfil his role in securing the Butler Danvers' succession. Mary conceived two sons by him: George Augustus (1793–1798) and George John Danvers (born 1794). Relations between Mary and Augustus Richard never developed and they agreed to live separately. (Given their age gap and the arranged nature of their marriage this was perhaps not surprising.) Augustus Richard stayed in Swithland and a house was bought for Mary in London at Upper Seymour Street, Portman Square. Perhaps that was her side of the bargain. She lived in London until her death in 1802.

Augustus Richard meanwhile led a colourful life. In 1795 he fought a duel in Hyde Park after a dispute at the theatre. *The Times* reported that:

> On Wednesday a duel was fought in Hyde Park, between the Hon Mr Butler and another gentleman in consequence of a misunderstanding the evening before at the play. After firing two pistols each the seconds interfered and the business was adjusted to the satisfaction of all parties.[78]

In 1801, he again made headlines.

> Butler Danvers and Mr Penn started on Monday from Hyde Park Corner to decide a bet of a rump and dozen, upon the question of which making the best of his way on foot to the five mile stone at Turnham Green, would return with most expedition. They set off at ten minutes past one, Mr Danvers at full speed and Mr Penn also ran to keep up with him ... The run at the outset winded both, but Mr Penn took the lead on the return, and Mr Danvers being seized with a pain in his side at Kensington, the other came in easy, at eleven minutes past three, having gone ten miles in two hours and a minute ... It is now high fashion to run, or at least trot through the streets at six miles an hour. A running walk is absolutely necessary for any young man who has the least pretension to ton. You must lounge in a hurry and saunter with expedition. It is an old proverb – the more haste, the worst speed; but Bond Street daily shows us the more hurry, the less to do.[79]

In 1807, Augustus Richard, along with others, was acquitted 'on an indictment for a conspiracy', the nature of which is unclear.[80] On 7th April 1808, *The Times* reported that Hon Danvers Butler was summoned to appear at the Middlesex Quarter Sessions for assaulting Mr Hughes, a bookseller, in Wigmore Street.

The real tragedy, however, was that Augustus Richard had a fatal propensity for getting into debt. In 1796, for example, he was in court over a debt of £4,000 to a Mr Collier[81] and in 1797 once more in court over a debt of £500 to a Mr Norton for goods sold and delivered.[82] A reference in one of Joanna Southcott's accusations against money lenders indicates that Augustus Richard was one of many caught up in the ruinous money-lending practices of the day. In accusing the money-lender, a Mr King, Joanna Southcott described the way in which Mr King had used Augustus Richard as an excuse to another customer to give him further bills instead of money, because he had 'made use' of the money obtained from the lender in order 'to free Mr Butler Danvers from a sponging house'.[83]

From 1796 to 1802 Augustus Richard lived in Swithland with, it was alleged, a Miss Sturt as his 'Kept Lady'. The Swithland church register records, in an 1802 list of children who had been named or privately baptized but not yet brought to church, Mary Sophia Eliza, the daughter of a Miss Sturt or Short, 'supposed to be by Hon Augustus Richard Butler Danvers', and Emily, also a daughter of Miss Short or Sturt 'supposed to be by the same'. Records indicate that Augustus Richard and Eliza had three children before they were able to marry, and six thereafter.

In his will, Sir John Danvers had left his Leicestershire estates to his daughter for her life, to Augustus Richard for his life, and then to their son George John Danvers.

> To my daughter Mary Butler, wife of the Hon Augustus Richard Butler of Baker Street, Portman Square, Middlesex, all my manors, messuages, farms, lands, tenements and hereditaments (whether freehold, leasehold, or copyhold) in the county of Leicestershire – for and during her natural life, and after her decease, to Augustus Richard Butler if he survive her, and after the decease of the survivor of them, to my grandson John Danvers Butler.[84]

The non-Leicestershire estates, however, were bequeathed, subject to certain annuities, to Augustus Richard absolutely.

> And as to the rest residue and remainder of my estates and effects whatsoever both real and personal wheresoever, I give devise and bequeath the same to the said Augustus Richard Butler his heirs executors administrators and assigns.

Proud of his name, Sir John Danvers directed that his successors carry his name and arms.

> And I do hereby will and direct that the said Augustus Richard Butler and my said grandson, and all and every other person and persons who shall under and by virtue of any devise hereby made come unto the possession of any my said real estates, do and shall take and use my surname and family arms.

Augustus Richard changed his name to Butler-Danvers by royal warrant in September 1796 to comply with Sir John's wishes, but he took less care over the estates he had inherited.

Although appointed joint executrix of Sir John's will with her husband, Mary refused to act. For the last years of her life she lived apart from her husband at her home in Upper Seymour Street, Portman Square, London where she died on 11th May 1802. Her personal property, principally a small legacy that she had received from her mother, she noticeably left to her son, not to her husband.[85] For his part, Augustus Richard re-married – with breathtaking speed – to Eliza Bizarre Sturt, at 3pm on 17th May 1802 at St Mary le Bone, Middlesex. The marriage took place less than a week after Mary's death, and three hours after her burial at Bunhill Fields in London.[86] Augustus Richard and Eliza Sturt had been living together at Swithland Hall for some ten years and already had three children; they were doubtless keen to legalize their relationship as soon as possible.

Despite his free lifestyle, Augustus Richard dabbled briefly in politics. When a dissolution of Parliament was expected in 1800, radicals in Leicester put his name forward for Parliament, as a partner to John Manners of Buckminster. In the event, there was a by-election, not a general election, in which Manners was opposed by Thomas Babington of Rothley Temple, and which Babington won. Augustus Richard was persuaded to look for a seat elsewhere.[87] There is no record, though, that he did so.

At the turn of the nineteenth century, Swithland must have felt it was experiencing revolutionary change. Locally, the last male Danvers had died, a ne'er-do-well Irishman had inherited the estate and, to finance his debts, was rapidly selling it off. Nationally, imposed radical changes in agricultural practice affected everybody, with the enclosure of Swithland and Thurcaston in 1799 and of Charnwood Forest and Rothley Plain in 1808. (Preliminary allotments of the latter were made in 1815, although the final Award was not made until 1828.) Enclosure permitted more efficient use of the land, but the tenants suffered and the process was expensive. Augustus Richard cared little for his estates and tenantry, and was consistently and conspicuously profligate with his money.

Augustus Richard's financial transactions read like a rake's progress. As early as 1792 he had borrowed £11,000. Shortly afterwards he borrowed a further £1,375 to service the debt. In 1797, almost immediately after he came into his inheritance on the death of Sir John Danvers, he took out a mortgage on, and subsequently sold, all the properties outside Leicestershire which he had been bequeathed: the manor of Basmey, in the parish of Eaton Soken, Beds; the manor of Prescott, in the parish of Cropredy, Oxon; houses, cottages and land in Aston-in the-Walls, in Wappenham, in Appletree, Oxon. and in Canons Ashby, Northants; property in St Clement Danes and in Hanover Square, London. The Leicestershire estates were protected against sale because Augustus Richard had only a life interest, but the Enclosure Acts allowed him to raise further mortgages in order to pay off the costs of Enclosure. In June 1799 he took out a mortgage of £2,515 on land at Swithland; in July 1799 he took out a further mortgage of £1,569 on land at Thurcaston.[88] By December 1802 he was in debt to the tune of £13,500. The Leicestershire estates then only yielded £4,230 per annum, so, unable to pay his creditors, he parted with his life interest for £12,000 in order to discharge most of his debts.[89] Early in 1815, again hopelessly in debt, he borrowed £10,000 from his son, George John – with a promise that it would be secured by a life insurance policy.

In 1815 Augustus Richard became heir apparent to the Earldom of Lanesborough. The fourth Earl, Augustus Richard's brother's son, was a bachelor and a lunatic.[90] George John was clearly anxious that his father should not further dispossess him of the Lanesborough estates, so, in August 1815, as part of his own marriage settlement,[91] he ensured that his father executed a deed of covenant with him 'that if he, Augustus Richard Butler Danvers, became entitled to the Lanesborough estates, then (he) would settle those estates on George John Butler Danvers'. George John then agreed to allow the sale of all the Leicestershire property excluding Swithland, Thurcaston and Mountsorrel and a few other specific properties, in order to raise £28,000 to pay off his father's debts.[92] Some 600 acres in Quorn, Rothley, Barrow, Cossington and Woodhouse Eaves were sold at auction at The Crown Inn, Mountsorrel on 30–31st October 1815.[93] The properties included the former Kingston land at Rothley (sold to Richard Fowkes), Quorn Mill and farm (sold to the Farnhams), land at Roecliffe (sold to James Heygate) and woodland and land at Swithland Wood and Hallgates (sold to the Earl of Stamford and Warrington).[94] The overall intention was to secure the financial future of George John, his wife and heirs, by freeing the remaining estates from debt, paying for the promised life insurance policy, and preventing any alienation of the expectant interest in the Lanesborough estates.

Whether from choice or necessity, Augustus Richard spent the remaining years of his life living in France – possibly in order to evade his creditors, or perhaps because his son insisted. A later commentator observed that 'the late Honble A. R. Butler Danvers was in difficulties for years previous to his death'.[95] He died in 1820 in Boulogne-sur-Mer, France, and was buried in the British Protestant chapel there.[96] During his stewardship he had managed to lose the entire Danvers landholding outside Leicestershire and virtually everything in the county as well, except the core holding of the manors of Swithland, Thurcaston and Mountsorrel. Augustus Richard was succeeded by his far more conventional son, George John Butler Danvers, grandson of Sir John Danvers, who set about building up his estates and position.

George John Butler Danvers (1794–1866)

When George John Butler Danvers succeeded his father in 1820, at the age of twenty-six, the effects of the industrial revolution in the towns were beginning to reach out into the countryside. The social prestige of landowners was increasingly challenged by manufacturers and merchants who were content to invest the bulk of their capital in commerce and industry, which meant that the large estates in Leicestershire tended to remain in the hands of the older gentry. George John successfully applied himself to public service and to re-shaping the Swithland estate. He was educated at St John's College, Cambridge and married Frances Arabella Fremantle, third daughter of Col Stephen Fremantle, in August 1815. George John, who was described as a conservative in politics, served as Sheriff of Leicestershire in 1831 and was a Justice of the Peace in the county.

Fig 1.9 John Flower engraving, Swithland Hall c. 1826 [97] (Lantern Cross in foreground).

Fig 1.10 George John Danvers Butler Danvers, fifth Earl.[98]

Soon after he succeeded his father, George John was faced with claims that the estates were not rightfully his. On the death of Henry Danvers in 1687, the Leicestershire estates had passed to succeeding eldest surviving sons: Samuel, then Joseph, and then John. Henry Danvers' youngest child, William (1666–1740), had settled in Shepshed. In 1829, his descendants began to make claims that they were the rightful inheritors. Their grounds for claiming this were based on a number of different, and sometimes conflicting, allegations.[99] They alleged that the estates were settled in tail male, that is through male heirs only, so that, at Sir John Danvers' death, they should not have passed through his daughter, Mary Danvers; that George John had been born before Mary Danvers had married Augustus Richard and was illegitimate; that Mary Danvers' child had died and another secretly substituted after being 'brought to Swithland Hall in a parcel at night'; that Mary Danvers had never given birth to any children; that a will of Sir John Danvers, in which he had given his estates to William Danvers of Shepshed as his closest male heir, had been destroyed by David Chapman (a servant of Augustus Richard) and that another will, giving them to Mary and Augustus Richard, had been forged by Thomas Thomas (servant to Sir John).

The sudden emergence of these allegations

```
                    Henry DANVERS = Ann Sacheverell nee Coke
                    (1623–1687)    |    (d.1686)
        ┌──────────────────────────┴──────────────────────────┐
Samuel = Elizabeth Morewood                    William = Ellen Lacy
(d.1693) |    (d.1719)                       (1666–1740) | (d.1732)
   Joseph = Frances Babington                  Richard = Elizabeth Leaptrap
(1686–1753) | (1694–1759)                    (1704–1755) |
     John = Mary Watson                        William = Ellen Walker
(1723–1796) | (d.1798)                       (1733–1761) |
       Mary = Augustus Richard                 William = Sarah Lester
   (1753–1802) |   BUTLER                    (1758–1840) |
               |  (1776–1820)                             |
         George John                           John = Elizabeth Stokes
       BUTLER DANVERS                       (1790–1880) |
         (1794–1866)                              William
                                                  (b.1813)
```

may well have been connected with the fall from grace of David Chapman. Chapman apparently started as coachman to Augustus Richard, was then appointed steward, and became the largest single farmer in the village at the Hall Farm. He fell behind with his rent, however, and was evicted in 1827. His was just one of many depositions that were taken from residents of the locality and from people who had worked at Swithland Hall in order to back up the allegations. The claim must have been extremely divisive. The Shepshed Danvers, however, were mostly framework knitters and lacked the financial resources to mount a legal action. There was minor skirmishing for the next fifteen years. The allegations were finally tested before a special jury at Leicester Assizes in August 1844. George John brought two actions for non-payment of rent in respect of the Blue Bell Public House, Mountsorrel (Danvers v Danvers & Antill) and in respect of another house in Mountsorrel (Danvers v Danvers & Noon). The occupiers, various members of the Shepshed Danvers family, had apparently refused to recognize George John as their landlord. However, the special jury heard that this had not always been so: a few years previously they had so recognized him, having paid rent to George John's agent. The judge therefore directed the jury to return a verdict for the plaintiff, and awarded costs against the defendants. Another attempt was mounted by the Shepshed Danvers to prosecute their claim in 1864 in a Queen's Bench action heard in London; this was again refused.[100]

George John's first task as lord of the manor was to tidy up the family finances. Far from being an absentee landlord, he contributed significantly to the life of the village. Churchwardens' records, for example, indicate that he was a regular attender at the annual Vestry Meeting. He was a benefactor of Swithland church. He was also a great builder – helped possibly by the general prosperity of agriculture after 1837. Swithland Hall being in significant disrepair in the early 1820s, George John set about building a new hall on a new site. It was sufficiently complete in 1834 to permit occupation. George John was also responsible for building many of the cottages that lend

Swithland its present character. The semi-detached cottages at Nos. 140–142 Main Street date from about 1840, as does No. 144. The semi-detached cottages at Nos. 81–83 bear the date 1842 and the initials GJBD. In 1842 the school was enlarged. No. 146 was built in 1845. The semi-detached cottages at Nos. 123–125 were built in 1850, as was No. 127. The semi-detached cottages at Nos. 132–134 date from about 1860. George John's first wife shared his philanthropic nature, founding an infant school in Mountsorrel c. 1848.[101]

Augustus Richard, despite being heir to the Earl of Lanesborough, had never succeeded to the Earldom. In 1806 the title had passed from Robert Herbert Butler, third Earl and elder brother of Augustus Richard, to Robert Herbert's eldest son, Brinsley. The fourth Earl also appears to have had a propensity to fall into debt: in 1768–69, the records of the Irish High Courts show judgments against him for £600, £800, £1,000, £3,226 and £4,363. At some point he was declared a lunatic, and his affairs were made subject to the scrutiny of the Lord High Chancellor of Ireland. This did not prevent a further judgment against him in 1827, this time for £48,000, although the debt was discharged in 1834. He lived until 1847, dying unmarried and insane,[102] leaving his affairs to be settled under a will made over forty years previously in 1806. Since Brinsley's younger brother had predeceased him, George John became the fifth Earl of Lanesborough. On his succession to the title in 1847, George John served for seventeen years as a representative peer for Ireland in the House of Lords. His improved finances and aristocratic status encouraged him to add two new wings and two gatehouses to Swithland Hall, all of which was completed in 1852.

In November 1851, following the death of his first wife, George John married Frederica Emma, youngest daughter of Charles Bishop and widow of Sir Richard Hunter of Delaney House, Sussex. Both he and his Countess subscribed generously towards the creation of a Swithland Village Library in 1854. George John died in July 1866 at his London lodgings at 8 Great Stanhope Street, Park Lane, London.[103] He and his Countess were buried in the Danvers aisle in Swithland. He left no children, and was succeeded by his nephew, John Vansittart. (In 1848, shortly after the fifth Earl succeeded to the title, John Vansittart Danvers, Charles Henry Danvers and their three sisters, Frances Georgina Danvers, Emily Rosa Danvers and Harriet Eliza Danvers, were granted the same rank and precedence as if it had been their father who had succeeded to the title.)

Fig 1.11 Frederica Emma, fifth Countess.

John Vansittart Danvers Butler (1839–1905)

The sixth Earl of Lanesborough, John Vansittart Danvers Butler, inevitably saw himself more as a Butler than as a Danvers, and was more interested in his Irish estates than in his Swithland ones. This did not, however, prevent his representatives from building up his holdings in Mountsorrel, especially in those areas where granite had begun to be quarried.[104] Not long after his succession, England experienced a depression in agriculture which continued until the Second World War and affected agricultural rents. The sixth Earl nevertheless maintained an expensive lifestyle, as well as following the Butler tradition of public service.

John Vansittart Danvers was born in India in April 1839 where his father, the Hon Charles Augustus Butler Danvers was serving in the Madras Artillery. He was educated at Rugby, subsequently entering the Royal Navy, becoming a sub-lieutenant in 1859 and lieutenant in 1860. In July 1863 he was appointed flag lieutenant to Sir Charles Fremantle, Commander-in-Chief, Devonport, and was promoted to commander in 1866. In October 1871 he was placed on the retired list at that rank, and promoted to captain on the retired list under an Order in Council in 1881. In 1864, he married Ann Elizabeth, daughter of Rev John Dixon Clarke of Bedford Hall, Northumberland.

Described as of a retiring disposition, John Vansittart took no major interest in the affairs of Leicestershire, except as a subscriber to various philanthropic institutions. He was sufficiently interested in cricket to play for Leicestershire in 1875, and to serve as president of the Leicestershire County Cricket Club from 1879–85, but resided only intermittently at Swithland Hall, leaving the estate to be managed by his agent Mr Clough Taylor. Instead, John Vansittart devoted most of his time to his Irish estates and his horses. He was Deputy Lieutenant of County Cavan from 1876–1900, and in 1870 was elected as an Irish representative peer.

In 1883 the Lanesborough estates were reckoned to consist of 7,946 acres in County Cavan, 6,606 acres in County Fermanagh and 1,845 acres in Leicestershire[105] – a total of 16,397 acres, worth £17,419 per year.[106] There was also a significant income in the shape of royalties deriving from the granite quarries at Mountsorrel. John Vansittart appears to have lived in a style in keeping with his income. He

Fig 1.12 John Vansittart Danvers Butler, sixth Earl, 1879.

Fig. 1.13 The sixth Earl, funeral cortege, 1905, Dale Walk.

was not present in Swithland at the time of the 1871 Census, but in 1881 his household included nineteen servants living at the hall: a governess, housekeeper, two kitchen maids, a scullery maid, two housemaids, two nurses, two coachmen, a butler and under butler, two footmen, a page boy and two grooms. In 1891, the household included sixteen servants living at the hall: a cook/housekeeper, a lady's maid, two nurses, three housemaids, two kitchen maids, a scullery maid, a butler and under butler, two footmen, a hall boy and a coachman.

At the beginning of the twentieth century, throughout all of England, the intrusion of urban life into the countryside became much more evident. Although John Vansittart managed to purchase the last remaining major outside landholding in Swithland – the church's glebe[107] – he was forced to cede a significant acreage of his lands for the construction of Swithland Reservoir and the Great Central Railway, both of which were built under private acts of parliament.

John Vansittart died aged sixty-six at Lanesborough Lodge, Belturbet, Co. Cavan in September 1905, but he was buried in Swithland with due ceremony. His coffin, covered with the white ensign, was wheeled on a bier from Swithland Hall to the church by eight bearers chosen from employees on the estate. He was succeeded by his son, Charles John Brinsley Butler, Lord Newtown Butler, who was then a major in the 2nd Battalion of the Coldstream Guards.

Charles John Brinsley Butler (1865–1929)

The seventh Earl, who spent much of his life as a soldier, was more English than his father. During his time agricultural rents continued to be depressed so that many country houses, including his own Swithland Hall, could not be supported by their estates. This did not prevent the seventh Earl, however, from indulging in later life his penchant for actresses and house parties.

Charles John Brinsley Butler was born at Devonport and educated at Eton. He had an extensive military career – becoming a captain in 1898, major in 1904, and lieutenant-colonel in 1919. He first joined the Irish Militia and received a commission in the 4th Irish Fusiliers. He joined the Coldstream Guards in 1888, rising to the rank of captain in 1898 and major in 1904. He volunteered for active service when the South African War (Boer War) broke out and served throughout the campaign from 1899 to 1902. He subsequently joined the regular army and by 1904 was a field officer in the Guards. In 1908, he served as Assistant Military Secretary to the Duke of Connaught, Commander-in-Chief and High Commander, Mediterranean. In 1909, he became Military Secretary to Earl Grey, Governor-General of Canada, before retiring with the rank of lieutenant-colonel in 1913. When the Great War broke out he joined up, receiving the command of a battalion of the Brigade of Guards. In 1915, he was lieutenant-colonel of the 10th London Regiment, but in the summer of 1917 he suffered from ill-health and returned home, finally retiring from the army in 1921.

In 1891, Charles John Brinsley married his first wife Dorothea Gwladys, daughter of General Sir H. Tombs VC, by whom he had a son and two daughters. Their son, John Brinsley died in 1912 of tuberculosis at the age of twenty-one. Their eldest daughter, Eileen Gladys, married the Duke of Sutherland. Their youngest daughter, Moyra Elizabeth, belonged to the circle of friends of the Prince of Wales. The Countess died in 1920. Shortly afterwards, Charles John Brinsley married the actress Dorothy Kate Watkins, née Brand, daughter of a theatrical impresario. Kate Brand, who appeared on the London stage at the turn of the century, was married to Captain Guy Watkins and Charles John Brinsley was cited as the co-respondent in their divorce suit. The wedding at the Register Office, Princes Row, Buckingham Palace Road, London, was followed by a 'benedictory service' behind locked doors at the church of St Jude-on-the-Hill, Hampstead. The Earl had intended that the service take place in the Chapel Royal, Savoy, but the chaplain refused to conduct a religious service for the wedding.[108] Shortly after their marriage, Dorothy Kate attended a New Year's Eve dance in Swithland Village Hall, but for the most part she lived in London, making only occasional visits to Swithland Hall.[109] It was not a happy marriage.

In civilian life, Charles John Brinsley served as a representative peer of Ireland in the House of Lords. He never took an active part in Leicestershire affairs, but led a retired life at Swithland, where he served as chairman of

Fig 1.14 Charles John Brinsley Butler, seventh Earl, with his mother and brothers, [standing left to right]: Henry Cavendish, Francis Almeric, Brian.

the Parish Meeting from 1925 until his death. He had a reputation as an all-round sportsman and was particularly interested in golfing, shooting, fishing and cricket. From 1913 to 1918 he followed his father's interest in cricket by serving as President of the Leicestershire County Cricket Club. In his retirement, he formed the Swithland Cricket Club who played in Swithland Park; he attended their matches and sometimes played. His last appearance for the team was in 1927, when he collapsed while playing. Swithland Reservoir, where he held both the shooting and fishing rights, was a favourite spot for both duck shooting and pike fishing. The seventh Earl was also a keen supporter of the Rothley Golf Club. It was said that he 'used to love strolling over the course, and regarded it as a second garden, taking a great pride in its appearance.'[110] The Charnwood Archery and Lawn Tennis Club was formed during his time as Earl and played on a site behind the rectory – on what is now known as the Rectory Spinney. There was a fine pavilion and grass tennis courts. Charles John was President of Swithland Cricket Club, President of Rothley Golf Club, President of the Old Coldstreamers' Association and President of the Charnwood Archery and Lawn Tennis Club.

Despite his commitment to the local community, Charles John left his estates considerably more impoverished than when he inherited them. The downturn in the prosperity of British agriculture during his stewardship cannot have helped him. He undoubtedly had greater resources at his command than many, but he chose to spend them on entertaining, rather than on improving his estate. Mains sewerage, for example, had been installed in the village in 1896, but most of the Swithland estate houses had to wait until 1938 to be connected. One of the seventh Earl's hobbies was watercolour

Fig 1.15 Funeral cortege for the seventh Earl, 1929, passing the Danvers Chapel.

painting; he was adept at drawing caricatures and cartoons – with which he would entertain his guests. Unfortunately his name appeared on more than one occasion on police court sheets among those summoned for non-payment of rates.[111] He died in 1929 and was succeeded by his brother.[112]

Henry Cavendish Butler (1868–1950)

The eighth Earl, Henry Cavendish Butler was a gentler character than his brother. Irish by birth, he was educated at Winchester and went on to farm in New Zealand, where he was appointed to the governor's staff. In 1894 he returned to England and married Isabel Daniell, who died in 1905. During the First World War, he held an appointment at the War Office. In 1917 he married for a second time, to Grace Lillian Abdy, daughter of Sir Anthony Abdy Bt. They lost their second son during the Second World War. The Hon Patrick Danvers Butler, a captain in the Scots Guards, was killed at Anzio in 1944.

Across Leicestershire, the financial burden of maintaining a large household, together with the cost of meeting heavy death duties with every succeeding generation, had led to the diminution or total dismemberment of many large estates. The Rothley Temple Estate was sold up in 1892. The Stamfords sold their Bradgate Leicestershire estates in 1925. The Beaumanor Estate at Woodhouse was sold in 1946. Henry Cavendish, however, managed to keep the Swithland Estate together by living in more modest circumstances. He was well known, for example, in Leicester, to which he frequently made shopping expeditions on the bus with his carrier bag.

A keen sportsman, Henry Cavendish hunted with the Quorn before the 1914–18 war. He was known as a good shot and an enthusiastic gardener, associating with several Leicester horticultural associations. He supported the Scout Movement, and, from 1939–49, was Chairman of the Leicestershire Scouts Council. Locally, he served as President of the Charnwood Tennis Club, which was based behind Swithland Rectory.[113] He was Chairman of Swithland Parish Meeting from 1930–50 and Vice-President of the Mountsorrel branch of the British Legion. In August 1950, he collapsed when going into lunch and died on Tuesday 22nd August, aged eighty-two.[114] He was buried at Swithland on 25th August. 'By special family request, Mrs B.R. Gimson, who was organist at the church for seventeen years, played Lord Lanesborough's favourite hymn'.[115] He was succeeded by his elder son, Denis Anthony Brian, Lord Newtown Butler.

LEFT
Fig 1.16
Henry Cavendish Butler, eighth Earl.

ABOVE
Fig 1.17
The eighth Earl and his Countess, in fancy dress.

Denis Anthony Brian Butler (1918–1998)

The ninth Earl inherited an estate badly in need of extensive modernization. Born in 1918, Denis Anthony Brian was educated at Stowe School. He joined the Leicestershire Yeomanry, rising to the rank of lieutenant in 1939. In that year he married Bettyne Ione Everard, who came from a local brewing family. They had two daughters, the elder of whom died in 1950 aged only six years. Sadly, the marriage was dissolved in the same year.

In January 1951, the Earl delighted his local friends and parishioners by entertaining the Hollywood film star Yvonne de Carlo at Swithland Hall one weekend. Chaperoned by her aunt, she was guest of honour at the annual

Fig 1.18 Denis, Lord Newtown Butler, with Yeomanry colleagues.

Yeomanry Ball. Born Peggy Yvonne Middleton on 1st September 1922 at Vancouver, British Columbia, Canada, de Carlo began a screen career in 1942 that continued into the 1990s.[116] Inevitably, they enjoyed some local and press speculative attention at the time, but both denied romance, though a friend said of Denis that he 'fell for her in a big way'. Journalist, Donald Zec quoted de Carlo as saying: 'The Oyl certainly knows how to en'ertain'. Another of the Earl's film star friends to bring celebrity to Swithland was Belinda Lee (1935-1961). She was a Rank Studios starlet of the 1950s who appeared in 'Life with the Lyons' (1954), 'The Belles of St Trinians' (1954) and 'Man of the Moment' (1955). Described as a 'sultry blonde bombshell', Belinda Lee left Rank soon afterwards and went to the continent where she made a series of sexy Italian films before being killed tragically in a car accident.

Fig 1.19 The ninth Earl entertaining Yvonne de Carlo, 1951.

The ninth Earl settled to pursue a life of considerable public service. From 1953 to 1964 he was Chairman of the Guide Dogs for the Blind Association in Leicestershire, serving as its president from 1964 to 1986. He was a member of Barrow Rural District Council. He was appointed Deputy Lieutenant for Leicestershire in 1962 and a Justice of the Peace in 1967. In addition, he was a member of the Gas Consumers Council 1973–78, a member of Trent Regional Health Authority from 1974–82, Vice-Chairman 1978–82, and Chairman of the Loughborough and District Housing Association 1978–85. He particularly enjoyed his involvement with the Mainline Steam Trust (Great Central Railway) of which he was a founding member, and he served for some years as its president.

At Swithland Hall the ninth Earl collected a substantial 00-guage electric model railway. A friend, describing the size of the installation, spoke of 'dozens of tracks; trains going in all directions; stations, bridges, village scenes ... One watched in amazement when an express hurtled into a tunnel and disappeared out of sight! It had, in fact, gone through the wall into the next room. And there was Denis – in the centre – controlling this incredible display like a real-life signalman ... and enjoying every minute of it'.[117]

An enthusiastic and knowledgeable shot, the ninth Earl maintained a pheasant and wildfowl shoot in the village for many years. Maintenance of the estate, however, became an increasing burden and it did not prove possible to assemble the necessary resources. It is supposed that the cost of his divorce settlement, together with the financial pressures of maintaining hall and estate, led in July 1954 to the sale of the land comprising the Swithland Estate. Some land and properties were sold to sitting tenants; the remainder was sold at auction.

Almost seven hundred years previously, in 1255, Robert le Waleys had acquired manorial rights in Swithland. Now the estate, built on that holding, was split up and the manor of Swithland, of which generations of le Waleys, Walcotes, Danvers and Butlers had been the lords, was finally dispersed.

Denis Anthony Brian retained Swithland Hall, a few cottages, and the woodland, but, shortly after the death of his mother in 1983, he sold the hall and most of its contents and moved to Kegworth, Leicestershire. The sale of the furniture and effects attracted some considerable attention when a valuable sculpture, a bust by Bellini, was not properly attributed at the time. The Earl is reputed to have been discreetly compensated. In 1994 he moved from

Fig 1:20
The ninth Earl at Kegworth, with John Leatherland.

Fig 1:21 The Lanesborough tombs, Swithland churchyard.

Kegworth to Roxburghshire, Scotland, where he married Julia Meston, an assistant and friend since the 1950s. He died there in December 1998 – the last Lord of the Manor of Swithland and, since he had no male heirs, the last Earl of Lanesborough. He was buried in Swithland churchyard. His alabaster memorial tablet stands in the family chapel.

The End of the Line

While Sir Joseph Danvers was possibly the most successful of all the lords of the manor, others contributed significantly to the shape and development of Swithland. Robert le Waleys began the holding. Francis Danvers re-united it after it had been split for many years. Sir Joseph and Sir John added to the landholding and the church in ways that lasted for one hundred and fifty years. Augustus Richard Butler saw through the enclosure, but lost most of the money. George John Butler Danvers recovered some of the losses, erected a new hall, a new school building and many village homes; he also inherited the Earldom of Lanesborough. Succeeding Earls preserved the Swithland Estate intact and free from development. Sadly, however, the economic challenges of maintaining a large hall and its estate finally proved impossible, and Swithland parted company with its last 'Lord of the Manor' in 1983.

Many signs of the Danvers' and Butler Danvers' stewardship remain in the village, not least in Swithland Hall – now in the ownership of Mr and Mrs Adam Page and happily restored to good repair. With the end of the Danvers family line, however, it might be asked whether the hall has become just another big house or if it still holds its power to symbolize and remind the present generation of all the past significance of the 'Lords of the Manor of Swithland'.

Notes to Chapter 1

1. John Nichols, who quotes Wyrley, in *The History and Antiquities of Leicestershire*, notes that the brook runs to Quorn.
2. Known as Rothley Plain, this 'detached part of Newtown Linford' was transferred into Swithland ecclesiastical parish in 1999.
3. John Nichols, The *History and Antiquities of Leicestershire*, vol. 3, part 2, Swithland, 1790.
4. Lincs RO, Rolls of Hugh de Wells, Bishop of Lincoln 1209–1235.
5. J. Finberg, *Exploring Villages*, 1958, 1998 edn. p. 53.
6. *Dictionary of National Biography, 1885–1900*, vol. 28, William Hunt.
7. Unfortunately none give a reference.
8. Or 1098, source information varies.
9. Their son, also named Simon de Montfort, called the first English Parliament.
10. Curia Regis Roll 109, Trinity, 15 Henry III, 1231 in G.F. Farnham, *Charnwood Forest and its Historians*, 1930, p. 91 .
11. Saer de Quincy is credited with re-writing Magna Carta from Henry I's Charter and the Saxon Code.
12. T.R. Potter, *The History and Antiquities of Charnwood Forest*, 1842, pp. 136ff. (Nicholls mistakenly dates Robert le Waleys acquisition of manorial rights at 1270, vol. 3, part 2, p. 1047, saying 'this appears from the Visitation of 1619').
13. ibid.
14. G.F. Farnham, *Charnwood Forest and its Historians*, 1930, p. 92.
15. ibid., p. 95. De Banco Roll 129 Trin, 27 Edw 1, m.40.
16. Leics. RO. DE1625/1 Charter, 26th June 1316. Reproduced with permission.
17. National Archives, SC 8/108/5377, P. Lloyd, The Coroners of Leicestershire in the early fourteenth century.
18. 1372 (46 Edw3) De Banco Roll.
19. 1380 (3 Rich2) Assize Roll.
20. cf 1458 Inquisition, Edward Grey, Lord de Ferrers of Groby, 'In Swithland, 27 virgates of land, which the heirs of John Walcote, chivaler, hold by a twentieth part of a knight's fee, worth 5s'.
21. Leics. RO, DE1625/2, Charter, 20 July 1405, naming William Bypsham and Elizabeth his wife as first party.
22. G.F. Farnham, *Charnwood Forest and its Historians*, 1930, p. 93. Coram Rege Roll 607 m. 36.
23. Leics. RO, DE1625/3, Charter, 25 September 1427.
24. Leics. RO, DE1625/4, 2 June 1435, gift, moiety of manor of Swytheland, which belonged to Margaret late wife of Thomas Assheton ... to hold for life, then to pass to John Davers and his heirs... See also T.R. Potter, *The History and Antiquities of Charnwood Forest*, p. 137, reference to deeds of 1431 and 1460 confirming John Danvers' inheritance.
25. Kinderton was one of the baronies of the County Palatine of Chester, and held for a long time by the Venables family.
26. A grant 7 April 1535 by John Danvers of Swithland to (trustees) of manors of Swithland and Shackerstone, to suffer his sons John and Edmund to take the profits of his manors and lands, until John, son of his deceased son Francis should attain the age of 21, etc.. Several Kingstons are remembered in memorials in Rothley church.
27. The site of this house in Fowke Street is now occupied by 'The Grange'.
28. A memorial to Joanne Comyn, d. 1350, who inherited Smisby on the death of her husband William Shepy, is in St James Church, Smisby, to which she had added a new nave and chancel.
29. Sixteen sons and daughters of Henry Kendall and Elizabeth Armstrong are listed in J. Charles Cox, *Notes on the churches in Derbyshire*, 1877, vol. 3, Appleton, Repton and Gresley Hundreds: Smisby (Derbyshire Records Office). There is an impressive memorial to Henry and Elizabeth and family in the chancel of St James' Church, Smisby.
30. Details of the transactions listed and referenced in Chapter 8, The Story of the Land.
31. G.F. Farnham, *Charnwood Forest and its Historians,* Quorndon Records: Bridget Worley had married 1. Matthew Farnham (Quorn) 2. Arthur Barford (Shakerstone).
32. R. Cust, 'Honour and Politics in Early Stuart England: the case of Beaumont v. Hastings', *Past and Present* 149, 1995.
33. See Appendix A: Wills, Francis Danvers, 1631.
34. Leics. RO, Mss of Earl Cowper KG, vol. 1, p. 296.

35. Subsequently demolished in Sir Joseph Danvers' re-ordering of the Danvers Chapel in 1727.
36. For full inscription see Chapter 4, The Parish Church.
37. For a fuller account of William's activities during the Civil War, see Chapter 6.
38. See, for example, Long Clawson parish records 1641–1680; Thomas Garton, b. and Mary Hincklinge, s., both of C. married at Swithland before Justice Danvers, 2 December 1654.
39. Cf. Chapter 5, The Clergy.
40. Leics. RO, 2D31/107, Settlement of 6 August 1657.
41. B.G. Grant Uden (ed.), *The Recipe Book 1659–1672 of Archdale Palmer, Gent. Lord of the Manor of Wanlip in the County of Leicestershire*, 1986.
42. ibid.
43. cf. Chapter 6, Civil War.
44. Leics. RO, 2D31/67, cf. Settlement by Jacinth Sacheverell (of 8 October 1647) father-in-law of Ann Sacheverell nee Coke, on her second marriage to Henry Danvers. (Re Manor of Cabbleston, Staffs).
45. Thurloe's State Papers, iv. p. 629.
46. T. Crosby, *English Baptists*, iii, pp. 90–97.
47. Family memorial, St Leonard's Church, Swithland.
48. Leics. RO, 929.2-538L, June Danvers, Danvers Papers, 1984, 929.2-538L.
49. The house still stands in Cheyne Walk showing very little exterior change.
50. This figurative reference is presumably to the East and West Indies.
51. Edward Pearce, *The Great Man: Sir Robert Walpole – Scoundrel, Genius and Britain's First Prime Minister*, 2007, p. 322.
52. ibid., quoting Cobbett (Parliamentary History of England), p. 322.
53. Horace Walpole, quoted in Romney Sedgwick, *The House of Commons, 1715–54*, vol. 2, 1970, p. 604.
54. J.B. Owen, *The Rise of the Pelhams*, p. 19, quoted by Pearce, ibid., p. 411.
55. A copy hangs in the Grey family house at Dunham Massey (now in the care of the National Trust).
56. Christie's Sale Catalogue, contents of Swithland Hall, 1978.
57. MGC archives; handwritten history. In 1877, the Mountsorrel Granite Company leased the 'old Charity School on Castle Hill from Lord Lanesborough, and turned it into a Cottage Hospital for quarrymen and for their families'. Accommodation for a matron was provided in the old schoolhouse. Doctor Herbert Skipworth was paid £25 per month to be Medical Officer.
58. Board displayed on remaining building. See also Leicestershire Charities Report 1837 (Leics. RO).
59. Leics. RO, DE1750, Box 7; Appendix A: Wills.
60. Quoted in Firth, *Highways and Byways in Leicestershire*, 1926.
61. William Gardiner, quoted by Firth, *Highways and Byways in Leicestershire*, 1926.
62. John Throsby, *Select Views in Leicestershire*, 1790, p. 207.
63. ibid., p. 93.
64. John Nichols, *The History and Antiquities of Leicestershire*, vol. 3, part 2.
65. See Chapter 3, The Parish Church.
66. Leics. RO DE1750, Box 25, Copy of bargain and sale, 1759.
67. ibid., Conveyance in trust for burial ground, 13 June 1759.
68. According to Eliza Conybeare (Rothley Historical Society, Chronicle 3), Mountsorrel was disparished in the reign of Henry II, for some offence against his authority; as a result half of the village was linked to Rothley and Rothley Peculiar, and the other half to the Barrow 'group'.
69. Leics. RO, DE1750, Box 32, Lease for 21 years, 17 August 1778.
70. A replica has since been built and sited in the market place, opposite the old Butter Market.
71. Archives: Mountsorrel Granite Company, a hand-written history.
72. ibid., A similar causeway was laid in Leicester in 1774. By then the demand for stone 'caused several men to be regularly employed wresting rock from the hill'.
73. See Appendix A, Wills: Sir John Danvers.
74. John Nichols, *The History and Antiquities of Leicestershire*, vol. 3, part 2, p. 1049.
75. Spencer and Spencer, *Leicestershire and Rutland Notes and Queries and Antiquarian Gleaner*, vol. 3, 1895. Accessed on-line.
76. John Nichols, *The History and Antiquities of Leicestershire*, vol. 3, part 2.
77. *Leicester Journal*, Friday 30 September, 1796. No. 2286.
78. *The Times*, 8 June 1795, p. 3, col.d.

79. ibid., 14 May 1801, Sports and Sporting: Pedestrian match between Mr Butler and Mr Penn.
80. ibid., 18 June 1807.
81. ibid., 15 November 1796.
82. ibid., 11 November 1797.
83. Joanna Southcott, 1807, An account on Bills of Exchange wherein the deceit of Mr John King and his confederates, under the pretence of lending money is exposed, and their arts brought to light.
84. Appendix A: Wills, Sir John Danvers.
85. Appendix A: Wills, Mary Danvers.
86. Guildhall Library MS1092/3-4, the Hon Mrs Mary Danvers, aged 48, brought from Edgeware Road, and buried in a vault in Bunhill Fields on Monday 17th May 1802 at 12 o'clock.
87. A. Temple Patterson, *Radical Leicester: A History of Leicester 1780–1850*, 1954.
88. Leics. RO, DE1750, Box 1, Mortgage of allotments in Thurcaston, 26 July 1799.
89. Leics. RO, DE311/45/4/2, Related indenture 7 Dec 1802, lists all Leics. lands with names of tenants.
90. cf. Leics. RO, DE1750, Box 24, Bill filed in Chancery by George John Danvers, plaintiff, March 1856.
91. Leics. RO, DE1750, Box 7, Indenture of 28 August 1815, marriage settlement between George John Butler Danvers and Frances Fremantle.
92. Leics. RO, 3D42/54/83, Copy conveyance, 1 July 1815.
93. Leics. RO, 5D33/355, Particulars of sale of Danvers estates at Quorndon, Rothley, Barrow, Cropston and Charnwood Forest. 30/31 October 1815.
94. Leics. RO, DE311/45/5/1-1, Copy (1819) of Conveyance in Trust for sale of 3/4th July 1815 of 7 farms and lands in Newtown Linford, Cropston, Quorn, Barrow, Rothley, Charnwood Forest.
95. Leics. RO, DE1750, Box 7, Papers for the opinion of Mr Wood in case of Danvers v. Danvers and Antill.
96. ibid., Certificate of burial, 29 April 1820.
97. T. Danvers, Memorials of the Danvers Family of Swithland and Shepshed (unpublished), suggests that the building drawn by John Flower c. 1826 may not have been the old Manor House next to Hall Farm, but was rather Hall Farm itself, temporarily being used as the Manor House while the new hall was being built.
98. National Portrait Gallery, photographs of the 5th Earl and Countess reproduced with permission.
99. Leics. RO, June Danvers, Danvers Papers 1984, 929.2–538L. Miscellany of papers transcribed by June W. Danvers of Murray, Utah, USA, giving details of these allegations and claims.
100. Various members of the Shepshed Danvers family have persisted, and still persist, in the belief that William Danvers of Shepshed (1758–1840) whose great-grandfather was the youngest son of Henry and Ann Danvers, was in fact the rightful heir to Sir John Danvers.
101. The building was later used as 'the parish room'.
102. Leics. RO, DE1750, Box 24, Mar. 1856, Bill filed in Chancery by George John Danvers, Earl of Lanesborough, referring to 'the said Brinsley, fourth Earl of Lanesborough, died on 14 Jun 1857, having been many years a lunatic'.
103. Leics. RO, *The Leicester Journal*, Friday 13 July 1866, p. 5.
104. Leics. RO, DE1750, Boxes 12, 13, 27, various documents 1850s–1900s.
105. ibid., Box 33. In 1874 the Earl of Stamford and Warrington's hereditaments in Swithland/Newtown Linford (the White House, etc.) were conveyed to the Lanesborough estates.
106. H.A. Doubleday & H. de Walden, (eds), *The Complete Peerage*, 1929.
107. Leics. RO, DE1750, Box 30, 1898 Deeds, map of sale of Glebe.
108. *Leicester Daily Mercury*, Wed 28 June 1922.
109. ibid., Tuesday 8 October 1935, (obituary).
110. *Leicester Mail*, 19 August 1929, (obituary).
111. ibid.
112. ibid., 22 August 1929, p. 5 (funeral notice).
113. PRO, IR58/51189, 1910 Land Tax valuation.
114. *Leicester Advertiser*, 26 August 1950 (obituary).
115. *Leicester Mercury*, 25 August 1950.
116. Yvonne de Carlo died in Los Angeles in January 2007.
117. Eulogy, the Funeral Service for the ninth Earl, Swithland, December 1998.

– CHAPTER 2 –

Groby Peculiar

The title of successive Lords of the Manor of Swithland to their lands and their right to hold a manor court was held from the Lord of the Manor of Groby. All manor courts were part of a system of temporal courts that were ultimately responsible to the king. The authority of the manor of Groby, however, within which Swithland lay, was not restricted to secular matters but extended to ecclesiastical matters as well. In this the manor was 'Peculiar' and its eight ecclesiastical parishes were among a minority of parishes in the Church of England where jurisdiction in ecclesiastical matters was not exercised by an archdeacon or bishop, but, until the 1850s,[1] reserved to the lord of their manor. Peculiar jurisdiction in Leicestershire was exercised in the parishes of the manors of Groby (Anstey, Glenfield, Groby, Newtown Linford, Oaks in Charnwood, Ratby, Stanton under Bardon and Swithland) and Rothley (Barsby, Chadwell, Gaddesby, Grimston, Keyham, Mountsorrel, Saxelby, South Croxton, Somerby and Wartnaby), and also in the peculiar courts of St Margaret, Leicester (covering the chapelry of Knighton) and the old parish of Evington.

From pre-Reformation times until 1858, church courts exercised considerable powers over both clergy and laity. For most of England there was a hierarchy of ecclesiastical courts. The court of first instance was the Archdeacon's Court, from which appeal lay to the Bishop's Court (consistory) then to the Archbishop's Court (prerogative). Further appeal lay to the Court of Arches (in the Province of Canterbury) or to the Chancery Court (in the Province of York). Final appeal, until 1533 and the Reformation, was to the Pope. After the Reformation, while the ecclesiastical court structure was retained, final authority no longer lay with the Pope.

Before 1839, all of Leicestershire fell into the single archdeaconry of Leicester within the vast diocese of Lincoln. In 1839 ecclesiastical responsibility for the Archdeaconry of Leicester was transferred to Peterborough Diocese, and then, in 1927, to the newly-created Diocese of Leicester which was divided into two Archdeaconries – Leicester and Loughborough.

Much of the business of the ecclesiastical courts related to the issue of marriage licences and the granting of wills. About a third of all court cases related to probate disputes, fifteen per cent to matrimonial matters, fifteen to dilapidations, faculties, pews and tithes disputes, and ten to defamation. The rest were mostly related to the behaviour of the clergy and other church officers.

Geoffrey Chaucer, in *The Friar's Tale*, painted an evocative picture of a fourteenth century Archdeacon's court:

> In my part of the world lived an archdeacon
> Once on a time; a man of high position,
> A stern executant of the retribution
> The law imposes upon fornication,
> Slander, and witchcraft, and church robbery,
> On procuration and adultery,
> Forging of wills and breaching of contract,
> Usury and simony and neglect
> Of sacraments, and other kinds of crime
> We need not enter into at this time.
> He'd castigate whoremongers most of all;
> If he caught them at it, how he'd make them squall!
> And as for those who hadn't paid their tithes,
> He came down on them like a sack of bricks
> If any parish priest reported them;
> He never missed a chance to take a fine.
> For a skimped tithe, or scanty offering,
> How piteously he'd make the people sing!
> Before the Bishop caught them with his crook,
> They'd be put down in the archdeacon's book,
> Whereupon, being in his jurisdiction,
> He had it in his power to penalize them. [2]

'Peculiar' Courts were exempt from the jurisdiction of bishop and archdeacon and under the authority of a lord of the manor, or of a royal estate, a university or cathedral – or some other authority – often as a residual inheritance from a pre-Reformation abbey. In his peculiar jurisdiction, therefore, Groby's lord of the manor, through his commissary, exercised most of the functions that the archdeacon and bishop exercised elsewhere.

At various times, the Bishop of Lincoln[3] seems to have had doubts about the legitimacy of Groby Peculiar. A note on a clergy list of circa 1663 states of Swithland that 'this is pretended to be a peculiar, but there have been several Institutions to it, one, particularly in Queen Elizabeth's reign'.[4] And another note from the eighteenth century – this time about Groby – records that:

> ... in 1772 the mandate for Mr Hooley's induction to Ratby rectory was directed to the Commissary of Groby Peculiar or his Surrogate or Deputy ... Mr Stockdale insists this was irregular. Note: the Bishop of Lincoln's right to institute & issue a mandate to the Archdeacon of Leicester was allow'd by Lord Stamford in 1784.[5]

It is possible that the peculiar jurisdiction over Groby was simply established by one of its lords of the manor by force majeure. John Nichols, writing at the beginning of the nineteenth century, described Groby Peculiar Court and its powers.

> The Lord of the Manor of Grooby is entitled to an exempt ecclesiastical jurisdiction, which he exercises by a commissary or conservator, who is empowered to appoint surrogates, proctors, and apparitors. The Court of the Peculiar has cognizance in all spiritual and ecclesiastical causes, and in matrimonial causes and divorces, and all other causes of which cognizance belongs to the ecclesiastical courts according to the law of this realm; and the correction and punishment of excesses and crimes of all persons in the Peculiar, as well clergy as laity, whose reformation belongs to the ecclesiastical court. The commissary is also empowered to hold synods and visitations of the clergy and laity; and to grant matrimonial licenses, faculties, and lawful dispensations. Also the proving and disproving of the testaments and last wills of all persons dying within the Peculiar, and the committing of the administration of the goods of deceased persons belong to the court of this Peculiar; which is entirely exempt from the authority or interference of the bishop; and archdeacon, and the appeal therefrom immediately lies to the Court of Arches.[6]

Groby Manor Court met in the church at Newtown Linford.

> The old church ... one of whose bells is said to have hung originally in Ulverscroft priory tower, was the place of assembly of the court of the Peculiar of Groby, that curious ecclesiastical *imperium in imperio*, whose commissary exercised in the seven neighbouring parishes many of the functions of the bishop of the diocese.

> Here on court days the clergy and churchwardens would meet, to adjudicate upon those who had committed such misdeeds as ringing a bell with their 'spurs on, their girdle or hat', and declining thereafter to pay the 'stated sum' by way of fine. When the business was over, the apparitor went to the church door and made proclamation thus: 'O yes, o yes, this is to give notice that the court is adjourned to the Horns Tavern, in this place, and so stands adjourned.' To the Horns Tavern at the upper end of the village they then proceeded, and there they dined, on a pike from Groby Pool, roasted and stuffed, and a fat buck from Bradgate Park, both provided by Lord Stamford. After dinner they fell to speech-making.[7]

According to John Nichols, three rectors of Swithland – Gilbert Smythe, Abel Brooksby and Henry David Erskine – served as officers of Groby Peculiar Court. He lists the officers of the court[8] between 1565 and 1846.

List of officers of Groby Peculiar Court 1565–1846

COMMISSARIES	SURROGATES	REGISTRARS
1565 Richard Browne	1595 William Ludyard	1609 Henry Presgrave
1575 William Stoughton	1608 Gilbert Smythe	1658 William Heyward
1591 John Chippendale	1672 John Herrick	1666 Edward Nowell
1622 John Presgrave	John Rogers	1672 George Saville
1646 John Angel	1675 Nicholas Folkingham	1672 John Birkhead
1666 Thomas Case	1679 John Burrows	1683 Thomas Wadland
1670 Richard Werge	1682 Theophilus Tapper	1698 Thomas Levet
1672 William Foster	1683 Samuel Collins	1720 John Ward
1701 George Newell	1685 Joseph Darby	1731 Richard Stephens
1741 John Wilson	1687 Robert Alefounder	1745 Norrice Cradock
1751 Joseph Hooley	1689 John Coleman	1764 Thomas Pares
1784 George Foster	1697 William Fox	1801 Samuel Miles
1799 William Pares	1705 Edward Stokes	*1846 William Matts*
1810 Robert Martin	1715 Reuben Clark	
1827 Henry David Erskine	1735 Abel Brooksby	
1835 Robert Martin	1741 John Tomlinson	
1846[9] Robert Martin MA	1747 Walter Crompton	
	1750 Joseph Hooley	
	1799 Robert Martin	
	1846 Rev William Close MA	

In their time, the church courts were influential agents of social control, regulating the moral behaviour of the English laity. Some of the influence of the church courts was lost during the Civil War and Commonwealth period, when, with the abolition of the episcopate, magistrates took over many of their functions. As time passed, more and more jurisdiction passed from the church courts and peculiar courts to the secular courts. Sorcery and witchcraft were decriminalised in 1736. Benefit of clergy, the right of clergy to be tried in ecclesiastical courts for criminal offences, was partially abolished in 1576 and finally abolished in 1827. Tithes were translated into rentcharges in 1836. Perjury was an ecclesiastical offence until 1823; defamation remained an ecclesiastical offence until 1855. Brawling in consecrated precincts and laying violent hands on a clergyman while taking a service remained ecclesiastical offences until 1860. Jurisdiction over probate work was transferred to new temporal courts in 1858.

The records of Groby Peculiar include two early eighteenth century examples of the exercise of jurisdiction by church courts on the moral behaviour of Swithland residents. The people concerned would most likely have been denounced by the churchwardens, following an order by William III that every parish priest should see that churchwardens present to the ecclesiastical courts all those guilty of adultery and fornication in the parish.

In 1702, Groby Peculiar Court issued the following 'Order of Pennance' which it 'enjoined' on Elizabeth Lee.

> She is appointed to be present in the parish church of Swithland
> upon Sunday or Lords Day being the eighteenth of June instant:
> after the Gospel be ended, having a white Rod in her hand, and
> covered with a white sheet from the shoulders to the feet, standing
> upon some form of bench near the reading desk where the
> minister readeth prayers, and shall say as followeth: 'Whereas I
> good prosper not, having the fear of God before my eyes, to the
> great displeasure of Almighty God and danger of my own soul and
> evil example of others: I do hereby humbly acknowledge my
> offence in committing the crime of incontinency or ante nuptial
> fornication with my now husband William Lee before our inter-
> marriage together and I do heartily acknowledge my said offence
> and are heartily sorry for the same, desiring Almighty God for the
> merits of Jesus Christ my Saviour to forgive me this and all other
> my sins and offences, and also to assist me with the grace of his
> Holy Spirit that I fall not into the like sin again; and I do desire all
> you present not only to take example by this my punishment to
> avoid the like dangers, but also to join with me in humble and
> hearty prayer, saying as our Father hath begun: Our Father, which
> art in heaven, &c'.[10]

Elizabeth Whatnall married William Lee on 3rd June 1702. She performed her penance on 18th June. Thomas, son of William and Elizabeth Lee was baptised on 11th August. Sadly the child died shortly afterwards and was buried on 22nd October. William and Elizabeth had another son, Richard, in 1704. If they had further children, it was not at Swithland as they would appear to have left the parish shortly afterwards.

A later Order of Penance also appears to have had an unhappy sequel. In 1737, the registrar of Groby Peculiar Court sent this order to the rector of Swithland.

> An order of penance enjoined by Rev John Tomlinson Clerk
> Surrogate to the worshipful George Newell Esq Bachelor of Laws
> Commissary of the Peculiar of Groby lawfully constituted. To be
> performed by Squire Whatnall and Mary his wife of Swithland in
> the Peculiar jurisdiction aforesaid for their having committed the
> crime of fornication together before their intermarriage which
> after they have humbly done you the Rector of Swithland or your
> Curate for the time being shall duly certify to us or our surrogate
> in one months time from the date hereof. Given under the seal of
> our office this 14th day of April in the year of our Lord 1737. R.
> Stephens, Registrar.
>
> The said Squire Whatnall and Mary his wife shall upon Monday
> the twenty fifth day of this instant April repair to the church of
> Swithland at the time of Morning Prayer and there standing before
> the Reading Desk in the face of the congregation there assembled
> being in their own clothes, immediately after the end of the second

lesson, shall with an audible voice make their humble confession as followeth:

'Whereas we Squire Whatnall and Mary Whatnall not having the fear of God before our eyes but being led by the instigation of the devil and our own carnal concupiscences have committed the grievous crime of fornication together before our intermarriage to the great dishonour of Almighty God, the breach of his most sacred laws, the scandal and evil example of others, and the danger of our own souls, without unfeigned repentance of the same. We humbly acknowledge and are heartily sorry for this our offence, we ask God and this congregation pardon and forgiveness for the same in Jesus Christ and beseech him to give us his grace not only to avoid such like sin and wickedness but also to live soberly, righteously and godly all the days of our lives, and to that end we desire all present to join with us in saying the Lord's Prayer'.[11]

John Oliver, curate, certified that the penance had been carried out on Monday 25th April 1737. Unhappily, Mary Whatnall died later that same year; she was buried on 8th December. Squire Whatnall remarried Ann Lovett of Swithland in 1741, subsequently bringing six children to Swithland church to be baptised. The order illustrates that penance was not reserved exclusively for the poor, as Squire Whatnall was listed as a freeholder in the Poll Book of 1741, with the right to vote.

Successive Lords of the Manor of Groby carefully guarded the rights and privileges of Groby Peculiar, notably when Charnwood Forest was enclosed. At the beginning of the nineteenth century, those who lived at the centre of Charnwood Forest had no established church building, though a non-conformist meeting-house had been erected at Bardon Park about 1690. When enclosure of the Charnwood Forest was first contemplated, Thomas Babington MP, of Rothley Temple, persuaded the Bishop of Lincoln and the drafters of the Enclosure Bill that they should provide for the establishment of several churches to serve the area. A large part of the centre of the forest, however, lay within Groby Peculiar, and the Earl of Stamford insisted that any church built in this area should be answerable to his peculiar. A clause was included in the bill providing for some 200 acres of the Charnwood Forest to be set aside for the maintenance of future ministers.[12] The rents were to be invested in government securities and allowed to accumulate until they were needed for the construction of a church, a parsonage or as glebe. After the Charnwood Forest and Rothley Plain Enclosure Act received the Royal Assent on 18th June 1808, it was agreed that the first church to be built should be at Oaks-in-Charnwood. Since as yet no funds had accumulated for the construction of the church, money was raised by subscription among the leading families. The church at Oaks-in-Charnwood was consecrated by the Bishop of Lincoln on 18th June 1815, coincidentally the same day as the Battle of Waterloo. As agreed, the vicar and churchwardens were answerable to Groby Peculiar and not to the bishop.

The other two new Charnwood Forest churches at Woodhouse Eaves and Copt Oak, both of which were completed in 1837 and built on land outside the manor of Groby, answered to the bishop.

The Earl of Stamford's pains over churches in Charnwood Forest were almost the last hurrah of Groby Peculiar. In 1846 Rev Robert Martin was still commissary, Rev William Close was surrogate, Roger Miles was registrar and William Matts was apparitor. They were most probably the last officers of the court when its jurisdiction ceased in 1851.

Notes to Chapter 2

1. Peculiar jurisdiction in Groby Manor ended in 1851.
2. Geoffrey Chaucer, *The Canterbury Tales*, The Friar's Tale, c. 1390, trans. David Wright, OUP, 1986.
3. The Archdeaconry of Leicester was within the Diocese of Lincoln until 1837.
4. Leics. RO, Speculum, 1883–1884.
5. Leics. RO, Speculum: Note on Peculiars of Groby.
6. John Nichols, quoted in T.R. Potter, *The History and Antiquities of Charnwood Forest*, 1842, p. 115.
7. R.E. Martin, Introduction to Farnham: *Charnwood Forest and its Historians*, 1930.
8. See also T.R. Potter, *The History and Antiquities of Charnwood Forest*, 1842.
9. The 1846 officers have been added to Nichols' list.
10. Leics. RO, ID41/49/3, Miscellaneous court papers, Groby Manor Peculiar.
11. ibid.
12. Leics. RO, Enclosure Award, QS42/ map QS47/2, Charnwood Forest and Rothley Plain.

– CHAPTER 3 –

Local Government

Today, local government in the parish of Swithland is a two-tiered instrument, as it is across the nation. The parish church is governed by the incumbent, churchwardens and the Parochial Church Council and relates to the wider government of the Church of England through its synodical structures. Civic jurisdiction is exercised through Swithland Parish Meeting, Charnwood Borough Council and, in respect of wider local government matters, through the Leicestershire County Council.

Each year, therefore, two annual meetings of Swithland parishioners are held, one in the church and one in the village's Memorial Hall. The meeting in the church is the 'Meeting of the Parishioners' (Vestry Meeting), which is immediately followed by the 'Annual Parochial Church Meeting'. The one held in the Memorial Hall is the 'Swithland Parish Meeting'. The agendas are quite different.

Annual Church Meeting 1999
In 1999 the Meeting of the Parishioners (Vestry Meeting) had four items of business: prayers, minutes of the 1998 meeting, election of churchwardens and election of deputy wardens.[1] Everyone who lived in the parish was entitled to attend and vote, but only twenty-seven people turned out. The Annual Parochial Church Meeting that followed had a different agenda.[2] Compulsory items were the minutes of the 1998 meeting, the report of electoral roll officer, the annual financial report and presentation of audited accounts, the fabric report, the Parochial Church Council report, elections of members of the laity to the Parochial Church Council and to the Deanery Synod, and the election of sidesmen. Other items on the agenda that year were the church's plans for marking the new millennium, plans for possible pastoral re-organisation involving Swithland, Woodhouse and Woodhouse Eaves, a progress report on the planned extension to the church and the chairman's report. The priest-in-charge (the benefice being 'in suspension') was in the chair and twenty-seven members of the congregation attended. Only members of the church's electoral roll were entitled to vote, to receive reports and elect Parochial Church Council members, Deanery Synod representatives and sidesmen. The church annual meeting has no other

decision-making powers. All other decision-making is the province of the incumbent and the Parochial Church Council.

Swithland Parish Meeting 1999

Some twenty residents attended the 1999 Swithland Parish Meeting in the Memorial Hall. The agenda included the election of the chairman, the presentation of accounts, the replacement of lamp-posts, repairs to the war memorial, a grant from the parish rate towards the maintenance of the Memorial Hall, and a variety of other issues raised by residents – kerbstones, dog-fouling and Neighbourhood Watch. Three visitors were in attendance: the Chief Executive of Charnwood Borough Council, who reported on recent flooding in the village, council tax and the coming local elections, the local beat policewoman for Swithland and Rothley who also addressed the meeting and the District Councillor for Swithland and Woodhouse Eaves.

Local Government in Church and State: the Historical Context

Current forms of local government are largely the product of Victorian legislation. County government was established just over one hundred years ago, with district councils a little earlier. Previously, although mayors and corporations had long run the towns, public affairs in rural areas had been decided by the manorial courts and by justices of the peace. Within the smaller local parish scene the community largely regulated its own affairs, both civil and ecclesiastical, subject to law.

Parish vestry meetings, which date back to at least the fourteenth century, managed local ecclesiastical affairs such as church rates. The hundredal[3] and manorial courts had long administered the organisation of the agrarian and social life of the manor, including judicial issues, and interpreted its customs. From the sixteenth century, however, the manorial court began to decline, and the vestry meeting took over its duties in addition to its own. The vestry meeting became the annual meeting of parishioners (ratepayers) and fixed all the rates for the coming year, as well as electing or appointing the parish officers, who included churchwardens, overseers of the poor, surveyors of highways (way-wardens), constables, parish clerks and sextons. Since the Middle Ages, individuals had been chosen or elected to these offices and undertook their responsibilities on behalf of the local community. The vestry meeting paid them, controlled their activities and 'allowed' their accounts.

In March 1758, Thomas Turner of East Hoathly in Sussex, made this note in his diary:

> Mon 27 Mar.
> After dinner I went down to the parish meeting at Jones's, where I made up the accounts between Mr Joseph Burges the present overseer and the parish, and there remains due to the parish £11 7s. 6d. There was the most unanimity at this vestry that I ever did see at any one before, there being not the least discord

imaginable; nor that I observed above 2 oaths sworn during the whole time of the vestry, which was from between 12 and 1 o'clock to ten. We stayed till about 10.10 and then came home, and all sober. We spent 3d. apiece after the money allowed by the parish was spent... The officers nominated for the year ensuing were Jos. Burges, churchwarden, Jos. Fuller, electioner; Tho. Fuller, overseer, Jn. Cayley, electioner.[4]

This pattern of vestry government continued until 1894, when the civil functions of the vestry were passed to the new local government authorities which legislated for parish councils and parish meetings. The legislation may have been prompted by a desire to reduce the powers of the Lord of the Manor and of the incumbent. It also met the objections of non-conformists to government by the established church.

While larger villages are governed by parish councils, Swithland and some other smaller villages opted to work with a Parish Meeting. The Parish Meeting consists of the local government electors for the parish, all of whom are entitled to attend and vote. Its purpose is to discuss parish affairs and exercise any statutory functions conferred on it. It must be called annually between 1st March and 1st June and meet on at least one other occasion in the year. At the annual meeting the chairman must be elected, and the audited accounts presented. Money to cover its expenses may be precepted from the borough council. It has a number of possible powers and functions, relating to land use, burial grounds, charities, licensing, lighting, rights of way and war memorials.

Swithland Parish Meeting

The first Parish Meeting in Swithland was held on 4th December 1894 in the School Room, and minutes of meetings have been kept since that date.[5] Its business consisted of appointing James Murray Dixon, the rector, as its chairman, and Edwin Pepper, farmer and churchwarden, as rural district councillor. In the parish, Leicester City Council was completing the construction of Swithland Reservoir. One of the conditions attached to these works was the diversion of Swithland's sewage. It was the construction of Swithland's sewerage scheme that occupied the attention of the first few meetings of the Parish Meeting. The meeting fired off a strong protest to the Rural District Council in 1896, complaining about delays in completing the work and the damage done to the roads by constructors' traffic.

Most chairmen of the Parish Meeting served for quite a number of years. James Murray Dixon served from 1894 until 1924. He was followed briefly by William Green. In 1926 the seventh Earl of Lanesborough was presiding, although there is no record of his election. The eighth Earl is recorded as having been elected 'President' in 1930; he continued to preside until his death in August 1950. The ninth Earl succeeded him as chairman of the meeting, as well as to his Earldom. The Parish Meeting minutes record that he was elected 'in succession to his father, the late Earl of Lanesborough'.

Meetings were perhaps not called as regularly as a strict interpretation of the law might enjoin. The ninth Earl served as chairman until 1977 when 'he insisted that the Parish had a new chairman'. Mr T. Willoughby Garton, estate agent and valuer, was elected, and continued to serve until 1997 when Mrs Sarah E. May, dental surgeon, was elected to replace him.

Chairmen of Swithland Parish Meeting

1894–1924	James Murray Dixon
1924–1925	William Green
1925–1929	Charles John Brinsley Butler, 7th Earl of Lanesborough
1930–1950	Henry Cavendish Butler, 8th Earl of Lanesborough
1951–1977	Denis Anthony Brian Butler, 9th Earl of Lanesborough
1977–1997	Thomas Willoughby Garton
1997–	Sarah Elizabeth May

Between 1902 and 1944, the Parish Meeting elected or nominated a parish representative to be a manager, later known as a governor, of the village school.

1902	Thomas William Loseby
1907	J.T. Bates
1910	A. Turner
1929	Samuel Hoult (Mr Turner having died)
1934	Archdeacon Mackay
1937	Mr Banbury

The 1944 Education Act still required representation from the Parish Meeting on the school's Board of Governors. The following were listed as having been elected as managers:

1947	Mr Banbury, Mr Dransfield, Lord Lanesborough
1952	Lord Lanesborough, Lady Lanesborough
1955	Earl and Countess of Lanesborough, Ben Bunney, Mr Banbury, Mr Dransfield, and the new rector, the Revd. Harcourt

During the Second World War, the Parish Meeting was further charged with the election of air raid wardens. Mr L. Berridge (senior warden); Mr S. Briers and Mr Harrison (sub-wardens) were elected. The meeting was also required to elect a rural district councillor. The following names were recorded in the Parish Meeting Minutes.

1894	William Henry Cuffling
1902	William Lowe (re-election)
1953	Samuel Briers (re-election)
1958	Mr Walker

'Assessors of taxes' were also elected at the meeting. (These were rating assessors, who evaluated rates according to the value of the property.)

1895   J.T. Bates, E. Tyers, J. Woods, B. Hemsley, S. Bunney, W. Bunney
1905   J.T. Bates, Wm. Hemsley, E. Pepper, C. Tyers, J. Barnett, A Preston
1906   Wm. Henry Berry, instead of J.T. Bates
1937   John Mackay, I. Berridge (S. Hoult having left the village)

The powers of parish meetings have always been limited. In Swithland, the meeting has never had responsibility for the village hall, a burial ground or a playing field. It has, however, exercised its powers with respect to footway lighting. In June 1946, it agreed to ask the Leicestershire and Warwickshire Electric Company to install six lights to illuminate Main Street. In October 1951, it asked for three additional lights. At the time, the meeting was pressing the Highways Authority to introduce a 30mph speed limit through the village. In order to secure the speed restriction, the meeting agreed in January 1953 to yet another street light so that the lights should not be more than 200 yards apart – an essential qualification at the time. By March 1955 the chairman could report that the speed limit was in force – although it was noted that few motorists observed this speed limit.

    For the most part, the Parish Meeting has been a democratic forum through which pressure could be brought on other public bodies. Since 1954 the most contentious issue has been housing development. As early as November 1955 the meeting was expressing dismay that planning permission had been granted for housing on the allotments, opposite to the White House. It was told that outline permission had been granted by Leicestershire County Council, and that detailed permission was allowed on appeal by the Ministry of Housing and Local Government. In the first decade of the third millennium issues of new housing remain contentious, not least the erection of 'Phoenix Barn' on previously uninhabited land between 1 and 67 Main Street. Another contentious issue was raised in 1994. Against the majority opinion of the Parish Meeting, a Swithland Conservation Area was created by the borough council. It covers the housing area of Main Street (Wood Lane Cottage to the Hall's North Lodge, and the grounds and gardens of all the properties.)

Vestry Meeting and the Parochial Church Council

After 1894, St Leonard's Church vestry meetings continued to elect churchwardens and other church officers, while the day-to-day business and decisions of the parish church, including financial business, was largely the responsibility of the incumbent and the elected wardens. The general body of parishioners had little or no say in these matters, except insofar as they took part in the annual election of churchwardens. Those urban parishes, which by then had Parochial Church Councils, had them only at the will of the incumbent; these early councils had no powers, excepting those the incumbent delegated to them.

    The Church of England Assembly (Powers) Act 1919 gave Parochial Church Councils a legal status for the first time and defined their composition and procedures. The basis of the scheme was the annually revised church electoral roll. Those on the roll are entitled to vote at the

Annual Parochial Church Meeting and to be elected to the Parochial Church Council, which is responsible for the financial affairs of the parish church, the care, maintenance and insurance of its fabric and goods and the care of the churchyard. It has other responsibilities, including all matters relating to ecclesiastical property and the benefice house, cover of any interregnum and a voice in the forms of services used and any proposed pastoral re-organisation.

In recent years, apart from the day-to-day running of the parish church, matters that have most exercised the Swithland Parochial Church Council have related to concerns about the future of the benefice and the benefice house. Since the establishment of the new benefice of Woodhouse, Woodhouse Eaves and Swithland in 1999, Swithland's Parochial Church Council has felt freer to focus on mission as well as maintenance, and to respond more confidently to the changing patterns of church life in diocese and nation.

Parochial church councils are part of the wider structures of government of the Church of England. Under the terms of the 1919 Act, parishes not only elected lay church members to help govern the life of the local church, they also elected lay members to deanery governing bodies who in their turn elected to the National Church Assembly. This was a huge change in the life of the Church of England. For the first time, lay men and, in time, lay women, were involved in decision-making at all levels in the Established Church. Hitherto, it had only ever been clergy-men. Swithland's first Parochial Church Council met in April 1920 and elected its first two lay church members to represent the parish at the new East Akeley Ruri-decanal Conference, 'and if so ordered by higher Authority, the Diocesan Conference'.[6] 'Mr A. Turner, proposed by Mrs Hoult and seconded by Mr Lloyd; and Mrs Hoult, proposed by Mrs A. Pepper and seconded by Mr Lloyd, were duly elected'. Elections were held annually.

In 1970, new Church of England synodical structures replaced the system of a National Church Assembly, Diocesan and Ruri-decanal Conferences. Parochial church councils are now invited to elect lay representatives to the house of laity of the Deanery Synod for a period of three years, and that body of lay representatives elects lay representatives to the Diocesan Synod and also to the General Synod.[7] In 1970, Swithland elected Mrs Lois Godfrey and Bill Harris to the house of laity of the Akeley East Deanery Synod. The same year Mrs Godfrey went on to be elected to Diocesan Synod and to General Synod. At the time, she was one of very few women to serve the church in this capacity and at this level. Swithland has not since sent a representative to General Synod, though Mrs Christine Smeaton, a member of Swithland's congregation from 2000 until her death in 2008, was a lay representative from Leicester Diocese on General Synod between 1980 and 1995. When Mrs Smeaton first stood for election, her nomination was seconded by Bob Osborne, one of Swithland's representatives on the Deanery Synod.[8] In 1996, Swithland's elected deanery representatives were Mr P.C. Barrett, Mr C.B. Byford and Mr R.B. Osborne (who also served on the Diocesan Synod).[9] In 2010, Swithland elected lay representatives Mrs J. Cranage, Mrs R. Page and Mr C.B. Byford to the Deanery Synod.

Swithland Parish Officers

Surviving records of the administrative history of Swithland village are patchy, in fact not going back much further than the mid-nineteenth century. The village, however, would have been governed by the same system as all other villages and served by similar office holders. The incumbent (parish priest) exercised moral supervision, with the elected and nominated churchwardens as his principal officers. Other officers, also chosen at the Vestry Meeting, had their own particular roles.

Almost all of these parish officers have now disappeared. Today, the churchwardens are the only officers left from the days when local government was effectively parish government, and even their powers and responsibilities have significantly changed.

Churchwardens

Churchwardens have traditionally been responsible for maintaining the fabric of the nave of the parish church, and its furnishings. The seventeenth century poet Christopher Harvie described their role in one of his poems.

> The Churches guardian takes care to keep
> Her buildings alwayes in repair,
> Unwilling that any decay should creep
> On them, before he is aware.
> Nothing defac'd,
> Nothing displac'd
> He likes; but most doth long and love to see
> The living stones order'd as they should be.[10]

The office of churchwarden was legally established by the thirteenth century. As the parishioners' representatives for parochial business, wardens have been elected annually at the Parish (Vestry) Meeting from at least the fifteenth century. They have traditionally acted as guardians of the parochial morals and trustees of the church's goods. Historically, wardens have been of two types: the rector's warden, appointed by the incumbent, and the peoples' warden, elected by the meeting of parishioners at the annual Vestry Meeting. This traditional distinction no longer applies – both wardens are now elected by the meeting.

Swithland has almost continuous records[11] of the names of its churchwardens from 1824, with some additional names from earlier years recorded, for example, in the church registers and churchwardens' accounts. Since 1851, the churchwardens have made annual returns to the Archdeacon describing the state of the church building and fabric. In 1863, for example, questions were asked of churchwardens Thomas Bates and William Cuffling regarding, among other things, the state of repair and the condition of the building ('good', 'in good order'); the state of the contents (mostly 'in good repair' or 'in good order'); the registers ('kept in the chest in the chancel'); finance (church rate 'two pence in the pound', collections 'given to poor in the parish'); Sunday services ('two, 11 and 3 pm. Most of

Swithland Churchwardens

1692	Henry Lovett	John Lovett
1701/2	Robert Hind	William Peak
1703	George Bolter	Robert Prier
1706	John Mee	George Bolter
1707	George Bolter	John Mee
1708	George Bolter	Robert Gilbert
1735	John Prior	John Walker
1803	Stephen Pryor (d.1803)	
1814	William Hind	
1817	William Hind	
1824	Matthew Simpson	
1828	Daniel Bates	William Hind
1835	Daniel Bates	William Simpson
1846	John Oldershaw	William Simpson
1851	Thomas Bates	William Simpson
1862	Thomas Bates	William Cuffling
1865	George Harris	William Cuffling
1872	William James Bates	William Cuffling
1876	William James Bates	Joseph Matts
1884	William James Bates	William Lowe
1886	Edwin Pepper	William Lowe
1889	Edwin Pepper	6th Earl of Lanesborough
1905	Edwin Pepper	Countess of Lanesborough
1907	Edwin Pepper	William Henry Berry
1911	Edwin Pepper	Thomas Beers
1918	William Paterson	Albert Pepper
1920	William Paterson	Albert Cook
1923	Percival George Lloyd	Elizabeth Hodges
1926	Percival George Lloyd	Walter Kilby
1945	Joseph Dransfield	Walter Kilby
1954	Joseph Dransfield	Mary Elizabeth Kilby
1960	George Ronald Clark	Mary Elizabeth Kilby
1964	Waldron Harris	Mary Elizabeth Kilby
1967	Waldron Harris	Gweneth Mary Gimson
1973	John Alexander Beachell	Gweneth Mary Gimson
1975	Sydney Ratcliffe	Gweneth Mary Gimson
1982	Robert Mee	Gweneth Mary Gimson
1993	Bernard Sidney Durham	Gweneth Mary Gimson
1996	David John Pugh	Gweneth Mary Gimson
2001	Graham Kenneth Sharp	Gweneth Mary Gimson
2006	Peter William Henry Mason	Gweneth Mary Gimson
2008	Sally Elizabeth Allen	Gweneth Mary Gimson
2009	Sally Elizabeth Allen	Graham Kenneth Sharp

the parishioners attend'); the minister's house ('in fair repair'); schools ('a day and Sunday school').

Originally a quarter of the church's endowment was appropriated for repairs. But from the early seventeenth century churchwardens could, with the agreement of the Vestry Meeting, levy a Church Rate for the maintenance of the church. The rate was charged on land in the parish, and was payable even if the owner or occupier did not live there.

As 'officers of the Ordinary',[12] churchwardens were required to monitor the spiritual welfare of parishioners and the conduct of the clergy. They were, for example, to see that all parishioners attended church every Sunday, reporting absentees to the Bishop. The wardens' responsibilities for clergy conduct required that twice a year they were to report to the Bishop on their minister: whether the parson read the Thirty Nine Articles twice a year, and the Canons once a year, preached every Sunday, read the Common Prayers, celebrated the sacrament, read the Homilies, preached in his gown, wore a surplice, visited the sick, buried the dead, catechised children, baptised with Godfathers, married according to law, and led a sober life. Wardens were also to ensure that no-one preached unless they had a bishop's licence. In 1921, William Paterson and Albert Cook were able to report that although the church and chancel were 'not in good repair', their cleric was resident, employed no curates and regularly performed his services and duties – 'no complaints'. In addition, the clerk, the sexton, the bell-ringers etc. did their jobs properly and were 'mostly' churchmen and communicants.

Churchwardens were also responsible for keeping order in both church and churchyard. They were required to apprehend anyone who interrupted or disturbed the minister. They were responsible, along with pew keepers, for placing parishioners in their seats in church. Quarrelling and brawling in church or churchyard was to be stopped, indeed the wardens had to ensure that everyone behaved in a sober, orderly and reverent manner in church, kneeling at the prayers, and not wearing a hat.

From 1601 until 1834, it was the churchwardens' task, in conjunction with the parish overseers, to arrange poor relief in the parish. Wardens acted as trustees for the people in the administration of gifts and revenues to the church. A 1662 Prayer Book rubric, for example, refers to the churchwardens' responsibilities for taking collections at regular intervals and giving alms to the sick and destitute: '(They) shall receive the Alms for the Poor and other devotions of the people, in a decent bason to be provided by the parish for that purpose'.[13]

One of the most important responsibilities of churchwardens was to act as sequestrators during an interregnum or clerical vacancy in the parish. The task of the sequestrators was to gather the income of the benefice, for example from ecclesiastical fees, and apply it in the manner required by the circumstances of the case. John Prior and John Walker are recorded as acting in this capacity in 1735 between the rectorships of Abel Brooksby and Philip Alston. William Hind acted as a sequestrator in 1814 between the rectorships of John Llwyd and Francis Bruxby, and in 1817 between the rectorships of Francis Bruxby and Henry David Erskine.

Once elected and sworn in, churchwardens used to enjoy a considerable degree of autonomy; they were remarkably free from both clerical and parochial restraint. They were not, for example, bound to obtain the advice or consent of any of the minister, the parishioners, or the Archdeacon, before carrying out the majority of repairs. They did, however, require the consent of the vestry if they wished to set a Church Rate to pay for them. Swithland churchwardens' accounts exist from 1834. It was clearly their custom to present them each year to the Vestry Meeting, even after church rates were stopped in 1878. In 1919, however, the churchwardens' financial responsibilities were largely taken over by the Parochial Church Council.

Wardens were elected annually. Re-election was possible and in some parishes quite usual. Most Swithland wardens remained in office for more than one year. Edwin Pepper, for example, served for thirty-two years from 1886 to 1918 and Gweneth Mary Gimson for fifty-one years from 1967 to 2008. It used to be customary for one warden to be nominated by the rector and the other by the parish. Today the parishioners, with the consent of the minister, should elect both wardens. Only if they are unable to agree should each make an appointment.

Swithland churchwardens have been drawn from all walks of life. Matthew Simpson (1791–1849) was an agricultural labourer; from 1889–1907, first the Earl and then the Countess of Lanesborough were wardens. In the nineteenth century Swithland churchwardens were mainly drawn from local farmers. Daniel Bates (1788–1858) farmed Pit Close Farm; William Simpson (1795–1860), son of Matthew and Elizabeth Simpson, farmed Forest End Farm; John Oldershaw (b. 1801) farmed Longlands Farm; Thomas Bates (1803–1870) farmed Kinchley Hill Farm; William Cuffling (1823–1876) farmed Hall Farm; William James Bates (1840–1896) farmed Forest End Farm; William Lowe farmed Rothley Plain Farm; Edwin Pepper farmed Longlands Farm and from 1908 to 1916 was landlord of the Griffin Inn. The one exception to this herd of farmers was Joseph Matts, tailor and draper, who was churchwarden from 1876 to 1884.

The trend changed after the 1914–18 war. William Paterson (1871–1926) was head gardener at Swithland Hall; Albert Cook (1877–1947) was lodge keeper at the hall; Percival George Lloyd (1872–1945) was head gamekeeper. More recently, Swithland wardens have numbered among their ranks bank managers and other professionals and retired members of the armed forces. Since 1954, Swithland has always had a female, as well as a male, warden.

Two Swithland churchwardens went on to be ordained. Joseph Dransfield became vicar of Harby, Leicestershire in the early 1960s, and Waldron Harris (1913–1979) was ordained in 1972 as a non-stipendiary minister and licensed to assist at Swithland.

Some wardens are particularly remembered. Among his other eccentricities, warden John Beachell (1973–75) once dispatched a pigeon that had become trapped in the tower-ringing chamber with a 12-bore shotgun. In terms of longevity of service, however, the record of the Kilby family is quite remarkable. Between them, they gave a period of continuous service as peoples' warden for eighty-two years. Walter Kilby was first elected

Fig 3.1 Gweneth Gimson, Bernard Durham, churchwardens, at the installation of the Revd Anne Horton as priest in charge, May 1994.

in 1926, in the wake of the church restoration controversy. He served during the difficult 1942 to 1955 interregnum, when there seemed no prospect of a new appointment to the benefice. At his death in 1954 he was succeeded in post by his wife, Mary Elizabeth Kilby, and, after her death in 1967, by their daughter, Gweneth Mary Gimson née Kilby, who retired in 2008.

Since the introduction of Parochial Church Councils in 1919, the responsibilities of churchwardens have changed. Now, the care, maintenance, replacement and insurance of the fabric of the church are the responsibility of the Parochial Church Council. Financial matters are the joint responsibility of the incumbent and the Parochial Church Council, though the wardens, as agents for the incumbent and the council, are still required

*Fig 3.2
Gweneth
Gimson MBE,
Buckingham
Palace, 2009.*

to ensure that the collection is taken, counted, recorded and handed over to the treasurer, or to some other authorised person. The wardens are not now necessarily the sequestrators for the parish during an interregnum.

Parish Clerks

Parish clerks and sextons were traditionally the lowest officers in the church. Usually appointed by the incumbent or the officiating minister, they were employed for relatively menial tasks.

The office of parish clerk began as a temporal one coming within the jurisdiction of the common courts. Originally, the clerk may have been a candidate for holy orders, but in the later Middle Ages he was little more than a salaried verger – serving the priest at the Mass, and responsible for the decent appearance of the church. One of his duties was the house-to-house sprinkling around the parish of the holy water that was consecrated by the priest each Sunday – hence clerks were sometimes known as holy-water bearers. Water sprinkling stopped at the Reformation, but the clerk acquired an enhanced role when the Reformers envisaged a higher level of participation by the congregation in the new church services. Not all the members of the congregation were literate, so a major part of the clerk's duties consisted of saying or singing the psalms and making the prayer book responses with or on behalf of the congregation. In the eighteenth century many churches had three-decker pulpits. The parish clerk would sit in the lowest seat and the parson in the middle seat, ascending to the third tier in order to preach. Swithland church contained its own version of the classical three-decker pulpit, with the middle and lower seats placed alongside each other.

The clerk's other duties were various. Some duties carried fees: attendance at burials and tolling the bell, for example, transporting a corpse into or out of the parish, attendance at weddings, whether by Banns or Licence, and at churchings. Clerks often kept the drafts of the parish registers. Sometimes they wound the church clock.

To be eligible for the post of parish clerk, a man had to be at least twenty years old and able to read, write and sing. Women were not normally eligible until the twentieth century, although parish records elsewhere indicate some were appointed.[14] Clerks were supposed to be licensed to their office by the Archdeacon, but many were not. A country clerk would combine his duties with most types of trade. Continuous records of Swithland parish clerks date only from 1807, but we know that John Parker (1639–1720), a shoemaker, served at sometime as parish clerk in Swithland. So did John Johnson (1733–1807), whose occupation is unknown.

Swithland Parish Clerks

Source: Swithland churchyard memorial stones	
	John Parker
– 1807	John Johnson
Source: churchwardens' accounts; memorials	
1807–1825	Stephen Clark
1826–1849	Thomas Johnson
1850–1854	Matthew Hodges
1855–1865	Stephen Clark
1866–1882	Charles Lynes
1884–1895	Thomas Hodges

Sometimes the job of parish clerk remained within the same family for years. Thomas Johnson (1774–1850), a slate cleaver, was followed by Matthew Hodges (1790–1854) an agricultural labourer. On Hodge's death, the post passed to schoolteacher Stephen Clarke (b.1822). When Clarke left the school in 1865 the post passed to his successor, Charles Lynes (1834–

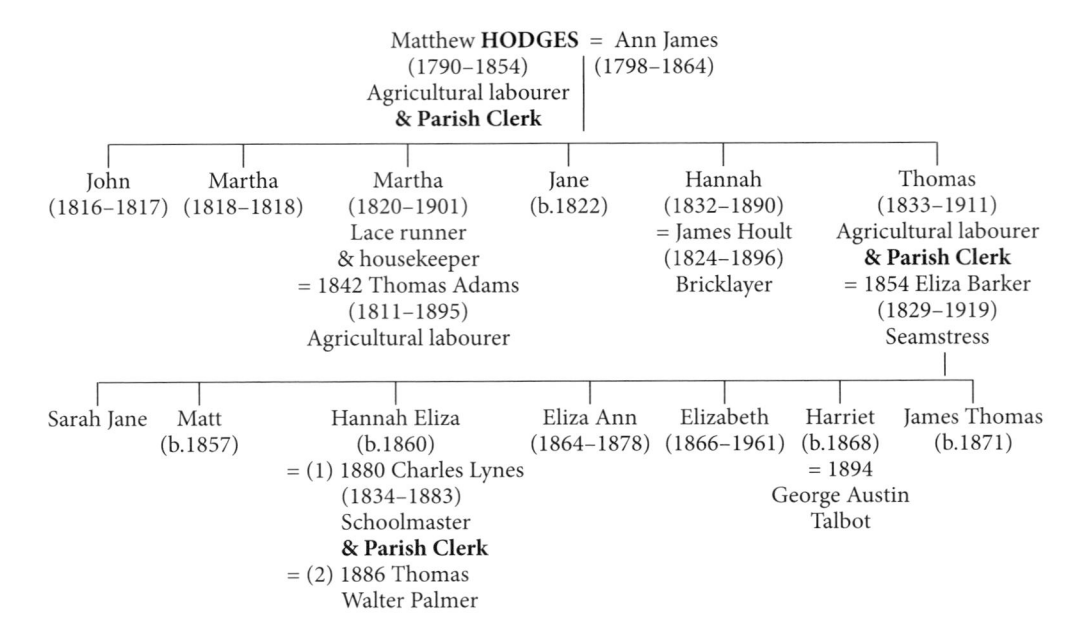

```
                    Matthew HODGES = Ann James
                    (1790–1854)     (1798–1864)
                    Agricultural labourer
                    & Parish Clerk
```

- John (1816–1817)
- Martha (1818–1818)
- Martha (1820–1901) — Lace runner & housekeeper = 1842 Thomas Adams (1811–1895) Agricultural labourer
- Jane (b.1822)
- Hannah (1832–1890) = James Hoult (1824–1896) Bricklayer
- Thomas (1833–1911) Agricultural labourer & Parish Clerk = 1854 Eliza Barker (1829–1919) Seamstress

Children of Thomas and Eliza:
- Sarah Jane
- Matt (b.1857)
- Hannah Eliza (b.1860) = (1) 1880 Charles Lynes (1834–1883) Schoolmaster & Parish Clerk = (2) 1886 Thomas Walter Palmer
- Eliza Ann (1864–1878)
- Elizabeth (1866–1961)
- Harriet (b.1868) = 1894 George Austin Talbot
- James Thomas (b.1871)

1883), who would later marry Matthew Hodges' granddaughter. On Lynes' death, it passed to his father-in-law Thomas Hodges (1833–1911).

Changing liturgical patterns in the second half of the nineteenth century, as well as more widespread literacy, tended to displace parish clerks from their traditional role in leading the people's responses during church services. This change, and the ending of the compulsory church rate in 1878, prompted a decline in the office and an adjustment of duties. Parish clerks had to rely entirely on fees and voluntary subscriptions, or on the generosity of the incumbent. In Swithland, the clerk was paid from churchwardens' funds. After 1895, the parish clerk became a local government officer. At that point Thomas Hodges, who had served the Swithland Vestry Meeting as clerk since 1884, began to be described in the church accounts as sexton and caretaker, rather than as a clerk.

Sextons

Elizabeth Smith, daughter of Thomas and Eliza Hodges (1866–1961) had inscribed on her tombstone the phrase 'churchwarden and sexton'. She was warden between 1923 and 1926, but there is no official record of her appointment as sexton. She may, however, after her father's death, have continued to exercise his parochial clerking duties. She died in 1961, aged ninety-six, 'after long and faithful service in the parish'.

Sidesmen

Despite the fact that virtually every English parish church seems to have had them, sidesmen have never received formal recognition in either canon or secular law. They would seem to have been appointed initially to support the churchwardens. In 1566 in Bredwardine, Worcestershire the duties of sidesmen were defined as 'to be joined with the said wardens for placing of seats, things to be done about the church lands and necessary affairs about the church'.[15]

The first written mention we have of the election of sidesmen at St Leonard's Church is in the minutes of the 1926 Vestry Meeting, when seven were elected; Mr A. Turner, Mr M. Bates and Mr A. Minkley were nominated by the rector and Major Dixon, Mr H. Copson, Mr M. Paterson and Mr Spence were nominated by church members. Their task was not described. In 1999, sixteen were elected by the Annual Parochial Church Meeting: Mrs S.E. Allen, Mrs L.J. Bate, Mrs E.D.P. Brook-Lawson, Mrs P.D. Copson, Mr D. Freestone, Mr S.B. Godley, Mrs O.M.F. Harris, Mr M. Harrison, Mrs J.H. Northam, Mr J.H. Morris, Mr H. Rowntree Clifford, Mr L.J.P. Sambrook, Mr B.H.O. Vann, Mrs M.E. Whyte, Mr T.N. Whyte and Mrs Z.S. Willson. The primary role of sidesmen today is to welcome worshippers, issue them with service and hymn books, and, if appropriate, show them to a seat. More recently, health and safety policy additionally requires knowledge of evacuation procedures in case of emergency, and the ability to use the appropriate fire extinguisher.

Non Ecclesial Vestry Officers

Not every parish officer is related to the church institution. From sixteenth century times, three officers in particular were found to be necessary to serve the needs of the community in general; the constable, the overseers of the poor and the surveyors of the highway. These originally served voluntarily and were appointed on an annual basis. Their expenses were covered by a charge on the parish, with ultimate responsibility for the carrying out of their duties resting with the justices of the peace. Their activities are therefore rarely, if at all, mentioned in ecclesiastical records.

Parish Constables

The office of parish (or petty) constable dates back to manorial legislation and may even be older than the office of churchwarden. Always a secular office, the constable was determined at the annual manor court leet or the parish meeting. He might be assisted by other officers such as headboroughs and tithingmen. His duties related to the maintenance of law and order and the enforcement of national legislation within the area of his jurisdiction. He arrested and detained offenders, and had to have at his command stocks, a whipping post and a parish lock-up – facilities commonly maintained by the wardens at the expense of the parish. The position of constable was voluntary, but his expenses were recompensed by the parish. Constables were not very popular among the parishioners.

A letter of 1636 contains a passing reference to the Swithland parish constable of the day. Sir William Danvers of Swithland began his letter of August 15th to Sir John Coke at Melbourne thus:

> The Constable of our town brought me this warrant from John
> Cobly, the postmaster of Loughborough, as he styles himself.[16]

From the early eighteenth century, constables were paid the allowances due to them out of the Poor Rate.[17] Their duties included ensuring that local means of punishment and imprisonment were maintained in good order; inspecting the alehouses; collecting the county rate; dealing with strangers, beggars and paupers; and caring for the parish bull.

Many of the constables' duties related to the enforcement of the Poor Laws. They might be charged to remove a pauper from one parish back to another, which was seen to be financially responsible; or in summoning non-ratepayers to appear before the magistrate, charged with the offence of not paying rates to the churchwardens and overseers.

From 1894 until 1928, the Swithland Parish Meeting chose the men amongst them who would serve as parish constables.[18] Copies of the lists of first the eligible,[19] and then the elected men had to be put up on the doors of all churches and chapels in the parish.

Swithland Parish Constables

1895	E. Pepper, E. Tyers, F. Bunney, John Adams
1899	S. Bunney, B. Hemsley jnr, John Adams, Walter Bunney
1902	John Adams, John Hodges, Charles Pratt, Ben Hemsley jnr.
1907	John Adams, John Hodges, Fred Bunney, Charles Pratt
1908	W. Hemsley, Samuel Hoult, Charles Pratt, John Hodges
1909	Wm. Woolley, Chas Pratt, Geo. Frith, Fred Bunney, John Adams
1910	W. Woolley, G. Frith, Alwyn Bunney, F. Bunney, H. Minkley
1911	G. Frith, F. Bunney, F. Copson, H. Minkley
1912[20]	F.W. Taylor, H. Minkley, Geo. Minkley, Richd. Wales, Jn. Hemsley, Ben Wesley, Fred Bunney, Chas Pratt
1928	W. Ball, C. Wainwright, A. Copson, A.E. Bunney

More recently, local men have been appointed as special constables by police authorities and given specific duties. Jim Carpenter, for example, who moved into the village c. 1947, when he became Lord Lanesborough's gamekeeper, was a special constable from about that time until his retirement. Family members remember his being on duty when there were fishing matches between the Leicester and Loughborough Police, and also his involvement with special duties at the East Midlands Airport on one occasion when HM The Queen visited Leicestershire. During the Second World War, Jim was a member of the Home Guard.

Overseers of the Poor

Care for the poor has been seen as obligatory for all Christians since the earliest days of the church. Before the Reformation, a percentage of the tithe and glebe used to be given for the support of those whose poverty derived from no fault of their own, though in years of general crop failure or epidemic sickness, that system may well have broken down. Some wealthier members of the parish made provision for the poor of their community in their wills. The numbers of able-bodied poor, however, rose to such a level from the late fifteenth century that national action was taken – Henry VIII requiring each parish to install a poor man's box for donations. In 1563, Elizabeth I's government required each parish to appoint 'two able persons' to gather and collect alms weekly from church-goers. Later legislation was more pro-active, requiring parishes to elect overseers – assistants to the wardens – to set the idle to work. In 1598, the first Poor Law was passed, requiring the parishes, through their elected overseers, to take responsibility for those paupers who could legitimately claim the parish as their birthplace. The overseers were empowered to call upon the wardens to levy a Poor Rate.

The 1601 Poor Law Act established a system of parish support across England. The act made it compulsory for each parish to provide for the eligible poor of their parish by levying a rate on all occupiers of property within the parish. Two residents were elected each year by the vestry to act as overseers. Originally unpaid, they worked with the churchwardens to find work for the poor, or give monetary relief.

Christopher Harvie's poem, 'The Overseer of the Poor', first published in 1640, annexed to George Herbert's 'The Temple', gives a snapshot of a seventeenth century overseer.

> The Churches Almoner takes care, that none
>   In their necessity
>   Shall unprovided be
> Of maint'nance, or imployment; those alone,
>   Whom carelesse idleness,
>   Or riotous excesses,
> Condemnes to needlesse want, he leaves to be
> Chasten'd a while by their own povertie.[21]

The appointment of overseers of the poor in 1662 legislation, passed in the form of the Settlement Act, allowed the churchwardens and overseers of the poor of any parish, on complaint being made to the Justice of the Peace, to remove persons who they considered would become a charge on the parish rate to their last place of legal settlement. The concept of legal settlement was determined by the criteria of whether a person was a native of a parish, a householder there, sojourner, apprentice or servant for the space of forty days.

From 1697, those benefiting from parish relief were to wear a letter 'P' on the shoulder of the right sleeve of their coat. The poor were classified as the impotent poor (the aged, decrepit, lame, blind, insane, infants), the poor by casualty (the maimed, those undone by fire, or overcome with children), and the self-inflicted poor (rioters, idlers, drunkards). In principle, the impotent poor were to be relieved, the poor by casualty were to be found work, and self-inflicted poverty was not to be relieved. However, both policy and practice changed over the years. Knatchbull's Act (1722) reflected a tendency to deal stringently with the able-bodied poor, and to grant them relief only if they were living in a workhouse or poorhouse in which they could be set to work. Gilbert's Act (1782) further allowed the able-bodied poor to be found work outside the workhouse.

From at least 1750 to 1834, the Swithland overseers rented three cottages from the Danvers/Butler-Danvers estate. These cottages could well have been located on land where the village war memorial was erected in 1920, since, in nineteenth century documents, the adjacent field is called Workhouse Close.

Poor harvests at the end of the eighteenth century and beginning of the nineteenth century led to a steep rise in the price of bread. For many agricultural labourers this brought the prospect of destitution and starvation. Throughout England, there was a crisis in the poor law system. The authorities feared bread riots. Some magistrates urged overseers to grant relief to labourers whose wages were insufficient to maintain themselves and their families. Occasionally, the magistrates would publish scales of relief – according to an applicant's earnings, the size of his family, and the price of bread. The most famous scale was that drawn up by the Berkshire justices, meeting at the Pelican Inn, Speenhamland, near Newbury, at Easter 1795. In addition to cash supplements, some parishes bought corn, which was sold to the poor at reduced prices.

Landowners and farmers bore the chief burden of the Poor Rate. They could stand the increase during the Napoleonic War, when prices, rents and profits were good. At the end of the war, however, depression hit agriculture. The concern of Swithland landowners to minimise the cost of the Poor Rate is reflected in an 1813 agreement to prevent people from establishing Swithland as their place of settlement:

> We who have hereunto subscribed our names being respectively resident in or parishioners of the parish of Swithland in the county of Leicester do hereby severally and respectively agree one with the other that if at any time or times hereafter either of us shall by any act or means cause or be the means of any person or persons obtaining a settlement in the said parish and thereby lawfully claim the aid and assistance of the parish of Swithland for his or her support or of the Officers or Officer thereof commonly called the Overseers of the Poor such of us who having been the cause or means of such person or persons settlement shall for every claim so to be lawfully made forfeit and pay to the Overseers of the said parish for the time being the sum of ten pound and we do hereby severally and respectively further agree that such penalty or penalties forfeiture or forfeitures shall and may be recoverable in any of His Majesty's Courts of Record at Westminster by the Overseer or Overseers for the time being of the said parish for the sole use and benefit of the poor of the said parish at our joint expense.
>
> Dated this 24th day of November 1813.
>
> (Signed) Augustus Richard Butler Danvers, David Chapman, Matthew Simpson, William Bunney, Daniel Bates, James Ward, Thomas Hales, Thomas Pryor, Edward Dexter and Barfoot Richardson.[22]

Parliamentary enquiries were held into the poor law system, which eventually led to reform. In 1817 Matthew Simpson, as Swithland's overseer, signed a return required by Parliament as to the money spent from the Poor Rate during the period 1801 to 1817.[23] On average some £237.23 per annum was spent in these years on the support and relief of the poor. Simpson was paid a fee of £3 per year for his work.[24]

The legislation that emerged was the Poor Law Amendment Act of 1834. The new poor law combined parishes into unions and called for the building of union workhouses. Some of the overseers' duties were given to 'Guardians of the Poor,' with the overseers as assessors and collectors of the Poor Rate. Swithland became part of the Barrow Union,[25] whose workhouse was in Linkfield Road, Mountsorrel. The following parishes were included in the union: Anstey, Barkby, Barkby Thorpe, Barrow upon Soar, Beaumont Leys, Beeby, Belgrave, Birstall, Bradgate Park, Cossington, Cropston, South Croxton, Gilroes, Leicester Abbey, Leicester Frith, Maplewell Longdale, Mountsorrel, Newtown Linford, Queniborough, Quorndon, Ratcliffe on the Wreake, Rearsby, Rothley, Seagrave, Sileby, Swithland, Syston, Thrussington, Thurcaston, Thurmaston, Ulverscroft, Walton on the Wolds, Wanlip and Woodhouse.

At any one time up to forty-five Swithland residents may have been receiving poor relief. In the three months to 25th June 1840, some nine Swithland paupers were maintained in the Union House. They were not resident for the whole period, since the parish was charged for only four hundred and twenty days at a cost of £7 15s. In addition, thirty-six paupers were listed as receiving out-relief at a cost of £26 18s. 7¾d.[26]

A schedule[27] of the paupers receiving relief from the Barrow Union includes the following residents of Swithland: Thomas Ainsworth, Sarah Bloomfield, Mary Bostock, Catherine Brex, Thomas Brex, Elizabeth Brookhouse, William Brookhouse, William Brookhouse Jnr., Catherine Brown, Jane Brown, Thomas Brown, Ann Bunney, Samuel Bunney, William Bunney, Elizabeth Burton, Henry Burton, James Burton, John Burton, Joseph Burton, Kezia Burton, Mary or Miriam Burton, Rachel Burton, John Deacon, Esther Fewkes, Ann Greasley, William Greasley, William Heron, Ann Hill, Thomas Hill, Ann Horner, Thomas Horner, Mary Jackson, Sarah Johnson, Richard Kirby, Jane Pearson, Ann Preston, Ellen Preston, Elizabeth Preston, Hannah Preston, Jane Preston, John Preston, Joseph Preston, Mary Preston, Richard Preston, Zachariah Raynor, John Roe, Elizabeth Simpson, Elizabeth Swain, Jonathan Swain, John Thompson, George Thorpe, Samuel Thorpe, Thomas Thorpe, Ann Vesty, Hannah Vesty, Thomas Vesty, Francis Wakerlin, Esther Wells, James Wells, Daniel Whatnall and Michael Whatnall.

Among Swithland people living at the Union Workhouse in Mountsorrel at their death were Joseph Simpson (1791–1866), an agricultural labourer, and his wife Elizabeth (1786–1869). Others who were at the 'Union House' at their death were Thomas Ward (d. 1871) and Jane Bunney née Thompson (1827–1908), the widow of George Bunney, another agricultural labourer.

Swithland Overseers of the Poor

1801–1817	Matthew Simpson[28]	
1895–1896	Charles Bunney	William James Bates
1896–1900	Charles Bunney	Edwin Pepper
1900–1907	Samuel Bunney	Edwin Pepper
1907–1908	William Hemsley	Edwin Pepper
1908–1909	William Hemsley	Samuel Hoult
1909–1915	Alex Preston	Samuel Hoult
1916	William Bates	Samuel Hoult
1917–1918	Michael Bates	Samuel Hoult
1918–1921	John Bunney	Samuel Hoult
1921–1922	Ambrose Copson	Samuel Hoult
1922–1924	John Frisby	Samuel Hoult
1924–1926	John Bunney	Samuel Hoult
1926	Matthew D. Bates	Samuel Hoult

Until 1865, the union's costs were allocated to each parish according to the number of paupers and other costs associated with that parish. The act also appointed a Poor Law Commission to supervise overseers and the Boards of Guardians of the workhouses. In 1847 a Poor Law Board replaced the Commission. It was absorbed into the new Local Government Board in 1871.

Following the creation of Parish Meetings (Local Government Act 1894), the Swithland Parish Meeting took over the vestry's responsibility for appointing overseers. The real work of collecting rates appears to have been done by an assistant overseer, who received a payment for his work. In 1908, when the previous assistant overseer resigned, Albert Pepper applied for the job. He was appointed at a rate of £8 per annum. In March 1918, Albert Pepper applied to have his remuneration increased by £4 – the meeting agreed an increase of £2. Whether as a result of this decision or not, Albert Pepper resigned in November 1918, and was replaced by Alwyn Bunney at a salary of £10 per annum. In 1923 his remuneration was increased by twelve shillings, but he was required to find a bondsman for £100, and to show a certificate of his bond to the overseers. Overseers of the Poor continued to be appointed by the Parish Meeting until 1926.

In 1919, control of the poor law system passed to the Ministry of Health. Throughout these changes, administration of local poor law relief remained in the hands of the Board of Guardians until 1930, when these boards were dissolved by the Local Government Act (1929). After this date, the Ministry of Health took responsibility for poor relief, administering it via public assistance committees. From 1930, arrangements for the relief of poverty were changed. Boards of Guardians were abolished by the Local Government Act (1929) and the Barrow Union ceased to exist. Public assistance committees under the Ministry of Health administered poor relief.

Surveyors of the Highways

This parochial role was set up in Queen Mary's reign, when an act required every parish to elect 'two honest persons' to be surveyors and orderers of the highways. These men could conscript able-bodied parishioners to do the work. If the surveyors failed in their duty, they could be punished by the justices at the Quarter Sessions. There are references in the Swithland Enclosure Award (1799) to 'Surveyors of the Highways'. Swithland has no records indicating the appointment of such officers. The Highways Act of 1864 allowed for the grouping of parishes under a Highways Board, which assumed responsibility for maintaining the highways in its district in good repair.

Swithland's Parish Meeting minutes record periodic concern for the cleanliness of the village street. In the early part of the twentieth century, Swithland had a resident roadman in the person of John (Old Jack) Tomlin.[29] Tomlin, who died in 1929 aged eighty-one, was married to Sarah Annie Maria (known as Annie), parish midwife, who pre-deceased him in 1921, aged seventy-one. They had at least one son, George Edward, who married Nellie Foulk in 1909.

In 1933, when asked by the rural district council, the Parish Meeting declared clearly that Swithland 'does not need a paid scavenger'.[30] By 1937, however, the villagers did acknowledge the need for 'scavenger' services, with a request that rubbish be collected weekly. There was also criticism of a roadman that year who was apparently collecting rubbish, but then tipping it into local hedges and ditches. In 1950, a 'foreign' working party was being employed to clean the road; their standards did not satisfy the meeting, who were still asking for regular roadmen to prevent people from 'dumping rubbish in the hedge along the Leicester Road' and 'by the railway bridge'. There was some relief expressed in 1958 that 'Mr Hubbard is now the roadman for Swithland' and that he was keeping the village clean and tidy.

Fig. 3.3 'Old Jack' Tomlin, road-sweeper, outside The Griffin, c. 1920.

Town Crier

For some years, a member of the Bunney family served as Swithland's town crier. The 1925 Parish Meeting minutes record that Joe Bunney agreed to serve free in that capacity, 'in consideration of it having been in his family so many years'.[31]

Almost all of these parish officers have now disappeared. Today, the churchwardens are the only officers left from the days when local government was effectively parish government, and their powers and responsibilities have significantly changed.

Notes to Chapter 3

1. A deputy warden has no legal status within parochial structures, but can be a helpful convenience in some parishes.
2. Church of England Rules governing the annual Meeting of the Parishioners are given in the Churchwardens Measure 2001. Required agenda items for the Annual Parochial Church Meeting are listed in the Parochial Church (Powers) Measure 1956.
3. A 'hundred' is an ancient administrative division of a county originally containing a hundred families. It ceased being a census reporting unit after 1851 as its administrative importance diminished. The unit eventually lost its administrative and judicial functions.
4. D. Vaisey (ed.), *The Diary of Thomas Turner 1754–1765*, 1994.
5. Leics. RO, DE3689, Swithland Parish Meeting 1894–1985.
6. Meeting, 16 April 1920, Swithland Parochial Church Council minutes book, 1920–52.
7. All licensed clergy are members of the Deanery House of Clergy; they elect their own representatives to the House of Clergy in the Diocesan and General Synod.
8. Christine L. Smeaton, 'Melon Soup and Tomato Juice', *Biograph*, 2007, p. 165. When Mrs Smeaton was elected to General Synod, she was a member of Newtown Linford Church.
9. The number of representatives relates to the size of a church's electoral roll. Swithland, with an electoral roll of over 100 members, may send three representatives to Deanery Synod.
10. Harvie, 'The Synagogue', annexed to George Herbert, *The Temple: sacred poems and private ejaculations*, London, Bell and Daldy, 1857.
11. Leics. RO, ID41/23/1-7, Partial records of wardens admitted 1896–1919.
12. The Diocesan Bishop.
13. Book of Common Prayer, rubric, Holy Communion Service.
14. Since 1672, a woman has been permitted to carry out the duties of churchwarden, sexton, Overseer of the Poor or rate-collector.
15. N.J.G. Pounds, *A History of the English Parish*, chap 5, pp. 186–7.
16. Leics. RO, L920COW, Manuscripts of Earl Cowper KG, vol. 11, Letter, August 15, 1636, Danvers to Coke.
17. In 1912, the Swithland Parish Meeting agreed to pay its constable £1 p.a..
18. Leics. RO, DE3689, Swithland Parish Meeting Minute Book, 1894–1985.
19. All resident males aged between 25 and 55, rated to the poor or county rate, who were not exempt.
20. The number doubled this year at the request of the Chief Constable.
21. Harvie, 'The Synagogue', annexed to George Herbert, *The Temple: sacred poems and private ejaculations*, London, Bell and Daldy, 1857.
22. Leics. RO, DE1750, Box 9, 24 Nov 1813, agreement.
23. Leics. RO, QS93/2/190, The Poor Rate, Swithland Parochial Returns 1801–1817.
24. Overseers of the Poor paid out of the Poor Rate.
25. Leics. RO, G/2/9C/1-18, Barrow-on-Soar Poor Law Union Parochial Ledgers, Nov 1837–March 1927.
26. ibid.
27. Leics. RO, G/2/28/1, Barrow-on-Soar Poor Law Union: Index of paupers relieved.
28. Leics. RO, QS93/2/190, The Poor Rate, Swithland Parochial Returns 1801–1817.
29. The Tomlins were not listed on the 1901 Swithland Census.
30. Leics. RO, DE3689, Swithland Parish Meeting Minute Book, 1894–1985.
31. ibid.

– CHAPTER 4 –

The Parish Church

For over eight hundred years, the central importance of religious belief to the lives of countless Swithland people has been expressed in the context and care of their parish church. Here, where the living still worship God, they are surrounded by many generations of the dead who worshipped in Swithland church before them. And, because our Christian understanding of God continues to evolve, the building has been adapted, and will continue to be adapted, to reflect fresh insights of faith.

St Leonard's Church stands at the eastern end of the village, next to the

Fig 4.1 St Leonard's Church, Swithland, 1995, by Tony Danvers.

Manor Park, and not far from the site of the old Swithland Hall. The church stands quietly – a little back from the Main Street – in a churchyard that is bordered by mature trees. The blue-grey and pink rubble stonework of its tower, nave and chancel lend it an unspectacular solidity. It is the oldest building in the village and the repository of much of the village's history. It is also the centuries-old expression of Christian belief and worship.

St Leonard of Limousin

The church is dedicated to St Leonard of Limousin (or Noblac), a fifth century Frankish monk. This relatively unusual dedication, popular in the twelfth century, may well be linked with the presentation of the living[1] of Swithland, which was originally in the hands of the French Benedictines at the Abbey of St Evroult, Normandy.[2] St Leonard, coming from the Limousin region of France, was one of their 'local' saints. He was venerated as the patron saint of prisoners and captives, which made him particularly popular among the early crusaders, among whom were members of the de Grandmesnil family.

Leonard, who died c. 559, was a Frankish nobleman who refused a bishopric in order to become first a monk and then a hermit at Noblac (now Saint-Léonard) near Limoges.[3] The many miracles attributed to him, both during his lifetime and after his death, inspired a widespread cult throughout Europe. As the patron saint of people in captivity, Leonard's emblem is a loosed padlock and chains. His patronage is also said to extend to women in labour, as well as to people and beasts afflicted with disease.

Fig 4.2 Chancel boss in St Leonard's Church, 1925, showing loosed padlock and chains symbolising St Leonard.[4]

For centuries, parishes in England have celebrated the anniversary of their patron saint. St Leonard's Day is 6th November. Swithland School records from the nineteenth century show that the children were given his feast day as a holiday and that a wake or feast for everyone was celebrated in the village.

St Leonard's Church in the Thirteenth Century

There has probably been a church building in Swithland from at least 1189, the earliest known written reference to the settlement at Swithland.[5] Documents in the keeping of the Diocese of Lincoln indicate that Roger, a chaplain, had the living of Swithland before 1206 and was still in Swithland in 1220.[6] Another document of 1225 indicates the church to be in the patronage of the Abbey of St Evroult.[7] The earliest structure was probably

*Fig 4.3
The ruins of
St Evroult
Abbey, 2009.*

a single rectangular cell, possibly with a small chancel to the east, and the altar at the east end of the chancel.

A document of 1277 refers to a chapel built by Robert Waleys, then Lord of the Manor of Swithland, recording that the Abbot of St Ebrulph gave leave that, by licence from the Bishop of Lincoln, Waleys might have a chaplain at his own expense in the chapel recently built in his court at Swithland.

The thirteenth century arcades within the present building and the remaining clerestory windows above them indicate there were two side aisles. There are three bulls-eye (vesica-shaped) clerestory windows, one incorporating Norman decoration, above the arches on the south side of the present nave, and part of another such window in the first of the arches on the north side. These windows would have been above the roof level of the north and south aisles. The aisles were probably some nine feet wide, with virtually flat roofs. Traces of a string-course on the south face of the south arcade may indicate the height of the original aisle roof. The earliest chancel would have been smaller than it is today and the nave roof probably of thatch – more steeply pitched than now – and with eaves at a lower level. A tower was added in the thirteenth century – smaller than we see today, as the first string-course indicates.

Within this small medieval parish church, those who lived within the parish gathered together on Sundays and Saints Days for the celebration of the Mass. The worshippers stood throughout the services, as mediaeval churches had no seats for worshippers, although there might have been some benches against the walls for the infirm.

Fifteenth Century Modifications

Subsequent adaptation and restoration means that little remains to show how the late medieval church in Swithland once looked. At some point in the fifteenth century the tower was increased to its present height, though the battlements and pinnacles were probably added later.[8] It is likely that there were also some additions to the interior of the church. The presence of an oak sill built into the south arcade wall may indicate that at one time there was a rood beam and gallery crossing the western face of the chancel arch. This might also have been the time when the Danvers family appropriated the south aisle for the burial of members of their family, though we have no evidence of any burials until that of Francis Danvers in 1631.

The only fifteenth century monument that does survive relates to the Ferrers family not to the Danvers. A monumental brass of 1455, commemorating Agnes Scot, originally lay at the head of the nave, just below the chancel step. 'On a flat gravestone inlaid with plates of brass, in the body of the church, near the entrance into the chancel,' says Mr Burton, 'is the picture of a woman veiled'.[9] The brass depicts a woman with her hands clasped together in prayer, dressed in a simple hood and flowing gown. The inscription on the brass suggests that Agnes Scot was an anchorite nun, connected to the Ferrers family, who were Lords of the Manor of Groby from 1265 to 1445.

> Hoc in conclave jacet Agnes Scot camerata,
> Antrix devota Dominae Ferrers vocitata:
> Quisquis eris qui transieris, queso, fune precata;
> Sum quod eris, fueramque quo des: pro me, precor, ora.

The English translation displayed in the church reads:

> Enclosed in this tomb lies Agnes Scot
> Called the devout mother of Lady Ferrers
> Whoever thou shalt be, who shall pass by; pour out prayers I beg:
> I am, what thou shalt be: I used to be, what thou art:
> Pray for me, I pray.

Nothing is known of Agnes Scot's link with Swithland, but, as such brasses were relatively costly, it is probable that she was well-connected – the inscription indicates her link to the Ferrers family and the translation 'devout mother of Lady Ferrers' a spiritual relationship. She must also have been important enough to Swithland as well; she was buried in a place of honour, she was commemorated both by the brass memorial and also in the stained glass above the church's altar. William Burton described the chancel window in 1622.

> In the East window of the chancel is her picture in glass, drawn to the life, in the same habit, with a ring on her finger.[10]

It is possible that Agnes was venerated before the Reformation in the same way as was her fellow anchoress, Julian of Norwich. The east window portraying Agnes has since been removed, possibly at the time that the present window was put in. At some point after Burton's visit in 1622, possibly during the Reformation years, Agnes' brass was moved to the floor to the immediate left of the south entrance to the church (which was in 1804, according to Nichols, 'in the present vestry'). It is now on the west wall of the south aisle.[11]

Reformation

The effects of the Reformation were as much practical as theological and affected the church's buildings, ministry, liturgy and organization. The sixteenth and seventeenth centuries therefore saw great changes inside all European church buildings. Even small villages like Swithland would not have escaped, though no visible evidence of protestant modification to Swithland church has survived later restoration. The only evidence of work in the sixteenth and seventeenth centuries is the re-roofing of the church. Timber framing was added to the nave walls, thus raising the height of the eaves and lowering the pitch of the roof.

Fig. 4.4 John Nichols' sketch of the monumental brass to Agnes Scot, 1455.

The Reformation effectively began in Europe in 1517 when Martin Luther's ninety-five 'theses' were nailed to the church door in Wittenberg, Germany. Change came more slowly in England, being at first more political than theological. Henry VIII, wanting a divorce from his first wife, declared himself Supreme Governor of the Church in England in 1532. By 1536 he had dissolved most of the country's monasteries. At least one Swithland parishioner was directly affected. 'Robert Clarcke of Swithland, a layman, was buried in Swithland in 1551. He was in receipt of a pension of 30sh. from Ripon Abbey'.[12]

Liturgical change was not Henry's priority. It was his son, Edward VI (1548–1553), who was the principal enforcer of the English Reformation. Thomas Cranmer's two prayer books, introduced in 1549 and 1552, displayed the outward expression of the theological beliefs of the English Reformers. The emphasis in Cranmer's prayer books moved from the sacrifice of the Mass to the Communion of the 'Lord's Supper'. Believing that church services should be 'understood of the people', Cranmer wrote his new services in English, not in Latin. The Reformers' emphasis on the place of the Bible in the life of every believer meant that the devotional focus within the church building moved away from the altar to the lectern and pulpit. From 1531 a Bible, in the English tongue, had to be provided in every church. Seating facing these new liturgical points of focus was gradually introduced and, by the late sixteenth century, permanent long benches with backrests began to be introduced into church naves. The only material reminder of those days still left in Swithland church is a small piece of wood carved with the date of 1589. It is now displayed within the chancel arch, bearing a plate inscribed with the names of former rectors. Those who placed it there in the 1920s advised that the wooden panel was part of the 1880 pulpit structure, thus possibly dating the pulpit.[13]

Swithland holds in its archives two large and now rather fragile matching volumes: an English Bible and a Book of Common Prayer, both inscribed on the outer cover 'Swithland, Leicestershire'. There is no indication, however, as to when these were printed or received.

Seventeenth Century Memorials

One of the distinctive features of the seventeenth century was the proliferation of family memorials in English churches. These effectively replaced all the ecclesiastical art, statues and pictorial displays of biblical and traditional Christian stories that were destroyed at the Reformation.

In 1622, William Burton recorded of Swithland church that the east window of the chancel contained the coats of arms of Ferrers (gueulles 7 masclets or) and Walleis (argent a lion rampant queue fourche gules), that the east window of the south aisle contained the arms of Ferrers of Groby (gueulles 7 masclets voided or), Montfort of Leicester (gueulles a lyon rampant queue fourche argent), Norton (vert a lyon rampant or), and Audley (gueulles fretty or), and that the south window contained the arms of England (gueulles 3 Lyons pass: gard: or) and Wake (gueulles 2 barres or 3 bizants in chief).[14] Burton does not mention a north aisle.

The south aisle of Swithland church may have been important for the Ferrers family, but it would seem already to have been established as a burial place for members of the Danvers family by 1631. In his will, Francis Danvers asked '... for my bodye, my desire is that it be buryed in the out Isle of Swithland church neere my wyff'.[15] His son, William Danvers, obediently buried him there and erected a large monument in his honour. Burton[16] described the monument as consisting of blue stone and alabaster raised a yard from the ground on which lay a plain Barrow stone wrought to the blue marble. Above the tomb were family coats of arms. The head of the tomb was in white, the arms and inscription set in a blue stone bordered with black, and bordered again with white chamfered alabaster. At the head of the tomb was a brass plate with the inscription:

> Franciscus Danvers, armiger, dominus iuius villae, qui er priore uxore
> Eliza Skeffington, filia Johannis Skeffington, de Fisherwick, armigeri,
> Duobus audas filius, Wiliemo et Johanne, filiaque una, Elizabetha:
> hos, ut et alteram conjugem, Brigettam Worley, filiam Edmundi Worley,
> Superstites relinquens, placide in domino obdormit undecimo die Junii,
> anno domini MDCXXXI,
> Aetatis suae septuagesimo primo.
>
> From exile home returned my flesh and spirit
> Their fathers houses, earth and heaven I inherit.

On another side:

> On earth to toyle and trouble not dejected
> There's certaine and uncertaine ...
> ... changed earth for heav'n, time for eternity.

On another side:

> True faith in God, to man firme faithfulness
> Honour of vertue, succour or distress
> Just holiness, prudent simplicitye
> With Danvers Liv'd, and in this grave do lie
> With Danvers dead, and yet not so for they
> Immortall are, and make him live for aye.

Francis Danvers' tomb was demolished by Sir Joseph Danvers in 1727, when he enlarged the south aisle. The plate, however, survives, now mounted on a slate ground and moulding, and currently positioned on the south wall of the south aisle.

Another local historian, John Nichols, refers to a flat memorial stone to an infant son of Samuel Danvers on the floor of the Danvers aisle.

> Here lieth the body of Francis Danvers,
> The son of Samuel Danvers, Esq, of Swithland;
> Who died December 1697, aetatis suae 4º.

The stone has not survived, but Francis Danvers is commemorated in a small brass plate on the floor of the current front pew of the 'Danvers Chapel'.[17]

Other people were buried in the church during the seventeenth and eighteenth centuries. Seven engraved slate stones,[18] dating from 1691 to 1724, record the burials of a small group of Presbyterians, including the Rev Michael Matthews and members of his family. These stones were noted by Nichols as situated at the nave crossing opposite the south door, but were removed during the 1925 restoration to a position outside the church, at the side of the north porch where they lie flat and at the mercy of the elements.

In the sanctuary, a traditional burial place for incumbents who die in office, there are eight gravestones that date from 1700 to 1742. These not only mark the burial places of Thomas Jackson, rector, and his family, but also the Raworths of Mapplewell.

> Here lieth the body of Thomas Bodle,
> Son of Thomas Bodle, and
> Grandson of the said Thomas Jackson;
> Who died 19 May, 1700
>
> —
>
> Here lieth the body of Johanna Jackson,
> Late wife of Tho. Jackson, rector;
> Who departed this life June 26, 1700, aged 68.
> Here lieth also interred Agrilla, the youngest daughter
> Of Johanna Jackson above-written,
> And wife of Mr Richard Bacon, of Markfield.
> She hath left three children, one son, and two
> Daughters; and, after a pious care of her family,
> She departed this life October 13, 1727, aged 51.
>
> —

Here lieth the body of Thomas Jackson,
Rector of Swithland 24 years;
Who departed this life Nov.6, 1700, aged 63.

—

Here lieth the body of Anne Bodle,
Wife of Thomas Bodle, of Markfield, gent.
And daughter of Thomas Jackson, late rector of
This place. She departed this life
March 26, 1702, anno aetatis 31, Salutis 1702.

—

Here lieth the body of Sarah Raworth,
The wife of John Raworth, of Mapplewell,
third daughter of William Yeomans of Derby.
She departed this life the 6th day of May, 1722,
In the 69th year of her age.

—

To the memory of John Raworth,
Who departed this life the 17 day of June, 1731,
In the 80th year of his age.
It's my desire by my wife to lie here.
Stir not our bones until that Christ appear;
Until the day that Christ do come, and say,
"Arise, my Saints, and come you all away."
This ordered by Anne Raworth his loving wife.

—

Here lieth the body of
William Raworth, of Mapplewell, gent.
Who married Anne, the daughter of
Robert Smalley, of Mountsorrel, gent.;
By whom she left issue one daughter named Anne.
He departed this life Feb.15, 1733, aged 46.

—

Here lieth Anne Raworth,
Daughter of Mr William Raworth, of Mapplewell;
Who died June 7, 1744, in the 12th year of her age.

A ninth stone, which marked the burial places of Abel Brooksby, rector, and his wife Alice was also, according to Nichols, in the chancel of the church. This stone is not among the others in the sanctuary floor. Maybe the stone was in the chancel rather than sanctuary, or broken, covered or removed before the 1920s restoration work, as, unlike the others, it is not noted in Albert Herbert's church plans.

Here lieth the body of Abel Brooksby, A.M.
Who was rector of this parish 34 years.
He departed this life 13th July, 1735, aetatis 60.

> Also here lieth the body of Alice Brooksby,
> The wife of Abel Brooksby;
> Who departed this life June 4th, 1742, aged 70 years.

Eighteenth Century Re-Ordering

Major alterations were made to the church in the early eighteenth century. These changes reflected social power rather than ecclesiastical or theological perception. The family at the manor were well established by 1721, and increasingly well monied. They wished their place in society to be reflected in the architecture of the church.

The north aisle had been demolished some time previously, and the arcades along the north of the nave blocked up. In 1727, Joseph Danvers caused the small south aisle to be pulled down and replaced with the more magnificent present aisle: a carved tie beam on the east wall shows the arms of Joseph Danvers and the date.

The rebuilt Danvers aisle was almost double the size of its predecessor; its height too was substantially increased. The new aisle incorporated an un-opened round-topped window at the west end as well as open and glazed windows along the south wall.[19] One of the windows on the south wall formed a half moon above the entrance door for the congregation. The doorway has been subsequently blocked, but the half window survives. On the way to their seating area, the villagers would have walked past the west wall to Danvers' family chapel on their right, at the east end of the south aisle. The chapel was separated from the remainder of the church by that wall and possibly by railings along its north boundary. Although described as a chapel, there was no altar[20] and no east window, but a new door in the east wall provided access to the Danvers chapel for the manor household. The chapel area was now elevated some three feet above the level of the rest of the church, presumably because of burial vaults below. Until this rebuilding, the only access to the church had been through a south door, and possibly also through the west door at the bottom of the tower door. The positioning of village footpaths and the burial stones from 1673, as well as the positioning of the mediaeval font, suggests that the south door was the main door.

At about the same time the chancel was enlarged, and the nave and chancel of the church fitted with round topped or 'venetian' windows, like the ones in the new aisle. These included two chancel windows in the same style as the new south aisle.[21] The pulpit and sounding board (tester) were positioned on the north wall, facing the new south aisle.

In his new family chapel, Joseph Danvers erected a carved slate wall memorial with a square brass plate in the centre, commemorating his great grandparents William and Elizabeth Danvers, his grandparents Henry and Anne Danvers, his parents Samuel and Elizabeth Danvers, and also himself and his wife.

> In memory of William Danvers, of Swithland Esquire who
> married 4th November 1618 Elizabeth daughter of Thomas

Babington of Rothley Temple, Esquire, by Catherine eldest daughter of Henry Kendall of Smithsby in Derbyshire, Esquire, and has issue 16 children. He died 30th August 1656 and his widow died in 1678.

Henry Danvers Esquire Son and heir of William was married 18th March 1644 to Anne, the third daughter of Sir John Cooke of Melbourne in Derbyshire, Secretary of State, and had issue 7 children. He died in 1687. His wife was learned in the Hebrew and Greek Scriptures. She died in 1686.

Samuel Danvers Esquire, son and heir of Henry, was married 20th December 1683 to Elizabeth, only daughter of Joseph Morewood of London, Merchant, by Elizabeth Blundell, co-heiress of Woodcock, Esquire, of Shinfield, Berkshire and had issue nine children. He died in 1693. His widow married John Danvers of Prescott in Oxfordshire, Esquire, without issue. She died 11 December 1719.

Joseph Danvers, Esquire, Son and heir of Samuel, was married 7 December 1721 to Francis, the second daughter of Thomas Babington Esquire, by Margaret Hall, daughter of Henry Hall of Gretford in Lincolnshire, Esquire, and has had issue 5 children. He rebuilt this chapel in 1727 and erected this monument.

> Lectori candido:
> God, who to thee reason and knowledge lent,
> Will ask how two such talents have been spent.
> Search not to find what lyes too deeply hid,
> Nor to know things whose knowledge is forbid.
> Look forward what's to come, and back what's past;
> Thy life will be with praise and prudence grac'd.
> Dame Fortune's smiles unguarded man surprise;
> But, when she frowns, he armes, and her defies:
> When well at ease and happy, live content;
> And then consider why that life was lent.

Fig 4.5 St Leonard's Church, 1790, by Nichols, showing the new south aisle.

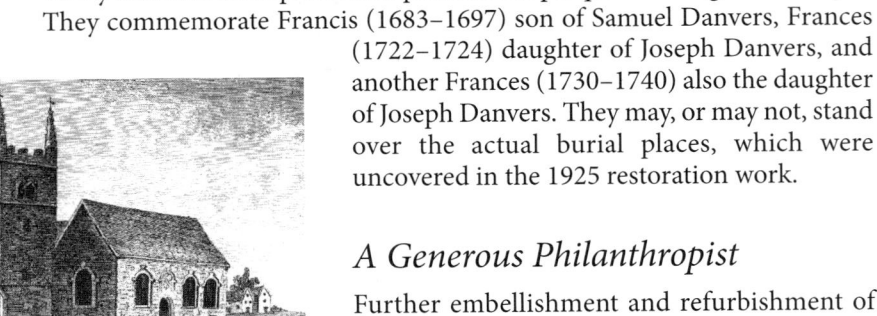

Today there are three plain brass plates in the parquet flooring of the chapel. They commemorate Francis (1683–1697) son of Samuel Danvers, Frances (1722–1724) daughter of Joseph Danvers, and another Frances (1730–1740) also the daughter of Joseph Danvers. They may, or may not, stand over the actual burial places, which were uncovered in the 1925 restoration work.

A Generous Philanthropist

Further embellishment and refurbishment of the church was carried out by Sir Joseph's son later in the eighteenth century. Sir John Danvers gave a new font to the church in 1760 – a marble bowl and pedestal by Haywood. It replaced the mediaeval stone font which was of considerable size: a bowl of 41½ inches in diameter, 21 inches deep outside and 15 inches inside, which stood on four side pillars.[22] This mediaeval font, which stood near the south aisle door, was eventually taken out and lay forgotten for many years in the adjacent rectory grounds. In 1953, churchwarden Joseph Dransfield recorded its fate:

> It lay at one time in the old rectory grounds and then to Hall Farm, Swithland, which was then farmed by the then rector the Rev J.M. Murray Dixon 1884–1925, & used as a pig trough!!! And was rescued by the 8th Earl of Lanesborough who placed it in the centre of the Rose garden at the Hall.[23]

The ninth Earl took the mediaeval font with him when he moved from Swithland Hall to Kegworth, and subsequently, on his removal from Kegworth, to Roxburghshire. It is hoped that this remaining link with Swithland's earliest Christians will one day be restored to the parish.

Sir John Danvers gave the church its six bells between 1760 and 1764. They are still rung every week. Each is inscribed 'Gift of Sir John Danvers Bart' and was made by Joseph Eayre of St Neots, Huntingdonshire. The third bell, however, must have become cracked soon after installation as it was re-cast by Edward Arnold of Leicester in 1793.

Another gift from Sir John at about the same time was a fine service of silver communion plate, consisting of two alms dishes, a flagon, two chalices, two patens, a salver and two candlesticks. The candlesticks and salver, hallmarked as having been made in 1701 and 1727, were originally secular pieces. The flagon, patens, cups, and one alms dish are hallmarked as made in 1757. The other alms dish is dated 1768. Each piece is engraved with the sacred monogram – a cross above and three nails below, within a circle of glory. Sir John, or another member of the family, also gave the church an oak chest, made around 1760, possibly to hold its records or valuables.[24] The chest, now sensitively restored, still has its original iron clasps.

Fig 4.6 Swithland's mediaeval font.

The church organ bears the date 1765 and was another gift of Sir John, who commissioned Johann Snetzler – a notable organ builder of the day – to build it to stand at the centre of a west end gallery in St Leonard's Church.

Johann or John Snetzler (1710–1785) was born in Shaffhousen in Switzerland, but moved to London as a young man. He became a respected organ builder, working throughout England and Ireland. Snetzler's Swithland organ was a single manual instrument, hand blown, with a Gothic pinnacled front. The keyboard was of blackwood with ivory-plated sharps.[25] William Gardiner, a near contemporary, wrote in 1838:

> When Snetzler was building the very excellent organ in St Martin's church, Leicester, he was applied to by Sir John Danvers to erect one in his church at Swithland, which now remains a specimen of the great talents of that mechanic. For a long time it has not been used; when I saw it thirty years ago, though saturated with damp, and covered with dust, I found it in tune and in playable condition. The reason was evident. In the first place, there was not a reed stop or mixture in it; and the other stops, both wood and metal, were substantially made.[26]

The only difficulty with Gardiner's account is that St Martin's organ was built in 1769–74, some years after the 1765 date on Swithland's organ.

It was William Gardiner who also recorded Sir John's liking of the colour red. 'He was remarkably fond, like the Chinese, of painting everything red, so much so that every door, window, shutter and gatepost in the towns of Swithland and Mountsorrel was so decorated.'[27] Local historian John Throsby confirmed Sir John's predilection for the colour red (roddle) when he described Swithland church in 1790. 'The church has three aisles, six bells, and a little organ, the case of which is painted with roddle. To this colour it would seem Sir John is wonderfully partial; the seats of the church, the window frames of the church, those of the parsonage house, his own, and doors, all shew roddle, roddle, roddle.'[28]

In 1764, Sir John gave the church its tower clock. Made by Joseph Eayre of St Neots, Huntingdonshire, the clock has a single face and is on the north side of the tower. It was originally positioned above the second string course of the tower.

In Sir John's day the family chapel was decorated with streamers and escutcheons. In it he placed a wall-mounted monument that purported to give his pedigree. The inscribed brass plate, mounted on slate and surrounded by carved slate mouldings, traces the Danvers family back to Norman d'Alverse, a Brabanter, who came to England in aid of William the Conqueror. Unfortunately, many of the details are inaccurate. Sir John probably erected this monument between 1753 and 1759, since inscribed on the churchyard tomb of Sir Joseph Danvers (d. 1753) and his wife Dame Frances (d. 1759) is the advice 'For further particulars relating to this ancient family you may consult the monuments of this church'. These 'further particulars' give both the names and the arms of the families concerned.

> **Norman d'Alverse**, a Brabanter. He came to England in aid of William the Conqueror anno domini 1066 and married one of the daughters of Torold, son of Jeffery the Saxon.

Hugh Danvers lived at the time of Henry I and married Felice, daughter and heiress of Thomas Sankville of Frolesworth Co Leicester.
Bertram Danvers of Frolesworth Co Leicester married Alice, relict of Robert de Barton.
Hugo Danvers of Frolesworth Co Leicester was born in the 18th of Henry III.
Stephen Danvers Lord of the Manor of Frolesworth Co Leicester. He was born 43 Henry III.
Robert Danvers was born the 8th of Edward I.
Nicholas Danvers married Isabella the daughter of Sir Robert Burdett Knight, 14 Edward II.
Joan Danvers daughter and heiress married Joseph Armery of Maldon Co Essex 15 Edward III.
Robert Danvers of Shakerston Co Leicester.
William Danvers of Shakerston Co Leicester was born the 6th of Edward II.
Henry Danvers.
John Danvers was born the 29th of Edward III.
John Danvers was born the 16th of Richard II.
John Danvers by the right of his wife of Swithland Co Leicester was born the 30th of Henry VI and married Elizabeth the daughter and co-heiress of Sir John Walcot Knight.
Thomas Danvers married Alicia, the daughter of — Venables, Baron of Kinderton 20 Henry VII.
John Danvers married Margaret the daughter of Sir Ralph Shirley Knight of Staunton Harold Co Leicester.
Francis Danvers married Margaret daughter of — Kingston in the county of Gloucester.
John Danvers of Swithland Co Leicester was born 2nd of Edward VI married Isabella, the daughter of Richard Coke of Trusley Co Derby.
Anna Danvers married Fr Mulso of Tywell Co Northampton.
Elizabeth Danvers married — Mounsal of Burton Latimer Co Northampton.
Dorothy Danvers married Arthur Beresford of Shakerstone Co Leicester.
Francis Danvers married Elizabeth daughter of John Skeavington of Fisherick, Stafford, died 1631.
John Danvers married the daughter of — Allen & died Oct 26th 1674 aged 77 years.
Francis Cumberford of Oxley Co Stafford married **Elizabeth Danvers**.
William Danvers married Elizabeth daughter of Thomas Babington of Rothley Temple Nov 1618 died 1656.
William Danvers married the daughter of William Harpur of the county of Derby.

Ann Danvers married Gabriel Taylor, Gentleman, of Wales.
Catherine Danvers married Josias Beesly, Gent on the 31st of March 1655.
Elizabeth Danvers married William Palmer of Wanlip.
Henry Danvers married 13 of March 1664 Ann the third daughter of Joseph Coke of Melbourne Knight and relict of Henry Sacheverell of Morley Co Derby.
Samuel Danvers married Elizabeth the daughter of Joseph Morewood, Merchant, London, by Elizabeth Blundell co-heiress of — Woodcock of Shirfield Co Berks December 20th 1683 died 1693.
Anna Danvers married John Palmer of Wanlip.
Eleanor Danvers.
Joseph Danvers was married December 7th 1721 to Frances the second daughter of Thomas Babington of Rothley Temple Co Leicester.
Frances Danvers.
Catherine Danvers became the third wife of Edward Lancelot Lee Esq of Coton Co Salop.
Lucy Danvers married Honble Col John Grey uncle to the Earl of Stamford & died 1799.
John Danvers was married October 10th 1752 to Mary Watson the daughter and heiress of Joel Watson Esquire of London, Merchant.

Susannah Danvers	**Henry Danvers**
Mary Danvers	**Joseph Danvers**
William Danvers	**John Watson Danvers**

From exile home return'd my flesh and spirit
There Father's houses, earth and heaven inherit.

Another eighteenth century slate and brass memorial, presumably also erected by Sir John, commemorates five of his children – all of whom died young. The slate is ornamented with three cherubs' heads above and a carved skull and crossed palm leaves below. The brass plate is inscribed to the memory of John Watson Danvers (d.1768, aged 13), of Joseph Danvers (d.1756, aged 3 months), of Henry Danvers (d.1759, aged 20 months), of William Danvers (d.1762, aged 3 months), and of Susannah Danvers. (The burial places of three of these children are also marked by brass memorial plates which are inset into the 1925 floor of the chapel: John Watson, Joseph, and Henry.)

> To the memory of John Watson Danvers Esquire, Mr Joseph Danvers, Mr Henry Danvers, Mr William Danvers, and Mrs *(sic)* Susannah Danvers, five of the children of Sir John Danvers Bart by Mary, Lady Danvers his wife who was the daughter and heiress of Joel Watson Esquire of London, Merchant, which children all died young and were buried in this chapel in leaden coffins. God's will be done.

The Parish Church

Some years before he died, Sir John Danvers erected a memorial to himself in the family chapel. Throsby, describing one of his 'Excursions' to Swithland in c. 1790, said that 'the most extraordinary thing here is a large monument, erected by and to the memory of the living Sir John Danvers, Bart., fearful that posterity, or perhaps his only daughter, should forget him'. The monument has a blue marble background on which is a white marble tablet between two Ionic columns and pediment surmounted by a vase. It was originally placed on the wall facing the east door of the Danvers chapel, but is now situated on the north wall of the nave. The tablet is inscribed.

> The Body of Sir John Danvers, Bart, who departed this life about the 18th century, was deposited under the blue stone at the foot of this memorial. He was the only son of Sir Joseph Danvers Bart by Frances his wife, daughter of Thomas Babington of Rothley Temple in this county, Esquire. Sir Joseph was the son of Samuel Danvers Esquire by Elizabeth Morewood, an heiress of Overton, in the county of Derby; who, surviving her husband, married John Danvers of Prescott Manor in the county of Oxford, Esquire, the only son and heir of Sir John Danvers of Whichwood Forest, in the said county, knight. Sir John was the only brother and heir of Henry Danvers, Earl of Danby, a general officer, and Knight of the Garter, and founder of the Physic Garden at Oxford, a past friend and loyal adherent of Charles the First, in whose reign and service he died without issue. These two brothers were sons of Sir John Danvers Knight[29] by Elizabeth, daughter of John Nevill, Lord Latimer, son-in-law of Queen Katherine Parr. The Earl was a friend of the king; but Sir John was a friend of the constitution; and in the violent struggles which ensued, sided with that band of patriots, who thought Liberty could not be too dearly bought, though at the expense of Royal blood. His death, happening before the Restoration, sheltered him from prosecution; but his son, who was an infant when the king was beheaded, saw his paternal estates, to the amount of ten thousand pounds a year, in the counties of Oxford and Wiltshire in the hands of strangers. The small portion of his patrimony which escaped the rapacity of the Court, that son left to Sir Joseph Danvers for life, and to Sir John in tail. He was happy in his choice; Sir Joseph was an able supporter of the Protestant cause. He was in Parliament nearly thirty years in the reign of George the Second; he was a deputy lieutenant and acting Justice of the Peace for this county, and with his wife lies buried in a tomb in this churchyard. Sir John, his son, thought proper to tread in the steps of his Protestant ancestors, and seized every opportunity of shewing his attachment to their religion and civil principles. His bounty beautified this Church and rebuilt the Parsonage. In all political contests he uniformly gave his support to the friends of the Protestant interest and assertors of Revolution principles, deeming them in conjunction

the best pledges and securities for his temporal welfare and eternal happiness.

Et genus & proavos & quae nos fecimus ipsi Vix ea nostra voco. Stemmata quid faciunt quid prodest Pontice longo Sanguine Censeri pictosque ostendere vultus Majorum. Nobilitas sola est atque unica Virtus.

Enjoying the idea of Sir John writing his own epitaph, Throsby added a footnote.

The little stone is certainly there,[30] but Sir John is in London – not food for worms and reptiles, but regaling, perhaps, over the famed sirloin of old England.

The Nineteenth Century Interior

The Ecclesiastical Census of 1851 describes a church with 230 sittings (sittings for children 60, free sittings 80, other sittings 90). The persons 'attending divine service' on Sunday 30th March, 1851 were:

Morning – General congregation 46: Sunday scholars 34
Afternoon – General congregation 66; Sunday scholars 34.[31]

In 1805, a white marble tablet surmounted by an urn had been erected on the south wall of the chancel to commemorate Mary Llwyd, wife of rector, John Llwyd. This was the first wall memorial to be erected in the church to someone other than a member of the Danvers family.

Mary Llwyd died on 24th August 1805 being about 72 years of age. She was the wife of the Reverend John Llwyd Rector of this parish and the only surviving issue of John Major Esquire formerly of the Borough of Leicester by Katherine his wife who was one of the daughters of William Byrd heretofore of Claybrooke in this County, Esquire, of whom she was the sole remaining descendant.

In the 1860s, George John Butler Danvers, now fifth Earl of Lanesborough, replaced Sir Joseph's south aisle windows with new ones. He also caused the floor of the nave to be tiled. He had the Lanesborough arms placed at the top of the two windows of the family chapel, arguably changing it from a 'Danvers' chapel into a 'Lanesborough' chapel. The north and south chancel windows were blocked up (if they had ever been glazed), and the nave windows gothicized. The only 1727 windows left untouched were the small window over the south door and the window frame at the west end of the south aisle. A new porch entrance was added to the Danvers chapel.

George John, perhaps not surprisingly, erected no memorials to his father or mother, or to his father's second wife.[32] His father, Augustus Richard Butler Danvers, died in Boulogne in 1820 and was buried there, his mother Mary died in London and was buried in Bunhill Fields. When George John died in 1866, however, he continued the Danvers tradition of being buried in a vault below the family chapel.[33] His first wife, Frances Arabella, who died in 1850, was buried in Dublin. Her husband set up a white marble wall memorial to her in Swithland church. It is mounted on a blue marble surround and situated on the south wall of the Danvers chapel.

> Sacred to the memory of Frances, Countess of Lanesborough, who departed this life Oct 5th 1850 at Lanesborough Lodge near Belturbet, Ireland, and was buried at St Anne's Church, Dublin, on the 9th of that month in a vault belonging to the Lanesborough family. Blessed are the dead which die in the Lord.

George John's own memorial is in the form of a brass plate surrounded by blue marble, inscribed in each corner with the emblems of the four evangelists.

> Here rests the body of George John Danvers Butler Danvers, 5th Earl of Lanesborough and Baron of Newtown Butler, eldest son of the Honble Augustus Richard Butler Danvers by Mary daughter and heiress of the late Sir John Danvers Baronet of Swithland, Born 6th December 1794, Died 7th July 1866. Frederica Emma, youngest daughter of the late Charles Bishop Esquire and Relict of Sir Richard Hunter, widow of the above named George John Danvers, Earl of Lanesborough, Born 13th February 1808, Died 3rd October 1870.

In 1867 George John's second wife, Frederica Emma, who was to be buried alongside him, caused a new stained glass window depicting the Resurrection and the Ascension to be set up at the east end of the church in memory of her husband,[34] possibly displacing the window which commemorated Agnes Scot.

Also worshipping at Swithland in the middle of the nineteenth century was the Heygate family from Roecliffe Manor. James Heygate (1747–1833) was a London banker who took advantage of land coming onto the market as a result of the Charnwood Forest Enclosure Award and purchased land from the Enclosure Commissioners. He bought the land at Roecliffe from Augustus Richard Butler-Danvers in 1815 and erected the country mansion known today as Roecliffe Manor. His son, William Heygate (1782–1844), completed the building. William Heygate was a partner in the London banking firm of Pares & Heygate of Aldermanbury, London, and held high office in the City. In the course of his career, he served as a Sheriff of the City of London in 1811–22, Alderman 1812–1843, Lord Mayor in 1822–23 and City Chamberlain in 1843–4. In addition, he was elected a Member of Parliament for Sudbury in 1818, which he served until 1826. He was created a baronet in September 1831. On his death in 1844, he was buried at St Margaret's, Leicester. His wife, Lady Isabella Heygate, however, was buried in Swithland churchyard in 1859.

In January 1864, Sir William's son, Frederick William Heygate (1822–1894), also entitled Sir William, wrote to the rector, George Napleton Treweeke, offering to finance some improvements to the western end of the south aisle.

Fig 4.7 Christ's Resurrection, east window, 1867.

> I offer to replace the present unsightly window over the vestry in which I have so long sat with a stone window exactly similar to the adjoining ones in Lord Lanesborough's chancel and to glaze it.
> I will remove all the present woodwork round the vestry and with the materials (adding what is necessary) erect two seats open at the end, one along the west wall, the other in front of it. I will also turn the present three remaining seats facing the organ, so as to look toward the east, similar to the other seats under the organ loft.
> I will put down tiles in the open passage leading from where the font will be to the west wall.
> In consideration of my doing the above should my offer be accepted, I ask only that my family and establishment may be considered to have a priority of possession of the two open seats first named. I mean that along the west wall and the one in front thereof.
> Of course this would not confer and could not confer any legal right to any sittings in the church nor should I ask such a thing ...[35]

Heygate's offer was accepted and a stained glass window, given by his four sons in memory of Sir William senior and Lady Isabella Heygate, was installed in 1864.[36] In the left-hand light of the window is a depiction of Martha and the text 'I know that he shall rise again'; in the right-hand light Jesus is portrayed with the words 'I am the Resurrection and the Life'; in the top light there is an angel and the legend 'Alleluia'. Later, in 1897, a plain memorial plate on the west wall of the south aisle was erected by William Unwin Heygate, in memory of his three brothers, Sir Frederick William Heygate, Major Edward Nicholas Heygate, and Robert Henry Heygate.

> In affectionate memory of Sir Frederick Heygate aet 72 Baronet of Bellaven Co Derry and late of Roecliffe, Leics, JP DL and for many years MR for the Co Londonderry. Also of Major Edward N. Heygate RE JP aet 68 of Buckland, Herefordshire. And of Robert H.J. Heygate Esq MA aet 59 of Oaklands, Herefordshire. Erected by their surviving brother W.U. Heygate of Roecliffe in this county 1897.

The mid-nineteenth century appeared to be a good time for Swithland church, at least in the eyes of the churchwardens, Thomas Bates and William Cuffling. Their returns for the 1863 Episcopal Visitation state that the building was in decent repair and kept in good order. It was not insured, but it was properly drained. No alterations had been done without licence. The chancel was in good repair, the state of the communion table was good and bread and wine were provided. There was no table of degrees set up, nor was there a book for entering the names of strangers who may preach in the church. The registers were kept in a chest in the chancel, and copies of registers were sent to the registry. The church was kept free from profane and secular uses. The pews were all free, with the exception of two, and were 'conveniently arranged'. The money collected in the offertory was given to the poor of the parish, but no replies were given to the questions relating to by whom the offertory was collected and what was the average amount.

People behaved in an orderly manner in church and churchyard, and the wardens used all diligence to prevent any profanation of the Lord's Day. The churchyard was well fenced; there were no encroachments or cattle feeding. No order in council had been given to discontinue burials and no trees had been cut down in the churchyard. The minister's house and outhouses were in fair repair. The rector, George Treweeke, was resident for at least nine months, he had no curates, performed the services properly and instructed the poor children properly too. There were two Sunday services, at 11am and 3pm. 'Most of the parishioners attend'. Holy Communion was administered four times a year, after the morning service, with an average attendance of twenty. There was a day school and a Sunday school. The church had a clerk who did his job properly and was paid properly. 'The parish does not give sums of money to charity.' Annual repairs amounted to about £11, the church rate was granted – at two pence in the pound. The wardens had nothing they wished to raise with the bishop.[37]

During the Victorian period, many English churches were 'restored', often substantially. Swithland church, however, remained largely unaltered during the late Victorian period. On the death of Rector George Napleton Treweeke in 1876, a white marble memorial tablet was placed on the north wall of the chancel.

> This tablet was erected by the Parishioners of Swithland in loving remembrance of the Reverend George Napleton Treweeke 20 years Rector of this Parish. Born September 8th 1821 Died at Southsea August 20th 1876. 'Thy Will be Done' Matt, vi.10.

But there was little other change.

According to a newspaper description dated June 1880,[38] the nave of Swithland church was still fitted with some box pews, presumably with doors. Photographs indicate that these pews faced the pulpit on the north wall. Swithland's 'three-decker' pulpit was in a prominent position on the north wall, half way down the nave. The preacher, who stood five feet above the ground when preaching, could therefore be seen by all. Below him was his reading desk from which he read the service, and next to that his clerk's reading desk.

When Treweeke was rector, the main Sunday morning service was 11am Matins, presumably followed by Litany and Ante-Communion, which liturgical practice suited the lay-out of the church. If hymns were sung, they might have been accompanied by a small band of villagers seated in the gallery at the west end of the church. There is no evidence that the organ was used at the time for accompanying hymns, but there is no record of a village band either. Evensong was at 3pm, possibly earlier in the dark winter months. Treweeke celebrated Communion once every quarter, presumably at Christmas, Easter and Whit Sunday. Because of the infrequency of Holy Communion services, and the fact that all the pews faced north, the altar at the east would have appeared less prominent.

Eighteenth-century chancels were generally screened off from the nave, though most roods had disappeared with the Reformation. In Swithland, in

1880, there was one step up to the chancel, which was separated from the nave by wrought iron railings and a gate across the chancel arch – the arch only eight feet in width at this time. According to the wardens, the church chest was kept in the chancel for the safe-keeping of the registers.

The main entrance to the church for the villagers remained the 1727 door in the south aisle. Just inside the church, on the floor to the immediate left of the entrance, was the brass monument to Agnes Scot. The pews on that side faced north, some boxed, some benches. The Snetzler organ was still in the wooden west gallery. The nave walls were covered with plaster, and the nave lit by two brass candelabra, each with twelve candles and the Danvers wyvern crest in the centre. These were probably a gift from the Hall.

On the right of the door in the south aisle, a stone wall divided the elevated Danvers chapel from the remainder of the south aisle. On its north side the Danvers chapel was separated from the remainder of the church by wrought iron railings and a gate. The chapel was lit by another brass candelabrum for twelve candles, which was subsequently moved to the nave. Inside the chapel, on either side of the eastern entrance door, were the monuments to William Danvers, John Watson Danvers and others. On the chapel's west wall was the pedigree of Sir John Danvers, together with the memorials to Sir John Danvers and to Francis Danvers. Above these wall monuments hung hatchments, a flag, and streamers.

Hatchments – funeral escutcheons – were erected to mark the deaths of the gentry. Swithland's hatchments are for John Danvers of Prescott (d.1721); Sir Joseph Danvers (d.1752); Lady Frances Danvers (d.1759). To these were subsequently added hatchments to Frances Arabella Butler, Countess of Lanesborough (d.1850); George John Butler Danvers, 5th Earl of Lanesborough (d.1866); and Frederica Emma Butler, Countess of Lanesborough (d.1870). Customarily, hatchments were first hung at the front of the house of the deceased, and later moved to the church. As neither John Danvers of Prescott nor Frances Arabella Butler were buried at Swithland, their hatchments are likely to have hung first where they died and subsequently moved to St Leonard's Church.

The hatchments show:

> **John Danvers of Prescott** (d.1721) who married Elizabeth, nee Morewood, widow of Samuel Danvers of Swithland.
> Arms and crest of Danvers-Nevill impaling Morewood. All black background.
> Crest: a wyvern or and gules.
> Arms – dexter: quarterly 1 & 4 gules, a chevron wavy, between three mullets (molets) of six points, radiant, or pierced azure; 2 & 3 gules on a saltire argent an annulet sable. Arms – sinister: vert an oak tree eradicated argent fructed or.

> **Sir Joseph Danvers,** 1st baronet (d.1753) who married Frances, daughter of Thomas Babington of Rothley Temple.
> Arms and crest of Danvers-Nevill impaling Babington. Dexter background black.

Crest: a wyvern or and gules.
Arms – dexter: quarterly 1 & 4 gules, a chevron wavy, between three mullets (molets) of six points, radiant, or pierced azure; 2 & 3 gules on a saltire argent an annulet sable. Arms – sinister: argent ten torteau, four three two and one, a label of three points azure.
Motto: Never fear.

Dame Frances Danvers (d.1759), daughter of Thomas Babington, who married Joseph Danvers.
A lozenge. Danvers-Nevill impaling Babington. All background black.
Crest: a wyvern or and gules.
Arms – dexter: quarterly 1 & 4 gules, a chevron wavy, between three mullets (molets) of six points, radiant, or pierced azure; 2 & 3 gules on a saltire argent an annulet sable. Arms – sinister: argent ten torteau, four three two and one, a label of three points azure.

Frances Arabella Butler (d.1850), Countess of Lanesborough, daughter of Col Stephen Francis William Fremantle, who married, 1815, George John Butler Danvers, 5th Earl of Lanesborough (d.1866).
Arms of Danvers-Butler impaling Fremantle. Sinister background black.
Countess's coronet.
Arms – dexter: quarterly 1 & 4 gules, a chevron wavy, between three mullets (molets) of six points, radiant, or pierced azure; 2 & 3 argent three covered cups in bend between two bendlets engrailed, sable. Arms – sinister: vert three bars ermine surmounted by a lion rampant gules in chief two plates argent. Supporters – dexter: a cockatrice vert, beaked or, ducally gorged or. Supporters – sinister: a wyvern, ducally gorged and chained or.

George John Butler Danvers, 5th Earl of Lanesborough (d.1866) who married, 1851, Frederica Emma, youngest daughter of Charles Bishop.
Danvers-Butler impaling Bishop. Dexter background black.
Earl's coronet.
Crest – dexter: a wyvern vert, wings elevated and tail nowed, or, gorged with a plain collar and chained or. Crest – sinister: a demi-cockatrice vert wings elevated, argent, combed beaked wattled and ducally gorged, or.
Arms – dexter: quarterly 1 & 4 gules, a chevron wavy, between three mullets (molets) of six points, radiant, or pierced azure; 2 & 3 argent three covered cups in bend between two bendlets engrailed, sable. Arms – sinister: ermine on a bend engrailed cotised vert three besants. Supporters – dexter: a cockatrice vert wings elevated, argent, combed beaked wattled and ducally gorged, or.

Supporters – sinister: a wyvern vert, wings elevated and tail nowed, or, gorged with a plain collar and chained or. Motto: Liberté, toute, entiere.

Frederica Emma Butler, Countess of Lanesborough, (d.1870), youngest daughter of Charles Bishop, who married, 1851, George John Butler Danvers, 5th Earl of Lanesborough.
A lozenge. Danvers-Butler impaling Bishop. All black background. Countess' coronet.
Arms – dexter: quarterly 1 & 4 gules, a chevron wavy, between three mullets (molets) of six points, radiant, or pierced azure; 2 & 3 argent three covered cups in bend between two bendlets engrailed, sable. Arms – sinister: ermine on a bend engrailed cotised vert three besants.
Supporters – dexter: a cockatrice vert wings elevated, argent, combed beaked wattled and ducally gorged, or. Supporters – sinister: a wyvern vert, wings elevated and tail nowed, or, gorged with a plain collar and chained or.

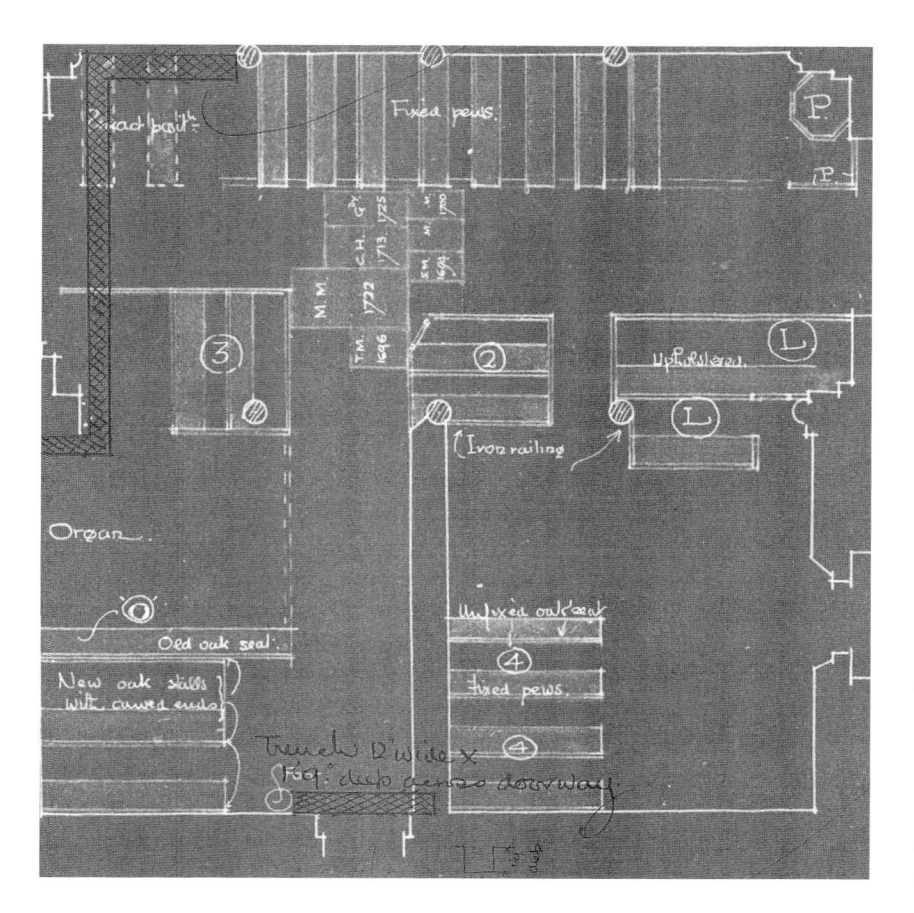

Fig 4.8 A sketch of the interior c. 1920 indicating layout of seating and nave burials.

Fig 4.9 Interior of St Leonard's Church, c.1920, facing east.

A 1880 newspaper description of the nave[39] referred to its old fashioned layout, which the writer clearly thought needed some updating.

> The nave is seated with once popular but now fast disappearing box pews. The pulpit bears the date 1589, and is of the old fashioned high barrel type, the preacher ascending a stair to deliver his sermons above, and leading the services from a primitive looking desk immediately below. This primitive piece of ecclesiastical furniture reminds us forcibly of the boasted 'good old times', when the service was little better than a duet between the parson and the clerk. The unusually conspicuous position it occupies moreover does not tend to diminish its congruity. In order that worshippers in the chapel may see and hear, the pulpit is reared about the middle of the north wall of the nave, and is therefore almost directly opposite the south door.

The sixth Earl, however, opposed any changes.

> To place both pulpit and reading desk in their conventional position under the chancel arch, it was proposed that part of the partitional south wall of the nave be removed; but this is supposed to be against the wishes of the Earl of Lanesborough, and has been allowed to drop.

Presumably the 'new' incumbent, Kingsford Beauchamp Sidebottom (1877–83), had proposed these changes. Reading between the lines of a visitation return submitted by Sidebottom in 1882,[40] we get the impression he wanted to make some changes in order to deepen the spiritual life of his parishioners. He reported that the Lord's Supper was administered 'once a month' (which was more frequently than had been the case in 1863 when Treweeke was rector) and said that he intended to try 'again' more frequent communion. (This would explain the desire to move the pulpit and reading desk so that the focus of attention in the church was oriented eastward towards the altar as well as to the pulpit and reading desk).

Sidebottom also reported that he felt there was a slight decrease of intemperance in the parish. He did not use the shortened services sanctioned by the diocese, and there was no 'Scripture Reader' or other form of lay agency for church work in his parish. He could not keep his young people in Sunday School after they left the Day School. He had 'tried Bible classes and communicants meetings with ill success' and was 'going to try the former again'. He had presented two candidates for confirmation last time, but had rejected four 'as showing unfitness'. There was one dissenting place of worship within the parish, but only one family 'professedly dissenters, and they are Baptists'. Sidebottom relinquished the living in 1883. His successor also found his congregation to be resistant to change.

Fig 4.10 Interior of St Leonard's Church, c. 1900, facing west.

Restoration

The new rector, James Murray Dixon, arrived in 1884. By 1894, convinced of the need for major restoration to the church, he began to raise funds for this purpose. His wardens were in agreement. In the 1905 Bishop's Visitation, churchwarden Edwin Pepper submitted their report.

> The church is not in good repair. The Chancel needs repairing. The Communion Table and its covering, the Linen Cloth, the Kneeling Cushions for Communicants and other furniture are not in good order … There is no fund out of which the fabric of the church is maintained in good repair. The necessary expenses are provided by collecting from house to house. I think it right to bring to the bishop's notice that the Church needs restoring very badly.[41]

Clearly there were problems. There were structural defects, and the interior layout of the church meant that those seated in the south-west corner had their view almost totally obstructed by the wall to the Danvers chapel. The writer of the *Leicester Chronicle* article in 1880 had remarked on the church's mantle of green ivy.

> This plant has grown luxuriantly on the tower and chancel and even springs and flourishes in a window-sill, from which it might be supposed impossible to extract moisture or nutriment.[42]

Postcard photographs from the end of the nineteenth century depict the tower and chancel smothered in ivy. They also show the access footpaths to the church on the south side and the absence of paths on the north side, the

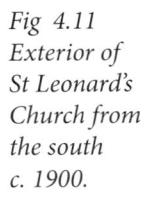

Fig 4.11 Exterior of St Leonard's Church from the south c. 1900.

Fig 4.12 Exterior of St Leonard's Church from the south-east c. 1900.

main entrance to the church through the south door and notice board beside, and the walled-up eighteenth century windows in the chancel.

Murray Dixon's incentive for restoration may also have been influenced by the inappropriateness of the interior for the kind of worship over which he wanted to preside. The nineteenth century Oxford Movement had called for a revival of reverence, piety, prayer, and commitment, urging that worship in parish churches should be restored to its pristine splendour. Leaders such as Newman, Keble and Pusey sought to re-establish the Eucharist as the most important part of a person's worship. The focus of Swithland church on the pulpit, rather than on the altar, did not chime well with such intentions.

Despite the opposition of John Vansittart Danvers Butler, the sixth Earl,

Fig 4.13 Exterior of St Leonard's Church from the north c. 1900.

to any major re-ordering of the interior of the church in 1884, Dixon was ready in 1902 to form an appeal committee to raise funds for church restoration. They were, however, not able to begin restoration work until 1917. Meanwhile the churchwardens kept up the pressure. In 1914 Edwin Pepper and Thomas Beers again reported to the Bishop.

> The church is not in good repair. It is not provided with a lightning conductor. It is insured against fire. The Chancel is in need of repair. The Communion Table and other furniture is not in good order ... I wish to draw to the attention of the bishop that the church is very badly in need of restoration.[43]

A start was made on the tower. When the walls were stripped of ivy, the tower was found to be in a dangerous condition, and repairs effected. The bells were re-hung in a steel frame. The clock was renovated and repositioned and the tower roof was entirely renewed. A ringing chamber was constructed in the tower to which a new external stair turret was built to give access. The turret also acted as an additional buttress to the tower. A vestry was created at the base of the tower below the ringing chamber. The tower door was re-fashioned and a stained glass window inserted into the lancet window showing St Michael, Captain of the Host, on whose shield bearing a Cross is the inscription 'In this sign conquer'.[44] The window was dedicated to Captain Nigel John Latham Wickham of the Connaught Rangers, who died in the Great War in 1916. He was fiancé to one of the rector's daughters. The tower restoration was completed in 1918, and thanksgiving services were held on Thursday 9th May 1918, with the Bishop of Peterborough preaching at the afternoon service and the Bishop of Leicester in the evening.

The work to the tower had cost more than had been anticipated. Further restoration work was therefore delayed, though some interior re-ordering proved possible. In 1920, Dixon donated the carved oak screen across the tower arch in memory of his son Henry Otto Murray Dixon who had died in action in 1917. The screen was dedicated by the Archdeacon of Loughborough on Easter Tuesday, 6th April 1920. Next, Murray Dixon repositioned the pulpit at the north-east corner of the nave, next to the chancel arch. Finally, he removed the organ from the gallery, which was demolished, and placed it against the southern buttress of the tower arch.

In 1921 churchwardens, William Paterson and A. Cook, reported that the church and chancel were 'not in good repair – the roof was defective'. They were, however, able to report that the church was insured by the Royal Exchange Assurance for £1,000, and that the premium – recently increased – had been paid, and that they were also insured under the Workmen's Compensation Act (1906).[45]

In 1924 Dixon addressed the problem of the Danvers chapel wall, the remaining box pews and the structural integrity of the remainder of the church building. His architect, Albert Herbert, toyed with a scheme that would have demolished Joseph Danvers' south aisle, and rebuilt smaller north and south aisles. If the idea had gone ahead, Swithland would have had a more symmetrical church – resembling the original mediaeval shape – but at the cost of losing the 1727 extension. Whether Herbert's drawings were any more than feasibility studies is not known.

Nevertheless, major works were undertaken. A row ensued which overflowed into the press.[46] Dixon resigned at the point when the chancel roof had been completely removed and work had begun in the nave and the south aisle, but sufficient finance had not yet been raised. Thanks, however, to a financial gift after Dixon's departure from one wealthy Swithland parishioner, Archibald Turner of The Cottage, 1 Main Street, restoration was finally effected. It had been a traumatic episode in the life of the church as well as a major structural undertaking.

An Interesting Complication

For some reason, no detailed records were kept by architect or Parochial Church Council as to what was intended and uncovered by the restoration work done between 1919 and 1925. All that was recorded in the church council minutes was a March 1923 decision taken by the council to the rector's all-embracing resolution

> ... that the Church restoration Committee has your sanction and approval to deal with the fabric & furniture of the church as they shall think most desirable.[47]

For a picture of what was done, we are indebted to notes taken by a visitor staying with relations in Anstey – Charles William Danvers of the Shepshed branch[48] of the Danvers family. Charles Danvers had his own agenda. He and his family were still attempting to prove the validity of the fraud they believed had been perpetrated by the Lanesborough family in order to inherit the Swithland estates. It was in pursuance of more evidence, therefore, that Danvers visited the church while the restoration work was in hand, asked questions of various people involved and wrote up his notes.[49] He pursued two lines of enquiry: whether the Swithland and Shepshed church registers had been tampered with, and to discover which Danvers family members were buried in the vaults.

In 1919 Charles Danvers met with Murray Dixon asking questions about the registers. Dixon appeared to encourage him in his surmise that the Swithland registers had at some point been tampered with. 'Glancing over the printed duplicate (of the Swithland registers) and seeing but one entry in the name of Danvers recording the death of Elizabeth, widow of William, I remarked 'you don't appear to have many of the name of Danvers registered here'. 'No' (Dixon) says, 'not when considering the years they resided here'. Charles visited again on several occasions. He was looking for Danvers' memorials and found, as he thought, too few. 'Even the blue Stone of history, marking the spot where the body of Sir John Danvers lay, I had not been able to discover nor the stone to Francis Danvers who died 1697, which was recorded in Nichols History of Leicestershire'.[50]

Danvers next recorded visits were in June 1924. 'On June 20th 1924, I ...

found that the body of the church floor had been lowered at the time about nine inches also that the steps leading up into the chapel had been removed'. He visited again on the August 29th. 'I saw that some of the chapel floor ... had been lowered some two feet and on a level with the church floor and ... exposed to view a great part of the brickwork of the vault in which Sir John Danvers Bart body lay.' His next visit was to Mr A. Turner, chairman of the Swithland Church Committee at his Elastic Mills, Deacon Street, Leicester. Turner told him several tombstones had been found in the portion of the floor that had been levelled, tracings had been taken, and that they were to be placed in the positions they were found on the new floor level. 'Also owing to the vaults which would have to be opened, no further groundwork could be done for it was feared that the vaults were very nearly full and that many coffins would have to be moved'.

After a further visit in April 1925 he found that 'another portion of the Chapel floor had been lowered. Part had been lowered by some twelve inches forming a step whilst the other part was by two feet, the same as the first portion ... Also a part of the West wall of the chapel had been pulled down ... the 1631 memorial to Francis Danvers was removed and a semi archway constructed in its place'. In pursuance of his suspicions of fraudulent activity, Charles sent several letters detailing them to, among others, the Bishop of Peterborough and the Home Office. Danvers must have felt the latter's final reply as a body blow.

> 25th May 1925. Sir, With reference to your statement dated the 11th last, regarding the Lanesborough Danvers Chapel, I am directed by the Secretary of State to say that on the information available he does not think it necessary to take any action in the matter. Your Obedient Servant E. J. Eagleston.

Murray Dixon resigned as rector on 30th July 1925. Shortly afterwards, disagreements over the church restoration burst into the local press. On Wednesday 16th September 1925, ten days after Murray Dixon's open letter to the parishioners,[51] the *Leicester Mercury* carried an inflammatory headline on the front page. 'Earl resents church dismantling. Family chapel at Swithland wrecked and tombstones displaced'. The article reported that:

> Swithland Parish Church has been reduced almost to ruins, and the congregation now worship in a disused Wesleyan chapel. Great indignation is felt by the parishioners at this remarkable state of affairs. The rector commenced an ambitious scheme of restoration in 1924, but when he resigned last July work stopped. The church is completely dismantled, the roof is almost off, and tombs and monuments have been interfered with. The Earl of Lanesborough is indignant over the 'wild cat scheme' and says despite a warning from the Lord Chancellor that it was private property, his family chapel has been practically pulled down, and the tombstones of his ancestors' graves removed from their setting. He says he would rather play golf than worship at the old Nonconformist chapel.

The newspaper's 'Special Correspondent' then 'elaborated'.

> An extraordinary impasse has arisen in connection with Swithland church, and people in the district are wondering at the delay in the work of restoration, begun without authority last year.
>
> In July of 1924, the Rev Murray Dixon, who had held the living for forty years, decided that the church needed restoring and work was accordingly begun, it being the intention to install a heating system, alter the chancel, build a new porch, as well as erect north and south aisles.
>
> No faculty was applied for at the time, and builders and the architect, Mr Herbert, of Messrs. Tait and Herbert, Leicester, proceeded with the task. The church was, to all intents and purposes pulled down.
>
> Trouble arose when the Ecclesiastical authorities were informed that the projected scheme had already commenced, whereupon, after some delay, a faculty was granted by the Chancellor of the Diocese (Mr Justice Lawrence).
>
> Having been informed that the faculty was granted, the bishop of Peterborough was actually forced to license a disused Wesleyan chapel at Swithland for the benefit of those who had no place of worship to attend.
>
> The work of restoration might have been long completed if matters were not complicated in July of this year, when it was announced that the Rev Murray Dixon had resigned from his benefice.
>
> His resignation was accepted, and the freehold of the church and the residence being vested in the beneficiary, no-one had authority to proceed with the work, which immediately ceased, it is stated, with the resignation of the rector. For many years, Mr Dixon had been collecting for a Restoration Fund, and on his retirement he handed over a considerable sum to trustees, among whom is the rural dean, the Rev Canon Briggs of Loughborough.
>
> Meanwhile, Church of England worshippers are compelled through force of circumstances to utilise the Wesleyan chapel. As a matter of fact, the greatest indignation is felt in Swithland by people who describe the situation as being 'most unsatisfactory, and without any explanation'.
>
> The church at present is completely dismantled, the roof is almost off, and the various tombs and monuments have been interfered with. The interior of the building is a chaotic mass of broken glass, rafters, bricks and debris, over which one has to climb to get from one end of the church to the other.

There followed statements from the Archdeacon of Loughborough and the seventh Earl of Lanesborough. The Archdeacon said that 'the laws governing church property were stringent, and in this case, until a new incumbent was appointed by the Lord Chancellor, no further work could be done at the church'. He said he did not know when an appointment would be made. The Earl of Lanesborough thundered that he was very angry. 'This was from the first to the last a wild cat scheme, and it has left me without a church or a parson. I have nowhere to worship...' When reminded that a Church of England service was being held in Swithland at the former Wesleyan Chapel, the *Leicester Mercury* correspondent reported that 'the Earl smiled, and said he would rather play golf'.

The newspaper article brought a swift rejoinder from the architect Mr Albert Herbert, challenging some of the contents, but conceding that monuments had been removed from the Danvers chapel. On 18th September, the newspaper carried a letter in which Herbert asserted that

> ... a faculty was obtained before any building contract was obtained or any work was ordered by me, although it is admitted that certain repairs and minor works had previously been put in hand ... Every portion of the roof is covered in except that of a new porch, which is now being erected. The church has not to all intents and purposes been pulled down. It is a fact that some monuments have been removed from the Danvers chapel, though not under my instructions.

In the same edition, there were two other letters. One expressed admiration for the 'late vicar' for having the courage to pull down the west wall of the chapel, which completely hid the congregation in the south-west portion of the church. The other sought to inform Lord Lanesborough that many parishioners and visitors to Swithland were grateful to the Wesleyans for lending their chapel.

The article also brought a rejoinder from Dixon. In a letter printed on 23rd September, he asserted that he was prepared to challenge practically every statement in the original article. The church was not being pulled down.

> I have not seen a vestige of broken glass, and not a stone of the church has been removed save where four new windows are placed in the chancel, the roof of which, being past satisfactory repair, is being replaced with a new one.

As to the work of restoration being a mad cat scheme, he wrote:

> ... the plans were passed in a much elaborated form in Bishop Carr Glyn's time, and revised and simplified with the concurrence of Bishop Woods, and had there been no outside interference, all the work contemplated could have been carried out in a comparatively short time. So far as I am aware, no work except clearing away rubbish was entered upon without a faculty.

As to the Danvers chapel, he commented:

> I can say positively that there was no disturbance to the (so called) Danvers chapel, other than that which was done by the

Earl of Lanesborough himself, or on his written authority, which I have in my possession, and in compliance with the terms of the faculty granted.

The effect on the church building of this incredible saga was that by the conclusion of the restoration work the old south doorway had been blocked-up, a new north doorway opened and a porch erected. Two thirds of the Danvers chapel floor had been lowered to the same level as the rest of the church floor, with the remainder only lowered by about one foot. Virtually all the old pews had been taken out and replaced by chairs, though some of the newer pews were retained as choir stalls in the chancel. Two box pews[52] were retained for the Earl of Lanesborough and his family at the front of the Danvers chapel and open pews were placed on the other side for his household. The railings across the chancel arch were removed and used to give a west boundary to the Danvers chapel where the wall had been, and the chancel arch was widened. The chancel roof was rebuilt. Two new flat-headed windows were inserted into both the north and south wall of the chancel. The tiled flooring through the whole church was taken up and replaced by oak blocks. The chancel floor was raised, giving three steps from nave to chancel in place of one. Plastering was removed from most of the interior walls. A group of slate tombstones to Michael Matthews and his family – that had been found under the floor at the aisle crossing – were lifted and placed outside the church, next to the new north porch. The west wall of the Danvers chapel was completely demolished. Of the monuments that had been positioned on that wall, the tablet to Sir John Danvers was placed on the north wall of the nave, Sir John's pedigree and the memorial to Francis Danvers were placed on the south wall where the old south entrance had been blocked-up. The brass to Agnes Scot was moved to the west wall of the south aisle. The organ was moved to the south-west corner of the church, and the

Fig 4.14 Interior of church showing new chancel arrangements, 1927.

opportunity taken to refurbish and enlarge it. Taylors of Leicester added another manual and a pedal board. The font was moved adjacent to the south side of the tower arch. A heating system, powered by an external coal boiler, replaced the stove in the centre of the nave. A new coal boiler was incorporated and its slate chimney built against the south side of the tower.

Shortly after the completion of the work, Archibald Turner, whose financial support had made the completed restoration possible, died. He is remembered in a plain tablet of Hopton stone on the north wall of the nave.

> This tablet was erected by the parishioners of Swithland in grateful memory of Archibald Turner who gave so generously to the restoration of this Church. At rest 26 April 1928.

Charles Danvers of Shepshed pre-deceased Turner in March 1927. He had certainly stirred things up in Swithland, but had found no evidence to support his family's conviction that they were the true heirs to Sir John Danvers' estates.

Later Twentieth Century Changes

After the earlier extensive changes, little further structural work was done to the church until the end of the twentieth century. Some new memorials were erected. The memorial to John Mackay (rector 1931–39, died 1942) was placed on the north wall near the pulpit; one to James Murray-Dixon (rector 1884–1924, died 1944) and his wife on the north wall of the chancel; and one to James Alexander Vazeille Boddy[53] (1895–1954), Parochial Church Council member and sidesman, on the west wall of the south aisle.

The introduction of twentieth century amenities must have made quite a difference to the look and feel of the church. Electricity was introduced in 1936. The three eighteenth century brass candelabra were adapted for electric light and hung in the nave, and two new plain wood rings with four lights, designed by Albert Herbert, were placed in the Danvers chapel. In the 1960s, the coal boiler was replaced; mains gas was brought in through the lych-gate, the old subterranean coal pit filled-in, and a new, functional – though rather unattractive – boiler house built at the west end of the south aisle (necessitating the removal of several tombstones to stand against the churchyard wall). The old coal oven chimney was left in place, and the new boiler connected to the 1928 hot water radiator system.

In the early 1950s modern light oak pews replaced the chairs and in 1961 the bells were re-hung. In 1962, 'under the Town and Country Planning Act (1962), the Church of St Leonard, Swithland, situate in the Rural District of Barrow upon Soar, (was) included in the list of buildings of special architectural interest in the area'.[54] In 1982 the choir stalls were removed from the chancel to the Danvers chapel.

In addition, many gifts of new furnishings were and continue to be made. The church frontals and other vestments and linen were given by Mary Kilby and her daughter Gweneth Gimson, who also gave the churchwardens' staves in memory of her father Walter Kilby. The oak stand for the Book of

Remembrance was given in 1995 by Alan Hardwicke in memory of his mother, and the Book of Remembrance was given by Audrey Benson in memory of her husband, Roy Benson. The oak chair in the sanctuary was given in memory of Percy Barrett, who chaired the church's finance committee for many years and oversaw the funding for the millennium extension. The best white chasuble and stole, bearing St Leonard's symbol of padlock and chains, were given to celebrate the completion of the extension. They were designed by Jill Woolley of Woodhouse Eaves, and embroidered by her and a team of church members.[55] A small oak table for the chancel was commissioned and purchased thanks to legacies from church members, Sydney Elson, Brian Vann and Kathleen Waltho. The tower flood-lighting was given in memory of churchwarden David Pugh. These and many other generous gifts have beautified the church and improved its facilities.

In the early 1980s a plan to build a raised hexagonal meeting room at the western end of the south aisle came to nothing. It was felt increasingly, however, that the church needed additional space to give meeting rooms for church groups and children's work, kitchen facilities and a toilet. Through the generosity of many members and friends of the church, a two-storey extension, incorporating these facilities as well as a new heating system for both church and extension, was built in 2000.[56] This Millennium Extension now stands in a long history of adaptations to a key building where generations of Swithland people have offered prayer, praise, and thanks to God.

Significantly, during the building works, the bricked-up eighteenth century window to the 1727 aisle was opened and glazed, thus connecting the eighteenth and twenty-first century extensions. The stained glass window was commissioned and dedicated 'in thanksgiving for the life and service of Robert Brian Osborne,[57] 1944–1999'. This window incorporates the armorial bearings of significant figures who have contributed to the history of village and church.

The Churchyard

For most of its history the church has stood in a rectangular plot of ground, with the rectory adjacent on its western side.[58] Until 1800, Swithland's Lower Green lay between the churchyard and the carriageway. Public access to the churchyard then was from a path south of the churchyard, with a gateway to the rectory in the west churchyard wall and to the Hall through a gateway in the east churchyard wall.

The Normans generally constructed the principal entrance to churches on the south side, where they also buried the dead. All the early burials in Swithland churchyard were therefore on the southern side of the church though, in the archaeological investigations for the Millennium Extension, an early unmarked brick grave was discovered at the east of the church. The earliest graves were unmarked, but gradually the richer and more socially important parishioners had their burying places marked. During the

Figs 4.15 Memorial stone to John Prier, May 1673.

seventeenth century, therefore, the numbers of headstones multiplied. The Swithland local slate industry was well placed to provide local memorials, especially as a primitive slate engraving industry was based in the village. As a material, slate is significantly harder than sandstone or limestone, and the inscriptions longer lasting. The first slate headstones in Swithland churchyard date from 1673 and are probably the earliest slate memorial stones in Leicestershire.[59]

HERE LYETH IN
TERRED THE BODY
OF JOHN PRIER THE
SONNE OF ROBART
PRIER WHO DEPART
ED THIS LIFE THE 8TH
DAY OF MAY 1673
BEING OF THE
AGE
OF 15 YEARES

HERE LYETH IN
TERRED THE BODY
OF DORATHIE
HALL WHO DEPA
RTED THIS LIFE
THE 17TH DAY OF
OCTOBER ANNO
DOM 1673

Later headstones show greater sophistication in engraving as techniques improved. Among the monuments on the south side of the church are groups of several members of the same family, the Priors, Gilberts, Newbolds, Wesleys and Clarkes. These were among the more affluent farmers and artisans of the village who could afford the cost of a headstone. Perhaps the finest slate memorial in the churchyard is the tomb to Sir Joseph Danvers Bt – with its carved pictures and inscriptions. The work to the tomb is said to have been done by a member of the Hind family who ran the local slate industry. There are also two seventeenth and eighteenth table top tombs to members of the Hind family. These are certainly impressive, but they lack the finesse of the Danvers tomb. The last members of the Hind family to be buried in Swithland, Henrietta Maria Louisa (d.1900) and Sarah Jane (d.1922), the Hind sisters,[60] are buried under a marble table top tomb on the north side of the church.

The north side of the churchyard began to be used for burials in the nineteenth century. Most of the headstones continued the tradition of inscribed slate memorials. Originally, these may have been decorated with a red, black and gold border: but subsequent weathering has removed all signs of decoration.

The Earls of Lanesborough are buried to the east of the church. The fifth Earl (d.1866) and his Countess, were buried in the Danvers chapel, but John Vansittart (d.1905) sixth Earl, Charles John (d.1929) seventh Earl, Henry Cavendish (d.1950) eighth Earl, and their Countesses, are buried in a line of graves, marked with granite crosses and substantial footstones, as in 1998

*Fig 4.16
St Leonard's Church, north side, before 1918.*

was the ninth and last Earl, Denis Anthony Brian. The six year old elder daughter of the ninth Earl, Georgina Ione (d. 1947) is also buried there.

Swithland Lower Green (one time 'common land') lay adjacent to the churchyard on the north side against Main Street. At the Enclosure Award in 1799, the Lower Green was allotted to Augustus Richard Butler Danvers, but must have been transferred to the church at some point, as in the latter part of the nineteenth century it was used as one of the entrance drives to the Rectory. It changed hands again, though, in 1924 when Murray-Dixon sold the old rectory and grounds to the seventh Earl of Lanesborough.

Fig 4.17 The Lych Gate, 1929.

In 1887 the old western entrance to the churchyard from the Rectory had been blocked off, leaving the point at which the churchyard touched Main Street as the only access. Here, in 1929, a lych-gate, designed by Albert Herbert, was erected in memory of Archibald Turner, who had contributed handsomely towards the restoration of the church. It was given by the employees of his elastic web manufacturing company in Leicester and Peterborough, and dedicated after Evensong on 15th June 1929 by the Bishop of Leicester.

By the 1920s, the Church Council was expressing concern at the lack of space for further burials, even though cremation was becoming increasingly popular. Numerous schemes were proposed – only to founder. The problem was finally solved in 1985 when 0.171 acres of land fronting Main Street – the old Lower Green – was acquired from the Earl of Lanesborough by compulsory purchase. The churchyard wall on the northern side was removed and a new wall built to enclose the additional land.

Patronage

From the first building of a chapel in Swithland, the Benedictine Abbey of St Evroult in Normandy had the right to present priests to the living, a right which they deputed to their daughter abbey church at Ware, Herts. The Benedictines held the advowson until the fourteenth century when it was transferred to the Crown. At some point, the right of the Crown to present to the living was delegated to the Lord Chancellor. When the living of Swithland was incorporated into the multi-benefice of Woodhouse, Woodhouse Eaves and Swithland in 1999, it was agreed that the patronage rights of the new benefice should be exercised alternately by the Lord Chancellor (patron of

Swithland) and the Leicester Diocesan Board of Patronage (patron of Woodhouse with Woodhouse Eaves). When the Prime Minister proposed to abolish the office of Lord Chancellor in 2003, Swithland opted that its patronage should revert to the Crown. In the event, the Government found they could not abolish the office without an act of parliament. This step was not taken. There is still a Lord Chancellor, and patron of Swithland, though he or she does not now have to sit in the House of Lords.

Charities

There is evidence of two charitable foundations for the poor of Swithland. In 1838, a Charity Commissioners report referred to a 'lost charity', saying that 'the Parliamentary Returns record that – Biddle gave £2, the interest thereof for four poor widows, and it is added that the money had been misapplied, but was then paid out of the poor rates. This does not, however, appear to have been done for upwards of thirty years. This charity must therefore be considered to be lost'. The date of this charity is unknown and the only references to a Biddle or Biddles in Swithland do not relate to a charity. There are records of an Elizabeth Biddles who was buried in the churchyard on 31 January 1635; a Robert and Margaret Biddles, whose daughter Margaret was baptized in 1636; a Henry and Edward Biddle who lived in the village in 1680;[61] a Robert Biddle, grazier of Mountsorrel, who married Ann Bramley of Rothley Plain in 1797; and a Thomas Biddles who in 1838 owned three roods of land in Rothley Plain.

The other charity linked to Swithland church is the 'Charity of Miss Sarah Jane Hind for the Poor of the Parish attending Swithland Church'. This charity was founded by the will of Miss Sarah Jane Hind of Ibstock, dated 10th November 1916, will proved 13th May 1922. Miss Hind bequeathed 'to the vicar and churchwardens for the time being of the parish of Swithland the sum of £200 free of duties with a direction that this amount should be invested and the yearly income arising therefrom or a sufficient part thereof be applied to maintain in good repair and order the two monuments of the Hind family in Swithland churchyard, and distribute the residue of such yearly income, if any, amongst such of the poor attending the parish church of Swithland as the vicar and churchwardens in their absolute discretion consider most deserving, and in the event of the said monuments not being maintained in good repair and order within six calendar months after being required in that behalf in writing by the Trustees of the Charity to be formed known as the Hind Sisters Homes (who are entitled to the whole of the residue of the estate), then the said sum of £200 and the investments representing it to that Charity to be applied for its general purposes'.

In May 1922, Messrs Fishers, solicitors to Miss Hind's executors, expressed doubts as to whether the direction to repair the family monuments could be supported in law, even though the provision had been inserted at Miss Hind's direct instructions. In August 1929, the rector of Swithland, the Revd F.J. Oliver wrote to Miss Hind's cousin to say that he was forbidden by a ruling of the courts to spend the money on anything other than to help the poor of the parish of Swithland. (The High Court had decided that the capital or income of the charity could not be used for the purpose of maintaining the monuments.)

In 1973, no payment from the charity having been made since 1963, it was felt that the objects of the charity were no longer capable of being carried out, there being no 'poor' in the parish of Swithland. The charity's funds were invested in 3½% War Loan Stock, giving an annual income of £7 only. At the suggestion of the chairman of the trustees of the Hind Sisters Homes, it was agreed to close the Swithland charity and transfer the assets to the Hind Sisters Homes. In its latter years, the Hind Charity for the Poor of Swithland was looked after by Mr Walter Kilby, Mrs Walter Kilby and Mrs Ben Gimson.[62]

Notes to Chapter 4

1. The right of an individual, originally the founder of the church, to nominate or 'present' a person as rector.
2. Hugh de Grandmesnil, Norman landowner, had re-founded the Abbey of St Evroult in 1050 and presented it with certain livings including Swithland. The abbot of St Evroult had delegated the right of presentation to Swithland and their eight other Leicestershire livings to the abbot of their daughter house at Ware in Hertfordshire, by the beginning of the 12th century. After 1340, the living of Swithland became the gift of the Crown.
3. Earliest 'life', 11th century.
4. Photograph by Steve Godley.
5. 1204 Inquisition Post Mortem into the lands held by Robert Fitzparnel, fourth Earl of Leicester, recorded the value of Swithland in 1189 on the death of the third Earl.
6. Lincs. RO, Rolls of Hugh de Wells, Bishop of Lincoln 1209–1235.
7. G. F. Farnham, *Charnwood Forest and its Historians*, 1930, p. 92. 'In the Matriculus of Hugh Welles, c.1225, the patron of Swithland church was the abbot of St Evroult.'
8. They are pictured in John Nichols' sketch in The *History and Antiquities of the County of Leicester*, vol. 3, part 2, 1798.
9. Quoted by John Nichols, The *History and Antiquities of the County of Leicester*, vol. 3, part 2, 1798.
10. William Burton ms, c. 1622 (Quoted by John Nichols, Swithland entry).
11. This brass was seen to be one of the church's treasures in the Second World War. Bill Lloyd, a local farmer, told of how he slept with her brass safely hidden under his bed.
12. Lincs. Record Society, vol 53. The state of ex-religious and former chantry priests in the Dio. of Lincoln 1547–74. p. 140.
13. *Leicester Chronicle & Leicestershire Mercury*, June 1880.
14. W. Burton's, *Description of Leicestershire*, entry for Swithland, 'in the hundred of West Goscote', 1622.
15. Leics. RO, 5D33/338, Will of Francis Danvers of Swithland, gent. 16 May 1631 (The phrase might also indicate that the south was the only aisle by 1631).
16. See Nichols, vol. 3, part 2, 1798.
17. The 'Danvers Chapel' is not a private chapel, but is under faculty jurisdiction like the rest of the church.
18. Details of inscriptions recorded at the beginning of Chapter 7: Dissent.
19. cf. Throsby's sketch, 1790. Subsequent work in 2000 indicated that the west window to the 1727 Danvers aisle was never opened.
20. Burton, 1622, refers to 'the east window of the south aisle', which indicates the possibility of an altar before the changes of 1727.
21. Photographs from the early twentieth century show these windows bricked up. Whether these had ever been glazed is unknown.
22. There are four indentures at the base of the bowl – where, presumably, side pillars supported it.
23. Dransfield's note book, Parish Archives.
24. In 1863 the chest was being used to hold the church registers. Most of the silverware is lodged in the bank.

25. The original keyboard was still in the church's possession until the 1960s. Unfortunately, during Walters' incumbency, a diocesan 'representative', the Revd Robert Symonds, then vicar of St Mary de Castro, took it away for 'diocesan safe-keeping'. It would appear that, without diocesan or parish authorisation, Symonds later 'gave' the keyboard to his organist for building into a new harpsichord.
26. William Gardner, the memoirs of, *Music and Friends*, vol. 1, 1838.
27. ibid.
28. John Throsby, 1790, *Excursions in Leicestershire*, p. 92.
29. cf. Chapter II, People: Sir John Danvers, regicide.
30. No longer visible; uncovered and reburied in 1925 restoration.
31. Leics. RO, HO129/416, Ecclesiastical Census, 1851.
32. Died 1811; place of burial not known; her family home Critchill Manor, Dorset.
33. Subsequently, Earls and their Countesses were buried in the churchyard and not in the church.
34. East window, 1867, designed by Henry Holiday when he was designer at the Heaton, Butler and Bayne studios in London. Heaton was much influenced by Edward Burne-Jones, working in his studios until 1861. The uppermost light is purported to be by Ninian Comper.
35. Swithland Church Archives.
36. 1864, an apprentice window from the William Wailes Studio, Newcastle.
37. Northants. RO, Misc L 601, Episcopal visitation documents 1863.
38. *Leicester Chronicle and Leicestershire Mercury*, 19 June 1880, supplement p. 4.
39. ibid.
40. Peterborough Diocesan Records, Episcopal Visitation, 1882.
41. ibid., Episcopal Visitation, 1905.
42. *Leicester Chronicle and Leicestershire Mercury*, 19 June, 1880, supplement p. 4.
43. Peterborough Diocesan Records, Episcopal Visitation, 1914.
44. Window by Charles Eamer Kempe, c. 1855 (brought to Swithland from elsewhere).
45. Peterborough Diocesan Records, Bishop's Visitation, June 1921.
46. See Chapter 5: The Clergy.
47. Swithland Church Archives, PCC minutes, March 1923.
48. The Shepshed branch of the family are descendants of William Danvers (1666–1740), the youngest son of Henry (1623–1687) and Ann Danvers (née Coke).
49. For a more complete account of the Shepshed Danvers family, and of their attempts to prove their claims to the Danvers' estates, see T. Danvers, 'Memorials of the Danvers Family of Swithland and Shepshed', 2010, Private publication.
50. Charles Danvers' notebooks.
51. Quoted in Chapter 5: The Clergy.
52. Made up from parts of old box pews to fit the particular location.
53. Boddy, James Alexander Vazeille, OBE, DL, JP (17 July 1895–14 August 1954) lived at Orchard House, 70 Swithland Lane.
54. The Link, September 1966.
55. Jill Woolley, Judith Copson, Olga Harris.
56. The architect was Martyn Jones of Martyn Jones Associates, Medbourne, Leics, and the builder was Johnson of Lubbenham, Leics.
57. Osborne was Parochial Church Council secretary when he died. He oversaw all the faculty application work for the Millennium Extension. The three coats of arms at the base of the window relate to his life and achievements. The central arms are those of his father, Sir Cyril Osborne, MP, and those to right and left are of the Worshipful Companies of Bakers and of the Worshipful Company of Framework Knitters, for both of which Osborne had served as Master. The window was commissioned from Norman and Underwood, Leicester and the design and work supervised by Angus Wallace.
58. Though the earliest clergy housing in the village may well have been on the site where Keeper's Close was built.
59. cf. note in Chapter 10: Swithland Slate.
60. The 'Hind Sisters Homes' in Station Road, Cropston, was founded as a result of their generosity.
61. Leics. RO, DE718/A/49, 12 April 1680, Contents: A note of goods of John Bent left in the house of Henry and Edward Biddle.
62. Some correspondence (1922/26/29/62/73) and bank statements (1962–74) relating to the charity are lodged in the Swithland Church Archives (Rectory Chest).

– CHAPTER 5 –

The Clergy

The importance of church life to the village has given to its successive rectors a central role in the life of the community. The title 'rector' was in general use in the twelfth century, and described the priest of a benefice whose patron had allowed the full benefice profits to pass to whoever was presented to the living. When the benefice at Swithland was identified,[1] the landowner, Hugh de Grandmesnil, who had been gifted the land by William the Conqueror, himself gifted the parish church and its *beneficium* to the Benedictine Abbey of St Evroult, in Normandy.[2] The abbot was thus entitled to present priests to the living, subject to their being given a license to officiate by the bishop of the diocese – in Swithland's case, the Bishop of Lincoln. (In some benefices, the monastery was the original 'rector', receiving the benefice income and passing a proportion on to its priest. It is possible that Swithland's first priests were of this category.)

At some point, the Abbey of St Evroult passed the responsibility of filling its English livings to the Abbey of Ware. Ware was one of the manors gifted to Hugh de Grandmesnil by William I in 1066. Hugh founded the Benedictine priory there as a daughter house to St Evroult. He and his family lived there when they were in England. Family members continued the tradition of founding religious houses and gifting them to St Evroult. In 1190, for example, the priory of Charley in Charnwood Forest was founded and gifted to the Abbey of St Evroult by the Countess Parnel of Leicester, Hugh de Grandmesnil's great grand-daughter. St Evroult transferred it to Ware c. 1204. A document of 1206 lists all the English parishes in the gift of the Abbey of Ware. In Leicestershire those parishes included Belgrave, Burton Overy, Carlton Curlieu, Desford, Noseley, Great Peatling, Sileby, Swithland and Thurcaston.

The first known priest at Swithland was named Roger, though we do not know when he was instituted. A 1220 paper relating to his appointment[3] describes Roger as *capellanus,* a chaplain, who had been presented to his living by the Abbot of Ware. From the fourteenth century, however, after the Crown had appropriated to itself the living of Swithland (among others) from the Abbey at Ware, the priests of Swithland were inducted as rectors, thus presumably receiving all the rights and income of the benefice.

Parish priests were in something of a privileged position in English society, since the church and the king had separate courts and systems of law. The 'benefit of clergy' exempted a clerk in holy orders from punishment in the king's courts, although for other purposes he was subject to the law of the land. He was entitled to certain tithes and customary dues, but though the mediaeval church is supposed to have had huge wealth, the priests who officiated in the parishes only received a relatively meagre income.

A Benedictine Living

Capellanus Roger was already in Swithland in 1220. In Bishop Hugh's matriculus of 1220, Swithland is described as being under the patronage of the Abbot of St Ebrulph (Evroult); Roger, the then rector, was instituted by Hugh, who paid the abbot one mark *de novo*. A rent of 10s. was also formally paid from Swithland to the priory of Hinckley.[4] It does not appear that priestly training then was over-rigorous. Of Roger it was reported that 'nothing stood in the way (of his appointment) except his being insufficiently learned'.[5] The Bishop of Lincoln, Hugh de Wells, directed that 'he is to study and, if then found competent, is to be admitted. Otherwise to be wholly dismissed from the benefice'. It is likely that Roger was trained by the Benedictines, as were his immediate successors, Roger de Turkillestone (1224[6]), Geoffrey de Warwick (1239), William de Merston[7] (1266[8]), John de Sutton (1275[9]) and Peter de Ilminston (1278[10]).

Ware Abbey seems to have moved its priests around the parishes over which it held the right of patronage.[11] On the death of Peter de Ilminston in 1286, it appointed Gilbert de Roubir to Swithland. Gilbert resigned in 1295 on his institution to Carlton Curlieu, where the abbey also held the right to appoint, but he only stayed there for three years before moving on to Shillington, Bedfordshire, yet another St Evroult parish. Reginald of St Evroult (1295) who had been appointed to replace Gilbert de Roubir at Swithland, was moved to Carlton to replace the latter in 1298. The frequent movement of priests ended with the appointment to Swithland of Alexander of Bowden (1298). He appears to have stayed some forty-two years before resigning in 1340.[12]

Appropriated by the Crown

In 1340 England was at war with France. (The Hundred Years War lasted from 1337 to 1353.) The king had taken over the property rights of the Priory of Ware. It was Edward III, therefore, not the Prior of Ware, who, in 1340, presented William Waleys[13] to the Bishop of Lincoln, for induction to Swithland. The prior may have regained his rights by the time of the appointment of Richard de Birchy in 1356, since he was sufficiently involved to initiate a court action in 1361 against the estate of William Waleys, 'late parson of the church of Swithland' for £6. But when de Birchy resigned within months of his appointment, the link with the Priory of

Ware appears to have ceased. Richard de Mitford, de Birchy's successor, was appointed by the Crown in 1356 – as were Robert de Calmont (1360), William Wylde[14] (1362) and all subsequent rectors.[15]

In the fourteenth century, the majority of churchmen, especially parish clergy, were little better off than the peasants among whom they lived. Some were able to improve their position by holding two or more livings in plurality. In 1298, when Gilbert de Roubir moved from Carlton to Shillington, he was allowed to hold in plurality the church at Staindrop, and the sequestrations at Chistleton and Laxfield. It was not uncommon for rectors to be absent from their parishes, and to appoint a curate in their place. In 1377, a priest named John is recorded as being chaplain at Swithland during the rectorship of William Wylde.[16]

The position of parish clergy was not helped by their being subject to taxation by Pope as well as king. A few churchmen did control huge endowments; the revenues of some bishops and abbots rivalled those of the wealthiest laymen and the king required them to subscribe to the cost of government, especially in time of war. But it was not only bishops and abbots who were taxed. At some time between 1371 and 1381, Henry, 'a priest at Swithland', fled the country rather than pay the clerical poll tax of two shillings.[17] (The Abbot of Garendon, who was the clerical tax collector in the Archdeaconry of Leicester asked for 'more time' to collect the money from him and from others.)

The large endowments of the church were one of the targets of John Wyclif, whose ideas found significant support in Leicestershire. Wyclif spent most of his life as an obscure Oxford teacher. From 1371, offended by the disparity of income between rich and poor clergy, he began to advocate a return to apostolic simplicity for clergy. He also desired the translation of the Bible into English and its accessibility to all. He rejected the doctrine of transubstantiation (the real presence of Christ in the sacred elements of the Mass). The displeasure of the ecclesiastical authorities, however, forced Wyclif to retire to his living in Lutterworth in 1381 and he was condemned as a heretic in 1382. He attracted a number of followers who were dubbed Lollards (mumblers). The term was not new; it was a loose term of disparagement that had been applied previously to heretics. Leicester became a notorious centre of the Lollard heresy, thanks in no small measure to the zeal of William Smith, a self-educated blacksmith, and William Swinderby, an unbeneficed Mass-priest. The heresy rumbled on for some years.

It is possible that the influence of the Lollard movement may have been felt in Swithland during the rectorships of Robin de Wibbertoft (1398), Robert Skyfington (1400), William Tarrutt (1405) and Roger Crosseby (1405). Crosseby had been a chantry priest in the Cathedral Priory of Coventry, another centre of Lollardy, before his appointment to Swithland. And, although the Lollard uprising of 1414–15 (Oldcastle's Rebellion) did not attract huge numbers, it is known to have recruited men from Belton-in-Charnwood, Mountsorrel, Sileby and Leicester.

Following the defeat of Oldcastle's rebellion, the Lollard movement fizzled out. The disparity in wealth between rich and poor clergy was not addressed. The poor position of the parish clergy remained unimproved through the rectorships of Thomas Wright (1427), Bartholomew Dulwich (1446), William Harrison (1458), Thomas Scott (1465), William Plabys (1465), Robert de Vynes (1472), Lawrence Orrell (1480), Richard Woods (1491), Richard Russell (1495), Michael Eden (1499) and Christopher Marshall[18] (1506). The holding of livings in plurality also continued. William Hebb (1516) was reported in July 1518 as being non-resident in Swithland; he had another living in Essex.

Reformation

From the early 1520s, the ideas of the German and Swiss Reformers began to trickle into the country. These Protestant beliefs took time to become established, even after the dissolution of the monasteries from 1536 and the imposition of the Prayer Book from 1549. Edmund Smythe (1528) may have managed to stay in post throughout the political upheavals of Henry VIII's divorce, Protestant reform under Edward VI, Catholic restoration under Mary I, and the Elizabethan settlement, though there is documentary evidence of a priest, William Gibs, or Gibbe, as being rector of Swithland in 1525 and 1534.[19]

In the latter part of the sixteenth century, efforts were made to improve the educational qualifications of the clergy. Potential ministers were encouraged to go to university; a requirement of 1575 insisted that men must be at least twenty-three years of age before being made deacon. In 1576, a visitation of the Leicester Archdeaconry described Michael Hudson (1567) as 'ignorant of Latin, in some way versed in sacred learning'. In 1576 Hudson had been resident in the parish, but in another survey of 1585 he is listed as absent.

Michael Hudson was single, even though clerical celibacy had been abolished in 1549. His successor Gilbert Smythe[20] (1588) was, however, married as well as university educated, though that did not seem to prevent him from being involved in a dispute with a Christopher Monke in 1620, whose background is unknown.[21] Monke had filed a petition before the local circuit judge, before justices Sir William Dixie and Mr Staresmore, before the Mayor of Leicester's court, and by Petition to the King, accusing Smythe of 'pilfery, foreknown perjury, suspected sorcery, and murder',[22] declaring that Smythe and his sons were responsible for the death of his son and injuries to his wife. Smythe filed a counter complaint on 26th July 1620, asserting that Monke had publicly slandered and disgraced him by:

> Saying that I am a Connier (dissembler), and have forsaken the true God; that I am a sorcerer, and the means of the breaking of his wife's arm and of his son's cutting of his own throat; that I and my three sons are felons and perjured. He hath thereby much disgraced the word of God in my mouth. He has adventured my life, goods, and reputation thereby, and the undoing of my wife and family who live by my breath.

Monke did not succeed with his claim. In July 1620 he complained in a petition to the king that he had made many efforts to get the crime cleared up, but had been put off. He intimated that the local justices dare not deal with Smyth, but that 'money and friends (had lulled) the Judges asleep'.

Gilbert Smythe's successor, Joseph Smith (1623)[23] was also involved in litigation. He brought a case against Daniel Baker of Swithland concerning the payment of tithes.[24] Smith was a sporting parson and belligerent with it. The Earl of Stamford caught him hawking on his land in 1638, and wrote indignantly to John Lambe, secretary to the Archbishop of Canterbury, William Laud.

> I desire your favour to acquaint the Archbishop with this relation. About a fortnight since, as I came from hunting, I heard, not far out of my way, certain falconers. It being within my royalty I made the more haste to see who they were, and there I found one parson Smith, of Swithland, and his company; he with a hawk upon his fist and speaking unto his dogs. So I repaired unto him and told him that I wondered how much he durst be so bold to take his pleasure within my royalties, having been often discharged. He answered that the laws of the realm allowed it him, and so long as the King lived, he would take his pastimes at his pleasure. I replied that within his own lands and liberties he might do what he pleased, but he had no property in mine, there I discharged him absolutely. Besides some other unmannerly speeches, he told me that he would halt there, whereupon I was very much moved at it, and did make offer to catch off his hawk's neck, but he cast off his hawk from his fist and bore at me with his other hand, and so caught hold of my shoulder. I, for my own defence, caught hold of a riband he wore across his body like a gallant, believing he might have pulled me off from my horse, but the riband, not owing any fidelity to its function, brake, and so we parted. I told him that I would complain to his Grace; he replied that he would meet me anywhere. I told him that then he must appear in a canonical garment; for when we met he had none such upon his body. I considered that he was a clergyman, and although I was very much moved and had a good hunting pole in my hand, yet, remembering his function, I forbore to strike him, believing that his Grace will consider that there is a distance betwixt so mean a man, both in learning and gravity, as Smith is, and a peer of the realm. I beseech you, let me leave this business to your care.
>
> PS. – Smith keeps greyhounds, crossbows, guns, and, as I am informed, all sorts of engines for destroying game.[25]

Interregnum

In 1642 Parliament established a Committee for Plundered Ministers; they oversaw the ejection of all clergy from their livings who were unwilling to consent to the ecclesiastical changes.[26] As one of these so-called 'delinquents', Smith was ejected from his living early in 1643. Given that the Danvers family supported Parliament, Smith's position in Swithland could have been very difficult. Yet despite their taking different sides in the war, Smith did receive some help from William Danvers. On 18th March 1643, Danvers wrote to Sir John Coke:

> Parson Smith was never imprisoned, nor any goods of his seized to the Parliament's use, but I, hearing of his wife's great distemper, have procured him a safeguard for his body and goods, and have assured his friends that spoke to me for him, that he shall come and go safely to his family.[27]

Smith's difficulties grew worse as the parliamentary forces gained the upper hand. On 15th March 1645, the Committee for Plundered Ministers

> gave him leave to show why he, having been sequestered from Swithland for delinquency & since presented to Hathern, should not be sequestered from Hathern.[28]

On 20th April 1646 he was charged before the County Committee on nine articles. It was alleged

> that he still prayed for the bishops and read Common Prayer, though the Directory had been presented to him; that he was a frequenter of alehouses, a swearer, who spent his time hunting and hawking; that for two years or so he lived in the royal garrison at Leicester; that he kept scandalous curates at Swithland, paying them only 40s per annum; that he employed himself more in fisicke than in divinity, yet had preached against the Parliament's Party; that he was at Leicester when it was taken by the enemy.[29]

The allegations sound exaggerated, but similar charges, of drunkenness, swearing etc., were levelled by the Puritans against many of the clergy that they wished to displace. Words such as 'delinquency' and 'scandalous' were 'technical terms' which simply meant that the accused persisted in the old styles of churchmanship. It is also difficult to see how Smith could have spent two years with the royalist garrison at Leicester. The royalists held it for a short period at the beginning of the war in 1642 and it was held again for one month after the Siege of Leicester in 1645. Apart from this, the town was held throughout the civil war by a parliamentary garrison.

Smith was fined £600 in 1649 after being judged a 'delinquent'.[30] The fine had not been paid by the following year, when he became embroiled in a dispute with Lady Lucy Grantham over Sileby Rectory. Smith must have owned the rents from the parsonage house and impropriate tithes. In 1640 he had borrowed £450, which he secured by leasing the rents to Lady

Grantham in 1646 for twelve years. Lady Grantham had started to receive the rents, but had then leased back the parsonage to Smith for seven years at £36 per annum. When Smith's assets were sequestrated, she no longer received the tithes and complained to the County Committee. She offered to pay off Smith's fine of £600 so that the sequestration was lifted, and she could then receive parsonage rent and tithes. The County Committee agreed to the proposal, which would leave her in receipt of rents and tithes until both fine and debt were paid off. However, in 1651 Lady Grantham was back, alleging that Smith was forcibly keeping her out of possession of the parsonage. In 1652 the Committee finally agreed to evict Smith, on condition that Lady Grantham allowed £20 per year towards the payment of a minister for Sileby.

Smith having been evicted, local commissioners appointed Richard Battie to the living at Swithland. The precise date of his appointment is uncertain, but he is listed as being in post in a survey of 1653. He remained in post at the Restoration and is recorded as attending a visitation in 1662.[31] He died in 1662.

Restoration

The (restored) Crown then appointed William Kimes to Swithland[32] (1663). He had been curate at Belgrave and Birstall before the Civil War and had been appointed vicar of Birstall by parliamentary sequestrators in 1648, but he apparently found no difficulty in swearing allegiance to the king, or in passing the narrow doctrinal test of the 1662 Act of Uniformity. Elsewhere in Leicestershire, three quarters of the parishes changed hands as a result of the Act.

Swithland's next rector, Thomas Jackson[33] (1676), was a local man who was educated at Cambridge during the Civil War and became vicar of Sileby in 1660. For a brief period, in addition to his responsibilities at Sileby, Jackson acted as curate at both Mountsorrel and Quorn. Frustratingly for the local historian, Thomas Jackson was somewhat negligent at keeping proper registers of baptisms, marriages and burials in his parishes. While the Bishop's Transcripts for the Peculiar of Groby seem to have been returned, it appears that Jackson only kept a rough record of such ceremonies, enough to make out his yearly 'bills'. He died in 1700 and is buried with his wife and members of his family in the sanctuary of Swithland church.

In the years following the Civil War, the ecclesiastical authorities failed to tackle the disparities between rich and poor livings. At the end of the seventeenth century over half the livings in England and Wales were worth less than £50. Swithland was among those that were relatively poorly endowed. In 1707 the value of the rectory was assessed as being worth £45 16s 10d.[34]

General and several tythes	£37 0s 0d
Glebe	£6 0s 0d
Rate tythes & composition	£2 16s 0d

With the launching of Queen Anne's Bounty in 1704, an effort was made to improve the value of small livings. Otherwise, it helped if clergy possessed a private income.

Abel Brooksby[35] (1700) was the son of a Leicester mercer. Shortly after coming to Swithland, he married Alice Palmer of Leicester and they had seven children. He was the first rector to keep systematic records of baptisms, marriages and deaths. He came to the parish almost directly from college, and remained until his death thirty-five years later. He may also have served as curate of Birstall in 1707 and of Newtown Linford in 1728 and 1732. At one point he acted as surrogate of Groby Peculiar Court, and, like his father, became a freeman of Leicester (1721). At his death in 1735 he owned land in Solihull and in Church Bicknell, Warwickshire; his possessions were valued at £47 15s 0d at probate. During his cure, Joseph Danvers substantially extended the south aisle of the church in 1727. According to John Nichols, Abel Brooksby is also buried in the chancel of Swithland church. When he died, the sequestration order named Joseph Prior and John Walker as churchwardens and therefore sequestrators during the interregnum.[36]

An Absentee Rector

After a succession of resident rectors, Philip Alston[37] (1735) was probably the last to have been almost entirely absent from the parish. By an agreement of 14th December 1737,[38] he leased the parsonage house with the glebe land and tithes to Joseph Danvers for twenty-one years at £20 per year. Danvers agreed to maintain the parsonage in repair, and to nominate, appoint, and pay a resident curate to live there. In 1737, John Oliver was signing official forms as curate and, in 1742, John Dickinson. From 1754 to 1759 George Cardale signed the registers as curate. Cardale was also rector of Wanlip and Rothley, but three of his daughters were baptized at Swithland in 1751, 1754 and 1756, suggesting that he was resident in Swithland at the time. In 1760 John Llwyd was signing as curate.

It was during Philip Alston's time as rector (and George Cardale's as curate) that Joseph Danvers erected, in 1745, the fine tomb for himself and his wife that now lies next to the churchyard wall. In his will, Joseph Danvers bequeathed 'to the Revd Mr. George Cardale Five Pounds, to buy him a Gold Ring and a Black Cloth Gown'.

Enclosure

John Llwyd[39] (1761) was another priest who spent his whole ministry at Swithland, a period of fifty-three years. This was a time when parson and squire co-operated far more than had previously been the practice. In Swithland, Llwyd farmed the glebe land while Sir John Danvers re-built the rectory and generously endowed the church. In 1799 the Enclosure Award allotted some 184 acres to Llwyd as rector 'in lieu and full satisfaction of and for all the tithes both great and small and other dues and payments belonging to the said rectory, except Easter offering, Mortuary and Surplice fees'.

Llwyd may have been in poor health in 1813 when Rev Robert Martin (1775–1832) of Anstey Pastures expressed an interest in the living of Swithland. In 1812, he had written to the Privy Council Office to enquire about the rectory of Newtown Linford; he was told that this lay in the gift of the Earl of Stamford, and was not in the gift of the Crown. The following year Martin gained the support of Lord Stamford in respect of his interest in the living at Swithland. Stamford wrote to the Prime Minister, Lord Liverpool, in January 1813 requesting his support.[40] On 1st April 1814, shortly after John Llwyd's death on 16th March 1814 and burial on the 24th, Martin again wrote to Stamford. Stamford approached the Lord Chancellor on 4th April and again on 9th May and advised Martin that he had done so.

> London, May 9th, 1814
> Sir, I have this day renewed in person my application in your favour to the Lord Chancellor. He received me very graciously, told me some information which had been mentioned to him in regard to the living of Swithland, and that he was making inquiries concerning it, but he hoped to give me an answer in a few days.[41]

Martin, however, was disappointed. Francis Bruxby (1814) was presented to the living of Swithland at the age of seventy-nine. Perhaps not surprisingly, Bruxby only stayed for three years before resigning. When he died in 1822, he was buried in Swithland churchyard.

Glebe Land

A valuation document of 1815[42] indicates the extent of the Rectory Glebe and the way it was farmed.

Let to W Hind from Lady Day 1814–15 and from Lady Day 1815 to Mr W Bates

	acres-roods-perches	
2 closes called Homesteads	7-1-0	mown
2 closes called Field Closes	4-0-0	grazed
4 closes called Rye Closes	11-2-0	1st now seeds mown 3rd followed, other 2 grazed
4 meadows	3-0-0	mown
Carr	2-2-0	mown
TOTAL	28-1-0	

Let to Wm Bates

1st Park Close	8-3-0	barley seeded
2nd Park Close	8-2-8	grazed
1st Cattle Piece	2-2-0	oats
2nd Cattle Piece	2-3-4	wheat
1st Bacon Bushes	4-1-5	grazed

2nd Bacon Bushes	4-1-9	grazed
Lammas Close	6-3-0	mown
Levett Lammas Close	6-3-0	fallow
Picks Close	6-1-3	beans
Leicester Ford	5-0-0	grazed
Black Furlong	10-0-0	grazed
Grescott Sick	5-2-0	grazed
Purgatory	5-2-0	quere grazed or oats
	TOTAL 76-0-29	
Rothley Plain	2-2-20	pared and burnt for turnips
Great Exlands	14-0-0	grazed
1st Little Exlands	5-3-0	oats or beans
2nd Little Exlands	6-0-0	fallow
3rd Little Exlands	4-2-0	grazed
1st Coulsabys	7-1-0	mown
2nd Coulsabys	8-0-0	mown
Pingle	4-2-0	barley & seeded
	TOTAL 50-0-0	
Let to William Hind		
Ferney Butts	8-3-0	barley & seeds
Hays Nook	9-0-7	grazed
Goss Close	10-0-30	mown
Hays Close	2-2-3	grazed
Wood Close	9-3-15	far part fallowed, remainder beans
	TOTAL 40-1-15	

An Aristocratic Rector

The Hon. Henry David Erskine (1817) was a high-flying priest with first-class social connections. He was the second son of Thomas Erskine, Lord Chancellor in 1806, who became Baron Erskine of Restormel Castle, Cornwall. Henry David Erskine was educated at Harrow and Trinity College, Cambridge. In 1813 he married Lady Mary Harriet Dawson, third daughter of the first Earl of Portarlington, by whom he had two sons and six daughters. Both his sons and three of his daughters were baptized at Swithland – the youngest in 1826. Lady Harriet died at a relatively young age in 1827 and is buried in Rothley Temple Chapel. Her tombstone is inscribed: 'Beneath this stone are entombed the mortal remains of the late Lady Harriet Erskine, wife of the Honorable and Reverend Henry David Erskine, rector of Swithland in this County'.[43]

Lady Harriet may have been buried in Rothley Temple Chapel because Erskine was the Commissary of Rothley Temple Peculiar. In this appointment he would seem, however, to have disappointed at least one young lady. Eliza Conybeare (née Rose), grand-daughter of Thomas Babington, the owner of Rothley Temple, wrote: 'The Lord of the Manor, the owner of Rothley Temple, appointed a Commissary, who is said to be our Bishop. In my childhood he was a Mr Erskine, the Clergyman of Swithland. What Episcopal functions he performed I do not know. He certainly did not confirm, and he certainly did not stop abuses. This was happily changed by Act of Parliament in 1851 and now Rothley is subject to the Bishop as any other parish in the Diocese'.[44]

Erskine's family connections may have helped him secure an additional living in order to supplement his income. In January 1828 Minnie Dawson-Damer, the adopted daughter of the king's paramour Mrs FitzHerbert, wrote to William IV. In her letter, she refers to

> the very sudden death of my sister-in-law Lady Harriet Erskine without a day's previous illness, and leaving her husband, Your Majesty may know as a son of the late Lord's, with eight children… and with her death nothing remaining to them but his small living,[45] as the allowance Lady Caroline Damer[46] kindly made her has I feared ceased with her.

At the beginning of the nineteenth century, St Martin's, Leicester (now Leicester's cathedral church), was a Crown living. Whether as a result of such lobbying or not, Erskine was appointed to the living of St Martin's, which he held from 1830[47] to 1841. He remained, however, resident at Swithland. The additional income allowed him to employ curates at St Martin's as well as servants in his household, three were recorded in the 1841 Swithland Census.

Erskine and his daughters were remembered by Mrs Eliza Conybeare, grand-daughter of Thomas Babington (d. 1837), in an autobiographical document 'Phases of English Life' written in 1874.[48] She remembers

> the Erskines of Swithland (he was the Rothley Commissary) a motherless family of five magnificent, high-born, open-hearted rowdy Irish girls, who were a power in the neighbourhood, made much of (though their ways were frowned upon) by all the families around, who compelled hunts for their special benefit from the Master of the Quorn hounds, and did all manner of wild things.

Erskine was something of a philanthropist and social reformer. An active supporter of the establishment of the Dispensary in Loughborough in 1819, he served as chairman of various committees associated with the venture. He also worked for the Leicester Fever Hospital (now part of the Leicester Royal Infirmary). Erskine supported the campaign to abolish black slavery in the British Empire. He was described as 'a great promoter of Mechanics' Institutes'. At the close of the old Grammar School in Leicester, he was involved in setting up in 1834–35 the Leicester and Leicestershire Proprietary School in Prebend Street, Leicester.[49] From about 1830, Erskine was on friendly terms with Ambrose March Phillips de Lisle, the worker for Christian Unity, and used to visit him at Garendon and at Grace Dieu Manor.

*Fig 5.1
Dean Henry
Erskine,
Princeton
University
Library.*[50]

The Swithland Enclosure Award in 1799 had allotted the rector 184 acres in Swithland. The Charnwood Forest and Rothley Plain Enclosure Award in 1828 allocated to the rector of Swithland three further pieces of land:

> A parcel (0.75 acres) 'in the manor of Rowcliffe', opposite the road entrance to Swithland Wood Farm;
> A parcel (14.75 acres) in Woodhouse Eaves, at Hemp Pit Hill on Brand Hill Road;
> A parcel (2.5 acres) in Rothley Plain, part of the field immediately past the railway bridge.

In 1834 Erskine agreed to an exchange of land with George John Butler Danvers, which included land adjacent to the parish boundary in the parish of Thurcaston.

Erskine resigned from Swithland in 1841 and moved to take up an appointment in Yorkshire. He became Dean of Ripon in 1847. C.L. Dodgson (Lewis Carroll) photographed him there and also two of his daughters. Erskine died in 1859, two months before his daughter Anne married the divorced barrister Robinson Fowler. A contemporary local diarist recorded their 'wedding at Winteringham Church this week. Miss Erskine, daughter of the late Dean of Ripon, was married to a Mr Fowler, who has been divorced, his wife having run off with a Duke's son'. They were married by the rector, Thomas Read, Anne's sister Louisa's husband.

Henry Campbell (1841), who was presented on 23rd June and inducted on 29th June, succeeded Erskine as rector of Swithland, but within weeks he had resigned. In his place Edward James Paget (1841) was inducted on 29th August. Paget was a relative of the Marquis of Anglesey, and may have enjoyed similar social connections to Erskine. Paget was wealthy enough to be employing five live-in servants in 1851: a butler, cook, nurse, nursery maid and housemaid.[51] He was also able to employ curates from time to time. Given that between 1844 and 1867 the value of the living at Swithland was assessed at £300 per annum, a private income must have been helpful.

Curates

From April to July 1846, John Butler Sanders, one of Edward Paget's curates and a retired Royal Navy chaplain, signed the parish registers. There are occasional entries in the registers signed by Richard Waterfield, rector of Thurcaston from 1837 to 1864, and George Napleton Treweeke signed himself as 'curate' in 1857–58.

Until 1839, the term 'curate' was almost always taken to designate a clergyman in whom was vested the sole charge of a parish in the absence of a non-resident vicar or rector. Strictly speaking 'curate' means the person responsible for the cure of souls in the parish. The Pluralities Act 1838 changed the law concerning the holding of plural livings, and, consequently, the role of curates. The act outlawed the possession of virtually all third benefices, as well as the holding of a second benefice unless it was less than ten miles from the first. Although an incumbent could be legally non-resident by exemption or by episcopal licence (e.g. because of incapacity of mind or body), the circumstances under which non-residence was allowed were tightened. Furthermore, curates could not live more than three miles from the church to which they were licensed.

Following the Pluralities Act, the pattern, where curates were employed, was that of an assistant curate working in the parish of a resident incumbent. Indeed, by the end of the nineteenth century, the term 'curate' was usually understood to mean a clergyman who assisted and worked under the direction of a resident incumbent. Whilst the Pluralities Act, by limiting pluralities, opened more opportunities for curates to become incumbents, there were disadvantages for those who remained curates. The Stipendiary Curates Act 1813 had laid down a relatively generous scale of minimum stipends for sole charge curates. But the Pluralities Act left the stipend for assistant curates to local discretion, and did not guarantee a minimum.

During Paget's rectorship, the 1851 Ecclesiastical Census was taken. It indicated that there were 230 'sittings' in Swithland church: 60 sittings for children, 80 free sittings, and 90 other sittings. On Sunday 30th March 1851, some 80 people attended morning service (46 general congregation, 34 Sunday scholars), and 100 attended the afternoon service (66 general congregation, 34 Sunday scholars). Paget resigned as rector of Swithland in 1858 in order to take up the living of Steppingley, Bedfordshire.

Stepfather to the Earl

George Napleton Treweeke succeeded Paget as rector of Swithland. In April 1853 Treweeke had married Letitia Rudyerd Ross Butler, the widow of Charles Augustus Butler Danvers. This made him stepfather to John Vansittart Danvers Butler, the heir to the fifth Earl of Lanesborough. This family connection cannot have disadvantaged him in securing the rectory at Swithland. In 1871 he and his wife were employing three servants at the rectory. His household included his stepdaughter, Harriet Eliza Danvers Butler, the sixth Earl's sister.

In 1860 Treweeke supported a move to sell some of the glebe. Mr Alfred Ellis, who had purchased the Brand from the Hind family, offered to purchase the rectory land at Hemp Pit Hill, Woodhouse Eaves. The Lord Chancellor, as patron, blocked the sale. Mr Ellis' agent rightly pointed out that a higher income could be secured by investing the sale proceeds in fixed-interest Government Consolidated Loan Stock:

> ... the proposed arrangement is altogether in favour of the Church as the purchase money, if invested in £3 per cent Consols till it could be laid out on the purchase of land, would be nearly double the present rent which is the best rent for the property.[52]

With some prescience, the Lord Chancellor's Secretary pointed out that land was the best long-term investment. The Lord Chancellor's objection was that:

> He considers land as the best security for the future income of the living. When land has once been sold, it is not generally to the interest of the existing incumbent to re-invest the purchase money in land, as he can probably obtain a higher interest for the money elsewhere. Unless therefore at the time of sale, provision is made for the immediate re-investment of the money in land, the probability is that such re-investment will never be made, and that the living will lose all the advantage that might accrue to it from the increase in the value of land.[53]

The hint was taken. An exchange of land, rather than a sale, took place with Alfred Ellis in 1863. Four fields at Anstey Pastures, adjacent to Gynsills House (and now part of the site of County Hall), were exchanged for the land at Hemp Pit Hill.[54]

Treweeke appears to have been absent for two brief periods during his rectorship. In 1861 John Longhurst was resident in the parsonage house and acting as curate. In September 1874 Frederick William Horner was signing the parish registers. Horner was licensed by the Bishop of Peterborough as curate in May 1874 at a stipend of £100 and required to live in the glebe house. From October 1874 to December 1875 the parish registers were signed by Thomas Ward Goddard. He too was licensed as curate by the Bishop of Peterborough in December 1874 and was required to live in the glebe house. From May to December 1876 William Agar, curate, was signing the registers.

Replies to the Bishop's Visitation in 1872[55] indicate that Treweeke was resident in the parish during that year, and employed no curate. There were usually two full services on Sundays – at 11.00am and at 3.00pm – at which Treweeke preached. The average number attending services each Sunday was about one hundred and fifty. Holy Communion was celebrated four times per year. Children were not catechised by the rector, but received instruction in the course of their school education. Treweeke died in 1876 at Southsea, and was succeeded by Kingsford Beauchamp Sidebottom.

A Poor Living

Between 1850 and 1884, Swithland Rectory was stated to be worth £385 gross (£300 net) plus parsonage house; until 1898 it also had 207 acres of glebe land. For a man without private means, this would have caused difficulties. Curates' pay (if such could be afforded) could amount to a sizeable proportion of the value of the benefice, and was not deductible as expenses before tax. Glebe houses had to be maintained, or heavy delapidations payments paid on leaving the parsonage. There was an expectation that a proportion of the benefice's revenues would be used for relieving the poor. Rates and land tax could absorb between a quarter and a third of modest gross incomes.

Sidebottom did not have Treweeke's economic resources. In the 1881 Census, he is shown as employing a single domestic servant. An old inhabitant of Swithland described him as

> ... a poor but proud rector who was generous to a fault. It is said that he directed his wife to give away his best coat, and then for reasons of dire necessity she had to request its return. He was an assiduous visitor to the church school, and loved the children, whom he often invited to the rectory for tea.[56]

Sidebottom lost an infant daughter Frances in 1878, and a son Maurice died in 1884, aged nineteen, both of whom were buried in Swithland churchyard. He remained at Swithland until 1884, when he moved to become vicar of Exning with Landwade, near Newmarket. There he changed his name to his wife's maiden name of Venner.[57] The modest value of the living caused a short interregnum, whilst another rector was found.

Fig 5.2 The old rectory next to the church.

One consequence of the parson's increasing power in the local community during the nineteenth century was that he could become divorced from the needs and aspirations of the majority of his poorer parishioners. That may have been hinted at in the letter M.A. Joel wrote from Brook House, Swithland, to the Bishop of Peterborough on 4th August 1884:

> My Lord Bishop,
> May I call on your Lordship's attention to the fact that the parishioners of the little village of Swithland in Leicestershire are entirely without spiritual aid, and have been since March last...
> The village is small, the present income £300 – dissent is rife in the villages around – our clergy apathetic. Can you not, my Lord, help us to a priest who will not think the poorest of his parishioners' souls beneath the trouble of attending to? I may add that our only religious service now is on Sunday afternoons. Hoping you will help us speedily in our need. I am, My Lord Bishop, Your Lordship's obedient
> M.A. Joel.[58]

The Bishop of Peterborough[59] moved to appoint James Murray Dixon to the living of Swithland. Dixon, who was born at Watlington, Oxon in 1852, was

Fig 5.3 James Murray Dixon (right of picture) in the old rectory garden.

proud of being a first cousin to Queen Mary.[60] He trained for the priesthood at St Bees Theological College in Cumbria.[61] In 1882, at Marshfield St Mary's Church near Bath, Dixon, then curate at St Mary the Virgin, Lapworth, married Etheldreda Trevelyan, daughter to one of the Trevelyans of Nettlecombe in Somerset.[62] He applied for the rectory of Swithland in 1884. As a cleric who did not live in the diocese to which he hoped to be appointed, he was required to provide three references as to his suitability. Dixon's referees were the vicar of Highworth, the rector of Stanton Fitzwarren and the vicar of Marston. On 23rd June 1884 the Bishop of Gloucester countersigned his application. Dixon was duly presented by the Lord Chancellor on 11th July. On 12th July he wrote to the Bishop of Peterborough from South Marston near Swindon insisting that responsibility for delapidations to the rectory should be resolved before he was instituted.

> I cannot arrange to be at Peterborough on Monday – there is the matter of delapidations to be settled. As soon as this is done, I shall be glad to be instituted at once.[63]

On 15th July, he amplified his concerns.

I am myself ready and willing to be instituted and shall be glad when I can go to Swithland. But I have no intention of making myself liable for the delapidations at Swithland. There will be very little income to be had, and at the time I accepted the living I stated that I would not hold it unless I could obtain the amount allowed for delapidations from the outgoing rector. I have the surveyor's report by me, and the amount allowed is £78. Now when has this to be paid? Because until it is, I must decline to be instituted. I shall have to live on my private means at Swithland, so could not think of finding this money as well.

The matter of delapidations was somehow settled. Dixon was instituted later in 1884, and remained rector for the next forty years. His private income allowed him in 1891 to employ eight servants: a lady's maid, nurse, nursemaid, cook, house maid, kitchen maid, coachman/groom, and a gardener – all were resident at the rectory. By the end of Dixon's time at Swithland, however, his resources were significantly reduced.

Controversy

Dixon was as much a countryman as a parson; he drove a four-in-hand, rode to hounds and conducted his services with his dog asleep under the pulpit. As a young man before ordination he spent some time on a ranch in Texas. He enjoyed working with horses, and was fortunate in that when he came to Swithland the sixth Earl of Lanesborough shared the same passion. Dixon made occasional trips to Ireland to purchase Irish Hunters for the Earl. He had a good relationship with the sixth Earl with whom he dined regularly. The Earl gave him a silver cigarette case bearing a roughly engraved inscription 'To the Bishop of Swithland'. His grand-daughter was told by parishioners that 'when there was a wedding or funeral to take, occasionally grandfather could not be found, so someone would have to dash over to the 'Manor' House to remind him – then down he would come, put on his necessary clerical attire but underneath would be seen riding boots shedding mud upon the church floor and with his dog at his heel'.[64]

Murray Dixon was a man of trenchant views, who was not afraid to express them, yet he was also described

Fig 5.4 The Revd. James Murray Dixon.

as charming and tolerant towards those who held other opinions.[65] He did, however, have a reputation for not visiting in the parish, and his tenure was dogged by controversy.

In 1887, he altered the way through the churchyard to the church entrance. It would appear that he prevented people walking along the bridle road between the church and his rectory, in favour of an entrance off the Main Street, where the lych-gate now stands. The matter caused some controversy. The Bishop of Peterborough was consulted, as was the Leicester Footpaths Association. Charles Bunney wrote to the Association from Swithland.

> Many of the parishioners will not go to church until they know adequately whether he can stop the road or not. As regards the churchwardens, I do not suppose you will get any reply at all from them. If you do I am afraid that it will not be in our favour for Mr Dixon has been buying them over to himself. He had them to dine with him a few evenings ago. I find the tone of one quite altered to what it was before. I asked this one at a meeting last Friday evening whether Mr Dixon had any authority to stop the road. His answer was I am not come here to answer legal questions.[66]

Bunney's misgivings were well placed. The Bishop prevaricated. The churchwardens, Edwin Pepper and the Earl of Lanesborough, found nothing wrong in Dixon's actions. The changes remained.

In 1891 the Leicester Footpaths Association again came into dispute with Dixon. By then he had fenced off another bridleway between the rectory and Swithland Woods and claimed that no right of way existed. The association took him to court and won. During the dispute, William Cuffling wrote to the association from Hall Farm in February 1891, describing Dixon as 'the most cantankerous man in this country if he cannot have his own way'.[67]

In 1894 the Local Government Act established parish councils and meetings. Dixon was elected the first chairman of Swithland Parish Meeting, and continued in that office for thirty years.

Sale of the Glebe

The continued depression in English agriculture, which had started in about 1870, reduced the income from the glebe. This may have persuaded Dixon to sell off Swithland's glebe land. In 1898 he sold most of it to the Earl of Lanesborough. In so doing he also sold a pre-emptive right to the Earl to purchase the remainder in the event that it was put up for sale. The 1898 sale included virtually all the glebe land at Swithland, the land at Thurcaston that had been acquired in the 1834 land exchange, the piece in Rothley Plain, and the four fields next to The Gynsills at Glenfield.[68] At the same time, ground next to the school was purchased by the Ecclesiastical Commissioners to build a new rectory, and the remaining proceeds of sale invested in fixed-income government stock – Consols, then yielding £200 per annum income.

The old rectory and surrounding land – some 14.757 acres – was purchased by Dixon from the Ecclesiastical Commissioners on 5th August 1897. Initially, part was let, but Dixon also used the old rectory as a grain store and the floors eventually collapsed under the weight. By the end of the Great War, the building was almost entirely derelict.

In 1903 Dixon took over the tenancy of Hall Farm, to which most of the former glebe land had been added. This meant he was farming 399 acres. But the enterprise was not successful. His farm labourers did not receive their wages as promptly as they should, and tradesmen were left with their bills unpaid for even longer. He also fell out with Charles John Brinsley Butler, the seventh Earl – possibly over improvements to the farm. In November 1909 they had agreed to settle all matters concerning Dixon's tenure of Hall Farm without proceeding to law, on condition that cross receipts be given.[69] The Earl paid £417 14s. Dixon acknowledged that this was the only sum that he proposed claiming from him 'for value received' in connection with Hall Farm up to 25th March 1908. The Hall Farm tenancy was taken up by Ambrose Copson, who had previously been Dixon's steward.

Church Restoration

For a considerable part of his incumbency, Dixon was intent on restoring the church. In 1881 the churchwardens had advised the Bishop of Peterborough, in their answers to the triennial visitation questions, that the church was in good repair. By 1894, however, Dixon had started raising money for restoration. In 1902 a formal appeal was launched for the restoration, under a committee consisting of the Earl of Lanesborough, the rector, Mr R.F. Martin of The Brand, Edwin Pepper and Samuel Bunney. A handbill advised that:

> At the present, the condition of the fabric is such that the Rural Dean of the Deanery of Akeley East has described it as one of the last two which are a disgrace to the deanery. The Lord Bishop of the Diocese, also, at a later date, when visiting the parish, recognised the grave necessity for Restoration.

Mr Arthur Reeve was appointed architect; he estimated that the cost would be £3,500. In 1905 churchwarden Edwin Pepper replied to the Bishop's visitation enquiry saying that the church was not in good repair and that it needed restoring very badly. But raising the necessary money was a painfully slow process. By 1919 Dixon had only collected £1,291. In 1917 a start was made on the church tower, which was found to be in a dangerous condition when overgrowing ivy was removed. That work was completed in 1918. The actual cost, however, was some £633 against an estimate of £350. The Bishop of Peterborough and the Bishop of Leicester preached at the afternoon and evening thanksgiving services respectively on the completion of the restoration on 9th May 1918.

Some of the cost of the tower restoration had to be met by a temporary loan from the church restoration fund. Much had been financed, however, with a loan of £300 from the Earl of Lanesborough that would need to be repaid. At the end of 1919 the restoration fund was less than half way towards the estimated target of £3,000. Nevertheless, Dixon pressed on.

In 1917 Dixon suffered the loss of his son, who was killed in action at Vimy Ridge. Following the tower restoration, he gave the oak screen across the tower arch in his son's memory. It was erected without application for Faculty permission. At about the same time, he moved the organ from the western gallery, and repositioned it at the west end of the church and the pulpit from the middle of the nave to the chancel arch.

At the same time as Dixon was trying, but failing, to raise enough money to restore the church, villagers had decided to erect a Memorial Hall in the village as a permanent memorial to those who had died in the 1914–18 war. Among those who had fallen was Brian Danvers Butler, brother of the seventh Earl, as well as Dixon's son, Henry Edward Otto Murray Dixon. The Earl gave the 3,136 square yards of land required, and the building was erected with a considerable amount of self-help by residents, and opened on 3rd June 1920. Dixon, however, felt himself unable to join the celebrations at its opening. He wrote in the July church magazine:

> Whilst God's house stands in this parish an object of shame and reproach to us after 25 years of hard effort to raise £3,000, a village hall, for man's amusement, can be provided at a cost of £1,000 to £1,500 – probably a considerably larger sum – in less than two years after its conception, and now displays itself – regarded under these circumstances – a monument of even greater disgrace to the village than the dilapidated church, because it stands for the exaltation of man over God.
> On the occasion of its opening ceremony, I was sorry not to identify myself with my parishioners in, what was to them, an epoch making day.[70]

In November 1920, James Murray Dixon began proceedings to change his surname. Baptised James Murray, he retained his Christian names and chose to be named James Murray Murray-Dixon.

In 1922, disagreements over the church restoration may have caused Dixon to become disillusioned, as he described Swithland as an undesirable place in which to live. He wrote to the Earl of Lanesborough's solicitors, hinting at changes, and offering the old rectory for sale.

> Swithland having become an undesirable place to live in, I propose making changes, and beg to offer the Earl of Lanesborough the refusal of the Old Rectory property according to the agreement entered into between the late Earl of Lanesborough and myself. I will be glad to hear if the present Earl desires to entertain the idea of purchase before offering it to a business firm, & if so, to be acquainted with the name of the appointed valuer.[71]

Valuers were appointed, and the old rectory, together with the remaining glebe, was sold to the Earl in March 1923.

Parochial Church Councils had been introduced by law in 1919, and the first meeting at Swithland was in April 1920. Opposition to the manner in which the restoration of the church was to be conducted did not come from this source. Church restoration was mentioned positively in the minutes of July 1923. Dixon proposed the all-embracing resolution 'that the Church Restoration Committee has your sanction and approval to deal with the fabric & furniture of the church as they shall think most desirable'.[72] The resolution was carried, and work was put in hand.

There were, however, moments of happiness. In 1923 Murray-Dixon had the joy of marrying his daughter Eleanor Margaret Trevelyan to Henry James Walsh.

Resignation

The war had brought great sadness to the rectory household, with the eldest son dead, and another suffering from severe post-war traumatization. Dixon must also have experienced much stress over church restoration challenges. In March 1923 he tendered his resignation as chairman of the Parish Meeting, though he had agreed to act until 'further arrangements could conveniently be made'. For some parts of 1923 and 1924 he was absent from the parish. The parish registers were signed by Geoffrey Frisby as 'priest-in-charge' in November 1923 and December 1924. Dixon wrote to the Parish Meeting in February 1924, regretting that owing to illness he would not be able to attend. The meeting expressed regret at 'the long illness of the Rector', and wished him a speedy recovery.

An emergency meeting of members on the Church Electoral Roll in January 1924, chaired by vice-chairman Mrs Archibald Turner and attended by fifteen others, considered arrangements for services during the alterations to the church. No suitable church building being available, it was unanimously decided that an evening service be held in the chapel, and that nurse Prior, a friend of Mrs Turner, be asked to conduct the service. A note in the minutes, written by Hon Secretary Millicent Nettleton, records the extraordinary statement that the churchwardens had no need to attend these services, and that parishioners might worship where they wanted.

> This decision freed the organist, caretaker & wardens from duty until such time as the church services could be resumed, and left parishioners free to attend any church they might choose to worship in.[73]

In April 1924, the council considered the question of where parishioners might receive Communion at Easter:

> It was felt that a Celebration was much to be desired on Easter Day. The Bishop's reply was awaited re the licensing of a building for such a purpose.[74]

In December, another emergency meeting of those on the Electoral Roll considered the question of the possible licensing of the Methodist Chapel

Fig 5.5
James and Etheldreda Murray-Dixons' Diamond Wedding Anniversary, 1942. Back left to right: Charles Edward Dixon, Helen Dixon, Rosamund Dixon, Patrick Hamilton, Cynthia Hamilton, John Underhill-Faithorne, Barbara Nicholson. Front left to right: Kate (Kitty) Dixon, James, Etheldreda, Amy Knott (bridesmaid).

by the bishop. Some, however, wished to continue using the schoolroom. A majority voted to use the chapel.

Dixon was still absent in January 1925, but by July he had returned and presided over a Parochial Church Council meeting. Disagreements continued. The vice-chairman, Mrs Turner, sent a letter of resignation. The council unanimously agreed on 21st July that the rector should carry on the work of restoration. At another meeting on 30th July, however, Dixon advised that he had resigned his office, and that the restoration of the church was no longer in his hands.

On 5th September 1925, Dixon wrote an open letter of farewell to his parishioners, apologising for his departure, and hinting that it might not have been voluntary.

> I have left you in a manner never contemplated – contrary to all my hopes and desires. I offer my apologies to you all ... for my abrupt

departure, but a combination of circumstances and conditions thus compelled me. I would not have left you without a church, or without endeavouring to gain some knowledge of who was likely to follow me had not my resignation been forced upon me.[75]

After his retirement, Dixon lived for another nineteen years, dying in 1944 at the age of ninety-one. In 1942, he and his wife celebrated their Diamond Wedding Anniversary.

The Murray-Dixons were buried together in St Leonard's churchyard. Making arrangements for his own funeral, Dixon travelled back to Swithland to request farmer John Leatherland to meet his coffin at the boundary of the parish along the road from Cropston, and to convey it, by dray, to the church. On the funeral day, John Leatherland junior, twelve at the time, remembers his father instructing him to grease the dray wheels so that they would run smoothly and silently. John did that, but obviously inadequately. To his great mortification, the wheels squeaked all the way, seemingly getting louder the nearer they got to the church! As soon as the coffin was removed and the dray turned round, the squeaking stopped, but that did not stop John's father rebuking his son for not greasing the wheels properly.

A plaque commemorating James and Etheldreda Murray-Dixon was placed in the church; it was paid for by donations from parishioners who remembered them.[76]

> In affectionate memory of James Murray Murray-Dixon priest for forty-one years Rector of this parish who died May 12 1944 aged 91 years also Etheldreda his wife daughter of the Reverend Edward Otto Trevelyan of Nettlecombe Somerset who died January 27 1943 aged 87. A tribute from parishioners and friends.

Young Gweneth Kilby, who would have been about thirteen when her family first started worshipping at Swithland in 1925, commented that Murray Dixon 'had been greatly admired but was thought to be more of a farmer than a parson. He rode to hounds and did all country pursuits. His dog always accompanied him to church and lay under the pulpit until the appropriate moment at the end of the service when rector and dog left the church'.[77]

A 'Low Church' Rector

In the place of the seventy-two year old Dixon, Frederick James Oliver, still in his twenties, was appointed rector towards the end of 1925. It was his first incumbency. The simplified church restoration scheme was completed, financed with the help of a substantial donation of £1,300 from parishioners Mr and Mrs Archibald Turner in 1927. Archibald Turner (1861–1928) died shortly afterwards. His widow, Gladys Marie, subsequently fell out with Oliver. It is said that the style of churchmanship at Swithland was not entirely to her taste. There was also some disagreement over the wording on the lych-gate to Swithland churchyard, which was erected as a tribute to her husband. It has further been alleged that she would have liked greater influence on parish affairs than Oliver was willing to concede her. The breach was sufficient for Mrs Turner to arrange for a bus each Sunday for the duration of Oliver's tenure to take those parishioners of her persuasion to worship at St Mark's, a 'high' church in Leicester. In 1932 her daughter, Lois Mary Gladys Turner, married the curate at St Mark's, Frederick Lindesay Godfrey. Mrs Turner herself remarried in 1946. Her husband was the vicar of St Mark's, Canon Albert Linwood Wright.

In Swithland, efforts were made to raise money to improve the available stipend, but without huge success. Whether because of the lack of support from Mrs Turner and the St Mark's contingent, or whether because of the small stipend, Oliver resigned in 1931 to take up a post with the Church Missionary Society in London. He died in a road accident not long afterwards.

An Eye for the Girls

An ex-colonial archdeacon, John Mackay succeeded Oliver as rector. Mackay had started life as an architect, but he had offered his services to the Church Missionary Society in 1893, beginning his missionary service as a layman in the Yoruba Mission, Diocese of Lagos, Nigeria. After ten years work there, he was ordained in 1904, and moved to work in Oshogbo, Nigeria for fifteen years. His wife's poor health[78] led him to resign from service abroad, and in 1919 he became rector of Norton-sub-Hamdon, Somerset. But in 1925 he returned to Oshogbo as secretary to the mission there, and was at once appointed Archdeacon of Yoruba County. Five years later he came home for good – to Swithland.

At Mackay's prompting the parish started an annual 'Sale of Work and Bring and Buy' fund-raising event at the Memorial Hall in support of the Church Missionary Society's work in Nigeria. The sale was always held on the third Thursday in November, and continued for thirty-nine years from 1934 until 1973. Proceeds went to endow a John Mackay ward in the Ado Ekiti Hospital in Nigeria.

Mackay listed his main recreation in a local Who's Who directory as lawn tennis. He served on the committee of the Swithland Tennis Club and was often seen playing social tennis at residences in the area. His socializing may have included an over-easy rapport with the opposite sex. He is remembered as 'having an eye for the girls' and is alleged to have had an affair with a parishioner.

In 1936 the income from the endowment of the living at Swithland was £282, out of which the Rev J. Murray-Dixon, the former rector, drew a pension of £68 per annum. The Diocesan Board of Finance proposed to try to increase the income by taking advantage of the Ecclesiastical Commissioners' augmentation scheme. But the improvement was, at best, modest. In 1940 Mackay announced his decision to resign from the living as the burden of keeping up the large rectory and expensive grounds on so small a stipend had become increasingly acute. He moved to Swithland Lane, Rothley, and helped with services until his death in 1942.

A Long Interregnum

There followed a sixteen year long interregnum. Three people especially – churchwardens Percy Lloyd and Walter Kilby, and Parochial Church Council secretary (and later churchwarden) Joseph Dransfield – helped to keep the church alive. Other local clergy and readers helped them maintain church services.

From 1941 to 1946 the Rectory was occupied by the military as a recuperation home. The diocese sold it in 1947. It was bought back by Mrs Linwood Wright, who eventually gave it back to the church 'provided it was used to house a parish priest for Swithland'. Between 1946 and 1954, however, Bishop and diocese attempted to combine Swithland with Old Woodhouse (1946), Woodhouse Eaves (1948) and Rothley (1954), although all their attempts failed. In March 1955 the Parochial Church Council was informed that Cecil Copp Harcourt had been appointed priest in charge.

A Link with Diocesan Responsibilities

Harcourt was instituted as rector in 1956. The appointment became possible partly because of the centralisation and equalisation of stipends, and partly because the living of Swithland was combined with the job of a diocesan officer. Harcourt served the diocese as bishop's advisor on race relations. That link with diocesan responsibilities became the pattern for subsequent appointments.

Harold Alexander Maxwell, Assistant Bishop of Leicester was instituted as rector in 1959. At one time he had served as an assistant bishop in China. Maxwell was an extrovert who had something of the showman about him. Some people have said that he was somewhat superficial in his relationships and selective in his social company; also that his high church leanings were firmly stamped on by the Countess of Lanesborough. Maxwell did, however, succeed in introducing a greater sense of professionalism into the management of the church. Under his vigorous leadership, the PCC met more frequently, a CEMS branch was formed in the parish, the team of bellringers was enlarged, services for parents and children were held at Swithland Camp, and the Sunday School was re-invigorated.

Thomas Geoffrey Stuart Smith, Assistant Bishop of Leicester, succeeded Maxwell in 1966. He was a quiet, sincere and involved individual, who was open to change. Some ladies have indicated that he had 'wandering hands' in the presence of the opposite sex. He had been an enthusiastic cricketer in his younger days. He introduced a family service and some of the newer authorized forms of worship, and was another ex-colonial bishop, having served in the Church of South India. It was Stuart Smith who encouraged the founding of the Swithland Men's Club to replace the Church of England Men's Society branch in the village, and the club continues to thrive. Unhappily, he suffered a disabling stroke, and although he struggled on with help for a short time, was forced to resign.

The next rector, Edward Wilson Carlile (1973), stayed only briefly.

Carlile, a chartered accountant before being ordained, was the grandson of the founder of the Church Army. Before reading theology, he had qualified as a chartered accountant. For eleven years he had served as the chief secretary of the Church Army. As well as being rector of Swithland, Carlile was given a diocesan responsibility for developing multi-faith relations in Leicester. He occasionally indicated his feelings that his diocesan responsibility was not valued by many of his parishioners, which may have influenced the brevity of his stay at Swithland.

Both Stuart Smith and Carlile were assisted by Lindesay Godfrey and Waldron (Bill) Harris. Frederick Lindesay Godfrey, a one time curate of St Mark's, Leicester, had married Lois Mary Gladys Turner, the daughter of Archibald Turner, in 1932. They came to live in Swithland in 1965 on Godfrey's retirement from the ministry and he assisted at Swithland until his death in 1984. Waldron Harris was an ophthalmic surgeon who held appointments in Persia, South Africa and Arabia, before coming to Leicestershire in 1959, where he practiced locally. He lived first on Loughborough Road, and subsequently on The Ridings, Rothley. Harris served as churchwarden from 1964 to 1973. After training on the Leicester Diocesan Ordination Course, he was ordained deacon in 1972, serving as honorary assistant curate at Swithland. In 1973 he was ordained priest, and continued to assist in Swithland in a non-stipendiary capacity until his death in 1979.

The link of the cure at Swithland with a diocesan responsibility continued with the appointment of Francis Raymond Walters (1977). He was a kind, diffident and scholarly man, who also served as diocesan Director of Education. The Rectory's ample size – a disadvantage to a single person – was filled by his family of one son and five daughters. They considerably augmented the choir. Under Walters, the parish continued to thrive. Walters was a gifted teacher; he was a tutor at Queen's Theological College, Birmingham, then for several years chaplain at Leicester University. For some time during his ministry at Swithland, Walters was assisted by Lay Reader, Andrew Lintern Ball, an assistant teacher of Chemistry at Loughborough Grammar School.

Walters was widely respected. He was appointed an honorary canon of Leicester Cathedral. But he was never made rector of Swithland, remaining priest-in-charge throughout his fourteen years in the village. This 'suspension of the living' was in order to facilitate what has come to be called pastoral re-organisation – the amalgamation of parishes. The parish of

Fig 5.6 Canon Raymond Walters.

*Fig 5.7
Canon Anne
Horton.*

Swithland was seen as too small to justify a full-time rector without any other diocesan or parochial responsibilities. Parishioners felt, however, that the size of the congregation at Swithland compared well with much larger parishes, so they were not prepared to agree quietly to amalgamation with another benefice, preferring to continue as a small parish pastored by an ordained diocesan officer.

In 1987, the Diocesan Pastoral Committee again suggested a union of benefices – this time with Woodhouse and Woodhouse Eaves. The Bishop of Leicester approved a draft scheme in December 1987. A vigorous campaign of objection was mounted in Swithland and an appeal made to the Church Commissioners. A sub-committee of the Commissioners' Pastoral Committee visited Swithland in October 1989; they recommended that the scheme should not be approved and it was dropped. In 1991, the Diocesan Pastoral Committee again returned to the subject. This time, a union of benefices with Newtown Linford was projected. The union was opposed by both parishes and dropped in December 1991. Meanwhile Walters resigned in 1991, with Swithland's future unresolved, and an interregnum of nearly three years followed. In October 1993, the Bishop of Leicester suggested a union of benefices with Thurcaston – with the parsonage house at Swithland. It was opposed by Thurcaston, and withdrawn in February 1994.

In 1993, when the Church of England agreed to the ordination of women to the priesthood, Anne Horton was already serving as Diocesan Director of Training. In May 1994, a week after she was ordained priest, she was licensed as priest-in-charge of Swithland, whilst continuing in her diocesan post.

*Fig 5.8
The Rectory,
157 Main
Street.*

Union of Benefices

In 1999, because of the continuing reduction in stipendiary clergy numbers, the parish finally agreed to enter into a union of benefices with Woodhouse and Woodhouse Eaves, provided that the incumbent had freehold, lived in the rectory at Swithland,[79] and that the first incumbent should be the current priest-in-charge of Swithland (if still in post at the time of the union). The benefice scheme became law in December 1999 and Anne Horton was instituted rector of the new benefice on 9th February 2000. From 2001–04, she was assisted by Peter Sheridan, non-stipendiary honorary assistant priest. In 1998, Robert Brian Osborne was accepted for training for Reader ministry in the parish of Swithland, but died suddenly in May 1999, while still in training. In 2000, Gary Lee, Lay Reader, transferred his licence from the parish of Oaks in Charnwood with Copt Oak to Woodhouse, Woodhouse Eaves and Swithland. In 2002, Valerie Joyce, Lay Reader at Rothley offered to become a link Lay Reader in the benefice, and Jean Curd was authorized as a Pastoral Assistant for Swithland.[80] Ruth Page from the Swithland congregation was authorized in 2005 as a Pastoral Assistant in the benefice.[81] From July 2007 until October 2010, Stephen Delaforce was licensed as a non-stipendiary assistant curate to the benefice.

Swithland has been fortunate in having a priest – for most of the time a freehold rector – serving the parish church and living in the village for eight hundred years. The present incumbent is, as far as we can tell from the records, the fifty-fifth so to serve.

Notes to Chapter 5

1. The date is not known. Swithland is not singled out as a village in Domesday, but would have been included in the general survey under Hugh's adjacent lordships.
2. Hugh, with his brother Robert, (monk at, later Abbot of, St Evroult) re-founded the Abbey, c. 1050. He went on to endow the abbey with his lands in Leicestershire, including 'Swithland'.
3. W.P.W. Phillimore (ed.), *The Rolls of Hugh de Wells, Bishop of Lincoln, 1209–1235*, Lincoln Record Society, vol. 3, 1912.
4. J. Nichols, *History and Antiquities of the County of Leicester*, Swithland entry, reference to Burton MS.
5. W.P.W. Phillimore (ed.), *The Rolls of Hugh de Wells, Bishop of Lincoln, 1209–1235*, Lincoln Record Society, vol. 3, 1912.
6. ibid., vol. 2.
7. G.F. Farnham, *Leicestershire Mediaeval Village Notes*, p. 272. Relating to ancient deeds, before 1274, reference to 'William Brun, rector of the Church of Swithelond', as witness.
8. F.N. Davis (ed.), The Rolls of the Bishops of Lincoln: Richard of Gravesend 1258–1278, Lincoln Record Society, vol. 20, 1925.
9. ibid.
10. ibid.
11. Leicestershire parishes in the gift of Ware included: Belgrave, Burton Overy, Carlton Curlieu, Desford, Noseley, Great Peatling, Sileby, Swithland and Thurcaston.
12. There may, of course, have been others for whom the presentation papers have been lost.
13. Very probably a relation of John Waleys, Lord of the Manor of Swithland in 1340.
14. G.F. Farnham, *Leicestershire Medieval Village Notes*, p. 209, De Banco Roll 1363 (37 Edw3), mentions William Wylde, parson of Swithland church.
15. The Alien Benedictine Priory at Ware was suppressed by King Henry V in 1414 and all the buildings except the church were demolished.
16. Lincs. RO, E179/35/14, Experimental Taxation of the Clergy 1371–81, p. 16.
17. ibid, p. xxii.
18. cf. Appendix A: Wills. Christopher Marshall bequeathed 3s 4d to various parishes, including Swithland.
19. Leics. RO, 1D21/12/2, lists of clergy attending Bishop's or Archdeacon's visitations in 1525, 1533, 1534, 1536.
20. Lincs. RO, 1588/53, Presentation Deed, 8 June 1588.
21. Leics. RO, Records of the Borough of Leicester, July 1620.
22. The reign of James I was marked by religious tension between Protestant and Catholic. Monke's charges may be linked with this.
23. Lincs. RO, 1623/23, Presentation Deed, 10 July 1623.
24. Leics. RO, 13D28/18, Papers in suit Joseph Smith, vicar of Swithland v Daniel Baker of same, 7 Aug 1623.
25. Calendar of State Papers, Domestic Series, 1638–9, pp. 81–82.
26. Later, until the dissolution of the Rump Parliament in 1653, the Committee served as a Board of Ecclesiastical Commissioners, with extensive powers. Its powers were then transferred to the Trustees for Maintenance of Ministers, by ordinance of 2 September 1654.
27. Leics. RO, Mss. of Earl Cowper KG, vol 2, p. 33x.
28. A.G. Matthews, *Walker Revised*, Oxford 1948.
29. ibid.
30. A royalist.
31. Leics. RO, 1D41/12/6, Clergy List 1662. Beside the Swithland entry is written 'Battie procurationem exhibuit', meaning 'Battie appeared at the visitation as a proctor in place of the Rector and exhibited the clergyman's licence and orders for him'.
32. Lincs. RO, 1662/58, Presentation Deed, 3 January 1663.
33. Lincs. RO, 1676/42, Presentation Deed, 7 March 1676.
34. Lincs. RO, Ben 8/44, Groby Peculiar, Lincs. Summary of Certificates 1707.
35. Lincs. RO, 1700/45, Presentation Deed, 29 November 1700.
36. Leics. RO, ID41/29/240, 19 July 1735, sequestration: Swithland, vacant by death of last incumbent.
37. Lincs. RO, Presentation Deed, 28 July 1735.
38. Leics. RO, DE1750 Box 22, Indenture, 14 Dec 1737.
39. Lincs. RO, 1761/11, Presentation Deed 4 June 1760.
40. Leics. RO, DE 718 (DG6), D6, D7, D8, D9, correspondence, Earl of Stamford and Warrington and Revd. Robert Martin.
41. ibid, D9.

42. Leics. RO, DE1750, Box 9, 27 Feb 1815, Valuation of Estate belonging to Swithland Rectory by Samuel Stone.
43. There is apparently more, but the stone is 'hidden under pulpit'.
44. 'Rothley Temple in the Olden Time', Eliza Conybeare, 1874, Rothley History Society, Chronicle 3.
45. In 1822, the value of the Swithland living was £10 4s 7d.
46. Lady Caroline was a cousin of Lady Harriet's father.
47. Lincs. RO, 1830/1, Presentation Deed, 14 March 1830.
48. 'Rothley Temple in the Olden Time', Eliza Conybeare, 1874, Rothley History Society, Chronicle 3.
49. The school was to be later known as the Leicester and Leicestershire Collegiate School.
50. Morris L. Parrish Collection. Department of Rare Books and Special Collections. Princeton University Library. Photograph by Charles Lutwidge Dodgson.
51. Swithland Census 1851.
52. Leics. RO, 3D42/57/59, Copy of correspondence re: proposed sale of glebe land, 1860.
53. ibid.
54. Leics. RO, 3D42/57/78, Plan with Conveyance, 25 Oct 1851, showing Hemp Pit Hill as Swithland glebe.
55. Peterborough Diocesan Records, March 1872, Bishop's Visitation.
56. S.R. Meadows, *Swithland*, 1965.
57. The memorial stone in Swithland churchyard to their two departed children uses the surname Venner.
58. Leics. RO, 7D55 965/1-8, this and related letters.
59. The archdeaconry of Leicester had been transferred from the diocese of Lincoln to the diocese of Peterborough in 1837.
60. Dixon's great great grandmother was Princess Mary Anne of Cambridge, the younger sister of Queen Mary's mother, the Princess Mary Adelaide, who married Francis, Duke of Teck. The Princesses Mary Adelaide and Mary Anne were daughters to Prince Adolphus, Duke of Cambridge, the youngest surviving son of George III and Queen Charlotte.
61. By the beginning of the 1800s, the Church of England was badly in need of well trained clergy. The instruction given at the Universities of Oxford and Cambridge was of indifferent quality, and outside the financial reach of many. The foundation in 1816 of St Bees, the first Church of England Theological College, heralded a change which was to transform clergy training in England.
62. Her father, the Rev. Edward Otto Trevelyan, the 5th son of Ven. George Trevelyan, was brother to Charles Edward Trevelyan, 1st Baronet of Wallington, Northumberland.
63. Leics. RO, 7D55 965/1-8, this and related letters.
64. Information in this paragraph contributed by Murray-Dixon's grand-daughter, Shelagh Guild.
65. Meadows, *Swithland*, 1965.
66. Leics. RO, DE295/59/16, Leicester Footpath Association.
67. ibid.
68. In February 1908, Charles John Brinsley Butler sold the land at Glenfield to the trustees of the will of James Ellis. Part was sold in June 1925 to Thomas George Hunt, a shoe manufacturer of Anstey Frith. It now forms part of the site of County Hall.
69. Leics. RO, DE1750 Box 30. Letter/agreement, 19 November 1909, signed 7th Earl and Murray Dixon.
70. Swithland Church Archives, Joseph Dranfield's notes and records.
71. Leics. RO, DE1750 Box 30, Telegram, Murray Dixon to Messrs Peake, Bird, Collins etc. 9 March 1922.
72. Swithland Church Archives, PCC minutes, March 1923.
73. ibid., April 1924.
74. ibid., Dec. 1924.
75. Swithland Church Archives, Joseph Dransfield, notes.
76. ibid.
77. G.M. Gimson, talk given to Swithland Mothers' Union, May 2003.
78. In later years Mrs Mackay was considerably disabled by arthritis.
79. Under the terms of the pastoral scheme, the benefice house of Woodhouse with Woodhouse Eaves (the vicarage of Woodhouse Eaves) was passed to the Diocesan Board of Finance for disposal. It was sold in 2003.
80. The lay ministry of pastoral assistant was approved for the diocese of Leicester in 1998. Unlike Reader ministry, which is under bishop's licence, pastoral assistant ministry is authorised in the Diocese of Leicester by the bishop, after selection and two years of ministry training.
81. Further lay ministers were called from the congregations at Woodhouse and Woodhouse Eaves. William Leeson, St Paul's, pastoral assistant; David Clarke, St Paul's, parish evangelist; Terry Casey, Woodhouse, Reader.

– CHAPTER 6 –

Civil War

Members of the Swithland Danvers family were heavily involved as active and committed participants in England's Civil War and its aftermath. Like many of the main families of Leicestershire, they supported Parliament over and against the King.

Civil War in Leicestershire

In 1629, quarrels between King and Parliament over finance and the royal prerogative led Charles I to dissolve Parliament and attempt to rule alone. At first all seemed to go smoothly for him, but, underneath the surface, trouble was brewing. Britain was not a united kingdom. An attempt to force the Book of Common Prayer on Scotland caused a revolt. Charles' initial attempts to put down the uprising failed. With no money and inadequate troops, he was forced to recall Parliament. Members of the 'Short' Parliament of April–May 1640, however, refused to approve any new taxation before their own grievances were addressed. Three weeks after its recall, the King, frustrated, dissolved Parliament, but his action solved nothing. When the Scots invaded the north of England, Charles had no choice but to recall Parliament in November 1640. Members, however, refused him their support. Instead they drew up a long indictment of his reign. By 1642, relations between King and Parliament had reached a desperate state. On 3rd January 1642, Charles, believing that Parliament was trying to violate his sacred rights, tried to impeach the five most revolutionary members of the Commons: Pym, Hampden, Holles, Strode, and Leicestershire's Hazelrig. He attempted, but failed, to arrest them. For Charles, this was a position of no return. The more extreme members of the House of Commons took refuge in the City of London and called the militia out against the King. On 10th January, Charles, with his wife and children left London by night. Subsequent discussions with Parliament came to nothing. The Civil War had begun.

In Leicester and Leicestershire the initial hope was to maintain neutrality. This proved impossible. County, like country, was divided. As Lucy Hutchinson, wife of one of the commanders of the parliamentarian forces, commented: 'Every county … had the civil war within itself'. The Royalist cause in the county was championed by Henry Hastings (later Lord Loughborough) of Ashby and Castle Donington. Other supporters included Beaumont of Grace Dieu, Farnham of Quorn, Nevill of Holt, Poultney of Lubenham, Shirley of Staunton Harold, Skeffington of Skeffington, Skipworth of Cotes, Turpin of Knaptoft, Turville of Aston Flamville, and Wright of Barlestone. The parliamentary side in Leicestershire was led by the Lord-Lieutenant of Leicestershire, Henry, first Earl of Stamford (c.1599–1673), from whom the manor of Swithland was held, and his son Thomas, Lord Grey of Groby (1623–1657). Stamford was supported by Ashby of Quenby, Babington of Rothley, Cave of Stanford, Danvers of Swithland, Dixie of Bosworth, Faunt of Foston, Hartopp of Buckminster, Heselrige of Nosely, Herrick of Beaumanor, Packe of Prestwold, Palmer of Wanlip, Pochin of Barkby, Smith of Edmundthorpe, and Villiers of Brooksby.

On 5th March 1642 the House of Commons, presuming the royal prerogative, nominated the Earl of Stamford as Lord Lieutenant of Leicestershire. Though the raising of troops under Stamford had been forbidden by Charles, Stamford came to Leicester on 5th May to make arrangements for ordering the militia. On 12th June, Henry Hastings, youngest son of the Hastings family, arrived in Leicester and persuaded the mayor to ignore Stamford's commission, but when the king visited Leicester on 22nd July, he received a polite, but cool welcome from the Mayor and Corporation. He passed through the town again in August, staying overnight at the Abbey Mansion before leaving for Nottingham. By June, it was clear that any reconciliation between King and Parliament was impossible. On 25th August, Charles raised his standard at Nottingham and armed conflict began.

Within days of the start of the war, Charles I's nephew, Prince Rupert, attacked Bradgate. His men broke up the furniture, turned the horses and cattle loose, and carried off arms and ammunition. Rupert's troops were reputed to have disarmed many of the inhabitants thereabouts, and to have taken away many of their goods. During the winter of 1642–43, Lord Grey of Groby secured Leicester for Parliament. Belvoir Castle, however, was taken for the king and a royalist garrison occupied Ashby Castle.

Throughout 1643 and 1644 the principal engagements of the Civil War were fought outside the East Midlands. Apart from the royalist garrisons, the county – thanks to Grey's position in Leicester – had largely been secured for Parliament. Grey, however, was reluctant to move from his base, fearing a breakout from Ashby and Belvoir, so there was constant skirmishing. Goods and supplies which could only be moved by armed convoy were liable to attack. Raiding parties from each side roamed the countryside. On 22nd September 1644, a party of Ashby horse entered Rothley church during the sermon, and took three men back to the castle – presumably to hold them for ransom. The following Sunday, they entered Loughborough church and tried to kidnap the preacher as he stood in his pulpit, but he was rescued by members of the congregation.

March 1644 saw a skirmish at Cotes, just outside Loughborough. The royalists had planned to gather a force at Ashby in order to relieve the besieged town of Newark. The force included some fifteen hundred horse and six hundred musketeers that Henry Hastings had gathered at Ashby by stripping outlying garrisons. Hastings' instructions were to link with forces under Prince Rupert, and also with a force of one hundred horse and six hundred musketeers who had been recruited in Nottinghamshire by Major General Porter. The parliamentarians, however, heard of these preparations and sent a force of two thousand horse from Newark, under Sir Edward Hartopp, to intercept Porter's troops and prevent them from reaching Ashby. They were to be reinforced by Grey's regiment at Leicester. An initial clash took place at Mountsorrel where royalist cavalry fought with a parliamentary advanced guard of horse from Leicester. Over the 17th and 18th March, a small battle took place at Cotes Bridge, just outside Loughborough. Colonel Grey and the Leicester foot drove the royalists off Cotes Bridge, allowing the parliamentary cavalry to cross and engage the royalist cavalry, whom they drove from the field. This success, however, was not followed up. Instead of pressing on with his main body, Hartopp ordered his cavalry to retire. The royalists drew off into the meadow on the west bank, where they faced the roundheads until nightfall. Following rumours that Prince Rupert had reached Ashby, Hartopp's horse returned to Newark in considerable haste and Grey's forces scuttled back to Leicester. This left the way clear for Porter's troops to march on to Ashby. The combined royalist force then went on, as originally planned, to relieve the siege of Newark on 20th March.

There was a brief local revival for the royalists in 1645. In March they won a battle at Melton Mowbray. In May, the king, who had left his headquarters at Oxford to relieve Chester, learnt that the siege there had been raised and attempted to relieve the pressure on Oxford by attacking Leicester. On 27th May a royalist army of about six thousand approached Leicester from the north. They were opposed by a Leicester garrison of about two thousand. John Bunyan, author of *Pilgrim's Progress*, is reputed to have been among the parliamentarians caught up in the siege. The King's cavalry under Prince Rupert was based at Queniborough. Charles set up his headquarters at Aylestone. Overnight, emplacements were built around the town to hold the royalists' heavy guns. The town corporation refused to surrender, and the town was bombarded and attacked on 30th May. By the next morning it had been taken and thoroughly sacked. Among those taken prisoner was Thomas, Lord Grey of Groby, the parliamentary leader in Leicestershire. Some one hundred and forty wagons of plunder were taken away to Newark. There were later allegations of the unwarranted slaughter of inhabitants, but this may have been puritan propaganda.

Before leaving Leicester for Oxford, the king imposed a tax of £2,000 on the town. He left a garrison of twelve hundred men to repair the fortifications. The royalist occupation of the town did not, however, last long. The Battle of Naseby on 14th June proved a significant setback. The King and Prince Rupert passed through Leicester in their flight from Naseby without stopping and Leicester surrendered to Cromwell's forces on 18th June. Some outposts in the county held out for a little longer: the garrison at Belvoir until January 1646, and that at Ashby until March 1646. But Leicestershire had effectively been secured for Parliament by July 1645.

Charles I surrendered to the Scots in April 1646. In January 1647 they handed him over to the Parliament's commissioners. In due course, the king was put on trial. Thomas, Lord Grey of Groby, was one of those who sat on the commission that tried him and who signed his death warrant.[1] Charles I was beheaded in 1649.

Swithland's Civil War

William Danvers of Swithland actively supported Parliament throughout the Civil War. Shortly after the outbreak of armed conflict, it was planned to move William Danvers' cousin, Sir John Coke of Melbourne Hall, Derbyshire, to Swithland for his greater security. Coke, a former Secretary of State, was a puritan and parliamentarian despite having two bishops in his family.

Sir John Coke was at Swithland at the end of January 1643. His son John Coke wrote to him there on 30th January. 'I thank God for the continuing of your good health, but I am sorry that the cause of your removal from Melbourne continueth still'.[2] Sir John's security, however, could not be assured. In early 1643 William Danvers moved his household from Swithland to Leicester. He had been appointed Steward to Lord Stamford and to Lady Exeter, while Stamford was away from Bradgate, and Lady Exeter away from Newark. On 18th March William wrote to Sir John. 'I thank God my wife and I and all our good friends here are in good health'.[3] In April Sir John was at Melbourne and Danvers still in Leicester. Danvers had been appointed to a committee with the task of raising money to support the parliamentary army and at some point raised a local troop. By October, however, he had left his family at Leicester, and was staying in London. On 11th October, John Coke wrote to his father, Sir John, at Melbourne: 'Cousin Danvers is still here. Some of his troop, among other of the Lord Gray's, were this week quartered at Tottenham'.[4]

In November, William's wife Elizabeth was at Swithland and pregnant again. (She and William Danvers had sixteen children.) She wrote to Sir John Coke, apologising that she could not receive him at Swithland. Apparently all her goods were at Leicester and she was short of coal, the supply of which was uncertain.

> I am heartily sorry that times are such as constrain you to remove from Melbourne at this unseasonable time of the year, and I am as sorry I cannot accomplish your desire of having you at Swithland ... I am ill provided of fuel and other necessities to entertain Your Honour at Swithland; and the great House in Leicester is so full, having three families besides myself in it, and being very unquiet because it is so near the street. But if Your Honour please to come to Leicester, I think the Newark the safest and quietest place in Leicester and Mr Wadland's house the fittest, because the judges lie there every assizes.[5]

She added that her husband was still 'at London with my Lord of Stamford upon some good employment'. The day before, Sir Edward Hartopp, Sir

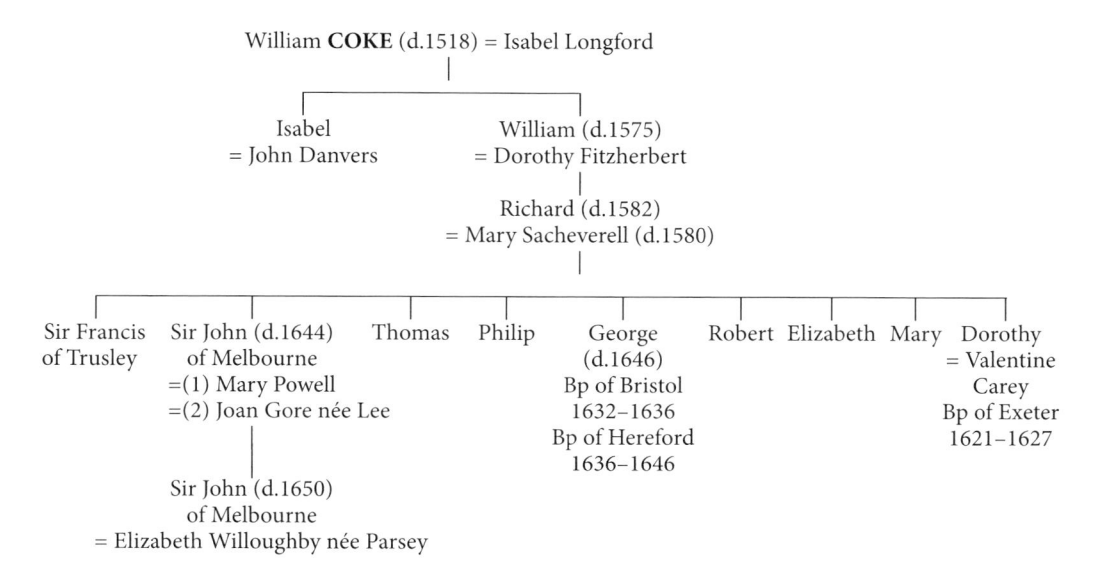

```
William COKE (d.1518) = Isabel Longford
                │
        ┌───────┴───────┐
      Isabel         William (d.1575)
   = John Danvers   = Dorothy Fitzherbert
                           │
                     Richard (d.1582)
                   = Mary Sacheverell (d.1580)
                           │
```

Sir Francis | Sir John (d.1644) | Thomas | Philip | George (d.1646) Bp of Bristol 1632–1636 Bp of Hereford 1636–1646 | Robert | Elizabeth | Mary | Dorothy = Valentine Carey Bp of Exeter 1621–1627
of Trusley | of Melbourne =(1) Mary Powell =(2) Joan Gore née Lee | | | | | | |

```
              Sir John (d.1650)
                of Melbourne
         = Elizabeth Willoughby née Parsey
```

John's son-in-law, had also written to Sir John at Melbourne, confirming that Swithland was not secure, and questioning whether Leicester was better.

> I am confident you will find neither security nor accommodation at Swithland… And being the general opinion and conclusion that the main armies on both sides are drawing into these parts for the enlargement of their quarters, I question whether Leicester will be convenient for you.[6]

Poor Sir John was forced to undertake the considerable journey to his own house at Tottenham, at the great age of eighty-one. He did not long survive, dying there on 8th September 1644.

In December 1643 William Danvers had lent Parliament £1,000 to enable Lord Grey to buy arms and ammunition for the defence of Leicester. At some time before July 1644, he had been promoted to the rank of captain in the parliamentary army and in October 1644 was named as one of those in Leicestershire responsible for raising money for the new parliamentary army in Ireland. In February 1645 he was among those raising money for Sir Thomas Temple's army, and in March 1645 he was appointed a member of Leicester County Committee.

Parliament set up local committees to take over the property of royalist supporters, which helped finance the war. Depending on the level of their involvement, royalists were subject to heavy fines. These sequestrations often resulted in the forced sale of land in order to pay. In 1654 the Hastings family was forced to sell their substantial holding in Buddon Wood to Peter Cheveney. At least one resident of Swithland had already suffered in this way. Francis Blankley of Swithland was discharged from his sequestration on 30th August 1645 by order of the House of Commons after having compounded with the local Sequestration Committee. Despite the financial penalty, Blankley was still resident in Swithland in 1664, when his house was assessed as having three hearths for Hearth Tax purposes. He was buried in Swithland churchyard in 1679. After his death, around 1690, Samuel Danvers purchased Francis' house and land from his heir William Blankley. Near neighbour, Edward Farnham of Quorn was also subjected to sequestration. His offence was that in February 1642 he left his house in Quorn in order to reside at Ashby, a royalist garrison. There he was joined by his wife. They remained there for two and a half years until 1645 when they returned to their house in Quorn. For this 'offence', he was fined £480 in March 1646 as a 'delinquent'.

A Royalist Rector

Swithland's rector at the start of the Civil War was Joseph Smith. Smith, a native of Norfolk, had matriculated at St John's College, Cambridge in 1609, obtaining his B.A. in 1613. He had been rector since 1623, but was ejected from office in 1645 because he was a royalist.

Parliament had abolished the episcopacy on 3rd January 1645, and, on 23rd May 1646, ordered the adoption of a presbyterian system of church government. The use of the Book of Common Prayer was forbidden. In its place, Parliament established a 'Directory for the Worship of God in the Three Kingdoms'. From 1647, those caught using the Prayer Book were punished by a fine of £5 for the first offence, £10 for the second, and imprisonment for one year for the third. Not to observe the Directory risked a fine on a minister of £2, and to say anything in opposition to the Directory was punishable by a fine of up to £50.

Parliament began to dismiss church ministers who were deemed 'malignant, delinquent or scandalous'.[7] Committees were authorized to make enquiry and to sequester the livings of those parsons who did not meet their requirements. Joseph Smith, although ejected as rector of Swithland, somehow managed to be appointed rector of Hathern in 1645. Nevertheless his allegiance came under enquiry. On 20th April 1646 he was summoned before the county committee and charged with royalist practices. It was alleged

> ... that he still prayed for the bishops and read Common Prayer – even though the Directory had been presented to him; that he was a frequenter of alehouses, a swearer, who spent his time hunting and hawking; that for two years or so he had kept scandalous curates at Swithland, paying them only 40 shillings per annum; that he employed himself more in fisicke than in divinity, yet he preached against the Parliament's party; and that he was at Leicester when it was taken by the enemy.[8]

Despite the charges against him, Joseph Smith managed to retain the rectory of Hathern until 1652, when he moved to become rector of Great Coates, Lincolnshire. He died there in 1662, doubtless having rejoiced to live to see the restoration of the monarchy in 1660.

Justice of the Peace

During the Commonwealth years following the end of the Civil War, William Danvers served as one of Leicestershire's Justices of the Peace. The 1653 Marriage Act made provision for marriages to be conducted by JPs, instead of church ministers. Danvers conducted marriages between December 1653 and his death in 1656. The Thurcaston Parish Register, for example, records that in December 1653 'John Fletcher and Elizabeth Johnson, both of Thurcaston [were] marryed before Wm Danvers Esq one of the Justices of the Peace of this county'.[9] The Tilton register records that 'Thomas Frisbie of Tilton and Mary Watts of Thrussington [were married] 6 June 1655 before William Danvers and Thomas Pochin, Esqs, Justices'.[10] The Hoton register records marriages 'before William Danvers JP' in 1654 and 1656, and the Melton Mowbray register shows William Danvers to be officiating at marriages there in 1653 and 1654. All these were civil marriages, and the Melton ones would probably have taken place at the Melton market cross. The Long Clawson register records that 'Thomas Garton, batchelor, and Mary Hicklinge, spinster, both of Long Clawson, were married at Swithland before Justice Danvers 2 Dec 1654; Robert Hicklinge & Sarah Julian, both of Clawson, [were] married at Swithland 21 Dec 1654'.[11] And the Belgrave register records that Robert More of Belgrave and Jane Sanderson of Leicester were married on May Day 1656 'before two Justices, Mr Danvers & Mr Pochin, Att the Angell'.

The new arrangements were not to everyone's taste. Nathaniel Tovey, rector of Aylestone from 1654 to 1658, wrote in his register:

> How the Register for marriages hath been discontinued in this Book, I knowe not. I conjecture some leaves have been torne out in the unruly times of warre. When I entered upon this parsonage marriages were (by I know not what order) taken out of the hands of the ministers, and put into the hands of Justices of the Peace. But now about the month of June 1659 there came out an Act which impowred ministers agayne to marry.[12]

As a Justice of the Peace, William Danvers was responsible for swearing in those appointed as parish 'registers', for whose appointment the Act provided. They were to be responsible for recording births, marriages and deaths. A note in the Humberstone Parish Register records:

> This is to signify unto whome it may concerne that Anthony Palmer of Humberstone, being elected parish Register for the parish of Humberstone aforesaid by the inhabitants of the said parish, did before me William Danvers Esq, one of the Justices of the Peace for the county, upon the third day of December instant [1653] take his oath for the faithful discharge of the said office.[13]

A similar entry in the Wymeswold Parish Register records the election and swearing in of James Brecknocke in December 1653 before Justice Danvers.

William Danvers died in 1656. Doubt and disillusion with the new order had begun to surface across the country. The people in general had not been won over. The Worcestershire Association reported in 1656 that 'the people understand not our public teachings, though we study to speak as plain as we can, and that after many years of preaching'. Within the puritan ranks, too, there was dissatisfaction. Danvers' eldest son, Henry, was among many who came to question Cromwell's later political judgment and policies, urging rebellion rather than quiescence to the Protectorate. Just before William Danvers died, he took the precaution of making a comprehensive settlement[14] to ensure that his younger children were provided for.

Fifth Monarchist and Radical

William's son and heir, Henry Danvers (1622–1687) was very different from his father, becoming noted – some might say notorious – for his religious and for his political zeal.

At the start of the war, Henry was in his mid twenties and living as a Staffordshire gentleman – his estate in Staffordshire was worth some £300 per year. Like his father, he espoused the parliamentary cause, and soon became a colonel in its forces. Whilst living in Stafford, Danvers, who had been an Independent,[15] became a Baptist – joining a General Baptist congregation that had the 'noted controversialist' Henry Haggar as its minister.[16] Danvers was himself already making a contribution to national political and religious thinking and, from 1847, was at the centre of discussions formulating a proposed Leveller constitution. He contributed to the various tracts and papers of the day. His 'Certain Quaeries Concerning Liberty of Conscience' (1649), for example, urged religious toleration.

During the Interregnum, Henry Danvers served on the County Committee in Staffordshire from 1650–52,[17] where he also became a Justice of the Peace. In March 1650 he was commissioned a major in the Leicestershire militia, and two months later also received a commission as a colonel in the Staffordshire militia. He served as Governor of the town of Stafford from 1650–51, and was described at that time as 'well beloved of the people, being noted for one who would not take bribes'.[18]

During the latter part of Danvers' time in Stafford, his religious views became more extreme. He moved to identify with the Fifth Monarchists, millenarian enthusiasts whose interpretation of the prophecies in the biblical books of Daniel and Revelation led them to expect the imminent establishment on earth of a fifth monarchy, the Kingdom of Christ. Believing that there had already been four great monarchies in human history – Assyrian, Persian, Macedonian and Roman – they considered that the puritan revolution in England should pave the way for the coming of the fifth and final monarchy. This time of preparation, they said, would last a thousand years, during which time the 'saints' – the godly people in the nation – should govern the country. It was this sense of responsibility for establishing a theocratic regime in preparation for the Second Coming, in which godly discipline would be exercised over the unregenerate masses, that set the Fifth Monarchists apart from other millenarians. They set out their expectations in a petition to Parliament in 1649.

> A kingdom and dominion, which the church is to exercise on earth; that extends to all persons and things universally, which is to be externally and visibly administered; by such laws and officers, as Jesus Christ our mediator hath appointed in his kingdom. It shall put down all worldly rule and authority (so far as relates to the worldly constitution thereof) though in the hands of Christians: and is to be expected about this time we live in. This kingdom shall not be erected by human power and authority, but Christ by his spirit shall call and gather a people, and form them into several less families, churches and corporations; and when they are multiplied, they shall rule the world by general assemblies; or church-parliaments, of such officers of Christ, and representatives of the churches as they shall choose and delegate, which they shall do, till Christ come in person.

The Church of Rome had earlier condemned millenarian ideas as heretical, and several sixteenth century Protestant reformers regarded millenarianism as a thing of the past. A few seventeenth century Protestants, however, interpreted the contents of chapter twenty of the Book of Revelation in terms of a future earthly reign of Christ and, following the execution of Charles I in 1649, millenarian views gained wide currency.

In March 1652 Henry Danvers was appointed a Justice of the Peace for Leicestershire. In July 1653, after the dismissal of the Rump Parliament, he was elected to the Barebones Parliament (the nominated Assembly) as the Member for Leicester. He was appointed to serve on committees dealing with tithes, Scottish affairs and prisons. While in London, he served as joint elder of the General Baptist Church of Edmund Challenge, like him a Fifth Monarchist.

Danvers' short parliamentary career came to an end in 1654 with the dissolution of the Barebones Parliament, but not his religious struggle. He profoundly disagreed with Cromwell over the establishment of a Protectorate; it went against his Fifth Monarchist principles. Believing that his fellow countrymen must establish the reign of the saints, he urged Christians of the same mind to rise in rebellion. Not all his fellow Fifth Monarchists shared his views. Danvers was not involved in Thomas Venner's plot to topple Oliver Cromwell, although some of his friends were. He was, however, briefly imprisoned in April 1657 for suspected complicity.[19] Later that year he was involved in raising Norfolk and Suffolk to arms 'to bring in the kingdom of Christ'; there was blood shed at North Walsham.

In 1659 the Rump Parliament was restored. Danvers was appointed a member of the Staffordshire County Committee and Commissioner for Middlesex. He appears to have been totally captured by his millenarian vision that the long awaited thousand years would come only when the saints ushered them in by establishing a godly society. In millenarian eyes, the existence of a sovereign was a curse on his subjects; Christians should openly

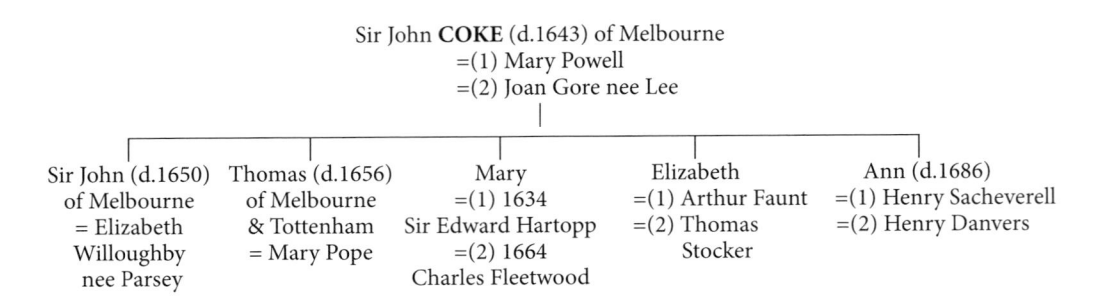

```
                    Sir John COKE (d.1643) of Melbourne
                           =(1) Mary Powell
                           =(2) Joan Gore nee Lee
```

Sir John (d.1650) of Melbourne = Elizabeth Willoughby nee Parsey	Thomas (d.1656) of Melbourne & Tottenham = Mary Pope	Mary =(1) 1634 Sir Edward Hartopp =(2) 1664 Charles Fleetwood	Elizabeth =(1) Arthur Faunt =(2) Thomas Stocker	Ann (d.1686) =(1) Henry Sacheverell =(2) Henry Danvers

or secretly resist it as best they could. When, therefore, in 1660, General Monck succeeded in engineering the restoration of the Stuart monarch, Danvers and his like-minded friends were committed to resistance.

Henry Danvers succeeded his father in 1656 and prudently placed his estate of manors and lands in Leicestershire, worth £400, in the hands of trustees, hoping to ensure its safety.[20] Even before his father's death, Henry's principal residence was at Stoke Newington, London, where his daughter Elizabeth is thought to have been born in 1647. Stoke Newington was a notorious centre of dissent. A large Elizabethan mansion there – later known as Fleetwood House – was the residence of Sir Edward Hartopp of Buckminster, Leicestershire, one of the leaders of the parliamentary army during the Civil War. Hartopp had married Mary Coke, daughter of Sir John Coke of Melbourne, Derbyshire, and it was her sister, Ann, who became Henry Danvers' wife in 1647.[21] Following Sir Edward Hartopp's death in 1658, Mary Coke re-married in 1664; her second husband – and she was his third wife – was the former parliamentary general, Lt. Col. Charles Fleetwood. They lived in half the house, while Mary's son, Sir John Hartopp, occupied the other half.[22] Henry and Ann Danvers spent the first years of their early married life amongst the Hartopp household. At some point they purchased a substantial residence of their own in Stoke Newington; in the 1670 Hearth Tax returns, their house was listed as having thirteen hearths.

In 1661 Henry Danvers was living in hiding, reportedly in Stoke Newington, and planning a rising. Government agents thought, wrongly, that he was involved in the 1662 Tong Plot to restore the republic, assassinate Charles II and the Dukes of York and Albemarle, and establish national liberty of conscience. Whilst in hiding, Danvers published a new tract, 'The Mystery of Magistracy Unvailed' (1663), arguing for the selection of godly magistrates by lot, and their rule in accordance with the principles of Mosaic Law. In November 1663, he was in Holland, plotting an insurrection in England. The Government, believing that Danvers had agents in Leicestershire for this purpose, issued a warrant for his arrest. In January 1664 he was alleged to be involved in another plot against the English government. Some weeks later he was reportedly 'visiting his wife in secret at Stoke Newington, disguised in a rural garb and a long beard down to his breast'.[23] In June he was said to be conniving with rebels in London, and preaching in Leicestershire. His wife was also active. She travelled to London in July to report the latest schemes to Frances, Lady Vane, who was a key contact with the London revolutionaries.

The authorities finally succeeded in arresting Danvers in August 1665, but a friendly crowd rescued him in Cheapside, London. Samuel Pepys' diary entry for the 5th August 1665 described

> ... a great Ryott upon Thursday last in Cheapside. Collonell Danvers, a Delinquent, having been taken, and in his way to the Tower was rescued from the Captain of the Guard and carried away – only one of the Rescuers being taken.[24]

On 30th August, Danvers was charged with high treason for complicity in the Rathbone Plot – a conspiracy to assassinate the king, seize the Tower of London, set fire to London, establish a republic, and redistribute property. Rathbone and some of his co-conspirators were arrested. Eight were executed, but Danvers escaped. One of Danvers' servants from Maddersall in Staffordshire, when interrogated on 9th September, admitted receiving books from Henry's brother Charles Danvers – also a Fifth Monarchist and a London merchant – but he denied knowledge of the whereabouts of his master. The Sheriff of Leicestershire was ordered to secure Danvers' estate, pending the outcome of his trial. Danvers fled to Ireland and continued to conspire against the Government. He remained a fugitive at large, despite further warrants for his arrest in March 1667 and in May 1670.

During this period, Danvers became minister to the Particular Baptist congregation that met at the 'Chequer' near Aldgate in London.[25] He wrote more pamphlets on religious themes, and entered into argument with other dissenters. 'Theopolis, or the City of God' (in which he argued that Christ's appearance would only come at the end of the millennium) and 'A Confession of My Faith' were published in 1672. In 1673 he wrote his 'Treatise on Baptism' – a work of one thousand pages – in which he attacked infant baptism, questioned accounts of the slaughter of Anabaptists in Germany in 1535, and denounced the open-communion principles of John Bunyan.[26] (The unlawfulness of infant baptism was one of the cardinal principles of the Baptists). But the work drew replies from well-known dissenters such as Richard Blinman,[27] John Bunyan, Richard Baxter[28] and Obadiah Wills, who accused Danvers of being an apologist for the slaughter of the Munster Anabaptists. Danvers wrote rejoinders: 'Innocence and Truth Vindicated' (1675), 'A Second Reply' (1675), and 'A Third Reply' (1676). In the middle of the controversy, he also wrote 'A Treatise on Laying On of Hands' (1674).

In November 1675 Danvers was reported to be preaching on foot throughout the country. A Staffordshire landowner informed the Privy Council in November 1675 that:

> Colonel Danvers has been preaching to his party in this country at all their meetings and went throughout the kingdom, as I am informed, on foot. 'Tis strange a person of his quality and estate should come 100 miles on that account. All the factious parties are very stirring at present, more than of late.[29]

Danvers was arrested in January 1676, as he was leaving his conventicle near Aldgate, London. This time, he was not rescued by the mob but was committed to the Tower on the charge of treason. There his health deteriorated so rapidly that he was discharged in April 1676 on payment of £1,000 security, and confined to his house.

Undaunted, Danvers continued to preach illegally. The Conventicle Acts of 1664 and 1670 had banned any religious gatherings outside the bounds of the national Church, but between 1681 and 1682 Danvers was openly preaching and ministering to a London conventicle of some seven hundred people. He continued to plot against the Government. In 1679, 'he huddled with Titus Oates'.[30] In 1682, he was reported to have conspired with the Green Ribbon Club members and with the Rye House plotters.

In September 1684 the Privy Council decided that it wanted to interrogate Danvers, but decided not to press the search when it was learnt that his whereabouts was unknown. But in December 1684 Danvers published what the Government perceived to be a seditious libel about the death of the Earl of Essex, 'Murther Will Out'. (Essex was among those who had been imprisoned after the discovery of the Rye House Plot. Danvers alleged that Essex did not commit suicide in prison, but had been murdered.) On 30th December, the Government issued a warrant for Danvers' arrest for treasonous activity, with a reward of £100 offered for his apprehension. Edward Bedingfield wrote to the Countess of Rutland on 1st January 1685:

> Some dayes past were severall damnable libells thrown at many persons dores, it contains a sheet or two of paper in substance a compendium of Ferguson's letter concerning the Earl of Essex's death, but still more black and bitter than that letter. Great perquisition has been made for the discovery of its author, and just now I hear they are thec'd out and the original seized on in the cabinet of Collonell Danvers who lives at Newington, but he is not yet seized on, through his house beleagur'd and his bed was found warme, so as they imagine him in some secret place from which they'll famish him.[31]

Danvers was not starved out, he had already escaped. Further warrants were issued on 20th January, 26th January, 8th February, and 4th July. But he remained at large.

In 1685, when it was evident that James II would succeed to the throne, Danvers joined a conspiracy to plan an insurrection to coincide with the coronation. The plans were changed to take account of the Duke of Monmouth's attempt to raise England. Monmouth landed from Holland at Lyme Regis, but failed to break through James' western defences. (Troops loyal to James had been withdrawn from London for this defence.) Monmouth had given Danvers and another man authority to lead the rising in London to build on his own attack. But despite having a number of men in London ready to rise, Danvers refused to act, being uncertain of Monmouth's success. The rebellion failed. On 27th July 1687 a royal proclamation commanded Danvers and others to appear before his majesty or to surrender themselves in twenty days.[32] He fled to Holland – this time for good. During his exile he was a major investor in a scheme to employ radical English exiles in cloth manufacturing. He died in Utrecht at the close of 1687.[33] His burial place, as that of his wife Ann, is unknown.

Some fifty years later T. Crosby described Henry Danvers as 'a worthy man, of an unspotted life and conversation, joint elder to a baptized congregation near Aldgate'.[34] Not everyone shared that opinion. The Earl of Arran judged him 'a dangerous fellow'; the nineteenth century Whig historian, Thomas Macaulay, whose views were somewhat biased, referred disparagingly to 'the craven Danvers'.[35] He described him as 'hot-headed but faint-hearted, constantly urged to the brink of danger by enthusiasm, and constantly stopped on that brink by cowardice'.[36] The facts, however, do not justify Macaulay's accusation of cowardice. Henry Danvers was convinced that his religious beliefs should govern his political behaviour, and never gave up the attempt to bring that about.

In some respects, Henry Danvers' career echoed the activities of the Grey family. Thomas Grey had also fallen out with Oliver Cromwell during the Commonwealth, and was briefly imprisoned. Like Danvers, he joined the Fifth Monarchists. His father, the Earl of Stamford was a more cautious man; he finally lost patience with the Commonwealth and supported the Restoration. He was imprisoned in 1659, but released on the accession of Charles II. Nevertheless both Charles II and James II regarded the Grey family with suspicion and Bradgate House was regarded as a possible centre for treacherous activity. Thomas Grey, again like Henry Danvers, joined Monmouth's rebellion in 1685. He was arrested at Bradgate, taken to London, and imprisoned in the Tower on a charge of high treason. He was later given bail and included in a general pardon, remaining in discreet seclusion at Bradgate for the remainder of James II's reign.

Rehabilitation

Throughout his adult life, Henry Danvers spent little time in Leicestershire. His children would appear to have been raised in Stoke Newington, whilst his mother, Elizabeth Danvers, managed the Swithland estates, which her son's revolutionary activities had undoubtedly placed in jeopardy. But the family's rehabilitation started even before Henry died. Unlike his father, Samuel Danvers was prepared to conform to the religious settlement of the day. His three eldest sons were baptized at Stoke Newington church between 1685 and 1688 according to the rites of the Church of England. Fifty years later, Henry's grandson, Joseph, was playing a prominent part in local and national administration.

Henry Danvers' son and heir, Samuel, was born in 1652 – possibly in Stoke Newington, possibly in Swithland – and grew up during the years when his father, with his mother's support, was actively challenging Oliver Cromwell. In 1683 he married a rich London grocer's daughter, Elizabeth Morewood. Elizabeth was to play an important part in ensuring a secure future for her husband's family and their children.

Fig 6.1 Prescott Manor in 1998.

She was the daughter and only child of Joseph Morewood, so when her father died in 1686 she inherited his entire estate, including premises in Hope, Brough and Thornhill in Derbyshire. It was an astute marriage; he benefitted from her money and land and she benefitted from his social position. With Samuel's father Henry dying abroad in exile in 1687, the marriage was timely. Elizabeth married again in 1710, some seventeen years after her husband died. This too was an astute marriage, not just for Elizabeth but for her family, and especially for her son Joseph.

Fig 6.2. Sir John Danvers' shield in the panelled room at Prescott Manor.[37]

Elizabeth's second husband, Sir John Danvers (1651–1721) of Prescott Manor, Cropredy was a wealthy bachelor aged fifty-eight, who had worked for the Government as a Commissioner of Revenue for some years and who came from another branch of the Danvers family. His wealth enabled him to 'indulge a taste which he had inherited for building and gardening. He added greatly to the old manor house at Prescott, especially one room, which was apparently built to receive the magnificent oak panelling which he bought out of Warkworth House. His arms and initials appear over the fireplace in the panelled room and over the present entry to the house'.[38]

Sir John died in 1721 and is buried in Cropredy church, where a fine memorial testifies to his worth. His memorial hatchment, however, hangs in the Danvers' chapel at Swithland Church. He left his entire estate to Elizabeth's son Joseph Danvers, Samuel's heir to the manor of Swithland. The Swithland Danvers family had emerged from the troubled years of the Civil War well placed for the future.

Notes to Chapter 6

1. As was Sir John Danvers of Oxford.
2. Leics. RO, mss Earl Cowper KG, volume II, letter 30 January, 1643.
3. ibid., letter 18 March, 1643.
4. ibid., letter, 11 October, 1643
5. ibid., letter, 12 November, 1643
6. ibid., letter, 11 November, 1643
7. i.e. Royalist
8. A.G Matthews, *Walker Revised*, 'Leicestershire'.
9. Leicestershire Phillimore Parish Registers (Marriages)
10. ibid.
11. ibid.
12. ibid.
13. ibid.
14. Leics. RO, 2D/31/107, Tripartite indenture, 6th August 1656, William and Elizabeth Danvers, settlement on their younger children, William, Charles, Margaret, Elizabeth, Anne, Diana.
15. One who believed that membership of the state should be separate from membership of the church, and that religion should be free to take any number of forms provided it was neither Catholic nor Episcopalian
16. *Victoria County History of Staffordshire*.
17. Calendar of the Committee of Compounding, etc., letters August 12th, 20th 1650; March 31st 1652.
18. Lichfield RO, The Gentry of Staffordshire 1662–1665, manuscript transcription.
19. Thurloe's State Papers, iv, 629; Rapin, *History of England*, ed. 1730, xii, 124.
20. T. Crosby, *English Baptists*, iii, p. 90–97.
21. Leics. RO, 2D 61/37, Settlement 8 Oct 1647, by Jacinth Sacheverell, father in law of Ann Sacheverell née Coke, on her second marriage to Henry Danvers, son of William Danvers.
22. Benjamin Clarke, *1894, Glimpses of Ancient Hackney and Stoke Newington*, London Borough of Hackney, 1986.
23. R.L. Greaves, *Saints and Rebels*, Mercer University Press, 1985.
24. R. Latham and W. Matthews (eds.), *Diary of Samuel Pepys*, 5 August 1665, vol. 6, 1972.
25. Walter Wilson, *The History and Antiquities of Dissenting Churches and Meeting Houses*, vol. 1, pp. 393–95. (Particular Baptists believed that salvation was for the elect alone).
26. Dr Williams Library, London, 1082.M.15. Henry Danvers: 'A Treatise on Baptism. Whereas that of believers and that of infants is examined by the Scriptures with ... The history of

Christianity amongst the ancient Britains and Waldenses And... A brief answer to Mr Bunyan about Communion with persons unbaptised'. 1673.

27. Dr Williams Library, Richard Blinman, 'An essay tending to Issue the Conversie about infant baptism ... occasioned by a Tender made by Henry Danvers in his late Book against infant baptism'. 1674.

28. Dr Williams Library, Richard Baxter, 'More proofs of infants Church-membership and right to baptism in three parts. The first... with the defence... against the exceptions of Mr Tombes… The second is a confutation of… Mr H Danvers… The third part is Animadversions on Mr Danvers' reply to Mr Willes…', 1675.

29. Calendar of State Papers, Charles II, 1675–6, Letter from Sir Henry Broughton to Sir Joseph Williamson, 27 Nov 1675.

30. R.L. Greaves, *Saints and Rebels*, Mercer University Press, 1985.

31. Leics. RO, Historical Manuscripts Commission, mss of the Duke of Rutland, letter, 1 January 1685, vol 2, p. 84.

32. N. Luttrell, *A Brief Historical Relation of State Affairs from September 1678 to April 1714*, vol. 1, p. 355; Salmon vol. 1, p. 238.

33. *Gentleman's Magazine*, ccxix, p. 358.

34. T. Crosby, *English Baptists*, 1740.

35. T. Macaulay, *History of England*, vol 1, 1848, p.175.

36. ibid. pp. 422, 459, 408.

37. Danvers arms quartered by Neville arms. Photograph 1998 by kind permission of the late Mrs Anne Crossman.

38. F.N. Macnamara, *Memorials of the Danvers Family*, Danvers and Webster. Centennial Edition 1995, pp. 8–32. Prescott Manor is owned by the family of the late Richard Crossman MP, who was an heir to the Danvers family, as was his wife Anne.

CHAPTER 7

Dissent

For most of Swithland's history, the parish church has been the sole focus of Christian life and worship in this small community. During the eighteenth and nineteenth centuries, however, members of the Presbyterian, Baptist and Methodist communities added their contribution to the spiritual history of the village and the church.

Presbyterians in Swithland

To the left of the north porch to Swithland church, in poor repair and almost hidden, lie seven slate gravestones, commemorating the Revd Michael Matthews (1661–1723), members of his family and an apparently unrelated eleven year old boy. Michael Matthews' name, however, does not appear amongst the list of the incumbents of the Parish Church. So who was he, and why are his remains interred in Swithland?

>Here lieth the body of Thomas,
>The son of Michael Matthews
>Who died May 7, anno 1691
>—
>Hic situm est corpus
>Sam^{lis} Matthews, qui ob^t 9º Martij, 1694-5.
>—
>Hic sit^m est corpus
>Thos, alter^s filii Mich^{lis} Matthews,
>Qui ob^t 23º Nov 1696.
>—
>Hic situm est corpus
>Nathanaelsis filii Mich^{lis} Matthews,
>Qui obiit 23º Sept. anno 1700.
>—
>Here lieth the body of Christian Hood,
>Of Longdon in Staffordshire; who departed this life,
>At Mountsorrel, the 27th Nov. 1713, aged 80.
>—

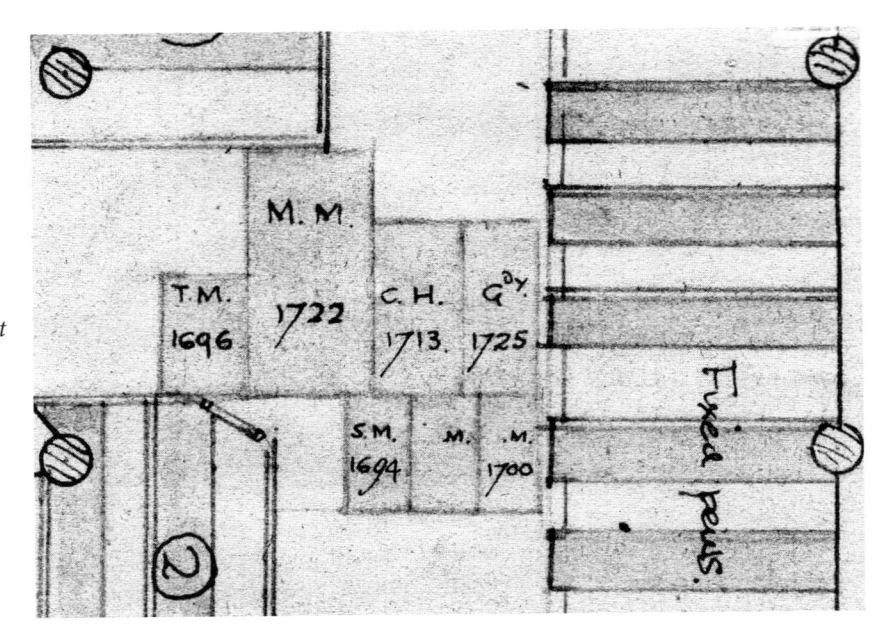

Fig 7.1 The Matthews' family graves at the nave crossing of St Leonard's Church, as discovered during restoration work in the 1920s.

Hic jacent reliquiae rev^{di} viri Michaelis Matthews;
Qui, Evangelium assidue concionando,
Juventutem pariter erudiendo,
Vitae suae ministerio functus, obdormivit nonis Ap.
Anno Salutis MDCCXXIII, aetatis suae LXII.
ITEM SARA MATHEWS, UXOR EJUS,
OBIIT V NON. MAII MDCCXLIV, ANN AET. LXXXI.

—

Under this stone was buried the body of William,
The eldest son of Nicholas Grundy[1], gent.
By Hannah his wife, third daughter of Henry Lycet,
Of Hansacre, in the county of Stafford, gent.
He died the 31st day of October, 1723, aged 11.

Originally these gravestones were set in the nave crossing of the church. The stones were discovered during the church restoration of 1924–28 and removed to their present situation. The burial of this group of people inside St Leonard's Church is unusual in that they were all Presbyterians, and none of them lived in Swithland. Michael Matthews was a Presbyterian minister and a regionally important figure at a time when toleration of religious dissent was first allowed.

Between 1649–60, under the Commonwealth and Protectorate of Oliver Cromwell, the Church of England was disestablished and outlawed. In its place, Presbyterian ecclesiology was introduced in place of the episcopate, the thirty nine Articles were replaced with the Westminster Confession, and the Book of Common Prayer by the Directory of Public Worship. The

Presbyterian order was never established in the entirety for which Cromwell and his followers hoped. Despite the pressure, about one quarter of English clergy refused to conform, and with the restoration of the monarchy in 1660, the Church of England was restored.

The part played by the Swithland Danvers' family during the Civil War and its aftermath has already been recorded. William Danvers and his family were on the side of Parliament, with Henry Danvers in particular being considerably more radical than Cromwell's own Presbyterians.

In 1660, with the end of the Commonwealth, Charles II – waiting to be called back to England – issued a declaration at Breda, promising 'a liberty to tender consciences'. His parliaments, however, were far less tolerant than he. They initiated a period of persecution on everyone who refused to conform to the practice of the re-introduced Book of Common Prayer. Religious dissent was penalised in the series of enactments known as the Clarendon Code. (The Earl of Clarendon was Charles II's Lord Chancellor.) The Corporation Act of 1661 banned from membership of municipal corporations anyone who refused to take the sacrament according to the Prayer Book rite. The Act of Uniformity (1662) further required assent to the Prayer Book as a qualification for many public offices. The Conventicle Act (1664) banned all meetings for religious rites (other than those of the Church of England) of more than five persons, except members of the same household. The Five Mile Act (1665) forbade any non-conformist minister from going within five miles of a town or city unless he swore an oath not to endeavour any alteration of Government either in church or state.

Many clergy were ejected from their parishes in 1662 for refusing to conform to the requirements of the Act of Uniformity. In practice, much depended on the climate of local opinion. Many of the ejected Presbyterian ministers, for example, not only attended their parish church, but also continued to act as pastors to such people as desired their services. In a few cases, they were even able to maintain a regular meeting for their former parishioners. In many parishes, however, opposition was such that they were unable to continue their ministry, either openly or in secret. Those families unwilling to conform were therefore faced with the problem of how to educate their children, now barred access to the universities. Some of the ejected ministers set up schools or academies for this purpose. One such was the academy in the manor house at Sheriffhales, near Shifnal, Shropshire, and it is here that we first come across Michael Matthews.

The founder of the academy at Sherriffhales was the Revd. John Woodhouse[2] (1627–1700.) Woodhouse was employed as a chaplain to Lady Grantham in Nottinghamshire during the Protectorate, but 'was silenced' in 1662. In 1667, however, he married Mary – the wealthy daughter of Major William Hubbart of Saxelby, Leicestershire – and is recorded as preaching at Saxelby in 1669. In 1675 he was licenced – as of Wartnaby, Leicestershire – to teach grammar in the dioceses of Lincoln, Lichfield and Hereford, and then from 1676 to 1697 his wife's money allowed him to run an academy 'of note' at Sherriffhales,[3] on the Staffordshire–Shropshire border. Woodhouse died in 1700, and is buried at Rearsby, Leicestershire, where he possessed an estate.

Fig 7.2 Sherriffhales Academy, now a local house.

The curriculum for the Sherriffhales' scholars was comprehensive.[4] Greek, Latin, Hebrew, mathematics, history, geography, natural science, logic, ethics and metaphysics were all taught. Every student had to read certain standard theological books, and students for the ministry had to read an extended list. They were taught how to analyse biblical texts and encouraged to adopt a 'plain and familiar way of preaching as most compatible with a faithful and diligent aim at usefulness in saving immortal souls'.[5] There were weekly law lectures for law students, and, for those who would become country gentlemen, there was instruction in land surveying, composing almanacs, manufacturing sundials and dissecting animals. Every day each student had to give an account of the previous day's lecture before listening to the next one, and once a week had to give a public declination of Latin, Greek and Hebrew verbs.

Michael Matthews seems to have been studying for the ministry at the Sherriffhales academy. In September 1689, living at Sherriffhales and described as 'gent', he married Sarah Hood (1663–1744) at Shenstone parish church, Staffordshire. Michael was the son of a clergyman; he matriculated from Jesus College, Oxford on 21st April 1658, taking his BA on 22nd March 1658/9.[6] Sarah was the daughter of Thomas and Christian Hood[7] of Longdon by Lichfield, and was baptised there in January 1664, although at the time of her marriage, she lived at Sutton Coldfield. Longdon was a centre of dissent. During a brief period of relative toleration, the house of Christian Hood[8] at Longdon was licensed in 1672 for Presbyterian meetings. Under the Declaration of Indulgence of 1672, licenses were also given to 'teachers' who would be allowed to speak, and in May 1672 Christian Hood and Edward Broughton were licensed as Presbyterian preachers and teachers at Longdon.[9] Later, however, there was a period of intense religious persecution and from 1678 to 1686 enforcement at Longdon was particularly strong.

Michael and Sarah Matthews were married by licence at Shenstone – not at Longdon – on 19th September 1689, probably because the persecution there was less severe. Shenstone was the home of William Grace,[10] son of John Grace of Shenstone, who served as vicar of Shenstone 1635–51 and as rector of Rearsby, Leicestershire from 1644. Grace was restored to Rearsby 1660–62, and also to Shenstone 1662–65, but he was denounced by his Shenstone churchwardens in 1665 for holding conventicles. He then moved to Syston, Leicestershire. In 1669 he was preaching in Rearsby, and in 1672 in Rugeley, but he had returned to Shenstone by 1690, where the pulpit suppliers were informed that he was 'blind and indigent can go noe where to preach'.[11] With the passing of the Toleration Act in 1689, dissenters gained the freedom to worship in their own way, although the obstacles to their entering public service remained. The Toleration Act also marked the end of aspirations for a comprehensive national church. After 1689 non-conformists ceased to be part of the national church, and became a dissenting sect.

Michael Matthews was ordained at Hemphill, Nottinghamshire in August 1690 by members of the Wirksworth classis (an assembly of Presbyterian elders, also called a presbytery). Later that year he was in Leicestershire, preaching in Swithland, and receiving £15 per annum from the Presbyterian Common Fund.[12] Matthews' wife was a Hood of Longdon in Staffordshire, who were probably related to the Hoods of Bardon Park, Leicestershire.[13] This would explain the move to Leicestershire. Matthews may have been recommended to the 'dissenting' Danvers family[14] by the Hoods of Bardon, who held secret Presbyterian worship meetings at their manor house, until the law was relaxed and they were free to worship publicly in the new chapel they built in the 1690s. Another Swithland connection was the ownership of the rents of Shenstone Rectory by the Danvers family.[15] No records of the number of dissenters in Swithland survive, but visitations in nearby villages show a significant presence, and Robert Gilbert's family in Swithland was later to avow friendship with Matthews.[16]

Michael and Sarah Matthews were living in Swithland when their infant son, Thomas, died in 1691. The family was apparently significant enough locally for the child to be allowed burial in the nave of Swithland church, rather than in the churchyard. Matthews was still living in Swithland when, in 1693, he was one of the recipients of books from the estate of Richard Baxter, a noted Puritan.[17] Under Baxter's will, the books in his library were given to such young students as his executors might nominate. A manuscript note records that books were sent to Michael Matthews, Swithland, Leicester on 8th April 1693. In 1694 Matthews was appointed master at the charity school at Woodhouse founded by the Presbyterian Thomas Rawlins. Rawlins' father, Thomas Rawlins, who was born in Woodhouse, was a baker of St Botolph's in Bishopsgate in the City of London. A strict Presbyterian,

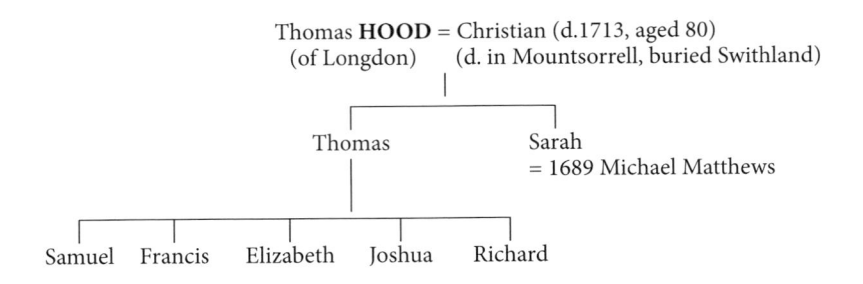

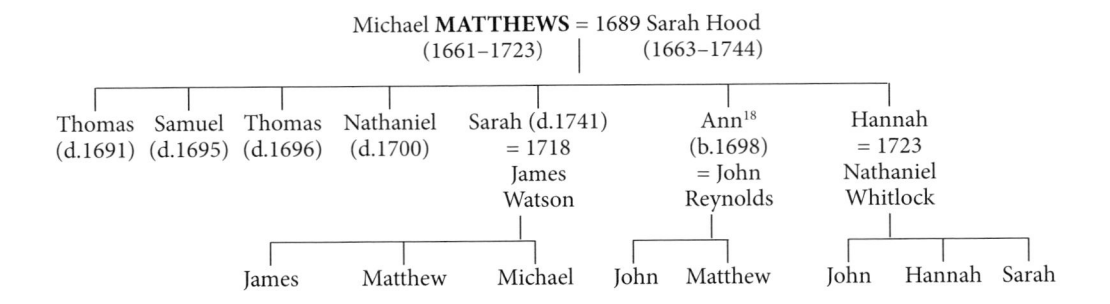

```
                    Thomas HOOD = Christian (d.1713, aged 80)
                    (of Longdon)   (d. in Mountsorrell, buried Swithland)
                                     |
                    ┌────────────────┴────────────┐
                  Thomas                        Sarah
                    |                         = 1689 Michael Matthews
    ┌───────┬──────┼──────────┬───────┬────────┐
  Samuel  Francis  Elizabeth  Joshua  Richard
```

```
                Michael MATTHEWS = 1689 Sarah Hood
                    (1661–1723)   |    (1663–1744)
  ┌──────┬───────┬───────┬───────┼──────┬─────────┬─────────┐
Thomas Samuel Thomas Nathaniel Sarah(d.1741) Ann[18]   Hannah
(d.1691)(d.1695)(d.1696)(d.1700) = 1718    (b.1698)  = 1723
                                 James    = John    Nathaniel
                                 Watson   Reynolds  Whitlock
                              ┌───┬───┐   ┌───┬───┐ ┌────┬─────┬─────┐
                            James Matthew Michael John Matthew John Hannah Sarah
```

Rawlins senior played a prominent part in the Civil War, and died during the plague of London in 1665. His property interests in Barrow, Woodhouse and Woodhouse Eaves passed to his son, Thomas Rawlins. In 1691, Thomas Rawlins the son made over part of his estate to trustees to provide £24 per annum for a master to teach freely. A Mr Chambers was appointed the first Master in 1691, and he continued until 1693 when Matthews took over. Despite Matthews' residence in Woodhouse, three other of his sons were buried at Swithland, alongside their brother in the nave of the church: Samuel (died 1695), Thomas (died 1696) and Nathaniel (died 1700). Matthews remained at Woodhouse until 1704, when he resigned as Master of the school. He had evidently taken boarders, including gentlemen's sons, a practice to which Rawlins objected.

In 1694 or 1695 Matthews also became minister of the Presbyterian congregation at Bardon Park[19] and the Meeting House there. John Hood (1647–1715) of Bardon Hall looks to have built the Meeting House in about 1694 for Matthews to minister from. The chapel, which was registered in 1702,[20] could well be the oldest surviving non-conformist meeting house in Leicestershire. Under the Toleration Act of 1689, protestant dissenters were given freedom to worship in public providing they registered their meeting places with a bishop, archdeacon, or at the quarter sessions, but there were often delays in registration. This may have been

Fig 7.3 Bardon Meeting House, John Throsby, 1790.

because the English public were not always as 'tolerant' of Dissenters as the name of the act would imply.

On 21th August 1702[21] Matthews, with John Doughty and Samuel Lawrence, fellow ministers, 'set apart to the office of a presbyter' William Woodhouse, minister at Rearsby.[22] (William was the son of John Woodhouse, who had presided over the Sherriffhales Academy in Staffordshire when Matthews was a student there.)

On leaving the school in Woodhouse in 1704, Matthews moved to Mountsorrel to minister to the Presbyterian congregation there. In 1708, Matthews was one of twelve who, at Mountsorrel on 15th September, 'set apart' Thomas Flavel to minister at Daventry.[23] Matthews built a meeting house on the Green at Mountsorrel

> ... upon his own freehold there and at his own proper costs and charges erect a Building or Meeting House containing four bays to the end and intent that the congregation or people might with more ease and greater conveniency assemble together for religious worship.[24]

Visitation inquiries indicate a not insignificant dissenting presence in Mountsorrel in 1676. Under Matthews, these figures were set to rise.

Returns to Seventeenth Century Visitation Inquiries

	1603 Communicants	1603 Recusants	1676 Conformists	1676 Recusants	1676 Dissenters
Barrow			303		
Cossington	61	0			
Loughborough	1,200	0	1,046	2	75
Mountsorrel	366	0	216	0	30
Quorn	270	0	270	0	28
Shepshed			366	6	4
Sileby	341	0			
Thurcaston	200	0	89	0	0
Cropston			53	0	0
Anstey			140	0	0
Wanlip	54	0	45	0	4
Woodhouse			177	0	1
Beaumanor Park			23	0	0
Maplewell			15	0	0
Wymeswold	351	0	100	2	80

(Recusants = Roman Catholics; Dissenters = Protestant non-conformists)

According to Dr Evans,[25] the congregation at Mountsorrel grew to number some two hundred and eighty people, almost twice as many as worshipped at the neighbouring Loughborough Presbyterian Church. The size of the meeting house can be judged from the ecclesiastical census which was carried out over one hundred and fifty years later in 1851. The space for public worship then consisted of 60 free sittings plus 50 in the gallery, some 60 other sittings, and standing room in the aisle for 70. Hensman recorded that Dr Isaac Watts was said to have preached there.

In the years that followed Matthews' move to Mountsorrel, he presided over what may have been at the time the main dissenting school in Leicestershire. The school was kept in the large vestry of the chapel, and the ministers lived in a substantial house adjoining the chapel.[26] The incumbent's return in 1719 for the Mountsorrel chapelry stated:

> There is a private school kept by Mr Matthews the presbyterian minister by whom a great many gentlemen's sons and others are educated and trained contrary to the doctrine of the Church of England. Neither he nor any of his family which is near fourty persons do ever come to church.[27]

Matthews is reputed to have been 'annoyed by the interference of the ecclesiastical authorities (in respect of the school) on the ground that he had not obtained a licence from the Bishop'.[28]

One of Matthew's Swithland pupils was Henry Gilbert, whose father Robert viewed Matthews as 'his loving friend'.[29] Henry Gilbert (1685–1716), studied at Clare College, Cambridge, and went on to become the minister of a dissenting church near York. In 1705 Matthews wrote from Mountsorrel to the trustees of the Presbyterian Throckmorton Trotman Fund.[30] Throckmorton Trotman (d.1663), a London merchant, had left houses in London to trustees, the income from which was to be used to pay for the education of poor scholars at the universities to fit them for the ministry. Matthews commended Henry Gilbert to them. Gilbert wished to study philosophy at Clare Hall (later Clare College), Cambridge, but did not have the necessary financial resources.

> This may certifie whom it concerns, that Henry Gilbert of Swithland in Leicestershire, being well qualified with school learning, and desirous to proceed in the study of philosophy, offered himself to Mr Lawton of Clare Hall, fellow, and was by him, and other Fellows, mentioned in his certificate, examined and approved for Admission, into the number of ye sizers of Clare Hall, in Cambridge, upon the 20th day of June last. Wanting only 6 pounds cautionary money, which he could not procure, till he has assistance from the charity of some Friends. The truth of which I am well assured of.[31]

Matthews' plea for help from the fund was successful. Henry Gilbert received a grant in 1705, enabling him to attend Clare Hall, Cambridge.[32] Moreover, Gilbert repaid the trustees' investment in him by going on to become minister of the dissenting chapel built in 1715 in Wheelgate, Malton, Yorkshire,[33] though sadly dying in 1719 at the young age of thirty-one.

Notwithstanding Rawlins' disagreement with Matthews about admitting boarders into the school at Woodhouse, on his death in 1710 Thomas Rawlins bequeathed £2 10s a year in his will:

... unto such poor old people as should be settled in a religious exercise in Mr Matthews' meeting house in Mountsorrel, to be distributed to such of them as should most want, by the two eldest trustees of the charitable use he had theretofore settled at Woodhouse.[34]

By 1715, Matthews had the assistance of James Watson, described in 1722 by Philip Doddridge, the great hymn-writer, as 'an incomparable preacher'. 'It is everybody's opinion that he (Watson) deserves a much better place than Kibworth[35] yet his present settlement in Mountsorrel is much worse'.[36] It is possible that Watson stayed in Mountsorrel because he married Matthews' daughter, Sarah, in Mountsorrel chapel in 1718. Between them, Matthews and Watson not only served Mountsorrel and Bardon Park, but also took turns with other ministers to supply Wanlip.[37] Watson also served the congregation at Willoughby-on-the-Wolds. Another Presbyterian minister, who worked with Matthews and Watson at Mountsorrel and Bardon Park from 1723 until his death in 1727, was Abel Ragg (or Page), another friend of Philip Doddridge.

In 1715 Matthews preached at the funeral service for John Hood of Bardon Park. The sermon was published: 'The great Privilege of a dying Believer, or living Christian in a dying hour; being a Funeral Sermon on the much lamented death of John Hood Gent who departed this life at Bardon Park, Leicestershire, 19 Jan 1714/15, in the 58th year of his age'. The work was dedicated to 'Mrs Hood the relict, and Mrs Willington, sister of the deceased'.[38] Matthews paid tribute to Hood: 'I bless God that I have had the comfort of his Acquaintance and Friendship so long as above 20 years.'

> How great a loss have I and you of his prayers for the success of the Word of God! It hath often put life into me, when I have found him on a Lord's day, at this duty, to hear how earnestly he prayed for a blessing.
> And oh that all of you would do the like! Such was his life, and his end was like it ... His dying frame was full of submission to the will of God, that all might be sanctified to him, and he might be disposed of according to the good pleasure of God; calling to prayer, and himself praying with and for his Family, a few hours before he departed.[39]

The fact that Matthews built his meeting house at his own expense suggests that he was not without resources. From his will,[40] made out in 1721, it is clear that he owned property and land in Mountsorrel, Rothley, and Woodhouse,[41] as well as a substantial estate at Longdon, Staffordshire. He left his 'messuages, lands, tenements and hereditaments' in Mountsorrel and Rothley to his wife for life, and then to his son-in-law James Watson and daughter Sarah Watson. An estate at Longdon, Staffs, which he had purchased from his wife's brother, Thomas Hood, and from his son Samuel Hood, was charged with annuities of £20 per annum to his wife, £5 per annum to his second daughter Ann Matthews, and payments of £100 to

Sarah Watson and £35 each to two children of Thomas Hood. A close in Longdon called Aldrith Field was left to James and Sarah Watson. An estate at Longdon, held on lease from the Earl of Uxbridge, and occupied by his brother-in-law Thomas Gee who had married his sister Anne, was bequeathed to Sarah Watson. An estate in Woodhouse and Woodhouse Eaves, in the occupation of Gabriel West, was left to his second daughter Anne Matthews, and a mortgage on lands in Woodhouse and Woodhouse Eaves was given to Abraham Chambers, gent. There were also cash bequests of £100 to Sarah Watson and £350 to his youngest daughter Hannah Matthews.

Michael Matthews' will[42] directed that his body be buried at the discretion of his executrix and widow, Sarah Matthews. He was living at Mountsorrel South End at his death in 1723 and his will was proved in Rothley Peculiar Court, but Matthews was buried alongside his children inside Swithland church. The Latin inscription on his grave stone translates:

> Here lie the remains of the Reverend Mr Michael Matthews
> Who, in assiduously and passionately declaiming the gospel
> Likewise in instructing young people,
> Having performed his life's service, fell asleep on 5th April
> In the year of our salvation 1723, at the age of 62.
> Likewise Sara Matthews, his wife,
> Died 3rd May 1744, aged 81.

After Matthews' death in 1723, the Mountsorrel Meeting House reverted to his widow Sarah Matthews and his son-in-law James Watson. In 1729 they offered to make it over to a body of fifteen trustees. The conditions attached to the transfer were, however, so onerous that the deed was not completed. Having candidated for the pulpit at the High Pavement Chapel in Nottingham in 1728, James Watson moved to become minister of the Great Meeting in Bond Street, Leicester in 1730. The congregation at Mountsorrel thereafter used the services of Samuel Statham, minister to the congregation at Victoria Street, Loughborough. As a gift from the Danvers family, Sir John of Swithland set up an endowment to Matthews' Mountsorrel Meeting House of about £6 per year, the payment of which appears in the account book of the Mountsorrel congregation from 1765 to 1842.

The joint pastorate with Victoria Street survived until 1842. James Watson remained minister of the Great Meeting, Leicester, where he was revered for his teaching, pastoral skills and compassion for the poor until his death. Both he and his wife died on the same day, 3rd August 1741, and were buried in the meeting house yard at Leicester where a slate memorial was erected to them.[43] In 1742, the deed for the Mountsorrel Meeting House was finally drawn up, and the transfer of the property was completed by Matthews' widow Sarah and grandson, Michael Watson, their signatures being witnessed by Dr Philip Doddridge.

Towards the middle of the nineteenth century the Presbyterian community in Mountsorrel, like most Presbyterian congregations across Leicestershire, had almost ceased to exist. Thomas Crompton Holland,

Presbyterian minister at Victoria Street, Loughborough, considered the Mountsorrel Meeting House would be better off in the hands of the Baptists. In 1842 Matthews' meeting house was handed over to the New Connexion of General Baptists. In 1856 the Baptists built a new chapel to the north of the present Memorial Hall in Mountsorrel. They adapted Matthews' meeting house on the green for use as a Sunday School. In 1926 modern Sunday School premises were built by the Baptists at the rear of their chapel and Matthews' meeting house was sold. An ecumenical Christian centre for young people, Sorrel Café, now (2011) stands on the site. Michael Matthews' removal from Swithland and his subsequent ministry elsewhere, however, did not signal the end of non-conformity in Swithland.

Swithland Baptists

By the south wall of Swithland churchyard stands a memorial stone to Matthew Eyre.[44] It was made by 'Pollard Quorn.'

> To the Memory of MATTHEW EYRE
> He was born on the 4th of March 1739
> and died October 11th 1783
>
> POLLARD QUORN

In the neighbouring village of Quorn, in the grounds of the Baptist Chapel, there are other stones signed by Pollard, including one to William Johnson signed POLLARD SWITHLAND. And thereby hangs a tale. Who was this Mr Pollard of Swithland, and why are there more signed Pollard stones in Quorn than there are at Swithland?

In 1723, the same year that Michael Matthews died, Benjamin Pollard was born in the village of Swithland and baptised in the parish church. His son, also Benjamin Pollard (1754–1818), was likewise born in the village and baptised in the parish church, as an infant. It was this Benjamin, however, a noted slate dealer and engraver, who left the Established Church, joined a Baptist community, and, in time, became a dissenting Baptist minister.

From about 1779, the Pollards were part of a small Christian community of Baptists living and worshipping in Swithland. The group was part of a larger community of Baptists who met at Loughborough and Quorndon.[45] Much of our knowledge of these Swithland Baptists comes from a first hand account of the Loughborough and Quorndon meetings which was recorded in a series of minute books, the earliest of which dates from October 1790.[46] The scribe from 1790 to 1816 was Benjamin Pollard of Swithland.

By trade Pollard was a slate mason. He was born in Swithland in 1754 and he and his wife Catherine (m. 1784) lived there until they moved to Quorn in 1790. By then Pollard was already established as one of the pastors of the Loughborough and Quorn meeting. Although he was paid by the church for his ministerial labours, he continued in slate work and also owned a stationery business. Some of his, or his family's, work in engraved slate headstones can still be seen in Quorn Baptist Church's burial ground.

The late eighteenth century was a time of expansion and growth for English Baptists. General Baptist witness in Leicestershire began with a meeting of six people in 1745 at Barton in the Beans. Within fifteen years, however, numbers had increased to such an extent that the church had subdivided into six meetings with over nine hundred and fifty members in all. These meetings were based at Barton, Hinckley and Longford, Melbourne, Kegworth, Loughborough and Kirby Woodhouse. In 1760, the Loughborough church meeting had fifteen members. Ten years later it had grown to two hundred and forty members and thirty candidates.

The Loughborough Baptist Church first met in a converted barn; the first meeting house proper was built in 1791 in Woodgate, Loughborough, at a cost of £900. The church drew its membership from a wide area: Quorn, Leake, Wymeswold, Widmorepool, Grimston and other near-by villages. Two pastors served the church, together with one ruling elder and five deacons. The first pastors of the Loughborough meeting were Joseph Donisthorpe, one of the pastors at Barton in the Beans, and John Grimley. Donisthorpe died in 1774, when he was succeeded by Benjamin Pollard. 'In a few years, the Lord of the Harvest sent other labourers into this part of the vineyard. Mr. B. Pollard of Swithland was discovered to possess ministerial abilities, and in March 1779 (at the age of twenty-four years) was, after satisfactory trial, requested to employ them for the advantage of the church. With this request he complied; and his labours were acceptable and useful'.[47]

Pollard soon developed something of a reputation as an effective preacher. In 1779, for example, he attended the execution of a man convicted of robbing the mail. He had previously visited the man in gaol, giving him spiritual advice and praying with him. On the day of the execution, Pollard and his friend Mr Tarratt addressed the crowd. We are told that such was the effect of their preaching 'that many hearing, believed, were baptised and joined the local Church'.[48]

When the second 'founding' pastor of the Loughborough meeting, John Grimley, died in 1787, there was urgent need of a new minister. Benjamin Pollard was his natural successor.

> It was thought necessary to obtain as soon as possible a successor
> to the deceased pastor, and the eyes of the whole church were
> turned towards Mr Benjamin Pollard, who had laboured amongst
> them as an assistant preacher for eight years; and was highly
> esteemed. He was accordingly called to the pastoral office; and
> publicly ordained at Quorndon on November 27th 1787, when Mr
> N Pickering addressed the people, and Mr S Deacon, the minister,
> from John xxi 13, 'Feed my lambs'.[49]

Preaching in Quorn began at Mr Robert Parkinson's house in 1766. In 1770, the first Quorn Meeting House was built at a cost of £270. In 1780 a preaching station was established at Rothley, and in the same year Baptist preaching at Woodhouse Eaves is recorded. By 1782, the Loughborough meeting – which oversaw all these developments – had reached such a membership size that it was agreed to divide the church into two, Leake and Wymeswold forming one meeting, and Loughborough with Quorn and its neighbouring villages the other.

In 1787, sixteen Swithland parishioners were members of the Baptist meeting at Quorn: Benjamin Pollard senior, John Pollard, Ann Pollard, William Johnson, Benjamin Pollard junior, Catherine Pollard, John Stableford, Sarah Stableford, William Johnson, Ann Johnson, Ann Spencer, William Johnson junior, Mary Johnson, Ann Clarke, Robert Preston and Sarah Pollard.[50] Other members came from Thurcaston, Cossington, Seagrave, Rothley, Wanlip, Sileby, Mountsorrel, Rushey Fields, Anstey, Newtown Linford, Woodhouse, Barrow, Burton, Hoton Hall, Coats (Cotes), Woodthorpe, Shepshed, Haythorne, Thorpe, Quorndon and Loughborough.

The Loughborough-Quorn church continued to prosper, and more divisions followed. Work was begun in Mountsorrel and Swithland in 1788. Between 1792 and 1796 preaching stations were opened at Barrow and in some of the other villages. In 1802, the Rothley meeting began its separate existence, and the church at Quorn separated off in 1803. In time the church in Loughborough also divided, with Woodgate and Baxtergate becoming separate meetings in 1842.

In the early days, though, non-conformist Christians faced real opposition. There was, for example, some antagonism in Swithland.

> Edward Johnson, a worthy General Baptist, and a member of the same (Loughborough) Church, had been turned out of a profitable farm at Swithland, on account of his religion; and had settled at Woodhouse Eaves … Not deterred by the persecution he had already suffered, he cheerfully opened his house, in 1780, for the preaching of the gospel. Many attended; and a foundation was laid, on which a separate interest has since been raised.[51]

Johnson's tombstone at Woodhouse Eaves Baptist Church affirms the respect in which he was held, and the lasting results of his generosity. It is a fine example of Swithland slate engraving, and was carved by Benjamin Pollard.

> To the memory of Edward Johnson, who died Jan. 22nd 1807 aged 84, is this honourable testimony gratefully inscribed; who for many years gave the use of his Dwelling House for the preaching of the Gospel; and as a more effectual provision of perpetuating the CAUSE he espoused, gave this ground; in which his remains are deposited & also, by his last will and Testament, gave Five Pounds to the poor of this congregation. Examples worthy of imitation! 'Faith without works is dead'.[52]

By 1788, attitudes to the Baptists in Swithland would appear to have been less confrontational. In that year 'they began to preach in a licensed dwelling-house at Swithland'.[53] Two years later the Quorn community had outgrown its first meeting house and had begun planning its enlargement. On 12th September 1790, the seventy-five church members present at the meeting at Quorndon, twenty-one of whom lived in Swithland,[54] unanimously agreed to forward the new building plans. The minister, Benjamin Pollard noted on October 3rd: 'It was also agreed to buy this book in which to minute down these, and other Matters of Importance, which may in future concern this church.'[55]

The meeting house was the focus of non-conformist congregational life. Most were rectangular buildings of austere and simple design. On the long side, facing the entrance, there was a high pulpit, sometimes surmounted by a sounding board and furnished with a pulpit cushion. Worship, though 'free' and 'non-liturgical', had its own traditional pattern. The long services included prayers, hymns, the reading of scripture and the preaching of The Word. Church meetings tended to follow on from worship. The church minute books recorded the decisions made at these meetings, together with something of the discussions.

The Quorn minute books are revealing. Besides the new building work, there were other major 'Matters of Importance' that occupied the attention of the Quorn meeting in the 1790s and early 1800s. Many of these related to the consequences of church growth. Who were to be their ministers? How many should there be and how much should they be paid? Which members were to assist with the preaching? How could they raise enough money to pay, not just for the work and ministry in their own community, but also for new buildings and new work in other Baptist congregations? Should the Quorn meeting become a meeting in its own right, and divide from the Loughborough meeting?

There were other matters too. We read, for example, about women being given 'the duty and privilege to give their silent vote in the church. For 51, against 1, neuters 23' (23rd January 1791).[56] An issue which divided church members in 1793 was the question as to whether the dead should be buried in the meeting house or in the outside burial ground. Theological matters were also periodically raised in meetings, often in debating whether or not their ministers were preaching the 'orthodox' Christian gospel.

The church minute books give us an insight into the life of what appeared to be a tightly integrated and inward-looking Christian community. There was regular discussion over matters relating to membership: baptisms, exclusions and reinstatements. Relations between church members often caused concern. Decisions were made as to who should preach where and when, and who should collect money for the work of the wider church and where. The meeting also appointed 'helpers', who visited and exhorted the people and prepared candidates for baptism.

Although the Quorn records cover some fifty years of the life of the meeting, most of what we can discover of the lives of its Swithland members comes from the earlier years of the records. There are, for example, lists of members in Swithland for 1787, 1790 and 1795,[57] but no further listings after that. Brothers Benjamin and John Pollard clearly exercised great influence within the little Swithland Baptist community, so it is possible that when Benjamin and his family removed to Quorn, fervour in Swithland gradually diminished.

The Swithland members, though, made their mark on the life of the church. Although part of the Quorn meeting, they also met separately in Swithland village. In 1794 they were using Robert Preston's house for local meetings. 'Church agreed to pay toward more for Br Preston's house to preach in at Swithland in consequence of a Promise made to the landlord and a raisment in the Rent so that we must now pay £1-10-0 for year' (17th April, 1794).[58]

John Pollard, younger brother of Benjamin, exercised a somewhat spasmodic preaching ministry in the life of the church. The records show that on several occasions he 'declined the ministry' (of preaching). On one occasion the reason for his reluctance was 'ill usage from some persons having spoken against him preaching behind his Back and not to his Face'.[59] John was a 'ruling elder' at Rothley in 1801, where he preached regularly for about a year, but then he 'removed his dwelling to a distance' and a new minister had to be called. In 1808 John Pollard accepted an invitation from the church at Under Cauldwell in Derbyshire, and went to labour among them, 'but his anticipations in regard to secular matters[60] not being realized led to his soon leaving them, though very much to their mutual regret'.[61]

Another ministerial roll was that of 'helper'. John Pollard was a 'helper' in Swithland for a time, as was William Johnson Jnr.[62] Within their own local community, the 'helpers' visited and exhorted the people, had the task of conversing with candidates for baptism and, when the baptisms had been ratified by the church, fixed the times for them.

The records indicate that the little Swithland community did not always relate happily with each other. John and Sarah Pollard, for example, had an edgy relationship with John and Sarah Stableford. In 1795 we read that 'the difference between Sr. Stableford and Br and Sister Pollard of Swithland yet continues, and Sister Stableford will not rest without Investigation, and Br John and Sister Pollard will not submit to it. Br Bates, Br Noakes and Br Miller appointed to examine the business'.[63] There was also a sad business relating to Sarah Stableford in 1793, when she took personally an anonymous letter addressed to the church about 'the impropriety of Burying in the Meeting-Houses'.[64] The letter coincided with the death of one of her children who she wanted to be buried in the meeting house. The majority of the meeting, however, voted that burials should take place outside. The tombstone of her son, William, is still to be seen outside in the Quorn meeting's burial ground.

Another Baptist family group in Swithland at the time was the Johnsons. One couple, William and Ann, between them presented a fair number of 'cases' for the church meeting to consider. William, for example, had a reputation for tale bearing. 'William Johnson's case (of Swithland) was brought before the Church, when his Penitence was pretty evident but as it appeared there was some offence through Reflections, tale bearing etc., it was thought best for this to be looked into by a committee' (8th June 1794). Four years later he was excluded for 'aiding a Poacher in catching fish and supplying him with other game' (25th August 1798). At one stage both he and his wife were excluded from the meeting, she because of 'drinking strong liquor to excess'.[65] There are graphic descriptions in the minute book of the evidence church members gave to justify their accusations.⁶⁶ 'She seemed different ... winking and blinking with a variety of odd gestures and motions.' 'Br. Willson declared he had seen her disguised several times, once especially, when Wm Palmer, Br. Smart etc. were drinking Tea there, when she could hardly hit either the Tea pot or cups, and Mrs Palmer and Br. Smart both noticed it.' 'Sr. Garret nursed her in part of her late affliction. Her conversation stammering, violent language, reeling talk were proof to her of it, also from the quantity of liquor consumed, viz. one Quart bottle of Brandy and two Quart bottles of Rum in a short time, I think in ten days.'

Benjamin Pollard, however, continued a tireless worker for the church. He and his wife Catherine removed from Swithland to Quorn in 1790. At this time, Pollard was being paid £10 per annum for his ministry. This was a third of what was being paid to Brother Truman, Pollard's assistant minister from 1790, and a 'settled' minister. Pollard, who ran a business, was obviously not seen as a full-time minister. In 1791, though, he told the meeting that he could not cope with all the preaching, and that 'it was inquired who must assist'. His brother, John Pollard, also from Swithland, was proposed. Feelings were clearly mixed, for when the motion for Br. John Pollard's continuing to preach was put, '57 were in favour, 9 against and 22 neuters'.⁶⁷

In the early 1790s, Benjamin Pollard was constantly out and about, in Lincolnshire as well as in Leicestershire, preaching and collecting money. The church at Quorn was active in financial support for the building of the new Loughborough Meeting House. All these additional labours of Pollard were recognised by his brethren. On Christmas Day 1792 he was given a present of £10 'for his lost time last year in collecting £729 for the Loughborough Meeting House'.⁶⁸ His achievement was impressive; it represented a major percentage of the £900 the new meeting house cost to build.

In 1797, tragedy struck the church meeting. An intoxicated driver accidentally killed Pollard's fellow minister, Br. Truman, who was returning home from preaching at Loughborough. After his death, the congregation struggled for some time to resolve questions about the ministry at Quorndon. Various avenues were explored, none satisfactorily. Pollard's notes on the church meetings give the impression of a community that gradually began to show signs of division and unhappiness. While his brethren discussed and debated the problems of what ministry was needed and could be afforded, Pollard himself shouldered the extra burdens of ministry within the church. They did, though, acknowledge this by extra Christmas annual payments of £10. His minutes, however, indicate that the increased weight of ministry was causing him stress. At one 'disorderly' meeting in 1799, he recorded that he rebuked, 'too sharply', one of his brethren for openly criticising the church for 'too much bokening'.⁶⁹ The pressures on him increased, as the meeting failed to agree on or appoint an 'outside minister'. This meant that Pollard was effectively acting as the full-time minister for the Quorn community. In 1800, he was being paid £40 per annum for his work, with the proviso that if a 'settled' minister were to be appointed he would give up part of his salary.

By 1805, Quorn meeting had nearly two hundred members, and the

Loughborough meeting as many more. There were eight places of public worship, all of them well attended. Membership was drawn from some thirty villages. This growth, and the financial pressures on members, led to a debate on whether the one Loughborough/Quorn church should divide. There was dissatisfaction in the brotherhood over the burden of supporting all three ministers, who between them served both the Loughborough and Quorn congregations. 'Each church', said the Quorn contingent in 1801, 'should bear its own burdens'. They did not see why they should contribute to the salaries of the two who ministered solely to the Loughborough community.

In August 1801, Pollard, by way of encouraging his growing church to divide, presented the Quorn meeting with something of an ultimatum. It is recorded in the church meeting minutes that 'the Pastor then stated the insupportable burden lying on him from so extensive a church so destitute of officers, in so divided and disordered a state, in conjunction with the weight of his business, difficulties of his family ... and assured the Church that unless some steps were taken for his Relief he must inevitably sink under the weight'.[70] The Quorn meeting voted overwhelmingly for division at that time, but there was significant opposition to taking that step within the Loughborough meeting, and a final agreement to divide was not reached until 1803.

The records of the years that follow the division, however, did not show a happier church community at Quorn. It is clear from the way he wrote up the meetings that Pollard was getting increasingly weary and dispirited. He was distressed by various accusations of his brethren. In a rare lapse of objectivity he wrote: 'Shall I (Pollard) exchange with Br Pickering on August 26th and he break bread here? But as there has been much grumbling about my going out so much, it is to be considered next month' (15th July 1810).[71] 'Deacon's account £13-9-4 – bad, this caused much talk. Br Mansfield wished to give up his office, but as all seemed satisfied, it drop. I thought it did not lie with Deacons but myself, as most of Money is for me. I conceive this tardiness is for a want of respect to myself; which, with my want of success in my work as a Minister caused me to press church to look out for a younger Minister, to which several objected, but Br Gamble thought it would be better, thought I had been long enough in one place, and that another Minister with or without me would be very useful. Much said. Put off another month.' (29th December 1811)[72]

The records from Pollard's remaining years show his increasing depression and bitterness. On Christmas Day 1814, he wrote: 'Br. Pollard asked to bate £10 of his salary as church finances so bad, to which I made but little reply, but they wished me to make up my mind by the next church meeting. From after conversation with Br. Gamble, I learnt that I am very extensively thought by the brethren to be a *Worldly-Minded Man*. It is wondered how I can find in my heart to take money off poor men who work hard from Monday morning to Saturday night. Br. Gamble afterwards said he didn't expect the Cause to revive in my hands – and he queried whether I had not better decline the Ministry in this place'.[73] And, a month later, 'I inform church that I shall not abate my salary ... which brought much conversation ... many reflections on my neglect etc. etc. etc. ... Johnson said

I *never* call on a friend, preach but three times per week, and am too well paid'. The following Christmas Day, in 1816, Pollard wrote for the last time in the church meeting minute book: 'Letter from the Pastor declining the work of the Pastorate on account of ill health'.[74]

Benjamin Pollard died in 1818. Despite affirmation from the majority of his brethren, he remained a focus of animosity from some. Edward Pywell, who took over the pastorate from Pollard, wrote: 'The subject of erecting a stone to the memory of Br. Pollard was resumed. Br. W Johnson, carpenter, thought it would be a waste of money, Br. Pearson observed we did not need an Idol to worship, and he could not bring his mind to approve of it. Others advocated the measure – it was put and carried by a large majority'. (3rd May 1818)[75] A stone was erected. The monument on the east wall of Quorn Baptist Chapel reads:

> To commemorate the departed worth of the Rev. Benjamin Pollard, 38 years minister of the church and congregation assembling in this place, whose laborious services for many years extended to more than 30 villages. As a preacher, he was energetic & powerful. As a pastor diligent, faithful & affectionate. As a husband and parent, most tender and kind. He was the honoured instrument of turning many to righteousness, and of training them by precept and example for a blessed immortality. He was called to the reward of his labours on the 6th April 1818 aged 64 years.

To which was later added:

> Catharine, relict of the above, died January 14th 1837 aged 81.
> 'Looking unto Jesus'.

References in the Woodhouse Eaves Baptist Meeting records indicate that there was still a small Baptist presence in Swithland at least until 1841. In 1825 there was a fortnightly meeting at Swithland on the morning of the Lord's Day. The minister, Mr Stephen Taylor, who was based at Woodhouse Eaves, also served the brethren at Swithland and, on occasion, at Markfield.[76] In 1829 Br William Johnson resigned his office as deacon. In 1838, Henry Hind was approved for baptism and fellowship.[77]

Methodists in Swithland

The only evidence remaining of both the Presbyterian and Baptist presence in Swithland village lies in its churchyard. The memorial to the Methodist presence in the village, however, lies in a building. Their meeting house still stands, albeit now a private dwelling, at the Woodhouse end of Swithland village within the Forest End complex of cottages. What is the story of this third and last phase of a distinct non-conformist presence in Swithland?

John Wesley first came and preached in the locality of Swithland in 1783. The following year he was to 'ordain' men for the Methodist mission in America. In 1786 he came and preached again. The 'preaching house' on both occasions was Stonehurst Farm, Mountsorrel, just a couple of miles from Swithland. At the time, Baptist witness in the area was strong and developing rapidly. In 1788, for example, local Baptists began to preach in a licensed dwelling house in Swithland. Arguably, Swithland village was too small to sustain two 'alternative' Christian congregations. But as Baptist witness in Swithland declined after the turn of the century, centering more on Rothley and Woodhouse Eaves, so Methodist witness in the village seems to have expanded.

Unlike the Baptist movement, Methodism began as a 'spiritual movement' within the Established Church. Baptists were 'Dissenters'; Methodists, at least in the early years of the movement, saw themselves quite differently. The 'founder', John Wesley (born 1703), was an ordained priest in the Established Church and always professed that he lived and died as a member of the Church of England. Before his death in 1791, however, various developments made it impossible for Methodism to remain Anglican. Not only were Church of England clergy increasingly opposed to Methodism, often 'excommunicating' members of the Methodist societies in their localities, but also, from 1784, John Wesley began to 'set aside' men for the Methodist ministry, first in America and Scotland, and then, not long before he died, in England. The decision of the Methodist Conference in 1795 to secede from the Church of England was a natural consequence of these and other developments.

The first reference to a Methodist living in Swithland is in a 'bargain and sale' document of 1801.[78] Daniel Bates of Swithland and his brother William Bates of Rushey Fields were amongst a group of seven men, trustees, who bought a piece of land for the Methodist church in Woodhouse Eaves, where they had earlier built a chapel for Methodist worship. (Bargain and Sale of Premises at Woodhouse Eaves 3 July 1801 between John Getlepp of Woodhouse Eaves, Cowherd (1) and Joseph Foulks, John Squire, Jonathan Tillson of Woodhouse Eaves, Framework Knitters, and Daniel Bates of Swithland and William Bates of Rushey Fields, William Smith of Mappelwell, Yeoman and Joseph Spencer (2)).

A vivid impression of the Woodhouse Methodist community in its earliest years is given in an obituary of Benjamin Squire, who died in 1820 at the age of ninety-five. Squire was one of the first members of the Woodhouse Eaves Chapel.

> He first heard the word from a Methodist preacher at Markfield and then travelled far and wide to hear the word. He did so, and heard Mr Wesley and Mr Whitfield and others of the Old Veterans in the Cause, and the word was spirit and life to his soul. He was set at liberty while returning home from Mountsorrel. He felt his mind powerfully impressed with these words: 'Stand still, and see the salvation of the Lord'. He first invited the Preachers to Woodhouse, and gladly received them under his humble roof. Frequently did he climb the adjacent Forest Hills to watch for their arrival, and 'on the Mountains their feet appeared beautiful' to him. The Preaching was long in his own house, and he witnessed the prosperity of the work of the Lord.

Not until 1819, however, is there any evidence of an official Methodist 'class' in Swithland. The Loughborough Methodist Circuit Membership Book (1803–24)[79] gives tantalising glimpses of the early days of that little congregation. We know that there was a class of eight people meeting in Swithland in that year, and that Richard Preston was its class leader. In 1820 the names of members of the class are listed as: Richard Preston (leader), William Brookhouse, Elizabeth Brookhouse, Matthew Hodges, Thomas Bruxby and Samuel Thorpe. In 1823, Richard Preston's little class had as members William Brookhouse, Elizabeth Brookhouse, Samuel Thorpe, William Morris, John Burton, William Bramley and Elizabeth Bramley. These are the only Swithland references from the circuit records to those early years. William Brookhouse and William Bates were previously members of the Woodhouse Eaves Class from 1813–15 and 1814–15 respectively, which may indicate that Swithland might have been a Methodist 'church plant' from Woodhouse Eaves. Richard Preston, however, was not listed as a member of any of other circuit congregations before taking up the leadership in Swithland in 1819, so it sounds as if it might have been his spiritual gifts that enabled the formation of the Swithland class.

By 1825, the Methodist congregation at Swithland was an established part of the Loughborough Circuit. The Circuit Stewards' Accounts 1825–75[80] indicate the Swithland class as paying a regular quarterly contribution to the circuit. Their financial contributions were relatively small compared with other chapels. Swithland were paying 10/- a quarter in 1825, which rose to 15/- in 1832, but then declined. During these early years, the congregation used an old malt office as a chapel, which they fitted up as a Wesleyan Chapel in 1828. Circuit records of 1833 indicate a service at Swithland every Sunday at 6pm. Diocesan records contain a meeting house certificate for 1849.[81] Local preachers travelled from Mountsorrel, Quorn, Loughborough, Woodhouse and Shepshed to take services. In the 1851 Census,[82] the building was described as being used exclusively for public worship. It had one hundred and twenty 'sittings' of which seventy were free. The number attending Divine Service on the evening of Sunday 30th March 1851 was sixty-four. This is the only statistic we have that might indicate that the little congregation grew. In 1856 a purpose-built chapel was erected on the site. Fronting on to Main Street, it was set back 21 feet from the road. The chapel was built right up to the two side boundaries and to the rear boundary of the site. It consisted of a single room, 26.5 feet by 19 feet.

After 1856, evidence from the Loughborough Circuit Quarterly Meeting minute books of 1854–96[83] points to a story of continuing decline. In 1856, for example, Swithland was listed as one of the congregations that refused to promise a regular quarterly contribution to circuit funds. In addition, Swithland was rarely represented at the quarterly meetings. Although the minutes rarely identify the chapels of members, they do show that in 1857 Mr William Cuffling was appointed to collect Swithland's contribution towards the reduction of the circuit debt. After that date, and the first quarterly meeting he is recorded as attending, Mr Cuffling is only listed as attending two more such meetings. He was, however, a key member of the

Swithland congregation, coming originally from the Methodist Societies at Quorn (1813–14) and Mountsorrel (1815–23) Chapels. He offered refreshment hospitality in his home after services in spite of its distance from the chapel: he had become tenant of Hall Farm, Swithland in 1851. He is recorded in 1860 as volunteering to preach on occasion. William Cuffling died in 1876 and was buried in Swithland churchyard.

In 1873, Swithland was again requested to contribute towards a fund for paying off the circuit debt. The amount of £1, relative to other allocations, indicates that Swithland was one of the smallest congregations in the circuit. By 1877, Methodism in Swithland was causing concern to the other members of the circuit. In the quarterly meeting minutes of June 1877 it is recorded: 'After some serious conversation, the cause there, and the work of God, it was resolved that a few of the brethren attend when the Superintendent preaches, and investigate the state of affairs at Swithland'. And from the meeting on 24th September: 'Some conversation having taken place respecting the state of the cause of God there' (at Swithland) 'the meeting expressed a sincere hope that the brethren appointed there for the future will endeavour to take their appointments, and try to improve the place'. Despite the hopes, it would seem as if there was little response. In March 1882, another Mr Cuffling made an appearance at a circuit quarterly meeting. In 1886, he appears to have been succeeded as the Swithland representative by Mr Charles Bunney. Like his predecessor, Bunney attended quarterly meetings very infrequently. During the 1880s there was a service at Swithland each Sunday evening at 6pm and a quarterly gathering on a Monday evening at 7pm.

In spite of the apparent feebleness of Methodist witness in Swithland at the time, Mr Joel of Brook House, who appears to have seen himself as one of the leading members of the village community, was either sufficiently fearful of free church growth in the wider area or else being politically astute when he wrote to the Bishop of Peterborough in 1884.[84] He urged the bishop to make haste to appoint a new incumbent to Swithland as 'dissent is rife in the villages around'.

In 1888, though Methodist numbers in the Loughborough circuit had risen to eight hundred and six, membership at the Swithland Chapel was just three, making it by far the smallest congregation in the circuit, with an annual income of just over £1. (The two highest memberships that year were recorded as three hundred and twenty-seven at Loughborough and ninety-three at Shepshed.) After 1888, numbers in the circuit generally showed signs of gradual decline, e.g. Loughborough two hundred and sixty-five in 1890, Shepshed fifty-nine, Swithland two. But of all the seventeen societies in the circuit, Swithland was a particular cause of concern. Matters came to a head in 1894. A record of the January quarterly meeting records: 'Swithland Chapel. A conversation took place respecting the very unsatisfactory state of the Society and Congregation at the above, when it was moved by Mr Richards, seconded by Mr Mayes and carried that the Secretary be requested to write to the Society Steward informing him that unless an improvement was made, the quarterly meeting is considering the desirability of closing the Chapel'. It would appear that no such improvement was forthcoming, for the next quarterly meeting in March decreed that 'it be worked for the ensuing Quarter by Mission Bands, and that the question (of closure) be again considered at the June Quarterly Meeting'.

The discussion continued at the next quarterly meeting in June. 'The question of the desirability or otherwise of continuing Services at Swithland was continued from last meeting. A letter was read by the Chairman from the Rev R Brewin offering on behalf of a Friend the sum of £5, and on his own behalf the sum of £1, towards the cost of an Evangelist for Swithland for work amongst the navvies employed at the New Water Works.' Considerable discussion ensued, concluding in a resolution to send the thanks of the meeting to the Rev R. Brewin for his kind offer, and to set up a committee to make enquiries and act if necessary. At the September quarterly meeting, the committee reported that they thought it advisable to take no action regarding the question of a resident Evangelist for Swithland and neighbourhood. The meeting then resolved by a majority of twenty-five to one that 'Services in Swithland Chapel be suspended for the present'. At the same meeting, details of membership numbers in the circuit churches were listed. Swithland had only two members and no juniors.

Fig 7.4 Swithland Wesleyan Methodist Chapel.

In 1891 the trustees of Swithland Wesleyan Chapel, who included Charles Bunney, farmer, and Thomas Hill, labourer, began to keep a minutes and accounts book.[85] The book records the annual accounts and gives one or two clues that fill out the history of this little chapel. There is, however, evidence only of decline. In 1891 the annual turnover was £8 12s 6d, and only two meetings are recorded: a Whitsunday Festival Tea and Evening Meeting, and the Chapel Anniversary Service in August. In 1898, the trustees agreed that local preachers should be asked whether the chapel should be re-opened to hold services during the summer months. The following year it was agreed that such services should be held, if possible, and the chapel was re-opened for Divine Worship. From then on, two or three services a year were

Fig. 7.5 Interior of Swithland Wesleyan Methodist Chapel, Easter 1924.

recorded: a June Tea Meeting, the Harvest Festival and the Chapel Anniversary. There was a mention of a chapel outing in 1906. 'Services of Song' seemed to be in fashion from 1908 to 1910.

In 1894 the chapel keeper was Mr Boyer. In 1899 Mrs Hubbard was caretaker, and Mr Boyer chapel keeper. Mr Hubbard, chapel keeper, left Swithland in 1900, when the services of Mr Charles Pratt were secured. Mrs Pratt cleaned the chapel in 1900. In 1903 Mrs Bunney was cleaning it and in 1931 and 1945 Miss Bunney. In 1949 the Misses Bunney were thanked for their services as caretakers. Mrs Edenbrow was caretaker in 1955.

There were occasions during the later history of the chapel when it was able to offer some hospitality to the members of the Church of England in the village. During 1924 and 1925, when major restoration work was taking place in the parish church, Anglican worship was conducted in the Methodist Chapel. This was an encouraging sign of ecumenism, at a time when even Methodist Union was still some seven years away.

In 1947, major repairs to roof, chimney, floors, ceiling and windows were effected, and electric light and power were installed. Fundraising for the repairs achieved £107 7s 3d, of which £35 was a grant from the General Chapel Fund. The total cost of repairs came to £164 2s 1d. Chapel services at Easter and Harvest continued until October 1964, when the building was sold. At the time of the sale, all the trustees of the Swithland chapel lived in Woodhouse Eaves. The last entry in the minutes was signed by the superintendent minister, Dennis Robson. It recorded that the final balance in hand was £7 8s 11d.[86]

When the Wesleyan chapel was sold in 1964 it was described[87] as having its internal walls plastered, and with wooden wall panelling, in keeping with its religious use. It had only three windows, and therefore a dark interior. There was electric light and one power point. The planning authorities noted that it was not a site that could be developed. At the rear the chapel abutted immediately onto cottages, and it was built right up to the two side boundaries. The only possible adjacent land that might be purchased in order to develop the site was on the south-west of the building. The firm valuing the property wrote that

> ... the only land which we consider likely to be available for extension purposes was on the south-western side, and upon enquiry of the lady owner of this land whether she was prepared to sell, she informed us that she had obtained planning permission for a house on the plot in question and 'would not sell one inch of her land'.

At the time of the proposed sale, the Methodist Church offered the rector of Swithland the courtesy of consultation. Bishop Alex Maxwell was appreciative of the gesture, but said that the church needed no extra accommodation since the Memorial Hall offered sufficient accommodation for church meetings and social activities. In 1964 the chapel was sold for £1,750 to Mrs Linwood Wright, 'an Anglican lady who had been supportive of efforts to keep it open in the past and who had indicated that after purchasing the building she would see to its repair and redecoration before reopening it as a Private Chapel'. The major part of the proceeds of the sale of the Swithland chapel was passed to the trustees of the Woodhouse Eaves chapel whose members had financially 'carried Swithland' for some years.

From Mrs Linwood Wright the chapel passed to her son-in-law, Canon Lindsay Godfrey, who incorporated it into the adjacent dwelling-house. Until his death in 1984, the chapel was regularly used for mid-week Church of England Holy Communion Services.

One Church

Since 1964, the parish church has been the only active ecclesiastical building in the village of Swithland. A long, divisive and often tumultuous chapter in English religious history would seem to have ended.

The Great Meeting (Unitarian) Chapel in Leicester, where Michael Matthews' son-in-law ministered, the Baptist chapels at Quorn and Woodhouse Eaves, with each of whom the Swithland Baptists were linked, continue to thrive, as does the Methodist church in Woodhouse Eaves. It is good to be able to conclude by affirming that in 2010 ecumenical respect and friendship is healthy and growing between the parish churches in Swithland, Woodhouse and Woodhouse Eaves and the Baptist, Catholic and Methodist congregations in Swithland's neighbouring villages of Woodhouse and Woodhouse Eaves.

Notes to Chapter 7

1. William is the only Grundy buried in Swithland. In 1711, however, a Nicholas Grundy of Thornton is mentioned in an indenture indicating he owned land in the open fields of Swithland. The house of Nicholas Grundy in Thornton, Leics. is mentioned in Spencer and Spencer, *Leicestershire and Rutland Notes and Queries and Antiquarian Gleaner*, vol. 3, p. 233, 1895, in connection with (Presbyterian) preaching in his house in 1673.
2. A.G. Matthews, *Calamy Revised*, Oxford 1934, p. 544.

3. A. Gordon (ed.), *Freedom after Ejection, A review (1690–1692) of Presbyterian and Congregational Nonconformity in England and Wales*, 1917.
4. H. McLachlan, *English Education under the Test Acts*, Manchester, 1931. McLachlan acknowledges the manuscripts of Joshua Toulmin (1740–1815).
5. A.G. Matthews, *Congregational Churches of Staffordshire*, 1924.
6. A. Gordon (ed.), *Freedom after Ejection, A review (1690–1692) of Presbyterian and Congregational Nonconformity in England and Wales*, 1917.
7. National Archives, CR 1908/23/1-6; 1661 Agreement for conveyance and release from Thomas Hood of Longdon, yeoman, and Christian his wife and Margaret Hood widow, mother of Thomas.
8. Presumably Sarah's mother and the Christian Hood who is buried in Swithland church.
9. Notes recorded by Maureen Piper of Longdon from the records of Longdon Green Presbyterian Chapel, registered in 1696. The chapel fell into disuse and was demolished in the 1970s.
10. A.G. Matthews, *Calamy Revised*, Oxford, 1934.
11. A. Gordon (ed.), *Freedom after Ejection, A review (1690–1692) of Presbyterian and Congregational Nonconformity in England and Wales*, 1917.
12. ibid.
13. This document in the Warwickshire Records Office indicates a relationship: CR 1908/23/16 Assignment of mortgage by John Taylor of Colton, clerk with the concurrence of Thomas Hood and Walter Landor to John Hood of Bardon Park, Leics., gent., of lands in Longdon called Two Pease Closes, Two Cow Closes, the Asches, the Pingle and the moiety of Great Meadow, 26th April 1699.
14. Swithland's Samuel Danvers, both of whose parents had been involved in Baptist and Fifth Monarchist activities, had just inherited the manor on the death of his father in 1687.
15. Possibly an inheritance from the years Henry Danvers held office in Staffordshire.
16. Leics. RO, DE1750, Box 22. Will, 1697, Robert Gilbert of Swithland. Gilbert describes Matthews as 'my loving friend'.
17. T.G. Crippen (ed.), *Transactions of the Congregational Historical Society*, vol. 5, p. 299.
18. Ann, baptized 3rd Sep 1698 at Woodhouse.
19. Common Fund records show that Richard Southwell was ministering at 'Braddon' in 1690. This is the earliest documented evidence of a congregation at Bardon.
20. David L. Wykes, 'Bardon Park Meeting House', *Leics. Arch. & Hist. Transactions*, vol. LXIV 1990, pp. 31–34.
21. E.W. Hensman in Alice Dryden (ed.) *Mountsorrel – Memorials of Old Leicestershire*, 1911.
22. Joshua Toulmin, *Protestant Dissenters*, London, 1814, p. 230.
23. Certificate in Somerset House.
24. E.W. Hensman in Alice Dryden (ed.) *Mountsorrel – Memorials of Old Leicestershire*, 1911.
25. John Evans, *List of Dissenting Congregations and Ministers in England and Wales 1715–29*.
26. Leics. RO, DE 2463 N/U/207/93/1-3, Notebooks: Loughborough and Mountsorrel Unitarian Meetings, –1864.
27. Brian Simon (ed.), *Education in Leicestershire 1540–1940*, 1969.
28. Leics. RO, DE 2463 N/U/207/93/1-3, Notebooks: Loughborough and Mountsorrel Unitarian Meetings, –1864.
29. Leics. RO, DE1750, Box 22, Will, 1697, Robert Gilbert of Swithland.
30. *Transactions of the Congregational Historical Society*, vol. 14, p. 76.
31. ibid.
32. ibid., p. 89.
33. George Eyre Evans, *Vestiges of Protestant Dissent*, 1897, p. 164.
34. Leicestershire Charities Report, 1837.
35. Watson was invited to become the minister at Kibworth in 1722.
36. W.H. Burgess, *History of the Loughborough Unitarian Congregation and Mountsorrel Chapel*, 1908.
37. John Evans, *List of Dissenting Congregations and Ministers in England and Wales 1715–29*.
38. John Nicholls, *The History and Antiquities of the County of Leicester*, vol. 3, part 1.
39. ibid.
40. Leics. RO, DG9/1092, Matthews' bequest to dau. Ann of his Woodhouse and Woodhouse Eaves property; see also Appendix A: Wills.
41. Leics. RO, DG9/1091, Conveyance to Matthews of a messuage and three closes (14a.) in Woodhouse Eaves.
42. Made 16 Jan 1721, Rothley Peculiar Court Register 1721; see also Leics. RO DG9/1092.

43. Gordon Bolam, *Three Hundred Years 1662–1962*, 1962.
44. Eyre's wife Elizabeth, and son and daughter Joseph and Elizabeth are buried in the Great Meeting burial ground, Leicester.
45. Leics. RO, MF17, Records of Quorndon and Loughborough Baptists, 1786–1837, include birth and registration details of children of Swithland members, as do records, MF 17 Rothley and Sileby Baptists 1791–1837, MF18 Woodhouse Eaves Baptist, 1799–1837.
46. An earlier minute book has been lost.
47. A. Taylor, *The History of the English General Baptists*, vol. 2, 1818.
48. Wilfred E. Mee, *Quorn Baptists*, 1960.
49. A. Taylor, *The History of the English General Baptists*, vol. 2, 1818.
50. Leics. RO, N/B/258/15, Quorn Baptists, Members Register, 1787–1839.
51. A. Taylor, *The History of the English General Baptists*, vol. 2, 1818.
52. His memorial, together with that to his wife Elizabeth, now stands in the entrance to Woodhouse Eaves Baptist Church.
53. A. Taylor, *The History of the English General Baptists*, vol. 2, 1818.
54. Leics. RO, N/B/258/15, Quorn Baptists Members Register, 1787–1839: Benjamin and Ann Pollard, Ann Wilson, John and Sarah Pollard, Robert Preston, William Johnson, Elizabeth Ffukes, Thomas Ffukes, Benjamin and Catherine Pollard, Elizabeth Gee, Ann Johnson, John and Sarah Stableford, Thomas Wilde, William and Ann Johnson, Ann Clarke, Ann Bird, Alice Eyre.
55. Leics. RO, N/B/207 A80, Loughborough, Woodgate Minute Book 1790–1800, 'A Minute Book for the General Baptist Church at Loughborough, Quorndon etc.'
56. ibid.
57. Leics. RO, N/B/258/15, Quorn Baptists Members Register, 1787–1839.
58. Leics. RO, N/B/207 A80, Loughborough, Woodgate Minute Book 1790–1800.
59. ibid., 24 September 1797.
60. Presumably either accommodation or payment.
61. J.R. Godfrey, *Historic Memorials of the Barton and Melbourne General Baptist Church*, 1891.
62. Leics. RO, N/B/207 A80, Loughborough, Woodgate Minute Book 1790–1800, 16 February 1794.
63. ibid., 19 April 1795.
64. ibid., 10 February 1793.
65. ibid., June 1800 (William and Ann Johnson were, however, 'restored' on December 21, 1800).
66. Leics. RO, N/B/207 A80, Loughborough, Woodgate Minute Book 1790–1800.
67. ibid., 23 January 1791.
68. ibid., 25 December 1792.
69. ibid., 10, 15 February 1799.
70. Leics. RO, N/B/258/1, 16 August 1801.
71. ibid.
72. ibid.
73. ibid.
74. ibid., last entry in minute book.
75. Leics. RO, N/B258/2, Quorndon Baptist Church Meeting Minute Book 1817–23.
76. Leics. RO, DE4798, Woodhouse Eaves Baptist Church Book.
77. ibid.
78. Leics. RO, N/M/207, Bargain and sale of premises at Woodhouse Eaves, 3 July 1801.
79. Leics. RO, N/M/207/6, Loughborough Methodist Circuit Membership Book, 1805–24.
80. Leics. RO, N/M/207/4, Loughborough Methodist Circuit Stewards Accounts, 1825–75.
81. Peterborough RO (Northampton), X953, Meeting House certificate, 1 June 1849.
82. Leics. RO, HO129/416, Ecclesiastical Census 1851.
83. Leics. RO, N/M/207/1, 2, Loughborough Methodist Circuit Quarterly Meeting Minutes 1854–82, 1882–96.
84. Leics. RO 7D55 965/ 1–8, this and related letters.
85. Leics. RO, N/M 207/139, Swithland Methodist Trustees Minutes and Accounts book, 1891–1964.
86. ibid.
87. Leics. RO, N/M 207/590, Papers re sale of chapel in 1964.

– CHAPTER 8 –

The Story of the Land

Until the twentieth century Swithland's economy had been based principally on agriculture. For a brief period the local slate industry provided employment opportunities, but only a few Swithland residents were involved. Other Leicestershire villages saw the development of cottage industries such as framework knitting, but Swithland remained predominantly a farming community, with its needs reflected both in the local landscape and in the settlement patterns.

In mediaeval times the agrarian economy in England was largely based on the open field system, with virtually the whole of the arable land of a settlement in several large 'open' fields.[1] The boundaries of these open fields were fenced against the incursion of livestock; inside, they were entirely open and uninterrupted. Open arable fields were made up of roughly rectangular blocks called furlongs, shots, flats or wongs. In their turn, furlongs were composed of long narrow strips or parcels, called acres, selions or lands. Perhaps these had originally been something approaching a furlong (furrow-long) in length by four poles in width, and containing in the region of an acre (a day's work) of land. But the strips were not of standard length, neither were the furlongs. Furlongs varied considerably in size, even in a single manor.

Open field lands were owned or tenanted by a number of people normally occupying the village location adjacent to them. In some villages the houses, cottages, or crofts would be grouped in a central area. In Swithland, for example, dwellings were sited on either side of the village's main street, as were the three open fields. The cottages would have consisted of one or two rooms, and been built in timber, wattle and daub. They might have had a yard for stacks and poultry, with an outhouse for beasts. Each dwelling stood in its own small enclosed piece of ground – a toft – which could be used for pasture, as an orchard, or for growing vegetables. Because of the need for access to water, the majority of cottages in Swithland were on the southern side of the road – the side on which the brook flows. Landholders and tenants had scattered parcels or strips of land distributed throughout the arable open fields, intermingled with those of their neighbours. They would have at least one strip in each field.

Up to enclosure in 1799, Swithland had three open fields, the Over (or Forest) Field, the Middle (or North) Field and the Exlands (or South) Field.[2]

The arrangement of three open fields suited the rotational agrarian practice of two thirds arable and one third fallow each year. A typical pattern might have been wheat, followed by barley, followed by fallow. The open fields became a common pasture after the crop had been lifted, and during the fallow year. The fallow year allowed the fields to be rested and also to be manured by grazing animals. In addition, both arable and common meadow land was pastured by the stock between harvest time and the time when the seed was sown in the spring.

Meadow – land outside the open fields – from which a hay crop could be taken for winter fodder was provided by the narrow water meadow by the side of watercourses. Pasture, for livestock grazing during the summer, consisted of the arable fields in their fallow year and, after harvest, of meadow land after haysel,[3] also of one or two closes set aside for rearing stock, and waste (rough, uncultivated) ground. Swithland's waste included a parcel of 2 acres (Pyehill), the upper and lower greens and roadside verges. Swithland residents also had rights on Rothley Plain and Charnwood Forest, both of which were entirely unenclosed waste.[4]

Farming the open fields was carried out collectively. Not every peasant could afford a plough or the horses to pull it. Pasture had to be saved from over-grazing, and rights to meadow hay controlled. The whole system required considerable co-operation between all concerned. Strict rules covering the nature of crop cultivation, the number and type of animals, and the control of livestock, were necessary. Each parish had its own customs, and the administration and implementation of this system in Swithland would have been the responsibility of its manorial court, run by the lord of the manor or his steward.

In 1387, over one hundred years after the 1255 grant of land to Robert le Waleys, John Walcote held the same twenty-seven virgates.[5] The living quarters of his manor hall would not necessarily have been over-large, since only the bailiff needed to be housed. There would, however, have been extensive outbuildings including possibly a granary, bakehouse, brewhouse, dairy, barns, cowshed, cart shed, pigsty, dovecote and sheepcote. Adjacent to the manor house would have been an orchard and enclosed vegetable garden. The remainder of the demesne land would have consisted of arable, meadow and common pasture. Most of the labour on the lord's demesne was provided by tenant peasants in lieu of their rent, but a small amount of wage labour might have been provided by the sons and daughters of tenants.

John Walcote's twenty-seven virgates covered between half and three quarters of the land in the parish; its exact location, however, cannot now be identified. Nor is there any indication, at the time of the division of the manor of Swithland in 1429, as to which parts were held by the Danvers family, and which parts by the Shepeys. Together their holding was substantial, but not complete. The manor of Groby retained a holding in the parish. Both Garendon Monastery and Ulverscroft Priory also held land in the village; the Priory held a croft (Tickhill Croft) and a copse (Puttocks). A small amount of glebe land belonged to Swithland Rectory. Others too held land. In 1540 Edward Able, as well as John Danvers, is recorded as being a leaseholder of Groby Manor. In 1515, Elizabeth Brigman and Alice Dawson, daughters of Thomas Mason of Swithland, sold a virgate of land with toft (homestead) and croft in Swithland; the toft and croft were described as lying between the land of the Prior of Ulverscroft on the west, and the land late of Edmund Shepey on the east, and extending from the king's highway as far as the land of John Danvers on the north. An Inquisition Post Mortem of 1564 on Richard Turvill of Thurlaston states that his father was seized of 'a large close in Swithland called Turville Leys', though it seems possible that this might be a slight mis-description, since Turville Leys is located in Woodhouse parish, just outside Swithland's parish boundary.

The open field system gave rights to peasant farmers and maintained an equilibrium, but it was not without its tensions. In order to increase his income, the lord of the manor sometimes extended arable cultivations at the expense of common pastures. More often the lord attempted to enclose part of the arable land for animal husbandry. The great monasteries in particular pioneered sheep farming on a large scale, starting a substantial wool trade; manorial lords also joined the profitable trade of animal husbandry. Enclosure, however, reduced the number of peasant livings, and it was not uncommon for peasants to break down the hedges as they tried to restore the old forms of arable husbandry. Occasionally, there was more widespread unrest beyond the boundaries of a single manor.

At the end of the Middle Ages, Leicestershire was mostly under arable cultivation. Although the demesne land was by then entirely enclosed, the open field system was still working, even where arable farming still predominated. Many of the smaller peasant holdings had been fragmented into even smaller units. These were occupied by cottagers and labourers who supplemented the produce of their holding with earnings from casual farm work. Some of the larger units became even larger; husbandmen farmed at most 40 to 50 acres, but those yeomen who had been able to acquire some personal wealth farmed on a larger scale.

At the dissolution of the monasteries between 1536 and 1539 virtually all monastic land was confiscated and passed to the king and his heirs. The land belonging to the Priory of Ulverscroft was surrendered to the Crown on 15th September 1539. The Garendon and Ulverscroft land was sold by Henry VIII in 1543 to Thomas Manners, Earl of Rutland. The Ulverscroft land was resold by Manners to Sir Andrew Judd, an alderman of the City of London who in 1550 sold it to Henry Grey, Marquis of Dorset, later Duke of Suffolk, who added it to his manor of Groby.[6] The monastic land in Swithland must subsequently have been sold to the Danvers family because, by 1658, all the lands in Swithland that had belonged to the Prior of Ulverscroft had been acquired, either directly or indirectly, by William Danvers. By then, a market for land had developed in England. The Shepeys, however, do not appear to have increased their landholding in Swithland. When Edmund Shepey died in 1509, his will[7] recorded that he was seized of a moiety[8] of the manor of Swithland: 7 messuages, 4 cottages, 4 virgates of land, 40 acres of meadow, 40 acres of pasture, 10 acres of wood, and 20 shillings rent.

Early Enclosure

The century following the dissolution of the monasteries saw significant prosperity in agriculture. The price of wheat increased by three and a half times; the price of other farm produce also increased. This prosperity allowed John Danvers to rebuild the manor house at Swithland in the late 1550s, and to purchase Rothley Hall as well as another estate in Rothley from Edmund Kingston in 1570.

Landowners continued to convert arable land into more profitable pasture by enclosure, and to amalgamate holdings into larger units – engrossment. It is likely that some such enclosure took place in Swithland. This practice, however, reduced the requirement for labour and was resisted. Legislation was passed to prevent such decay of tillage and depopulation: a statute of 1489 against depopulation was followed by further acts of 1515 and 1536. The legislation was, however, only spasmodically enforced. The last attempt at enforcement came in the 1630s when bad harvests caused alarm, and the Privy Council instituted yet another investigation into enclosure.

In 1635, on the 18th December, William Danvers wrote to Whitehall to his cousin, Sir John Coke, then Secretary of State, denying any such activity.

> My Lord of Stamford tells me that I am certified to the Council Board, by an inquisition taken by Mr Savage and Mr Window, for decay of tillage and depopulation. I have rested 30 acres for 3 years, 10 acres in a field, but I have made neither hedge nor ditch in a field, neither have I decayed the farm or tenement. There is as many houses, as many people, as many farms in our town as ever there was; neither is there any in our town that is indigent or beggarly. I wonder I should be thus dealt withal.[9]

His plea did not stop the inquiry. On 10th June 1637 he wrote again to Sir John.

> I am summoned…to appear at the Council Table this term at London for my enclosures and depopulations and decay of tillage, here at Swithland. I will never do these things. Neither did my father or my grandfather that have lived here these fourscore years. But what was in tillage, within the memory of any man alive is now tilled by us, the inhabitants of Swithland. We have planted some more families than formerly there have been, and they live now better than they ever did, and not one of these that troubles or charges either the town or country, saving two old people that are relieved by us. [The] messenger hath summoned three poor men of this town at this time also, that in this kind are as guiltless as your Honour is of any such thing. I humbly entreat you to stop these unjust clamours and false accusations against us. I cannot travel as far as London, unless there be some great necessity in it. As I hear from your Honour I shall direct my course. Your Honour's poor kinsman.[10]

In fact, the commission condoned enclosure as much as it condemned, for enclosure brought benefits to the Crown in the shape of fines.

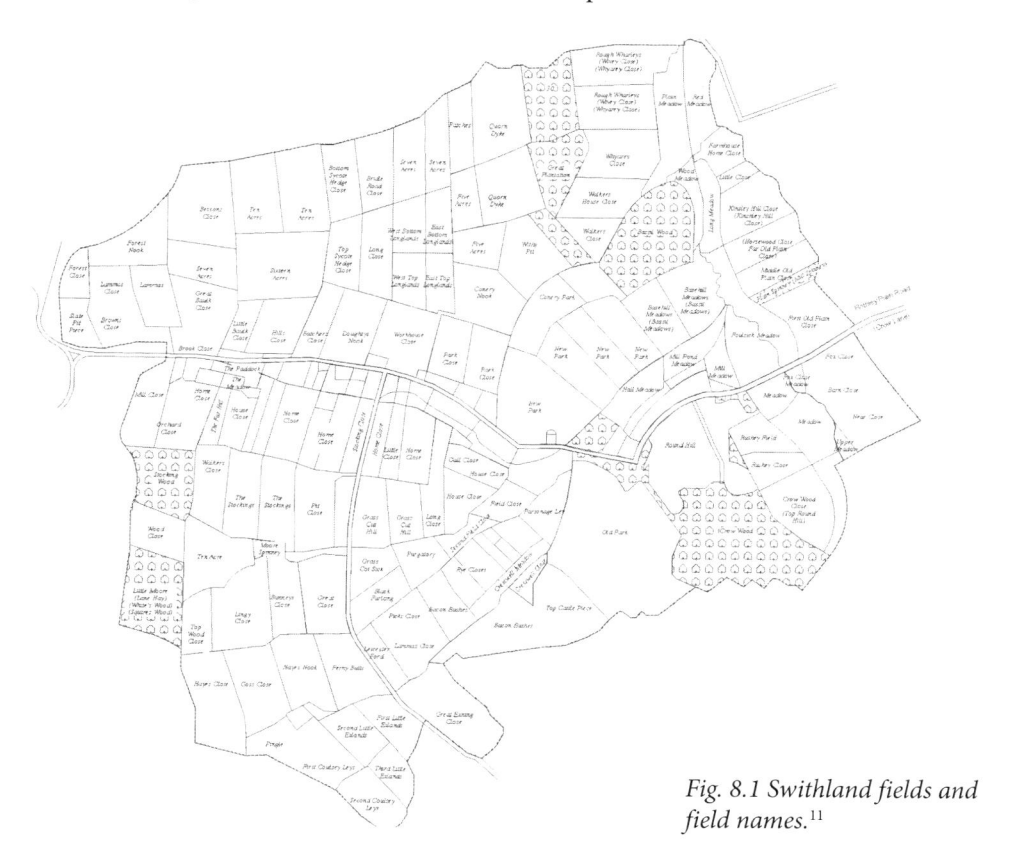

Fig. 8.1 Swithland fields and field names.[11]

Seventeenth Century Transactions

At the height of the increase in land prices, Henry Kendall[12] started to sell off parts of his estate in Swithland. In the space of a few months in 1622 he sold:

> Horsewood Leys Close (occupied by John Jarret of Mountsorrel, mercer) to Henry Parker of Rothley, yeoman[13]
>
> Rye Close (occupied by William Warden and Thomas Warden) to Francis Sutton of Swithland, blacksmith[14]
>
> Milne Close, to Robert Hinde of Swithland, tanner[15]
>
> A messuage, Gilberts Close and Gilberts Croft [8 acres in all] (occupied by Elizabeth Gilbert and Arthur Gilbert) to Arthur Gilbert of Swithland, husbandman[16]
>
> A messuage (occupied by Robert Browne), 5 closes (Little Wharleys alias Brownes Wharleys Close, Broome Croft Close, Stockinge Close,

> Baron Buske Close, Little Barsell Meadow alias Browne Barsell meadow) and other pieces of property to Robert Browne of Swithland, husbandman[17]
>
> Kinsley Hill Close and other closes (20 acres meadow, 40 acres of pasture, 4 acres of wood) to Francis Smalley of Mountsorrel, mercer.

In the same year, Kendall also sold Oxe Lersowe Close (occupied by George Thornton) to George Thornton of Mountsorrel, innholder.[18] (It is likely that Oxe Lersowe Close is located in Quorn parish, just beyond Swithland's parish boundary).

Henry Kendall died in 1627 and was buried in his church at Smisby, where the family erected an impressive marble memorial. In 1629 his son, Henry Kendall, sold the remainder of his half of the manor of Swithland to Francis Danvers for £400.[19] The indenture of sale does not name or describe in detail the land that was sold; plans were not attached to conveyances until the nineteenth century. It was simply described as consisting of 4 cottages, a garden, an orchard, 20 acres of land, 18 acres of meadow, 150 acres of pasture and 11 acres of wood and common pasture. Of the enlarged holding a significant part was farmed by his son, and the remainder let to tenants in modest blocks. At Francis Danvers' death in 1631, his son William farmed 40 acres of meadow, and 200 acres of pasture as well as the woodland; the tenanted estate in Swithland consisted of nine holdings of an average size of 19 acres, none of which had more than 35 acres of land.[20] (William Danvers' tenant Daniel Baker may also have been his steward, as a deed of 1634[21] styles Baker as acting for Danvers in the lease of land at Rothley.)

> Messuage & 35 acres (occupier: Henry Bolley);
> Messuage & 20 acres (occupier: Daniel Baker);
> Messuage & 20 acres (occupier: Richard Kirke);
> Messuage & 18 acres (occupier: John Baker);
> Messuage & 20 acres (occupier: Arthur Hebb);
> Messuage & 24 acres (occupier: John Lakin);
> Messuage & 16 acres (occupier: Francis Sutton);
> Messuage & 10 acres (occupier: Thomas Warden);
> Messuage & 10 acres (occupier: Nicholas Ball);
> and 16 cottages.

Consolidation

The Civil War turned the recession in agriculture to a slump. Heavy taxes were levied by each side to pay for the war; many men were no longer available to work on the land since they had been conscripted to fight. Many of the estates belonging to royalists had to be sold off in order to pay for the fines imposed by the victorious parliamentarians. The Danvers family, as committed parliamentarians, escaped such fines, and may even have profited from sales of royalist land.

The first overview of land holding in Swithland is provided by a survey of the manor of Groby towards the end of the Commonwealth period in 1658 (see p. 192).[22] It confirms the predominant position of the Danvers. The list may not be totally reliable as the land purchased from Kendalls appears to have been included in the Waleys inheritance and Turville Leys is listed as part of Swithland, rather than of Woodhouse. In addition to the land listed, there would have been a small amount of glebe land in the village, probably about 8 acres, which belonged to Swithland Rectory. Clearly, however, William Danvers owned by far the largest area of land, although, because of the Kendall sales of 1622, a number of others owned smaller portions.

For the century after the Civil War, agricultural prices remained broadly stable. The steady change throughout Leicestershire from arable to grassland continued. The easiest method was enclosure, but change could be made even within the open field system, since the open field farmer could leave his strips under grass, and tether his livestock. Many of the yeoman farmers prospered. Inventories made at the deaths of several Swithland residents indicate that it was not just the lords of the manor who were involved in animal husbandry.[23]

> 1722 Robert Prior, labourer: 3 cattle, 0 horses, 10 sheep, 0 pigs
> 1738 Edward Johnson, yeoman: 20 cattle, 2 horses, 80 sheep, 2 pigs
> 1745 Thomas Perkyns, husbandman: 16 cattle, 7 horses, 100 sheep, 0 pigs
> 1746 Robert Hews, yeoman: 21 cattle, 6 horses, 50 sheep, 0 pigs
> 1765 John Perkins, yeoman: 15 cattle, 8 horses, 100 sheep, 0 pigs

The pattern of estate management adopted by both the Stamfords and the Danvers was to lease their land for a long period of years. Quite frequently, the manor of Groby let land for a life, or for more than one life. Robert Hind, for example, in 1622 leased his land for his life and for those of his children, and in 1646, Robert Whitley leased his land for twenty-one years. A 1677 statement of rents due to the manor of Groby on leasehold land in Swithland mentions leases to Jempson (for two lives) at 12s 0d, Robert Hind (for two lives) at 7s 0d, and to Robert Whyte (for one life) at 2s 8d.[24]

The same pattern was adopted by the Danvers. In 1697, Elizabeth Danvers leased a close in Swithland (Lovett's Yard) to John Bennett, labourer, for ninety-nine years. She attached a condition that he 'will erect and get up upon some convenient part of the said premises one or more bay or bays of building for a dwelling house'.[25] On 28 February 1794 Henry Hind (1726–1801) entered into a lease for the lives of Henry Hind of Newtown Linford (69), Robert Hind of Leicester (59) and Thomas Hind of Swithland (33).[26] In 1733, Sir Joseph Danvers entered into a number of leases for land in Mountsorrel.[27] In 1741 he leased a messuage with barn, outhouses, orchard, garden and homestead to Henry Hind of Newtown Linford for sixty years.[28] In the same year, Joseph Danvers leased another messuage with barn, outhouses, orchard, garden and homestead to Joseph Ayres of Swithland for forty years.[29] In 1753 Sir John Danvers let a messuage on Swithland's Upper (Forest) Green to Joseph Johnson of Nottingham for sixty-three years.[30]

Survey of Manor of Groby 1658: Swithland

FREEHOLDERS
  William Danvers (inherited from Waleys):
      Lordship of Swithland
      A capital messuage
      9 other messuages
      9 cottages
      Seventeen Yard land
      A windmill
      Browns Hey
  William Danvers (purchased other than from Kendalls):
      North Hey Close
      Little Lyns spring wood
      Ballards (19 acres)
      Pickhill Croft
      Puttocks
      A messuage and half Yard of land
      Little Moore Wood alias Lane Hey Wood or White's Wood
      A messuage
      A messuage & parcel of ground
  William Danvers (purchased from Kendalls):
      A capital messuage
      3 messuages
  Rebecca Parker (purchased from Kendalls):
      2 closes (Horsewood Leys)
  Ralph Smalley (purchased from Kendalls):
      4 closes
      1 messuage, 5 closes, and 30 acres of land
  Emmanuel Smith, clerk (purchased from Kendalls):
      1 messuage, 1 close, and 6 acres of land
  Henry Squire (purchased from Kendalls):
      1 messuage, 1 close, and 17 acres of land
  Arthur Gilbert (purchased from Kendalls):
      1 messuage, 1 close, and 8 acres of land
  Margery Sutton (purchased from Kendalls):
      Rye Close
  Thomas Hind (purchased from Kendalls):
      Milne Close
  Michael Bosse (purchased from Kendalls):
      Turvey Leys Close

LEASEHOLDERS (FROM MANOR OF GROBY)

Robert Whitley	Fox Closes (22 acres)
Robert Hind	Messuage, two crofts, 7 acres and 1 selion of land in the open field (Lady Land)

WASTE

Manor of Groby	Pyehill (2 acres)
	Forest Green (1 acre)
	Town Street & Church Green (1 acre)
	Learke Lane (2 roods)

TENEMENTS ON THE WASTE

Manor of Groby	5 tenements (various tenants)

During these years, major landholders were consolidating and improving the land that they already owned. At Swithland, Joseph Danvers set about buying up land that was not already in his ownership. It was, however, to be a slow process. Some pieces were to pass through several hands before the opportunity arose for Danvers to buy. In 1651 Joseph Blankley of Kimboulton, Notts, mortgaged a close called Cattail Piece to William Pollard.[31] The principal was not repaid, and Pollard took possession. In 1672 Ann Sculthorpe, wife of William Sculthorpe of Newark, yeoman, daughter and executrix of William Pollard, sold the close to Nicholas Langstaffe of Burley, Rutland, yeoman, and Jane his wife.[32] In 1679 the Landstaffes sold to Richard Blackwell of Swithland, yeoman.[33] In 1709 Blackwell's daughter and executrix, Jane Branston of Swithland, sold it to Thomas Boley of Mountsorrel, cordwainer.[34] His wife and executrix, Elizabeth Boley, sold the piece in 1747 to Joseph Prior on trust for Joseph Danvers.[35]

Similarly, a close called Rye Close (6 acres), next to the 'parsonage ley', had been purchased in 1622 from the Kendalls by Francis Sutton of Swithland, blacksmith.[36] In 1658 it was owned by Margery Sutton. In 1675, it is mentioned in Jane Blakwing's will.[37] In 1694 Sarah Templar, relict of Benjamin Templar, sold Rye Close to Stephen Clarke for £70.[38] Stephen gave Rye Close in 1711 to his third son, William Clarke on his marriage to Mary Beaumont.[39] In 1732 William Clarke died, leaving Rye Close to his son, John Clarke,[40] and in 1741 it was included in John's marriage settlement with Elizabeth Case. In 1779 Elizabeth Clarke of Swithland, widow, sold the close to Sir John Danvers.

In other cases, small outstanding parcels of land still in villagers' hands, were further subdivided. It was not uncommon, for example, for land to be divided between children on the death of the parents, thus the opportunity for purchase away from a family did not immediately arise. On her death in 1675, Jane Blakwing left cottages in Markfield and Cropston, as well as closes in Swithland (Cattel Piece and Lint Close): they were divided between her three granddaughters.[41] Similarly, Jane Blakwing's daughter, Jane, wife of Henry Braunston, divided her property in 1732 between her three sons (Henry, William and John) and her daughter (Ann Wesley).

> Henry Branston, one messuage and 16 lands in the open fields;
> John Branston, one close (Stocking close);
> William Branston, one messuage and 16 lands in the open fields; and
> Ann Wesley, one messuage and four lands in the open fields.[42]

Eventually the Braunstons did sell. William sold his property to Joseph Prior in 1734;[43] Henry sold part of his property to Prior in 1742,[44] and the remaining messuages to Sir John Danvers in 1765.[45] Jane Wesley sold her inheritance (from William Wesley) to Sir John in 1775.[46]

Smaller Landholders

The Danvers were not the only potential purchasers of land in the village. Some of the more prosperous yeoman families also sought to increase their holding. The Gilbert family[47] and Joseph Prior, as well as the Braunston family, built up modest holdings.

The Gilbert Family

Arthur Gilbert, husbandman, purchased land from Henry Kendall in 1622,[48] and, in 1633 from Henry Fletcher.[49] In 1722 his grandson, Robert Gilbert (1679–1759) acquired from Eleanor Brown, sister of William Squire of Swithland, a messuage and 8½ acres of land in the open fields.[50] Robert Gilbert, a tenant of Sir Joseph Danvers, signed a lease in 1733[51] for twenty-one years on Crisps/Millers Close (10½ acres), on 110 lands in the open

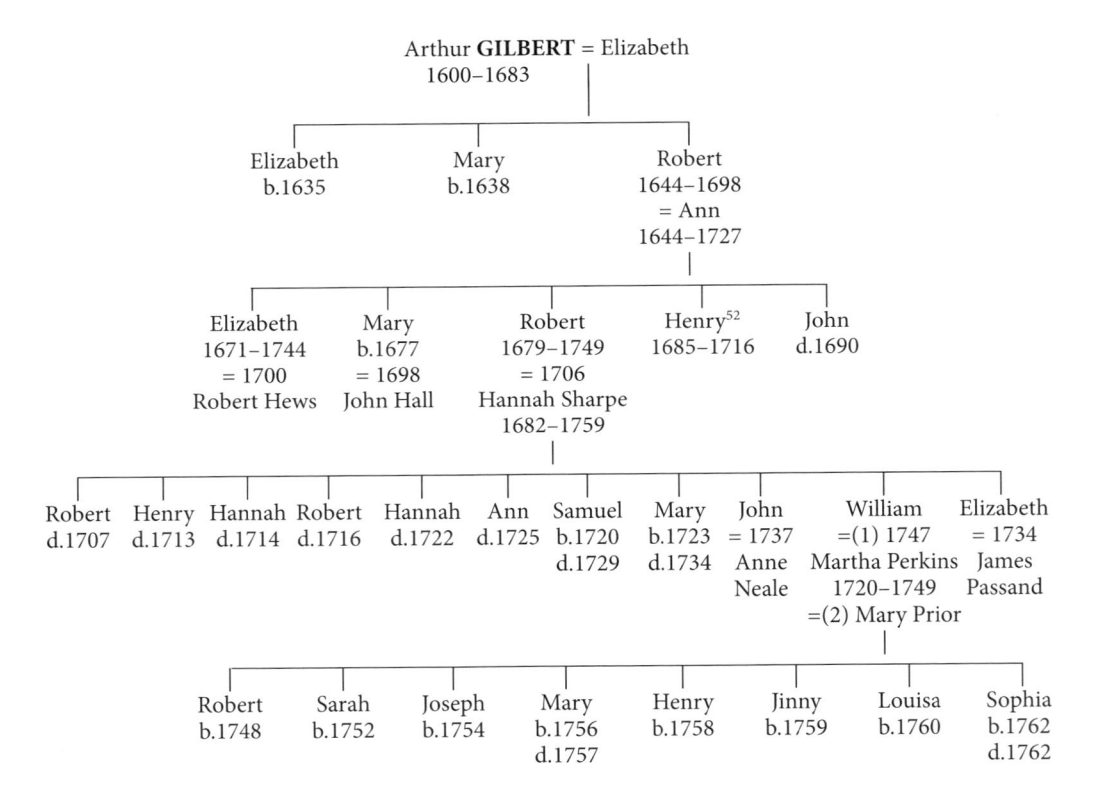

```
                    Arthur GILBERT = Elizabeth
                       1600–1683
       ┌───────────────────┼───────────────────┐
   Elizabeth             Mary              Robert
    b.1635              b.1638            1644–1698
                                          = Ann
                                          1644–1727
   ┌──────────┬──────────┬──────────┬──────────┐
Elizabeth   Mary      Robert      Henry[52]    John
1671–1744  b.1677    1679–1749   1685–1716    d.1690
= 1700     = 1698    = 1706
Robert     John      Hannah Sharpe
Hews       Hall      1682–1759

Robert Henry Hannah Robert Hannah Ann  Samuel Mary   John        William          Elizabeth
d.1707 d.1713 d.1714 d.1716 d.1722 d.1725 b.1720 b.1723 = 1737    =(1) 1747        = 1734
                                          d.1729 d.1734 Anne     Martha Perkins   James
                                                        Neale    1720–1749        Passand
                                                                 =(2) Mary Prior

      Robert   Sarah   Joseph   Mary    Henry   Jinny   Louisa   Sophia
      b.1748   b.1752  b.1754  b.1756  b.1758  b.1759  b.1760   b.1762
                              d.1757                            d.1762
```

fields (35½ acres), 31 lands in the North Field, 36 lands in the West Field, and 43 lands in the South Field. Following the death of Robert Gilbert,[53] Sir John Danvers acquired the remaining Gilbert interests in 1761 when he purchased 2 messuages and 9 acres of land in the open fields from Robert's son, William Gilbert.[54]

Joseph Prior

In 1712, Joseph Prior (1687–1786) purchased a messuage from William Porter, labourer.[55] In 1734 he acquired William Braunston's interests[56] (10 lands). In 1738, he purchased 3 tenements and a backside from William Perkins, tailor.[57] In 1742, he bought part of Henry Braunston's interests.[58] He also acquired a messuage from John Clarke. In successive deeds, Joseph Prior is described first as a slatter,[59] then as a farmer, and lastly as a gentleman. By 1742, Prior was steward to Joseph Danvers. Finally, in 1764 he sold his entire land holding to Sir John Danvers. His tombstone in Swithland churchyard describes him as:

> Land & House Steward to Sir Joseph and Sir John Danvers
> Baronets, which place he enjoyed many years, and died possessed
> of a good fortune and a good character.

The 'good fortune' that he possessed at his death amounted to £563 14s 0d, of which £315 was in bonds and mortgages and £105 in bank bills.[60]

The Smalleys and Kinchley Hill Farm

One of the largest holdings in the village not in the hands of the Danvers was the 65 acre property at Kinchley Hill Farm. It was owned by the Smalley family.

Francis Smalley of Mountsorrel, mercer, had purchased some land at Kinchley Hill in 1622 from Henry Kendall.[61] The land was bequeathed in 1655 to Francis' son, Ralph Smalley. At his death in 1666, Ralph left the land to his brother's eldest son, also called Ralph, but entailed it. (It was left to Ralph's male heirs in succession, and in default to his brothers' male heirs in succession, and in default again to his sisters.) At this Ralph's death, it therefore passed to his son – another Ralph. Despite the entailment, the land was left, after the third Ralph Smalley's death in 1730,[62] to his widow for life, and then to John Fisher of Cossington and Ralph Tebbutt[63] of Frisby-on-the-Wreake, plumber and grazier.

In order to purchase the land, Joseph Danvers needed to buy up the interests of all the remaindermen. He mounted an examination of the title. On 13th February 1742, Joseph Prior, his steward, wrote to Joseph Danvers at Great Chelsea that he had had the church register at Shepshed examined. The purpose was to establish who might still have a legal interest in the land:

> I have enclosed the extracts taken from the registers of
> Shepshead, which I did not get attested till John Tomson had try'd
> to make out the marriage of John Smalley with Pentecoast, but
> their marriage is not registered. John has enquired of several old
> people, and some which was servants to the said John and
> Pentecoast, who most of 'em say they were married by licence, by
> Mr Rose at that time vicar of Shepshead, and in a room at the old
> Drs house, but he cannot meet with any body that was present at
> the marriage, they say Smalley of Mountsorrel threaten'd to
> prosecute the parson for that marriage, and think that was the

reason he did not enter it in the register, the servants say they have heard the Dr and his wife say that they were married in the Green Chamber at the old doctors house.[64]

Other church registers were also being examined. On 13th February, Joseph Prior again wrote to Joseph Danvers at Great Chelsea:

I was misinformed as to their keeping a register at Mountsorrel, there has been kept there of late, but there is no old ones. I was there yesterday and took extracts of all that could be found relating to the Smalley family, I have the extracts attested by the minister and churchwardens, and have inclosed a copy, the oldest there reaches no higher than the death of Mr Ralph Smalley who was the father of Robert and Penticoast. Mr Greasley who assisted me says he thinks they are all registered at Barrow. But we can't get any thing from there till Mr Foster is at home.[65]

In 1747 Sir Joseph purchased the interests of some of the remaindermen.[66] But when Sir John Danvers took legal advice on the position in 1756, he was advised that no title had passed.[67] The Smalley land was not in fact secured until 1828, and then only in an exchange for other land.[68]

Consolidation

The most successful members of the Danvers family, Sir Joseph and Sir John, tried most assiduously to consolidate their holding in Swithland.

At some time between 1733 and 1742, Joseph Danvers acquired the land of William Barnett, William Braunston (part), John Walker and John Gilbert, and between 1734 and 1779 the Danvers acquired the lands of Thomas Gimson, Robert Howes, Robert Gilbert[69] and John Clarke.[70] In March 1755, William Perkins the tailor sold to Sir John 'two messuages, cottages or tenements now divided in four dwelling houses in Swithland near Braunstone's Lane, now in the tenure or occupation of William Pollard, John Braunstone, Charles Fernelow, otherwise Ferneley, and William Westley.[71] In 1764 Joseph Prior sold out to Sir John Danvers for £400.[72] In 1767 Henry Braunston sold him two messuages in Swithland.[73] In 1783 the land of Bartholemew Mountney & John Squire (Stocking Close, 2 acres) was purchased.[74]

By 1783, there were only six landowners in Swithland:

Sir John Danvers
The Earl of Stamford & Warrington: Fox Close[75] and Barn Close (25 acres) on the boundary with Rothley Plain; a messuage, four closes and land in the open fields (9 acres)
Rev John Llwyd, rector: Glebe (8 acres)
John Clarke: a cottage and 1 close[76] (Mill Close, 5½ acres)
Mrs Elizabeth Smalley: 65 acres
Jonathan Grundy

Of the whole village only about 120 acres were not owned by Sir John Danvers.

Enclosure

Landowners throughout England sought to make better use of their land at this time. Sir Joseph and Sir John were both 'improvers' of their estate. In 1759–60, Sir John Danvers erected two magnificent barns[77] at Hall Farm that still stand, and there are other outbuildings at Hall Farm also dating from this time. At nearby Dishley Grange, Robert Bakewell (1725–1795) exercised a wide influence on methods of raising pedigree livestock. This required larger farming units, as well as more scientific methods. Disparities in the size of tenanted holdings started to become greater, as is evidenced by Assessments for Land Tax.[78]

Swithland: Land Tax Assessment 1773[79] (Assessments over £1)

PROPRIETOR	OCCUPIER	TAX (£-s-d)
Sir John Danvers	Sir John Danvers	9-04-02
	Edward Johnson	5-12-06
	John Newbold	4-07-00
	John Clarke	3-16-06
	John Hall	3-12-00
	Nathaniel Hall	3-12-00
	Richard Jesson	3-06-00
	Stephen Prior	1-04-09
	William White	1-04-00
Rev John Llwyd	Rev John Llwyd	5-04-01
Earl of Stamford	John Dawson	1-02-06

Although the open field system had provided some flexibility in adapting to changing systems of husbandry, there was a strong incentive to enclose. Quorn was enclosed in 1763, Mountsorrel in 1781, and Cropston in 1782: Sir John Danvers was among the petitioners in each case. But it was not until 1798, after the death of Sir John Danvers, that applications were made for parliamentary approval to enclose Thurcaston and Swithland.

There had long been a movement towards enclosing land for pasture, and combining two or more farms into larger units. It had begun, perhaps, with mediaeval desertions, but the process was in full flow from 1600, and went on extensively throughout the seventeenth century. During the eighteenth century the process was almost totally completed under a series of parliamentary acts. Swithland (1799) was one of the last Leicestershire parishes to be enclosed.

Enclosure was expensive. Landowners were expected to meet the costs of the Commissioners who were appointed to allot the land to be enclosed; they also had to meet the cost of fencing. In Swithland, the potential cost may have persuaded John Adderley, successor to Mrs Jonathan Grundy, to sell his land in 1798 to Augustus Richard Butler Danvers. Landowners believed, however, that enclosure would increase agricultural productivity. They may have been encouraged by the high price of food during the Napoleonic War of 1793–1815.

When they were enclosed, Swithland's open fields were said to occupy about 350 acres – about a third of the parish. The three open fields were named the Over Field (or Forest Field), the Middle Field (or North Field) and the Exlands Field (or South Field). The Over and Middle Field formed a continuous block north of Main Street. The Exlands Field was situated astride the road to Thurcaston. Contemporary deeds indicate the names of some of the furlongs within these fields.

OVER FIELD	MIDDLE FIELD	EXLANDS FIELD
Cover Croft	Bottom	Black
Brand Nook	Cunory Nook	Coulsey Ley
Green	Long Land	Ferny Butts
Lint Style	Quorndyke	Gallclose Side
Sicut Hedge	Nether	Galloway Side
Welewong	Warleys Nook	Grescott Hill
		Hayes Nook
		Little Exlands
		Leicester Ford
		Moor End
		Picks Close
		Ryde Leas
		Townside

Enclosure also eliminated the frustrations of tithe collection, since land was allocated to the rector in lieu of tithes. The law of tithing was complex; it could and did lead to arguments. In principle, farmers paid a tenth of their produce to the rector. Great tithes were payable on the produce of the soil: grain, hay, and wood. Small tithes were payable on the increase in animal livestock, on their products (especially wool), and on other minor produce. Originally, tithes were intended for the assistance of the poor and for the upkeep of the church as well as for the maintenance of the clergy. But by the sixteenth century, they were regarded as being solely for the support of the rector. Usually, crops could not be removed from the field until the tithe portion had been collected, so could be damaged during the delay. There were practical difficulties in collecting tithes in kind, and in taking the produce to market for sale. There were frequent disputes about liability. As a result, it was not uncommon for landowners to agree a 'modus' or compensation – in which a money payment was made, rather than payment in kind. The Smalley land at Kinchley Hill was assumed by the Enclosure Commissioners to be subject to such a composition.

From July 1798 to January 1799, the Swithland Enclosure Commissioners held a series of meetings to direct the enclosure and agree the Award.[80] They met sometimes at the house of William Bishop, at The Three Crowns Inn, Leicester, and sometimes at the house of John Phillips, 'at the sign of the

Wifforn at Swithland'. They appointed Robert Harvey Wyatt to survey the land. In July 1798 they ordered that the Fallow Field be ploughed three times at the usual time. By November, Wyatt's survey had been completed, and the proposed roads were staked out. In December, the Commissioners ordered 'all owners and occupiers of all the open field land within the Lordship of Swithland to take away all their beasts, sheep, and other cattle before 14th January next, and that all right of common shall cease from that time'.[81]

The process of allotment started with all the land in the area – even the village greens and whether in the open fields or otherwise, all were thrown into the hotch pot. The Commissioners then allocated the land on the basis set out in the Enclosure Act. Having set out the roads and carriageways, land was firstly allotted to the rector in lieu of tithes. Next a special allotment was made to the Surveyors of Highways. Small allotments were then made in respect of manorial rights. Finally, the majority of the land was allotted between the proprietors – the existing landowners.

The award gave 839.28 acres to Augustus Richard Butler Danvers,

Fig 8.2 Swithland Enclosure Award Map, 1799.

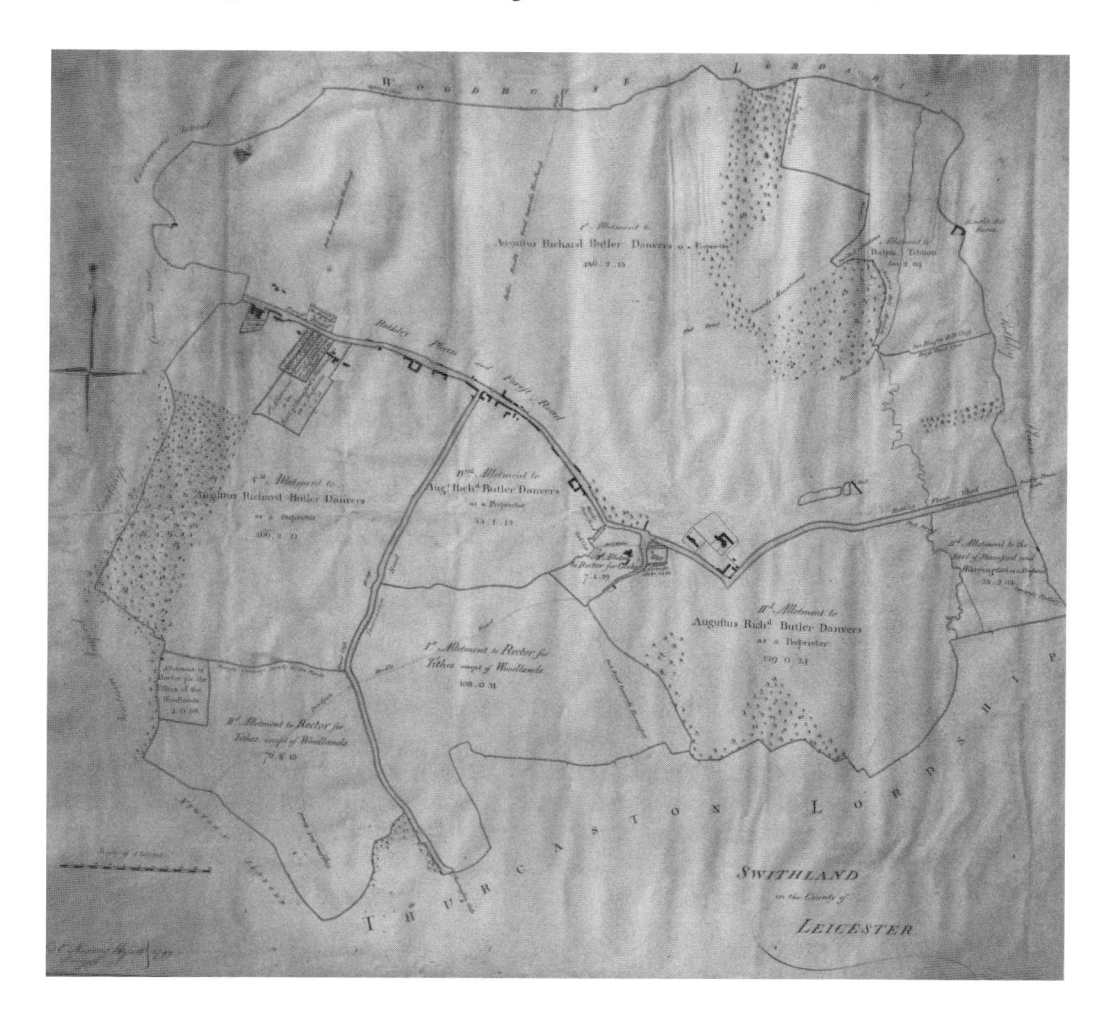

192.49 acres to John Llwyd (rector), 60.53 acres to Ralph Tebbutt (successor to Mrs Elizabeth Smalley), 34.12 acres to the Earl of Stamford & Warrington, 1 acre to the Surveyors of Highways, and 0.93 acres to William Clarke.

Enclosure must have been one of the most momentous events in the history of the village. Within a few short years it transformed the physical landscape, altered its farming beyond recognition, and changed the entire culture and habits of the community.

After enclosure, the new owners were required to fence the blocks of land that they had been allocated. The open fields of Swithland may have occupied only a third of the total parish land area. When the parish was enclosed, however, these large fields, with their patchwork of gently curving strips, were replaced with a landscape of hedged closes, often in formal rectangular shapes. Many of the new closes were named after the furlongs on which they lay.

In most parishes, enclosure worsened the position of the poor. The peasant farmer was displaced, and the peasant society collapsed. Before enclosure, cottagers and labourers with no land had been able to rent a strip in the open fields to meet some of their needs; after enclosure, this was denied them. The right to graze one or more cows on common land was lost. The opportunity to glean after harvest was lost. With the conversion of land to pasture, the number of people employed on the land fell. The position was worsened by an agricultural slump between 1816 and 1837. Several tenants, who were then on a single year tenancy, were evicted. The most notable was David Chapman, who was evicted from his 206 acres at Hall Farm in 1829. Others to leave their holding included Thomas Hales (103 acres), William Leake (68 acres) and William Bunney (63 acres).

The crumbling of the old system showed itself most obviously in the calamitous rise in poor rates. Before 1834, each parish was responsible for the welfare of its own poor. The overseers were careful to support only those who were entitled to assistance by virtue of establishing that the parish was their 'place of settlement'. A report in 1797 stated that in Leicestershire the rise in poor rates was caused by the poor being thrown out of work by the enclosures. To a small extent, the unemployment numbers in Swithland may have been mitigated by the growth of the nearby slate industry. There are, however, indications that the population fell in the years following enclosure. According to the 1801 Population Census there were 322 residents occupying 58 houses; the 1841 Census recorded a population of 306 in 56 houses of which 8 were empty.[82]

Elsewhere in England, enclosure provided a pool of labour for the development of industry. In Leicestershire a large proportion of the labour force that had been displaced from the land found employment in hosiery, but hosiery was never a major source of employment in Swithland. In any event, the hosiery business had its own problems. Towards the end of the eighteenth century, the adoption of trousers for men reduced the demand for stockings. Furthermore, the rise in corn prices put bread beyond knitters' means, increasing mechanisation took work away from them and the Napoleonic wars stopped exports. Knitters were brought to the edge of starvation. In 1773 a mob in Leicester destroyed a newly invented knitting machine, which they saw as a threat to their livelihood. The Luddite Rebellion took its name from a half-witted Anstey youth named Ned Ludd, who smashed a stocking frame in retaliation for a punishment he had received. At Loughborough, a factory night-watchman was shot and wounded during a riot in which fifty-three machines were wrecked. The Government made machine breaking a capital offence.

Enclosure changed the look of the countryside as the greater part of the open field arable land was converted to permanent pasture. In the place of fragmented holdings of land scattered in open fields, land was allocated in blocks. This meant that larger farming units could be developed, and more land be put down to grass. In Swithland in 1801, some 327½ acres were in arable cultivation: 103 wheat, 83 barley, 78 oats, 49½ turnips, 11 peas and beans, and 3 potatoes. During the nineteenth century the arable area fell, since more money could be made from livestock husbandry and there was an engrossing of farms by large graziers at a much-enhanced rent. The Swithland Hall Estate was consolidated into a small number of principal farms, and a scattering of smallholdings. Augustus Richard Butler Danvers reduced the quantity of land that was farmed directly, rather than being let. He also undertook some rebuilding. He enlarged the farmhouse at Hall Farm and let the farm.

Swithland Hall Estate: Holdings above 10 acres (Area: acres-roods-perches)

OCCUPIER/TENANT	DESCRIPTION	1807	1815	1820
Hon A.B. Danvers	In Hand	78-0-00		
David Chapman	Farm & lands	160-0-00	191-3-29	206-0-29
Matthew Simpson	Farm & lands	137-0-00	132-2-22	133-0-00
Thomas Hales	Farm & lands	108-0-00	98-3-20	
Matthew Simpson (ex Hales)				103-0-00
William Leake	Farm & lands	68-0-00	78-0-00	
Matthew Simpson (ex Leake)				68-0-00
Michael/William Bunney	Farm & lands	58-0-00	58-1-10	
Matthew Simpson (ex Bunney)				63-1-00
Daniel/Jenny Bates	Farm & lands	66-3-34	102-3-10	
William Bates		30-2-30		
Joseph Bostock				95-0-00
Thomas Prior	Several parcels	34-3-09	34-3-09	
Henry Snow				28-2-00
Sarah Prior	Several parcels	18-1-12	18-2-21	18-1-21
John Lakin	Public House &c	18-0-00	18-0-30	18-0-00
Samuel Hardy/Edward Dexter	Water Mill &c	10-0-00	10-0-00	10-0-00

Source: 1807 Claims re: Charnwood Forest & Rothley Plain Enclosure Award; 1815 Mortgage Agreement by Augustus Richard Butler Danvers; 1820 Valuation Report by Mr Samuel Stone.[83]

In the course of the century that followed enclosure, the Butler-Danvers family continued to buy up land in Swithland which was not yet in their ownership. The 61 acres of Smalley/Tebbutt land at Kinchley Hill was finally acquired in 1820. William Bates had taken over the tenancy of the farm in 1818 from Richard Burchnell, and remained in occupation, but as tenant of George John Butler Danvers. The Earl of Stamford's estate in Swithland was acquired in 1873.[84]

Apart from Augustus Richard, the greatest beneficiary of enclosure had been the rector, in compensation for the loss of tithes. John Llwyd continued to farm the glebe he had owned before enclosure. The additional land that he acquired as a result of enclosure was let. Following his death in 1814, the land was let[85] to William Hind (68.59 acres), and to William Bates (126.2 acres). In 1834 some of the glebe was exchanged with George John Butler Danvers. The then rector, Henry David Erskine, swapped land in Swithland for land in Thurcaston parish which adjoined his glebe, south of Exning spinney. The request for the exchange may have been connected with the construction of the new Swithland Hall for George John, as it allowed him to extend the park in front of his new residence. Successive rectors continued to let their glebe land: in 1891 both Benjamin Hemsley and Edward Tyers were farming parts of the glebe.

Revival

From 1837 there was a general revival in agriculture in England. It reached a boom period in the decade after 1853 and continued until 1874. The village economy was dominated by the tenants of the larger holdings, who provided employment for landless agricultural labourers. In the 1841 Swithland Census five people described themselves as farmers and two as cottagers. The farmers were major village employers. Between them they employed thirty agricultural labourers and thirty-two servants. Although farmers looked to security from their landlord, they preferred to hold their farms on annual tenancies because of fluctuations in the prices of farm produce. The landlord generally provided the fixtures (the buildings, fencing and field drainage); farm improvements, for such works as drainage, were encouraged by government loans. In Swithland, George John Butler Danvers undertook quite extensive improvements to many of the farms, particularly in the decade from 1841 to 1851. For their part, the larger and more progressive tenants increased the productivity of their holdings through mechanisation and more scientific methods. Greater use of fertilisers was helped by the construction of the railways, which made manures and artificial fertilisers cheaper to transport.

Principal Farms

By 1851 the pattern of principal farms in Swithland had clearly emerged, the three largest being Hall Farm, Forest End Farm and Longlands Farm. Land to the south-east of the parish was farmed from Hall Farm – the largest single unit. Land in the west belonged to Forest End Farm. Longlands Farm lands were at the north of the parish. Of the two smaller farms, Kinsley Hill was at the north-west end of the village, and Exning Farm at the centre. There were also a number of smallholdings, such as Pit Close Farm and Brook Farm.

Swithland Hall Estate 1851[86] *(Area: acres-roods-perches)*

FARM	TENANT	AREA IN SWITHLAND
Hall Farm	William Cuffling	270-0-39
Forest End Farm	William Simpson	206-3-35
Longlands Farm	Isaac Leake	158-1-38
Kinsley Hill Farm	Thomas Bates	68-2-17
Spinneys &c in hand	Earl of Lanesborough	67-0-34
Exning Farm	Daniel Bates	49-0-25
Griffin Inn	George Harris	15-1-25
Brook Farm	Benjamin Petts	11-0-36
Swithland Mill	Edward Dexter	8-3-24
Pit Close	Benjamin Hemsley	6-0-23

Hall Farm and Longlands Farm – the Cuffling Family

The Cufflings were typical of the more entrepreneurial Victorian farmers. William Cuffling senior was born in Stanton-under-Bardon in 1790, but moved to Mountsorrel. In 1830 he was running a business as a baker and corn dealer, but by 1841 he had taken the tenancy of a 126-acre farm in Mountsorrel employing ten labourers. His eldest son, William Cuffling junior, who married Mary Ann Dakin and had twelve children, ran a 130-acre farm at Mountsorrel before moving in 1851 to take over the 290 acres of Hall Farm, Swithland. By 1871 the farm had expanded to 320 acres and William junior was employing five men and two boys. In the same year his son John began a ten year tenancy of Longlands Farm, Swithland. When William Cuffling died in 1876, his wife Mary Ann continued at Hall Farm, farming it with the help of her sons, John and William Henry, until her death in 1900. William Henry carried on the tenancy until his death in 1902.

Fig 8.3 Mary Ann Cuffling (nee Dakin), widow of William Cuffling, c. 1880.

Swithland: Church and Estate

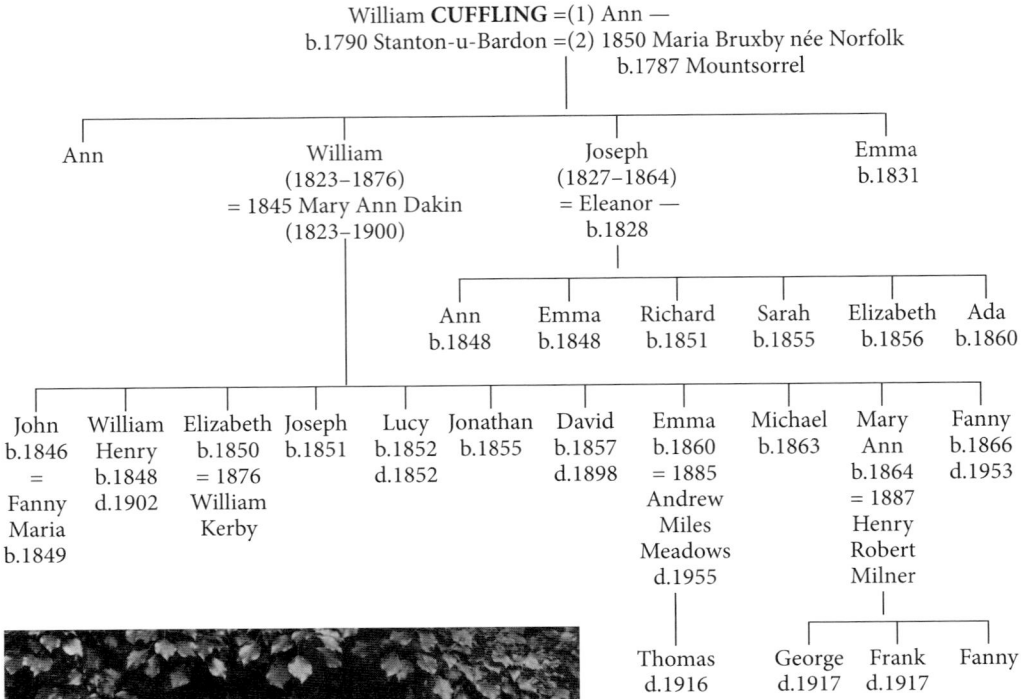

```
William CUFFLING =(1) Ann —
b.1790 Stanton-u-Bardon =(2) 1850 Maria Bruxby née Norfolk
                              b.1787 Mountsorrel
```

- Ann
- William (1823–1876) = 1845 Mary Ann Dakin (1823–1900)
- Joseph (1827–1864) = Eleanor — b.1828
- Emma b.1831

Children of Joseph and Eleanor:
- Ann b.1848
- Emma b.1848
- Richard b.1851
- Sarah b.1855
- Elizabeth b.1856
- Ada b.1860

Children of William and Mary Ann Dakin:
- John b.1846 = Fanny Maria b.1849
- William Henry b.1848 d.1902
- Elizabeth b.1850 = 1876 William Kerby
- Joseph b.1851
- Lucy b.1852 d.1852
- Jonathan b.1855
- David b.1857 d.1898
- Emma b.1860 = 1885 Andrew Miles Meadows d.1955
  - Thomas d.1916
- Michael b.1863
- Mary Ann b.1864 = 1887 Henry Robert Milner
  - George d.1917
  - Frank d.1917
  - Fanny
- Fanny b.1866 d.1953

Brothers William Henry and Jonathan both had periods of managing the adjacent water mill, Jonathan from 1875–80 and William Henry from 1891–94. Their sisters Emma and Mary Ann both lost sons in World War One. Emma's son, Thomas Meadows, was killed in 1916 and Mary Ann's two sons, George and Frank, in 1917. Their names are recorded on their grandmother's grave stone.

Fig 8.4
Fanny Cuffling, William Henry Cuffling and Mary Ann Milner (née Cuffling).

Plate 1: Approximate Location of Swithland Open Fields at Enclosure, 1799.

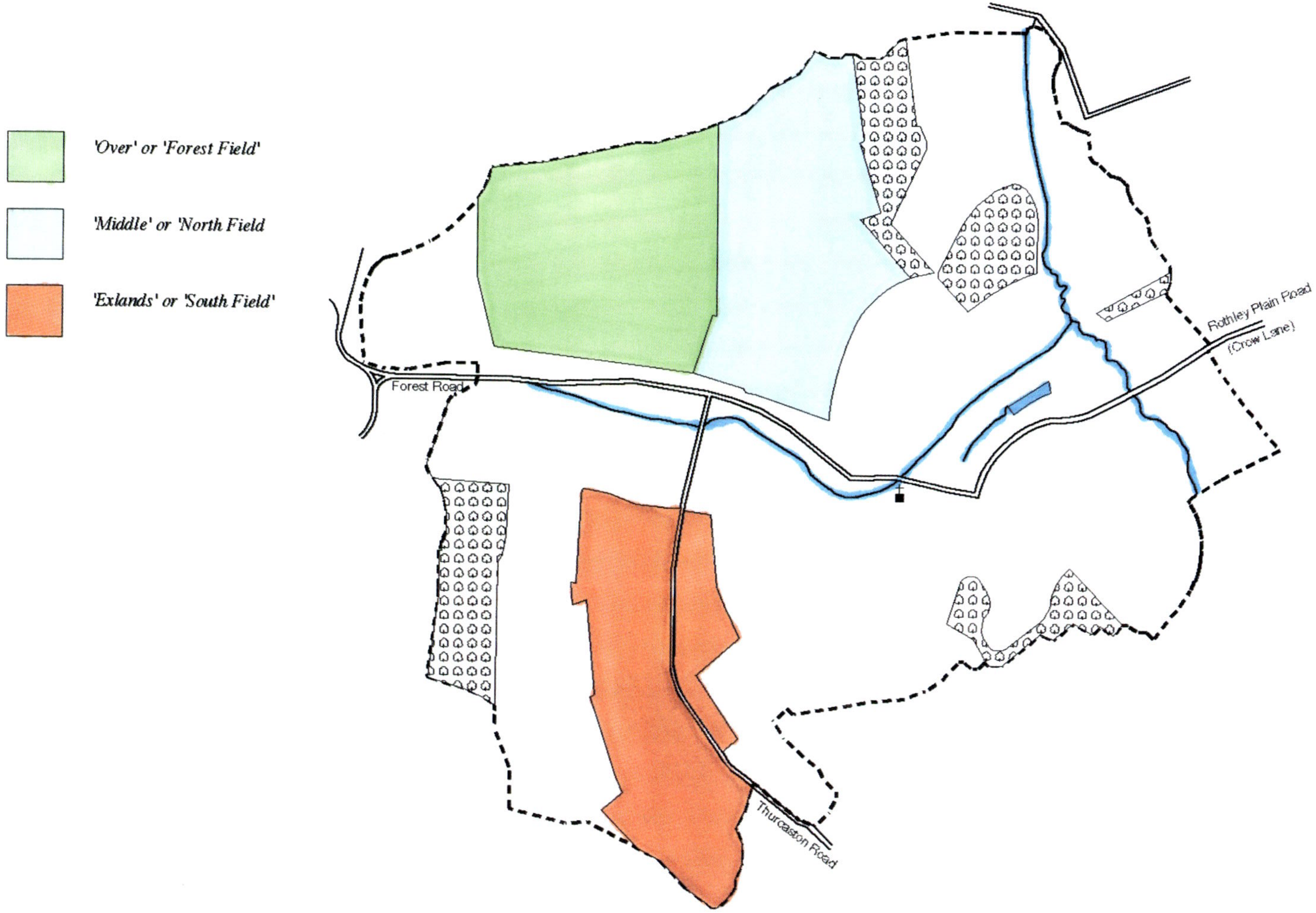

'Over' or 'Forest Field'
'Middle' or 'North Field
'Exlands' or 'South Field'
Forest Road
Rothley Plain Road
(Crow Lane)
Thurcaston Road

*Plate 2: Swithland Land Ownership after Enclosure, 1799.
(Acres–Roods–Perches)*

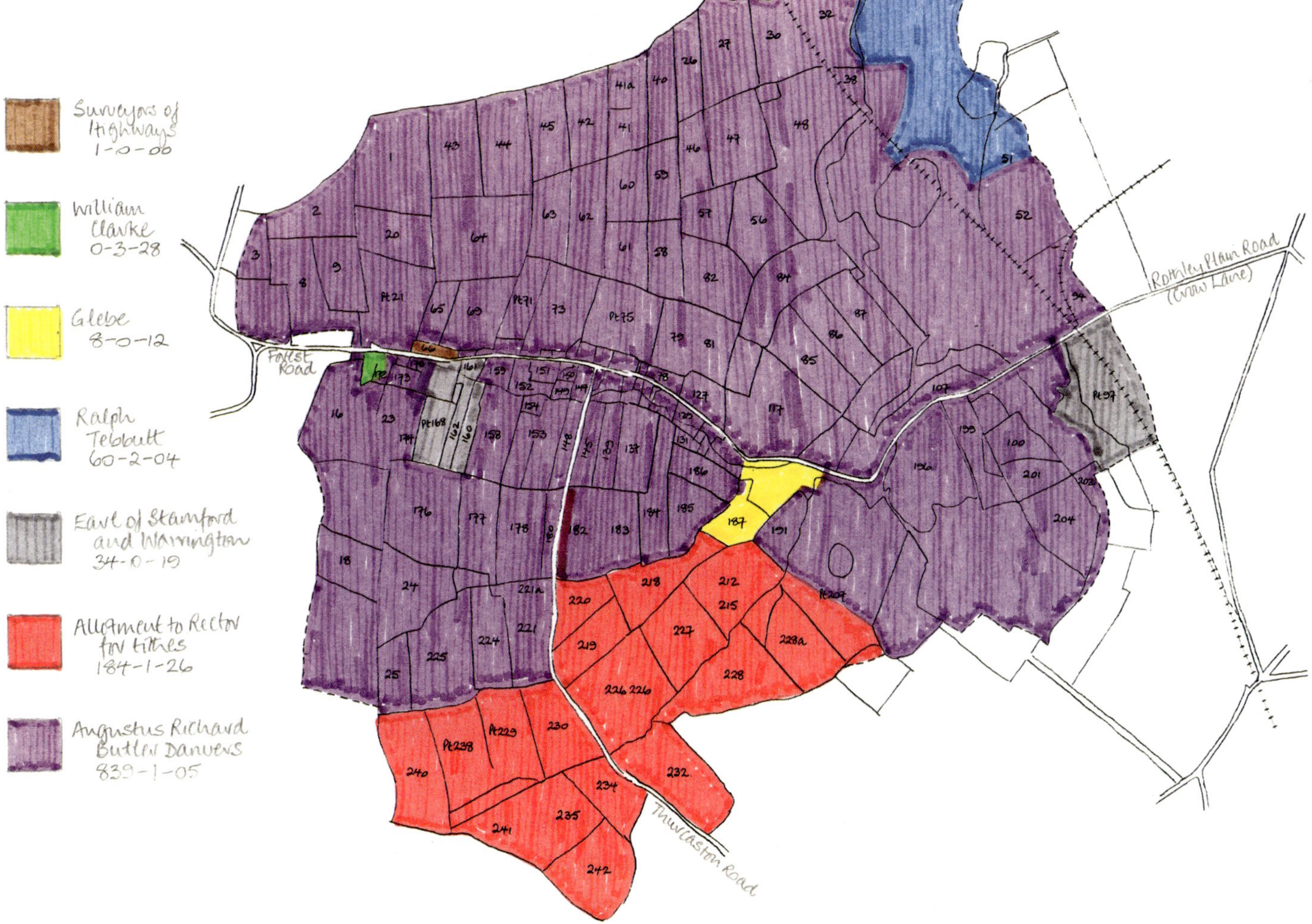

Colour	Owner	Area
Brown	Surveyors of Highways	1-0-06
Green	William Clarke	0-3-28
Yellow	Glebe	8-0-12
Blue	Ralph Tebbutt	60-2-04
Grey	Earl of Stamford and Warrington	34-0-19
Red	Allotment to Rector for tithes	184-1-26
Purple	Augustus Richard Butler Danvers	832-1-05

Plate 3: Swithland Land Ownership, 1834.

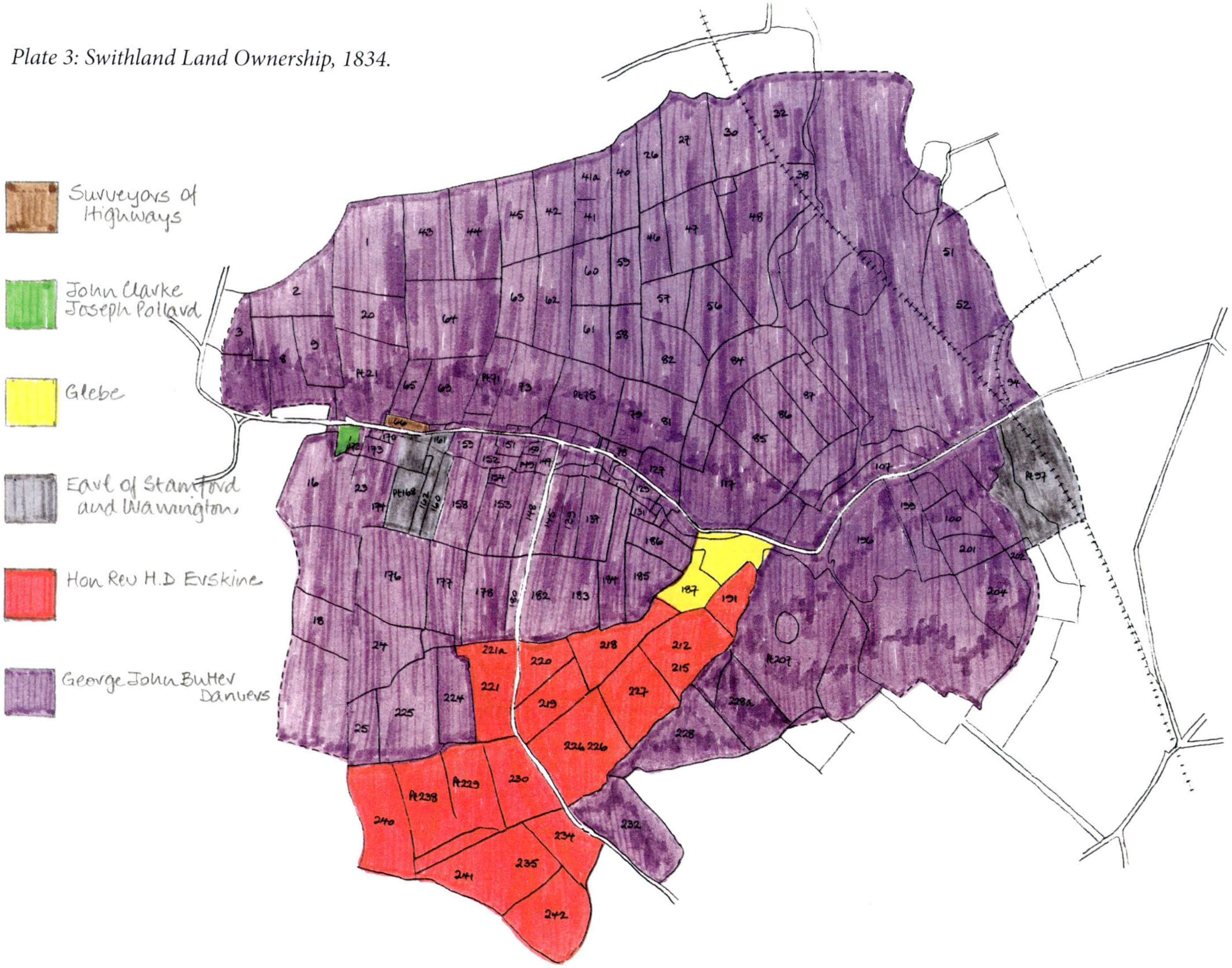

- Surveyors of Highways
- John Clarke Joseph Pollard
- Glebe
- Earl of Stamford and Warrington
- Hon Rev H.D Erskine
- George John Butler Danvers

Plate 4: Swithland Hall Estate Tenant Farmers, 1903

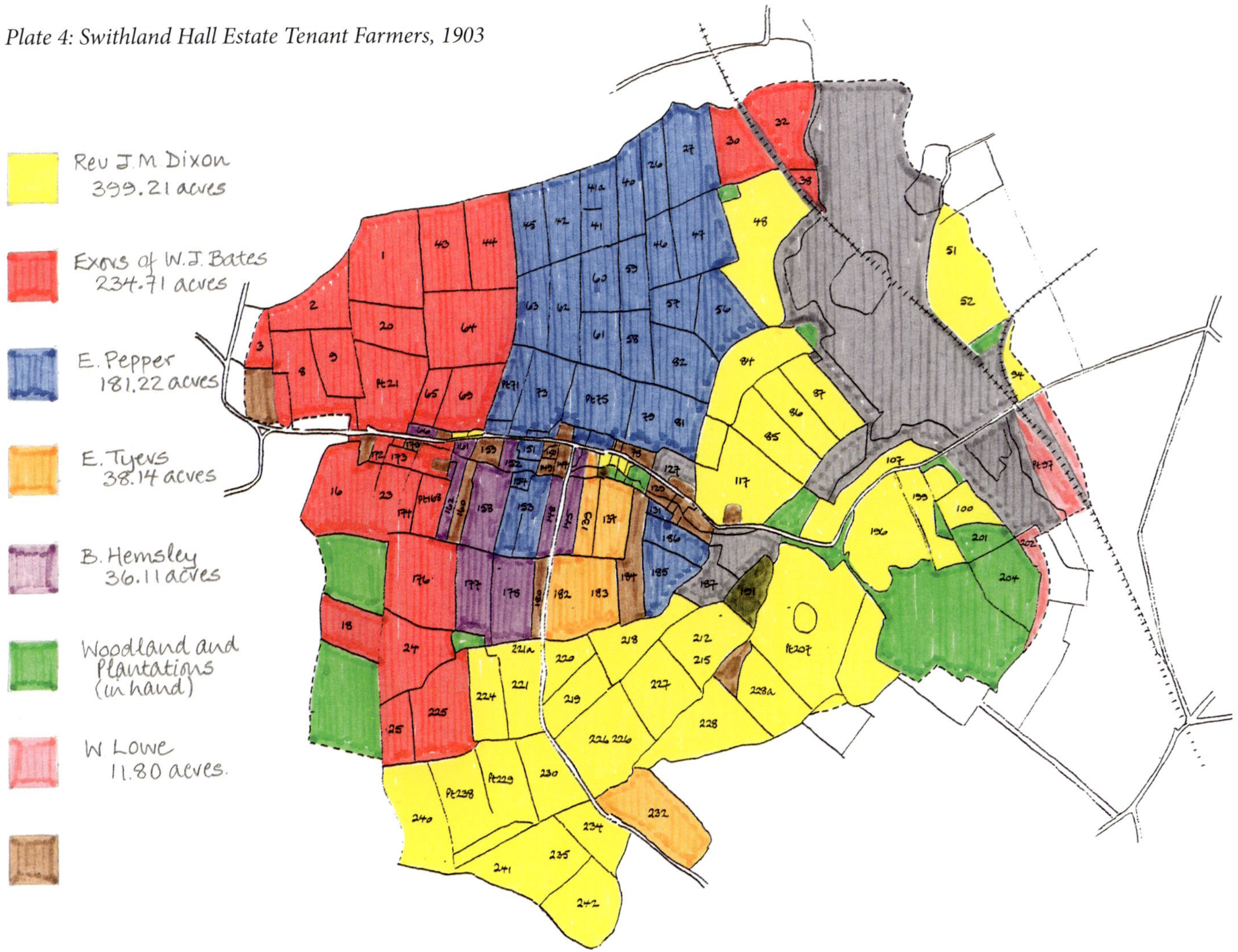

- Rev J M Dixon — 399.21 acres
- Exors of W J Bates — 234.71 acres
- E. Pepper — 181.22 acres
- E. Tyers — 38.14 acres
- B. Hemsley — 36.11 acres
- Woodland and Plantations (in hand)
- W Lowe — 11.80 acres

Plate 5: Land Tax Survey of Swithland Hall Estate, 1909.

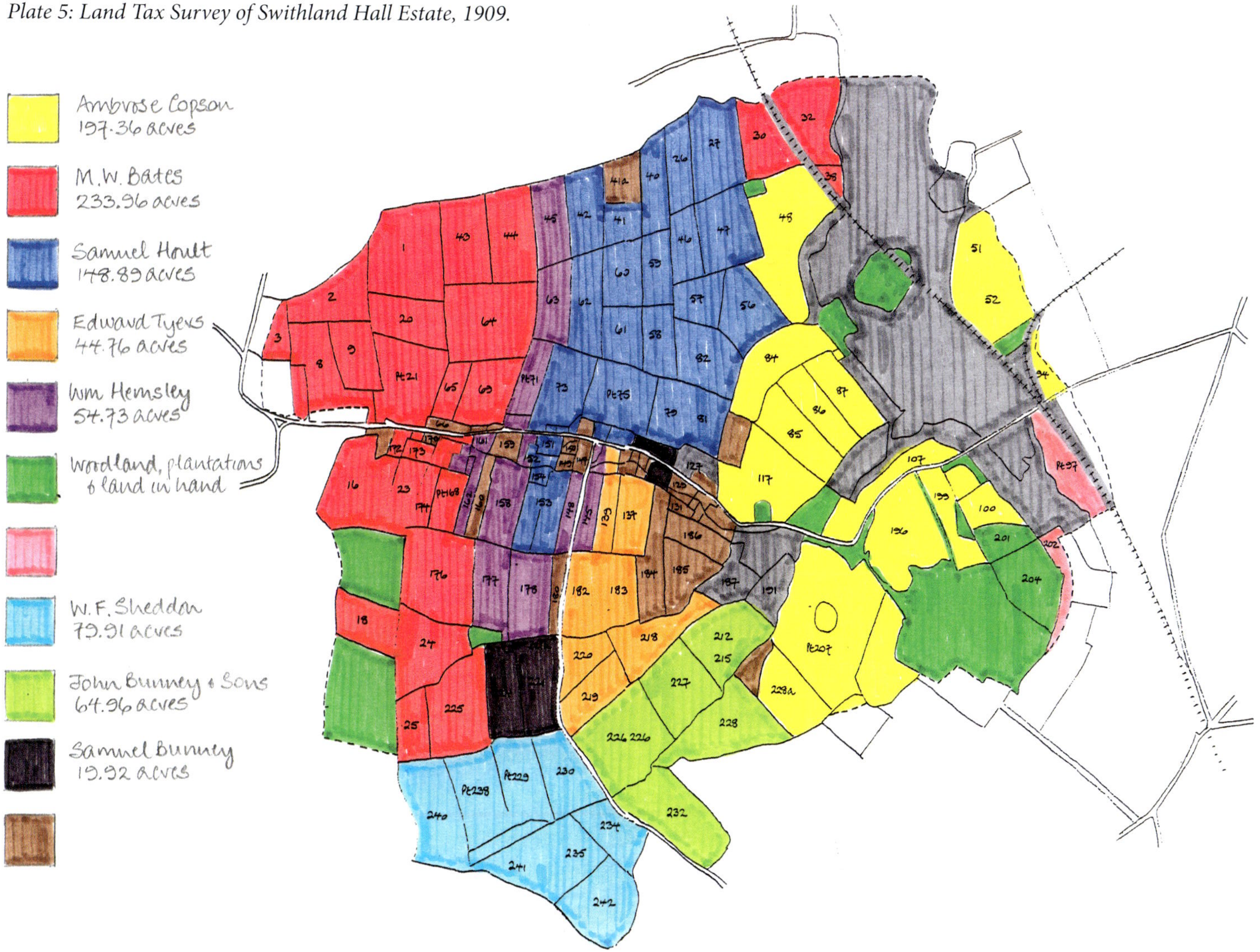

Plate 6: Survey of Swithland Hall Estate Tenant Farmers, 1921.

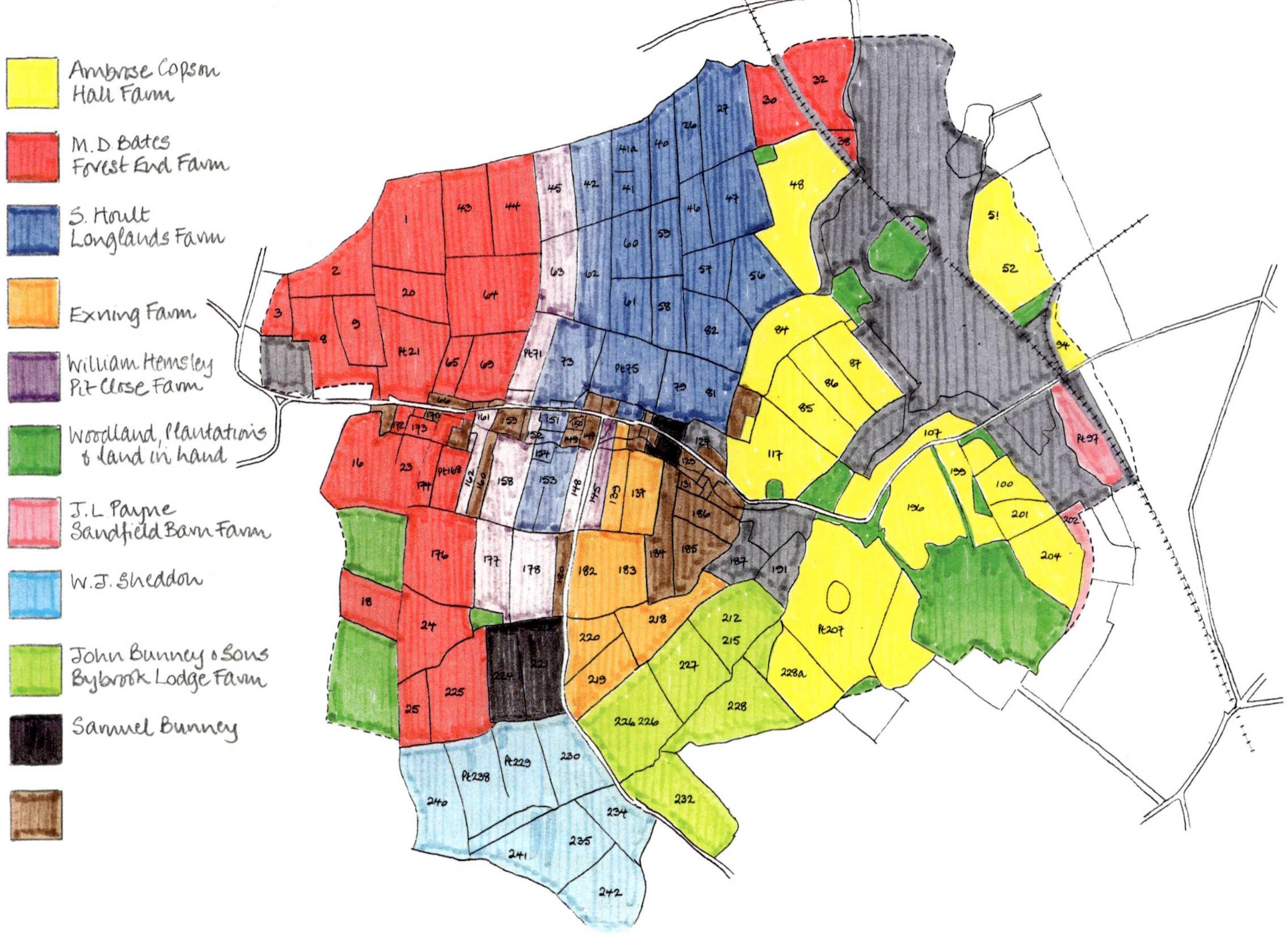

- Ambrose Copson, Hall Farm
- M. D Bates, Forest End Farm
- S. Hoult, Longlands Farm
- Exning Farm
- William Hemsley, Pit Close Farm
- Woodland, Plantations & land in hand
- J. L Payne, Sandfield Barn Farm
- W. J. Sneddon
- John Bunney & Sons, Bybrook Lodge Farm
- Samuel Bunney

Plate 7: Swithland Hall Estate Farms, 1954.

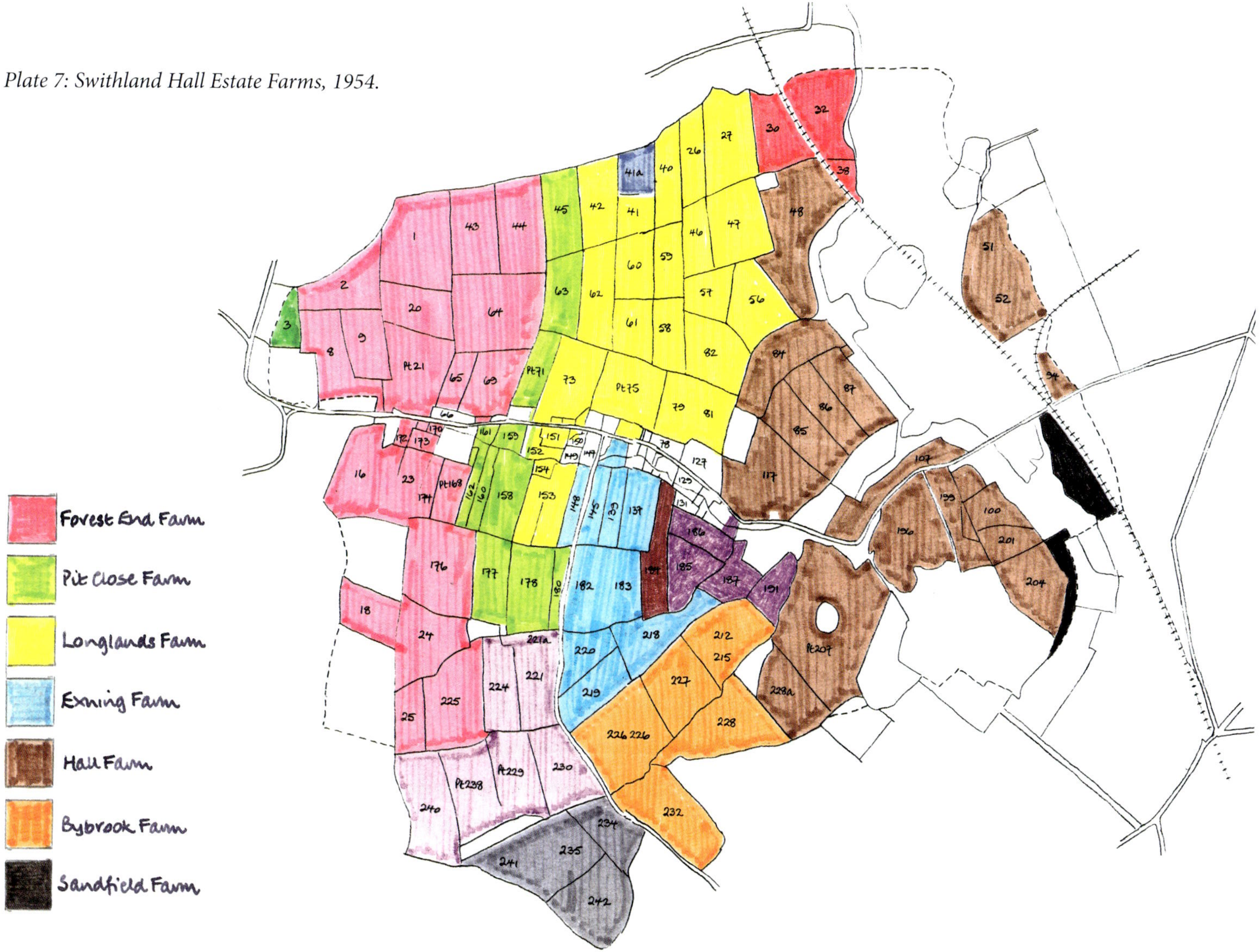

Plate 8: Swithland World War II Sixty Year Celebration Party 16th July 2005.

Kinchley Hill and Forest End – the Bates Family

Fig 8.5 The farmyard at Forest End.

The Bates family was another of Swithland's Victorian farming families. Thomas Bates was born in Woodhouse, but in 1818 his father took the tenancy of Kinchley Hill Farm, where Thomas succeeded him as tenant in about 1840. On Thomas' death it was farmed by his widow Juliana until her death in 1877, then briefly by his grand-daughter Catherine Anne until 1881, and finally by his daughter Juliana Ann, until the farm was lost in the construction of Swithland Reservoir.

Meanwhile in about 1870, Thomas Bates' son, William James had taken on the tenancy of Forest End Farm. At his death in 1896 the farm was run by his widow Ann assisted by their son Matthew Daykin. The family connection with Forest End continued, as Matthew Daykin took over the tenancy until 1932.

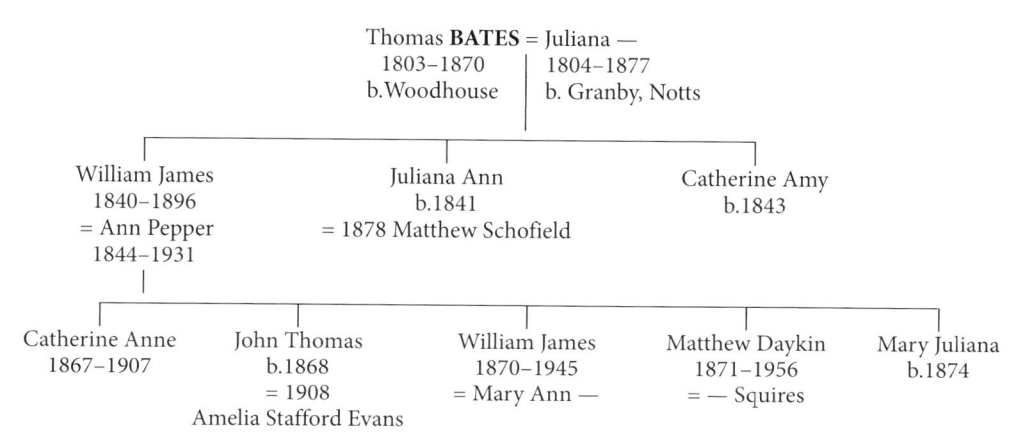

```
                    Thomas BATES = Juliana —
                     1803–1870   | 1804–1877
                     b.Woodhouse | b. Granby, Notts
    ┌───────────────────────┼───────────────────────┐
William James           Juliana Ann              Catherine Amy
 1840–1896                b.1841                    b.1843
= Ann Pepper       = 1878 Matthew Schofield
 1844–1931
    │
┌───────────┬───────────┬───────────┬───────────┐
Catherine Anne  John Thomas   William James   Matthew Daykin   Mary Juliana
 1867–1907      b.1868        1870–1945       1871–1956         b.1874
                = 1908        = Mary Ann —    = — Squires
           Amelia Stafford Evans
```

Fig 8.6 Jack Leatherland of Pit Close Farm with his son John.

Pit Close Farm – The Hemsleys and the Leatherlands

In 1851 Pit Close was the smallest farm in the Swithland estate, being listed then as just over 6 acres. By 1954 it had been extended to about 50 acres. Daniel Bates farmed it between 1830 and 1858, though in 1851 twenty-five year old Benjamin Hemsley was listed as the tenant farmer. Between 1859 and 1875 it was farmed successively by William Howson and John Warren. The tenancy came back into the Hemsley family in 1880, with first Benjamin (1857–1938) and then his brother William (1865–1938) listed as tenant farmers. William's nephew John Leatherland succeeded to the tenancy in 1936 and passed it down to his son John in 1967. John Leatherland junior farmed Pit Close until he retired in 1996. When the estate was sold in 1954, Pit Close Farm was bought by Dr Maurice Barton who sold it on to Tom Boyden in 1973. The Leatherlands continued as tenant farmers until 1996, when they bought the farm.

Decline and Sale

During the golden age of Victorian agriculture in the 1850s and 1860s, the industry was buoyed up by high prices and expanding markets. Output per acre soared with the introduction of field drainage, crop rotation, artificial fertilisers and new machinery. But from 1874 an agricultural depression started. It was provoked by the cheap imports of foodstuffs from overseas, and was not to end until after the Second World War. Cheap grain from abroad made arable husbandry less profitable, so the general trend was for land to be turned over to grass. On the other hand, the milk trade was helped by the growth of the railways, which made urban markets more accessible, so that dairying tended to expand at the expense of grazing. Nevertheless, these remained difficult times. Tenants could only make a success of farming by drastically reducing costs, working in the fields themselves and accepting a lower standard of living. Landlords too were affected, as farms could no longer be let at the same rents.

For most of the nineteenth century, the Earl of Stamford retained his 25 acres on the Swithland–Rothley Plain border and the 9 acres around the White House in Main Street. In 1873, at the start of the depression, he sold these holdings to John Vansittart Danvers Butler, the sixth Earl of Lanesborough.[87] The land near the White House became part of Forest End Farm; the other land continued as part of Rothley Plain Farm, which the sixth Earl had purchased at the same time.

The last years of the nineteenth century saw the creation of Swithland Reservoir on the edge of the village, and the extension of the Manchester, Sheffield and Lincolnshire Railway through the village. Both projects required the acquisition of areas of estate land. Almost immediately after these significant land losses through compulsory purchase to Leicester Corporation and the Great Central Railway, John Vansittart Danvers Butler succeeded in buying up almost all the remaining ground in the village. First he purchased the small area at Forest End, allotted at the enclosure to William Clarke, and then, in 1898, from Rector Murray Dixon, some 154 acres of glebe land.[88]

At the beginning of the twentieth century, then, Swithland was still very much an estate village. The only parts of the village not owned by the Earl were the church, rectory and some 14 acres of glebe around the church, the Methodist chapel and the reservoir and railway. The glebe land that the Earl did buy was added to Hall Farm, which Murray Dixon farmed as tenant for a short time. In 1906, the seventh Earl exchanged land with Frederick Merttens, the Earl acquiring land on the boundary with Thurcaston. This allowed the creation of Bybrooke Lodge Farm, or Bybrooke Farm. The following year, Lanesborough sold the ex-glebe land at Anstey Pastures to Herbert Ellis and others.[89]

While the railways helped agriculture by bringing urban markets closer to remote farms, they also took away the farmers' best labourers, attracted by 'better' prospects in the towns. Farmers were no longer major employers. Between 1871 and 1911 the proportion of the national workforce engaged in agriculture nearly halved. The trend may have been a little slower in Swithland as the Great Central Railway was not built until 1898, nevertheless, whereas there were thirty-two agricultural labours in the village in 1841,[90] the number had dropped to twenty-three by 1891.[91] During this period of agricultural depression, both landowners and farmers were trying to survive on ever reducing incomes. Field drainage was practically discontinued, land was far less intensively farmed, bills for cake and fertiliser were reduced, fewer stock were kept on the same acreage, and fewer labourers were employed. The condition of the land deteriorated.

Hall Farm – the Copson Family

There were some, however, who took up the challenge of farming in Swithland in these difficult years. Ambrose Copson came to Swithland in 1903 as steward or bailiff to Rector James Murray Dixon at Hall Farm. In 1908, after Dixon's unsuccessful tenancy, Copson himself took on the tenancy. Allied to his dairy herd was a milk round, which was managed by his sons, Alfred Ernest and Harry. Shortly after the Great War, Harry and his wife Vera ran Hollycroft Dairy at 104 Main Street, with Alfred Ernest and his wife Edith who lived at Corner Cottage, 122 Main Street. Ambrose's second son, Charles, took on the tenancy of Brickyard Farm, Rothley in 1923. At a time when betting was illegal, it was not unknown for roundsmen to act as bookmakers' runners. It is supposed that, in the course of their milk rounds, Harry and Alf gave way to the temptations of betting and drinking – at a level that could only be sustained through defrauding their father. The result was that Ambrose found difficulty in paying his debts. Ambrose was forced to leave Hall Farm in 1932, and lodged with Alf and Edith at Corner Cottage. His difficulties, however, continued. One Christmas Day he fell out with his son and daughter-in-law, and was ejected from the house. He was offered shelter by Jack Leatherland at Pit Close Farm, where he lodged until his death shortly afterwards in 1943.

The End of the Estate

In the first part of the twentieth century owners of land multiplied in Leicestershire as large estates were reduced in size or sold off. Small disposals of properties in Swithland were occasionally made. In 1903, Archibald Turner purchased some land (a detached part of Newtown parish) from the Earl of Stamford and Warrington, between the Swithland triangle and the parish boundary; in 1908 he took out a twenty-nine year lease from the Earl of Lanesborough on the adjacent property known as The Cottage. In 1917, the freehold interest in The Cottage was bought by his wife, Gladys Marie Turner.[92] In 1920 the Earl gave a small area of land to the village for the construction of a war memorial and Memorial Hall. On Sunday 4th December 1921, the war memorial was unveiled by Captain R. Gee VC, MC, MP and dedicated by the Archdeacon of Loughborough, the Ven P.H. Bowers.

Effectively, however, at the turn of the century, the integrity of the Swithland estate, unlike many others, was largely retained. It was, however, subject to substantial mortgages. In 1921, a report on the estate was presented to enable Lord Lanesborough to borrow £20,000.[93] There was little or no new building, but in 1924 the Earl of Lanesborough did acquire the remaining 14 acres of glebe.

Prosperity began to return to agriculture after 1945, though it was too late to save the estate. Meanwhile, the traditional patterns were maintained. The combination of rent payment day with lunch for the tenant farmers at the Griffin Inn was one such tradition. David Hunt, for example, was invited by Lanesborough's land agents, Frank Newman & Son, to attend the

AMBROSE COPSON Tenant of Hall Farm, Swithland 1903–34

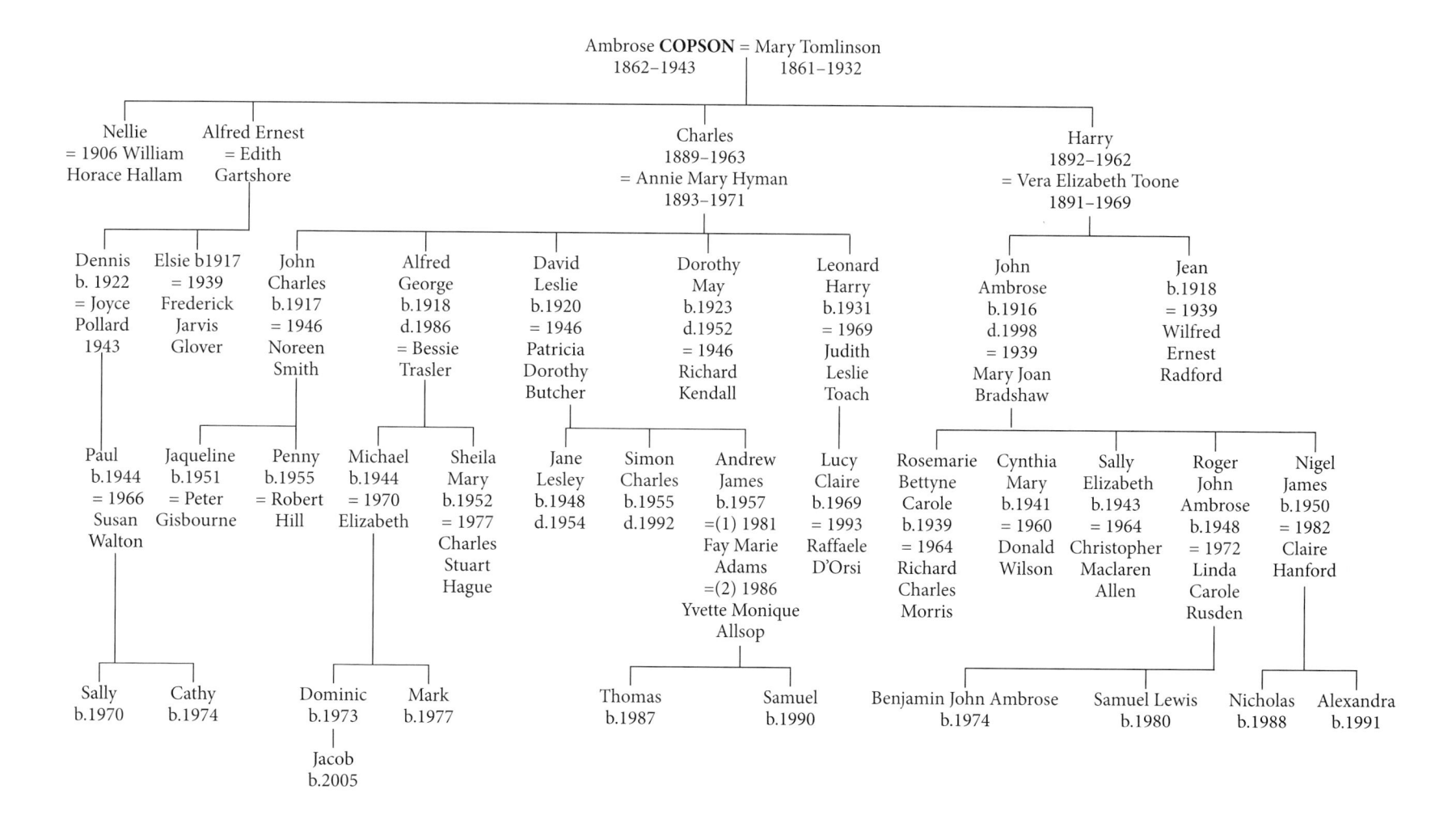

Ambrose **COPSON** = Mary Tomlinson
1862–1943   1861–1932

Nellie
= 1906 William Horace Hallam

Alfred Ernest = Edith Gartshore

Charles 1889–1963 = Annie Mary Hyman 1893–1971

Harry 1892–1962 = Vera Elizabeth Toone 1891–1969

Dennis b.1922
= Joyce Pollard 1943

Elsie b.1917
= 1939 Frederick Jarvis Glover

John Charles b.1917
= 1946 Noreen Smith

Alfred George b.1918 d.1986
= Bessie Trasler

David Leslie b.1920
= 1946 Patricia Dorothy Butcher

Dorothy May b.1923 d.1952
= 1946 Richard Kendall

Leonard Harry b.1931 = 1969 Judith Leslie Toach

John Ambrose b.1916 d.1998 = 1939 Mary Joan Bradshaw

Jean b.1918 = 1939 Wilfred Ernest Radford

Paul b.1944
= 1966 Susan Walton

Jaqueline b.1951
= Peter Gisbourne

Penny b.1955
= Robert Hill

Michael b.1944
= 1970 Elizabeth

Sheila Mary b.1952
= 1977 Charles Stuart Hague

Jane Lesley b.1948 d.1954

Simon Charles b.1955 d.1992

Andrew James b.1957
=(1) 1981 Fay Marie Adams
=(2) 1986 Yvette Monique Allsop

Lucy Claire b.1969 = 1993 Raffaele D'Orsi

Rosemarie Bettyne Carole b.1939 = 1964 Richard Charles Morris

Cynthia Mary b.1941 = 1960 Donald Wilson

Sally Elizabeth b.1943 = 1964 Christopher Maclaren Allen

Roger John Ambrose b.1948 = 1972 Linda Carole Rusden

Nigel James b.1950 = 1982 Claire Hanford

Sally b.1970

Cathy b.1974

Dominic b.1973

Mark b.1977

Thomas b.1987

Samuel b.1990

Benjamin John Ambrose b.1974

Samuel Lewis b.1980

Nicholas b.1988

Alexandra b.1991

Jacob b.2005

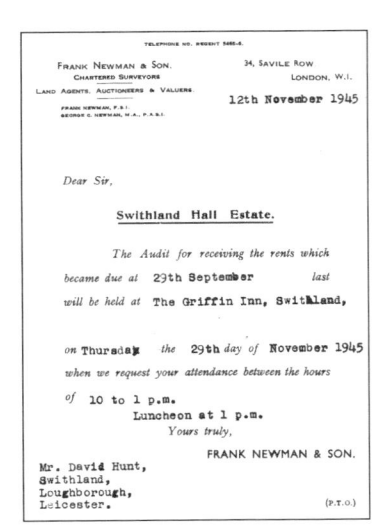

Fig 8.7 Invitation to the 1945 Michaelmas Annual Audit.

Michaelmas annual audit at the Griffin Inn, Swithland on Thursday the 29th November 1945 between the hours of 10–1pm, with luncheon at 1pm. Hunt, who tenanted land near Exning Wood, the gardener's house and the old Hall kitchen gardens, as well as the old rectory premises and grounds, was charged the half yearly rent of £55 18s. 0d.[94]

In 1954 the ninth Earl decided to sell most of his land holding in Swithland, Mountsorrel, Rothley and Thurcaston. He retained Swithland Hall, the woodland and plantations, and a few cottages (the lodges to the Hall, Keepers Lodge and Hall Gardens) but put up some 15,376.566 acres for auction. The properties were offered

Fig 8.8 Swithland Estate tenants 1945 at the Griffin Inn.
Back row [left to right]: David Hunt Snr (Cropston land & later Hall Gardens), Fred Chantrell (Bybrook Farm), Harry Banbury (Hall Farm), Charles Pratt (136, Main Street), Fred Copson, (140, Main Street), Ben Bunney (Exning Farm), Roland Payne Jnr (Sandhills Farm, Rothley), Harry Copson (104, Main Street), John Wallis, (Thurcaston).
Front Row [left to right]: Bill Pepper, Samuel Hoult, (Longlands Farm), Len Payne Snr (Sandhills Farm, Rothley), George Walker, (Forest End Farm), Frank Newman Agent, Frank Newman's son, Samuel Briers, (Griffin Inn)

to sitting tenants (see page 212 for tenants of Swithland farms) for sale before the auction, by private treaty, and many took up the offer. The remaining other properties and lots simply went under the auctioneer's hammer on Thursday 22nd July 1954 (see page 213 for sale details).

Swithland Hall Estate: Principal Farms 1851 (Acres in Swithland)

FARM	1903	1909	1921	1944	1954
Hall Farm	399	197	236	234	173
Forest End Farm	235	234	234	201	186
Longlands Farm	181	149	147	148	147
Exning Farm	38	45	45	51	49
Bybrooke Farm	-	65	65	186	66
Pit Close Farm	36	55	54	49	51

Source: Survey of Swithland Hall Estate 1903;[95] Land Tax Valuation 1909;[96] Survey of Swithland Hall Estate 1921;[97] MAFF Agricultural Census 1944; Swithland Hall Estate Sale Particulars 1954.

The sale of the Estate did not mean the end of farming in Swithland. Here, though, as elsewhere in the country, farms were retained in hand, rather than being tenanted; mixed farms were replaced by more specialist husbandry; farm units were increased in size in order to remain viable; many of the farm buildings proved inappropriate for more mechanical means of production. The land attached to Exning Farm was amalgamated with that of Bybrook Farm; Forest End farmland was farmed from Rushey Fields Farm, Woodhouse. Both farmhouses were converted to private residences. Longlands Farm was farmed in conjunction with other land outside the parish. Hall Farm, the largest unit, was the only farm of sufficient size to continue on its own, but in order to survive, Brian Beeby, the owner from 1984, had to diversify – first into livery stabling, and then, from 2000 into sourcing, bottling and distributing Swithland Spring Water.

Swithland Hall, together with the land nearest the Hall, was bought in 1979 by Adam Page. Some land nearest to the Hall was purchased at the same time, and additional land in 1999. Thus the integrity of the Hall as a private dwelling place with a certain amount of agricultural land surrounding it has, for the time being, been maintained.

Tenants of Swithland Farms

KINCHLEY HILL FARM:

1766–1775	Richard Fowkes	1818–1832	William Bates
1777–1781	John Hill	1841–1870	Thomas Bates
1782–1795	John Johnson jr of Beaumanor	1871–1877	Juliana Bates
1796–1798	Ralph Tebbutt jr	1878–1881	Catherine Anne Bates
1799–1817	Richard Burchnall of Cropston	1881–1894	Juliana Bates

HALL FARM:

1753–1796	[Sir John Danvers]	1877–1880	David Cuffling
1797–1803	[Augustus Richard Butler Danvers]	1881–1900	Mary Ann Cuffling
1804–1829	David Chapman	1900–1902	William Henry Cuffling
1830–1832	William Whatoff	1903–1908	James Murray Dixon
1841–1851	George Morris	1908–1932	Ambrose Copson
1851–1876	William Cuffling	1935–1956	Harry Banbury

FOREST END FARM:

1815–1827	Matthew Simpson	1912–1925	Mary Juliana Bates and Matthew Daykin Bates
1828–1854	William Simpson		
1861–1863	Charlotte Simpson	1928–1932	Matthew Daykin Bates
1871–1896	William James Bates	1935–1956	George Douglas Walker
1900–1908	Ann Bates Matthew Daykin Bates		

LONGLANDS FARM:

1846–1854	John Oldershaw	1908–1935	Samuel Hoult
1861–1863	Edward Wildman	1941	Mary Ann Cockerill
1871–1881	John Cuffling	1944–1975	A.W. Cockerill & Sons
1883–1904	Edwin Pepper		

EXNING FARM:

1801–1817	William Leake	1861–1875	George Harris
1818–1827	Matthew Simpson	1880–1916	Edward Tyers
1828–1832	William Simpson	1922–1935	Benjamin Bunney
1851–1854	Henry Thompson	1941–1956	Charles Benjamin Bunney

PIT CLOSE FARM:

1830–1858	Daniel Bates	1908–1935	William Hemsley
1859–1863	William Howson	1936–1967	John William Leatherland
1871–1875	John Warren	1967–	John William Leatherland, jnr
1880–1904	Benjamin Hemsley		

BYBROOKE FARM:

1871–1891	Charles Bunney	1932	John Morris
1895–1925	John Bunney	1934–1944	Frederick Chantrell

Source: conveyances, land tax return, census, commercial directories, farm surveys.

Sale of Swithland Hall Estate 1954

LOT	PROPERTY	ACRES	TENANT
1	Forest End Farm, Swithland (no.60)	186.101	Mr G. Walker
2	Pit Close Farm Swithland (no.106)	50.777	Mr J.W. Leatherland
3	Longlands Farm, Swithland (no.112)	147.297	Mrs A.M. Cockerill & Sons
4	Exning Farm, Swithland (no.130)	48.819	Mr C.B. Bunney
5	Hall Farm, Swithland (no.227)	223.487	Mr H.A. Banbury
6	Bybrook Farm, Swithland	146.643	Mr F. Chantrell
7	5 enclosures	60.462	Mr G.L. Sibson
8	Arable land	5.303	Mr G. Walker
9	Enclosures	3.981	Leicester Corporation
10	Arable & pasture land	5.303	Mr G. Walker
11	2 enclosures	23.849	Mr G.L. Sibson
12	9 cottages, Swithland	0.938	Various
13	Forest House, Swithland (no.54)	0.339	Mrs M.E. Wainwright
14	Allotment gardens	1.030	Various
15	Cherry Tree cottage, Swithland (no.83)	0.235	Mr E. Minkley
16	Holly Croft, Swithland (no.104)	0.720	Mrs M.J. Copson
17	118 Main Street, Swithland	1.546	Mrs C.A. Pratt
18	122 Main Street, Swithland	0.943	Mr A.E. Copson
19	123-125 Main Street, Swithland	0.398	Mrs T. Smith & Mr C.E. Baxter
20	127 Main Street, Swithland	0.268	Mr J. Bunney
21	Frontage land	0.888	Mrs A.M. Cockerill & Sons
22	132 Main Street, Swithland	0.239	Mr H.A. Banbury
23	134 Main Street, Swithland	0.253	Mr & Mrs H.M. Harrison
24	136–138 Main Street, Swithland	0.496	Mr R.S. Harrison & Mr A.E. Stevenson
25	140–142 Main Street, Swithland	0.338	Mr S. Bunney & Mr A.E. Hubbard
26	Paddock	1.201	Mr I.L. Berridge
27	160 Main Street, Swithland	1.483	In hand
28	School House & School	0.230	Miss Dixon & Leics County Council
29	Hall Gardens, Swithland (no.217)	3.550	Mr D. Hunt
30	4 enclosures	20.945	Mr S. Briers
31	Pasture Lane	6.715	Mrs Pratt
32	Pasture Lane	2.734	Mr C.B. Bunney
33	Pasture Lane	2.445	Mr J.W. Leatherland
34	3 enclosures	34.104	In hand
35	4 enclosures	27.146	Mr D. Hunt
36	Enclosure	5.129	Mr F. Chantrell
37	Sandfield Farm, Thurcaston	72.511	Mr A.L. Whittle
38	Gravel Pit, Thurcaston	7.151	Swithland Sand & Gravel Co
39	Vine House Farm, Thurcaston	129.904	Mr C.H. Green & Mr T.H. Green
40	Frontage land, Thurcaston	1.887	Mr C.H. Green & Mr T.H. Green
41	Frontage land, Thurcaston	4.243	Mr C.H. Green & Mr T.H. Green
42	Enclosure	3.247	Mr A.L. Whittle
43	Bybrook Farm	38.828	Mr S.A. Wallis
44	Corner site	0.807	Mr S.A. Wallis
45	4 enclosures	36.480	Mr H.A. Bunney
46	3 enclosures	12.218	Mr G.L. Sibson
47	Allotments, Thurcaston	1.936	Mr R.C. Seal
48	78 Rectory Lane, Thurcaston	0.124	Mr H.B. Shortland
49	4 cottages	0.390	Various

Notes to Chapter 8

1. Modern 'fields' are not fields in the mediaeval sense, but 'closes'.
2. Leics. RO, QS47/1/44 and DE40/54 Swithland Enclosure Award. Names as cited in the award.
3. The hay-making season.
4. Rothley Plain and Charnwood Forest were enclosed in 1829.
5. John Nicholls, *The History and Antiquities of the County of Leicester*, III, 2, p. 1047, Swithland: Esch.45EdwIII.No.22,Leic.
6. Incomplete references in G.F. Farnham, 'Charnwood Forest, The Charnwood Manors', in *Leicestershire Archaeological Society Transactions*, 1928/29.
7. Will of Edmund Shepey Esq of Smythsby Co Derby proved 23 November 1509.
8. One of two approximately equal parts.
9. Leics. RO, Mss of Earl Cowper KG, vol 2, p.103.
10. ibid., p.159.
11. This is a compendium of field names. Names changed or were adopted at different periods of history.
12. Leics. RO, DE4211, Newspaper article from 1950 by 'JC' on the Kendall family (general information). See also Smisby parish website. Kendall died in 1627.
13. Leics. RO, 44'28/676.
14. Leics. RO, 44'28/677.
15. Leics. RO, 44'28/678.
16. Leics. RO, 44'28/680.
17. Leics. RO, 44'28/681.
18. Leics. RO, 44'28/679.
19. G.F. Farnham, *Charnwood Forest and its Historians*, p. 94.
20. Leics. RO, C142, 487, Ch (2) No. 16, Inquisition Post Mortem.
21. Leics. RO, 2D 31/10, Deed of 4 June 1634, Daniell Baker on behalf of William Danvers of Sweathland.
22. Leics. RO, DE1982/181, 1658, Survey of Groby Manor.
23. Leics. RO, DE73/299, 437, 515, 497, 612.
24. Leics. RO, DE1982/181.
25. Leics. RO, DE1750, Box 22, lease, 1697, Elizabeth Danvers to John Bennet.
26. Leics. RO, DE 1982/182, Estate Book.
27. Leics. RO, DE1750, Box 31.
28. ibid., Box 22, Counterpart lease, 1741, Joseph Danvers to Henry Hind.
29. ibid., Box 22, Lease, 1741, Joseph Danvers to Joseph Ayres.
30. ibid., Box 22, Counterpart lease, 1753, Sir John Danvers to Joseph Johnson, house in Swithland.
31. ibid., Box 18, mentioned in Agreement Quadropartite, 12 Oct 1747, conveyance to Joseph Prior in trust for Sir Joseph Danvers.
32. ibid., Agreement Quadropartite 1747.
33. ibid.
34. ibid.
35. ibid.
36. Leics. RO, 44'28/677.
37. Leics. RO, DE73/248, Will, Jane Blakwing, dated 1675, proved 1696. 'And my will is that when my grandchild Henry Branson shall enter on the close that I bought of Mrs Templar called the Rie close...'
38. Leics. RO, 13D28/12/33, Indenture 7 Aug 1694 between Sarah Templar and Stephen Clarke of Swithland.
39. Leics. RO, DE1750, Box 16, Settlement after marriage, 18 Nov 1711.
40. Leics. RO, DE73/388, Will, William Clarke 1732, also DE1750 Box 19.
41. Leics. RO, DE73/248, Will, Jane Blakwing, dated 1675, proved 1696.
42. Leics. RO, DE73/393, Will, Jane Braunston, 1732.
43. Leics. RO, DE1750, Box 24, Conveyance, William Brawnston to Joseph Prior, 1734.
44. ibid., Box 18, Conveyance, Henry Brawnston to Joseph Prior, 9 June 1742.
45. ibid., Box 17, Conveyance.
46. ibid., Box 25, Indenture, 11 Dec 1775, messuage with shop yard, garden and close and four pieces of land, one 'called west or windmill field'.

47. ibid., Box 26, Thomas Hinde to Robert Gilbert, the Mill Close, 1684.
48. ibid., Box 26, Conveyance to Arthur Gilbert, 19 July 1623.
49. ibid., Box 24, Conveyance, Henry Fletcher to Arthur Gilbert, 16 October 1633.
50. ibid., Box 5, 1722 lease, within papers relating 1761 lease.
51. ibid., Box 22, Counterpart 21 years lease, Joseph Danvers to Robert Gilbert, 1750.
52. Henry Gilbert (1685–1716), studied at Clare College, Cambridge, and became minister to a dissenting church near York, before dying at the young age of 31. cf. Chapter 7: Dissent. See also, Appendix A: Will of Henry Gilbert of York, 1716, Leics. RO, DE1750, Box 24.
53. Leics. RO, DE1750, Box 5, Copy of Will, Robert Gilbert, 1749.
54. ibid., Box 5, 3rd/4th April 1761, Conveyance of an estate in Swithland, William Gilbert to Sir John Danvers (includes the Gaul Close).
55. ibid., Box 22, Lease, Joseph Prior and William Porter, 1712.
56. ibid., Box 24, Conveyance, William Brawnston to Joseph Prior, 1734.
57. ibid., Box 16, Indenture, Joseph Prior and William Perkins.
58. ibid., Box 22, Assignment of mortgage, Ann Coley to Joseph Prior, 1742.
59. ibid., Box 22, William Porter, labourer, bound unto Joseph Prior, slatter, for £60, 1712.
60. Leics. RO, DE73/630, Will and inventory, Joseph Prior, 1766.
61. Leics. RO, 13/28/1/23, refers to Kinsley Hill Close, Swithland, which had been purchased by Francis Smalley in 1622 from Henry Kendall, Francis Danvers and Cornelius Smith, on which Smalley had built a farmhouse.
62. Leics. RO, 13/28/1/21, 12 March 1730, Admeasurement of Mr Smalley's land in Swithland by Samuel Wylde.
63. Leics. RO, 3D42/84/84/1-27, Documents 1775–1779 relating to Tebbutt family property at Ratcliffe on the Wreake, Swithland and Woodhouse.
64. Leics. RO, DE1750, Box 16, Letter 3rd February 1741, Joseph Prior, steward, to Sir Joseph Danvers.
65. ibid., Box 16.
66. ibid., Box 5.
67. ibid., Box 16, Legal opinion, 11 June 1756.
68. ibid., Box 3, Deed of Exchange, G.J.B. Danvers Esq and Mr Ralph S Tebbutt, 28 February 1828.
69. ibid., Box 5, Conveyance, William Gilbert to Sir John Danvers, 3rd/4th April 1761.
70. ibid., Box 16, Conveyance, 16 April 1779, Rye Close, Elizabeth Clarke, widow of John, to Sir John Danvers £110.
71. ibid., Box 16, Conveyance £106, William Perkins to Sir John Danvers.
72. ibid., Box 18, 1765, Conveyance, Mr Prior to Sir Jn Danvers, Bart, an estate in Swithland.
73. ibid., Box 5, Conveyance, Henry Branston to Sir John Danves, 14 August 1767.
74. ibid., Box 5, Conveyance, Mountney and others to Sir John Danvers, 20/21st March 1783.
75. cf. Leics. RO, DE1982/164, Lease, 1669, Fox Close, for 21 years, from Henry Earl of Stamford to Robert Jempson of Swithland.
76. Leics. RO, DE1750 Box 17, Conveyance, 1718, Mill Close and Cottage, Stephen Clarke to Samuel Clarke, both of Swithland. And in 1750 a bond for £320, and conveyance, Mill Close, John Clarke to Sir Joseph Danvers.
77. The design has been attributed to Robert Bakewell, Dishley Grange.
78. See also Leics. RO, MP41 QS62/299, Swithland Land Tax Returns 1773–1832.
79. Land Tax was first established in 1692. From 1780, under 20GeoIII c.17, duplicate returns had to be lodged with the clerk to the peace – to be used to establish voters' qualifications. The Reform Act 1832, which inaugurated Electoral Registers, rendered unnecessary the deposit of duplicate assessments. In 1798 the tax was fixed at 4 shillings in the pound and made a permanent charge on the land. Although Land Tax was paid on some offices of profit, on tithes and on some buildings, it was largely a tax on land.
80. Leics. RO, 3D42/5/8/9, Swithland Enclosure Award 1798.
81. ibid.
82. cf. Chapter 5: Local Government. In 1840, nine Swithland paupers were living in the Barrow Workhouse; 35 residents (including a William Bunney) were receiving out relief.
83. Leics. RO, DE1750, Box 9, Valuation of Swithland by S. Stone, May 1820.
84. Leics. RO, DE453/198 a&b.
85. Leics. RO, DE1750, Box 9, Valuation of estate belonging to Swithland Rectory by Samuel Stone, 27 Feb 1815.

86. ibid., Box 29, Settlement on marriage of Earl of Lanesborough and Lady Hunter, 22 Nov 1851.
87. Leics. RO, DE453/198 a&b, Stamford & Warrington's Swithland estate sold to sixth Earl of Lanesborough, 1873. See also Leics. RO, DE1750, Box 33, Conveyance, 1874, freehold hereditaments: Rothley Plain farm and a farm in Swithland (Stephen Simpson, tenant).
88. Leics. RO, DE1750, Box 30, 1898, Parts of glebe sold by Murray Dixon to sixth Earl.
89. ibid., Sale, 1907, Lanesborough to Ellis, Anstey Pastures.
90. 1841 Census.
91. 1891 Census.
92. Leics. RO, DE1750, Box 30, Sale details.
93. ibid., Report on Swithland Hall Estate, 1921.
94. In the Ladyday rent notice of 1958 Hunt was being charged the same amount of rent (£35) on Old Hall gardens and cottage (£30) and Rectory Gardens (£5) as he was in 1945. He was no longer tenanting the land near Exning Wood, because he had bought it in the estate sale of 1954.
95. Leics. RO, DE1750, Box 30.
96. Leics. RO, IR58/51189.
97. Leics. RO, DE1750, Box 30.

– CHAPTER 9 –

Woodland

Buddon Wood and Swithland Wood lie to the north-east and south-west of Swithland village. Both woods contribute to the setting and attractiveness of the village and are part of its history. All of Buddon Wood and parts of Swithland Wood were, at one time, owned by the Danvers of Swithland.

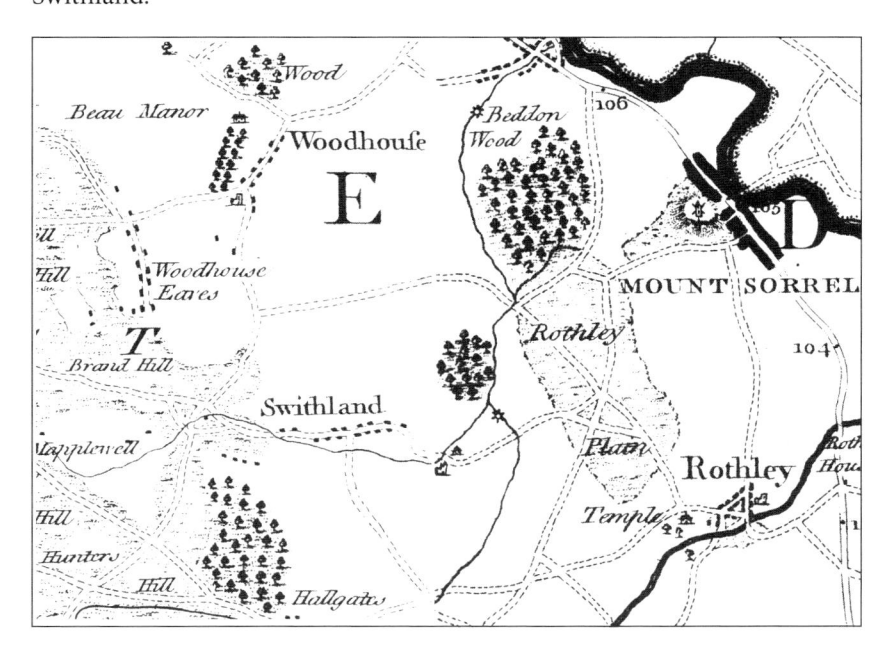

Fig 9.1 Buddon and Swithland woodlands, 1777, John Prior's map of Leicestershire.

Buddon Wood

The extensive area of Buddon Wood rises prominently at the north-east border of Swithland. It is one of the oldest woods in Leicestershire. At the time of the Domesday Survey (1087) it belonged to the manor of Barrow-on-Soar, of which Quorn was part. In the early part of the twelfth century the wood was part of the hunting park of the Earl of Chester.

At Roger de Somery's death in 1273, the wood was partitioned between his four daughters. Later in the Middle Ages, the greater part of the wood was acquired by the Erdington family, descendants of de Somery. When Thomas Erdington died in 1467, that part of the wood passed to the Crown and was granted to William Hastings, Earl of Huntingdon. In 1654 the sixth Earl of Huntingdon sold his part to Peter Cheveney for £2,100[1] in order to pay the sequestration fine the Parliamentarians had imposed on him. This part of the wood then remained with the Chaveney family until the death of Henry Chaveney in 1725. The 'Huntingdon section', having passed via William Busby[2] and heirs to Jane Symes,[3] was purchased by Sir John Danvers in 1770.[4]

A second part of the wood, to the south of the 'Huntingdon section', appears to have been owned by the Walcotes of Swithland and was divided at the same time as the manor of Swithland was divided. At his death in 1631, Francis Danvers owned one of these two parts, and in 1633 his son William Danvers purchased the second part from Henry Kendall of Smisby for £60. The remaining section of the wood – some 100 acres – was purchased by Sir Joseph Danvers in 1752 from Judith Letitia Bury of Headon, Notts. By 1770, therefore, the entire wood had been re-united in a single ownership, and it remained with the Danvers/Lanesborough family into the twentieth century.

John Throsby, writing in 1790, called the wood 'a fine embellishment to this part of Leicestershire'.

> Budden, or Button Wood, has been long admired: it is formed on a grand scale, either as a beauty for a background, a middle object, or taken in part on the foreground of the picture. In any point of view it is a fine embellishment to this part of Leicestershire.[5]

Fig.9.2 'Button Wood view', John Throsby, 1790.

During the nineteenth century, Buddon Wood was run as commercial woodland. A typical advertisement appeared in the 17th January 1840 edition of the *Leicester Journal*.

> The Annual Sale of Oak Timber with the Bark and Underwood will take place at the Griffin, in Swithland, on Friday, the 31st of January 1840 at two o'clock. By Auction. By B. Payne & Son. Joseph Cresswell gamekeeper of Swithland will shew the lots, of

whom printed particulars may be had; of the auctioneers or at the office of Mr T. Miles surveyor, Leicester. Dinner on the table at one o'clock.

At the end of the nineteenth century a very small part of the wood was compulsorily purchased for the construction of Swithland Reservoir. In 1925, the Lanesborough estates extended the quarrying rights of the Mountsorrel Granite Company to include the right to work Buddon Wood. Some quarrying was begun in the late 1930s, but activity ceased until the end of the Second World War. Leicestershire County Council gave planning permission to the Granite Company in 1946 to quarry the reserves below the wood. The quarry at Broad Hill in Mountsorrel reached the end of its workable life in the 1960s, and quarrying was started again at Buddon Wood. Redland Aggregates Ltd, who had purchased the Mountsorrel Granite Company, invested substantially to create the largest granite quarry in Europe. They operated with the benefit of a permission that had been granted in 1946. Then, because of the desire to re-build the country's infrastructure at the conclusion of war, controls were minimal. The effect of their operations has been that the core of Buddon Wood has been destroyed, and the height of the hill on which is stood notably reduced. Extensive landscaping has been put in place, but the substance of the wood has effectively disappeared.

Swithland Woods

Swithland Woods[6] lie at the western edge of the parish of Swithland. Today the woods are owned by the trustees of the Bradgate Park and Swithland Wood Trust and held for the quiet enjoyment of the people of Leicester and Leicestershire. Like Buddon Wood, it has an interesting history.

At the Norman Conquest this whole area of woodland and wood pasture was part of the lordship of Groby. In the mid-twelfth century, when the village of Swithland was established, the Lord of the Manor was ordering the clearing of woodland so that it could be put to the plough. Swithland's western boundary may therefore mark the extent of land that could easily be cleared. This westward expansion continued throughout the thirteenth century and possibly into the fourteenth, when much of the area of Swithland Wood was cleared and put to the plough. Indications of ridge and furrow cultivation can still be detected below the present tree cover.[7] The rocky terrain, however, meant that the land was unproductive and marginal, so when the Black Death of 1348 killed about a quarter of the population of Europe and land became difficult to let, the most marginal land was abandoned. The stony ploughlands within Swithland Wood reverted firstly to grass and then to scrub, with some self-seeded trees.

Today we think of Swithland Woods as one wood, but its gradual establishment is a story of several adjacent woods, four in Newtown Linford civil parish (Stamford's Woods) and two in Swithland (Danvers' Woods). The names given to these sections have not always been consistent and there has sometimes been some variation in the regime within a section, but the various woods were divided by ditches or earth banks, some remains of which are still evident.[8] The woodbank and slate wall that marked the southern boundary of the wood can also still be seen.

Danvers' Woods

Danvers' two woods lie within the parish of Swithland: Stocking Wood to the north and White's Wood (variously known over the years as Little Moore, Lane Hay and Squire's Wood) immediately to the south of it. Both woods were held by the Waleys and Walcote families whilst they held the lordship of Swithland. When the manor of Swithland was divided in 1429, both areas went to the Shepeys. By 1511 a wood was clearly established on the northern parcel as an Inquisition Post Mortem on lands owned by Edward Shepey showed 10 acres of wood in Swithland – an area later known as Kendall's Stocking Wood. The Shepey inheritance, including this wood, duly passed to the Kendall family and, in 1629 was sold to Francis Danvers. Francis Danvers clear-felled Kendall's Stocking Wood in 1630 and established White's Wood on the ground to the south that he had recently acquired. The northern parcel of land was still in pasture at the death of William Danvers in 1656, when it was known as North Hey close. This close was subsequently replanted. In a survey of Groby Manor in 1658, Danvers is recorded as owning 'a parcel of wood lying on the east side of Great Lyns called Little Moore, or Lane Hey, sometimes White's Land'.[10] John Danvers' marriage settlement of 1752[11] mentions both Squires or White's Wood and Kendalls Stocking Wood. At the Swithland Enclosure Award, both parcels are shown as woodland.[12]

Still evident in the woods, there are some distinctive slate boundary stones, engraved 'S' on one side and 'D' on the other. These stones, which mark the boundaries between Butler Danvers' land and that of the Earl of Stamford,[13] must have been put in place at about this time. The northern part of White's Wood was clear-felled shortly after the Enclosure Award, leaving the indentation that remains today.

In Newtown Linford parish, at some point after 1754, Sir John Danvers planted an area of pasture at the south-west corner of the present wood, now known as Hallgate Wood.[14] This was fully established woodland by the turn of the century, when it passed from Augustus Richard Butler Danvers to the Earl of Stamford.[15] At the north-west corner, another parcel of land, later called Little Linns, was also owned for a time by the Danvers. Probably planted before 1512,[16] it had become pasture by 1540.[17] Little Linns reverted

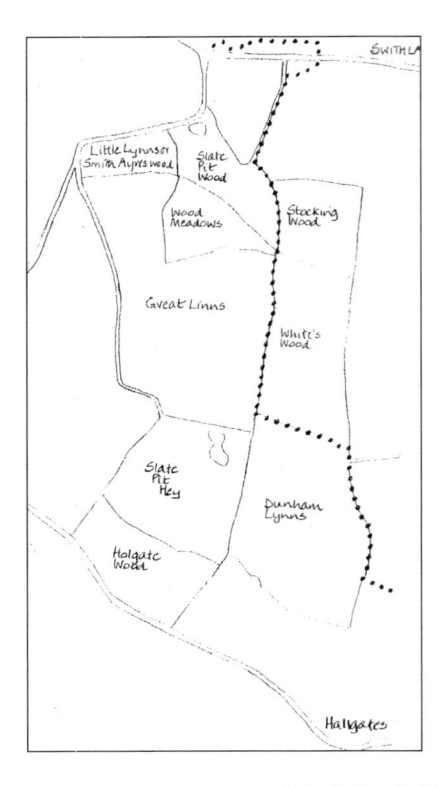

Fig. 9.3 The old woods within Swithland Woods.[9]

again to woodland in about 1600 and was described as 'springwood'[18] in 1656. The Inquisition Post Mortem on William Danvers in 1656 lists Little Linns amongst his property. Similarly, it was held as a wood by Henry Danvers in 1677 and mentioned in John Danvers' marriage settlement in 1752.[19] Little Linns Wood was sold to the Earl of Stamford in 1819[20] with the name of Smith Ayres Wood.

Stamford's Woods

This Danvers-owned ring of woods enclosed six other separate parcels of woodland which were owned and managed by the Earls of Stamford.[21] To the south of White's Wood, a parcel called Dunham Linns was planted shortly before 1670, and has remained woodland ever since. Slate Pit Hay was wood pasture in 1540,[22] when it was in the hands of the Danvers family, but was described as wood by 1677.[23] Great Linns South was described as pasture in 1657, but as a wood in 1677. Great Linns North was planted before 1512.[24] Slate Pit Wood was planted not long after 1677, was cleared between 1754 and 1759 and replanted by 1800.[25] The Earls of Stamford actively worked their woodlands. Estate records and advertisements for the sale of timber suggest that the favoured regime was coppicing, which took place at about twenty-one year intervals. An advertisement in the *Leicester Journal* of January 1784 advised:

> The Sale in the Manor of Grooby will be in Dunham Linns near Swithland Slate Pits, consisting of about 50 acres, which will be sold in pieces as usual, at the home of Wm Hughes, victualler in Newtown Linford, on Tuesday the 3rd day of February as soon as dinner is over. Dinner on the table at 1 o'clock. At the same time will be sold nine Oak and two Ash trees standing in Mr Hind's meadow adjoining the spring wood. The Bark will be sold at the same place on Thursday following.

Fig 9.4 [left to right] Benjamin Hemsley snr., Benjamin Hemsley jnr., and Joe Bunney working in Swithland Woods, c. 1900.

Sale of the Bradgate Estate

The woods were managed by the Greys until 1921 when Mrs Katherine Henrietta Venezia Grey, niece and inheritor to the seventh and last Earl of Stamford and Warrington,[26] sold a substantial part of The Bradgate Estate.

Fig 9.5 Swithland Woods in the early twentieth century.

One of the lots comprised Hallgate Farm, Swithland Wood Farm, two small grass enclosures, and 144 acres of Swithland Wood.

Swithland Wood was sold to local timber merchant William Gimson for £7,300.[27] The trustees for the sale, under a settlement made by the Earl's will dated 26 June 1875, were Katherine Grey, Harry Alfred Payne, the Hon. George Nicholas de Yarburgh-Bateson and Sir Edward Richard Henry. Some of the most valuable timber was felled.[28] But soon afterwards, members of the Leicester Rotary Club persuaded Gimson to sell the wood to them for £3,000, so that it could be kept for the use of the public.[29] The Rotary Club made an appeal for money, and the wood was purchased in August 1925.

The club decided not to become involved in forestry schemes, but to leave the wood more or less untouched. There was some discussion in the club about raising an endowment so that it could be given to the National Trust. But, in 1929, when nearby Bradgate Park became the property of the people of Leicester and Leicestershire through the gift of Charles Bennion and the Bradgate Park Trust was set up to administer the park, rotary club members decided that this trust was a more suitable body to take responsibility for Swithland Woods. They therefore approached the trustees in 1930 and transferred Swithland Wood to them in May 1931.[30] Words carved on the rock face of the first quarry record the gift.

Swithland Wood
Secured as a national heritage by the Rotary Club of Leicester
1931

Ecclesiastically speaking, only a relatively small part of Swithland Woods lies within the parish of Swithland, the rest is extra-parochial (not part of any ecclesiastical parish). Stocking Wood and White's Wood have always been part of Swithland parish. Wood Meadow, a roughly triangular area towards the north of the wood, was a detached parochial area of Newtown Linford ecclesiastical parish until 1998, when it was transferred into Swithland ecclesiastical parish. Also transferred to Swithland ecclesiastical parish from Newtown Linford in 1998 was the area on the western edge of the woods which contains Swithland Wood Farm and the adjacent caravan and chalet site.

Fig 9.6 The Great Slate Quarry, Swithland Woods.

Bluebell Service

In 1928, members of Swithland church asked the Leicester Rotary Club to allow an outdoor service in the wood. The then rector, Frederick James Oliver, and his churchwardens Walter Kilby and Percy Lloyd, had conceived the idea of an outdoor service among the bluebells. Oliver wrote to Mr Bedingfield on 31st March:

> I am given to understand by Mr Viccars of Rothley that you are the Secretary of the Swithland Woods Committee of the Rotary Club. He referred me to you in the matter of a 'Bluebell Service' which it is proposed should be held in the Woods about Whitsunday.
>
> This idea rose out of a conversation I had with one of your members, Mr Gimson of Rothley; he felt that the Rotary Club might be able to lend us their help and co-operation in arranging it.
>
> Would you be so kind as to bring this matter before your Committee and ask for the permission of the Rotary Club to hold the service? We should be very grateful if they would allow us to do so.[31]

Permission and support was duly given, one of the rotarians going so far as securing 'the services of eight wind instruments'. Rotarian Rev Allan Ritchie agreed to give an address – 'a brief lesson and a ten minute address as you suggest,' he wrote to Mr Oliver. The first service was conducted by Oliver on Whitsunday, May 20th at 3.30pm. The following year the arrangements were similar. The year after, 1930, Mr Oliver wrote to Mr Bedingfield regretting that 'the Rotary Club do not desire to co-operate in the arranging of the Service this year'.[32] They had no objection, however, to his carrying on as usual and arranging it himself, which he duly did. The 'Bluebell Service' has continued an annual fixture ever since.

Fig 9.7 The Bluebell Service, 1998.
[from left to right] Bob Osborne, David Pugh, John Roberts, Janet Roberts, Mary Hancock, Margaret Dixon, Canon Anne Horton, Revd Howard Ketton, Salvation Army band.

ORDER OF SERVICE
Sunday 20th May 1928[33]

Hymns
    City of God, how broad and far
    I vow to thee, my country
    O worship the King (tune Hanover)
Collects
Lesson – Rev AM Ritchie
Hymn   Lead, kindly light
Address – Rev AM Ritchie
Hymn   Jesu, lover of my soul
Short Litany – Rev A King, Vicar of Woodhouse
Address – Rev FJ Oliver, Rector of Swithland
Hymn   Abide with me
Benediction

In the early years a harmonium was wheeled into the woods to accompany the singing; Mrs Kitty Burrows accompanied at first, then Miss Gweneth Kilby. More recently members of the local Salvation Army band regularly provided instrumental support, and, since 2008, a band of students from Welbeck Sixth Form Defence College, Woodhouse.

Swithland Wood Farm and Camp

Land to the west of Swithland Wood was for many years part of the 'waste' that was Charnwood Forest. When the forest was enclosed under the 1808 Charnwood Forest and Rothley Plain Enclosure Act, virtually all the land up to Slate Pit Hill Road was allotted to the Earl of Stamford. In the early nineteenth century, the farmhouse on the western edge of the wood, now called Swithland Wood Farm, may have been used by some of those engaged in slate extraction, but at the beginning of the twentieth century its 72 acres was farmed by Mr Charles Illesley.

Many farmers in the Charnwood Forest area at this time allowed small groups of townsfolk to camp on their land in the summer. The forest air was thought to be healthy, and farming was experiencing a depression, so any supplement to their income was welcome. Like other local landowners, Illesley allowed people to camp on the land near his farmhouse. The first visitors stayed in bivouacs and bell-tents, but after the Great War, campers were allowed to build wooden chalets enabling them to stay for longer visits. The 'camp' also accommodated recovering soldiers from World War One. Swithland School records show that from 1922 children from 'Illsley's Camp' were occasionally on its attendance roll. In 1921, when the Stamford estate was split up and sold, Swithland Wood Farm was sold at the same time as Swithland Wood. The farm was purchased by Arthur Lane. Of all the forest camp sites, Swithland's became the most successful and most enduring. Camp committees were established to organise the social events.

> At one time two events arranged by the camp committee were the 'Sports' on Bank Holiday Monday and the End of Season Supper which was always held on the last Saturday in October ... Tables were placed in the Grey tea-room and after supper, singers and

Fig 9.8 Swithland Wood Camp Farm, c. 1920.

Fig 9.9 Fairey family members outside their Swithland Camp chalet, c. 1940.

comedians entertained us. Then there was dancing until midnight, and watches were put back, and the merriment continued for another hour only, otherwise we should have encroached on the first hour of the Sabbath.[34]

Given the paucity of the ground and the size of the holding, it is not surprising that in 1942 Arthur Lane's primary source of income came from rents from the camp, rather than from agriculture. After he died, the farm and the camp were run by his daughter. Planning restrictions now prevent the expansion of the camp, but for those who continue to own chalets, it remains a quiet haven in which to enjoy the countryside of Charnwood Forest.

Notes to Chapter 9

1. Hastings Collection, California.
2. Leics. RO, DE1750, Box 28, Settlement, Henry Chaveney to William Busby, 5 February 1722, tripartite indenture 1725.
3. ibid., Release and conveyance, Messrs Garnier and Keck to Mrs Jane Symes 12 February 1766.
4. Leics. RO, DE1750, Box 1, Bargain and sale, 7 June 1770, Mrs and Miss Symes to Sir John Danvers, Bart.
5. John Throsby, *Select Views in Leicestershire*, 1790.

6. S.F. Woodward, *Swithland Wood: A Study of its History and Vegetation*, 1992, 3.6.1. The name 'Swithland Wood' first appeared in a schedule of 1772.
7. ibid., 2.3.8.
8. ibid., 2.3.7.
9. Sketch, R.B. Osborne.
10. Leics. RO, DE1982/181, Survey of Groby Manor, 1658.
11. Leics. RO, DE311/7/2/, Marriage settlement, John Danvers and Mary Watson, 1757.
12. Leics. RO, QS47/1/44, Swithland Enclosure Award, 1799.
13. S.F. Woodward, *Swithland Wood: A Study of its History and Vegetation*, 2.3.9.
14. Leics. RO, QS47/1/44, Swithland Enclosure Award 1799, described Hall Gates Wood; LRO QS47/2, Charnwood Forest Enclosure Map 1828, described as Holgate Wood.
15. Leic. RO, DE311/45/5/1-2, Copy (1819) of Conveyance in Trust for sale of 3rd/4th July 1815, of seven farms and lands in Newtown Linford, Cropston, Quorn, Barrow, Rothley, Charnwood Forest.
16. Public Records Office National Archives, transl. Farnham, 1930, p. 115, Minister's Accounts, Henry VIII No 1824, 1512, Groby and its members.
17. Northants RO, T(S) 40/4, Account compiled 1539/40 by William Chesledon, 'Swithland, a pasture called Litell Lynds in the tenure of John Smythe'.
18. Leics. RO, DE1982/181, Survey of manor of Groby, 1658.
19. Leics. RO, DE311/7/2, Marriage settlement, John Danvers and Mary Watson, 1757.
20. Leics. RO, DE311/7/7/1&2, Lease and release, 8 and 9 September 1819.
21. These woods, too, have been variously named over the years: Great Lynns or Great Dunham Linns; Little Lynns or Little Dunham Linns; Dunham Lynns, or Dunham Linns Spring, or Slate Pit Wood; Slate Pit Hay or Old Slate Pit Wood.
22. Northants RO, T(S) 40/4, Account compiled 1539/40 by William Chesledon, 2 references: 'Swithland ... eight acres of pasture called Sclatepitthey'; '£12 13. 4d for divers trees called *polis* sold this year in Sclatpitt Hey'.
23. Leics. RO, DE1982/181, Survey of manor of Groby, 1677.
24. Public Records Office National Archives, Farnham, 1930, p.115 tr. Minister's accounts, 1512.
25. Leics. RO, DG20/Ma/236/2, c. 1800 map, part of Newtown adjoining the parish of Swithland'.
26. The seventh Earl died, and Mrs Grey inherited, in 1883.
27. *Leicester Evening Mail*, 28 July 1921.
28. Leics. RO, 21D69/21/1, Leicester Rotary Club papers, letter from Ferrers, 1925.
29. Leics. RO, 21D69/20, Leicester Rotary Club papers, minutes of Swithland Wood Committee.
30. Leics. RO, 21D69/20, Minutes of Swithland Wood Committee.
31. Swithland Church Archives, Correspondence between Oliver and Bedingfield, 1928.
32. ibid.
33. Swithland Church Archives, Service Order.
34. *Leicester Mercury*, 30 March 1998, Mr Leicester's Diary, quoting Leslie Sherwood, Leicester Living History Unit's newsletter.

– CHAPTER 10 –

Swithland Slate

Fig. 10.1 Millennium Commemoration Slate. [from left to right] Mrs May Musgrove, Mrs Sarah May (Parish Meeting), Miss Beatrice Bunney, Canon Anne Horton.

To mark the beginning of the third millennium, the people of Swithland commissioned an engraved slate panel to be set up in the grounds of the village Memorial Hall. The panel acknowledged the place within Swithland village history of those who, over the centuries, had worked the Swithland slate pits. The 34 inch square tablet, which was carved by local craftsmen,[1] was unveiled by village representatives, Miss Beatrice Bunney and Mrs May Musgrove in July 2001. The engraving, inspired by an eighteenth century lithograph, depicts a slate quarry being worked. The inscription reads:

This memorial commemorates all those who worked in the
Swithland Slate industry from the 13th century until its closure in
the late 19th century.
Placed here by the people of Swithland AD 2000

Swithland[2] slate could be said to be Swithland's main claim to national fame. The rock is pre-Cambrian, formed over fifty million years ago. Depending on the location of the quarry, the stone is coloured light-grey, blue-grey, green-grey or purple. The greatest concentration of slate quarries around Swithland was immediately to the west of the village, in Swithland Woods, at the Brand and just north of the 'Swithland triangle'. Quarrying in the Swithland area ceased in 1887, but the water-filled quarry sites remain to remind the visitor of what used to be a flourishing local industry, as, across the whole of Leicestershire, do the Swithland slate roofs, churchyard memorials and material used for house and wall building.

The earliest evidence of the use of Swithland slate is from Roman times. Archaeological evidence indicates that the slate, levered from outcrops or shallow quarries, was used for roofing and wall cladding. Diamond shaped roof slate tiles of the Roman period have been found all over the Charnwood area. Written records, which detail the use of slate in building work locally, date from c. 1300, such as a 1305 entry in the Mayor of Leicester's accounts. In 1343, a Chancery Inquisition Post Mortem lists, in property belonging to Henry de Ferrers of Groby (1303–1343), the quarries or 'sclates' in Swithland and Groby Park.[3] Swithland slates were used in 1377–78 for the repair of Leicester Castle, when the builders purchased some 1,500 slates from Swithland for 4s. 7½d.[4] Swithland slates were used in 1439 for further repairs. Other important local buildings incorporated Swithland slate. The Leicester Guildhall and Rothley Temple both had Swithland slate roofs, and slate from Groby was used for the construction of Kirby Muxloe Castle. From the late-fifteenth century, slate started to be used for purposes other than for roofing. Between 1491–1510 the drains and cellars installed at Bradgate were of Swithland slate and local slate was also used in the arches and floor of the Newarke in Leicester.

Slate was also used to create artifacts. From the late-seventeenth century, it became a popular stone for gravestones and this led to a flourishing slate engraving industry. The earliest identified gravestones made from Swithland slate date from 1673. The small tablet commemorating John Prier, died May 1673, which stands in Swithland churchyard is possibly the earliest one in Leicestershire. In the eighteenth century, many further uses for the stone were found, including sundials, clock faces, milestones,[5] datestones, paving slabs, fireplaces, troughs, presses, sinks, dairy cupboards, milk cisterns and gateposts. In 1944, Robert Martin wrote that 'many of the older farmhouses have slate troughs for salting bacon and for holding milk, and with slate slabs for the dairy pavings. The presses in which the famous Leicestershire cheeses were made usually had slate stone weights descending on to slate slabs, in which were channels for the escape of the whey'.[6] These artifacts were not just to be found in Leicestershire. The geographical position of the quarries, reasonably near the River Soar, allowed for slate to be shipped to Lincolnshire, Nottinghamshire and Derbyshire. The advent of the canals in the eighteenth century gave added impetus to the trade.

Seventeenth Century Slaters

But what of the slaters themselves? John Dodsworth was the first Swithland man known to have worked with slate. In 1611 Dodsworth, then aged about sixty-four, described himself in a Chancery Court deposition as tenant of 'certain slate pits from the manor of Groby'.[7] In 1646 the Earl of Stamford granted a lease to George Daft, William Hitch and Peter Bellamy of 'all slate pits, mines and quarries of stone in the forest of Charnwood'.[8] A further lease was granted in 1665 to George Daft of Mapplewell, John Wane of Cropston, Henry Squire of Swithland and Edward Callis of Woodhouse.[9] In 1690 'all the quarries and slate pits in Newtown Linford parish' were leased by the Earl of Stamford to William Perkins, John Lovett, Henry Lovett and John Hackett of Swithland. A lease on Brand Hill, which contained a 'delph' of slates was held by William Nicholles. Then in 1688, William Palmer of Wanlip granted to Henry Hind, Stephen Hind and John Bennet a lease for ninety-nine years on 'that area called Brand Hill for getting of slates in the forest of Charnwood'.[10] This lease may well mark the beginning of the direct involvement of the Hind family in slate quarrying. The Hinds were to dominate the industry for the next one hundred and sixty years.

The Hind Family

It may have been the need for oak bark that first brought members of the Hind family to the Bradgate and Swithland area. Some members of the sixteenth century Hind family were tanners and Leicester was well known for its long-established leather industry, which, until synthetic agents replaced it, consumed large quantities of the bark of local coppiced oak for the tanning process.

Various members of the Hind family became notable citizens of Leicester. Several were appointed Freemen of Leicester.[11] John Hynd (1540–1595), a tanner, became a freeman in 1565, chamberlain in 1572, coroner in 1584, and mayor[12] in 1589–90. His eldest son John Hynde (1576–1641), also a tanner, became a freeman in 1599, was elected councillor in 1599, chamberlain in 1607, alderman in 1611, and served twice as mayor – in 1622 and in 1638.

Records show that there were Hinds living in Swithland from at least 1620. The 1620 Lay Subsidy Roll lists Robert Hind as living in the village, and in 1622 he appears in a list of leaseholders from the Earl of Stamford in connection with a piece of ground called 'Ladyland' in the town and fields of Swithland.[13] In the same year Robert Hind, tanner, paid Henry Kendall £64 for a close of land called 'Milne Close',[14] though it was probably Robert Hind's son, Henry, who started the family interest in slate quarrying. Thomas Hind, a labourer and churchwarden of Swithland in 1633, may have been a member of the same family.

Before 1688, members of the Hind family were employed on the Earl of Stamford's Bradgate estate engaged in wood-keeping and in recording the visits of wood and slate collectors to the Swithland quarries.[15] Robert Hind's son, Henry, seems to have started the family business in slate quarrying. By 1700, two groups held leases for 'the getting of slates' in the Swithland area. Hind's group (Henry Hind, Stephen Hind and John Bennet) held the northern area of Brand Hill, while Perkins' group (William Perkins, John Lovett, Henry Lovett and John Hackett) held the southern area of Swithland Woods.

During the eighteenth and early-nineteenth centuries, the Hind family firm continued to expand. In 1706 Henry and Stephen Hind bought out their partner John Bennet in the Brand Hill lease. The area changed ownership again in 1727 when Archdale Palmer and John Palmer sold their interest to John Raworth.[16] The area of the Hinds' concession was increased by leases on those parts of Brand Hill which lay in Mapplewell manor: from William Raworth of Mapplewell in 1732[17], and from Francis Barber of Greasley, Notts, in 1755.[18] The Mapplewell land was eventually purchased by Henry Hind in 1777.[19] The Hind family appears to have worked the northern part of the Brand until about 1740, and the southern part from then until 1811.[20] In addition, the Hinds took over land from the Perkins group in 1738 by leasing Slate Pit Hill in Swithland Woods from the Earl of Stamford. (Perkins' group had worked the quarry, but to no great depth). In 1787 Henry Hind also took on the lease of the slate quarry in Groby from the Earl of Stamford.[21]

The original method of producing slates was for the stone to be dug out and kept until the winter. It was then sprinkled with water and exposed to the frost. In the spring and summer, the quarried stone was cleaved into slates. The great innovation the Hind family introduced to slate quarrying, in about 1740, was the use of gunpowder for blasting. It was an important element in allowing slate to be quarried to a far greater depth than before. In 1802, Nichols described the slate operations at the Brand.[22]

> The slate pits are very deep, extensive, and employ a great number of hands... an immense excavation has, within the last 50 years, been made... [Blue slates] are raised as blocks, first blasted from an almost seamless rock. The blocks are first cleft into slabs; and the slabs afterwards into slates... There are two large pits, which cannot be less than 40 yards from the surface to the bottom. The depth of soil to the stratum of the slate is from 10 to 15 yards. The blocks which form the materials of workmanship are blasted out of the rocks by what is called Drilling; which is performed in the following manner: A hole is bored with an iron drill to the depth of from three feet and a half to one foot. The hole is then dried out, and powder deposited at the bottom of the hole; a wire is then inserted until it comes into contact with the powder, upon which the hole is rammed very hard with clay to the mouth; then the wire is drawn out, and the orifice made by it which leads to the body of the powder is filled with powder; a small piece of touch paper with fire at one end is then applied to that part of the powder in the orifice made by the wire, and burns gradually, in order for the men to get out of the way. When it reaches the body

of the powder, the explosion instantly takes place... When the blocks are loosened, they are drawn up by a machine in pieces from one hundred weight to a ton and a half. When the rocks are blasted a good deal of water often flows out; and there are springs of water at the bottom of the pits, from whence the water is raised up by machines for that purpose... The blocks are sawed with hand saws, and are kept in a proper state for the operation of the saw with constant supplies of sand and water.[23]

Despite their economic success, the Hinds kept a careful and respectful relationship with their landlords. A letter[24] of 13th October 1780 from Henry Hind of Swithland to 'The Honorable Sir John Danvers, Baronet, at Swithland' reads:

> May it please your Honor,
>
> It gives me some pain to write to you on the affairs that you was pleased to mention to me on your return from the Quarry the other day, and I hope your Honor will not be displeased that I make those affairs known to you as near as I can inform, especially as you then said we must have some talk about these affairs.
>
> I have spoke with Thos Burton and viewed the Ridbands[25] which appear to have been got some time and who positively affirms that he asked leave to get a few in Mapplewell Grounds to bind up a rid of Goss or two for his own use which is all I know of it.
>
> Upon further consideration of the water course which your Honor was also pleased to mention. That course has been taken out of the Forrest in my time, with a piece of ground to it by old Thos Pollard which my father told me came out of Lord Stamford's Royalty, and I don't doubt but you may remember Lord Stamford's Jury going by the old Brook Course through the Middle of that Yard &c, &c, &c.
>
> And also another piece was added to the Yard in my time by the same person taken from your own Royalty.
>
> However this may be - it is not my intentions to dispute with your Honor as a gentleman to whom I owe much honor and great regard, on Accounts of favours received, and 'tis only for peace is the cause of these, and from which consideration I would wish to enforce by my endeavour to promote your Publick House which of late has been much neglected by my men though not by my wishes. You will also further observe that the last time that I was at Groby Court as thirdborough the Jury was interrogated on the occasion of making preventments &c, yet notwithstanding the necessity, or how far . . . right or wrong my Conscience said Peace.
>
> I am, Hond. Sir, your obedt. Servant at Comd.
> (signed) H. Hind.

The letter appears to reflect concern by Sir John about the diversion of a stream, probably at Swithland triangle. Hind attempted to assure him that the manorial boundary was unaffected and that a recent Groby Manor Court had confirmed the old course of the brook as the boundary. Sir John may also have been concerned about obstructions to the water in the stream. Hind reminded him that at the court, which he attended as a thirdborough (head man or petty constable), an acceptable arrangement had been agreed by the Court Jury. Hind's letter may also indicate that some quarrying was already going on at the western end of Swithland, next to the house at Swithland triangle.

Another matter of concern to Sir John was that the workers at the slate quarries were neglecting his public house, known in 1778 as the Wifforn,[26] presumably frequenting another, perhaps the hostelry on Brand Lane known at one point as 'the Slatesplitters Arms'.[27] An advertisement in the *Leicester and Nottingham Journal* in 1779[28] shows that the landlord there was offering amenities as much for passing trade as local trade. The house offered accommodation for the carriages of those visiting the slate quarries and also pasture for the droves of cattle that came through the villages.

One of the visitors to the slate quarries was John Throsby on one of his Leicestershire excursions. Describing his visit he wrote, 'In this lordship are excellent slate pits, part of which, I believe, has been purchased lately by Mr Hind of this place, and the others he rents of Lord Stamford. One of these pits I dreaded and remembered well; whilst, some few years since, viewing a steep precipice here, whose large rocky sides struck me with sensations of the sublime, I was near falling into another'.[29]

Towards the end of the eighteenth century, the Hinds' pitmen had an unexpected windfall.[30] They won a huge musical clock in Cox's Lottery, a prize reputedly worth £500.[31] The clock was said to be six feet high, 'standing on a solid brass frame with twisted glass pillars; the machinery supported by two oxen of cast brass, elegantly gilt, and adorned with pearls and precious stones, and containing a capital set of chimes, a spring clock and an infinite variety of movements'. It was purchased from them by Sir John Danvers and was among the household effects that were sold off in 1798 following his death, in a sale that 'attracted the notice of the neighbourhood for fifteen days'.

Housing

The men who worked in the slate quarries needed housing as well as hostelries. In Swithland, the boom in the slate quarrying industry had encouraged William Clarke, a husbandman, to embark on building a small 'housing estate' at the western end of the village.[32] The complex came to be known as Forest End. By 1788 three dwellings had been built, and by 1800 the site contained ten dwellings. In about 1819 Clarke sold five of the cottages to William Johnson the younger, who altered them to form nine cottages, so that by 1825 there were fourteen dwellings in all at Forest End. These dwellings had little more than one room upstairs and one room downstairs and were mostly built in slate, brick and thatch. The Hinds also built cottages for their workmen along Brand Road. The Woodhouse 1851

Census lists Thomas Bramley, William Bramley, John Raynor, Thomas Beston, George Bunney, William Spencer, Thomas Preston, William Clarke and Edward Voce as slate workers living along Brand Road, Woodhouse. Some of the names are familiar as members of Swithland families.

There are occasional references in the Swithland Parish Registers to slatepitmen. John Beasley and Thomas Beston were described as such in the last decade of the eighteenth century; a John Johnson worked as a slate cleaver. Census returns, too, show a small number of residents working in the slate industry.

Swithland Slate Cleavers, Quarry Labourers, Engravers &c [33]

1841	William Bunney, Thomas Johnson, John Morris, Benjamin Petts, Robert Raynor, George Thorpe, Samuel Thorpe.
1851	Thomas Lines, John Morris, Joseph Pollard, Robert Raynor, Joseph Shaw, Samuel Thorpe, William Thorpe.
1861	Samuel Bunney, Thomas Hill, Arthur Shaw, Charles Shaw, Joseph Shaw, William Shaw.
1871	John Adams, Samuel Bunney, Walter Bunney, Henry Burton, William Firth, Thomas Hill, Robert Raynor.
1881	Henry Burton

In the main, however, employment for those living in Swithland village was in agriculture, domestic service and framework knitting, rather than in slate. In any event, by the time of the 1841 Census, the slate industry was already in decline.

The Hinds had originally constructed a dwelling for themselves adjacent to their slate extraction operation at Brand Hill. The first Henry Hind died in 1732, and the business was taken up by his son Henry (1691–1773). Henry Hind II was born at Woodhouse Eaves, but moved at a young age to live near Bradgate. Towards the end of his life he moved his residence to Rushey Fields. In 1741 he took out a lease for sixty years from Joseph Danvers of Swithland of a 'messuage or tenement in Swithland, with the barn and outhouses, orchard, garden and homestead, lately in the occupation of widow Porter'. This is likely to have been for operational purposes as by 1773 the lease had been surrendered. In 1764 Hind was leasing the Bradgate Lodge house and yard, close to the south end of Swithland Woods, from the Earl of Stamford.[34] The lodge house, now called Hallgates, together with its enclosed yard, gave Henry Hind a workshop and storage area, with accommodation close by. He was succeeded by his son Henry (1726–1801). In 1787 Henry Hind III leased a messuage and land in Swithland, 'The White House', from the Earl of Stamford.[35] It was here that his son, the next Henry (1760–1820) was first based.

Developing Business

The opening of the Leicester Navigation Canal between Leicester and Loughborough in 1794 gave a considerable boost to the local slate industry, and further local extensions to the canal system also helped. Production of Swithland slate continued to grow. Somehow, the Hind family influence was always present. On 31st July 1801, an advertisement appeared in the *Leicester Journal*:

> Swithland New Slate Quarry, Messrs Shenton and Johnson beg leave to express their warmest thanks for favours conferred upon them since the commencement of their Business, and to assure their friends of their best Exertions to serve them with Articles of the first Quality, and at the shortest notice.
>
> Slates, Gravestones, ornamented and plain Chimney Pieces, Cheese-Presses complete, Milk Stones, Salting ditto, Sink and Hearth ditto, Slabs, Soughing, Hovel and Walling Stones, Window Sills etc. For accommodation of their friends an assortment of various articles in the above branches will be kept on sale at the Public Wharf in Belgrave Gate and Attendance given every Market Day at the White Hart, Leicester, and at the Anchor, Loughborough. B.B. Welch Slates at the above Wharf, also salt on lowest terms.

From c. 1800 to 1813, William Johnson, in partnership with Francis Shenton, a slater and engraver from Mountsorrel, worked a quarry on the edge of Swithland village, on the west of Brand Hill, which straddled the boundary between land belonging to the Marquis of Hastings and land belonging to Augustus Richard Danvers Butler Danvers. William Johnson, who would seem to have worked for the Hinds for several years as their quarry manager, lived at Hallgates before opening this 'new' slate quarry with Shenton. He used Forest Farm as a slate and workshop area.

Henry Hind had a hard business head when it came to dealings with his landlord, the Earl of Stamford. In 1807, the Earl of Stamford called in Robert Wyatt of Barton-under-Needwood to assess the true values of the Swithland and Groby slate quarries. Wyatt received little help from the Hinds. He reported to the earl:

> ...it is extremely difficult to obtain a correct account of either the expenses or receipts, without working at the quarry for some time, as interested parties will not disclose them.[36]

Nevertheless, he delivered an assessment to the earl in November 1807 that a rent of £156 was reasonable. The earl's steward, William Martin, advised Henry Hind accordingly. Martin reported to the earl in February 1808:

> I then offered Mr Hind the slate quarry with the house and the land he now holds at Mr Wyatt's valuation: he seemed quite surprised at the height of the value and immediately said he must give up all thoughts of taking it and would resign the property into your Lordship's hands.

Martin ascertained that the highest rent which Hind would contemplate was £100, and, despite Wyatt's valuation, recommended acceptance. The rent was agreed at £100.

Johnson abandoned his lease on the quarry at Swithland triangle in 1813, when he transferred his operations to a new quarry on the north-east edge of Swithland Wood, adjacent to Roecliffe Road. By then it would seem he was no longer working with Shenton, since the December 1813 advertisement in the *Leicester Journal and Midland Counties General Advertiser* selling the lease was issued in Johnson's name alone. Johnson operated his new quarry at Slate Pit Hill from 1813 until his death in 1832. The lease was then taken up until 1838 by William Bramley, Johnson's nephew and deputy quarry manager. Thereafter, however, quarrying ceased at Slate Pit Hill, though Bramley continued in the slate trading business until the mid 1850s.

From 1815 Johnson's old pit was occupied by Wilmot, but major extraction soon ceased. In 1822, the Hastings trustees sold their 2 acres of land on this site to Thomas Bainbrigge Herrick of Beaumanor, and in 1827 William Herrick sold the land to George John Danvers Butler Danvers, thus the two parts of the quarry came into the single ownership of Butler Danvers.[37] The cottage adjacent to the site – where 1 Main Street now stands – was occupied by John Pollard, the slate engraver from 1801 to 1817 and from 1818 to 1827 by Richard Preston. From 1828 to 1830 James North occupied the site, then, after 1830, Thomas Thirlby. All these men were simple quarry workers, rather than serious quarry operators.

The Hinds meanwhile continued to operate both The Brand and the Groby quarries, and to dominate the local industry. For all their mechanical expertise, however, they were unable to quarry at a depth lower than 120 feet as they could not keep the lower levels free from water. In 1811 operations ceased at The Brand, although the house there was retained. The Hinds moved their quarrying operation to Swithland Wood, where they re-opened the Old Slate Pit or Great Pit. At the same time, they continued to operate the old quarry at Groby.

Henry Hind IV had moved his residence from the White House, Swithland to Quorn Court, and from thence to Loughborough. Henry's son – yet another Henry (1786–1822) – did not long survive him, and the family business was taken over by his second son, William Hind (b.1788). As well as renting the White House and its 9 acres from the Earl of Stamford, William also rented glebe land in Swithland. In 1814 he was renting five closes – about 40 acres of land – at the side of the bridleway (then a private carriage road) from Leicester Lane to Swithland Wood. William Hind served as a churchwarden at St Leonard's in 1814 and 1817 and from 1828 to 1835. As churchwarden he also acted as a sequestrator when there were vacancies at the Rectory.

Twenty-one members of the Hind family are buried in Swithland churchyard, some of them under the two table tombs on the south side of the church. Henry and Sarah Hind of Ibstock Manor are buried, with their two daughters, in a table tomb on the north side of the church. The two

Fig 10.2 The Hinds table tombs.

daughters, Henrietta and Sarah, are associated with the foundation of the Hind Sisters Homes in Cropston, the older sister Sarah making provision for them to be built in memory of her sister, Henrietta, who pre-deceased her aged only thirty years. Other Hind family members are buried in Quorn churchyard: Henry Hind (1822), eldest son of Henry and Mary Hind; John Hind (1802–1880) and six members of his family.[38]

Fig 10.3 The Hind sisters' tomb.

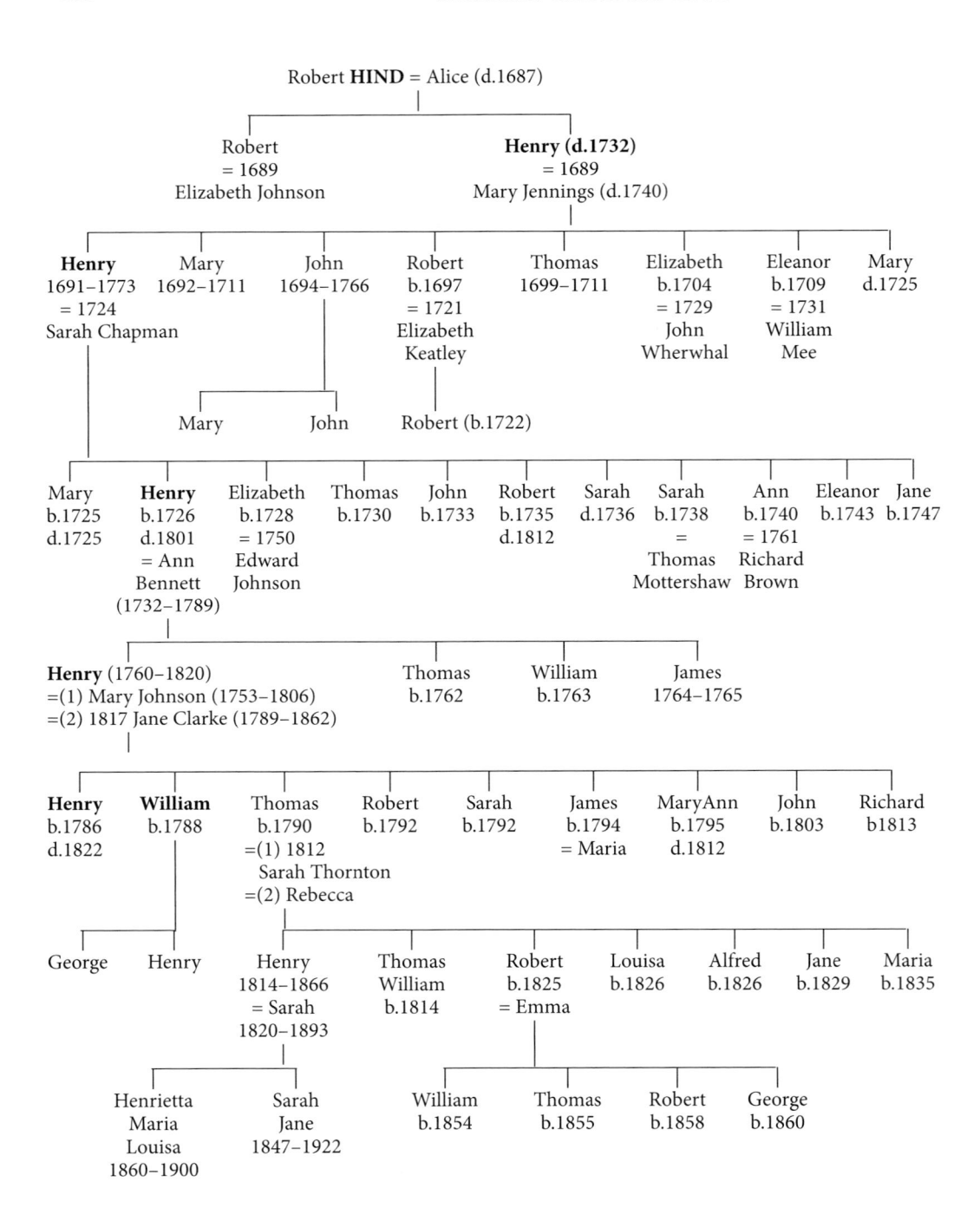

Robert **HIND** = Alice (d.1687)

- Robert = 1689 Elizabeth Johnson
- **Henry (d.1732)** = 1689 Mary Jennings (d.1740)

Children of Henry and Mary Jennings:
- **Henry** 1691–1773 = 1724 Sarah Chapman
- Mary 1692–1711
- John 1694–1766
  - Mary
  - John
- Robert b.1697 = 1721 Elizabeth Keatley
  - Robert (b.1722)
- Thomas 1699–1711
- Elizabeth b.1704 = 1729 John Wherwhal
- Eleanor b.1709 = 1731 William Mee
- Mary d.1725

Children of Henry and Sarah Chapman:
- Mary b.1725 d.1725
- **Henry** b.1726 d.1801 = Ann Bennett (1732–1789)
- Elizabeth b.1728 = 1750 Edward Johnson
- Thomas b.1730
- John b.1733
- Robert b.1735 d.1812
- Sarah d.1736
- Sarah b.1738 = Thomas Mottershaw
- Ann b.1740 = 1761 Richard Brown
- Eleanor b.1743
- Jane b.1747

Children of Henry and Ann Bennett:
- **Henry** (1760–1820) =(1) Mary Johnson (1753–1806) =(2) 1817 Jane Clarke (1789–1862)
- Thomas b.1762
- William b.1763
- James 1764–1765

Children of Henry:
- **Henry** b.1786 d.1822
- **William** b.1788
- Thomas b.1790 =(1) 1812 Sarah Thornton =(2) Rebecca
- Robert b.1792
- Sarah b.1792
- James b.1794 = Maria
- MaryAnn b.1795 d.1812
- John b.1803
- Richard b.1813

Children of William:
- George
- Henry

Children of Thomas:
- Henry 1814–1866 = Sarah 1820–1893
- Thomas William b.1814
- Robert b.1825 = Emma
- Louisa b.1826
- Alfred b.1826
- Jane b.1829
- Maria b.1835

Children of Henry 1814–1866 and Sarah:
- Henrietta Maria Louisa 1860–1900
- Sarah Jane 1847–1922

Children of Robert b.1825 and Emma:
- William b.1854
- Thomas b.1855
- Robert b.1858
- George b.1860

Final Years

A new quarry just to the north of the old Groby quarry was operated from 1833 by William Parsons and Abraham Gill, Leicester architects and surveyors. Gill died unexpectedly in December 1834, and Parsons surrendered his interest almost immediately. In February 1835 the Hinds took over the Parsons and Gill quarry, abandoning the old Groby quarry.

The construction of the canals meant that Welsh slate became available in Leicestershire from 1795. In 1831 a transport tax on carriage of goods by sea was repealed. This meant that Welsh slate, transported initially by sea to Liverpool, and then by canal throughout England, could now be supplied at lower cost. The market was flooded with cheap Welsh slate, and by the 1840s the Swithland slate industry was struggling. Welsh slates were lighter; so roofs could be built less substantially and therefore more cheaply than if Swithland slates were used. The construction of the Midland Railway further helped the Welsh industry. The Hind quarries continued to trade until the competition from the Welsh slate industry became too great. In 1849 William Hind gave up his leases both on the Great Pit in Swithland Woods and in Groby quarry, retiring to Whetstone.

In 1851 he sold the house at The Brand, as well as the land, slate pits, tenement, blacksmith's shop and garden, and several closes and tenements, to John Ellis. Thomas Rudkin, builder, took over Hind's quarry leases in 1850: from 1851 to 1853 in partnership with Fielding Moore of Glenfield, and from 1853 to 1865 on his own.

In the field in front of the Hind house at Whetstone Pastures,[39] William Hind erected an impressive obelisk made from the largest (reputedly) single block of stone of Swithland slate ever quarried. His intention, it is said, was that it should be inscribed thus:

> I, William Hind, of Whetstone Pastures
> Went through life with sore disasters
> But in spite of all my fate
> I bought these lands by selling slate.[40]

The seventeen and a half foot (above ground) obelisk still stands in the grounds of his old house, but the inscription was never carved on it.

The Ellis family, John Ellis & Co, took over the working of the slate quarries, applying modern business methods and machinery. In 1860 they re-opened the Brand quarry; in 1864 they took over the Great Pit; and in 1866 they took over the Groby quarry. New water pumping equipment allowed them to quarry to a depth of one hundred and ninety feet.

The operation of slate quarries was always hazardous. In 1828 Joseph Hemsley was killed 'by a blast at the Pitts'. In 1861 it claimed the lives of two more people in an accident reported in the *Leicester Advertiser*.

> The slate pit at Swithland was the scene of a deplorable incident, resulting in the death of a man and a boy and a horse. The pit was being worked by Messrs Bunney and Shaw and three boys. Last

Saturday, Shaw noticed trickles of earth running down from the bank about him but work still went on. After three loads had been drawn up to the crane, the bank upon which Bunney and one of the boys were standing suddenly collapsed. The two men, the boy and the crane horse were all buried, but after two hours Shaw was recovered alive. During the course of the day the other bodies were recovered.[41]

Both Samuel Bunney and Joseph Shaw were Swithland residents. Samuel Bunney (1819–1861) was buried in Swithland churchyard; the boy elsewhere. In 1861 Joseph Shaw (b. 1816) and three of his sons, Charles (aged 19), William (aged 16) and Arthur (aged 14), were all working at the quarry. By 1871, Shaw was no longer living in Swithland.[42]

The construction of Cropston Reservoir between 1866 and 1870 consumed large quantities of slate, mostly from Groby. But this business provided only a temporary reprieve. The Brand quarry was closed again in 1865. Local pride deprecated this development.

Every (Swithland) slate is worth three Welshmen, both in respect of durability and picturesqueness, although an age of cheapness and bad taste prefers, of course, the flimsier article.[43]

Finally, in 1887 the Ellis' pulled out. The Great Pit was abandoned, and the lease of the Groby quarry surrendered. The working of waste tips continued for a short time. The Groby quarry was operated from 1888 to 1897 by Charles Wesley, one of Ellis' workers. But slate production in the Swithland area ceased in 1887, and the quarries were left to flood.

Ellis sold The Brand in 1887 to Robert Martin of Anstey Pastures. Charles Wesley continued to trade in worked-up slate from Groby from 1897 to 1908, but there was no more slate production. In 1921, under the will of George Harry, seventh Earl of Stamford and Warrington (d. 2 Jan 1883), Swithland Wood was sold by his trustees. In 1925 it was purchased by the Leicester Rotary Club, and handed over to a body of trustees for public leisure purposes.

Engraved Slate Headstones

It had long been thought that the earliest engraved slate headstone in Leicestershire was that which marked the grave of the Revd Elias Travers DD, rector of Thurcaston 1628–41, now sited in Thurcaston church. Recent research,[44] however, suggests that the date of the Travers' memorial might be significantly later than 1641, possibly as late as 1686–88. This would make the two earliest engraved slate gravestones in Swithland churchyard the earliest slate headstones in Leicestershire – those to John Prier (d. 8th May 1673) and to Dorathie Hall (d. 17th October 1673). The carving on these small stones is unsophisticated and there is no indication as to the engraver.[45]

The majority of slate engravers produced gravestones as a sideline and normally engaged in some other branch of the building industry. For a few craftsmen, however, the making of gravestones became their principal means of livelihood: Thomas Wood of Bingham, Joseph Butchnell of Leicester, John Bettoney of Oadby, James Sparrow of Radcliffe, William Charles and the Winfields of Wymeswold, and the Hinds. These men, and those who followed them, developed the craft into a fine art. The first known slate cutter (engraver) of the Hind family was John Hind (b.1694) who served as an apprentice to William Heafford. John Hind was elected a warden of the Slaters, Plasterers, and Tallow Chandlers Guild of Leicester in 1718–21 and again in 1744. He was steward of the Guild in 1723, 1729 and 1740.

With the frequent use of the family name, Henry, through several generations of Hinds, it is difficult to know exactly which member of the Hind family engraved those stones that are signed 'H. Hind' or 'Hind'. Robert Hind (b.1697), another son of Henry senior, was by 1754 signing his headstones with the addition of 'of Whetstone'. This reference did not indicate the whereabouts of his workshop, only that the family had diversified into farming at Whetstone Pastures.

The Hinds received commissions for memorial stones from a wide area. As well as numerous Hind stones in Leicestershire, others have been identified in Newark parish church, Nottinghamshire, Brixworth churchyard in Northamptonshire and at Folkingham in Lincolnshire.[46] Among the Hind memorials are two works that are among the most interesting products of Swithland slate carving. These are the panel representing the Last Judgement on a slate to William Hunt at Rothley; and the box-tomb, made entirely of slate, to Sir Joseph Danvers at Swithland.

Monuments to Sir Joseph Danvers (1745) and William Hunt (1794)

The 1745 table tomb for Sir Joseph Danvers in Swithland churchyard has two side panels in delicate relief, carved with scenes, each forming a multiple picture to bring out the meaning of the adjacent texts. The north panel shows a ship in full sail, a church below a hill, a castle and a fort – illustrating the couplet:

> When young I sailed to India, east and west,
> But aged in this port must lye at rest.

The church looks like Swithland church, and the hills are probably intended to be those of Charnwood. The second panel is of a scene of ploughing and building. A field is being ploughed by a three-horse team with a ploughman and a boy holding a stick. A path leads from a gate in the field fence to a country house in process of construction. The house is surrounded by scaffolding and ladders, and built up to the first floor. Nearby are a mason and tradesmen, including a carver at work on a slate tablet with his hammer and chisel. It illustrates the text:

> Be cheerful, O man, and labour to live,
> The merciful God a blessing will give.

Fig 10.4 Sir Joseph Danvers' tomb, 1745, with slate carvings showing the detail of a ship (top left) and horse (top right).

The 1794 Hunt memorial stone in Rothley churchyard shows Christ in heaven, holding a trumpet and surrounded by angels, amid the thunder and lightening that has riven the spire of a country church, which is about to topple on the tombs below. The panel is particularly interesting because, with the exception of the spire, it appears to be an accurate representation of Swithland church, showing the Danvers chapel as it had been built in 1727.

Fig 10.5 Detail of 1794 carving, The Doom, W. Hunt tombstone, Rothley.[47]

The Pollard Families of Swithland and Quorn

There are comparatively few signed engraved slate headstones in Swithland churchyard.[48] The earliest is that to Matthew Eyre (1739–1783), signed 'Pollard Quorn'. The Pollard family, originally from Swithland, were involved in the

Stonemasons/Slaters listed in Commercial Directories 1794–1841

Weston's Directory	1794	John Clay of Friar Lane
Fowler's Directory	1815	Shenton, Hull & Pollard, stonemasons, London Rd
Pigot's Directory	1822–23	Shenton, Hull & Co, stonemasons, Granby St
Combe's Directory	1827	Hull & Pollard, statuaries & masons, Granby St
Pigot's Directory	1828–29	Joshua Shenton, (merchant), slater, Humberstone Gate
		Samuel Shenton, slater, Humberstone Rd
		Hull & Pollard, stonemasons, London Rd
Pigot's Directory	1830	Hull & Pollard, stonemasons, London Rd
		Joshua Shenton (merchant), slater, Humberstone Rd
Pigot's Directory	1831	Joshua Shenton, slater & slate merchant, Humberstone Gate
		Samuel Shenton, slate & school slate mfr, Humberstone Rd
		Thomas Shenton, slater, Coulson St
		Hull & Pollard, stonemasons & statuaries, London Rd
Pigot's Directory	1840	Samuel Hull, stone & marble masons, Granby Gate
		Thomas Shenton, slater, Humberstone Rd
Pigot's Directory	1841	Samuel Hull, stonemason, Granby St

POLLARD Family from Swithland and Quorn

John **POLLARD** d.1729 = Elizabeth d.1750

Thomas b.1704 d.1778
=(1) Elizabeth 1693–1738
=(2) 1738 Hannah Wrencher 1713–1776

William d.1769
=(1) 1729 Elizabeth Peake d.1756
=(2) 1762 Isabella Ferneley

Children:
- Ann b.1733 =1762 Joseph Lewin
- William b.1738 =1761 Elizabeth Prior b.1740 d.1809
- Thomas b.1742
- Edward b.1746

Children of William b.1738 and Elizabeth Prior:
- John b.1731 =(1) 1760 Mary Lewin =(2) 1774 Alice Caudwell
  - Elizabeth b.1764
  - Edward b.1769 =1787 Anthony Woodford
  - John b.1762
  - Ann b.1764
  - William b.1766
  - Catherine b.1768
  - John b.1770
  - Sarah b.1770
  - Mary b.1775
  - Jane b.1777

Sarah b.1733

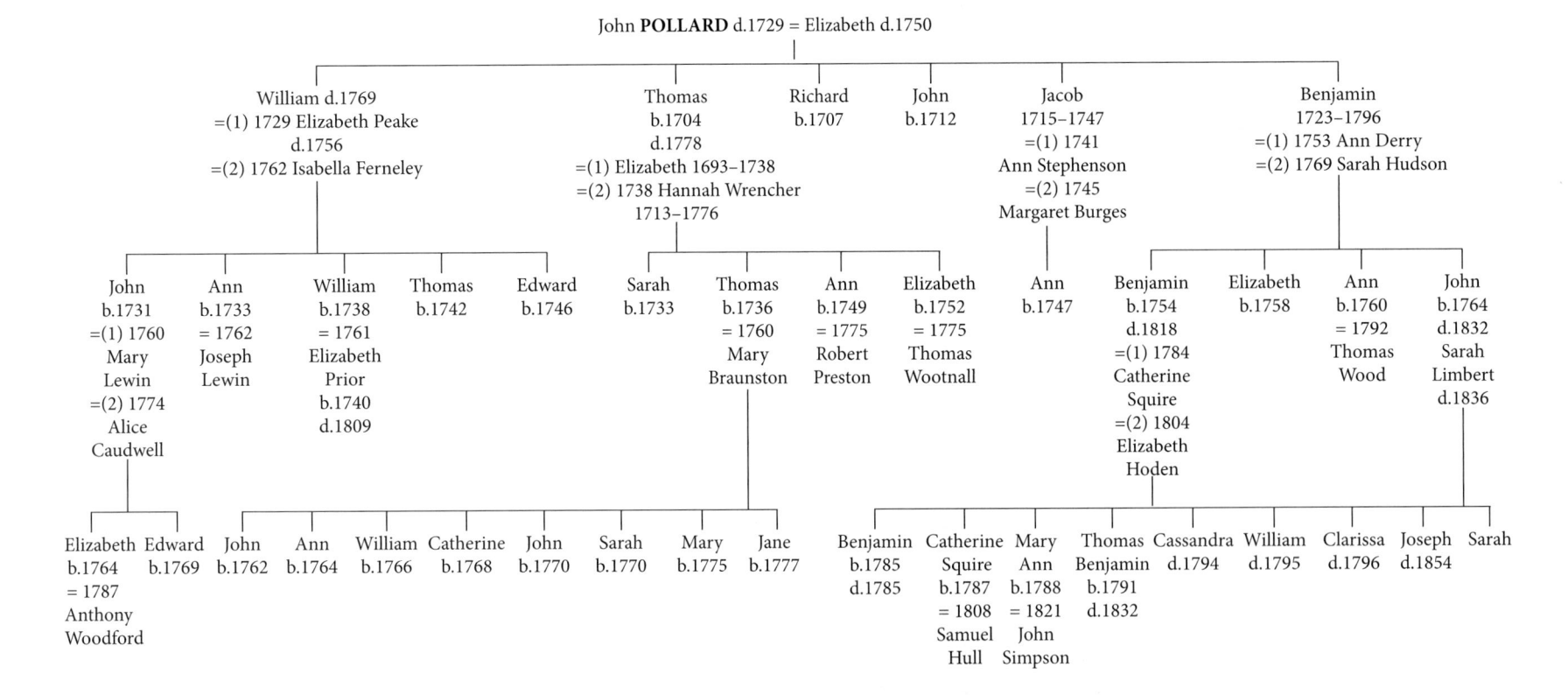

Thomas b.1736 =1760 Mary Braunston

Ann b.1749 =1775 Robert Preston

Elizabeth b.1752 =1775 Thomas Wootnall

Richard b.1707

John b.1712

Jacob 1715–1747
=(1) 1741 Ann Stephenson
=(2) 1745 Margaret Burges

- Ann b.1747

Benjamin 1723–1796
=(1) 1753 Ann Derry
=(2) 1769 Sarah Hudson

- Benjamin b.1754 d.1818 =(1) 1784 Catherine Squire =(2) 1804 Elizabeth Hoden
  - Benjamin b.1785 d.1785
  - Catherine Squire b.1787 =1808 Samuel Hull
  - Mary Ann b.1788 =1821 John Simpson
  - Benjamin b.1791 d.1832
  - Cassandra b.1794
  - Thomas d.1832
  - William b.1795
  - Clarissa b.1796
  - Joseph d.1854
  - Sarah
- Elizabeth b.1758
- Ann b.1760 =1792 Thomas Wood
- John b.1764 d.1832 Sarah Limbert d.1836

selling and engraving of slate from 1680 to 1867. Members of the Pollard family were Baptists,[49] which is possibly why finer examples of their engravings are in the burial ground at Quorn Baptist Church.[50] Matthew Eyre's headstone would have been engraved by Benjamin Pollard (1754–1818). His brother, John Pollard (1764–1832) was, at his death, in partnership with Francis Shenton of Mountsorrel and Samuel Hull of Loughborough.

Shenton, Hull & Pollard had by far the largest share of the minor statuary business in Leicestershire during the nineteenth century. They were also builders, dealt in roman cement, salt, lime, timber, and made school slates. Their firm built St George's Church, Leicester in 1826, designed by William Parsons, and also the obelisk on Naseby Field. The original partners Pollard and Shenton were later joined by Hull. When the Shentons left the firm, Pollard and Hull stayed in business together until c. 1835, when Pollard left Samuel Hull to work on his own.[51] John's son, Joseph Pollard (1795–1854) of Swithland continued their family business alone, specializing in slate engraving.

Since the closure of the Swithland slate pits at the end of the nineteenth century, the memorials in Swithland churchyard have mostly used slate from other sources – in the main Welsh slate – although some pieces of Swithland slate have been found locally and re-used for memorial stones. It was, for example, possible to use pieces of Swithland slate for the dedication tablet for the Swithland Church Extension in 2000 and for the memorial stone for Robert Brian Osborne, d. 1999. The engraver for both stones was James Salisbury of London.[52]

Fig 10.6 Swithland Church Millennium Extension plaque, 2000 (above left).

Fig 10.7 Memorial stone for Robert Brian Osborne, d. 1999 (above right).

Notes to Chapter 10

1. From Central Memorials, Shepshed.
2. The term 'Swithland' slate is usually used to include slate quarried in Groby, Newtown Linford and Woodhouse Eaves as well as in Swithland.
3. G.F. Farnham, *Leicestershire Medieval Village Notes*, p. 362, Chancery Inquisition Post Mortem.
4. Mary Bateson (ed.), *Records of the Borough of Leicester, 1103–1603*.
5. In 1745, Hinds of Swithland had a contract to supply milestones for the Market Harborough to Loughborough Road. They lost the contract in 1817 when the surveyors of this turnpike road ordered that the Swithland slate stones be replaced by iron milestones. (J. Lee and J. Dean, 'Leicestershire Historian', millennium edition, Leics. Archaeological and Historical Society).
6. R. Martin, Forward to 'Swithland Slate Headstones, Albert Herbert, 1943–44', Transactions, Leics. Archaeological and Historical Society.
7. Leics. RO DE1982/237, Interrogatores 1611 (copied 1810), Thomas Babington v. Henry, Lord Grey of Groby.
8. Leics. RO, DE1982/16, 1646.
9. Leics. RO, DE1982/18, 1665, 21 year lease.
10. Leics. RO, 3D42/62/1, 1688.
11. H. Hartopp (ed.), *Register of Freemen of Leicester*, vol. 1, 1196–1770.
12. H. Hartopp, *Roll of the Mayors of the Borough and Lord Mayors of the City of Leicester, 1209–1935*.
13. D.A. Ramsay, 'Leicestershire Slate', Leicestershire Industrial History Society (LIHC) Bulletin 9-1986.
14. Leics. RO, 44'28/678.
15. Leics. RO, DE1982/181, 3D42/62/1-11, Collection of Hind documents 1720–1817.
16. Leics. RO, 13D28/6/25, Mortgage by John Raworth of Mapplewell.
17. Leics. RO, DE1982/181, 3D42/62/1-11.
18. ibid.
19. ibid.
20. Leics. RO, 3D42/57/66, Abstract of title of trustees to Alfred Ellis citing 1851 sale from Hinds to Ellis of Slate Pit House, land, slate-pits etc. to John Ellis. Also 1851 Conveyance.
21. Leics. RO, DE1982/165, 26 Mar 1787, 20 year lease from George Harry, Earl of Stamford to Henry Hind – messuage, closes, land in open fields in Swithland; stone or slate quarry in Groby near Turnpike Road, stone or slate quarry called Old Slate Pitt Hill in Charnwood Forest with liberty to dig for slate.
22. Nichols considerably over-estimates quarry depths.
23. J. Nichols, *History and Antiquities of Leicestershire*, vol. 3, part 2, p. 1050. Nichols' sources include Throsby's 'Leicestershire' (1777), Marshall's 'Remarks on the Agriculture of the Midland Counties, vol 1', and in conversation, Revd Aulay Macaulay, as well as Mr Hind and Mr Johnson, who were working the pits when Nichols was writing.
24. Leics. RO, DE1750, Box 22, Danvers papers.
25. Long, narrow, flexible pieces of timber.
26. Now known as The Griffin Inn, Swithland.
27. The building has since been demolished.
28. *Leicester and Nottingham Journal*, 30 January 1779, p. 3 col. 3.
29. J. Throsby, *Supplementary Volume to the Leicestershire Views, containing a Series of Excursions to the Villages and Places of Note in that County*, 1790, p. 92.
30. F. Burgess, 'English Sepulchral Monuments: Swithland Slate Carvers', *The Monumental Journal*, vol. 22, No. 12, December 1955.
31. J. Throsby, *Select Views in Leicestershire*, 1790, p. 206.
32. cf. Chapter 12: Village Buildings and Families.
33. Census returns, Swithland.
34. Leics. RO, DE1982/182, Earl of Stamford's rent books.
35. Leics. RO, DE1982/165, Counter-part lease for twenty years.
36. Leics. RO, Leics. Industrial History Society, Bulletin, No. 9, 1986.
37. Leics. RO, DE1750, Box 17, William Herrick to George John Danvers Butler Danvers, Conveyance 11 May 1827. See also DG9/157.
38. Quorn Village On-Line Museum, St Bartholomew's Village Graves Transcriptions C50, C59.

39. Sold by the Hinds to William Herbert in c. 1910. The house is now a residential care home; members of the Herbert family still farm Whetstone Pastures Farm.
40. A. Herbert, 'Swithland Slate Headstones, 1943– 44', Transactions, Leics. Archaeological and Historical Society.
41. *Leicester Advertiser*, 2 Nov. 1961.
42. Swithland Census, 1871.
43. F.T. Mott, *Charnwood Forest*, 1868.
44. Margaret Grieff in 'Leicestershire Historian', 2009, Leicestershire Archaeological and Historical Society.
45. The signing of slate memorials only became standard practice in the 1760s.
46. D.A. Ramsey, The Leicestershire Slate Industry, 2000, private publication.
47. Photograph taken by Terry Sheppard.
48. In his paper, Swithland Slate Headstones, Albert Herbert points out that engravers did not begin to add their names to the stones until c. 1750.
49. cf. Chapter 7: Dissent.
50. The Quorn website 2003 listed transcriptions of all the churchyard memorials in the Baptist, as well as Church of England churchyards.
51. Frederick Burgess, *English Churchyard Memorials*, 1963.
52. James Salisbury also engraved the alabaster wall tablet for the ninth Earl of Lanesborough, which is placed on the south wall of the Danvers chapel.

– CHAPTER 11 –

Reservoirs and Railways

Until the eighteenth century Swithland had scarcely been touched by the industrialisation that had gone on elsewhere. The local slate industry had influenced the material of its buildings, and also to some extent its housing patterns, with some dwellings for slate-workers built at the Woodhouse end of the village. In the main, however, Swithland remained an agricultural estate village. The numbers of Swithland residents who were engaged either in the quarries or in slate engraving was relatively small, and in any case, the industry began to go into serious decline from the 1830s.

Swithland Reservoir

Towards the end of the nineteenth century the water needs of the urban centre of Leicester began to impact on outlying villages such as Swithland. In 1801 the population of Leicester had only been some 16,953 people, but by 1840 it had increased to 50,806 and was still rising. These people needed water, and the Leicester Waterworks Company was formed to investigate Leicester's water supplies. In 1847 parliamentary approval was secured for the construction of Thornton Reservoir, which was completed in 1854. With Leicester's population still rising, parliamentary approval was given for the construction of Cropston Reservoir in 1866; it was opened in 1870. In 1878 Leicester Corporation acquired the Waterworks Company. Attempting to satisfy ever-increasing demand, the Corporation tried to acquire a further source of water at Blackbrook in 1880, but lost out to Loughborough. The Corporation then turned its thoughts to Swithland. In 1888, boreholes were sunk to test the ground beneath the proposed embankment.

In 1889 the Corporation opened negotiations with Farnham of Quorn and Lanesborough of Swithland, the landowners concerned. Mr W.E.J.B. Farnham of Quorn House agreed terms that included the reservation of shooting, fishing and sporting rights on the 55.38 acres the Corporation wished to acquire from him. By November 1889, though, they had still not reached an agreement with the Earl of Lanesborough in respect of the 225.25 acres required from his estate. The Corporation therefore applied to Parliament for compulsory powers. The Earl of Lanesborough petitioned against the Bill, and was represented at the House of Lords Select Committee hearing, but his petition failed. The Leicester Corporation Waterworks Act received the Royal Assent in May 1890.[1] The Act gave power to the Corporation to:

> ...compulsorily purchase land and construct a reservoir at Swithland; take water from the Swithland Brook, Lingdale Brook, Hallgates Brook and Bradgate Brook; raise the level of the Rothley-Swithland road; divert the Mountsorrel-Woodhouse road; erect a pumping station, filter beds and associated works; and install a pipe from the pumping station to Anstey to connect into the Corporation's water supply network.

Clauses protecting the Earl were placed into the act: sporting rights were reserved and a portion of Brasil Wood was reserved. The Corporation was required to divert the sewage from Swithland village away from the reservoir and to bear the costs.

The Earl, however, continued to fight. Despite the parliamentary powers, he managed to delay the building of the reservoir while he attempted to negotiate better terms. He was served with notice to treat for about 225 acres, but in the absence of agreement on the compensation, the matter went to arbitration. The value of the timber had been agreed at £2,700. The Corporation submitted a valuation of £18,700 for the land; the Earl's representative claimed £51,312. On 19th March 1892, Mr Ralph Clutton, the umpire, awarded £27,800.

The Corporation's troubles were not, however, at an end. Steps had to be taken to obtain possession of the land from the tenants. A small piece of land at Kinchley Hill, measuring about 1 rood and 28 perches (0.425 acres), belonged to the Surveyors of Highways of the parish of Newtown Linford. It was purchased for £250. The mineral rights to some 40 acres of land purchased from the Earl of Lanesborough had been vested in the Lord of the Manor of Groby; these were acquired from the Countess of Stamford and Warrington for £100. Two closes of land in Rothley Plain, measuring about 5.82 acres, were also required for the reservoir; they were purchased in September 1893 from the Revd A.N. Bates of Humberstone.

On 5th July 1894 Alderman Edward Wood JP (Chairman of the Leicester Water Committee 1889–1908) cut the first sod in Swithland in, according to the press, 'the most propitious weather'. There were between two and three hundred people present. Some of the visitors were taken on the contractors' temporary railway line to view the valley that was to be submerged. The company was then entertained to lunch by Alderman and Mrs Wood in a marquee. The contractors, the London company of J.B. Aird & Son, presented Alderman Wood with a wheelbarrow of polished oak, silver mounted. The engineer, Mr J.B. Everard, presented the traditional silver spade. The cost of constructing the reservoir came to £133,511. It had been designed to collect the rainfall from a drainage area of 3,500 acres, and to store 490 million gallons of water.

A number of rights of way were affected by the construction. Most were

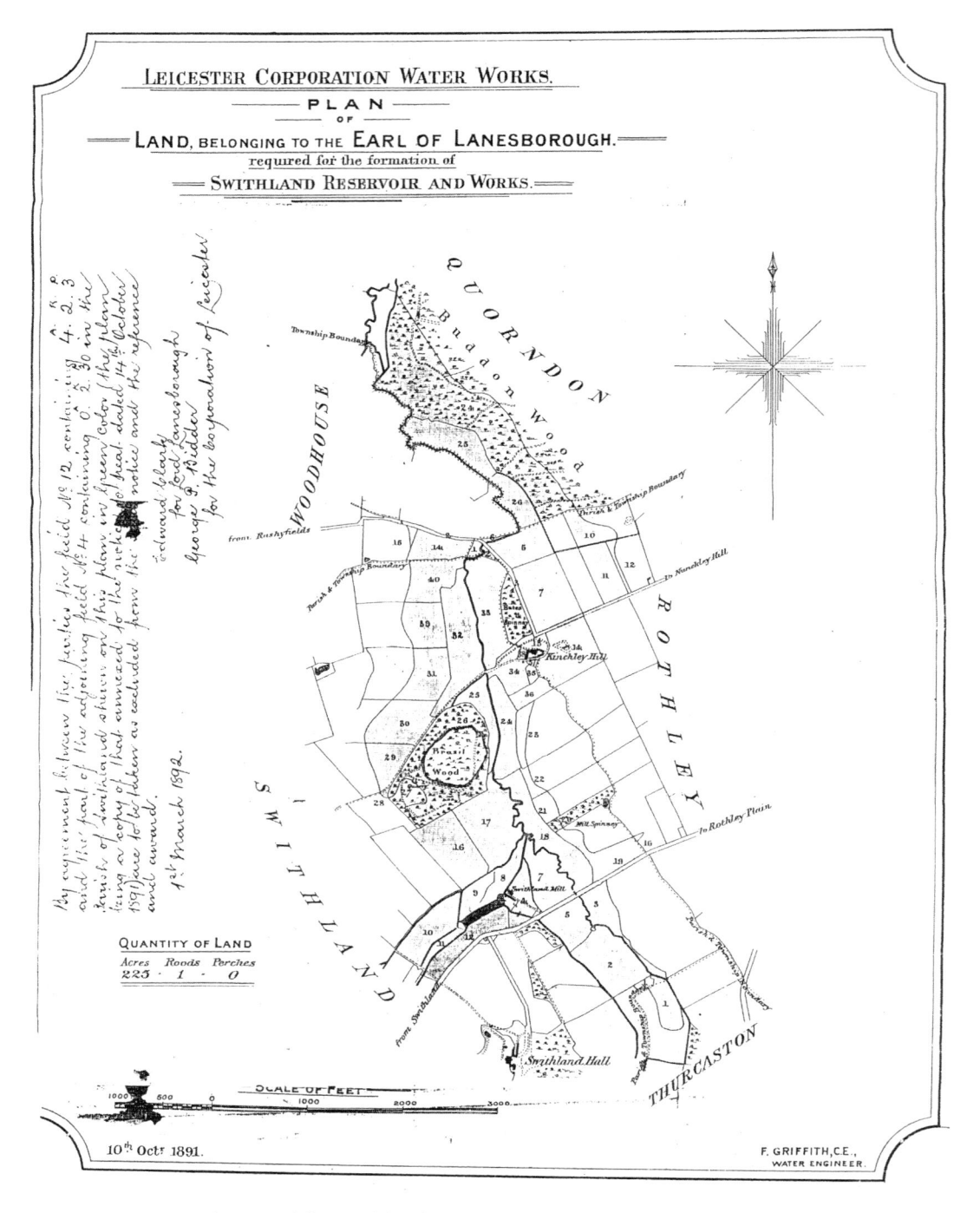

Fig.11.1   Land required for Swithland Reservoir and works, 1891.

diverted, but a footway from Mountsorrel to Swithland was stopped up. Since the reservoir cut off the water to Quorn Mill, compensation had to be paid to the miller – Messrs M. Wright & Sons were paid £1,500. The Act also required the Corporation to bear the cost of diverting Swithland's sewerage away from the reservoir; it was pumped to a field north of the village. Even this construction of Swithland's new sewerage system did not go without difficulties. In January 1896 the Swithland Parish Meeting protested to the Rural District Council, which had agreed the details of the contract with the City Council. Residents were concerned about the time already occupied in the general construction of the new system and the unsatisfactory way in which the work was being conducted. They alleged that the roads were in a disgraceful state as a result of contractors' traffic, and specifically cited the bridle path that led past the new sewerage farm, the facts that the storm water system had been disrupted and that a number of village wells had dried up as a result of the works. The reply from the Rural District Council was deemed unsatisfactory. In February 1898, the Parish Meeting was still urging the Council to put pressure on the Highways Board to repair Main Street.

Swithland Mill and Kinchley Hill Farm were both lost in the building of the reservoir. The mill was converted into a boat house. Kinchley Hill farmhouse was used for some time as two dwelling-houses, but then allowed to fall into ruin and finally demolished in 1975. One of the families who lived in Kinchley Hill farmhouse during those years was the Allen family.

In 1905, Mr William Allen of Woodhouse Eaves was appointed outdoor foreman at the Swithland Water Works. He was responsible for supervising all the workmen outside the Engine House, and was expected to 'work in harmony with Mr Cook who is in charge of the Engine House and Pumping Station'.[2] His wages on appointment were 24 shillings per week, with another shilling per week after a period of six months.

The Victorian red-brick buildings of Swithland Water Works, visible from the road across the dam, still look much as they did when they were built, apart from the engine house chimney, which was demolished. When first designed, the grounds were planted as an arboretum: at least one specimen of every tree suited to the latitude was planted. The formal gardens around the filter-beds were planted with over one hundred species of heather. Today the grounds, though no longer kept to their original standards, continue as a fine natural habitat for vegetation and wildlife.

Fewer than four years after the construction of the reservoir, the additional capacity provided by Swithland Reservoir was deemed inadequate for Leicester's

Fig.11.2 Water works, engine house and pumping station at Swithland Reservoir.

Fig.11.3 The formal gardens around the filter beds of Swithland Reservoir.

needs and the Corporation had to seek further parliamentary powers. In 1898 they applied to be supplied with water from the River Derwent in Derbyshire. As a result Leicester joined with Nottingham, Sheffield and Derby to form the Derwent Valley Water Board. In 1912 and 1916 the Howden and Derwent Reservoirs were built to meet extra demand, then in 1945 the Ladybower Reservoir was opened. By the mid 1950s, industrial expansion and the ever-rising population meant that even more capacity was needed. The River Dove Water Board was formed in 1955 and intakes constructed to take supplies from the River Dove to the Staunton Harold and Foremark Reservoirs. At the same time, the old steam pumps at Swithland were replaced by electrically-driven pumps. The old water work buildings became redundant, but, apart from the tower, still stand.

Fig.11.4 Olive Allen, daughter of the outdoor foreman at the water works, relaxing by the reservoir with her fiancé Eric North, c. 1920.

Since the creation of the Water Authorities in the act of 1973, Severn Trent Water has managed Leicestershire's water supplies with over ninety per cent of Leicester's water now coming from the rivers Dove and Derwent. A hundred years after its opening, Swithland is now a relatively small reserve reservoir. The grounds around the old buildings are now closed to the public, but the reservoir area has become an important local attraction, to birds, bird-watchers, steam railway enthusiasts and tourists alike.

Fig 11.5 Olive Allen (rowing) and friends.

The Great Central Railway

The second major impact of nineteenth century industrialisation on Swithland was the coming of the railway. In 1836, the Midland Counties Railway had opened a line running from Derby, Leicester, Rugby and Nottingham. The network was extended in 1844, linking the Midlands with London and Birmingham. Locally, the Mountsorrel Granite Company took advantage of the link, and applied to build a branch line to connect their quarries with the Midland Counties main line at the station in Barrow upon Soar. An act of Parliament was applied for and passed.[3] The line was constructed in 1860 and ran from the north end of Mountsorrel, along a new bridge across the Soar, to Barrow.

The Manchester, Sheffield and Lincolnshire Railway also planned to develop its rail network through Leicestershire. The company was formed in 1847 with the amalgamation of several smaller railway companies. In 1873, under the ambitious management of Sir Edward Watkin MP, the company put forward their first scheme to extend their railway to London. Watkin's initial and far-sighted vision was of a railway linking the industrial centres of Manchester and Sheffield with the expanding markets of continental Europe, via a Channel tunnel. The other railway companies, however, were not interested, and Watkin had to be content with a 'London Extension'.

The Manchester, Sheffield and Lincolnshire Railway (Extension to London) Bill was submitted to the 1890–91 session of Parliament. Residents were probably not aware of it at the time, but Swithland would have been very much affected. It was proposed that the railway line cut straight through the centre of the village, as is shown in the 1891 deposited plans.[4]

There were immediate objections from the Earl, but not because of the effect of the plans on the village. Mr Clough Taylor appeared on his behalf before the House of Commons Standing Committee on 10th June 1891 to

Fig.11.6 Railway viaduct across Swithland Reservoir, 1925.

object to the railway being built 'in front of Lord Lanesborough's residence'. More importantly for the success of the project, however, Watkin was opposed by the London & North Western Railway, by the Midland Railway, and by the Great Northern Railway, and the Bill was thrown out of Parliament. New plans were drawn up and, after the Great Northern Railway was promised a new joint station at Nottingham, opposition was withdrawn. A new Manchester, Sheffield and Lincolnshire bill was successful, receiving the royal assent in March 1893.[5] This time, however, the proposed alignment

Fig 11.7 Rail bridge at Swithland, under construction, 1897.[6]

of the railway was to be across Swithland Reservoir[7] rather than through the village, and Anstey was not to be connected.

The cost of the construction was high; as against an estimate of £6m, the complete cost of the 'London Extension' was £11.5m.[8] The East Leake to Aylestone section of the railway alone – 16 miles 36 chains – built by the firm of H. Lovatt of Northampton, cost £548,835. Swithland Reservoir had to be emptied to allow the construction of the two viaducts carrying the railway line across it. Swithland station yard was built at the southern end of the reservoir and sidings were laid, principally for the Mountsorrel Granite Company's traffic. The Company had applied for a short branch line to be constructed linking the 'London Extension' with the Mountsorrel quarries and the 1860 Mountsorrel-Barrow branch line.[9] Originally called 'the Nunckley Hill Railway', its single line of standard gauge ran from the Mountsorrel side of Swithland sidings across the fields, passing the Nunckley Hill quarry, going under Swithland Lane (at the top of Halstead Road) and down towards the new Mountsorrel quarry.[10]

The Manchester, Sheffield and Lincolnshire Railway Company had intended originally to open a station at Swithland and provision was made for an island platform there. Steps to the proposed platform were built in the archway of the bridge over the road from Swithland to Rothley Plain. The planned station, however, never materialised. Instead, a station was built in Rothley Plain, adjacent to Frederick Merttens' new housing development between Swithland Lane, The Ridgeway and Westfield Lane.

Fig.11.8 Steps up to the proposed Swithland Station, now bricked up.[11]

The 'London Extension' to the Great Central Railway[12] opened to freight traffic in July 1898, and the first passenger train ran from Marylebone Station in March 1899. The company advertised their services under the slogan 'rapid travel in luxury' and for one hundred and fifty years trains steamed through Leicestershire on the Great Central Line. After the Second World War, however, the increasing use of the private motor car and heavy lorries together with the development of the motorways, led to a decline in the use of the railways. Lord Beeching's cuts in the 1960s led to the closure of long stretches of the Great Central Line in 1966, including those parts that ran through Leicestershire.

In 1969 a group of local rail enthusiasts were inspired to recreate the nostalgia of the old railway steam days. The ninth Earl of Lanesborough was one of the restored Great Central Railway's most resolute supporters. He was the first president of the Main Line Steam Trust and a director of Great

Fig.11.9 View across Swithland Reservoir to railway viaduct in the distance (drained for cleaning and re-commisioning in 1928, and showing the course of the old Cropston Overflow).

Fig 11.10 Aerial view of the reservoir, 2010.

Central Railway plc. He did much to ensure the re-opening of the old line and the success of the new venture. It is now possible to travel again from Loughborough to north Leicester by steam train, and the Great Central Railway is now an important Leicestershire tourist attraction.[13]

Notes to Chapter 11

1. Leics. RO, QS/80/3, Leicester Corporation Waterworks Act 1890.
2. Letter of appointment, still in the hands of the family.
3. Leics. RO, QS 73/123, 1858.
4. Leics. RO, QS 73/288, Railway Plans 1890. (An artist's sketch of the effect that the proposed line would have had on Swithland village was printed in the Summer 1994 edition of 'Main Line', the magazine of the Main Line Steam Trust.) QS73/294, plans 1891.
5. Leics. RO, QS73/302, Manchester, Sheffield and Lincolnshire (extension to London) Act 1893.
6. Leics. RO, S.W. Newton, collection of photographs, Great Central Railway Construction, 1890s, reproduced from archives with permission.
7. Leicester Corporation sought to protect their new reservoir, so obtained a number of protective measures in the act.
8. www.gcrailway.co.uk.
9. Leics. RO, DE1750, Box 32, 1896 lease, Lanesborough to Mountsorrel Granite Company; 1897 receipt from MGC for £1,897 – being part of a sum not exceeding £10,000 to be paid by Lord Lanesborough and Lord Newtown-Butler for construction of the Nunckley Hill railway, May 4 1897.
10. The line was closed and the track lifted in the mid 1960s, but in 2007 a project was set to restore the Nunckley Hill railway, the 'Mountsorrel Railway Project.'
11. Leics. RO, S.W. Newton, collection of photographs, Great Central Railway Construction, 1890s, reproduced from archives with permission.
12. In August 1897, the Manchester, Sheffield and Lincolnshire Railway changed its name to the Great Central Railway. From 1923 it became part of the London and North Eastern Railway. It was nationalised in 1948, and closed in March 1963.
13. www.gcrailway.co.uk.

– CHAPTER 12 –

Village Buildings and Families

In 1901 there were fifty dwellings in Swithland, twenty-two of them with fewer than five rooms. There were one hundred and ninety-five inhabitants, including children, eighty-eight of whom were males and one hundred and seven females.[1] A hundred years later there were eighty-five properties in Swithland, virtually all with five or more rooms and one hundred and sixty-seven electors. The change, of course, lies in the size of the buildings and the wealth of the owners. Yet, with one or two exceptions, someone walking round the village today can still see the evidence of many of those 1901 dwelling places, much of which dates from the mid-nineteenth century. The village of Swithland does, however, go much further back into history.

Mediaeval Swithland

The oldest building still standing in Swithland is St Leonard's Church, which has a probable late twelfth century foundation. After the church, the oldest and least changed secular buildings in the village are the two eighteenth century barns at Hall Farm. Imagination is therefore required to visualise what mediaeval Swithland looked like.

It looks as if there were two groupings of buildings. The church, the manor house and the priest's house (rectory) were situated together at the lower end of the village, with the rest – mainly labourers' dwellings – probably sited higher up the village in closer proximity to the open fields and to the stream flowing through the village. As far as the first cluster of buildings go, village tradition has it[2] that, opposite the church, on the site of the old game-keeper's cottage (now a modern development, Keepers Close) there was a mediaeval 'hospice' or resting place for monks living in, or travelling through, Swithland. The old manor house also stood opposite the church, where Charnia Grove, another modern housing development, now stands. While it is not impossible that Swithland might have had at least one[3] other significant mediaeval building, in addition to the manor house and the rectory, it would most likely have been sited nearer the church end of the village. Whatever the speculation, the remains of any other mediaeval building in Swithland would have been lost in the domestic rebuilding that followed the 1799 Parliament Enclosure Act.

Higher up the village, on the north side of Main Street and opposite the former Methodist Chapel, lay two of the village's open fields – 'over' or 'Forest' field and 'middle' or 'North' field. A small cluster of buildings is shown on the roadside of this area on the 1799 enclosure map, but nothing of that now survives above ground. A 1901 'six inch county series' map of the village shows 'fish ponds' on land slightly higher up the village, opposite the Swithland triangle. The group of mediaeval dwellings of the common villagers would have been little more than hovels or huts. Even in the sixteenth and seventeenth centuries, most ordinary villagers would have lived either in one-room structures of mud, built with reeds laid on branches, or in weak timber structures with the framework filled in with mud. Heating and cooking would have been by a fire on the bare earth floor, with smoke filtering out by degrees through the roof. Water was taken from wells, ditches and ponds.

It is impossible to link any individual residents with particular dwelling sites, excepting of course with the manor and the church. While there is some documentary evidence relating to sixteenth century land occupation in wills, conveyances etc, it is equally impossible to identify where exactly the land was situated. The earliest written documents that record villagers by name relate to their ability to pay taxes and tithes, to fight for their 'lord' and country, and to put their names, or marks, on legal documents. From these we know the names of some of the people who lived in Swithland between 1327 and 1622 but not where they lived. Written church registers were not required to be kept until the sixteenth century, though, until 1700, that was done more in the breach than in the observance, and graves were not marked with inscribed stone markers until the late 1600s.[4]

> 1327 LAY SUBSIDY ROLL
> Roger Edwyne, Richard Ivotes, Thomas de Oudeby, William Pullehare, Roger son of John, Roger le Reve, Robert le Warde.
>
> 1332 LAY SUBSIDY ROLL
> John Bercar, Roger son of John, Richard le Clerk, Richard Ivotes, William atte Waynhouse, John Waleys.
>
> 1377 LAY SUBSIDY ROLL/POLL TAX (56)
> Robert Alden & wife, Nicholas Badeworth & wife, Adam Bagworth & wife, John Barker, William Boney & wife, John Brume & wife, Margaret Can, Emmota Doney widow, Roger Drake & wife, Richard Drake servant, Robert Gardon & wife, William Gofray servant, William Hallebowe & wife, John Har servant, William Honwode & wife, William Howton & wife, John Hunte & wife, Aleyne Hunte & wife, William Lodebrok & wife, Henry Nyk & wife, Alice Ruddle, William Ryngsted & wife, Thomas Slater & wife, Thomas Smyth, John Souter servant, Robert Souter & wife, William Sowter & wife, John Squyer & wife, Henry Taylhor & wife,

Joan Tayllor widow, John Tresscher & wife, John Walcote Esq & wife, Ralph servant of John Hunte, William servant of Loddebrok.

1424 GAOL DELIVERY ROLL
John Broun, William Donne, John Nyk, John Sclater, William Sclater, John Wales, Thomas Wyre.

1524 LAY SUBSIDY ROLL
Edward Abell, Thomas Abell, John Bower, Robert Brett, John Brown, Robert Broun, Richard Byarde, William Bychemand, Elizabeth Cotys, John Danvers, Richard Hews, John Hull, Richard Kardall, John Martin, William Mason, Ralph Neubold, John Sands, William Sclater, John Smythe, John Webster.

1540 MUSTER
Archers: Edward Beaumont, John Bryan, Richard Byrde, Edmund Davers, John Dodsworthe, William Hull, Richard Smith, John Starke, Thomas Stoley;
Byllmen: Thomas Abell, John Alyn, John Boley, John Browne, Thomas Browne, Richard Brygeman, John Davers, Roger Darker, John Gilbirde, Robert Jackson, William Morley, John Ormyson, John Skyeton, Robert Smythe, Thomas Sutton.

1545 LAY SUBSIDY ROLL
Thomas Abell, — Gille, John Hall, William Hardwyn, Raynold Harreson, Robert Jacson, Henry Smythe, Richard Southe, Thomas Sutton, John —.

1571 LAY SUBSIDY
John Danvers, John O'Godard, John Smythe.

1620 LAY SUBSIDY ROLL
Davie Blankley, Francis Danvers, Robert Hinde, Richard Rearke.

1622 CONVEYANCES
Francis Sutton blacksmith, Robert Hynde tanner, Arthur Gilbert husbandman, Robert Browne husbandman

Hearth Tax to Enclosure

The lay subsidy rolls indicate that Robert Hinde, a tanner, was living in Swithland in 1622. The Hind family were still living in the village until the nineteenth century, on the site of 78 Main Street, the White House. In the seventeenth century the Hind dwelling would have been small and primitive. Hearth tax records in 1664 list it as having one hearth. The village Hearth Tax returns give an indication of the housing stock in Swithland at the end of the Civil War. This tax was established by an Act of 1662 (14CarII c.10) and levied an annual due of two shillings for every hearth. Exemptions were made for the poor and those whose homes were worth less than twenty shillings per annum. Inmates of hospitals and almshouses were also

Swithland Hearth Tax, 1664 and 1666

	Number of hearths	
	1664	1666
William Baker	1	1
Thomas Bird		1
Richard Blackwell	1	1
Eleanor Blankley	2	
Francis/Richard Blankley	3	3
John Browne	1	
William Browne	1	
Richard Bull	1	
Robert Charley	1	
John Clarke	1	1
Hugh Coates (ex Robert Blastocke)	1	1
John/Mary Crispe	1	2
Mrs Danvers	8	7
Joseph Franke		1
Arthur Gilbert	1	1
Robert Glenn	1	1
William Greene	2	
Henry Hall	1	1
John Hinde	1	1
Henry Hinde	1	2
John Hodson	1	2
William Hollin	1	1
John Howson	1	1
John Hughes	1	1
Mr Kines (ex Richard Battie)	4	4
Thomas Major	1	
Widow Nicholas/Nicholls	1	2
William Perkin	1	1
John Pick		1
Edward Porter (ex George Hewes)	1	1
Robert Prior	1	
Ralph Robinson	1	
William Sheppard	1	
Thomas Shaw	1	1
George Shutlewood/Shitlewood	1	2
William/John Siston (ex Anthony Siston)	1	1
William Smith	1	1
Henry Squire	1	
Henry Squire	1	
Samuel Sutton	1	1
Thomas Watson		1

exempted, as were private ovens, kilns, and the like. The tax was met with opposition, its levying was hampered by concealment of hearths and the unwillingness of local officials to co-operate; it was abolished in 1688. Swithland returns show that only three houses had more than one or two hearths: the Danvers' manor house had seven or eight hearths, the Rectory had four, and a house belonging to the Blankleys, possibly a former residence of the Shepeys/Kendalls, had three hearths. All other dwellings had a single hearth, at most two. In 1670 there were forty-one Swithland households paying Hearth Tax.

Some early wills of Swithland inhabitants give clues as to the dwellings they inhabited as well as some details of their land and their beasts. There are hints, for example, of an early grocery shop in the inventory of the effects of Elizabeth Ward of Swithland[5] (d. 1727).

Inventory of Goods and Chattles of Elizabeth Ward, late of Swithland

	£-s-d
In the house: 1 table, 6 chairs, 4 pewter dishes, 4 plates, a fire grate, a warming pan.	1-1-6
In the kitchen: 3 kettles, 2 tubs, 3 barrels, 1 table, 1 pail.	1-8-6
In the chamber over the house: 1 bed, 4 chairs, 1 trunk, a small table.	2-2-6
In the chamber over the shop: 1 bed, a press, 2 chairs, 1 box, a small table.	2-5-0
In the shop: grocery ware & other shop goods.	8-5-6
Purse & apparel	2-4-0
Lumber with other things seen and unseen	1-3-6
Debts good and bad	1-2-6
	19-13-0

Robert Gilbert's will[6] (1749) mentions 'the parlour and chamber over the parlour at my house in Swithland … also a bed and sufficient furniture out of my household goods for these two rooms...' And William Westley, a carpenter, in his 1775 will, mentions a shop at his Swithland messuage.[7]

Nineteenth and Twentieth Century Swithland

With some exceptions, most of the buildings now thought of as Swithland's 'older' buildings were erected in the first half of the nineteenth century, when farms and cottages were adapted to post-enclosure agriculture. The decade 1840–50 saw a significant level of building in which new stone-built cottages replaced earlier less substantial structures. The builders made use of the distinctive local blue-grey slate quarried in the nearby pits. Their use of this local stone, as well as of Mountsorrel granite, gives Swithland buildings their distinctive character.

By the end of the nineteenth century, the Earl of Lanesborough owned virtually the entire village. The estate had no particular need to add to the housing stock, and, importantly, it did not choose to sell parts for speculative housing development. As a result, Swithland's nineteenth century houses were preserved and improved rather than demolished, so the size of the village remained consistently small. As the fortunes of the Swithland Hall Estate declined, along with the recession in British agriculture, the housing stock remained largely un-modernised. Although mains sewerage was installed in the village in 1896, most of the houses remained unconnected until the 1930s, and the villagers used earth closets. While most village houses used candles or oil/paraffin lamps for lighting until mains electricity came to the village in 1938, the Hall installed its own electrical generator.

Shortly after the end of the Second World War, local authority housing was erected in the form of three pairs of semi-detached cottages or council houses (Nos. 91–99). It was intended that these be made available for people employed in local agriculture. Increasing mechanisation meant, though, that they were not all needed for that purpose, and so they became part of the local authority's housing stock. The majority are now owner-occupied, having been initially purchased by their longstanding tenants under right-to-buy legislation in the 1980s.

Following the sale of the Swithland Hall Estate in 1954, old properties were refurbished and new building took place. From 1966, the older village buildings have been listed.[8] The slate industry having long been closed, new dwellings have typically been built with rendered walls, occasional granite stone features, and, in the main, Welsh slate roofs. Initially, planners tended to prefer bungalows to houses so that the newer dwellings should not over-dominate the older ones, but that restriction seems no longer to stand. Swithland was designated a Conservation Area in July 1993, introducing some restrictions on building styles. More recently, larger houses have become normative, more and more being built mainly with red-brick, but with some granite facing and slate-like tiling.

Kinchley Hill Farm (1622)

Little trace is now left of the small farm that stood at the base of Kinchley Hill.[9] When the reservoir was constructed in 1895, the farmhouse with its outbuildings remained above water so was inhabited for a while, but most of its surrounding farmland was submerged.

The first building on the site was constructed in 1622 by Francis Smalley, a mercer of Mountsorrel. He purchased from Henry Kendall some 65 acres of meadow and pasture land in Swithland on the north-eastern boundary of the parish, next to Rothley Plain.[10] There he built Kinsley Hill farmhouse. He did not live there himself – he had significant other land interests – but he let it to tenants, such as husbandman Thomas Briesley of Mountsorrel (1649). When Francis Smalley died in 1653, the land and farmhouse passed to his son, Ralph Smalley (d. 1666) and then to his brother's son – also named Ralph. The land continued to be let. The second Ralph Smalley died in 1737, leaving the farm to his wife for life, and then to his sons-in-law, John Fisher of Cossington, gent, and Robert Tebbutt.[11]

In 1777 Elizabeth Smalley leased the land to her son-in-law John Fisher.[12] The holding was described as consisting of 65 acres; the Little Rough Close, the Corn Close, Bassell Meadow, Red Meadow, Rough Wall Leys. When Elizabeth died in 1784, ownership of the land passed to her son-in-law Ralph Tebbutt,[13] who was in 1766 a plumber and grazier of Frisby-on-the-Wreake.

By 1782 he had become 'a gent. of Ratcliffe-on-the-Wreake'. In 1783, his son Ralph Smalley Tebbutt moved to Mountsorrel, where he built for himself an Adam-style house at the corner of York Road (later Sileby Road) known as Mountsorrel Hall. From 1796 – the year of his marriage[14] – to 1799, Ralph Smalley Tebbutt, 'farmer and grazier' farmed Kinchley Hill as his father's tenant.[15]

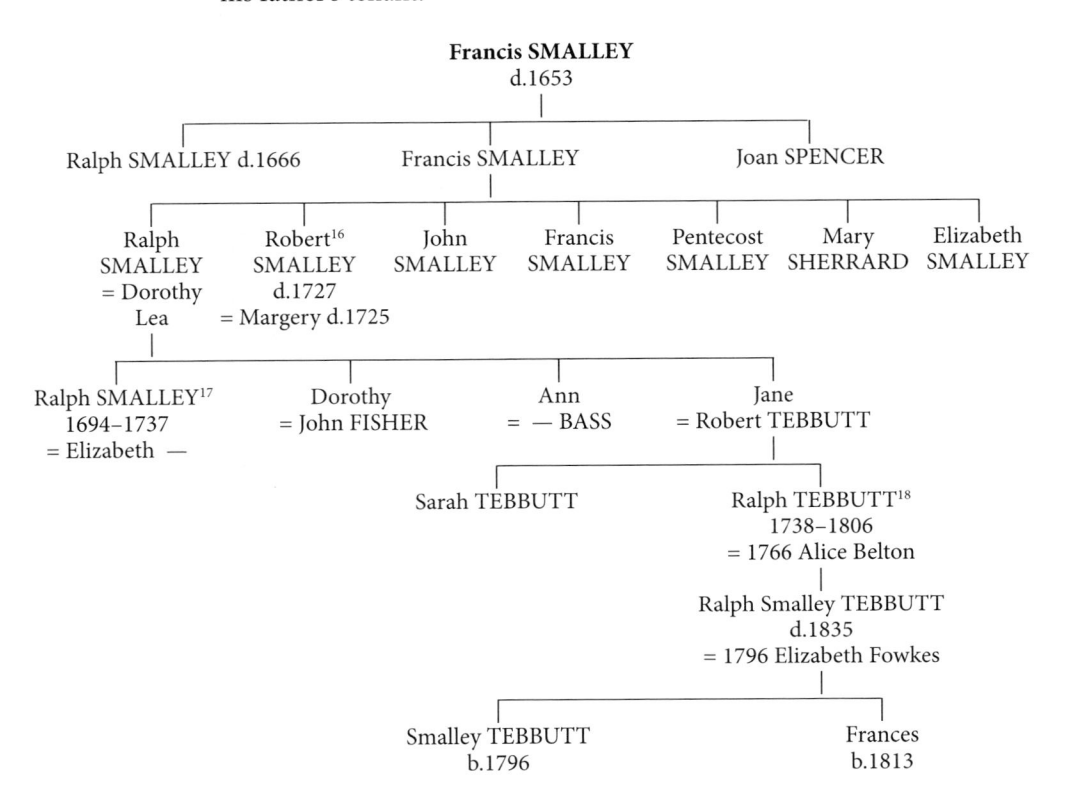

Francis SMALLEY
d.1653

Ralph SMALLEY d.1666 — Francis SMALLEY — Joan SPENCER

Children of Francis SMALLEY and Joan SPENCER:
- Ralph SMALLEY = Dorothy Lea
- Robert[16] SMALLEY d.1727 = Margery d.1725
- John SMALLEY
- Francis SMALLEY
- Pentecost SMALLEY
- Mary SHERRARD
- Elizabeth SMALLEY

Children of Robert SMALLEY and Margery:
- Ralph SMALLEY[17] 1694–1737 = Elizabeth —
- Dorothy = John FISHER
- Ann = — BASS
- Jane = Robert TEBBUTT

Sarah TEBBUTT (daughter of Ann = Bass)

Ralph TEBBUTT[18] 1738–1806 = 1766 Alice Belton (son of Jane = Robert TEBBUTT)

Ralph Smalley TEBBUTT d.1835 = 1796 Elizabeth Fowkes

- Smalley TEBBUTT b.1796
- Frances b.1813

The 1799 Swithland Enclosure Award allotted the Tebbutts their 65 acres, describing it as consisting of Kinchley Hill Close, the Little Rough Close, the Corn Close, the Bassell Meadow, the Red Meadow, and the Rough Wall Leys. The house was described as standing near to the public road from Mountsorrel to Woodhouse. The enclosure award also confirmed a footpath to Swithland at the side of the house.

Sir Joseph Danvers tried to buy the land in 1742.[19] It would seem that he purchased a reversion expectant from Ralph Tebbutt and John Fisher, but failed to secure a good title because the land had been entailed some time previously.[20] The farm finally came into the ownership of the Butler Danvers of Swithland Hall in an exchange under the Charnwood Forest and Rothley Plain Enclosure Award 1818–28. A conveyance of 1828 [21] describes the land as consisting of:

The Kinchley Hill Close (now called the House Close)
The Little Rough Close (now called the Little Close)
The Corn Close (now called the Upper Close)
The Wood Meadow (now called Long Meadow)
Bassell Meadow (now called Wood Meadow)
Red Meadow (now divided into 2 closes called the Plain Meadow and Red Meadow)
Rough Wall Leys (now called the Whyary Close)

Kinchley Hill Farm was tenanted by members of the Bates family from 1818 to 1894, when it was compulsorily purchased by the Leicester Corporation for the construction of Swithland Reservoir. The farmhouse was then converted into two residences for Corporation employees. William Allen of Woodhouse Eaves was appointed to the position of outdoor foreman at the Swithland Water Works in 1905[22] and his family lived in one part of the farmhouse for some years. The Allens left in 1953, and the farmhouse fell into disrepair and was demolished in 1956.

Fig 12.1 Kinchley Hill Farmhouse, c. 1950.

Kinchley Hill Farm Tenants

1622	Francis Smalley built house
1766–1775	Richard Fowkes
1777–1781	John Hill
1782–1795	John Johnson jr of Beaumanor[23]
1796–1798	Ralph Tebbutt jr
1799–1817	Richard Burchnall of Cropston[24]
1818–1832	William Bates
1841–1870	Thomas Bates
1871–1877	Juliana Bates
1878–1881	Catherine Anne Bates
1881–1894	Juliana Bates
1901	1. Joseph Barrett; 2. Charles Clowes
1909	1. Joseph Barrett; 2. Charles Clowes
1924	1. William Allen/Collis; 2. James Simpson
1931	1. William Allen; 2. Collis
1933–1953	1. William Allen

Swithland Water Works (1895)

Fig 12.2 Swithland Water Works, with the foreman's house on the right.

Swithland Reservoir covers land in the parishes of Swithland, Woodhouse and Quorn, but the buildings, now listed,[25] at Swithland Water Works lie in the parish of Woodhouse. Designed by Hawkesley of London, they were built in 1895 and are of red brick. The grounds were laid out as an arboretum; one species of every tree that was known to flourish at this latitude was planted. The borders of the formal garden design were planted with over one thousand varieties of heather.

Swithland Hall (1837, 1852)

The 1799 Enclosure Map suggests that the post-medieval[26] (and probably medieval) site of Swithland Hall lay near the present Hall Farm on the other side of Main Street to the church. Local historian John Throsby, describing the Hall in 1790 in Sir John Danvers' day, complained that it was almost impossible to portray pictorially, being

> ...so beset with barns, stables, and something like outhouses, eight feet high stone walls one within another, pigeon houses and high gates, in some places lofty trees, and in a variety of other obstacles which are mortifying in the extreme to a picture maker.[27]

There was a clock over the coach house and stable, under which were inscribed the lines:

> Each day you see me turn about,
> Time fleeth, and the lamp burns out

An undated note[28] indicates the size of the main rooms in Sir John Danvers' manor house and something of its size.

Dining Room	27' x 19'6" wide x 10'2" high
Drawing Room	24' on square & bow 4'9" x 19'6" wide x 18'4" high
Breakfast Room	18' x 16'6" wide x 9'9" high
Best bedroom	13'9" on square & bow 4'9" x 19'6" wide x 8'6" high
Best dressing room	13'9" x 13'9" x 9'9" high
Room over dining room	19'9" x 14'6" x 7'7"
Small room over dining room	14' x 12'
Sir John's room	18' x 16' x 8'
Sir John's dressing room	11'9" x 7'6" square
5 best Lodging rooms	
2 dressing rooms	
4 servants rooms above stairs	

In 1796, Sir John Danvers died and the manor came into the ownership of an Irishman, Augustus Richard Butler Danvers, who had married Sir John's surviving child Mary Danvers in 1792. Augustus Richard was a young spendthrift under whose management the manor and house deteriorated rapidly. When he died in 1820, the building was virtually unliveable in, though it might be that his son and heir George John Danvers Butler Danvers (1794–1866) had not given up on it continuing as his family home. In 1822 and again in 1832 he applied, both times successfully, to the Quarter Sessions to have the main street to the south of the Hall diverted to run to north of it.[29] The new road would have come off Main Street at a point just above Keeper's Lodge and rejoin it at the site of the present North Lodge. The section of the road in front of the church (and manor house) would have become a private road so the old, and what would be the new, Hall sites would not have been divided by a main public carriageway. Possibly because the decision was taken to build a new Hall, the road diversion was never pursued. The map attached to the 1821 publication shows Swithland Hall slightly south of its position on the Enclosure Map. The old Hall was evidently still standing.

An unproven tradition maintains that the old Hall was burnt down in 1822. It cannot, however, have been totally destroyed. Not only is it pictured on the sketch map accompanying the 1832 application for a road diversion, but an 1830 inventory and valuation 'at Swithland Hall'[30] would seem to indicate a possibly empty and part-derelict building, but with various identifiable rooms, among them a butler's pantry, kitchen, housekeeper's closet, wine and ale cellars, larder and dairy – 'all the brick work, roof etc. complete' – laundry, wash house, 'White Room', 'Lady Kaye's Room', nursery, drawing room, as well as stables, groom's house and garden house. One of the outbuildings, situated just in front of the old Hall, looks as if it might have been adapted as the Hall, then, in the course of time, the remains of the previous old Hall were demolished leaving now no trace of

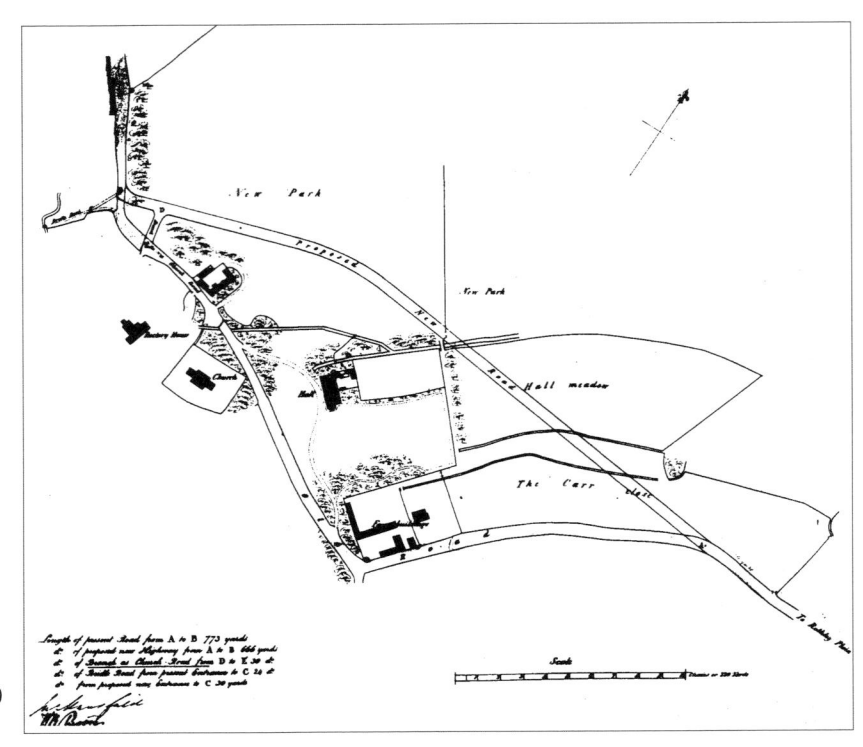

Fig.12.3 Proposed road diversion to the north of Swithland (Old) Hall, 1821.

that building. Seventeenth and eighteenth century garden walls, however, do survive on the northern and western sides of the site.

In his 1826 painting of the Hall,[31] artist John Flower (1793–1861) seems to use some artistic licence. The Hall looks very different from Throsby's description and drawing of some thirty years earlier, and may not, it has been suggested, be that building at all, rather the Hall Manor Farmhouse adapted for the Hall family's use at a time when the old Hall was uninhabitable.[32] Flower's engraving (Fig. 1.9) portrays the mediaeval lantern cross in the foreground and Buddon Wood to the rear, which would make sense were the Hall he painted the adapted Manor Farmhouse. The most striking feature of the building in Flower's picture is a canopy all round the building to the first floor level, the only evidence of that particular feature

Around 1832, George John Butler Danvers commissioned James Pennethorne (1801–1871) to build a new residence in the 'Old' Park. Pennethorne, said to be the son of Thomas Pennethorne, a cousin of Mary Ann Nash, the second wife of John Nash, was born in Worcester in 1801. He was brought up by Mrs Nash, who was believed to be the mistress of the Prince Regent. In 1820 he entered Nash's architect's office, and was placed under the charge of Augustus Charles Pugin.[33] From 1824 to 1826, he completed his architectural education with travel in France, Italy and Sicily, and then returned to Nash's office to begin a career as a government architect. It was, therefore, relatively early in his career that he received the commission to build Swithland Hall.

The new Hall was a two-storey house, and was built on a new site well away from the old Hall. It was cement rendered, with 'banded rustication'[34] to the ground floor. The most striking feature was the entrance on the east side, under a Greek Doric portico of four short sturdy pairs of columns. The main rooms looked westwards towards the hills of Charnwood Forest. Already standing in the park was the old Lantern Cross which Sir John Danvers had removed from Mountsorrel; some landscaping was carried out to provide a suitable setting. Spinneys were planted to the south (The Rough) and east (Crow Wood) of the house, small copses established to the north (Black Spinney and Cook's Plantation), and a wooded walkway (Dale Walk) constructed between the Hall and the church. Carriageways connected the Hall to Main Street, Swithland, at a point adjacent to the water mill, and to Station Road, Cropston. The house was ready for occupation in 1834.

Pennethorne went on to design a number of London public buildings: Christ Church, Albany Street (1836–37), the Museum of Economic Geology (1847–48), the Public Records Office (1851–66), Somerset House, west wing (1852–56), the State Ball Room, Buckingham Palace (1853–55), Duchy of Cornwall Offices (1854–55), and University of London, Burlington Gardens (1866–70). He also carried out various schemes of road improvements, including New Oxford Street, Endell Street, Buckingham Gate, Kensington Palace Gardens, and Commercial Road, Stepney. Swithland Hall was perhaps the only complete house outside London that he built. He was knighted in 1870, and died the following year.

George John Danvers Butler Danvers succeeded to the earldom of Lanesborough in 1847, and in 1852 added two wings to the Hall, and the two lodges. At some point, an ice house – a round, stone built structure with a domed ceiling let into an earth bank – was built at a distance from the Hall. In winter it was filled with ice to conserve food. The ice house still remains, long unused, but in remarkably good condition.

Fig 12.4 Swithland Hall, front view, c. 1900.

Fig 12.5 Swithland Hall, rear view, c. 1900.

At the end of the nineteenth century, and through the early years of the twentieth, Swithland Hall hosted many house parties of some size and magnificence. Both the sixth and seventh Earls maintained considerable households. In 1921, a report by land agent Frank Newman, described the Hall as a plain but somewhat dignified country manor house with modern sanitary arrangements, electric light generated on the premises by an oil engine, and mains water. He considered the property to be 'quite comfortable and in good order', except the domestic quarters, which were particularly poor and in shabby condition. Unfortunately, neither the eighth or ninth Earls were able to raise the Hall to its former glory, but both were generous in allowing the house and grounds to be used for charity events. During the 1939–45 war, the house's extensive cellars were used for the storage of the Quarter Sessions records and archives.

When the ninth Earl moved away in 1967, there was some uncertainty as to the future of the Hall and it was placed on the market. (Many similar houses elsewhere in the country were being lost through demolition at this time.) Swithland Hall was, however, purchased by Mr Adam Page as a private residence and business offices. The Pages extensively restored and refurbished the house and put the grounds in good order. At the beginning of the twenty-first century, therefore, Swithland Hall still stands as a fine example of an historic English country home.

The Lantern Cross[35]

The mediaeval lantern cross in the grounds of Swithland Hall used to stand at the bottom of Baron Lane (now Watling Street) in Mountsorrel, where it was described as being 'hid by a paltry building'. It has a long slender shaft of eight sides, is fluted with carved heads, quatrefoils and other ornaments in the flutes. The cross is raised on three steps with a winged figure at each corner of the pedestal. Sir John Danvers, who was also Lord of the Manor of

Fig. 12.6 North Lodge to Swithland Hall.

Mountsorrel as well as of Swithland, removed the cross from Mountsorrel in 1793, erecting it on his own land at Swithland. As a replacement he gave Mountsorrel its attractive, classical and more functional 'Butter Market'. Mountsorrel tried to recover the mediaeval cross in the late twentieth century, but it was judged too fragile to be moved. The land on which it stands is currently owned by Mr Brian Beeby of Hall Farm.

North Lodge, 250 Main Street (1847)[36]

North Lodge was built for George John Danvers Butler Danvers by James Pennethorne as part of the second phase of the construction of Swithland Hall, the South Lodge being built at the same time. North Lodge stands on Main Street at the foot of the drive to the Hall. Initially it was occupied by George Rockley, a gardener's labourer. From about 1860 it was occupied by William Cook (1833–1916) who was employed as a garden labourer, in addition to his duties as lodge keeper. With the construction of the railway station at Rothley, one of the lodge keeper's responsibilities was to issue passes for those who wished to use the Hall driveways in order to walk from Swithland to the station. According to the 1901 Census, three of the Cook children living at North Lodge worked at the Hall, William Bowman as a

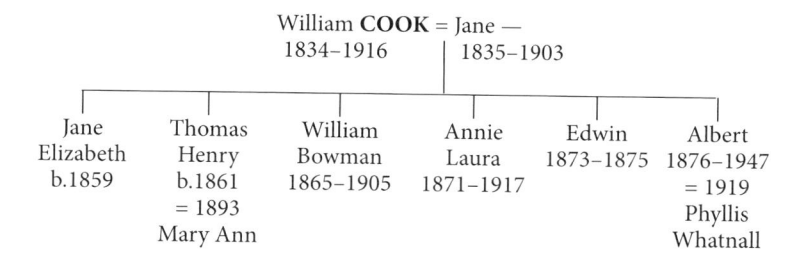

```
                    William COOK = Jane —
                     1834–1916  |  1835–1903
   ┌───────────┬───────────┬───────────┼───────────┬───────────┬───────────┐
   Jane        Thomas      William     Annie       Edwin       Albert
   Elizabeth   Henry       Bowman      Laura       1873–1875   1876–1947
   b.1859      b.1861      1865–1905   1871–1917               = 1919
               = 1893                                          Phyllis
               Mary Ann                                        Whatnall
```

groom, Albert as a gardener and Annie as a dressmaker. When William died in 1916, Albert took over the responsibilities as lodge keeper, and remained at North Lodge until his own death in 1947. Albert Cook was buried on the same day as the wedding of Miss Gweneth Kilby to Mr Ben Gimson. It was reported by the bride that one of the pallbearers had so enjoyed their wedding reception that he fell into the open grave! The lodge was not included in the sale of the Swithland Hall Estate in 1954 but was retained as a house for the gamekeeper. Since 1947, house occupants have included Messrs Frecknall, Partridge, Ryan, Smith, Hutchinson and Shakesby.

Swithland Water Mill (Eighteenth Century)

Until the end of 1894, a water mill stood to the north-east of Hall Farm, presumably adjacent to Mill Spinney. The earliest record of a mill in Swithland comes from a 1315 De Banco (plea) Roll, but the entry does not indicate its situation. The distribution of mills in medieval times was influenced by the right of the Lord of the Manor to insist that his tenants ground their corn at his mill, but by 1700 this seigneurial right, the milling soke, had declined. In 1658, a Survey of Groby Manor[37] recorded that William Danvers 'lately died seized of... one windmill'. In 1752 Sir John Danvers' marriage settlement referred to two water mills and a windmill. A 1770 Groby Manor Estate book recorded that Sir John Danvers was making payment for the watercourse to Swithland Mill, and John Prior's 1777 map of Leicestershire shows one watermill near Hall Farm but no other mills. A Butler Danvers mortgage deed of 1802 mentions two watermills and a windmill.

Henry Guildford, a miller, was living in Swithland between 1703 and 1719. William Whatnall, described as a miller, was working in 1717. A deed of 1722 mentions a William Whittle of 'Sweadland', miller. Another miller, John Newbold, was buried at Swithland in 1788. There is, however, no indication whether they worked one of Swithland's watermills or its windmill.

It is possible that Swithland's windmill may have been located at the west end of the village, as there are successive deeds concerning a field in that area described as Milne Close or Mill Close. In 1622 it is referred to as 'Milne Close'; in 1684 and 1716 as 'Mill Close'. A conveyance of 1775 refers to 'that piece or parcel of arable land called west or windmill field containing one rood or thereabouts', but does not indicate where that field lay. A valuation of 1903 shows a field called Mill Close just south of Main Street, alongside

Swithland Water Mill Tenants

1765–1774	William White	1815–1863	Edward Dexter
1776–1780	Samuel Hardy	1870–1871	Thomas Dann
1781–1784	William Tyler	1875–1880	John Cuffling
1785–1787	John Stevenson	1881–1884	John Payne
1788–1797	Joseph Porter	1891–1894	William Henry Cuffling
1798–1802	William Buckley	1894–1895	Henry Goodman
1803–1814	Samuel Hardy		

the western boundary of the parish. No windmill at this location, however, is shown on Prior's map of 1775, or in the 1799 Swithland Enclosure Award. Both Prior's map and the enclosure award do, however, show the watermill adjacent to Hall Farm, where the millers appear to have had the use of two closes amounting to about 10 acres, as well as the mill house and millpond.

During the nineteenth century, the diversion of rivers into water storage reservoirs and for urban flood prevention schemes deprived a number of millers of their supply of water. They were forced to convert to an alternative power source or close. Leicester Corporation's need for water storage, and their construction of Cropston Reservoir in 1875, took away some of the water from Swithland Mill. The Earl of Lanesborough was paid £855 4s 9d by the Corporation as compensation for his water rights to Swithland Water Corn Mill and Quorn Mill. Twenty years later, with the construction of Swithland Reservoir, Swithland's watermill was put out of operation totally. The mill at Quorn was also affected and its water supply impounded; the miller was awarded £2,750, paid in 1893, by way of compensation. Swithland's last miller was Henry Goodman from Poplar in London, but his employment did not last long. His three children of school age, Gertrude, Henry and Eleanor, were admitted to Swithland School in November 1894 and left on 11th January 1895.

The Swithland mill house survived as a boathouse, a one-storey building with a steep pitch roof, slate and rubble gable end, and sidewalls of brick. What remained of the water wheel indicated that it was a breast-shot wheel with wooden buckets.

Hall Farm (Eighteenth and Nineteenth Century)

A colourful carved stone panel of Sir Joseph Danvers' coat of arms stands proudly just below one of the first floor windows of Hall Farm, indicating that the oldest parts of the present building probably date from the early eighteenth century. The farmhouse was substantially rebuilt in the early nineteenth century. The adjacent barns, however, erected by Sir Joseph in 1749–50, remain much as they were when they were first built.

Hall Farm has had some interesting tenants. David Chapman, who was evicted in 1827 for falling behind with his rent, was one of the witnesses called by a Shepshed branch of the Danvers family to support their claim to the title. George Morris was also the village blacksmith. The Cufflings were a farming family who between them tenanted the farm for over fifty years. Some members of the family were involved with the Methodist chapel in the village, among them William Cuffling who was openly critical of Rector Murray Dixon, who himself farmed Hall Farm after the Cufflings ended their tenancy. Rector Murray Dixon took on managing the farm for some years in order to increase his income, but discovered that farming was not his forte. Ambrose Copson, tenant from 1908–32, was a member of the relatively extensive Copson family, some of whose descendants still have links with the village.

Fig 12.7 The Cuffling family outside Hall Farm

Fig 12.8 Hall Farm dairy cart.

Hall Farm Owners and Tenants

	OWNERS	TENANTS
1753–1796	Sir John Danvers	
1797–1803	Augustus Richard Butler Danvers	
1804–1829		David Chapman
1830–1832		William Whatoff
1841–1851		George Morris
1851–1876		William Cuffling
1877–1880		David Cuffling
1881–1900		Mary Ann Cuffling
1900–1902		William Henry Cuffling
1903–1908		James Murray Dixon
1908–1932		Ambrose Copson
1933–1935		Ralph Hallam
1935–1956		Harry Banbury
1956–1964	Harry Banbury	
1964–1984	Norman Beeby	
1984–	Brian Beeby	

At the beginning of the twenty-first century, Hall Farm was one of two remaining working farms in Swithland, but although there is still some arable farming, the work has mainly diversified away from traditional agriculture and into livery stabling and the production of Swithland Spring Water.

Fig 12.9 Hall Farm workers.

Fig 12.10 Ambrose Copson with his grand-daughter Rosemarie.

Hall Farm Barns (1749, 1750)[38]

Two almost unaltered eighteenth century barns stand on the Hall Farm corner on Main Street. Each is built of granite and slate, with some red brick and a Swithland slate roof. One has an inscription carved on an interior roof beam 'Sir Joseph Danvers Baronet, 1749'; the inscription in the other is simply '1750'. Behind and at right angles to the 1749 barn is a single-storeyed stable of the same period.

Hall Estate Gazebos

The two round 'towers' standing on Main Street, one by Hall Farm and one near the school, were part of the Swithland Hall Estate buildings. They were built from Mountsorrel granite and Swithland slate and were reputedly used by the nineteenth century estate gamekeepers for 'spotting' poachers. They were also used as 'lock-ups' for lawbreakers and local drunks, a wooden staircase leading up to a convenient grill. The bibulous had to sit on a bottom step till a return to sober reality came with the dawn.[39] Village lock-ups fell into disuse after the passing of the County Police Act (1939), after which local police stations were built with their own cells. Charnwood Borough Council lists these 'towers' as eighteenth century constructions, suggesting that, as they originally stood at either end of the old manor house grounds, they were most probably initially folly boundary towers or gazebos.[40]

Fig 12.11 The Gazebo near Hall Farm.

Hall Gardens, 217 Main Street

Fig 12.12 Hall Gardens house before demolition c. 1990.

After the demolition of the remains of the old manor house, various buildings and outbuildings were left, including a cottage (possibly incorporating the remains of the Old Hall building) that came to house the gardener for the (new) Swithland Hall kitchen gardens.[41] From 1841 to 1901 the tenant of Hall Gardens is listed on the census returns as a gardener – Andrew Paterson, for example, was gardener in 1851. Other tenants and Hall gardeners have included Peter Grieve, Richard Rodgers, Mr Paterson, Arthur Pentelow, Edmund Ratcliffe and David Hunt. The property was still being used as the Hall's kitchen garden up to and through the Second World War. One of the 'old' villagers[42] who worked up at the Hall, describing the walled garden with its greenhouses in the years just before the Second World War, said there was a wonderful variety of fresh fruit and vegetables grown for the Hall; she especially remembered the peach trees, the morello cherries and the asparagus bed.

The Hall Estate sale catalogue (1954) described a brick built and slated house at the centre of the holding, standing well back from the road, screened by an orchard and by ornamental and timber trees, under-planted with spring flowering bulbs and approached by a gravel drive. The house comprised on the ground floor, a sitting room, a living room with single oven, a scullery, store room, wash-house and WC, and, on the first floor, five bedrooms approached by two stair cases. Other buildings in the grounds included a large brick-built and slated workshop with a loft, a mushroom house and a blue-brick manure house, and five glasshouses, one of which was a vinery, with Muscatel and Black Hamburg grapes. The extensive productive walled garden contained trained fruit trees, and yards of raspberries, black and red currants and gooseberries. In the 1950s, David and Ada Hunt and their family ran a market-garden business from there. Charnia Grove[43] now stands on the old site of the Hall Gardens. The five detached houses were built in 1990s.

The Old Rectory (c. 1760)

Fig 12.13 The old rectory, late nineteenth century photograph.

A rectory stood adjacent to the church from at least 1650, and probably for some time before. In 1650 The Rectory was valued at £40.[44] Hearth Tax returns of 1664 and 1666 indicate that it was the second largest dwelling in the village, having four hearths. The Rectory was rebuilt by Sir John Danvers, probably during the 1760s. John Throsby, visiting Swithland in 1790 on one of his excursions, reported that 'the church is in good order; the parsonage house, if possible, better. An excellent room, an hospitable clergyman of the name of Lloyde (educated about the middle of the eighteenth century), and a bottle of good port wine, were good things during a heavy shower of rain'.[45]

The Rectory was clearly spacious enough to host the rector's family and servants. In 1841, Rector Erskine, who had five daughters, was listed by the census as having three female servants living in. In 1851, Rector Paget had five servants, including a butler. In 1861, curate John Longhurst and his wife were living in The Rectory; they had seven unmarried children but, on a curate's stipend, could only afford one servant. In 1871, the Treweeke's had three servants, two of whom were members of Swithland's Baum family, but in 1881 the less well-off Sidebottoms had just one. In 1891 the Murray Dixon household employed a coachman, gardener, lady's maid, nurse, cook, housemaid, kitchen maid and nursemaid, though by the time they moved into the 'smaller' new rectory, they were reduced, in 1901, to just four servants, none of whom had been with them ten years previously.

On 5th August 1897, with a new rectory built for him next to the school and opposite the Griffin Inn, James Murray Dixon purchased The Old Rectory and its surrounding 14.757 acres from the Ecclesiastical Commissioners. Initially he let out part of the building and used another part as a grain store, but the floors eventually collapsed under the weight.

Charles Illsley lived, briefly, in the habitable part in 1909, Thomas Beers, gardener to The Rectory from 1910–15 and Charles Driver from 1916. By the end of the Great War, however, the entire house was virtually derelict. It was demolished in 1918, but the entrance from Main Street is still evident.[46]

Keeper's Cottage, 207 Main Street

An old thatched cottage once stood on this site that, until the Hall Estate was sold off in 1959, housed the Hall's gamekeeper. The first redevelopment of the site kept the old footprint of the original cottage and outbuildings, but all that was lost in the 2003 development 'Keeper's Close'. The place where one of the old village pumps stood is still, however, evident.

Gamekeepers 1829–1959

1829	Thomas Vestey (1778–1833)
1834–1841	Joseph Cresswell (b. c.1806)
1849–1851	William Jeffcoat (b. 1807)
1861–1875	George Handley (1808–1878)
1880–1896	William Bunney (1827–1907)
1900–1904	Thomas Johnson
1908	William Knox
1909–1945	Percival George Lloyd (1872–1945)
1945–1959	Jim Carpenter

The old Keeper's Cottage was a popular postcard view in the early years of the twentieth century. One was purchased and sent in 1912 to Miss C.

Fig 12.14 Postcard view of Keeper's Cottage, c. 1910.

Fig 12.15 Keeper's Cottage, 1950s.

Fig 12.16 (above) [back left to right]; Percy Lloyd, Harold Sharpe; [middle left to right]: Phyllis Lloyd, Dorothy Sharpe; [front left to right]: Rodney Lloyd, Paul Sharpe, VE Day 1945.

Fig 12.17 (right) Jim Carpenter, keeper, with son David.

Lynes[47] at the House of Mercy in Chester. Harriette's message paints a little portrait of village life at the time.

> Dear C, You will be surprised to see where I am if you have not heard from Dransfield. I did so want to see the snowdrops and at last I have managed it. They are nearly over, and the violets are coming on. I am staying with Lizzie H. Her mother keeps wonderful. Went up to Mr Bates last night, heard all about FC, will tell you in a letter all about it. Am wondering how you are. I do hope better. But the weather has turned to cold again here. Am going home on Wednesday all being well if there are any trains. Perhaps you will send me a line before I go back. Have got Ella with me. With love from Harriette.[48]

Fig 12.18 The village pump outside Keeper's Cottage.

The School House (1843)[49]

The 1799 Enclosure Map indicates that quite a substantial, long, narrow building was standing on the same site as the present school. It is quite possible that there was a Sunday or even a day school there; certainly Sir Joseph Danvers had bequeathed money for that purpose in his will. Had it been a Sunday school, it would have been run under the auspices of the

Fig 12.19 Swithland School and School House, c. 1910.

parish church and rector. Two lay school masters were, however, resident in Swithland in 1830, Joseph Barry and John Clarke, so a day school on the site at that time looks to have been a possibility.

The school may well have been the first fully red-brick edifice to have been built in the village. In 1843, George John Danvers Butler Danvers adapted or rebuilt the school building as a day school and his coat of arms with that date is displayed above the main front entrance to the school. This single storey building comprised a master's house to the left of the principal door and accommodation for teaching seventy-five children to the right. The first school master we know to have lived there, with his parents and siblings, was Stephen Clark who, in the 1841 Census was twenty years old. (Stephen Clark, senior, was a shoemaker). In the 1851 Census, Stephen Clark, 29, is recorded as living on his own in the School House, with his parents and their family living in Long Close, 118 Main Street. From 1851 until 1988[50] a school teacher lived in the School House in the village, but in 1994 the school teacher's accommodation was turned into classrooms.

Brook Farm

Brook Farm and Cottage

TENANT FARMERS		COTTAGE	
–1793	Samuel Clarke		
1794–1842	James Ward	1841	John Bowler
1842–1864	Benjamin Petts	1851	William Emerson
1864 –	Joseph Pratt (from Long Close)	1871	Thomas Clark

At the turn of the nineteenth century a smallholding of 4.19 acres and a cottage stood where the car park of the Griffin Inn now stands. Brook Farm was managed until 1793 by Samuel Clarke and from 1794 to 1842 by James Ward. The Swithland Enclosure Map refers to the holding as 'Ward's Homestead'. James Ward's daughter, Mary, had married Benjamin Petts in 1829, and on Ward's death in 1842, Petts took over farming the homestead.

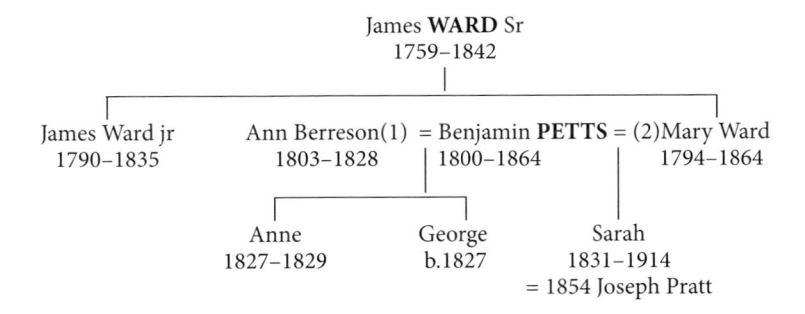

```
                        James WARD Sr
                          1759–1842
                              |
   ┌──────────────────────────┼──────────────────────────┐
James Ward jr    Ann Berreson(1) = Benjamin PETTS = (2)Mary Ward
 1790–1835         1803–1828    |   1800–1864        1794–1864
                        ┌───────┴───────┐                |
                      Anne            George           Sarah
                    1827–1829         b.1827         1831–1914
                                                  = 1854 Joseph Pratt
```

Village Buildings and Families

In 1851 Brook Farm consisted of 11 acres. There had been some re-adjustment of land, and Petts' holding included Creswell's Close and Long Close. In 1861 Petts was farming 23 acres. Petts' daughter married Joseph Pratt and after Petts died in 1864 Joseph and Sarah Pratt went to live at Long Close Cottage at No. 118, farming the land from that holding. Brook Farm continued for a short period as a residence, but it eventually fell into disrepair and was demolished.

An adjacent cottage to Brook Farm housed agricultural workers. In 1841 John Bowler lived there, in 1851 William Emerson and in 1871 Thomas Clark. That cottage also fell into disrepair, and was eventually demolished.

The Griffin Inn, 174 Main Street

Fig 12.20 The Griffin Inn, early twentieth century.

A hostelry has existed on the site of The Griffin Inn, opposite the school, for at least three hundred years. The present building is thought to date from about 1700, and there were probably earlier buildings on the site. Until the end of the twentieth century, there was an evident 'coaching entry' to the inn yard. Recent major alterations have, however, removed this feature, and have changed the character of the courtyard.

The name 'The Griffin' is thought to be a misnomer for the 'Wyvern', which was the crest of the Danvers family. (The Lanesborough crest also included a cockatrice.) The griffin is an imaginary animal consisting of a compound of a lion and an eagle: the lower part of a lion (tail and hind legs) joined to an upper part of an eagle (head, fore-part, legs, talons and wings). The griffin has four legs, whereas the wyvern and cockatrice have only two. The body of both wyvern and cockatrice end in a large long tail and both have wings. The wyvern has the legs and feet of an eagle, and the head of a serpent – with tongue extended and barbed; the cockatrice has the legs and feet of a cock, and the head of a cock – also with tongue extended and barbed.

The Griffin Inn Tenants

1773–1783	William Clarke	1922–1925	Joseph Frisby
1783–1802	John Phillips [Schraeder]	1928–1959	Samuel Briers, Eric Briers
1803–1837	John Lakin	1967–1983	William Feasey
1838–1850	John Wright	1987–1993	Norman Jefferson
1851	Suzannah Wright	1993–1995	Richard Dimblebee
1851–1854	George Harris	1995–2000	Alan Birchenall
1860–1881	Thomas Chapman	2002–date	John Cooledge
1884–1900	Henry Lovett		
1903–1916	Edwin Pepper		

The first known tenant of the public house was William Clarke. It was in his time, in 1780, that Henry Hind, manager of the slate quarries, was in correspondence with Sir John Danvers about Sir John's public house at Swithland. Sir John was anxious that Hind's slate-pitmen should patronise it and not the hostelry on Brand Lane.[51]

Clarke was succeeded in 1783 by John Phillips, otherwise John Phillips Schraeder. The Leicester gossip, William Gardiner, writing in 1838, recounts a visit he paid to the inn about 1790.

> In one of our rambles through the forest (with Sir John Danvers), we regaled ourselves at the only inn he permitted on his domain. My friend, the Abbé Dobler, was with me; and, recollecting that the landlord was an old Prussian coachman of Sir John's, I requested my friend to speak to him in German, which he did as he was handing us some radishes and bread-and-butter. On hearing his native tongue, the old coachman was so astounded, that the spartan dish fell from his hand, and, as soon as he could speak, he told my friend that he had not heard a word of German for more than forty years. It is impossible to describe the pleasure the old man evinced during our stay; and when we would have discharged our reckoning, we were told that we had nothing to pay, and he hoped he might have the honour of receiving us as friends as often as we visited the forest.[52]

John Phillips Schraeder married Rebekah Sutton of Quorn on 8th November 1765 in Quorn parish church. Little more is known of him, except that he was landlord in 1799 when the Swithland Enclosure Commissioners met at his house 'at the sign of the Wifforn'.

Schraeder's successor, John Lakin, farmed 18 acres as well as keeping the public house. Throughout the nineteenth century other tenants worked on a smallholding in addition to keeping the inn. In 1851 George Harris was farming 15 acres. Thomas Chapman was sometime a butcher and latterly a publican and grazier. Edwin Pepper was the tenant of Longlands Farm before taking over The Griffin; for a brief period he continued at Longlands, farming all 181 acres, as well as running The Griffin, but eventually he concentrated solely on the public house and its 11 acres of smallholding.

In the 1870s, when Thomas Chapman was advertising the merits of 'The Griffin Hotel' to 'Picnic parties and visitors to the charming village of Swithland and Charnwood Forest', he spoke of its 'large dining room, one of the olden time, capable of accommodating two hundred people'. For most villagers then, however, this large, high-roofed brick building behind the roadside elevation of the inn was seen as the Club Room, where the larger village gatherings took place until the erection of the Memorial Hall in 1920. In 1947, The Griffin Inn was passed from the manor estate to Everards, the Leicester brewers. The publican between 1928 and 1959 was Samuel Briers. He was a police officer in London before he came to Swithland, and was proud to tell of his experience as the arresting officer of suffragette Emmeline Pankhurst.[53]

Fig 12.21 Samuel Briers, arresting police officer, with Emmeline Pankhurst.

Rose Cottage, 160 Main Street (Early Nineteenth Century)

From at least 1622 to 1928, Rose Cottage was the site of the village smithy. The present building of slate and granite rubble with some red brickwork is listed as 'early nineteenth century.' Rose Cottage did not, however, seem to get the complete 1840s makeover that some of the other estate buildings received.

Fig 12.22 Rose Cottage, c. 1900.

Swithland Blacksmiths

1622	Francis Sutton	1839–1888	George Morris
1702–1712	John Walker	1842–1851	John Morris
1708–1721	William Barnet	1842–1850	John Dudley
1801	George Lovatt	1896	Samuel Hill
1802–1816	Francis Morris	1912	William Thompson
1813–1818	William Potter	1916–1928	Richard Walker

The (1898) Rectory, 165 Main Street

The large three-storey red brick rectory was built in 1898 for James Murray Dixon who, after his move, bought the dilapidated old rectory beside the church from the Ecclesiastical Commissioners to house Hall Farm labourers and store grain. Dixon, his wife and children moved into the new rectory just before the 1901 census. It was one of the few village buildings with a second floor, giving quarters for their four servants. At some time Otto Murray Dixon used one of the upper rooms as his studio.

Rectors who lived in the 1898 Rectory

1900–1925	James Murray-Dixon	1959–1965	Alex Maxwell
1925–1930	Frederick Oliver	1966–1973	Geoffrey Stuart Smith
1931–1939	John Mackay	1973–1976	Bill Carlile
1955–1958	Cecil Harcourt	1977–1991	Raymond Walters

Fig 12.23 Otto Murray Dixon outside the 1898 rectory, c. 1910.

During the Second World War, there was a long interregnum at The Rectory, and the house was used as a convalescent home for soldiers. After the war the benefice was still vacant, and the diocese, which hoped to amalgamate Swithland with another benefice, sold The Rectory in 1947 to a private buyer, against the expressed wishes of parishioners and church council. In 1955, however, Mrs Linwood Wright of The Cottage, 1 Main Street, Swithland, bought the house back and gave it to the parish in 1963, on condition that it be used as a house for a resident priest in Swithland, which it was until Walters retired in 1991. At that point the diocese attempted, yet again, to sell the house with no promise of buying another, or of housing a priest in Swithland. Local campaigning foiled this attempt, and, by agreement with the parish and Church Commissioners, the old house was sold and a new rectory built in its grounds. The next priest-in-charge moved to live there in 1994. In the 2000 creation of a multi-benefice of Woodhouse, Woodhouse Eaves and Swithland, it was formally agreed that the rectors of the new benefice should live in the parsonage house in Swithland.

The 1898 house was set in 3 acres of ground. A small part of the land was sold to Leicestershire County Council in 1963 in order to extend the school playground.[54]

Langton House (The Laundry), 146 Main Street (1845)

As the inscribed tablet over the door indicates, this cottage was re-built in 1845 on the instructions of George John Danvers Butler Danvers. Francis and Mary Raynor were living there during the 1871 and 1881 census. A laundress worked from this cottage between c. 1881 and c. 1901. In 1909 W. Sharman lived there, in 1931 Harold Peach, in 1936 H.M. Bowes-Lyon and D.D. Longmore and from 1939 to 1959 Peter and Barbara Berridge. James and Marjorie Hall (during the 1960s) were succeeded by John and Margery Lumley who lived there until John's death in 2005. The house is currently (2010) owned by Gareth and Harriet Jones.

Thatched Cottage, 144 Main Street (c. 1840)[55]

Charles Bunney (1823–1900), who lived at Thatched Cottage from c. 1861, was tenant farmer at Bybrooke Farm from 1871–91. After his death, Thatched Cottage continued to be lived in by members of the Bunney family, probably first by his son Samuel (1851–1918) and his wife Emma and then, after his mother's death in 1934, by Alwyn Bunney and his wife Clara. As well as managing his smallholding at No. 144, Alwyn ran a milk round from Astills Dairy, Cropston. Astills Farm was managed by his cousins Annie Margaret and Dorothy; the Leicestershire War Agricultural Committee reported in 1941 that their holding was 'well managed and this is reflected in the condition of the land and the stock', but that they did not have 'the knowledge and experience of an arable farmer'.[56] From 1939 to 1953 Thatched Cottage was the home of Bill and Peggy Lloyd, who moved

Fig 12.24 Thatched Cottage (No. 144) and the Laundry (No. 146), a laundress in the doorway.

Fig 12.25 Samuel Bunney outside Thatched Cottage with his horse, Polly.

there from Exning Farm, where they had been lodging with Charles and Ellen Bunney. Walter and Evelyn Shrive followed the Lloyds, living in Thatched Cottage until c. 1974.

Fig 12.26 Samuel Bunney and his son Alwyn on the left with their sheep, c. 1890.

140–142 Main Street (c. 1840)[57]

Originally No. 140 Main Street was one of a pair of cottages re-built by George John Danvers Butler Danvers in the early 1840s. Henry Bunney, a gardener, lived here in 1871 with his wife Mary and children William, Letitia and Sarah. His widowed and blind mother-in-law was then living with them. By 1881, Henry's brother George, also a gardener, had replaced him and lived there with his wife Jane and their two sons, Fred, then an agricultural labourer, and Walter, a bricklayer. In the 1930s, Sid and Annie Bunney lived at No. 140, buying the house when the estate was sold in 1954.

No. 142, the other half of 140, was lived in by estate workers until the 1954 sale. In 1861 Joseph Preston may have lived there; in 1871, it was the home of William Brookhouse, an eighty-one year-old ex-soldier living on a pension. Brookhouse was followed by Thomas and Jane Raynor (1881 Census), then by Mary Raynor (1891 Census), George Frith (1909 valuation), Elizabeth Tyers (1924), Hannah Frith (1931), and, from 1933 to 1965, by Albert Hubbard and his wife Elizabeth.

136–138 Main Street

This pair of eighteenth century cottages was among the first restored by George John Danvers Butler Danvers, probably in the early nineteenth century. Thomas Hodges and his wife Eliza lived at No. 136 between 1871 and 1901. They described themselves on the 1891 Census as an agricultural labourer and a seamstress, then, in 1901, Thomas, 67, was a labourer and a road repairer. George Spence, who lived with his wife Violet at No. 136 in the 1920s and 30s, was at one point tower captain at St Leonard's Church. The Spences were followed into No. 136 by Ralph and Lilian Harrison (c. 1950–66). Dorothy Brown followed the Harrisons (c. 1969–70) and the house is now owned (2010) by Nicholas Burrows.

Next door at No. 138, John Adams, an agricultural labourer (1871 Census), was followed by Thomas Johnson a gamekeeper (1881, 1891 Census), then by George Clowes, a waterworks labourer (1901 Census). In 1924, Joseph and Jane Bunney lived there. Mr and Mrs J. Hornsby, who shared the accommodation with Mr and Mrs A. Stevenson during the 1930s, were related to the Hornsby family of model railway fame. The Stevensons were still living at No. 138 in 1974. The house is now owned (2010) by Norman Reynolds.

137 Main Street

This two-storey slate and granite rubble stone cottage, with dormer windows and Swithland slate roof built at the side of the street, has been assumed to date from 1718[58] on the strength of an engraved slate tablet on its southern elevation carrying the inscription 'JPE 1718'. No building, however, is shown in this location on the 1799 Swithland Enclosure Award Map, which shows considerable accuracy in other respects. The style of the building is less sophisticated than the several cottages erected in Swithland in the 1840s by George John Danvers Butler-Danvers. The house is likely, therefore, to have been built c. 1820, possibly incorporating material from another house, which might have included the slate date plate.

For most of the nineteenth century, the cottage was occupied by members of the Raynor family. Francis Raynor (1806–1888) was an assistant gardener; Zachariah Raynor (1792–1861) was an agricultural labourer; his son Thomas Raynor (1836–1913) was also a general farm labourer.

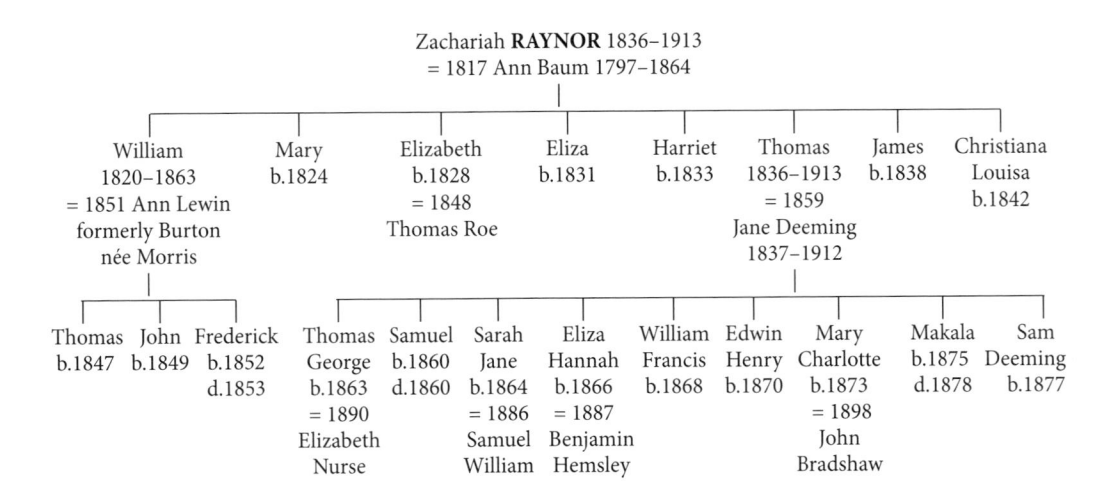

Zachariah **RAYNOR** 1836–1913
= 1817 Ann Baum 1797–1864

| William 1820–1863 = 1851 Ann Lewin formerly Burton née Morris | Mary b.1824 | Elizabeth b.1828 = 1848 Thomas Roe | Eliza b.1831 | Harriet b.1833 | Thomas 1836–1913 = 1859 Jane Deeming 1837–1912 | James b.1838 | Christiana Louisa b.1842 |

William's children: Thomas b.1847, John b.1849, Frederick b.1852 d.1853

Thomas's children: Thomas George b.1863 = 1890 Elizabeth Nurse | Samuel b.1860 d.1860 | Sarah Jane b.1864 = 1886 Samuel William | Eliza Hannah b.1866 = 1887 Benjamin Hemsley | William Francis b.1868 | Edwin Henry b.1870 | Mary Charlotte b.1873 = 1898 John Bradshaw | Makala b.1875 d.1878 | Sam Deeming b.1877

Fig 12.27 Nos. 142–130 Main Street and opposite, No. 137.

Tom and Elizabeth Underwood lived at No. 137 from c. 1924 until Tom's death in 1936. Roger and Ada Hearst lived in the cottage from c. 1950 until the 1990s.

Fig 28 No. 137 Main Street, garden view from footpath, 1990s.

132–134 Main Street

The 1984 listing of this pair of cottages dates them to c. 1860, when older cottages on this site were restored by the fifth Earl.

It is just possible that the Baum family lived at No. 132 before the Burton family, but the early census returns are not specific enough. A John Baum, who lived in the village in 1841 was a 'labourer in woods' and in 1851 a 'timber dealer'; he died in 1881 and his youngest son George moved back into the village as a joiner. According to the 1891 Census, Henry Burton, a slate cleaver, lived at No. 132; he was followed, by George Minkley, according to the 1901 Census a 'waggoner on farm'.

Between 1881 and 1918, Samuel (1852–1918) and Emma Bunney kept a shop at No. 134. They described themselves in the 1891 Census returns as, respectively, 'provision dealer' and 'mistress'. In the 1901 Census, Samuel was listed as 'grocer and grazier'. They were followed into the cottage c. 1918 by Joseph and Hilda Harrison, Hilda was Samuel and Emma's youngest daughter, then in c. 1969 by Joseph's son Ralph and his wife Lillian. Ralph Harrison kept racing pigeons, livestock and poultry and grew vegetables. They farmed two fields next to Leicester Lane called Bunneys Closes, which lie next to the Pit Close field. Harrison also farmed what is called The Pollards, also known as Strip, and the field on the opposite side of Main Street. Lillian Harrison (d. 2010) was affectionately known in the village as 'the egg lady' as she sold their eggs, as well as their vegetables, from her cottage door for many years.

Exning Farm, 128–130 Main Street

Exning Farm is sometimes called Exlands Farm, the name deriving from the fact that some of the farmland originally lay in the Exlands open field. Exning was another of the post-enclosure farmhouses and built mainly from local granite and slate. The amount of land farmed there varied over the years; Exning Farm was affected by various changes in land ownership. Daniel Bates farmed the land at some point before Edward Tyers took up the tenancy between 1871 and 1881. Tyers farmed Exning for about thirty years. From c. 1930–65 Charles Benjamin and Ellen Bunney farmed there. They sold the property to architect Roland Smith in 1965, who converted the farmhouse into two private dwellings, Nos. 128 and 130 Main Street.

Pit Close Cottage, 124 Main Street (Possibly Seventeenth Century)

Pit Close Cottage is an attractive thatched cottage at the junction of Main Street and Leicester Road. It has been claimed that it is the oldest surviving secular building in Swithland.[59] There was certainly a complex of buildings on the site at the end of the eighteenth century; four building 'blocks' are clearly marked on the 1799 Enclosure Map. The present cottage, and some outbuildings at right angles to the village street, stand on two parts of that 1799 footprint. Other buildings were evidently demolished after 1799.

Fig. 12.29 Pit Close Cottage, early twentieth century, offering 'tea and hot water'.

Joseph Doughty, a carpenter, lived in the cottage from c. 1828 to c. 1861. In the 1828–30 Swithland Hall Estate rental books, Doughty is listed as renting there a 'cottage, garden and shop',[60] which indicates that there were probably only the two buildings on the site at the time. Members of the Hemsley family[61] lived at Pit Close Cottage from at least 1891 to 1953, and possibly from some time before. Other members of the family lived at Pit Close Farm. It is likely that the name 'Pit Close Cottage' refers to the farm dwelling's link between the cottage and the farm. At the beginning of 1954, Pit Close Cottage was semi-derelict, but it was purchased and restored by Mr Walter Payne, a Leicester cobbler who lived there until the 1970s, when it was bought by Willoughby and Jo Garton.

Workhouse Close

In the nineteenth century, a field adjacent to the site where the village war memorial now stands was called Workhouse Close. We know that from at least 1750–1834 the Swithland Overseers of the Poor rented three cottages from the Hall Estate and it is likely that those cottages were situated somewhere near Workhouse Close. The 1799 map does show a complex of buildings opposite Exning Farm that would appear to have been demolished before the 1840s, as they were not part of George John's renovation programme.[62]

Memorial Hall (1920)

The village Memorial Hall, formally opened in 1920, was built as a permanent memorial to those inhabitants of Swithland who fell in the Great War. It is a wooden chalet-like building, surrounded by a verandah, standing in generous grounds and providing space for outdoor village

Fig. 12.30 Memorial Hall.

events. The old village stocks were rescued and re-positioned in one corner of the grounds.[63]

In an indenture dated 12th February 1929, the seventh Earl of Lanesborough formally gifted the site of Swithland Village Hall to the trustees of the Swithland War Memorial Fund. The first trustees were named as the seventh Earl of Lanesborough, Disney Charles Barlow, Ambrose Copson, Frank William Orr and the Revd F.J. Oliver, rector.

> This indenture made the twelfth day of February one thousand nine hundred and twenty nine Between the Right Honourable Charles John Brinsley Butler (7th) Earl of Lanesborough (hereinafter called 'the Vendor') of the first part The Equity and Law Life Assurance Society whose registered Office is at 18 Lincoln's Inn Fields in the County of London (hereinafter called 'the Mortgagees') of the second part and the said The Right Honourable Charles John Brinsley Butler (7th) Earl of Lanesborough, Disney Charles Barlow of the Chase Woodhouse Eaves in the County of Leicester Esquire, Ambrose Copson of the Hall Farm Swithland in the said County of Leicester Frank William Orr of 6 Bedford Row in the County of London Esquire and Frederick James Oliver MA of the Rectory Swithland in the County of Leicester Clerk in Holy Orders or other the Rector for the time being of the Parish Church of St Leonard's Swithland in the said County of Leicester the Trustees of the Swithland War Memorial Fund (hereinafter called 'the Trustees') of the third part.[64]

The terms of the Trust Deed covered a variety of uses. One 'permits the Rector of Swithland to have and enjoy without payment the sole and exclusive use of the said buildings on every Sunday of each year for

Village Buildings and Families

ecclesiastical or religious purposes and also the like use without payment on such other day of the week as the Trustees may from time to time determine for any ecclesiastical purpose or for the purpose of mission services, Sunday schools, or Meetings, or for any object or purposes having in view the spiritual, moral, social or intellectual wants of professing members of the Church of England'. Another allows that the trustees 'shall permit the said buildings to be used for lectures, concerts, dramatic performances and other public or private entertainments and for meeting classes and other assemblies connected with Parliamentary, Municipal, Parochial or other Elections, or with religious, philanthropic or other Societies or purposes or as a Reading Room and Club for the use of persons resident in the parish of Swithland, and otherwise for the benefits of the inhabitants of the said Parish ... but in no circumstances shall any intoxicants be sold upon the said premises ... nor shall any gambling or playing baccarat roulette or any games of chance or hazard with dice (except backgammon) or other unlawful game be permitted therein.' The trustees may, however, at their discretion, allow those hiring the hall for private parties or wedding receptions to consume, but not sell, intoxicants on the premises, provided the hirer has previously obtained the appropriate licence from the local authority.'

Though the grounds were gifted to the trustees by Lord Lanesborough, the labour involved in the initial build of the hall was provided by parishioners. John Leatherland, for example, remembers that his father was one of the labourers involved in digging the foundations. Archibald Turner gave generously towards the building, but fundraising events were also staged. One such was held on 17th July 1920, a 'Swithland Hall Fête in aid of the Funds for the Swithland Memorial Hall.' It was opened by one of the Earl's daughters, the Duchess of Sutherland.

The War Memorial, which stands in the grounds, bears the names of those parishioners who gave their lives in the two world wars. It was unveiled and dedicated on Sunday 4th December 1921. Captain R. Gee, VC, MC, MP

Fig 12.31 War Memorial.

unveiled the memorial and the Archdeacon of Loughborough, the Ven P.H. Bowers MA, dedicated it. His dedicatory prayer read:

> To the glory of God, and in proud and loving memory of Brian Danvers Butler, Sidney Mark Collis, HEOM Murray Dixon, Bernard Hornsby, John Thomas Minkley, we dedicate this cross, in the name of the Father, the Son and the Holy Ghost. Amen.[65]

Post Office Cottages, 123–125, Main Street and Lanesborough Cottage, 127 Main Street (c. 1840)

Fig 12: 32 Post Office Cottage and Lanesborough Cottage.

Fig 12.33 Another view from the opposite direction of Post Office Cottage.

The two Post Office cottages, now extended and converted into one dwelling, probably date from the substantial re-building works carried out by George John Danvers Butler-Danvers in the 1840s. They, with Lanesborough Cottage, replaced an older range of buildings on approximately the same site.[66]

One of the early occupants of No. 125 was Elizabeth Wakerley (née Hefford), the widow of Francis Wakerley, an agricultural labourer, whom she had married in 1825, but who died between 1841 and 1851. Elizabeth Wakerley worked as a laundress from about 1840 to 1875, assisted by her daughter, also Elizabeth, who was married in 1870 to George Handley, an agricultural labourer.

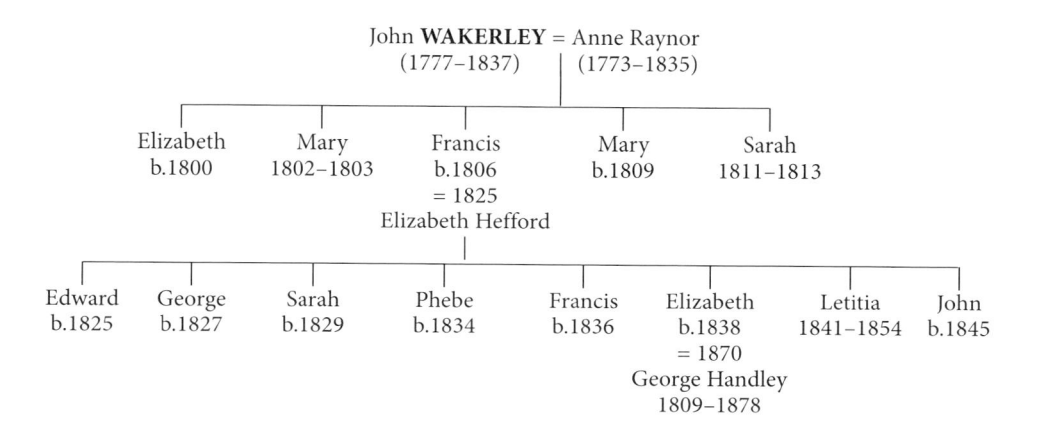

```
                    John WAKERLEY = Anne Raynor
                      (1777–1837)   (1773–1835)

   Elizabeth    Mary      Francis      Mary      Sarah
   b.1800    1802–1803    b.1806      b.1809   1811–1813
                          = 1825
                      Elizabeth Hefford

  Edward  George  Sarah  Phebe  Francis  Elizabeth  Letitia    John
  b.1825  b.1827  b.1829 b.1834 b.1836    b.1838    1841–1854  b.1845
                                          = 1870
                                       George Handley
                                         1809–1878
```

By 1881, the house was occupied by bricklayer John Hodges and his wife Sarah Jane. From 1896, the telegraph, together with a shop, was run from No. 125 by John Henry Hodges (1852–1920), but from 1904, in name as well as practice, by the redoubtable Sarah Jane Hodges (1854–1947). Rector Murray-Dixon's obituary for John Hodges was published in the parish magazine.[67]

> Our village life has lost a landmark in the removal from our earth's sphere of our dear old blind friend John Hodges. For many years he had groped in darkness; yet his cheerfulness was well sustained, and I think I never heard him complain about his affliction, on the other hand he was always ready to apply himself to any useful piece of work of which he was capable, one of his chief delights being to help in the production of the Church music, by acting as organ blower, for which service, by the way, he received the disgracefully inadequate sum of five shillings a year. We shall all miss him, but our loss is his gain; for we like to think of him, by the mercy of God, now in the light and with the fuller knowledge of the love of God in Christ, to whom he drew near, while here on earth, in the Blessed Sacrament of the Altar.
> JMMD, Rector

Fig 12.34
Sarah Jane 'Granny' Hodges (on the right) with a friend.

Fig 12.35
Joe Bunney (1870–1960), Swithland's town crier.

The Hodges were followed into No. 125 by Charles Baxter, then Edmund Wright (1959) and John Beachell (1964).

From c. 1841–c. 1901 the Bowler family lived at No. 123. Both John Bowler and his son John, who followed him, were agricultural labourers. The Bowlers were succeeded by Thomas and Elizabeth Smith. Elizabeth, who died in 1961, was the daughter of Thomas Hodges, Swithland's parish clerk, and she may well have succeeded him in that position.

Thomas, a servant, and Frances Woolston may have lived at 127 Main Street (Lanesborough Cottage) in 1851. They were followed by William and Martha Bunney, whose family was to live in the cottage for about one hundred years, c. 1861–c. 1959. William was, according to the 1861 Census, a labourer and his wife and daughter were lace runners. His son Walter is listed in the 1901 Census as a caretaker at the slate quarries. (Forty years earlier, Walter's cousin, Samuel Bunney, had been killed in an accident at the same quarries.) Walter's son, who followed him into No. 127 was Joseph Bunney, who was for many years the village crier. Mr and Mrs Brook moved into No. 127 after Joe Bunney's death in 1961. The current owners (2010) are Mr and Mrs Hosking.

Corner Cottage, 122 Main Street
Gladys Cottage, 120 Main Street (c. 1800)
Long Close, 118 Main Street

Three cottages[68] forming a long range stand at the junction of Main Street and Leicester Lane opposite the village Memorial Hall. Though much restored, they are thought to have been built before 1799, since they appear on the Swithland Enclosure Award and it is possible they were a part of the improvements to village housing effected by Sir John Danvers.

George Morris, a gardener, listed on the 1851 Census, was an early occupant of Corner Cottage (no. 122). Joseph Woods, agricultural labourer and later postmaster, moved to the house on marrying Morris' daughter Catherine in 1860, and remained there until his death in 1909. From 1876, Joseph Woods oversaw Swithland's first telegraph office in Corner Cottage, which he ran until 1896. After 1896, the telegraph with the post office and a shop was run from No. 125 by John and Sarah Hodges. From c. 1924–c. 1953, Corner Cottage was occupied by Alfred (Fred) Ernest Copson,

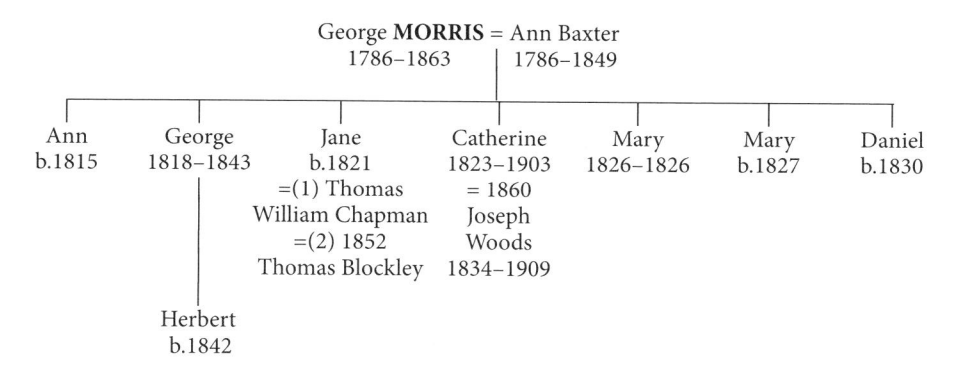

```
                George MORRIS = Ann Baxter
                 1786–1863    | 1786–1849
   ┌──────┬──────┬──────┬──────┼──────┬──────┬──────┐
   Ann    George  Jane   Catherine  Mary   Mary   Daniel
   b.1815 1818–1843 b.1821 1823–1903 1826–1826 b.1827 b.1830
                  =(1) Thomas = 1860
                  William Chapman Joseph
                  =(2) 1852   Woods
                  Thomas Blockley 1834–1909
          │
          Herbert
          b.1842
```

dairyman, and his wife Edith. Fred's father Ambrose Copson lived with them for a while towards the end of his life. John and Dorothy Scott then bought Corner Cottage and lived there until c. 1974. The current owners (2010) are Bill and Pam Howlett.

No. 120 Main Street has seen a succession of different tenants. Thomas, a gardener's labourer, and Dorothy Brooksby were living there at the 1851 Census, then in 1861, Joseph, agricultural labourer, and Jemima Bunney. From 1871 the tenants were James, agricultural labourer, and Harriet Bunney. It was the home of John and Jane Hornsby from the beginning of

Figs 12.36 Outside No. 120 Main Street, early 1930s, [from left to right]: Renée Hemstock, Ada Leatherland, Dolly Hemstock (holding Mary), Mrs Mitchell (and daughter).

Fig 12.37 Dolly Pratt of Long Close, c. 1900.

the twentieth century until the Second World War. They were followed by Joseph and Gladys Handley who lived there until the 1980s. No. 120 takes its name 'Gladys' Cottage' from Mrs Gladys Handley. The current owners (2010) are Alexander and Lorraine Toll.

Long Close, No. 118, was the home of Stephen Clarke (1792–1875), a shoemaker, in 1851 and 1861. From 1864, Joseph Pratt, cottager and agricultural labourer, lived there. He had previously been living at Brook Farm, but farmed the land attached to Brook Farm from No. 118, which became known as Long Close. On Joseph's death in 1902, the smallholding was taken over by his son, Charles Benjamin Pratt. Dorothy Ann (Dolly) Pratt was his daughter. The Pratts were followed by Tom and May Musgrove in 1951.

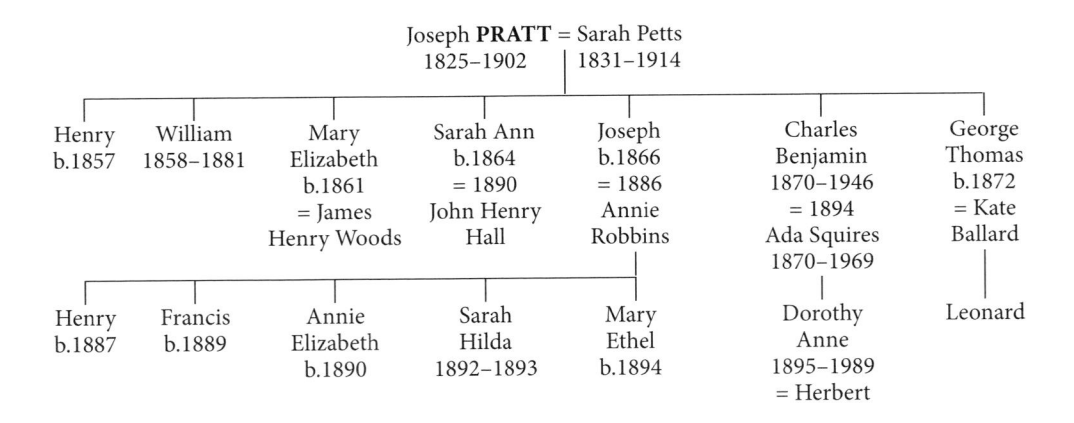

```
                    Joseph PRATT = Sarah Petts
                    1825–1902    | 1831–1914
 ┌──────┬────────┬──────────┬──────────┬────────┬──────────┬──────────┐
Henry  William  Mary        Sarah Ann  Joseph   Charles    George
b.1857 1858–1881 Elizabeth  b.1864     b.1866   Benjamin   Thomas
                 b.1861     = 1890     = 1886   1870–1946  b.1872
                 = James    John Henry Annie    = 1894     = Kate
                 Henry Woods Hall      Robbins  Ada Squires Ballard
                                                1870–1969
 ┌──────┬────────┬──────────┬──────────┬────────┬──────────┬──────────┐
Henry  Francis  Annie       Sarah      Mary     Dorothy    Leonard
b.1887 b.1889   Elizabeth   Hilda      Ethel    Anne
                b.1890      1892–1893  b.1894   1895–1989
                                                = Herbert
```

Longlands Farm, 110–112 Main Street (pre 1799)

The long farmhouse of Longlands Farm also dates from the end of the eighteenth century as, like the cottages at 118–122, the building is recorded on the 1799 Enclosure Award map. Longlands was one of the five major farms that emerged after enclosure with much of its land previously forming part of Swithland's Middle (or North) Field.

The 1851 Census returns show John Oldershaw as the tenant farmer of

Village Buildings and Families

Longlands Farm Tenant Farmers

1846–1854	John Oldershaw	1908–1935	Samuel Hoult
1861–1863	Edward Wildman	1941	Mary Ann Cockerill
1871–1881	John Cuffling	1944–1975	A.W. Cockerill & Sons
1883–1904	Edwin Pepper		

Longlands' 216 acres. He was unmarried, but had something of an extended family living with him, including his fifteen year old nephew Vincent Oldershaw, described as an agricultural labourer, his niece and nephew Mary Ann and Edward Dexter, Elizabeth and Ann Eggleston, two unmarried farmer's daughters and two servants, Mary Mills and Joseph Crooks. They were followed into Longlands by Edward and Frances Wildman, with their three children, aged three, two and six months in 1861, and then, by the 1871 Census by John and Fanny Cuffling. The 1891 Census returns indicate that the school mistress Elizabeth Huntley and her sister Annie were boarding at Longlands Farm with farmer Edwin Pepper and his family and not living in the school house. Samuel Hoult followed Edwin Pepper and then the Cockerills farmed the land from 1939 to the 1970s. The national farm survey reported of Longlands in 1941 that it had been 'recently taken over by the present tenants and the farm appears to be gradually coming up to 'A' standard'.

In 1954 the Swithland Hall Estate sale particulars describe Longlands as 'a valuable mixed farm with house and buildings built of Swithland slate, and situated in the Main Street of the village.' Further details included:

Fig 12.38 Longlands Farm 1935, with Pit Close Farm in the distance.

On the Ground Floor: entrance hall, two sitting rooms with beamed ceilings, living room with single oven Combination range, and beamed ceiling, scullery with Crane Enamelled Boiler, WC, bathroom with lavatory basin (h. and c.), dairy and cellar. On the First Floor, four bedrooms and a box room. All services were connected. The farm buildings comprised cow sheds with water bowls (27 cows), six calf pens, cooling place, blacksmith's shop, three-stall stable, barn, three-bay open implement shed, crewyard, store place and garage. There was also a garden and orchard. Land attached (147 acres) was mainly arable with some grass and pasture.

Longlands Farm and land was bought in the estate sale by Lady Osborne of Kinchley House, Kinchley Lane. Since then the buildings have been modernised and adapted, initially in creating two homes from the one farmhouse. The outbuildings were turned into several dwellings c. 2005, but the 1954 footprint has been maintained. The land is now contract farmed.

Pit Close Farm, 106 Main Street (Eighteenth Century)

Fig 12.39 Benjamin and Eliza Hemsley, c. 1900.

Pit Close Farm is recorded on the 1799 Enclosure Act, so there were farm buildings there from at least the end of the eighteenth century. According to the 1841 and 1851 Censuses, Daniel Bates with his wife Frances farmed 86 acres at Pit Close; in 1861 William and Edith Howson were farming the same acreage; but in 1871 John and Martha Warren farmed just 29 acres. In 1881 Benjamin Hemsley was listed as farming 58 acres; he was followed by his son William in 1908.

Hemsleys had lived in Swithland since at least 1800, in various village dwellings including Pit Close Cottage and Pit Close Farm. The 1841 Census records Benjamin (65, agricultural labourer) and his wife Mary (70) as resident, possibly in one of the Forest End cottages. In 1851, their grandsons Benjamin (born in Woodhouse) and Joseph (born in Swithland) lived in the village and worked as agricultural labourers, though an 1851 document records Benjamin as farming just over 6 acres.[69] The 1861 Census described Benjamin as a cottager, who may then have been living in Pit Close Cottage with his wife Ann (Dorothy) and their four young children. His brother Joseph, listed as an agricultural labourer, also still lived in the village with his wife and young children. By the 1871 Census, Joseph and family had moved away, but

Village Buildings and Families

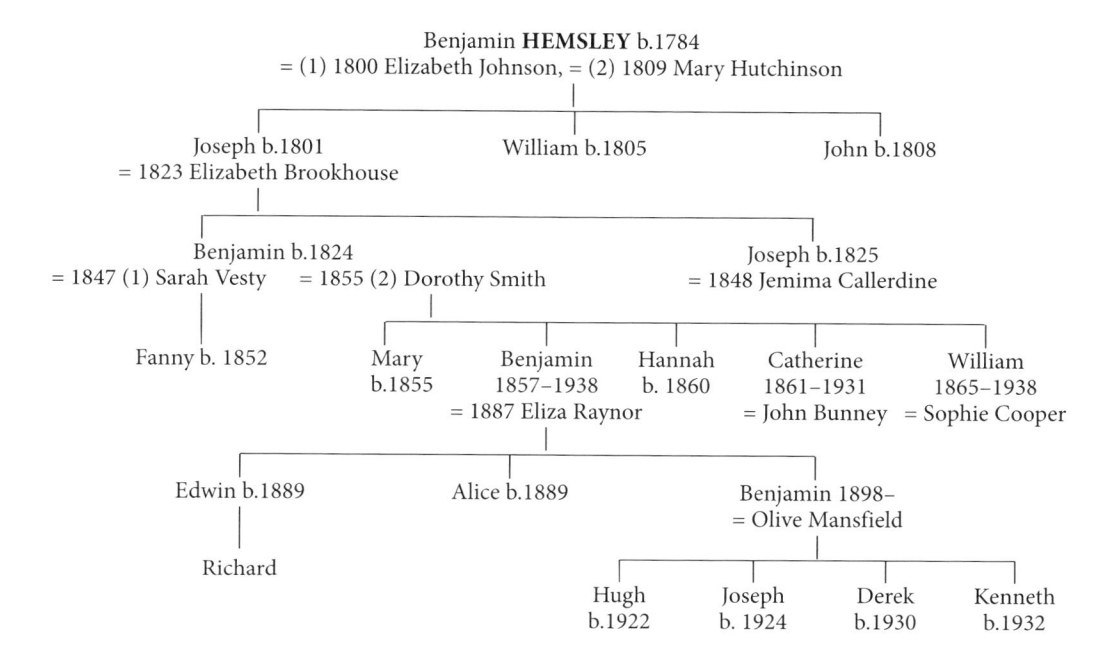

```
                    Benjamin HEMSLEY b.1784
         = (1) 1800 Elizabeth Johnson, = (2) 1809 Mary Hutchinson
                                |
   ┌────────────────────────────┼────────────────────────────┐
Joseph b.1801              William b.1805                John b.1808
= 1823 Elizabeth Brookhouse
   │
   ┌────────────────────────────────────────┐
Benjamin b.1824                        Joseph b.1825
= 1847 (1) Sarah Vesty  = 1855 (2) Dorothy Smith    = 1848 Jemima Callerdine
   │                        │                            │
Fanny b. 1852    ┌──────┬──────────┬──────────┬──────────┬──────────┐
              Mary    Benjamin   Hannah    Catherine    William
              b.1855  1857–1938  b. 1860   1861–1931   1865–1938
                      = 1887 Eliza Raynor  = John Bunney  = Sophie Cooper
                            │
              ┌─────────────┼──────────────┐
          Edwin b.1889  Alice b.1889   Benjamin 1898–
              │                        = Olive Mansfield
           Richard                         │
                           ┌──────┬──────┬──────┬──────┐
                         Hugh  Joseph  Derek  Kenneth
                        b.1922 b. 1924 b.1930 b.1932
```

Benjamin (now an 'agricultural labourer') and his family were still resident. By 1881, Benjamin was at Pit Close, a 'farmer' of 58 acres and Joseph was still an 'agricultural labourer'. He and Jemima had moved back into the village, perhaps into Pit Close Cottage.

In 1936–37, Jack Leatherland and his wife Ada, who had been farming at Quorn, took over the tenancy of Pit Close Farm from Jack's uncle by marriage William Hemsley. Their son, John, and his wife Joan took over the tenancy in 1967, and farmed there until John's retirement in 1996.[70]

Fig 12.40 John (Jack) and Ada Leatherland, Pit Close Farm.

Pit Close Farm Tenant Farmers

1830–1858	Daniel Bates	1908–1935	William Hemsley
1859–1863	William Howson	1936–1967	John William Leatherland
1871–1875	John Warren	1967–	John William Leatherland, jnr
1880–1904	Benjamin Hemsley		

At the time of the Swithland Hall Estate sale, the farm was 50 acres. The 1954 sale catalogue described the accommodation at the farmhouse:

> ...on the Ground Floor: entrance hall, two sitting rooms with beamed ceilings, a living room and a pantry; on the First Floor: three bedrooms; outside a WC and a dairy. All mains services were connected. Outbuildings: three calf pens, stable for five horses, cowshed for ten cows, a barn and a corrugated iron implement shed.

Fig. 12.41 Pit Close Farmhouse, c. 1951.

There was also a slate built cattle shed. The holding was bought from the estate in 1954 by Dr Barton, with the Leatherlands continuing to tenant farm. Barton sold to Tom Boyden in 1973, who then sold to John and Joan Leatherland in 1996. John retired from farming the property in 1996, selling his farming equipment in September 1996. The building was Listed Grade II by the Borough Council in 1984.

Fig 12.42 John and Joan Leatherland, 1996.

Village Buildings and Families

John LEATHERLAND = Jane Stevenson
|
Joseph Leatherland b.1775 = 1807 Ann Marshall
[Vict] Golden Fleece, South Croxton;
|
Thomas Leatherland b.1812 = (1833) Mary Greaves b. c.1813
Blacksmith, innkeeper South Croxton;   Barsby, Ashby Folville, Leicestershire
|
Joseph Leatherland b.1834 = (1864) Mary Smith b. 1831
Master Blacksmith, South Croxton;   Dressmaker, Thurnby, Leicester
|
William Henry Leatherland b.1869 = 1895 Mary Cooper b.1868
Blacksmith, Syston;   Syston
|
John William Leatherland b.1903 = 1930 Ada Mary Haddon b.1902
b. Quorn, Farmer, Pit Close Farm, Swithland from 1937
|
John William Leatherland Jnr b.1932 = 1954 Joan Margaret Derrick b.1931
Farmer, Pit Close Farm, Swithland;   b. Breaston, Derbyshire
|
Ann Leatherland b. 1960

Holly Croft, 104 Main Street

Fig 12.43 Holly Croft, first house on right, 1920s.

A building on this site is shown on the 1799 Swithland Enclosure map. In 1954, when the Swithland estate properties were sold, it was described as 'house, buildings and land, substantially brick built and slated. The accommodation comprised: on the ground floor – entrance, lobby, sitting room, living room with inglenook, kitchen, pantry and dairy, WC; on the first floor 3 bedrooms; outside coalhouse, storeroom, brick and slate built

2-stall stable. Main services of electricity, gas, water and drainage connected – also Kitchen Garden and Croft.'

Church registers indicate that Prestons have lived in Swithland since the end of the seventeenth century. At the end of the nineteenth century the Preston family lived at 104 Main Street; the census records indicate that branch of the family lived in Swithland from 1841, probably in the same house, but the early census records do not positively identify families with particular dwellings. According to the census returns, Joshua Preston, a bricklayer, was born in Swithland. He was married to Mary (Watson) and had four children, Eliza, Harriet, George, Ann and Emma. By 1851 they had five more children: Denby, Charlotte, Lucy, Alex, Thomas. In 1881 Alex and his sister Eliza lived in the same house, which might have been No. 104, with their nieces Harriet and Cecilia Johnson. By 1891 Alex, a builder, had married May, and he, May and Eliza shared the house.

Fig. 12.44 Jack Copson.

From the 1920s to the 1950s the Copson family, first Harry and Vera and then John (Jack) and Joan, lived at No. 104, known then as Holly Croft. They ran a dairy, selling milk, butter and cream from the Hall Farm herds. In 1941 Jack Copson described himself as a producer-retailer and a part-time farmer. He farmed 12 acres, most of it grass for grazing or mowing. In 1941 they had seven or eight cattle, one sow, one horse, seventy-eight hens and eight ducks. The Copsons were followed into Holly Croft in the 1960s by Grahame and Daphne Briers. Mr and Mrs Blackbourn owned No. 104 until 2010 when it was bought by Duncan and Angela Keates.

The White House, 78 Main Street (c. 1780)

The property known as The White House[71] is built on the only piece of land in Swithland that was once owned by the Earls of Stamford and Warrington. It is a whitewash rendered two-storey structure with a Swithland slate roof, gabled cross wings and two brick ridge stacks. Most of the building is of eighteenth century origin – possibly with an earlier core. It is one of the few houses in the village whose history is known to date back to over one hundred years before enclosure.

The 1658 survey of Groby manor lists Robert Hind as leaseholder of a messuage, two crofts and 7 acres on 'Lady Land' in Swithland. The Hearth Tax returns of 1664 and 1666 suggest that this was not a hugely substantial dwelling, as in 1664 Henry Hind is listed as occupying a house with a single hearth. The number increased to two hearths in 1666, but the increase is likely to be attributable to more accurate reporting than to building activity.

Fig 12.45 The White House, from the front, 1947.

Succeeding generations of the Hind family continued to lease the house and land, although they may have sub-let it for some periods. Henry Hind (1726–1801), a leading member of the slate quarrying family, was living there between c. 1755 and c. 1787. In 1787 he signed a lease for twenty years from George Harry, Earl of Stamford, on the messuage, several closes (Home Close, Small Meadow, The Pingle, Hays Close), and land in the open fields. The lease required that Henry should rebuild part of the house, and hints that part had already been rebuilt.

> Henry Hind shall and will before 29th September 1788 at his own costs and charges take down all the old parts of the said messuage or tenement, and rebuild the same in addition to the new part of the messuage or tenement in the form and with such materials and in such manner as specified in a plan and particular agreed between Henry Hind and the said Earl [of Stamford] ... the Earl allowing the said Henry Hind wood in the rough sufficient for the roof and door and window frames of such additional building.[72]

Henry's son, also Henry Hind (1760–1820), lived at the house from c. 1786 to c. 1803. He subsequently moved his residence to Quorn Court, and then to Loughborough, but he leased the Swithland property from Stamford until 1811, when the lease was taken over by his son William Hind (b. 1788). William lived there until 1835, and looks to have retained the lease until his retirement from the slate industry, and from the area, in 1849. The smallholding then appears to have been let to a succession of farmers.

The house and land was sold by George Harry, seventh Earl of Stamford, to Lord Lanesborough in 1874.[73] The land was stated to be in the tenure of Stephen Simpson, and to consist of 9 acres. Simpson and his wife Harriet, the daughter of Swithland tailor Joseph Matts, who married Simpson in 1862, did not live in Swithland.

Land belonging to the White House in 1874

		Acres-roods-perches
The Far Hill	Pasture	2-2-00
House close	Pasture	3-3-37
House, buildings, yard, garden & orchard		0-3-26
The Paddock	Pasture	0-3-37
The Meadow	Pasture	1-0-04

Having bought the land, the Earl of Lanesborough incorporated it into Forest End Farm. The house was then divided into two – the first recorded tenants being bricklayer James Hoult (1824–1896) and his wife Hannah, née Hodges (1832–1890). In 1909 William Woolley, who farmed at Rothley Plain, was a tenant, and from 1933 quarryman and farm labourer Horace Minkley lived there – one of the large and extended family of Minkleys in Swithland. The Minkleys were followed by the Carters (1947–1959) and the Brook-Lawsons (1959–2005).

As befits the home of significant Swithland slate-quarriers, the house and grounds showed significant slate features. Until 2006, for example, when the Brook-Lawsons sold The White House, there was a unique Swithland slate staircase to the right of the front door.

Fig 12.46 The slate staircase in The White House, 2005, Mrs E.P.D. Brook-Lawson.

Penny Cottage, 81 Main Street and Cherry Tree Cottage, 83 Main Street (1842)

The two cottages, Penny Cottage and Cherry Tree Cottage – Grade II Listed in 1982 – were probably built by George John Danvers Butler Danvers. The gabled porch with Tudor arch and wood mould at Penny Cottage has the date 1842 inscribed on a stone shield. In 1851, the cottages were occupied by Frances Matilda Burton, an unmarried seamstress, and Robert Ward, slate cleaver. Shortly afterwards, Cherry Tree Cottage was occupied by William Haywood Gamble (1820–1891), grocer and sometime groom at the Hall. Gamble and his wife Sarah kept a grocery shop there from about 1860 until Gamble's death in 1891. Sometime after the 1901 Census, Herbert Minkley moved in, and it remained the Minkley family home until Herbert and Mary Ann Minkley's youngest daughter, Irene Elsie, died in 1999. After their father died in 1938, Mary Ann lived there with her sons Herbert and Charles Edward (Ted) until her death in 1953, then Charles Edward on his own until he died in 1982. His sister Irene and her husband Robert Mee[74] then moved into the cottage, sharing their home with Brian Vann, son of Irene's elder sister Doris. The current owners (2010), Jeff and Alison Wright and their daughter Beth, moved in into Cherry Tree Cottage in 2003.

Penny Cottage may have been occupied at the 1881 Census by James Hoult, a bricklayer, and his wife Hannah; in 1891 Edwin, coachman and domestic servant, and Hannah Gibbs lived there. By 1896 John Adams (a gardener), his mother Martha, his wife Eliza and their children Emily, Florrie and Albert were in residence. In the 1920s and 30s George and Alice Adnett lived there; they were followed in the 1940s and 50s by Joseph and Gladys Heighton, then the Simpsons, Nicholas Hackett and Cyril and Betty Deacon. The current owners (2010) are Peter and Ann Swann.

In the 1954 Swithland Hall Estate sale catalogue Cherry Tree Cottage was described as having accommodation on two floors comprising living room with beamed ceiling, kitchen and two

Fig 12.47 William Hayward Gamble of Cherry Tree Cottage.

Fig 12.48 Wedding group, Emily Adams of Penny Cottage to Charles Sherman, 1896.

Fig 12.49 Cherry Tree Cottage.

bedrooms, with a washhouse, coal house and closet outside. Electricity was from the public supply, and water was obtained from a pump (access shared by the occupier of Penny Cottage). Penny Cottage was sold separately (in a lot with Forest End Farm); at the time no main services were connected to the cottage.

Cherry Tree and Penny Cottages have remained semi-detached dwellings, but both have been developed since 1954.

Harold Balm's Backside

Cherry Tree and Penny Cottages seem to have replaced an earlier building or row of buildings, which might have included the home of Harold Balm or Baum whose land provided a reference point for property descriptions in many conveyances.

Papers relating to land belonging to the Braunston family suggest that Harold Baum was living in Swithland in the 1730s, but nothing is known of

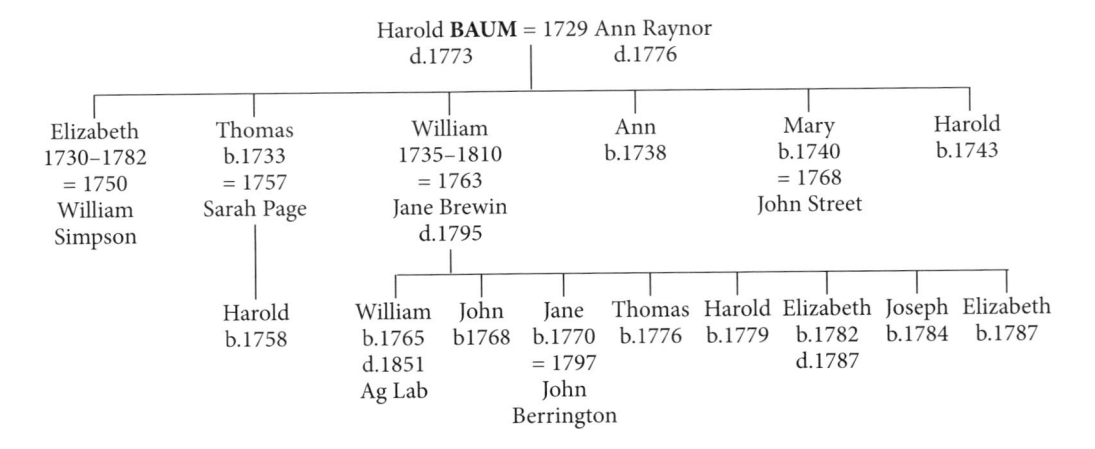

```
                    Harold BAUM = 1729 Ann Raynor
                        d.1773  |   d.1776
    ┌───────────┬───────────┬───────────┬───────────┬───────────┐
Elizabeth   Thomas      William        Ann        Mary       Harold
1730–1782   b.1733      1735–1810      b.1738     b.1740     b.1743
= 1750      = 1757      = 1763                    = 1768
William     Sarah Page  Jane Brewin                John Street
Simpson                 d.1795
            │           │
          Harold    ┌────┬────┬────┬────┬────┬────┬────┐
          b.1758  William John Jane Thomas Harold Elizabeth Joseph Elizabeth
                  b.1765 b1768 b.1770 b.1776 b.1779 b.1782  b.1784 b.1787
                  d.1851       = 1797                d.1787
                  Ag Lab       John
                               Berrington
```

BRAUNSTON Family from Swithland

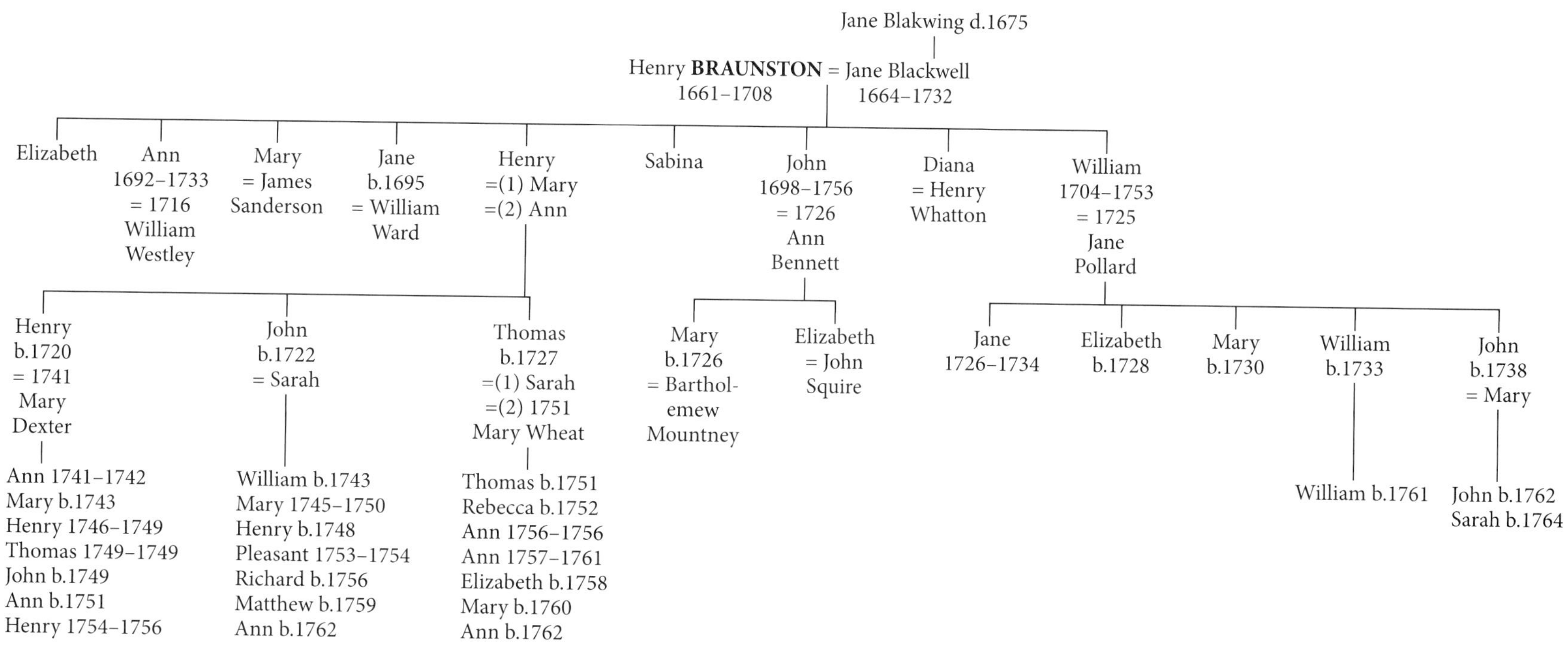

Jane Blakwing d.1675
|
Henry **BRAUNSTON** = Jane Blackwell
1661–1708   1664–1732

Children of Henry Braunston and Jane Blackwell:

- **Elizabeth**
- **Ann** 1692–1733 = 1716 William Westley
- **Mary** = James Sanderson
- **Jane** b.1695 = William Ward
- **Henry** =(1) Mary =(2) Ann
- **Sabina**
- **John** 1698–1756 = 1726 Ann Bennett
- **Diana** = Henry Whatton
- **William** 1704–1753 = 1725 Jane Pollard

Children of Henry (=(1) Mary =(2) Ann):
- **Henry** b.1720 = 1741 Mary Dexter
- **John** b.1722 = Sarah
- **Thomas** b.1727 =(1) Sarah 1751 =(2) Mary Wheat

Children of John b.1698 and Ann Bennett:
- **Mary** b.1726 = Bartholemew Mountney
- **Elizabeth** = John Squire

Children of William 1704–1753 and Jane Pollard:
- **Jane** 1726–1734
- **Elizabeth** b.1728
- **Mary** b.1730
- **William** b.1733
- **John** b.1738 = Mary

Children of Henry b.1720 and Mary Dexter:
- Ann 1741–1742
- Mary b.1743
- Henry 1746–1749
- Thomas 1749–1749
- John b.1749
- Ann b.1751
- Henry 1754–1756

Children of John b.1722 and Sarah:
- William b.1743
- Mary 1745–1750
- Henry b.1748
- Pleasant 1753–1754
- Richard b.1756
- Matthew b.1759
- Ann b.1762

Children of Thomas b.1727:
- Thomas b.1751
- Rebecca b.1752
- Ann 1756–1756
- Ann 1757–1761
- Elizabeth b.1758
- Mary b.1760
- Ann b.1762

Children of William b.1733:
- William b.1761

Children of John b.1738 and Mary:
- John b.1762
- Sarah b.1764

him apart from his name. In 1732 Jane Braunston of Swithland, widow, bequeathed to her son William in her will, amongst other things, one strip of land in the Over Field 'against Harold Balm's Backside'. In 1734 William Braunston of Swithland, framework-knitter, and Jane his wife, released to Joseph Prior of Swithland some messuages and some lands lying in the Over Field[75] including 'an old rood land which shoots down to a certain place called Harold Balms Backside, the land of John Walker lying on the west side, and the land of William Westley lying on the east'.[76]

Forest End Farm, 60 Main Street

The building that is now No. 60 Main Street was once the farmhouse building for Forest End Farm. It has been significantly adapted since it was sold by Swithland Hall Estate in 1954 to the then tenant, George Walker. In the 1954 estate sale catalogue, Forest End Farm was described as 'a useful mixed farm, the homestead being conveniently situated on the farm and in Main Street, Swithland'. There were 186 acres of arable and grassland. The farmhouse was built 'of Swithland slate' and the accommodation included:

On the Ground Floor: Entrance Passage, Living Room with inglenook, two Sitting Rooms with beamed ceilings, Kitchen, Dairy, WC, Storeroom.
On the First Floor: four Bedrooms, three Storerooms with separate Staircase leading from the Kitchen.
Outside: Garage, Coalhouse, Garden and Vegetable Garden.
Services: Mains water, gas, electricity and drainage.
The Buildings include: Cooling House, Cowsheds, Loose Box, Stabling, Open Implement Shed, Barn, Root Place, Crew Yard, two Calf Pens, four Pig Styes, Tractor Shed, Implement Shed.

One of the outbuildings was later converted into a separate dwelling at 62 Main Street.

Forest End Farm was created after the enclosure act was passed but there look to have been some buildings on the site in 1799. Matthew Simpson was the first recorded tenant farmer (1815–27) and the tenancy remained with his family until the 1860s. William Bates, whose parents farmed at Kinchley Hill until the reservoir flooded the land, took over the tenancy c. 1871, and the farm remained in his family's hands until George Walker took it over in 1935. George and his wife lived there until 1959. Lindesay and Lois Godfrey lived there for some years from 1965. The present owners (2010) are Cedric and Joan Brown.

Fig 12.50 William James Bates, tenant farmer at Forest End Farm 1871–96.

Forest End Farm Tenant Farmers

1815–1827	Matthew Simpson	1912–1925	Mary Juliana Bates and Matthew Daykin Bates
1828–1854	William Simpson	1928–1932	Matthew Daykin Bates
1861–1863	Charlotte Simpson	1935–1956	George Douglas Walker
1871–1896	William Bates		
1900–1908	Ann Bates Matthew Daykin Bates		

Pollard (Forest) House, 54 Main Street (1830s)

Fig. 12.51 Approach to Swithland from Woodhouse Eaves, with Pollard House in the distance.

The history of Pollard House is linked with the group of Forest End houses next door – they were all built on the same plot of land. But in 1831, part of that plot was sold to John Pollard, slate engraver, who bequeathed it to his son Joseph who built the large house with outbuildings that we see today. When Joseph Pollard died in 1854, the house was sold[77] to Joseph Matts.[78] Matts was a tailor with a shop in Newtown Linford as well as in Swithland. In the 1871 Census Matts is also listed as 'a farmer of eighteen acres'. In 1879, Joseph Matts conveyed Pollard House to his son, John Matts,[79] who sold it in 1887 to Charles Theophilus Parker, a Lanesborough trustee.[80] The sixth Earl of Lanesborough formally acquired it in 1897.[81]

One of the first tenants was Joseph Barrett, a carter. He and his wife Emily were living there at the time of the 1901 Census with their niece Amelia Evans (24) and their nephew George Read (20) who was a wheelwright apprentice. The Barretts were followed into the tenancy by Charles and Mary Ellen Wainwright; Charles had married Frederick Bunney's daughter in St Leonard's Church in 1907.

A 1909 description of this brick, stone and slate house indicates that it

Fig 12.52 Joseph Matts, tailor and draper, living at Pollard House in 1871.

had five bedrooms, two attics, two sitting rooms, a kitchen, a tea room (Barrett supplemented his income by offering 'tea' to tourists), and a wash-house. The photograph of Forest End and Pollard House (fig. 12.53) shows a three-storey house, since demolished, behind Pollard House and a cart on the other side of the road. The cart may have been the one that belonged to Joseph Barrett.

When Pollard House, then known as Forest House, was sold in the 1954 estate sale, it was in the tenancy of Mrs Mary Ellen Wainwright, daughter of Fred Bunney of Swithland and widow of Charles Wainwright, coal merchant. The property included an 'enclosure of garden ground situated immediately opposite' on which land Charles had kept his wagons and horses. It was advertised as a 'substantially built detached residence, with a wide entrance from the road to a yard at the rear, and sufficient space for the erection of a garage'. Main services of electricity, gas, water and drainage were all connected. On the ground floor were two sitting rooms, an office, and a living room with a single oven combination range and a dairy. On the first floor were three double bedrooms and two single bedrooms, and on the second floor three attic rooms. Outside were the WC and a coalhouse. The house is currently (2010) occupied by Mr and Mrs Stephen Mellor.

Fig 12.53 (from left to right) Pollard House, Forest End Cottages, Methodist Chapel.

Forest End Cottages, 34–54 Main Street

In 1954, Lot 12 in the Swithland Hall Estate sale comprised nine freehold cottages. These were 'brick and slate built and with gardens at the front and rear, being Nos. 36–52 (even numbers), Main Street, Swithland', at the time let to Miss Bunney, Messrs Woodcock, Stone, Walker, Simmons Bros. and others on various tenancies and producing a gross annual rent of £95 14s. 0d, with the tenants paying rates.

During the eighteenth century, a small 'housing estate' had been developed on this site, presumably to meet the housing needs of quarry workmen from the nearby slate pits. For many years the development was known as Forest End. The properties that remain comprise the complex of houses, Nos. 36–54 Main Street, though No. 50 has since been demolished.

The first cottages were built on Mill Close, a field of about 8 acres adjoining the parish boundary, which was owned in 1684 by Thomas Hinde of Houghton-on-the-Hill, baker. Thomas was the son of Thomas Hinde of Swithland, tanner. Hinde had let the field to a John Woodford, but in 1684 he passed the tenancy to Robert Gilbert of Swithland, husbandman. Soon after, however, Hinde must have sold the close, with the purchaser erecting a dwelling on part of the land. By 1715 Stephen Clarke (1645–1726) of Swithland, husbandman, owned Mill Close and the house; in that year he sold part of the close, containing a homestead, to his son William Clarke (1681–1732). In 1718 William appears to have sold the other part to Samuel Clarke.[82] Samuel's son John sold on to Sir Joseph Danvers in 1750.[83] On William Clarke's death in 1732, he bequeathed[84] his interest in Mill Close to his son, William (b. 1720), who in his turn left it[85] to his son, also William (b. 1756). This William Clarke, again a husbandman, began to erect other cottages on his part of the close. By 1788 there were three dwellings, occupied by William Clarke himself, Robert Pearson and Benjamin Pollard. William Clarke then took out mortgages[86] in 1788, 1789 and 1794 in order to erect further cottages. By 1800 ten dwellings had been built. Five of them were occupied by Samuel Pitts, John Pollard, Richard Wilson, Stephen Clarke and William Clarke.

Swithland was enclosed in 1799. The Enclosure Award allocated the three roods and twenty-eight perches (4,477 square yards) of land on which his cottages were built to William Clarke. His apportionment is clearly marked on the Enclosure Map. In the course of the next century, the cottages underwent several changes of ownership.

In 1800 William Clarke mortgaged five of his cottages to William Johnson.[87] The property enterprise may not have been as successful as he had hoped because in about 1819 he sold the five cottages to William Johnson. Johnson then altered his five cottages, which had been occupied by Samuel Pitts, John Pollard, Richard Wilson, Stephen Clarke and William Clarke, to form nine cottages, so that by 1825 there were fourteen dwellings on the small site, nine owned by Johnson and five by Clarke. Other buildings were also erected on Johnson's site for the purposes of a bakehouse, a malthouse, a stable, and a shoemaker's shop. In 1828 the malthouse was

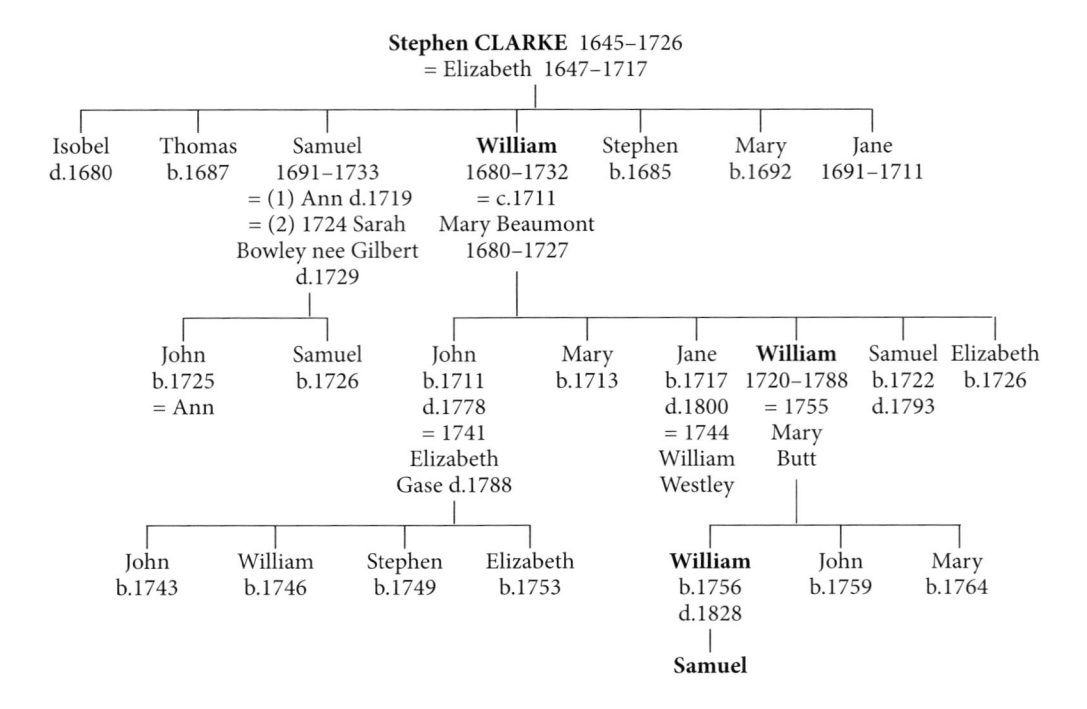

```
                           Stephen CLARKE  1645–1726
                           = Elizabeth  1647–1717
   │        │         │          │           │         │         │
 Isobel   Thomas   Samuel     William    Stephen    Mary      Jane
 d.1680   b.1687   1691–1733  1680–1732   b.1685   b.1692   1691–1711
                   = (1) Ann d.1719  = c.1711
                   = (2) 1724 Sarah  Mary Beaumont
                   Bowley nee Gilbert  1680–1727
                   d.1729
           │          │        │        │        │          │         │
         John      Samuel    John     Mary     Jane      William    Samuel  Elizabeth
        b.1725    b.1726   b.1711   b.1713   b.1717    1720–1788   b.1722   b.1726
        = Ann              d.1778             d.1800    = 1755     d.1793
                           = 1741            = 1744     Mary
                           Elizabeth         William    Butt
                           Gase d.1788       Westley
              │         │         │         │              │         │         │
            John     William   Stephen   Elizabeth      William     John      Mary
           b.1743    b.1746    b.1749    b.1753         b.1756     b.1759    b.1764
                                                        d.1828
                                                          │
                                                        Samuel
```

fitted up as a Wesleyan chapel.[88] When Johnson died in 1827, he bequeathed most of his property to his wife, with the remainder to his children.[89] The Johnson property was conveyed on in 1829 to William Middleton and in 1846 to Thomas Raven.[90] On William Clarke's death in 1828,[91] his five cottages passed to his son Samuel Clarke. Part of Samuel Clarke's land was bought by John Pollard in about 1831, and it was on this parcel of land that Pollard (or Forest) House was built.

In 1852, six years after Thomas Raven of Quorn acquired the Johnson cottages,[92] he bought the five Clarke properties.[93] He bequeathed them in 1856[94] to William Ackroyd of Quorn, but not before giving part of the ground to the Wesleyan Methodists who erected a chapel to replace the old 'malthouse' chapel. Ten years later, Ackroyd sold his interests on to George John Danvers Butler Danvers, fifth Earl of Lanesborough, shortly before the Earl's death in 1866.[95] One of the tenants, Susannah Sharpe Potter (1805–1889), wife of Richard Potter (1804–1857), kept a shop from her cottage from 1860 to 1880. She was a grocer and tea dealer.

Towards the end of the nineteenth century, the fourteen cottages were adapted into four lodgings and six cottages and gardens. As late as 1910, a survey described all the dwellings as 'lodgings'; some consisted of only one room upstairs and one room downstairs plus a scullery, while others had two upstairs rooms with one or two downstairs rooms and a scullery. In these small dwellings families of some size were raised. In the 1841 Census, for example, eight persons are recorded as living in each of the households of Samuel Thorpe and Zachariah Raynor, while William Carter presided

Village Buildings and Families

Forest End: Heads of Household [96]

CLARKE COTTAGES:
- 1828 Mary Preston, William Brookhouse, James Clarke, William Hutchinson, William Bunney.
- 1844 John Clarke sr (cottager), John Hampson, Joseph Thompson, James Clarke (butcher), Thomas Hill (quarryman).
- 1851 Henry Brown (rag & bone gatherer), Thomas Hill (quarryman), James Clarke (butcher), John Thompson (agricultural labourer).
- 1852 John Thompson (agricultural labourer), Thomas Hill (quarryman), William Raynor (agricultural labourer), 2 houses unoccupied.
- 1861 Joseph Shaw (quarryman), James Bunney (agricultural labourer), Martha Clark, Thomas Hill (quarryman), Thomas Raynor (agricultural labourer), Thomas Raynor (agricultural labourer), Anne Hodge.
- 1866 Thomas Hill, George Brown, Thomas Brookhouse, George Goodall, James Hoult.
- 1871 Mary J. Godbald (agricultural labourer's wife), George Brown (agricultural labourer), Thomas Hill (former quarryman), Charles Boyer (agricultural labourer), James Hoult (bricklayer).

JOHNSON COTTAGES:
- 1800 Samuel Pitts, John Pollard, Richard Wilson, Stephen Clarke, William Clarke.
- 1825 William Preston, William Clarke, Joseph Brookby, Thomas Preston, Zachariah Raynor, Thomas Raynor, widow Thornton, Henry Burton, 1 unoccupied.
- 1851 John Thorpe (agricultural labourer), George Thorpe (agricultural labourer), John Morris (stone quarry labourer), Joseph Hemsley (agricultural labourer), Thomas Adams (agricultural labourer), Robert Raynor (slate cleaver), Samuel Thorpe (stone quarry labourer), Zachariah Raynor (agricultural labourer), William Bunney (agricultural labourer).
- 1852 Daniel Weston, Zachariah Raynor, Samuel Thorp, Robert Raynor, Thomas Adams, William Bunney, George Thorpe, John Thorpe, 1 unoccupied.
- 1861 John Thorpe (agricultural labourer), George Thorpe (agricultural labourer), Henry Squires (coal dealer), Mary Thorpe, Thomas Adams (agricultural labourer), Robert Raynor (agricultural labourer), Susannah Potter (grocer and tea dealer), John Spencer (agricultural labourer), Henry Bunney (agricultural labourer).
- 1866 widow Carter, John Spencer, Susan Potter, Robert Raynor, John Adams, Martha Thorpe, George Thorpe, widow Thorpe, Ann Raynor.
- 1871 John Adams (quarryman), George Bunney (agricultural labourer), Mary Thorpe (former laundress), Thomas Adams (agricultural labourer), Robert Raynor (slate cleaver), Susannah Potter (grocer), John Spencer (agricultural labourer), Edward Bunney (agricultural labourer).

Forest End: Tenants 1909 (Head of Household only) [97]

4 LODGINGS, EX CLARKE, NOS. 36–40 MAIN STREET

3 up 3 down - brick & thatch. Occupier = George Clowes. Rent £4-0-2 /week

2 up 1 down + scullery – brick, stone & thatch. Occupier = Thomas Hill Rent £3-5-0 /week

1 up 1 down + scullery – brick, stone & thatch. Occupier = Charles Boyer Rent £3-5-0 /week

2 up 1 down + scullery – brick, stone & slate. Occupier = Samuel Gazy Rent £4-11-0 /week

6 COTTAGES & GARDENS, EX JOHNSON, NOS. 42–52 MAIN STREET

2 up 1 down + scullery - brick, stone & slate. Occupier J.R. Preston
3 up 1 down + scullery - brick, stone & slate. Occupier Sarah Brown
2 up 2 down + scullery - brick, stone & slate. Occupier Fred Bunney
2 up 2 down + scullery - brick, stone & slate. Occupier Matthew Daykin Bates
2 up 1 down + scullery - brick, stone & slate. Occupier Charles Burgess
4 up 2 down + scullery - brick, stone & slate. Occupier William James Bates

Fig 12.54 Beatrice Bunney and her mother Ethel May Bunney outside No. 46.

over a household of seven. Many of the Forest End tenants in those early years were among those who received relief from the Barrow Poor Law Union.

Various other village families have lived in the Forest End cottages over the years. No. 52 was occupied at one time by Daniel Bates (d. 1858). More recently, No. 50 (now demolished) was occupied by Mr and Mrs Charles

Frecknell; No. 48 by John and Joan Leatherland 1954–67;[98] No. 46 by Annie Bunney and Beatrice Bunney.[99] Nos. 40 and 42, three-storey buildings now demolished, were occupied at various times during the twentieth century by, amongst others, Mr and Mrs Mutch and Mrs and Mrs Meakin; No. 38 by Bert and Jean Stone and their son John; No. 36 by Mr and Mrs Woodcock, then by Tom and May Musgrove. The current (2010) residents of Nos. 38–40 are Peter and Sandra Kinder; Peter Harvey and Dinah Harratt live in No. 36.

Sough Mouth Spring

Sough Mouth Spring used to supply water[100] for the villagers until mains water was installed in the early twentieth century. Some of the older villagers living near the spring continued to use it, being suspicious of the new piped supply.

Fig 12.55 Nos. 50 and 48 Main Street (No. 50 now demolished).

Wood Lane End or Lane End Cottage, 24 Main Street

Wood Lane End Cottage is the last cottage at the Woodhouse Eaves end of the village. It stands next to a footpath to Swithland Wood, on land that at the time of enclosure was part of the Newtown Linford lordship. The cottage is relatively modern, being built on land bought from the Earl of Stamford and Warrington in 1903 by Archibald Turner,[101] for his wife when they moved to Swithland. She encouraged him, however, to lease an old slate-worker's cottage with its land on the other side of the road. They restored and extended that cottage and moved into it in 1908.

Wood Lane End housed the Turners' tenants. One of the early dwellers was Olive Margaret Ellis, Mrs Turner's sister, who sent a postcard of the very new looking Wood Lane End to Nurse C. Kirby in Clapham, London. She wrote: 'Dear Nurse, Hope to have a line when you can spare time, don't quite forget us in our little stone cottage, thought this would remind you we are inside it.' Olive Ellis was twenty-nine when she married Godfrey Leveson Brooke-Hunt in September 1914. In

Fig 12.56 Sough Mouth Spring, 1999.

Fig 12.57 Wood Lane End Cottage, postcard sent by Olive Ellis in 1911.

1947, as a widow, she returned to Swithland and lived as friend and companion to Gladys Linwood Wright for the next thirty years. She died in Bath in 1985, her sister having pre-deceased her in 1977.

For some years the cottage was divided into two flats, the upper flat being accessed by an exterior staircase. Over the years the various tenants at Lane End Cottage have included Elizabeth Baxter and Ethel Adkin (1901 Census), Horace Moore, gardener at 'The Cottage' and his family in the 1930s, Edith Evelyn Bunney and Phyllis Liddle, from c. 1945–52, Muriel Turner and John Gregory (1970s). The current owners (2010) are Richard Wollaston and Yvonne Dulson.

Fig 12.58 Wood Lane End Cottage, during Moore's tenancy, showing exterior staircase.

The Cottage, 1 Main Street

Figs 12.59 The Cottage, c. 1977.

The Cottage, 1 Main Street, at the western end of the village, has been considerably altered over the years and almost nothing of the original remains. Its history was for many years inextricably linked with the local slate industry. At the beginning of the nineteenth century a dwelling on the site lay next to the boundary between the land of Augustus Richard Butler Danvers and the Marquis of Hastings. From about 1800 William Johnson, in partnership with Francis Shenton, was quarrying next to the house and astride the boundary. The house was tenanted by John Pollard the slate engraver between 1801 and 1817, then by Richard Preston from 1818–27. It was then occupied by slate workers for most of the remainder of the century – Henry Burton, a slate cleaver and his wife Mary were resident when the 1871 and 1881 Census returns were collected. In 1891 it was listed as unoccupied.

```
            Henry BURTON = Mary —
             1824–1895   |  1817–1884
          ┌──────────────┴──────────────┐
      Alice Mary                 Elizabeth Lockton
       b.1854                         b.1857
                                  = George Baum
```

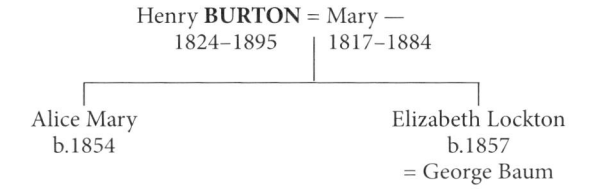

Archibald Turner took out a twenty-nine year lease of the land and cottage from the Earl of Lanesborough in 1908, though he had an interest from 1903. His wife, Gladys Marie Turner, bought the freehold interest in The Cottage in 1917. The Turners restored and extended the old slate-worker's cottage, adding a wing extending the house to the rear by building into the hillside. The site included an old slate quarry,[102] which, when the The Cottage was sold in 1975 was described as 'a rock pool of water of over one third of an acre in extent.'[103]

Archibald Turner was a member of Swithland church, and a generous contributor. A plaque in the north wall of the nave reads: 'This tablet was erected by the Parishioners of Swithland in grateful memory of Archibald Turner who gave so generously to the restoration of this Church. At rest 26 April 1928.' The Church's lychgate was erected in his memory, and dedicated during Evensong at 6pm on Saturday 15th June 1929. 'The Lychgate has been erected in memory of the late Mr Archibald Turner, by his Staff and workers.'

Fig 12.60 Gladys Turner, 1917.

Archibald **TURNER** = Gladys Marie Ellis = Albert Linwood **WRIGHT**
1861–1928 | 1883–1977 | 1875–1950

Lois Marie Gladys
1904–1963
= 1932 Frederick Lindesay Godfrey

Between about 1930 and 1945, Nurse Emmeline Prior lodged with Mrs Turner as a companion after her husband's death. Mrs Turner, helped by Nurse Prior, founded the Bluebird Guild, a village organisation for Swithland women of all ages. Gladys Turner later married again, c. 1946, to Albert Linwood Wright, previously vicar of St Mark's, Belgrave, Leicester. Mrs Linwood-Wright hosted periodic village events at The Cottage, some in support of the Bluebird Guild, others in aid of charitable fund-raising. After Mrs Wright's death in 1977, Bill and Jean Adderley, founders of Dunelm Mill, bought The Cottage. The current owners (2010) are Roy and Nicola Coley.

The last public event at The Cottage was in 1969 when Mrs Linwood Wright was eighty-six. She wrote:

Dear friends

Just to give you a final word about our 'Mingle' at the Cottage on Saturday June 21st at 2.30 pm. It will be our last, for at 86 years it is time to stop! but it is a great happiness that the two churches that have meant so much in my life, St Mark's Leicester, and my own Swithland, are joining together for this occasion. We know all our old friends and neighbours will support us, and indeed many have already made generous promises of help. But we so hope that all those who have come to the village more recently will join us too, and help to give a warm welcome to the strangers within our gates, whether from Overseas or as passers-by. We also hope to make a little money for our two Churches and for 'Christian Aid', and hope to enjoy music from our own 'Folk Formula', some International dancing, bargains and food delights from the stalls and a good tea; so come and mingle with us?

Gladys M Wright

PS There will be a 'miniature flower' (4" x 4") competition to be judged by pennies, and the House will be open and decorated. There will be no formal opening, but we shall dedicate our humble, small effort to that majestic and greatest of all 'Mingles,' that of the Holy, Blessed and Glorious Trinity, at 3pm. in the Marquee.[104]

Fig 12.61 The marriage of Lois Turner to (Frederick) Lindesay Godfrey, 1932.

Residents of The Cottage, 1 Main Street

1871 (Census)	Henry & Mary Burton
1881 (Census)	Henry & Mary Burton
1891 (Census)	unoccupied
1903 (Survey)	A. Turner
1909 (Valuation)	A. Turner
1924	Turner/Moore
1931	G.M. Turner/Hind/Jarvis/Prior/Randles
1933	G.M. Turner/Green/Prior/Stockwell
1936	G.M. Turner/Green/B Harrison/E Prior/Stockwell
1939	G.M. Turner/B Harrison/A Moore/E Prior
1945	G.M. Turner/B Harrison/Prior
1947	A.L. & G.M. Wright/Brooke-Hunt
1948	Wright/Brooke-Hunt/B. Harrison
1950	A.L. & G.M. Wright/Brooke-Hunt
1951	G.M. Wright/Brooke-Hunt/B. Harrison
1952	Wright/Brooke-Hunt/B. Harrison
1953	Wright/Brooke-Hunt
1956	Wright/Brooke-Hunt
1959	Wright/Brooke-Hunt
1964	Wright/Brooke-Hunt
1966	Wright/Brooke-Hunt/Eade
1969	Wright/Brooke-Hunt
1974	Wright/Brooke-Hunt/Esther R. Thomas

Swithland Brand

Thomas Hodges (1834–1911), parish clerk of Swithland, told Robert Martin of the 'Brand' that his father Matthew Hodges (1790–1854) could remember there being a gate across the road at the Woodhouse end of the village, to prevent the stock on the open forest from coming down into the street.

> The cattle ran free on the Forest, being rounded up twice a year for marking. It is probably owing to this custom that the name 'Brand' occurs in three places on the outskirts of the Forest, near Breedon, Thorpe Acre and Swithland, the cattle being collected there to be marked with their owner's sign. When I was a boy, the old people used to speak of 'the Swithland Brand', though the second name only is now used.[105]

Notes to Chapter 12

1. 1901 Census, Swithland.
2. The tradition was passed by word of mouth from the eighth Earl of Lanesborough to the gamekeeper's family who inhabited Keeper's Cottage at the time. It is certainly true that, until the fourteenth century, Swithland Rectory was served by Benedictine monks, and the original footprint for Keeper's Cottage, now completely lost, indicated both dwelling place and barn or stabling space.
3. In 1429, when the manor of Swithland was divided, it is possible that Shepeys (later the Kendalls) as well as the Danvers had their own manor dwelling in Swithland.
4. Earliest Swithland grave marker was to John Prier, 8 May 1673. It is possibly the earliest one in the county.
5. Leics. RO, DE73/326, Will and inventory: Elizabeth Ward, Swithland, 1727 (Groby Peculiar Court).
6. Leics. RO, DE73/517, Will of Robert Gilbert, Swithland, 1749.
7. Leics. RO, DE73/689, Will of William Westley, Swithland, 1775.
8. Charnwood Borough Council website.
9. What remains is sited on private Severn Trent land, and approached from Kinchley Lane.
10. Leics. RO, 13/28/1/23, Reference to purchase, Francis Smalley from Henry Kendall, Francis Danvers, Cornelius Smith.
11. Leics. RO, 3D42/84/4, Reference to terms of will in 1777 lease (Elizabeth Smalley to John Fisher).
12. ibid., 21 year lease 'if she should live so long' from Elizabeth Smalley of Mountsorrel, widow, to John Fisher of Cossington, gentleman, 6 March 1777.
13. John Fisher having presumably died.
14. Leics. RO, 3D 42/84/3, Marriage settlement, Ralph Smalley Tebbutt and Elizabeth Fowkes.
15. Leics. RO, 3D 42/84/11, 5 October 1797, lease 'from year to year'.
16. There is a memorial to Robert and Margery Smalley in Barrow parish church.
17. Ralph and Elizabeth Smalley are buried in Barrow parish church and commemorated by a double tablet left of the altar.
18. Memorial in Mountsorrel, St Peter's Church.
19. Leics. RO, 13/D/28/1/86, Letter from Joseph Danvers of Chelsea to Mr Woodroffe, attorney, Loughborough, 1743, concerning some proposal of Mr Tebbuttt and Fisher to purchase the reversion expectant after the life of Widow Smalley.
20. Leics. RO, DE1750, Box 16, 11 June 1756, Legal opinion of William Henry Ashurst.
21. ibid., Box 3, Exchange of land between George John Danvers Butler Danvers of Chesterfield Street, Mayfair, and Ralph Smalley Tebbutt of Leicester, 28 Feb 1828.
22. Note of appointment, in the ownership of the North family of Rothley. (Olive, daughter of William Allen, married Eric North of Swithland Lane, Rothley.)
23. Leics. RO, 3D 42/84/10, Lease, Tebbutt to Johnson.
24. Leics. RO, 3D 42/84/12, Lease for life, Ralph Tebbutt to Richard Burchnall, 1 May 1799.
25. Charnwood Borough Council, listed 1984, Swithland Reservoir buildings.
26. Leics. RO, 87/82, Danvers Papers, transcr June W Danvers. With assertion that the Manor House was rebuilt in Queen Mary's and Queen Elizabeth's time by John Danvers.
27. John Throsby, *Select Views in Leicestershire*, 1790.
28. Leics. RO, DE1750, Box 9, Note on size of rooms in Sir John Danvers house.
29. ibid., Box 23, QS48/1/62,63 & QS48/1/87.
30. ibid., Box 9, Inventory and Valuation of Fixtures etc. at Swithland Hall, 23 February 1830.
31. John Flower, *Views of Ancient Buildings in the Town and County of Leicester*, 1826.
32. Tony Danvers, author of a book about the Shepshed branch of the Danvers family, has suggested that Flowers' drawing could be a picture of Hall Farm which might have been used as the manor house at a time when the 'old' manor could have been inhabitable. (George John was living in Chesterfield Street, Mayfair in 1828.)
33. Father of Augustus Welby Pugin.
34. Charnwood Borough Council, listed 1979.
35. ibid., Grade I listed, 1 June 1966.
36. ibid., Grade II listed, 1979.
37. Leics. RO, DE1982/181, Survey of Groby Manor, 1658.

38. Charnwood Borough Council, Grade II listed, 1984.
39. Swithland Church Archives, S.R. Meadows, *Swithland*, 1965, printed Willsons (Printers) Ltd, Leicester. Now out of print.
40. Charnwood Borough Council, Grade II listed, 1966.
41. The walled kitchen gardens of the Old Hall were on the other side of the road, on land adjacent to the eighteenth century rectory.
42. Phyllis Lloyd (d. 2007), spoken memories.
43. The villagers' desire to retain the old name Hall Gardens was over-ridden by the local council.
44. S.R. Meadows, *Swithland*, 1965.
45. John Throsby, *Select Views in Leicestershire*, 1790, p. 92.
46. Leics. RO DE1750, Box 30, Letters March, April 1922. Murray Dixon offered the 'refusal' of the Old Rectory property to the sixth Earl in 1898; the matter was raised again with the seventh Earl in 1922.
47. The Lynes family used to live in the School House, when Charles Lynes was the school teacher.
48. Swithland Church Archives, card post-marked Swithland 9th March 12, Loughborough.
49. Charnwood Borough Council, Grade II listed, 1984.
50. Swithland Burial Registers, School teacher Mrs Sheila Joy Bryan died in 1988.
51. The public house on Brand Lane (possibly 'The Slatesplitters' Arms) is no longer there and should not be confused with the Wheatsheaf Inn on Brand Hill.
52. William Gardiner, memoirs of, *Music and Friends*, vol. 1, 1838.
53. Permission to use the photograph has been kindly given by family member, Grahame Briers.
54. Swithland Church Archives, held at the Rectory.
55. Charnwood Borough Council, Grade II listed, 1966.
56. Public Records Office National Archives, MAF 32/398/157, 429334, Farm Survey Records, Swithland, 1941.
57. Charnwood Borough Council, Grade II listed, 1979.
58. The building was listed by Charnwood Borough Council in 1984.
59. S.R. Meadows, *Swithland*, (1965), states that it was built in 1425, but offers no evidence for his claim. He also suggests that it was used as a laundry for the Old Hall for three hundred years. (This may have been told him by 'old' villagers.) Its listing note (Grade II, 1966) claims seventeenth century.
60. Leics. RO, DE1750, Box 9, Swithland Hall estate rent book 1828–30.
61. There were already some Hemsleys living in Swithland in 1800 – Benjamin (of Woodhouse) married Elizabeth Johnson (of Quorn) in 1800. Their three children were dedicated in Rothley Baptist Chapel.
62. The Barrow Poor Law Union, which served Swithland, was established by the 1834 Poor Law Amendment Act and was formed on 11 September 1837. A new Barrow-upon-Soar Union workhouse was erected in Rothley parish near Mountsorrel in 1838–40.
63. Now disintegrated and removed.
64. Swithland Archives, Indenture 12 February 1929, between the seventh Earl, the Equity and Law Life Assurance Society and the trustees of the Swithland War Memorial Fund.
65. Local Church Archives, service leaflet.
66. Leics. RO, 1799 Enclosure Map.
67. Swithland Church Archives, J. Dransfield, Notes.
68. Charnwood Borough Council, Grade II listed, 1984.
69. Earl of Lanesborough's marriage settlement (1851)
70. When John Leatherland retired in 1996, he sold his cattle and other agricultural effects, but bought the farmhouse and outbuildings.
71. The White House was also known for a short while as 'The Laurels'.
72. Leics. RO, DE1982/165, Lease, 1787.
73. Leics. RO, DE453/198, Stamford's Swithland Estate sold to Earl of Lanesborough.
74. Churchwarden, St Leonard's, 1982–93.
75. The 'Over' or 'Forest' field was one of the three Swithland open fields, and ran alongside that part of Main Street on that side of the road.
76. Leics. RO, DE1750, Box 16, indenture 17 May 1734, William Braunston and Joseph Prior.
77. ibid., Box 30, Conditions of sale, 1855.
78. ibid., Box 30, Conveyance to Joseph Matts, mortgage, abstract of title 1855.
79. ibid., Box 30, Conveyance to John Matts, 25 Oct 1879.

80. ibid., Box 30, Conveyance 27, Jan 1887, John Matts to Christopher Theophilus Parker.
81. ibid., Box 30, Conveyance 30 Sept 1897, C.T. Parker to John Vansittart Danvers Butler.
82. ibid., Box 17, Conveyance 20 Dec 1718, Mill Close and cottage, Stephen Clarke to Samuel Clarke, about 5½ acres, 'in the tenure of occupation of Stephen Clarke'.
83. ibid., Box 17: 21 Dec 1750, bond for £320 to Sir Joseph Danvers, Mill Close 5½ acres.
84. Leics. RO, DE73/388, Will, William Clarke 1732.
85. Leics. RO, DE73/758, Will, William Clarke, 1788.
86. Leics. RO, DE1750, Box 19, Bundle no. 11, William Clark to Miss Harcourt, mortgage 1788 and deeds for security 1788, 1789, 1794.
87. ibid., Box 29, Conveyance 1800, Clarke to Johnson.
88. For the story of the Chapel, see Chapter 7: Dissent.
89. Leics. RO, DE1750, Box 29, Will of William Johnson, 19 November 1827
90. ibid., Box 29.
91. ibid., Box 29, Copy of will, William Clarke, 1828.
92. ibid., Box 29, Conveyance 1846, Middleton et al to Raven, 9 messuages.
93. ibid., Box 19, Bundle 11, Conveyance, 1852.
94. ibid., Box 29, Will of Thomas Raven of Quorndon, 1856 (Raven d. 5 Sept.1858).
95. ibid., Box 29, 1866 Conveyance, William Ackroyd to Lord Lanesborough.
96. Source: conveyances and census returns.
97. Source: 1909 Land Tax valuation.
98. Ann Leatherland born at 48 Main Street in 1960.
99. Annie Bunney d. 1977; Beatrice Bunney d. 2007.
100. There were also two parish pumps in the village, one standing in front of the old Post Office and the other down towards Keeper's Cottage.
101. Leics. RO, HMC Records of British Business and Industry: Archibald Turner & Co Ltd, elastic web and hosiery manufacturers, Leicester, records: 1841–1954. Archibald Turner's was the only Leicester firm to exhibit in the Paris Exhibition of 1878, when Leicester goods were held to be as good as those produced by either France or Spain.
102. For its history see Chapter 10: Swithland Slate.
103. Sale catalogue, 1975.
104. Swithland Church Archives, The Link, June 1969.
105. R.E. Martin, Introduction xiv, in G.F. Farnham, *Charnwood Forest and its Historians*, 1930.

– CHAPTER 13 –

Education

In the Middle Ages, apart from the children of the manor and the rectory, few Swithland children would have learnt to read or write. In the wake of the Reformation, however, schools were founded, but not in the small villages of Leicestershire, rather in its market towns and larger villages: such as Leicester, Loughborough, Melton Mowbray, Lutterworth, Hinckley, Billesdon and Hallaton. Gradually, however, the scene changed. Church records of the seventeenth century record that there were village school masters in at least seventy Leicestershire villages, including Mountsorrel and Quorn. Many of these school masters were the parish incumbent or curate, who had first refusal of the post.

Thomas Rawlins and Michael Matthews

During the eleven years of England's Commonwealth (1649–60), leading reformers envisaged the development of an organised system of schools under parliamentary control. With the restoration of the monarchy in 1660, however, these hopes were dashed. But the dissenters in particular continued a strong commitment and involvement in education in England. One such dissenter was the Presbyterian Thomas Rawlins, who founded a school at Woodhouse in 1691, when he made over part of his estate to trustees to provide £24 per annum for a master to teach freely.

The first documented link between Swithland and any kind of formal education for children is with Michael Matthews[1] (1661–1723), Presbyterian minister and school teacher, who is buried inside Swithland church. In 1694 Matthews was the third[2] person to be appointed master at Rawlins' new school, where he taught until 1702. When he fell out with Rawlins for taking in fee-paying boarders to the detriment of the education of the children of the poor, Matthews moved to Mountsorrel. Here he built a meeting house and school which flourished for several years at the beginning of the eighteenth century.

One of the Swithland children who later attended Rawlins' school was John Prior (1729–1803), son of Joseph Prior, Sir Joseph Danvers' steward. John was Swithland born and bred, and he did so well at the school that in

1744, at the age of fifteen, he was appointed master there. (During his time, his father Joseph Prior was the schoolmaster (1744–50.) John's appointment, however, prompted a petition from the villagers of Woodhouse against appointing too young a master at the school. In fact, he is held to have run the school with 'singular ability' for nearly twenty years. He resigned in 1763 when he was presented with the living at Ashby de la Zouch parish church, and was also appointed Master of the Ashby Grammar School.[3]

Sir Joseph Danvers and His Schools

In the early years of the eighteenth century there was some effort on behalf of the established church to claim the educational field. The Society for the Propagation of Christian Knowledge (SPCK), a voluntary organisation, was established to co-ordinate and promote charity schools teaching Anglican doctrine. Its input into Leicestershire may, however, have only been slight and temporary. In Swithland, it was Sir Joseph Danvers, Lord of the Manors of Swithland, Mountsorrel and Thurcaston who made the first educational provision for Swithland children. Sir Joseph was one of a new class of landowner–industrialists. He owned the gravel pits at Mountsorrel and had gained considerable wealth in London. Such men often provided a building and an annuity for a school teacher for the benefit of a dependant village. In 1742, Sir Joseph erected a school in Mountsorrel for poor boys from Mountsorrel and Swithland.

Joseph Danvers' school stood on a site below Castle Hill, north-west of The Green, near the site of the old Chapel of St Nicholas in Mountsorrel. A plaque on the wall of the building still records:

> This English school for poor boys out of Mountsorrel and
> Swithland given by Joseph Danvers Esq 1742.

Sir Joseph appears to have been closely involved in the enterprise. A letter dated 3rd February 1741 to Joseph Danvers at Chelsea from his steward, Joseph Prior, refers to the search for an appropriate building for the school:

> Mr Stone [land agent] says that he has not found anything yet that will suit you for Mountsorrel school... Freeman, the schoolmaster, lives at your house and teaches two boys from each end of Mountsorrel. Freeman was with me last night and told me that until you had settled the school to your own mind, if any three poor boys would come to him from Swithland, he would teach 'em gratis. I thought this offer was very kind and told him I would acquaint you with it. Will Johnson[4] would be glad to have one of his boys go, but I told him I would not do any thing in it without your orders.[5]

The Mountsorrel school may have been endowed with further land for the payment of the schoolmaster. In 1782, when Mountsorrel was enclosed by Parliamentary Act, it is thought that the endowment land for the Mountsorrel school was allotted to Sir John Danvers on condition that he paid £4 per annum for the Mountsorrel school's maintenance. An inquiry of 1837 into local charities reported:

> No further information could be obtained respecting the origin of this charity beyond what is stated in the inscription on the school house. There is a house with rather more than an acre of ground attached, which is supposed to have been appropriated by Mr Danvers for the use of the schoolmaster. It appears that for a long period of years, an annual sum of £4 is paid in consequence of the Commissioners having on the inclosure allotted to Mr Butler Danvers, on that condition, the land bequeathed by Sir J Danvers, which looks as if a certain quantity of land had been devised for the support of the school, but it could not be ascertained that this was the case.[6]

As was the pattern elsewhere, the Lord of the Manor had the right of nomination to the free places. In addition to these students, the Mountsorrel schoolmaster was at liberty to take paying pupils.

> The Master is appointed by Mr Danvers and is required for the above salary to teach gratis, reading, writing and arithmetic, to 12 poor boys who are nominated by Mr Danvers. Of that number, eight are selected from the parish of Mountsorrel, and four from the parish of Swithland. The full number is always kept up. The master also has upon an average about 30 pay scholars.[7]

Sir Joseph Danvers had also hoped to construct a school in Swithland. In a 1752 codicil to his will, he bequeathed money for the construction of a school 'on the green beside the forest in Swithland'.

> I give the remaining one hundred pounds... to my wife and the Overseers of the Poor of Swithland and I do hereby desire my wife will give one hundred pounds out of her own substance to the said Overseers, and the said two hundred pounds are hereby given in Trust half thereof to be laid out in Trust for erecting a Cottage containing three bays with a lean-to for the use of a school master or school mistress to live and teach young children both boys and girls to read and spin and knit upon Swithland upper Green next the forest, the remaining half to be put out at Interest and the interest to be paid yearly for the said School Master or School Mistress for teaching any poor children out of Swithland to read knit and spin such exercises being very useful in bad weather after they are grown up to be Man or Woman, and it is hereby intended that the said school shall be too full of scholars the said School Master or School Mistress to be placed in the said school by the said Sir Joseph Danvers and the owner of the Lordship and Manor of Swithland from time to time may demand and take so much for their labour in teaching quarterly as the said Sir Joseph or the said owners of the Lordship of Swithland shall together with the said Overseers shall from time to time agree upon to be fit.[8]

The site that Sir Joseph had in mind was probably a small plot on Swithland's Upper Green – the ground between the brook and Main Street, north of No. 78 Main Street (The White House). There is no documentary evidence that a school was ever built there, or that there was any later planning for a school building or for separate educational provision for children in Swithland village until George John Butler Danvers built Swithland School in 1843. Having said that, it is not impossible that sometime before 1799 a school, possibly a Sunday School, was run in Swithland under the auspices of the parish church, possibly even on the site of the present school, opposite the Griffin Inn. Certainly, a substantial building is visible on that site on the 1799 Enclosure Map. A few years later, during the 1830s, Joseph Barry and John Clarke, both schoolmasters, were resident in Swithland, so may have taught there.

Local Schooling in the Nineteenth Century

According to the plaque over the front door, Swithland's red-brick Day School was built in 1843 by George John Butler Danvers. This was a time when increasing numbers of school buildings were being set up for younger children. In 1847 George John's wife, Frances Arabella Butler Danvers, provided for an infants' school in Mountsorrel; it was housed in the building on the Loughborough Road that was later known as the Parish Rooms. In 1871, two new schools were built in Mountsorrel: St Peter's School in Watling Street and Christ Church School, on Rothley Road. (The old Joseph Danvers' school building in Mountsorrel was leased in 1878 to the Mountsorrel Granite Company as a private or village hospital and later came to be used as a private residence.)

In the late seventeenth and early eighteenth century the countryside was generally being neglected by the well-off. Some villages still paid for schoolmasters or school dames, but most of them did very little, save mind the children. However, from the late eighteenth century, the Sunday School movement paved the way for day schools. Anglican societies and diocesan authorities began to promote education in the parishes; the National Society for Promoting the Education of the Poor in the Principles of the Established Church was founded in 1812. The main problem with mass education at the time was that school time conflicted with work time. Children were expected to work, even in rural communities, as many families could not afford to maintain them unless they did. This dilemma began to be solved by the creation, during the 1780s, of Sunday Schools. Here children received training in basic literacy, numeracy and religious instruction on the one day of the week when their labour was not required. Considerable numbers of children throughout the country enrolled.

In 1843, George John Butler Danvers adapted (or built) the school building still standing today. (His coat of arms is displayed over the front door.) He may have taken advantage of the building grants of up to half the cost of school buildings that the Government began to make after 1833. The 1843 building comprised a master's house and accommodation for seventy-five children, and Stephen Clark was appointed its first head teacher at the age of twenty-two. The schoolroom is not likely to have been lavishly furnished – probably little more than long rows of desks facing the schoolmaster's desk. School days were normally broken for two hours at noon, when children would return home for a meal. Schooling was not free, although the Government introduced grants from 1846. Indeed, it was through the need to regulate these grants that school records began to be required. From 1862, grants were paid on results: on attendance, and on the results of an annual test of reading, writing and arithmetic. Children were grouped into six 'standards', covering the six years of school life from age six to age twelve. A curriculum for each standard was laid down, and tests were conducted by an independent inspector; the Church of England also appointed a diocesan inspector to examine children on religious instruction.

The First Pupils

The first entry in the earliest of Swithland's Attendance Register that has survived is that of Harriet A. Lynes, daughter to Swithland schoolmaster Charles Lynes. She was registered by her father in 1865, and, in 1867, was joined by six more pupils, mainly aged three to four years old, and most of them from modest backgrounds. The school gradually began to grow.

Swithland School Register [9]

PUPIL	START	AGE	LEFT	PARENT	PARENT'S OCCUPATION
Harriet A. Lynes	1865	4	1875	Charles Lynes	Schoolmaster
Mary H. Lynes	1867	5	1877	Charles Lynes	Schoolmaster
Eliza Ann Hodges	1867	4	1875	Thomas Hodges	Agricultural labourer
Sarah Ann Pratt	1867	4	1876	Joseph Pratt	Cottager/agricultural labourer
Sarah A. Raynor	1867	3	1875	Thomas Raynor	
Sarah Bunney	1867	3	1875	Henry Bunney	Agricultural labourer
Mary Ann Godbald	1867	4	1875	George Godbald	Farm labourer
Charles W. Lynes	1868	3.7	1879	Charles Lynes	Schoolmaster
Eliza Hodges	1868	3.9	1877	Thomas Hodges	Agricultural labourer
Sarah Ann Spencer	1868	4.0	1875	John Spencer	Agricultural labourer
James Henry Woods	1868	3.1	1878	Joseph Woods	Under gardener
Fanny Cuffling	1869	3.2	1879	William Cuffling	Farmer
William Hemsley	1869	4.0	1877	Benj. Hemsley	Farm labourer
George Brown	1869	4.0	1876	George Brown	Agricultural labourer

Education Acts 1870–1902

The Education Act 1870 gave powers to school boards to make school attendance compulsory. The effect of the legislation was not felt in Swithland, however, until 1875. In 1873 and 1874 some nine children were admitted to the school each year. But in 1875 there was a rush of thirty children, followed by nineteen in 1876, seventeen in 1877, and twenty in 1878, before dropping to single figures in subsequent years. Children were required to attend school until the age of ten, whilst those aged between ten and thirteen were allowed to leave once they reached standard five.

Religious instruction was given by the rector; all the children attended church on Ascension Day and Ash Wednesday. The children were also instructed in needlework. Gradually, the curriculum was broadened beyond literacy and numeracy, but the equipment was not lavish: slate writing boards were only discontinued and replaced entirely by paper in July 1904.

Under the 1870 act, schooling was not free; fees not being abolished until 1891. The school log[10] records that in 1886 several children were sent home for school and coal money. The school log records also include several references to 'the relieving officer', requiring a signed certificate of attendance for Jabez Tebbutt, son of Edward Tebbutt of Thurcaston. Jabez, who was admitted, aged ten, in September 1874 – his former school being Wanstead National School – was eventually sent to Wakefield in August 1876 in a dispute over the parish to which he belonged.[11] (In 1876, an education act had been passed establishing school attendance committees to encourage as many children as possible to take advantage of educational opportunities and parents were made responsible for ensuring that their children received basic instruction. The committees could help to pay the school fees if parents were too poor to do so themselves – but this was not compulsory).

Good attendance may have been assisted by legislation on child labour in agriculture: the employment of children aged seven and under in agriculture was prohibited in 1867, and the age was raised to ten in 1873. Nevertheless, children were frequently withdrawn from school to help on the farm or in some other way. The school log records that: in July 1876 William Hemsley was kept from school to help get the hay; in November 1876 Joseph Pratt was kept at home to tent the birds; in January 1882 fifteen boys were kept from school 'for beaters to shooters', and in February 1883 many boys were absent 'helping the keeper in shooting'. There are several references to the school closing early so that children could take tea to the hayfields or cornfields, and to low attendance around harvest time. In September 1889 some eleven children were absent 'on account of gleaning in the cornfields' – not, perhaps, that the children required too much encouragement to be absent. In March 1889 the school was not opened until the afternoon as 'the majority of the scholars attended the meet and afterwards ran after the hounds', and in June 1893 several children were reported away at the Rothley Wake.

As early as 1875, children were being kept from school to prevent the spread of disease. Periodically the school had to close as a result of epidemics of contagious diseases. The log contains references to outbreaks of scarlet fever, whooping cough, scarletina, measles, typhoid fever, mumps, blister pox, ringworm and influenza. More general concern about the health of working class children throughout England resulted in legislation in 1906 to allow local authorities to provide school meals, and in 1907 to introduce

Fig 13.1 Swithland School c. 1900, headmistress, Mrs Blackwell on the right.

school medical inspection. From 1909 there are references to visits to Swithland by the medical officer.

In 1893 the school leaving age was raised to eleven, then in 1899 to twelve. This did not vastly increase the number of children on the roll at Swithland. In 1910, the Board of Education in Whitehall advised that the school capacity had been reduced from seventy-five to fifty-eight pupils, but actual numbers were far fewer. At the turn of the century, there were twenty-five children on the register, and the number remained between twenty and thirty children until 1939.

County Council Control

In 1902 a new education act abolished local school boards, and gave the County Council the responsibility of financing elementary education through the rates, as well as the power to finance technical and secondary education. Voluntary schools like Swithland were thereafter funded by the County Council as local education authority schools, even though they were denominational. Gradually the Council's controlling hand became more influential. In 1905, for example, the Council directed that children under five were not to be admitted, and the appointment of Mrs M.S. Minkley as caretaker in 1909 required Education Authority approval. Swithland School continued to be run by a board of managers, chaired by successive rectors, but increasingly it was answerable to the Council's education department, based then at Greyfriars, Leicester. Among the early school managers were Edwin Pepper, H. Clough Taylor, Archibald Turner, William Green and William Frisby.

The school year included breaks in the summer, at Christmas, at Easter and at Whitsuntide, but holidays were not extensive, except for the summer harvest. In 1902–03, for example, the year started after the Whitsuntide holiday:

> SWITHLAND SCHOOL: SCHOOL HOLIDAYS 1902–03
> School opens: 2nd June 1902
> School closes: 1st August
> **Harvest holidays**
> School opens: 15th September
> School closes: 23rd December
> **Christmas holidays**
> School opens: 1st January 1903
> School closes: 9th April
> **Easter holidays**
> School opens: 20th April
> School closes 29th May
> **Whitsuntide holidays**

There were also occasional holidays. In June 1902, for example, Swithland children enjoyed three days holiday for the Coronation of King Edward VII.

School Life 1902–26

The school continued to be inspected annually, both by an H.M. Inspector and a Diocesan Inspector, until 1907. After this date there was an annual diocesan inspection, but H.M. Inspectors called less frequently. Because the school grant was partly dependant on attendance, punctuality was important. Mrs Blackwell, in particular, would cane children who were late. In the three years between June 1901 and April 1904, some seventy canings were administered: twenty for lateness; nineteen for talking; eleven for having dirty hands or face and eight for careless work.[12] Her successor, Mrs Lane, was equally concerned about punctuality, but offered incentives as well as punishments. In May 1905 she allowed the children to leave twenty minutes early 'on account of such good attendance', and in June, children received prizes for good attendance. Indeed, despite the attentions of the Board of Education in Whitehall, and of the County Council, there was scope for some local colour. At Christmas 1907, Mrs Archibald Turner visited the school and gave prizes for drawing. For several years afterwards she visited at Christmas and gave presents to the children. In July 1905 and 1906 and in September 1907 the children were allowed a day's holiday in order to make a trip to the seaside at Grimsby and Cleethorpes, for which they had saved during the previous year.

Fig 13.2 Swithland School, teacher's house and school, 1920s.

From 1911 Swithland School was run by the well-liked and respected Millicent Nettleton. As well as being head teacher for twenty-eight years, she also served as Hon Secretary to the Parochial Church Council for twenty years. Mrs Nettleton was required to teach all the children without help, although the school log does refer to occasional 'monitors': Norman E.V. Gibson from 1911–14 and Mary Beers from 1914–15. When a close relative of Mrs Nettleton died in 1920, the school had to close for the three days that she was away – having, of course, first notified the education authorities.

From time to time, important local and national events impinged on the life of the school. In December 1912, for example, it was closed for the afternoon – with the permission of Mr Brockington, County Director of Education – for the interment of John Brinsley, Lord Newtown Butler, son of the seventh Earl of Lanesborough. He had died at the young age of nineteen. During the First World War there was an influx of children temporarily staying in the village area and enrolling in the school for a period. On 11th November 1918 the children were dismissed for the afternoon by the chairman of managers, Rev J.M. Dixon, in honour of the Armistice ending the Great War. On 3rd June 1920 the school was closed for the day for the opening of Swithland Memorial Hall. On the occasion of the wedding of the rector's daughter in 1923, the children, dressed appropriately, were in attendance.

Using its powers under the 1902 Education Act, the County Council could give scholarships for children to go to grammar schools, such as the Thomas Rawlins School which had been re-founded at Quorn in 1892. Thirlby Hoult was an early Quorn pupil, leaving Swithland at the age of eleven in 1921. He was followed by John Ambrose Copson 1928 (twelve), Dorothy Adnett 1927 (eleven), Ethel Hoult 1928 (eleven), Kathleen Bunney 1929 (eleven), and Jean Copson 1929 (eleven). These pupils had to walk to Rothley to take the entrance examination. A few pupils, like John Charles Copson 1928 (eleven) and Edwin Glover 1928 (ten), attended Loughborough Junior Technical

Fig 13.3 A class at Mountsorrel School, including Olive Allen (on the right in the third row back), from Kinchley Hill Farm, in the 1920s.

School – a higher elementary school – from 1909–17 and then a junior technical school from 1917. Other children stayed at Swithland until they reached the school leaving age, which was raised to fourteen years in 1922.

In the 1990s, Jack Copson, a pupil from 1921–28, recorded his memories of life in Swithland for the Leicestershire Oral History Archive. He recalled that boys were expected to raise their caps to the Earl and Countess of Lanesborough and to Mrs Nettleton wherever they encountered them, and that fairly strict discipline was imposed on the children by both parents and the school teacher. One day, he and Ted Lloyd had been discovered by Mrs Nettleton in the act of preparing to fire their catapults at some roadside pigeons. The next morning they were called out after prayers at the school and given six strokes of the cane each on the hand – without any explanation. For her part, Mrs Nettleton must have forgotten to make an entry in the school's Punishment Book: indeed there are only two entries for the period 1920–30. There appears to have been a happy atmosphere in general at the school during her regime. A report by H.M. Inspector Mr A.T. Kerslake in July 1925 said:

> The children in this school are well-mannered, cheerful, responsive and industrious. They take an evident pleasure in their school life and manifest a delightful sense of humour. The work in all subjects reaches a high level, Arithmetic and Written Composition being worthy of special praise.[13]

During Mrs Nettleton's regime, annual trips to the seaside continued, but were funded from the proceeds of a Hallowe'en Dance at the Village Hall organised by Mrs Nettleton and Mr and Mrs William Green. Children were transported by local omnibus to Rothley Station, and thence by train to Skegness, Mablethorpe or Cleethorpes. Other joys are highlighted. On 25th September 1926, for example, the school log recorded that 'Children attend match on Cricket Field in which several Notts and Leics players took part'.

Fig 13.4 Swithland scholars at the wedding of Margaret Dixon and Henry James Walsh, 27 June 1923. BACK (left to right): John Botterill, Keith Paterson, Gladys Lloyd, Kathleen Glover, Dorothy Lloyd, Tom Adnett, John Glover. MIDDLE (left to right): Renee Minkley, Pat Hoult, Jean Copson, Dorothy Adnett, Elsie Copson, May Bunney. FRONT (left to right): Eric Adnett, Jack Copson, Geoff Hoult, John Copson, Mary Bunney, Lewis Glover, Ted Lloyd, Ernest Adnett.

Fig 13.5 Swithland School, 1929.
BACK (left to right): Joan Harrison, Mary Bunney, Beatrice Bunney, Elsie Copson, Roy Lloyd, Betty Sellars, Winnie Bloxham, Leslie Copson. MIDDLE (left to right): Bryan Pepper, Norman Pepper, Denis Copson, Molly Copson, Dorothy Minkley, Ralph Harrison. FRONT (left to right): Frank Spence, George Minkley, Brian Green.

Primary School Status

The Hadow Report of 1926 recommended to the Government that education within the elementary system be re-organised into three stages: infant (ages five to seven), junior (seven to eleven) and senior (eleven to fourteen). In 1935 the County Council re-organised its elementary schools into primary schools, which were to educate children until the age of eleven, and modern schools which, with the existing grammar and technical schools, were to provide for secondary education. In March 1934, aged fourteen, Winifred Violet Bloxham was the last Swithland pupil to leave school without progressing to secondary education. In October 1935, the older children at Swithland transferred to South Charnwood Central School. Dorothy Copson 1935 (twelve), Dorothy Minkley 1935 (twelve), Maurice Bunney 1938 (eleven) and Patricia Staynes 1939 (eleven) were among the first Swithland pupils to make the bus journey to South Charnwood.

During the Second World War, the numbers on the school roll fluctuated as evacuee children were billeted in homes in the village to escape the threat of bombing in the towns. There were twenty-six children on the roll in March 1939, but this quickly rose to thirty-seven in September 1939 when six evacuee children from Sheffield, and four other children, not under any evacuation scheme, but staying in the village for an indefinite period, were admitted. The Sheffield children were accompanied by their own teacher, a Miss Phillips, but the group returned to Sheffield in November 1939.

Fig 13.6 Swithland School, 1939.
BACK ROW (left to right): Shirley Staynes, Janet Marshall, Audrey Marshall, Pamela Marriott. 2ND ROW (left to right): Alf Ringrose, Faith Banbury, Barbara Bunney, Pearl Pentelow, Margaret Adkin, Patricia Staynes, Philip Pentelow, Margaret Ringrose. 3RD ROW (left to right): Sheila Haynes, Josephine Staynes, Dorothy Rudkin, Patricia Lloyd, John Adkin, Margaret Rudkin, Edith Sills. FRONT ROW (left to right): Neville Hyman, Colin Minkley, Peter Lloyd, Harry Woolley, John Leatherland jnr, Leonard Copson, Leonard Holliday.

Fig 13.7 Mrs Millicent Nettleton (seated), headmistress 1911–40, watching a game of cricket at Swithland.

Throughout the war, other evacuee children attended for short periods, as directed by the local billeting officer. Thirteen evacuee children from Bromley, Kent were admitted together in July 1944, but they returned home in October and November the same year.

In November 1937 Millicent Nettleton asked the Education Authority for 'a suitable girl to assist … i.e. one who has obtained her school certificate'. From March 1938, she was assisted by Joan Harrison, who was employed as a monitress. Joan Harrison left in October 1940, having passed her Pupil Teacher's Examinations, and was replaced as monitress by Miss Birch from Leicester, who left in December 1941. In January 1942, Amy Holden was appointed supplementary teacher; she stayed in the village from Monday to Friday.

In November 1939, Mrs Nettleton suffered a severe stroke that left her incapacitated: she was not able to resume her duties, but resigned, and left the area. She lived for a further twenty years, dying in 1961, and is buried in Swithland churchyard. For a short period Mrs Joan Naylor acted as temporary head teacher, until Miss Winifred Dixon took over in 1941.

Schooling continued to be interrupted by outside events, not least relating to the progress of the war. On 20th November 1940, according to the school log: 'Only fourteen children present this morning. Very inclement weather and an air raid last night partly accounts for this low attendance'. The school took part in money raising events such as 'Wings for Victory Week' and 'Salute the Soldier Week'. Occasionally there was an organised collection of rose hips from around the village, which were sent on for processing 'to provide vitamin C'. On 9th May 1945 the school was closed for two days in celebration of the cessation of hostilities in Europe. Two Belgian refugees, Georges Gillis who had lodged at Forest End, and Andrée Raiwet who had been three and a half years at Bybrook Farm, finally returned home in July.

Even before the war, the school was admitting children beyond the village of Swithland. Of the children on the registers from 1935–38, just over a half

Fig 13.8
Miss Winifred Dixon and pupils c. 1959. [3rd row left to right]: unknown, Nigel Copson, David Hall, Geoffrey Price; [2nd row left to right]: Jane Orton, Elizabeth Adkin, Alison Hickling, Lynn Haynes, Lynn Southam; [front left to right]: Sheila Copson, Rosemary Martindale.

lived in Swithland. After the war the trend was even more pronounced: fewer than a third of admissions 1947–50 were from the village, with two-thirds of the children coming from the Swithland Lane area. Most children left to go to South Charnwood Secondary Modern or to Quorn Rawlins Grammar, but a few transferred to the Loughborough Endowed Schools or to private schools. A re-organisation in 1948 of nearby grammar schools, at the insistence of the local education authority, turned Quorn Grammar from a co-educational school into a girls school, and Humphrey Perkins Grammar School at Barrow into a boys school. Boys from Swithland who would previously have gone to Quorn, now went to Barrow: James Stanley Allen was the first Swithland pupil to attend Barrow in 1949.

Aided or Controlled Status

The 1944 Education Act gave to church schools the option of becoming 'aided' (where the education authority aided managers to run the school) or 'controlled' (where foundation managers controlled schools run by the authority). The advantage of aided status was that the so-called foundation managers – those appointed by the church – retained a majority on the Board of Managers. The disadvantage was that the foundation managers were expected, with the help of Government grants, to bring the buildings up to standards that the Education Committee had decreed. This was a daunting prospect for trustees with no foundation funds on which to call, and may have contributed to the high number of Leicestershire schools opting for controlled status. The County Council adopted a plan for re-organisation in 1946, but managers were given until 28th September 1950 to apply for aided status. The Swithland managers were advised by the Education Authority that, under the Council's Plan, it was proposed to close Swithland School in 1953–54, when Swithland children would be expected to go to Woodhouse Eaves. Unsurprisingly, therefore, the managers opted for the school to become 'controlled'. In fact, Swithland School was not closed, but the managers had irrevocably chosen controlled status, which meant that foundation governors would be in a minority on the new Boards of Managers.

The number of children on the school roll at the end of the war was forty, and numbers continued at that level until Winifred Dixon resigned as head in 1961. In September 1950, the last of the school's unqualified assistants, Miss Holden, left. She was succeeded in October 1950 by Mrs Neale of Thurcaston, a qualified teacher, who taught the infants. The accommodation was cramped. In June 1956, a report from an H.M. Inspector recorded in the school log observed:

> This school building consists of one room of approximately 12 x 36 feet divided into two equal portions by a sliding partition. The floor is of stone, heating is by stoves and electric light has been installed. The furniture consists of heavy dual desks… The small porch cloakroom contains two washbasins and the scullery equipment for the school meals service...

> At the time of the inspection there were 21 juniors and 19 infants on the roll. They are friendly helpful and courteous to their fellows and to the adults with whom they work. More than 30 stay regularly for the school meal, which is served on the desks...

Despite talk about an extension to the school, however, nothing materialised.

More changes in the provision for secondary education locally were seen in 1959. Shepshed Secondary Modern School opened, and children from Swithland, who had not secured a place at one of the local grammar schools, transferred there rather than to South Charnwood. Thus, in July 1959 Malcolm Pollard left to attend Loughborough Grammar School; Graham Price, Roger Copson, Richard Orton and Stuart Musgrove went to Barrow Grammar School; Mary Bream left for Quorn Grammar School; and John Stone, Robin Cook and Christine Orton were the first from Swithland to attend Shepshed Secondary Modern School.

Winifred Dixon had been unwell for some time before she resigned as head teacher in April 1961, after twenty-one years in post. She retired to the Lake District, enjoying twenty years of retirement before dying in January 1981 at the age of eighty. Assistant teacher Mrs Neale retired in July 1964 after fourteen years service, and in the following September Mrs Evelyn Dexter of Woodhouse Eaves replaced her. Miss Dixon's successor was Eric George Waller. He canvassed for better facilities at the school; the Education Department conceded that the accommodation was sub-standard, and a new office extension was built at the rear of the school. Waller also set about introducing progressive teaching methods.

The Leicestershire Plan

In 1967, Leicestershire re-organised secondary education again. The county had been operating a bi-partite system with twenty-five per cent of pupils allocated to grammar schools and seventy-five per cent to secondary modern schools. This required primary pupils to take an examination in their last year, the Qualifying Examination for Secondary Schools (QESS), otherwise known as the 11+ exam. This was an intelligence quotient (IQ) test, which, together with an assessment based on head teachers' recommendations and the school Order of Merit, was used to select for secondary education. Under the 1967 Mason Plan, named after the county's director of education, selective education for secondary children was abolished and replaced by all-ability comprehensive middle schools (high schools) for pupils aged from eleven to fourteen, with upper schools for pupils over fourteen years old. All Swithland pupils now transferred at eleven years to the re-named Hind Leys High School at Shepshed.

Eric Waller left in August 1967 to become head at Braunstone Millfield County Primary School. Miss Joyce M. Powell took over as acting head teacher for one term until Mrs Sheila Joy White (later Bryan) was appointed permanent replacement. Assistant teacher Evelyn Dexter resigned at the end of 1968 to emigrate to Australia, and was replaced by Mrs Hodgkiss, from January 1969 to March 1970, followed by Mrs Barbara Harrington in April 1970.

One of Mrs Bryan's early pre-occupations was the dramatic fall in the number of pupils on the school's roll. Waller's progressive methods may have alienated some parents. In 1963 there had been forty-three pupils, but by 1968 this had fallen to twenty-seven. Some education authorities had adopted a policy of closing schools of this size. Mrs Bryan acted quickly to re-establish confidence in the school and numbers stabilised at between thirty and forty pupils. Her challenge was the greater because the number of pupils from Swithland itself continued to be low: of children admitted between 1970–74 only twenty-one per cent lived in the village, thirty-two per cent came from the Swithland Lane area, and the remainder were drawn from Anstey, Birstall, Rothley, Quorn, Mountsorrel, Woodhouse, Woodhouse Eaves, Newtown Linford and Cropston. Additionally, almost one half of this cohort left for private education – principally at Fairfield, the junior section of the Loughborough Endowed Schools, which could take children at the age of eight, and later lowering this to five years old.

Lack of space at the school did not help. By 1980, given the changed criteria used by the Department of Education and Science, the managers could justifiably request the provision of another classroom. A demountable or 'mobile' classroom finally arrived in January 1982, and the infant class was able to move into it in March of that year. These new mobile classrooms helped allow the Education Authority to address the problem of falling rolls in Leicestershire high schools. Following the 'baby boom' immediately after the war, birth rates had fallen, and the numbers at some high schools had dropped to a level that placed in jeopardy the proper delivery of the

Fig 13.9 Swithland School, 1977. On the left is Mrs Barbara Harrington, assistant teacher and the right, Mrs Sheila Bryan, head teacher.

curriculum. The authority therefore proposed that some high schools should take children from the ages of ten to fourteen. Since this would remove the top year at primary schools, it was agreed that, in these areas, primary schools could admit children aged four. From 1983, Swithland became a '4–10' age primary school. And, because staffing standards required a nursery nurse for nursery-age children, a qualified NNEB nursery nurse was appointed.

National concern about standards in education led to legislation in the 1980s for the introduction of a compulsory National Curriculum, attainment tests and more local management of schools. Unfortunately Sheila Bryan's indifferent health in later years may have impeded the school's adaptation to the new requirements. In October 1979 Mrs Bryan underwent an operation, with Mrs Georgina Moorhead taking over as acting head until February 1980. From January to May 1983 Mrs Bryan was on sick leave receiving medical treatment, and again in November 1987. Mrs Harrington took over as acting head, but she retired in March 1988. Mrs Vivienne James, a member of the permanent unattached supply staff at County Hall, took over as acting head, and was assisted by Miss Linda Washington. Mrs Bryan finally resigned in September 1988, and died shortly afterwards. She is buried in Swithland churchyard.

Stability and Growth

The cumulative effect of changes and uncertainties led to a crisis of confidence among parents. Numbers on roll fell to twenty-six in January 1989. The Department of Education and Science was making tentative suggestions that, in order to teach the National Curriculum properly, the minimum size of a primary school should be fifty-two pupils. The County Council considered the closure of the school, but consented to the appointment of Mrs Caroline Webb as head teacher for a fixed period of two years, during which the school's future would be re-assessed. Mrs Webb succeeded in stabilising pupil numbers, despite the fear of some parents that the school would inevitably close. In 1991 Mrs Betty Wood became head teacher on a permanent contract, and, with phenomenal success, set about restoring numbers and confidence.

Mrs Webb had not chosen to live in the schoolhouse, and Mrs Wood chose also to retain her own home. The schoolhouse was therefore available as an additional teaching area for the school. There was some uncertainty as to ownership, which was not helped by the absence of any trust deed. When the Swithland Estate had been offered for sale in 1954, the school was included in the lots, but was withdrawn before auction. A note in the school log in spring 1963 recorded that the schoolhouse and school had been purchased from Lord Lanesborough. With the agreement of all the possible interested parties, the house was converted in early 1994, and the capacity of the school thereby increased.

In October 1994 there were sixty-one pupils on roll in the three classes, and when Betty Wood moved to another post in June 1996, numbers had risen to seventy-four. Beryl Wheeler was appointed head teacher in August 1996. During her years at Swithland, pupil numbers continued to grow, necessitating the replacement of the single mobile classroom with a double-mobile in 1997. The school was then able to be divided into four classes, and by August 1998 there were ninety-one children at the school. By 2003, the school had stabilised at just under one hundred pupils, with a planned admission agreement that would not see numbers rise much above this level. Mrs Wheeler retired in 2006, having raised the school's Ofsted standards to 'very good'. Standards continued to rise to 'excellent' under head teachers Carolyn Beaton (2006–08) and Christine Lethbridge (from 2009).

A School with a Future

The latter part of the twentieth century saw considerable interest in education from Government. Fortunately, with the recent growth in pupil numbers, Swithland is now spared any anxiety from debates about a minimum viable size. That it has survived, in spite of a small population base from which to draw pupils, is testimony to the excellent work of its teaching staff. Many Swithland children have succeeded in life thanks to their start at St. Leonard's School. It remains one of the few public institutions remaining in the parish – bringing life to the village, through the merits of a pupil-friendly educational experience.

Head Teachers at Swithland School

1843–1865	Stephen Clarke	1961–1967	Eric Waller
1865–1883	Charles Lynes	1968–1988	Sheila Joy White (Bryan)
1883–1884	John Hindley Mee	1988–1989	Vivienne A. James
1884–1888	Charlotte Moore	1989–1990	Caroline Webb
1888–1897	E. Lily Huntley	1991–1996	Betty Wood
1897–1904	Mrs J. Blackwell	1996–2006	Beryl Wheeler
1904–1911	Gertrude Conway Layne	2006–2008	Carolyn Beaton
1911–1940	Millicent Nettleton	2009–	Christine Lethbridge
1941–1960	Winifred Dixon		

Notes to Chapter 13

1. See Chapter 7: Dissent.
2. D. Wix and I. Keil, *Rawlins: The First 300 Years*, list of school masters, p. 18.
3. J.D. Welding (ed.), *Leicestershire in 1777*, 1984. Prior was also curate at Woodhouse and Quorn, 1755–63.
4. William and Jane Johnson had a daughter and four sons: Mary b.1730, William b.1732, Joseph b.1733, John b.1737 and Henry b.1738. Whether or not Will Johnson's son was one of the Swithland boys educated at Mountsorrel is not known.
5. Leics. RO, DE1750 Box 16, Letter 3 February 1741, Joseph Prior, steward, to Sir Joseph Danvers.
6. Leicestershire Charities Report, 1837.
7. ibid. (Sir Joseph Danvers' school probably closed a few years after this report, given that new schools were opened in the 1840s in both Swithland and Mountsorrel).
8. Leics. RO, DE1750, Box 7, Will, Sir Joseph Danvers, 1753.
9. Local Swithland archives.
10. Parish Archives, Swithland School Log Books from 1875.
11. School Log entry, 11 August 1876.
12. Parish Archives, St Leonard's School punishment book.
13. Recorded in School Log, July 1925.

CHAPTER 14

Family Connections

There are some people, famous, infamous, and one simply mysterious, whose stories are caught up with the history of Swithland families and who should have a place within the village history. These include John Danvers of Chelsea and Oxford (1588–1645), who signed the death warrant of Charles I, his brothers, Charles and Henry, and his first wife, Magdalen Herbert, mother to George Herbert (1593–1633) and good friend and inspiration to another poet-priest, John Donne (1572–1631). Two famous sons born in the village were John Prior (1729–1803), Leicestershire teacher and map-maker, son of Sir Joseph Danvers' steward, and Otto Murray Dixon, a son of the rectory and noted wild-life painter, whose untimely death on the battlefield was seen as a national loss. There was also Louie Burrows of Quorn, for a short while engaged to the Nottinghamshire novelist and poet D.H. Lawrence (1885–1930), whose brother, sister-in-law and niece lie in Swithland churchyard. And finally, there are the 'Hind sisters', last of the line to live in the village, but who gave their names to the Hind Sisters Homes in Cropston. Pre-dating all of them, however, is the mysterious fourteenth century lady, whose brass may be found fixed to the west wall of the church, but who is buried in an honorary position at the east end of the nave, the anchoress Agnes Scot.

Agnes Scot

At first sight, the inscription on Agnes Scot's brass is all we know about her.

> Hoc in conclave jacet Agnes Scot camerata,
> Antrix devota Dominae Ferrers vocitata:
> Quisquis eris qui transieris, queso, fune precata;
> Sum quod eris, fueramque quo des: pro me, precor, ora.

The Latin is in places ambiguous, but a very rough interpretation might read: 'Agnes Scot, anchoress/hermitess, lies in this tomb, a cave-dweller, recognised as devout by Lady Ferrers. Whoever you are who pass by, I beg you. I am what you will be; I was what you are now. I beseech you, pray for me'. The wording of the translation given on a notice in the church describes her as 'devout mother of Lady Ferrers', but this has to be an interpretation, as the word 'mother' is not part of the Latin text. The translator was seeking to portray her as a spiritual mother, someone who supported and directed the spiritual life of others. Whoever this lady was – nun, anchoress or hermit – she was clearly seen by the Lady Ferrers of Groby as a holy woman, and not just worthy of a special burial place, but also worthy of portrayal on the main east window, the most important window of the church and traditionally the place for pictures of Christ and the saints or of biblical scenes; worthy of remembering, perhaps even worthy of offering our prayers. What was it that was, and remains, so special about her?

Recent research has sought to place Agnes Scot within the late mediaeval tradition of English holy women, especially in this midlands region.[1] Kelcey Wilson-Lee believes that, in comparison with only eighteen other monuments commemorating late mediaeval women religious in England and one in Scotland, the monument to Agnes Scot is highly unusual. Other monuments seem to fall into two categories: abbesses and nuns, required to live in religious communities, and lay widows who took vows of chastity after their husbands' deaths, who were not. There are differences and similarities in the memorials to these two groups of women. The differences identified relate to the portrayal of their dress, and also to the presence or absence of ecclesiastical accoutrement, such as crosiers, rings of office, ecclesiastical heraldry. Women religious in general are portrayed wearing simpler, more loose-fitting robes than the gentry widows (vowesses); high level women religious, like abbots and bishops, often hold a crozier or wear a ring. Agnes Scot wears a simple, belted, long gown with loose sleeves, (and, in the old east window, a ring) but her brass shows no personal accoutrements (though her window contained the arms of her patroness, Ferrers of Groby). Unlike all the other abbesses and nuns, however, Agnes, while veiled, is not wearing a wimple, which would seem to indicate that she led an enclosed, rather than an open to public view, life. The inscription, however, would seem to indicate a solitary religious, living the life of a hermit rather than one living with the support of a community, such as at nearby Grace Dieu or Langley Priory, or at Kingsmead Priory in Derbyshire – a female house linked to Darley Abbey, which was under the patronage of the Ferrers family.

> Cave-dweller (antrix) suggests that Agnes was a hermitess, rather than an anchoress (camerata) as we would normally think of one. Anchoresses lived enclosed in cells attached or very close to churches – in urban, village or monastic settings. Cave-dweller instead implies a non-urban reclusive existence, in this case probably in the wooded upland area near Swithland or Groby. The description of Lady Ferrers' support given in the monument's inscription does not suggest that Agnes was part of an established religious community, but rather that she lived alone ... The greatest difficulty in labelling Agnes a 'hermit' is that there were not supposed to be female hermits in fifteenth-century England...[2]

However, Roberta Gilchrist does allow that 'the informality of privately founded hermitages may have encouraged the participation of religious women as inmates'.[3]

We are left still wondering who Agnes Scot was, and where and how she lived and prayed, but increasingly aware that in her we had a very special and unique person in English spiritual history living and dying amongst us.

Charles, Henry and John Danvers: Traitor, Murderer, Regicide

The Danvers family of Swithland was just one branch of the wider Danvers family whose history has been traced back to Helge of Alvers (or Auvers) born c. 1000 AD in France. Helge's son, Sir Roland de Alvers (b. 1065), came over to England with William the Conqueror and established his household in Little Marlow and Dorney in Buckinghamshire. By c. 1300, when the family name had evolved to Danvers,[4] the three main branches of the family were living in Little Bourton, Little Marlow and Winterbourne. Two hundred years later, the main family base had moved from Buckinghamshire to Oxfordshire, with Culworth, Dauntsey and Prescote the primary places of residence, where it remained until the sixteenth century. The modern Swithland branch of the Danvers family[5] was descended from the Culworth branch c. 1420. (Other Leicestershire Danvers lived in Frolesworth and Shackerston.) The Oxfordshire and Swithland branches of the Danvers line were united on 3rd January 1710 when Elizabeth Danvers, widow of Samuel Danvers of Swithland, married John Danvers of Prescote (1651–1721) whose father, Sir John, one of the Dauntsey Danvers, was among those who had signed the death warrant of Charles I. In marrying John Danvers of Prescote, Elizabeth had united herself to a family with a relatively infamous past. Usefully, however, she had married money and respectability.

Elizabeth's new father-in-law was the youngest of three brothers, Charles, Henry and John. Their father, Sir John Danvers (1540–1593) of Dauntsey, Wiltshire, was a notable man in his day. He played an important part in the national preparations to defend England against the Armada, and he had married Elizabeth Nevill, daughter and co-heiress of the last Lord Latimer. John and Elizabeth Danvers produced three sons, Charles, Henry and John.

Their eldest son, Charles (1568–1601), was educated at Oxford and at the Middle Temple. He was MP for Cirencester from 1586–87 and from 1588–89. He served in the English army in the Netherlands during this time, and was knighted there in 1588. In 1594, however, he was implicated, together with his brother Henry, in the death of a Wiltshire neighbour, Henry Long. Henry Long had apparently been committed to prison for theft by Charles Danvers' father. To avenge the insult, the Longs killed one of the Danvers' servants, and abused the whole Danvers family, and especially Charles. At some point, Henry Long appears to have issued a challenge to Charles, as a consequence of which Henry Long was shot, in 1594, possibly by Charles' brother, Henry. The two brothers took refuge with the Earl of

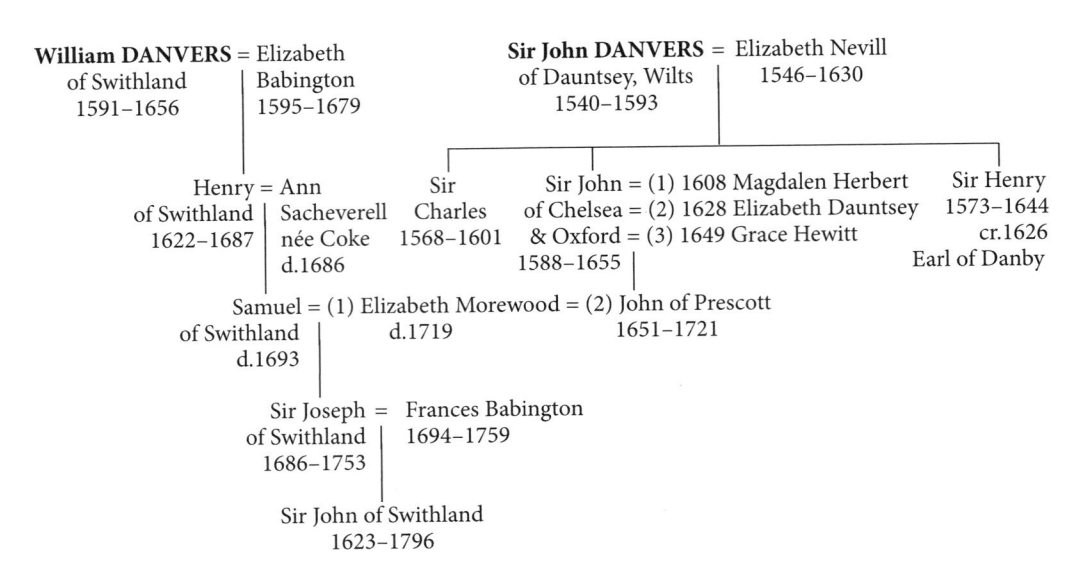

```
William DANVERS = Elizabeth          Sir John DANVERS = Elizabeth Nevill
  of Swithland   | Babington           of Dauntsey, Wilts | 1546–1630
    1591–1656    | 1595–1679              1540–1593       |
        |                                                 |
   ┌────┴────┐                      ┌──────────┬──────────┴──────────────────┬──────────┐
  Henry = Ann         Sir        Sir John = (1) 1608 Magdalen Herbert      Sir Henry
of Swithland | Sacheverell     Charles    of Chelsea = (2) 1628 Elizabeth Dauntsey   1573–1644
 1622–1687   | née Coke       1568–1601    & Oxford = (3) 1649 Grace Hewitt            cr.1626
             | d.1686                        1588–1655  |                         Earl of Danby
        |
   Samuel = (1) Elizabeth Morewood = (2) John of Prescott
 of Swithland |      d.1719                  1651–1721
    d.1693    |
        |
   Sir Joseph = Frances Babington
  of Swithland | 1694–1759
    1686–1753  |
        |
   Sir John of Swithland
       1623–1796
```

Southampton, but they were outlawed and fled to France. Both were pardoned in 1598, and Charles went on to serve with the Earl of Essex in Ireland in 1599. In 1601, however, Charles was involved in a conspiracy by the Earls of Essex and Southampton to 'persuade' Elizabeth I to change her government. Their plot was discovered, Danvers confessed his part, and was beheaded, with the Earl of Essex, on Tower Hill on 6th February 1601. He was buried in the Tower Chapel[6] and his estates were forfeited to the Crown, but James I restored Charles' estates to his brother Henry in 1605.

The middle brother, Henry Danvers (1573–1644) was educated at Christ Church, Oxford. He, too, fought with the English army against France, and was knighted by the Earl of Essex in 1591 before the Battle of Rouen. Following Henry Long's murder, Henry was also forced to live in exile in France between 1594–98, but he served with distinction during this time in the army of Henry IV of France. (It was at this time that he acquired the large scar, near his left eye, which can be seen in Van Dyck's 1635 portrait of him.)[7] In 1603, shortly after the accession of James I, Henry was created Baron Danvers of Dauntsey, and in 1605 was restored as heir to his father by Act of Parliament. This allowed him to take possession of the family estates which had been forfeited to the Crown by his brother's involvement in Essex's Rebellion. James I also appointed him Lord President of Munster (1607–15), and Governor of Guernsey. Henry was something of a philanthropist, founding the Oxford Physic Garden in 1621 – the first botanical gardens in England – when he presented land and money to Oxford University. His foundation was commemorated with a grand gateway.

> The Physic Garden is situated to the south of Magdalen College. We pass through a small court to the grand entrance, designed by Inigo Jones, and executed by Nicholas Stone. It is of the Doric order, and ornamented with rustic work. It is moreover adorned with a bust of the founder Lord Danby, a statue of Charles I, and

another of Charles II. These statues were purchased for £34 being the fine imposed on the university by Anthony Wood. On the face of the corona and the frieze is the following inscription: Gloriae Dei optimi maximi Honori Caroli I. Regis in Usum Academiae et Reipublicae Henricus Comes Danby, Anno 1632.8 The same inscription is on the garden front. The Garden, which is five acres in circumference, is surrounded by a noble wall, with other portals in the rustic style at proper distances. The ground is divided into four quarters. On the right and left, at the entrance, are two neat and convenient green-houses, stocked with a valuable collection of exotics. The quarters are filled with a complete series of such plants as grow naturally, disposed in their respective classes. Without the walls, on the east, is an admirable hot-house, where various plants, brought from the warmer climates, are raised. This Garden was instituted by the Earl of Danby above-mentioned, A.D. 1632; who having replenished it with plants for the use of students in botany, settled an annual revenue for its support.[9]

In 1626 Henry Danvers was created Earl of Danby,[10] and in 1633 a Knight of the Order of the Garter, in which robes he was painted by Van Dyck in 1635. Danby was a steady royalist. He died aged seventy-one in 1644, 'at his howse in Cornbury-parke'[11] and was buried in the church at Dauntsey that he had restored. He died unmarried, so the barony of Danvers and the Earldom of Danby became extinct.

> Sacred marble, safely keep
> His dust; who under thee must sleep,
> Until the graves again restore
> Their dead, and time shall be no more;
> Meanwhile, if he (which all things wears)
> Does ruin thee, or if thy tears
> Are shed for him; dissolve thy frame,
> Thou art requited: for his fame,
> His virtue, and worth shall be
> Another monument to thee.[12]

Looking back at Danby's life from the vantage of the 1680s, John Aubrey described Sir Henry as 'tall and spare; temperate; sedate and solid'.[13]

John (1588–1655), the third and youngest son of John and Elizabeth Danvers, and knighted by James I in 1608, has been described as an aristocratic and strikingly handsome playboy. 'His complexion was so exceeding beautifull that the people would come after him in the street to admire him.'[14] In February 1609, he married, aged only twenty, Magdalen Herbert,[15] a widow twice his age, and the mother of ten children – including the poet-priest George Herbert (1593–1633). George Herbert would later pay poetical tribute to his step-father[16] when he penned a short poem on the sight of his portrait.

Passe not by.
Search and you may
Find a treasure
Worth your stay.
What makes a Danvers
Would you find?
In a fayre body
A fayre mind.
Sir John Danvers' earthly part
Here is copied out by art;
But his heavenly and divine,
In his progenie doth shine.
Had he only brought them forth,
Know that much had been his worth.
There's no monument to a sonne,
Read him there, and I have done.[17]

Magdalen's fortune allowed Sir John, in 1618, to buy some land in Chelsea from Thomas, Earl of Lincoln, where, in 1622, he built a substantial mansion called Danvers House. Samuel Pepys described the house in 1661 as 'the prettiest contrived house that I ever saw in my life'. The house stood close to the River Thames, near to Old Chelsea Church. According to Aubrey, the chimney piece in Sir John's personal chamber was formally in the chamber of Sir Thomas More, whose old house stood nearby. Around the house,[18] Sir John created a celebrated Italian garden, the first of its kind in the country.

In 1610 he was elected MP for Arundel, in 1614 for Montgomery, in 1621 for Oxford University, and in 1624 for Newport, Isle of Wight. In April 1625, he was again elected Member of Parliament for Oxford University, for which he was re-elected in January 1626 and again in February 1628.

After his first wife, Magdalen, died in 1627, John married Elizabeth Dauntsey in July 1628. Through this marriage he had five children. He also came into possession of the estate of Lavington, Wiltshire, where he laid out gardens even more elaborate than those at Chelsea. However, he soon fell into debt. From 1630 to 1640 he was struggling with creditors. In 1639 he refused to contribute to the king's expedition against the Covenanting Scots, and passed into outright opposition. He was elected to the Short Parliament for a fourth time by Oxford University.

In 1642 he took up arms for Parliament, and was granted a colonel's commission, but he played no prominent part in military affairs. On the death of his brother, the Earl of Danby, in 1643, Sir John went to live at Dauntsey. Danby had left much of his property to Henry, Sir John's son by Elizabeth Dauntsey, but had also made generous disposition to Sir John himself. Nevertheless, Sir John set about trying – unsuccessfully – to overturn Danby's will, and to disinherit his own sisters.

In January 1649 he married for a third time – to Grace Hewitt, by whom he had another son, John. Later that year John Danvers was appointed a member of the Commission to try King Charles I, and was among those fifty-nine people who signed the King's death warrant. At the Restoration of Charles II in 1660, forty-one of the 'regicides' were still alive; fifteen escaped abroad and nine suffered the full penalties of treason. Sir John, fortunately, it may be said, had died in April 1655 and was buried at Dauntsey. Although he died before the Restoration, Sir John's family did not escape the consequences of his actions. He was among those named in the Bill of Attainder against the regicides, and his estates were forfeited.

After that forfeiture in 1660, little of the Danvers' estates survived. Most went to the Earl of Clarendon, although in 1662, the manor of Prescote, Oxfordshire, which had been in the family since 1419, was granted by the King to Sir John's widow, Grace, together with lands at Charlebury and Ascot.

Fig 14.1 Sir John Danvers, Regicide.[19]

> Charles R.
>
> Our pleasure is that you forthwith prepare a Bill for our signature, containing a Grant of all that Manor or Capital Messuage called Prescott or Prescott Farm together with the Tythes and Mills thereof, and all Lands Tenements and Hereditaments thereunto belonging lying within the parish of Cropredy in the County of Oxon and of all that Messuage Tenement or Farm lying in Shorthampton within the parish of Charlebury in the said County now or late in the tenure or occupation of Richard Harris or his assignees, And all that other messuage Tenement or Farm lying in Shorthampton aforesaid, now or late in the tenure or occupation of Richard Browne or his assignee, And all that Messuage Tenement or Farme lying in Chilson within the parishes of Charlbury and Ascott or one of them in the said county of Oxon, now or late in the tenure or occupation of Thomas Bland or his assignees, And of all houses Lands Tenements and Hereditaments to the said several Messuages Tenements or Farms in Shorthampton and Chilson belonging or appurtaining, All which premises were forfeited unto us and vested in us by an Act of the present Parliament intitled an Act declaring the pains penalties and forfeiture imposed upon the estates and persons of certain notorious offenders excepted out of the Act of free and general pardon indemnity and oblivion, as part

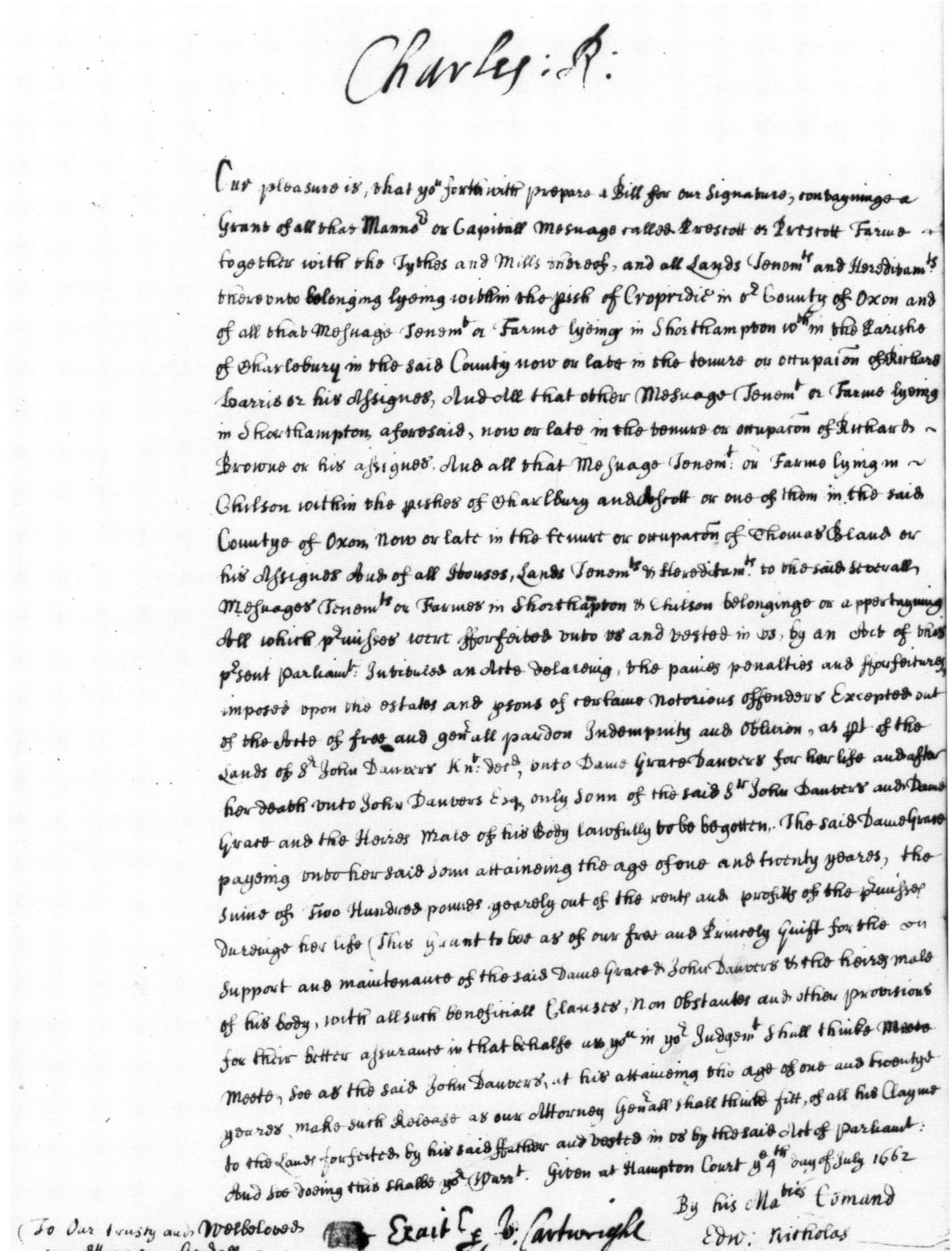

Charles R.

Our pleasure is, that you forthwith prepare a Bill for our Signature, contayninge a Grant of all that Mannor or Capitall Mesuage called Prescott or Pretscott Farme together with the Tythes and Mills thereof, and all Lands Tenem:ts and Hereditam:ts thereunto belonging lyeing within the parish of Cropredie in o:r County of Oxon and of all that Mesuage Tenem:t or Farme lyeing in Shorthampton w:th in the parishe of Charlebury in the said County now or late in the tenure or occupaçon of Richard Harris or his Assignes, And all that other Mesuage Tenem:t or Farme lyeing in Shorthampton aforesaid, now or late in the tenure or occupaçon of Richard Browne or his assignes. And all that Mesuage Tenem:t or Farme lyeing in Chilson within the p:ishes of Charlbury and Ascott or one of them in the said County of Oxon, now or late in the tenure or occupaçon of Thomas Claud or his Assignes And of all Houses, Lands Tenem:ts & Hereditam:ts to the said sev:all Mesuages Tenem:ts or Farmes in Shorthapton & Chilson belonginge or app:teyning All which p:misses were fforfeited unto us and vested in us, by an Act of this p:sent parliam:t Intituled an Acte declaring the paines penalties and fforfeitures imposed upon the estates and p:sons of certaine notorious Offendo:rs Excepted out of the Acte of free and gen:all pardon Indempnity and Oblivion, as w:ll of the Lands of S:r John Danvers Kn:t dec:d, unto Dame Grace Danvers for her life and after her death unto John Danvers Esq: only sonn of the said S:r John Danvers and Dame Grace and the Heires Male of his Body lawfully to be begotten. The said Dame Grace paying unto her said sonn at attaineing the age of one and twenty yeares, the sume of Two Hundred pounds yearely out of the rents and profitts of the p:misses dureinge her life (This grant to be as of our free and Liberely guift for the Support and maintenaunce of the said Dame Grace & John Danvers & the heires Male of his body, with all such benefinall Clauses, Non Obstantes and other provisions for their better assuranc:e in that behalfe as yo:u in yo:r Judgem:t shall thinke meete, Soe as the said John Danvers, at his attaineing the age of one and twentye yeares make such Release as our Attorney gen:all shall thinke fitt, of all his Claymes to the Lands forfeited by his said ffather and vested in us by the said Act of parliam:t: And soe doeing this shall be yo:r Warr:t Given at Hampton Court the 4:th day of July 1662

(To our trusty and welbeloved our Attorney gen:all.)

Exam:d p: B: Cartwright

By his Ma:ties Comand
Edw: Nicholas

Fig 14.2 Charles II Grant to Grace Danvers, 4 July 1662.

of the lands of Sir John Danvers Kt deceased, unto Dame Grace Danvers for her life and after her death unto John Danvers Esq, only son of the said Sir John Danvers and Dame Grace and the heirs male of his body lawfully to be begotten. The said Dame Grace paying unto her said son attaining the age of one and twenty years, the sum of two hundred pounds yearly out of the rents and profits of the premises during her life. This grant to be as of our free and princely gift for the support and maintenance of the said Dame Grace and John Danvers and the heirs male of his body, with all such beneficial clauses, non-obstants, and other provisions for their better assurance in that behalf as you in your judgement shall think meet, so as the said John Danvers, at his attaining the age of one or twenty years, make such release as our Attorney General shall think fit, all of his claim to the lands forfeited by his said father and vested in us by the said Act of Parliament. And so doing this shall be your warrant. Given at Hampton Court, the 4th day of July 1662.

To our trusty and wellbeloved	By his Majesty's Command
Our Attorney General	Edw Nicholas

After Grace Danvers' death, John, her son with Sir John Danvers of Chelsea and Oxford, succeeded to the restored estate. It was this Sir John (of Prescott) who, as a bachelor of forty-two years, married the widow of Samuel Danvers of Swithland in 1693. During his lifetime, John Danvers of Prescott built quite a substantial fortune. His epitaph in Cropredy church states that he 'served many years with great honour and integrity in several Commissions of the Revenue in the reigns of King William, Queen Anne and King George'. At his death in 1721, two years after Elizabeth's death, he held the manor of Basmey (Eaton Soken, Beds), as well as the manor of Prescott, and land at Charlebury and Ascot, Oxon. He may have gained part of his wealth through the Salt Office where he was one of the commissioners of the tax on salt.[20]

In a first codicil to his will, he made no less than twenty-seven specific cash legacies, amounting to some £7,180. He and Elizabeth had died without heirs. Sir John willed his manor and Lordship of Prescott, together with lands in the parishes of Prescott, Cropredy and Appleby, to Joseph Danvers of Swithland – Elizabeth's eldest son by Samuel Danvers – together with his plate, books, saddle horses, household goods, furniture and pictures at Prescott.[21]

The treatment of Sir John Danvers of Chelsea and Oxford obviously rankled in the family for many years. On the monument which Sir John Danvers of Swithland (1723–1796) erected to himself in Swithland church in 1790, he refers to Sir John Danvers, the regicide, describing him thus:

> He was a friend of the constitution; and in the violent struggles which ensued, sided with that that band of patriots, who thought Liberty could not be too dearly bought, though at the expense of Royal blood. His death, happening before the Restoration,

sheltered him from prosecution; but his son, who was an infant when the king was beheaded, saw his paternal estates, to the amount of ten thousand pounds a year, in the counties of Oxford and Wiltshire in the hands of strangers. The small portion of his patrimony which escaped the rapacity of the Court, that son left to Sir Joseph Danvers for life, and to Sir John in tail.

The estates at Dauntsey were permanently forfeited, but the charge of rapacity may have been an exaggeration. In any event the displacement of James II, and the accession of William I at the English Revolution in 1688, seems to have marked the end of the Danvers' antipathy to the monarchy, and their re-integration as pillars of society.

Lady Magdalen Danvers, George Herbert and John Donne

Lady Magdalen Herbert (née Newport), the first wife of Sir John Danvers of Chelsea and Oxford has an interesting history of her own. Magdalen Newport's first husband was Sir Richard Herbert of Montgomery Castle (d. 1596), with whom she had ten surviving children. One of those seven sons and three daughters was the poet-priest George Herbert (1593–1633). Magdalen was herself a cultured and highly lettered woman, but it was the academic career of her eldest son, Edward, which first took her and her younger children up to Oxford in c. 1599, where she met John Donne, who, according to Isaak Walton, greatly appreciated 'the Beauties of her body and mind'.[22] A friendship between the two developed, which continued after Donne's marriage to Ann in 1601 and Magdalen's second marriage to Sir John Danvers in 1609. According to Walton, John Donne and Magdalen were never lovers, though they exchanged letters frequently, and Magdalen seems to have inspired several of Donne's poems.[23] It is possible that Magdalen once had hopes of a relationship with Donne, which he, by then married to Ann, had to deny her. (One of the four letters, written in 1607, which Walton made public gives that impression.) Magdalen Herbert married the twenty year old John Danvers in 1609, but she remained friendly with John Donne until her death in 1627. In 1625, during a time when the plague was virulent in the City, Donne stayed in Chelsea with Lady Magdalen and Sir John Danvers. Donne called her house a 'secular monastery'.[24] He admired Magdalen then for her holiness of life and her social goodness. 'When every (other) doore was shut up', Magdalen offered the afflicted who called on her 'releefe applicable to that very infection from this house'. When she died, in 1627, Donne preached the commemorative sermon for her at Chelsea, which moved him at times to tears.

George Herbert was Lady Magdalen's third son by her first husband. According to Walton, Herbert and Donne had 'such a Sympathy of inclinations that they coveted and joyed to be in each other's company'.[25] There was also a very affectionate relationship between George Herbert and his Danvers relations. In 1619, Herbert, hoping at the time to win the orator's place at Cambridge, wrote appreciatively, though diplomatically, to his step-father.

I hope I shall get this place without all your London helps, of which
I am very proud, not but that I joy in your favours, but that you may
see, that if all else fails, yet I am able to stand on my own legs.[26]

Walton's *Life of George Herbert* says of his relationship with his uncle Henry, Earl of Danby, that, when Herbert was ill in 1629, Danby 'loved Mr Herbert so very much, that he allow him such an apartment (in his house at Dauntsey) as might best suit with his accommodation and liking. And in this place, by a spare diet, declining all perplexing studies, moderate exercise, and a cheerful conversation, his health was apparently improved to a good degree of strength and cheerfulness.'

Shortly afterwards George Herbert married Jane Danvers, one of his step-father's cousins, after just three days acquaintance. It was a happy marriage, though sadly short-lived, as Herbert died three years later.

John Prior (1729–1803)

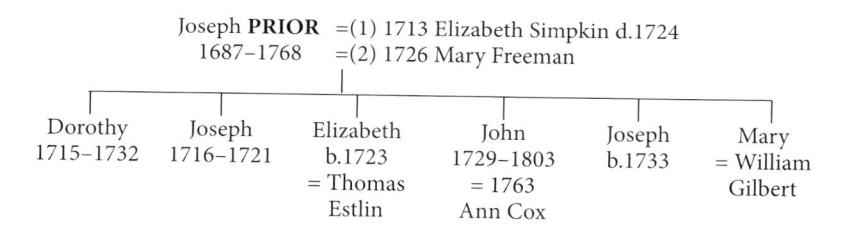

```
Joseph PRIOR    =(1) 1713 Elizabeth Simpkin d.1724
1687–1768       =(2) 1726 Mary Freeman

Dorothy    Joseph     Elizabeth   John        Joseph     Mary
1715–1732  1716–1721  b.1723      1729–1803   b.1733     = William
                      = Thomas    = 1763                 Gilbert
                      Estlin      Ann Cox
```

John Prior, the second[27] son of Joseph Prior, Sir Joseph Danvers' steward, became a noted and respected figure in Leicestershire. Born at Swithland in August 1729, he went to Rawlins' School at Woodhouse, where from 1744 until 1750 his father was schoolmaster.[28] John did so well that at the age of fifteen he was appointed master there, succeeding his father. Five years later he took holy orders, serving as a curate at Woodhouse and Quorn from 1755 to 1763, while continuing the teaching post at Rawlins' School. In 1763, with the benefit of the patronage of Francis, Earl of Huntingdon, Prior was appointed master of the grammar school at Ashby.[29] In the same year, he married Ann Cox (Cock) of Quorn with whom he had a son, John, and three daughters. Their son followed his father in holy orders, becoming first curate at Willesley, a small village near Ashby, in the gift of the Hastings/Abney family. Ann Prior died in 1774, just after her husband took the degree of Bachelor of Divinity at Emmanuel College, Cambridge in 1772. In 1782, the Earl of Huntingdon presented him to the living of Ashby-de-la-Zouch, adding the vicarage of Packington in 1792.

John Prior was a man of many interests and skills, being both an able mathematician and a talented musician. He was said to be knowledgeable in musical theory and a good performer on the violin. The story goes that when the Earl of Huntingdon said to his friend that Prior was 'a poor preacher', the friend replied 'but you should hear him fiddle'.[30] His classical abilities are evidenced by the publication of his appendix to the *Eton Latin*

Fig. 14.3 Dedication page of Prior's Map of Leicestershire, 1777.

Grammar. He was over sixty years old when he took up the study of Hebrew in order to read the Old Testament in its original language.

Possibly Prior's greatest claim to fame was his publication in 1777 of a one inch to the mile map of Leicestershire. The surveying was done between 1775 and 1777 by one of Prior's former pupils, Joseph Whyman. It was the first scale survey of the county since Elizabethan times, showing in particular the network of roads and lanes in the county, as well as local landmarks such as churches, houses, wind and water mills etc. In Swithland, for example, the church, the manor house, the water mill and village housing is shown, and there appear to be buildings on the north edge of Swithland woods that are not shown on the Enclosure Map. Perhaps these were slate workshops, which were no longer needed when the Hinds ceased working the quarries at the north end of the wood. Prior's particular contribution was to manage and finance the production of the map, and to that end he raised subscriptions from people across the county. The Earl of Huntingdon wrote to Lord Romsey at the Society of Arts in 1778.

> My Lord, A map of the county of Leicester, executed by the Revd Mr Prior, being to be laid before the Society of Arts etc. immediately after the holidays, I take the liberty of troubling your Lordship with my testimony in favour of the author and his work. Mr Prior is Master of a Grammar School at Ashby de la Zouch, where I placed him, and where he has behaved so meritoriously that I intend to present him to the living when it becomes vacant. Those parts of the county that are within my knowledge are very exactly delineated and the remainder is universally allowed to be done with equal accuracy. He has a family of children and (as yet) a small income, and for his learning and good morals deserves reward and encouragement.[31]

John Prior died on 15th October 1803. Up to eight days before his death he was teaching at the Ashby Grammar School, although there were only three or four pupils. His monument is set up on the north side of Ashby parish church. Prior's obituary in the *Gentleman's Magazine* describes his mild and unassuming temper, perfect freedom from ambition, love of music, and relish for the calm delights of literature, friendship and domestic society. 'Humility was the highest characteristic of his mind; and with abilities of the highest order, both natural and acquired, he was perhaps of all men, the least obtrusive' (John Nichols).

John and Ann's son John, also ordained, and their daughter Mary are buried in Quorn churchyard.[32] Mary Prior's name appears on a tombstone erected for her grandparents John and Elizabeth Cock (Cox), whose son Ward Cock was uncle to Mary and John Prior. Ward Cock's entry is followed by: 'And was followed by his niece Mary Prior, daughter of the late Revd J Prior vicar of Ashby De La Zouch on 2nd September 1819 in the 52nd year of her age'. Her brother has his own stone: 'In memory of the Revd John Prior for many years Minister of Willesley, in the County of Derby, son of the late Revd John Prior vicar of Ashby de la Zouch, nephew of the late Ward Cock and grandson of the late John and Elizabeth Cock of Quorndon, who departed this life on the 1st of February 1833 in the 68th year of his age.'

Otto Murray Dixon (1885–1917)

Henry Edward Otto Murray Dixon was the eldest son of the Revd James and Etheldreda Murray Dixon. Born in Swithland on the 4th August 1885, his interest in nature and his artistic talents were evident from a young age. He would have been about fifteen when his family moved from the old rectory into the new purpose-built one next to the school. An old family retainer said that:

> The new Rectory was three storeys high, and Otto had the top two rooms, one as a studio and one as a bedroom. He spent a lot of

time in his studio and was not to be disturbed whilst working. He even missed his meals. On fine days he would go fishing on the local reservoir in his boat, taking his painting materials with him. He also went to Buddon Wood which was situated at the end of the reservoir to pick bee orchids which he took home to his mother. He also used to take his mother to Swithland Woods to hear the nightingales.[33]

Otto Dixon's passion was natural history, and his great talent was to portray the birds and animals around him in sketch and watercolour. Leonard Copson, whose grandfather Ambrose Copson had acted as Hall Farm bailiff for Otto Dixon's father, the rector, described a family heirloom he inherited – an oil painting executed by Dixon in 1906. It was of a white calf standing on yellow straw against a brick wall. 'He (Rector Dixon) had ideas about cattle breeding and these ideas resulted in the picture I now possess. He decided to breed Lincoln Red cattle, and in order to do this purchased two Lincoln Red heifers and a Lincoln Red bull. The first calf born to one of those heifers, after mating with the bull, turned out not to be the expected colouring, but pure white ... Harry Dixon, as my father used to refer to the artist, spent a lot of time down at Hall Farm, and chose to paint this unexpected phenomenon.'[34]

Otto Dixon studied drawing at the Leicester School of Art, Calderon's School of Animal Painting and the Royal Academy Schools. A family member described 'long hours of patient observation spent in swamp, field and wood. He always drew from life ... carried on at all hours of the day and night under most trying atmospheric conditions. The woods and large stretches of water in the neighbourhood of his home afforded him peculiarly valuable opportunities for the study of plant life (he found several species of plants unique to Leicestershire) and the observation of a large variety of waterfowl and shore birds.'[35] He presented part of his collection of plant specimens, birds and eggs to Leicester Museum, who also have on loan from his family a significant collection of his artwork. He was highly thought of by fellow artists, including such significant figures as Alexander Thorburn and John Millais.

At the outbreak of war in 1914, Dixon joined the United Arts Corps from which he transferred on obtaining his commission in the 4th (Ross Highland) Battalion Seaforth Highlanders in November 1915. Some of his paintings from The Front were printed in the *Illustrated Sporting and*

Fig 14.4 Otto Murray Dixon, 4th Battalion Seaforth Highlanders, 1915.

Fig 14.5 Fox and Rabbit by Otto Murray Dixon.

Dramatic News and *The Field* and his letters home contained sketches and descriptive notes of the birds and plant life around him. He also found comfort in his ability to visualize natural objects and scenes. 'It is a blessing' he wrote in 1916, 'having a memory for natural objects. I can recall the wild flowers of any month to mind in every detail, butterflies and birds too, and often I do so when I get to bed – it is such a rest'.[36] Murray Dixon was wounded in the attack on Vimy Ridge, 9th April 1917 and died the following day.

His obituary in the *Ross-shire Journal*, Friday 4th May 1917, reads:

Fig 14.6 Woodcock and Wren by Otto Murray Dixon, 1915.

Fig 14.7 Hooded Crows on a French cornstack by Otto Murray Dixon, 1916.

2nd Lieut. Henry Edward O Murray Dixon, Seaforths, who
died on 10th April of wounds received in the battle of Arras the
previous day, was born in 1885, and was the eldest son of the
Rev. J and Mrs Murray Dixon, of Swithland Rectory,
Loughborough, Leicestershire. His whole life was devoted to
artistic pursuits and natural history, and he attained a very high
position among bird painters. Yet his works of art embraced
many subjects. He was fond of botanising, and wild flowers
filled his soul. Scotland, with its varied scenery and wild-life,
appealed to and fascinated him. He was an all-round man; fond
of hunting, a cautious stalker, good shot and keen fisherman.

His was of a high-strung, and a somewhat sensitive nature,
but he was as brave as a lion, yet tender hearted and
affectionate. 'Murray Dixon was all right when tried. I
thought he would be; and he was such a nice boy,' writes a
superior officer of his battalion. 'He loved nature, and
worshipped nature's God,' says one intimate with him in a
singular degree.

On the outbreak of war, Lt Murray Dixon had joined the
United Arts Corps. Subsequently he was given a commission
in the Seaforth Highlanders, and after a strenuous training
with the 4th (Res.) Seaforths, went to France the early days of
January this year.

As a son, it has been said of him, he was all that his parents
could desire; as a friend, loyal and true; as a man, a hero!

Louie Burrows (1888–1962) and D.H. Lawrence

Just outside the north porch of Swithland church stands a memorial stone to Alfred and Kathleen Burrows and their daughter Kathlyn. Alfred Burrows farmed at Cropston Hall for many years, as his descendants still do. Louie (Louise) Burrows was Alfred's sister, and was for a short while romantically linked to the author D.H. Lawrence.

On 3rd December 1910, Lawrence proposed to Louie Burrows on a railway train that was travelling through Swithland. Writing to Rachel Annand Taylor, another friend, later that day, he said

> I have been to Leicester today.[37] I have met a girl who has always
> been warm for me – like a sunny happy day – and I've gone and
> asked her to marry me: in the train, quite unpremeditated,
> between Rothley and Quorn – she lives at Quorn. When I think of
> her, I feel happy with a sort of warm radiation – she is big and dark
> and handsome.[38]

Two days later, he wrote more fully to Arthur McLeod:

> We had been talking very sympathetically, and had got to Rothley,
> next station to Quorn. 'And what do you think you'll do, Bert, –

after Christmas?' said Louie. I said I don't know. 'What would you like to do?' she asked, and suddenly I thought she looked wistful. I said I didn't know – then added 'Why, I should like to get married'. – She hung her head. 'Should you?' I asked. She was very much embarrassed and said she didn't know. 'I should like to marry you' I said suddenly, and I opened my eyes. She flushed scarlet. – 'Should you?' I added. She looked out of the window and murmured huskily 'What?' 'Like to marry me?' I said. She turned to me quickly, and her face shone like a luminous thing. 'Later,' she said. I was very glad. The brakes began to grind. 'We're at Quorn' I said, and my heart sank. She suddenly put her hand on mine and leaned to me. 'I'll go to Loughborough' she said. The five women rose. 'I can come back by the 8.10' she said. The five women, one by one, issued forth, and we ran out among the floods and the darkness. There were such floods at Loughboro – I saw them going up.[39]

Lawrence immortalised the encounter in poetry as well as in letter. In his preface to his *Collected Poems,* 1928, he said that Louie was 'the woman of 'Kisses in the Train', and 'The Hands of the Betrothed'.[40] Louie and Lawrence had known each other from about 1900; they both attended the Pupil-Teacher Centre at Ilkeston from 1902, the Day Training College of University College, Nottingham, and both qualified as teachers.

Louie was born in Ilkeston, Derbyshire, in 1888, the eldest of eight children. In 1890 her family moved to Cossall, Nottinghamshire. Alfred, her father, worked first as a draughtsman in Ilkeston and then as a lace manufacturer in Nottingham. His hobby was woodcarving: he ran a voluntary woodcarving class in the village, which made a reredos for Cossall church, where he was choirmaster. In 1907 Alfred Burrows moved his family to Chaveney Road, Quorn, where he took up a post of peripatetic teacher of handicrafts with Leicestershire County Council. He called his house there 'Coteshael' – the mediaeval spelling of Cossall.

Louie's teaching career began in 1908. She taught in Leicester, Ratcliffe-on-the-Wreake and Gaddesby before becoming headmistress of Quorn Church of England Primary School. Lawrence visited her both at Cossall and Quorn, and they corresponded regularly. Their engagement lasted eighteen months before Lawrence broke it off in February 1912.[41] The following month he met and fell in love with Emma Maria Frieda Johanna Weekley, née von Richthofen (1879–1956), wife of Ernest Weekley, head of the Modern Languages Department at Nottingham University College. On 3rd May 1912, Lawrence and Frieda eloped together to Germany and married in July 1914.[42]

Lawrence's novel *The Rainbow* is said to have been based on the Burrows family.[43] The novel is set in Cossethay – clearly drawn on the village of Cossall. Alfred and Ann Burrows are the Will and Anna Brangwen of the novel. Louie Burrows is Ursula Brangwen. Yew Tree Cottage is Alfred Burrows' home, Church Cottage in Cossall. The novel was first published in 1915, but was suppressed within six weeks. At a short hearing at Bow Street Magistrates Court on 13th November it was ordered to be destroyed. An American edition, containing a number of cuts, was published in December 1915. The book did not become available in England until 1926. It has also been suggested that Swithland Hall may well have suggested to Lawrence the name of the Crich estate, Shortlands, in *Women in Love*. In an earlier version of the novel, Lawrence had called the estate Shortland.[44]

Alfred Burrows retired from teaching in 1929. He served as a diocesan Lay Reader in the archdeaconry of Loughborough, based at St Bartholomew's Church, Quorn, from 1929. He died at Quorn in 1948. He was less than pleased that his family had been used and depicted in such a way by Lawrence, of whom he was somewhat critical. But Louie, who had been deeply unhappy when the engagement was ended, remained loyal. For many years she remained single, but in 1940 she married Frederick Heath, a retired shoe manufacturer. They lived at The Cedars in Cropston, before moving to Greetham in Rutland. Louie died in 1962 and is buried in Thistleton, Rutland.

Fig 14.8 Louie Burrows, a family portrait.

The Hind Sisters

A table tomb to the left of the path that now runs from the lych gate to the church porch marks the burial spot of the two 'Hind Sisters'. Henrietta and Sarah Jane Hind, neither of whom married, were the only children of Henry and Sarah Hind, also buried there, and descendants of the slate quarrying Hind family. At the time of the sisters' deaths the family lived in Ibstock, but their worshipping links were with Swithland. The younger Hind sister, Henrietta, died in 1900 aged forty, but her older sister, Sarah Jane, lived until 1922.

In her will, Sarah Jane Hind bequeathed most of her estate for the building of a settlement of ten cottages, with a warden's cottage, for retired ladies of limited means, not requiring nursing care, who were members of the Church of England. Miss Hind decreed that the homes be built in memory of her sister. The charity, known as The Hind Sisters Homes, is administered by a board of trustees. The homes, which were officially opened in 1928, were built along Station Road in Cropston. An inscription on a bronze plaque mounted on the front elevation of the homes reads: 'These houses were erected in memory of Sarah Jane & Henrietta Maria Louisa Hind, Daughters of Henry Hind, one time owner of the Brand Slate Quarries at Swithland, in accordance with the will of the survivor, Sarah Jane Hind'. Sarah Jane Hind also left a small amount of money to be invested to support the poor of the parish of Swithland, and to maintain her family tombs.[45]

Notes to Chapter 14

1. Kelcey Wilson-Lee, Dissertation, 'A Fifteenth Century Brass at Swithland, Leics, and the Commemoration of Female Religious in Late-Medieval England', 2008.
2. ibid.
3. Gilchrist is Professor in Archaeology at the University of Reading, and author of *Gender and Material Culture: Archaeology of Religious Women*, 1997.
4. The spelling of the Danvers family name gradually evolved from de Alvers to de Anuers, then from d'Anuers to Danuers and Danvers. By the thirteenth century, most were listed as Danvers.
5. An earlier Swithland branch had died out during the fourteenth century.
6. Though, according to Aubrey: 'I find in the register of the Tower Chapel only the burial of Robert, Earl of Essex that year: wherefore I am induced to believe that his body was carried to Dauntsey in Wiltshire to lie with his ancestors'. Richard Barber (ed.), *John Aubrey, Brief Lives*, 1982, p. 84.
7. The original Van Dyck portrait passed to Danby's nephew John of Prescott who bequeathed it to his stepson Joseph Danvers of Swithland. Joseph gave or sold it to Sir Robert Walpole whose collection, including this portrait, ended up in the hands of Catherine the Great. It now hangs in the Hermitage Museum in St Petersburg. A copy hangs in the house at Dunham Massey, until 1976 the seat of the Earls of Stamford and Warrington.
8. To the glory of God and the greatest honour of King Charles I Henry Earl of Danby [gave this garden] for the use of both the University and the state in the year 1632.
9. *The Universal British Directory*, 1791.
10. Danby Castle in Yorkshire had been acquired by Henry's father, Sir John, when he married Lady Elizabeth Nevill in c. 1568.
11. Inscribed on Danby's tomb.
12. George Herbert, Epitaph, inscribed on the east side of Danby's tomb.
13. Richard Barber (ed.), *John Aubrey, Brief Lives*, 1982.
14. John Aubrey, *The Natural History of Wiltshire*, printed by John Britton, 1847.
15. According to John Aubrey (*Brief Lives*, p. 86) 'for love of her wit' and that 'the Earl of Danby was greatly displeased with him for this disagreeable match'.
16. According to John Aubrey (*Brief Lives*, p. 85) this poetical tribute was made to the father, Sir John of Dauntsey.
17. George Herbert, 'Collected Poems'. At the time of writing, Sir John had yet to beget progeny of his own. Herbert's poems were published as *The Temple* by his friend, Nicholas Ferrar in 1633.
18. The house was partly demolished in 1696 to make way for the construction of a new road, Danvers Street: it was entirely demolished in 1716, although Danvers Street remains.
19. National Portrait Gallery collection, reproduced with permission.
20. John Danvers of Prescott was a Salt Office commissioner from 1702–14.
21. Public Records Office/National Archives PROB 11/582, Will of Sir John Danvers of Prescott, 1721.
22. Izaak Walton, *The Life of Dr John Donne*, 1640.
23. 'The Autumnall' and 'The Relique' are both thought to have been inspired by Magdalen.
24. Letter, Donne to Sir Thomas Roe, 25 November 1625 in John Hayward (ed.), *Complete Poetry and Selected Prose* [of John Donne], Bloomsbury, 1929.
25. Izaak Walton, *The Life of Dr John Donne*, 1640.
26. Letter to Sir John Danvers in George Herbert, *The Complete English Works*, (Everyman's Library, A. Pasternak (ed.), new edition 1995).

27. The eldest by Joseph Prior's second wife, Mary Freeman.
28. Don Wix and Ian Keil, *Rawlins: The First 300 Years*. Information from plaque listing names of schoolmasters 1691–1864, now hanging in one of the oldest rooms in the present school buildings.
29. John Prior was succeeded as master of Rawlins' school by Samuel Wylde (1763–70). Wylde drew the map 'Perambulation around Charnwood Forest' (1754), giving the only two prints to William Herrick and Sir Joseph Danvers. Nicholls says he was 'a man of genius and abilities, but intemperate as to drinking'. (John Nichols, *The History and Antiquities of the County of Leicester*, Vol. III, i, p.113.) Wylde also wrote 'a book on arithmetic' (possibly *The Practical Surveyor*, 1725).
30. J.D. Welding, *Leicestershire in 1777*, 1984.
31. ibid.
32. Quorn Village On-Line Museum, St Bartholomew's Village Graves Transcriptions A93, 94.
33. Hamilton family letter. Recollections of Miss Elsie Ind who joined the Murray-Dixon household aged twenty in 1912 as a cook, and served with the family for sixty-four years.
34. Letter, Copson to McDonald Booth, Dec. 1980, in possession of Christopher Hamilton.
35. Chap XVIII, 'The Work of the late HEO Murray Dixon' in H. Frank Wallace, *A Highland Gathering: Being Some Leaves from a Stalker's Diary*, 1932.
36. ibid.
37. Lawrence's mother was ill in a hospital in Leicester.
38. James T. Boulton (ed.), *The Letters of D.H. Lawrence*, vol 1., 1901–13, CUP, 1979.
39. ibid.
40. ibid., Footnote, p. 29.
41. ibid., Letter dated 4 February 1912.
42. James T. Boulton (ed.), *Lawrence in Love, letters to Louie Burrows*, University of Nottingham, 1968.
43. George H. Ford, *Double Measure: A study of the novels and stories of D.H. Lawrence*, 1965, p. 116.
44. ibid., Footnote p. 117.
45. See Chapter 4: The Parish Church, Charities.

– CHAPTER 15 –

Myths and Legends

Mortal Body's Guard

On the eastern wall of Swithland churchyard, surrounded by iron railings, stands the striking slate table tomb of Sir Joseph and Dame Frances Danvers. The tomb was built in 1745. Sir Joseph died in 1753, and Dame Frances in 1759. The tomb catches the attention, partly for its being built eight years before its first inhabitant died, partly because of the fine slate engravings by a member of the local Hind family, and partly because of its position. Standing at the eastern-most edge of the churchyard, it seems to be built into the church wall, giving some the impression that a small part of the grave lies outside the churchyard, on Danvers' own land. There is no evidence that the churchyard boundary has been changed, and the design of the tomb – with a blank face positioned where the wall meets the tomb – does suggest that it was designed to be let into the wall. This latter feature began to give rise to a certain amount of public speculation – but not until 1880, one hundred and forty years after the erection of the tomb.

This first attempt to 'explain' the position of the tomb[1] puts forward two theories: first that Sir Joseph might have been 'half a Non-Conformist'; second that he wanted to stand up on Judgement Day and view his fine manor house. Forty-five years later, an article in the *Leicester Mercury* in 1925 went a little further suggesting that Sir Joseph wanted to 'arise' upon his own land. Later that year, another suggestion was mooted, which seemed to have caught the public imagination then and is still popular today. Paul Dare, in his 1925 book on Charnwood Forest, claims that Sir Joseph wanted his 'favourite dog' to be buried with him. By 1967, the dog seems to have been given a name – Bodyguard.

Joyce Lee and Jon Dean, in their book on the *Curiosities of Leicestershire & Rutland*, (1995), enlarged on Dare's legend, but without citing any evidence.

> Family pets have long been accorded their own gravestones and sometimes elaborate memorials, but here at Swithland, tradition has it that local squire Sir Joseph Danvers (1686–1753) went one step further. Unwilling to be parted in death from his favourite dog, he wanted the animal to be able to share his grave. However the parson

would not agree. In the end, a compromise was reached, resulting in one of the most unusual and eccentric graves in Leicestershire. The land next to the churchyard belonged to Danvers' own estate – consequently he had his tomb built into the churchyard wall, part of it inside the churchyard, part extended outside onto his own land, so that he could be buried on the consecrated side, with his dog in the adjoining un-consecrated ground.

Most of Sir Joseph's Swithland ancestors were buried in the south aisle of the church. The first Danvers we know to be buried there was Sir Francis, Sir Joseph's great-great grandfather, who died in 1631. In 1727, Sir Joseph enlarged and rebuilt the south aisle to create a more impressive chapel for his family. It is certainly intriguing, then, that Sir Joseph chose to be buried in the churchyard rather than in his new family chapel, and at its eastern-most point. The most recent legend of the dog is one possible explanation, but then so are all the others. But are they all myths and legends, or is there some truth behind one or all of them? The answer to these questions may never be known, but the historical facts as well as the various legends are all well worth the telling.

Those who described the churchyard soonest after Sir Joseph's death saw nothing to wonder at. John Throsby, writing in 1790, forty years after Sir Joseph died, just wrote 'In the church-yard is a tomb to the memory of Sir Joseph Danvers, Bart. who died in 1753 and was born in 1686'.[2] John Nichols, writing in 1804,[3] simply described it as 'a handsome slate tomb surrounded by iron rails'. Elsewhere in his history, Nichols does not shrink from reproducing local legends and myths, but when describing Danvers' tomb he does not even mention that it was built into the churchyard wall, let alone speculate as to why that might be. A newspaper article of 1880[4] is the first to speculate as to the positioning of the grave.

> The most noticeable tomb is that which encloses the remains of the late Sir John Danvers[5] who died in 1753 … The features connected with this place of sepulchre that have excited the most speculation are two. In the first place, the tomb extends across the boundary wall into the adjoining un-consecrated park. In the second, there is a singular looking aperture in the slate at the back. Some of the rumours as to the object of this arrangement are curious. One has it that Sir John was half a Nonconformist, or desired to make provision for the possibility of being able to rise to his feet and view the old hall.

Likewise, Breedon Everard's *Charnwood Forest* (1907) refers to the position of the grave, but again there is no speculation about a possible dog. Another newspaper article about Swithland church, in the *Leicester Mercury* in September 1925, developed the old 1880 story adding a phrase about arising 'on his own land'.

> According to tradition, [the tomb] was so placed in order that the occupier of the tomb, Sir Joseph Danvers, may arise upon his own land on Judgement Day.

The first time the dog theory finds expression is in M. Paul Dare's *Charnwood Forest and its Environs* (1925). Writing one hundred and eighty years after the tomb was built, Dare suggested that 'according to local tradition, Sir Joseph desired to have a favourite dog buried with him'. The theory, inevitably, proved popular with the dog-loving English, and soon became the preferred story. It is repeated in Firth's *Highways and Byways in Leicestershire* (1926), and in C.N. Hadfield's *Charnwood Forest: A Survey* (1952). A journalist, in a newspaper article of 1967, adds further 'details' to the speculation. 'Sir Joseph Danvers ... insisted on being buried in the churchyard rather than in the family vault in the chapel. This is simply because he wished to be buried next to his dog Bodyguard.[6] As the dog could not be buried on consecrated ground, Sir Joseph had part of the tomb built outside the churchyard itself'.

There are many reasons for discounting the dog theory. First, of course, is its relative modernity; had there been any truth in the story, it would have been in circulation long before 1925. Another reason is the position of the man himself. Sir Joseph was a man of substance and influence. He was not just Lord of the Manor of Swithland, he had been Sheriff of Leicestershire in 1721, a Member of Parliament from 1722 to 1747, and a baronet from 1746. He had served Leicestershire both as a deputy lieutenant and as a Justice of the Peace. The lower clergy of his day tended to co-operate with their squires and patrons, not stand up against them, especially when they were paid by them. In 1745, the year Sir Joseph erected his tomb, the rector, Philip Alston, was absent and there was a curate living in Swithland and managing parish affairs. In 1737 Alston had contracted with Sir Joseph that he should rent the rectory and glebe to a curate, who Sir Joseph would appoint and pay. The curate in 1745 was George Cardale, the rector of Wanlip. Cardale held this curacy at Sir Joseph's pleasure. Sir Joseph paid him! This would not seem the strongest position from which to argue about the presence of a dog in consecrated ground. And then of course there is no reference on the tomb to a dog. Rather, inscribed on the four corners of the tomb, above the year 1745, are the four words: 'Erected', 'Mortal', 'Body's', 'Guard'. These words advise the reader that Danvers erected the tomb in 1745 to be his own mortal body's guard.

It was not unknown for animals to be buried in consecrated ground, but that does not seem to have been the Danvers' tradition. Sir Joseph's son, Sir John, had a favourite canine companion which he buried in the Old Hall gardens. The elaborately engraved slate stone to his pet's memory now stands in the grounds of the 'new' Swithland Hall.

Sir Joseph's will of 1753 simply directed that his 'body be deposited in the New Vault in the Church Yard of Swithland... in a private manner in the forenoon' and that everyone of his tenants and their wives who dwelt in Swithland should be given a pair of black gloves each and walk at his funeral.[7] The rest is speculation.

So the questions remain. Why was Sir Joseph buried in the churchyard and not with his ancestors inside his fine new chapel? And why is his tomb positioned as it is? Frustratingly, we shall probably never know the truth of the matter.

Swithland's Grey Lady

Swithland's rectory stood next to the church until 1896, and this eighteenth century rectory is the place where the legend of the Swithland Ghost, or the Grey Lady, is set. We do not know when the legend about the Grey Lady began to circulate orally, but, like the story of Sir Joseph and his dog, it first appeared in print in the twentieth century, at a time when dramatic myths and stories were in vogue.

The following anonymous and somewhat dramatic version was printed in the *Loughborough Echo* in 1934. The writer tells his story as if from the lips of the Grey Lady herself.

> There are countless folk who will have nothing to do with stories of ghosts, and decry with infinite scorn the tales they have heard of the appearance of the spirits of the dead in gloomy churchyard or ancient manor house. Very wise these people deem themselves when they opine that a ghost has to be seen to be believed. Fools that they are, they will never understand that we have to be believed, ere we may be seen. For truly we are sensitive and have our due and proper pride; moreover we can sense in a moment that dire atmosphere of scepticism which daunts the courage and must ever damp the enthusiasm of the most resolute ghost. This appalling scepticism is a modern growth and largely accounts for the rarity of ghostly visitations in latter years. It is grossly unfair that such a state should exist. Will mortals ne'er realise our trials, our difficulties, and our rights?
>
> For to die in bed is a happy and restful fate, but to be the victim of a horrible murder, to see a madman, with gruesome intent vividly expressed in staring eyes creeping stealthily towards you, such an experience can never be erased from the mind, such a memory can never fade. Therefore, instead of remaining peacefully in the grave, I cannot rest, but needs must haunt the neighbourhood in a vain seeking after unattainable peace. But I have anticipated; you shall forthwith hear my story which is like unto the tale which every genuine ghost can unfold.
>
> My father was surely to blame for the events of that terrible day. He was a masterful man, and once his mind was made up he would ne'er change his decision. We had been from home for some weeks in distant Yorkshire, and were due to return immediately. The house, our dear old rectory, was left in the charge of the butler, a man I ever did loathe, but who seemed to possess some strange power over my father. Without any warning I suddenly received orders to proceed a day ahead of the rest of the family to see that all was well in the house for the homecoming. Surely every body must fain agree that it was a most improper errand for a young gentlewoman of scarce twenty years, to make a long journey alone and entirely unprotected.

But my father would pay no heed to our feeble protestations and thus perforce I set out on the stage coach at six of the clock on a misty June morning. At three in the afternoon I alighted at the 'Plough', in Loughborough Market Place, and sought a private conveyance which would carry me to Swithland village.

I had not been long home when I was sorely beset with uneasy misgivings. Parker, the butler, though properly respectful in manner, yet made me vaguely apprehensive. For his eyes were blood shot and heavy in appearance, moreover he reeled somewhat in his gait, so I began to fear that he must be grievously sick. But I pretended that I perceived nothing strange in his manner, and hoped that all would be well in spite of my fears and suspicion.

I retired to my room that evening determined that I would not sleep but would watch through the hours of the short summer night until the day did break. I locked my door and lay down on the bed to rest my weary limbs. I did not disrobe, but remained in my dress of grey brocade ready for any unexpected happening that might arise.

Alas my resolve to stay awake was a vain one. Wearied by my long journey, I fell into a restless sleep from which I was rudely awakened. The door was opening slowly but steadily. I sprang hastily from the bed, but ere I could defend myself I was roughly seized. I struggled with all my power, but my frantic efforts were entirely unavailing. What chance indeed has a girl against a man endowed with a madman's strength?

Here this narrative abruptly ended!

This story, as do all good stories, grew in the telling. S.R. Meadows, for example, in his 1965 booklet about Swithland, says that the story refers to 'a nameless lady' who lived in the old Rectory some one hundred and fifty years previously.

The story begins in Yorkshire, where the Grey Lady was staying on holiday with her father, who was mainly to blame for the disturbing event that followed. Much against her better judgement, the daughter was persuaded by her over-bearing parent to proceed a day in advance to the Rectory, which had been left in the charge of an unreliable butler. Proceeding by stage coach, our Grey Lady alighted at the Plough at Loughborough, and was then carried by private conveyance to Swithland village. On arrival there, her worst forebodings were confirmed, for she found the family butler in a sullen drunken condition, and it was evident that he had spent most of his time in the rectory wine-cellar. Without delay she retired to her room, without disrobing, but, prepared for any emergency, lay down to rest in her dress of grey brocade. Falling into a deep sleep, she was rudely awakened by the maddened butler, who grasped her roughly by the throat, and strangled her with the four-poster bed cord. Then, sobered by the enormity of this horrible deed, the murderer, filled with remorse, rushed into the pantry, seized a large carving knife, and put an end to his own wretched life. On the following day, the family, on their return, found the two bodies.

Since that day, and until about sixty years ago, we are informed[8] that strange wailings and screamings have been heard at night in the village, the butler has been seen, in gory disarray, emitting bitter cries of remorse, while the lady, in her dress of grey, has haunted the vicinity. She was noticed at village parties, and guests had remarked on her old-fashioned dress, supposing she was a lady of former days.[9]

Meadows' local researches found a 'contradiction of opinion' in the village. He was able, however, to quote two reputable ladies.

Lady Lanesborough (the eighth Earl's Countess) informs us that she has spoken to two villagers, who swear they have seen the spectre of the Grey Lady. Again Mrs Hamilton recalls that her father, the Revd. Murray-Dixon, hurried into the rectory one Ascension Day to inform his family that he had just seen the ghost of the Grey Lady glide through the garden wall. She recalls, also, that one of the farm labourers refused to draw water from the farmyard brook after seeing the apparition hovering over the water.[10]

Canon Walters, Swithland's rector from 1977–91, wrote in the March 1986 parish magazine to record the recent death of Mrs Hamilton of Braziers Hall, Stowmarket. 'Rosamund Murray-Dixon, the last of the Revd Murray-Dixon's family, lived at the Old Rectory to the west of the church. She was one of two people I have known of who have seen the Swithland Ghost. Mrs Hamilton saw her standing on the black and white flag floor, which some senior residents will also remember from the Old Rectory'.[11]

Meadows concluded that, as the ghost had not been seen for many years, 'let us hope that the Lady in grey brocade has ceased her wandering, and has found the rest she richly deserved'.[12] That may have been wishful thinking, as the current rector has also spoken to someone who thought he had seen the Grey Lady. In the late 1990s, a bell-ringer who rang regularly with the Swithland band, arrived at practice one night and told his fellow ringers of a strange grey lady he had seen walking up the church path ahead of him and disappearing just beyond the north porch. This gentleman had never heard about Swithland's Grey Lady until his fellow ringers told him about her that night.

A possible 'yes' to seeing the ghost, however, does not imply the historical truth of the gruesome legend! It has to be said that there was no mention of a murder at Swithland Rectory in any local publication c. 1805 (one hundred and fifty years before Meadows wrote his Swithland booklet). Also that the rector of Swithland at the time was one John Lloyd and he and his wife had no children, let alone a daughter! This is probably no consolation to those who enjoy the legend and who may feel left with the question, 'If she was not the rector's daughter, then who was she?'

Black Annis

The eighteenth century historian John Nichols linked Black Annis, a legendary Leicestershire apparition, with the anchoress Agnes Scot who is buried in St Leonard's Church. In his entry on Swithland church's monumental inscriptions,[13] Nichols wrote, quoting a pre-1727 manuscript attributed by him to Mr Burton:

> On a flat gravestone, inlaid with plates of brass, in the body of the church near the entrance to the chancel, is the picture of a woman veiled ... This Agnes Scot, as I guess, was an Anchoress; and the word Antrix in (her) epitaph coined from *antrum*, a cave, wherein she lived; and certainly (as I have been credibly informed) there is a cave near Leicester, upon the West side of the town, at this day called *Black Agnes' Bower*.

According to the stories, 'Black Annis' lived in a cave known as 'Black Annis Bower' that she is said to have clawed from the rocky hills with her own bare hands. Writing to the editor of the *Leicester Chronicle* in 1874, a correspondent said:

> Little children, who went to play on the Dane Hills were assured that she lay in wait there, to snatch them away to her bower; and that many like themselves she had scratched to death with her claws, sucked their blood, and hung up their skins to dry.[14]

'Black Annis' was also blamed for the disappearance of babies from nearby homes, supposedly reaching through the windows to steal them. Other stories have her haunting the underground chambers of Leicester Castle, which she could reach through a tunnel from her bower.

Some have suggested an early pagan link with the goddess Danu or Anna,[15] and that her bower may mark an Iron Age shrine. She has also been linked with what used to be, until the early eighteenth century, the Leicester tradition of 'hunting the cat': a mock hunt with a dead cat soaked in aniseed being dragged through Leicester's streets from Annis' bower to the Lord Mayor's front door.

In the early seventeenth century, John Herrick composed a poem 'On the Cave called Annis' Bower, being the answer to a very young Lady's Enquiries about the story of Black Annis'. Herrick does not make any link between the Black Annis of his poem and Agnes Scot of Swithland.

> Where down the plain the winding pathway falls,
> From Glenn-field vill, to Lester's ancient walls,
> Nature or Art with imitative power,
> Far in the Glenn has plac'd Black Annis' Bower.

An oak, the pride of all the mossy dell,
Spreads his broad arms above the stony cell;
And many a bush, with hostile thorns array'd,
Forbids the secret cavern to invade;
Whilst delving vales each way meander round,
And violet banks with redolence abound.
   Here, if the uncouth song of former days
Soil not the page with Falsehood's artful lays,
Black Annis held her solitary reign,
The dread and wonder of the neighb'ring plain.
The shepherd griev'd to view his waning flock,
And traced the firstlings to the gloomy rock.
No vagrant children cull'd the flor'rets then,
For infant blood oft stain'd the gory den.
Not Sparta's Mount, for infant tears renown'd,
Echo'd more frequently the piteous sound.
Oft the gaunt Maid the frantic Mother curs'd,
Whom Britain's wolf with savage nipple curs'd;
Whom Lester's sons held aghast the scene,
Nor dared to meet the Monster of the Green.
   'Tis said the soul of mortal man recoil'd
to view Black Annis' eye, so fierce and wild;
Vast talons, foul with human flesh, there grew
In place of hands, and features livid blue
Glared in her visage; whilst her obscene waist
Warm skins of human victims close embrac'd.
   But Time, that Man more certain, tho' more slow,
At length 'gainst Annis drew his sable bow;
The great decree the pious Shepherds bless'd,
And general joy the general fear confess'd.
   Not without horror they the cave survey,
Where hung the monstrous trophies of her sway.
'Tis said, that in the rock large rooms were found,
scoop'd with her claws beneath the flinty ground;
in these the Swains her hated body threw,
but left the entrance still to future view,
that children's children might the tale rehearse,
and Bards record it in their tuneful verse.
   But in these listless days, the idle Bard
Gives to the winds all themes of old regard;
Forgive, then, if in rough, unpolished song,
An unskilled Swain the dying tale prolong.
   And you, ye Fair, whom Nature's scenes delight.
I Annis' Bower your vagrant steps invite,
Ere the bright sun Aurora's car succeed,
Or dewy evening quench the thirsty mead,
Forbear with chilling censures to refuse

> Some generous tribute to the rustic Muse.
> A violet, or common daisy throw,
> Such gifts as Maro's lovely nymphs bestow;
> Then shall your Bard survive the critic's frown,
> And in your smiles enjoy his best renown.

In December 1837, a melodrama 'Black Annis' Bower' or 'The Maniac of Dane Hills' was performed at Leicester's old Theatre Royal. The play was written by a local actor, Mr Higgie. The following year the company staged another melodrama that purported to tell the story of Black Anna. Entitled 'The Broken Heart', or 'The Rose of Newarke', this Civil War romantic drama was set in the days of the Battle of Newarke and the Siege of Leicester. It told the tragic story of two lovers, Mariana and Valentine. Valentine's friend Norland lusts after Mariana and kills Valentine when they are called to arms. He seduces Mariana. She, however, has an encounter with Valentine's ghost, who tells her the truth; she finds his body buried on the Dane Hills. She becomes demented, roams the hills, tries to seduce Norland, who escapes her, then murders her, and, in his turn, is struck down by a bolt from heaven.

Another Agnes

Among the other legends of the county that some have tried to link with Agnes of Swithland is one that has as its heroine the Lady Agnes, the daughter of Lord Ferrers of Groby Hall, and is set some five hundred years ago. Lady Agnes was desired by Lord Comyn of Whitwick, a huge, violent man. Under threat of being abducted, Lady Agnes left the castle with the intention of seeking sanctuary at Grace Dieu Priory. She took a circuitous route through Charnwood, pursued by Comyn's men, but she became lost in the forest. She might well have died, had she not stumbled upon the holy well at Holywell Haw, where the monks of the hermitage gave her assistance. She escaped Comyn, and, when she later married Edward Grey, the couple went back to the hermitage, after their wedding at Ulverscroft, to thank the monks and to make an endowment of two hides of land and three fallow deer annually.[16]

Unfortunately the legend does not correspond with fact, as it was Elizabeth Ferrers, and not Agnes, who married Sir Edward Grey in 1446. And any wish to link it with Swithland is made more difficult by the dedication of the Swithland memorial stone to Agnes Scot and not to Agnes Ferrers.

Agnes Scot

There is no reason to believe that Agnes Scot was anything other than an anchorite nun who was sufficiently well thought of and well connected for someone – presumably the Ferrers family – to see that she was buried in an honorary place in Swithland church (at the entrance to the chancel) and to go to the cost of commemorating her in both brass memorial and stained glass. For, when the seventeenth century historian, Burton, described Swithland church in one of his manuscripts, he spoke of the church's east window where was 'her picture in glass, drawn to the life, in the same habit, with a ring on her finger'. Burton may well be to blame, however, for popularising the legendary link between the Dominican nun and the Black Cat. In this he has a lot to answer for!

Maybe the last word on the subject, to those who would know of Agnes Scot, should be her own tombstone request to pray for her soul, rather than to speculate about her story.

> Enclosed in this tomb lies Agnes Scot
> Called the devout mother of Lady Ferrers.
> Whoever thou shalt be: who shall pass by;
> Pour out prayers, I beg:
> I am, what thou shalt be: I used to be, what thou art:
> Pray for me, I pray.[17]

The Mowde Bush Stone

> The court of East Goscote was originally held at Mowde Bush Hill in Syston Parish. When the Hundred of Goscote was divided into East and West, the court of East Goscote was transferred to Mountsorrel, where what was still called the Mowde Bush Court was held within the present century by Sir John Danvers. In order that the court might be properly constituted, a turf was duly cut on Mowde Bush Hill and carried to Mountsorrel whenever a sitting was held.[18]

Bob Trubshaw, in his booklet *Standing Stones and Mark Stones of Leicestershire and Rutland*,[19] refers to this story about Sir John Danvers, and also to 'another tradition recorded in the nineteenth century – that persons from neighbouring districts would bring a turf to put on it'.[20] The story does not explain the point of cutting the turfs and bringing them to the Court. Did the turf represent the various lands they held or symbolize something equivalent to a tythe?

The Mowde Bush Stone was situated 'from time immemorial' until 1994 near Sileby, Leicestershire (129:649110) on an ancient ridgeway from Tilton. The stone stood about three feet above the ground, with the same amount buried below ground. Its longer axis pointed north-south. If the Hundred Court of Goscote met there, the name is possibly a derivative from 'Moot' Stone. It has also been suggested that the stone might have marked a place of observation or for a beacon fire[21] and that 'the site and orientation of the stone points to an earlier usage than tradition assigns to it'.[22]

Notes to Chapter 15

1. *Leicester Chronicle and Leicestershire Mercury*, 19 June 1880, supplement, p. 4.
2. John Throsby, *Supplementary Volume to the Leicestershire Views, containing a Series of Excursions to the Villages and Places of Note in that County*, 1790, p. 94.
3. John Nichols, *The History and Antiquities of the County of Leicester*, London 1802.
4. *Leicester Chronicle and Leicestershire Mercury*, 19 June 1880, supplement, p. 4.
5. The journalist got his facts wrong. It was the late Sir Joseph, not the late Sir John.
6. This new theory was possibly inspired by the four words that are inscribed separately on the four sides of the tomb: erected, mortal, body's, guard.
7. The will of Sir Joseph Danvers, 17 October 1753 (See Appendix A).
8. No informants are named!
9. S.R. Meadows, *Swithland*, 1965.
10. ibid.
11. Swithland Parish Archives, *The Link*, March 1986, Rector's letter.
12. S.R. Meadows, *Swithland*, 1965.
13. John Nichols, *The History and Antiquities of the County of Leicester*, vol. 3, part 2, p. 1051, published 1804.
14. Letter to the Editor, *Leicester Chronicle*, 1874.
15. Alice Dryden (ed.), *Memorials of Old Leicestershire*, 1911; Charles Billson & others, *Vestiges of Paganism in Leicestershire*, 1994, p. 188ff.
16. A 'poetic version' of this legend may be found in T.R. Potter, *The History and Antiquities of Charnwood Forest*, 1842.
17. This English translation of the Latin inscription hangs below the brass in St Leonard's Church.
18. J. Spencer and T. Spencer, *Leicestershire and Rutland Notes and Queries*, 1895.
19. Part of the Leicestershire and Rutland Earth Mysteries series, Part 3, 1991.
20. The story is to be found in Alice Dryden (ed.), *Memorials of Old Leicestershire*, 1911; A.R. Horwood, *Pre-Historic Leicestershire*, p. 49.
21. J. Plant, FGS Report of the British Association 1879/80, p. 112.
22. Alice Dryden (ed.), *Memorials of Old Leicestershire*, 1911; Charles Billson & others, *Vestiges of Paganism in Leicestershire*, 1994, p. 188ff.

– CHAPTER 16 –

Rothley Plain

> From the ash tree and stones in Red Meadow hedge to the
> highway from ye nether end of Swithland leading to
> Mountsorrel to the stile that goes into Mountsorrel, West Field
> and Bounds thereof to ye top of Rothley Lane, abutting on
> Rothley Temple and to Thurcaston Fields and upon
> Rileys and Fox croft.
> *(Survey of Groby Manor, 1658)*

Rothley Plain has been known as such since before Domesday, but today only the occasional road sign recalls the old name. Rothley Plain is historically and sociologically more closely linked to Newtown Linford and to Swithland, than it is to Rothley, within whose civic electoral district it currently lies. Covering about 412 acres, it stretches north to south from Rushey Lane, at the Mountsorrel end of Swithland Lane, to the bend at the Thurcaston end of Swithland Lane (adjacent to the Homestead) and from east to west from the bend on The Ridings to a point a little way along the road into Swithland village.[1]

For much of its history, Rothley Plain was a detached enclave of the ecclesiastical parish of Newtown Linford, the land having belonged through most of its history to the Greys of Groby and to their heirs, the Earls of Stamford and Warrington. A small part of the north-east corner, though, would appear to have been part of the early mediaeval manor of Swithland. When new housing development began in the early twentieth century, the church at Newtown Linford handed over their responsibility for pastoral care of this area to the ecclesiastical parish at Swithland, initially by a 'gentleman's agreement' between the rectors, but, by 1946, more formally through an episcopally-authorised agreement.[2] That arrangement was legally recognized by the Church Commissioners in a pastoral scheme of December 1999, such that Rothley Plain now falls within Swithland's ecclesial parish. For civic electoral purposes, however, in 1884, the plain was transferred from Newtown Linford to Rothley.

Domesday

Rothley Plain was woodland waste at the time of the Norman Conquest. The 1086 Domesday Survey describes it as 'wood', a word which does not imply that the plain was as densely planted with trees as was the 'forest of Buddon Wood' just to the north. Buddon Wood was kept densely wooded to better serve as an enclosure for animals of the chase. Rothley Plain, however, was manorial 'waste' – uncultivated open land on which grazing took place.[3]

In 1086 Rothley Plain belonged to the King. Some time later it became part of the manor of Groby, passing to the Ferrers family and to the Greys (later to become Earls of Stamford and Warrington). The fact that they were lords of the manor did not mean that they were free to use the land as they willed. Local inhabitants had rights of common and were entitled to graze their livestock there. Determining who had that right was under the jurisdiction of the Swanimote Court,[4] a meeting of the local swains.

The lords of the manors of Whitwick, Shepshed and Groby all convened courts in their manorial areas. The Groby Swanimote gathered at the Copt Oak. Another local court was the Goscote Hundred Court, which met at Mowde Bush Hill in Syston parish, though when the hundred was divided into East and West Goscote, the court of East Goscote moved to Mountsorrel.[5]

Swithland residents enjoyed rights of common both on Rothley Plain and in Charnwood Forest. A seventeenth century entry from the Court Rolls of Groby Manor records: 'All the whole township of Swithland, which are known to be ancient houses both of husbandmen and ancient cottyers are intercommoners with all manner of lawful cattle, both in the Forest of Charnwood and Rothley Plain without stint'.[6] Those who wished to collect fallen timber had to pay the fee of one woodhen; the 1656 manor records indicate that fifteen Swithland residents paid their fees yearly in or about the month of February.

The inhabitants of Rothley (including those who lived in the south end of Mountsorrel) had, from an early date, paid for the right of pannage[7] on Rothley Plain. Groby Manor accounts of 1512 record that the manorial income included 'for 3s 4d rents and farms of the tenant of the lord there (of Rothley manor) having common in the foreign woods of the lord (of Groby) yearly'.[8] In 1611, however, a dispute arose between Thomas Babington of Rothley and Lord Grey of Groby over grazing rights on the plain. Babington claimed the right, as Lord of the Manor of Rothley, to free warren on the plain for his livestock. He pastured some beasts there. Grey instructed that they be driven off. The matter went to the Chancery Court, which was asked to determine whether 'the owner of Rothley Temple have common on Rothley Plain for his beastes and cattell sauns number levante and cowchante'.[9]

Depositions were taken from some of the older local residents. They were asked, at a special meeting of the court at Mountsorrel, to give testimony on oath of previous practice, and what had been the decisions of the Swanimote Court. Among the witnesses were Swithland residents Edmonde Gilbert, husbandman (reputed to be aged sixty-six), John Dodworth, labourer (seventy-four) and John Whitehead, husbandman (one hundred and ten). John Dodworth attested that three years previously a jury of the court had found against Babington. John Hobey, shepherd to the late Sir John Babington, told the Swanimote that twenty-five years earlier Sir John's sheep had been intercepted, and that, in order to avoid their being impounded, Sir John had promised not to put them on the Plain. Another witness, John Parker of Rothley, a husbandman of about fifty-one years of age, testified that the court had, on three occasions in his memory, declared that Babington's ancestors had no right of common there. Lord Grey won his case.

In 1658, a survey of Groby Manor showed that the inhabitants of Rothley paid 3s 4d to the Lord of the Manor of Groby for 'pawnage' in Rothley Plain. The survey provides one of the earliest descriptions we have of the extent of Rothley Plain:

> From the ash tree and stones in Red Meadow hedge to the
> highway from ye nether end of Swithland leading to Mountsorrel
> to the stile that goes into Mountsorrel, West Field and Bounds
> thereof to ye top of Rothley Lane, abutting on Rothley Temple and
> to Thurcaston Fields and upon Rileys and Fox croft.[10]

Another survey in 1677 recorded that Rothley inhabitants paid 3s 4d every Michaelmas to the lord or to his Receiver.[11]

A legal opinion of 1728 records a further dispute.[12] Francis Smalley had bought land at Kinsley Hill (Kinchley Lane) in 1622, and his successors in title and their tenants had enjoyed the Plain for cattle grazing. On 27th June 1728, however, cattle had been 'drifted' (collected) and a Swainmote Court was held. In the absence of verderers, the Court was held before Thomas Carter, steward of the Court for Harry Earl of Stamford, and some freeholders. The jury noted that a number of people, including the tenant of Mr Ralph Smalley, were being threatened with distraint and impounding of their cattle on the grounds that they had no right of common. Ralph Smalley took legal advice from John Belfield, who advised that the Court could not be properly held without verderers as a jury, and that Smalley's ownership of Kinsley Hill farm gave him a right of common on the Plain. Smalley evidently won the case, since he was allotted land on the Plain in the subsequent enclosure award.

Warreners and Commoners

Through the seventeenth and eighteenth centuries the Plain became less wooded. Local historian William Burton described in 1622 'the vast and decayed Forest of Charnwood' and there is no reason to suppose that Rothley Plain was any different. At some point a rabbit warren was established. In 1316, Oliver Waleys had secured the right of free warren on his lands in Swithland by Royal Charter from Edward II and Groby Manor must have secured a similar right on Rothley Plain. By the seventeenth century, there were some residents on the Plain. In 1657, Samuel and

Elizabeth Whitley were living there. From 1668 George Hews the younger held the old cottage or tenement and the warren of coneys on Rothley Plain from Groby Manor.[13] The lease had in fact been granted to Lewis Ganoys Cooke, but, with the permission of the lessor, it was assigned firstly to George Hews the younger, then to Mr Henry Farnham, and then to Robert Whitley.[14]

Newtown Linford's church registers suggest there was more than one dwelling on the Plain. Alice, the daughter of the same George and Alice Hewes 'of Roadley plaine' was baptised at Newtown Linford in February 1671.[15] In 1703, Michael Coy and Mary Oarton, both 'of Roadly Plain', were married; in 1705, Rebecca, the daughter of Joseph and Elizabeth Hall was baptised; in 1706 Peter, the son of Michael and Mary Coy was baptised and in 1717 Edward, the son of Richard Knight was baptised. In 1797 Robert Biddle of Mountsorel, grazier, married Ann Bramley of Rothley Plain. In addition, the records of Groby Peculiar include probate in 1742 of the will of Robert Whitley of Rothley Plain, yeoman.

The existence of warrens was not regarded with favour by commoners, especially when a lord of the manor tried to extend his warren at the expense of the common land. Local historian John Nichols records that there was considerable unrest around Charnwood Forest between warreners and commoners in 1749, which led to widespread civil disturbance.[16] At that time there were at least five large warrens in Charnwood. In January 1749 the inhabitants of a number of forest villages met at Charley Knoll, and began to tear down the fences of warrens where it was believed that the warreners had encroached, notably at Woodhouse Eaves and at Newtown Linford. Their actions were followed by a crowd (allegedly of colliers from Coleorton) who dug up the warrens.

A further incident at Warren Hill saw warrener William Whittle and his assistants attacked. They attempted to defend themselves. In the scuffle, Whittle, the only person with a gun, discharged it into the air. One of the rioters, William Stevenson, received a wound to the head and died. Whittle and several others subsequently stood trial at the 1749 Lent Assizes at Leicester accused of Stevenson's murder. When it was proved that Stevenson's injury was inflicted with a fork, and a grant to Mr William Herrick of Beaumanor to keep a warren was produced, the defendants were acquitted. Nevertheless the unrest continued. Two troops of dragoons were drafted into the area to keep order, and substantial numbers of rioters detained and imprisoned before quiet was restored. The commoners did manage to establish that the Forest was free common for twenty-six neighbouring villages. Such was the disaffection, however, that a petition was drawn up shortly afterwards and presented to William Herrick. It protested at the decay of common caused by the enlarging of the rabbit warrens and was signed by the officiating ministers of twenty-two villages (including Swithland, Rothley, Mountsorrel, Quorn, Woodhouse, Newtown Linford, Cropston and Thurcaston).

By the eighteenth century, brickmaking of some sort had started on Rothley Plain. In 1757 John Dawson of Rothley took out a lease for the lives of his wife, Elizabeth (d. 1787), and two children, Elizabeth (d. 1822) and Mary, of Rothley Plain warren.[17] His lease included a tenement on Rothley Plain (the warren house), the warren and a 'brick kiln'. There were later to be several small brick kilns on the Plain, using the clay that lay on top of the granite stone. John Dawson remained in the warren house until 1782, Thomas Pagett lived there from 1783–89 and Richard Fowkes from 1790–1820.

Enclosure

At the turn of the nineteenth century, Rothley Plain remained uncultivated, open common land. In 1794, however, 'A Review of the Agricultural Reports of the Midland Counties'[18] was published, which effectively encouraged landowners to apply for enclosure. 'Charnwood Forest contains about 15,000 or 16,000 acres, three-fourths of which might be made into very useful land: and if inclosed, would make some valuable farms.' Agricultural 'experts' who had viewed the land expressed their shock at the sight of so much cultivable land in Charnwood being put to such poor use. The woods had mostly vanished. The higher parts of Charnwood Forest were abandoned to fern and gorse. The lower and better tracts were covered with black heath that yielded scanty sustenance to a wild herd of forest sheep. What was true for Charnwood Forest applied also in great measure to Rothley Plain.

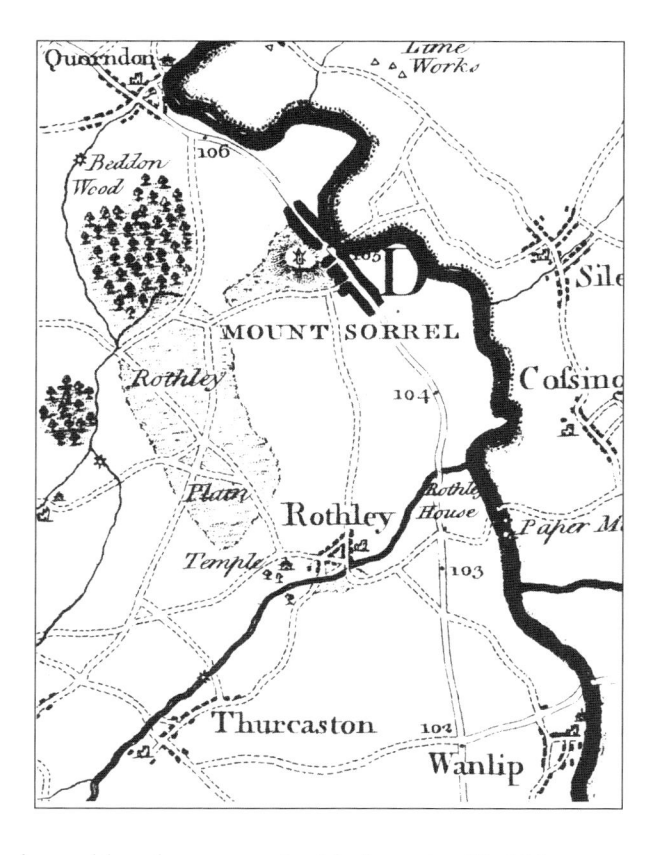

Fig 16.1, Rothley Plain, 1777, John Prior's Map of Leicestershire.

The leading landowners applied to Parliament to have both Charnwood Forest and Rothley Plain enclosed. Adjacent areas had already been enclosed: Woodhouse in 1668, Quorn in 1763, Barrow in 1761, Rothley in 1781, Mountsorrel in 1782, and both Swithland and Thurcaston in 1799. The Charnwood Forest and Rothley Plain Enclosure Act was passed in 1808.

Early in the enclosure arbitration, another dispute broke out over the parochiality of Rothley Plain. Thomas Babington, MP of Rothley Temple, claimed that it was in Rothley; the Earl of Stamford and Warrington claimed that it was in Newtown Linford. For both men the issue was important as it would affect the amount of land they would be allotted. The Commissioners decided that Rothley Plain was in the parish of Rothley, but the Earl of Stamford appealed against their decision and the matter went to court at the Lent Assize for the county of Leicester in 1811.[19]

One of the arguments Thomas Babington's counsel put forward was that Rothley Plain had been described in the Domesday Book as part of Rothley.

> The king holds Rothley. King Edward held it. 5c of land.
> In Lordship 2 of them and 2 ploughs
> 29 villagers with a priest and 18 smallholders have 6 ploughs
> A mill at 4s; meadow 37 acres;
> the lord's woodland 1 league long and ½ league wide;
> The villagers' woodland 4 furlongs long and 3 furlongs wide.

Rothley Plain, he argued, was the wood of '1 league long and ½ league wide'. Parish boundaries were fixed at about that time, therefore Rothley Plain was in the parish of Rothley. Counsel for the Earl of Stamford denied that parish boundaries were fixed at that time. The only resident in the area, he said, was a warrener, who in living memory had paid his tithes to Newtown Linford, and not to Rothley. The jury found for the Earl of Stamford. Babington took legal advice, but was persuaded against further appeal. The Enclosure Commissioners continued their work. They seem to have found this particular award a considerable undertaking. In addition to the 412 acres of Rothley Plain, they were required to award 10,726 acres of Charnwood Forest. They finally made their award in 1829.[20]

Fig. 16.2 Enclosure Map, Rothley Plain, 1829.

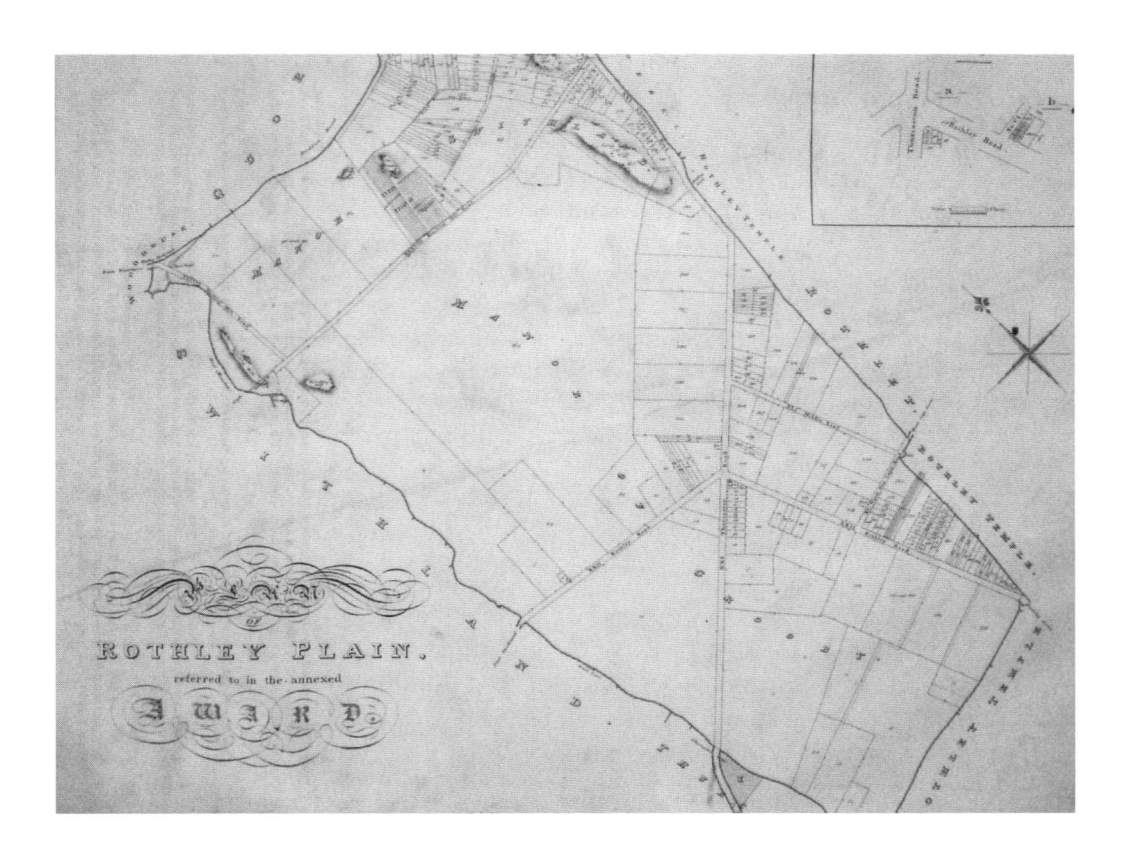

The Commissioners described the geographical area of the Plain as:

> ... beginning at Rothley Style, and leadeth southwardly and westwardly by the fences of enclosures in Rothley and Rothley Temple belonging to Richard Fowkes and Thomas Babington to a mere at the south corner of the Plain adjoining Rothley West field; northwardly by the fences of old enclosures in Thurcaston to a mere at Thurcaston Gate and northwardly by the fences of the old enclosures in Swithland to a mere by Hood's Barn and to a stile by the Red Meadow Gate by the fence to other ancient enclosures in Swithland and Woodhouse to Rushey Fields Gate; eastwardly by the fence of ancient enclosures in Woodhouse the forest of Buddon Wood and ancient enclosures in Quorndon the fence of Mountsorrel Hills ancient enclosures in Mountsorrel and Rothley Temple to Rothley Style.

As directed by the Act, the Commissioners first set out the public roads, some of them remaining approximately on the same alignment as those on John Prior's map of 1777. These were Thurcaston Road (Swithland Lane), Rothley Road (The Ridings), Quorndon Road (Wood Lane) and Kinsley Hill Road (Kinchley Lane). Six 'private carriage roads' were then created to provide access to some of the allotted land. Three of these roads have since become public highways: Water Gap Lane (Cross Lane), Middle Road (Gipsy Lane) and Rushey Lane. The other three private roads have, with the amalgamation of land holdings, ceased to exist.

Land was then allotted. There was a special allotment of just over 2 acres to the Surveyors of Highways of Newtown Linford. The parishes were then effectively the 'highways authority' and were expected to maintain the roads in the parish and the allotment to the Surveyors was of plots where stone could be quarried for road maintenance. Some 25 acres were allotted to the Lords of the Manor of Groby (the Earl of Stamford and Warrington) and of Swithland (Augustus Richard Butler Danvers). These allotments were in respect of payments for the right of common and the loss of other income as lord. Next, about 37.5 acres were allotted to the Earl of Stamford as improprietor (the person entitled to the tithes) of Newtown Linford. (At some time, the church must have sold the tithes, either directly, or indirectly, to the Stamfords.) The allotment was to compensate him for the loss of the tithes, which were not payable after enclosure. Next, some 60 acres were simply sold by the Commissioners. The remaining land was allotted to those persons who had rights of common on the Plain. These were principally those who owned freehold property in Swithland and Rothley, including in the south end of Mountsorrel.

The largest single beneficiary of the Enclosure Award was the Earl of Stamford, who was allotted 158.48 acres, including his 20 acres as Lord of the Manor of Groby. Augustus Richard Butler Danvers (who had died in 1820 while the Commissioners were carrying out their work) was allotted 46.54 acres, including 4 acres as Lord of the Manor of Swithland. Those with smaller allotments included Thomas Babington with 34.66 acres (5 acres of which he purchased from the Commissioners) and Richard Fowkes with 25.66 acres (16 of which he purchased from the Commissioners). Some of the allotments were extremely small. The trustees of Mountsorrel School, for example, were awarded five perches (151 square yards).

After Enclosure

In the years following the Enclosure Award, the major landowners, the Stamfords, the Lanesboroughs and the Babingtons, added to their holdings by buying up adjacent smaller holdings. The allotments to Stamford and to Butler Danvers bounded their existing holding in Swithland. Most of the land was put to the plough. By 1838, these were the owners and tenants of the land in Rothley Plain.[21]

Rothley Plain: Owners and Tenants in 1838

OWNERS	TENANTS	ACRES-ROODS-PERCHES
G.J. Butler Danvers	G.J. Butler Danvers	3-2-10
G.J. Butler Danvers	Thomas Bates	22-0-18
Rev John Dudley	Richard Place	19-3-37
John Bunney	William Cufflin	1-0-03
Thomas Castledine	Thomas Castledine	8-1-17
Rev W.Q. Wilde	Thomas Castledine	8-1-20
Richard Wale	William Cufflin	3-3-21
J.S. Mansfield	William Cufflin	5-3-01
G.J. Butler Danvers	Robert Adderley	1-3-04
John Adderley	Robert Adderley	3-3-31
Thomas Babington	John Astill	4-3-28
Matthew Babington	Rev Ackworth	0-0-27
Earl of Stamford &c	Thomas Burbage	147-0-27
Thomas Biddles	Thomas Biddles	0-3-00
Walter Barrs	Walter Barrs	1-1-07
William Thornton	John Barker	0-1-07
		236-1-18

In the years following enclosure, Lord Stamford mostly farmed his holding as a single unit, Rothley Plain Farm. The farm was based on the house and buildings now called The Homestead on Swithland Lane. William Thornton, whose wife Anne Thornton (d. 1820) and infant daughter Jane (d. 1817) are buried in Swithland churchyard, was tenant farmer there in 1836; in 1838 the farm was occupied by tenant Thomas Burbage, in 1841 by Maria Burbidge, who employed Joseph Reynolds as her farm bailiff, and from 1843 by Joseph Skevington (1809–1867) until his death in 1867.[22] His son Joseph continued at the farm until 1879. In 1874, George Harry, seventh Earl of Stamford, sold all his Swithland and Rothley Plain interests to the

Lanesboroughs.²³ William Lowe took over from Skevington as tenant of Rothley Plain Farm.

As well as farming, some small-scale brickmaking continued at the top of Kinchley Hill Lane and at the Swithland Lane crossroads. In 1840, William Place the elder, of Mountsorrel, sold some land (now the garden of 2 Kinchley Lane) that had been allotted to him in the Enclosure Award, on which there was 'a valuable brick kiln'.²⁴ In 1857, John Woolley of Mountsorrel started a brick and pipe making business at what came to be Brickyard Farm, near the junction of Swithland Lane and The Ridings. An advertisement for its sale by auction in 1862 suggests that the brickyard, of which Woolley was tenant, had by then extended to 1 acre.²⁵ In January 1859, two closes between Rushey Lane and Kinchley Lane – Far Brick Kiln Close and Near Brick Kiln Close – were sold to William Perry Herrick of Beaumanor by the Trustees of Spring Hill College, Yardley, Worcs.²⁶ In February 1859 an advertisement was placed in the *Leicester Journal* 'for sale of brick kiln close, in occupation of Mr Joseph Cuffling, who is under notice to quit 6 Apr next'. It was advertised for sale again in the Journal on 28 Nov 1862, when it was in the occupation of John Weston. There were various legal complications²⁷ to be sorted regarding Joseph Cuffling's position with respect to this and other land in Rothley Plain, including the Homestead, but in 1865, after Cuffling's death, the land, now released for absolute purchase, became the property of the Earl of Lanesborough.²⁸

Meanwhile, in 1847 a row of three cottages, Newtown Cottages, had been built near the junction of Swithland Lane and The Ridings. One of the residents, Eleanor Goddard, was buried at Swithland in June 1850.²⁹ In 1851 the three cottages were occupied by Daniel Warner, miller, John Holmes Sibson, cordwainer and Benjamin Harwood, also a cordwainer.

At the turn of the century, George Jackson, a Scotsman, had been working the Mountsorrel stone quarries at Hawcliffe Hill that he leased from Augustus Richard Butler Danvers. Using techniques that he had seen in Scotland, he sought to dress the stone with steel-faced tools. The enterprise did not flourish. The lease was taken up in 1842 by Mr William Martin, and then, from 1858 until his death, by Mr John Martin.³⁰ Martin moved the centre of quarrying from Hawcliffe Hill to Broad Hill. As the century progressed, some small-scale quarrying of granite also took place at various locations in the north part of Rothley Plain. Most of this quarrying was adjacent to Kinchley Lane, where a few quarrymen's cottages were built and where Martin built a new house for himself and his family. The Martins were the largest, but not the only, extractors of granite on the Plain. William Wale, previously of Mountsorrel, and latterly of 28 Sparkenhoe Street, Leicester, leased his Rothley Plain granite quarry, lately in the occupation of Joseph Lockwood and Joseph Cuffling, to John Martin of Groby Pool House on 29th September 1856, for ten years at £4 pa.³¹ In 1876 the Mountsorrel Granite Quarry, in which the Martin family was a principal shareholder, took over the rights to the Broad Hill quarry.

The construction of Swithland Reservoir in 1894 by the Leicester Corporation barely affected Rothley Plain, though a small amount of land in the north-east of the area, at the bottom of Kinchley Hill, was compulsorily purchased. Only a small amount of Rothley Plain land was required for the construction of the Great Central Railway. Initially, the main impact on the area from railway and reservoir was the construction of a mineral railway line. In 1894, the Earl of Lanesborough ceded to Mountsorrel Granite Company the right to quarry for stone in Nunckley Hill (previously known as Long Cliff Hill). When, shortly afterwards, the Manchester, Sheffield and Lincolnshire Railway Company secured permission to build their railway line from Nottingham to London, the parliamentary approval included permission to construct a single line track – the Nunckley Hill Railway – to connect the Hawcliffe Hill and Broad Hill quarries at Mountsorrel and the Nunckley Hill quarries in Rothley Plain, with the new main line at Swithland sidings. This connection with the main line railway was to be of major significance.

At the beginning of the twentieth century, the Lanesboroughs owned most of the land to the north and west of Rothley Plain. The Earl had acquired the major Stamford block in 1874, and had been slowly buying up other interests ever since. In 1896, he bought further land on the Plain, including the small Swithland Glebe Field, Woolley's brickyard and Newtown Cottages.[32] He let Nunckley Hill Spinney, at the top of Kinchley Lane, to the Mountsorrel Granite Company. John Woolley continued to farm 32 acres adjacent to the brickyard until 1903, with William Lowe farming the remaining former Stamford land from Rothley Plain Farm. Nunckley Hill Spinney, at the top of Kinchley Lane, was leased to the Mountsorrel Granite Company.

The Development of Rothley Temple Estate

The Rothley Temple Estate owned much of the land to the east of Swithland Lane and some of its estate farms rented land on the Plain. When, in 1892, the estate was sold at auction to Frederick Merttens, William Clarke tenanted Lodge Farm, Rothley. The land he farmed included 10 acres in Rothley Plain. Thomas Moore was tenant of Westfield Farm, Rothley; his land included 23 acres in the Plain. William Hyman ran a market garden on the 9 to 10 acres around his house, Linford Cottage, land of which lay in both Rothley Plain and the Rothley Temple Estate. William Hickling was tenant of yet another estate smallholding, of which 5 acres were on Rothley Plain.

Frederick Merttens bought the Rothley Temple Estate with the intention of turning it into a housing development. The type of development he planned had already been established in other places such as Hampstead and Letchworth. For rich industrialists and members of the rising middle classes, the ideal of their own small 'estates' within a residential development set in rural ground away from the towns and cities that provided their wealth, was becoming increasingly attractive.

As a young man, Merttens (1849–1935), an émigré from Prussia, had first travelled to South America before settling in Manchester. Here he founded a successful export business, Merttens & Schneider, Cotton Factors.

He was only forty-three when he bought the Temple Estate, which was sold in one lot at auction on 30th May 1892. It provided him with a country seat for himself, Rothley Temple, as well as land suitable for property development.

> His commendable enterprise in attempting to establish a model suburban settlement on his estate is being watched with much interest by those who share his views on the housing question and the possibilities of discriminate town planning. His object is to establish a settlement with ample gardens, broad avenues and houses of artistic design containing modern conveniences and comforts.[33]

In the event Merttens only lived at Rothley Temple for a relatively short period, the death of his business partner forcing his return to Manchester. Rothley Temple was let. In the years that he was 'in residence', Merttens restored the Temple Chapel (1896), created a billiards room – now the Wilberforce Room – added the south and kitchen wings, as well as a lodge, entrance gate and stables. Merttens never returned to Rothley, but went to live near Bilton, Rugby.[34] His ideas for the housing development, however, proceeded. Merttens donated his extensive collection of Rothley Temple records, some 1,500 relating to the manor and soke of Rothley, to Leicester Museum in 1928, on condition that a strong room would be provided to contain it.[35] Merttens died in 1935. He and his family are commemorated, at his request, by plaques on the walls in the Temple Chapel.[36]

Fig 16.3 The Rothley Temple Estate, 1892, from sale details.

In 1960, ownership of the manor, house and chapel passed to Clive Wormleighton, a member of the modern Order of Knights Templar and Preceptor of Leicester in 1974, who converted the house into Rothley Court Hotel.

When Merttens bought the Rothley Temple Estate in 1892, it comprised some 850 acres. By subsequent purchases and exchanges[37] he increased this to over 1,100 acres. He was confident that there was a demand for the type of development he envisaged, not least because the proposed new

Fig. 16.4 Railway Cottages, built in 1897, from a 1933 postcard.

Nottingham to London railway would have a station nearby, which would ensure the development's success.[38] Like the Garden Cities' Association formed in 1898, Merttens promoted the concept that his development would 'combine the advantages of town by way of accessibility and all the advantages of the country by way of environment without any of the disadvantages of either'. He started on the new development shortly after 1897. By 1898, the local railway construction had been completed and was open to passenger traffic. There were already some new houses nearby, as the railway company had built a row of cottages at the southern end of Swithland Lane in 1897.

Roman Remains

Merttens' housing development began with the building of an entirely new road adjacent to the Rothley Railway Station. It was to be called Templars Avenue but was later renamed The Ridgeway.[39] There were, however, archaeological complications. During the excavation work in 1896 for the new 'London Extension' to the Manchester, Sheffield and Lincolnshire Railway line, Saxon and Roman remains were found on land near the new Rothley Station. Archaeologists were therefore ready and waiting when the diggers came in to build The Ridgeway in 1901. They were not disappointed. The excavations revealed a floor, an under-floor heating structure, wall foundations and a well. It was concluded that these must be the remains of a bath suite belonging to a large Roman villa. The excavated area was scheduled as an ancient monument in 1976, and later geophysical surveys indicate that the villa area also extended across the field on the other side of The Ridgeway.

Meanwhile, the building of The Ridgeway continued. The necessary services were constructed: water supply, drainage, gas and electricity.

Building sites were identified and offered for sale. In terms of location, their saleability was unquestionable. The railway station was nearby. The historic relationship with Rothley Temple, the surrounding countryside, with mature trees and working farms, all served to satisfy the romantic longing for a country life away from the pollution, squalor and smells of Leicester city. Even the names of the first houses reflected the rural romanticism behind the development – Uplands, The Spinneys, The Coppice. And those houses would be substantial, with room for servants. One third of the land nearest the station was to be left as open countryside. Any washing left out to dry must not be soiled by the soot and ash from the steam engines!

The Ridgeway: First Houses

The first three houses on The Ridgeway were completed by 1902. Uplands (No. 45), and The Spinneys (No. 33) were both on the southern side of the road and The Coppice (No. 62) on the northern side. Each was designed by Leicester architect Thomas Henry Fosbrooke (1861–1925). Fosbrooke, a Fellow of the Society of Antiquaries, had a 'particular passion for Gothic art',[40] and was responsible for the restoration of the old Town Hall and for the Leicester Guildhall, which colleagues saw to be 'his permanent memorial in Leicester'.[41] Fosbrooke was 'a man greatly liked... He delighted in airing agnostic opinions in religion; but he was always the first to cherish the monuments of the past, and his conduct was shot through with Christian charity'.[42]

The second three houses to be built were Three Oaks (No. 39), Holly Lodge (No. 60) and Paigles (No. 54). While Fosbrooke designed Three Oaks, the other two were designed by J. Stockdale Harrison. Harrison was a fashionable Leicester architect, who lived for a while (c. 1881) at Rockside, Maplewell Road, Woodhouse Eaves. He later (1910) gained a prestigious commission to design Edinburgh's baroque Usher Hall.

UPLANDS, the first house to be built, was designed for Leicester solicitor Robert Harvey (1854–1920.) The house's Arts and Crafts style was typical of other early houses on the estate. There were large gardens and stables, an impressive drive to the front door, and accommodation for servants. Uplands first owner, Robert Harvey, qualified as a solicitor in 1878, and became a partner in Harvey and Clarke, solicitors of Millstone Lane, Leicester. In politics he was a Liberal and was elected as councillor for

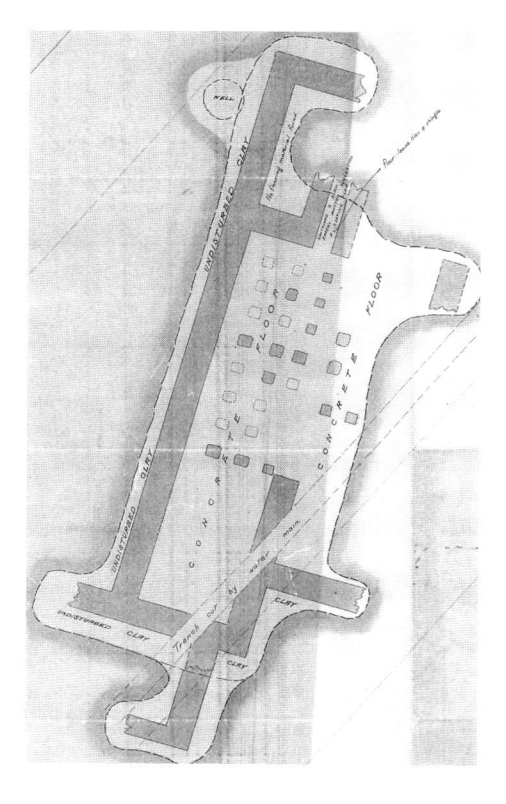

Fig 16.5 Site of Roman villa, Rothley, sketch plan of excavated remains, 1901.

Fig 16.6 The Oak, 'New Road' (The Ridgeway), looking towards The Ridings, 1911.

East St Margaret's ward in 1888, and was said to be a 'good and fluent speaker, with a large fund of energy'.[43] When he became Leicester's Coroner in 1890 he resigned from local government. A man of strong principles, he refused to hold inquests at a public house, only in board houses, coffee houses or other non-alcoholic establishments. As coroner he was seen as 'acute and correct in his deductions, and sifts right down to the bottom of death causes, wherever any public advantage is to be held'.[44] Public health was clearly an important cause: Harvey was seen as hammering 'at the nail of the improper feeding on infants, incessantly inquiring into and deprecating juvenile insurance'.[45] He was involved in various movements that worked for the improved culture of the community, such as the Literary and Philosophical Society (president 1892) and, as an accomplished amateur musician, the Leicester Orchestral Union (founder member 1854).

Fig 16.7 'New Road' from The Ridings, Holly Lodge on the right, 1911.

The next occupant of Uplands was George Cecil Gorham Gee (d. 1970). Son of Harry Simpson Gee and brother of Percy Gee, Cecil was a director of Bagworth Colliery and also of the family firm Stead and Simpson. There were several shoe factories in Rothley, one of which was owned by Stead and Simpson. (This factory was later used by Hunt's Boot and Shoe Company, Hunts Star Works, which expanded to employ over one hundred workers in the 1920s and 1930s.) Gee served as High Sherriff of Rutland in 1920 and of Leicestershire in 1930. He was a governor of the University College, Leicester (of which his brother Percy was a generous benefactor), a trustee of Oakham School, treasurer of the Diocese of Leicester and a lay canon of Leicester Cathedral. For a time he served as chairman of Rothley Parish Council. In the Great War he served in the 4th Battalion of the Leicestershire Regiment and continued after the war as a member of the Leicestershire Territorial Army Association.[46] On his death in 1970, the Bishop of Leicester paid him tribute.

> With the death of Lay Canon Cecil Gee the last link is broken with the original group of laymen who were responsible for the founding of the diocese in 1926. He became a Lay Canon in 1935, and in the course of his long life (he reached the great age of 95) he served the diocese in almost every capacity open to a responsible layman. Great, however, as was his service and also his generosity, he will be remembered most for his radiant and sunny personality. He loved roses. He loved cricket. He loved children. Throughout his life he showed joy and he gave joy. Now he has entered into the fullest joy, the joy of his Lord.[47]

In 1947, Gee swapped houses with relatives, the Wessel family of Newlands, Swithland Lane. Robert L. (Bobby) Wessel worked for Corahs and rose to become a director. His mother was a Corah, but his father was Danish-born. Harry Wessel, like so many in Victorian times, travelled to South America to make his fortune. He did so in spectacular fashion. He served as Danish Ambassador to Chile and, on his return to Denmark, was so well thought of by the Chilean government that he was appointed to serve as Chilean Ambassador to Denmark.

THE SPINNEYS was perhaps the most substantial of the first three houses built along The Ridgeway. It was built in a more traditional style than were Uplands and The Coppice. According to the 1909 brochure it was erected for Arthur Henry Bennett, but ownership of The Spinneys remained with the Rothley Temple Estate until June 1913 when, with other properties on the Estate, it was sold at auction. John Bennett, who rented The Spinneys until 1913, was a solicitor with a practice at 6 Market Street, Leicester. His partner in the firm of Bennett & Ironside was Alfred Allen Ironside, who married Edith Lead, the daughter of William Henry Lead who lived first at Holly Lodge and then at West Lawn, both on The Ridgeway.

After the Great War, John Williams Wilkes moved from Loughborough Road, Belgrave into The Spinneys. Wilkes Bros & Co. were the quality shoe manufacturers Solito Shoes of Bruin Street, Leicester, who later expanded

*Fig 16.8
The Spinneys,
2000.*

to wholesale under the Gypsy King and Gypsy Queen trademarks. Wilkes bought land on both sides of Woodgate, Rothley; the more substantial of the two plots covered an area bounded by Woodgate, Howe Lane, Town Green Street to the corner, and back up to Woodgate. His land incorporated cottages as well as a small farm, but he sold on the land fairly quickly to Harry Hames of Victoria Mills, Hosiery Manufacturers of Rothley.

Wilkes was followed into The Spinneys in 1935 by Cecil R. Coleman, managing director of Corah and later of Woodfords & Wormleighton, another knitwear manufacturer. Cecil Coleman is probably better remembered as the buyer of the Launde Abbey Estate which he then restored and gifted to the Diocese of Leicester. Shirley Ellis bought The Spinneys in 1946 after the Second World War. His family had been involved in the textile trade since 1800. Ellis was chairman of the family company of Donisthorpe's,[48] Bath Street, Leicester, dyers and suppliers of cotton thread. Ellis' father had been managing director of Donisthorpe's, and Shirley Ellis knew Frederick Donisthorpe. Both had a love of shooting, and, in Shirley Ellis' case, golf. In 1931, on his marriage, he bought land at Brownhill Crescent, Rothley, where he built Anmer, splendidly adjacent to the Rothley Golf Club. (Ellis once met King George at Sandringham, and named his house Anmer after a village on the Sandringham Estate).

THE COPPICE stands at the intersection of The Ridgeway and The Ridings. It was built for Reginald Edensor Stanley Richardson (b.1868). Son of the founder, Richardson was managing director of John Richardson & Co Ltd. of Leicester, a family pharmaceutical and wholesale manufacturing chemists founded in 1869. The company was based in Friar Lane, but manufacturing took place in Pocklington's Walk.

(William) John Spurway followed Richardson into The Coppice.

Spurway's father, John Spurway (d.1912) who was in the wool trade before expanding to carpet manufacture, had moved to Leicester from Kidderminster, and set up a retail company based at 51 Highcross Street, Leicester. (His property was part of the structure of the old Free School of Queen Elizabeth's day.) Spurways, which claimed to be the largest floor covering company in the Midlands, specialized in oriental and other carpets. In 1920, Spurway moved to Aberfeldy, a newly built dwelling at 28 The Ridings. He was succeeded at The Coppice c. 1920 by Albert William Hanford who removed there from Red Walls, 32 The Ridgeway. In 1926 only Miss Hanford was living at The Coppice.

Mr Archibald Chamberlain Garner followed the Hanfords into The Coppice in c. 1940. Arthur Harry Swain (b. 1880) lived there after the Garners. Swain, whose father James Christopher Swain was a pioneer of the boot and shoe industry, was an insurance broker who founded AH Swain & Co. Ltd, with offices near to St Martin's, Leicester. In 1936, Swain became Lord Mayor of Leicester.[49] After his death, his widow remained at The Coppice until her re-marriage to Mr Rudkin, when she moved to Cossington and rented out The Coppice.

THREE OAKS was also designed by Fosbrooke, who seems to have been its original owner. In c. 1924 it was bought by Gerald Hugh Robert Johnson, a yarn merchant of 27 Friar Lane, Leicester. Alfred Davies was living there in 1928; he had the telephone phone put in – Rothley 5. The house then passed into the hands of Norman Fawcett, managing director of Fielding Johnson and chairman of the Midland Master Spinners Association. Fawcett sold on in 1931 to Arthur and Kathleen McCurry. Arthur Llewellyn McCurry (1898–1974), who was born in Belfast, was the premier eye surgeon in the Midlands, working at the Leicester Royal Infirmary. He served as chairman of the Leicestershire and Rutland Branch of the British Medical Association and was a former president of the Leicester Medical Society. They left the house in 1950.

HOLLY LODGE was built for the Leicester printer, William Henry Lead (1850–1937). William Henry's great grandfather, Leonard Lead (1756–1821) was, according to a 1798 source, a Derbyshire charcoal burner, a 'wood collier' of Belper. His second son, Leonard (1786–1869), apprenticed in Derby in 1800, was an artist for Crown Derby and a noted flower painter. His son William was a printer, in which profession he was followed by his

Fig 16.9 William Henry Lead of Holly Lodge, with son William and grandson David.

Fig 16.10 Holly Lodge, 2000.

son William Henry Lead of Leicester. Lead's daughter Edith married Alfred Allen Ironside, whose second daughter still continues the connection with Rothley. William Henry was a freemason and a member of Rothley Golf Club. Lead died in 1937; his funeral was held at Rothley but he was buried at Welford Road Cemetery. Mrs Lead continued to live at Holly Lodge until 1947. From 1955–1971, Mr and Mrs Victor Burton lived there.

THE COTTAGE (or PAIGLES) was also designed by J. Stockdale Harrison. It was built for Edward John Holyoak, a partner in the family firm of Leicester solicitors E.J. and F.G. Holyoak of the Priory Chambers, St Martin's. After leaving Cambridge, Holyoak was articled to William Napier Neeve, and admitted as a solicitor in 1881. A man who listed his recreations[50] as lawn tennis, football and cricket, Holyoak is remembered in Belgrave, Leicester as being one of those who established the Belgrave Recreational Ground and Eleemosynary Charity. The Holyoaks moved away in 1935.

By 1951 William Bentley had taken over possession of Paigles. His was one of the two Leicestershire families[51] to dominate and shape the British textile machinery industry, witnessing both its pre-eminence in engineering in the first half of the twentieth century and also its slow demise. Percival Arthur (Percy) Bentley, William Bentley's father, was a graduate engineer who invented 'electric earth clocks', taking a patent out in 1910. Unfortunately his attempts to manufacture and market them through his company, the Bentley Manufacturing Company of Forest Gate, Clarendon Park Road were halted by the outbreak of war in 1914, and not reintroduced after the war. His son, William, saw a more profitable business in designing and building hosiery machines, starting a new future in that industry with the Komet machine. Over the next thirty years, the Bentley Group consolidated the hosiery machine industry, taking over Cottons, Wildt, Blackburn, Mellor, Bromley and Grieve. In 1946, Dr Wildt had apparently taken advice from financier Charles Clore and his investment company; it is said that Clore was furious when Bentley's hostile take-over bid succeeded. Within twenty years, however, fortunes reversed when the Bentley Group was taken over by Clore's Sear Holdings.

Garden Cities and Suburbs

From the mid-nineteenth century, reformers and political theorists had begun to develop an interest in what came to be known as 'the Garden City Movement'. Rural England and agriculture were in serious decline as the century ended, and agricultural land prices dropped. Industrial concerns, on the other hand, were expanding, and those who owned them were becoming wealthy. Financially astute business men, such as Merttens, took advantage of the situation and offered the newly rich industrialists their own country estates. There was also a romantic nostalgia for country life among the monied middle-classes, and developers like Merttens arguably helped them realize their fantasies by creating 'new village' building developments. Some of the first 'garden city' developments, such as Bournville and Hampstead, were motivated by a concern for peoples' well-being, but others, like Rothley Garden Suburb, were unashamedly commercial.

In 1898, Sir Ebenezer Howard had published 'Tomorrow: a peaceful path to real reform'. His proposals were ambitious: nothing less than an organized attempt to move large numbers of the population away from the over-crowded cities to the sparsely-settled rural districts.[52] While there was much that was idealistic, Howard's initial approach was essentially pragmatic, assuming private enterprise rather than civic policy, for while there was a real concern in the country to address urban misery, there was little support in Britain for the more radical approach of Marx and Engels in their 1848 Communist manifesto.

Several 'village associations' were set up in the middle of the nineteenth century with the intention of building around the London metropolis. A development around Ilford, for example, had been proposed in 1848. Their stated ideals were very similar to those of later 'garden city' prospectuses. 'Air and space, wood and water, schools and churches, shrubberies and gardens, around pretty self-contained cottages neither too large to deprive it of country character, nor too small to diminish the probabilities of social intercourse'.[53] Forty years later, two garden city developments were realized by private philanthropy, one at Port Sunlight near Birkenhead (1887) and the other at Bournville (1889).

These relatively small projects encouraged the larger creations of the garden cities of Letchworth (1903) and, later, Welwyn (1920–49). In 1907, the Hampstead Garden Suburb development had been instigated by Henrietta Barnett. Her intentions were altruistic, and a response to the threatened ruin of 'the sylvan restfulness of the most beautiful open space near London'.[54] Through the Hampstead Heath Extension Council, heath extension land was purchased and given to the London County Council to provide for people of all classes a beautiful and healthy place to live in. It was a social experiment, the broad lines of which were that it should be accessible to all, including the handicapped and weekly wage-earners, be relatively spacious, with a garden for every house, and with woods and public spaces which would be open to all. Everything should be planned so that 'none should spoil each other's outlook or rob its neighbour of beauty'.

Sir Raymond Unwin, given the responsibility of planning the suburb, applied ideas to his planning of street and housing layout that originated in the eighteenth century landscape gardens. He also aimed to achieve 'an intricate balance of different types of house for different classes of people', arranging them in such a way as to keep the classes 'just sufficiently apart from one another to enable the larger house to be commercially viable'.[55]

A Charming Country Estate

All this must have influenced Merttens' thinking. Whilst his initial concept for the Rothley Temple land may have been that of the 'country estate', his more realisable marketing of the Rothley Plain properties as 'Rothley Garden Suburb' in 1909 was clearly directed at a wider group of potential buyers, who he needed to attract as the initial development of his estate had proceeded relatively slowly. With the economy in decline, even those with money could not afford to be spend-thrift, and by 1906 only nine houses had been commissioned and completed. While some saw those years as a bad time to build, Merttens had the confidence to continue to acquire more land and so to increase the size of his development. There was sand and gravel in abundance on the estate, and brick and tile companies nearby.[56] The main building contractors, William Moss and Sons, a Loughborough firm, had proven experience of building work in the Hampstead Garden Suburb. In 1903, the sixth Earl of Lanesborough had agreed an exchange giving Merttens Rothley Plain farmhouse and its surrounding outhouses and land. Another opportunity arose with the seventh Earl in 1906 and Merttens acquired another 46 acres, a triangle of land bounded by Swithland Lane, The Ridings and Swithland parish boundary. By 1906, therefore, Merttens owned most of Rothley Plain to the south of the Nunckley Hill mineral railway, with the remaining Lanesborough interests in the Plain being concentrated on the north side.

It was said of Merttens in 1907 that 'his object is to establish a settlement with ample gardens, broad avenues and houses of artistic design containing modern conveniences and comforts. The initial stages of the enterprise have been successful. Houses have already been erected from designs by the best London architects, and further work of a similar character is proceeding'.[57] With the land that he needed in his possession and houses gradually going up,[58] Merttens was in a position to run his new and aggressive marketing campaign. He commissioned various London architects to produce designs which might prove more attractive to those with smaller purses than the first buyers along The Ridgeway. He engaged George E. Clare as his resident estate architect and surveyor, set up an estate office at the southern end of Swithland Lane and, in February 1909, printed the first of his advertising brochures.[59]

It was targeted at 'commercial and professional men, clerks, tradesmen and others who have learned to appreciate the rest, comfort, pure air and rural pursuits associated with a country home'. Merttens even made a virtue of the Roman remains, telling his potential customers that 'the Rothley

Fig 16.11 Rothley Garden Suburb, 1909 plan.

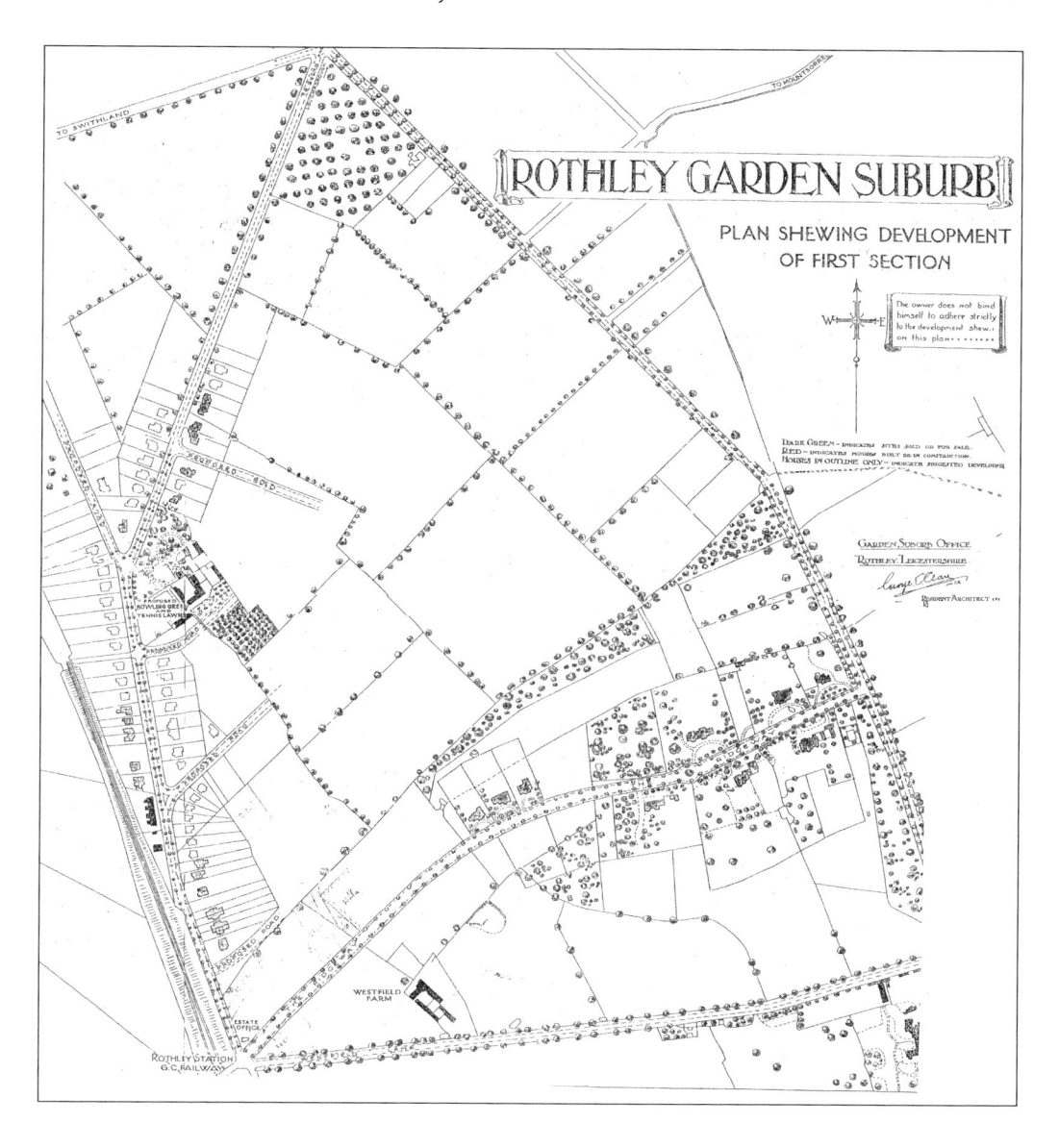

Garden Suburb is situated amidst a lovely chain of hills and dales, forests, lakes and charming country lands. The neighbourhood is full of interest, and the very building sites now offered are on the ground of an old Roman Settlement'. As well as the beauty of the countryside, the use of reputable local firms[60] was described as one of the strengths of the project. Emphasis was placed on the quality of design and construction, which was guaranteed by a requirement that all plans would have to be vetted by the estate architect, George Clare. Among the other virtues cited were the all-inclusive construction costs, potential savings in expensive city rates and the modern amenities of mains water, gas and telephone communication. It was claimed

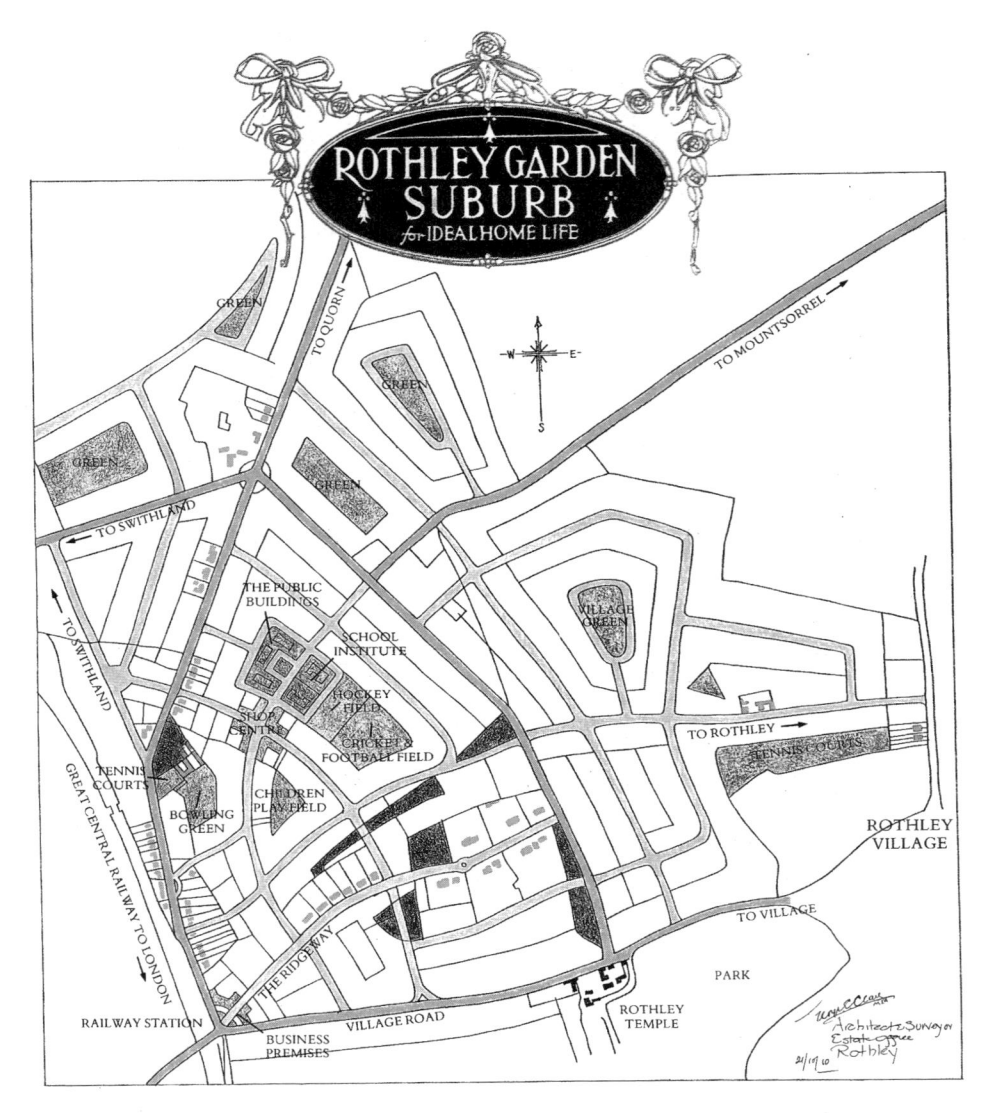

RED INDICATES : BUILDINGS ERECTED
LIGHT YELLOW INDICATES : PROPOSED & MADE ESTATE ROADS
DARK YELLOW INDICATES : OLD PUBLIC ROADS
DARK GREEN INDICATES : PLANTATIONS TO BE RETAINED
FOR PUBLIC BENEFIT
LIGHT GREEN INDICATES : OPEN SPACES PROPOSED TO PRESERVE
FOR D°

Facsimile of the **Rothley Garden Suburb Plan** from 1910

Fig. 16.12 Rothley Garden Suburb, 1910 plan.

that the postal service was so good that a letter posted on the estate at 4.50pm would be delivered in London that same evening.

The map attached to the brochure indicated several proposed and completed new roadways linking in with the old. From the station corner, where the Estate Office stood – between the road to Quorn (now Swithland Lane) and the road to Rothley (Westfield Lane) – a new road (The Ridgeway) already gave access to dwellings built or in process of building and joined the road from Rothley Temple to Swithland (The Ridings). Four proposed beginnings of roads going off to the right of Swithland Lane were shown, and another, at the Homestead bend, was proposed to go off to the left at that point and connect with the road into Swithland village. It was proposed to incorporate tennis lawns and a bowling green on the land between the road and the Homestead complex of buildings.

In 1910 a second brochure was issued with a more developed plan. It included information about mortgages, thereby acknowledging that some potential buyers might have difficulty raising immediate capital. The new plan showed the network of roads yet to be made criss-crossing the whole estate area. The plan showed how private dwellings would link with the public amenities yet to be built. Merttens did not offer those social facilities that could be accessed in nearby villages, rather he offered new leisure facilities with which he hoped to attract his 'looking for a better life-style' clients. Next to the Homestead he built tennis courts in 1909 and, just off Westfield Lane, an eighteen-hole golf course the following year. He also promised a bowling green and allotments,[61] though these never materialised. His brochure was, however, able to refer to Charnwood Preparatory School at 27 Swithland Lane, at the time under a Miss Marsden.

The 1910 plan promised public buildings, a school institute, a shop centre, play, cricket and football field as well as various 'greens'. Also clear from the 1910 plan is that Merttens was considering the possibility of infill development inside The Ridings, Westfield Lane and the Swithland Lane road to Quorn. Two roads were planned to turn into the development area from Westfield Lane. There was already in existence an unofficial short cut to the golf course running from The Ridgeway to Westfield Lane, through Westfield Farm. (The track was closed once a year to ensure that it could not be taken as an official highway right.)

This more up-front marketing had the effect of increasing the rate of construction. In the four years between 1908 and 1912, four more houses were built along The Ridgeway, making a total of thirteen houses in all, and seventeen more houses were built along Swithland Lane, making the number there thirty-eight.

Architects

The architects chosen by Merttens to promote his 'garden suburb' were marketed as having proven 'garden city credentials', having designed and sold homes, large and small, in Hampstead Garden Suburb. There were architects from London: Messrs Michael Bunney & Meakin, 33 Henrietta

Street, Strand, London; Mr E. Guy Dawber, 22 Buckingham Street, Adelphi, Strand, London; Mr Geoffry Lucas, 14 Hart Street, Bloomsbury, London; and Mr Arnold Mitchell, 17 Hanover Square, London. Leicester architects were also advertised, including Messrs. Langley & Baines, 16, Friar Lane; Mr Clement Ogden, 7 St Martin's (opposite Parr's Bank); Mr William Mann, 15 Kimberley Road. Mertenns' resident estate architect was George E. Clare of Clare & Ross, Chelmsford and London.

Michael Bunney (1874–1927), whose practice had offices in London and in Gloucestershire, concentrated on small domestic buildings. His designs were much to the fore in the development of Hampstead Garden Suburb and in Gidea Park, Essex. With Horace Field, to whom he was articled, Bunney produced a book of measured drawings and photographs of the small English domestic buildings of the seventeenth and eighteenth centuries. Bunney's early days were spent in Venice, where his father, an artist, was making, with the encouragement of John Ruskin, topographical watercolours of Venetian and other Italian buildings.[62]

Sir (Edward) Guy Dawber (1861–1938) designed Red Walls, 32 The Ridgeway. A leading British architect in the early twentieth century, Dawber was mainly famed for his work on the restoration and conservation of some of Britain's finest country homes and gardens (such as Armscote Manor, Warks. and Eyford Park, Glos). He had a particular interest in the local architecture of the Cotswolds.[63] He also became known as a 'traditional' architect whose work included St John's Chapel of Ease in his hometown of Matlock Vale, the war memorial at Moreton-in-Marsh (1921) and, with Joan Beauchamp Proctor, the reptile house at London Zoo (1927). Dawber was made president of the British School of Architecture (1925–26), president of CPRE (1926) and knighted in 1926.

(Thomas) Geoffry Lucas (1872–1947) designed a pair of houses in Swithland Lane. He is perhaps best remembered for his work in connection with the garden city movement, but he also designed churches and church fittings. Lucas designed a group of inexpensive cottages at Paddock Close, Letchworth (1905) that were described as 'The £150 House'. Of these houses he said, 'Although simple, an effort has been made to obtain dignity, and an architectural treatment, without extravagance'. 'Whilst a similarity in style can be seen, their simplicity forms a marked contrast with the more opulent houses which he was designing for private patrons at this time'.[64] Lucas was made a Fellow of the Royal Institution of British Architects in 1911.

Arnold Bidlake Mitchell (1863–1944) designed The Gables, 68 Swithland Lane, winning first prize at an Ideal Home Exhibition for the design. He was a gifted 'Arts and Crafts' architect who began practice in 1886, specializing in parish-halls, houses, and schools. His most renowned works include St Felix School, Southwold, Suffolk (1902), the School of Agriculture, Cambridge (1909–10), and University College School, Frognal, Hampstead, London (1905–07). His domestic works included properties in Hampstead Garden Suburb.

George E. Clare, MSA, was Merttens' resident architect for the latter stages of his project. An Essex architect, he had co-authored with Walter G. Ross *Ideal Homes for the People* (1902), which addressed building appropriate and inexpensive accommodation for the working classes in rural districts using Clare's own 'patent concrete and fire-proof timber construction' method. Clare was a particularly appropriate architect at a time when a stagnating national economy was having a discouraging effect on the housing market. His 'method' promised to cut building costs significantly and that would have been attractive. He designed several homes along Swithland Lane, and restored Rothley Plain Farm (now known as the Homestead, 65 Swithland Lane) and its four outbuildings, (Nos. 57–63 Swithland Lane) all of which are now listed buildings. In 1910, the partnership of Clare & Scott, 2 Berridge Street, Leicester, co-operated with Tuckers of Loughborough in a stand at the 1910 Ideal Home Exhibition. They showed various designs for 'an up to date Weekend Cottage' – a four bedroomed house with an additional room for the maid, for whom there would be a separate entrance. The design incorporated a sunken tea-lawn on the west side of the house, 'to catch the afternoon sun', and, on the east side, a motor house. Laid out gardens at the front would be matched with larger gardens behind the house, featuring a tennis lawn surrounded by formal gardens. It was a house of 'compactness and convenience to reduce the service labour to within the limits of one useful maid'.[65]

Developments along The Ridgeway 1908–14

MYAMIN (No. 36) later called The Lawns, was probably built to another of T.H. Fosbrooke's designs. He lived there himself until his death in 1926, when he was succeeded by the Winks family. Their son, Lieut. Jack Greville Winks is commemorated on Rothley's War Memorial (1939–45).

WEST LAWN (No. 44) was built for Miss Rose Ellen Paget, a member of the banking family of Pagets. The house was called West Lawn after the nearby Westfield Farm.[66] Thomas Paget founded Pagets Bank in 1825. Originally known as Paget & Kirby of Leicester, the bank prospered through the nineteenth century to such an extent that Thomas Tertius Paget, son of the founder, died a millionaire. Thomas Paget, the founder, was well known as a farmer and stockbreeder, but rose to be elected as MP for the county of Leicester and was twice elected Lord Mayor of Leicester. After the death of his father in 1862, Thomas Tertius became senior partner. He became High Sherriff of Leicester in 1869 and was elected a Liberal MP for South Leicestershire in 1880. He caused the Leicester Opera House to be built. After he died in 1892, his remaining partners felt the pressure of being the last private bank in Leicestershire, and sold Pagets Bank to Lloyds Bank. Pagets had just the three branches – in Loughborough, Market Harborough and Melton Mowbray; they only opened on market days. Remarkable today, but it was the custom of Pagets Bank to balance the cash once a year rather than every day after transactions. Miss Paget was succeeded into West Lawn by Alfred A. Ironside, a Leicester solicitor. After his death, Claude and Gertrude Brown bought the house in c. 1951. At about the same time his daughter and son-in-law, the Bett family, moved to Swithland Lane. Brown was managing director of En-Tout-Cas, Leicester, manufacturers of sports tracks and tennis courts, and a director of British Runways Ltd.

Fig 16.13 Architect's drawing of Red Walls, from the 1909 brochure.

RED WALLS (No. 32), which had a guide price in 1909 of £1,250, was designed by Guy Dawber and built for Albert William Hanford of Hanford & Miller, hosiers of Derby Road, Loughborough. Hanford & Miller was established in Loughborough by c.1900. The Hanfords later moved into 'the Coppice' following John Spurway. In 1924, the Payne family from America bought Red Walls and they lived there until 1937. Payne was a member of the American company which partnered the British United Shoe Machinery Company. (BUSM was chaired by Charles Bennion, one of Leicester's significant benefactors, best remembered for his gifting Bradgate Park for the enjoyment of the people of the city and county of Leicester.)

FAIRFIELD (No. 26), designed by G.E. Clare in 1910 for Mr Joseph Arthur Hilton, had a large garden with tennis courts. Hilton was a son of Mr Stephen Hilton, JP, Mayor of Leicester in 1904, and Stephen H. Hilton & Son was the original company from which Hiltons' shoe retailers emerged. The Hiltons were followed into Fairfield in 1934 by George Hunt and his family. Hunt's family company, T.G. Hunt & Son, Boot and Shoe manufacturers, was founded in 1885 and based at Premier Works, Melton Road. Their brand names were Stiletto, Grey Heron and Fidelity. With the death of Hunt in 1955, the house was sold.

ST BERNARD'S (No. 28) was built c. 1912 for Samuel Francis Burford FCS. Burford had moved to Rothley Garden Suburb from Kirby Muxloe. He was public analyst at the corporation buildings in Horsefair Street, Leicester. Walter Reed Cook and his family were the next occupants, c. 1927–31. Cook was a dyer (W.R. Cook) with possible connections with Walter Cooke (Leicester) Ltd., bleachers of Rugby Street, Woodgate. The next owners were Mr Keyworth Houston, FSA, FRGS and Mrs Catherine Alice Houston, 1931–67. Brand, Edwards & Branson of Bowling Street, Leicester, drew up the plans for the extension of the house for them. Mrs Houston, a family member of the owners of Griffin & Spalding department store in Nottingham, collected fine china. Such was the quality of her collection, that on her death, the collection went to London for auction. Mr Houston was a talented musician who had an organ built in the 'Music Room'. A fastidious man, it was said that when his newspaper was delivered, he insisted that it should be ironed, and even then he wore white cotton gloves when reading it. Like his wife, Houston was a collector – of wine glasses, art, furniture and books.[67]

PIPERS END was the name of the six-bedroomed house for which G.E. Clare drew up plans in 1912, but it was never built. No. 23 The Ridgeway, named variously *WOODCOTE*, Causeland and Ditton was built for Joseph Langton of S & E Langton, estate agents of Halford Street, Leicester who lived there until 1937.

HERONGATE (No. 30) was designed in 1914 by William Mann for Arthur Oliver, director of George Oliver (Footwear), Leicester. As a young man, Arthur Oliver was a keen cricketer. The annual large dinner of the company's cricket team was attended by the good and great of Leicester.

Developments along Swithland Lane 1908–14

CHARNWOOD PREPARATORY SCHOOL No. 27 Swithland Lane – the house had no other name – was advertised as a 'select private elementary school'. According to Merttens' brochure, the school was 'under Miss Marsden'. From 1912–17 the teacher was Miss Florence Rich.[68] Trades directories indicate that Miss Ellen Braginton was in charge from 1919–27, but when she retired to the south coast the school was closed down. According to local memories, those pupils who arrived by carriage were

Fig 16.14 Charnwood Preparatory School, garden view.

Fig 16.15 Charnwood Preparatory School classroom.

Fig 16.16 Newlands, 2000.

dropped off at the front of the school and the pony traps continued around the short crescent and back onto Swithland Lane. The Misses Winifred and Edna Harrop lived at No. 27 from 1928–35.

NEWLANDS (No. 90) was built in 1909, and was possibly one of the first houses to be built to the designs of resident architect George E. Clare. Built for G.A. Pochin, it is arguably one of the more successful of Clare's designs on the development.[69] In 1920 the house was bought by Lt. Col. Thomas Paget Fielding Johnson. His family connections are in themselves a small history of industrial Leicester, as were the powerful connections with the Unitarians. Leicester Unitarians in the 1800s had the banking wealth of the Pagets, the legal ability of Samuel Stone, the hosiery fortune of the Biggs family, the engineering skills of the Gimsons and the solid business interests of the Fielding Johnsons, the Coltmans and of Brewin & Whetstone. The Fielding Johnson family could look back in their family heritage to both the Earls of Denbigh (Fieldings) and the Earls of Buckingham (a Fielding married a Villiers). Thomas Fielding Johnson senior joined his uncle's family spinning company. His philanthropic contribution to Leicester was enormous. His interests ranged from health (he endowed the Fielding Johnson Hospital, Regent Road and the Leicester Royal Infirmary) to education (endowing the University College and the Wyggeston Schools) and to politics (he was a JP for many years, and at one time Lord Mayor of Leicester). His son, Lt. Col. Thomas Paget Fielding Johnson, whose Paget name came from Alfred Paget, solicitor of Leicester (he had elected to practice law rather than banking) carried on his father's interests as well as serving as an officer in the Leicestershire Regiment. Johnson sold the house in 1924, offering it in two lots, the second he described as pasture land and 'ripe for immediate development'. From the 1940s the Wessel family[70] occupied Newlands. In 1947 they moved to Uplands on The Ridgeway in a direct house exchange with relative Cecil Gee.

INGLEDENE (No. 86) was built in 1912, also from a design by Clare. It was originally sold to Mr E. Walker who lived there until c. 1924. He was followed by Stanley Adams. *WAYSIDE* (No. 88) was designed by T.M. Wilson, built by Mr R. Moss and bought by Mr Pegg c. 1914. *GRAYRIGG* (No. 80) was built in 1909 and first belonged to a Mr Leech. James Eatough lived there between c. 1941 and 1970. According to Swithland's parish magazine, Mr Eatough was 'a well known figure in Footwear circles, and had completed forty-three years as director of his Earl Shilton firm, Eatough's Ltd.'[71]

FAIRVIEW (No. 3) was the nearest to the railway station of a set of smaller houses and semi-detached properties. It was designed by George E. Clare, and, according to the prospectus, sold to W. (1909) or J. (1910) Sharpe Esq. George Sharpe was living there from 1909–c. 1920. *BRENTWOOD* (No. 5) and *CLAREMONT* (No. 7), *WOODLANDS* (No. 9) and

Fig 16.17 Fairview, 3 Swithland Lane, sketch by G.E. Clare.

STANSWELL (No. 11) were two semi-detached pairs of houses. 'Claremont' was first occupied (1912) by the Lane family, who also owned adjacent 'Brentwood' (1914). 'Claremont' first passed to the McDonalds (1920) and then to the North family. The Norths, who still live locally, have had a long and continuous connection with Rothley Plain. David North was one of a group of pioneers who went out to Canada with his family in 1913 to settle. By 1924, however, North had changed his mind and they returned to England. When he bought 'Claremont', he was working for Lloyds Bank, High Street, Leicester. His son Eric, initially a farmer, retailed provisions from his own home, which was next door to the station on Westfield Lane. The family business continues to thrive under Eric's son, David North and his son Dominic. 'Stanswell' was build for Mr Jelley, who stayed there until 1948. Next to 'Stanswell,' three other houses were all built at about the same time (1912): *CHARNWOOD HOUSE* (No. 15), *CHURSTON* (No. 17) and *WINDYCROFT* (No. 19). Windycroft was the home of Charles Frost.

THE SHRUBBERY, (No. 38), originally known as Greenfields, was the first of the houses to be built immediately adjacent to the railway cottages on the west side of Swithland Lane, and was the home of George Clare, the estate's resident architect (1912). Next to Greenfields stood a group of 1912 houses: *REDHOLM* (No. 40) later to be known as *THE WHITE HOUSE*, first lived in by a Mr Dicks; *CLONMELL* (or Holmwood) and *THE LAURELS*, which were a semi-detached pair of houses (Nos. 44 and 46), as were *CRAFERS* (or Midrise) and *SUNNYDENE* (Nos. 48 and 50), which were first occupied by Mr Garner and later by the Kilby family (1924). In 1941 Sunnydene was the home of retired Canon Frederick Hedley Joscelyne,

Fig 16.18 The Shrubbery, from a 1913 sale catalogue.

whose daughter Adeline was to marry, in 1944, her widowed neighbour, Albert Herbert at The Gables (No. 68). Adeline Herbert was one of the first women Readers in the Leicester diocese, licensed to minister in Quorn from 1970.

THE GABLES (No. 68), Swithland Lane, was an interesting and relatively small house.[72] Designed by Arnold Mitchell, whose original 1909 design won first prize in an Ideal Home Exhibition competition. Mitchell was a highly regarded architect in Europe and in Eygpt, whose practice enlarged worldwide. Initially built as an 'estate starter', the tenant in 1913 being a Mr G Taylor, The Gables was first offered for sale in 1913 at £950. It was perhaps appropriate that it was eventually bought, in 1916, by a fellow architect, also highly thought of in Leicestershire, one Albert Herbert. He enlarged the house considerably.

Albert Herbert (1875–1964) came from a Whetstone yeoman family. He was the third son of Henry Herbert, a building contractor. Herbert was educated in Leicester, trained as an architect under James Tait, worked for three years with London architects Lanchester & Richards and then returned to Leicester to administer his own practice. Most of his commissions were in the East Midlands, though some were international. He was among those who finally persuaded Leicester City Council not to demolish the Jewry Wall (1937). His profound interest in mediaeval architecture involved him in much ecclesiastical work, including fifty-seven major church restorations. Two larger ecclesiastical commissions were the completion of Northampton's Roman Catholic Cathedral (1963) and of the Church at Mount St Bernard's Abbey, Leics, where he was described in a local obituary as 'resolving in that building one of the most difficult architectural problems, the marriage of stillness and light'.

It was said of Herbert that 'his plans and drawings were remarkable for

Fig 16.19 The Gables in 1916, with Albert Herbert's son in the foreground.[73]

their accuracy and singular purity of line. As a youth he had roamed the streets of Leicester, frequently before breakfast, sketching and making measured drawings of interesting architectural features. In London he submitted himself to the discipline of the life class. In his maturity and old age he was never without his sketch book (his tailor provided a special pocket for it). And what he drew, he remembered. He was a helpful and illuminating conductor of excursions, presenting a re-creation of the whole life of a building, an experience that greatly enriched his hearers'.[74]

Herbert was the architect for St Leonard's Church, Swithland during the 1920s. The restoration work he presided over as architect was significant, and also sensitive to the integrity of the building.[75] He is buried in Swithland churchyard, along with his two wives, Dorothy (d. 1938) and Adeline (d. 1977).

ORCHARD HOUSE (Egerton) No. 70 Swithland Lane, was built at the same time as The Gables. The first owners were the Etchells. A later owner was James Alexander Vazeille Boddy,[76] member and vice-chairman of Swithland Parochial Church Council (1944–54). Boddy was the only son of the Revd. Alexander Boddy, vicar of All Saints, Monkswearmouth, the pioneer of the British Pentecostal Movement, who was descended from Mary Vazeille, whose second husband was John Wesley.[77] The Boddys gave the name Vazeille to their three children. Boddy is commemorated by a plaque on the north wall of the nave in Swithland church.

BRICKYARD FARM, ROTHLEY PLAIN FARM AND THE HOMESTEAD
After Merttens acquired Rothley Plain Farm in an exchange of lands with Lord Lanesborough, farming ceased there. Merttens had agreed to build a new farmhouse and outbuildings on the site of the old Swithland Lane brickworks. The new farm, Brickyard Farm, was managed by Stephen Richardson until 1922. Richardson was succeeded by Charles Copson in 1923.

It probably fell to estate architect, George E. Clare, to re-design the late eighteenth century Rothley Plain Farmhouse and its outbuildings into appropriate new dwellings for the new estate. Four smaller houses were created from the farm barn and buildings, Nos. 57–63 Swithland Lane. When, in 1974, Rothley Temple Estates marketed these cottages, all four had tenants:

No. 57   Mr B Hemsley, paying weekly rent of £ 1.04.
No. 59   Mrs K Pickthall, paying weekly rent of £ 0.94.
No. 61   Miss S. Marshall, paying weekly rent of £ 0.98.
No. 63   Mr G Baker, paying weekly rent of £ 1.04.

The re-designed Rothley Plain farmhouse was newly named *THE HOMESTEAD* (No. 65) and was bought in 1912 by Arnold Viccars, a director of Paton & Baldwin, manufacturers of knitting yarn. (Viccars' father, William Purdon Viccars of Anstey Pastures, was managing director of J. & J. Baldwin & Partners, later Paton & Baldwin). Arnold Viccars had many gifts and skills. He had a deep interest in education, especially adult education, and served as a member of council and governor of various colleges and schools. He had

Fig 16.20 (Above, left to right) 61, 59 and 57 Swithland Lane, 2011 photograph.

Fig. 16.21 (Left) The Homestead.

a special concern for the welfare of those he worked with, both employers and employees. He was a member of the Society of Artists, the Leicester Archaeological Society, and president of the Leics. and Rutland Folk Dance Society. As a trustee of Bradgate Woods, he was concerned with the possible reforestation of Charnwood. Viccars lived at The Homestead up to the time of his death in 1945. His funeral service was held at St Leonard's Church, and his memorial service at Leicester Cathedral. (His widowed daughter, Mary Leeson, lived in Brownhill Crescent for many years.) The Homestead was next bought by Harry Gee. The farmhouse and the adjoining four cottages were listed by Charnwood Borough Council in 1984.[78]

JUST NORTH OF THE HOMESTEAD, more houses were built. *WESTOVER* or Freshfield (No. 71 Swithland Lane) was built in 1909, to a design of Michael Bunney. It was described in a sales catalogue for 1934 as being 'in the best part of Swithland Lane'.[79] *BRENDON* (No. 73), sometimes known as Lexden, was built in 1912, as were *LYNTON* (No. 77) and *EASTFIELD* or Forest View (No. 79).

The first owner of Brendon was Charles Stibbe. Charles' father, Godfrey Stibbe, had left Holland for Glasgow in order to set up a yarn agency, but moved, first to London and then in 1890 to Leicester. In the 1920s, he patented various knitting techniques. Stibbe soon realized that it would be more profitable to sell machinery, and set about an agency arrangement with Wildman and with Spiers & Tompkins. Over the next fifty years his company was to keep and expand the yarn and fabric merchant business, to import and assemble machinery, and, in the 1930s, to build their own machines. Over the next thirty years, the Stibbe Group consolidated by expanding their own range of machines and by buying S.A. Monk. By the 1950s, the Stibbe and Bentley Groups were the only British builders of knitting machines. Stibbe was a member of the Leicester Rotary Club. In 1918, when he was secretary he marked his secretaryship 'by offering a pair of socks to any Rotarian who could find a mistake in the roster! It is not recorded whether any socks were won, but throughout his membership he frequently gave items of knitwear or hosiery from his own factory to important visitors. Only occasionally were they paid for by the club'.[80] In 1946, Harry Hay Gimson's family became the owners of Brendon.

MAPLECOTE and *NILGIRIS* (Nos. 81 and 83, Swithland Lane) are a pair of cottages built in 1912. Nilgiris was bought by the Gimson (engineering) family. All the Gimsons were exceptionally gifted in their chosen fields of interest – the most notable family member being Ernest Gimson, a leading and influential member of the Arts and Crafts movement, both as a designer and maker of fine furniture. Other members of the Gimson family were involved in engineering (originally Josiah and Benjamin – the Vulcan Engineering Works), timber (Harry – the Gimson Timber business) and fine china and pottery.

Maplecote was bought first by a Mr Backhouse, who was followed in 1923 by Walter and Mary Kilby and their young children Cedric and

Gweneth. Walter Kilby, Mary Kilby and Gweneth Kilby served Swithland church successively as church wardens in an uninterrupted line from 1928 to 2009. Walter Kilby and his brother Frank (who lived at Sunnydene from 1924) worked at Stead and Simpson. Gweneth Kilby married Ben Gimson, 'the boy next door', in 1947. They lived first at Eastfield (No. 79 Swithland Lane) then at The Gables (No. 68) before finally moving to live in the Ernest Gimson house, Lea Cottage, at Ulverscroft.

Fig 16.22 (Left) Miss Gweneth Kilby in Maplecote's back garden.

Fig 16.23 (Above) Maplecote, Ben and Gweneth Gimson after their wedding, 22 March 1947.

EASTFIELD or Forest View (No. 79) was built in 1912. It was bought first by Mr Savage who sold it to Mr Ramsey after the First World War. The next buyer, in the early 1920s, was Clarence Sadd, a banker. Sadd started work in Manchester at the Midland Bank when he was fifteen, but rapid promotion came his way, including the position of manager at Leicester's Granby Street branch. In 1933 he moved to the bank's head office in London, rising to director, chief executive and finally vice-chairman. He was knighted in 1945.

As treasurer of the Lawn Tennis Association, Sadd was instrumental in reviving Wimbledon after 1945. It was said of him[81] that 'he was an early exponent of the need for cultivating personal relations within banking'. When Sadd took the train from Rothley Station he would sometimes give 6d to Charles Hodkinson, the station manager, to keep the train waiting while he walked up and down the platform to see who was also on the train so he could join him in the same carriage. Ben (son of Josiah) and Gweneth Gimson, moved into Eastfield after their marriage in 1947.

The 1913 Sale

Some of the homes in Rothley Garden Suburb were let initially to their occupants and only later sold. The auction catalogue lists the particulars of a sale of seven lots on Wednesday 18th June 1913 by Messrs. Warner,

Sheppard & Wade, auctioneers: The Spinneys, The Ridgeway, 2 acres occupied by A.H. Bennett Esq.; The Gables, Swithland Lane, 1,800 sq. yards occupied by G. Taylor Esq.; The Shrubbery, Swithland Lane, 1,400 sq. yards occupied by G.E. Clare Esq.; plots of land on The Ridgeway, 3,500 sq. yards, and Swithland Lane, 1,200 sq. yards, 1,350 sq. yards and 1,400 sq. yards. A note in the catalogue advises that the 'houses were built to start the Rothley Temple Building Estate, and having served their purpose will be offered at reserved prices far below their cost'. All lots were served by Leicester Gas and Water. The particulars of the sale catalogue were printed by W.H. Lead, printer and lithographer, who was one of the first to buy an establishment on the estate – Holly Lodge, The Ridgeway.

Inter-War Development

The First World War effectively stopped all building development on Rothley Plain and it did not re-start until the 1920s. The estate was administered from the offices at the western end of The Ridgeway by land agent J. Bruce Galloway, who lived first at 71 Swithland Lane and then at 11 Brownhill Crescent. Galloway was also secretary of Bradgate Woods Ltd. and the managing director of Rothley Temple Estates. There is a memorial mural tablet in his memory in Rothley Temple Chapel, saying simply 'John Bruce Galloway, 1886–1949, Guide and Friend'.

In 1925, the estate land was transferred to a private company, Rothley Park Estate, Ltd. The pattern of ribbon development had resumed on both The Ridgeway and on Swithland Lane – where building now began to extend beyond the cross-road with The Ridings. Building also began on Westfield Lane, including Brownhill Crescent. The farmland adjacent to the housing development was let to new tenants – Charles Copson took over Brickyard Farm from Stephen Richardson in 1922. And, at the end of the war, Harry Hyman moved from his small holding at Linford Cottage to become tenant of Westfield Farm.

Along The Ridgeway 1918–39

On The Ridgeway only four more new houses were built after 1912. On the northern side, *COVERTSIDE* (No. 38), was built for Frederick Mawby. Mawby's company interest was Buswell & Mawby leather mercers, of Nichols Street, Leicester. Arthur Pateman and his family moved in c. 1928 and lived there for some twenty-five years. He was the chairman of Imperial Typewriter Co. Ltd, which started in 1902 and became a limited company based in Wharf Street, Leicester in 1908. The unique selling point for the Imperial was that the typewriter could be easily split into two major parts – the keyboard mechanism and the main frame. It was, therefore, just a quick change of part for a different language to be typed. Following a visit to the works from the King and Queen, sales soared. Over ninety percent of their sales were for export.

On the other side of The Ridgeway, *RICHMOND* (No. 19) was designed for Charles Edwin Smith. In order to add a nursery, the house was extended

Fig 16.24 Sir Cyril and Lady Osborne, with daughters Jill and Hazel at West Acre.

in 1921 by architects Harding & Williams of 13, New Walk, Leicester. The Smith family remained at Richmond for over twenty-five years. Charles Smith was in business with his uncle, John Hardy Smith, in the partnership Staines & Smith. When the partnership dissolved, Charles joined J. Hardy Smith & Sons, leather suppliers, at St Mark's Works, Foundry Lane, Leicester. The company was later sold to British BATA. Smith was followed at Richmond in 1952 by James Stanley Hartridge, a director of British Thread Mills, sewing cotton and thread manufacturers, of East Park Road, Leicester.

WEST ACRE (No. 25) was built for the Hanfords. It was bought in 1935 from Mrs Freda Mary Hanford by Cyril Osborne, a stockbroker and MP for Louth (from 1945). The Osbornes moved from West Acre in 1956 to Kinchley House, Kinchley Lane, at the north end of the Plain. Cyril Osborne was taught his trade by Sir Arthur Wheeler, at one time the most influential stockbroker in the Midlands. During the First World War, Wheeler dedicated his energies to selling war bonds, and for this he was created a baronet in the 1920 New Year Honours List. In the late 1920s Wheeler sought to consolidate the hosiery industry by creating the British Hosiery Trust. Family companies Allens of Macclesfield, Aristoc of Derbyshire,

Byfords of Leicester and Woodford, and Wormleighton of Leicester merged their interests into this trust. After a few years, however, the trust failed and was broken up with the families taking back ownership of their companies. Thirty years later, two of those families were again joined, this time more happily, by a marriage between an Osborne and a Byford. Wheeler, however, was ruined by the Depression, when he was declared bankrupt and in 1931 was jailed for twelve months for fraud. After his release he retired from business.

Along Swithland Lane 1918–39

Most of the inter-war development in Rothley Garden Suburb took place along Swithland Lane. Thirty six new houses were built between 1930 and 1951. Most of these were much less ambitious than those built in the early stages of the development. The plots were smaller and the residences less substantial. Instead of a country estate, their style seems to have had more in common with a suburban development – reflecting the changed economic and social circumstances that had come about after the Great War. Those who bought these properties continued to be from the professional classes or to own manufacturing companies, especially knitwear and hosiery, boots and shoes. There were, though, some slightly more substantial houses built in the middle part of Swithland Lane, among them *BRACONDALE* and *DANEWAY*, both built c. 1924.

BRACONDALE (No. 72) was built for Harold D.M. Barnett, partner in Harding & Barnett, a firm of Leicester solicitors. His son, Geoffrey Barnett, also qualified as a solicitor and followed his father, not only in business, but also in the ownership of Bracondale (1945). In 1941, whilst in the army, Geoffrey Barnett had married Isabel Morag Marshall (1918–1980), a qualified doctor. Isabel Barnett, who gave up her medical career in 1948, rose to public prominence as a television personality in BBC's 'What's my Line?' programme. In the early 1950s, Geoffrey was chairman of Barrow RDC for three years, and served as Lord Mayor of Leicester 1952–53. He was knighted in 1953 for his political and public services to the city of Leicester. About this time, the Barnetts moved from Bracondale to live in the White House, Cossington. *DANEWAY* (No. 76) was built for Leicester timber merchant Harry Hay Gimson at a time when he had a growing family of three children. After the war, in 1946, he and his wife moved to Brendon. *BERESFORD* (No. 155) was built a little later, c. 1933. When it was sold in 1945, it was done 'under instructions from Alderman A.H. Swain'.[82]

The Ridings, Westfield Lane and Brownhill Crescent

There were no properties at all on The Ridings on the 1808 Enclosure map. In 1808 the land there belonged to the Earls of Stamford, who exchanged with the Earl of Lanesborough in 1874, then in 1903 Lanesborough did an exchange deal with Merttens. But Merttens' 1909 plan focused along The Ridgeway and Swithland Lane, and it was not until after the Merttens land was conveyed to the Rothley Temple Estates in 1925 that new building was started along The Ridings. Linford Cottage, No. 120 The Ridings, was already built by then. On the 1925 conveyance document the property and land there was described as 'Linford Cottage and Paddock, Orchard and Buildings, Paddock'. At the time it was tenanted from Merttens to H. and J.L. Hyman, who also had the tenancy of Westfield Farm.

The only additional development the Temple Estates made along The Ridings between 1921 and 1929 was to build three new houses – there seems to have been no evidence of plans at the time for any more. *ABERFELDY* (No. 28) was built for Mr Spurway c. 1920, then bought by Sydney Burton c. 1924. Burton was a director of the box-manufacturing company, Jane Cox of York Street, Leicester. *BRYNGARTH* (No. 23 The Ridings), opposite The Ridgeway, was built in 1927 for Walter J. Basford, managing director from 1927–45 of F. Hewitt & Son, Ltd, publishers of the *Leicester Mercury*. (A subsequent managing director, Mr C.T. Barton, was later to buy Fairfield on The Ridgeway.) On the same side of the road, on the bend in The Ridings where the original Rothley Plain borders on to Rothley Temple land, *PAX* (No. 75), a three-bedroomed dormer house, was built. It was owned by the Packe family (which may be why the house was named Pax).

Westfield Lane saw very little housing development after the First World War; fifteen houses had been built by 1929, then only another five before 1951. Brownhill Crescent, though established as a road off Westfield Lane, also saw a modicum of housing development, at least in the first half of the century.

Rothley Garden Suburb: Number of Houses Completed (cumulative)

	1908	1912	1929	1951
Brownhill Crescent	0	0	3	7
Gipsy Lane	0	0	0	0
The Ridgeway	9	13	17	17
The Ridings	0	0	4	4
Swithland Lane	21	38	73	99
Westfield Lane	0	3	15	20

Source: Ordnance Survey; Sale Particulars; Register of Electors

ROTHLEY PLAIN FOOTBALL CLUB had their ground nearly opposite to Cross Lane on The Ridings. Eric Hyman of Linford Cottage, (No. 120 The Ridings) played with, among others, Fred Stacey and Harry Hancock. At some point in the 1930s the club re-organized itself and changed its name to Rothley Plain United F.C.. The playing ground, which was on the corner of The Ridings and Cross Lane, was known as Hickling's Field. Dr T. Maitland Gibson, who had played for Leicester City whilst a medical student, was one of the vice-presidents of the club. The club goal-posts were held at Linford Cottage. Players included Les John, Alf Copson, Steve Dimmock (a goalkeeper who had once had a trial with Aston Villa), and Morris, Bert and Cliff Staples. On the side of the field nearest to 'Pax' was a small track known as Tea Pot Lane; it led nowhere! A little brick hut had been built in the small field next door to Hickling's Field which served as an allotment or kitchen garden for Mr Exton from Rothley village.

The 'North End' of Rothley Plain

During the first half of the twentieth century, the area of Rothley Plain north of the Nunckley Hill mineral railway saw little change. The land adjacent to the Swithland boundary was incorporated into Hall Farm, Swithland; it was farmed by Ambrose Copson until 1932, and then by Harry Banbury. An area of land between Kinchley Lane and the mineral railway was farmed initially by John Woolley from The Laurels, Swithland, until it, too, became part of Hall Farm.

North of Kinchley Lane, Lord Lanesborough let land to the Mountsorrel Granite Company. Their principal quarry in Rothley Plain, Nunckley Hill, continued in production until 1924. Shortly afterwards, the company's chairman, Charles Martin, built himself a substantial residence on Kinchley Lane, *KINCHLEY HOUSE* (No. 12). The granite for its construction came from the Broad Hill quarry in Mountsorrel and was transported on the mineral railway.

Broad Hill became the principal centre of the company's activities, although it owned rights on other land in the area that it later developed, including Buddon Wood. The expansion of the Broad Hill quarry, across the old Mountsorrel-Woodhouse Road, may have been a factor leading to the construction of Halstead Road. At the quarry, meanwhile, the production of setts and kerbs was gradually phased out in favour of crushed stone for the construction industry, and sett-making ceased in 1936.

Kinchley House became the venue for Sunday School outings from Mountsorrel. Sometimes the children would ride in an open mineral wagon and be taken from Mountsorrel to Swithland Sidings for an outing and picnic at the Reservoir. Rothley Common, sometimes known as Mountsorrel Common, was a further attraction for a weekend outing. Two former railway carriages were put on the Common and served as huts. A charabanc from Leicester would bring parties of people to visit and picnic there.

The 1950s and Beyond

The Rothley Temple Estate was sold in 1973, twenty years after Swithland Hall Estate in 1954. The Estate had remained substantially intact until then. In 1973 it still owned 786 acres, including the golf course, several houses in Town Green Street, Rothley and in Swithland Lane, and five farms: Brookfield Farm (156 acres); Park Farm and Southfields Farm (265 acres); Westfield Farm (71 acres); Brickyard Farm[83] (111 acres). The sale marked the end of an era.

There was an attempt, at the end of the 1980s, to 'complete' the garden suburb with a whole new development, The Gallops, to fill in the undeveloped land bordered by Westfield Lane, The Ridings and Swithland Lane. The plans, put forward by David Wilson Estates (on behalf of Rothley

Temple Estates), provided for forty-four country houses, a parkland setting with 'treed walks', stables and paddocks, tennis club, new spinneys and woodland. There was much opposition, and planning permission was not granted.

It would appear that significant amounts of undeveloped land was bought up by potential developers in 1973, so it is likely that other proposals will come forward in due season. Certainly social and economic changes in the last sixty years have had their effect – local industries have declined, family companies of past years have been taken over by much larger concerns, even professional practices have merged in the face of competition. New industries and professions continue to develop. Those seeking to buy homes in the Rothley Plain area today, though, probably share many characteristics with their predecessors – not least that they look for larger, more luxurious houses, with space and privacy, set in attractive countryside. Much of the change since the 1960s has been characterized in part by home-owners with extensive grounds either selling part of the grounds for infill housing, or, when buying, modernizing and extending the properties they have bought. When The Gallops proposals were put forward, many indicated unease about new development in the remaining open spaces, yet there is little evidence of commitment, from planners or buyers, to retaining the 'Arts and Crafts' vision of the original development.[84] Very few properties on the estate have been listed, so the constant modernization and extension of properties, together with the new-build styles, is gradually destroying the overall architectural integrity of the area.

Notes to Chapter 16

1. Swithland Lane, house numbers 65–171 and 68–164 inside Rothley Plain (now in Swithland ecclesiastical parish); house numbers 1–63, 2–66 lie inside Thurcaston and Cropston ecclesiastical parish; house numbers beyond 171 lie inside Mountsorrel ecclesiastical parish. The Ridings house numbers 120–128 and 125–137 lie inside Swithland ecclesiastical parish; the houses beyond the bend and along The Ridgeway, lie in the extra-parochial area of Rothley Temple; Kinchley Lane and Rushey Lane lie in Swithland ecclesiastical parish, land which was part of Swithland's mediaeval manor.
2. Correspondence, Swithland Church Archives.
3. William Marshall, Review and Abstract of the County Reports to the Board of Agriculture, 1818 wrote: 'The county's only wastes of any account are known by the name of Charnwood Forest and Rothley Plain; they are both of them properly commons, or sheep-walks.'
4. The court was part of English forest jurisdiction. It was held three times a year before the forest verderers by the steward of the court. The Swanimote (Swainmote) got its name because the swains – local freeholders – were the jurymen. They ruled on matters such as who had grazing rights and what restrictions should be placed on the number of animals in order to conserve the area.
5. J. Spencer & T. Spencer, *Leicestershire and Rutland Notes and Quotes*, 1895.
6. Leics. RO, DE1982/181, Volume containing various surveys, rolls etc. of various manors including Groby Manor.
7. The right to feed swine and other livestock.
8. G.F. Farnham, 'Charnwood Forest, The Charnwood Manors', *Leicestershire Archaeological Society Transactions*, 1928/29, p. 111
9. Leics. RO, DE1982/237, Interrogatores, 1611, copied 1810, Babington v Grey.

10. Leics. RO, DE1982/181, Survey of Groby Manor, 1658.
11. ibid., List of copyholders and leaseholders in Groby lordship, 1677.
12. Leics. RO, 13D 28/1/23, Case of Ralph Smalley, with the opinion of John Belfield, concerning the right of common on Rothley Plain, 1728.
13. Leics. RO, DE1982/181, Lease, 20 Jan 1668.
14. ibid., 1677 copies and leases.
15. Newtown Linford Church Registers.
16. John Nichols, *The History and Antiquities of the County of Leicester*, vol. 3, part 1, p. 131.
17. Leics. RO, DE1982/182, John Dawson, lease dated 12 Dec 1757 (Estate Book).
18. See also Monk, Agricultural Report for Leicestershire, 1794.
19. Leics. RO, 2D31/406/1-20, Letter and papers relating to Rothley Plain.
20. Leics. RO, QS47/2/4, Enclosure Award, Charnwood Forest and Rothley Plain, 1829.
21. Leics. RO, DE1982, Earl of Stamford & Warrington Lease Books, 1838.
22. Leics. RO, DE453/171(a)(b), 1843 Survey, farm 'in the occupation of Joseph Skevington'.
23. Leics. RO, DE1750, Box 33, Conveyance, 1874, Stamford to Butler, land including Rothley Plain Farm and farm in Swithland (Stephen Simpson, tenant). See also Leics. RO, DE453/198, Sale, 1873.
24. *Leicester Journal*, 17 Jan 1840.
25. ibid., 21 Mar 1862.
26. Leics. RO, DG9/394, Sale of land, 11 January 1859.
27. Leics. RO, DE1750, Box 1, Devisees in Trust for Sale under will of Mr Joseph Cuffling to Earl of Lanesborough, 27 Oct 1862 and other documents related to the Brick Kiln closes, and other small parts of 'old enclosure' property in Rothley Plain, which were gradually 'collected' by the Danvers/Lanesboroughs.
28. ibid., Box 12, Mr Cuffling's trustees, to Lanesborough, copy of purchase agreement, 1865.
29. Swithland Parish Records.
30. Mountsorrel Granite Company archives, Leicestershire and Warwickshire Granite, paper, JBF Earle.
31. Leics. RO, DE1750, Box 1, Lease of a granite quarry to John Martin, 29 Sept 1856; Box 32, lease of stone quarries, 30 Jan 1858.
32. ibid., Box 33, Conveyance, 1896.
33. *Leicestershire: Historical, Biographical and Pictorial*, Alan North, London 1909.
34. In 1921, he was recorded as living at Bilton Rise (formerly Plex House) Old Bilton, Rugby, Warks. In 1924 he is recorded on the house deeds for Linford Cottage as living at 'Rodeley' Bilton, Rugby.
35. A. K. B. Evans, 'The custody of Leicester's archives from 1273 to 1947', *Leicestershire Archaeological and Historical Society Transactions* 66, 1992.
36. Frederick Merttens of Rothley Temple and Rugby (1849–1935); Fritz Roel Merttens (1898–1919); Margaret Joanna Merttens (1867–1954); John-Bernard Merttens (1907–1909); Inez D.H. Merttens (1909–1938).
37. Leics. RO, DE1750, Box 14, Agreement to land exchange between sixth Earl of Lanesborough and Merttens, 5 July 1906.
38. Merttens donated the land for Rothley Station to the railway company.
39. On early postcards, though, it is just called 'New Road'.
40. A. Hamilton Thompson, 'The Leicestershire Archaeological Society in the Present Century', *Transactions 1939–40*, vol. 21, part 2, p.124.
41. ibid, p. 140.
42. Leicestershire Archaeological Society website.
43. *The Wyvern: A Topical Critical and Humourous Journal*, 7 April 1893.
44. ibid.
45. ibid.
46. Leics. RO, *Who's Who in Leicestershire*, 1935, Ebenezer Bayliss & Sons Ltd.
47. Leicester Diocesan News and Views, July 1970.
48. See also Shirley Ellis, *A Mill on the Soar – a personal and company narrative*, privately printed and published, 1978.
49. Leicester City Council website, Lord Mayors of Leicester.
50. Leics. RO, *Nottinghamshire, Leicestershire and Rutland – Social and Political Leaders*.
51. The other family were the Stibbes, who were to live along Swithland Lane.
52. Howard's overall ambition was not fully realised until the New Town programmes some

thirty years later. Loughborough's Shelthorpe Estate was probably one of Leicestershire's earlier developments along a more philanthropic line.

53. *Edinburgh Magazine*, Dec. 1848
54. Quoted on the Hampstead Garden Suburb website.
55. ibid.
56. G. Tucker & Sons Ltd, Brick and Tile Manufacturers, Loughborough.
57. *Leicestershire: Historical, Biographical and Pictorial*, Alan North, London, 1909.
58. By 1908, nine houses had been built on The Ridgeway, and twenty-one on Swithland Lane.
59. *Rothley Garden Suburb, For Ideal Home Life*, February 1909, sales brochure.
60. Frank Sleath of Rothley, Tuckers of Loughborough, Hyman's Nursery, Rothley, etc.
61. *Rothley Garden Suburb, For Ideal Home Life*, February 1909, sales brochure.
62. *The Builder*, 11 February, 1927, p. 237.
63. D.W. Galsworthy & E. Guy Dawber, *Old Cottages, Farm Houses and other Stone Buildings in the Cotswold District*, Batsford, 1904.
64. Wikipedia 2009.
65. Ideal Home Exhibition, 1910, catalogue.
66. The house opposite was named West Acre.
67. Leics. RO, DE 6153/3, Sale Catalogue, St Bernard's, 1967.
68. Leics. RO, County Hall records.
69. Its sale in 2008/9 has occasioned significant building changes.
70. cf. entry for Uplands.
71. *The Link*, September 1970.
72. The Gables has been extended at least twice since it was built (post 1920), both times by its owner, the architect Albert Herbert.
73. Herbert sent this postcard to his son in 1916.
74. Leics. RO, *Leics. Archaeological and Historical Society Transactions*, XL, 1964–5.
75. Though it looks as if, from some plans of his in the Swithland Church Archives, he toyed with the idea of pulling down the eighteenth century south aisle, replacing it with what might have been there in the Middle Ages, and also constructing a new matching north aisle to the church, on the assumption that one might have been there in the Middle Ages. It didn't happen!
76. Boddy, James Alexander Vazeille, 17 July 1895–14 August 1954. Lieut. 64 Squadron, 18th Battalion Durham Light Infantry; WWI; married Marjorie d'Arcy 1920; Exec. Council, Royal British Legion; Deputy Lieut. Leics; Home Guard WWII; OBE 1953. One of Boddy's sisters, Jane Vazeille Boddy, a CR sister in Grahamstown SA, was elected Mother Joanna Mary CR in 1934.
77. Sadly, the Wesleys' marriage was not a very happy one.
78. Charnwood Borough Council website, listed buildings, Rothley.
79. Leics. RO, DE4674/470.
80. Thompson and McIntosh. A History of the Rotary Club in Leicester, accessed at www.rotary-leicester.org.uk
81. *The Times*, obituary, 3 October 1962.
82. Leics. RO, DE4674/2104, Sale catalogue.
83. Brickyard Farm and its land together with the row of three terraced cottages (Nos. 57, 59 and 61 Swithland Lane), were sold by auction on 29th September 1983.
84. Rothley Ridgeway Conservation Area was approved by Charnwood Borough Council in 2010. The following properties were listed: 57–63 Swithland Lane; Lodge, Turret, Gate Piers and Gates at Rothley Court Hotel; Nos. 33, 54, 60, 62 The Ridgeway; outbuilding between 57 and 65 Swithland Lane; Rothley Court Hotel and the Chapel; Rothley Station; Site of Roman Villa, The Ridgeway; The Homestead, 65 Swithland Lane.

– CHAPTER 17 –

The Old Order

During the hundred years preceding the First World War, life in Swithland showed few outward signs of change. The working lives of nearly everyone who lived in the village revolved around the Hall, its estate and the village itself. This remained the situation certainly up until the First World War, and, to a large extent, through the inter-war years. A contemporary hymn spoke of 'the rich man in his castle, the poor man at his gate, God made them high and lowly, each in his own estate'.[1] The description was certainly appropriate to Swithland, though the Earls would probably have argued that 'the rich man in his castle' tag was not quite as accurate as they would like it to have been. Each resident, however, was very clear as to the boundaries of their 'own estate'.

Local building work in nineteenth century Swithland reflected this traditional order. Before 1840, the only buildings in the village were the Hall, the Church, the Rectory and all those others that housed local workers or catered for village needs. In the 1830s, the fifth Earl had built himself a fine hall on a new site. Between 1840 and 1860 he rebuilt and re-furbished the village school and then the homes of those who worked on his estate. His successors, however, did little or nothing to change or improve the estate. Only one other new house was built in the nineteenth century – a new rectory for Rector Murray Dixon in 1898.

In 1903, however, 'new money' made its first move into Swithland. Archibald Turner and his wife moved into a new, but relatively, small house at the Woodhouse end of the village. The land was available for sale to Turner as it did not belong to the Hall Estate. Originally thatched with heather, No. 24 Main Street, variously known as Wood Lane End and Lane End Cottage, was the Turners' home until 1908, when they bought another property on the other side of the street. The Cottage, No. 1 Main Street, was also one of the few Swithland properties that did not belong to the Hall Estate. When the village was enclosed in 1798, this land was jointly owned by the Hon. A.R.B. Danvers and the Marquis of Hastings. The slate quarry on the site and an old workman's cottage were let to slate-workers. The Pollards of Swithland owned an adjacent plot, and sited one of their slate engraving workshops there. The Turners re-designed and extended the old slate industry buildings on that site as their new home, and soon began to contribute to the life of Swithland village and church.

A few years earlier, just a mile down the road towards Rothley, other new 'rich men's castles' began to be built on Rothley Plain. The financial good fortune of the urban industrialists and their desire to display that fortune in their home circumstances led to the development and steady expansion of the new 'garden suburb' there. This expanding estate of attractive privately-owned houses stood in stark contrast to the village and the Swithland Hall Estate, where the effects of national rural depression and depopulation through the latter years of the nineteenth century were increasingly evident.

Census

The ten-yearly census returns from 1841–1901 give some information about life in Swithland in the last half of the nineteenth century. Had we access to the earlier returns, which were administered locally by the overseers of the poor and the clergy and now lost, we might know a little more than we do about Swithland in the first thirty years of the century. We know from other sources that in 1801 three hundred and twenty-two people lived in Swithland's fifty-eight dwelling houses, but no more. These early censuses recorded information about each dwelling and its inhabitants, their names and ages, their birth place and the occupation of the head of household. At first the questions were fairly basic, but in 1811 questions were asked about why some of the houses were unoccupied, in 1821 people's ages were recorded, and, from 1831, their occupations. From 1841, however, the census was administered and archived nationally, and eventually made available for public information.[2]

The 1841 Census, taken in June, showed that fifty-six of Swithland's dwellings were inhabited and eight, including the Hall, were not. The population of two hundred and ninety-five people consisted of eighty-nine adult males (fifteen years and over), of whom nine were aged sixty-five and over, and one over eighty years old. There were eighty-six adult females, eight of them over sixty-five and two over eighty. Of the under fifteens, there were fifty-seven boys and sixty-three girls. Only eighteen people, six per cent of the inhabitants, were born outside of Leicestershire. Of those who listed their occupation, there were five farmers and thirty agricultural labourers. Other 'independent' or working males were listed as two cottagers, a carpenter, shoemaker, blacksmith, butcher, slate cleaver, gravestone engraver, gamekeeper, clergyman, bricklayer, gardener, miller and a labourer in the woods. There were five labourers at the slate quarries and two labourers at the stone pits. The thirty-two servants included nineteen males (sixteen of whom were farm servants, two at the Griffin Inn, and one at the Mill) and thirteen females, employed mainly at the Rectory, the Hall and in the farmhouses. Ten ladies, mostly widows, described themselves as 'independent'.

The 1851 Census included additional questions about the relationship of each individual to the head of household, and whether any were blind or dumb. More detailed information about places of birth was required. Details were also noted of inhabitants who were living on vessels in inland waters or at sea (including the Royal Navy and the merchant navy), those serving abroad with the forces, or with the East India Company, and of British subjects residing overseas. The Swithland returns of 30th March listed fifty-nine inhabited houses in the parish. The Earl and his family were not in residence. Of the two hundred and eighty-three people resident there were eighty-nine adult males (fifteen years and over), three of whom were aged sixty-five years or more, but none over eighty years. There were eighty-eight adult females; four were over sixty-five and none over eighty. Of the under-fifteen year olds, there were fifty-two boys and fifty-four girls. One hundred and sixty-two (fifty-eight per cent) of inhabitants had been born in Swithland, thirty-two who were either heads of households or their wives. Eighty-six of the other residents (thirty per cent) had been born in Leicestershire, and only thirty-five people (twelve per cent) outside the county. There were twenty-three domestic servants; forty-nine agricultural and outdoor labourers, eleven ladies with independent occupations (school mistress, dressmaker, two lace workers, seamstress, chairwoman, four laundresses, a bonnet maker), seven farmers, twelve other labourers (slate quarries, stone pits, bricklayers), twelve other male workers (rag and bone gatherer, schoolmaster, carpenter, three shoemakers, a blacksmith, a (gravestone) engraver, a gamekeeper, a clergyman, a publican and a miller). Ten boys aged fifteen years and younger were listed as working – one of them was fourteen, two were thirteen and one was twelve. Only five girls, two aged fifteen years and three aged thirteen years, were working.

In 1861 fifty-four dwellings were inhabited and the population totalled two hundred and fifty-one persons. Eighty-five males over fifteen years old were listed and eighty-six females. There were forty-three boys younger than fifteen – of whom thirteen were Bunneys – and thirty-seven girls. There were six Bunney households in the village that year. Forty-seven per cent of the listed residents were born in Swithland, thirty-seven per cent in other parts of Leicestershire and sixteen per cent outside the county. There were thirty-eight labourers, twenty-five of whom were agricultural, seven gardeners or gardener's labourers, and six quarrymen. There were twenty-four domestic servants, nine farmers, three millers, a shoemaker, four blacksmiths, two butchers, a gamekeeper, a clergyman, a slate cleaver, an engraver, three bricklayers, a woodsman, two game-keepers, a keeper's son, a schoolmaster, a coal-dealer, a tailor and draper, two cordwainers, a shepherd, an inn-keeper, a lodge-keeper, a brewer and a groom. Of the working ladies, three were lace runners, three laundresses, and one a shopkeeper. There was a school teacher, a school mistress, a dress-maker and a cotton-winder. Two of the single ladies, one of whom was blind, described themselves as 'retired'. Despite the Earl not being in residence, there were obviously more villagers employed on the Swithland Hall Estate, both as indoor and outdoor staff. For the first time, three of the young village boys are listed as 'school boys'.

Minor changes were made to the census questions between 1871 and

1901. From 1871 until 1911 people were asked whether any inhabitant was an 'imbecile or idiot or feeble-minded'. Swithland recorded none. In 1871 and 1881 people were asked whether they were employed or unemployed (the latter question was not asked again until 1931). From 1891 a distinction was made between employers and employees, and from 1901 there was a question about residents working from home.

In Swithland in 1871, fifty-three households are listed and two hundred and forty-two people. There were seventy-seven adult males, two of whom were over eighty, and seventy-nine females. One of the females was recorded as being blind. Of the children under fifteen years of age, forty-seven were boys and forty-nine girls. Forty-five males were listed as outdoor labourers, twenty-seven in agriculture, six in gardening, seven in the quarries and five bricklayers. There were eight farmers and twenty-five indoor servants. The self-employed and other males included an engine-driver, five blacksmiths, a tailor and draper, two tailor's apprentices, a threshing-machine proprietor, a retired carpenter, five joiners, a stone mason, a woodman, a retired soldier (Chelsea Pensioner), a schoolmaster, a pupil teacher, a publican, a gamekeeper, the rector, two millers, a coachman, a groom and a grocer. There were twelve self-employed females, a post-office mistress, a seamstress, two dressmakers, five laundresses (one retired), a grocer, a trimming maker, a sewing mistress, and eight females not working, excluding wives of householders. Again, the Earl and his household were not in residence.

The 1881 Census recorded forty-seven households which housed eighty-five men and seventy-five women, forty-three boys under fifteen and forty girls. Of these, five were farmers and thirty-eight were in indoor service. There were thirty-four outdoor labourers, twenty-five in agriculture, one slate cleaver and eight gardeners; twenty-eight men were self-employed and there were eight other males. Their occupations were listed as: a tailor and draper, a journeyman tailor, another tailor, three bricklayers, three blacksmiths, a printer, two gamekeepers, a joiner, a grocer, a horse-dealer, a schoolmaster, an inn keeper, the rector, two coachmen, three grooms, a butler and an under-butler, two footmen, a page boy and a miller. There were seven self-employed females: a shop-keeper, three laundresses, a seamstress, the post-mistress, and the sewing-mistress. The Earl was in residence that year, which accounted for the larger percentage of indoor staff in the census.

In the 1891 Census, forty-eight households were listed, but there was a significant population drop. Only two hundred and eight persons were recorded, some forty fewer persons than in 1881, mainly in the under fifteens. Seventy-eight adult males were resident, seventy-six adult females, twenty-seven boys under fifteen and twenty-nine girls. There were five farmers, thirty-five outdoor labourers, twenty-six of whom were agricultural workers, three worked in the quarries and six in gardening. Of the self-employed and other males there were two grooms, two coachmen, a farm bailiff, a bricklayer, a builder, a mason, a provisions dealer, a farm dealer, a blacksmith, a licensed victualler, the rector, two gamekeepers and a threshing-engine driver. The twenty-four domestic and indoor servants were mostly at the Hall. Of the self-employed and other females listed, two were seamstresses and three laundresses; there was a school-mistress, a charwoman, the postmistress and a shop-mistress. Forty children were listed as scholars. The Earl and his household were in residence.

In 1901, the two hundred and fourteen residents inhabited forty-six dwellings, with four dwellings unoccupied. There were seventy-eight adult males, seventy-seven adult females, twenty-nine boys and thirty girls. There were five farmers and three graziers. Among the twenty-nine outdoor servants, seventeen were farm labourers, two were quarry men etc, and five were gardeners. There was one waterworks labourer, a road repairer, and three wood-fellers. Nineteen males were self-employed or in a profession: the rector, two carters, a blacksmith, wheelwright and apprentice, two gamekeepers and an under-gamekeeper, a builder, a bricklayer, a grocer, a carpenter, a commercial traveller, a traveller in the boot trade, a licensed victualler, two coachmen and one groom. In all there were twenty-four indoor servants (fifteen at the Hall), and seven self-employed and other females – the school teacher, another school mistress, the sub-postmistress, two laundresses and two dressmakers. Of the boys and girls, forty-one were listed as scholars and twelve were under school age. Two under-fifteen year old boys laboured as agricultural boys and one as a stable boy. The Earl was again in residence and with a full household.

Full census details after 1901 are not yet available (2010). The 1911 Census included a new question about the fertility of marriage, a question prompted by a concern about falling birth rates. It also distinguished between occupation and industry. In 1921, people were further asked about their education and how they travelled to work. In 1931, the onset of widespread economic depression reduced the scope of the census, and some of the questions that had been introduced in 1911 and 1921 were dropped. The outbreak of war in 1939 meant that no census was taken in 1941, but peacetime prompted another expansion in 1951. Questions regarding place of work, educational standards, fertility and household amenities were introduced. This broadening of scope has continued to characterize each subsequent census and to reflect sociological change. In 1961, for example, a question about educational and professional qualifications was included, in 1981 one about the number of cars and vans owned by each household, and in 2001 a question about each individual's health.

Place of Birth

Over the years, a decreasing percentage of Swithland inhabitants were born and bred in the village. In 1841, the census simply distinguished between those born inside or outside Leicestershire, and showed that ninety-four per cent of Swithland residents were Leicestershire folk. In 1851, a more specific question revealed that fifty-eight per cent of residents were born in Swithland, thirty per cent elsewhere in Leicestershire and twelve per cent outside the county. In 1861, forty-seven per cent had been born in

Swithland, thirty-seven per cent elsewhere in Leicestershire and sixteen per cent outside the county. In 1871, the respective percentages were thirty-nine, forty-one and twenty per cent. In 1881 and 1891, the number of residents born in Swithland (forty-four and forty-two per cent) only just exceeded those born in Leicestershire (thirty-seven and thirty-six per cent), while the numbers of residents born outside the county was gradually increasing (eighteen and twenty-two per cent). The fact that the Earl was in residence when the census was taken in 1881, 1891 and 2001 may have slanted these percentages, as the servants employed by successive earls came increasingly from outside village and county. By 1901, the sixty-one Swithland born residents were in the minority for the first time. Sixty-three inhabitants were born elsewhere in Leicestershire, and sixty-nine outside the county. Future census details will most likely continue to reflect this trend. In 2001, for example, only three or four of those living in the village were also born in it.

Occupations

Until 1901, agriculture was the major source of employment in Swithland, though after 1881 the number of working farms in the village began to decrease. Domestic service was the second most important source of employment, particularly when the Earl was in residence. In 1841, it was usually just the head of the household's occupation that was listed, and those women listed in any distinct capacity were either 'independent' or 'servants'. From 1851, however, everyone who worked was questioned about their occupation, giving a much fuller picture of village life. The majority of

Fig 17.1 Forest End Farm, harvesting team, c. 1900.

women saw themselves as in full-time work, either in their own or in other households. For some women, their occupation was closely connected with their husband's. They described themselves as rector's wife, farmer's wife or daughter, or gardener's wife. Others exercised various professional skills such as laundress and lace-worker, while some were more specialised. Miss Sarah Jefferat, for example, the gamekeeper's sister, worked as a dress and straw-bonnet maker.

Domestic labour differed according to the status and wealth of the employer and his household. In 1841, for example, ten out of the fifty-six households had live-in servants. Swithland Hall, even with the family away, maintained seven servants. George Morris at Hall Farm and William Simpson at Forest End Farm maintained five servants each, farmers Thomas Oldershaw and Thomas Bates of Kinchley Hill Farm each maintained four, the Rectory and the Griffin Inn employed three each, and Daniel Bates (Exning Farm), Edward Dexter (the Mill) and Eleanor Gregory, an independent lady, just the one. In 1851, up at the Hall – again even with the family away – there were resident a housekeeper, housemaid, stillroom maid, a footman and groom. William Simpson at Forest End Farm said he employed five servants (three outdoors and two indoors), one of whom was his sister and another his son. The rector employed a butler (male), a cook, a nurse, a nursery maid and a housemaid. Of such employment differentials was social status defined.

A summary comparison of all occupations listed from 1851 to 1901 shows only marginal change overall. In 1851, thirty-seven per cent of all occupations related to agriculture, twenty-five per cent to traditional village roles, twenty-one per cent to domestic service, seven per cent to work in quarries or woods and seven per cent to garden labour. Some had specific professional skills. Joseph Pollard, for example, who lived and worked at the Woodhouse end of the village (where 1 Main Street now stands), was a skilled gravestone engraver. In 1901, thirty-four per cent of the working villagers were still involved in agriculture, sixteen per cent in traditional village roles, forty per cent in domestic service and six per cent in the woods or quarries. There were a few 'new' occupations each year. In 1901, for example, two people were working at the waterworks, one was repairing roads and two were commercial travellers.

Other sources of information add to the picture of the occupations of Swithland village residents in the nineteenth century. Swithland Hall Estate rental books of 1830 indicate that Joseph Doughty kept a shop, though there is no information as to what he sold, and that John Williamson kept a butcher's shop. County annual trade directories also list a small number of local traders. Joshua Preston was variously described as a mason, a shopkeeper and a bricklayer in Swithland in 1846, 1849 and 1854, though in the census returns he is just described as a bricklayer. Susannah Potter was a grocer and tea dealer between 1861 and 1881, and Sarah then William Gamble kept a grocer's shop in the village between 1861 and 1864. Joseph Woods and then Catherine Woods kept the village post office from 1876–81. Mrs Maria Johnson is recorded in 1895 as keeping a shop; in 1896,

Wright's *Directory* lists Samuel Bunney as a farmer and shopkeeper, Joseph Wood as a cottager and sub-postmaster, and John Henry Hodges as a bricklayer and sub-postmaster. After 1900, *Kelly's Directory* is the primary source of information. The following names are listed: Samuel Bunney (1896–1916), William Bunney (1900), Joseph Barnett (1900–8), Emma Bunney (1922–8) and Sarah Jane Hodges (1928–41).[3] Personal memories, too, contribute to our knowledge of those years. Neighbours remember that around 1928 Charles Wainwright, the local coal merchant,[4] kept his wagons and horses in stables built on land opposite his home at Forest (Pollard) House. The stables fell into disrepair, and although there was still a building there in 1955, there is no trace of it today. The entrance to his yard could still be seen in 2007, however, by a white gate set in the stone wall.

Child Labour

In 1841 ten boys and five girls of fifteen years and under were listed as working. Of the ten boys, six were fifteen, two were fourteen and two thirteen. Three boys were agricultural labourers, six farm servants and one a servant at the mill. Four of the five girls employed were fifteen, and one was twelve. Two of them worked at the Hall in domestic service, the other three in farmhouses. Similar numbers of twelve to fifteen year olds and younger were labouring in 1851. The youngest children working were twelve year old farm servants John Charles and Samuel Worth, and thirteen year old John Preston who was a bird-tender. In 1861 the youngest working child was thirteen year old William Cuffling, a farmer's son. 1871 saw ten year old James Spencer working as a farm boy. In 1891 there were fewer younger children working. By then children were recorded on the census return as 'scholars'[5] and seventeen boys and twenty-one girls under the age of eleven, and four girls and three boys who were eleven years or over were so registered. By 1901, with the school leaving age now twelve years old, only two Swithland boys were listed as working. Fourteen year old Albert Adams was a horse boy, and Charles Pepper, the same age, was a farmer's son.

Life and Leisure in Nineteenth Century Swithland

For most villagers, life would have focussed around their daily work. There were, however, some opportunities for leisure. Since at least 1700, the Griffin Inn has been an important village social centre, at least for the men. The inn offered more than alcohol. The large brick building at the rear[6] once served as the village meeting room. When advertising the inn in the 1870s, the landlord described a 'large dining room, one of the olden time, capable of accommodating two hundred people'.

A different aspect of attention to the villagers' welfare was the founding of the Swithland village library in 1854. The school had been rebuilt in 1843 and the library, of some two hundred and sixty books, was probably housed there.[7] The cost of purchasing those first books was raised by public subscription. Some £9/15/- was raised, £2 being donated by the Earl of

Lanesborough, £2 by the Countess, £1 by Rector Edward Paget, £1 by Lady Heygate of Roecliffe Manor, 10 shillings by schoolmaster Stephen Clarke and the same amount by the Sunday School children. The remainder was subscribed by thirty-six residents. The money was collected by Stephen Clarke. The books bought – only the titles are listed – covered a wide range of subjects and included *Agricultural Chemistry, Beveridge's Sermons, Comfort for the Afflicted, Domestic Fowls, Eminent Anglo-Saxons, Foxe's Book of Martyrs, Garden Flowers, Homer's Iliad, Jamaica, Last Hours of Christians, Mohammed, Robinson Crusoe, Self Improvement, Successful Men, Tales of Shipwrecks, Thrift, Uncle Tom's Cabin, The Vicar of Wakefield*. The borrowers were mainly the women of the village; the rector's footman was one of the very few male borrowers. There were six regulations for borrowers. Subscriptions were to be paid in advance; a book was not to be kept for more than fourteen days before renewal; subscribers keeping a book longer than the specified time would be fined 1d for each succeeding week; books were exchanged on Monday evenings between 4.30pm and 5.30pm; subscribers were not allowed to lend books belonging to the library to any person not residing in the same house; any book soiled or injured had to be paid for.

Another little volume in Swithland church archives records the accounts of a 'club' organised in the village between 1859 and 1884. It appears to show the financial records of some sort of local savings society for the village 'cottagers' (mainly women, but some men) supported by Lady Lanesborough. Approximately thirty members subscribed one shilling monthly and Lady Lanesborough gave about £5 each year. Joseph Matts certified 'paid' or 'received' at each year end. Either he was the club accountant, or else, given that he was a tailor and draper resident in the village (at Pollard House, Forest End) it was a savings club for new clothes made by Mr Matts. Joseph Matts, who was a tailor and draper in Newtown Linford, had moved into the village in 1855.

There were also local sporting activities. A village cricket team, for example, was active in the 1880s. Swithland Cricket Club started under the patronage of the Hall with matches played in the park, just behind the church. E.E. Snow noted that the sixth Earl 'laid out the ground which was in the park at the back of the church. Many cricket house parties were given by the sixth Earl, and later by the seventh and eighth Earls'.[8] Snow also mentioned the cricket game played there against Rothley on Boxing Day 1939, when snow lay on the ground. The village club later moved its ground to a field behind the White House, and then over the road to land behind the Memorial Hall, where the pitch was smoothed down by a horse drawn roller. The team probably played throughout the year.

According to Rodney Lloyd, a descendant of estate gamekeeper, Perceval Lloyd, the Lloyd boys, and one of the Lloyd grandsons Frank Spence, were a significant part of the Swithland cricket team in the 1920s and 30s. Other team members at the time included the Patersons, the Copsons, Cedric Kilby and Sid Bunney who acted as a groundsman. The pitch was in the Hall grounds opposite the entrance to Hall Farm. The team first played in dark blue caps sporting a golden griffin, but Rector Mackay disapproved of the

The Old Order

Fig.17.2 Swithland village cricket team c. 1880.
Back: Fred Bunney, Sutton, Clowes, Bowler, unknown, Morgan, John Hodges, unknown
Middle: unknown, unknown, Fred Bunney jnr, Joseph Bunney.
Front: unknown, unknown, Vesty Ellis.

Fig 17.3 Swithland village cricket team, c. 1930, outside Keeper's Cottage.
Back: Fred Lloyd, Mac Paterson are second and third from the left.
Front: Harry Copson is fourth from the left.

connection with the inn, so the team, amid much furore, was renamed the Swithland Park Cricket Club and issued with pale blue caps. The Second World War, however, put an end to village cricket and although an attempt was made to re-start the Swithland village cricket club after the war, it was finally disbanded at the end of the 1940s.

There was also a village football team. Games were played on a 5 acre area beside the bridle path near the present grain-driers belonging to Longlands Farm. The team, who called themselves the St Leonard's Football Team,[9] was still playing in the 1930s.

During the 1880s, Swithland held its annual village Wake on or near the patronal feast day of St Leonard, 6th November. There are brief references in the school log book. One entry, for example, on 8th November 1880 told of a 'Half Holiday, p.m, being the Feast'. In his publication of 1965, Meadows records memories of the Wake in the late 1880s shared by older villagers. 'Outside the Griffin Inn, in the glare of naptha flares, there were stalls with spinning jennies, skittle games, swings, roundabouts, coconut shies, and even the inevitable Italian organ grinder with his monkey. Later in the evening, a celebration dance was held in the Griffin Club room, the music being supplied by a solitary melodeon player who came from Mountsorrel. He knew but one tune, which he adapted for every kind of dance, but, as an old resident remarked, this always sounded just like a Polka'.[10]

Communication, Transport and Facilities

In the 1880s the post was brought from Loughborough by Faulks the postman driving his pony and trap. Faulks spent most of the day delivering and collecting the mail, and, before returning, usually enjoyed a good meal at the Hall.[11] *Kelly's Directory* for 1899 refers to the Swithland post office and to Mrs Sarah Jane Hodges the postmistress. Letters would arrive from Loughborough at 8am (8.20am on Sundays) and were dispatched at 5pm (11.45am on Sundays). Postal orders could be issued at Swithland, but not paid. The nearest money order and telegraph office was at Woodhouse Eaves.

Before 1899, all journeys into Leicester were made by carrier's cart. These journeyed twice weekly between Woodhouse and the city. Directories from 1899 inform us that four carriers in Woodhouse Eaves (Joseph Taylor, Joseph Hardy, Henry Preston and Harry Murcott) were journeying to Leicester and back on Wednesdays and Saturdays, and to Loughborough on Thursdays, and also that Richard Whatnall offered an additional carrier service to and from Loughborough. The arrival of the new Central Railway in 1899, however, provided for a more comfortable and quicker journey between the village and both Leicester and Loughborough. The nearest railway stations were Quorn and Rothley. Rothley was the station favoured by Swithland villagers, but as there was no public right of way across the fields, Mr Clough Taylor, the agent for Swithland Hall Estate, issued tickets allowing holders to walk from the village to the station, via the church, Dale Walk, the Hall drive, and the top lodge. This rather feudal system ended after the First World War with the coming of a regular bus service to the village from

Leicester. The first motorbus was a Prestwell's conveyance and was known affectionately as 'the Boneshaker'.[12] Cycling, too, became an increasingly popular form of transport.

Before mains water came to village in the 1930s, there were two village pumps accessing local springs. Suf (sough) Mouth Spring supplied all the water for the cottages at the Swithland Woods end of the village. The expression, 'suf mouth', is said locally to have a connection with wine or quarry ventilation, though 'suf' was a word used generally for a small drain or a beck. Access to the spring was well built with slate, and it is still evident today beside the roadside opposite Forest End. It fell into gradual disuse and decay after mains water became available. One village pump, dated 1861, was in the vicinity of the old Post Office and the other was outside Keeper's Cottage.

Fig. 17.4 Cyclists visiting Swithland Woods c. 1912.

Village Families

The nineteenth century was the last full century to see local families staying for any length of time in a small village like Swithland. Two of these families, about whose history some family research has been done, were initially newcomers. Both the Browns[13] and the Bunneys moved into Swithland in the latter part of the eighteenth century because there were labouring jobs available in the village.

The Browns

The Brown family came to Swithland in the 1750s. Over the course of one hundred and twenty years, they brought some fifty children to the church to be christened. William (buried 1802) and Ann Brown appear to have moved into the village c. 1757, William probably to take up a labouring job. All ten of their children, seven girls and three boys, were baptised at Swithland, with at least two, Jane and Lucy, dying in infancy. Two of their sons, William and Samuel, married, and saw one or more generations of their families living and working in Swithland. They all seem to have lived in one of the cottages at Forest End.

William (junior) a labourer, (born in 1769) fathered eleven children by three wives, being successively married, in St Leonard's Church, to Elizabeth Beston (m. 1790, d. 1801), Elizabeth James (m. 1801, d. 1808) and Elizabeth Matthews (m. 1808). He had four sons (Thomas b. 1790, William b. 1793, John b. 1795, and Samuel 1798) by Elizabeth Beston; two sons and two daughters (Daniel b. 1804, Daniel b. 1808, Elizabeth b. 1803, Sarah b. 1806) by Elizabeth James, who died giving birth to her second son; and, by Elizabeth Matthews, a son and two daughters (Diana b. 1809, Jane b. 1811 and Anne b. 1818). Samuel, (b. 1773, William and Ann's second son), who married first Sarah and then Elizabeth, fathered ten children, (by Sarah: Ann 1805, Samuel 1806, Mary 1809, Eliza 1811, Elizabeth 1815; by Elizabeth: Catherine 1819, Henry 1823, Jane 1826 and Isaac 1827).

Both brothers, William and Samuel, saw one of their sons marry and settle in Swithland. William's son James, an agricultural labourer, married Sarah Pickering. They had ten children, one of whom, George 1835–1907, married to Sarah, saw his own family of nine children begin life in Swithland. Sarah survived George, dying in 1917. She must have been one of the last members of the Brown family to live in Swithland. Samuel's son Henry, listed as a rag and bone man in the 1851 Census, married Priscilla, by whom he had two sons: the second, another Henry, became apprenticed to Joseph Matts, the tailor and draper, who lived a few doors away in the house next to Forest End Farm.

The Bunneys

There have been Bunneys living in Swithland since the eighteenth century. David and Elizabeth (née Pitts) Bunney, married in Swithland in 1794 and with their descendants, ensured a Bunney presence in Swithland right up to the present day.[14] Nothing is known of David and Elizabeth, but by the time of the 1841 Census, their younger son William, with Martha his wife and their seven children were living in the village, as was their widowed and re-married daughter-in-law Sarah (originally a Swithland Baum) with the three children of her first marriage to Samuel Bunney. (Her second husband, John Thorpe, was an agricultural labourer.) William Bunney was a labourer at the slate quarry, who in 1841 was probably living at Forest End, though by 1861, he and his wife had moved to 127 Main Street.

By 1851 there were three Bunney households at Forest End, Swithland: William (now agricultural labourer) and Martha; William (their son, agricultural labourer) and Elizabeth; Charles (their nephew, agricultural labourer) and Elizabeth. Ten years later, three more of William and Martha's sons George, Henry and James (all labourers) had set up their own households, all at Forest End. By 1871, William had died, but his younger son Walter, a slate quarryman, and his wife had moved in with his mother. William and Martha's grandson, George's son Edward, an agricultural labourer, also added to the Bunney households in the village. The total number of Bunney households though remained six, as it would appear that William and Elizabeth had moved away.

And so the family story went on. There were still six Bunney households in Swithland in 1881, but the employment status of the heads of the households was improving. George's son Fred (under-gamekeeper at the Hall) had moved into Forest End, marrying Sarah in 1882; James and Harriet had moved into 120 Main Street Street; George, now a gardener, and Jane had taken over Henry and Mary's house at 140 Main Street; Charles and Elizabeth were living in 144 Main Street, with Charles employed as tenant farmer at Bybrooke Farm. Their son Samuel, who had married Emma, lived at 134 Main Street and ran a grocery and provisions shop. William and

Elizabeth had moved back into the village, to Keeper's Cottage, as William had become gamekeeper for the Hall.

In 1891, Fred (agricultural labourer) and Sarah were still at Forest End; James (labourer) and Harriet still at 120 Main Street; George (agricultural labourer) and Jane at No. 140; Charles, now widowed, at No. 144; Samuel and Emma at No. 134; and William and Elizabeth at Keeper's Cottage. John Bunney, Charles and Elizabeth's son, having married a Hemsley in 1884, had moved into Pit Close Cottage. In 1901 there were seven Bunney households. Fred (under-gamekeeper) and Sarah, James (general labourer) and new wife Mary, Walter (caretaker at slate quarry) and Mary Ann, Samuel and Emma, and Jane, George's widow, were all still living at the same addresses. William and Elizabeth still lived in the village, though not at Keeper's Cottage as William had retired as gamekeeper. There was also a Louisa Bunney (widowed), living, possibly at 144 Main Street, with her eight year old niece Gwendoline.

In the years that followed, 144 Main Street remained a Bunney home till at least 1933, as, until 1974, did No. 140, No. 134 until Samuel died c. 1918, and No. 127 until c. 1961 when Joseph Bunney died. No. 120 passed out of the family c. 1909, James having died in 1906. One of the Forest End cottages also remained with a Bunney family. Charles and Ellen Bunney moved into part of Exning Farm c. 1924 and lived there until 1969. At the estate sale in 1954, Charles Benjamin Bunney bought Exning Farm (No. 130), Joseph Bunney bought 127 Main Street, and Sid Bunney and Mr A.E. Hubbard bought 140–142 Main Street. Up until 2007, when Beatrice May Bunney died, there were still two houses in Main Street belonging to descendants of the Bunney family. Some family members still live in the locality of the village in 2011.

For over one hundred years members of the Bunney family acted as Swithland's town criers. When Joe Bunney was interviewed in 1960,[15] on his ninetieth birthday, he showed the reporter the seven pound bell, muffled, which he had last used in 1940 when he had summoned the villagers to a defence meeting. The same bell was used by his father Walter and grandfather William Bunney.

The 'County Set'

There were gradations of social order within the local community. The life of a local country gentleman, for example, was very different from the life of a tenant famer, which was also different from the life of an estate worker. It was also different from the life of the Earl and his family. The 1896/1897 diary of William Francis Martin[16] of The Brand, near Swithland, paints an interesting picture of his life during his twenty-first year. Martin's father was managing director of the Mountsorrel Granite Company, and in 1892 the family had removed to The Brand from Anstey Pastures. The diary shows that William Martin's life was a mixture of work (with the Granite Company), social life and sport.

There are references in Martin's diary to various friends and neighbours. He dined regularly, for example, at Roecliffe Manor, Beaumanor, Barrow

Lodge, and Swithland Hall. Apart from the Hall family, the Murray Dixons (at the Rectory) were the only Swithland village family who fell into his sporting and social round.

> *Wednesday 16th September 1896*
> Cubbing at Outwoods. 6.30 fine. Met 2 M Dixons on way. Many there, did not kill.
> *Monday 21st*
> Fine frosty morning up 5.30 cubbing at Barkby ... Rode there with Rev Murray Dixon and his brother who was dead late. Parsons horse has been thrown down by a groom looking over a stone heap. 1 knee badly cut but will heal alright. Back 11.30 and cycle to Sorrel for lunch.
> *Saturday 26th*
> To shoot at Ulverscroft with E de L, Selves and 2 Everards. 20 brace, 1 couple rabbits, 1 hare. Rain at intervals. Rev Murray Dixon taken bad with a kind of 'flu.

Young Martin and his friends were involved in the local cricket matches, as well as in hunting, cubbing and other sports. He also rode one of the newly fashionable bicycles.[17]

> *Friday 23rd April 1897*
> Tea with Barrow folks. Polo on cycle afterwards and collision with GHM on the road home, nothing much damaged. Asked by J Boss to play v. Swithland, could not because WJM coming up to tent peg.
> *Saturday 24th*
> Have caught cold. Down 8.50 per cycle, got it repaired in fitters shop. Round with GB to site of smash. Up with him to wheat field where Marshall and another are clearing still, Tyler being ill.
> Made tracing of Fox's Cottage for G Blunt. 12 noon over to Garendon and brought back lance for WHM's use. Telegraphed him that I had it. Only Gerald turned up finally on Sobersides who is very good for pegging. Had some rifle practice and down and watched match. Swithland 32, Maplewell 50. Great victory for Maplewell.

Not that it always went that way!

> *Saturday 12th June 1897*
> Home for lunch and to Maplewell v. Swithland. They 44 and 10 for 6 wickets, we 23. Match played till 6.30 instead of 7 as agreed on. Self, run out without getting a ball, not out really.

Martin was involved in the formation of the Woodhouse and Swithland Rifle Club in 1902. It was arguably more of a Woodhouse club, with its shooting ground at Broombriggs Farm, Woodhouse Eaves. Colonel Curzon was president and William Francis Martin was captain. By 1907 the club had sixty members, using .22 rifles in competition with other clubs.

Hall Life and Leisure

The social life around the Hall was something different again. In some ways, the late nineteenth and early twentieth century was something of a golden age for the big country houses and the country house life style.

The sixth Earl, who inherited the Swithland Estate in 1866, was totally different to his more seriously-minded predecessor. He was Irish, and although he showed little real interest in the management of the Swithland part of his estate, leaving that to his estate manager, he certainly spent some time at Swithland Hall – not so much maintaining it, as using it as a social base. It was in his time that the Hall witnessed a flowering of 'county' sport and leisure activity.

John Vansittart had an obvious interest in cricket.[18] Many country houses sported their own cricket teams and grounds and Swithland Hall was no exception. The Earl formed his own team, the Lanesborough Cricket Team, of which Mr Clough Taylor, his Swithland agent, was chairman. In February 1895, the Earl hosted a concert in front of a fashionable audience to raise money for his new cricket field in the Hall grounds just behind the church. They raised £3. Another concert was held two years later. It was reported in the *Loughborough Monitor and News*, February 1897.

> Swithland Cricket Club Concert
>
> A concert in aid of the new cricket ground was given in the club room on Wednesday evening, before a large and fashionable audience, amongst whom were the Countess of Lanesborough, Lady Winifred Butler, Miss V Fitzwygram, the Honourable BD Butler, Rev JM Dixon, Mr & Mrs Clough Taylor and many other residents in the neighbourhood. The chair was taken by Rev J Murray Dixon, president of the club. The programme was very creditably performed by the various ladies and gentlemen taking part, the several accompaniments being kindly undertaken by Miss Seale (Newtown Linford), Miss Camm (Rushy Fields), Mr T M Green: Overture, Miss Booth: song, 'Anchored Corner', Mrs Clough Taylor: song 'I fear no foe', Mr F Squire: song 'Douglas Gordon', Miss Moss: comic song. 'You can't think of everything', Mr J Camm (encored): song, 'When we Meet', Miss Wesley: song 'The Old Brigade', Mr B Moss (encored); song (in character), 'Whacky, Whacky, Whack', Miss Booth (encored): song 'Jolly Company', Mr C Orton: duet (pianoforte and violin), Mr and Mrs Sale: song 'After the Ball', Mr B Moss: song 'Coming through the Rye', Mrs Clough Taylor: (encored) Irish comic song 'Miss Holigan's Christmas Cake', Mr Granshaw (encored): song, 'No thank you, Tom', Mr F Squire: song, 'Going to Market', Miss Moss: comic song, 'They wouldn't do that in London', Mr J Camm (encored). At the close, Mr H G Clough Taylor proposed a hearty vote of thanks to the performers for their kind and generous help. The amount realised after paying expenses was £8.

In the late 1890s, the sixth Earl built a pavilion on estate land behind the rectory and school. The new pavilion was in the New Park Field, Park Close, and faced 3 acres of ground which had been especially landscaped for croquet and tennis. It was magnificent, with modern amenities, changing rooms, toilets, a kitchen and a room where tea and luncheon could be taken. There was a large clock on the top, facing the four tennis courts. Croquet was played on both banked lawns. (In the early days of the development of croquet, the lawns were usually a field which had been cut carefully with a scythe and then marked out.)

At the new Swithland grounds, in order to improve viewing, four thatched wooden huts were erected on the bank overlooking 'twelve first class (croquet) lawns'[19] with steps down to the lawns. In 1898, Charnwood Forest, the name of the club, founded an annual tournament which was played at Swithland each year at the end of July. The competition took place over three or four days, sometimes even longer, with guests staying at the Hall or boarding in the village. At the Earl's invitation, croquet and tennis players came from a wide area to compete. Villagers may well have enjoyed watching, but pavilion activities were always part of the life of 'the Hall', never of the village.

Croquet was introduced into England from Ireland in 1852 as a country house pastime, with the rules being administered by the Wimbledon All England Croquet Club. By the beginning of the twentieth century, the English game needed new blood, new tactics and new ideas. This was provided by players such as Cyril Corbally and C.L. O'Callaghan, who came over from Ireland. (O'Callaghan may well have had a social connection with the Earl of Lanesborough.) Leading Irish lady players such as Nina Coote also came over to reinvigorate the English game. She competed at Swithland many times.

> From the *Croquet Association Gazette*
> July 14th 1904 saw the first large competition hosting the Championship of the Midlands. Visitors enjoyed a glimpse of the prettiest part of Leicestershire. Played over four days, the players were mostly from the Midlands area, the locals having their chance in the handicap singles and doubles. There is a photo of Mrs R. Hulton and T.N. Brown in the final. Mr Abbot Robinson was Hon Secretary.[20]

By 1905, the venue at Swithland had grown in importance nationally and the tournament ran over six days. At one time there was an hourly train service from Leicester, as well as from Loughborough to Rothley. Mr Barnett and Mr Alfred Pepper from Swithland met the trains with carriages. Luncheon at the Pavilion was 2/6d and tea 1/-. The Grand Hotel in Leicester offered discounted terms for visitors to the tournament at 4/ 6d and 9/- for a single and double room respectively, and provided a free bus service to Swithland. The members of the committee in 1905 were Colonel the Hon. M. Curzon, Captain W. Heygate, Colonel T. Henry, the Hon. B. Butler, E. Warner, Captain Lillingston, R.W. Tuckett Esq and Major Pochin, who also acted as secretary. The local members did well in the handicap singles that year, with the Hon. Brian Butler reaching, though failing, in the final of his Class.[21] Contemporary reports said the venue deserved to host the Gold Medal meetings. Responding, the Club offered to hold the tournament over a fortnight, pointing out that a special train service from Leicester would ensure easy access to the really unique position of these grounds.

In 1905 it was very hot and there were local restrictions on watering. It was said that cabbage leaves and long drinks were in great demand! In 1913, however, it was so cold that visitors wished they had brought their winter clothes. One local player was the envy of all; she had a fur coat, with fur outside and inside, which she not only sat about in but played her match in without any apparent detriment to her game! The report added that 'apart from the actual croquet, various amusements were provided for the players and spectators, such as Pekinese dogs, the taking of wasp's nests and the Hon. H. Butler's most cheering presence'.

For the two years before the Great War, Major Childers of the Holt, Woodhouse, club secretary, and Colonel William Du Pré, a distinguished national and international player, joined the committee. Du Pré, who won the world championship on numerous occasions, played in nearly all the Charnwood tournaments. Although he was Member of Parliament for High Wycombe from 1914–23, croquet was his principal interest and he was still playing in 1938, becoming national mixed double champion that year. Du Pré was also passionate about golf. It was said that his love of croquet filtered through to his golf. A *Daily Telegraph* reporter, commenting on the Colonel's putting in 1920, wrote, 'The Colonel stands facing the hole and swings the club between his legs'. After the war, croquet as a national sport went into decline, and the local croquet competitions at Charnwood Forest ceased. But as croquet declined, lawn tennis became increasingly popular.[22]

Fig 17.5 Swithland Pavilion: Croquet and tennis lawns, 1904.

Unlike croquet, lawn tennis was not the sole prerogative of the country house set. Families from the well-off industrial middle classes, who had settled locally, also wanted to play. Members of the Charnwood Forest Lawn Tennis Club society, however, were reluctant to open their lists to those 'in trade' – however wealthy. The membership list of 1915 reads like a Who's Who of Leicestershire: the Earl of Lanesborough, president; the Countess, the ladies' captain; the ground committee headed by Captain Heygate and the bankers Parrs of Leicester. Leicestershire family names on the membership list included Everard, Farnham, Fielding Johnson, Herrick, Lady Joyce, Martin, Packe, Paget, Pochin, Abel Smith and Turner. Even the officers of the 17th Regimental Depot were only 'honorary members'. Swithland tennis players not on this exclusive list started their own village tennis club and played on courts beside the new Memorial Hall in 1920.

Archery was also played on the Park Close grounds, with the targets stored at the end of the pavilion. The society was renamed the Charnwood Forest Archery and Lawn Tennis Society. It was reported that 'the Charnwood Forest Archery Society met in Swithland Park every year and is attended by the elite of the County'. These 'elite' would enter the grounds to the Pavilion via the track by Keeper's Cottage, and through some large gates at the back of the school. Percival (Bill) Lloyd, the gamekeeper's son, used to earn a half-penny or penny tip for opening the gate for them!

Navvies, Tourists, Campers, Invalids and other Visitors

Various groups of people have either visited or passed through Swithland at some stage in its history. At the end of the nineteenth century, navvies were called upon to assist with the construction work on reservoir and railway. From the early years of the twentieth century, visitors and tourists from the city and beyond were a significant feature of village life at weekends and during holiday periods. There were several convalescent and charitable homes on the edge of the village, which offered hospitality and fresh country air. There were other visitors too, such as the Leicestershire Caravan Mission to Village Children.

Navvies

One group of people working locally at the end of the nineteenth century were the navvies, the necessary work force employed for building the reservoir and the railway. These men and their families might have been expected to impinge more on Swithland than they did. But these peripatetic bands of labourers, who travelled round the country following the work, had little impact on Swithland village life.

Other places were affected more directly. Thomas Hardy wrote in 1895 of the social changes the navvies brought to his local county of Dorset. He pointed to the recent supplanting of the class of stationary cottagers, who carried on the local traditions and humours, by a population of more or less migratory labourers, which has led to a break of continuity in local history, more fatal than any other thing to the preservation of legend, folk-lore, close

Fig 17.6 A Navvy family settlement outside Swithland, 1897.[24]

Fig 17.7 Swithland navvies, 1897.

inter-social relations and eccentric individualities. For these the indispensable conditions of existence are attachment to the soil of one particular spot by generation after generation.[23]

The navvies who were engaged in building Swithland's reservoir and adjacent railway lived in their own temporary settlements. At nearby Manton in Rutland, where work on the Midland Line began in the 1870s:

> ... men (with their wives and families) crowded in from all parts of the country, and the question had to be solved where the newcomers were to be lodged. It was clear that they were too many for the villages lying near ... The difficulty, however ... was soon settled

> ... Soon the hills and dales, for fifteen miles, began to echo with the sound of the mattock, the hammer and the axe. Hut villages seemed to grow up like mushrooms. Taking your stand on anyone point of the line above ground, I do not think there was a single spot from which you could not see a hut, or the smoke of it anyhow, rising from one of the little chimneys ... Over two hundred of these erections were made, mostly of wood, a few of bricks, and some even of sods of earth.[25]

Sydney Meadows, in his booklet on Swithland (1965), quotes one of Rector Murray Dixon's daughters (Mrs Hamilton) remembering that 'Italian workmen were employed' as navvies in the 1890s. And in 1894, when Swithland's Methodist Chapel was threatened with closure, the members considered a mission link to the navvies employed at the New Water Works and suggested that an Evangelist for Swithland be appointed to work amongst them. This suggestion was never taken up.

Tourists

From the early years of the twentieth century, charabancs brought people out from Leicester to Swithland Woods during the summer and at bank holidays to enjoy the walking and the views. Merttens in his advertising literature for Rothley Plain Garden Suburb had described Swithland as 'quite a miniature Lake District'. Teas were available from many of the farmhouses and cottages, with some offering boarding. Villagers erected signs advertising teas, such as a bread and jam tea for 9d and a fruit and jam tea for 1/3d. At Forest (Pollard) House, No. 54, there was an especially good trade to be had, as it was one of the houses nearest to Swithland Woods. In the summer, the family made the attic their bedroom so they could hire out their own bedrooms for boarding.

Many postcards of local scenes record something of this tourist economy. Fred from Bartholomew Street in Leicester, for example, sent his friend John a postcard of Swithland Woods in August 1904 asking if Mabel remembered this place.[26] Another card picturing the slate pits pre-1902 simply reads: 'This beats our river view almost. So glad you're getting well quickly'. And a 1915 postcard of the reservoir from a young lady to her 'dearest' (stationed in Andover) conveyed the news that she had had 'a ripping time at Swithland and Cropstone. Just waiting at Rothley for train. Feel done in and filthy, should love a wash. Spent nearly 3/- this holiday. Shall go on skint after tomorrow. Yours as ever, F. xxxxx'

Campers

During the same period, many Leicester people enjoyed coming out and staying in a tent on the camp site at Swithland Wood Farm. One of those early campers recorded his memories in the Leicester Living History Unit's newsletter. His family went by train to Rothley and then walked four miles to the campsite. As a child of two, young Leslie (Sherwood) was first pushed there in a mail cart which had a basket of provisions strapped on to the back.

Fig 17.8 Swithland Camp, c. 1920.

He remembered that 'two events arranged by the camp committee were the 'sports' on Bank Holiday Monday and the End of Season Supper ... Tables were placed in the Grey tea-room and after supper, singers and comedians entertained us. Then there was dancing until midnight, and the merriment continued for another hour only, otherwise we should have encroached on the first hour of the Sabbath'.[27]

Convalescents

Various convalescent and other homes were built locally; Swithland Convalescent Home for Women on Brand Hill, Woodhouse Eaves was just one. A postcard of the recreation room in the home sent by Dorrie on 27th August 1917 reads:

> Dear Elsie, You will see where I am. I am feeling in the pink here, the weather is grand. Where have you been for your holiday? Give my love to Mable. Best love, Dorrie XX

Leicestershire Caravan Mission to Village Children

A single undated photograph, possibly from the 1920s, indicates that Swithland was occasionally visited by the Leicestershire Caravan Mission to Village Children. This was an evangelistic movement that was started in the south of England in 1892 by members of the Children's Special Service Mission (CSSM), a voluntary Christian group that organised seaside beach mission services for children.[28] Initially there were only one or

Fig 17.9 Leicestershire Caravan Mission visiting Swithland, c. 1920.

two CMVC caravans, containing living quarters and room to carry a tent, but by 1913 there were thirteen caravans, mainly in the south of England and by 1921 twenty-two caravans. By then there is evidence that there were country CMVC evangelists as well as county caravans.

End of an Era – The First World War

There are very few references in Swithland's own records about the impact of the First World War on daily life. The East Akeley Deanery magazine for November 1914 reported that local villages had set up various voluntary aid societies or working parties to support the troops. The Swithland Voluntary Aid Society was set up on 8th August, 1914 co-ordinating local support work for a group of neighbouring villages. The president was the Countess of Lanesborough and her vice-presidents Mrs Heygate, Mrs King and Mrs Martin. Captain Heygate was the chairman, Colonel Winter the secretary, and Miss Ellis the treasurer. There was a committee of ladies from Woodhouse, Woodhouse Eaves and Swithland, Rothley, Quorn, Mountsorrel, Oaks in Charnwood, Copt Oak, Thringstone, Thurcaston, Cropston, Cossington and Thrussington. The society was dissolved in October 1914, because all the villages decided to set up working parties of their own, but their achievements in those first three months were impressive.

> £100 given by Mr Faire, towards a motor ambulance, 700 articles had been made for the St John's Ambulance Base Hospital in Leicestershire, £20 had been collected for the Belgian Relief Fund, £20 for Lady Jellicoe's Fund for the Fleet, and £3 towards blankets for Lord Kitchener's appeal. £16 had been spent on making shirts for the 5th Battalion Leics. Regiment, 116 pairs of socks had been sent to the Queen's Women of the Empire Guild, 63 shirts to the men of the Royal Artillery at the Front and about 1050 articles for the Red Cross Society, making a total of about 2000 articles with £159 collected and distributed.[29]

There is a brief reference in the Swithland School Log to the end of the war. The entry for 11th November 1918 records that 'School re-opened today (it had been closed since Oct. 25th because of influenza). 16 children present. In honour of the day children were dismissed by the Rev. J Murray Dixon soon after assembling for afternoon school'.

The most powerful impact of the war, however, was felt in the Swithland village homes where family members had been killed in action, or had returned home injured or traumatised by what they had experienced. The names of the Swithland dead are engraved on the village War Memorial.

> Brian Danvers Butler
> Sidney Mark Collis
> HEOM Murray Dixon
> Bernard RD Hornsby
> John Thomas Minkley

Brian Danvers Butler was the fourth son of John Vansittart Danvers, sixth Earl of Lanesborough. The only one of the Earl's children to be baptised in Swithland, he was killed in action, aged forty, at Orchard Trench in France on 18th August 1916 while serving as temporary lieutenant in the 7th Battalion of the Kings Rifle Corps. He is buried at the Thiepval Memorial, Somme. He was unmarried.

Sidney Mark Collis is commemorated with the Swithland dead because he was lodging in Swithland when the war started. He came from Quorn, and enlisted in Mountsorrel. A private, serving with the 13th Labour Battalion (formed August 1916) of the Leicestershire Regiment, Collis was killed in action in France at Flanders on 26th March 1918. He is buried in the New British Cemetery at Noyen.

Otto Murray Dixon, (1885–1917) the rector's eldest son, was a notable painter, particularly of wildlife.[30] In his memory, his family gave Swithland church the carved oak screen that divides the nave from the tower vestry. He is buried in the Aubigny Communal Cemetery Extension, Pas de Calais. His father recorded his death in the Swithland church registers. 'Henry Edward Otto Murray Dixon, at the age of 31, in the 1914–18 war: 'By someone – somewhere in France – a man of peace, he fell in war giving his life for others'. Otto was not the only one of the Murray Dixon boys to be damaged by the war. One of his brothers suffered severe traumatisation.

Bernard Hornsby was the son of John and Jane Ann Hornsby who lived at 120 Main Street from c. 1909 until 1930. Bernard, who was born in Birstall, was a private in the 6th Battalion Leicestershire Regiment. He died on 22nd April 1918, of wounds received at Flanders, France. He is buried in the Roisel Communal Cemetery. His sister, Ivy Annie, married Arthur Stevenson in 1935 and they lived at 138 Main Street. His father, John (Jock) died in 1940, aged eighty-two and is buried in Swithland churchyard.

John Thomas Minkley, whose family moved into Swithland in the closing years of the nineteenth century, was born in Wanlip and enlisted in Leicester. He was a private in the 2nd Battalion Leicestershire Regiment and was killed in action in Flanders, France on the 20th November 1914. He is buried in Le Touret Military Cemetery, Pas-de-Calais. The Minkleys were another large Swithland village family; the last local member, Brian Vann, died in 1999.

Six other men who died in the First World War are commemorated in Swithland church and churchyard. John Cleaver Needham, in whose memory an Order of Holy Communion service book was given to the church, was a corporal in the Household Cavalry and Cavalry of the Line, Leicestershire Yeomanry. Needham, who came from Syston and enlisted in Leicester, was killed in action in Flanders, France on 13th May 1915 and is buried in Bedford House Cemetery, Ypres. Herbert Percy Meakin, to whose memory the church altar cross is dedicated, and the two pairs of Kerry oil candles, was a captain in the 3rd Battalion Coldstream Guards. He was killed in action at Hers, France on 25th September 1916, and is buried at Thiepval, Somme. Nigel John Latham Wickham, who is commemorated by the stained glass window above the tower west door, was a captain in the Connaught Rangers. He died on 18th April 1916, and is buried in the Noeux-les-Mines

Communal Cemetery, Pas-de-Calais, France. The lancet window shows St Michael, Captain of the Host, on whose shield bearing a Cross is inscribed: 'In this life conquer'. The inscription reads: 'Dedicated by his betrothed[31] to the memory of Nigel John Latham Wickham, captain, the Connaught Rangers, who gave his life for another April 18th 1916'.

The names of three grandsons of Mary Ann Cuffling who died in the Great War are inscribed on her tombstone in Swithland churchyard. Thomas Miles Meadows was the son of Emma (Cuffling) and Andrew Miles Meadows who lived in Welford, Rugby. Meadows, who was born in Thrussington in 1893, was a lance corporal in A Company of the 7th Battalion Northamptonshire Regiment. He died of wounds on 6th April 1916 and is buried in the Berks Cemetery Extension, near Ypres, Belgium. George W. Milner and Frank H. Milner were the sons of Mary Ann (Cuffling) and Henry Robert Milner. George, their eldest son, was born in Gloucester in 1889 and was a private with the 25th Battalion Canadian Infantry. He was killed in action on the 11th April 1917, and is buried in the Lapugnoy Military Cemetery, Pas-de-Calais. Frank, born in Melton Mowbray in 1892, was a private in the 50th Battalion Canadian Regiment, and was killed in action on 26th October 1917. He is buried in Tyne Cot Cemetery, Passchendaele.

The First World War hastened the end of the Victorian/Edwardian era. By the end of the war, Russia had had a communist revolution and murdered its emperor; the Austro-Hungarian and Ottoman empires no longer existed; Kaiser Wilhelm II had abdicated, and gone to live in Holland; the Middle East was notionally controlled by the French and the British; the Jews were looking for a homeland, unfortunately in the same territory where Arabs sought to establish their own independent kingdoms; Ireland was moving towards independence and/or civil war; British women over thirty years old had gained the parliamentary franchise and all of them had a far greater measure of work opportunity; socialism, having conquered Russia, was seen as a viable political option in Italy, Germany, France, Spain and Britain; and America, no longer Britain with her Empire, had become the essential ingredient in the Allied victory over Germany and the natural broker of the Peace. For the families who lived in Swithland, however, change was far less revolutionary and came much more slowly.

Notes to Chapter 17

1. C.F. Alexander, 'All things bright and beautiful', in *Hymns for Little Children*, 1848.
2. Information from census returns is made publicly available after one hundred years.
3. Leics. RO, Various trade directories, including Wright's and Kelly's.
4. Wainwright and Co, the family firm, was based in Woodhouse Eaves from c. 1899.
5. Under the terms of the 1880 Education Act the school leaving age was 10; in 1893 and 1899 the leaving age was raised first to 11 and then to 12 years.
6. Now incorporated into the building.
7. A list of the books is held in Swithland Church Archives.
8. E.E. Snow, *Country House Cricket Grounds of Leicestershire and Rutland*, ACS Publications, 1998.

9. S.R. Meadows, *Swithland*, 1965.
10. ibid.
11. ibid.
12. ibid.
13. Brown family tree research, notes supplied by Mrs Elizabeth Jones.
14. Bunney family tree, see Appendix E.
15. *Leicester Mercury*, 10 Monday October, 1960.
16. Mountsorrel Granite Company archives.
17. The first commercially successful English safety bicycle was produced about 1885. By 1890, bicycles had air-filled rubber tyres. The back-pedal brake and adjustable handle bars were also added about this time.
18. The sixth Earl played for Leicestershire in 1875, and served as president of Leicestershire County Cricket Club between 1879–85.
19. To give an idea of the importance of the Swithland croquet lawns, the largest croquet grounds in England today have only eleven lawns.
20. *Croquet Association Gazette*, Report, 27 July 1904, p. 139.
21. In the following years, play was dominated by well known and nationally recognized players.
22. So much so that the Wimbledon All England Croquet Club was taken over by the Wimbledon All England Tennis Club, and the croquet club had to find a new home.
23. Quoted from C. Harvie & H.C.G. Matthew, *Nineteenth Century Britain*, OUP, 2000.
24. Leics. RO, figs 17.6, 17.7 reproduced from S.W.A. Newton Collection with permission.
25. D.W. Barrett, *Life and Work among the Navvies*, 1880. (Barrett was Vicar of Nassington, diocese of Peterborough.)
26. Local archives.
27. *Leicester Mercury*, Mr Leicester's Diary, 30 March 1998.
28. CSSM and CMVC were non-denominational organisations which merged into the Scripture Union.
29. Leics. RO, East Akeley Deanery Magazine, November 1914.
30. See also Chapter 14: Family Connections.
31. Captain Wickham was engaged to Rosamund, the youngest Murray Dixon daughter.

– CHAPTER 18 –

Transition

After the Great War, Britain saw an increasing national confidence and the desire everywhere to restore and to build. In Swithland, restoration work on the church was started in 1917. Rector Murray Dixon held thanksgiving services in 1918 – not just for the end of the war but also for the restoration work to the church. Inevitably, the temptation was to look back. Murray Dixon was very mindful of family loss and injury, and especially of his son Otto, who had died from wounds received in battle in May 1917. In November 1920, he held an Armistice Day service 'with special tender reference to such as belonged to us'.

> A Special Service was held in the Church on November 6th, on the eve of the Sunday appointed for the commemoration of Armistice Day. It being the Feast Day[1] of our Church, it was thought desirable to associate with the memory of our Patron Saint that of our Glorious Dead, with special tender reference to such as belonged to us. Upon this occasion, the Revd AW Taylor, Rector of Thurcaston, preached a very helpful sermon, taking his text from the book of Wisdom iii, 1. The service was appallingly disgracefully attended, for which neglect I search in vain for a justifiable excuse, and can only regret that owing to their apathy the majority of my parishioners should have suffered the loss of so great spiritual help and comfort.[2]

He did find, however, one matter to rejoice in.

> During the course of the service, a beautifully illuminated record of the achievement of the St Margaret's Guild of Ringers on the bells of our Church, was accepted by the Rector and hung in the Church. It embodies three striking features. A 5040 change peal in Bob Minor in 2 hours and 51 minutes. An artistic marvel in etching by Mr Ernest Morris, the leader of the team, set in a frame, displaying artistic workmanship, the handicraft of Mr William Patterson, the Rector's Churchwarden …
>
> The record of the ringing should stimulate the young men of

the village with enthusiasm to attain to equal honours, and this pleasing design, which I hope may be treasured in our church, should have this voice for all, 'What man hath done, man may do', and move us all to strive to rise to greater heights of physical and spiritual activity and efficiency.[3]

There appears to have been something of a conflict between the rectory and the village at this time, or at least between the rector and certain parishioners, which may explain something of the rector's bitterness. He wrote disapprovingly of the effort that had gone into building the new Memorial Hall which opened in 1920. Having failed, over some time, to raise the necessary money to restore the dilapidated church building, Murray Dixon was clearly distressed that money for the new Memorial Hall had been raised with relative speed and ease. Enough monies to complete the church restoration work were to be donated eventually, but not until Murray Dixon had resigned from the Rectory in 1925 and left the village.

A different perspective on the new Memorial Hall was expressed by Mrs Gladys Turner, the wife of Archibald Turner of 'the Cottage'. She described the day of the opening ceremony in an article in the August 1920 edition of the parish magazine.[4]

> Thursday June 3rd 1920, on which Lady Betty Butler, accompanied by Lord Lanesborough, came to open our Village Memorial Hall, will be a day long remembered in Swithland, for it brought with it a very great deal of happiness for all, and also the fulfilment of a long-felt wish for a sorely needed gathering place for the village, which has now been made possible by the effort of all in the place, and by the kindness and generosity of many friends and neighbours, who will always find a warm welcome awaiting them at any gatherings that may be held there.
>
> The day from start to finish was a great satisfaction, and must have amply rewarded those who gave so freely of their time and strength to make it such a true success. God's blessing was asked on the Hall after the opening, and that it may rest on it through the years, it will be our great desire to ensure.
>
> Gladys M Turner

Free tickets for the opening ceremony were given to all who lived in the village. Visitors were charged 1/6 for the day's entertainment, which consisted of a tea (to be paid for by all who partook of it), a social, and a dance, which commenced at 8pm.[5]

From its opening, the Memorial Hall served as a rendezvous for all sorts and groups of villagers. In the mid 1920s, Mrs Turner, with her companion Nurse Prior, started the Bluebird Guild, an organization for the women of the village, which met regularly in the Memorial Hall. Guild members went on outings, heard lectures, and, in a variety of ways, contributed to the communal welfare of the village.

Social Change in the Community

Change was in the air in the post-war years, not least in relation to the 'authority figures' within local communities. The Local Government Act of 1894 had transferred powers relating to non-ecclesiastical matters from the vestry meeting to a new structure of parish councils and meetings. Most villages, neighbouring Rothley for example, were governed by parish councils, councillors being elected by the villagers. Smaller villages, however, might choose, as did Swithland, to be governed by a parish meeting, which was chaired by someone elected by all the villagers.

For its first thirty years, the Swithland Parish Meeting elected its rector as chairman, then, for the next fifty years, successive Earls of Lanesborough. The authority of rector and Earl within Swithland's village community remained in the main unquestioned, at least until the 1940s. After World War Two, however, in Swithland as elsewhere, authority began to be shared more widely. Swithland's rich 'incomers', for example, used to exercising authority in their professional and business capacities, saw themselves as on a par with squire and parson. In this was much potential for conflict. In Swithland, for example, where the Earl was the major employer until the mid 1950s, estate workers were used to 'doffing their caps' whenever they met him. It must have been very tempting for the powerful and moneyed newcomers to expect a similar deference from their more 'working class' neighbours.

Since most of the land in Swithland was owned by the Hall Estate, only one such new 'industrialist' moved into the village between 1903 and 1955 – Archibald Turner and his wife. They had little competition, therefore, in establishing their 'position' within village and church life. It would appear that while they might have enjoyed a reasonably civilised relationship with the Hall, relationships were at times somewhat cooler with the Rectory. Archibald Turner, who made his money from the elastic web and hosiery manufacturing business he managed in Leicester, waited until after the rector's resignation before he made his £1,300 donation to the Church's Restoration Appeal. For this the congregation expressed their due gratitude, in plaques on the lych-gate and on the inner north wall of the nave.

While these old and new authority figures negotiated their positions, the villagers also were adjusting to social and economic change. Their life-style, of course, was very different. This is evident from two accounts of village life in the 1920s and 30s. In 1989 Jack Copson[6] (1916–1998) recorded an interview with the county's oral history archivists. In 1969, an anonymous villager recorded his or her memories in the parish magazine.

Village Life between the Wars

Jack Copson was the son of Harry and Vera Copson, and grandson to Ambrose. Ambrose, the first Copson to move into Swithland, was born in Sutton in the Elms, Leicestershire. He was tenant farmer at Hall Farm from 1903–32. Ambrose had three sons, Alfred (Fred) Ernest, Charlie and Harry.

From 1922, middle son Charles farmed Brickyard Farm, which lay on the Rothley Plain edge of Swithland village. He eventually passed on the tenancy to his son Leslie. When Brickyard Farm was sold by the Rothley Estate in 1983, Les Copson retired from farming, and moved with his wife Pat to Mountsorrel. From the 1920s to the 1950s, Charles' other two brothers, Fred and Harry, ran the Hollycroft Dairy from 104 Main Street. Jack, Harry's son, grew up in the village and went to the village school. He lived with his wife and family in Main Street.[7] In 1989 he was encouraged by the County Oral History archivists to record for posterity some of his memories of Swithland village life in the 1920s and 30s.[8]

Copson told his interviewer that most of the houses in the village then belonged to the Swithland Hall Estate and were therefore tied cottages. Nearly every working man was employed by the Earl either as a farm labourer[9] or in some other capacity on the Estate or up at the Hall. (A few villagers

Fig 18.1 (Above) Francis Almeric Butler (left) with Fred Copson, c. 1922.

Fig 18.2 Shooting Party: the seventh Earl and his second Countess (right of picture), c. 1922, Charles Copson leading the horses.

Fig 18.3 The eighth Earl with his daughter Freda, Wedding in 1931.

worked independently, such as the roadmen.) There were fourteen men working as gardeners in the large Hall gardens opposite the church. Nobody was very well off. Harry Copson, Jack's father, for example, earned 19 shillings for a week's work in the 1920s. The most anyone earned then was two pounds a week. While the outdoor estate workers usually came from the village community, those who worked 'indoors', up at the Hall, usually came from 'outside', which resulted in quite a few of Swithland's marriages.

Jack described life at Hall Farm in the days when his grandfather Ambrose, 'a cantankerous old man', was tenant farmer. The rent was 17 shillings an acre, and it was almost impossible to make farming pay. Some six or seven men lived in the farmhouse, and Ambrose's wife Mary had to look after them all. Lighting in the 1920s was by oil lamp, and everyone went

*Fig 18.4 Swithland men at work on the Rectory garden c. 1925.
Back (left to right): George Lloyd, Joe Lines, Fred Lloyd, Nat Wilson, Revd Frederick Oliver. Front (left to right): Ted Lloyd and Roy Lloyd.*

*Fig 18.5: Swithland men relaxing, 1920s.
Standing (left to right): Herbert Minkley, Joe Lines. Kneeling: Mac Paterson. Sitting (left to right): Fred Lloyd with dog, John Leatherland snr, Les Bunney, Bill Lloyd.*

to bed with candles. There was just the one cold-water tap in the kitchen, and two black ranges, one in the kitchen and one in the living room. Water was heated in a copper. Breakfast was porridge, bacon, egg and fried bread, with tea served up in pint cups. Sides of ham were hung from the beams; supper was usually a piece of bacon cut from a ham. Other dishes regularly eaten included jam or currant roly-poly puddings – wrapped in a cloth and steamed in the copper.

In the 1920s and 30s Hall Farm was part arable and part dairy. While other Swithland dairy farmers sold their milk in Leicester, milk from Hall Farm was sold locally. The pony and trap daily retail milk round was run by Jack's uncle and father, Fred and Harry Copson, from Hollycroft Dairy, 104 Main Street. The daily routine began at 5.30am, when the cowman arrived to milk the cows. He milked into buckets, transferring the milk to bowls covered by a cloth. Thirty gallons of milk were required before the cart was full enough to begin the twice-daily milk round. Any milk over and above that was used to feed the calves or made into cream and butter by Mary, Ambrose's wife and Jack's grandmother. She used to make eighty pounds of butter each week, churning it herself, though when Jack was old enough, he would help her. The butter and cream was also sold on the milk round.

The arable acreage of Hall Farm cropped wheat, barley, oats, mangles (mangolds), turnips and cow cabbage (a variety of kale). The crops fed both the villagers and their cattle. Mangles were staple food for cows and were harvested in April. Barley was grown to feed the pheasant chicks (there were regular shoots on the Estate). Hay was harvested in the early summer, and wheat from the end of August.[10] The wheat was hand-scythed, the scythed crop being gathered into shocks and left to stand for three weeks before being carried by horse and dray to the farmyard for stacking. The wheat was then drum thrashed, the drum being driven by a large steam engine. Two men stood on the stack, one on the drum, and two more men cut the bands. The wheat was fed into the drum, straw coming out one end and grain the other. Two men stood by with eighteen-stone sacks to collect the grain, which was carried seventy yards to the barn for stacking. The straw was tied with string and stored for animal fodder.

There were two shops in Swithland in the 1920s, the Post Office and a general shop. Four or five visiting bakers made hand-cart deliveries in the village, likewise two or three greengrocers and butchers. The hardware man visited the village on Tuesdays.

There were a good number of children living in the village, with attendance at the village school of some forty children, aged from four plus to fourteen years. There was just the one class, and the schoolmistress, Mrs Nettleton, was held in much respect. She was not averse to using the cane. She, and their parents, taught the children to 'know their place'. Caps should always be doffed to the Earl and Countess, as well as to Mrs Nettleton. One of the joys for the boys of reaching the age of ten was that they were given responsibility for a small plot of garden in the school grounds. Here they grew vegetables and flowers and were expected to write about it in their school journals. The girls had to do needlework instead.

Fig 18.6 Swithland men outside the Post Office, 1920s. (left to right): Reg Reader or George Botterill, Joe Lines, Les Bunney, John Leatherland snr, Ken Paterson and his dog.

The boys soon took their place among the men of the village. At nine years old they joined the village men's club gatherings at the Memorial Hall. On Monday, Thursday and Friday evenings the men gathered socially for billiards, table skittles, shove ha'penny, cards and dominoes. Wednesday nights saw the village women meeting at the Memorial Hall as the 'Bluebird Guild' for social and sewing time. Tuesday evenings were devoted to dancing classes, and on Saturday nights there was always a Whist Drive.

While the Memorial Hall served as a social centre for all the villagers, The Griffin Inn was the place where the men went for their beer. There were just the two rooms, one being the old 'club room'. And there would seem to have been a variety of ways – more or less legal – in which the men raised their beer money. According to Jack Copson, Joe Bunney, the estate timber man, might have been 'tempted' to sell the occasional tree for beer money. Other men poached and sold rabbits and pheasants. Rabbits were netted or snared; pheasants were caught using flashlights. While rabbits sold for 9d each, a pheasant could raise four shillings. It also made a good Sunday lunch. Leonard Copson, one of Jack's cousins, remembered his parents teaching him to refer to a poached pheasant as 'beaky', if ever his school teacher should ask him what he had for lunch.

The weekends gave everyone some precious leisure time. Sunday was for church-going, morning and evening services, with Sunday School in the afternoon. Saturday afternoons, however, were free times, even during harvest. In the summer, the cricket pitch on the Hall land behind the church was a focal point. Two cricket teams used the pitch: the village team played on Saturdays, while the Earl's cricketing friends played on Thursdays. There were annual special village events too, such as May Day, when the village May pole was set up, Midsummer Revels and Hallowe'en.

The latter was much enjoyed, with people dressing up. Jack Copson remembered Nurse Prior dressing up as a witch. There were turnip lanterns, games and prizes.

In the days before electricity was installed in the village, homes were lit by oil lamps and candles. Most homes usually had just the one tap, in the kitchen, where there was a kitchen range kept alight all year through, and a copper for the hot water. Hurricane lamps were used to light the cow-sheds.

Breakfast was an important meal, cooked every day in the Copson household by Jack's grandfather: porridge, bacon, egg and fried bread with a pint mug of tea.

Pig slaughtering was an important annual event. Every home had its own pigsty. The slaughterer, Joe Stockwell, came from Woodhouse Eaves, and slaughtering was always done at night.

In 1969 another 'old villager' – sadly anonymous, but apparently female, and possibly a member of the Bunney family – recorded some of her memories from the same period in the church magazine.

> I remember old Tom Hill, who lived up behind the Chapel, telling me he walked to work every day to Mountsorrel granite quarry on a breakfast of half a dried herring and a piece of bread, with another bit of bread and cheese for his mid-day snack. The one bright side of this meagre diet must have been that the bread was home made, as each villager gleaned his own corn and took it to Woodhouse Eaves windmill to be ground.
>
> The farmers had to provide bundles of faggots at hedge-cutting which were used on baking day for the fire in the communal beehive oven opposite the Chapel. The ashes were removed and each family's loaves put in, with, I expect, the odd pot of rabbit stew if they were lucky.
>
> Transport was always a problem, and any luckless child who had to have his tonsils out had to be taken by the milk-float as far as Rothley Station, go by train, walk to Leicester Infirmary, have the operation, and, on being discharged, often in a semi-conscious state, be carried back to the same station, and chance getting a lift back the last three miles. If he was lucky enough to have an appointment for the right day, he might go by Carrier's Cart, with its wonderful assortment of shoppers and produce, and return with even more parcels and commissions, for the Carrier was the equivalent of our Mail Order catalogue.
>
> My highlights were the visit of the barrel organ, and the magic of the Christmas Waits and Handbell Ringers getting nearer and nearer and the fun of singing myself when I was older.
>
> In a way we were among some of the pioneers of Religious Drama, for we produced a wonderful 'Spectacular' called 'Two Christmas Eves' which started with revelry in the hall of the Lord of the Manor, and ended with a version of the first Christmas. Its cast included almost every person in the village and it was so

successful that we did it in Loughborough Town Hall. Lots of us will also remember the many Church Pageants we took part in.

Another pioneer venture was the School for Mothers, with its monthly health talk and baby weighing, and the Blue Bird Guild, with its Long Vision nights and all sorts of other activities, which was like an early Women's Institute.

The coming of modern transport suddenly plunged the village into change. Over half of the houses were built since cars made it possible for people to live here and work elsewhere. It has perhaps tended to make us less dependant on home-made pleasures and, alas, has given us less chance to do things together or even get to know each other's names, but a happy village can still be a very real 'Family' in an increasingly unfriendly world.[11]

The 'old villager' referred to the Christmas pageant of 1928. On Friday 21st December 1928 the *Loughborough Echo* printed an enthusiastic report.

A pageant or a play, whichever word you prefer, representing the Babe in Bethlehem and the legend of Good King Wenceslas is appropriate to this season. And when the news came that the presentation would be given by the villagers of Swithland, interest was enhanced. Happily today we hear more and more of these village societies who foster legend and story by public performances and of these, fewer will have a higher place in art and accuracy than the one seen on Saturday evening in Loughborough Town Hall. For this we are greatly indebted to Mrs Archibald Turner, who also, we understand, wrote or arranged the scenes and the tableaux. The crowded audience gave witness to this by spontaneous applause, and indeed, for the equable narration of the scenes it would have been better if no encores had been given in the second part. First came the legend with appropriate music and carols sung by a Loughborough choir, and one witnessed with pleasure one incident followed by another – the three ships that came sailing by, the bringing in of the boar's head, the carousing feast, the merry making for the children, the Yule log – an easy succession of scenes associated with Christmas tide, in which all the villagers showed encouraging form towards a successful evening being spent. We desire to single out a special feature in the legend – the jester, who was, we may say, the life and soul of the stage performance.

The 'other Christmas Eve' dealt with the ever welcome story of the Babe of Bethlehem, the arrival at the inn, the shepherds' adoration, the three wise men, and the reverent gifts of children. Some were in active form, some were seen in tableaux, some in Christmas hymns, some in libretto, but all of these illustrating, with the reverence, the care and the love that such narrative requires, the ever new Story of the Nativity. How lavishly Mrs Turner must have spent her time in the production, and how freely the visitors gave their aid, not only in the scenes, but in the preparation of home made costumes. Almost with regret we were reminded that only one evening was allotted to this presentation.

At the close, Canon Briggs warmly complimented the performers and their leader, and Mrs Turner acknowledged the compliment. The proceeds were in aid of the Parish Church Sunday School and the Swithland Blue Bird Guild.[12]

Villagers Miss Beatrice Bunney, Mrs May Musgrove and Les Copson, interviewed in 2000, still remembered the occasion. Mrs Musgrove was able to name some of the performers. The Jester: Miss Lois Turner; Dame Trot: Mrs Cissy Hubbard; Harpist: Miss Emma Minkley; Joseph: Mrs Patterson; King: Mrs Sally Minkley; King: Mrs Vera Copson; King: Miss Alice Hemsley; Yule Log Boys: Roy and Ted Lloyd; Boar's Head: Evelyn Bunney; Harpist's helper: Mary Bunney; Mary: Miss Kathleen Hoult; Angels: May and Elsie Copson; Angel Gabriel: Kitty Minkley; Shepherd: Mrs Sidney Bunney.

The Gamekeeper's Family

The early twentieth century saw various newcomers to Swithland who worked for the Swithland Hall Estate. Whilst the Lanesboroughs employed some who already lived in the village, many of their household staff owed their appointments to those serving in similar establishments elsewhere. Some of them moved on, but others stayed to bring up their families in the village. Among them was gamekeeper Percy Lloyd (c.1872–1945), the first of the Swithland Lloyds. Percy's brother Bert (Herbert), gamekeeper with the Lillingstones at Ulverscroft, had recommended him to the seventh Earl for the position of keeper at Swithland. Percy and Bert were the sons of Fred Lloyd, an Oxfordshire gamekeeper. Percy moved into Keeper's Cottage in 1905 with his wife Hannah King and their four children, and remained living in the cottage until his death in 1945. Five more children were born to them in Swithland, making nine children in all: Violet (1898–1943), Emily May (b.1901), Fred (1903–1978), George (b.1905), Bill (1908–1995), Gladys (1911–1997), Dorothy (1912–1995), Ted (1915–1995) and Roy (b.1918).

Four of the Lloyd children married and left the village: (Emily) May married a Canadian soldier and emigrated, Gladys and Dorothy married and moved into Mountsorrel and Cropston respectively, remaining, with their families, part of the Swithland village and church family. Roy, after his marriage, however, settled in Somerset and Devon.

Violet married George Spence from Littlethorpe, who drove a Sentinel steam lorry. They lived in a cottage next to the old Swithland pinfold all their lives. Fred, an excellent cricketer, first followed in his father's footsteps as an under-keeper at Swithland Hall, but, after the break up of much of the Estate, worked for the Water Board at Cropston. He never married, living on at Keeper's Cottage with his father after his mother's death, and then with his sister Gladys. George started out as a gardener at the Hall, first living in the gardener's cottage opposite the church, then with his wife and family in a cottage on Kinchley Lane, and finally settled in Cotes. William (Bill) worked at Swithland Reservoir, walking across the fields to work each day. He married Peggy, who worked at the Hall, and they lived in an estate house until they both moved to work for the Osborne family, first at West Acre, The Ridgeway, and later at Kinchley House. Bill and Peggy retired to Longlands Farm, where their son Peter and his wife Mary had been running a poultry business in the village. After Bill's death in 1995, Peggy moved away to Cambridgeshire to live with her son and his wife. Ted Lloyd lived in Swithland all his life, apart from the war years. He became a bricklayer on leaving school, although he was always a gamekeeper at heart. He married Phyllis Yates in 1942; she had come to Swithland Hall to work for Lady Lanesborough as a teenager in the 1930s. In 1948, they moved into the newly-built council house at 101 Main Street and lived there until Ted died, aged eighty, in 1995.

Phyllis Lloyd died in 2007 and there are now no Lloyds living in the village. Ted and Phyllis' son Rodney and his family, however, still maintain a Swithland worshipping connection. Rodney married Sherrin Rutter at Swithland in 1971, their daughter Emma married Matthew Ross at Swithland in 2005 and Emma's son Edward was baptised at Swithland in 2006. Rodney remembers his days at the village school in the 1940s and 50s, playing in the street, helping John Leatherland on Pit Close Farm, playing cricket for Woodhouse Eaves, singing in St Leonard's Church choir, ringing the bells and joining the beaters on shooting days at Swithland Hall.

Tourist Attraction

After World War One, Swithland villagers benefitted by their village's status as a tourist attraction. As city dwellers became country tourists, many of the residents advertised teas, or let rooms in their homes to boarders, which must have been a welcome boost to the village economy. Mr Illsley, who farmed Swithland Wood Farm, set up a campsite on his land. Initially, Leicester city dwellers travelling to the campsite caught the train to Rothley and then walked to the woods, but later there was a bus from Leicester that they could catch. Tents on the campsite gradually became wooden bungalows and chalets, and eventually small caravans appeared.

Bell Ringing

One of the Sunday activities for the men[13] of the village was bell-ringing. St Leonard's six bells were given by Sir John Danvers between 1760 and 1764.[14] Living memory goes back to ringing in the 1920s. Villager ringers were in the majority then, which meant that the bells were rung mainly for evensong, as the men were mostly at work in the morning. Older ringers were always glad to pass on their skills to new members of the tower. From at least the 1920s, Thursday night was practice night, and it still is. Gweneth Gimson (then Kilby) of Swithland Lane remembers being taught to ring by Ted Lloyd, in the days when the band included Roy Lloyd, Frank Spence and

George Lloyd. Villager May Musgrove recalls that during the 1930s the tower captain was Bill Lloyd, and that he taught her to ring. Another learner at the time was Peggy Lloyd, and band members included Joe Bunney, Charlie Pratt and Mr Raynor. John Leatherland recalls that his father, John Leatherland senior, a ringer, was at one time tower captain. One of the village traditions was to ring the bells to welcome newly weds back from their honeymoons.[15]

Mr George Spence, who married Violet Lloyd and lived in 136 Main Street, was tower captain in the mid 1930s. Spence was presented with a 'silver bar for careful lorry driving, without accident, for six years', and his colleagues pride in him was shared with the whole deanery in its monthly magazine.[16] In Spence's time, the belfry windows were made fit to open. He reported to the PCC in 1936 that 'the ringers found the belfry unbearably hot in the summer months owing to lack of ventilation.'[17] George died, sadly as a relatively young man, in 1937.

During World War Two, there was the inevitable break from ringing, but, at the end of the War, there was great joy when the ringers returned from war service and the bells were heard again.

The Telephone

It was not until 1928 that a Swithland resident was connected to the telephone. The very first telephones in the United Kingdom date back to the late 1870s, but a unified telephone system was not available in most of Britain until 1912. It took longer for rural areas to be connected, and Kelly's directories record its increasing popularity. The directory had always been a bit of an arbiter in declaring 'who was who' locally, as it listed in its pages the principal private residents in town and village as well as the commercial businesses. In Swithland in 1899, for example, principal private residents included the Earl, the farmers and graziers, shopkeepers and a bricklayer. When the telephone connection was established locally in the 1920s, the directory recorded that information too.

The first users locally were the gentry and those who ran businesses. In 1925, local telephone holders were:

>Allen, Charles Maclaren, carrier, TN Woodhouse Eaves 3
>Le Fevre's Shop, TN Woodhouse Eaves 4
>Dr Tuckett, TN Woodhouse Eaves 5
>The Golf Club, TN Woodhouse Eaves 9
>Mr Heath, The Oaks, TN Woodhouse Eaves 21
>Lady Rowena Paterson, Bird Hill, TN Woodhouse Eaves 22
>Mr Fielding Johnson, Maplehurst, TN Woodhouse Eaves 26

In 1928, one Swithland 'private resident' was named by Kelly, the rector, but he was not connected to the telephone. There were, however, two Swithland commercial listings that were connected: William Green, land agent to the Earl of Lanesborough (TN Rothley 1), and Samuel Briers, of The Griffin Inn (TN Woodhouse Eaves 31).

A mile away in Rothley Plain, however, forty-two of the sixty-four private residents listed by Kelly in 1928 had telephone connections.

NAME	ADDRESS	TELEPHONE
Adams, Stanley	Ingledene, Swithland Lane	Rothley 29
Aitken, Geo.	Brieryshaw, Rothley Plain	Rothley 75
Ashwell, Geo.	Coburn, Swithland Lane	
Bailey, Mrs	Berhampore, Swithland Lane	
Baker, Arthur	Billinge, Swithland Lane	Rothley 97
Barton, Clement	Forest View, Swithland Lane	Rothley 120
Barton, Maurice	Toneham, Rothley Plain	Rothley 84
Beal, Mrs	Glenarrif, Swithland Lane	Rothley 54
Bone, Arthur	Mill Hill Cottage, Rothley Plain	
Chambers, Andr	Glenmona, Swithland Lane	
Chambers, Arthr	Nilgiris, Rothley Plain	Rothley 51
Davies, Alfred	The Oaks, Swithland Lane	Rothley 5
Eastwood, Jos.	Holmecroft, Swithland Lane	
Frost, Chas.	Windycroft, Swithland Lane	Rothley 52
Gee, Capt. C.G.	Uplands, The Ridgeway	Rothley 31
Gimson, Harry	Daneway, Rothley Plain	Rothley 109
Goddard, G.H.	Latharna, Swithland Lane	Rothley 143
Goddard, Owen	Merok, Rothley Plain	Rothley 80
Hammond, Herbt	Chaseside, Rothley Plain	
Hanford, Albt	The Ridgeway	Rothley 91
Hanford, Miss	The Coppice, The Ridgeway	Rothley 53
Harris, John H.	The Bungalow, Swithland Lane	
Harrison, John E.	Swithland Lane	
Heatherill, Jas	Swithland Lane	
Hoggett, C. Francis	Rathnay, Swithland Lane	Rothley 33
Holton, the Misses	Hillsborough, Rothley Plain	Rothley 67
Hopkins, Herbert	The Firs, Rothley Plain	Rothley 87
Hunt, Wm Robinson	Midrise, Swithland Lane	Rothley 47
Johnson, Gerald	Three Oaks, The Ridgeway	Rothley 32
Kibart, Arthur	Brentwood, Swithland Lane	
Kilby, Walter	Maplecote, Swithland Lane	
Lane, Harold	Harcla, Swithland Lane	
Lanesborough	Swithland Hall	Rothley 1
Langton, Jos	The Ridgeway	Rothley 62
Lead, William H.	Holly Lodge, The Ridgeway	
Martin, Chas H.	Kinchley House	Rothley 69
Moore, Wm	Lynton, Swithland Lane	Rothley 127
Morgan Fred H.	Covertside, The Ridgeway	Rothley 104
Oliver, Fred. J.	Swithland Rectory	
Oliver, Arthur C.	The Ridgeway	Rothley 112
Oram, Thos.	Sunnycroft, Swithland Lane	Rothley 11
Paget, Mrs	The Ridgeway	Rothley 78
Paine, John S.	Red Walls, The Ridgeway	Rothley 48

Palfreyman, Arth	Fairview, Swithland Lane	Rothley 55
Pegg, Geoffrey	Wayside, Swithland Lane	Rothley 21
Pettipher, Walt.	The Chestnuts, Swithland Lane	
Potter, Mrs	Woodside, Swithland Lane	
Price, William E.	Grey Rigg, Swithland Lane	Rothley 89
Pye, William J.W.	Northfield, Swithland Lane	Rothley 90
Riley, Alfred	Sandbeck, Swithland Lane	Rothley 125
Royce, David C.	The Laurels, Swithland Lane	
Russell, Robert	Nithsdale, Swithland Lane	
Sadd, Clarence D.	Rothley Plain	Rothley 73
Simpson, Albert	Charnwood House, Swithland Lane	
Smith, Chas. E.	The Ridgeway	Rothley 30
Stibbe, Chas	Lexden, Rothley Plain	Rothley 13
Stone, Frank F.	Budden View, Rothley Plain	
Storer, Thos	Brewood, Rothley Plain	
Taylor, Rev A.W.	The Gables, Swithland Lane	
Viccars Wm A	The Homestead	Rothley 18
Wagstaffe, Sid. H	Birkin	Rothley 118
Walker, David A	White Cottage, Swithland Lane	Rothley 136
Wallace, Henry A	Newlands, Swithland Lane	Rothley 35
Wilkes, John	The Spinneys, The Ridgeway	Rothley 9
Wykes, Percy	The Woodlands, Swithland Lane	

Two Communities with One Spiritual Home

Today it is hard to believe that two communities of people, the one in Swithland village and the other on Rothley Plain, could have lived so close to each other and yet have such different standards of living. The fascinating thing was that both communities happily shared a spiritual home in St Leonard's Church. The Parochial Church Council records indicate something of the way in which these two communities grew together, even though for a number of years the morning congregation mainly came from Swithland Lane and the evening congregation, largely because of morning farming duties, from Swithland village.

Whilst new forms of local government had been established in 1894, it was another twenty-five years before Parliament passed comparable legislation for church governance. In 1919, however, the Church of England Assembly (Powers) Act was passed, involving, for the first time, lay church members in all aspects of decision making in the Church of England, locally, regionally and nationally. The village hierarchical order, though, remained. Not surprisingly it took some time for people to adjust to the consequent social changes. Incumbents, for example, continued as ex-officio chairmen for church meetings in their benefice. And in Swithland, in the absence of a rector, the congregation first turned to their other traditional authority figure, the Earl of Lanesborough, appointing him as acting chairman of church meetings right up until 1954.

Despite that courtesy, Swithland's ecclesiastical community moved relatively quickly into a more democratic form of church government. After Murray-Dixon's resignation, the power base in the village clearly shifted, but not, as they might have expected, towards the Turners at The Cottage in Swithland's Main Street. Increasingly it was church-going families who had moved into the new housing development on Rothley Plain, many of them business and professional people, who worked with the Swithland villagers to ensure the future of their parish and parish church.

Events worked with them. The challenge from 1939–55 of a long interregnum at St Leonard's Church necessitated and raised up strong congregational leadership. The pattern of 'newcomers' working together with 'old' villagers for the good of all did much to ensure the successful future of the village community in Swithland when it had to adapt to the sale of Swithland Hall Estate in the 1950s.

Change in the Church

The Church of England Assembly (Powers) Act of 1919 required that parochial church councils be set up for all benefices in the Church of England. Swithland's church records date from 1920. The first church meeting and church council minutes book[18] gives electoral roll lists for 1920, 1930 and 1933. Dates of removals and additions were not recorded, nor, on the whole, were detailed addresses. It would appear, though, that the first Electoral Roll (listed in PCC secretary Mrs Nettleton's clear handwriting) comprised eighty-seven persons, (with four insertions, italicised below, in another hand) and that the number had risen to ninety-nine in the 1930s.[19] Every member of the 1920 roll lived in Swithland village.

The 1920 electoral names were:

Adnett	George Voiles	Swithland
Adnett	Alice	
Bates	Ann	Forest End Farm
Bates	Mathew Dakin	
Bates	Mary Juliana	
Bates	William James	
Bates	Mary Ann Lucy	
Bates	Beatrice Amy	
Bunney	Emma	
Bunney	Hilda May	
Bunney	Frederick	
Bunney	Sarah Ann	
Bunney	Annie Violetta	
Bunney	Edith Evelyn	
Bunney	Walter	
Bunney	Mary Ann	
Bunney	Johnson	
Bunney	Joseph	

Bunney	Jane	
Bunney	Alwyne Everard	
Bunney	Annie	
Bunney	May	
Brown	George	
Cupit	Robert William	
Copson	Mary	Hall Farm
Copson	Ambrose	Hall Farm
Copson	Harry	
Copson	Vera	
Cramp	John	
Cramp	Lavinia	
Cook	Albert	
Frisby	Joseph	*removed by request*
Frisby	Adeline Elizabeth	*made by letter*
Frisby	Adeline	*dated 26th Jan. 1927*
Hoult	Samuel	
Hoult	*Kathleen Grace*[20]	
Hoult	Ethel Martha	
Hodges	Elizabeth	*re-entered as Mrs Smith*
Hornsby	Jane Ann	
Hornsby	Ivy Annie Elsie	
Hodges	Sarah Jane	
Hansford	Olive	
Ind	Elsie	
Lloyd	Percival	
Lloyd	Hannah	
Lloyd	Violet	
Murray-Dixon	Etheldreda	The Rectory
Murray-Dixon	Charles Edward Trevelyan	
Murray-Dixon	Eleanor Margaret Trevelyan	
Minkley	George	Swithland
Minkley	Mary Sophia	Swithland
Minkley	Horace	
Minkley	Alice May	*Palmer*
Minkley	Herbert	
Minkley	Mary Ann	
Minkley	John William	
Minkley	Albert Frederick	
Minkley	Muriel	
Minkley	Alfred	
Minkley	Emma	
Moore	Horace George	
Moore	*Alice*	
Moore	Edward James	The Cottage
Moore	Margery	The Cottage
Nettleton	Millicent	

Pepper	Edwin	Swithland
Pepper	Emma	
Pepper	Albert Edwin	
Pepper	Kate	
Preston	Mary	
Paterson	Emily Elizabeth	Hall Gardens
Pratt	Charles	
Pratt	Ada	
Pratt	Dorothy	
Smith	Thomas	
Smith	*Elizabeth*	
Smith	Susan	
Turner	Archibald	The Cottage
Turner	Gladys Marie	
Tarry	Alice	The Hall
Taylor	Frederick William	
Taylor	Sarah	
Tyers	Elizabeth	
Tomlin	John	
Tomlin	Annie	
Underwood	Tom	
Underwood	Elizabeth	
Hubbard	Elizabeth	
Wilford	Doris	
Wainwright	Charles	
Wainwright	Mary Ellen	

Added later, still by Mrs Nettleton, thirteen names:

Prior (1923)	Emmeline	The Cottage
Spence (1923)	George	Swithland
Lloyd (1923)	Frederick P.	
Lloyd (1923)	George L.	
Harrison[21]	Hilda M.	Swithland
Paterson	Laurie	Hall Gardens
Turner	Lois M. G.	The Cottage
Bunney	Dorothy	Swithland
Spence	Violet	
Walsh	Elinor M.T.	
Davenport	Margery	
Lanesborough	Charles J Brinsley Butler	Swithland Hall
Bates	Edith	Forest End Farm

Through the 1920s, more and more families living in Rothley Plain and The Ridgeway joined the electoral roll of St Leonard's Church. Among the first were Mr and Mrs Walter Kilby of Maplecote, Swithland Lane. They were followed by: Mr and Mrs Arthur Bone of Mill Hill Cottage, Swithland Lane;

Mr and Mrs Sidney Wagstaffe, first of The Bungalow, 63 Swithland Lane, and later of Birkin, 140 Swithland Lane; Mr and Mrs Harry Gimson of Daneway, 76 Swithland Lane; Mr and Mrs Simmons of The Byeways, 135 Swithland Lane; Mr and Mrs Herbert Hammond, Chaseside, 146 Swithland Lane; Mr and Mrs Arthur McCurry, Three Oaks, The Ridgeway; and Mr and Mrs Albert Herbert, of The Gables, 68 Swithland Lane.

Additions and deletions to Swithland's electoral roll were recorded through the 1920s. The first set, not in Mrs Nettleton's handwriting, comprised:

Lloyd	Percival William	
Lines	Joseph Henry	
Minkley (1923)	Herbert	
Botterill	George	
Paterson	Malcolm	
Burgoyne	Bessie	
Copson	Alfred Ernest	
Copson	Edith	
Bunney	Annie Maria	
Bunney	Ellen	
Oliver	Frederick James	
Oliver	Marian	
Kilby	Walter	Maplecote, Swithland Lane
Kilby	Mary E.	
Minkley	Kathleen	
Cook	Charles Herbert	
Cook	Eliza	

The next set of entries was in Mrs Nettleton's hand.

Bone	Barbara Wellington	Swithland Lane, Rothley
Bone	Minnie Laura	"
Bone	Arthur W	"
Heatherill	Margaret Scott	"
Wagstaffe	Charlotte	Birkin, Rothley Plain
Wagstaffe	Sidney Herbert	"
Wilson	Nathaniel	Swithland
Standage	Arthur	"
Minkley	Horace	"
Minkley	Olive Agnes	"
Leake	H. Elizabeth	"
Taylor	Leslie	
Taylor	Edith Helen	
Herbert	Edna Minnie	*Mrs G Lloyd*
Beeby	William	
Beeby	Annie Elizabeth	
Minkley	Evelyn	
Minkley	Charles Edward	

Adnett	Thomas George	
Gimson	Alice W.	Rothley Plain
Gimson	Harry H.	Rothley Plain
Jordan	Frances May	Atkin Street, Leicester (Camp weekends)

Swithland's first Parochial Church Council meeting took place on 13th April 1920 in the schoolroom. The minutes, and those of subsequent meetings, show a church community keen to come to grips with their new responsibilities. The rector, James Murray Dixon, chaired the meeting, and Mr Paterson recorded the minutes. There was a good deal of general discussion with regard to various matters and points of order. The chairman ruled that any such persons as were on the Electoral Roll were eligible to attend the Parochial Church Meetings. Various resolutions were over-ruled by a suggestion from the chairman that a list of names of those eligible to serve on the Parochial Church Council be now taken in which a selection might be taken at a later meeting.

The following list was made of 'Candidates properly proposed and seconded by members of the Parochial Church Meeting, assembled in the room: viz – Messrs Horace Moore, Joseph Frisby, Archibald Turner and Mrs Turner, Mrs Nettleton, Mrs Hoult, Mrs S. Bunney, Miss Hodges, Mr P. Lloyd, Mrs E. Pepper, Mrs Paterson, Mrs A. Pepper, Mrs Pratt, Mr S. Hoult, Miss Bates, Miss Annie Bunney, Mrs A. Copson, Mrs Lloyd, Mrs G. Minkley, Mrs Frisby, Mrs Adnett, Mrs A. Minkley, Miss V. Lloyd, Miss Frisby, Mrs H. Minkley, Miss Underwood, Miss Tarry, and Miss Ivy Hornsby, after which the meeting was adjourned'.[22]

The meeting reconvened three days later on the 16th April. Of the twenty-eight names proposed at the 13th April meeting as candidates for the Church Council, some names were removed at the beginning of the meeting as being ineligible under the rules: Mr S. Hoult, Mrs S. Bunney, Mrs Pratt, and Mrs A. Copson. Elections were then held. Mr A. Turner and Mrs Hoult were elected as parish representatives to the Ruri-decanal Conference. Fifteen people were further elected to serve on the Parochial Church Council: Mrs Frisby, Mr Lloyd, Mr Frisby, Mrs A. Pepper, Mrs Paterson, Miss A. Bunney, Mr A. Minkley, Mrs Adnett, Mrs Lloyd, Mrs Nettleton, Mrs Turner, Miss Bates, Mr H. Moore, Mrs G. Minkley and Mrs H. Minkley. The elected members then convened as the Parochial Church Council and elected the following officers: Mrs Turner, vice chairman; Mr Paterson, secretary; and Mr Turner, treasurer.

The minute books show that at first, while the compulsory annual church and council meetings were held every April, the council slowly began to meet more frequently. In 1921 in Swithland, the wardens still seemed to be taking responsibility for the church finances, even though the 1919 Church of England Assembly (Powers) Act had transferred most of their financial responsibilities to the Parochial Church Council. At the 1921 annual meeting, Mr Turner, as treasurer, proposed through the chairman: 'that which is known as the Swithland Quota to the Diocesan Fund be raised and paid by the churchwardens before the council has legal authority'. No vote was taken, but the rector agreed to discuss the matter with the churchwardens.[23] By 1922, however, the council had taken up some of its new financial responsibilities, and had elected a Standing Committee to manage them. 'It was proposed and seconded that the funds for the upkeep of the churchyard and the appointment of one to keep same in order be left to the standing committee. Carried'. Later that year the council set up a finance committee which recorded in June that the appointment of an organist should be left in abeyance – Miss Illsley was the temporary organist at the time – and also that two church members, Mr A. Turner and the Earl of Lanesborough, were prepared to give an annual donation to the church (£15 and £10 respectively).

At the church council meeting prior to the annual meeting in 1923, there was a discussion as to the amount of the fund in hand available for repairing or restoring the nave of the church. It was agreed that a discussion about finance be held at the coming annual meeting, but that before then the Finance Committee should meet and draw up a balance sheet to present to the annual meeting. This was duly accepted and passed at the annual church meeting on 4th April. At this meeting Mr Lloyd was re-elected as rector's warden and Miss Hodges was elected as people's warden. Miss Hodges had been acting as caretaker of the church, but resigned from this post at the meeting. Mr Albert Cook was re-appointed to take care of the churchyard.

A Church Restoration Committee was in place by 1923, and the church council had approved a motion proposed by the rector that the Church Restoration Committee 'had its sanction and approval to deal with the fabric and furniture of the Church as they shall think most desirable'. Mr Turner asked whether the Parochial Church Council thought that the restoration should be carried out as a whole. The rector replied that that should be left to the committee. The need was dire. 'There were holes in the roof, small trees growing out of the slates and water continually falling on the floor'.[24] The years that followed saw the Parochial Church Council struggling to cope with a restoration scheme begun by one rector and completed under another. Their struggles opened up something of a power struggle, resulting in resignations from the council and tensions both in church and local community. This was not helped by the vocal involvement of the local press. Eventually the church's financial challenges were resolved when, in 1927, Mr and Mrs Turner made a generous donation to the church 'to commemorate the Restoration of the Diocese of Leicester, and a Thank Offering for twenty-five years of happy married life'.[25] The new young rector, Frederick Oliver, must have been hugely relieved that the primary financial burden on the church had been lifted and that the restoration programme had been completed.

Newcomers From 'The Lane'

Oliver must also have been encouraged by the presence in his church community of relative newcomers Mr and Mrs Walter Kilby from Swithland Lane. The Kilbys seem early to have won the trust and confidence of the

Fig 18.7 Walter, Mary and Gweneth Kilby.

congregation at St Leonard's, as Walter was soon elected as People's Warden and his wife Mary as a member of the Church Council. Two months later, Mr Turner, who was still the Council's treasurer, proposed that Walter Kilby become the secretary to the Free-Will Offering Scheme.

The Kilby family had moved into Maplecote, 81 Swithland Lane c. 1923. Previously they had lived in Woodhouse Eaves, worshipping at St Paul's Church, where Walter Kilby served on the Parochial Church Council. After a period of walking his family the two miles or so through Swithland to St Paul's Church and back, Kilby decided to make St Leonard's Church his family's church. He believed they might be able to make a useful contribution there. It was a significant and important decision for his family and for the church.

Kilby, who worked in the shoe trade, quickly became a natural and acceptable leader in a church where the lives of the majority of the members were still very much built round a traditional agricultural estate. They elected him People's Church Warden in 1926, which was only three years after his family began to attend the church. He served as warden for twenty-seven years; on his twenty-fifth anniversary, co-warden Joseph Dransfield organised a thanksgiving gift from church members – a television set and aerial. After Kilby's death in 1954, his widow Mary was elected as People's Warden in his stead. And when Mary Kilby died in 1967, their daughter Gweneth, who had married Unitarian next-door neighbour Ben Gimson, was elected as People's Warden, and held office until March 2009 – fifty-two years after first being elected. The Kilby family's fine tradition of service, particularly important through times of interregnum, together with their sound financial sense, has been a major guarantee of the church's continuing strong presence in Swithland.

Albert Herbert, an esteemed Leicester architect, had bought and extended The Gables in Swithland Lane as a home for himself and his wife. He was soon adopted as the architect to St Leonard's Church.[26] As a member of the church, he initially worked with the Parochial Church Council to complete the 1920s restoration project. He accepted election to the Church Council in 1936, but resigned in 1941 when he moved away from the parish. Herbert's continuing advice to and work for the church until 1953, however, ensured a sound structure for the church building and, thanks to the continuing financial commitment of church members, the building has been maintained in good condition ever since.

New Ideas and New People

Swithland soon discovered that, in Frederick Oliver, they had an enthusiastic young rector who was eager to move the church forward spiritually. In 1927 he proposed the formation of a Church of England Young Men's Society, a Communicants' Guild and a Women's Guild. In the first of these proposals he was supported by Walter Kilby who advised Church Council members of the work and procedures of Young Men's societies that he had been involved with. The Church Council, however, although clearly more confident and focussed in the new regime, was not yet ready to lend its support to these new ideas. Some members of the council, too – notably Mr and Mrs Turner – were suspicious of Oliver's churchmanship and his agenda for what might have seemed like 'change'. Council members were, however, ready to welcome new members into church life, among them the Bones and the Wagstaffes who lived along Swithland Lane. Mr Bone became the church's auditor, and Mrs Wagstaffe was elected to the Parochial Church Council in 1927.

At the end of 1927 a proposal from the diocesan authorities was put to the Parochial Church Council: that Swithland be transferred from East Akeley to Guthlaxton[27] Deanery. The Church Council strongly rejected the suggestion, advising both the archdeacon and the ruri-decanal council of their feelings. The matter was raised again at the next Ruri-Decanal Council, when Swithland was pleased to find that they had the support of their deanery colleagues. In March 1928 the Parochial Church Council secretary recorded, with some evident satisfaction, 'nothing further heard of the matter up to present'.

By the time Oliver resigned in 1931, not only had all debts in relation to the church restoration work been paid off, but the organ had also been restored, with the £450 costs raised and paid. Financial affairs were under control and a free-will offering envelope scheme had been launched. A memorial lych gate to Archibald Turner (d. 1928) was erected in 1929.[28] A small choir had also been formed, some work set up amongst the children of the congregation and the annual Bluebell Service started. 'It was just a casual word one day in 1928. The Rector and Father walked out of church and mentioned bluebells. Why not have a Service in the woods? And that is how it all began. I know that is true because I was there. Mrs Burrows played the harmonium for the first service and I played afterwards'.[29]

Concern for a necessary extension to the churchyard had led to various conversations with the Earl. According to Mr Turner, the Earl had offered some twelve feet of land on the Rectory side of the churchyard. In 1929 the rector said that the Earl had 'promised' a ten yard width of land on the south side of the church. Neither offer, however, came to anything, presumably, in part, because the seventh Earl died in 1929. Discussions on raising additional monies to augment the living suffered the same fate, possibly because monies kept getting diverted to other, apparently more pressing, financial demands. This was unfortunate, as it may have contributed to Rector Oliver's resignation in 1930. 'He couldn't afford to stay' said one parishioner. There was also, of course, the church's reluctance to rise to some of the new spiritual challenges that Rector Oliver put before them. Surprisingly, no mention of Oliver's departure, or subsequent tragic death,[30] was recorded in the Parochial Church Council minute books. The council did, though, record its delight in 1931 when it heard that Archdeacon John Mackay might be willing to take up the living.

At his first Parochial Church Council meeting, Mackay stressed the importance of regular attendance at church and especially at Communion. He also urged regular giving, commending in particular the Free-Will Offering Scheme. Both themes were constantly re-iterated during his time as rector. Certainly, during his ministry, the church's finances remained satisfactory, but that was arguably due more to the Earl of Lanesborough's annual donation of £25, than to regular generous giving by parishioners in general. Another of Mackay's priorities, presumably because of his own past ministry, was the parish's support for work of the church overseas. In that he was well supported by the Parochial Church Council. Their minutes of meetings through these years do communicate a sense of purpose and efficiency, but Mackay did not always seem to receive the amount of support he might have expected. At one stage he even had to cut the churchyard grass himself. The fact that he resigned because of financial problems, citing the heavy 'burden of keeping up the large Rectory and extensive grounds', and indeed died not long after his resignation, may seem to indicate a Parochial Church Council whose members, with a few notable exceptions, talked while their rector worked.

The rather predictable business of the Parochial Church Council continued to plod along in the 1930s, regardless of the war, and with an obviously tiring rector. Tennis cheered him up, however. Gweneth Kilby remembered 'He was well known for preaching and his love of tennis. He was a very good tennis player and he and I were partners at all the local tournaments. We cycled to them most Saturdays in the summer with our racquets fastened on the front. He was over six feet tall in long white flannels and I was very small in the shortest white pleated skirt. We must have looked a funny pair, but we did win tournaments and it was great fun'.

After Mackay's departure, Parochial Church Council discussions rather lost focus, and the church went into financial deficit. Regular giving was not a congregational strength; church finances depended on 'appeals' when in deficit, and the occasional 'Bring and Buy' sale.

Joseph Dransfield, who joined St Leonard's congregation in the late 1930s when he was living at Hall Farm, was an important player in the significant years between the resignation of Mackay and the appointment to the benefice, after a seventeen year interregnum, of Cecil Copp Harcourt. Dransfield had great leadership potential; the long years of the interregnum gave scope for that potential and enabled his vocation to Christian ministry to develop. A sidesman from 1938, he was elected to the Parochial Church Council in 1941 and made Rector's Warden in 1946. From the beginning, Dransfield was an enthusiastic contributor to Church Council discussions, emerging as the main encourager for fund-raising activities for church restoration work and for diocesan appeals. As warden with responsibility for fabric matters, his reports to the Parochial Church Council were always thorough, and the records he kept of the progress of the Church Restoration Fund were punctilious. He and Walter Kilby, his co-warden and church treasurer, made a good team.

Dransfield also contributed to the life of the village school as a member of the board of managers. And, in the days when there was no distinctive parish magazine, he contributed what was effectively the equivalent of 'the rector's letter' to the Swithland column in the deanery magazine. His contributions give a flavour as to life in Swithland church and village in the 1930s. Not every issue of the magazine has survived, but from those of the late 30s that have, a picture emerges of a church which supported various charities[31] through sales of work and special collections and where Mrs Herbert, Mrs Wathes, Mrs Gimson and Mrs Stanley Adams were regulars on the sanctuary flowers rota, 'quietly beautifying the church on Friday mornings'. Dransfield advertised the times of services and gave the names of the preachers. On Easter Day 1938, there were ninety-five communicants, a 'record number'. He listed those who contributed to the new Boiler Fund in 1938; their gifts totalled £45 15s. 3d. He noted special services such as those on Armistice Day with the 'usual short service at the War Memorial',[32] a Christmas Toy Service where the children brought toys for distribution to poor children in Leicester, and the annual Eastertide Egg Service, to which the children brought eggs to be taken to the Royal Infirmary.

> The number of eggs brought by the children was 302, and four chocolate eggs. A letter of warm appreciation and thanks from the Governor of the Royal Infirmary mentioned the fact that some two thousand eggs are used in the Infirmary each week.[33]

In a file that is part of the parish archives, Dransfield also kept his own records of Swithland happenings, particularly those relating to the raising of money for special purposes, together with his Swithland history research notes. He died in 1963, before he was able to put together his proposed booklet on Swithland. That task was taken up by Sydney Meadows who published a history of Swithland, based on Dransfield's notes, in 1965.

In 1960, Dransfield stood down as Rector's Warden, and offered himself to the Bishop of Leicester for ordination. After his ordination, he served in the parish of Harby, Leicestershire, but died in 1963 and was buried in the churchyard there. His memorial stone reads:

> In loving memory
> Reverend Joseph Henry DRANSFIELD
> died Dec 10 1963
> *In glory everlasting*

The 'Long Interregnum'

Swithland's long interregnum began with the resignation of John Mackay in 1939. The Bishop gave no indication that he would appoint a successor. For two or three years, the Parochial Church Council showed signs of faltering. Despite treasurer Kilby's careful husbandry, there was a deficit budget, and the 1942 diocesan quota (fourteen guineas) could not be paid in full. From 1942, the Rectory was used as a military 'hospital', fuelling fears that the appointment of a new rector would be long-delayed. The Parochial Church Council, normally chaired by the Earl of Lanesborough, focussed almost exclusively, and perhaps understandably, on the church's fabric,[34] its finances and the future of the ministry in Swithland.

In December 1945, the church council secretary wrote to the Bishop of Leicester, reminding him that the living had been vacant for more than six years, during which the parish had carried on paying its Diocesan Quota, while also keeping up its efforts for the Church Missionary Society and other church obligations. They told him that during the war there had been little visiting of the sick and distressed and that the celebration of Holy Communion was presenting special difficulties.

One of the difficulties of attracting a new incumbent for Swithland was the depressingly low level of the stipend. Clergy for whom the stipend was the only source of income could not afford to take up a living as poor as Swithland, which could only offer c. £250 p.a.[35] At a Parochial Church Council meeting in December 1936, Archdeacon Hurrell explained the Board of Finances' proposals to raise diocesan stipends that were insufficient for purpose (such as Swithland's) up to a minimum level of £300 pa. The Archdeacon asked Swithland Parochial Church Council to contribute an annual sum of money to the Board of Finance towards the grant of £43 that the board had, for some years, been making in order to bring the living of Swithland up to a diocesan minimum of £300 p.a.[36] Envelopes were distributed among the worshippers and parishioners. Mr Cecil Gee, a member of the board who lived locally, and was linked to Rothley church, came and 'occupied the pulpit' for the morning and evening services on the Sunday when the envelopes were presented. The total amount given by church members on this occasion was £15 6s. 10d. It was not enough.

In 1945 diocesan authorities informed the Parochial Church Council that 'the main difficulty in the way of an appointment' to Swithland Rectory was the size and state of the rectory house. Churchwarden Joseph Dransfield told the church council in 1946 that 'the endowment of the living had been further depleted, and that Swithland would have to be joined with another parish, most probably Old Woodhouse. St Leonard's would be the mother church and the new rector would reside in Swithland. The churchwardens had been instructed by the Ecclesiastical Commissioners to put the Rectory in order for the new incumbent when appointed'. For some reason, however, that amalgamation did not proceed.

In 1947, the Diocesan Dilapidations Committee asked the Church Council for approval to sell the Rectory. There is no record that the Parochial Church Council ever gave their consent, but it was sold, over their heads, for £5,008 12s 2d after paying expenses, to Arthur Everard Leigh Boulter. In 1948, still without a rector, and now without a parsonage house, the Parochial Church Council was told that, in view of the shortage of clergy, and the financial straits of the church, the bishop was proposing a union of benefices with Woodhouse Eaves. He would be holding a Commission of Enquiry. The Council was asked to consider whether there was enough work in the parish for a full-time clergyman, and whether the available sum of £186 per year was sufficient.

At a meeting in July 1948, the Parochial Church Council agreed unanimously to carry on as present. Nevertheless, the Bishop decided to recommend the scheme of union to the Church Commissioners. In March 1949 the Church Council resolved unanimously that the union was unacceptable. They agreed to appeal to the Church Commissioners; if a union were inevitable, they felt that it should be with Rothley. Early in 1950, the Council learnt that the Bishop's scheme had been withdrawn. In May 1954, the diocesan pastoral committee came up with yet another scheme, proposing a union of benefices between Swithland and Rothley. Swithland Parochial Church Council requested a public meeting to enable church members and villagers to meet with representatives from the diocesan pastoral committee. At the subsequent Church Council meeting, in a secret ballot, members voted sixteen to four to reject the scheme.

The Bishop capitulated. In March 1955, he wrote to the churchwardens stating his intention to install Cecil Copp Harcourt as priest-in-charge of Swithland. He would live at the Rectory, which had been bought back by Mrs Linwood Wright, previously Mrs Turner, and offered by her for use by the church on condition that it was used to house a parish priest for Swithland. In 1962, Mrs Linwood Wright gave the Rectory to the parish, with the same provisos.

Sadly, Walter Kilby did not live to see this successful resolution to the seventeen year-long battle with the diocese. He died, suddenly, in November 1954. The church's silver processional cross was presented to the church, in his memory, by his widow.

So ended the 'long interregnum'. It is worth noting that, through all those long years without a parish priest, Swithland consistently paid the full diocesan quota, maintained a full weekly provision of services and kept the building and churchyard in good repair. Another church community might have given in. St Leonard's, however, 'grew up' during those long years of fighting for its independent identity. The increasing confidence and maturity of its members as lay Christians ensured the future of the church in Swithland parish.

The Second World War and Social Change

Until 1939 the two great bastions of Swithland village life were the family at Swithland Hall and the agricultural economy. After the Second World War, however, this all changed. After a brief post First World War period of revival, the 1920s saw widespread rural depression. Prices of farm products fell, the level of rural income declined and rural populations decreased. The vitality of all communities with economies based on agriculture consequently diminished.

A counter-cultural movement in the 'green revolution', however, was spreading ever-more widely. Prime examples locally of this 'green revolution' were the new building developments in Rothley Plain and Rothley Temple. Between 1918 and 1926, while the countryside appeared to preserve its traditional appearance, the number of new small landowners in the rural areas on the edge of the city of Leicester grew steadily, arguably effecting the greatest transformation in landholding and use since the Norman Conquest. While most of those who had traditionally owned or earned their living from the land became increasingly impoverished, those whose economic fortune rested in the new worlds of industry and commerce became increasingly well-off. It was these families who bought up the land and property that was being off-loaded by the impoverished rural landowners. It may have been this turnaround in fortunes that fuelled the apparently bitter social division in Swithland referred to in the local papers of the 1960s and 70s.[37]

National Farm Records

Arguably the last hoorah of the traditional English small-holding was uttered during the Second World War with the Government's desire to make Britain as self-sufficient as possible, at least food-wise. Forgetful of the lessons of the First World War, British agriculture had been allowed to decline. A second world war brought in a second food crisis. In 1940, therefore, a National Farm Survey was begun, creating a record of every farm in Britain, noting the state of its buildings, soils, fencing and roads. Nothing like this had been attempted since William the Conqueror set out to discover the wealth of his new conquest, recording those facts in his *Domesday Book*. The survey makes interesting reading, not least in that every dwelling with potential space for growing food was listed, and not just the traditional farms. In this time of national emergency, every landowner was seen as a potential farmer and listed as such.

In the Rothley Plain area of the parish, the following houses and farms were included in the national farm records of 1944: Toneham, Rothley Plain, farmer Dr M. Barton, 74.6 acres; Brickyard Farm, farmer Chas. Copson, 82.6 acres; Linford Cottage, farmer H.M. Hyman, 12.5 acres; West Acre, The Ridgeway, farmer C. Osborne, 6.7 acres; Erin Cortref, Kinchley Lane,

Rothley Plain, farmer B.R. Rouse, owner Mountsorrel Granite Company, 10.4 acres; Rothley Plain nursery, farmer E.H. Whittle, Wantoma, Cross Lane, Rothley, owner J.T. Green Esq., 15 acres; Sandfield Farm, farmer L.F. Whittle, owner Swithland Hall Estate, 80 acres; The Upland, The Ridgeway, G.C.G. Gee, 7.6 acres; Temple Farm, Farmer S.W.T. Hoult, owners: Gimson, Fawcett and Kilby, 16.5 acres; Aberfeldy, The Ridings, Mrs G.M. Burton; Oakleigh, Cropston Road, Mr E.E. North; Wood Farm, Swithland, Farmer C.B. Lane, 124.5 acres.[38]

In Swithland, in addition to the farms and smallholdings, four others were listed. Samuel Briers at The Griffin Inn was described as having 15 acres of grass and 5 acres of oats and poultry – 'no great use is made of the land and no income is made out of it'. David Hunt farmed land in Anstey, Charles Pratt had 8 acres of grazing land – 'no great use of this land; an outlying field could be put to another farm without upsetting the tenant' – and Mr Berridge of Langton House had 1½ acres of grass and a few hens.[39]

Evacuation

With the coming of war, the countryside was seen to be a safe haven for the children of towns vulnerable to enemy bombing. A significant number of child evacuees were allocated to Swithland, especially during the first few months of the war. The children billeted in Swithland are listed in the school records. Many, but by no means all, were staying with their grandparents.

In the autumn of 1939, Robert and Barbara Burrage and Kenneth and Vera Hollocks from East London were staying at 'the White House', and Patrick Godfrey[40] from Bow was staying at The Cottage with his grandmother. During 1940, Mrs Stevens from Forest End hosted William Fenn and Sylvia Moughton from Yarmouth, and Mrs McCrum, of Reservoir House, Cropston, hosted her granddaughter Maureen McCrum and Peter Davie. Meanwhile Kenneth Hyman from Liverpool was staying at Linford Cottage (The Ridings), Robert Jelley, also from Liverpool was staying at Stanswell, Swithland Lane, Pamela Lane, from London, with the Lanes of Swithland Wood Farm, and Jean Lowe from Sunderland, Ernest Gregory from Northamptonshire and Donald Whitmore from Coventry with Mrs Leatherland at Pit Close Farm. There were fewer evacuees from afar after 1941, but among them were John Theobald from London (with Mrs Pratt, Main Street), James Adkin from Essex, Sylvia Fay from Cheshire (Swithland Wood Farm), Peter Gladwin from Essex (with Mrs Chorlton, Main Street), and Ruth Rubens and Alan Howard from London. A number of children were also evacuated to Swithland from Leicester during 1940 and 1941. Their hosts included Mrs Howden from Cropston, Mrs Pratt and Mrs F. Copson of Main Street, Mrs Briers at The Griffin Inn, Mrs Foster of Rothley Plain and Mrs Minkley at the White House.

In 1944, thirteen children[41] came to Swithland School for a few months from Bromley, Kent, and stayed with various Swithland families: Mrs Lloyd at Thatch Cottage, Lord Lanesborough at Swithland Hall, Mrs Chorlton, Mrs B. Bunney of Exning Farm, Miss Hemsley, Mrs J. Copson of Hollycroft, Mrs Leatherland, Mrs Wainwright at Forest House, Mrs Cox, Main Street,

Mrs Bryan of Delafield, Swithland Lane, and Mrs Carr of Three Oaks, The Ridgeway. Swithland also hosted two visitors from Belgium: Andrée Raiwet (1942–45) who stayed at Bybrooke Farm and Georges Gillis (1944–5) who stayed at Forest End. An air raid shelter was built in the school grounds, but there are no references in the school log as to its use.

It has to be admitted that the children were received with mixed feelings. A villager, who was a child herself at the time, recalled:

> Towards the end of the war we got some evacuees in our village. They came on a bus and were put in the village hall, which was like a community centre, to see who would take them into their homes. These were children from the East End of London who had suffered in the German bombing raids. We were astounded to see they were even poorer than we were. My mother said she could only take one girl as our house was already quite full. I think she hoped there would be no girls left when it came to her turn. When all the children had been allocated, there stood Margaret and her five brothers. She was about ten years old and refused to go anywhere without her brothers. Eventually she was persuaded to come to us, and the boys were given to two ladies who had a big house ... Margaret transferred her mothering instincts to me, and it was she who took me to school when I was small ...

Second World War Time Memories

John Leatherland, of Pit Close Farm, a youngster during the war years, has another set of memories. Pit Close housed several lodgers during the war years – among them Fritz Appel, a German prisoner of war, who stayed and worked at Pit Close. The Leatherlands described Fritz as 'a very nice man'. He kept in touch with his friends in the village after the war ended. Both Ada Leatherland and Miss Dixon sent him and his family food parcels after the war, as his hometown of Kassel had suffered from severe bombing and was one of the last major towns in West Germany to be rebuilt.

Occasionally members from the Free French and American armed services on local night manoeuvres would stay in Pit Close Barn. Fred Garland and Arthur Wardale, armed security guards at Swithland sidings, were also wartime lodgers at Pit Close. Their job was to watch the railway and to protect those trains

Fig 18.8 Fritz Appel, after the war, with his family.

carrying ammunition. By contrast, the ammunition that was stored in rows of Nissen huts on one of Lord Lanesborough's fields along Leicester Lane[42] was largely unprotected. The huts, which just had canvas hangings at front and back, were only inspected periodically.

John Leatherland also remembers helping his father with 'scavenging' during the war. 'Scavenging', the collection and removal of refuse, including 'night soil' (human waste), was a necessary task in the days before modern methods of sewage disposal came to the village. It was also a helpful additional source of income. John Leatherland senior, using his old car and trailer, collected the night soil in buckets from the big houses locally, the campsite at Swithland Woods, local army camps, and the German prisoner of war camp at Garendon Park (where petrol for transporting it was sometimes given by way of payment). Swithland's night soil collection was tipped out every morning into fields on the other side of the road from Pit Close Farm, as these fields did not drain into the reservoir.

Jim Carpenter, gamekeeper at Swithland Hall from 1946 to 1959, served as a special constable during the war years and was a sergeant in the Home Guard. John Leatherland senior was the village's ARP (air raid precautions) warden, one of whose jobs was to keep a check on blackout compliance. Jack Copson also served in the Home Guard during the war. The Swithland Home Guards belonged to the Forest Company: Charnwood Forest, of the Charnwood Battalion of the Loughborough Group. One observation post was situated in quite a deep hole, now ploughed in, in the field known locally as 'the balk',[43] which was next to Mole End Cottage.

The Home Guard was formed in 1940, in response to a broadcast call on 14th May from the Secretary of State for War, Anthony Eden. He said 'We want large numbers of men, who are British subjects, between the ages of seventeen and sixty-five to come forward now and offer their services. The name of the new force, which is to be raised, will be the Local Defence Volunteers. This name describes its duties in three words. In order to volunteer, give your name at your local Police Station'. The Lord Lieutenant was automatically chairman of the county volunteer force.[44] He helped chose the volunteers' officers, usually prominent local citizens who often had previous military experience. He chose Brigadier-General Sir Thomas Cope of Market Bosworth as Leicestershire's County Commandant. As the first Area Commandant for the Loughborough Group, Cope chose Major Charles Hamilton Martin, one of the Barrow-on-Soar Martins, a director of the Mountsorrel Granite Company, and at the time the Chairman of Leicestershire Yeomanry OCA (Old Comrades Association).

Immediately after the evacuation from Dunkirk (27th May–7th June 1940) there was great fear across the country that Germany would invade Britain. Farmers, for example, were instructed to place obstructions on all their fields over 300 yards long, to prevent any landing of invading aircraft. Patrolling seemed to be the main activity in those early months. One of the Quorn LDV team remembers that they 'used to patrol at night in twos along the railway to Rabbit Bridge, near Swithland Reservoir, because they thought the Germans would land and put poison in the water. But there was that much undergrowth we would never have seen them'.⁴⁵ From the end of July, the name 'Home Guard' came into use, but uniforms and weapons remained in short supply until late 1940.

In October 1940 the Home Guards were formally organised. The Charnwood Battalion headquarters was the Drill Hall at Mountsorrel⁴⁶ and the Forest Company headquarters was at Maplehurst, Maplewell Road, Woodhouse Eaves. The Forest Company Commander was J.R. Leeson, and his second in command was A.F.P. Wheeler.⁴⁷ There were four platoons: Woodhouse Eaves and Woodhouse, Swithland, Ulverscroft and Charley. The platoon commander for Swithland was G.E.L Alexander. In February 1941 there had been some renaming. The local battalion was re-named the 10th (Charnwood) Battalion, with five companies, A, B, C, D, E – with the old Forest Company presumably having become 'E' Company. 'E' Company had its HQ at the Schools, Woodhouse Eaves. The 10th Battalion HQ was by then at the Coppice, on the Ridgeway, Rothley Plain, and the battalion commander was Lt-Colonel C.H. Martin, OBE.

From late 1940, German bombers began to fly over the Midlands more frequently. From then, blackout measures were seen to be more important and the law was enforced much more vigorously, especially after Leicester was blitzed on 19th November.

The Home Guard was stood down officially on 3rd December 1944. The 10th (Charnwood) Battalion had planned to hold their parade on the playing fields of Loughborough College, but thanks to wet weather, had to assemble in Loughborough's Odeon cinema.

Fig 18.9 Home Guard Jim Carpenter.

> A service was conducted by their padre, Revd F.C. Hargreaves. After the King's Message had been read by Brigadier-General R.S. Abbott, Lt-Col C.H. Martin, the CO of the 10th Battalion, addressed his men. His speech was met with three cheers. Afterwards, both battalions marched past the saluting base in the Market Place to music provided by the Brush Band. Members of the women's Home Guard Auxiliary also attended, but did not parade. From there, the various companies dispersed and marched through their respective villages.⁴⁸

Those living along Swithland Lane during the war years remember a fairly quiet start to the war and the willingness of people to help with the war effort. Gweneth Kilby writes:⁴⁹

> Soon after the declaration of war, every house in the Lane was visited by an official wanting to know how many bedrooms we were not using. Mother had two, so we had two evacuees from Leeds – boys aged 9 and 10. They had to walk to Rothley School. After a year, they moved into a house nearer the school. They

> were very good but missed their parents so much. Although I
> was at work in Leicester during the day, travelling to and fro by
> train and carrying my gas mask, I volunteered to man the Air
> Raid Office, and in my part of the Lane it was a few houses away.
> This meant that after work I went to the Office three nights a
> week. With another volunteer, I walked up and down the Lane
> every half hour looking for lights in houses and listening for the
> warning bell, which announced a raid. I also went to the
> ambulance depot in The Ridgeway, and learnt how to drive an
> ambulance (a converted large van). We used to listen anxiously
> when we heard the bombs dropping, or the sound of our boys
> going over in their planes. I remember being out in the Lane one
> night when the air raid bell went off, and hearing the bombs
> being dropped in Leicester. They were aiming for the Midland
> Railway Station, but instead completely demolished houses
> nearby, in one of which lived Ben's parents.[50] They were luckily in
> their shelter, but many people lost their lives. In Swithland Lane,
> I do not think anyone had an air raid shelter, because we did not
> feel near enough to Leicester. At Church, I remember, we had to
> cover all the church windows with black-out curtains, and
> Evensong was moved forward to 3pm. to save lighting up at
> night. When the war was over, there was a large 'street party', but
> we didn't go to it, as my brother Cedric's death was so recent.[51]

Shortly after the outbreak of the war, churches were forbidden to ring their bells. The reason for this was that the bells would be rung across the country in the event of an invasion. After 1943, however, this interdict was lifted. Many of Swithland's ringers were still serving abroad, but one of the village farmers, John Leatherland, remembers being asked by Gweneth Kilby to ring the one bell before church services, until the rest of the ringers came home when all six bells could be rung. He also remembers the 'end of the war' big fire that was built on the top of the field next to 'Mole End' – Forest End farmland – and the celebratory fireworks that were let off.

Bereavement

The war was indiscriminate as to whose lives were taken. Swithland lost several of its sons. At Swithland Hall, the eighth Earl's second son, the Hon Patrick Danvers, a captain in the Scots Guards, was killed at Anzio in 1944.[52] He was twenty-four. To compound the family tragedy at Swithland Hall, the six year old daughter of the Earl's elder son, Georgina Ione Butler, died in December 1947.

> We all offer our very deepest sympathy to Lord and Lady
> Newtown Butler on the tragic loss of their elder daughter, and our
> prayers will be with them in these immediate days when they will
> feel the loss the most, for she has always been a care. Taken ill on
> Christmas morning, and called home, appropriately enough, on
> Holy Innocents Day to enjoy the health and happiness denied her

here, we laid her to rest on the last day of the old year in the sunswept sweetness of the churchyard. May light perpetual shine upon her and peace.[53]

The little stone angel, which stands on the Lanesborough Chapel window sill, was given in her memory.

The death, also at Anzio, of Cedric Kilby, the son of Walter and Mary Kilby, was another tragic loss. The Swithland parish column in the deanery magazine for July 1944 records:

> Mr and Mrs Kilby have been officially notified that their only son, Captain Cedric Kilby, Sherwood Foresters, was killed in action at Anzio. He was twenty-eight years old. During the long months of suspense, we had earnestly hoped and prayed that good news would eventually reach his family, and the announcement of his death has caused deep sorrow. Cedric Kilby was educated at Wyggeston School, where he won his colour for cricket and football. He was also a violinist in the school orchestra. Before joining the army nearly four years ago, he was a sidesman, and most regular in his attendance at St Leonard's, where his unassuming personality endeared him to all. To Captain Kilby's young widow, to Mr and Mrs Kilby and to Miss Kilby our honorary organist, we extend our deepest sympathy.[54]

Most of the Swithland war dead are buried in France. There is just one war grave marker in the churchyard at Swithland. It stands in memory of Sergeant Robert Dashwood Frost, 1818309, 102 Sqdn, Royal Air Force Volunteer Reserve, whose family lived at Windycroft, Swithland Lane. He died aged twenty on 30th July 1945.

Fig 18.10 Cedric Kilby, killed in action, 1944.

Coronation

In 1953, Swithland, along with the rest of the nation, joyfully celebrated the coronation of Queen Elizabeth II. Village plans were discussed in the Parish Meeting.[55] Lord Lanesborough, chairing, volunteered 'tea and sports' at Swithland Hall on Saturday 6th June, for the children of the parish and those who sing in the church choir, and for all the old age pensioners. All of them would receive a commemorative mug. Everyone else would come and help with the tea and sports. The meeting responded with enthusiasm – a house to house collection would be organised to defray expenses, as would a whist drive at the Memorial Hall, for which generous prizes were promised. It was assumed that everyone would decorate their own houses, but the front of the Memorial Hall would also be decorated with the red, white and blue bunting that Mr Berridge had been able to secure. Two strings of flags would be hung across the road as well. The customary practical concerns were expressed: whether a coronation grant might be given by the District Council; that a roadman be organised to clean up the village before the Coronation. But come the day, cometh the joy. And Sally Copson, then aged ten, remembered it well:

> We went to the party at Swithland Hall. All the children from the village and the school were there. There were games on the lawn and tea. Lord Lanesborough's coronation robes were on display. We were a bit disappointed because we thought they were rather moth-eaten! During the afternoon we were taken into the Hall to see Lord Lanesborough's train set. Yvonne de Carlo, the film star, was at the party. She was staying at Swithland Hall, and came to church the following Sunday with Lady Lanesborough. We were all given a coronation mug and a copy of the New Testament as a memento of the day.[56]

The village children enjoyed yet another coronation celebration. A little note in the school log book records: 'On June 9th, as a Coronation Treat, the children had a picnic and games in a field'.[57]

Notes to Chapter 18

1. St Leonard's feast day is 6th November.
2. From the Swithland church magazine, which was printed January–December 1920; this entry copied into J. Dransfield's notebook.
3. ibid.
4. Swithland Parish Archives, Joseph Dransfield, Notes, Easter 1950.
5. Swithland Parish Magazine, August 1920, copied into his notes by J.H. Dransfield.
6. The Copson family connection with Swithland goes back over one hundred years, and although there are now no Copsons living in the village, there are still family members living locally, some of whom maintain the family connection to St Leonards Church.
7. Members of the Copson family bought 104 Main Street (Hollycroft Dairy) and 122 Main Street in 1954, at the sale of the Hall Estate, but have since sold the properties.

8. Leics. RO, East Midlands Oral History Archive: Leicester Oral History Archive Collection, John Copson, accession no. 887; 202/1/2/3, collection no. LO/251/202.
9. The three largest farms were Hall Farm, Longlands Farm and Forest End Farm.
10. The time of harvesting was obviously dependant on the weather. Les Copson remembered one harvest that was not completed until the beginning of new year.
11. Church archives, Anon, 'the third oldest local born inhabitant', *The Link*, June 1969.
12. This newspaper article, re-printed in *The Link* March 2000, was discovered thanks to the energies of Jean Curd, editor and Paschal Griffin, researcher.
13. Ladies were gradually included!
14. The third bell was recast in 1793 by Edward Arnold of Leicester. In 1961 all six bells were re-hung by Taylors of Loughborough, as a gift from Colin McLeod of Bybrook Hall.
15. From research conducted by Janet Beeby of Hall Farm, deputy tower captain from 2005.
16. In the November 1936 edition of the East Akeley Deanery Magazine.
17. Parochial Church Council Archives: Minutes, April 1936.
18. Swithland Church Archives, Parochial Church Council minutes book 1920–54.
19. For some reason, men's names were recorded in black ink, and ladies in red!
20. Later insertion, not dated.
21. Re-entry due to marriage, née Hilda May Bunney
22. Swithland Church Archives, Parochial Church Council minutes, 1920–54.
23. Messrs Paterson and A. Cook were wardens in 1920. As elected wardens through the vestry meeting, they were ex-officio members of the PCC. Paterson was also elected secretary to the PCC.
24. 'G.M. Gimson, churchwarden 1967–2009', a talk given to Swithland Mothers Union, May 2003.
25. PCC minutes, 7th February 1927.
26. PCC minutes, January 1925.
27. This seems odd, as Guthlaxton deanery lay in the south of the diocese. Probably there was an error in recording the PCC minutes, and Goscote was the deanery proposed. (Adjacent village Rothley lay in Goscote Deanery.)
28. There was some disagreement over the inscription. Mrs Turner wanted wording that was a little too 'high church' for Rector Oliver.
29. G.M. Gimson, 2003 talk to Swithland church members.
30. Mr Oliver died in a traffic accident not long after leaving Swithland.
31. e.g. the 'Medical and Overseas Missions' and the 'Church of England Waifs and Strays Society'.
32. East Akeley Deanery magazine, November 1938.
33. ibid, May 1938
34. The state of the roof continued a concern even after major restoration work, costing c. £1,700, was completed in 1951.
35. The income from the endowment of the Swithland living was £282, from which the Revd. J. Murray-Dixon drew a pension of £68 pa. until his death in 1944.
36. East Akeley Deanery magazine, December 1937.
37. e.g. Paul Brown, article on Swithland, *Illustrated Chronicle*, 1967; Julia Wright, article on Swithland in the *Leicester Advertiser*, 18 July 1975.
38. Public Records Office National Archives, MAF 32/394/153, 1944 Farm Records.
39. Public Records Office National Archives, MAF 32/398/157, 1941 Farm Records.
40 Son of Rev. Lindesay Godfrey, vicar of St Matthew's, Stepney and Mrs Lois Godfrey (née Turner).
41. Alan Parsons, Michael Vane, Dorothy Dewberry, Shirley Spice, Basil Lee, Margaret Lee, Derek Lee, David Lee, Brenda Parsons, Anthony Dewberry, Douglas and Barbara Matthalie and Brian Hunter.
42. 'Ammunition Field', as it was known locally, was on the right hand side of Leicester Lane on the way to Cropston – two or three fields up from Corner Cottage.
43. Maybe related to the definition of balk as 'a strip of ground left unploughed as a boundary line between two ploughed portions'.
44. In 1940 this would have been the Territorial Army. Mass conscription had called up most of the TA's Leicestershire yeomanry, hence the need for the new volunteer force.
45. An interview with Quorn LDV member Chris Long in A.J. Ruddy, *To the Last Round: the Leics. and Rutland Home Guard 1940–45*, p. 26.

46. ibid., Appendix A.
47. Sir Arthur Frederick Pullman Wheeler of Woodhouse Eaves, 2nd Baronet (1900–1964).
48 A.J. Ruddy, *To the Last Round: the Leics. and Rutland Home Guard 1940–45*, p. 79, citing *Leicester Mercury*, 4.12.1944, p. 3.
49. A note to Canon Horton
50. Gweneth was to marry Ben Gimson in 1947.
51. Capt. Cedric Kilby, killed in action, Anzio 1944.
52. The enamelled English alabaster memorial tablet on the south wall of the Lanesborough Chapel in St Leonard's Church bears the Lanesborough crest and arms, and is inscribed: In loving memory of Patrick Henry Stanley Danvers Butler, Captain 1st Battn Scots Guards, younger son of the 8th Earl of Lanesborough. Born 27th December 1920. Killed in Italy at Anzio Beachhead 28th February 1944. The plaque was the gift of his parents, the Earl and Countess of Lanesborough, and was dedicated by the Rev. W.A. King, rector of Woodhouse, on All Souls Day 1947.
53. Leics. RO, East Akeley deanery magazine, 1942–47, vol. 46–51, January 1948.
54. ibid., July 1944.
55. Leics. RO, DE3689, Swithland Parish Meeting Minute Book, 1894–1985.
56. In conversation with the author.
57. Local archives, Swithland School Log book, 1927–64.

– CHAPTER 19 –

A Mile Worth a Million Pounds

> A mile worth a million pounds.
> A one street village, changed in a decade from feudalism to a
> retreat for the rich and retired.[1]

In October 1955, Swithland Parish Meeting was told that a building licence had been issued to a Mr Lilley by Barrow Rural District Council for the erection of two houses on the allotments site. Consternation ensued amongst those who had worked allotments there for the past twenty years. The chairman, the Earl of Lanesborough, who had sold the site to the would-be developer, defended himself, saying that he had sold the site for a very low price (£150) for allotments and not for a building site. All agreed to fight the project, with the village representative on the Rural District Council saying that 'nothing had been said to him'. Six months later, it transpired that nothing could stop the building project. The villagers would lose their allotments and four, not two, new houses would be built. Change, so long put off in Swithland, was about to take everyone by storm.

The Sale of Swithland Estate

The ninth Earl could not afford to keep up the Estate, though he did try for a while to keep up the Hall. There was no male heir, so he had no real incentive to retain it. In 1954, therefore, he put up the Estate for sale,[2] which meant that Swithland would cease to be an estate village. Many of the properties were bought by sitting tenants. The remainder were bought by more moneyed outside interests. The sale changed, not only the ownership of the land, but also the whole social fabric of the village.

Over two hundred people crowded into the sale room at the King's Hotel in Loughborough for the auction of the final twenty-five lots, which were mostly of land rather than property. Examples of auction prices paid for those properties sold that day were Pit Close Farm and farmland £3,100, 122 Main Street £950, 136 and 138 Main Street £355. All twenty-five lots realised £59,470.

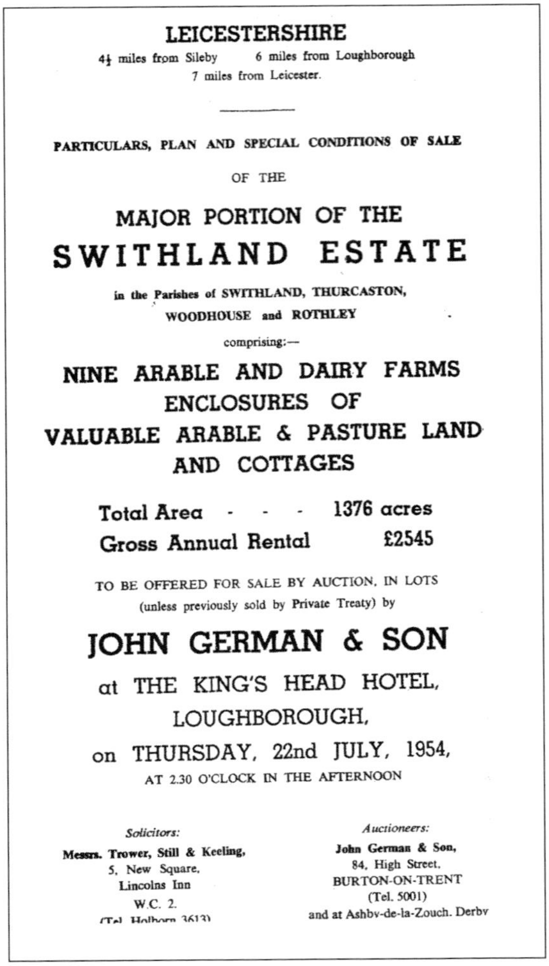

LEICESTERSHIRE

4½ miles from Sileby 6 miles from Loughborough
7 miles from Leicester.

PARTICULARS, PLAN AND SPECIAL CONDITIONS OF SALE
OF THE

MAJOR PORTION OF THE
SWITHLAND ESTATE

in the Parishes of SWITHLAND, THURCASTON,
WOODHOUSE and ROTHLEY
comprising:—

NINE ARABLE AND DAIRY FARMS
ENCLOSURES OF
VALUABLE ARABLE & PASTURE LAND
AND COTTAGES

Total Area - - - 1376 acres
Gross Annual Rental £2545

TO BE OFFERED FOR SALE BY AUCTION, IN LOTS
(unless previously sold by Private Treaty) by

JOHN GERMAN & SON

at THE KING'S HEAD HOTEL,
LOUGHBOROUGH,
on THURSDAY, 22nd JULY, 1954,
AT 2.30 O'CLOCK IN THE AFTERNOON

Solicitors:
Messrs. Trower, Still & Keeling,
5, New Square,
Lincolns Inn
W.C. 2.
(Tel. Holborn 3613)

Auctioneers:
John German & Son,
84, High Street,
BURTON-ON-TRENT
(Tel. 5001)
and at Ashby-de-la-Zouch. Derby

Fig. 19.1 Swithland Estate, sale by auction, 22 July 1954.

Soon after the sale, house values soared, despite the poor state of repair of many. The Earl of Lanesborough had been chairman of the local planning authority, Barrow Rural District Council. He had been unable to secure, or unwilling to seek, planning permission for housing development and sold all his land in the village as agricultural land. Almost immediately after the sale of the Estate, however, the planning authorities began to allow infill housing, though they did impose some conditions on the design of new houses built.[3] The first new development was a row of five detached houses (Nos. 173–181 Main Street) between the school and Keeper's Cottage. Further roadside infill housing was built in subsequent years.

The first purchasers must have been delighted with the rewards on their initial financial outlay. The site of the allotments, for example, which were bought for £150 would see four houses built on that one plot. Another plot, sold for £30 in 1954, was worth over £3,000 in 1967. House prices in the village continued to inflate. Fifty years after the estate first came on the market, the average house price in Swithland was £500,000 and rising, thus making the 1969 Swithland 'mile worth a million' a mile worth nearer £100 million. In those fifty years the village changed from a somewhat run-down and impoverished rural estate to a highly sought after and expensive rural retreat. But what was the effect of that rapid change on the villagers?

Two Communities?

In April 1967, journalist Paul Brown claimed he had discovered much discontent at the changes, and not just from the old residents.[4] 'Swithland is a quiet country village with a rural atmosphere', one anonymous newcomer told him, 'we want to keep it like that, and we have paid through the nose for the privilege'. An old villager told him that the village as a village was spoilt. 'In the old days when someone was ill we used to go across and get them a cup of tea and wash the pots, help out and cheer them up. Now these days they do not want to know'. The article stirred up some correspondence. To complaints about not joining in village activities, a correspondent to the *Illustrated Chronicle* responded:

> I am fairly sure that the majority of villagers in Swithland would be unwilling to hear my views on life or want to discuss the controversial issues of the day – they want us all pressed into the mould of their own choosing. So they must remain in their isolated little pockets, living on nostalgia, unaware of the exciting opportunities and horizons in their midst.

Other newspaper articles on Swithland at the time painted a slightly more positive picture. Anne Coltman, writing in June 1967 for the *Leicester Advertiser*, had discovered a keen team of bell ringers and some thriving church organisations, with support apparently coming from both 'old' and 'new' communities. The school was said to have an active Parents' Association and The Griffin Inn was described as an hospitable pub. At the village post office and general store, Mrs Musgrove spoke about the various activities at the Village Memorial Hall, of which committee she was both secretary and treasurer.

Just two years later, in 1969, Pru Barlow, again for the *Leicester Advertiser*, met up with various new and old villagers in her quest to discover Swithland's current identity. Newcomer, Maurice Carr, chairman of the Swithland Church Men's Club, said that 'townspeople who move into a village are usually even more village-y than the villagers', and Mrs Hilda Price, who described herself as an 'older newcomer', was quoted as saying that the village was 'still a nice place but not quite the same'.[5] Ten years later, in 1975, yet another newspaper article spoke of 'two totally different communities, the business and professional people and the older section of the population who have their roots in the country'. The correspondent, Julia Wright, had conversed with the Earl, who had sold off the Estate. He had apparently described the village as 'a city dormitory' which will 'soon become part of Leicester'. Of others interviewed, 'oldest' Swithland resident Mrs Annie Bunney, regretted the absence of youngsters in the village, Mrs Sheila Bryan, school headteacher, spoke of the school's long waiting list and Rector Bill Carlile said that Swithland was a 'very busy community'.

The truth of the matter was that Swithland was gradually adjusting to its new identity, and even for a small village this takes time and good will. Over the years, however, the village gradually developed a new identity and sense of community, and these, though ever developing, are still strong. Despite the fears of the 1960s, there is still care and support between neighbours in the village, though some residents value a more private life than others. The parish church and the Memorial Hall continue as strong focal points of village life. And St Leonard's School thrives,[6] making its own important contribution to village community life. The price of properties in Swithland does, however, militate against young families moving into the village, and that, as well as the temptation to assume that a private education is necessarily better than a state one, can mean that the number of Swithland scholars from the school's catchment area remains relatively low.

Rural Suburb

The recent history of Swithland is a story of incipient gentrification, with newcomers influencing the developing ethos of the local community, while working with those already living there to evolve a new community identity which has continued far more coherent than the press articles of the 1960s and 70s predicted.

Not all change in the village, though, came as a result of the sale of the Estate or of the social aspirations of those who bought into the village. The challenging and changing economics of agriculture, for example, was also a factor for change. The old farmhouses, farm buildings and land were no sooner on the market than they were snapped up by those who could afford to build their own 'country estate'. Fifty years after the sale of the Estate, virtually all the Swithland farms had gone. That there still remains one farm unit in the village, as well as agricultural land owned locally but contract-farmed, is entirely due to the willingness of their owners to diversify and to adapt to new circumstances. Another factor for change, in Swithland as elsewhere, was the effect of two world wars. In Swithland, the second had the greater effect, coincident as its aftermath was with the sale of the Hall Estate. Just as in the rest of the country, after the immediate post-war austerities of the late 1940s, the joys of better housing, greater social mobility, cleaner air, better consumer choice and all the long-awaited dividends of painful post-war earnestness were also felt in Swithland.

As in many other villages across Britain, a new phenomenon had emerged from the old. Swithland, for so long an 'estate village', had become effectively a 'rural suburb'. One of the 'new' residents said to reporter Pru Barlow in 1969 that a fortunate and distinctive feature of this particular developing mile of rural suburbia was that enough new residents 'were prepared to get involved in the life of the village', and work with and through the organisations that were part of the village before they arrived. In November 1936, for example, the parish column in the East Akeley deanery magazine described village Harvest Festival traditions, charities supported by sales of work and the activities of the bell-ringers. Seventy years later, many of the same traditions and activities still take place, with the support and encouragement of newcomers and more long-standing inhabitants alike. More recently, however, the effect of Swithland village being given the status of 'conservation village' in 1993 is still being worked out. The restrictions this imposes on new building development can encourage a 'not in my backyard' mentality.

With decreasing numbers of old villagers alive to share their personal stories of these transitional years, and newer villagers not living in the village long enough to accumulate significant contemporary community memories, Swithland's various written records become increasingly important for telling the village story. Parish Meeting and Parochial Church Council minutes have been kept since the 1890s and 1920s. An East Akeley Deanery magazine which nearly always included a short paragraph about Swithland was kept from 1936 to 1957 (though the Leicestershire Record Office has only an incomplete collection). Swithland Church's Parish Magazine, of which there is an almost complete collection, has been published monthly from 1965 to 2000 when it became a 'benefice' magazine. It continues to include news items and information from both church and village life for all three parishes in the benefice. Parish magazines might only cover those things seen by successive editors to be important, but they have enabled a greater coverage of the history of church and village life than has any other documentation.

Swithland in the 1950s

At the turn of the decade, six new council houses were built at the top end of the village. Now Nos. 91–101, they were first numbered 1, 3, 5, 7, 9, 11. In the 1950 Electoral Register, where the housing is not numbered – rather named (if it had a name) – it looks as if the Barnes, the Ortons, the Cooks and the Lloyds had moved in by 20th November 1949, the 'qualifying date'. By the publication of the 1952 Electoral Register, Harold and Elsie Edenbrow were living at No. 1, Neville and Hilda Price at No. 3, Robert and Florence Barnes at No. 5, Charles and Jessie Orton at No. 7, Charles and Olive Cook at No. 9 and Ted and Phyllis Lloyd at No. 11. When the 1953 Electoral Register was published the numbers were as they are now, and 'The Cottage' had become No. 1 Main Street.

Fig 19.2 The Cook children and friends, with the new council houses in the background.

Fig 19.3
From the
Cradle to the
Grave, 1955,
Confirmation.

Swithland was without a rector from 1939 until 1955, so churchwarden Joseph Dransfield wrote the parish column in the deanery magazine. Not content with news, he added views and introduced a short 'spiritual' paragraph to accompany the various facts, figures and rotas. It is interesting to read between the lines and see in those paragraphs evidence of Dransfield's developing vocation towards ordination. In 1954, for example, introducing the first performance of the pageant 'From the Cradle to the Grave',[7] he wrote:

> The object of the pageant is to teach the Faith and especially the ordered use of the Sacraments of the Church in ordinary life. It tells also of the care of Mother Church for each individual

member, and of the value of each individual soul in the sight of God. Religion is not something which we 'use' on Sunday only when we are in our 'Sunday best', and put away again in the cupboard for another week, but something that is with us in the house, the factory, the building site, or the mine, wherever we might be, and not only in our work, in which so much of our waking life is spent, but in the hours of leisure too, be it spent on the sports field or elsewhere. All find their place and bear witness. For it is when we are very busied with the affairs of daily life, when we are off guard, we proclaim what we really are and believe, when we come to church, we come to bring ourselves and the whole of our lives and offer them to God, and He will help us live victoriously. It (the pageant) will be a genuine act of worship by each person taking part, and should carry its message to the hearts and minds of those attending.[8]

The 1955 repeat performance saw these people taking part:[9]

Narrator, Rev C.C. Harcourt; Mother Church, Mrs Lucy Spence; Bishop, J.H. Dransfield; Parish Priest, Rev D. Rowe; Crucifer, David North; Crucifer and Acolytes, Alfred Banbury, Gordon Harrison, John Haines; Parents and Child, Mr and Mrs Dixon; Godparents, Mr and Mrs R. Mutch; Confirmation Candidates, Christopher Vielage, Rodney Lloyd, Anthony Cook, Sally Copson, Gillian North, Rosemary Harrison.
Marriage: Bride, Mrs Phyllis Lloyd; Groom, Mr Ted Lloyd; Best man, Mr Maurice Bunney; Bridesmaids, Gillian Briers, Allison North; Father of Bride, Mr C.R. Simmons; Churchwardens, Mrs B.R. Gimson, Mrs M.E. Kilby; Verger, Mr Sidney Bunney; Angel of the Valley, Miss B.M. Bunney; Cantor, Mr A. Boughton; Men Workers, Mr R. Harrison, Mr A. Copson, Mr L. Copson, Mr J. Leatherland; Women Workers, Mrs R. Harrison, Mrs Musgrove, Mrs J. Leatherland, Miss W.A. Simmons, Mrs Stone; Men Sports, Mr A. Taylor, Mr R. Simmons, Mr D. Carpenter, Mr A. Carpenter; Women Sports, Miss F. Banbury, Miss Sheila Gregory, Miss Hazel Rudkin, Miss Margaret Rudkin; Boy Scout, Roger Wardle; Girl Guide, Cynthia Copson; Child's games, Roger Copson, Keith Handley, Richard Orton, Gillian Smith, Margaret Handley; Bells in Belfry, Mr F. Lloyd.
The choristers were Jennifer Wardle, Olga Gregory, Edith Sills, Freda Haines, Margaret Simpson, Jean Davenport, Miss EE Bunney, Mrs Copson, Mrs Hulse, Mrs Wardle, Mr Wardle, Mr J. Copson, Mr Sills, Mr G. Jones, Mr Rudkin. The sidesmen were Mr W. Rudkin, Mr C. Minkley, H.A. Banbury and I. Hammond. The producer was Mrs G.M. Wright and the Organist Mr Gamble.

*Fig 19.4
From the
Cradle to the
Grave, 1955,
Wedding.*

Another pageant, 'The Instruments of the Passion', was presented in Holy Week, 1956.[10] 'It makes us realise the awfulness of sin and the cost God paid for our Redemption'. Pageants were popular community activities in Swithland in the 1950s and 1960s. Several were staged and are still remembered by villagers who were there. Many were 'all age' affairs, others just staged by the village children. A Sunday School pageant, 'The Yew Tree and the Flowers', was presented at the Sunday School Festival in July 1954. This was produced by Mrs Linwood Wright and Miss Beatrice Bunney. The narrator was the Revd. Lindesay Godfrey, then vicar of Coleorton, who had married Lois Turner, Mrs Linwood Wright's daughter, in 1932, and who would eventually spend his retirement years in Swithland. Another Sunday School pageant was staged in 1955.

Fig 19.5 Sunday School Pageant. Back centre: Miss Beatrice Bunney; Front [left to right]: Roger, Nigel and Jane Copson, Helen Simmons.

Ministry among the children of the parish was strong in Swithland in the 1950s. From 1949, Mrs Dorothy Rudkin hosted Swithland's weekly Sunday School[11] (the 'kindergarten' was started in 1955) at the Rudkin's home in Rothley Plain. Miss Beatrice Bunney and Mrs Rudkin were the teachers and Mr Walter Rudkin played the piano.[12] There were monthly Sunday afternoon children's services and special services, with Gweneth Gimson playing the organ from 1954, outings, an annual party and the Sunday School Festival. In 1955, Rosemarie Copson wrote a letter to thank Mr Dransfield, Miss Bunney, Mrs Rudkin and their helpers for the Christmas party and presents the children had been given.

The formality of Sunday services was then seen to require robed choirs, and Swithland had a robed choir of both adults and boys. In 1950 it cost £117 to re-robe St Leonard's choristers in cassocks and surplices.[13] But they had fun together too, including a regular choir outing. In January 1955, for example, they all went to the pantomime together. A Swithland Youth Fellowship was formed about this time, with organist Ernest Gamble leading; they met every Friday evening at the Memorial Hall. Rector Harcourt saw the fellowship as a rallying point for the young people of the parish, and urged them to attend the 8a.m. service once a month. He trained some of the boys as servers, which got a bit of criticism from the choir, as they felt

Fig 19.6 [left to right] Sally, Cynthia and Rosemarie, Copson, Sunday School Festival.

he was 'poaching' choristers for this purpose! Despite these initiatives, the parish column in a 1955 issue of the East Akeley Magazine reported that attendance at services was 'worryingly low', with average attendance at Mattins of only ten worshippers and fifteen at Evensong.

The Swithland branch of the Mothers' Union, which was reported in the deanery magazine as meeting monthly in 1942, continued to be an important organisation within the church through the 1950s and beyond. They met regularly at the village Memorial Hall, with guest speakers, such as, in February 1955, Miss Hilda Ellis. In 1955 Mrs Mary Kilby was the enrolling member.

Annual special services such as the Bluebell Service continued to be held, the Bishop of Leicester, for example, preaching at the Bluebell Service in 1955. In December 1956, Rector Harcourt instigated Swithland's first service of Nine Lessons and Carols. One of Harcourt's passions were the traditional 'Countryside Services', and so, during his ministry, Swithland enjoyed Plough Sunday, Lammas and Harvest services. These were reportedly popular. Rotas continued for sanctuary flowers and sidesmen, and in 1955 a new organisation was set up; the St Leonard's Guild was a team of ladies who worked together on a rota system to clean the church each week.

As far as bell-ringing in Swithland went, the 1950s are remembered as a time of dearth. A few villagers rang, among them John Leatherland (senior), who was at one point tower captain.[14] Swithland became more and more reliant on outside ringers and visiting bands. Bells were rung for funerals and weddings, but it was not possible to get a regular team together for Sunday services. The end of the decade, however, saw the beginnings of a ringing revival with the advent of tower captain Ray Brown, who had moved from Barrow on Soar to live in Swithland Lane, and Percy Wells, who built the Tower House, Main Street in 1959 and whose campanological enthusiasm was catching.

> Methods such as Bob Doubles and Bob Minor, Grandsire Doubles and Steadman Doubles were rung at Thursday practice nights, and bells were rung for most services and on New Year's Eve. Rodney Lloyd recalls the revival of bell ringing being helped by several ringers from outside the village, notably from Barrow. Regular ringers included Alf and Michael Copson, Ray, David and Michael Brown, the Ellway and Clark brothers, Sally Copson and Lesley Ryall.[15]

Money was a constant concern for a church which was never without its maintenance challenges. The Church Finance Committee, set up in 1953, commended the 'free-will offering' scheme and also the use of covenants. That year just £149 had been raised in the collection plate; by 1957 the annual collection had increased to £420. The first two covenants to the church were taken out in 1954; by 1976 there were thirty covenanting givers. There were regular articles in the church magazine encouraging members to give freely and generously to the church. A 'Friends of Swithland' free-will offering scheme was set up at the end of the decade with some sixty-one books of envelopes in use. But the church looked outwards too. Charities supported by St Leonard's during the 1950s were the Church of England Children's Society and the Church Missionary Society.

Perhaps the four most significant events for the church in this decade were the decision in 1954 not to unite with Rothley parish church, the death of Walter Kilby in November 1954, the gift of the Rectory back to the parish by Mrs Linwood Wright and the appointment in 1955, after a long seventeen years interregnum, of a priest-in-charge, the Revd. Cecil Copp Harcourt. Walter Kilby had served the church at Swithland faithfully and loyally for twenty-eight years. Without his strength of purpose, it is questionable whether there would have been a church for Harcourt to be appointed to. But appointed he was; it was an occasion of joy, huge relief and a renewed sense of purpose for the parish. And, with the usual short interregna, the church has had a resident priest ever since.

From The Link: *Church Missionary Society*

Swithland church had established a link with the Church Missionary Society in the time of Archdeacon Mackay (1931–39). He had worked as a CMS missionary before coming to Swithland. Parishioner Pearl Pentelow recalled being taken by Mackay, with other senior pupils from Swithland School, to a CMS missionary exhibition at Loughborough in 1939.[16] She attributed the beginnings of her own vocation to missionary work to that visit. Subsequent rectors, Alex Maxwell (1959–65) and Geoffrey Stuart Smith (1966–73) had also served as CMS missionaries. During the years of their ministries, a number of Swithland parishioners worked in various ways to raise money for the work of CMS. Sheila Gregory, for example, reported on the missionary working (sewing) party meeting which met eight times in 1960, and raised £250 for CMS HQ, an 'increase on the previous year'. The Sunday School was also involved. A Lent project for 1968 saw them 'getting to know' by pictures, letters, lessons and film-strips, the children in the Atunda-Olu school for physically handicapped young people in Lagos, Nigeria. They collected and sent £10 10s 3d towards buying a bus to take the children to and from their school.

Autumn 1966 saw the beginning of a twenty-six year parish missionary support link with CMS missionary, Miss Sheilagh Jebb. An invitation from the Rectory in the October parish magazine ran '24th October. Rector and Mrs Stuart Smith at Home at the Rectory 8pm. to all who would like to meet Miss Sheilagh Jebb, CMS missionary who is linked with this parish. Miss Jebb is the Matron of Ile Abize Hospital at Ado Ekiti in W. Nigeria'.[17] St Leonard's supported the link with Sheilagh Jebb from 1966 to 1987. Olga Harris (née Gregory), who acted as Miss Jebb's Swithland contact person, faithfully focussed Swithland's support and friendship for Miss Jebb, reporting regularly to the church via *The Link*. Her reports told two stories: one of a missionary's overseas ministry and of Anglican church life in Africa, the other of the wider church's changing understanding of mission during those twenty-six years.

Miss Jebb was a nurse for whom her medical work was her primary employment. As a Christian nurse, however, she was also encouraged to see Christian education as part of her ministry. Her regular letters, printed in *The Link* magazine, kept Swithland in active touch with the work of the Anglican church in Nigeria, the Yemen, Northern Sudan, Sierra Leone and the Gambia, as well giving church members insights into a changing understanding of missionary work and of the church's attitude towards people of other faiths.

Another member of the congregation who was dedicated to promoting the work of the Church Missionary Society in parish and deanery was Mrs Phyllis Tyldesley. In May 1970 Rector Stuart Smith wrote: 'We congratulate Mrs P. Tyldesley on being made an Honorary Life Governor of the Church Missionary Society. This is in recognition of her devoted services to the whole missionary cause in parishes and deanery, particularly the Deanery CMS Women's Committee. She is entitled to attend and vote at meetings of the general committee in London. Thus we now have a personal link with the headquarters of that great Society'.[18]

In 1972, Sheilagh Jebb paid a visit to the parish, speaking at the family service and meeting members of the congregation socially afterwards. She continued to make regular short visits to the parish during her biennial furlough periods. From 1984 Miss Jebb was based at the Anglican Training Centre at Farafenni in the Gambia. Her work was mainly related to health education, but she also taught English to various people, including a team of Chinese doctors. Her regular letters to the church were published in *The Link*. In them, Miss Jebb wrote of some of her special people: Ellen, a young girl with leprosy, whose leg had to be amputated; student converts to Christianity standing up for their faith despite ill-usage from non-Christians. We read of the Bishop of Gambia's hopes of setting up a school of evangelism at the training centre and of the baptism of a young Sierra Leonian teacher, the son of a Muslim chief with eight wives.

In 1984, the Parochial Church Council agreed two annual occasions for encouraging some financial 'missionary' support for the work of the church overseas and at home. Church plate collections on Advent Sunday would benefit the work of the church overseas, and those on the first Sunday of Lent would benefit the work of the wider church at home. In view of already well established links, the missionary charity so supported was the Church Missionary Society. At Advent 1984, the plate collection of £101.95 was sent. This traditional support continues to this day.

When Miss Jebb finally retired in 1990, Swithland no longer had such close contact with a link missionary, but by then the church mission scene had changed considerably, the church at home being seen as much a mission field as the church overseas. It is arguable, however, that something important has been lost. Maybe the new millennium will offer the opportunity for a challenging link between the church in Swithland and another church beyond our boundaries and culture.

Swithland in the 1960s

The sixties was a decade of radical change even in Swithland. Many new houses were built. Keeper's Cottage was sold in 1959; it would eventually be taken down and re-built into a modern home, though honouring the footprint of the old cottage.[19] Three new houses were erected at the end of the 1950s between the School and Keeper's Cottage, Nos. 173 (Wells) 175 (Bailey) 179 (Fanshawe) and Nos. 177 and 181 for the Hacketts and the Whytes by 1964. Mr Marsden, a builder, who had bought the four plots next to the Rectory in the Estate sale, sold the two plots nearest to the Rectory to John Woolley.[20] Woolley built No. 153 Main Street, naming it Elmleah because of the elm boarding on the outer end gable; he and his wife Norah moved in there in 1960. A bungalow for Mr Len Shipman, a director of Leicester City Football Club, was eventually built on the adjacent building plot. Bungalows numbered 141 (the Olivers) and 143 (the Browns) had been built by 1969. A small cottage had already been created by 1959 for the Tomblins at 135, adjacent to Roger and Ada Hearst at 137, and by 1964 house numbers 129 and 131 had been erected for the Stubbings and the Butterleys. Further up the village, houses were also built on the old allotment site, No. 67, the house nearest the old footpath, for Mr and Mrs Maurice Carr and No. 71 for Mr and Mrs Dingley, then No. 75 for the Harris' and No. 77 for the Deacons. On the other side of the road, three of the building plots below The Griffin Inn had been bought by publican Samuel Briers (the tenant at the time of the sale) who built bungalows there, including No. 178 for himself, into which he had moved by 1969. The Carnalls had moved into No. 180 by 1964. Above Rose Cottage, two bungalows were built, No. 154 for the Fisks and 152 for the Hastings. In 1965 Charles Benjamin Bunney sold Exning Farm to Roland Smith, who converted it into two houses, No. 130 for himself and his wife, and 128 for Mr and Mrs Andrews. The

Fig 19.7 Elmleah, 153 Main Street, built for John Woolley.

stack yard was sold separately, and Troutbeck House, No. 126 Main Street, between the Exning farmhouse conversion and Pit Close Cottage, was built for the Smiths by 1964. Four more new houses were built above Hollycroft at the same time: Nos. 100 (the Wrights), 96 (the Selbys) and 82 (the Ingrams); No. 102 (the Jackmans) was erected by 1969. And, just below Forest End Farm, Mr and Mrs George Walker built another new house, No. 66, incorporating some of the farm buildings from Forest End.

Newcomers started buying into some of the older houses too, adapting them for their different ways of life. In 1963, Canon Lindesay Godfrey and his wife moved to live in the parish. They lived in The Granary, the house created from an amalgamation of the old Methodist Chapel with an adjacent Forest End house. After six years ministry as warden of Launde Abbey, Godfrey had just been appointed Leicester Diocesan Missioner, a post without a 'house for duty'. He held this post until his retirement in 1972, after which he continued to live in Swithland and to assist in ministry in the parish until his death in 1984. A deeply spiritual priest, Godfrey's presence in Swithland proved a blessing to many people, not least to the rector.

Sydney Meadows, first editor of Swithland's new parish magazine, introduced a series of interviews with leading church people across the diocese in *The Link* starting with the Bishop of Leicester, Ronald Ralph Williams. In June 1968, he interviewed Canon Lindesay Godfrey. The article began:

> Where can we find a clergyman who has rowed for his college, gained a Half Blue for boxing, plays golf occasionally and has done a 'hole in one', worked his passage back from Canada on a cattle boat, and today spends part of his limited leisure time mending watches and clocks?

And ended:

> I left Canon Godfrey with a feeling that I had talked with one who is charitable to all in full measure and who is filled with solicitude for his less fortunate fellowmen.

Newcomers to both village and church, if they were willing, contributed their energies into Swithland's community life and transformed it. A 1968 skittle match at The Griffin, for example, gives some indication of the changes to village social life. Ten years previously, this social combination of people from Swithland village and Swithland Lane would have been much less likely.

> THE BATTLE OF SWITHLAND
> On Monday July 5th, the Swithland Lane 'Marauders' invaded the Griffin Hostelry, to vie their skill against the Swithland 'Natives'. Here are the teams who battled:
> SWITHLAND Messrs R. Copson (Capt), N. Copson, J.A. Copson, M. I. Carr, J. Carpenter, R. Orton, J Davies, Fanshawe, Smith, Porch, I. Carnall, Dr. Hall and Jane Orton
> SWITHLAND LANE Messrs G. Willson (Capt), J. Ashton, G

Wood, J. Wainwright, H. Bate, A. Ellway, G. Taylor, L. Hannibal, D. Copson, A. Copson, D. Buswell, W. Garton, J. Tucker.

After a thirsty session, the 'Marauders' gained the spoils by two legs to one leg. As a climax to a happy evening, five members of the Copson clan challenged any other five comers and were victorious.[21]

Some aspects of old village life continued more or less unchanged through the 1960s. Hall Gardens, in part the remains of the old Hall, had not been sold with the rest of the estate, and tenants David and Ada Hunt carried on running their market garden business from it, together with their son, David. Even after the sale of the gardens, David and Janet Hunt managed the village newspaper round until 1997, when it was handed over to the Mercury Newshop in Rothley. Another 'old' villager, Mrs Lily Harrison, continued to advertise 'eggs for sale' from her Main Street home until the 1990s, and Sid Bunney continued in his office as church sexton until 1971.

Change, though, certainly beckoned within the life of the church. New rector, Bishop Alex Maxwell (1959–65) and his Parochial Church Council sought spiritual re-invigoration for Swithland. Joe Dransfield, through whose energies the church had thrived during the forties and fifties, resigned as churchwarden in 1960 and offered himself to the bishop for ordination. At the 1960 annual church meeting, members suggested that the Sunday School and youth club, both active during the first half of the fifties, needed new impetus, that the parish would benefit from starting a 'young' wives group, to complement the older Mothers' Union, and that a wider agenda of social events would benefit everyone. Earlier initiatives had already ensured that the church bells were safe to ring. New ringers had been recruited and trained, and a team of twelve were ringing regularly.

During this decade, after much discussion, new oak pews replaced woodworm damaged chairs, and the bells underwent serious restoration work. Costs for all of this were recovered through donations and fund-raising events. At Christmas 1962, the new rector sent a letter of welcome to every house in the parish. It followed up a letter earlier in the month from the Bishop of Leicester, and indicated a diocesan outreach initiative. The glossy black and white folded Swithland outreach leaflet had a photograph of the church on the cover. It contained the letter from Alex Maxwell and his churchwardens, Mrs M.E. Kilby and Mr G.R. Clark, a brief history of the church, and information about the regular church services and the church fellowships, which offered all parishioners a welcome. In September 1963, both parish and diocesan officials responded positively to a request from the school for transferring a small part of the rectory land to the school, to enlarge the size of the playground.

In 1965, a new parish magazine was launched[22] with an initial mixed reception, and, in the same year, Sydney Meadows' small booklet on Swithland was published. Joe Dransfield, who had begun it, had died before he was able to complete it. *Swithland* was a successful and appreciated publication. It was printed by Leicester printer George Willson, who lived in Swithland Lane, and initial sales showed a profit of £140.[23] In April 1967, a complimentary copy of a new parish magazine, *The Link*, was distributed to every house in the parish with the hope of attracting new subscribers. Also in 1967, Swithland's first *Reservoir Recipe Book* was produced, with all profits going towards Christian Aid. A second edition of the cookbook was produced in 1971, again with profits supporting Christian Aid. In May 1972, Canon Godfrey's booklet *About Prayer* (a collection of short articles originally printed in the Diocesan Prayer Fellowship monthly leaflet) was on sale in the village, again raising money for Christian Aid. This was something of a best-seller in Swithland, with Bishop Ronald also commending it for sale across the wider diocese in his January 'News and Views' letter.

Rector Maxwell, as Assistant Bishop of Leicester, brought a wider perspective of national church life into Swithland parochialism.[24] He was assisted in his efforts by the diocesan missioner, Canon Lindesay Godfrey who had married into the village. When in 1963, Maxwell proposed a parish 'School of Discipleship', he invited Canon Godfrey to conduct it. Maxwell suggested that some subjects for consideration would arise from the theme of the 1963 Anglican Congress in Toronto: Mutual Responsibility and Inter-Dependence in the Body of Christ. A first meeting was held in Canon Godfrey's home with representatives from surrounding parishes invited to attend; a subsequent one just for Swithland parishioners was held a month later. This led into a Lenten Course with an average weekly attendance of twenty-eight people. Various actions resulted: Christian Aid Week support, Mrs Godfrey becoming co-ordinator; the renewal of a Youth Fellowship; and the introduction of a Bible study group.[25]

Swithland lay representatives had attended a diocesan conference in 1965 at Swanwick in Derbyshire. A possible union of the Church of England with the Methodist Church was raised at that conference, and discussion about this possibility continued in Swithland, and across the national church, over the next few years, with Swithland's congregation responding positively. In 1969, there was some reflection, notably in the rector's magazine letters, over the failure to approve an Anglican-Methodist Covenant in England.[26] (There was inadequate support from the Convocations and Church Assembly.) Its failure was much regretted in Swithland, the magazine editor speaking out strongly against the Bishop of Leicester who had opposed the measure.[27]

In 1962, responding to a diocesan initiative of 'consolidation and advance', St. Leonard's Church had circulated a 'welcome leaflet', visiting every home in the parish. The leaflet advertised nine fellowships: the Sunday School, a Youth Club, the Young Wives, the Church of England Men's Society, St Leonard's Guild of Church Cleaners, the Altar Flower Ladies, the Bell Ringers, the Choir and the Mothers' Union.

The re-constituted Sunday School, for four to twelve year olds, which had previously met in a private house, now met in St Leonard's School on Sunday afternoons (excepting fourth Sundays) from 2.30–3.15pm, under the supervision of Mrs Waller, the schoolmaster's wife. Mrs Tyldesley took over in 1967. By 1969, there were fifty children on the books. The parish magazine reported on the annual prize-giving, clearly a highlight of the year.

The inclement weather did not deter the many parents and friends who filled our Church on the occasion of the Annual Prize-giving on Sunday January 12th. We had the joyful experience of listening to a service conducted in turn by all of the pupils, even to the very young, who delighted us with their action songs. Readings, prayers and hymns were beautifully rendered by the leaders: Adrian Ashton, Simon Copson, Huw Weeks, Carol Gourlay and Anne Smith, while the soloists were Linda Squires, Shelley Adcock, Simon Ashton and Peter Davies, accompanied by Anne Smith, Sheila Copson and Simon Copson on Guitar and Recorder, with our Organist, Mr Carnall, in his usual place. Lady Lanesborough graciously presented the prizes, graded according to attendance, (one mark for each attendance) with due allowance for sickness and excusable absence. One scholar, Ann Leatherland, received the double gold star award for full attendance, while 10 Gold Star, 28 Silver Star and 7 other prizes were presented. Gold Crossbearer Badges went to Adrian Ashton and Simon Copson, and Book tokens were presented to Sheila Copson, Helen Ashton, Susan Lapham (Teachers) and Tina Adcock (Monitor Teacher). Even Mrs Tyldesley was not forgotten, for she received a gift at the hands of one of the pupils.[28]

The Youth Fellowship had been started in the late fifties by organist Ernest Gamble. Meeting fortnightly on Friday evenings in the Memorial Hall, it was open to 'boys and girls in the parish who attend Church or Chapel and are between the ages of 12 and 21'. In 1962, when the secretary was Miss Sally Copson, of 99 Main Street, a youth service included the showing of a 'coloured film', New Day. Reports were regularly made to Parochial Church Council meetings, whose minutes show that at one point council members were concerned because the Youth Fellowship lacked structure. The election of a 'committee', with chairman, secretary and treasurer, put their minds at rest! This Friday group may have re-constituted, however, as in 1965 there is mention of a Youth Fellowship meeting in various houses of the parish on Sundays after Evensong. By 1969, however, numbers attending had fallen so significantly that the club was forced to close for the winter months.[29]

The choir continued to play its important part in the church's worship, singing every Sunday morning, and at the various special choral evening services. The junior choir during those years showed encouraging growth, Mr Wally Egglestone frequently speaking on their behalf at Church Council meetings. There was, however, some anxiety about adult choir numbers in the early sixties: in 1962, choirmaster Mr R. Davy of 223 Swithland Lane 'urgently' needed more people to help lead the musical part of the church services. By the time choir mistress, Mrs Lorna Waller, wife of the head teacher of Swithland School, moved away from Swithland in September 1967, however, the choir was thirty strong, and had, in the Holy Week of that year, sung Stainer's Crucifixion with the choir of Woodhouse Eaves at services in both churches. The choir also led the singing at the annual Bluebell Service, where they were joined by choirs and clergy from neighbouring parishes. In 1968, Swithland were joined by the clergy and choirs from Anstey, Woodhouse Eaves and Newton Linford. The preacher that year was Canon R.A. Jones of Loughborough. There was a congregation of three hundred, a Salvation Army band led the singing, and £28 was donated to Vietnam relief. Mr Ian Carnall was Swithland's organist from 1967 to 1971. On his retirement, the rector paid him tribute:

> As you know, Mr Ian Carnall who has served our church so wonderfully as an organist for many years, has been obliged by ill health to discontinue.
> Although his health has improved a little, it seems unlikely that he will be able to resume the work regularly. He has maintained a high standard and we miss him very much.[30]

In 1962 the bellringers were a 'fine team under the captaincy of Mr Raymond Brown[31] of 34 Swithland Lane' but in need of 'men, women and young people'. The appeal must have born fruit, since in 1963 the bells were rung twice every Sunday by a team, mostly of youngsters trained by Mr Percy Wells. The bells were also rung for special occasions.

> Following the re-hanging of the bells, a quarter peal of Bob Minor was rung on 17th January 1963. A half muffled quarter peal was rung on 15th December 1964 in memory of Reverend J. Dransfield who had been church warden for 15 years before taking holy orders.

The 1962 renovation of the bells (including hanging on ball bearings and attention to the clappers) had been done by Taylor's of Loughborough at a cost of £437.[32]

In 1960, the church annual meeting suggested that a 'Young Wives' group be formed. Young wives groups began to be founded nationally in the 1940s, with the aim to reach out and help other young wives and mothers who were outside any religious organizations. Members of young wives' groups were encouraged to join the Mothers' Union, to which the groups were affiliated, when their youngest child entered the junior school. Swithland Young Wives, who were 'of any church affiliation within the Parish', met monthly at 8pm, usually at their leader's home. In 1962, their leader was Mrs R. Clark of 7 Gipsy Lane. By 1964, when Mrs G.M. Gimson had taken over as leader, meetings were generally held at her home, 'The Gables', 68 Swithland Lane. She reported a membership of thirty-two wives with an average attendance of twenty-five. A feature of the group's activities was the attendance at the Family Service.[33] The Mothers' Union, meanwhile, were meeting monthly at 3pm, generally in the Memorial Hall. The enrolling member in 1962 was the rector's wife, Mrs Grace Maxwell, who said that 'we have a good group already, and would warmly welcome others'.

The traditional pattern for the meetings of the various adult fellowships in the 1960s was receptive rather than proactive; members met to listen to

Fig 19.8 Outing to the Wedgewood factories, Swithland ladies, 1962.

'a speaker'. In November 1965, for example, the Young Wives listened to Miss N. Mense speaking on 'Australia' and, in December, to Lady Isobel Barnett who spoke on 'Some fascinating people I know'. The Mothers' Union in January 1966 welcomed Mrs M. Rees who spoke on 'Mission to Seamen'. Meanwhile, the Swithland branch of the Church of England Men's Society heard the Revd N. Robinson of South Wigston speaking on 'the Isle of God' and, in December, the Revd C.R. Bull JP on 'A Parson on the Bench'.

Outings and meals were also popular. In 1966, the Mothers' Union went on an outing to Harrogate and Harewood House, and the Young Wives had a dinner at Ashby-de-la-Zouch. In 1968, at the Mothers' Union Christmas Party, listening and eating were combined.

> The Christmas party held at the Rectory on the afternoon of Thursday December 12th attracted 22 members, who enjoyed a talk on Tunisia given by Mrs Tyldesley, illustrated with informative slides. The yuletide cake was quite a communal affair, as it was made by Mrs Woolley, almond iced by Mrs Lloyd, and received the last coat of sugar icing at the hands of Mrs Gregory. It was then duly cut by Lady Lanesborough, and everyone had a share, including our Rector, the only male present at this pleasing event.[34]

The men of the parish had their own organisation. A branch of the Church of England Men's Society was formed in 1959. By 1960 it had twelve members. Jack Copson was one of those first members. His membership and prayer card, signed by the President (H.A. Maxwell) and Secretary

(G.R. Clark) of the Swithland branch, indicate that he was admitted on 13th September 1959. The Society met once a month at 7.45pm 'in one of the men's homes'. The meeting in January 1966, for example, was held at Mr Hammond's home. In 1968, however, the decision was taken to disband the parish branch of the CEMS and to explore a fresh organisation. An open meeting was held in April, to which new Rector Bishop Stuart Smith invited all men of the parish. Forty men accepted his invitation. After viewing Trevor Weston's colour sound film on 'Swithland' (1963), which was much enjoyed, a general discussion led to the decision to set up a new society of 'men of Swithland parish and surrounding district'. A committee was elected[35] to take the proposals forward, and the Swithland Church Men's Club was born.

In November 1968, the Men's Club organised a communal bonfire night. 'Over one hundred parents with their children enjoyed an illuminating evening fortified by refreshments provided by Mrs Carr and Mrs Davies, to whom our special thanks are tended. This successful event was sponsored by our Men's Club, with their energetic secretary Mr Bate, and we hope this will be an annual fixture in the Swithland calendar'.[36] For some years the bonfire was hosted at the White House, by kind invitation of Michael and Trish Brook-Lawson, but it eventually returned to the field behind the Griffin. Because of prohibitive insurance costs and health and safety regulations, however, the Men's Club felt unable to continue the tradition after 2003.

In December 1968, the Men's Club took over the organisation of the previously established parish Christmas carol singing tradition, arranging two sessions in the week before Christmas, one through Swithland village, the other along Swithland Lane, and raising £45 for charity. The same year the Men's Club held its first Christmas Dinner, a tradition that continues to the present day.

> On Monday December 9th 1968, forty-one members and friends enjoyed an excellent dinner at the Griffin Inn, Swithland, when those present embraced the welcomed opportunity of meeting all those who have joined this recently formed club. The Chairman, Mr Maurice Carr, presided, and carried out the office of Toastmaster with honours, while Mr RG Smith briefly welcomed the guests, which included the Earl of Lanesborough, who replied to the toast. After dinner, we had the pleasure of listening to a Folk Song recital, with guitar accompaniment, given by Sheila Copson, Michael Collins and Wendy Latham, and a happy evening concluded with communal Carol singing. Our Chief Guest was so impressed by the occasion that he promptly decided to join us and we were duly honoured to welcome him as a new member.[37]

In 1962 the St Leonard's Guild of Church Cleaners, which was set up in 1955, comprised twenty-four ladies, who worked together in pairs to help clean the church every week.[38] Co-ordinator Miss Simmons, 207 Swithland Lane, was glad to hear 'of other people wishing to help'. Miss Simmons was still there in 1977, and still wanting additions to her then twenty ladies. Another 1962 team comprised the sixteen 'altar flower' ladies, under the leadership of Mrs B.R. Gimson of The Gables, Swithland Lane. She too indicated that she would be glad to 'hear of others'. Then, as now, church life was shaped by rotas! In November 1965 these included the flower list, the sidesmen, and the St Leonard's Guild.

> Flower List: Oct 31st, Mrs Beachell; Nov 7th, Mrs Butterley; 14th Young Wives; 28th, Mrs Harris, Dec 5th Mrs Wakeling.
> St Leonard's Guild. Nov 4th, Mrs Harris, Mrs Tyldesley; 11th Mrs Payne, Mrs Shrive; 18th Mrs Brook-Lawson, Miss Fewkes; 25th Mrs C. Copson, Mrs Boulton; Dec. 2nd, Mrs Sharpe, Miss Simmons.
> Sidesmen: Nov. 7th, Mr Symington, Dr Harris, Mrs Gimson, Mrs Harris; 14th Mr Corbin, Mr Banbury, Mr J. Copson, Mr Wakeling; 21st, Mr Tyldesley, Mrs Harris, Mr Minkley, Mr Lloyd; 28th Mrs Gimson, Mrs March, Mr Brown, Mr A. Copson; Dec. 5th, Mr Hammond; Mr Symington, Mrs Corbin, Mr Simmons.[39]

Church officers are rarely fêted in church histories, but the parish magazine does offer an opportunity for at least some local celebration of those committed people who have shared the responsibilities of leadership and service in the life of church and community. These are a selection of 1960s tributes to some wonderfully faithful people.

Churchwarden Mary Kilby died in July 1967. There were lengthy tributes in the September magazine. The rector wrote: 'I knew her to be a remarkable person. Not only was she on the Church Electoral Roll and Parochial Church Council longer than anyone else, but she became churchwarden in succession to her active service, and continued to hold that office for thirteen years, discharging it with a devotion which put many younger persons to shame. She made a point of being at the church in time to set out the vessels for Holy Communion. When I arrived at the church, she was always waiting to welcome me. She was a wonderful example of duty well done to the end. She will be missed'.[40]

In a letter to the editor printed in the December 1967 magazine, Walter Rudkin wrote:

> It is with great joy that I read in the Parish News of Swithland, that we have Mrs B. Gimson to fill the vacancy of Church Warden until the annual vestry meeting. This would have given both her parents much pleasure. It is now over forty years since I first came to Swithland and I have always attended this beautiful church which I have watched grow over the years. ... Until the present organist Mr Carnall came, Mrs Gimson was organist for many years and her interest in the Young Wives, the Church of England Children's Society and other causes, which includes her active work with the Meals service for the old people in Mountsorrel ... I do hope and pray that the whole Church and Parish will support Mrs Gimson in her new duties, and I trust that when the time comes, she will be officially elected as Church Warden.

His plea did not fall on deaf ears. Mrs Gimson was elected people's warden in 1967, and served until 2009.

Ian Hammond's 'retirement' as PCC secretary was noted in June 1968. 'From a schoolboy at Swithland Church School, to choirboy, sidesman, reader and finally the elected secretary of the Parochial Church Council, these are the stages in the Church life of Ian Hammond, recently retired as Secretary after sixteen years. Due to promotion in his business life, Mr Hammond took leave of St Leonard's congregation, armed with a gift of photographic equipment, a tangible reminder of his work for the parish'.[41]

Sid Bunney was sexton for some thirty-one years. When he retired in 1971, the rector wrote: 'By the time this is in your hands, we shall have lost the faithful services of Mr Sid Bunney. He has taken pride in keeping the churchyard in good order and has put into it a tremendous amount of hard work. But with advancing years it has become more and more difficult for him to carry on and now it has become too much. We owe him a big debt of gratitude'. Mr Bunney was given a shooting stick as a thank you present 'to rest on when he visits the churchyard'.[42]

Mrs Phyllis Tyldesley of the Old Cottage, Woodhouse, took over as Sunday School Superintendent in 1967. When she stood down for health reasons in 1971, there were fifty children on the roll. Speaking of her careful and devoted leadership, Rector Stuart Smith noted 'Before she took charge in 1967 there were very few children, and I was wondering how much longer it could last. But from the moment when Mrs Tyldesley took it over it has grown and thrived'.[43]

Three further random snippets from the end of the decade's parish magazines give the feel of times passing and changing. In 1966, the Parochial Church Council had entered the churchyard in the diocesan 'best-kept churchyard competition' and had been awarded a certificate of merit. Likewise, the parish meeting entered the village into Leicestershire's 'best kept village' competition and received an 'Award of Merit'.

The Harvest Supper, a popular Swithland tradition, now brought together families from the wider Swithland community. In 1968 the parish magazine reported:

> Everyone voted (it) an unqualified success, and the 109 seated guests greatly enjoyed the singing of Mr Egglestone, accompanied by our Organist, the sketch performed by Mrs Ashton, Mrs Adcock, Mr Adcock, and the group folk formula provided by Sheila Copson, Wendy Latham, Stuart Hague and Michael Collins. Elsewhere a well-deserved tribute has been paid to the Ladies.[44]

And in 1970,

> Harvest Supper. 100 guests. 'Following this, three of our readers delighted us all with selections from a potted Mikado, and the generous applause indicated that the soulful renderings of Gwen Gimson, firstly as the bashful Yumyum and then as the austere Katisha, supported by Bill Harris as the playful Koko, and John

Beachell as the ponderous Poohbah, were much appreciated. An evening to remember.[45]

Despite all the decade's exuberance and exhilaration, Swithland's rector was left in pensive mood. Decimal currency had been introduced in the United Kingdom in 1969, but Rector Stuart Smith, in his message to the parish, was clearly anxious.

> What will people put in the collection when there is no half-crown? Will they search in their pockets and purses for a sixpence to go with their two-shilling piece? Or will they be content to give two shillings, comforting themselves with the rather shallow thought that the cost of living is rising?[46]

Perhaps he was anticipating the financial challenges of the seventies?

From The Link: *Editors*

From November 1965, a Swithland parish magazine has been published every month. It was not the first parish magazine, just the first that lasted. The first Swithland church magazine that we know about was issued in January 1920 and continued for one year. At that point the rector, James Murray Dixon, was sorry to announce that the publication must cease, owing to a fall off in subscribers. 'Admittedly', he said, 'the subscription is high, but owing to the printing this could not be avoided on so small a number; (he himself) being the loser of ten shillings a month'.[47]

Parish magazines are probably unique in giving their readers something of a bird's eye view of the day to day life of a parish, its church, its community, and its priorities, at least from the perspective of those who edit and write for the magazine. Various subjects and themes recur reassuringly, in the main local though not always ecclesial, and sometimes personal. Just occasionally something larger from the national or international scene breaks through into the parochial consciousness. What is highlighted in a community magazine may only illustrate a very small part of the lives of the people in the community about which it reports, but its pages do give a flavour of Swithland parochial life. The parish archives hold an almost complete[48] set of copies of the parish magazine from November 1965 to the present day. Rector Stuart Smith began the rectory collection and all but one of his successors have kept it up to date. There were magazines prior to November 1965, but the rectory archives do not possess them. In earlier years, the parish contributed to a deanery magazine, of which some copies are part of the diocesan records collection.[49]

In the first issue, November 1965, the main news item was the pending retirement, on grounds of ill health, of the then rector, Alex Maxwell. The rest of that issue included the monthly notes, the flower list, St Leonard's Guild and sidesmen's rotas, marriages and deaths 'from the registers' and two articles, one by John Beachell on his visit to Japan in July 1964, and the other by Canon Lindesay Godfrey, advertising the pageant 'From the Cradle to the Grave'.[50]

The first St Leonard's Church, Swithland Parish Magazine, as it was called until March 1967, was a four page glossy printed leaflet.[51] It was edited by Waldron (Bill) Harris and contained the monthly Leicester Diocesan Leaflet and The Sign. In 1965 it was priced at 9d. With the arrival of a new rector in 1966, some changes were made. The Rt Revd T.G. Stuart Smith, in his March 1967 letter wrote:

> This is the last issue of the Swithland Parish Magazine in its present form. Naturally some people will miss the familiar cover with its nice etching.[52] But periodical changes are in the modern journalistic tradition. I hope you will like THE LINK, which will be the name of the magazine in future. The PCC and a special Magazine Committee which they have appointed have taken a lot of trouble in choosing the new set-up. It will contain a lot more both in the way of news and of articles and other matter. It will include the Leicester Diocesan Leaflet, but no longer The Sign. Here I want to express our deep gratitude to Dr W Harris, who was editing the magazine when I came to the parish. He has also acted as distribution manager; and all this on top of professional work which leaves him very little spare time. The editorship will now be in the hands of Mr S.R. Meadows, well known for his book on Swithland. Mrs Zoë Willson will be co-editor.[53]

The new editorial team of Sydney Meadows and Zoë Willson promised a big drive to increase circulation. The new magazine, *The Link*, at 6d each month, was 3d cheaper than the old one; this was possible because, for the first time, advertisements from local companies were incorporated into the magazine's cover pages. The front of the new glossy cover carried a photograph of the church (standard roses alongside the path) with coloured top and bottom panels. The eight inside pages had been typed and copied. The editorial invited 'news of special occasions, anniversaries and similar functions' and 'helpful suggestions or questions for our correspondence column'. Bishop Stuart Smith's letter indicated that a complimentary copy was being sent to all the houses in the ecclesiastical parish with the hope that the magazine would attract a greater number of regular readers. A full calendar for the month and the usual rotas were all included. A regular feature for the new magazine was editor Sydney Meadows' monthly interview with interesting people. The first interview, for March 1967, was with the Bishop of Leicester, Ronald Williams. Another new feature was a 'Women's Page and Parish News'. In 1967, for example, readers were advised that original 'young wife' Mrs Midge Groves was moving with her family to Cape Town, South Africa; that PCC members Mr and Mrs R.H. Corbin were also on the move, from Swithland Lane to Barton-on-Sea, only a mile and a half from Bishop Maxwell's retirement home; and that five people had been confirmed at Swithland on March 16th, Helen Ashton, Graham Paul Bate, Sally Christine Hannibal, Christine Anne Labrom and Rowena Anne Whyte.

As the years passed, the number of pages of advertisements doubled and the local content continued an interesting mixture of parish news and informative articles from a broader as well as parochial perspective. The monthly price of 6d was held until decimal currency came into force; from February 1971 the price was changed to 2.5p. By then the type face had been changed several times, but editorial policy on content remained the same. In January 1978, the monthly price of each issue rose from 5p to 10p a month, due to the rising costs of 'paper, ink and stencils'. In 1972, Sydney Meadows stood down from the editorial team, but Zoë Willson continued to edit *The Link* until October 1984, when she, with her supporting production team of Sally Allen and Jo Northam, relinquished their responsibilities. Lesley Walton was then persuaded by the rector to become the new editor. Lesley served as editor until September 1987. During her editorship, the contents of the magazine focussed on matters beyond the parish as well as those within it, embracing articles on, for example, Launde Abbey, aspects of spirituality and of Christian social concern, including Amnesty International. During this period the magazine moved from the duplicator to the photocopier, a development which led eventually to a change in the cover design. The new printing method also allowed for the introduction of appropriate art-work into the contents pages. In August 1987, for example, a cartoon appeared for the first time in *The Link* showing a church guide 'moving on' someone kneeling in prayer, 'I'm sorry, sir, but this chapel is reserved for sightseers'.

From September 1987 the rector edited the magazine. During his term of office, he maintained the customary diet of reports from church and village organisations, but included the occasional theological reflection. In February 1989 the magazine cover was changed again, to reproduce an original pen and ink sketch of Main Street, the work of Simon Harrington of The Ridings. The rector saw the new design as illustrating 'the Link between the Church and the Parish which the Magazine serves'. In March 1990, Rector Walters persuaded Norman Cutler to take over editing the magazine. Norman, with his wife Pam, produced the magazine until October 1998, when they passed the editorial baton to Mrs Jean Curd. In 1995, the Church Council agreed to make three issues of *The Link* each year 'community issues'. Content for those months was to have a broader interest, and the community issue would be distributed free to every household in the parish. Characteristic features of *The Link* under Norman Cutler's editorship included hagiological articles, informative material on Christian worship and spirituality, and delightful cartoons. There were several of these latter in a 'saints' series, not least the one in the last magazine edited by Norman, October 1998. Against a picture of trees and sun and flowers was set the caption: 'saints… often stand and stare'. Was this a weary editor's cri de coeur?

Under Jean Curd's editorship, the magazine embraced new computer technology, which has influenced both layout and content. In 2006, Swithland became part of a United Benefice with Woodhouse and Woodhouse Eaves. Two separate magazines were continued until the end of 2007. In February 2008 a united publication *Parish Matters* was launched which, while acknowledging the multi-parish nature of the benefice, continues to reflect the distinctive identities of the three parishes. The magazine continues to attract a wide readership and, while covering all expenses, to make a profit.

From The Link: *Advertisements*

In April 1967 the cover of *The Link* published these first advertisements on its inside pages:

> F. Sleath and Sons Ltd,
> Builders -Contractors -Plumbers -Decorators
> FUNERALS COMPLETELY FURNISHED

> The Double H. Store (Rothley) Ltd
> 5 Woodgate, Rothley, Leicester
> Domestic Hardware, Garden Implements, Ironmongery, Timber Supplies, Paints, Wallpapers, Fencing

> Howlett's of Quorn
> Express Summer Services
> G Howlett & Son (Quorn) Ltd.,
> 94 Barrow Road, Quorn, Leics.

> Peter Bowie
> Alpine Nurseries, Halstead Road, Mountsorrel

> Greeting Cards for all occasions
> Stationery
> M.F. Ward
> Post Office, 18a Woodgate, Rothley

The advertisers in May 1973 were:
> F. Sleath and Son Ltd, Rothley
> D.C. Hudson, formerly 'The Butcher Boy', Rothley
> The Little Shop for Ladies Fashions, Anstey
> Willsons Printers, Leicester
> The Royal Leics, Rutland and Wycliffe Society for the Blind
> Cropston Garage
> S. Bradshaw, Rothley
> JM Thompson, Newsagent, Rothley
> June, Florist, Loughborough
> Colin's, Taxi, Mountsorrel
> M.F. Ward, Post Office, Rothley
> Selby's Garage (Woodhouse) Ltd, Woodhouse Eaves
> Carr's, The Tailors, High Street, Leicester
> Howlett's of Quorn
> The Double 'H' Store, Rothley
> Kee Fuels Ltd, Leicester

The Link magazine continued to finance itself via advertisements until at least 1973, but by 1976 a decision had been taken not to include advertisements and not to have the covering pages printed professionally. *The Link* resumed taking advertisements in 1999, partly in order to fund the Parochial Church Council's new policy of distributing a free 'community' copy of *The Link* three times a year to all homes in the parish.[54] The advertisements in that first *Community Link* were sponsored by:

Le Fevre's Stores, Woodhouse Eaves
J & B Stone (Motor Services) Ltd, Barrow upon Soar
G.A. Gamble and Sons of Quorn, Funeral Directors
J. Oakland (Butchers), Rothley
Oakwood Pharmacy, Woodhouse Eaves
Anstey & District Funeral Services
A. Lockton, Security Systems
Rowena Garden Centre,
Rothley Pilbeam Academy of Dance
The Griffin Inn, Swithland
David North, Rothley
John E. Capewell, Electrical Contractor, Rothley

Swithland in the 1970s

Nationally, the 1970s were very different to the 1960s. While the decade began positively with fiscal growth and monetary expansion, there was trouble ahead. Inflation led to crisis. Oil prices quadrupled, the miners went on strike, the nation was reduced to a three day working week, unemployment almost doubled and the pound collapsed. After 1976 there was some recovery, but then came 'the winter of discontent' and seventeen per cent interest rates. It wasn't the best of decades. But what was happening in Swithland?

Swithland bellringers saw to it that the 1970s began on an upbeat note. For various reasons, the 1960s team had dwindled, and the bells had hung silent in their tower for some years except when a visiting team brought them to life. In 1970, however, members of the Swithland Church Men's Club committed themselves to building up a local team of ringers. Ringer John Beachell[55] described how their target was reached.

> As one of the objects of the Church Men's Club is to do things, it seemed to me that here was something we could tackle and, once more, Mr Wells took on the considerable task of training six, not so young, members of the Club, who had never pulled a bell rope before. Things were now moving in the desired direction and their services were reinforced by four others who were not beginners. Our target was to ring for Harvest Festival, and at 9am. on the beautiful Sunday of September 27th, six men assembled to ring in the congregation, trusting that they would not disgrace their master. The others came for Evensong, so all ten rang on a memorable day.[56]

The rector applauded their efforts. 'It was grand to hear the church bells ringing for the Harvest Festival services and each Sunday since. This is one of the achievements of the Men's Club, with the able tuition of Mr Percy Wells. We congratulate them'.

Just twelve months later, however, the ringers had the sad task of ringing the bells half muffled at both morning and evening services as a tribute to the late Mr Percy Wells, Master of the Bells, their teacher. Enthusiasm for the exercise, however, was maintained, and Keith Andrews, deputy tower captain, advertised for more ringers.

> Bell Ringing. Here's a chance to join Swithland's men at the top! If you missed the local evening paper quote: 'Life at the top means for a group of executives living around Swithland a climb up the stairs of the bell tower every Sunday to ring the bells of St Leonard's Church. Which disproves the cynic's theory that you can only reach the top rung of the ladder by pulling strings and shows that, in fact, you don't start pulling until you've got there.' Please help! More bellringers are urgently needed.[57]

The appeal succeeded, and a second team of new Swithland ringers was formed. One of them, Marc Wainwright recalled that ringers were each allocated a bell by the tower captain, Harold Williams. Tom Boyden, John Beachell, Tony and Sue Rowntree Clifford, Sarah Dixon, Peter Stobart and Keith Andrews were all members of the band. Bob Doubles and Grandsire Doubles were two of the methods rung.

As far as the wider history of Swithland village goes, the most important event of the decade had to be the contents sale at Swithland Hall organised by Christies on 16th and 17th October 1978. The sale caused great excitement locally, and catalogues are still treasured by villagers who attended, as are the items they succeeded in buying. The story has already been told of the great big valuation mistake relating to the Bellini bust,[58] but also up for auction were 1,493 other lots, pieces of glass, ceramics, pictures, books and ephemera, objects of art, furniture, some garden statuary, and the Earl's model railway and rolling stock. This last collection went for £1,400.

In the village meanwhile, a few more new houses were built and new families moved in. There was now new housing all down the north side of Main Street, the only 'gap' being the land between No. 1 (The Cottage) and No. 67. A further house, No. 89, had been squeezed in behind Cherry Tree Cottage by 1974 and six new bungalows (103, 105, 107, 109, 111, 113) were built below the council houses for the Williams, the Boydens, the Deakins, the Parkinsons, the Harrisons and the Hoskings.

Swithland observed the Queen Elizabeth II's Silver Jubilee in 1977 with enthusiasm. There were special services in Church on June 5th, the parish supported an open air diocesan service in Bradgate Park on June 26th, and the village Parish Meeting agreed the renovation of the Memorial Hall as its Jubilee Project. Every child of school age in the village received a Jubilee mug. Swithland School held a Jubilee Supper in the Memorial Hall, their Jubilee Sports Day saw the children wearing red, white and blue. Every child was also given a commemorative crown. Willoughby Garton, chairman of the Parish Meeting, sent a telegram to the Queen: 'On the occasion of the celebration of the Anniversary of the Silver Jubilee of the Accession of our Sovereign Lady, Queen Elizabeth the Second, the residents of Swithland, Leicestershire, send loyal greetings'.[59]

The 'Jubilee project' of renovating the Memorial Hall was a popular one. In 1977, Willoughby Garton of Pit Close Cottage, chairman of the parish meeting, and the new rector, Raymond Walters, ex-officio chairman of the trustees, took responsibility for furthering the project. In an order under the Charities Act 1960, the following trustees were re-appointed, the rector remaining an ex-officio trustee: Lord Lanesborough, Colin McLeod of Bybrook Hall and Sydney Radcliffe of Main Street, Swithland. A management committee was elected, Mrs Brook, Mrs Bryan, Mrs Copley, Mrs Garton (secretary), Mrs Jeyes (treasurer), Mr Bate (vice chairman), Mr J Copson, Mr Lumley (chairman) and Mr Stevenson.[60] The estimated cost of the necessary work to the hall, renovation, redecoration, modern conveniences, was £3,000. The Memorial Hall Restoration Fund was launched with a Jubilee Dance, which raised £221, and an Art and Craft exhibition, in the Swithland Room at the Griffin Inn, which raised £170.[61] The first statement of affairs, for year ending 31st December 1978 showed receipts of £3,695.99 and expenditure, mainly on building work, of £2,812.04. The management committee was innovative in raising significant amounts of money through lettings, social and other events. In the first year they organised a Saturday market, a country dance, a cheese and wine party, a pâté party, a mile of pennies, a sale of scrap, a play, a craft market and a Christmas Dance, as well as regular activities such as yoga classes and modem sequence and old time dancing classes. In addition, there was a 100 Club and grants from the Rural Council and the Parish Rate. The following year the turnover was £5,782.66, with significant grants from Charnwood Council and the Department of Education and Science. Thanks to the hard work of these and subsequent trustees and management committees, the Memorial Hall has remained in good condition and constant use to the present day.

Another significant innovation of the decade was the Village Fruit, Flower and Vegetable Show. In 1977, the Swithland Church Men's Club organised the first of these now annual shows, staging it at the Griffin Inn and the school on September 10th at 2.30pm. The chairman of the Men's Club, Keith Andrews, performed the opening ceremony, and, at the close, club member Jeff Harrison auctioned all remaining exhibits in aid of the Club's Charity Fund.[62] £60 was raised, £41 through the auction.

In the church, the Sunday School had developed a special friendship link with the Charnwood Children's Home in Woodhouse Eaves. In 1970 and subsequent years members sent Christmas gifts to all the children. They were able to 'adopt' one or two of the children, taking a special interest in them, praying for them, and sending birthday and Christmas gifts. Sunday School members were also encouraged to build on the church's long-standing links with the Church Missionary Society. In 1971, they sent representatives to the annual rally at Coventry, where Carol Gourlay read one of the lessons and Jackie Wainwright presented their Lent project gift of £28.64. After Phyllis Tyldesley stepped down as Sunday School superintendent in 1971, no immediate long term replacement was found. Various church members continued to act as teachers, including Shirley Herbert, Shelley Adcock, Jackie Wainwright, Tim Wright and Debbie Bryan.

The Youth Fellowship continued its sporadic career. In March 1977 a new Church Youth Group was formed, with monthly meetings and Shelley Adcock as the contact person. Meetings alternated between the Wainwright and Dixon homes. The following year a new Girl Guide Company was formed in Swithland, Christine Deakin, Christine Smeaton and Pat Wishart taking the initiative. The initial meeting of the 1st Swithland Girl Guides was held on 25th September 1978. Their first Church Parade was on Remembrance Sunday. The first twelve members of the company were Julie and Georgiana Bocock, Angela Smeaton, Jeanette Buswell, Kathryn Pollard, Rosemary Wishart, Rachel Deakin, Lisa Chell, Rachael Walsh, Joanna Smith, Gillian Walters and Susan Room. By June 1979 the company was twenty strong, holding its first weekend camp over 29th and 30th June, and planning to join the Cropston Guides for a week's camp during August. They were forced to close in 1982, however, as the new Woodhouse Eaves Guide Company attracted more than half the Swithland Guides into their company, but not before two of the Swithland Guides achieved the Queen's Guide Award.[63]

The Mothers' Union went out on a limb somewhat in September 1977, when they organised a 'coffee and shandy' morning at 72 Swithland Lane, with an especial invitation to 'all the retired gentlemen with a morning to spare'.[64] Like Swithland's other parish church organisations, the Mothers' Union supported overseas and charitable projects, such as a correspondence link with a young person in Nigeria in 1977 and also support for INFO, a residential hostel in Leicester for rehabilitated drug addicts.[65]

In 1976, the Young Wives decided that they were perhaps no longer 'young' and decided to change their name to 'Church Wives'. Highlights of their annual programme were the 'Summer Supper' at Lea Cottage, the home of their leader Mrs Gweneth Gimson, and the annual Advent Gift Service, where members brought Christmas gifts to church to donate to a local charity.[66] In 1977 Mrs Gimson was 'disappointed in the number of Church Wives who attended the annual service on Sunday November 20th held at the new time of four o'clock. A very interesting sermon was preached by the Rector, Canon Walters, and Mrs Gimson and Mrs Wishart read the lessons. Collections were taken by Mrs Allen, Mrs Dixon and Mrs Northam'.[67]

Rectors meanwhile came and went during this decade! In 1973 Stuart Smith retired because of ill-health and was replaced that same year by Bill Carlile, who only stayed for three years, perhaps because at heart he was an urban rather than a rural priest. He was remembered with affection by many. His farewell message included the words 'We shall always look back with gratitude to our three years in your midst, and this brief, yet stimulating interlude will have been of immense benefit to our urban ministry from which we seem unable to escape'. Ray Walters, the diocesan Director of Education, followed him as rector, moving to the parish in 1977. A quietly intellectual man, Walters encouraged church members in theological exploration, building on the parish's established traditions of study and discussion groups. In 1971, for example, Rector Stuart Smith had held fortnightly meetings in church for Questions and Answers, with a general theme of 'Christian Horizons for the Seventies'. When Ray Walters arrived, he started a monthly prayer group, in addition to the established pattern of study groups during Lent. In Lent 1978, the Passion and Resurrection Gospel narratives were studied. Walters also started a tradition of 'Compline and Address' on Saturday evenings in Lent, and preached themed Lenten sermons in both morning and evening worship. One year, for example, the Compline addresses focussed on 'the Passion sequence', Sunday morning sermons were on 'prayers of the Eucharist' and evening sermons on 'parables'.

There was change and development on the national church scene too, which impacted on Swithland. 1970 saw the publication of the New English Bible. Rector Stuart Smith commended it to his flock, encouraging them to 'try to learn as much as we can from it'.[68] Another national church development in 1970 was the admission of women into the Association of Readers. Three women were admitted in Leicester diocese, one of whom, Mrs Adeline Herbert, would serve at Quorn parish church. Adeline Herbert, the daughter of Canon and Mrs Joscelyne who had lived along Swithland Lane, was the second wife of Albert Herbert, who was at one time Swithland's architect. She, with him, is buried in St Leonard's churchyard.

Also in 1970, synodical government was introduced into the life of the Church of England. The rector's letter described the changes, particularly stressing the increased participation of the laity that would result. It is hard to realise the huge change in the life of the church this represented, as today we take lay participation in the decision-making processes of the church for granted. That year the annual church meetings were held at the Memorial Hall and were the first to be held under the Church of England's new synodical regulations. At the time, Swithland had two hundred and twenty-three members on its Electoral Roll. For the first time, these people could elect their representatives to the new Deanery Synod. They sent Lois Godfrey and Waldron (Bill) Harris. Those elected became part of the electorate for lay representation on the new Diocesan and General Synods. The November issue of News and Views, listing those elected to the General Synod, reported that Mrs Lois Godfrey of Swithland was one of the first members of the House of Laity on the new General Synod, and one of the relatively few women members. All other representatives from the Leicester diocese were male. The other lay members were John Baden Fuller, James Crompton and Mr P.C. Hyde Thompson; elected clergy members were Harold Lockley, Archdeacon of Loughborough, Canon Dudley Gundry, and the Rev. Eric Devenport. The Bishop and the Archdeacon of Leicester were ex officio members. Lois Godfrey enjoyed her first General Synod residential meeting at York, in July 1971, despite 'the long hours' and wrote a full report in the September issue of *The Link*. The agenda included discussions on confirmation and the admission to Communion of communicant members of other churches, Anglican-Methodist unity, recruitment to the Ministry, the World Council of Churches' grant to freedom fighters and the increase of civil strife.

Waldron (Bill) Harris was Rector's Warden from 1964–72. When the Bishop and diocese of Leicester agreed in 1972 to develop an auxiliary ministry of priesthood in the diocese. Dr Harris was among the first to be ordained as, initially, an auxiliary deacon. His ordination was seen as somewhat timely, coinciding as it did with the illness and forthcoming retirement of Rector Stuart Smith.

Nationally, the economic situation in the last half of the decade was depressing, as were the facts and figures relating to clergy income. In a 1977 diocesan synod discussion of clergy stipends and expenses, the Bishop of Leicester expressed his regret at the poor record of the parishes in Leicester Diocese when paying clergy expenses. He told the Synod that the average annual expenses falling on the clergy in 1977 were £500 and these were left to the individual parishes to pay. National statistics showed, he said, that the Leicester parishes were, on average, 'among the least generous in the land'.[69] In 1978, when Swithland's quota was £1,925 and the annual incumbent's stipend was £2,985, Swithland paid its rector £200 expenses. As the rectory at Swithland was, strictly speaking, a 'Sunday' post, the expenses paid by Swithland were far from being 'the least generous in the land'.

Each decade has its downs, as well as it ups. Swithland was to mourn the loss, among others, of Mrs Linwood Wright, Mrs Annie Bunney and Dr Waldron Harris. All were given affectionate tributes in *The Link*.

> On the 1st June 1977 Swithland lost one of its most illustrious residents. Mrs Linwood Wright lived at The Cottage for no less than 70 years after her marriage and established herself as a hostess of grace, dignity and generous hospitality. Her artistic gifts were amply shown in her home and in the events arranged in the house and garden throughout the years, especially through 'the Swithland Revels' which raised the sum of £700. Her home turned over to the 'Feed the Minds' Campaign in a floral display was one of her supreme efforts which will always be remembered as an inspiration to those who saw and took part in it. Her gifts of organisation, combined with the golden touch of diplomacy, stretched out into the factories of Luke Turner and Co. when her husband, Mr Arch Turner died, and from adverse circumstances then existing in the business, she was able to make a success of the firm. She was supported by loyal workers, many of whom showed their appreciation by attendance at the funeral. Looking at her past, her accomplishments included the founding with Nurse Prior of the Leicester Curzon Street Baby Welfare Centre, and the Bluebird Guild in Swithland. After her second marriage to Canon Linwood Wright, diocesan Canon Missioner, she was able to help him in promoting Christian Drama. At the great age of 94 years, 'the morning has broken' for her and none of those who knew her could end an appreciation without paying tribute to the devotion of her much beloved sister, Olive Brooke-Hunt, and the unceasing care, in the last few years, of Esther Thomas, friend and housekeeper.[70]

Fig 19.9 Swithland Revels at The Cottage in the 1950s.

Fig 19.10 Tug of War, Swithland Revels.

Mrs Annie Bunney also died in 1977:

> With the death of Mrs Annie Bunney, Swithland loses one of its oldest residents. She was a very familiar figure in the village having lived in her cottage for sixty years. One of the founder members of the Swithland Mothers' Union, formed in the early years after the restoration of the Church, she was a very regular churchgoer. She was also a member of the Missionary Working Party and a member of the Bluebird Guild. As a member of the Village Hall Management Committee, she helped run whist drives to keep the hall open. We extend our sympathy to Mr Sid Bunney, our faithful sexton until he retired, and to the rest of the family.[71]

And in 1979 the Revd Dr Waldron (Bill) Harris died. Bill Harris was one of a number of men who trained for auxiliary ordained ministry at Launde Abbey in the Leicester diocesan training scheme, an experiment in its day. He was ordained deacon in December 1972. Bill Harris was clearly respected and loved.

> How shall we ever forget the untiring and unselfish service of our former Churchwarden and honorary Curate, Dr Waldron Harris, affectionately called Bill. (The anonymous writer recalls) his deep inner faith, quiet personality and gentle ministry. He had a great sense of dry humour and many of us will remember him as one of the bashful three little maids in the Mikado, the playful Koko also in the Mikado, and the elegant Admiral Sir Joseph Porter in HMS Pinafore, performed at two of our Harvest Suppers.[72]

He married Olga Gregory in 1972, his first wife having died in 1970.

From The Link: *Church Services 1965–2007*

Every issue of *The Link* advertises the church services for that month. Looking back over the last forty years, there has been very gentle change in both pattern and style of services. St Leonard's has seen no sweeping change from 'ancient' to 'modern', rather the church community has embraced, for many years, a balanced mixture of services which seek to serve the spiritual needs of all its members. From 1968, services have been taken both from the Book of Common Prayer and from the new 'alternative' services authorised by the General Synod over the years. A regular monthly Family Service has been held since 1962. Series 2 Holy Communion services were introduced in 1968, Series 3 in 1971, the Alternative Service Book in 1980, and Common Worship in 2000. Rector Ray Walters encouraged a full Holy Week celebration from 1977, and this tradition has been continued. Walters also introduced a greater emphasis on music in worship which has also been maintained. Evensong had been celebrated every Sunday for many years, but with falling numbers, it was decided in 2001 to hold choral evening services for special occasions only – approximately once a month.

In 1962 the pattern of services varied according to the Sunday of the month. Holy Communion was celebrated at 8am on the first and third Sundays, with Mattins at 11am on the first, third and fifth Sundays. Holy Communion with Sermon was celebrated on the second Sunday at 11am, and at 10.30am on the fourth Sunday. This was because a Family Service was also held on the fourth Sunday at 9.45am. The Sunday School met at 2.30pm. every Sunday except the fourth Sunday. Evensong was at 6.30pm every Sunday, and on the third Sunday it was followed by Holy Communion.

By 1968, it was clear that the Family Service drew far more congregational support than did the traditional services. It was therefore decided to add a second family service each month, and to begin using the new Holy Communion Service (Series 2) for some services. Rector Stuart Smith commended the new service: 'Changes of this kind are necessary in a Church which is still alive'. Whilst acknowledging the 'inconvenience' of change to some worshippers, he foretold that 'some kind of revision in the Church's forms of worship will be found necessary every thirty years'.[73] After a few months of experimentation, it was agreed by the Parochial Church Council that the new Series 2 service would be used for all services of Parish Communion, and the Prayer Book service would be used for all 8am Sunday services.

By 1971, the pattern of worship at Swithland had seen further adjustment, with the second Sunday Family Service being replaced by a Parish Communion Service, since the rector felt that too few parishioners were taking Holy Communion. The Sunday School was held at the Memorial Hall at 9.30am on the 1st, 2nd, 3rd and 5th Sundays of the month.

> Every Sunday, the Prayer Book Communion service was said at 8am.
> 1st Sunday: 11am Holy Communion (BCP); 6.30pm Evening Prayer
> 2nd Sunday: 9.45am Parish Communion (series 2); 6.30pm Evening Prayer
> 3rd Sunday: 11am Morning Prayer; 6.30pm Evensong and Holy Communion (BCP).
> 4th Sunday: 9.45am Family Service; 10.30am Parish Communion (series 2); 6.30pm Evensong
> 5th Sunday: 11am Morning Prayer; 6.30pm Evensong.

Later that year, the Series 3 proposed order for Holy Communion was published. The Parochial Church had a preliminary discussion as to whether or not to use it.

Stuart Smith retired in 1973 and was followed by Edward Carlile. Unfortunately Carlile failed to keep copies of the parish magazine during his incumbency, so we have no record of the pattern of services and style of worship during his time.

When Ray Walters was appointed priest-in-charge in 1977, the Sunday School and Family Service aspect of worship was slightly adjusted. The Sunday School was held at the Memorial Hall at 10am on the 1st and 3rd Sundays of the month; there was a Family Service on the 2nd Sunday of the month, and a Family Communion on the 4th Sunday. With his interest in church music, Walters introduced a sung Eucharist on the 1st and 5th

Sundays of the month. Service times were tidied up: the main morning service (and the Sunday School) all started at 10am. Winter evening services, however, were moved to 4pm, initially because of work to replace the church boiler. The tradition was popular, and continues to this day.

A more major innovation during Walters' incumbency was the observation of the full tradition of Holy Week Services. On Palm Sunday, the 10am service included the procession of palms, and, in the evening, the Men's Club annual service was held. Holy Communion on the Monday, Tuesday and Wednesday of Holy Week was celebrated at 7.30am at Canon Godfrey's home, The Granary, with evening services on Tuesday, Maundy Thursday, and Easter Eve. There were services at 10am and 2pm on Good Friday. By 1988 the pattern had settled down to a Palm Sunday with Holy Communion Services at 8 and 10.45am, Procession of Palms and Mattins at 10am and Men's Club Evensong at 6.30pm. There were 7.30pm Holy Communion services at Church on Monday, Tuesday and Wednesday. On Maundy Thursday at 7.30pm the service of 'thanksgiving for the institution of the Eucharist' was held; on Good Friday there was Mattins, Litany and Ante-Communion at 10am and a Devotional Service at 2pm; the Paschal Liturgy was celebrated on Holy Saturday at 11.30pm; and on Easter Day, there was an 8am Holy Communion, a 10am Family Communion and 6.30pm Evensong. Walters also held celebrations of Holy Communion at 10am on Easter Monday and Easter Tuesday.

The tradition of observing the full Holy Week pattern of services has been maintained in subsequent years, with minor changes made in 2000 when Swithland became part of the larger benefice of Woodhouse, Woodhouse Eaves and Swithland. Currently there is an ecumenical Palm Sunday service at Woodhouse Eaves, with a procession of palms through the village to either the Baptist or the Methodist Church, with the Swithland Church Kidz Club members encouraged to attend this service.

In 1980, the Church of England introduced a new book of 'alternative services' to run alongside the *Book of Common Prayer* services. St Leonard's bought fifty copies of the *Alternative Service Book* (1980) ready 'for use in church in the Lenten period'.[74] Rector Walters staged a series of sermons during Lent that year introducing the new book. Sermons were preached on: Prayer Books – for whose benefit; the Daily Service; Prayer Book and Bible; Family Services; the Eucharist. The Parochial Church Council agreed to use the new alternative services for Parish and Family Communion and Family Services, but to continue to use Prayer Book forms for the 8am Holy Communion and for Morning and Evening Prayer. Walters also started a tradition of 'Compline with Address' on Saturday evenings in Advent and Lent, as well as 'sermon series' for morning and evening services during Lent.

Come the mid-nineties, come the end of the *Alternative Service Book* (1980), services from which were authorised only to the year 2000. The Church of England, having established that its worship should be both traditional (*Book of Common Prayer*) and contemporary, needed to reshape its 'contemporary' services. The 'alternative services' of 1980 were looking tired and thin. Three post-1980 seasonal worship publications, material from which was being increasingly used to enrich the alternative services, showed something of the way forward: *Lent, Holy Week and Easter* (1986), *The Promise of His Glory* (1991) and *Enriching the Christian Year* (1993). In the mid-1990s, the archbishops gave some eight hundred parishes permission to use draft forms of the authorized services in *Common Worship* on an experimental basis before they were presented to the General Synod. The services were adjusted in the light of feedback from this 'field testing'. Swithland was one of those parishes so authorized. From 1995, therefore, there were gradual changes in the liturgies Swithland used in its agreed 'contemporary' worship slots. Publication of the full range of *Common Worship* authorized services was completed in 2008.

Over the years, Swithland has also kept its own local festivals and worship customs, such as its Patronal Festival and Dedication Festival. With St Leonard's feast day being November 6th, the patronal festival used to be observed on the first Sunday in November, at about the same time as the village wake. The 'wake', however, has not been observed by village or church since the 1960s and the patronal festival has been assimilated into the All Saints observation. The church's Dedication Festival, however, is observed each year. Not knowing the actual date of its dedication, the festival was initially kept in October. Since 2000, however, the Dedication Festival has been kept on the fourth Sunday of June, this being the Sunday nearest to the anniversary of the dedication of the church's Millennium Extension.

Other occasional innovations during the last decades have been Flower Festivals, a Snowdrop Festival (2006) and, since 1996, a Christmas Eve afternoon 'Open Church' and family carols. A 'Christmas Crib' Festival was held in December 2009.

Swithland in the 1980s

The 1980s, according to Andrew Marr,[75] 'set the mould for Britain today – the defeat of grit, soot, smoke and clank; the triumph of credit and rampant consumerism ... an age of unparalleled consumption, credit, show-off wealth, quick bucks and sexual libertinism'. It was, of course, the era of Thatcherism. So what marked this decade in Swithland?

Swithland's new decade had begun with a heart-felt plea in the January issue of *The Link* from a lady who had lost something. 'At the Candlelight Dance in the Memorial Hall, Swithland, some lady unfortunately took away the wrong black velvet jacket and left her own. If you find you have the wrong jacket would you please contact J.B.' The subsequent February magazine failed to reveal whether or not J.B's plea was successful.

The eighties were the era of 'pâté parties' in Swithland, with the Ladies Group just one of the village organisations to organise them. The Swithland Ladies Group, which was launched in the 1970s,[76] was a village group, not a church organisation, and set up for the purpose of enabling villagers to get to know each other and to raise money for charity. Events in March 1970, for example, raised £222 16s 6d for the Multiple Sclerosis Society and the Good Samaritans. By 1976, pâté parties were all the rage. Miss Dorothy Peck, for example, hosted an annual autumn 'wine, cheese and pâté party' at her home, the Manor House (Hall Farm), raising money for charity. One of the founding members of the group, Mrs Norah Woolley, who then lived at 'Elmleah', died in 1980. Her obituary noted that she was also a member of the Swithland Mothers' Union and a leading flower arranger in the county.[77]

The newly restored Memorial Hall was in constant use. The wedding of the Prince and Princess of Wales in July 1981 offered a perfect opportunity for what might be described as the Swithland social event of the decade. Reporting afterwards, Willoughby Garton said: 'The village celebration on 29th July was certainly an occasion to remember. On a perfect summer's evening, over two hundred people, all of whom either lived in the village or belonged to one of the village organisations, enjoyed a wonderful evening of games and barbeque for the children, a celebration supper, including cutting of a wedding cake, musical entertainment and finally a disco. To commemorate the event a winter flowering cherry tree was planted (in the Memorial Hall grounds) by villagers led by Miss Dorothy Peck and Master Timothy Hardwicke'.[78] Later in the decade, the Memorial Hall began to be used regularly on Tuesday afternoons by the Swithland Mother and Toddlers group, founded in 1984 by Janet Beeby, Trish Lawrence, and Mandy Lynch. Another highlight of the decade was the hosting of a recording of the Radio Leicester Inter-village Quiz in 1985. A Swithland team was entered.

Other village and church organisations continued their regular activities. In 1981, the Youth Group built the November bonfire at the Griffin Inn, staged a dramatic presentation at the church morning service, held a debate, played 'Call my Bluff' and 'Blankety Blank' and held a Christmas season 'male dinner and female entertainment to close the celebrations'.[79] The Sunday School was re-started in 1984 by Janet Roberts with Janet Beeby, Margaret Hardwicke and Anne Gray. It met in the Memorial Hall from 10–10.45am on the first and third Sundays of the month.

St Leonard's School reported regularly in *The Link*. In December 1981, for example, it was announced that a Nativity Play was to be performed in the church on Tuesday December 15th. 'Written by Norman Harrington, the play presents the Christmas story from an unusual angle'. In 1984, to mark National Heritage Year, the school staged an 'open to visitors' exhibition on Chaucer and the Canterbury Tales. 'It was a very exciting day for all our class', wrote Ben Copson, aged nine years, 'We had twelve figures of Chaucer and the Canterbury pilgrims. We had loads and loads of visitors. Everyone did a picture of a pilgrim and made a book. I thought the exhibition was extra Ace. I liked the figures best because they looked alive. We were also selling Middle Ages Cookery Books and the infants had a travelling exhibition called 'Journeys''.[80]

Parish magazines keep readers up to date with every aspect of village life. Writing in the March 1988 edition of *The Link*, the rector reported on Mrs Harrington's impending retirement as infant teacher at Swithland School 'after many years of faithful and enthusiastic service'. 'Many remember', he wrote, 'her firm but kind presence in the classroom and acknowledge that they owe their grounding in education to the happy beginning they experienced with her'. In August 1988 he had also to report the resignation of headmistress Sheila Bryan because of illness, and then, sadly soon after, her sudden death.

Bellringing thrived in the village through the eighties. Keith Andrews became Tower Captain in 1980, with Percy Barrett as his deputy. Percy Barrett continued as deputy when John Roberts took over as tower captain in 1987; he taught many learners during the eighties and nineties including members of the Hardwicke, May, Capleton and Beeby families, all of whom became regular ringers for church services. Many of the young learners were undertaking the Duke of Edinburgh Award; learning to ring bells was a part of completing their award. During these years, various ringing traditions began which still survive. From 1983, a single bell has been rung every Sunday for the 8am Holy Communion service. From 1986, there has been a bell ringers' outing. The first was organised in September 1986 by John Roberts, when ringers visited towers in Northamptonshire.[81] This annual outing is still organised jointly with the Thurcaston band. The ringers also hold an annual dinner; this was started as a regular event in 1982 under Percy Barrett's organisation.[82] The annual Bellringers' service in June was started in 1983.

After a gap of nearly twenty years, a quarter peal was rung on 22nd November 1983 to mark the completion of repairs to the tower. This was a first quarter peal for four members of the team – Louise Holloway, Percy Barrett, Keith Andrews and John Roberts.[83] The other members of the team were Willoughby Garton and G. Lowe. Other special peals and quarter peals were rung during the decade. A quarter peal of Bob Minor on 9th November 1985, for example, was rung as a part of a Leicester and Syston District quarter peal day. *The Link* records a semi-muffled quarter peal on 8th June 1986, which was rung in memory of Alfred Copson, a keen member of the St Leonard's band in the 1960s who rang two peals in 1961. In May 1987, a peal of 5040 Plain Bob Minor was rung at Swithland in 2 hours 50 minutes by P.C. Barrett, V. Stevenson, J.M. Roberts, E. Atkinson, C.H. Robbins and H.J. William (conductor). 'This peal', wrote Percy Barrett in *The Link* magazine, 'was notable in a number of respects. It was the first peal in which Swithland ringers had taken part for over twenty years; the first peal on an inside bell for John Roberts and Eric Atkinson, and the first peal for Percy Barrett, rung three days short of the 81st anniversary of his grandfather's last peal rung at Lichfield Cathedral on 29th May 1906'.[84]

Within the church building some re-ordering work was done in the chancel. The rector, Ray Walters, had originally suggested enlarging the sanctuary, 'replacing the altar rails with new oak ones half way down the chancel (using the old rails to replace the iron railings marking off the Lanesborough chapel), lowering the sanctuary and chancel floor and moving the chancel pews'.[85] A faculty application, with slightly revised proposals, was submitted in June 1980. Two years later, with faculty permission finally given, the pews were removed from the chancel, the floor made good, the steps to the chancel lengthened and a movable rail installed for the use of those mounting the chancel steps. The work was followed by 'a thorough cleaning of the church'.[86]

Another major project was the restoration of the Snetzler organ between 1986 and 1987. The contractor, Martin Renshaw, undertook not only to clean and repair the instrument as necessary, but also to bring into use some of the original Snetzler pipe work, which was then purely decorative. The approximate cost of the work was £14,000. An organ restoration celebration concert was given on September 19th by James Dalton, organist of Queen's College, Oxford. He played music especially chosen to illustrate the work of Johannes Snetzler, with narration by Martin Renshaw. A further celebration concert with supper at the Village Hall was held on 23 October 1987, with Peter White, Leicester Cathedral's Master of Music, as the guest soloist. In December 1987, the BBC broadcast a programme of music played by Peter White on Swithland's newly-restored organ. St Leonard's own organist, Margaret Lintern Ball, wrote in the magazine that she was 'particularly looking forward to accompanying the Psalms, for the new stops on the organ mean that we should be able to 'Praise the Lord in the sound of the trumpet', hear the birds 'sing among the branches' and even experience a suggestion of 'lions roaring after their prey'.[87]

1986 saw the completion of many years of striving to enlarge the churchyard. In his magazine letter of January 1986, the rector was delighted to report 'that we have now obtained possession of the land between the churchyard and the road to extend the churchyard to serve the village for very many years. This is the fruition of plans which began as long ago as the 1920s'. A gradual development was promised 'so that its character as a country churchyard will be maintained.' The parcel of land measured 827 sq. yards, and had belonged, since the Enclosure Act (1798) to the Danvers/Lanesborough family. (It seems likely that this parcel of land was at one time Swithland's 'Lower Green'.) The work on the extended churchyard was completed before the end of 1989, with the large gate to the new area being donated by the ninth Earl.

The history to which the rector referred was indeed long and convoluted. The matter of extending the churchyard had first been raised in 1929; for the next fifty-six years the Parochial Church Council had pursued the matter, fruitlessly, with successive Earls of Lanesborough. In 2004, with permission granted by the local authority to remove all but the holly trees in that part of the new area nearest the road, the Parochial Church Council authorised a final clearing, levelling and grass-seeding operation opening the view to the new boundary wall.

The Link regularly records the baptisms, marriages and deaths of Swithland parishioners and to print short obituaries. The December 1981 issue, for example, recorded the passing of Ian Carnall, who had been organist of St Leonard's for ten years. Ian was also 'a founder member of the Church Men's Club, and the unofficial Music Maker and Accompanist at the Club's meetings and outings for many years'. Bishop Stuart Smith, a past rector, died in that same month. Like many of his predecessors, his remains are buried in Swithland churchyard. The January 1982 issue of *The Link* obituary affectionately remembered him 'on his cycle during his visits to both sick and new residents of the parish as well as his regular congregation'.

John Beachell, Swithland's Tower Captain from 1971–80, died in February 1983. His successor, Keith Andrews, paid tribute to a man who 'had bullied us into ringing the bells again in Swithland. It is a tribute to him that we now have a strong following in Swithland'. The Countess of Lanesborough, widow of the eighth Earl, died in August 1983. Her funeral was 'a significant stage in the history of the association of the Lanesborough family with Swithland. She was a faithful member of her church and is remembered with great respect and affection as a Christian lady. When her health permitted she was always in the family pew'.[88] Lady Lanesborough had been an active member of the Swithland Mothers' Union since 1932. Another sad loss to both church and village was the passing of Canon Lindesay Godfrey in August 1984. Zoë Willson, editor of *The Link*, paid him tribute in the September issue.

> His sense of humour frequently surfaced in the production of *The Link*. His homes, both at Forest End and at the Granary, where everyone was welcome, were the venues for many parish gatherings. One, in particular, the successful exhibition for Christian Aid, comprising fascinating exhibits of old Swithland, will be remembered. 'His prayer leaflets, and his second book compiled from them, will be a lasting memory of a person it was a privilege to have known.'

There are always miscellaneous snippets of abiding interest in parish magazines! This from the January 1987 edition of *The Link* might be judged as one appropriate 'end-note' to this summary of the parish in the 1980s.

> Swithland is one of the few parishes to have a parish bier, a four-wheeled handbarrow on which, in former times, coffins were borne to the grave. Our bier probably dates from the beginning of the twentieth century. In view of the absence of demand for its use, it is proposed to offer it on permanent loan to the Museums service.

And this, from the last magazine of the decade:

> After fifteen years, I would very much like to relinquish the responsibility for the War Memorial Weekly Flower Rota from Easter to Christmas. Would anyone be willing to take it on, or offer any suggestions? If so, please phone Jean Herbert.

This quiet but appreciated ministry was taken over by Margaret Hardwicke who still continues it.

From The Link: *Letter from the Rector*

An important part of every church magazine is the letter from the rector, or, in an interregnum, the churchwardens. Swithland's magazine is no exception. The message usually falls into two parts, a touch of popular theology, and some words about significant events and people. Just sometimes there is a personal touch, such as the rector's reflections on arriving and leaving the parish.

Most recent rectors have left Swithland at retirement time, which means that there is the occasional reference to ill health. Bishop Alex Maxwell, for example, had a heart attack in 1965, and retired 'through ill health' in 1967. In his farewell letter he said: 'This is the last letter I write as your Rector. It is a very sad thought to Grace and myself, for we have been so happy in this Parish and have made so many friends whom we are going to find very difficult to leave'.

Incoming rectors always arrive with new ideas and hopes. Geoffrey Stuart Smith, for example, was a retired bishop looking forward to the opportunities for pastoral care afforded by a small parochial charge. In his first letter he wrote: 'My most important task at present is to get to know you all. So do not be surprised to see me on your doorstep'.[89] Stuart Smith knew the value of affirming peoples' contributions to the life of the church: 'Our church is well kept and draws many expressions of praise from visitors. Our churchyard also is well kept, thanks to the untiring efforts of Mr Sidney Bunney'.[90] Stuart Smith must have been a good listener; his tribute to Mr Bunney continued: 'It is no light task to keep (the churchyard) all tidy at this time of year. It would, I suspect, be made a little easier if all those living in or near the village who have relatives buried in the churchyard would attend to the graves in which they have a particular interest'. He was also a wise educator and his magazine letters were a frequent source of Christian teaching. He introduced the Revised Standard Version of the Bible into St Leonard's Church in 1966 and set up a Bible Study group in the parish. He had inherited a parish church with a flourishing Sunday School and a monthly family service and he encouraged their development. 'Family Services', he said, 'have come to stay, and Sunday Schools are an important institution, but should be efficient to justify their retention'.

Stuart Smith encouraged Swithland church to be part of all diocesan pastoral initiatives, and stressed the importance of the whole church working together towards Christian Unity. In early 1972, however, he suffered a stroke, and May saw him writing from hospital: 'Progress is slow, but, I think, sure. Being very impatient, I often wish it could be quicker.' Sadly, his illness forced him to retire, first as Assistant Bishop (July 1972) and then as rector of Swithland (1973).

> I would end this letter to you on two notes. The first must be thankfulness that in the closing stages of my ministry God has sent me to Swithland. The other note must be one of penitence. Of course, in some respects I have failed. So I must add a little prayer which is very familiar to users of the Prayer Book, 'Lord, have mercy'. Let me add a short prayer for all of you, 'The Lord be with you.'[91]

Frustratingly, no one added any copies of *The Link* to the Rectory archives during the next interregnum or through Bill Carlile's brief incumbency (1973–6). The story from our records picks up, however, in

November 1976 as Bill Carlile prepared to leave Swithland. In the short interregnum that followed, Lindesay Godfrey wrote as priest in charge: 'We shall all miss Bill Carlile greatly as our Rector. We shall miss his stimulating sermons, his intercessions, his sheer kindliness to all of us who have come to know him, and above all his example of his devotion to our Lord Jesus Christ'.[92] Carlile's consequent letter of thanks to the parish concluded: 'We shall always look back with gratitude to our three years in your midst, and this brief, yet stimulating interlude will have been of immense benefit to our urban ministry from which we seem unable to escape'.[93]

Three months later, the name of Carlile's successor had been announced. The Revd Raymond Walters,[94] recently appointed Leicester Diocesan Director of Education, would also be priest-in-charge of Swithland. Ray Walters' first letter showed tact. 'We appreciate the generosity of the parish in providing central heating for the rectory'.[95] He referred to the time-consuming nature of his work as Diocesan Education Secretary, but said 'I shall always appreciate the opportunity of being at the fore front of the Church's work which is still, I believe, in the parochial ministry'. As usual, some of the new rector's priorities were outlined in his early letters, not least an emphasis on church families, church music and good liturgy. He appealed for new choristers and adults to volunteer as servers, 'Jeff Harrison having agreed to act as Head Server'. Fourteen years later he was regretfully writing his farewell letter: 'It is very hard to say goodbye. These have been years full of event and purpose in which we as a family have shared with you the enterprise of Christian living in the community, and we depart rich in memory and friendship for that time'.[96]

Three years later, his successor, the Revd Anne Horton, writing her first letter, reflected on 'the immensity and the responsibility of this new mutual commitment we are about to take on' and prayed that 'sharing our ministries, we may serve one another and make Christ known in this community'.[97]

From The Link: *Interregna*

The interregnum (the years between rectors) is a traditional feature of church life everywhere in the Church of England. During an interregnum, the traditional 'letter from the rector' in the parish magazine is often replaced by a letter from the wardens or some other church official, and services are taken by a variety of visiting priests and Readers.

It is clear from listening to parishioners how important and appreciated the ministry of visiting priests can be, especially when the wardens are able to ensure the same priests visiting over a period of time. In the 1960s, for example, Canon Percy Lidster was a popular visitor. When he died in 1980, Mrs Gimson wrote: 'Since 1938, during our several interregnums, he had been one of our regular visiting clergymen, and though he could preach to all kinds of congregations, he loved to talk to children at our children's services (as they were then called) and I am sure many of our teenagers will remember his amusing and interesting stories'.[98] The Revd John Elliott was another regular visiting priest. Chaplain at Loughborough School, Mr

Elliott visited Swithland on and off for over forty years. His last visit to the benefice, shortly before he died, was to stand with the family of Archdeacon Harold Lockley (another old friend of Swithland) as we buried him beside his wife in Woodhouse Eaves churchyard. Swithland was also much blessed in that Canon Lindesay Godfrey, a much loved retired assistant priest, lived and ministered in Swithland for many years. He over-saw the short interregnum 1976–77 and was generous in the use of his home for meetings and worship. Mid-week Holy Communion services, for example, were for a time held in his chapel at 'The Granary'.

Churchwardens have particular responsibilities during interregna and often write 'the letter' in the parish magazine. During the 1991–4 interregnum, the churchwardens were Gweneth Gimson and Bob Mee (later Bernard Durham). This interregnum covered some years of battling between Swithland parish and the Leicester diocese with respect to possible pastoral re-organisation, and the wardens' letters stressed the importance of supporting the church so that the new Bishop should be persuaded to re-appoint a resident priest. It was evident that the wardens were encouraged by a visit to the parish by the Bishop of Leicester early in the interregnum and also by the precedent-setting appointment of Assistant Bishop Godfrey Ashby as priest-in-charge of Newtown Linford. They were certainly elated by the news in July 1992 that they would, when the new rectory[99] was built in the grounds of the old rectory and when the right person could be found, have another resident priest. They were further encouraged by the November 1992 passing of legislation in the General Synod to enable the priesting of women in the Church of England, and hoping that 'the defections and schism forecast by the tabloid press will pass us by'.

Interregna, especially since lay ministries have been encouraged in the Church of England, bring out latent skills in many people. Articles in *The Link* 1991–94 showed that Swithland had a strong laity, with many people, not just the churchwardens, prepared to take on leadership roles. This was particularly evident with regard to administration, finance and worship. David Pugh headed up a Stewardship Campaign and chaired the Worship Committee and Roger Scoppie, the choir master, was responsible for choices in church music and hymnody. In a Christmas letter to the parish in 1992, Archdeacon Emeritus Harold Lockley wrote: 'Lay giving in Swithland, in terms of time, talents and money, have been decisive in maintaining the worship and life of the parish'.

All interregna have beginnings and endings, usually marked by the parish in a social gathering at the Memorial Hall. At Rector Bill Carlile's farewell, Mrs Gimson, one of the churchwardens, gave a 'prayerful farewell' to the rector 'on the unique occasion of a Swithland rector leaving to take a fresh appointment'. 'Within living memory', she said, 'all others have stayed until leaving to live in retirement'. She praised his courage. 'Never afraid to experiment, where one venture did not meet with the success he hoped, he tried another'.[100]

From The Link: *Decades of Charitable Support*

Virtually every copy of *The Link* has reported how, through one event or another, Swithland people, from both community and church, have been involved in raising money for charity. A few quotations per decade give the flavour of local generosity.

Swithland has been supporting Christian Aid since 1963, when Mrs Lois Godfrey agreed to be co-ordinator. Canon and Mrs Godfrey held regular fund-raising events for Christian Aid at Forest End, such as a 'history of everyday times' exhibition, with a 'trad' supper. The first *Reservoir Recipe Book* was gathered and printed in 1967, and copies sold for 5/- in aid of Christian Aid. For some years during the 1980s, the Swithland Youth Club took responsibility for organising the collections. During the 1990s, Pam Howlett volunteered to act as the village's Christian Aid co-ordinator, and she continued to do this quietly and efficiently until 2006, when she passed over the mantle to Baroness Byford. Other charities to have received long term support in Swithland have been the Church of England Children's Society and Missions to Seamen. For many years, Mrs Gweneth Gimson was responsible for organising the annual box collection for the Children's Society, various parishioners holding boxes at home. The Missions to Seamen charity was supported for some years by an annual street collection in the village. In the June 1987 issue of *The Link* the rector reported: 'Mrs Phyllis Lloyd tells me that the collection from the Village in aid of the Missions to Seamen amounted to £54.41, and we are grateful to all who supported this important Christian work'. Other charities benefiting from street collections spear-headed by Swithland residents over the years have been the Royal National Lifeboat Institution and LOROS.

Various village and church organisations have encouraged charitable donations. Miss Dorothy Peck of Manor House, Swithland, organised and hosted a pâté party in September 1980 and 'due to the generosity of many people, Swithland Ladies Group were able to send a total of £204 to the Leicester branch of the Parkinson's Disease Society'.[101]

Since its inception in 1977, the Swithland Fruit and Vegetable Show, organised by a committee of the Church Men's Club, has raised significant amounts of money for local charities, in part through auctioning the exhibits in the show. At the first show £101 was raised, with Jeff Harrison as auctioneer inspiring £41 of the total. Ten years later £500 was raised, which was split equally between Riding for the Disabled and the Leicester Mission for the Deaf. In 2010 the main beneficiaries of the £5200 raised were LOROS and Rainbows. In other ways, too, the Men's Club has continued its charitable fundraising through the decades. Each Christmas, for example, they raise money while eating and singing. The January 1990 issue of *The Link*, for example, reported that 'the Christmas Dinner was very well supported', that 'over £230 was made on the raffle for LOROS' and that 'due to the generosity of residents of Swithland and Swithland Lane on carol-singing nights over £400 has been shared between COPE and Swithland Church'.

The Annual Bluebell Service in Swithland Woods has also traditionally collected for a local charity. In 1988, for example, 'the largest collection ever taken' meant that £125.50 was sent to LOROS, the Leicestershire and Rutland Hospice. For many years the church has made annual donations to the *Church Times* 'Train a Priest' appeal and the Church Missionary Society.

In September 1990, the Leicester and Leicestershire Historic Churches Preservation Trust organised its first sponsored bicycle ride. Swithland was one of the churches open on the day, and it has participated by opening the church to visitors every year since. Swithland cyclists have also 'ridden for Swithland' on the day, raising money through sponsorship, half of which has gone to the Leicester and Leicestershire Historic Churches Preservation Trust and half to their own parish church. Since the mid-1990s, Swithland has supported the work of the Loughborough Christmas Shelter, both financially and with gifts of food. The annual Church Wives' Gift Service on Advent Sunday continues that custom. When the Christmas Shelter turned into a permanent shelter and base for work amongst the homeless in Loughborough, Swithland was able to extend and broaden its support; harvest gifts, for example, from both church and school have been donated both to the Loughborough shelter and to the Y Centre in Leicester.

Swithland in the 1990s

Nationally, the 1990s began on a low note. The boom years were over, and Britain's economy was wilting. Unemployment numbered over two million people; the interest rate was ten per cent and rising. Black Wednesday 1992 saw interest rates reaching fifteen per cent, with Britain pulling out of the European Exchange Rate Mechanism. It was a decade of Gulf Wars, which would spill over into the new millennium. Conservatism collapsed; New Labour swept into power with a prime minister who, at least according to one of his advisors, did not 'do God'. Arguably the British monarchy came near to collapsing too, part of the aftermath of the death in a car accident in 1997 of the Princess of Wales. Globally meanwhile, the rapid spread of the world wide web and internet communication was affecting everything. But if the decade in Britain began in the financial doldrums, it certainly ended in an atmosphere of dotcom consumerism.

Swithland's rector, Ray Walters, in his New Year's letter, wondered what the 1990s would hold. 'Decades' he wrote 'seem to acquire their own characteristics – the 'swinging sixties', the materialism of the eighties – what will the nineties be?' He went on: 'The Church has asked that the nineties be a decade of evangelism for Christian people, and it is still remarkable that there are those who do not appreciate that this is a competitive area to move into today'. As he called on Christians in Swithland to think evangelistically, he spoke, prophetically, of the increasing momentum of Islam in Britain, asking his parishioners to compare its growth with a 'tongue-tied and fearful' Christianity too often presenting the Christ 'not as living and reigning, but as encapsulated in quaint and antique trappings and language'.[102]

Various challenges were put before the church in Swithland in the nineties, not least at the beginning of the decade when they were challenged to raise £960 towards the diocesan contribution to the national Church commitment to set up the £18m Church Urban Fund.[103] Some of the money from Swithland came from individual donations, some from joint efforts and some from the creation and sale of a third *Reservoir Recipe Book*, a local publication of recipes and household hints, collected and edited by Olga Harris. The June 1992 issue of *The Link* reported that all the copies had been sold and £155 profit made.

In September 1990 the youngest daughter of the Rectory, Gillian Walters, left Swithland to spend a year in South Africa doing voluntary work within the Anglican Church. Gillian sent regular reports back to the parish via *The Link*. Based at Pretoria Cathedral, she was tasked with improving links between black and white families from the cathedral with those from their link parish in Garankuwa. She had a specific involvement with young people and street kids. 'I was taken to Mamelodi where some 350,000 live, the majority in dwellings made of plywood and corrugated iron. I tell you, I was scared! Outside Mamelodi there is a squatter camp called Stanza Village. This has grown up because of severe over-crowding in Mamelodi. These camps are grim. No running water, electricity or toilets. The primary problem – the black population lives on only 13% of the land. On Christmas Day we visited four families – and each time we arrived we were warmly embraced and shown into the house where a meal awaited us! This is one of the beauties (and dangers!) of African hospitality'.[104]

For many, one of the major ecclesiastical discussions in the Church of England in the nineties pertained to the ordination of women to the priesthood.[105] Across the parishes of the land, the issues were debated, voting took place and the results sent to the various diocesan authorities for analysis. Swithland began its discussions at a symposium after Evensong on Sunday 24th February 1990. Percy Barrett spoke for the proposal, Mrs Gillian Walters, the rector's wife, reluctantly, put the case against; the voting figures were forty-one in favour, five against and one abstention.[106]

A stewardship campaign was organised in 1992, with David Pugh as campaign chairman. The churchwardens, in their August letter in *The Link*, had indicated the importance of 'ensuring that when the successor to Ray Walters arrives, he finds a parish with all its affairs in order, thus enabling him to be concerned only with the spiritual life of the parish'. That successor was able to confirm that when the Bishop approached her about going to Swithland, he was able to assure her that it was just 'a Sunday job' as the parish had got everything else sorted!

In September 1994, the Parochial Church Council agreed to investigate further the possibility of constructing an extension to the church building. An article in *The Link* March 1995 paved the way for discussions at the Annual Church Meeting. 'We would like to be able to offer a Sunday School, but where could it meet that isn't too far from the worshipping congregation and the children's parents? We would like to encourage young families into church, but we cannot offer any crèche facilities. We would like to be able to build up the fellowship of the congregation after Sunday worship, but we have no meeting room or kitchen facilities to help us do this. There are times when quiet or private space would be invaluable, but there is nowhere to go. Our vestry accommodation is limited; likewise our storage space. We urgently need cloakroom facilities and hot water on tap. It is embarrassing directing members of our wedding and funeral congregations round to the back of the boiler house. When children from our school visit us, there are similar problems. Members of our congregations, too, would appreciate such facilities'. It took two sets of plans, six years of discussion, planning and fundraising, but, at last, on 25th June 2000, the church rejoiced in the dedication service for its Millennium Extension, presided over by the Bishop of Leicester, the Rt Revd Tim Stevens. The money, about £170,000, had all been raised by generous donations and local fundraising. It was fitting that the dedication plaque should read: 'to the greater glory of God; in thanksgiving for the generosity of friends and parishioners of St Leonard's'.

When the faculty permission for the extension came through in 1999, only about £40,000 still needed to be raised. Percy Barrett chaired the extension appeal committee, David Pugh taking responsibility for the appeal brochure. Letters were written to everyone who lived in the parish. As well as the committee, every organisation in the parish organised fundraising activities. The commemorative mugs, for example, were a fundraising initiative of the bellringers; these quickly sold out and have become collector's items! Other fundraising events included a lunch time drinks party, an evening bridge drive, musical evenings at Swithland Hall, a coffee morning and a Hallowe'en party. A team of cyclists agreed to represent Swithland in the 1998 'Leicestershire historic churches bicycle ride'. Half the money they raised through sponsorship went towards the appeal, the other half supported the 'historic churches' charity. By the time the extension was dedicated in June 2000, all the monies had been raised without any need to ask for trust or grant aid. It was a wonderful symbol of local generosity and faith.

In 1997, Swithland's ecclesiastical parish area was slightly enlarged. With the support of Newtown Linford Parochial Church Council, Swithland successfully applied for a change in formal boundaries, and took into its ecclesiastical care three additional small patches of land that were previously 'detached' areas of Newtown Linford parish. As Bob Osborne reported in the December 1997 issue of *The Link*: 'Swithland Wood Farm and Swithland Camp are now in Swithland! So is the house at 24 Main Street, Swithland. And so is the uninhabited triangular field in the middle of Swithland Woods'. The parish grew again in 1999. Under the pastoral scheme, which brought about the United Benefice of Woodhouse, Woodhouse Eaves and Swithland – another detached part of the parish of Newtown Linford, Rothley Plain – was also incorporated into Swithland ecclesiastical parish. This had long been sought for, as, under a long-standing and episcopally-approved agreement between the incumbents of Swithland and Newtown Linford, Swithland had exercised the pastoral care of Rothley Plain since the housing development began there early in the twentieth century.

Meanwhile, in the bell tower, Percy Barrett succeeded John Roberts as tower captain in 1997, with Graham Sharp taking over in 2000 after Mr

A Mile Worth a Million Pounds

Fig 19.11 Cycling for Swithland, September 1998.
[left to right]: Tom Capewell, Bob Osborne, Anne Horton, Joseph Thompson, Hazel Byford, Isabel Thompson, Christopher Roberts, Patrick Thompson, Philip Thompson, Edward Capewell.

Barrett's death. Through the decade, the tower traditions of an annual dinner, an annual church service and an annual outing continued as highlights of the ringing year. In 1996, ringer Jean Curd wrote a new 'bellringers hymn', which was sung for the first time at the 1996 annual service, and has been sung every year since. In 1997, it was adopted by the Leicester Diocesan Guild for use at bellringers services throughout the diocese, and in 2003, the hymn, entitled 'Ringing through the Year', was included in *Seasonal Worship from the Countryside*, a book of worship resources published by SPCK.

> Give praise to Him, our God on high,
> Ring out, let notes on breezes fly.
> By our labours through the year
> We seek to draw His faithful near.
>
> Our harvest's golden gifts now blest,
> Hail Autumn's languid span of rest,
> November comes with sombre sounds
> And echoes, muffled all around.

> On Christmas Eve in midnight air
> O'er frosty grass and branches bare,
> Sing out the songs of joyous praise
> And, heavenward, hearts of all men raise.
>
> In morning light of early spring,
> In praise of Jesus Christ our King,
> Let these tuneful voices swell
> With homage from each herald bell.
>
> When Lent is o'er, with Easter mirth,
> We celebrate our world's rebirth.
> Then Whitsuntide's ascending sound
> Through streams of warming air abound:
>
> As Summer's halcyon days roll on,
> We honour God in sound and song
> Come morning mists and evening dew
> Our lives we dedicate anew.[107]

In 1999, towers across the nation were encouraged to recruit new ringers so that that new millennium could be rung in with style, as indeed it was in Swithland, both at midnight and at noon on New Year's Day. In 2004, Graham Sharp successfully spearheaded a recruitment drive across the new benefice of Woodhouse, Woodhouse Eaves and Swithland, with the aim of raising enough new ringers to ring in two towers of the benefice most Sundays.

Fig 19.12 Swithland bellringers, 2000.
Front [left to right]: Val Capewell, Jean Curd, Rector, Percy Barrett (capt), Janet Beeby. Back [left to right]: Dan May, Graham Sharp, Peter Dobson, David Pugh, John Roberts, Laura Beeby, Philip Thompson, Willoughby Garton, Matthew Roberts, Marc Wainwright.

The Sunday School that re-started in 1984, continued into the 1990s under the leadership of Valerie Capewell and Janet Roberts. In 1994, when its members were old enough to be confirmed, the Sunday School closed for a short while, but it was re-activated in 1996 as the '5–10 Club', with Mrs Pam Cutler co-ordinating a team of mothers who were willing to share leadership. At first the '5-10 Club' met monthly in the school, but, after the completion of the Millennium Extension, it met in the 'Upper Room' on the fourth Sunday of each month in term time. Another group that was re-activated at the beginning of the nineties was the Swithland Youth Club, Graham and Jan Sharp hosting an inception meeting in May 1990 in the Village Hall.

The Memorial Hall was also the venue in June 1992 for a second round broadcast of the Radio Leicester 'County Questions' Quiz. A Swithland team, Willoughby Garton, Sarah May, John Lumley and Pat Griffin, had already beaten teams from Thurcaston and Cropston and Newtown Linford. In round two Swithland, with Richard Wilkinson playing instead of Willoughby Garton, faced teams from Seagrave and Swepstone. Sadly they came second. But 'it was an enjoyable and entertaining evening' and 'refreshments afterwards raised £10 for Groby Road Hospital'.[108]

Over the weekend of the 6–8 May 1995, village celebrations for the fiftieth anniversary of VE Day were staged at the Memorial Hall. There was a fancy dress 'forties dance', a special service in church, with flowers all in red, white and blue, followed by a procession to the War Memorial where a wreath was laid and two minutes silence observed. On the Monday afternoon, a children's party was enjoyed by nearly seventy children; in the evening, the adults enjoyed a hog roast. Throughout the weekend, an exhibition of 1939–45 memorabilia was on display in the hall itself. And the church bells were rung – both in the morning, a quarter peal (Peter Dobson's first) and also in the evening, after the two minutes silence had been observed.[109]

An audio-visual highlight of the decade was Paschal Griffin's hour-long video documentary on the village, filmed over 1989 and 1990, copies of which joined Sydney Meadows' 1965 history of the village as an important archive and a much sought after treasure for posterity. The proceeds from the video were donated to 'Link-Up', Groby Road Hospital Support Group. Paschal Griffin also made a video of the November 1993 Flower Festival in St Leonard's Church, 'The Messiah' in Flowers, which was presented by the Bradgate Flower Club and launched with a concert of music from Handel's Messiah by the Kingfisher Chorale. Profits contributed to the provision of new robes for Swithland's church choir.

In 1993, the building of a new rectory, in the grounds of the 1898 Rectory, marked the satisfactory outcome of Swithland's discussions with the diocese of Leicester over a continuing priestly presence in the village. On 14th May 1994, the Revd. Anne Horton was licensed and installed as priest-in-charge of Swithland, the first woman priest to be licensed to an incumbent status post in the Leicester diocese. She and the parish were, as she observed in her first official letter to *The Link*, 'making church history together'. She was much honoured on the morning of that memorable day to hear a celebratory peal of Cambridge Surprise Minor from the church tower, which was rung

Fig 19.13
The Rectory,
157 Main Street.

by 'leading ringers in the diocese, including two past presidents of the Leicester Diocesan Guild and two ladies'. In the evening, a team of Swithland ringers rang a quarter peal to herald the licensing service at 6pm.

The building of The Rectory in 1993 was followed, within the next two or three years, by the building of two new houses (Nos. 155, 159) adjacent to it and in a similar style – red brick with some granite facing. Another set of five houses, Charnia Grove, was also built in this decade, on the site of the old Hall Gardens. There was some opposition to this move in the village at the time, especially to the use of non-local stone and to the name of the development; it was felt that the older name of Hall Gardens should have been retained. Meanwhile another new house was built on land adjacent to the church, near the site of the eighteenth century rectory. David and Anne Carpenter moved into The Woodyard in 1994.

In April 1997, Sarah May was elected chairman of Swithland's Parish Meeting. Her predecessor, Willoughby Garton, had been chairman for twenty-one years. In her first report for *The Link* (September 1997) Mrs May reported that permission to site a 'VE memorial' seat had been requested from Charnwood Borough Council, that the village had reached the final of the Best Kept Village Competition (hamlet section), that planning applications could now be viewed at 126 Main Street, and that thinking had begun as to how the village should celebrate the new Millennium.

In 1998, Swithland Parochial Church Council was asked to consider the possibility of forming a united benefice with Woodhouse and Woodhouse

Eaves, the vicar of the Woodhouse parishes having just retired. The Parochial Church Council, supported by an extra-ordinary Parochial Church Meeting, which, while mindful of the parish's relatively recent twelve year struggle to remain a single benefice with a resident priest, agreed to explore this possibility, provided the rector of the new benefice lived in Swithland. The Council, mindful of continuing cutbacks in stipendiary clergy numbers and in the number of diocesan officer appointments being made in the diocese, felt it might be better to move into a united benefice of our own choosing, rather than being forced into a less happy 'marriage of convenience' later. The following two years saw these discussions pursued until, in December 1999, the new benefice of Woodhouse, Woodhouse Eaves and Swithland was formed. The current priest-in-charge of Swithland was inducted as the first free-hold rector of the united benefice, and the parsonage at Swithland was identified as The Rectory.

Fig 19.14 The Woodyard, 188 Main Street.

During the nineties, various people who had contributed generously to church and village life in Swithland moved away or died. Among those who moved away were Andrew and Margaret Lintern Ball who had been active members of the church for twelve years. Margaret had been the church organist and Andrew had served as a Reader in the parish. Rector Walters, bidding them farewell spoke of the quality of the music and singing that Swithland enjoyed, and to which Margaret and Andrew had contributed so generously. He also paid tribute to some of Andrew's more memorable sermon illustrations, and their joint efforts in helping keep the churchyard tidy and cared for.[110]

In September 1991, Ray Walters, who had served in Swithland for fourteen years, announced his retirement. The parish organised a special harvest supper and presentation at the Rothley Centre on the 25th October to mark his retirement. The editor of *The Link* wrote that 'we shall miss his challenge, unswerving and unshakeable, that we should continue, each according to his own light and his own calling, to uphold the Faith in our own lives and claim the Church as mother of us all and the rock on which alone our lives stand secure.'[111]

In August 1992, *The Link* recorded the death of Mrs Kitty Burrows, 'one of the oldest members of our congregation. As a child she had lived in the old Rectory adjacent to the church, long since demolished… In her early days she played the organ, and it was always a joy to her that she played the music for the first Bluebell Service. Her father and his men had taken the harmonium on a horse drawn cart and set it up amongst the bluebells'. Bob Mee, churchwarden 1982–93, died in July 1993; after his funeral the bellringers (Willoughby Garton, Keith Andrews, Percy Barrett, Eric Atkinson and Chris Newman) rang a semi-muffled quarter peal of Plain Bob Doubles. Previous rector, Ray Walters paid tribute to Bob's calm wisdom and his knowledge of village affairs. 'His professional skill in electronics was used to advantage in the care of the church. The Men's Club remember his help with the amplification of their Carol Singing at Christmas-time.'[112] In March 1994, Olive North, a member of the 10am congregation and of the Mothers' Union, died. She and her family were the last people to live in Kinchley Hill Farm House, when her father was the outdoor foreman at Swithland Water Works. She and Eric North did some of their courting by the reservoir's edge!

After the death in 1996 of one of Swithland's previous rectors, Bill Carlile, Barbara Harrington wrote an affectionate tribute in the September 1996 issue of *The Link*. 'My respect and affection for him grew from his weekly visits to Swithland School where I was teaching, when, every Friday morning, after talking to the children, he would have coffee with Sheila Bryan, the headmistress, and me. Our conversations were stimulating, down-to-earth and often hilarious. After Bill and Elizabeth moved to Belgrave, I took the opportunity of widening the school children's horizons by befriending four people from St. Michael's Parish. Bill chose our new friends carefully, thoughtfully and with great sensitivity. A gracious, unassuming gentle man, a saint with a sense of humour.'

Another old villager, David Hunt, died a year later. Bob Osborne paid him tribute in *The Link*. 'For many years, he and his parents lived at Hall Gardens, opposite the church. David and Janet were married in Swithland Church in 1962. He has been an ever familiar figure around the village. His newspaper round brought him into daily contact with many residents, striding up the street in all kinds of weather. His farming activities were (until recent housing development displaced them) based on Hall Gardens and the Woodyard. His tractor and fodder box were regularly seen travelling through Main Street. His interest in, and observation of daily happenings in the village were worthy of the best Neighbourhood Watch contact. We shall not only miss seeing him, but miss too his spirit of enquiry and his love of conversation'. Janet Hunt also wrote a little note in the same issue of *The Link*, thanking everyone for their support and friendship, and regretfully communicating her decision to end the family business of the newspaper round in Swithland, after forty years.[113]

December 1998 saw the death of Lord Lanesborough, the ninth and last Earl. His funeral service was marked by both a strong sense of affection between Earl and his old estate community and also by a tangible awareness that his passing marked the end of a very long era in the history of Swithland.

For, though the ninth Earl was 'a Butler', his family had married into that long family line which had provided Swithland's 'lords of the manor' since the fourteenth century. Gweneth Gimson wrote a personal reflection for *The Link*. She spoke of Lord Lanesborough's generosity and deep concern for others, including his former tenants, of his charitable work with the Guide Dogs for the Blind Association, his donations towards the upkeep of the Lanesborough Chapel and family monuments, and his interest in trains and the Great Central Railway. She also shared personal memories.

> During his school holidays, Lord Newtown Butler, as was then his title, and his brother Patrick were brought to church by their parents, and used the family chapel. Very often, if the regular organ blower did not arrive, he was instructed by his father to help. Alas, sometimes the music would stop. I know, for I was organist at the time. 'Was it accidental?' I hear you ask. That would be telling!! He did not get the 'going rate' for the job (six old pence per service) he just liked doing it, and the congregation was very understanding![114]

Bob Osborne died suddenly in May 1999. Born when his family lived along The Ridgeway, Bob was proud to be a 'local boy'. As Swithland farmer and county councillor, Bob had a profound understanding of and interest in the local community, past and present. At the time of his death he was master of the Worshipful Company of Bakers, a position he enjoyed and took very seriously. He was also a past master of the Worshipful Company of Framework Knitters. Both livery companies made a generous contribution to Swithland church to mark Bob's life and service; their part in his life was marked in his memorial window. As Parochial Church Council secretary since 1984, Bob efficiently looked after much of the church's administration. He managed most of the initial business relating to the Millennium Extension to the church; legal permission to proceed arrived in the post just a few days after he died. For some years Bob had been a member of the Leicester diocesan and deanery synods, and chaired the finance committee of the Leicester Diocesan Board of Education. In January 1995, Bob was authorised by the Bishop to lead

Fig 19.15 Bob Osborne, 1944–1999.

Morning and Evening Prayer, and began to develop skills in leading worship, occasionally preaching, leading study group sessions and assisting at funerals. In 1998 he was selected for training for Reader ministry, and began studying on the East Midlands Ministry Training Course. A few days after his funeral, Swithland bellringers rang a quarter peal for him. Percy Barrett, tower captain, who worked with Bob on the Church Council, wrote:

> Although Bob was never a bellringer, he was familiar with the ringing chamber as, for a number of years, he faithfully wound the church clock week by week. We remember with affection the cryptic and always amusing notes he used to leave for the ringers when they had omitted to restore the chimes of the clock after ringing.[115]

A 'chuckle', a 'chill' and a 'cheer' factor from *The Link* with which to close this decade. An article in *The Link*, August 1994, described a Sunday service of Evensong during a thunderstorm.

> Three short power-cuts plunged the church into total darkness as rain lashed the windows. Credit is due to the support team. Gwen Gimson, who, in between playing the organ was busy looking for vessels to catch the water that cascaded through a hole in the roof near the font. Bob Osborne seemed relieved that the lights stayed on while he read the first lesson. But the minor miracle that left the small congregation in awe occurred when the lights went out again and they wondered how the reader at the lectern would cope, when out of total darkness they heard the clipped voice of Percy Barrett intone the words 'Here endeth the second lesson'. Percy had, he assured us, just reached the end of the reading.

In December 1995, Gordon Geary, one of Swithland's visiting bellringers, contributed an article to *The Link* entitled 'Who was this Ghost?' He recounted a personal experience of 17th February 1992 when, taking one of his usual walks round the village, he passed by Swithland church. He said he saw a middle-aged woman walking along the road ahead of him, going into the churchyard and walking up the path, past the door of the church towards the stone wall by the shed, where she disappeared. 'She was wearing an old fashioned brown-grey baize cloak. Her face had a look of extreme urgency. I thought it strange that I could not see the bottom of her cloak. It was only when I told Percy Barrett of this happening that I learned what I had seen'. Swithland's 'grey lady', it was presumed.[116]

And, from the last parish magazine of the millennium year, a story about Swithland villager, Peter Osborne, 'taking New York in his stride'. Correspondent, Paschal Griffin, reported that Peter 'completed the New York City Marathon in a creditable time of 3hrs 46mins in November, and his efforts have resulted in a donation of £1,000 to Rainbows'.[117] Definitely something to cheer about!

From The Link: *Swithland v. the Diocese of Leicester*

Towards the end of the 1980s, the Leicester diocesan authorities fired a significant shot over Swithland's parochial bows. Their initiative heralded years of antagonism and conflict between parish and diocese. Parochial Church Council secretary, Bob Osborne, did not mince his words when he introduced the matter in the January 1987 issue of *The Link*. Summarising the diocesan position ahead of a parochial meeting on 21st January, he was blunt but accurate.

> The Parochial Church Council heard that the Diocese has now published a draft scheme by which the parishes of Swithland, Woodhouse and Woodhouse Eaves would be joined to form a new benefice, the incumbent of which would live at Woodhouse Eaves. Swithland Rectory would be transferred to the Diocesan Board of Finance for disposal. The immediate implication of this scheme is that Swithland would lose its resident priest. It would share a priest with two other parishes. Swithland Rectory would be sold, and the proceeds kept by the diocese. There would probably be fewer church services at Swithland. If the scheme were approved, there might be pressure in the longer term to form a single united parish with its own Parochial Church Council. There might also be pressure to retain only one of the three churches, with Swithland and Woodhouse churches declared redundant. The Parochial Church Council has been asked to comment on the proposals before the end of January. It will be meeting representatives of the diocesan Pastoral Committee before deciding its view.

The parish meeting on 21st January with three diocesan representatives, including the Archdeacon of Loughborough, was attended by seventy parishioners. Strong feelings were expressed, as a result of which the Parochial Church Council drew up a petition addressed to the Diocese opposing the proposals.[118] It was felt that the parish was prospering under the present arrangements and that the proposed union was likely to weaken it without any benefit to the diocese. Many felt that the diocese had no moral right to sell the Rectory and pocket the proceeds. The Archdeacon possibly realised that battle lines had already begun to be drawn up as he threatened parishioners with the opinion that opposition at Privy Council level was likely to be very expensive.

In February, some two hundred and thirty-five people signed a petition opposing the proposals. That petition was sent to the Bishop. 'Meanwhile', Parochial Church Council secretary Bob Osborne reported, 'the Diocese has conceded that it might not be free to sell the Rectory. The conveyance of the Rectory in March 1962 from Mrs Linwood Wright to the Church Commissioners includes a condition which appears to limit the Commissioners' freedom of action. The diocese is taking legal advice on the proper interpretation'.

Having heard that the Bishop had officially asked the Church

Commissioners to prepare a scheme along the originally proposed lines, with Derek Buxton (then priest in charge of the Woodhouses) as first incumbent, the Parochial Church Council set up a special committee in November 1987 to advise it on how diocesan proposals should be opposed. In February 1988, the Lord Chancellor's secretary, Nicholas Wheeler, made one of his occasional visits to Swithland, which meant that the parish's concerns could be conveyed directly to the patron of the living.

In September 1988, Percy Barrett reported to the Parochial Church Council that 'Operation Penpush' had been successfully completed and some three editions of the 'Crusade' had been distributed. The committee made a presentation to the diocesan pastoral committee in October, where it was distressed to hear 'no interest was shown in the overall support for the church in the parish'. The diocesan committee advised the Bishop to sign the draft scheme. The Parochial Church Council immediately agreed that 'representations to the Church Commissioners should be prepared without delay'.[119] These were lodged in January 1989. At the same time, the rector announced his resignation from the post of Diocesan Director of Education from June 1990.

On 13th March 1989, a question was asked in the House of Commons by MP Michael Latham regarding the re-organisation of benefices affecting the parish of St Leonard's, Swithland. Mr Latham asked Mr Alison (MP for Selby, representing the Church Commissioners) 'Will my hon. Friend confirm that Swithland Rectory in the constituency of my necessarily Trappist hon. Friend the Member for Loughborough (Mr Dorrell) was donated to the Church less than thirty years ago so that the Incumbent could live there? Given that a thousand ages let alone thirty years are but an instant in the sight of the Almighty, is it not unseemly for the rectory to be alienated so soon against the wishes of the benefactor?' To which Mr Alison replied 'This is one of the complications that have arisen as a result of the proposed reorganisation scheme. It will have to be considered actively by the pastoral committee and the board of governors when they consider objections to the scheme'.[120]

On 9th October 1989, representatives from the Church Commissioners Pastoral Committee visited Swithland and met with members of Swithland's Parochial Church Council. They also met with Canon Walters, Canon Buxton (priest in charge of Woodhouse and Woodhouse Eaves), Stephen Dorrell MP and members of the PCCs of Woodhouse and Woodhouse Eaves. Swithland's representatives felt that they had a received 'a fair hearing'. Bob Osborne commented 'it may be a little time before we know the decision. The only means of contesting an adverse decision is by application for leave to appeal to the Judicial Committee of the Privy Council'.[121] In the July 1990 edition of *The Link*, he was able to report that the Commissioners have decided that the draft pastoral scheme 'should not be made'. Their decision was based on the following points: Swithland is a self-supporting pastoral unit, it can afford, and has met, its commitments; the tradition of the church services are different from those in the Woodhouses; Swithland sought only what the diocese had allowed for thirty years; the characteristics of the parish are different from the Woodhouses; the expectations of the donor of the Rectory had not been fully taken into account; the pastoral arrangements for surrounding parishes, notably Newtown Linford, had not been finally determined.' It was the end of the matter, at least for the time being, but as the Parochial Church Council secretary warned, other 'pastoral arrangements for Swithland may be considered'.[122] The Parochial Church Council continued to affirm its view that the retention of a parsonage house in Swithland for occupation by a resident priest with responsibility for the cure of the parish was essential to any future pastoral planning.

Building of the new Rectory began on 21st April 1993; the new rector moved in on 26th April 1994, and was installed as priest-in-charge on Saturday May 14th by the Bishop of Leicester, the Rt Revd Tom Butler, and the Archdeacon of Loughborough, the Ven Ian Stanes.

From The Link: *Perspectives from the Wider Church*

Swithland's parish magazine has always been delivered together with the diocesan newsletter, *News and Views*. Until recently, this publication told something of the story of the national church as well as of the churches within the diocese of Leicester. Reading past issues alongside the parish magazine for the same month, something of the impact of national and diocesan thinking on the individual parish is evident.

Between 1960 and 1980, the bigger issues highlighted by *News and Views* were mainly national church issues, such as Anglican-Methodist relationships, Synodical Government, and the changing shape of the Church's ministry. In 1980, for example, it was becoming clear that cuts to stipendiary ministry numbers were inevitable. After 1980, there was a focus on the debate about the church's mission and ministry, and an attempt to involve parishes in the various discussions and changes.

St Leonard's has long been aware that the decreasing numbers of stipendiary clergy has meant that small village parishes can no longer expect to be allocated full-time incumbents just to serve them. This challenge is now far more widespread. It is not just a question of smaller numbers of people offering themselves for ordained ministry, nor yet the church's difficulties both in financing them as well as keeping their parish church buildings in good repair. The challenge today increasingly relates to the identity and task of the church as it responds to advancing secularism and the changing faith composition of the nation.

In 1995, Bishop Tom Butler spearheaded 'Mission 2001' through the diocese. Parishes were challenged to think through various key issues to help with the shaping of a mission strategy for the diocese as well as for the parish. Swithland organised six discussion sessions, hosted and led by members of the Parochial Church Council: witness in the world; witness to the world; developing our resources; relationship to God; relationship to each other; developing our gifts. A report was produced, for both parish and diocese, and the Parochial Church Council, through its committees, worked towards implementing its own recommendations. When a new Bishop of Leicester was appointed in 1999, he promoted his own suggestions as to the way forward: the 'Vision and Value' and 'Shaped by God' proposals were both supported by Synod and then implemented through the diocese. In October 2008, as part of the diocesan scheme, a 'mission partnership' was launched between the benefices of Woodhouse, Woodhouse Eaves and Swithland (with the Welbeck College Chaplaincy), Mountsorrel, Quorn, Barrow with Walton on the Wolds, and Prestwold with Wymeswold. These partnerships are to equip congregations to promote mission and outreach in both benefice and partnership areas. A further diocesan initiative of 2010, '2020 Vision', expects deaneries to accommodate further reductions in stipendiary clergy numbers.

New Millennium

The first six months of the new millennium in Swithland saw the building of a new church extension. Jean Curd, editor of *The Link*, reported on the initial archaeological investigations in November 1999. She witnessed the excavations, and was amazed not just at what was found, but at how the archaeologists were able so clearly to identify their finds.

> I watched and waited during the three cold days, recording the careful and at times strenuous work. I was amazed by the description Simon gave to each find. He could distinguish between a child, a teenager and an adult when just a tibia bone was found... In one instance he said it was a pity we did not know the name of a man who walked with a limp...There were no full skeletons, although a number of skulls were discovered. No artefacts were found. Each small bone was given an identity number, and these were all labelled, ready for a later re-interment by Canon Anne in another part of the churchyard.[123]

During the months that followed, Jean Curd kept a watching brief, compiling a photographic album for posterity.

> At the start of the extension, a daily journey from home to Church is almost like going back to work! My aim is to make a photographic record of the progress of the building. First on site are the archaeologists to oversee the cutting of the footings. Despite rain, frost or clear skies visits become a must – in case something exciting is about to happen, or has unexpectedly happened in the previous twenty-four hours.
>   At the gate, camera in hand, I cautiously plan my way to the builder's hut without being a 'nuisance' and quickly glance at the latest aspects of the building. A short informal chat with the site foreman starts each visit, a coffee if there is time (having once found a clean cup!), and then I listen to the workers' news on progress – this is certainly an exciting place and time.
>   Progress is swift once the footings and base are complete. The stone work facing and inner walls seemingly grow apace,

scaffolding leaps upwards as new walls are keyed in. Soon the roof of reclaimed Swithland slate is finished. The doors and windows are fitted. Inside church the pews are moved to make way for the new heating system. The hard work of knocking through the two metres of the 13th century tower wall between vestry and extension is finally complete. Then there is a problem as the west end wall of the Lanesborough Chapel is knocked through, ready to receive the Bob Osborne window. It was thought the wall contained a large blocked up window space but in fact the window had never existed - so no lintel! Eventually to solve the problem an extra girder is to be fitted. Walls up, roof on, now finally, after plastering, painting and fitting internal furniture, all is ready for our congregation to make full use of the 'Upper Room', kitchen and toilet facilities. Wonderful!

Amid the noise and bustle of this building site, nature serenely progresses from Winter to Spring and early Summer. Snowdrops have covered the ground, trees have burst into leaf, birds and wild life have ignored all disturbance. Soon the ground will recover and the churchyard will become a peaceful, beautiful place once more.

Six months later, the new church extension was ready for dedication and use. There was an article about the extension and a photograph in the diocesan newsletter *News and Views,* August 2000. The article, written by David Pugh,[124] was headed 'Bishop Tim dedicates extension to Swithland Church'.

Generous donations and a multitude of fund-raising activities by church groups enabled work to start last December on a two-storey building, and it was ready in time for 25th June when Bishop Tim knocked on the door of the extension to start the Dedication Service. The church was full to see him dedicate, in addition, a memorial window to Bob Osborne, who had been Parochial Church Council secretary for many years. At the end of the service, a memorial plaque was unveiled on the outside of the extension. Everyone was then able to appreciate the skills of the architect and builder in an extension that was modern internally, but which blended externally with the thirteenth century body of the church.

In the August 2000 parish magazine, various parishioners shared their memories of the service. Marjorie Whyte wrote: 'Many people had helped to create an aura of readiness for the event. Flower arrangements completed, pews polished, and cushions brushed. Well-polished silver[125] on the snow-white altar cloth was shining, with the crucifix gleaming in the centre, each piece seemed to be enjoying the attention of everyone'. Tom Whyte wrote: 'To us, the dedication of the new extension seemed a very fitting culmination of many years at St Leonard's. We very much missed, as everyone else did, Bob, but were delighted and touched to see Percy and hear his gallant reading of St John's Gospel. We thoroughly enjoyed the Concert, the Flower Festival, meeting Bishop Tim, and the celebration in the churchyard after the Dedication.' Don Freshwater, in his recollection, wrote: 'The first part of the service took place outside the church. From our position we could hear the choir singing their hearts out. The builder, Trevor Johnson, handed the key to the Rector who unlocked the new Church Door. Bishop Tim then knocked on the door with his crook, and after making the sign of the cross on the lintel said the prayer of blessing. With more great singing from the choir, the Bishop entered the church from the West End, and the service proper began. (After readings, prayers, sermon) we moved to the dedication of the beautiful new window which was dedicated to the memory of Bob Osborne who did so much, not only for the church as a whole, but especially for this new building'. Don concluded: 'One other person must be mentioned in this brief account and that is Mr Percy Barrett. It was wonderful to see him rise above his debilitating illness to attend this ceremony. His reading of one of the lessons was something that will long live in the memory. As one of the chief architects of the scheme to build this extension, it was very fitting that he should be there'.[126]

Another perspective was given in the Thompson family's report 'When the Bishop came to Church'.

Fig 19.16
The Osborne Memorial Window.

When we arrived at the church for the special Dedication Service, I thought that Jeff Harrison was the Bishop! I think he was quite pleased to be mistaken for him. All the children from the '5–10' Club sat up in front of the altar and behind the Bishop. We had a very good view of the congregation. We presented the Bishop with a picture of the church and a self-portrait of each member of the '5–10' Club. We went into the extension with the Bishop and Canon Anne, and he wet us with a branch – we all giggled. I liked giving out the cakes to the Bishop and Percy and everyone else at the end.

    Isabel (aged 6) (and Mummy) Thompson,
        and a bit of help from Emily (8) and Joseph (10)

Perhaps the 'last' reporting word on the extension should come from the concluding sentence of churchwarden David Pugh's report on the Dedication Service for the diocesan newsletter. 'We can now concentrate on extending the church spiritually in the new millennium.'[127]

Village Millennium

Swithland saw in the new millennium with hope and celebration. The celebrations began with a Millennium Eve party at the Memorial Hall, with rockets and champagne. There was a short service in church, then the church bells rang out at midnight – just five ringers, Percy Barrett, Marc Wainwright, David Pugh, Jean Curd and the rector, as everyone else was at the party! On New Year's Day, there was a short 11.30am. Church Service, after which Swithland bells joined the rest of the nation in ringing at noon. Percy Barrett, Laura Beeby, Peter Dobson, Gordon Geary, David Pugh and Marc Wainwright rang at Swithland, while another Swithland team rang the bells of St Mary in the Elms, Woodhouse: Janet Beeby, Val Capewell, Jean Curd, Willoughby Garton, Graham Sharp and Philip Thompson. January 2nd was a Sunday. A Millennium Civic Service was held at 3pm, with villagers processing down the Main Street from the Griffin Inn to the church, with Jeff Harrison carrying the church cross and leading the robed church choir.

Fig 19.17 Dedication of the Millennium Extension, 25th June 2000.

A book of Millennium Prayers, each one written or submitted by parishioners, was edited by Dr. Don Freshwater. Special millennium cards were designed by children from St Leonard's School and a card was sent to every parishioner. Commemorative New Testaments were given to all the pupils at the school, and to all the other young people in Swithland church and village. Alice and Adam Page generously hosted an Epiphany Luncheon at Swithland Hall for all parishioners and Swithland-linked folk who were 'over 70', and a commemorative photograph album of everyone attending was compiled by Alice for the parish archives.

As a permanent commemoration in the village, a Slate Millennium Memorial to all the Swithland slate workers through the last millennium was unveiled in the grounds of the village Memorial Hall by Beatrice Bunney and May Musgrove. Six months later, at the church, the new Millennium Church Extension was dedicated by the Bishop of Leicester on June 25th.

Beyond Millennium

In 1967 an outsider cynically described Swithland as 'a mile worth a million pounds'. As Swithland heads into 2011, many who are part of the village and its extended family today would want to say that the life of this small part of England is worth far more than a million – not so much financially (though of course it is) – but in the far more important attributes of community and friendship.

Village communities do change over the years and Swithland has changed and developed, and will continue to do so. For most of its history Swithland has focussed on the land, whether as land-workers or land-owners. Workers who lived locally in Roman times, around 200AD and perhaps around the settlement alongside Rothley Plain, were focussed on the possibilities of Swithland slate. Scandinavian raiders (800AD and beyond) pushing farther into England's mid-lands might have given our village its name – 'land cleared by burning'. We have no historical evidence of an Anglo Saxon community, but by Domesday Swithland was a minor settlement and, in 1197, Swithlanders laboured to clear the forest back and created a community around the church and manor house. By the thirteenth century an agricultural community was well established, as was the manor house with its lord recognised by the King himself. Through the fifteenth and sixteenth centuries Swithland lived through the division of its lands, returning to a single lordship under Francis Danvers in 1629. That unity was threatened first by the Civil War, when the Swithland Danvers identified with the Parliamentary side, and again when Sir John Danvers, with no male heir to succeed him, married his daughter to a reckless Irish man in 1792. Mercifully, their son was a 'good' man who restored the estate, but subsequent times of agricultural hardship and an increasingly impoverished family at the Hall again threatened the village's future. Rich industrialists from the city of Leicester bought their wealth into Swithland's midst at the turn of the twentieth century, however, and restored its fortunes yet again.

With the departure of the Earls of Lanesborough, the Swithland Estate properties and land was sold in 1954 and the Hall in 1978. Within the village's conservation area limits, there has since been both new build and restoration of old build. The Borough Council determined Swithland's character as a conservation village in 1993, thus it remains a rural suburb of a size and population much the same as it has always been, with St Leonard's Church and School, the Memorial Hall and The Griffin Inn focussing community life and activities. Many new and old villagers have worked to maintain a vibrant village community life. They hope and pray that there will always be newcomers who, like them, continue to value and develop the Swithland community and its networks of friendships into this third millennium.

Notes to Chapter 19

1. Paul Brown, *Illustrated Chronicle*, April 1967.
2. The estate included property in Cropston and Thurcaston as well as in Swithland.
3. Local stone facing on part of the elevation was encouraged, as was Swithland slate rooting. Since, however, supplies of Swithland stone and slate were limited, Mountsorrel granite and Welsh slate were permitted in some cases.
4. *Illustrated Chronicle*, April 1967.
5. *Leicester Advertiser*, 18 July 1969.
6. St Leonard's School, 2008 Ofsted inspection judged the school to be 'excellent' in all areas.
7. Presented at the Church's Dedication Festival on Sunday 5 December 1954 (repeated 1955, 1965).
8. East Akeley Deanery magazine, November 1954.
9. Parish Church Archives, 1955 document.
10. East Akeley Deanery magazine, March 1956.
11. Parochial Church Council minutes 1949, 1953.
12. *The Link*, August 1980.
13. PCC minutes, 1950.
14. At Leatherland's funeral in 1967 all his wreaths were arranged outside the church in the form of a bell.
15. Local research by Janet Beeby, ringer, of Hall Farm.
16. *The Link*, June 1970.
17. ibid., October 1966.
18. ibid., May 1970.
19. In 2006, a modern courtyard of houses was built on the site. The historic footprint was completely lost.
20. Woolley & Noel, Chartered Land Agents & Surveyors, Loughborough.
21. *The Link*, September 1968.
22. The deanery magazine had ceased publication.
23. Profits benefited cancer charities.
24. Subsequent rectors have continued in their efforts to bring a national perspective to bear on parochial discussion!
25. APCM, 1965, minutes.
26. *The Link*, March 1969.
27. In 2003, revised proposals for such a Covenant were agreed by both churches.
28. *The Link*, February 1969.
29. ibid., March 1969.
30. ibid., August 1971.
31. Brown resigned in 1965.
32. Parochial Church Council meeting minutes, Specification, 5th January 1962.
33. ibid., June 1964.
34. *The Link*, January 1969.
35. President: the rector; chairman: Maurice Carr, Hon. Secretary: Harold Bate, committee members: Wally Egglestone, Tom Whyte, and John Beachell.
36. *The Link*, December 1968.
37. ibid.
38. 1962 church outreach leaflet.
39. *The Link*, November 1965.
40. ibid., September 1967.
41. ibid., June 1968.
42. ibid., August 1971.
43. ibid., August 1971 (Shirley Herbert, 167 Swithland Lane, succeeded Mrs Tyldesley).
44. ibid., October 1968.
45. ibid., November 1970.
46. ibid., August 1969.
47. Parish Archives, J.H. Dransfield, Notes.
48. Missing from The Rectory archives are all magazines before Nov. 1965; Feb, March, April, June, Sept, Nov, Dec 1972; all magazines for 1973, 1974, 1975 and Jan–Oct. 1976; Feb. 1977; July 1980.

49. Now kept in the Leicestershire Records Office, Wigston.
50. First performed in 1954, the pageant was repeated on 7 November 1965.
51. Printed by G.H. Potts, Printer, Castle Donington.
52. St Leonard's from the road, with lychgate in foreground, showing original boundary wall.
53. Parish Archives, Magazine March 1967, rector's letter.
54. First *Community Link* published December 1998.
55. Tower captain from 1971.
56. *The Link*, November 1970.
57. ibid., November 1971.
58. See Chapter 1: A Considerable Lordship.
59. *The Link*, July 1977.
60. ibid., January and February 1978.
61. ibid., November 1977.
62. ibid., September 1977.
63. ibid., May 1982.
64. ibid., August 1977, Mrs G.M. Gimson.
65. ibid., December 1977.
66. At first for the Church of England Children's Home, Woodhouse Eaves; later for the Loughborough Christmas Shelter for homeless people.
67. *The Link*, December 1977.
68. ibid., April 1970.
69. *New and Views*, December 1977.
70. *The Link*, July 1977.
71. ibid., August 1977.
72. ibid., March 1979.
73. ibid., July 1968
74. ibid., February 1981.
75. BBC News webpage, 12th June 2007.
76. The Swithland Ladies Group was first mentioned in *The Link* in April 1970.
77. *The Link*, February 1984.
78. ibid., September 1981.
79. ibid., November 1981.
80. ibid., June 1984.
81. Thrapston, Ringstead, Great Addington, Little Addington (the Bell Inn, for lunch), Twywell, Cranford St John, Rothwell and Rushton.
82. *The Link*, August 1978 refers to a Ringers Dinner that year at the Bull's Head, Woodhouse Eaves.
83. During this time, much of the Swithland bands progress in method ringing was due to the teaching of Tim Payne from Syston.
84. *The Link*, June 1987.
85. Parochial Church Council minutes, 6 December 1979.
86. *The Link*, July 1982.
87. ibid., May 1987.
88. ibid., September 1983.
89. ibid., June 1966.
90. ibid., July 1966.
91. ibid., May 1973.
92. ibid., November 1976.
93. ibid.
94. Appointed Honorary Canon, Leicester Cathedral, May 1977.
95. *The Link*, April 1977.
96. ibid., November 1991.
97. ibid., May 1994.
98. ibid., June 1980.
99. In June 1992, the Parochial Church Council formally consented to the sale of the Rectory at 165 Main Street, the diocesan authorities having agreed that half the old garden would be used as three building plots, one of which would be used for a new rectory. (*The Link*, July 1992).
100. *The Link*, December 1976.
101. ibid., October 1980.

102. ibid., January 1990.
103. The Church Urban Fund, responding to the Church of England 'Faith in the City' report (1985) was launched in 1987 to help develop practical church-inspired projects.
104. *The Link*, September, November 1990, November 1991.
105. Ecclesiastical legislation had provided for the ordination of women to the diaconate in 1986. Continuing discussions led to the decision to ordain women as priests from 1993.
106. *The Link*, March 1991.
107. Words: Jean Curd, b.1940; Tune: Gott Will's Machen.
108. *The Link*, July 1992.
109. ibid., June 1995.
110. ibid., April 1991.
111. ibid., December 1991.
112. ibid., August 1993.
113. ibid., October 1997.
114. ibid., February 1999.
115. ibid., July 1999.
116. c.f. Chapter 15: Myths and Legends.
117. *The Link*, December 1999.
118. ibid., February 1987.
119. ibid., December 1988.
120. Hansard, 13th March 1989, reported in *The Link,* April 1989.
121. *The Link*, November 1989.
122. ibid., November 1990.
123. ibid., March 2000. All human remains were buried with prayers as near their family graves as possible. A new stone was erected to commemorate all whose earthly remains were not able to be identified.
124. David Pugh, one of the churchwardens, had acted as the church's liaison officer with the architect and builders throughout the building progress.
125. Marjorie's husband, Tom Whyte, was the church silver 'polisher' at the time!
126. Percy Barrett, lay chair of the PCC, and chair of the Finance Committee, spear-headed the fundraising for the extension, but sadly died in September 2000.
127. Diocese of Leicester, *News and Views*, August 2000.

– APPENDIX A –

Wills

This appendix contains the wills of:
 John Danvers, 1598
 Francis Danvers, 1631
 Samuel Danvers, 1693
 John Danvers of Prescott, 1721
 Sir Joseph Danvers Bt, 1753
 Sir John Danvers Bt, 1796
 Hon Mary Butler Danvers 1802
 Christopher Marshall, (rector 1506–16)
 Jane Blakwing, 1675 (proved 1696)
 Henry Gilbert of York, 15 June 1716
 Michael Matthews, 1721

Will of John Danvers of Rothley, 1598 [1]

In the name of God: Amen. I John Danvers of Rothley sick in body but perfect in remembrance, thanks be given to God, do ordain constitute and make this my last will and testament the fourth day of July in the year of our Lord God one thousand five hundred and ninety eight and in the fourtieth year of the reign of our Sovereign Lady Queen Elizabeth. First and principally I give and bequeath my soul to Almighty God my creator and to his son Jesus Christ my redeemer and to the Holy Ghost my sanctifier trusting in the blessed Trinity that I shall be saved through the mercy of my holy Saviour… And I bequeath my body to the earth to be buried in Rothley church at the discretion of my executor. Item, I give and bequeath to Joyce my wife my over house in Rothley and Adcocks farm and the sheep close and Alderley at Swithland for her maintenance during her natural life. Item, I give unto the said Joyce all the bedclothes and bedstead that hath been commonly used at the said over house and five of my best kine and my roan mare and all other things that be within the said house except my armour my own chests my guns my two scarves; and my books and all other things both at the over house and ?nether house which I have not given and bequeathed to my wife, I give and bequeath to my son Francis Danvers of Swithland whom I make my full and sole executor. And I make and appoint Francis Moulsoe my son in law my supervisor and overseer of this my last will and testament to see those things performed which I shall give and bequeath. Item, I bequeath to Francis Danvers my said executor all my said armour my chest my guns my two scarves my books and my vestry provided always that the great pot and lead at the one house did come unto me as heirlooms: and my will is that they should so return again after my mortal life ended. Item, my will is that my executor Francis Danvers shall pay unto Joyce my foresaid wife ten pounds of lawful English money within weeks after my funeral is ended toward the helping of her necessities. Item, all of the debt that Richard Tilley doth owe me I yield all my rights to my said wife so that my executor shall have nothing to do with it. Item, I give and bequeath to my daughter Anne Moulsoe my little sorrel mare and her foal. Item, I give to Francis Moulsoe my said supervisor my grey mare and her foal. Item, I give to Francis Danvers my executor my bay mare. The residue of my goods both moneable and commoneable I give them to the said Francis Danvers whom I have made my executor. And I desire Francis Danvers to be good and friendly to my two servants Zachary Heywood and Thomas Deacon and that he would be as careful as I myself would be if I were living and so my assured trusted that he will be. Thus I make an end of this my last will and testament leaving Francis Danvers my executor and Francis Moulsoe my supervisor. In witness whereof I have haven to set my hand and seal the day and year first above written. John Danvers. Read and sealed according to the true meaning hereof before us. Gilbert White his mark. Zachary Heywood.

Will of Francis Danvers, 1631[2]

In the name of the Father, the Sonne and of the Holye Ghost. Amen.
I, Francis Danvers of Swithland, Co Leicester, gentleman, being sicke in body but sound in mind thanks be to God, ordeyne this my last will, revoking all former wills etc.. Soul to God... And for my bodye, my desire is that it be buryed in the out Isle of Swithland church neere my wyff. And for my worldly goods as followeth. Item, I will that my son John Danvers have all the wood in the yard and barns of Shakeston with the slates there, and the great brass pot there, with the bed and furniture both of the bed and chamber over the little lodging parlour in Shakeston, whether it be now there or brought away, viz that bed and furniture which hath been usually used in or for the said chamber. Item, for my wyffe, she being an old woman and not fit to keep house free from debts, and hath as good as five score pounds a year to live on, notwithstanding all this, I give her all the household stuff that she brought from Shakeston, except that which I have given to my son John. I give her more her grey mare, four kyne, her sheepe, and would give her more but that I must consider them that have more need and pay my own debts. Item, for my daughter Elizabeth Comberford: she hath her portion the house that I bought of Mr Armstrong which was Mr Kendall's, her husband and she have the possession of my deed which I will she shall have according to the purport of the same. I will also that she and her husband shall have the £300 which my son John standeth bound to me to pay, and that the bond which I have from my son John for the same shall be

delivered unto them & my son John to pay the same according to the agreement betwixt me and my son Comberford at his marriage. Item, my will further is that if my said daughter Comberford die and leave no issue before 2 years be expired, then my son Comberford is to receive but £100, which he is to receive presently, and the other £200 are to be divided betwixt my son William Danvers and my son John Danvers, viz to William Danvers and his children £100, and to John Danvers and his daughter £100. I give to my daughter 2 beds with the furniture belonging to them, the bed in my chamber, and the best bed in the seeled chamber over the hall if it be not my wife's, if it be, she to have the best bed in the buttery chamber. Item, for my house and land that I have bought of my cosen Robert Barford at Skeffington, I give it to my son John Danvers and his heirs upon condition that he shall sell it and divide the money into three equal parts, one part to himself, another part to his sister Comberford, and the third part to my cosen Robert Barford's daughter that lives at Nailstone, that is his youngest daughter by his first wife. Item, for my mortgage of Yoxall which I have of my cosen Michael, I leave it to descend to my son William Danvers in satisfaction of anything which he may chance to claim in or out of any part of the house or land in Skeffington which I have devised to my son John Danvers as aforesaid. And my will further is that within one month of my decease, my said son William Danvers shall release all his right and title in and to the said houses and lands in Skeffington to my son John Danvers and his heirs, which, if he refuse to do, I devise all my lands in Yoxall, Co Stafford, to my son John Danvers and his heirs for ever, to be sold and the money thereof made to be divided equally between him, his sister Comberford, and the said daughter of Robert Barford. Item, I make my son William Danvers my sole executor, he paying my debts and discharging my funeral, and do make my cosen Thomas Gilbert and my cosen Henrye Gilbert, his son, my overseers; and I give either of them a colt. Item, my desire is further that Mary Hall alias Mekin have a lease of the house during her life that I bought of Richard Smyth, and is now widow Hampson's after her decease, upon a reasonable rent. In witness whereof to this my last will & testament I herewith have set my hand and seale the sixteenth day of Maye in the yere of our Lord one thousand six hundred thirty one by me   Francis Danvers.

Will of Samuel Danvers of Swithland, 1693 [3]

In the name of God: Amen. I Samuel Danvers of Swithland in the county of Leicester Esq being sick in body but of sound and disposing mind and memory (praises be God) do make and ordain this my last will and testament. And first I bequeath my soul into the hands of Almighty God and my body to the earth to be decently interred at the discretion of my executrix hereafter named in the hopes of a joyful resurrection through the merits of Jesus Christ the righteous. And as for my worldly estate wherewith it has pleased God to bless me I dispose thereof as followeth. Impris. I give and devise all that my messuage closes lands and tenements by me lately purchased of William Blankley and John Watts about or one of them and lying in Swithland aforesaid and also all other my lands and tenements in Swithland aforesaid which are not already settled to my beloved wife Elizabeth and her heirs in — nevertheless that she shall give and dispose of the same to and amongst my younger children in such proportions and at such times and in such manner as she shall think convenient. And as for my personal estate, I give and bequeath the same after my debts paid and funeral expenses defrayed to my said wife whom I make sole executrix of this my will and do appoint her guardian of all my children. And my will is that the child wherewith my wife is now enceint shall have such share in my said lands by me hereby divided or in the money which shall be raised by sale thereof as my said wife shall think convenient. In witness whereof I have hereunto set my hand and seal the second day of November anno domini one thousand six hundred ninety three. The mark of Samuel Danvers. Signed sealed published and declared by the said Samuel Danvers as his last will and testament in the presence of us and by us attested at his request and in his presence. Arch Palmer, Benj Blundell, William Palmer.

Will of John Danvers of Prescott 1721[4]

This is the last will and testament of me John Danvers of Prescott in the county of Oxon Esq.

First I give and devise all my manors messuages lands tenements and hereditaments whatsoever within the kingdom of Great Britain or elsewhere unto the heirs of my own body lawfully to be begotten

And for default of such issue I give and dispose thereof as followeth (that is to say):

As for and concerning all that my messuage and all those my cottages farms, lands, tenements, and hereditaments, with their and every of their appurtenances, in Chilson in the parishes of Charlebury and Ascot or one of them in the said county of Oxon, late in the possession of Elizabeth Witt deceased, I give and devise the same unto my old and faithful servant Thomas Gray for and during the term of his natural life; and I do hereby devise and bequeath that it shall and may be lawful for the said Thomas Gray, when he shall be in the possession of the said messuage farm and premises hereby to him devised by virtue if this my will, by one or more lease or leases to demise the same or any part thereof for any term or number of years determinable upon one two or three lives in possession and not in reverter remainder or expectancy under the rent of fifteen pounds per annum or more for the whole, or a just proportion thereof for any part so to be demised, to continue payable during such term so to be demised so as such lease or leases be not made dispunishable of waste and contain provisions of re-entry for non-payment of the rent and rents thereby to be reserved and so as the respective lessees seal and deliver counterparts thereof.

And as for an concerning the said messuages cottages, farm, lands and premises in Chilson aforesaid from and immediately after the decease of the said Thomas Gray, and as for and concerning my manor or lordship of Prescott in the said county of Oxon with its rights members and appurtenances, and all my messuages, lands, tenements, and hereditaments in Prescott and in Cropredy and in Appletree alias Appleby and elsewhere in the said county of Oxon and in the county of Northampton, from and immediately after my own decease and failure of issue of my body lawfully to be begotten, subject to the annuities hereinafter in this my will or by any codicil by me to be made charged thereon, I give and devise the same unto Joseph Danvers of Swithland in the county of Leicester Esq for and during the term of his natural life without impeachment of or for any manner of waste; and from and after the determination of that estate, I give and devise the same unto George Townsend the elder of Lincolns Inn in the county of Middlesex Esq and unto his heirs and assigns during the life of the said Joseph Danvers in trust to preserve the contingent estates hereinafter devised from being defeated or destroyed, but nevertheless to permit the said Joseph Danvers to enjoy the profits thereof during his natural life; and from and after the decease of the said Joseph Danvers unto the first son of the body of the said Joseph Danvers lawfully begotten or to be begotten and the heirs male of the body of such first son lawfully issuing; and for default of such issue to the second third fourth fifth and all and every other the son and sons of the body of the said Joseph Danvers lawfully begotten or to be begotten and the heirs male of their several and respective bodies lawfully issuing severally and successively and in remainder one after another as they and every one of them shall be in seniority of age and priority of birth – the elder of such sons and the heirs male of his body issuing to be always preferred and take before the younger of such sons and the heirs male of his and their body and bodies issuing. And for default of such issue, I give the same manor messuages and last mentioned premises in Prescott, Cropredy, Chilson and Appletree alias Appleby subject as aforesaid unto John Danvers, brother of the said Joseph Danvers, for and during the term of his natural life without impeachment of or for any manner of waste; and from and after the determination of that estate, I give and devise the same unto the said George Townsend and unto his heirs and assigns during the life of the same John Danvers in trust to preserve the contingent uses and estates hereinafter devised from being defeated or destroyed, but nevertheless to permit the same John Danvers to enjoy the profits thereof during his life; and from and after the decease of the same John Danvers unto the first son of the body of the same John Danvers lawfully begotten or to be begotten and the heirs male of the body of such first son lawfully issuing; and for default of such issue to the second third fourth fifth and all and every other the son and sons of the body of the same John Danvers lawfully begotten or to be begotten and the heirs male of their several and respective bodies lawfully issuing severally and successively and in remainder one after another as they and every one of them shall be in seniority of age and priority of birth – the elder of such sons and the heirs male of his body issuing to be always preferred and take before the younger of such sons and the heirs male of his and their body and bodies issuing. And for default of such issue, I give and devise the same manor messuages lands tenements and premises subject as aforesaid unto Charles Danvers woollen draper, eldest son of Charles

Danvers late Recorder of the Devises in Wiltshire deceased, for and during the term of his natural life without impeachment of or for any manner of waste; and from and after the determination of that estate, unto the said George Townsend and unto his heirs and assigns for and during the natural life of the said Charles Danvers in trust to preserve the contingent uses and estates hereinafter devised from being defeated or destroyed, but nevertheless to permit the said Charles Danvers the son to enjoy the profits thereof during his life; and from and after the decease of the said Charles Danvers the son to the first second third fourth fifth and all and every other the son and sons of the body of the same Charles Danvers lawfully begotten or to be begotten severally and successively and in remainder one after another as they and every one of them shall be in seniority of age and priority of birth and the several and respective heirs male of the several and respective body and bodies of all and every such son and sons lawfully issuing – the elder of such sons and the heirs male of his body issuing to be always preferred and to take before the younger of such sons and the heirs male of his and their body and bodies issuing. And for default of such issue, unto the right heirs of the said Charles Danvers the father for ever.

Provided always, and my will and desire is, that in case my personal estate not specifically devised shall not be sufficient for the payment of my debts legacies and funeral expenses, and the charges of the probate of my will, then and in such case the rents and profits of my said Lordship of Prescott, with other the premises in Cropredy, shall after payment of the several annuities hereby charged or by any codicil hereafter to be charged thereon in aid of my personal estate, be subject and liable thereunto, but not by sale thereof. Providing also and my will and desire is that it shall and may be lawful to and for the said Joseph Danvers, John Danvers and Charles Danvers respectively, when they shall respectively be in the actual possession of the said premises in Prescott and in Chilson, Appletree alias Appleby aforesaid by virtue of this my will, by any deed or deeds writing or writings or by their respective last wills and testaments in writing – such deed or deeds writing or writings or last will and testament in writing to be by them respectively signed and sealed in the presence of three or more credible witnesses – to limit or appoint the same or any part thereof to such woman or women as he or they shall respectively happen to marry for the term of her natural life or lives of such woman or women respectively for and as a jointure or in the nature of a jointure – subject nevertheless to the several annuities hereby charged or to be charged thereon as aforesaid, and to the payment of my debts legacies and funeral expenses, in aid of my personal estate in manner and form aforesaid – and also to let or demise the same or any part thereof from time to time for any term or number of years not exceeding seven years in possession and not in reversion remainder or expectancy so as upon every such lease to be made there be reserved and made payable for the same during the continuance of such lease and leases the best improved yearly rent that can be gotten for the premises so leased at the time of making such lease or leases, to be made payable half yearly without taking any money or other thing by way of fine for or in respect thereof, so as in such leases be contained provisees of re-entry upon non-payment of the respective rents thereby to be reserved, and so as such leases be not made dispunishable of waste and do contain therein such covenants as are usual in such like cases, and so as the respective tenants in such lease and leases seal and deliver counterparts thereof.

And as for and concerning my Manor of Basiney in the parish of Eaton Soken in the county of Bedford, and all other my messuages lands tenements and hereditaments situate lying and being in Eaton Soken aforesaid or elsewhere in the said county of Bedford (subject to one annuity of twenty pounds per annum granted out of the same by my mother to my cousin Mrs Mary Hewes for the term of her natural life or for a term of years determinable upon her death, and to another annuity of ten pounds per annum granted by me out of the same to my said cousin Mrs Mary Hewes for her life or for a term of years determinable as aforesaid – which said annuities I do hereby desire may be punctually paid in neat money free from any taxes and other payments that are or may be charged thereon by Parliament or otherwise) I give and devise the same unto the said John Danvers for and during the term of his natural life and from and after the determination of that estate I give and devise the same unto the said George Townsend and unto his heirs and assigns during the natural life of the same John Danvers in trust to preserve the contingent estates hereinafter devised from being defeated or destroyed, and for that purpose to make entries and bring actions as the case shall require, but nevertheless to permit the same John Danvers to receive and take the rents issues and profits thereof during his life; and from and after the decease of the same John Danvers, I give and devise the same premises in the said county of Bedford unto the first son of the body of the same John Danvers lawfully to be begotten and the heirs male of the body of such first son lawfully issuing; and for default of such issue to the second third fourth fifth and all and every other the son and sons of the body of the said John Danvers lawfully to be begotten severally and successively and in remainder one after another as they and every one of them shall be in seniority of age and priority of birth, and the heirs male of their several and respective bodies lawfully issuing – the elder of such sons and the heirs male of his body issuing to be always preferred and take before the younger of such sons and the heirs male of his and their body and bodies issuing. And for default of such issue, I give and devise the same unto the said Joseph Danvers for and during the term of his natural life and from and after the determination of that estate to the said George Townsend and his heirs and assigns during the natural life of the said Joseph Danvers in trust to preserve the contingent estates hereinafter devised from being defeated or destroyed, and for that purpose to make entries and bring actions as the case shall require, but nevertheless to permit and suffer the said Joseph Danvers to receive and take the rents issues and profits thereof during his life; and from and after the decease of the said Joseph Danvers, I give and devise the same unto the first son of the body of the said Joseph Danvers lawfully to be begotten and the heirs male of the body of such first son lawfully issuing; and for default of such issue to the second third fourth fifth and all and every other the son and sons of the body of the said Joseph Danvers lawfully to be begotten severally and successively and in remainder one after another as they and every of them shall be in seniority of age and priority of birth, and the heirs male of the several and respective body and bodies of all and every such son and sons lawfully issuing – the elder of such sons and the heirs male of his body issuing being always preferred and take before the younger of such sons and the heirs male of his and their body and bodies issuing. And for default of such issue to Sir Danvers Osborne of Chicksands in the county of Bedford Baronet and his heirs and assigns for ever.

Provided always and my will and desire is that it shall and may be lawful to and for the same John Danvers from time to time during his natural life by any deed or deeds writing or writings or by his last will and testament in writing – such deed or deeds writing or writings or last will and testament in writing to be by him signed and sealed in the presence of three or more credible witnesses – to limit or appoint all or any part of the same premises in the said county of Bedford so devised to him for the term of his natural life as aforesaid to any woman or women he shall happen to marry for the term of her or their natural life or lives for or as a jointure or in the nature of a jointure; provided also and I do hereby further direct and appoint that it shall and may be lawful to and for the said John Danvers and Joseph Danvers respectively when they shall respectively be in the actual possession of the said premises in the said county of Bedford by virtue of this my will from time to time to let or demise the same or any part thereof for any term or number of years not exceeding seven years in possession and not in reversion remainder or expectancy without taking any money or other thing by way of fine for or in respect thereof so as upon every such lease to be made there be reserved and made payable during the continuance of such lease and leases the best improved yearly rent that can be gotten for the premises so leased at the time of making such lease or leases, to be made payable half yearly, and so as in such leases be contained provisees of re-entry upon non-payment of the respective rents thereby to be reserved, and so as such leases be not made dispunishable of waste and do contain therein such covenants as are usual in such like cases, and so as the respective tenants in such leases seal and deliver counterparts thereof.

I give and devise to my cousin Mrs Mary Hewes one annuity or yearly payment of fourty pounds for and during the term of her natural life; and unto my said servant Thomas Gray one annuity or yearly payment of twenty pounds during his natural life; and unto old George Maunder the father now living at Prescott one annuity or yearly payment of four pounds during his natural life; I give and devise unto Mrs Margaret, the wife of Samuel Phillips the elder – at present an officer in the Revenue on Salt, one annuity or yearly payment of twenty pounds for and during her natural life;

Which said several annuities it is my will and desire shall be raised and paid out of the rents and profits of my lordship at Prescott and lands in Cropredy with the appurtenances, and that the same shall be liable to distress in case of non-payment, and that the said annuities shall be paid free of all taxes by quarterly payments, that is to say, at the feast of the Annunciation of the Blessed Virgin Mary, the Nativity of St John the Baptist, the Feast of St Michael the archangel, and the Birth of our Lord Jesus Christ, by even and equal portions – the first payment to be made on such of the said feasts as shall happen next after my decease.

And as for and concerning my goods chattels and personal estate, I give and dispose thereof in manner following:

First I give unto my said servant Thomas Grey my moiety of an annuity of fur and twenty pounds per annum payable at the Exchequer out of the excise on Beer ale and other liquors during his and his wife's life and the life of the survivor of them, for the which there is a tally or tallies and orders in their name, and for the same I paid a moiety of the purchase money;

I give unto the two eldest sons of Mr Charles Danvers woollen draper the sum of one hundred pounds apiece to be paid to them respectively by my executors immediately after the decease of my cousin Mrs Mary Hewes before mentioned if they shall then have respectively reached the age of one and twenty years; and if they or either of them [shall not have attained the age of one and twenty years at her decease] then it is my will and desire that the legacy of him or them being then so under the age of one and twenty be paid to his or their father for his or their use if he shall then be living, and in case their said father shall be then dead, be retained by executors, until he or they so under the age of one and twenty years shall arrive at that age and then be paid to him or them, together with interest for the same from the death of the said Mrs Mary Hewes until the time of such payment or payments respectively.

I give and devise unto my niece, the honourable Dame Frances Dereham widow, relict of Sir Richard Dereham Baronet deceased, the sum of one thousand pounds; and if my said niece happen to die before me, I give and bequeath the same thousand pounds to Sir Thomas Dereham Baronet and Richard Dereham his brother, the two sons of my said niece the Lady Dereham, to be equally divided between them, and if either of them die before me the share of him dying shall go to the survivor.

I give unto my grandnephew George Villiers, now student of Christ Church in Oxford, the sum of one thousand pounds towards enabling him to pay my executors the debt which shall be owing to me from him at the time of my death; and in case the said debt shall be discharged in my lifetime, then I desire my executors to pay the said legacy of one thousand pounds to the said George Villiers out of my personal estate.

I give unto my cousin Charles Danvers the woollen draper before named the sum of one thousand pounds; and if the said Charles Danvers happen to die before me, I give and bequeath the same one thousand pounds unto and amongst such of his children as shall survive him; and in case the said Charles Danvers die before me and have no children that survive me, my will is that the same thousand pounds shall be equally divided amongst all the brothers and sisters of the same Charles Danvers that shall be living at the time of my death; and I bequeath the same to them accordingly share and share alike.

I give unto the said Joseph Danvers two pictures of my father and mother reputed to be done by Hoskyns in water colours and set in gold; and also the picture of my uncle the late Earl of Danby in his garter robes, the great family piece of my father and his second wife and children, the little family picture of my father and his second wife and children, the picture of my grandfather Sir John Danvers and the picture of my grandmother his wife daughter of the Lord Latimer; I do earnestly desire and request that the said Joseph Danvers so far as in him lies and as far as the law will permit make such disposition of the pictures so devised to him as that the same may descend and go with my Lordship and house at Prescott so long as the same shall continue in his name and family.

I likewise give to the said Joseph Danvers all my gilt plate and books and such two of my saddle horses as he shall choose and also my household goods furniture and pictures at Prescott aforesaid.

I desire to be buried at Prescott Aisle in Cropredy church with as little ceremony and expense and may be at the discretion of my executors, but not exceeding two hundred pounds in the whole for my funeral and interment, comprising the charge of my tomb and inscription hereinafter mentioned; I would have a large stone laid over my grave and a white marble to be fixed upon the east wall of the said Aisle – with an inscription cut into the said marble mentioning the time of my death, age, name, and particular descent both by father and mother, from my grandfathers on both sides: that my father was the youngest son of Sir John Danvers by Elizabeth Neville daughter of the said Lord Latimer, my mother was the youngest of fourteen children of Thomas Hewes of Kimerton in the county of Gloucester Esq by his wife daughter of Sir Thomas Chamberlain of Presbury in the same county, and also mentioning my entail of Prescott Basmey and Chilson upon the family of the Danvers of Swithland, and without any other epitaph.

And I do appoint my executors to distribute the sum of fourty pounds to such of the poor as they shall think the greatest objects of charity within the three parishes hereinafter named, that is to say, within the parish of Cropredy twenty pounds, within that of Eaton Soken in Bedfordshire ten pounds, and ten pounds within that parish wherein I shall happen to die.

And as for and concerning the rest and residue of my goods chattels and personal estate plate jewels pictures ready money debts and securities for money (other than what I have particularly disposed of by this my will or shall be particularly disposed of by any codecil to the same) from and after payment of my debts legacies and funeral expenses and the charge of the probate of my will, I give and devise the same unto the said Joseph Danvers and John Danvers upon trust that they the said Joseph Danvers and John Danvers and the survivor of them do and shall with as much convenient speed as may be after my decease convert the same into ready money and lay out and dispose of the money so raised in the purchase of lands tenements or hereditaments in fee simple in that part of Great Britain called England; and when the same are so purchased, to be conveyed and settled on the same person and persons for the same or the like uses intents and purposes and for the same or the like estates and interests as I have hereinbefore devised my said Lordship of Prescott and lands in Cropredy aforesaid so far forth as the lives of parties and any accidents that may arise or happen in the meantime will admit.

And I do hereby constitute and appoint the said Joseph Danvers and John Danvers executors of this my will

Provided always, and my will and desire is, that in the meantime and until such purchase shall be made, it shall and may be lawful and I do hereby direct my said executors and the survivor of them and his executors and administrators from time to time until such purchase shall be made, to place out the money so to be laid out from time to time as the same shall be raised or got in at interest upon securities, and the interest thereof shall from time to time be paid out to the person and persons who for the time being would have been entitled to the rents and profits of the premises so to be purchased in case such purchase had actually been made; provided always, and my will and desire is, that my executors or the survivor of them or the executors or administrators of such survivor do and shall with as much convenient speed as may be after my decease lay before my honourable friend Sir Robert Eyre, one of the justices of the court of King's Bench, and my friend George Townsend the elder of Lincolns Inn Esq, or the survivor of them or the executors or administrators of the survivor of them a true and particular account of my goods chattels and personal estate and of all debts which I shall owe at my decease and of the legacies by me given to the end a computation or estimate may be made by them of what sum of money will remain after payment of my debts and legacies to be laid out in one or more purchase or purchases according to my directions hereinbefore contained for that purpose; and it is my will and desire that in making such purchase or purchases and placing out the moneys to be laid out therein at interest until such purchase or purchases shall be made according to my desire hereinbefore contained, my executors and the survivor of them and the executors or administrators of such survivor do from time to time take the consent and approbation of the said Sir Robert Eyre and George Townsend or the survivor of them or the executors or administrators of such survivor; and in case my said executors or the survivor of them or the executors or administrators of such survivor shall refuse or neglect to perform the trust hereby reposed in them or any of them with relation to the laying out the surplus of my goods chattels or personal estate or shall refuse or neglect to lay such accounts thereof before the said Sir Robert Eyre and George Townsend or the survivor of them or the executors or administrators of such survivor as are hereinbefore by me directed, then in such case I desire and request that the said Sir Robert Eyre and George Townsend or the survivor of them and the executors or administrators of the survivor of them… making such default therein to be prosecuted from time to time in such manner as the said Sir Robert Eyre and George Townsend or the survivor of them or his executors or administrators shall think most proper and advisable until my said executors and the survivor of them and the executors and administrators of such survivor shall have fully executed and performed my will in the particulars before mentioned; and my will and desire is that the said Sir Robert Eyre and George Townsend and the survivor of them and the executors or administrators of such survivor shall from time to time out of my personal estate be satisfied for paid and re-imbursed all such trouble costs damage loss and expense which they or any of them shall sustain or be put unto for or by reason of the premises or anything relating thereunto anything herein contained to the contrary thereof in any wise notwithstanding; providing always that neither of my said executors and trustees shall be answerable for the other of them but each for himself and his own acts only, nor for any more money than shall actually come to their respective hands by virtue of this my will or the trust hereby in them reposed, not for any loss that shall happen by defect or insufficiency of any security upon which such money shall be placed out at interest as aforesaid, or by the failing of any person or corporation in whose hands any of the trust money shall be placed out for safe custody, or for any other loss that shall happen in the premises without their respective wilful defaults or neglects.

Provided also, and I do hereby direct and appoint, that it shall and may be lawful to and for my said executors and trustees and the survivor of them and his executors and administrators in the first place to re-imburse him and themselves out of the trust estate hereby devised to them all such costs damages loss and expense as they or any of them shall sustain or be put unto for or by reason of the trust hereby in them reposed or any thing relating thereunto.

And lastly, I do hereby revoke all former wills by me at any time made.

In witness whereof I the said John Danvers have to this my last will and testament contained in thirteen sheets of paper whereof I have caused two parts to be written each of the same tenor and effort and set my hand and seal to each sheet of each part thereof this eighteenth day of October anno domini one thousand seven hundred and twenty.
(Signed J. Danvers)

Signed sealed published and declared by the testator for and as his last will and testament in the presence of us who have subscribed our names as witnesses thereunto in the testators presence and at his request. (Signed Ch Townsend, Nath Chambers, Richard Ditchfield)

The three witnesses above named subscribed their names in my presence (signed J. Danvers)

I John Danvers of Prescott Esq do add this codicil to my last will and testament bearing date the eighteenth day of October in the year of our Lord God 1720.

First I give and bequeath to Joseph Danvers in my will named the sum of five hundred pounds and unto his brother John Danvers in my will named one thousand pounds.

I give to my late wife's two daughters, viz Anne and Eleanor Danvers, the sum of one thousand pounds apiece of my capital stock in the Bank of England if I shall die interested in so much of the said stock, and if not, then I give them eleven hundred pounds apiece.

I give unto Robert Wakeman an infant the son of my old acquaintance

Mr Robert Wakeman a Turkey Merchant deceased in compassion to the great losses his said father sustained by trade the sum of five hundred pounds to be paid to the said infant Robert Wakeman at his age of one and twenty years together with interest for the same at the rate of five pounds per cent per annum from the time of my death until the same shall become payable; and I hereby authorise my executors to apply the said interest for his maintenance and education if they find it necessary.

I give the sum of five hundred pounds to be paid applied and disposed of to such person and persons and for such uses intents and purposes as Elizabeth the granddaughter of Sir William Temple deceased now wife of John Temple of Moore Park in the county of Surrey Esq shall notwithstanding her coverture and whether she shall be sole or married by any note in writing to be by her signed in the presence of two or more credible witnesses direct or appoint, to the intent that the same shall be disposed of by her for her own private and personal occasions and not to be subject to the control debts forfeitures or engagements of her present husband or any other husband she shall happen to marry.

I give the like sum of five hundred pounds to be paid applied and disposed of to such person or persons and for such uses intents and purposes as Dorothy another of the granddaughters of the said Sir William Temple and now wife of Nicholas Baron of Shrubland Hall in the county of Suffolk Esq shall notwithstanding her coverture and whether she be sole or married by any note in writing to be by her signed in the presence of the like number of witnesses direct or appoint to the intent that the same may be disposed of by her for her own private and personal occasions and not to be subject to the control debts forfeitures or engagements of her present husband or any other husband she shall happen to marry.

I give to Dame Martha Gifford widow the sum of one hundred pounds.

I give to my godson Robert Osborne the son of Sir John Osborne of Chicksands in the county of Bedford baronet the sum of one hundred pounds.

I give to my godson Sir Danvers Osborne in my will named the sum of five hundred pounds.

I give to my goddaughter Mrs Philadelphia Dyke sister of Sir Thomas Dyke of Horeham the sum of five hundred pounds, and to Elizabeth Dyke sister of the said Philadelphia Dyke one hundred pounds.

I give to Sir Robert Eyre one of the Justices of the Court of Kings Bench the sum of three hundred pounds.

I give to George Townsend the elder of Lincolns Inn Esq the sum of one hundred pounds.

I give to my godson Chamberlaine son of Mr George Chamberlaine late of Wardington deceased the sum of fifty pounds.

I give to Margaret the wife of Samuel Phillips to whom I have given an annuity by my will the sum of one hundred pounds; and if the said Margaret die before me, I give to her daughter fifty pounds.

I give to Grace the wife of James Baily clerk sister of the said Margaret Phillips the sum of one hundred pounds; and if she shall die before me, I give the sum of one hundred pounds to such of her children as shall be living at my decease equally share and share alike.

I give to Nicholas Mellichamp now an officer in the Revenue on Salt and who is son of Richard Mellichamp deceased the sum of one hundred pounds; and if the said Nicholas Mellichamp happen to die before me my will is and I hereby bequeath the same one hundred pounds in such case and not otherwise to be paid to and amongst such of his children surviving him as shall be alive at the time of my decease share and share alike.

I give to William Mellichamp late an officer in the Revenue on Salt the sum of fifty pounds.

I give to Dorothy Mellichamp sister of the last mentioned William Mellichamp the like sum of fifty pounds.

I give to William Mellichamp father of the last mentioned William and Dorothy Mellichamp the sum of one hundred pounds.

I give to the three daughters of Richard Browne deceased lately a Silkman in Cheapside the sum of one hundred and fifty pounds a piece; and in case any of them shall happen to die before me the whole to go to such of them as shall survive me.

I give to John Danvers, brother of Charles Danvers in my will named one hundred pounds.

I give to Joseph Parker now or late an officer in the Salt Duty fifty pounds.

I give to Mr John Hall haberdasher now or late one of the accomptants in the Salt Office the sum of one hundred pounds., and to each of the children of the said John Hall which shall be living at my death twenty pounds.

I give to Mr Stannier Vittar of Cropredy the sum of ten pounds.

I give to my servant Thomas Gray in my will named the sum of four hundred pounds; and to every other of my menial servants (except the said Thomas Gray) who shall be living with me at the time of my death and shall have served me six whole years next before that time two whole years wages more than what shall be then due for them; and to every one of my menial servants (other than the aforesaid Thomas Gray) who shall have served me above the space of two whole years next before the day of my death yet not six years before that time one whole years wages more than what shall then be due to them.

In witness whereof I the said John Danvers the testator have to this codicil whereof I have caused two parts to be written each of the same tenor and effect and each contained in three sheets of paper set my hand and seal to each sheet of each part thereof this nineteenth day of October anno domini one thousand seven hundred and twenty. (signed) J. Danvers.
Signed sealed published and declared by the testator as a codicil to his last will in the presence of us who have subscribed our names as witnesses hereto at his request and in his presence. Ch Townsend, Nath Chambers, Richard Ditchfield.

I John Danvers of Prescott in the county of Oxon Esq do desire that this present writing may be taken as an additional codicil and added to my last will and testament bearing date the eighteenth day of October anno domini one thousand seven hundred and twenty and deemed part of my said will.

Whereas in and by my said last will and testament I have in case of failure of heirs male of my own body to be begotten given and devised all that my messuage and all those my cottages farms lands tenements and hereditaments with their and every of their appurtenances in Chilson in the parishes of Charlbury and Ascot or one of them in the said county of Oxon late in the possession of Elizabeth Witt deceased unto my old and faithful servant Thomas Gray for and during the term of his natural life with power to make leases thereof in the manner in my said will mentioned with divers remainders over after the decease of the said Thomas Gray, now I do hereby give and devise the said premises in Chilson in the parishes of Charlbury and Ascot aforesaid and each of them from and after the decease of the said Thomas Gray unto my very good friend the honourable Sir Robert Eyre Kt one of the justices of His Majesty's Court of King's Bench and his heirs and assigns for ever subject nevertheless to such lease or leases as the said Thomas Gray shall make there in pursuance of the power to him in that behalf given in and by my said will, provided always and my will and desire is that in case the said Sir Robert Eyre shall happen to die in my lifetime then and in such case the said premises in Chilson shall go unto the same person and persons and for the same estates as the said premises were given and devised by my said will from and after the decease of the said Thomas Gray.

And whereas there is now remaining due and owing to me from Mr George Villiers student of Christ Church College in Oxon the principal sum of sixteen hundred pounds secured by one or more mortgage or mortgages of the manor of Burgh alias Burrowes in the county of Norfolk and divers messuages lands tenements and hereditaments in Burgh alias Burrowes aforesaid and in Aylsham in the county of Norfolk or one of them, now it is my desire that my executors do with as much convenient speed as may be after my decease call in and receive the said principal sum of sixteen hundred pounds and the interest thereof which shall be then due, and it is my will and desire that the said principal sum of sixteen hundred pounds be divided into four equal parts: one of which four parts I give unto the said Sir Robert Eyre, and another of the said four parts unto George Townsend of Lincolns Inn Esq as a recompense for the trouble they have promised to take upon them in seeing my will duly executed and performed pursuant to my desire and request to them in my said will, and out of other of the four said parts unto my old acquaintance and friend Erasmus Lewis Esq late Secretary to the right honourable the Earl of Dartmouth when he was Secretary of State to her late Majesty Queen Anne, and as to the remaining fourth part of the said sixteen hundred pounds I give and devise the same unto the President and Governors of Christ Church Hospital in the City of London upon trust to be by them or their successors laid out in the purchase of the freehold and inheritance in fee simple of lands tenements and hereditaments or to be from time to time placed out at interest upon mortgages or other securities and the rent and profits of the premises so to be purchased and the interest on the money so to be placed out, it is my will and desire shall be applied from time to time for the special use and benefit of the boys of the said Hospital who are or shall be educated there for the sea service and commonly called King Charles the Second's Foundation in putting such boys out apprentices to skilful masters or mates of ships at the discretion of the President and Governors of the said Hospital for the time being, provided always and my will and desire is that in case the said principal sum of sixteen hundred pounds or any part thereof shall be paid off in my lifetime shall be paid and made good to the said Sir Robert Eyre, George Townsend, Erasmus Lewis and the said President and Governors of Christ Church Hospital according to their respective proportions thereof before mentioned to be given to them respectively by my executors out of my personal estate.

In witness whereof I the said John Danvers have to this my codicil contained in two sheets of paper whereof I have caused two parts to be written each of the same tenor and effect set my hand and seal to each sheet of each part thereof this fourth day of March anno domini One thousand seven hundred and twenty. (Signed) J. Danvers.

Signed sealed published and declared by the above named John Danvers for and as an additional codicil to his last will and testament in the presence of us who have subscribed our names as witnesses thereof in the said testator's presence and at his request. Gerard Bothomley, Geo Townsend jr, Ch Townsend.

Will of Sir Joseph Danvers Bt, 1753[5]

I Sir Joseph Danvers of Swithland in the county of Leicester, Baronet, do hereby revoke and make void all former and other wills by me at any time hereintofore made, and declare this to be my last will and testament.

I desire that my body may be deposited in the new vault in the church yard of Swithland aforesaid in a private manner in the forenoon, and that every one of my tenants, being house keepers in Swithland at the time of my decease, may be paid ten shillings; and also that every such tenant and his wife who shall dwell at Swithland aforesaid shall have a pair of black gloves each, and walk at my funeral, and that there may not be any more company. And as to my temporal estate, I dispose thereof as follows.

First I will that my just debts and expenses of my funeral (to be performed in manner before directed) be fully paid and discharged.

Item, I give and desire all my messuages, farms, lands, tenements, tithes, and hereditaments situate at Wendover or Elsborough or in either of them in the county of Bucks now or late in the tenure or occupation of Thomas Atkins and Richard Mitchell, their undertenants or undertenant, and all other messuages, lands, tenements, tithes and hereditaments whatsoever in that part of Great Britain called England, also all my advowsons and right of presentations whatsoever unto my son John Danvers his heirs and assigns forever. Nevertheless I do hereby direct that my estate in Brough Hill and Hathersage in the county of Derby shall be subject to and chargeable with such annuity as is hereinafter mentioned.

Item, I give all that my messuage, or Mansion House, and all the outhouses, yards, gardens, and grounds thereto belonging, situate at Chelsea in the County of Middlesex, now in our occupation and which are held by sundry leases from Sir Hans Sloane and others unto my said son John Danvers his executors administrators and assigns upon this condition that my said son John Danvers his executors administrators and assigns shall permit and suffer Dame Frances my wife during the term of her natural life to have and enjoy the said messuage and premises at Chelsea aforesaid or such parts or part thereof as she shall choose to have without paying the ground rent reserved thereon or any part thereof, or any taxes charges or aseessments, parliamentary, parochial or otherwise for and in respect thereof; but in case my said wife shall choose to hold and enjoy during the time of her natural life the whole of the said Mansion House and premises, then I do hereby direct that my said son John Danvers his executors, administrators and assigns shall only pay the ground rent and land tax for and in respect thereof; but I will that my said son shall at his own proper charges and expense keep and maintain the said Mansion House and premises in good and sufficient repair during the life of my said wife.

Item, I do hereby give unto my said wife Dame Frances the use of all my household goods, plate and linen which shall be in my Mansion House at Chelsea aforesaid at the time of my decease, and also the use of such pictures as shall be there as she shall be desirous to have during the term of her natural life; and in case my said son John Danvers his executor administrators and assigns shall not permit my said wife for the time of her natural life peaceably and quietly to use, occupy, posses and enjoy my said Mansion House and premises in such part or parts thereof as she shall choose, and also the use of any household goods, furniture, plate, linen, and pictures as aforesaid, then I give the said Mansion House and premises held by lease from the said Hans Sloane and others, unto Dame Frances my wife, her executors administrators or assigns, together with all my household goods, furniture, plate, linen, and pictures which shall be therein at the time of my decease; but in case my said son shall permit my said wife to enjoy my household goods, furniture, plate, linen, and such pictures as she shall choose during the term of her natural life, then from and after her decease, I give the same to my son and his executors and administrators.

Item, I give all other my messuages or tenements and lands situate at Chelsea aforesaid and held by any lease or underleases from Sir Hans Sloane unto my said son John Danvers his executors administrators and assigns.

Item, I give unto my said wife Dame Frances my coach which I use at Swithland, with harness for a pair of horses, and also her watch jewels and other personal ornaments.

Item, I give unto my said wife Dame Frances, my son John, and daughter Catherine Danvers – to be equally divided amongst them – all such rents and arrears of rents as shall be due and owing to me at the time of my decease from any of my tenants.

Item, I give unto my said son John Danvers all my household goods, furniture, plate, linen, books and pictures, which shall be used or belong unto or found in my Mansion House at Swithland, and also all books which shall anyways belong unto me elsewhere.

Item, I give unto my said son John Danvers all my coaches, chariots, harness and other wheel carriages, and also all my horses and implements of husbandry, and also all my stock in husbandry alive and dead, which shall happen to be at Swithland aforesaid at the time of my decease, except my coach and harness and a pair of horses hereinbefore by me given to Dame Frances my wife.

Item, I give my daughter Catherine Danvers the sum of two thousand five hundred pounds, to be paid to her within one year after my decease.

Item, I give to William Palmer of Ironmongers Hall in the City of London gentleman, and John Hood of Bardon Park in the county of Leicester gentleman the sum of fifty pounds apiece as an acknowledgement of the trouble I have hereby given them; and in case either of them should die before me, or shall decline to act in any of the trusts hereby reposed in them, then I will that the legacy of him so dying or declining to act shall go to the other of them as shall survive and act in such trust.

Item, I give the Honourable John Gray and Lucy his wife twenty pounds apiece for mourning.

Item, I give to my brother Babbington and to his son and two daughters, Joel Watson of Clapham in the county of Surrey Esquire and to his daughter Cecelia, the sum of ten pounds apiece for mourning.

Item, I give to my nephew Thomas Babbington Esquire and to his two sisters, my sister Danvers, my sister Palmer and her son and daughter Norwood, ten pounds apiece for mourning.

Item, I give to Joseph Prior my steward the sum of fifty pounds.

Item, I give to my servant Thomas Brookhouse the principal sum of one hundred pounds which I lately lent to his father upon a mortgage or security of a messuage or tenement in Anstey in the said county of Leicester; and I do hereby order my executors to assign and transfer the said mortgage or security to my said Thomas Brookhouse his executors administrators and assigns in order that he and they may be fully entitled to demand and receive the said principal sum due thereon.

Item, I give to my said servant Thomas Brookhouse all my plain woollen clothes and linen.

Item, I give to the Reverend Mr George Cardale five pounds to buy him a gold ring and a black cloth gown.

Item, I give twenty gold rings to be disposed of by my son John Danvers to such gentlemen as he shall think proper.

Item, I give and devise unto my servant the said Thomas Brookhouse and his assigns, for and during the term of his natural life, one annuity yearly rent or sum of eight pounds of lawful money of Great Britain, free and clear of all taxes and deductions whatsoever parliamentary or otherwise, to be issuing and payable out of my estate in Brough Hill and Hathersage in the county of Derby the same yearly rent or sum to be paid halfyearly by equal payment, viz on Lady Day and Michaelmas Day, the first payment thereof to be made on such of the said Feasts as shall first happen after my decease;

and my will is that in case the same yearly rent or sum of eight pounds or any part thereof shall be behind or unpaid by the space of thirty days next after either of the said Feasts whereon the same is directed to be paid as aforesaid, then and so often it shall and may be lawful to and for the said Thomas Brookhouse and his assigns to enter into and upon all or any part of the said premises so charged with the payment thereof as aforesaid and distrain for the same or for so much thereof as shall be so in arrear and all full costs and charges which shall be occasioned by the non-payment thereof and the making of such distress.

Item, I will and desire my said son John Danvers within one month after my decease to give and distribute the sum of five pounds to and amongst such poor persons of the town of Swithland aforesaid, and also the sum of five pounds to and amongst such poor persons of the town of Thurcaston in the said county of Leicester, and also the sum of five pounds to and among such poor persons of the town of Mountsorrel in the said county of Leicester, and also fifty shillings to and amongst such poor persons of the town of Newtown Linford in the said county of Leicester; and also fifty shillings to and amongst such poor persons in the town of Rothley in the said county of Leicester, and as my said son John Danvers shall think fit objects to receive the same.

Item, after payment of all my just debts funeral charges and legacies, I give and bequeath all the rest and residue of my personal estate wheresoever unto the said William Palmer and John Hood their executors administrators and assigns upon trust to lay out and invest the money I shall leave, or which shall arise from the sale or disposition of the residue of my personal estate Government or real securities or in Parliamentary stocks or funds with the privity and consent of my said wife during her life or if at the time of my decease any part of the residue of my personal estate shall be standing out on real securities Parliamentary funds or public stocks and my said wife shall be desirous to leave the same securities stocks or funds continued, I will that my said trustees may from time to time as they shall see [expedient] with the privity and consent of my said wife during her life call in any money (part of the residue of my estate) which shall be standing out on any securities and with the like consent invest the money arising therefrom in other Government or real securities Parliamentary funds or public stocks. And I do hereby declare that it is my mind and will that the devise of the residue of my personal estate to the said William Palmer and John Hood is upon further trust that they the said trustees do and shall pay the interest or dividends arising therefrom unto my said wife Dame Frances and her assigns during the term of her natural life; and after her decease, I give and bequeath all the principal moneys together with all interest and dividends thereof (except such interest and dividends directed to be paid my said wife as aforesaid) unto my said son John Danvers his executors and administrators; and I do hereby order and direct that the said William Palmer and John Hood and the survivor of them his executors and administrators do and shall … monies as aforesaid … their hands and assignee and … the same securities stocks or funds on which the … part of the residue of my personal estate shall be invested unto him my said son John Danvers his executors administrators and assigns.

And my will is that it shall and may be lawful for my executors and each of them to compound and settle with any person … for or on account of any debt or demand due or to grow due to me or to my estate and to accept and take away any part thereof in full discharge of the same or any security for the same or any part thereof; and I do hereby declare that any said trustees and executors or any of them shall not be answerable or accountable for any damage or loss that may happen to any part of my estate by their or any of their management or disposition thereof or any part thereof either in placing or laying out the same as aforesaid or otherwise unless such damage or loss shall happen by their or any of their wilful default, and that they or any of them shall not be chargeable with or for any more monies that what they shall respectively actually receive out of or from my said estates or for the acts receipts payments and defaults of each other but each of them for his own acts receipts payments and defaults only; and it shall and may be lawful for them and each of them in the first place to deduct and retain out of my said estates or the produce thereof all such money as they or any of them shall expend or lay out in or about the execution of this my will and all or any of the trusts hereby reposed in them, and also to indemnify themselves and every one of them out of our said estate for all such full costs charges and damages as they or any of them shall expend or … or suffer, and also retain all such sum or sums of money as shall be reasonable for and on account of a loss of time or business done in or about the execution of all or any of the trusts hereby in them reposed or in or about any matter or thing hereinbefore contained.

And I hereby constitute and appoint my said wife Dame Frances Danvers my said son John Danvers and my daughter Catherine Danvers executors of this my will.

In witness whereof I have to each sheet of … will (the whole being contained in the three precedent sheets of paper) … and to the top of the first sheet and to the … in the year of our Lord one thousand seven hundred and fifty two. (Signed) Jos. Danvers.

Signed sealed published and declared by the said Joseph Danvers as and for his last will and testament in the presence of us who in his presence and at his request have subscribed our names as witnesses hereunto: Martha Thornton, William Swan, Jos Prior jr.

I Sir Joseph Danvers of Swithland in the county of Leicester Baronet do declare this to be a codicil and to be taken as part of my will being all wrote with my own hand writing.

Whereas my son John Danvers owes me five hundred pounds on his Bond with interest thereon, I hereby release and give to my said son all interest due thereon at my decease; and I do hereby give to my daughter the honourable Lucy Grey four hundred pounds – part of the principal money of the said Bond – to be paid to her order and for her use, not subject to the control of her husband; and I give the remaining one hundred pounds – part of the said five hundred pounds Bond – to my wife and the Overseers of the Poor of Swithland; and I do hereby desire my wife will give one hundred pounds out of her own substance to the said Overseers, and the said two hundred pounds are hereby given in trust – half thereof to be laid out in trust for erecting a cottage containing three bays with a lean to for the use of a schoolmaster or schoolmistress to live and teach young children both boys and girls to read spin and knit upon Swithland Upper Green next the forest, the remaining half to be put out at interest and the interest to be paid yearly to the said schoolmaster or schoolmistress for teaching poor children out of Swithland to read knit and spin, such exercises being very useful in bad weather if they are grown up to be men or women; and it is hereby intended that if the said school shall be too full of scholars the said schoolmaster or schoolmistress to be placed in the said school by the said Sir Joseph Danvers and the owners of the Lordship or Manor of Swithland from time to time may demand and take so much for their labour in teaching quarterly as the said Sir Joseph Danvers and the owners of the Lordship of Swithland shall together with the said Overseers from time to time agree upon to be fit.

And whereas I have given the use of my Mansion House and furniture at Chelsea to my wife during her life, and I do hereby confirm the same, that from and after the decease of my said wife I hereby give and devise to my daughter Katherine Danvers the yearly sum of thirty pounds during her life and being single and unmarried towards paying the rent of a house for her to live in either in Town or Country; and I do hereby order my trustees out of the residue of my personal estate after the decease of my said wife to pay the said sum of thirty pounds yearly to my said daughter Katherine Danvers so long as she shall continue single and unmarried.

In witness whereof I have to this codicil set my hand and seal this twenty eighth day of May in the year of our Lord one thousand seven hundred and fifty three. (Signed) Jos. Danvers.

Signed sealed published and declared by the said Sir Joseph Danvers baronet as a codicil and part of his last will and testament in the presence of us who in his presence and at his request have subscribed our names as witnesses hereto: Mary Prior, Jos Prior jr, Ann Sarson.

I the said Sir Joseph Danvers do hereby recommend and further direct that the charge of housekeeping at Swithland and all servants wages shall be paid for six months after my decease out of the residue of my personal estate in case … Frances Danvers shall desire the same. 17 Oct 1753.

I Sir Joseph Danvers do hereby give my old servant Joseph Prior senior the sum of fifty pounds over and above what I have already given. 17 Oct 1753.

Will of Sir John Danvers Bt, 1796

I, Sir John Danvers of Swithland in the County of Leicester, baronet, but now residing in the City of Bath, being of sound and disposing mind, memory and understanding, do make publish and declare this to be my last will and testament in manner following, that is to say: In the first place, &c.

I will that all my just debts, funeral expenses, and the costs and charge of proving this my will, shall be fully paid and satisfied;

And my further will is that I may be buried at the discretion of my executor and executrix hereinafter named in the church of Swithland aforesaid under an oblong slate stone, near to and in front of the new marble monument there lately by me erected and in front of the church door through which I and my family have been accustomed to enter.

I give and bequeath to all and every of my servants who shall be living with me at the time of my decease one year's wages over and above what may be due to them.

I also give devise and bequeath to my trusty servant and butler Thomas Thomas – for his many years care and fidelity towards me – an annuity or yearly sum of one hundred and fifty pounds to commence from the quarter day which may happen next after my decease, and to be paid to him the said Thomas Thomas by yearly payments home to the quarter day which may happen next preceding his the said Thomas Thomas's death; and I do hereby charge my estates both real and personal with the payment thereof.

I give devise and bequeath to my daughter Mary Butler, wife of the Honourable Augustus Richard Butler of Baker Street Portman Square in the county of Middlesex, all my manors messuages farms lands tenements and hereditaments whatsoever and of what nature or kind soever, whether freehold leasehold or copyhold situate lying and being in the county of Leicester aforesaid according to the nature of the several tenures and estates by which I hold the same for and during the term of her natural life; and from and after her decease, in case the said Augustus Richard Butler her husband shall happen to survive her, then I devise and bequeath the same manors messuages farms lands tenements and hereditaments unto him the said Augustus Richard Butler and his assigns during the term of his natural life; and from and after the death of the survivor of them, the said Augustus Richard Butler and Mary his wife, then I give devise and bequeath the same manors messuages farms lands tenements and hereditaments unto my grandson John Danvers Butler, son of the said Augustus Richard Butler and Mary his wife, his heirs executors administrators and assigns according to the nature of the several tenures or estates of which I held the same; but in the case of the death of my said grandson in the lifetime of his said father and mother or of the survivor of them under the age of twenty one years without issue, then I give and bequeath the same estates after the decease of my said daughter Mary Butler to the said Augustus Richard Butler his heirs executor administrators and assigns according to the several natures and tenures thereof respectfully.

And as to the rest residue and remainder of my estates and effects whatsoever both real and personal wheresoever, I give devise and bequeath the same to the said Augustus Richard Butler his heirs executors administrators and assigns.

And I do hereby will and direct that the said Augustus Richard Butler and my said grandson, and all and every other person and persons who shall under and by virtue of any devise hereby made come unto the possession of any said real estates, do and shall take and use my surname and family arms. And my will is, and I do hereby declare, that in case my said grandson shall happen to obtain the age of twenty one years in the lifetime of his said father or mother or in the lifetime of the survivor of them, that then and in that case he my said grandson shall have and be entitled to one annuity or yearly rent charge of eight hundred pounds, to be issuing and payable out of my said manors messuages lands tenements and hereditaments situate in the county of Leicester aforesaid until he, my said grandson, shall become entitled to the possession of the said estates and hereditaments under and by virtue of the devise and bequest hereinbefore made to him as aforesaid; and I do hereby charge and make chargeable the said estates and hereditaments with the payment thereof according to the several powers of entry and distress for the same according to law.

And lastly I do hereby nominate, constitute and appoint the said Augustus Richard Butler and Mary his wife joint executor and executrix of this my last will and testament, hereby revoking and making void all former and other will or wills by me at any time heretofore made.

In witness whereof I the said Sir John Danvers have to this my last will and testament in one side of one sheet of paper set my hand and seal this sixteenth day of September in the year of our Lord one thousand seven hundred and ninety six.

The mark of Sir John Danvers.

Signed sealed published and declared by the said testator Sir John Danvers by his subscribing his mark (being incapable to write his name from an unsteady hand) in the presence of us who in his presence, and in the presence of each other at his request, have subscribed our names as witnesses. Redhead Finchley. Zachery Bayliss. John Langley.

Proved at London 4th October 1796 before the worshipful John Tewell Doctor of Laws and surrogate by the oath of the Honourable Augustus Richard Butler one of the executors, to whom administration was granted, he having been first sworn duly to administer – Mary Butler, wife of the said Honourable Augustus Richard Butler the daughter and other executor having first renounced the execution thereof.

Will of Hon Mary Butler Danvers 1802

I Mary Butler Danvers of Upper Seymour Street, Portland Square, in the county of Middlesex, wife of the Hon Augustus Richard Butler Danvers, but living separately from my said husband, do under or by virtue of the power or authority given or secured to me in and by a certain indenture of six parts bearing date on or about the third of May seventeen hundred and ninety nine and expressed to be made between the said Augustus Richard Butler-Danvers and myself of the first party Dame Mary Danvers my late mother of the second party Henry Thorton Esq and John Wainwright of the third party, the Rt Hon Charles Lord Viscount Maynard and William Northey Esq of the fourth part John Edward Carter and Joseph Spencer Cardale of the fifth part, Thomas Smith of the sixth part, and under or by virtue of every right and all powers and authorities enabling me in this behalf make and publish my last will and testament as follows and do appoint the said Henry Thornton Esq to be executor hereof.

I direct all my just debts to be duly satisfied and paid.

I desire the said Henry Thornton to accept the sum of twenty pounds sterling.

I give and bequeath to my servant Sarah Robinson the sum of fifty pounds sterling , and also my wearing apparel and household linen, and I give to my servant Sarah Simmerton the like sum of fifty pounds, provided that the said Sarah Robinson and Sarah Simmerton shall respectively be in my service at the time of my decease.

All the residue of my estate, not hereinbefore disposed of, after payment of my debts hereinbefore mentioned, I give and bequeath unto the said Henry Thornton upon the same trusts for my dear son George John Danvers Butler-Danvers as in and by the last will and testament of the said Dame Mary Danvers my mother dated the seventh of December seventeen hundred and ninety six and a codicil to her said will dated the fourth day of July seventeen hundred and ninety nine are expressed in favour of my said son concerning the residue of my said mother's estate in the event of my dying in the lifetime of my said husband and in case my said son shall die before he shall become absolutely entitled to my said mother's estate then I direct that the said Henry Thornton shall stand possessed of the said residue of my estate upon trust for himself and his brothers Samuel Thornton and Robert Thornton Esquires in equal shares for their own absolute use and benefit.

In witness thereof I have to this my will set my hand and seal this third day of April eighteen hundred and two. (Signed Mary Danvers)

Witnesses: Wainwright, Grays Inn; Harriet Herrick, Edgeware Road; Sarah Playll, 57 Wills Street.

Will of Christopher Marshall, Rector of Swithland from 1506

I, Christofer Marshall, clerk, bequeath my soul to Almighty God who created it, to His Only Begotten Son who redeemed it and to the Holy Spirit who gave me and will give me life, to Blessed Mary the Mother of Christ, to Blessed Michael the Archangel and to all angels and to the orders of all angels and other saints so that it should be defended against the evil spirit and should enjoy their fellowship everlastingly. I leave my body, after my soul has left it, to be buried in the earth as it shall be decided. I will that five candles should be burnt about my body on the day of my burial and also at the day of my month's mind and my anniversary, while requiem and mass are being said and on each of the three days beforenamed I will that there should be said for my soul the requiem of the dead and a trentall of masses if conveniently it can be done from my property. I give to each priest saying requiem or celebrating mass 8*d*. I bequeath to be distributed for my soul in bread and ale and other food on the day of my burial 10*s*., on the thirtieth day 6*s*. 8*d*., and on the day of my anniversary 10*s*. I bequeath to each of twelve parish churches 3*s*. 4*d*., namely to Yolgraff, Wyrkesworth, Kyrkeyreton, Monyashe and Hope in the County of Derbey, and to Rothley, Oleppe, Thiraston, Baro, Sylebe, Cosynton and Swithland in the County of Leicester. I bequeath 12*d*. to each of the twelve chapels of Elton, Wyndstor, Alderwasloe, Cramforth and Carston in the County of Derbei, and to Austy, Newton, Querndon, Wudhowse, the two chapels of Montsorell and to Temple Chapel near Rotheley in the County of Leicester and 5*d*. to each curate and chaplain serving the said churches and chapels to say requiem and mass for my soul, and also 4*d*. a year for three years to those who use bede rolls and will pray for my soul with others named in their bede rolls on Sundays. I bequeath to each son and daughter of my brothers and sisters 12*d*. I bequeath to the parish church of Yolgraffe, County Derbei, a small chest with the books and other things it contains so that they may be used in the best way possible for the service of God, the good pleasure of the priest serving there and the edification of souls and also to be used for the instruction of those willing to learn at the discretion of the vicar and of other discreet parishioners. I will that Ursula Marshall, my kinswoman, should have 10 *li*. of my goods.

Be it knowen to my speciall frendes, Sir Wyllyam Sore, vicarye of Saynt Martyns nygh the Charyng Crosse, and to John Thatcher of the parysshe of Kensyngton that all my money wheche I have above my dettes payd lyeth in the pew or sete wheras Maister John Meawtes custumably knelith or sittith in the churche of Kensyngton under the seconde bord upon the which he knelith, under that end of the bord toward the qwer of the which money I will that the said Sir William and John Thatcher comunelly have the disposicion acording to my last will the which I have wretyn with myn owne hand desiryng thaem to my trew executors.

Sir Christofer Marshall. 1 May 1516.

[Proved 18 Sep. 1516 by Master Thomas Hedd and administration granted to Sir William Sore. John Thatcher on 19 Jan. 1517 renounced his power as executor in the presence of the vicar-general.]

'Register Palmer: Nos. 1–40', *London Consistory Court Wills 1492–1547: London Record Society 3* (1967), p. 1–25. Priests dying in the Diocese of London from the year 1514.

Will of Jane Blakwing, 1675[6]

In the name of God Amen. Jane Blakwing of Swithland in the Countie of Leicester widow doo make this my last will and testament in form and manner following

Imprimus I commit my sole into the hands of my Blessed Lord and Saviour Jesus Christ and my Body to be decently buried in the Church yard of Swithland at the discretion of my Executor hereafter nominated and as for my worldly goods I give them as followeth

Item – I give unto my grandchild Mary Branson my house at Markfield and the Apurtenances thereunto belonging for to enter thereon four years after my decease.

Item I give unto my grandchild Elizabeth Branson my house at Cropston and the Appurtenances thereunto belonging for to have it and enter therein four years after my decease.

Item: I give to my grandchild Ann Branson a Close commonly called and known by the name of Cattel piece for to have it and enter therein four years after my decease. And if please God that if any one or two shall die before they shall come to enter therein that it shall be divided equally to the longer survivor of them.

Item I give unto my sonne Henry Branson's daughter Sabina Branson the sum of fortie shillings when she comes to one and twenty years of age. And my will is that when my grandchild Henry Branson shall enter on the close that I bought of Mrs Templar called the Rie Close that he shall pay unto his two sisters May and Elizabeth the sum of five pounds apiece.

Item I give unto my brother Robert …. the sum of 10 shilling.

Last I make my daughter Jane full executor of this my last will and testament and Thomas Adkins of Anstey and William Howkins Trustees and overseers for the children to see that all things be done and performed according to the true intent and meaning of this my last will and testament. Made and sealed with my own hands this 13 day of November Anno Dominy 1675

Witnesse
Jane Blakwing
Edward Callis Senior
Abigail Smith
Edward Callis Junior

(27 October 1696 – John Colman. Surrogate)

Will of Henry Gilbert of York, 15 June 1716 [7]

I give and devise unto my dear mother Ann Gilbert for her natural life all my close or parcel of ground commonly called Mill Close lying and being in the parish of Swithland … and after the death of my said mother I give and devise the said close and premises with the appurtenances unto Michael Matthews of Mountsorrel, gent., John Burnham of Nuneaton, gent., John Vans of Loughborough, gent., Christopher Smalley of Atherstone, gent., John Jennings of Upper Kibworth, gent., …. upon trust .. to sell… for the best – upon such bargain as shall well and sufficiently secure the yearly sum of 20 shillings .. to be paid out .. for charitable uses as hereinafter mentioned: I bequeath to my sister Hews of Swithland, two guineas to be paid out of the purchase monies of the said close. And all the rest of the said purchase money I give and bequeath unto all my nephews and nieces living at my death equally to be divided among them, and the shares of such of them as shall not be of full age to be paid to their respective parents. All the rest of my goods and chattels and personal estate .. I give and bequeath unto my brothers Robert Gilbert and John Hall, and make them joint executors.

Extracts from Will of Michael Matthews, 1721

My body to be buried at the discretion of my executrix

Messuages, lands, tenements and hereditaments in Mountsorrel and Rothley, to my wife Sarah Matthews for life, afterwards to my son-in-law James Watson and Sarah his wife for their lives, and afterwards to the heirs of the body of James and Sarah Watson.

An annuity of rent charge £20 per year payable out of the estate at Longdon, Staffs, which I purchased of my brother in law Thomas Hood and Samuel Hood his son and heir to my wife,

The estate at Longdon so purchased to my wife for life, paying from the profits thereof £5 yearly to my second daughter Ann Matthews for and during the several lives of Gabriel West of Woodhouse and Mary his wife, £100 to my daughter Watson and any remaining profits to my two daughters Anne and Hannah the estate at Longdon, after the death of my wife to Anne and Hannah that close in Longdon, Aldrith Field, to James and Sarah Watson that estate in Longdon (occupied by my brother in law Thomas Gee) which I hold by lease from the Earl of Uxbridge for my own life, and the life of my sister Anne, the wife of Thomas Gee, to my daughter Sarah Watson, for her own benefit.

My estate at Woodhouse and Woodhouse Eaves (in the possession of Gabriel West) to my second daughter Anne Matthews and all such money as is or shall become due to me by virtue of a mortgage of lands in Woodhouse and Woodhouse Eaves from Abraham Chambers, gent.
£350 to my youngest daughter Hannah Matthews when she attains 21 years or marries.

And whereas the estate at Longdon was charged with the payment of £70 to

Francis, Elizabeth, Joshua and Richard Hood the younger, children of my brother-in-law Thomas Hood, – Francis and Elizabeth having received their share; Joshua and Richard still to be paid – £50 to Matthew Watson, second son of James and Sarah Watson

Residue of estate to my wife, Sarah Matthews

Sarah Matthews is named as executrix.

Notes to Appendix A: Wills

1. Public Records Office, National Archives, Wills, PROB11/92.
2. Leics. RO, 5D33/338, Will of Francis Danvers of Swithland, gent. 16 May 1631.
3. Prerogative Court of Canterbury, PAB1, 1694, folio 6.
4. Public Records Office, National Archives, PROB 11/582, Will of John Danvers of Precott.
5. Leics. RO, DE1750, Box 7, Will of Sir Joseph Danvers, 1753.
6. Leics. RO, DE73/248, Will of Jane Blakwing of Swithland.
7. Leics. RO, DE1750, Box 24, will of Henry Gilbert of York, 1716.

– APPENDIX B –

Incumbents and Other Ministers

Rectors and Priests in Charge

1220	Roger
1224	Roger de Turkillestone
1239	Geoffrey de Warwick
1266	William de Merston
1275	John de Sutton
1278	Peter de Ilminston
1286	Gilbert de Roubir
1295	Reginald of St Ebremar
1298	Alexander of Bowden
1340	William Waleys
1356	Richard de Birchy
1356	Richard de Mitford
1360	Robert de Calmont
1362	William Wylde
1398	Robyn de Wibbertoft
1400	Robert Skyfington
1405	William Tarrutt
1405	Roger Crosseby
1427	Thomas Wright[1]
1440	Thomas Wright
1446	Bartholomew Dulwich
1458	William Harrison
1465	Thomas Scott
1465	William Plabys
1472	Robert de Vynes
1480	Lawrence Orrell
1491	Richard Woods
1495	Richard Russell
1499	Michael Eden
1506	Christopher Marshall[2]
1516	William Hebb
1525	William Gibs (Gibbe)[3]
1528	Edmund Smythe
1534	William Gibs (Gibbe)[4]

1576	Michael Hudson
1588	Gilbert Smythe
1623	Joseph Smith
1647	Richard Battie
1663	William Kimes
1676	Thomas Jackson
1700	Abel Brooksby
1735	Philip Alston
1761	John Llwyd
1814	Francis Bruxby
1817	Henry David Erskine
1841	Henry Campbell
1841	Edward James Paget
1858	George Napleton Treweeke
1877	Kingsford Beauchamp Sidebottom
1884	James Murray Dixon
1925	Frederick James Oliver
1931	John Mackay
1955	Cecil Copp Harcourt
1959	Harold Alexander Maxwell
1966	Thomas Geoffrey Stuart Smith
1973	Edward Wilson Carlile
1977	Francis Raymond Walters
1994	Roberta Anne Horton

Biographical Notes on Rectors & Priests in Charge

Roger, chaplain, presented by the Prior of Ware to the Church of Swithland, as 'nothing stood in the way except his being insufficiently learned. Meanwhile he is to study and, if then found competent, is to be admitted. Otherwise to be wholly dismissed from the benefice'. [5]

Gilbert de Roubir. Gilbert of Rothbury, clerk in minor orders, presented by Fulk, Prior of Ware, to the Church of Swithland, vacant by the death of Peter. Ordained subd and instituted. Thame 21 Dec 1286[6] 'Mandate to Robert of Burton, sequestrator, to relax, until further notice, any sequestration imposed on the revenues of the churches of Carleton and Swithland, held by Gilbert de Roubir, Dorchester on Thames, 11 September 1294'.[7]

Reginald of St Ebremar. Reginald of St Evroult, clerk in minor orders, presented by Ralph, Prior of Ware, to the Church of Swithland, vacant because Sir Gilbert de Roubir has been inst to Carleton. Ordained subdeacon, and inst. London 28 May 1295.[8] beneficed priest 1296.[9]

Alexander of Bowden. Clerk in minor orders, presented by Ralph, Prior of Ware to the church of Swithland, vacant because Reginald of St Evroult has been instituted to Carleton Curlieu. Ordained subdeacon and instituted Brampton, nr Huntingdon, 20 September 1298.[10]

Roger Crossby. Rector of Swithland 1405. Exchanged the Chantry of the Holy Trinity and St Mary in the Cathedral Priory of Coventry for the Church of Swithland, 19 Dec 1405.[11]

Thomas Wright. Named as 'pastor of Swythelond' in 1427 legal document.[12]

William Hebb. Rector of Swithland 1516. Non-residence reported in July 1518.[13]

Michael Hudson. Rector of Swithland 1576 (value of living £10 6s 3d) presented by the Lord Keeper, ordained by the late Bishop of Lincoln, 40 years of age, not married, resides, ignorant of Latin, in some sort of way versed in sacred learning.'[14] In 1585, 'Sir Michael Hudson, rector. Absent.'[15]

Gilbert Smythe. Born 1559 at Ridge, Herts. Queens College, Cambridge. Matriculated 1579. BA 1583. Deacon 1584. Vicar of Ridge 1587–89. Rector of Swithland 1588–1623. Surrogate of Groby Peculiar Court 1608.

Joseph Smith. Born Norfolk. St John's College, Cambridge. Matriculated 1609. BA 1613. Rector of Swithland 1623–45. Listed as patron of Sileby 1641. Rector of Hathern 1645–52. Rector of Great Coates, Lincs 1652–67. Died 1667.

Richard Battie. Born 1604. Oriel College, Oxford. Matriculated 1617. Listed as minister at Swithland 1653.[16] Rector of Swithland ?1647–62. Died 1662.

William Kimes. Trinity College, Cambridge. Matriculated 1629. BA 1634. MA 1637. Priest 1640. Curate of Belgrave 1633–38. Curate of Birstall 1632–38. Appointed vicar of Belgrave by parliamentary sequestrators 1648. Rector of Swithland 1663–76. Died 1676.[17]

Thomas Jackson. Born 1637. Leicestershire School, Leicester; Peterhouse College, Cambridge 1654. Vicar of Sileby 1660–76. Curate of Quorn 1669–73 and Mountsorrel 1669–73. Rector of Swithland 1676–1700. Died 1700. Buried with his wife and other members of his family in Swithland church.[18]

Abel Brooksby. Born 1675 at Leicester. Eldest son of John Brooksby of Leicester, mercer. Leicestershire School, Leicester; Trinity College, Cambridge. Deacon 1699. Priest 1700. Rector of Swithland 1700–35. Married 1701 Alice Palmer of Leicester. Freeman of Leicester 1721. Surrogate of Groby Peculiar Court 1715–35. Died 1735. Buried with his wife in Swithland church.[19]

Philip Alston. Born 1708 at Woodburn, Beds. New College, Oxford 1727. Rector of Swithland 1735–60.[20]

John Llwyd. Born 1737 at Llandeei Velfrely, Pembs. Jesus College, Oxford 1761. Rector of Swithland 1761–1814. Married 1772 Mary Major of Leicester. Died 1814. Buried with his wife in Swithland church.

Francis Bruxby. Born 1735. Emmanuel College, Cambridge 1778. Rector of Swithland 1814–17. Resigned 1817. Died 1822. Buried at Swithland.

Henry David Erskine. Born 1786. Harrow School; Trinity College, Cambridge 1806. Married 1813 Mary Harriet Dawson. Rector of Loddington, Northants 1816–17. Rector of Swithland 1817–41. Vicar of St Martins, Leicester 1830–1841. Commissary of Groby Peculiar 1827–35. Rector of Kirkby Underdale, Yorks 1841–59. Listed as Commissary of Rothley Peculiar 1846. Prebendary of Warthill in York Minster 1845–47. Dean of Ripon 1847–59. Died 1859. Buried at Ripon.

Henry Campbell. Presented[21] to the Rectory of Swithland on the cession (*i.e. the surrender of the benefice before accepting another*) of his predecessor on 23rd June 1841. Inducted 29th June 1841. Resigned 1841.

Edward James Paget. Born 1812 at Reigate, Sussex. Christ Church College, Oxford 1828. Rector of Swithland 1841–58.[22] Resigned 1858. Rector of Steppingley, Beds 1864–69. Died 1869.

George Napleton Treweeke. Born 1822 at Penzance, Cornwall. Jesus College, Cambridge 1840. BA 1843. Deacon 1846. Priest 1847. Curate of Illogan, Cornwall 1846–51. Married 1853 Letitia Rudyerd Ross Butler née Freese. Curate of Thelbridge, Devon 1854–56. Curate of Swithland 1856–58. Rector of Swithland 1858–76.[23] Died 1876.

Kingsford Beauchamp Sidebottom. Born 1834 at Hampton, Middlesex. Durham University 1853. Deacon 1858. Priest 1862. Curate of Derryhill 1858–60. Curate of Todmorden 1860–61. Curate of Balham, Cambs 1861–62. Curate of Sevenoaks 1862–74. Curate of

St Jude, Islington, London 1875–76. Rector of Swithland 1877–83. Vicar of Exning with Landwade 1884–91.

James Murray Murray-Dixon. Born 1852 at Watlington, Oxon. St Bees College, Cumberland 1872. Deacon 1875. Priest 1876. Curate of St James, Ashted, Birmingham 1875–76. Married Etheldreda Trevelyan 1882. Rector of Swithland 1884–1925.[24] Resigned 1925. Died 1944. Buried with his wife at Swithland.

Frederick James Oliver. St Catherine's College, Cambridge; Ridley Hall, Cambridge 1919. Deacon 1920. Priest 1921. Curate of St Helen's, Liverpool 1920–22. Curate of St Mary's, Eccles 1922–25. Rector of Swithland 1925–30.[25] Resigned 1930.

John Mackay. Born 1870 at Woburn. Educated at Howard House School, and at Church Missionary College, Islington 1903. Married 1900 Sarah Caroline Grover. Deacon 1904. Priest 1904. Church Missionary Society missionary at Oshoglo, Western Equatorial Africa 1904–19. Rector of Norton-sub-Hamdon, Somerset 1919–25. Archdeacon of Yoruba County, Nigeria 1925–29. Rector of Swithland 1931–39. Resigned 1939. Died 1942.

Cecil Copp Harcourt. University of Toronto, Canada; Wycliffe College, Toronto. Deacon 1921. Priest 1926. Curate of St James, Keew 1921–25. Curate of St Luke, St Johns, New Brunswick 1926. Missioner at Aklavik 1927–29. Curate of St Paul's, Toronto 1931–34. Rector of Catwright 1934–38. Curate of St Nicholas, Leicester 1939–41. Vicar of Sileby 1941–48. Vicar of Locking, Somerset 1948–51. Rector of Ware, Somerset 1952–55. Priest in charge at Swithland 1955–56. Rector of Swithland 1956–58.

Harold Alexander Maxwell. University of Liverpool. BA 1922. MA 1946. Ridley Hall, Cambridge 1922. Deacon 1923. Priest 1924. Curate of St Benedict, Everton 1923–26. CMS missionary at Mienyang Diocesan School 1926–35. Vicar of St Thomas, Mienchu 1935–40. Lecturer at Union Theological College, Chengtu 1940–43. Assistant Bishop of West Szechwan 1943–50. Assistant Bishop of Leicester 1950–65. Vicar of Copt Oak 1950–52. Vicar of Ab Kettleby with Wartnaby and Holwell 1952–59. Rector of Swithland 1959–65.

Thomas Geoffrey Stuart Smith. Jesus College, Cambridge. BA 1924. MA 1927. Ridley Hall, Cambridge 1923. Deacon 1925. Priest 1926. Curate of St Mary, Bermondsey 1925–28. Chaplain, Ridley Hall, Cambridge 1928–30. Vice-Principal, Cam Nicholson Institute and Mission at Kottayan 1930–39. Archdeacon of Mavelikara 1939–47. Bishop of North Kerala, Church of South India 1947–54. Vicar of Burwell 1954–60. Rector of Danbury 1960–66. Assistant Bishop of

Chelmsford 1961–66. Assistant Bishop of Leicester 1966–73. Rector of Swithland 1966–73.

Edward Wilson Carlile. Born 1916. Kings College, London. Deacon 1943. Priest 1944. Curate of All Saints, Queensbury, London 1943–46. Assistant Secretary, Church Army 1946–49. Chief Secretary, Church Army 1949–60. Vicar of St Peter with St Hilda, Leicester 1960–73. Rector of Swithland 1973–76. Priest in charge at St Michael, Belgrave 1976–. Died 1996.

Francis Raymond Walters. Balliol College, Oxford. BA 1949. MA 1954. Wycliffe College, Oxford 1951. Deacon 1953. Priest 1954. Curate of Boulton, Derbys 1953–56. St Philip Cathedral Church, Birmingham 1956–64. Curate of Harborne 1958–64. Vicar of St Nicholas, Leicester and chaplain to Leicester University 1964–73. Rector of Appleby Magna 1973–77. Leicester Diocesan Director of Education 1977–90. Priest in charge at Swithland 1977–91. Hon Canon of Leicester Cathedral. Resigned 1991.

Roberta Anne Horton. Born 1944. University of Leicester, B Sc. 1966. Cert. Ed. 1967. Nottingham University BCS 1982. Lincoln Theological College 1979, Deaconess 1982, Deacon 1987, Priest 1994. Cambridge St James, Ely 1982–86; Christ the King, Leicester 1986–91; Diocesan Director of Training 1991–2000; Priest in Charge Swithland 1994–2000; Hon Canon Leicester Cathedral from 1994; Rector of Woodhouse, Woodhouse Eaves and Swithland from 2000.

Biographical Notes on Assistant Curates

George Cardale. Born 1715 at Bulkington, Warwicks. Nuneaton; St John's College, Cambridge. Matriculated 1735. BA 1738. MA 1741. DD 1759. Priest 1739. Rector of Wanlip 1739–69. Vicar of Rothley 1759–69. Died 1769.

John Butler Sanders. Born 1792 in London, the son of Rev John Sanders. St Paul's School; Trinity College, Cambridge. BA 1816. Chaplain in Royal Navy until about 1844. Retired or entitled to half pay from about 1848 to 1862. Died 1863 at Handsworth.

John Longhurst. Queens College, Cambridge 1820. BA 1824, MA 1828. Deacon 1823. Priest 1824. Curate of Knaptoft with Shearsby & Mowsley 1823. Curate of Kirkby Mallory with Earl Shilton 1824–53. Vicar of Dunton Bassett 1845–47. Resigned 1847. Curate of Swithland 1861. Vicar of Dunton Bassett again 1863–72.

Thomas Ward Goddard. Born 1836 at Peckham, Surrey, the elder son of Thomas Goddard, mercer, of Lee Park, Blackheath, Kent. Pembroke College, Cambridge. BA 1858. MA 1861. Deacon 1859. Priest 1860. Married 1864 Ellen Gibson, daughter of Rev John Gibson. Curate of St John's, Chatham 1859–61. Curate of Furneaux Pelham, Herts 1861–63. Curate of Felmersham, Beds. 1864–66. Curate of Sherington, Bucks 1866–71. Curate of Newnham, Hants 1876–76. Curate of Swithland, Leics. 1874–76. Curate of Ham, Hants. 1876–78. Curate of Rockford, Essex 1879–81. Rector of Bitteswell, Leics. 1881–90. Vicar of Nazing, Essex 1890–1922. Died 1923.

William Agar. Born 1820 at Great Yeldham, Essex. St Johns College, Cambridge. BA 1845. MA 1848. Deacon 1846. Priest 1847. Curate of Upton and St Peter's, Northants 1846–49. Curate of Overstone 1850–58. Other curacies 1858–65. Headmaster, Kimbolton Grammar School, Hants 1865–77. Curate of Eastleach Martin and Eastleach Turville, Glos 1877–80. Curate of Longworth, Berks 1880–82. Rector and Patron of Newton Bromswold, Northants 1882–99. Died 1899.

Geoffrey Frisby. St Chad's College, Durham. BA 1920. Ely Theological College 1920. Deacon 1920. Priest 1921. Curate of Higham Ferrers, Northants 1920–23. Resident at Swithland in 1924–25.

Stephen Robert Delaforce. Born 1952. Middlesex Polytechnic BSc 1980; Cranfield Institute of Technology MSc 1988; Nottingham University MA 2003; CEng MIMechE 1983; EMMTC 2004. Deacon 2007. Priest 2008. NSM Woodhouse, Woodhouse Eaves and Swithland 2007–10.

Biographical Notes on Other Clergy

Frederick Lindesay Godfrey. Born 1902. Son of Ernest Henry Godfrey. Merton College, Oxford. BA (Modern History) 1926. MA 1928. Wycliffe Hall, Oxford 1926. Deacon 1927. Priest 1928. Curate, Holy Apostles, Leicester 1927–29. Curate, St Mark's, Leicester 1929–32. Married 1932 Lois Mary Gladys Turner at Swithland. Curate, St Dunstan's, Stepney, 1932–35. Vicar of St Matthew's Stepney, 1935–43. Vicar of St Peter's, St Helier, Surrey, 1943–54. Warden of Launde Abbey retreat house 1957–63. Curate in charge of Loddington 1958–63. Hon Canon of Leicester Cathedral 1957–68; Residentiary Canon 1968–72; Canon Emeritus 1972–84. Diocesan Missioner 1963–72. Chaplain, Groby Road hospital 1964–70. Buried at Swithland 1984.

Waldron Harris. Born 1912 at Rochester, Kent. Educated at Rochester, St Thomas Hospital, London; St Deiniol's, Hawarden, N. Wales; St Augustine's, Canterbury. MRCS, LRCP 1937. DOMS 1944. FICS 1963. Served in RAF 1941–45. Practicing ophthalmic surgeon & consultant 1946–79. Churchwarden of St Leonard's, Swithland 1964–73. Deacon December 1972. Priest September 1973. Married 1939 Buddug Morgan (died 1970). Married 1972 Olga Gregory. Ashes buried at Swithland 1979.

Peter Sheridan. Born 1937. Saltley Training College, Birmingham, Cert Ed 1959; Leicester Polytechnic B.Ed 1982; Northern Ordination Course 1989. Deacon 1992, priest 1993. NSM Braunstone 1992–95; NSM Ratby cum Groby 1995–98; NSM Newtown Linford 1995–98; Team Vicar Bradgate Team 1998–2000; Permission to Officiate NSM Woodhouse, Woodhouse Eaves and Swithland 2001–06.

Notes to Appendix B: Incumbents and Other Ministers

1. Leics. RO, DE1625/3, Gift 25 September 1427, 'Thomas Writgth, parson of Swythelond', named as s a witness.
2. See Appendix A: Wills.
3. Leics. RO, ID21/12/2, Document refers to William Gibs, Gibbe as rector of Swithland in 1525 and 1534.
4. ibid., Visitation documents refer to William Gibs, Gibbe as rector of Swithland in 1525 and 1534.
5. W.P.W. Phillimore (ed.), *Rolls of Hugh de Wells, Bishop of Lincoln 1209–1235*, Lincoln Records Society, vol. 3, 1912.
6. Lincoln Records Society, vol. 76.
7. *Rolls and Registers of Oliver Sutton, Bishop of Lincoln 1280–1299*, Lincoln Records Society, vol. 60.
8. Lincoln Records Society, vol. 76.
9. ibid., vol. 69.
10. ibid., vol. 76.
11. A. Hamilton (ed.), *Visitations of Religious Houses in Diocese of Lincoln 1436–1499*, Lincoln Records Society.
12. Leics. RO, DE1625/3, Gift 25 September 1427 (Shepey moiety of Swithland passing to John Danvers son of late Margaret Assheton).
13. *Episcopal Court Book, Diocese of Lincoln, 1514–1520*, Lincoln Records Society, vol. 61
14. *Lincoln Episcopal Records in the time of Thomas Cooper 1571–1584*, Lincoln Records Society, vol. 2 (1912).
15. ibid.
16. Public Records Office National Archives, E336/28, Transcripts of Sherriff's returns listing church livings and incumbents 1651/2; shows 'Swithland (£10-4-5) Richard Battee.'
17. Leics. RO, ID41/28/536, Induction mandate.
18. Leics. RO, ID41/28/709, Induction mandate.
19. Leics. RO, ID41/28/921, Induction mandate.
20. Leics. RO, ID41/28/1206, Induction mandate
21. Leics. RO, 7D55 963/1, Presentation deed.
22. Leics. RO, 7D55 964/1, Presentation deed.
23. Leics. RO, 7D55 965/1-2, Presentation deed.
24. Leics. RO, 7D55 966/1-8, Presentation deed.
25. Leics. RO, 7D55 967/1, Presentation deed.

– APPENDIX C –

Swithland School Admissions 1865–1980 (July)

Place of residence = Swithland
 or A (Anstey), B (Birstall), BP (Bradgate Park), Br (The Brand), By (Bybrooks), c/o (c/o a Swithland resident), Cr (Cropston), CrWW (Cropston WaterWorks), H (Hoton) HGC (Hall Gates Cropston), K (Kinsley Hill), M (Mountsorrel), NL (Newtown Linford), Q (Quorn), RP (Rothley Plain), RT (Rothley Temple), SwCamp (Swithland Camp), SM (Swithland Mill), SwWdFm (Swithland Wood Farm), T (Thurcaston)

Book One

1865 H.A. Lynes
1867 M.H. Lynes, E.A. Hodges, S.A. Pratt, S.A. Raynor, Sarah Bunney, M.A. Godbald
1868 Chas W Lynes, Elizb Hodges, S.A. Spencer, Jas H Woods
1869 Fanny Cuffling, Willm Hemsley, Geo Brown, Eliza Raynor, Jas Pratt
1870 Mary Spencer, C.A. Bates,
1871 Willm Raynor, Wllm Adams, Caroline E. Lynes, Harriette Hodges, Harriette Godbald, Jas T Bates
1872 Elizb Mayne, Thos Milley, Chas Milley, Arthur Payne
1873 Chas Pratt, Jas Bampton, Fanny Godbald, E.M. McLean, W.J. Bates, W. Brown, Edw Chapman, Daniel Milley, Edw Raynor
1874 S.R. Dance *(RP)*, Chas F. Dance *(RP)*, Elizb Rouse *(RP)*, Jo Bunney, Leo Payne, Thos Reynolds *(T)*, Jabez Tebbutt *(T)*, Chas Ratcliffe
1875 Jas Thos Hodges, Walter Bunney, Fredk Moor, Arthur Moor, Henry Moor, Frank Handley, W.B. Cook, Ann Knight *(RP)*, Alfred Adams, Harriet Maud Johnson, Florence Johnson, Cicely Mary Johnson, Jane Ann Rouse *(RP)*, William Reynolds *(T)*, George Pratt, Harry Graham, Elizabeth Bunney, Thos Ratcliffe, Sarah J. Adams, Lavinia Bunney, M.J. Rebk Bunney, Arthur Payne, Alfred Payne, Elizb Milley, Fanny Moore, Matthew Daykin Bates, Joseph Bowler, Eliz Bunney
1876 Willm Milley, Willm Clark *(RP)*, Annie Laura Cook, Mary Bowler, Elizabeth A. Brown, Mary Charlotte Raynor, Chas Payne *(SM)*, John Sharp Disney, Thos Willm Underwood, Ellen G.B.

Underwood, Benjm B. Underwood, Emma A. Chapman, Elizb Chapman, Ada Rouse, *(RP)* Arthur Ellis, Emily Adams, Cecilia M. Johnson, Fredk Moore, M.A. Cuffling,

1877 M.A. Cockayne *(RP)*, Fredk A. Underwood, Mary Jane Adams, Clara Helen Hodges, Latitia Handley, Mary Spencer, Walter Remington, Walter Thos Ellis, Wm J. Cuffling, Harriet M. Johnson, Johnson Bunney, Sarah Elizb Ratcliffe, George Sharpe, J. Herbert Sharpe

1878 Mary Juliana Bates, Fredk James Bunney, Ellen Chapman, Annie M. Underwood, Richard Clark *(RP)*, Louisa Godbald, Matthew Thos Adams, Alfred Sharpe, Frank James *(BP)*, Zoë Hodges, John Willm Dance *(RP)*, Martha Bate, Willm U. Hackett *(HGC)*, Louisa M. Hackett *(HGC)*, Maud A. Hackett *(HGC)*

1879 Tom Moore, Edith Emily S Bunney, Geo Stockwell *(K)*, James Stockwell *(K)*, Mary Jane Bunney, Albert Taylor Hubbard *(RP)*,

1880 James Geo Dance *(RP)*, Mary S. Payne, Martha Bale, Martha Ann Adams, Albert Cook, Joanna Brown, Mary Cuffling, Sam Deeming Raynor, Louisa Alice Lynes

1881 William Curzon, Thos F. Johnson, Bill Clowes, Ernest Sharp, Annie Clowes, Martha Clowes

1882 Wm Henry Wilkins, Alwyne Everard Bunney, Edith Hodges, James Crowden Hubbard *(RP)*

1883 Charlotte Pepper, Fanny Simson Pepper, Albert Edwin Pepper, Millicent L.G. Hackett *(HGC)*

1884 Rose Ann Hodgkinson *(Br)*, Thomas Hodgkinson *(Br)*, Sarah Hodgkinson *(Br)*, Arthur Johnson, Mary A. Simpson, Florence Adams, Annie Hodges, John Henry Bird, Edith M. Pepper, Elizabeth Clowes *(K)*, Ellen Bunney

1885 Margaret Hubbard *(RP)*, Margaret Baum, Jessie McClure, Kate Clowes *(K)*, Florence E. Lynes, Annie M.D. Johnson, Mary E. Bunney

1886 F. Elizabeth Payne, Cath E. May Pepper, Lucy Grey, Ada Page, Arthur Lynes, Margaret E. Adams, Emma Brown, Albert Mawby, Ellis Mawby

1887 George Bunney, Fred A. Steele, John Young *(RP)*, Louis T. Pepper, Martha Gazy, Eliza Glazy, Bertie Hemsley, Herbert Gazy, Rose Bunney

1888 George Clowes, David Leake *(RP)*, Frances S Noon, Lizzie Noon, Eliza Seal *(T)*, Ruth Seal *(T)*, David Seal *(T)*, Winifred Bunney, Clara V. Noon, Gertrude Johnson, Hannah Holling, Emma Holling, Ada Holling, George Holling, Edith E. Burdett *(RP)*, Clara Burdett *(RP)*, Florence Hyman *(RP)*, Mary A. Hill

1889 Alfred Geary, Leonard Geary, Abraham Geary, Frank Geary, Hannah Leake *(RP)*, Harry Pratt, Edith Hyman *(RP)*, Agatha Hicks, Charles Henry Pepper, Mary Jane Gresswell, William Gresswell

1890 Lilly Hallam, Margaret Hyman *(RP)*, Annie V. Bunney, Sarah A. Gresswell, Annie M. Bunney, Ada Noon, Thomas Lee

1891 John Thos. Gresswell, Albert Adams, Maurice R. Bunney, Wilfred Bowler *(K)*, Frances Frith, Hilda M. Bunney
1892 Edwin Hemsley, Laura F. Bunney, Francis Pratt, Fredk Wm Pepper
1893 no records of admissions entered
1894 Helen E.T. Dixon, Rosamund M. Dixon, Harry Dixon, George Milner, Florence Selby, Elizabeth Selby, Fanny Milner, Elizabeth West, Nathan West, Thomas West, Gertrude Goodman *(SM)*, Henry Goodman *(SM)*, Samuel Randall, Olive Randall, Eleanor Goodman *(SM)*, Annie E. Pratt, Alfred E. Bunney, Olive Pepper, Alice M. Hemsley, Edith M. Hawkes, Ernest Hawkes
1895 Blanche Bent, Jane Elizabeth Picker, Florence Picker, Alfred Minkley, Frank Giles, George Picker, Emily Picker, Thirza Giles, Thomas Giles
1896 Gwendolen Polly Bunney, Lilian Elsie Bunney, Alice Stevens
1897 John Minkley, Frank Milner, Dorothy Elizth Bunney *(By)*
1898 Beatrice Alice Bunney, Martha Hughes, Herbert Bunney *(By)*, Dorothy Pratt, Wilfred Dean, William Minkley, Frederick Minkley, Ruby Hawkins
1900 Charles Robert Copson, Violet L. Minkley, Edith Emily Minkley
1901 Absalom Smith, Henry Smith, Fanny Smith *(children of travelling grinder John Smith)*, Jack Hughes, Charles Benjamin Bunney *(B)*, Chas Ernest Rivett Blackwell, Daisy Cross, Ernest Cross
1902 Evelyn Bunney, Philip Horton Blackwell, George Minkley, Horace Minkley, Willie Berry, Nellie Bennett, Harry Copson
1903 Bennie Bunney, David Bunney, Bennie Hemsley, Ella Berry, William Carter, Clara Carter, Lily Carter, Frank Carter
1904 Alice May Minkley, Muriel Minkley, Arnold W. Watson, Vernon Watson, Gertrude Ford, Fanny Buttery, Saml A. Bunney *(B)*
1905 Bernard C. Hornsby, Ivy A.E. Hornsby
1906 Ellen F. Walters, Lawson W Walters, Arthur Wm Boulter, Harriet Boulter, George Seaton Boulter, Frank Boulter, Beatrice Amy Bates, Alice Burgess, Margaret H. Paterson
1907 Florence Burton, Maud Burton, Harry Burton, John Burton, Doris Woolley, Wm Ernest Paterson, William J. Bates, Edith Gretchen Mills, Doris Minkley, Violet Lloyd, Emily May Lloyd
1908 Olive Woolley, Victor Knox, Maggie Knox, Minnie Sharpe, Ada Sharpe, Janet Paterson, Eric Baxter, Mabel Baxter, Albert E. Cousins, Doris Cousins
1909 Frederick Lloyd, Dora Preston, Arthur Sharman, Hetty Sharman, Willie Illsley, Kitty Illsley, Alfred Higgs, Charles Higgs, Jack Woolley
1910 June Tomlin, George S. Phillips, May Beers, George L. Lloyd, Herbert Minkley, Harold A. Burgess, Ellen Heggs, Laurie Paterson, Phyllis Lucy Beers, Frances Needham *(c/o)*, Gerald Phillips
1911 Leslie Everard Bunney, Mary Talbot *(c/o)*, Kathleen Minkley, Albert Edward Cousins *(c/o)*, Frances A Needham *(c/o)*, Florence E. Hepworth *(c/o)*

1912 Maud Annie Wells, Fanny Gertrude Bates, Frederick Needham, Elsie M Green *(c/o)*, Evelyn M Minkley, Ronald Crampton *(c/o)*, Malcolm Paterson

1913 Percival William Lloyd, M. L. Nicholson *(c/o)*, Amy Shepherdson *(c/o)*, John C Burgess, Charles Edw Minkley, Eileen V. Bunney

1914 Marjorie Henrietta Goward, Kenneth R. Paterson, Gertrude M. Farmer *(c/o)*, Kathleen P. Bates, Kathleen G. Hoult, John W. Leatherland *(c/o)*, Laurie Paterson, Frank Johnson

1915 Joseph Edw Buttery, William H. Buttery, Kathleen M. Holt, Frederick A. Holt, Charles Leslie Holt, Samuel Driver, Jim Driver, Lily Driver, Phyllis M. Bunney *(By)*, William Farmer *(c/o)*, Wesley Arthur Roland Black *(c/o)*, Lilian Underwood, *(c/o)* Gladys Mary Lloyd, Geo. Thomas Adnett, Kathleen M. Glover, Denis Crampton *(c/o)*

1916 Ed G. Hepworth *(c/o)*, Eric V Adnett, E. Keith Paterson, Percy Holt, Frank Tomlin *(c/o)*, Louis Tomlin *(c/o)*, Hilda Green *(c/o)*, Cyril Green *(c/o)*, Gladys E. Minkley, Millicent L. Nicholson *(c/o)*

1917 Kenneth J. Laundon *(c/o)*, Frank Johnson *(c/o)*, May Holliday *(c/o)*, Noelle Watson *(c/o)*, Millicent Hewitt *(c/o)*, Winifred Draper *(c/o)*, Irene Woolley *(c/o)*, Bernice Woolley *(c/o)*

1918 Dorothy F. Lloyd, Kathleen A. Talbot *(c/o)*

1919 Albt. John F. Glover *(RP)*, Florence A. Austin *(c/o)*, Ernest Adnett, Eileen M. Doubleday *(c/o)*

1920 Frank Butcher *(c/o)*, Mary Green, Sidney Ed Lloyd, John Ambrose Copson, Irene Elsie Minkley

1921 Ethel M. Hoult, Dorothy M. Adnett

1922 Horace Agnew *(c/o)*, J. Charles Copson, Kathleen M. Bunney, Elsie M. Copson, Jean Copson, Mary Smith *(RP)*, Ida Smith *(RP)*, Jack Shepherdson *(SwCamp)*, John R.S. Maycock *(SwCamp)*, Dorothy M. Maycock *(SwCamp)*, Joyce B. Maycock *(SwCamp)*, Arthur E. Johnson *(c/o)*

1923 Edwin L.G. Glover *(RP)*, Geoffrey C. Hoult, Harry Allen *(c/o)*, John Botterill, John Ch Copson *(RP)*, Herbert Brewin *(SwCamp)*, Jack Webster *(SwCamp)*, Herbert Roy Lloyd, Alfred Geo Copson *(RP)*, Harold Hepworth, James Hawkyard

1924 Leslie Bird, Nellie Bowden *(SwCamp)*, John J. Bowden *(SwCamp)*, Sidney Shepherdson *(c/o)*, Henry Farmer *(c/o)*, Aubrey R. Ed Reeve *(SwCamp)*

1925 Isabel A. Allen *(SwCamp)*, Beatrice Allen *(SwCamp)*, Mary R. Bunney, Winifred May Lane *(SwWdFm)*, H. Ray Bickley, Beatrice M. Bunney, David Leslie Copson *(RP)*, Margaret A. Lewin

1926 Joan L.M. Harrison, Violet W. Bloxham *(c/o)*, Betty May Sellars *(SwCamp)*, Winifred Gosling *(c/o)*

1927 Dennis Copson, Thom. Geo. Minkley, Brian Green, Frank A. Woolley *(T)*, Dorothy M. Copson *(RP)*, Dorothy K.M. Minkley

1928 Ralph S. Harrison, Joan E. Simpson, Norman Rue *(c/o)*, Stanley Ed Lockton *(SwCamp)*, Phyllis M. Low, Frank G. Spence, Henry Roy Knights

1929 James Morgan *(c/o)*, Gladys K. Knights, Bryan Cecil Pepper *(By)*, Norman Ch Pepper *(By)*, Charles H. Bilby *(c/o)*, Betty M. Sellers *(WE)*, Gladys N. Snodin *(By)*, Ralph E. Snodin *(By)*

1930 Doreen C. Frost *(Cr)*, Walter C. Littleworth *(Cr)*, Winifred V. Bloxam, G. Adeline Pepper *(By)*, Ian H. Hammond *(RP)*

1931 Gladys M.A. Dickens *(Cr)*, Edna M. Dickens *(Cr)*, John A. Townsend, Vera Baker *(SwCamp)*, Maurice E.C. Bunney

1932 Mary Marshall *(WE)*, James R.S. Barton *(RP)*, Jean Eliz Snodin, Alice Vera Ringrose, Wesson Tom Dickens *(RoecliffeLane)*, Barbara M. Gamble *(WE)*, Adella R. Welch *(Cr)*, William Stanley Adkin *(HGC)*, Kathleen M. Richards *(T)*, Marjorie D. Stone *(CrWW)*, Hubert Partridge, Joseph Hemsley *(T)*, Christine D. Johnson *(Cr)*, Robert B. Johnson *(Cr)*

1933 Margaret J. Gamble *(WE)*, Patricia A. Burrows*(Cr)*, Arnold Keith Harrison *(Cr)*, Patricia M. Staynes *(Cr)*, Leonard Horn *(SwCamp)*, Nellie D. Atkinson *(RoecliffeLane)*

1934 Margaret Adkins *(CrResLodge)*, C. Margaret Wheeler *(Cr)*, William Hadley *(Cr)*, Ernest Hadley *(Cr)*, Albert Hadley *(Cr)*, Sheila M. Chantrell *(By)*, Reginald W. Chantrell *(By)*, Shirley M. Staynes *(Cr)*, Barbara E. Bunney

Book Two

1935 Muriel Brenda Chantrell *(By)*, Patricia E.H. Ward *(c/o)*, Kathleen Emily Perry *(Cr)*, Audrey Marshall *(WE)*, Alfred Ringrose, Faith Kathleen Banbury, Percy Henry Arnett *(c/o)*, Joan Arnett *(c/o)*, Owen Arnett *(c/o)*

1936 Leonard Harry Copson *(RP)*, Jean Elizabeth Stone *(CropRes)*, Mary H. Minkley, Dorothy M. Rudkin *(RP)*, Gordon Edgar Bray *(RP)*, Peter William Lloyd, Colin Minkley, John Wm Leatherland, Janet Marshall *(WE)*, Harry H. Woolley *(RoeManor)*, Margaret Lily Leader

1937 Robert Edgar Adkin *(HGates)*, Gladys Muriel Dean, Vera Mary Croxton, Joyce Louisa Croxton, Sadie Alice Edwards, Joan Edwards, Terence Peter Clements, Pamela Anne Marriott, John Adkin, Pearl Mavena M Pentelow, Philip John L. Pentelow

1938 Sheila Ann Haynes *(RP)*, Margaret A. Ringrose, Leonard Ernest Holiday, Richard Geo Washington, Ivy May Washington, Neville Charles Hyman *(RP)*, Josephine Cecilia Staynes *(Cr)*, Gwen Margaret Rudkin *(RP)*

1939 Annie Patricia Lloyd, William David John Rutt, John Victor Whiles *(W)*, Edith Mary Sills *(RP)*, Robert Burrage *(c/o)*, Barbara Burrage *(c/o)*,Kenneth Hollocks *(c/o)*, Vera Hollocks *(c/o)*, Jean McClintock *(RP)*, Patrick L.A. Godfrey *(c/o)*, Leonard E. Sanson *(c/o)*, Peter Murray *(c/o)*

1940 John Roger Boulton *(RP)*, Maureen Alice McCrum *(CrRes)*, Kenneth Stanley Hyman *(RP)*, Robert Michael Jelley *(RP)*, Paul

William Murray *(Cr)*, William Fenn *(c/o)*,Sylvia Moughton *(c/o)*, Davie Peter Campbell *(c/o)*, Jean Lowe *(c/o)*, Pamela Ruth Lane *(SwWdFm)*, Ernest Henry Gregory *(c/o)*, Irene Frances Hardy *(SwCamp)*, Peter Frederick Hardy *(SwCamp)*, Patricia June Thompson *(c/o)*, Elizabeth Calladine *(c/o)*, Charles Calladine *(c/o)*, Mary Calladine *(c/o)*, June Black *(c/o)*, Jill Black *(c/o)*, Donald Whitmore *(c/o)*

1941 Gordon Blair *(c/o)*, Roma Goodger *(c/o)*, Winifred Maguire *(c/o)*, John Hewett *(c/o)*, Gillian Hosack *(c/o)*, John Maguire *(c/o)*, John Theobald *(c/o)*, Joyce Winifred Keeling *(c/o)*, Brenda Margaret Goodger, David Albert Asher *(RP)*, John Wilford Asher *(RP)*, Janet Black *(SwCamp)*, Patricia Allen *(SwCamp)*, Howard Selwyn Chapman *(Cr)*, Edward B. Ratcliffe, Doreen Hazel Rudkin *(M)*

1942 Andrée D. Raiwet *(c/o)*, Monica Eleanor Smith *(T)*, Dorothy Jean Neal *(c/o)*, David Lambourne *(T)*, Gordon Robert Harrison *(Q)*, Michael Theobald *(c/o)*, John Charles Simmons, Peter Geoffrey Gladwin *(c/o)*, James Stanley Adkin *(WE)*, Eileen Holiday, Joyce Mary Ringrose, John Edward Haynes, Derek Charles Ball, Sylvia Josephine Fay *(SwWdFm)*, Peter Bailey *(c/o)*, James Alfred Darey, George Patrick Darey,

1943 Jean Mapletoft, David Robert Smith *(RP)*, Pamela Mary Lloyd *(RP)*, Ida Ruth Asher *(RP)*, Brian Roy Minkley, June Margaret Pratt *(Cr)*, Alfred Banbury, Jacqueline Elizabeth Ann Pape *(c/o)*, Mary Lavinia Lambourne *(T)*

1944 David John Hunt, Bernard Arthur Stevenson, Georges Gillis *(c/o)*, Margaret Adrienne Hulse *(c/o)*, Charles Henry Wallace *(T)*, Freda Maureen Haynes *(M)*, David Reginald Simmons *(RP)*, Ruth Rubens *(T)*, Jennifer Ann Wardle *(RP)*, Alan Parsons *(c/o)*, Michael Vane *(c/o)*, Dorothy Dewberry *(c/o)*, Shirley Spice *(c/o)*, Basil Lee *(c/o)*, Margaret Lee *(c/o)*, Derek Lee *(c/o)*, David Lee *(c/o)*, Brenda Parsons *(c/o)*, Anthony Dewberry *(c/o)*, Douglas Matthalie *(c/o)*, Barbara Matthalie *(c/o)*, Brian Hunter *(c/o)*, Rosemarie Bettyne Carole Copson, Alan Howard *(c/o)*, Elaine Mildred Cooke *(c/o)*, David Hall *(c/o)*, Janet Mary Rudkin *(c/o)*, Neville George Pepper *(c/o)*

1945 Caroline Mary Cardwell *(RP)*, Dawn Elizabeth Felse *(RP)*, Robt Anthony Wessel *(RP)*, Richard Davison Crockett *(RP)*, David Paterson *(RP)*, Neville Percival, Norman Percival, Maureen McClintock *(RP)*, Diana Elizabeth Gristwood *(RP)*, Jennifer Flude *(Cr)*, Richard Flude *(Cr)*, Valerie Margaret Adnett *(T)*

1946 Margaret Handley, William Paul Sharpe *(Cr)*, Peter Wm Lawrence *(RP)*, José Barbara Hewitt *(Cr)*, Richard Adkin *(Cr)*, David Allen North *(R)*, Cynthia Mary Copson, Margaret Christine Simpson *(RP)*, David Morris *(c/o)*, Peter Morris *(c/o)*, John David Dixon *(RP)*, Michael Raymond East *(c/o)*,Sheila Walters *(c/o)*, Richard Walters *(c/o)*

1947 Roger Dixon *(RP)*, Jennifer Kinch *(Cr)*, David M. Boulter *(Cr)*, Geoffrey Turner *(Cr)*, Michael Lancashire *(c/o)*, Michael Hudson

(RP), Sarah Ann Boon *(R)* John Henry Crockett *(RP)*, John Adrian Simmons *(RP)*, Barbara Summerland, Martyn Graham Lindrea *(RP)*, Sally Wessel *(RP)*, Angela Mary Phillips *(RP)*, Gillian Rosemary North *(R)*, Raymond Ward *(M)*, James Andrew Symington *(RP)*, Francis Joseph Spieler *(c/o)*, Rosamund Hill *(RP)*, Patricia Mary Smith, Brenda Josephine Heighton

1948 Desmond Peter Maxwell *(RP)*, Sally Elizabeth Copson, Anthony Cook, Ann Patricia Cook, Gillian Ann Smith *(RP)*, Jacqueline Elizabeth Hudson *(RP)*, Robert Adkin *(Cr)*, Carole Frances Holland *(c/o)*, Patrick Bernard Wallace *(c/o)*, Clive Malcolm Hill *(c/o)*

1949 Malcolm Alfred Meakin, Michael John Lockyer *(RP)*, Jennifer Harris *(RP)*, Michael Walter Brown *(RP)*, Paul Cook *(M)*, Heather Joyce Edenbrow, Rodney Edward Lloyd, Derek Charles Ball, June Georgina Ball, Roger Neil Wardle *(RP)*, Michael Peter Tillotson, Janet Elizabeth Foster *(RP)*, Gerald Ernest Humphrey *(RP)*, Gillian Ruth Humphrey *(RP)*, John Malcolm Harmer *(RP)*, Joy Elizabeth Harmer *(R)*

1950 Michael John Copson *(RP)*, Sandra Victoria Ball, Guy Christopher Scott Baker *(RP)*, Barry Nigel Freestone *(RP)*, Nellie Patricia Bowers *(RP)*, Linda Ann Wormley *(RP)*, Robert Alan Wormley *(RP)*, Clive William Wormley *(RP)*, Bayoane Rosemary Romayne Twigger, David Patrick John Basham *(RP)*, Dorothy Ann Smith *(RP)*

1951 Alan Terence Simpson *(RP)*, Allison Elizabeth North *(R)*, George Alexander Noble Dean *(RP)*, Cedric Paul Simmons *(RP)*, Gordon Barratt *(Cr)*, Stewart John Hardy Symington *(RP)*, Jocelyn Mary Longhurst *(RP)*

1952 Carolyn Clare Ward *(M)*, Catherine Wallis *(By)*, David Brown *(RP)*, Terence Bexley *(c/o)*, Robin Cook, John Kemp Hives *(RP)*, John Hewitt *(R)*, Dawn Hewitt *(R)*, Virginia Beard *(Cr)*, Susan Symington *(RP)*, Nicholas Robt Harmer *(RP)*, Timothy James Harmer *(RP)*, Arthur Dean *(RP)*, Stuart Donaldson Musgrove

1953 Richard John Orton, Christine Ruth Orton, Peter Charles Bowler *(M)*, Diana Margaret Basham *(RP)*, Paul David Barratt *(Cr)*, Graham Dennis Price, Martin Greenwood *(RP)*, Judith Hickling *(RP)*, John Arthur Stone, Roger John Ambrose Copson, Jane Lesley Copson, Patricia Susan Simmonds *(RP)*, Patrick Simon Lane *(T)*, Keith Handley, Julie Margaret Tibbert *(RP)*, Christina Jayne Symon *(RP)*, Ian Christopher Fraser Symon *(RP)*

1954 Mark Andrew Lane *(T)*, Kevin Francis Dobbs *(By)*, Helen Joyce Simmons *(RP)*, Anthony Neil Ward *(M)*, Barry Payne, Kathryn Sonia Towers *(RP)*, William Cook, Diana Margaret Hooker *(Cr)*, Timothy Nevil Hooker *(Cr)*

1955 Paul Rodric Jessop *(RP)*, Nicolette Susan Woodcock, Carol Kathleen Simmons *(RP)*, Paul Cedric Harrison, Malcolm Anthony Pollard *(Cr)*, Susan Lorraine Mutch, Nigel James Copson, George Allen Bowler *(M)*, Lynn Marion Haynes *(M)*, Alison Margaret Hickling *(RP)*, Susan Hill *(R)*, Marion Christine Weatherall, Enid Mary Bream *(Cr)*

1956 Jane Elizabeth Orton, Geoffrey Neville Price, Beatrice Marie-Louise Schnedl *(RP)*, John Ashley Chapman *(Cr)*, Rosemary Elizabeth Martin *(Cr)*, Elizabeth Teresa Adkin *(Cr)*, Anthony Frank Storer *(Cr)*, Stephen Clive Cook, Rayner Paul Mott, Anne Mutch, Sheila Mary Copson *(RP)*

1957 James Christopher Brabbs *(Cr)*, Lynne Shelley Southam *(Cr)*, Barbara Kay Mott, Clive Louis Aucott*(M)*, Anthony Frank Dixon *(Cr)*, Stephen Brett Lane *(Cr)*

1958 Colin Clive Shaw, Raymond John Wm Shaw, Susan Melanie Bunney *(M)*, Margaret Ann Thwaites *(RT)*, Bernard John Fowkes *(Cr)*, Charles Anthony Barnes *(RP)*, Richard Fredk Watts *(R)*, Elizabeth Mary Simmons *(RP)*, Ian Hunt *(RP)*, Neil Hunt *(RP)*, Margaret Keightley *(R)*, David Keightley *(R)*, Jennifer Joan Towers *(RP)*, Glenda Joy Price

1959 Giampaolo Seira *(RP)*, Jacqueline Fowkes *(Cr)*, Christine Fowkes *(Cr)*, Richard John Timson *(Cr)*, Sarah Margaret Brookman *(W)*, Peter Barrow Williams *(Cr)*, Donald John Livingstone, Nigel John Williams *(RP)*, James Rodney Groves *(RP)*, Lorraine Grace Ruth Aucott *(M)*, Mark Anthony Egglestone *(Cr)*, Angela Mary Williams *(Cr)*

1960 Carolyn Mary Hart *(RP)*, Michelle Anne Goodman *(Cr)*, George Robert Willson *(RP)*, Richard Hambly *(RP)*, Jacqueline Henfrey *(Crc)*, William David Brookman *(W)*, Judith Mary Bunney *(M)*, Sally Kathleen Hardee *(Cr)*

1961 Simon Charles Copson *(RP)*, Elizabeth Joyce Thomas *(RP)*, Jane Wornley *(RP)*, Keith Wornley *(RP)*, Geoffrey Peter Watts *(R)*, Wendy Jean Shaltock *(Cr)*, Geoffrey Paul Shaltock *(Cr)*, Nigel Bruce Waller, James Edward Shilvock *(WE)*, Mark Ivor Wright *(RP)*, Andrew Brook-Lawson, Cheril Jane Dorman, Nicholas James Gardner *(RP)*

1962 Claire Keenan Barton *(RT)*, Andrew James Copson *(RP)*, Christopher Dickens *(RP)*, Gerard Mark Waller, Martin Parnell *(Cr)*, Norma Chapman *(R)*, Angela Kemm *(RP)*, Elizabeth Joan Storer *(Cr)*, Mary Fiona Brook-Lawson, Christine Mary Adcock *(RP)*

1963 Dallas Elaine Percy *(Cr)*, Stephen Murray Adcock *(RP)*, Mark William Bunney *(M)*, Linda Jane Squires *(Cr)*, Michael Fowkes *(Cr)*, Jeremy William Hercock *(Cr)*, Anthony Charles George *(Cr)*, Christopher John Thomas *(RP)*, Sonia Ingrid Kropp *(M)*, Mark James Vann Halman *(RP)*, Rosetta Ann Green *(T)*, Christopher Martin Wesson *(RP)*, Paul Nigel Stokes *(RP)*, Angela Jacqueline Stokes *(RP)*, Michael James Penny *(RP)*, Elinor Booth *(Cr)*, Peter Anthony Davies, Kathryn Jane Farmer *(Cr)*

1964 Lloyd Wright *(RP)*, Neil Scotney Henfrey *(Cr)*, Timothy William Shilvock *(WE)*, Michael James Carr, Richard Geoffrey Pratt, Malcolm Noel Dexter *(WE)*, Sally Chell *(Cr)*, Alec Roderick Rich *(Cr)*, Elizabeth Jane Green *(Cr)*, Bruce Keith Pollard *(Cr)*, Yvonne Jeanette Aucott *(M)*

Appendix C: Swithland School Admissions 1865–1980 (July)

1965 Timothy Warner *(Cr)*, Denise Jocelyn Beaumont *(RP)*, Nigel Kelsey Beaumont *(RP)*, Wendy Michelle Beaumont *(RP)*, Nicole Martine Beaumont *(RP)*, Sarah Louise Bunney *(R)*, Robert Mark Thorndyke *(Cr)*, Julie Ann Thorndyke *(Cr)*, Nigel James Davies, Jonathan Barry Hercock *(Cr)*, Ann Leatherland, Karen Mary Labrom *(RP)*, Robert John Squires *(Cr)*, Charlotte Anne Jay *(Cr)*, Julia Eve Jay *(Cr)*, Sally Ann Wainwright *(RP)*, Nicholas Charles Wainwright *(RP)*, Peter Robert Lloyd, Adrian Charles Ashton *(RP)*

1966 Mark Thomas Tyrrell *(RP)*, Simon Mark Ashton *(RP)*, Frances Cook *(Cr)*, Robert Walton *(Cr)*, Stephen Martin Beaumont *(RP)*, Joanna Bunney *(R)*, Paul Francis Reynolds *(RP)*, Niall Rory Dexter *(WE)*, Linda Penny *(RP)*, Julian Waller, Donovan Sinclair Howden *(Cr)*, Kathryn Deborah Lindsay *(Cr)*, Rona Christine Lindsay *(Cr)*, Amanda Jane Lindsay *(Cr)*

1967 Ian Barrie Thorndyke *(Cr)*, Timothy Bentley *(W)*, Katherine Bentley *(W)*, Joanne Chell *(Cr)*, Mark Charles Bird, Chantral Trudi Adcock *(Cr)*, Murray Warner *(Cr)*, Amanda Lloyd

1968 Deborah Sarah White, Mark Prince *(Cr)*, Helen Thomas *(RP)*, Sheena Rich *(Cr)*, John Dingley, Timothy Self *(RP)*, Anthony Rowntree Clifford *(RP)*, Susan Rowntree Clifford *(RP)*,

1969 Simon Harrington *(RP)*, Andrew David Price, Miranda Long *(WE)*, James Patrick Long *(WE)*, Mark Warde-Norbury *(R)*, David Crowther *(RP)*, Sharon Self *(RP)*, Catherine Louise Hern *(Cr)*, James Ward Andrews, Richard Briers, Kerry Jane Wesson *(RP)*, Jane Dingley, Jennifer Elizabeth Needham *(RP)*, Nicholas Butterfield *(RT)*, Annette Susanne Thompstone *(Cr)*

1970 Harold Worsley *(RP)*, Frederick Worsley *(RP)*, Alison Jayne Clark *(B)*, Sarah Ann Clark *(B)*, Helen Margaret Cox *(RP)*, Antony Paul Blackmore *(B)*, Catherine Jane Blackmore *(B)*, Claire Louise Willis *(A)*, Dorothy Juliet Catharine Jones *(RP)*, James Della-Porta *(RP)*, Jeremy Harrington *(RP)*, Edward Wheeler *(NL)*, Benjamin Michael G. Wright, Christopher J. Gidley Wright, David William Smith *(RT)*, Alistair Warde-Norbury *(R)*

1971 Matthew Benjamin Wheeler *(NL)*, John Charles Hirst *(WE)*, Edward Anthony Strange *(RP)*, Julie Bocock *(RP)*, Matthew Douglas Scott Farnham *(Q)*, Nicholas John Edward Northam *(RP)*, Simon Gregory Bolton *(M)*

1972 Ruth Michelle Eames, Caroline Jane Brown *(RP)*, Laura Jane Harrison, Lucy Anne Harrison, Rachel Elizabeth Clark *(B)*, Joanne Penny *(RP)*, Caroline Elizabeth Hunt *(W)*, Daniel Hall *(H)*, Timothy Hall *(H)*

1973 Noelle Sylvia Worsley *(RP)*, Helen Louise Moore *(Cr)*, Shaun Wilkins *(A)*, Rachel Deakin, Michael John Jeyes, Emma Katharine Whall *(WE)*, Georgina Bocock *(RP)*, Sarah Frances Northam *(RP)*, Andrew Anthony Jeffrey, Jonathan Wright, Samantha Louise Semple *(SwWdFm)*,

1974 Andrew Richard Evans *(RP)*, John Nicholas Hunt *(W)*, Michael

Eames, Sarah Willis *(A)*, Mark Wallet *(H)*, Paul Wallet *(H)*, Howard James Long *(WE)*, Helen Louise Briers, Susan Stephanie Keates *(A)*, Emma Jane Jordan *(R)*

1975 Marcus Harewood Caston *(NL)*, Alistair William Kershaw *(RP)*, Matthew Marshall *(WE)*, Jonathan Steven Peters *(RP)*, Verity Leigh Russell *(Q)*, Phillipa Dora Norwood *(WE)*, Laurence Charles Hyman *(W)*, Richard Andrew Buswell *(RP)*, Joshua Alwyn Rory Fothergill *(Ba)*, Emily Rose Hodgkiss *(WE)*, Jenny Louise Warrilow *(Cr)*, Annamaria Carril

1976 Alexander Chandler *(Cr)*, Jane Marie Wilkins *(A)*, Jessica Louise Salisbury *(Q)*, Duncan Rupert Keates *(A)*, Robin Oliver Mault, Aaron Clarkson *(M)*, Christine Smith *(Cr)*, Nigel Dorian Copely

1977 Sarah Louise Hunt *(Q)*, Wayne Anthony Kinch *(RP)*, Sandra Louise Wilkins *(A)*, Gillian Katharine Angela Walters, Nicola Jane Buswell *(RP)*, William George Jordan *(W)*, Jeremy Daniel Peters *(RP)*, Beverley Ruth Ellis *(RP)*, Eloise Ann Russell *(Q)*, Max Harrison, Rebecca Hodges *(RP)*, Nicola Jane Morris *(RP)*

1978 Philippa Thornton Knott *(RP)*, Rebecca Mary Wheeler *(NL)*, Suzanne Clare Ledger *(RP)*, Katharine Ledger *(RP)*, Karl Gray

1979 Simon Anthony Henig *(Lancaster)*, Alexander Charles Capleton *(RP)*, Juliette Mary Leverment *(Cr)*, Christopher Thomas Hodges *(RP)*, Jennifer Elizabeth McHugh, William Henry McHugh

1980 Stephen Smith *(Cr)*, Stefan James March *(R)*, Timothy Robert Hardwicke, Patrick James Knott *(RP)*

New Register from Autumn Term 1980

APPENDIX D

Parish Registers

A royal injunction of Henry VIII, dated 29th September 1538, by Thomas Cromwell, Vicar General, ordered all parochial clergy to keep parish registers.

> The curate of every parish church shall keep one book or register, which book he shall every Sunday take forth, and in the presence of churchwardens, or one of them, write and record in the same all the weddings, christenings and burials made the whole week before; and for every time that the same shall be omitted, shall forfeit to the said church three shillings and four pence.

The instruction was, however, widely disregarded. The injunction was renewed in 1547 and in 1559 under Elizabeth I.

These early records were often written on paper. In 1597 a constitution, made with royal approval by the archbishop and clergy of the province of Canterbury, enforced the regular keeping of parchment register books, and carefully stipulated their proper conservation. The entries from the old paper books were to be transcribed into the parchment registers. The constitution ordered the incumbent or churchwardens, one month after Lady Day each year, to make a copy of their register for the previous year up to Lady Day and send it for preservation to the Registry of their diocese. These copies are known as Bishop's Transcripts.

This order was also largely neglected. In 1603 it was reinforced by a further order, embodied in the 70th Canon of that year, requiring that, in every parish church and chapel within the realm, shall be provided one parchment book at the charge of the parish, wherein shall be written the day and the year of every christening, wedding and burial which had taken place in that parish since the time that the law was first made in that behalf, so far as the ancient books thereof can be procured, but especially since the beginning of the reign of the late Queen. Not all the returns were sent to the diocesan centres; some remained in the archdeaconry registries.

In 1653 an Act of Parliament during the Commonwealth directed that all persons should be married by declaration before a Justice of the Peace. The act made new regulations, appointing lay officials, called 'Registers' who would keep the registers, entering all births, marriages and burials, omitting any reference to baptism. William Danvers of Swithland (1591–1656), as a

Justice of the Peace, was one of those who swore in the new Registers, and presided at many of these new civil marriages. The Commonwealth regulations were set aside at the Restoration of the monarchy in 1660, and the previous regulations restored. The civil marriages which had taken place were acknowledged as legal (12Car2 c33), but marriage could thereafter only take place through the established church. The result was an increase in the number of clandestine marriages.

Further legislation of 1695 and 1700 ordered that dissenters' births be reported to the vicar, either to be added to his register or entered in a separate book. These laws were not universally effective.

Continuous proper registrations of baptisms, marriages, and burials for Swithland date from 1700. Some earlier bishop's transcripts do, however, survive: transcripts from the Swithland register for the years 1616, 1624 and 1633–38. Transcripts to the Peculiar of Groby, of which Swithland was a part, also survive for the years 1687, 1695, 1701 and 1706–08. In addition, there is a compilation, consisting of fifty-four mixed entries of births, baptisms, marriages and burials for the years 1676–81; the single sheet is entitled 'an account of what Christenings, Marriages and Burials that have beene (soe far as we can understand) in the parish of Swithland since Mr. Thomas Jackson took possession of that Rectory'. Finally, there are single page registers for the years 1684, 1692 and 1698.

The Swithland registers do not contain much additonal information above the statutory information that was required. There are many entries of children 'received into the congregation of Christ's flock' with notes of their private baptisms, or of their having been 'named'. An entry in 1788 records the baptism of Mary, Elizabeth and Martha Newby, with a note that they were 'at one birth'.

Before 1753 most non-conformists were in practice married in church, but not all. Lord Hardwicke's Marriage Act of 1753 (22Geo.2 c33) was intended as 'An Act for the preventing of clandestine marriages'. It ordered that all marriages, except those of Quakers and Jews, must take place in parish churches. The effect of the Act was to make common law marriage (which is what, technically, these non-conformist marriages had been) illegal.

Another Act of 1783 (23Geo.3 c67) imposed a stamp duty of 3d on the entry of any burial (except of persons buried from a workhouse or hospital, or at the sole expense of any charity) in the register of any parish, precinct or place in Great Britain. A similar duty of 3d was imposed on the entry of any birth or christening (except where parents receive any parish relief) in such a register. Payment of the stamp duty would have been an additional cost to the surplice fee paid to the minister. It is not surprising that some poorer residents failed to have their children baptised. In about 1802 the rector of Swithland compiled a list in the register of children who had been named or privately baptised, but not yet brought to church. In the list is a reference to John Deakin, 4 Feb 1801, 14 weeks old, and another [child] not yet named. A note records that the mother had said 'times were too hard to have a christening'. A later hand has added the comment 'and the silly rector received the excuse!!!'

From 1812, baptisms, burials and marriages had to be kept in separate books, in an approved form. The Parochial Registers Act 1812 required that registers of baptisms and of burials – be kept in separate books of parchment or durable paper by the incumbent – in a form specified in the act, and supplied by HM printers. Marriage registers were to be supplied by the Registrar General. The registers were to be kept in a locked iron chest in a dry and secure place in the incumbent's house or in the parish church.

Legislation passed in 1836 provided for the civil registration of births and deaths, and allowed marriages to be registered civilly. From 1837 therefore, parish registers record only the baptisms, marriages and burials that take place in the parish church. Before 1837, burials of non-conformists normally took place in parish churchyards, and the death recorded in parish registers, although some chapels had their own burial grounds. Non-conformist births were not usually entered in parish registers, since the Church of England recorded baptism, and not birth.

Occasionally, the Swithland registers give more information than bare names and dates. Thus, in the year 1828, Elizabeth Hemsley died of consumption; her husband Joseph Hemsley died less than four months later 'killed by a blast from the Pitts'; and her brother Thomas Brookhouse died five months after that 'killed by a fall from a tree'. In 1862 William Bunney was killed by lightening. Later Registers state the place of abode. A poignant entry by James Murray Dixon in April 1917 records the death of his son, Henry Edward Otto Murray Dixon, at the age of thirty-one in the 1914–18 war: 'By someone – somewhere in France – a man of peace, he fell in war giving his life for others'.

More recent legislation has provided for the placement of registers that are not being used in a Diocesan Records Office, or in an approved Records Office. The Parochial Registers and Records Measure 1929[1] gave authority to the Bishop to require that records be kept in a Diocesan Record Office. All but the current Swithland registers are now deposited at the Leicestershire County Records Office.

---

1. Updated, The Parochial Registers Measure 1978, amended 2003, Office of Public Sector Information website

St Leonard's Church, Swithland: Baptisms

ABBOT, Catherine: Mary 1745.
ADAMS, Albert Edward & [wife]: Albert Edward 1909.
ADAMS: Fay Marie (b1964) 1979.
ADAMS, John & Charlotte: George Handley 1865, William Henry 1868, Mary Jane 1873, Alfred James 1873, Charlotte 1875.
ADAMS, John & Eliza: Sarah Jane 1871, Emily 1873, Matthew Thomas 1874, Martha Ann 1876, Florry 1878, Joe 1880, Margaret Eliza 1883, Albert Edward 1887, Matilda 1888.
ADAMS, Thomas (labourer) & Martha: John 1846, Matthew Hodge 1851, William 1853.
ADNETT, George (farm labourer) & Alice: Dorothy Mabel 1916.
ALLEN, Christopher Maclaren (industrial chemist) & Sally Elizabeth: Rachel Elizabeth 1966, Charles Maclaren 1969.
ALLEN, Charles Maclaren (bank manager) & Joanne Elizabeth (bank manager): Georgia Elizabeth 2003, Joshua Maclaren 2001
ANDJELIC, Nigel Dursan Rade & **FOSTER-SMITH**, Sharon: Edward Rad March 1997.
ASBURY, Barrie Charles (catering manager) & Janet Pauline: Lisa Marie (b1974) 1980.
ASHER, Albert Henry Gordon (soldier) & Mabel Elen: Gordon Lionel 1916, Doreen 1920 & Joan 1920 (twins).
AXELRAD, Paul Peter (company director) & Penny Anne: Holly Emma 1986.
BABINGTON, Matthew Drake (clerk) & Hannah: Churchill 1821.
BAILEY, John Leggett (research chemist) & Margaret: Michael Leggett 1947.
BAINES, John Lewis (air force) & Shirley: Sally Joan Eleanor 1941.
BAKER, Daniel & [wife]: Edward 1625.
BAKER, George Henry (merchant) & Phyllis Harriett: Guy Christopher Scott 1945.
BAKER, John & [wife]: William 1625.
BALL, Derek Benjamin Owen (engineer inspector) & Georgina Mary: Sandra Victoria 1945.
BALL, Richard (husbandman) & Elizabeth: Mary 1635, William 1638.
BALL, William & Ethel Adelaide: Audrey Penelope (b1930) 1968.
BANBURY, Alfred Henry (farmer) & Phyllis Ann: Simonne Caroline 1961, Christopher Andrew Charles 1963.
BANBURY, Harry Andrew (farmer) & Kathleen Ada: Alfred Henry 1938.
BANCROFT, [husband](deceased) & Helen: Jean Mary (b1936) 1952.
BANCROFT, Harold James (engineer) & Eftig Judie: Diane Anne 1963, Kathryn Dawn 1964.
BARBER, Roger William (civil engineer) & Brenda: Jane Suzanne Walters 1951.
BARLOW, John (labourer) & Diana: John 1835.
BARNES, George (shop assistant supervisor) & Ida Patricia: Deborah Elizabeth 1967.
BARNET, William (blacksmith) & Anne: Anne 1708, John 1711, Mary 1712, Elizabeth 1715, William 1719, William 1721.
BARRY, Joseph (schoolmaster) & Rebecca: Thomas 1831, Walter 1834.
BARTON, Clement Thornton (newspaper manager) & Elfrida: Thelma Thornton (b1921) 1926, Barrie Keith Thornton (adopted) 1926.
BARTON, James Reginald Searle (doctor) & Sheila: Brian Guy James 1959.
BARVILL, David (labourer) & Sarah: Jane 1822, Elizabeth 1822.
BATE, Harold (company director) & Laura Joy: Graham Paul (b1953) 1962.
BATES, Daniel (labourer) & Jinny: Ann 1786, Daniel 1788, Jane 1790, Fanny 1793, Sarah 1795, James 1797, Hannah 1800, Catherine 1805.
BATES, Daniel (farmer/labourer) & Frances: Ann 1817, John Warren 1819, Frances 1821, Jane 1823, Daniel 1825, Catherine 1827, James 1829, Sarah 1831, George 1836.

Appendix D: Parish Registers

BATES, Roger Marshall (company director) & Hedvig Gudrun: Katarina Suzanne 1964.
BATES, Thomas (farmer) & Juliana: William James 1839, Juliana Anne 1842, Catherine Amy 1843.
BATES, William James & Ann: Catherine Anne 1866, John Thomas 1868, William James 1869, Matthew Daykin 1871, Mary Juliana 1873.
BATES, William James (farmer) & Mary Anne: Annie Jemima 1907, Kathleen Phyllis 1914.
BATTERHAM, Ivan Michael (caretaker) & Eileen Mary: Tina Marie 1988.
BAUM, George & Elizabeth Lockton: Mary Phoebe Ethel 1877, Archibald George Lockton 1879, Ellen Elizabeth Maggie 1880, Mary Alice Mabel 1883, Sophia Rosie 1885.
BAUM, Harold & Anne: Elizabeth 1730, Thomas 1733, William 1735, Ann 1738, Mary 1740, Harold 1743.
BAUM, Harold (labourer) & Elizabeth: William 1812, Thomas 1814, Thomas 1815, Catherine 1817, Thomas 1817, Jane 1819, Joseph 1824.
BAUM, John (labourer/woodman) & Phoebe: Edward 1833, Emma 1835, Caroline Jane 1838, William 1840, Frederick 1842, Laura Fanny 1844, Martha Ann 1846, Sarah Maria 1848, Joseph Frederick 1850, Mary Elizabeth 1852, George 1854.
BAUM, Thomas & Sarah: Harold 1758.
BAUM, William & Jane: William 1765, John 1768, Jane 1770, Thomas 1776, Harold 1779, Elizabeth 1782, Joseph 1784, Elizabeth 1787.
BAXTER, Bryan Reginald (schoolmaster) & Dorothy Vera: Joan Maureen 1933.
BAXTER, Charles Edward & Edith: Charles Eric 1903.
BEACHELL, Jeremy George (life insurance underwriter) & Julia Valerie: Paul Alexander 1965.
BEASLEY, John (slatepitman) & Mary: Samuel 1772, Mary 1774, [dau] 1776, William 1778, John 1780, Thomas 1784, Henry 1791.
BEEBY, Brian Joseph (farmer) & Janet Margaret: Laura Kate 1982, Jennie Mary 1983, David John 1985.
BEEBY, Edward (farm labourer) & Sarah: William (b1892) 1928.
BEEDELL, Timothy John (personnel officer) & Pamela Mary: George Mark Findhorn 1985.
BELL, Alfred Stanton (assistant publicity manager) & Sheila Mary: Joanna 1967.
BENNET, John (framework knitter) & Anne: Mary 1724.
BENNET, John & Elizabeth: Elizabeth 1758.
BENNET, John & Martha: Elizabeth 1726, Martha 1730, Martha 1732, John 1735, Thomas 1738, Elizabeth 1738, Elizabeth 1742.
BENNET, John (labourer) & Mary: Elizabeth 1709.
BENTLEY, Iain Ewart George (rose grower) & Clare Elizabeth: Frances Georgina 1992, James Anthony 1993.
BENTLEY, John & Ann: Elizabeth 1746, John 1752, Mary 1754, George 1756, Catherine 1758.
BENTLEY, John McDonald (electro-optical design engineer) & Jean Marjorie Florence: Katherine Jane (b1961) 1969.
BERRIDGE, Peter Lovell (hosiery manufacturer) & Barbara Nora: Fenella 1946.
BERRINGTON, John & Jane: John 1799, Jane 1801, Ann 1804, Mary 1806, Phebe 1809, Alice 1812.
BERRY, William Henry & Emma Jane: Gertrude Ella 1905.
BESTON, Thomas (slatepitman) & Mary: Mary 1789, Thomas 1799.
BIDDLES, Robert (husbandman) & Margaret: Margaret 1636.
BILBEY, Charles Henry (toolmaker) & Ethel May: Robert Charles 1944.
BINCH, Robert Walter (engineer) & Karen Anne: Cherie Louise 1991.
BIRD, Thomas & Mary: Mary 1684, Mary 1698.
BLACKBURN, Samuel (gamekeeper) & Ann Elizabeth: George Arthur 1856.

BLACKWELL, Ernest Samuel & Jane: Charles Ernest Rirett 1898, Philip Horton 1898, Gwladys Helen 1901.
BLAISSE, Folkert Boudevijn (economist) & Rosalind Mary: Pieter Lawrence 1976, Celina Judith 1977.
BLISSET, David Clive (insurance salesman) & Marsha Ann: Anna Clare 1980, William Harry 1982.
BLOOMFIELD, Henry (tailor) & Ann: Sarah 1782, Elizabeth 1784, Alse 1786, Ann 1789, William 1790, Mary 1793, William 1795, John 1798.
BLOOMFIELD, William & Sarah: William 1749 & Robert 1749 (twins), Robert 1750, Elizabeth 1752, William 1755, Henry 1757, Henry 1759.
BLOXAM, Harold Amos (factory hand) & Florence: Violetta Winifred (b1920) 1937.
BLUNDILL, Robert (labourer) & Mary: William 1719, Elizabeth 1723.
BOCOCK, Christopher George Frederick (motor vehicle sales manager) & Gillian Rosemary: Julie Louise 1966, Georgina Jane 1969.
BODLE, Thomas & Ann: Thomas 1700.
BOLTER, George (labourer) & Sarah: Elizabeth 1711, George 1712, Mary 1714, Sarah 1714, George 1717, Elizabeth 1717, William 1721.
BOLTON, James Edward (mining engineer) & Karen Marion: Lee James (b1980) 1984.
BOLUS, Oliver & Eileen Marjorie: Jeremy 1935.
BONIFACE, Roy (civil servant) & Norma Winifred: Sylvia Mary 1962.
BOSDEN, Kenneth Karl (computer consultant) & **BOCOCK**, Julie Louise: India Rose 1996.
BOSTOCK, Joseph (farmer) & Sarah: John 1817, Joseph 1818, Sarah 1822, Anne 1822, Elizabeth 1822, Mary 1827, George 1827, Johima 1827.
BOTT, William & Mary: Anna 1686, Katherine 1687.
BOWERS, Charles Neville Jenkins (costumiers manager) & Doris Lily Wilkins: Robert Charles 1950.
BOWLER, John & Mary: Charles 1869.
BOWLEY, Joseph Ernest (water works driver) & Jean Gwendolyn: Alan Roger 1953, Nigel Andrew 1956.
BRAMLEY, Thomas (stonemason) & Alse: Elizabeth 1792, Ann 1795, Sarah 1797, William 1799, Thomas 1803, Eliza 1809.
BRAMLEY, William & Elizabeth: Mary 1769, Thomas 1770, Ann 1773.
BRAMLEY, William (slate cleaver) & Elizabeth: John 1822.
BRAMWELL, Richard & Joanna: Layla 2002
BRANSON, Henry & Anne: Thomas 1727.
BRANSTON, Henry (framework knitter) & Mary: Henry 1720, John 1722.
BRAWNSON, Henry & Mary: Ann 1741, Mary 1743, Henry 1746, Thomas 1749 & John 1749 (twins), Ann 1751, Harry 1754.
BRANSTON, James (stockinger) & Elizabeth: John Thomas (b1827) 1847.
BRANSTON, John & Anne: Mary 1726.
BRAWNSON, John & Mary: John 1762, Sarah 1764.
BRANSTON, John & Sarah: William 1743, Mary 1745, Henry 1748, Pleasant 1753, Richard 1756, Matthew 1759, Ann 1762.
BRAWNSON, Mary: Elizabeth (by Thomas Pollard) 1760.
BRANSTON, Richard & [wife]: Richard 1617.
BRAWNSON, Thomas & Sarah: Thomas 1751.
BRAWNSON, Thomas & Mary: Rebecca 1752, Ann 1756, Ann 1757, Elizabeth 1758, Mary 1760, Ann 1762.
BRANSTON, William & Jane: Jane 1726, Elizabeth 1728, Mary 1730, William 1733, John 1738.
BRAWNSON, William & Mary: William 1761.
BREWIN, Francis & Ann: Francis 1759, John 1761, Frances 1761, Kitty 1763, Thomas 1767.
BREWIN, William & Elizabeth: Ann 1741, Lucy 1756.

BREWIN SMITH, Simon Andrew (sales executive) & Allyson Julie: Hannah Alice 1991, Harry William 1994.
BREX, Thomas (labourer) & Ann: Catherine 1820.
BRIERLEY, John & Ann: Jonathan 1754 & Mary 1754 (twins).
BRIERS, Grahame (horticultural engineer) & Daphne Golden Lann: Richard Leigh 1965, Stephen Andrew 1967, Helen Louise 1970.
BROOKHOUSE, William (labourer) & Elizabeth: William 1790, Francis 1792, John 1795.
BROOKHOUSE, William (labourer) & Elizabeth: Sarah 1838, William 1838, Elizabeth 1838.
BROOKHOUSE, William (labourer) & Hannah: Mary 1824, Maria 1825, William 1828, Ruth 1831.
BROOK LAWSON, Donald Michael (engineer) & Eva Dorothy Patricia: Andrew Michael 1956, Fiona Mary 1957.
BROOKS, John & Hannah: Ann 1750, Elizabeth 1756, John 1758, Hannah 1760.
BROOKSBY, Abel & Alice: John 1702, Abel 1703, Anthony 1704, Mary 1705, Alice 1707, Alice 1709, Elizabeth 1710, William 1712.
BROOKSBY, Charles & Ellen: Elizabeth 1753.
BROOKSBY, Thomas (labourer) & Dorothy: Thomas 1800, Ann 1802, Elizabeth 1804, Dorothy 1807, Mary 1809, Francis 1813, Jonathan 1816, Jonathan 1821, Sarah 1821.
BROOKSBY, Thomas & Mary: Thomas 1824, Anne Dennis 1826, Anne 1827.
BLOOMFIELD, Robert & Mary: Mary 1728.
BLOOMFIELD, William & Mary: Jane 1761, Sarah 1763.
BROWN, George & Sarah: Mary Ann 1863, George William 1865, James 1868, William Henry 1869, Elizabeth Anne 1871, Joseph 1873, Johanna 1876, Emma 1882.
BROWN, Henry (labourer) & Priscilla: Tom 1851.
BROWN, James (labourer) & Sarah: William 1835, James 1835, George 1835, Mary 1838, Thomas 1839, Diana 1840, Mary Ann 1844, Joseph 1844, John 1846, Thomas 1848.
BROWN, John (mason) & Catherine: Catherine 1708.
BROWN, John & Dorothy: Mary 1677.
BROWN, Michael Walter (soldier) & Diane Julie: Caroline Jane 1966, Tracey Karen 1969.
BROWN, Robert (labourer) & Elizabeth: Robert 1633, Mary 1638.
BROWNE, Robert (labourer) & Elizabeth: Alice 1717, Mary 1722.
BROWN, Samuel (labourer) & Elizabeth: Catherine 1819, Henry 1823, Jane 1826, Isaac 1827.
BROWN, Samuel (labourer) & Sarah: Ann 1805, Samuel 1806, Mary 1809, Eliza 1811, Elizabeth 1815.
BROWN, Thomas & Ellen Susannah: Joseph Thomas 1888.
BROWN, Thomas & Mary: William 1677, John 1678, Arthur 1679, Benjamin 1684.
BROWN: Wilfred (adult) 1971.
BROWN, William & Ann: Ann1757, Mary 1759, Sarah 1762, Elizabeth 1764, Jane 1766, William 1769, Catherine 1771, Samuel 1773, Robert 1774, Lucy 1776.
BROWN, William (labourer) & Elizabeth: Thomas 1790, William 1792, John 1795, Samuel 1798, Elizabeth 1803, Daniel 1808, Diana 1809, James 1813, Anne 1818.
BROWN, William & Mary Louisa: Ethel Sarah May 1891.
BROWN, William & Sarah: William 1803.
BUCHANAN, James Alexander (design engineer) & Sally Angela: Benjamin James 1989, Sarah Elizabeth 1991.
BUCKLEY, William (miller) & Elizabeth: William Kirk 1798, Mary 1801.
BUNNEY, Alfred Edwin & Ethel May: Beatrice May (b1921) 1934.
BUNNEY, Alwyn Everard & Clara: Ellen Vera 1908.

BUNNEY, Charles (labourer) & Elizabeth: Sarah Jane 1845, Joseph 1846, Edmund 1849, Samuel 1853, William 1855, John (b1855) 1857, Charles Edmund 1859, Lewis 1861, Benjamin 1862, Elizabeth 1864, Catherine Anne 1867.
BUNNEY, Charles Benjamin (farmer) & Ellen: Maurice Edwin Charles 1926, Barbara Ellen 1929.
BUNNEY, David (labourer) & Elizabeth: Samuel 1795, Ann 1797.
BUNNEY, Edith Emily Sarah: Gwendolen Polly 1909.
BUNNEY, Edward & Helen: Lavinia 1869, Mary Jane Rebecca 1871, Lucy Ellen 1876.
BUNNEY, Frederick & Sarah Ann: Mary Ellen 1882, Rosa Rebecca 1885, Annie Violet 1887, Alfred Edwin 1898, Lilian Elsie 1898, Beatrice Alice 1898, Edith Evelyn 1898.
BUNNEY, George (labourer) & Jane: Edward (b1849) 1856, Henry Thompson (b1853) 1856, Thomas 1856, Frederick 1858, Samuel 1861, Walter 1862, William George Daniel 1869.
BUNNEY, Henry (labourer) & Mary: James Carter 1856, Maria 1856, William 1861, Letitia 1861, Sarah Elizabeth 1865.
BUNNEY, James (labourer) & Harriett: Martha Lucy 1858, Samuel George 1861.
BUNNEY, John (farmer) & Katherine: Charles Benjamin (b1896) 1926, Sidney Oswald (b1891) 1926.
BUNNEY, Mary Ellen: Clarice 1914.
BUNNEY, Maurice Edwin Charles (farmer) & Margaret Beatrice: Susan Melanie 1953, Judith Mary 1956, Mark William 1958, Sarah Louise 1960, Joanna 1962.
BUNNEY, Samuel & Emma: Edith Emily Sarah 1876, Winifred Lilian Bertha 1885, Hilda May 1888.
BUNNEY, Samuel (farmer/slate cleaver/labourer) & Sarah: William 1816, Samuel 1819, Mary 1825, Charles 1825, Isaac 1831, Daniel 1832.
BUNNEY, Samuel (labourer) & Mary: Samuel 1846.
BUNNEY, Sidney Oswald (farmer) & Annie Maria: Mary Ruth 1921.
BUNNEY, Walter & Mary Ann: Joseph 1871, Johnson 1874.
BUNNEY, William (labourer) & Anne: Charles William 1841.
BUNNEY, William (labourer) & Elizabeth: Eliza Ann 1856, George William 1856, Fanny Elizabeth 1858, Frederick James 1872.
BUNNEY, William (labourer/slate cleaver) & Martha: William 1827, George 1831, Henry 1832, James 1834, Samuel 1834, Frederick Harry 1839, Walter 1839, Mary 1843, Fanny Elizabeth 1843, Walter 1846.
BUNNEY, William (farmer) & Mary: Anne 1810, Mary 1812, William 1815.
BUNNEY, William & Sarah: Samuel 1862, Eliza 1867, Betsy 1867, Fanny Sarah 1871.
BURBIDGE, Thomas (attorney & farmer) & Maria: Henry Theodore 1839, Frederick William 1840, Arthur Arnold 1842.
BURCHNALL, Osborne Frederick Benjamin (farmer) & Jennifer Mary: Nicholas William 1963.
BURCHNALL, Richard (farmer) & Betsy-Ann: Elizabeth 1803, Mary Ann 1805, Richard Sarson 1806, Joseph 1813, James 1813, Samuel 1814.
BURNABY, John & Rebecca: Mary 1762, Ann 1762.
BURNABY (so called); **MOOR**, Rebecca: Ann 1768, Hannah 1770, William 1775, Ann 1781.
BURROWS, Alfred (farmer) & Kathleen Mary: William Ralph (b1929) 1934, Rosemary Jill 1934, John Richard 1937.
BURROWS, Henry (husbandman) & Mabel: Ann 1635, Mabel 1635, Henry 1638.
BURTON, David (slate cleaver) & Mary: Johnson 1845.
BURTON, Henry & Dorothy: Joseph 1775, John 1786, Ann 1789.
BURTON, Henry (labourer/slate cleaver) & Elizabeth: William 1822, Francis 1824, Joseph 1826, Mary 1828, George 1830, Harriet 1832, Emma 1834, Anne 1837.
BURTON, Henry & Margaret: Henry 1747, Margaret 1748, Henry 1751, Thomas 1753, Hannah 1756.
BURTON, Henry (slate cleaver) & Mary: Alice Mary 1854, Elizabeth Lockton 1856.

Appendix D: Parish Registers

BURTON, Henry (labourer) & Sarah: Joseph 1827.
BURTON, Joseph (labourer) & Ann: John 1795, Thomas 1797, Henry 1799, William (b1804) 1807, Joseph (b1805) 1807, James (b1806) 1807, Francis 1808, Sarah 1830.
BURTON, William (labourer) & Elizabeth: Anne 1828, Anne 1830, John 1830, Margaret 1832, Fanny 1835, Augustus George 1838, Mary Ann 1847.
BUSWELL, Derek Alfred (director) & Rosemary Ann: Anthony Paul 1963, Jeanette Helen 1969.
BUTLER, Charles John Brinsley & Gwladys Dorothea: Eileen Gwladys 1892.
BUTLER, John Vansittart Danvers & Ann Elizabeth: Brian Danvers 1876.
BUTLER, Raymond (printer) & Barbara Mary: Barbara Elizabeth Irene 1959.
BUTTERY, Joseph William & Martha: Fanny Eliza 1898.
BUXTON, Lukas Warr (sales manager) & Carol Jane **GOURLAY** (business writer) Rose Mae 2001
CAPEWELL: John Edmund (adult) 1997(conditional on not having been previously baptized).
CAPEWELL, John Edmund (electrician) & Valerie Ann: Thomas Charles (b1982) 1986, Edward Jack (b1984) 1986.
CARDALE, George (clerk) & Elizabeth: Frances 1751, Jinny 1754, Lucy 1756.
CARTER, William (labourer) & Anne: Robert 1790, Thomas 1792, John 1794, Thomas 1796, James (b1801) 1806, William (b1804) 1806, Sarah 1806, William 1808, James 1810.
CARTER, William (labourer) & Sarah: Sarah 1831, Mary 1836, James 1836, Fanny 1839, Letitia 1841.
CHAMBERLAIN, Matthew & [wife]: William 1617.
CHAPMAN, David (farmer) & Anne: George 1808, David Augustus 1810, William 1812, Mary 1814, Henry 1818, Thomas 1822, Frances Matilda 1825.
CHAPMAN, George & Elizabeth: Thomas 1729.
CHAPMAN, Henry & Lydia: Ann 1768.
CHAPMAN, John & Catherine: John 1714.
CHAPMAN, Thomas & Ann: William 1869, Edward 1869, Emma Annie 1873, Helen 1874, Florence 1878.
CHAPMAN, Thomas (innkeeper) & Emma: Charles Wade 1860, Mary Elizabeth 1862.
CHAPMAN, Thomas William (groom) & Jane: William John 1848.
CHARLTON, George & Mary: Thomas 1802, Jane 1805.
CHARLTON, Thomas (labourer) & Elizabeth: Thomas 1828, Jane 1832.
CLARKE, David Childs (solicitor) & Hope Eleanor: Martin Childs 1935, Louise Childs 1937.
CLARKE, Henry (labourer) & Jane: Sarah Jane 1859.
CLARKE, Herbert Ezra (farm foreman) & Margaret Gwendoline: Jacqueline Ann 1964, Dianne Lorraine 1970.
CLARKE, James John & Elizabeth (alias **WISE**): see **WISE.**
CLARKE, John & Ann: John 1771, Ann 1779, Samuel 1781.
CLARKE, John & Elizabeth: Elizabeth 1676.
CLARKE, John & Elizabeth: John 1743, William 1746, Stephen 1749, Elizabeth 1753.
CLARKE, John (slate cleaver) & Joanna: William Watts (b1850) 1856, Maria (b1850) 1856, Mary Anne (b1854) 1856, Fanny 1856.
CLARKE, John (labourer) & Martha: Elizabeth 1815.
CLARKE, John (labourer) & Susan: John 1795, Richard 1797, William 1800, Sarah 1803, John 1805, James 1808, Ann 1814.
CLARKE, John (schoolmaster) & Susannah: John 1837.
CLARKE, Neil George (building contractor) & Karen Joy: Daniel Alan 1990, Emma Louise 1993, Laura Joy 1996.
CLARKE, Robert Jonathan (masseuse) & Melanie Tracey (Midland Bank): Marchella Sophie Maria 1998.

CLARKE, Samuel & Elizabeth: Elizabeth 1746, Samuel 1749, James 1755, Stephen 1757, Jinny 1760, Ann 1764, Elizabeth 1773, Samuel 1777.
CLARKE, Samuel (husbandman) & Sarah: Johnson 1725, Samuel 1726.
CLARKE, Stephen & Elizabeth: William 1680, Stephen 1685, Thomas 1687, Mary 1692.
CLARKE, Stephen (shoemaker) & Jane: Fanny 1786, Stephen 1792.
CLARKE, Stephen (labourer) & Jinny: Stephen 1777, Elizabeth 1778, James 1780, John 1782, Samuel 1784, Mary 1786, Jinny 1789, William 1791, Ann 1793, Stephen 1795, Ann 1799.
CLARKE, Stephen (cordwainer) & Sarah: Stephen 1821, Henry 1824, Sarah 1826, Fanny 1830, Samuel 1836, Jane 1836, Elizabeth 1838.
CLARKE, William & Ann: Samuel 1785, James 1786.
CLARKE, William (labourer) & Elizabeth: John 1768, Stephen 1769, Elizabeth 1771, Elizabeth 1773, Jane 1775, Jinny 1776, William 1778, Mary 1789.
CLARKE, William (cordwainer/shoemaker) & Elizabeth: Rupert Chawner 1814, Samuel 1817.
CLARKE, William (husbandman) & Mary: John 1711, Mary 1713, Jane 1717, William 1720, Samuel 1722, Elizabeth 1726.
CLARKE, William & Mary: William 1756, John 1759, Mary 1764.
CLARKE, William (labourer) & Sarah: Martha 1826, Sarah 1829.
CLARKSON, Ian Gordon (project manager) & Victoria Susan: Alistair James 1993, Charles Elliott 1996.
CLARKSON, William & Hannah: William 1764.
CLEAR, Charles Jeremy (chartered accountant) & Lesley Anne: Charlotte Emily 1979, Caroline Amy Wallis 1980.
CLEAVER, George & Mary: George Henry 1886.
CLIFF, Daniel (HGV driver) & Rebecca Louise **JOHN**, Emily Rose 2002
CLUSKEY, Andrew (dental surgeon) & Ann: Sarah Abagail 1979.
COCKERAM, James Alexander Neil (marketing director) & Jayne: Sam Richard 1989.
COCKROFT, Richard William (insurance broker) & Marjorie: Paul Ian 1952.
COLLARD, Jeffrey John (chartered accountant) & Denise Irene: Philip Edward 1990.
COLLETT, Maurice Anthony (sales director) & Carol: Mark Adrian 1981, Amy Elizabeth 1985.
COLY, Henry & [wife]: [son] 1624.
COOK, Elizabeth (a pauper): William 1789 & Mary 1789 (twins).
COOK, William (gardener) & Jane: Jane Elizabeth 1858, Thomas Henry 1861, William Boman 1864, Annie Laurie 1870, Edwin 1873, Albert 1876.
COOK, William & Mary: Elizabeth 1789.
COPSON, Alfred (engineer) & Bessie: Sheila Mary 1952.
COPSON, Charles (farmer) & Annie: Alfred George (b1918) 1955, David Leslie (b1926) 1955, Leonard Harry (b1931) 1955.
COPSON, David Leslie (farmer) & Patricia Dorothy: Simon Charles 1956, Andrew James 1957.
COPSON, Dennis (water dept) & Joyce: Paul (b1944) 1948.
COPSON, Harry (farm servant) & Vera Elizabeth: John Ambrose 1916, Jean 1918.
COPSON, John Ambrose (farmer/dairyman) & Mary Joan: Rosemarie Bettyne Carole 1940, Cynthia Mary 1941, Sally Elizabeth 1943, Roger John Ambrose 1948, Nigel James 1950.
COPSON, Leonard Harry (social worker) & Judith Leslie: Lucy Claire 1970.
COPSON, Rosemarie Bettyne Carole (bank clerk): Martin Jonathan 1961.
COX, Jonathan Stanley (insurance broker) & Emma Jane: Dominic James 1993.
COY, Michael & [wife]: Sarah 1709.
CRAMP, Thomas & Elizabeth: Thomas 1692.
CRAMPTON, Albert & Edith Emily Sarah: Ivy May 1903.
CRAVEN, Gary Robert James & Penelope Anne: Heloise Minda Ruth 1998.
CRESSWELL, Ann: Sarah 1792.

CRESSWELL, Sarah: Elizabeth 1813.
CRISPE, Robert (husbandman) & Joan: Ann 1634, Mary 1637, Elizabeth 1637.
CROSS, William & Elizabeth: William 1775, John 1777, Sarah 1779, Elizabeth 1781, Silas 1782, Thomas 1786.
CROCKETT, Jack Davison (representative) & Barbara: Richard Davison 1939.
CROXTON, William Harry (farm labourer) & Ada Mary Agnes: Raymond John 1937.
CUDBILL, Nicholas (hypnotherapist counsellor) & Pauline: Oliver Ashton Nicholas 1992.
CUFFLING, John & Fanny Maria: Mary 1871, William Joseph 1874, John Coleman 1875.
CUFFLING, William (farmer) & Mary Ann: Lucy 1852, Jonathan 1854, David 1856, Edmund 1858, Emma 1860, Michael 1862, Mary Anne 1864, Fanny 1866.
DABIN, Lee (managing director) & Marsha (inclusion worker): Amber Grace 2007
DAFT, George & [wife]: Mary 1633.
DANCE, Charles & Louisa: John William 1874, James George 1876, Lucy Louisa Mary 1878, Louisa Lucy Mary 1878.
DANN, Thomas Henry & Harriet: Herbert James 1870.
DANVERS, Joseph & Frances: John 1723.
DANVERS, William & Elizabeth: Matthew 1635, Charles 1638.
DAVIES, Andrew Christopher (barrister) & Sarah Louise (nurse): Oliver Barnaby 1998, Lucy Alice 2002, Benjamin Charles 2006.
DAVIES, William Ewart (engineering buyer) & Margaret: Susan May Sarah 1955, Judith Elizabeth 1957.
DAVY, Roger (teacher) & Yvonne: Elizabeth Anne 1960, John Roger 1962.
DEACON, John & Elizabeth: Mary 1797, John 1803.
DEAN, Nicholas Martin (sales & marketing directory) & Kirsty Anne (marketing director): Sophie Grace Elise 2009
DE PLANO, Emanuele Gianluca (company director) & Angela Mary (journalist): Celeste Elisabetta 2003, Giorgio Lucca, 2006.
DEWICK, Neil Edward (bricklayer) & Sarah Christine: Bradley Roy 1994.
DEXTER, Edward (miller) & Catherine: Thomas Stevenson 1835, Anne 1835, Esther 1835, Charlotte 1835, John Edward 1835, Fanny 1835.
DEXTER, George (labourer) & Elizabeth: Mary Anne (b1836) 1857.
DEXTER, Paul James (gardener) & **BOCOCK**, Georgina Jane: Jade Elizabeth 1986, Amy Louise 1989.
DINGLEY, John Brian (company secretary) & Dawn: Jane 1965.
DIXON, Frank Gerrard (representative) & Winifred Annie: Anthony Frank 1952.
DIXON, James Murray & Etheldreda: Henry Edward Otto Murray 1885, Rosamond Mary Trevelyan 1887, Edward Charles Trevelyan 1888, Gerald Donovan Trevelyan 1890, Eleanor Margaret Trevelyan 1893.
DIXON, Charles Edward (international development consultant) & Ruth Vargas: Josué Benjamin 2006.
DORE, Edward & Mary: Edward 1680.
D'ORSI, Raffaele (police officer) & Lucy Clare (née Copson, police officer): Ruby Isabella 2007
DOUGHTY, Joseph (carpenter/labourer) & Ann: Sarah 1810, William 1812, Mary Ann 1814, Elizabeth 1816, Martha 1820, Esther 1822.
DRAYTON, William & Elizabeth: [child] 1737, Henry 1739, Thomas 1740, Samel 1742.
DUDLEY, John (blacksmith) & Sarah: Mary 1842, William 1850.
DUNNE, Charles Thomas (cable jointer/police officer) & Lynn Marion: Charles Jonathan Robert 1971, Lucinda Marion 1974, Anthony Stephen Andrew 1976.
ELLWAY, Gerald David (transport engineer) & Susan Mary: Sarah Jane 1970.
EMMERSON, William (labourer) & Ann: Ann 1847.
ERSKINE, Henry David (clerk, rector) & Harriet: Caroline Stuart 1818, George David 1820, Fanny Louisa 1822, Anne Agnes 1824, Julia Henrietta 1826.

FANSHAWE, Gordon Lennox (company director) & Enid May Elizabeth: Caroline Mary (b1957) 1962.
FARMER, John Aird (sales representative) & Dorothy Violet: Jonathan Mark 1971.
FARMER, Joseph & Mary: Thomas 1756.
FARMER, Thomas (labourer) & Mary: Maria 1830.
FEASEY, Edward Eric (sales executive) & Judith Caroline: Samuel James 1985, Benjamin Timothy 1988.
FELCE, Francis Herbert (representative) & Betty Evelyn: Dawn Elizabeth 1939.
FELLOWES, Geoffrey Edward (motor mechanic) & Patricia Anne: Lisa Anne 1968.
FENNELOW, John & Mary: Jinny 1756, Ruth 1761, John 1763, Elizabeth 1765, Stephen 1768.
FERNELEY, John & Mary: Ann 1752, Mary 1754.
FIELDING, John & Alice: John 1680, Elizabeth 1682, Edward 1685.
FILLINGHAM, Geoffrey William & Joan: Kathryn (b1964) 1971.
FISHER, John (farm labourer) & Nancy Kathleen: John Edward 1940.
FLETCHER, James (labourer) & Florence: Irene Elizabeth May 1914.
FLINT, John William (servant) & Sarah: Eliza Jane 1850.
FLOWER, Scott Russell (scaffolder) & Samantha **SAUL** (health club manager): Matilda Alethia Saul-Flower 2010.
FLUDE, Harry (representative) & Edith: Jennifer 1938, Richard 1940.
FOX, Frederick Charles (butcher) & Ivy Idena: Noel William (b1922) 1935, Pamela Vera (b1932) 1935.
FRANKES, Samuel (mason) & Sarah: John 1727, William 1728, Elizabeth 1732, Sarah 1735.
FRASER, Thomas Monro (company director/throwster) & Sheila Margaret: William Donald Munro 1960, Adrian James Munro 1966.
FREARSON, William (labourer) & Isabella: William 1830.
FREEMAN, Samuel & Jane Elizabeth: Samuel 1892.
FRIEND: Paul Terence (adult) 1990.
FRIEND, Paul Terence (insurance surveyor) & Jennifer Mary: Jessica Laura 1990, Luke Gregory 1993.
FUKES, Thomas & Elizabeth: William 1778, Thomas 1780, John 1782, Mary 1785, Elizabeth 1786, Mary 1789, Dorothy 1792.
GAMBLE, William (labourer) & Ruth: William Vesty 1836.
GAMBLE, William Haywood (labourer) & Sarah: Isabella 1853, Joseph Charles 1857.
GARDNER, Francis Henry & Amanda: Sophie Rebecca 2002
GARNER, Elizabeth: William Harriman 1842.
GERRITY, Sean William Patrick (travel agent) & Alison: Lewis Royston 1984, Charles Thomas Patrick 1990, Jack Michael Sean 1992.
GILBERT, Arthur (husbandman) & Elizabeth: Elizabeth 1635, Mary 1638.
GILBERT, Graham (managing director) & Debbie: Rachel Natasha (b1991) 1995.
GILBERT, Robert & Ann: Mary 1677, Henry 1685.
GILBERT, William & Martha: Robert 1748.
GILBERT, William & Mary: Sarah 1752, Joseph 1754, Mary 1756, Henry 1758, Jinny 1759, Louisa 1760, Sophia 1762.
GILLETT, Leslie John (order co-ordinator) & Sadie Anne (administrator): Jessica Ann 2004
GIMSON, Benjamin Russell (company director) & Gweneth Mary: Jeremy Russell 1948, Jennifer Mary 1954.
GLOVER, Benjamin & Elizabeth: Thomas 1740, Thomas 1746.
GLOVER, Frederick Jarvis (gas fitter) & Elsie Mary: Pamela Ann 1941.
GLOVER, John (coachman/carter) & Edith Mary: Kathleen Mary 1911, Albert John Frederick 1914, Edwin Lewis 1918.
GLOVER, William & Elizabeth: William 1805, Robert 1807.
GODBALD, George & Emma: Mary Anne 1863.

GODBALD, George & Jane: Fanny Maria 1871, Hannah 1872.
GODBALD, George & Mary: Harriett 1868, Louisa 1875, Emma 1877.
GODBALD, John & Mary: Sarah Ellen 1878.
GODFREY, Christopher Martin Valentine (architect) & Micheline Marie Paule: Charlotte Louis 1971.
GODKIN, John Richard Hayman (chartered accountant) & Geraldine Sheila: Richard John 1968.
GODLEY, Stephen Barry (company director) & Philippa Louise (company secretary): Saskia Georgia 2001, Rhett Stephen 2004
GODWIN, Thomas & Mary: Elizabeth 1736.
GOODMAN, Stephen & Anne: Mary 1727.
GOURLAY, Simon Robert (sales manager) & **DEITH**, Gillian Mary: Jack Oliver 1989.
GOURLAY, Russell (chartered surveyor) & Daniella: Samuel Russell 1989, Thomas Jameson (b1988) 1989.
GRAHAM, James & Elizabeth Ann: James Harry 1871.
GRAY, John & Ann: Elizabeth 1784, Ann 1785.
GRAY, Malcolm James (accountant) & Ann Elizabeth: Alexander James Maynard 1981.
GREASLEY, George (labourer) & Elizabeth: George 1835, Charles 1838.
GREASLEY, William (labourer) & Anne: George 1809, Anne 1811, William 1814, Elizabeth 1817, Jane 1820, Elizabeth 1831.
GREEN, James (labourer) & Ada Elizabeth: Ivy Muriel 1918.
GREENE, William (butcher) & Alice: Alice 1637.
GREEN, William (land agent) & Mary Ann: Brian 1922.
GRIPPER, Mark Bradley (medical practitioner) & Susan Margaret: Ann Lindsey 1981, Hugh Jonathan 1983.
GUILDFORD, Henry (miller) & Mary: Mary 1703, Elizabeth 1705, John 1706, Henry 1709, Henry 1711, Elizabeth 1714, Samuel 1717, Anne 1719.
GUILFORD, Henry (labourer) & Mary: Elizabeth 1714.
HACKETT, John & Grizam: [dau] 1700, John 1702.
HAGUE, Charles Stuart (insurance associate) & Sheila Mary: Jemma Victoria 1935, Charles Spencer 1989.
HALE, Henry & Ann: Ann 1767, George 1769.
HALE, John & Mary: Hannah 1775, Joseph 1779.
HALE, Philip Raymond (police officer) & Jill Anne: Harriet Anne Isom 1988, Charlotte Hannah Isom 1990, Vanessa Rae Isom 1992, Georgina Olivia Isom 1996.
HALES, Thomas (farmer) & Helena: Hannah 1806, Anne 1808, Charlotte 1813, Maria 1814.
HALL, Francis & Ann: Francis 1676, Sarah 1680.
HALL, Henry (carpenter) & Ann: Jane 1633, Francis 1634, Mary 1635, Ann 1638.
HALL, John & Mary: Sarah 1758, Hannah 1762.
HALL, Joseph & [wife]: Joyce 1702.
HALL, Lewis Duval & Mary Kate: Frank Duval 1871.
HALL, Nathaniel (husbandman) & Elizabeth: Nathaniel 1712, Elizabeth 1714, Anne 1719, Francis 1721, William 1726.
HANDFORD, George (labourer) & Mary: Anne 1837.
HANDLEY, George & Elizabeth: Frank Handley Wakley 1871.
HANDLEY, James (labourer) & Christiana Louisa: William James 1860, Thomas 1862.
HANDLEY, James & Louisa: Christopher George 1863.
HANDLEY, Joseph James (farm worker) & Gladys Mary: Keith 1949.
HANNIBAL, Leslie Ernest (master printer) & June Silvia: Sally Christine (b1953) 1962, David Robert (b1955) 1962.
HARDY, Samuel & Elizabeth: Ann 1776, John 1778, Sarah 1780.
HARDY, Nicholas John (professional writer) & Maria Louise (retailer): Abigail Velvet (b 1989) 2000, Bethany Primrose (b 1991) 2000, Coco (b 1993) 2000

HARGRAVE, David Miles William (marketing manager) & Jane (physiotherapist): Emily Jane (b1993) 1996, Holly Rebecca 1996.
HARMER, John Malcolm (salesman) & Ann Gillian: Paul Doncaster 1974, Simon John 1976.
HARNER, William & [wife]: Ann Maria 1779.
HARRIMAN, Thomas (labourer) & Maria: Hannah 1838, Agnes Jessy 1841.
HARRINGTON, Norman Donald (landscape gardener) & Barbara Aileen: Simon Paul 1964, Jeremy Ian 1956.
HARRIS, Geoffrey Ernest (company director) & Glenis: Laura Francine 1977, Matthew Christopher 1979.
HARRIS, James & [wife]: William 1679, Ellen 1680.
HARRIS, Neil Christopher (chartered accountant) & Jayne Louise: Simon Thomas 1989, Lucy Victoria 1991.
HARRISON, Jeffrey Cecil (company director) & Valerie Anne: Max 1972.
HARRISON, Joseph Harry (labourer) & Hilda May: Joan Lilian Moyra 1922.
HARRISON, Paul Cedric (carpenter) & Susan Elizabeth: Carla Jane 1971.
HARRISON, Ralph Stone (butcher) & Lilian Rebecca: Paul Cedric 1949.
HASTINGS, John & Aline: Anna 1687.
HAWORTH, Christopher William (yarn merchant) & Margaret Joan: Charles David 1949.
HAYNES, John Henry (bus conductor) & Gladys Mary: Sheila Ann 1932, John Edward 1937, Freda Maureen 1939, Lynn Marion 1950.
HAZELL Malcolm (police officer) & Jayne: James Daniel (b1990) 1992, Thomas Edward 1992, Alexander 1997.
HEATH, Neil Andrew (planner/platemaker/checker) & Julie Anne: Luke Matthew 2001.
HEATON, Frank (cycle salesman) & Hilda Mary: Brian Howard 1929.
HEATON, William: Catherine 1634.
HEITCH, Edward & Mary: Anne 1733.
HEITCH, Joseph & Mary: Abraham 1745, Daniel 1747.
HEITCH, Richard & Ann: Richard 1698, Robert 1700, [son] 1701, [dau] 1704, Edward 1706.
HEITCH, Richard (carpenter) & Mary: Elizabeth 1710, Elizabeth 1711.
HEMSLEY, Benjamin & Eliza Hannah: Edwin 1889.
HEMSLEY, Joseph (labourer) & Jemima: Anne Eliza 1850, Joseph 1853, Harriett 1855, Elizabeth 1857.
HERCOCK, William Barry (company director) & Barbara Cleone: Timothy Rowland (b1963) 1970, Sally Elizabeth (b1963) 1970.
HERMANN, Oscar & Marguerita: Gertrude Dorothy (b1907) 1939.
HETTERLEY, John & Mary: John 1853.
HEYGATE, Frederick William (baronet) & Mary Ann: Isabella Mary Anne 1856, Maud Alice 1865.
HICKLIN, William (labourer) & Elizabeth: Elizabeth 1815.
HILL, John & Juliana: Juliana 1776, Jane 1779, Martha 1781.
HILL, Samuel & Cordelia: Mary Ann 1884.
HILL, Thomas (labourer) & Elizabeth: Elizabeth 1786, Thomas 1789, Benjamin 1791, Ann 1794, Thomas 1799.
HILL, Thomas (labourer) & Elizabeth: Mary Anne 1829, Eliza 1833, Hannah 1836, Anne 1838, Laura Fanny 1841, Thomas 1843, Charlotte 1846, Eliza 1848, Mary 1850, Fanny 1857.
HILL, Thomas (labourer) & Sarah: Mary Louisa 1841.
HILL, William (labourer) & Sarah: Anne 1839, [child] 1841, Benjamin 1843, Sarah 1846.
HIND, Henry & Ann: Henry 1760, Thomas 1762, William 1763, James 1764.
HIND, Henry & Mary: Henry 1786, William 1788, Thomas 1790, Robert 1792, Sarah 1792, James 1794, Mary Ann 1795, John 1803, Richard 1813.

HIND, Henry & Sarah: Eleanor 1743, James 1747.
HIND, Robert & Elizabeth: Henry 1617, Thomas 1625, Dorothy 1634.
HIND, Robert (framework knitter) & Elizabeth: James 1725.
HIND, Robert & Rachel: [son] 1701.
HIND, Stephen & Hannah: [dau] 1698.
HIND, Thomas (labourer) & Margaret: Thomas 1637.
HIND, Thomas & Mary: Dorothy 1635.
HIND, Thomas & Mary: John 1676, Peter 1680.
HIND, Thomas (farmer) & Sarah: Henry 1814, Thomas William 1814.
HODEN, George & Eleanor: Eleanor 1676, Ann 1679, George 1680.
HODGES, Graham Peter (garage proprietor) & Carol Christine: Rebecca Jane (b1972) 1979, Christopher Thomas (b1974) 1979.
HODGE, Hannah (lacerunner): John Henry 1851, Eliza 1853.
HODGE, James Thomas & Annie: William James 1897.
HODGE, Matthew (labourer) & Ann: John 1816, Martha 1818, Martha 1819, Jane 1822, Hannah 1831, Thomas 1833.
HODGE, Thomas (labourer) & Eliza: Sarah Jane 1855, Matthew 1857, Hannah Eliza 1860, Eliza Ann 1863, Elizabeth 1865, Harriett 1868, James Thomas 1871.
HOLBERRY, John Simon (sales director) & Fiona Catherine Macdonald (marketing director): Kate Olivia Joy 1997.
HOLIDAY, Ernest James (caretaker/roadman) & Winifred Sarah: Leonard Ernest 1933, Eileen May 1938.
HOLLIN, Thomas & Elizabeth: Thomas 1749, Ruth 1752, Richard 1767.
HOLLOWAY, Nicholas Frank (bank manager) & Alison: Jacqueline Ann 1991, Joanna Elizabeth 1991, William Ronald Frank 1992; Nicholas Frank (bank manager) & Clare Elizabeth: Francesca Alice 2006.
HOLLOWAY Christopher William (insurance area manager) & Jane Elizabeth (bank clerk): Benjamin James 1999
HOLLOWAY, Richard James (security manager) & Aisha (research nurse): Thomas Alexander James 1999, Joshua James, 2008.
HOLMES, Anthony Norman (motor trader) & Margaret Ann: Richard Anthony 1979.
HOLT, Charles Henry & Johanna: Charles Leslie 1907.
HOLT, Samuel & Ethel Martha: Kathleen Grace 1908.
HOLMES, Philip (company director) & Susan Patricia: Stephen Leslie 1960, Jonathan David 1960.
HOMES, Frederick William & Emily Jane: William Beesor 1874.
HOOD, Geoffrey Ivor (coal merchant) & Marjorie: Penny Anne 1950.
HOPKINS, William (servant) & Anne: William 1852.
HOSKING, Henry John (estate manager) & Jacqueline Ann: Nicholas John 1970.
HOULT, Samuel (farmer) & Ethel Martha: Samuel William Thirlby 1912, Ethel Martha 1917, Geoffrey Clark 1918.
HOWLETT, David (scientist) & Judith Mary (teacher): Benjamin William Rogers 1993, Naomi Catherine Rogers 1995.
HUDSON, Francis & [wife]: Francis 1695.
HUDSON, John (labourer) & Ann: Eliza (b1833) 1847.
HUGHES/HEWS, John (labourer) & Eleanor: George 1703, Robert 1706, John 1709, Thomas 1713.
HUGHES, John (labourer) & Elizabeth: Elizabeth 1716.
HEWS, John & Mary: Thomas 1676.
HEWS, Robert & Elizabeth: Robert 1754.
HEWS, Thomas & Elizabeth: Thomas 1747, Elizabeth 1751, Joseph 1756, John 1758.
HUGHES/HEWS, Thomas (carpenter) & Mary: Elizabeth 1706, William 1707, Elizabeth 1709, Thomas 1711, George 1717, Jonathan 1719.
HEWS, Thomas (millwright) & Mary: Mary 1714.
HUGHES, Thomas & Rosamund: Elizabeth 1763.

HULSE, Arthur Henry (bus/lorry driver) & Edith Muriel Olive: Henry Adam 1935, Margaret Adrianne 1939.
HUTCHINSON, Noel (farmer) & Jenifer: Timothy Staughton 1955.
HUTCHINSON, William & Jane: William 1759.
HUTCHINSON, William (mason) & Mary: William 1789, John 1791, Thomas 1792, Mary 1795.
INGRAM, Mary: Ann 1737.
ISOM, Thomas & Mary: Elizabeth 1802.
JACKSON, Elizabeth: Elizabeth 1740.
JACKSON, Peter Maitland (company managing director) & Jacqueline Mary: Matthew Peter James 1987, Samuel David Christopher 1990.
JAMES, Elizabeth: Ann 1798.
JAMES, John & Clara Helen: Cecil Topliss 1899.
JAMES, Samuel & Mary: Samuel 1773, [son] 1776.
JAMES, Thomas Henry & Martha Ann: John Charles 1900.
JARVIS, Neil Anthony (general manager/engineering) & Julie Ann (company director): Oliver James 2001, Benjamin Charles 2005
JESSON, Richard & Mary: James 1772, Mary 1774, Thomas 1776.
JOHN, David Neil (schoolmaster) & Fiona Mary: Rebecca Louise 1983, David Nicholas 1985, Edwina Daisy Gay 1990.
JOHNSON, Alan (carpenter) & Mandy Jane: Ted Matthew 2004, Felicity Grace 2008
JOHNSON, Arthur & Charlotte: Harriet Maud 1882, Cicely Mary 1882.
JOHNSON, Arthur (gardener) & Frances: Arthur Eric 1915.
JOHNSON, Edmund (husbandman) & Friza: William 1700, Mary 1703, [son] 1705, [son] 1709, Elizabeth 1711.
JOHNSON, Edward & [wife]: William 1698.
JOHNSON, Edward (labourer) & Elizabeth: Elizabeth 1719, Edward 1722, John 1725, Mary 1727.
JOHNSON, John (slatecleaver) & Ann: William 1793, Thomas 1793, Ann 1796, Elizabeth 1798.
JOHNSON, John & Dorothy: Joseph 1735, Elizabeth 1737, William 1739, Thomas 1742, Mary 1744, Dorothy 1747, Ann 1753.
JOHNSON, John & Elizabeth: Elizabeth 1762, John 1763, Frizzy 1765, Ann 1770, Thomas 1772, Joseph 1775, Jinny 1778, William 1782.
JOHNSON, Richard & [wife]: John 1617.
JOHNSON, Robert & Elizabeth: Jane 1760.
JOHNSON, Thomas Francis & Mary Jane: Doris 1902.
JOHNSON, Thomas James & Anna Maria: Arthur 1880, Anna Maria Davis 1882, Priscilla Gertrude 1885.
JOHNSON, Thomas & Frances: Sarah 1803, Francis 1806, Frances 1808.
JOHNSON, William & Ann: Jane 1760.
JOHNSON, William & Elizabeth: Sarah 1764, Alice 1766, Sarah 1768, William 1771, Elizabeth 1774, Ann 1776, Charlotte 1780.
JOHNSON, William (labourer/slate cleaver) & Elizabeth: Joseph 1809, Mary Ann 1812, Thomas 1815, William 1816, William 1818, Henry 1818.
JOHNSON, William & Jane: William 1732, Thomas 1733, Robert 1735, Robert 1736, Jane 1739, Joseph 1746.
JONES, Christopher (building engineer) & Caroline Mackenzie: Clare Catherine 1986.
JONES, David Gwynfor (senior technician) & Doreen Hazel: Sian Margaret 1966.
JONES, Gareth (engineer) & Harriet: William Ralph 2010
JONES, Stephen Mark (solicitor) & Elizabeth Anne: Amy Elizabeth 1991, William Stephen (b1990) 1991, Thomas Matthew 1997.
KARRAN, Roger Alexander (captain, RASC) & Bertha Joy: Rosemary Alexander 1941.
KERR, Finlay Robert (police officer) & Vicky (careers advisor): Harrison William Finlay 2010.

KETCHER, Sarah: Thomas 1776.
KINAL, Peter John (bank clerk) & Elinor Jane Waldron: Christopher Waldron 1979, Heather Jane 1981.
KINDER, Peter Charles (company director) & Sandra Elizabeth: Sophie Elizabeth 1988, Aimee Louise 1991.
KING, Paul Frederick (sales & marketing director) & Bertha Ines: Ian Paul Eduardo 1982, Richard Enrique 1984.
KINGHORN, George Robert (physician) & Sheila Anne: Robert Alexander 1978.
KIRBY, George & Mary: Thomas 1746, Martha 1750, John 1753.
KIRKE, William & Isobel: William 1720.
KIRTON, Graham Crawford & Erin Doris Amelia: John Christopher 1997.
KNIGHT, Richard (labourer) & Elizabeth: Edward 1713, William 1715, Edward 1718.
KNIGHT, Thomas & Hannah: Elizabeth 1742.
KNOPP, Gunta (market gardener) & Ingebord: Sonia Ingrid 1958.
LAKIN, John (husbandman) & Ann: William 1634, Henry 1638.
LAMB, Lawrence James (electrical engineer) & Doreen Ann: James Edward 1972, Andrew Laurence Peter (b1973) 1975.
LANE, Richard Elliott (nail manufacturer) & Elizabeth Joyce: David Viccars 1937, Elizabeth Ann 1939, Anthony Richard 1942, Rosemary Margaret 1945.
LAUNDON, John Harold Redfern (serving with King's forces) & Winifred Lilian Bertha: Alioyn Clarendon Redfern 1917.
LAURENCE, John & Sarah: Ann 1782.
LAWSON, Jonathan Mark (groundsman/contract supervisor) & Tina Marie: Jodi Louise 1988, Thomas Michael 1991; Magnus (motor trader) & Barbara WRIGHT (housing officer): Jessica Dawn Romayne 2008 (born 1998)
LEAGOE, Thomas (shoemaker) & Anne: [dau] 1720, Sarah 1722, Thomas 1724.
LEAKE, John (farmer) & Mary Anne: William Jarvis 1835, Mary Anne Alice 1835; Martin John (marketing manager) & Julia Caroline (sales development manager): Samuel Thomas 2007, Maisie Poppy 2011.
LEATHERLAND, John William (farm labourer) & Ada Mary: John William 1932.
LEATHERLAND, John William (farmer) & Joan Margaret: Ann 1960.
LEE, Samuel William & Sarah Jane: Sarah Makala Jane 1887, Thomas William 1887, Edwin Harry 1888, Annie Agnes Jane 1890.
LEE, William & Elizabeth: Thomas 1702, Richard 1704.
LEE, William Edgar (roadman) & Ada Mary: Edgar William 1928, Helen Mahala Mary 1929.
LEE, Zachariah (roadman) & Nellie Jacques: Beryl Margaret 1926, Norma Mary 1927.
LEEMING, Paul (sales manager) & Lynne Tracey (clinical scientist): Jonathon Paul 2005, Matthew Robert 2007
LESSLEY, Andrew & Sarah: Elizabeth 1760.
LEVIS, Benjamin (farmer) & Mary: Mary 1792, Ann 1794, Sarah 1796, William 1798, Alse 1799.
LEWIN, Benjamin & [wife]: Anne 1698, John 1700, Benjamin 1701.
LEWIN, Samuel (labourer) & Ann: Rebecca 1837, Bertha Ellen 1839, Thomas 1841, John 1843, Jane 1844, Jemima 1848, Ann 1848.
LISTER-KAYE, John Lister (baronet) & Matilda: Emma 1825, Lister 1827.
LIVINGSTONE, William John (farm labourer) & Isabel: Philip David (b1957) 1958, Robin 1958, Edward Macleod 1961.
LLOYD, George Lewis (gardener) & Edna Minnie: Annie Patricia 1934, Pamela Mary 1938, George Michael 1943.
LLOYD, Percival George (gamekeeper) & Hannah Matilda King: George Lewis 1909, Percival William 1909, Gladys Mary 1910, Dorothy Freda 1913, Sidney Edward 1916, Herbert Roy 1918.
LLOYD, Percival William (engine driver) & Doris Annie: Peter William 1931.
LLOYD, Peter (farmer) & Mary: Peter Robert 1957.

LLOYD, Sidney Edward (HM Forces) & Phyllis May: Rodney Edward 1944.
LOCKWOOD, [parents] (shoemaker): Joseph 1840.
LOVAT, George & Mary: John 1797.
LOVETT, Henry & [wife]: [son] 1705.
LOVETT, Henry & Dorothy: William 1685.
LOVETT, Mary: John 1720.
LOVETT, Thomas & Elizabeth: Anne 1747, Mary 1749, Thomas 1750, Isabella 1752.
LOVITT, Thomas (tailor) & Elizabeth: John 1790.
LOVETT, William (mason) & Anne: Anne 1724, William 1727, Thomas 1730, Sarah 1734.
LOVETT, William & Sarah: William 1747, Mary 1749, John 1751, Thomas 1752, Rebecca 1754, Alice 1755.
LOWES, George Albert (civil servant) & Barbara Ellen: Elizabeth Ann 1955, Robert John 1958.
LOWES, Simon Peverall (executive) & Shirley: Christopher Peverall 1985.
LUCAS, Simon James (insurance accounts manager) & Deborah: Phoebe Alexandra 1991.
LUETCHFORD, Peter (company director) & Clare Denise: Karl Peter (b1986) 1991, Tanya Clare 1991.
LYNCH, Kevin Paul (company director) & Lynda Anne: Vincent Mark 1986, Helen Louise 1988, Katherine Lucy 1990.
LYNES, Charles (schoolmaster) & Ann: Harriett Ann 1860, Mary Helena 1862, Charles William 1864, Caroline Eliza 1867, Louisa Alice 1876.
LYNES, Charles & Hannah: Florence Elizabeth 1881, Arthur Henry 1883.
LYNES, Richard & Ruth: Sarah 1802, Thomas 1805.
LYNES, Thomas (labourer) & Elizabeth: Sarah 1841, Elizabeth 1841, Ann 1843.
MAIN, Stephen & Clara : Clara 1869.
McCHRYSTAL, Ian Denis (company director) & Susan Joy: Charles Ian 1984, Emma Charlotte 1986.
McCLINTOCK, Patrick (taxi proprietor) & Myra May: Myra Maureen (b1936) 1952.
McCLURE, John & Sophia: Annie Mabel 1882.
McDONALD, Jon Lance (company director) & Beverley Marie: Ross Alexander Lance 1980, Charlene Dominique Toni 1981.
McGUNNIGLE: Michael Jonathan (account manager) & Linzi Joanne (business analyst): Daniel Michael (born 2004) Oliver John (born 2006), 2008
MANIAS, Antony (general manager) & Anne: Alexandra 1991, Nicholas Reinert 1994.
MARCH, Alfred & Margaret: Alan 1964.
MARSHALL, Frederick Donald (commercial traveller) & Millicent Lavinia: Mary 1926.
MARSHALL, John Jeremy (pharmaceutical industry executive) & Juliett Anne: Sarah Rachel 1964.
MARSTON, Nigel James (retail manager) & Lesley Carroll: Joshua Luke 1992.
MARTIN, Thomas & [wife]: Robert 1684.
MAY, Timothy Hugh Clare (builder) & Nicola Karen (clothes designer): George James, 2008
MEASOME, Francis (wheelwright) & Mary: Mary 1637.
MEE, John (husbandman) & Elizabeth: Ann 1703, John 1706, Elizabeth 1709.
MEE, John & Elizabeth: John 1754.
MEE, John (stockingweaver) & Mary: Anne 1715.
MEE, Richard William (sheep farmer) & Jane Elizabeth: Laura Elizabeth 1990.
MELLOR, Stephen & Theresa: Rosemary (b1982) 1995.
MERRIMAN, William & Martha: Annie 1875.
MILLEY, James & Mary Jane: Mary 1875.
MILTON, Alex Paul (doctor) & Emma Louise (teacher): Isabella Rose 2010
MILNER, Henry Robert & Mary Ann: George William 1892, Fanny 1892, Frank Henry 1892, John Alvaro 1896.

MINKLEY, George & Mary Sophia: Violet Lilian 1896, Horace 1898, Alice May 1903, Kathleen 1909.
MINKLEY, George Henry (carman) & Martha Mahala Sarah: Joyce Mary 1927.
MINKLEY, Herbert (general workman) & Mary Ann: Muriel 1903, Doris 1903, Herbert 1909, Evelyn Mary 1909, Charles Edward 1909, Gladys Elizabeth 1911, Marjorie 1913, Irene Elsie 1915, Thomas George 1920.
MINKLEY, Horace (quarryman/farm labourer) & Olive Agnes: Dorothy Kathleen Mary 1923, Colin 1931, Brian Roy 1939.
MINKLEY, John William & Elsie Mary: Kathleen Mary 1922.
MOORE, Charles & Emma: Charles Frederick 1866, Arthur 1868, Thomas 1875, Fanny 1875, Henry 1875.
MOORE, Horace George (gardener) & Alice: Gladys Mae 1926.
MOOR Joseph (labourer) & Hannah: Joseph (b1696) 1716.
MOOR, Sarah: John Burnaby 1738.
MORGAN, Leslie (teacher) & Erica Mary: Judith Erica 1964.
MORRIS, Francis (servant) & Jane: Harriett 1858.
MORRIS, Francis (blacksmith) & Mary: Francis 1802, Mary 1803, William 1807, Thomas 1809, Sarah 1815, Joseph 1816.
MORRIS, Ann (servant): Albert 1843.
MORRIS, George (farmer/labourer) & Ann: Ann 1815, George 1818, Jane 1821, Catherine 1823, Mary 1826, Mary 1827, Daniel 1830.
MORRIS, George & Catherine: Rosa Alice 1867.
MORRIS, George (blacksmith) & Mary: Fanny Agnes 1839, Ellen 1841, George 1850, Cordelia 1850, Frank 1850.
MORRIS, John (blacksmith) & Caroline: Emma Sophia 1842, Caroline 1848, Eliza Mary 1849, Frances 1849, John Edward 1849, Caroline 1851.
MORRIS, Jason Wayne (adult) 2001
MORRIS, Jason Wayne (audio shop proprietor) & Elke: Jacob Jay 2001
MOSS, Herbert Arthur & Ethel Mabel: Phyllis Adeline 1921.
MOULDS, Christopher James (soldier) & Rebecca: Brandon Thomas 2009 (born 2005), Nathan George 2009 (born 2006)
MUSGROVE, Stuart Donaldson (microbiologist) & Elizabeth Anne: Thomas William 1977, Joseph Anthony 1979.
MUSGROVE, Thomas Donaldson (carpenter) & Kathleen Margaret May: Stuart Donaldson 1947.
MUTCH, Robert (motor driver) & Betty: Ann (b1951) 1954, Valerie Jane 1954.
NEALE, Andrew Robert (internet consultant) & Justine Anne (marketing manager): Mary Elizabeth 2003
NEEDHAM, Frederick (shoe operator) & Alice Rachel: Ralph Ernest James 1912.
NEEDHAM, Henry Holyoak & Doris Olivia Bannister: Henry Conway 1921.
NESBITT, Peter John (company director) & Hazel Irene: Stephen John 1987, Laura Kate 1990.
NEWBERG, Savilla (servant): Sarah Jane 1853.
NEWBOLD, John & Elizabeth: Samuel 1772, Goodath 1775, Elizabeth 1779.
NEWBOLD, John & Sarah: Edward 1764, Edward 1766, Robert 1768.
NEWBOLD, Robert & Goodath: Francis 1732, Mary 1733.
NEWBY, John & Hannah: John 1784, Mary 1788 & Elizabeth 1788 & Martha 1788 (triplets).
NEWBY, John (labourer) & Mary: Elizabeth 1789, Mary 1797, Thomas (b1800) 1806, Mary (b1803) 1806, Hannah 1806, George 1809.
NEWBY, William & Hannah: Henry 1786.
NEWTON, Adam Killingworth (general manager) & Gaynor-Jo: Harry Miller 2004
NEWTON, Hayden Henry (director) & Sandra: Sarah Jane 1982, Jenna Louise 1985.
NICHOLAS, Edward & Mary: Sarah 1767.
NICHOLLS, William & Ann: Ann 1678.

NOON, Tom & Mary Elizabeth: Edith Gertrude 1888, Hilda 1890.
NORTH, David Allen (grocer) & Wendy Christine Helen: Nicholas Andrew (b1962) 1972, Dominic David James Paul (b1968) 1972.
NORTH, Dominic James Paul (chef) & Julie Ann **LOWE** (accounts manager): Lottie Olive 2009
NORTH, Nicholas (journalist) & Tracey: Sam Christopher 1992.
NORTHAM, John Malcolm (teacher) & Josephine Hartree: Sarah Frances 1968.
NORTON, Edgar & Annie Lizzie: Edith Gertrude 1886.
NURSE, Jacob (labourer & farmer) & Sarah: John 1789, Sarah 1793.
OLDERSHAW, Henry (farmer) & Mary: Elizabeth Ann 1848.
OLIVER, Alfred & Jane Elizabeth: Ena Miriam 1905.
OLIVER, Frederick James (clerk in holy orders) & Marian: Margaret 1927.
ORME, Robert Bryan Lewis (farmer) & Patricia Helen: Pauline Helen 1959.
ORTON, Charles Victor (waterworks) & Ruth Jessie: Jane Elizabeth 1951.
PAGE, John & Ellen: Cordelia Morris 1869.
PAGE, Sarah: Thomas 1756.
PAGE, Jason Robert Stoddard (company director) & Justine Rosalind (company director): Amelia Alice Cosima 2001
PAGET, Edward James (clerk, rector) & Emma Catherine: Horatio Edward 1843, Frances Elizabeth 1844, Eleanor Caroline 1845, Frederica Maria 1849, Charles Berkeley 1849, Edward Clarence 1851.
PALMER, Elizabeth: Elizabeth 1750.
PARKER, John & [wife]: John 1695, Elizabeth 1701.
PARKER, William & Ann: Thomas 1676.
PARTRIDGE, Lloyd Glyn (company director) & Caroline (company director): Olivia Catherine (b 1997) 2000, Guy Alexander 2000
PATTERSON, Andrew (gardener) & Ann: Isabella 1848, John 1850.
PATERSON, Kenneth Robert (gardener) & Olive May: David 1940.
PATERSON, William (gardener) & Emily Elizabeth: Malcolm 1908, Kenneth Robert 1909, Edmund Keith 1912.
PAVESI, Richard (management consultant) & Lucy Anne (doctor/medical advisor): Eliot James 1994, Alice Louise 1996.
PAYNE, John & Mary: Fanny Elizabeth 1884, Charles 1884.
PEAKE, William & [wife]: Elizabeth 1695.
PEBODY, John & Hannah: John 1700, [son] 1701, Elizabeth 1703, Hannah 1707.
PEBERDY, John (farmer) & Sarah: Emmeline Ethel 1859.
PELLICIER, Bruno (ski patroller, mason) & Amanda June (ski patroller): George Antoine 2004, Louis William 2008
PENNY, Christopher John (company director) & Marion: Sophie Frances (b1987) 1991, Emelia Frances 1991.
PENTELOW, Arthur William (gardener) & Jane: Veta Queenie Freda 1939.
PEPPER, Edwin & Emma: Thomas Lewis Mason 1884, Charles Henry 1886, Frederick Wiliam Zaccheus 1889, Doris Olivia Banniston 1891.
PERKINS, John & Lydia: John 1760, Rebecca 1761, Elizabeth 1763, Martha 1764.
PERKINSON, Thomas (labourer) & Elizabeth: William 1711, Elizabeth 1713, Thomas 1714, John 1717, Martha 1720, Richard 1723.
PETTS, Benjamin (labourer) & Anne: Anne 1827.
PETTS, Benjamin (labourer) & Mary: Sarah 1831.
PHIPS, Susannah (sworn to John Bates): John 1813.
PICKAVER, Andrew Nicholas (builder) & Sandra Jane: Andrew Barry Roy 1984.
PICKERING, George (butcher) & Deborah: George 1722, Benjamin 1722.
PICKERING, Joseph & Elizabeth: Anne 1813.
PITT, Samuel & Elizabeth: Anne 1780.
PLACE, William & Elizabeth: William 1779.
POLE, William & Mary: John 1684.

POLLARD, Benjamin & Ann: Benjamin 1754, Elizabeth 1758, Ann 1760, John 1764.
POLLARD, John (labourer) & Elizabeth: Thomas 1704, Richard 1707, John 1712, Jacob 1715, Benjamin 1723.
POLLARD, John & Elizabeth: Hannah 1775.
POLLARD, John & Hannah: John 1743.
POLLARD, John & Mary: Elizabeth 1764, Edward 1769.
POLLARD, Thomas & Elizabeth: Sarah 1733, Thomas 1736.
POLLARD, Thomas & Hannah: Ann 1749, Elizabeth 1752.
POLLARD, Thomas & Mary: John 1762, Ann 1764, William 1766, Catherine 1768, John 1770, Sarah 1770, Mary 1775, Jane 1777.
POLLARD, Thomas & Sarah: William 1741.
POLLARD, William & Elizabeth: John 1731, Anne 1733, William 1738, Thomas 1742, Edward 1746.
PORT, John (framework knitter) & Rebecca: Robert 1726.
PORTE, David Timothy (company director) & Veronica Lois: Lois Emily 1987, Charlotte Emma 1990.
PORTER, Edward & Mary: Catherine 1682.
PORTER, Joseph (miller) & Ann: Elizabeth 1788, Thomas 1790, Ann 1793.
PORTER, Thomas (labourer) & Catherine: Thomas 1711, John 1714, [son] 1716, William 1719, Anne 1721, Catherine 1723, Daniel 1725.
PORTER, Thomas & Elizabeth: Mary 1738.
PORTER, William & Ann: Henry 1678.
POTTER, George (railway porter) & Ann: George William 1854.
POTTER, William (blacksmith) & Elizabeth: William 1813, William 1814, Ann 1815, Elizabeth 1818.
POULSON, Mark David (accountant) & Angela Caroline (graphic designer): Harrison Neil 2010
POWELL, Harry George (clerk) & Margaret: Averil Evelyn Gertrude 1934.
PRATT, Joseph & Annie: Henry 1886, Francis 1888, Annie Elizabeth 1890, Sarah Hilda 1892, Mary Ethel 1894.
PRATT, Joseph & Sarah: Joseph 1866, Charles Benjamin 1869, George Thomas 1871.
PRATT, Nevill Joseph (education welfare officer) & Hazel Winifred: Kathryn Alison 1964.
PRESTON, Arthur (bricklayer) & Mary: Elizabeth 1862, William 1862.
PRESTON, Daniel (carpenter) & Jane: Emma 1831.
PRESTON, Eliza: Thomas Walter (b1851) 1859.
PRESTON, James Richard & Alice: Edith May 1909.
PRESTON, Joseph & Ann: Ann 1744, John 1745, Joseph 1747.
PRESTON, Joseph (labourer) & Alice: Thomas 1835, William 1835, Mary 1838, Joseph 1839, John 1839.
PRESTON, Joshua (bricklayer/mason) & Mary: Eliza 1831, Harriet 1839, George 1839, Aaron Denbigh 1839, Emma Rosa Matilda 1839, Charlotte 1843, Charlotte 1846, Lucy 1846, Robert 1859, Alex (b1851) 1859.
PRESTON, Richard & Jane: Ruth 1835.
PRESTON, Sarah Ann: Kathleen Nellie 1909.
PRESTON, Thomas (labourer) & Sarah: Ann 1815, William 1821, Sarah 1821, Thomas 1825, Martha 1828, Zipponah 1841.
PRESTON, William & Anne: Jinny 1770, John 1772, Martha 1774, Joseph 1775.
PRESTON, William (labourer) & Anne: Anne 1838, Arthur 1838, Simson 1838, George 1838, Mary 1838, William (b1821) 1847.
PRESTON, William & Frances: Bessie Anne 1866.
PRESTON, William & Mary: Jane 1739, William 1742.
PRICE, David Patrick Chester (engineer) & Marie Gertrude: Maaike Alicia Sophie 1968.
PRICE, Neville Earnest (farm worker) & Hilda: Andrew David 1964.

PRICE, Robert & Elizabeth: Robert 1746.
PRIDGEON, Christopher (factory manager) & Penny Anne: Rebecca Jane 1976.
PRIOR, Joseph (mason) & Elizabeth: Dorothy 1715, Joseph 1717, Elizabeth 1723.
PRIOR, Joseph & Mary: John 1729, Joseph 1733.
PRIOR, Robert & Elizabeth: Joseph 1679, Elizabeth 1680.
PRIOR, Robert & Elizabeth: Ann 1739, Elizabeth 1740, Mary 1742, Martha 1744, Robert 1747, Henry 1748, Samuel 1750, Robert 1755.
PRIOR, Samuel (mason) & Anne: Isabella 1700, Robert 1705, Elizabeth 1708.
PRIOR, Stephen & Sarah: Thomas 1773, John 1774, Sarah 1776, Sarah 1777.
PRIOR, Thomas (farmer) & Elizabeth: Thomas 1811, John 1814.
PUGH, William (manager) & Angela: Toby William John 2001
QUINTON, Richard & Mary: Ann 1788.
RAINER, Thomas (framework knitter) & Sarah: Anne 1817, Elizabeth 1817, Eliza 1817.
RANLME, Robert Mark Andrew (freight forwarder) & Lillibet: Nathaniel Patterson Kirby 1991.
RATCLIFFE, Thomas & Matilda: Herbert Ernest 1881.
RATCLIFFE, Thomas & Sarah Jane: Sarah Elizabeth 1875, Charles Edmund 1875, Thomas 1875.
RAWLINS, George & Mary: Mary 1727.
RAYNOR, Alan David (sales representative) & Angela Marjorie: David Edward 1965.
RAYNOR, Isaac (slatecleaver) & Joanna: Isaac 1856.
RAYNOR, Robert (labourer) & Mary: John Thomas 1837, Sarah Anne 1841, Robert 1843, Francis 1846, Frederick Petts 1850.
RAYNOR, Thomas & Christian: Thomas 1784, Elizabeth 1790.
RAYNOR, Thomas & Elizabeth: Mary 1755, Francis 1760, Zacharias 1762, Elizabeth 1766, John 1772, Ann 1775,
RAYNOR, Thomas (labourer) & Jane: Samuel 1860, Thomas George 1862, Sarah Jane 1864, Eliza Hannah 1866, William Francis 1868, Edwin Henry 1870, Mary Charlotte 1872, Makala 1874, Sam Deeming 1877.
RAYNOR, William (labourer) & Ann: Thomas 1853, John 1853, Frederick 1853.
RAYNOR, Zachariah (slate cleaver/labourer) & Anne: William 1820, William 1825, Mary 1825, Elizabeth 1831, Eliza 1831, Harriet 1841, Thomas 1841, James 1841, Christina Louisa 1842.
REEDER, Reginald Luard (farm labourer) & Winifred Lilian Bertha: Rosamond Mahala 1928.
REID, Andrew Ian (engineer's pattern maker) & Ann Barbara: Alastair Ian 1979.
RENALS, Ann (singlewoman): Harriet 1854.
RENSHAW, Derek Geoffrey (hairdresser) & Susan Irene: Lisa Dawn 1980.
RICHARDSON, Barfoot (butcher) & Elizabeth: Elizabeth 1813, John Lakin 1815, [child] 1818.
RICHARDSON, Paul (chartered accountant) & Valerie Edwards: Benjamin Paul 1981, Wendy Jane 1983.
RIGBY, Josiah & Hannah: Mary 1775, John 1777, Charlotte 1780, James 1784.
RILEY, Stuart Ian (auditor) & Audrey Louise: Amy Charlotte 1991.
RINGROSE, Alfred Roland (farm labourer) & Rose Hannah: Alice Vera (b1927) 1929, Alfred 1930, Margaret Ann 1933, Joyce Mary 1938.
ROBBINS, Edward & Florence: Sarah 1887.
ROBERTS, John Michael (electrical engineer) & Janet: Christopher James 1982.
ROBSON, John Percy (industrial chemist) & Patricia Mary: Timothy John 1957, David James 1960.
ROBSHAW, Paul Randall (company director) & Joyce Vera: Judith Caroline 1958.
ROCKLEY, George (labourer) & Mary: Sarah Smith 1848, William Smith 1849, Sarah Jane 1851.
ROE, Mary: Benjamin Assel 1795, John (a bastard by Matthew Simpson) 1803.

ROGERS, John Patrick Austin (company director) & Susan Margaret: John Mark Austin 1976.
ROGERS, Richard (gardener) & Dinah: Isabel 1853, Edmund 1854, Arthur 1856, Helen 1858.
ROLLS, Charles Richard (hotel manager) & Diane Anne: David Paul 1978, Christopher Peter 1981.
ROLPH, Malcolm Frederick (airline pilot) & Christine Therese: Charlotte Ashley 1986.
ROSE, Thomas Henry & Charlotte Lucy: Thomas William Edwin 1896.
ROSS, Edward Robert Charles (detective constable) & Laura Jane: Ian Harrison 1997, Natalie Jane 1999.
ROSS, Joseph (labourer) & Sarah: James 1851.
ROW, Thomas (labourer) & Elizabeth: Elizabeth Ann 1859.
ROWLINSON, Walter Bradley (hairdresser) & Julia: Carrie (b1918) 1964.
RUDKIN, John (farmer) & Sarah: Sarah Frances 1861, Sophie 1863, Emma 1863.
RUDKIN, Walter (gardener) & Mary Emma: Doreen Hazel 1936.
RUDKIN, William & Elizabeth: Elizabeth 1740.
RUSSELL, Nicholas Simon (production manager/sales manager) & Jennifer Mary: Alexander Benjamin 1987, Olivia May 1989.
SANDERS, Joseph & Elizabeth: Elizabeth 1728, Joseph 1732, Thomas 1736.
SAUNDERS, David Charles (company manager) & Dinah Susan: Louise Charlotte 1978.
SAUNDERS: Joseph & Phyabe: George 1739.
SCADDAN, Henry (butler) & Elizabeth: Caroline 1849, Henry 1852, Louisa 1854, Emma 1856.
SCHOFIELD, James & Juliana Ann: Juliana Bates 1879.
SCOPPIE, Roger Patrick (university administrator) & Hilary Gay: Oliver Marcus 1984, Imogen Flora 1989.
SCOTT, John William Fairfax & Dorothy: Caroline Elizabeth Fairfax (b1946) 1971.
SCRIVENS, Sally Ann 2007 (adult baptism from St Paul's, Woodhouse Eaves)
SEATON, James (labourer) & Harriett: Elizabeth Anne 1859, Zachariah Raynor 1859.
SENIOR, Keith Howe (insurance broker) & Margaret: Charlotte Samantha 1972.
SHAKESBY, Alan Peter (public service vehicle driver) & Susan Joan: Alison Clare 1976.
SHARDLOW, John (printer) & Rita: Christopher John 1955.
SHARP, John & Mary Ann: Ernest 1877, Frederick 1880.
SHARPE, John & Patricia: Kate (b.1983) 1997.
SHAW, Joseph (labourer/slate cleaver) & Elizabeth: Charles 1843, James William 1854, Arthur 1854, George 1854, Ann Preston 1855.
SHEARMAN, Charles Pinnell & Emily: Frances Emily 1896.
SHELLARD, Paul David (printing sales executive) & Sally Ann (accounts clerk): Steven Leonard (b.1994) 2005.
SHELTON, Samuel (labourer) & Ann: Sarah 1808, Ann 1810, Samuel 1813 & John 1813 (twins), Mary 1815, Thomas 1817.
SHEPHERD, Joseph & Mary: John 1758.
SHEPHERDSON, John Sidney & Annie Jane: Nancy May 1902.
SHERIDAN-KNOWLES, Paul John Sheridan (research technician) & Maxine Dawn Sheridan-Knowles: Emily Josephine 2006, born 2001.
SHILVOCK, Ronald Alfred Stanley (commercial traveller) & Sheila Kathleen: James Edward 1956, Timothy William 1959.
SHORT, Mary Sophia Eliza (supposed to be by Hon Augustus Richard Butler Danvers) 1803, Emily (supposed to be by Sam Offson) 1803.
SHORTER, Ernest Victor (farm labourer) & Dorothy: Jean Mary 1937.
SIBSON, Thomas & Mary: Thomas 1635.
SIDEBOTTOM, Kingsford Beauchamp (clerk) & Frances Elizabeth: Frances 1878, Beauchamp Henry 1879, Audrey Ann Florence 1884.

SIFTON, Anthony & Jane: Elizabeth 1634, Mary 1635, Michael 1635, William 1639.
SIMMONS, Charles Edward Rupert (builder) & Ethel Martha: John Charles 1937, David Reginald 1939, Patricia Susan 1948, Carol Kathleen 1950, Elizabeth Mary 1953.
SIMMONS, Reginald Alfred (builder) & Dorothy Rose: Cedric Paul 1946, Helen Joyce 1949.
SIMPKIN, Peter & [wife]: Elizabeth 1634.
SIMPSON: Charles Fred (b1913) 1933.
SIMPSON, Mary Ann (singlewoman): Henry 1854.
SIMPSON, Matthew (farmer) & Elizabeth: Matthew 1789, Joseph 1791, Anne 1791, John 1792, William 1794, Mary 1795, Mary 1803.
SIMPSON, Matthew (farmer) & Mary: Matthew 1821, Mary Anne 1825, Frances 1828, William 1831.
SIMPSON, Thomas & Elizabeth: Thomas 1743, John 1747, John 1748.
SIMPSON, William & [wife]: Sarah 1803.
SIMPSON, William & Mary: William 1863, John Thomas 1864.
SKELLINGTON, George & Grace Granger: George 1638.
SKERINGTON, Joseph Hellaby & Emma: Kate Hellaby 1878.
SKETCHLEY, Edward (labourer) & Harriet: Emma 1898.
SKETCHLEY, Elizabeth (servant): Fanny 1858.
SLATER, Peter Graham Nash (general manager) & Louise Margaret: Anthony Charles 1986.
SMITH, Andrew (economist) & Myrna: Mieke Kyra 1987, Kayleigh Lara 1989.
SMITH, Edward & Mary: Edward 1686, Mary 1692.
SMITH, Frederick William & Edith Winifred: Marjorie Hazel (b1922) 1968.
SMYTH, Joseph & Ann: Ann 1638.
SMITH, Kenneth Paul (police officer) & Suzanne Dawn: Samuel Joseph 1994.
SMITH, Michael James (building society chief clerk) & Susan Phyllis: Andrew Michael Lees 1975, Anthony James 1977.
SMITH, Michael (sports development director) & Catherine Nadine Krznaric: Maya Jean 2010, Magellan 2010
SMITH, Robert Alan (schoolmaster) & Sandra Elizabeth: Matthew Oliver 1970, Paul James 1972.
SMITH, Stuart Arthur & Doreen Margaret: Stephen James Adrian (b1954) 1963.
SMITH, Thomas & Elizabeth: Mary 1754, Thomas 1755, Elizabeth 1757.
SMITH, Thomas (labourer) & Mary: Sarah 1705, Ann 1708, Elizabeth 1711, Thomas 1715.
SMITH, Thomas Percival (chauffeur) & Florence Ethel: Gillian Ann 1944.
SMITH, William & Grace: Ann 1635.
SNOW, Henry (butcher & farmer) & [wife]: [child] 1818.
SOARES, William & Elizabeth: Elizabeth 1742, William 1745.
SPENCE, George (motor driver) & Violet Annie: Frank George 1923.
SPENCER, John (labourer) & Mary: Tom 1853, William 1856, Edward 1857, John Edward 1859, James 1861, Sarah Anne 1864, Mary 1866.
SQUIRE, Henry (husbandman) & Ann: Ann 1634, Frances 1637.
STABLES, Samuel & Jane: Samuel 1687.
STEPHENS, Edward & Mary: Edward 1685.
STEVENSON, Arthur Ernest (labourer) & Ivy Annie Elsie: Bernard Arthur 1939.
STEVENSON, Bernard Arthur (foreman of despatch) & Gillian Mary: Julia Anne 1963.
STEVENSON, John & Elizabeth: Hannah 1785.
STONE, Bert Henry (coach finisher) & Jean Gertrude: John Arthur 1948, Enid Glenys 1949.
STONE, Frederick (coach builder) & Elsie: Bert Henry (b1922) 1965.
STONE, John Arthur (garage proprietor) & Celia: Amanda Glenys 1978.
STUART-SMITH, David (civil engineer) & Elizabeth Ann: Caroline Frances 1968.
SUTTON, Francis (blacksmith) & Margaret: Samuel 1638.

SUTTON, Thomas & Mary: Mary 1779.
SWAINE, Thomas & Alice: Thomas 1676.
SWIFT, John (servant) & Eliza: Alfred 1842.
SYKES, Stephen Alan Howarth (company director) & Rachel Alison (housewife): Daniel Peter Howarth 2005, Harriet Christine Ramsay 2007.
SYMINGTON, Archibald & Mary Williamson: Reginald (b1905) 1956.
TALBOT, George Austin & Harriet: Margaret Austin 1895.
TAYLOR, Frederick William (gardener) & Sarah: Kathleen 1914.
TAYLOR, Gordon Maurice (hosiery manufacturer) & Barbara May: Joanna Jane 1965, Amanda Jane 1965, Virginia May 1970.
TAYLOR, Leslie (labourer) & Edith Helen: Ida Kathleen 1927, Leslie 1927.
TAYLOR, Rupert James (piano tuner) & Louise Georgina (occupational therapist/teacher): Claudia Rose Kennedy (born 2000) 2007
TEBBUTT, Ralph Smalley & Elizabeth: Smalley 1796, Frances 1813.
THOMAS, Maurice Anthony (bank official) & Barbara Miriam: Helen Barbara 1963, David Anthony 1967.
THOMPSON, John (labourer) & Hannah: William 1827, Catherine 1830, Richard 1832, Ann (b1838) 1847.
THORNTON, Joseph (labourer) & Mary: Jane 1817.
THORNTON, Thomas & Margaret: Mary 1809, Thomas 1809.
THORPE, Nicholas John (shoe components director) & Sandra Dora: Peter Lawrence 1965, Simon Nicholas 1968, Lisa Jane 1969.
THORPE, John (labourer) & Lydia: Mary Anne 1838.
THORPE, John (labourer) & Sarah: Louis Jabez 1841.
THORPE, Samuel (slate cleaver/labourer) & Mary: Thomas 1821, Elizabeth 1823, George 1841, Charlotte (b1831) 1847, Mary 1853.
THORPE: Sarah 1768.
THORPE, Simon Nicholas (sales engineer) & Julia (educational sales): Lawrence John 1999.
THORPE, William & Mary: John Clarke 1793, George 1803, Thomas 1803, Elizabeth 1807, Anne 1811, Richard 1811.
TILBY, Joshua & Hannah: John Henry 1809.
TILLIORYHAIT, Thomas Charles & Sarah Ann: John Thomas 1866.
TILLOTSON, Leonard (farm worker) & Sheila Mary: Diane Mary 1950.
TOBIN, Michael John (mechanical engineer) & Valerie Ann (teacher): Anna Grace 2001.
TOMAJER, Pietro (area sales manager) & Anna **MICHALSKA** (artist): Matteo Carlo Stan 2007, Gracie Isabella 2010.
TOONE, Andrew Shirley (school teacher) & Gaynor Mary: Benjamin Andrew Bourner 1984, Amanda Jayne 1987.
TOONE, Thomas John (tobacconist) & Sarah: John Henry 1858.
TORMEY, Richard John (electrical engineer) & Margaret Christina: Sally 1947, John 1947.
TOWNSEND, Henry (labourer) & Ann: Sophia 1813, Henry 1815.
TREVOR-ROPER, Richard Eric (accounts clerk) & Patricia Ann: Richard Patrick 1955.
TURNBULL, William Stuart (horse trainer) & Virginia May (horse trainer): Jack Henry 2009
TWIGGER, Harold (bricklayer) & Joan Lilian Moyra: Bayoane Rosemarie Romaine (b1945) 1953.
TYLER, Howard Vernon (solicitor) & Ruth: William Alec 1948, Vivienne Ruth 1950.
UNDERWOOD, William & Eliza: William 1877.
UPTON, George & Eliza: George William 1862.
UPTON, Joseph (labourer) & Eliza: Mary Louisa 1854, Eliza 1856, Thomas 1859.
UTECHT, Terrance (joiner) & Cheryl: Andrew Franz 1979.
VANN, Albert Edward (clerk) & Doris: Beryl Elizabeth 1927.

VARHAM, Richard Leonard (farm hand) & Margaret: Anthony John 1934.
VERSO, Alan Desmond (traveller) & Edith Joan: Andrew Jonathan 1962.
VESTY, Elizabeth: Thomas Choice 1795.
VESTEY, Isaac & Ann: Ann 1778.
VESTEY, Robert & Mary: Joseph 1765, Samuel 1767, Robert 1769, Catherine 1771, Mary 1773, Elizabeth 1776, Richard 1780, Ann 1781, John 1783, Sarah 1788.
VESTY, Samuel (labourer) & Anne: Robert 1828, Jane 1831, Jemimah 1836.
VESTY, Thomas (labourer) & Hannah: Thomas 1803, Hannah 1803, Sarah 1806, Mary 1807, Ruth 1813, Mariah 1815, William 1824.
VILLAGE, William Stanley (Royal Air Force) & Gwynnth Enid: Christopher John 1946, Peter James 1948.
VINE, Julian Terence (retail manager) & Linda Ann: Amelia Jasmine 2001
WAIN, Maurice Frederick (company director) & Nellie: Penelope Michelle 1947.
WAINWRIGHT, Hannah (servant): William 1841.
WAINWRIGHT, Marcus Beresford (marketing executive) & Vivienne Mary: Jacqueline Suzanne 1962.
WAKEFIELD, Harry Alfred (gardener) & Peggy: Christine Margaret 1947.
WAKERLY, Francis (labourer) & Elizabeth: Edward 1825, George 1827, Francis 1836, Elizabeth 1838, Letitia 1841, John (b1810) 1847.
WAKERLY, John & Ann: Elizabeth 1800, Mary 1802, Francis 1804, Mary 1809, [child] 1811.
WALKER, Christopher Edward (builder) & Susan: Nina Marie 1985, Jessica Anne 1987, Ryan Mark 1989.
WALKER: James 1617.
WALKER, John (blacksmith) & Sarah: John 1702, William 1705, Sarah 1707, Alice 1710, Thomas 1712.
WALKER, Thomas & Martha: Sarah 1753, Martha 1755, Thomas 1757.
WALLER, Eric George (head master) & Lorna Margaret: Julian Charles 1963.
WALTERS, David Graham (electrical engineer) & Dorothy May Elizabeth: Nigel Graham 1960.
WALTON, Mark Jonathan (company accountant) & Judith Shirley: Simon Jonathan 1986, Oliver James 1988, Georgina Joan 1990.
WALTON, William Joseph & Kate Louisa: Annie Louisa 1905.
WARD, James (farmer) & Mary: James 1826, Mary 1830, Katherine 1831.
WARD, John & Sarah: George 1809.
WARD, John William (works foreman) and Sarah Louisa: Patsy Pamela 1950.
WARD, Thomas & Elizabeth: Robert 1812.
WARD, Thomas (labourer) & Mary: George 1830.
WARD, William (labourer) & Mary: [son] 1701, Robert 1708, William 1711.
WARDLE, Harry (bricklayer) & Mary Rebecca: Roger Neil 1944.
WARRILOW, John Keith (shopkeeper) & Judith Ann: James Mark 1976.
WARRINGTON, Bernard (grocery manager) & Clarice: Michael Alan (b1945) 1954.
WATHES, Richard Charles (dairyman) & Mary Constance: David Richard 1936, Valerie Anne 1938.
WATLING, William (labourer) & Alice: William 1639.
WATSON, Benjamin & Ann: Sarah (b1802) 1807.
WATSON, Henry (labourer) & Mary: William 1714, [son] 1716, Mary 1719, Elizabeth 1724, Thomas 1727, John 1728.
WATSON, John & Clara Helen: Arnold Wainwright 1897, Cecil Topliss 1899, Ernest Vernon Henderson 1900.
WATSON, William & Ann: Henry 1773.
WEAN, Thomas & Jane: Jane 1745, Thomas 1748.
WELLS, William & Mary: William 1761, Elizabeth 1762.
WESLEY, George & Dorothea: Sarah 1827.
WESTLEY, Joseph (framework knitter) & Mary: Joseph 1723, William 1725, Mary 1728.

WESTLEY, William (carpenter) & Anne: William 1717, John 1718, William 1721, Anne 1724, Henry 1727, Jane 1729.
WESTLEY, William & Grace: Mary 1734, Mary 1735, Sarah 1738.
WESTON, John (labourer) & Jane: Jane 1824, John 1831, Fanny 1831, Rebecca 1834.
WHATNALL, Daniel (weaver) & Mary: Squire 1707, Mary 1712, Daniel 1714.
WHATNALL, Samuel & Mary: Daniel 1736.
WHATNALL, Squire & Ann: Mary 1742, William 1743, William 1745, Thomas 1748, Milly 1754, Richard 1761.
WHATNALL, Thomas & Elizabeth: James 1775, Thomas 1777, Hannah 1779.
WHATNALL, William & Susannah: William 1771, Mary 1773, Ann 1775, Richard 1780.
WHITE, Geoffrey Ralph (chartered accountant) & Julie Ann: Adam James 1990.
WHITE, John (architectural assistant) & Janice: Benjamin James 1976.
WHITE, Joshua & Elizabeth: John 1774.
WHITE, William & Ann: John 1765, Thomas 1766, James 1768.
WHITTLE, Samuel & Anne: William 1734.
WHITWELL, William (miller) & Sarah: William 1717, Anne 1719.
WHOWELL, Anna (investment banker): George Robert 2009 (born 2006); Alexander Robert Fisher 2009 (born 2008)
WHYTE, David Francis (business) & Lois Jean: Jason Francis 1971.
WIGNALL, Howard Ernest Edwin (factory manager) & Jane Mary: Jonathan Howard 1980.
WILD, Rebecca Elizabeth (secretary): Oliver Cameron 2003, born 1997
WILDMAN, Edward (farmer) & Frances: Nathaniel Hooke 1857, Edward 1859, Frances Ann 1860, Thomas 1862, Mary 1864, William 1866.
WILKINS, Timothy John (company director) & Joanne: Katie Grace 1996, Emily May 1998, Adam Charles 2000.
WILKINS, William & Alice Mary: William Henry Percival 1877, Alice Florence Mary 1879.
WILKINSON, Richard Alan (textile manufacturer) & Susan Helen: Jocelyn Mary 1986, Samuel Robert 1988, William David 1991.
WILLAT, Anthony (labourer) & Elizabeth: Anthony 1822.
WILLIAMS, Kenneth (gardener) & Margaret Katherine: Nigel John 1955, Catherine Theresa 1957.
WILLIAMSON, (butcher): Mary 1826, Sarah Anne 1828.
WILLIAMSON, Harry (quarry worker) & Doreen May: Judith Helen 1952.
WILLIAMSON-CARR, Elspeth May Louise (adult) 1999 (conditional upon not having been previously baptised)
WILLSON, George Herbert (master printer) & Zoe Sonia: Victoria Angela 1959.
WILSON, David (labourer/gardener) & Mary: David 1827, Charlotte 1829, Eliza 1831, Emma 1834, Darcey 1836, Henry 1838, Albert George Victor 1840, Mary Anne 1842.
WILSON, Donald (builders clerk) & Cynthia Mary: Sharon Marie 1962, Louise Jane 1963.
WILSON, John Robert (antiques dealer) & Raynor Joan: Emily Grace 1992.
WILSON, Richard & Elizabeth: John 1758, George 1761.
WISE, John (labourer) & Elizabeth: Joseph 1824, John 1825, Mary 1827, Sarah 1828, Thomas 1827.
WITHERS, Martin Bernard (company director) & Sally: Amy 1982.
WOOD, James (builder) & Joanne: Benjamin Joe 1991.
WOOD, William & Ann: Sarah 1775.
WOOD, William & Mary Ann: Henrietta Fanny 1884.
WOOD, Roger (engineer) & Fay: Callum Gregory Charles (b 1993) 2000.
WOODARD, Alan James (chemist) & Susan Melanie: Alexandra Helen 1982.
WOODCOCK, William (watchmaker/television engineer) & Hazel Veronica: Nicolette Susan 1950, William Martin 1957.

WOODFORD, John & Elizabeth: John 1676, Susannah 1679.
WOODFORD, John & Sarah: Anne 1684.
WOODHOUSE, Edward Victor (security officer) & Brigitte Anne: Hannah Elizabeth 1985.
WOODS, James Henry & Mary Elizabeth: Catherine Winifred 1892.
WOODS, Joseph (labourer) & Catherine: William 1862, George Morris 1853, James Henry 1855.
WOODWARD, William (farmer) & Elizabeth: Mary 1793, Ann 1795, Elizabeth 1803, Hannah 1813.
WOOLSTON, Thomas (butler) & Frances: Thomas 1849.
WOOLSTON, William (labourer) & Charlotte: Thomas 1835.
WOOTNALL, William & Susannah: James 1787.
WORSHIP, Edward & Sarah: Dan 1684.
WORSLEY, Norman John (regional manager of retail toy firm) & Sylvia Mary: Rosemary Linden 1976.
WORTH, Paul David (engineering manager) & Elaine Mary (consultant anaesthetist): Louise Elizabeth & William Edward 2007 (twins); Charlotte Mary 2008
WREGHITT, Christopher Michael (general manager/sales & marketing consultant) & Wendy Ann: Samuel James 1991, Katie Louise 1993.
WRIGHT, Benjamin Michael Gidley (company director/footwear agent) & Rosemary Ann: Oliver James Gidley 1990, Emily Louise 1994.
WRIGHT, Ivor William (fitter/engineer) & Jean Phyllis: Mark Ivor 1956, Lloyd 1959, Philip John 1964.
WRIGHT, John (licensed victualler/farmer) & Susan: Rhoda Anne 1840, Louisa 1842, Jane 1844, Mary 1846.
WRIGHT, John Michael Gidley (shoe manufacturer) & Jill Veronica: Christopher Jeremy Gidley 1965, Jonathan Mark Gidley 1969.
WRIGHT, Nicholas Edward Gidley (company director) & Nicolette Joya: Louis Harold Gidley 1993.
WRIGHT, Orson (shoe manufacturer) & Rosamund Leslie: Patricia Orson 1939, Jacqueline Orson 1943.
YEOMANS, John (labourer) & Elizabeth: William 1826, Hannah 1826, William 1827.
YOUNG, Nathan Edward (electrician) & Zoe (flight attendant): Poppy Anna 2001, Kitty Florence 2004, Jemima Gracie 2007.

Swithland Residents: Births registered at Quorn & Loughborough, Rothley & Sileby, and Woodhouse Eaves Baptist Chapels

BEEBY, Joseph & Elizabeth (daughter of William & Mary Johnson of Sawley): Sarah 15 Sep 1812, Eliza 6 May 1813.
BESTON, William & Sarah (daughter of John & Mary Johnson of Swithland): William Apr 1827.
BIRD, William & Ann (daughter of Moses & Ann Johnson of Quorn): Ann 24 Dec 1780, Thomas 20 Aug 1783, Mary Feb 1786, Rebecca 28 May 1788, John 29 May 1791, William 22 Oct 1794.
FLETCHER, Nathan & Mary (daughter of William & Mary Johnson of Swithland): Mary 11 Nov 1809, Thomas 23 Jan 1811, Richard 11 May 1812, Ann 3 May 1814, Sarah 12 Jun 1818, Betsy 26 May 1821.
HEMSLEY, Benjamin (son of John & Hannah Helmsley of Woodhouse) & Elizabeth (daughter of Moses & Hannah Johnson of Quorn): Joseph 26 Oct 1801, Thomas 24 Sep 1805, John 21 Mar 1808.
HULL, Samuel & Catherine (daughter of Benjamin & Catherine Pollard of Quorn &

Swithland): Thomas Pollard 1 Dec 1809, William Henry 10 Sep 1810, Catherine Pollard 31 Mar 1812, Edwin 4 Jan 1815, Emma 26 Apr 1816.
HUTCHINSON, William & Mary (daughter of Richard Benskin): Mary 6 May 1822, Anna 13 Oct 1824, Jennet 1 Feb 1829.
JOHNSON, William & Mary (daughter of William & Ann Parkinson of Quorn): William 9 Jan 1787, Mary 22 Oct 1788, Thomas 15 Feb 1792, Elizabeth 24 May 1795.
MORRIS, John & Sarah (daughter of Richard Lines): William 16 Sep 1831, Mary 28 Oct 1833, Sarah 24 Jul 1836.
POLLARD, Benjamin & Catherine (daughter of Thomas & Catherine Squire of Quorndon): Catherine Squire 11 Feb 1787, Mary Ann 29 Mar 1788, Thomas Benjamin 24 Feb 1791.
PRESTON, Richard & Jane: Daniel 28 Aug 1805.
PRESTON, Robert & Mary (daughter of William & Ann Parkinson of Quorn): John 24 Nov 1788.
PRESTON, Robert & Mary (daughter of William & Elizabeth Lygo of Anstey): John Nov 1788, William 4 Jun 1790, Stephen 24 Mar 1793.
PRESTON, William (eldest son of Robert & Mary Preston of Swithland) & Ann (daughter of John & Sarah Kirby of Swithland): Elizabeth 24 Aug 1814.
STABLEFORD, John & Sarah (daughter of William & Deborah Harrison of Rempstone): John 2 Mar 1787, William 18 Jan 1789, Thomas 21 Oct 1790, Deborah Harrison 18 Aug 1792, William 17 Mar 1794.
WARD, Thomas & Elizabeth: Elizabeth 23 Jan 1810, Robert 26 Jun 1812, Daniel 1 Jun 1815, William 24 Nov 1817, Mary 7 Jul 1820.
WILD, Thomas & Ann (daughter of Samuel & Elizabeth Clark of Swithland): Thomas 17 Nov 1794.
WOOD, Thomas & Ann (daughter of Benjamin & Ann Pollard of Swithland): Elizabeth 21 Dec 1792.

St Leonard's Church, Swithland: Confirmations 1947–2008

1947, May 22, at St Peter's Mountsorrel, by Asst Bishop of Leicester, J.J. Willis prepared and presented by Rev J.L. Joyce, Vicar of Rothley
 Peter William Lloyd (15)
 Faith Kathleen Banbury (19)
 Barbara Bunney (17)
 Dorothy Mary Rudkin (16)
 Olga Muriel Fay Gregory (14)
 Sheila Ann Haynes (14)

1950, May 16, at St Bartholomew's, Quorn, by Lord Bishop of Leicester, Guy Vernon prepared and presented by Rev J. Morris, St Peter's, Mountsorrel
 Derek Palmer (18)
 Jean Stanyon (16)
 Margaret Rudkin (16)
 Edith Sills (16)

1952, November 25, at St Peter's, Mountsorrel, by Asst Bishop of Leicester, H.A. Maxwell prepared and presented by Rev J. Morris, St Peter's, Mountsorrel
 John Edward Haynes (15)
 Gordon Robert Harrison (15)
 David Robert Smith (14)
 David Hall (13)
 Bernard Arthur Stevenson (13)

Hazel Doreen Rudkin (16)
Jennifer Ann Wardle (13)
Freda Maureen Haynes (13)
Jean Mary Bancroft (16)
Myra Maureen McClintock (16)

1955, December 12, at Swithland, by Lord Bishop of Leicester, Ronald Ralph Williams prepared and presented by Rev C.C. Harcourt

Roger Neil Wardle (11)
Rodney Edward Lloyd (11)
Barry Payne (12)
Tony Cooke (13)
David Allen North (14)
Terence Herbert Cooke (16)
Grahame Briers (16)
David Paterson (16)
John William Leatherland (23)
Leonard Harry Copson (24)
Maurice Edwin Charles Bunney (29)
David Leslie Copson (35)
Alfred George Copson (37)
Sidney Oswald Bunney (61)
Charles Benjamin Bunney (59)
Sally Copson (12)
Gillian Ann Smith (12)
Gillian North (13)
Cynthia Copson (13)
Angela Marjorie Kirke (14)
Margaret Christine Simpson (14)
Margaret Handley (15)
Rosemarie Copson (16)
Ann Payne (16)
Patricia Anne Trevor-Roper (21)
Joan Margaret Leatherland (24)
Molly Horsling (26)
Patricia Dorothy Copson (31)
Barbara Towers (31)
Muriel Allen (33)
Eve Bowler (34)
Betty Mutch (36)
Marjorie Wood (40)
Olive North (45)
Hilda Billy (47)
Ada Mary Leatherland (53)
Elsie Lily Nora Uptons (67)
William Paul Sharpe (15)

1957, March 21, at Emmanuel Church, Loughborough, by Lord Bishop of Leicester, Ronald Ralph Williams
prepared and present by Rev C.C. Harcourt

Reginald Symington (51)
Reginald Thomas Mattinson (60)

1957, December 7, at Leicester Cathedral, by Lord Bishop of Leicester, Ronald Ralph Williams
prepared and present by Rev C.C. Harcourt

Gerald Ernest Humphrey (13)
Michael Walter Brown (13)
Michael John Copson (13)
David Newman Hawthorn (13)

Richard Neil Clark (13)
　　　John Anthony Clark (15)
　　　Raymond Richard Brown (37)
1958, March 6, at Holy Trinity, Leicester, by Asst Bishop of Leicester, HA Maxwell
prepared and presented by Rev C.C. Harcourt
　　　Barbara Gillian Thornton (19)
1959, March 18, at Sileby Parish Church, by Lord Bishop of Leicester, Ronald Ralph Williams
prepared and presented by Bishop H.A. Maxwell (Rector)
　　　Alison Reed (14)
　　　Lesley Judith Ryall (14)
　　　Roderick Nigel Ellway (15)
　　　Gerald David Ellway (14)
1960, Feb 21, at St Peter's Church, Mountsorrel, by Lord Bishop of Leicester, Ronald Ralph Williams
prepared and presented by Bishop H.A. Maxwell
　　　Thomas Donaldson Musgrove (39)
　　　Bayaone Rosemary Twigger (15)
1961, May 30, at St Paul's, Woodhouse Eaves, by Asst Bishop of Leicester, H.A. Maxwell
prepared and presented by Bishop H.A. Maxwell
　　　Stewart John Hardy Symington (15)
　　　Susan Margaret Symington (14)
　　　Andrew Ross Clark (15)
　　　David Brown (14)
　　　Gillian May Briers (15)
　　　Hannah Mary Whyte (14)
1962, May 29, at Loughborough Parish Church, by Asst Bishop of Leicester, H.A. Maxwell
prepared and presented by Bishop HA Maxwell
　　　Alan Terence Simpson (16)
　　　Guy Christopher Scott Baker (17)
　　　David Francis Whyte (17)
　　　Anthony John Ellway
　　　Enid Mary Elizabeth Fanshawe
　　　Eva Dorothy Patricia Brook-Lawson
1963, May 13, at Mountsorrel, by Asst Bishop of Leicester, H.A. Maxwell
prepared and presented by Bishop H.A. Maxwell
　　　Nancy Mary Briers (47)
　　　Daphne Briers (21)
　　　Patricia Susan Simmons (14)
　　　Kathleen Carol Simmons (13)
　　　Penny Anne Wood (14)
　　　Margaret Basham (14)
　　　Roger John Ambrose Copson (14)
　　　Stuart Donaldson Musgrove (15)
　　　Richard John Orton (15)
1964, May 11, at St Leonard's, Swithland, by Asst Bishop of Leicester, H.A. Maxwell
prepared and presented by Bishop H.A. Maxwell
　　　Frederick Tyldesley (65)
　　　Carrie Rawlinson (45)
　　　Joy Bate (43)
　　　Barbara Aileen Harrington (32)
　　　Brian Richard Rawlinson (21)
　　　Valerie Edwards Bate (15)
　　　Lynn Marion Haynes (14)
　　　Sheila Mary Copson (12)

1965, at Leicester Cathedral, by Lord Bishop of Leicester, Ronald Ralph Williams
prepared and presented by Bishop H.A. Maxwell
    David Alexander Walker (81)
    Margaret Walker (67)
    Sydney Robert Meadows (68)
1965, Dec 4, at Leicester Cathedral, by Asst Bishop of Leicester, J.L.C. Horstead
    Bert Henry Stone (42)
    Alison Elizabeth Cameron (14)
1967, March 16, at Swithland, by Lord Bishop of Leicester, Ronald Ralph Williams
prepared and presented by Bishop T.G .Stuart Smith (Rector)
    Graham Paul Bate (13)
    Helen Ashton (14)
    Sally Christine Hannibal (13)
    Christine Anne Labrom (14)
    Rowena Anne Whyte (14)
1968, March 26, at Swithland, by Asst Bishop of Leicester, J.L.C. Horstead
prepared and presented by Bishop T.G. Stuart Smith (Rector)
    Mark Anthony Egglestone (13)
    David John Tucker (17)
    Susan Melanie Bunney (15)
    Judith Mary Bunney (12)
    Judith Shipley Bayes (14)
    Audrey Penelope Parker (45)
    Marjorie Hazel Tilley (37)
1968, October 8, at Swithland, by Asst Bishop of Leicester Bishop T.G. Stuart Smith (Rector)
    Percy Wells (of full age)
1968, Dec 8, at Leicester Cathedral, by Asst Bishop of Leicester, Bishop T.G. Stuart Smith (Rector)
prepared and presented by Bishop T.G. Stuart Smith (Rector)
    Charlotte Ironmonger (20)
    Jane Elizabeth Orton (18)
1969, at ?, by Asst Bishop of Leicester, Bishop T.G. Stuart Smith (Rector)
prepared and presented by Bishop T.G. Stuart Smith (Rector)
    John Derek Humphries (13)
    Jane Elizabeth Lapham (14)
1970, March 10, at Christ Church Mountsorrel, by Asst Bishop of Leicester, J.L.C. Horstead
prepared and presented by Bishop T.G. Stuart Smith (Rector)
    Christopher John McClintic (18)
    Christine Mary Adcock (14)
    Gillian Mary Needham (14)
    Tessa Jane Underwood (15)
1971, April 13, at Swithland, by Asst Bishop of Leicester, J.L.C. Horstead
prepared and presented by Bishop T.G. Stuart Smith (Rector)
    Michael David Rowntree-Clifford (15)
    Caroline Mary Fanshawe (13)
    Elspeth Ann Beynon Jones (13)
    Lucy Clare Stobart (13)
    Veronica Lois Wright (13)
1974, April 13, at the Cathedral, by Lord Bishop of Leicester, Ronald Ralph Williams
prepared and presented by Rev E.W. Carlile (Rector)
    Anthony Rowntree Clifford (15)

Appendix D: Parish Registers 631

1974, December 22, at Swithland, by Asst Bishop of Leicester, John E.L. Mort
prepared and presented by Rev E.W. Carlile (Rector)
    Howard Norman Worsley (15)
    Mark Thomas Tyrrell (14)
    Jonathan Peter Mark Cross (12)
    Elizabeth Anne Cross (14)
    Shelley Anne Adcock (15)
    Susan Angela Clifford (14)
    Jacqueline Suzanne Wainwright (12)

1976, Feb 17, at Swithland, by Asst Bishop of Leicester, T.S. Garrett
prepared and presented by Rev E.W. Carlile (Rector)
    Ernest Frank Lin Wilson (69)
    Robert Mee (58)
    Roy William West (55)
    Anthony Paul Buswell (12)
    Iain James Cox (12)
    Sarah Field Bentley (15)
    Andrew Ian Fergusson Wishart (12)
    Simon Paul Harrington (12)
    Sarah Rachel Dixon (12)
    Deborah Sarah Bryan (13)

1978, Feb 14, at Swithland, by Asst Bishop of Leicester, John Mort
prepared and presented by Rev F.R. Walters (Rector)
    James Ward Andrews (13)
    Jonathan Mark Crowther (16)
    David Simon Crowther (14)
    David Michael James Higgs
    Nicholas John Walters (13)
    Helen Dixon (13)
    Fiona Louise Higgs (14)
    Yolanda Page (18)
    Jacqueline Page (16)
    Lindsey Ann Stokes (14)
    Amanda June Taylor (14)
    Joanna Jane Taylor (14)

1979, May 17, at Rothley Parish Church by Asst Bishop of Leicester, John Mort
prepared and presented by Rev F.R. Walters (Rector)
    Guy Charles Andrews (12)
    Rachel Elizabeth Allen (12)
    Laura Jane Harrison (13)
    Lucy Anne Harrison (12)
    Susan Mary Wood (13)

1979, June 12, at St David's, Broom Leys, by Lord Bishop of Leicester, Richard Rutt
prepared and presented by Rev FR Walters (Rector)
    Judith Angela Rosenberg (27)
    Jill Wright (23)

1980, May 1, at Swithland, by Lord Bishop of Leicester, Richard Rutt
prepared and presented by Rev F.R. Walters (Rector)
    Fay Marie Adams (17)
    Diana Joy Belcher (37)
    Sarah Frances Northam (11)
    Gillian Katherine Angela Walters (12)
    Rosemary Ann Wishart (13)
    Carol Anne Wood (12)

1980, Dec 23, at Leicester Cathedral, by Asst Bishop of Leicester, John Mort
prepared and presented by Rev F.R Walters (Rector)
    Nicholas John Edward Northam (14)

1981, May 1, at Swithland, by Lord Bishop of Leicester, Richard Rutt
prepared and presented by Rev F.R. Walters (Rector)
- Charles Maclaren Allen (12)
- Charles Dixon (13)
- Jeremy Ian Harrington (15)
- Jeanette Helen Buswell (13)
- Rachel Deakin (13)
- Mandy Jane Elson (12)
- Philippa Louise Elson (14)
- Elizabeth Louise Holloway (14)

1983, July 4, at Swithland, by Lord Bishop of Leicester, Richard Rutt
prepared and presented by Rev F.R. Walters (Rector)
- Lucy Clare Copson (13)
- Julie Elizabeth Roberts (17)
- Virginia May Taylor (13)
- Rebecca Mary Walton (12)

1985, Mar 29, at Swithland, by Asst Bishop of Leicester, John Mort
prepared and presented by Rev F.R. Walters (Rector)
- Stephen John Bence (14)
- David Anthony Roberts (15)
- Roger Patrick Scoppie (30)
- Hilda Marion Statham (49)
- Jenny Warrilow (14)

1988, March 6, at Thorpe Acre Parish Church, by Lord Bishop of Leicester, Richard Rutt
prepared and presented by Rev F.R. Walters (Rector)
- Max Harrison (15)
- Timothy Robert Hardwicke (14)
- Richard James Holloway (16)
- Helen Jane Lawson (24)

1990, Dec 3, at Leicester Cathedral, by Asst Bishop of Leicester, Godfrey Ashby
prepared and presented by Rev F.R. Walters (Rector)
- Paul Terence Friend (41)
- James Warrilow (14)
- John Ralph Whitehead (15)
- Michael Peter Whitehead (15)
- Jennifer Mary Friend (30)
- Sarah Jean Page (20)
- Caroline Ruth Page (15)

1995, Mar 26, at Swithland, by Lord Bishop of Leicester, Thomas Butler
prepared and presented by Canon R.A. Horton (Rector)
- Derek Ambrose Freestone (68)
- Richard Grove Hardwicke (15)
- Matthew John Roberts (14)
- Mark Adrian Collett (14)
- Thomas Charles Capewell (12)
- Christopher James Roberts (12)
- Edward Jack Capewell (9)
- Carol Collett (47)
- Rebecca Louise John (11)
- Laura Emily Robinson (11)

1995, April 15, at Leicester Cathedral, by Lord Bishop of Leicester, Thomas Butler
prepared and presented by Canon R.A. Horton (Rector)
- Rosemary Mellor (13)

1997, Nov 29, at Leicester Cathedral, by Lord Bishop of Leicester, Thomas Butler
prepared and presented by Canon R.A. Horton (Rector)
- John Edward Capewell (65)
- Kate Zillah Sharpe (15)

1999, June 27, at Swithland, by Asst Bishop of Leicester, William Down
prepared and presented by Canon R.A. Horton (Rector)
    Elspeth Mary Louise Williamson-Carr (35)
    Amymay Louise Williamson-Carr (12)
    Abigail Louise Williamson-Carr (10)
    Andrew James Bruce (12)
    Amanda Susanne Bruce (10)
1999, Nov 27 at Leicester Cathedral, by Lord Bishop of Leicester, Timothy Stevens
prepared and presented by Canon R.A. Horton (Rector)
    Richard William Davis (50)
    Helen Anne Syme (41)
    Zöe Young (26)
    Nathan Edward Young (25)
2001, Jan 7, at Swithland, by Asst Bishop of Leicester, William Down
prepared and presented by Canon R.A. Horton (Rector)
    Hollie Anne Davis (14)
    Rebecca Grace Hackett (13)
    Sophie Elizabeth Kinder (13)
    Aimée Louise Kinder (12)
    Betty Celia Smith (70)
2002, June 9, at St Paul's, Woodhouse Eaves, by Asst Bishop of Leicester, Colin Scott
prepared and presented by Canon R.A. Horton (Rector)
    Neil Anthony Jarvis (adult)
    Julie Ann Jarvis (adult)
    Patricia Morris (adult)
    Emily Johanna Mason (13)
2002, June 23, at St John the Baptist, Old Dalby, by Asst Bishop of Leicester, Colin Scott
prepared and presented by Canon R.A. Horton (Rector)
    Pauline Janet Hunt (adult)
2004, Nov 27, at Leicester Cathedral, by Asst Bishop of Leicester, Colin Scott
prepared and presented by Canon R.A. Horton (Rector)
    Christopher Robert Jerald Craven (14)
    Benjamin Joe Wood (14)
    Harry William Brewin-Smith (11)
    Laura Yasmin Mason (12)
    Hannah Alice Brewin-Smith (13)
    Louise Georgina Kennedy Taylor (adult)
2005, Nov 26, at Leicester Cathedral, by Asst Bishop of Leicester, Colin Scott
prepared and presented by Canon R.A. Horton (Rector)
    John Paul Bernard Sheridan (adult)
    Maxine Dawn Sheridan-Knowles (adult)
2004, Feb 18, at Swithland, by Asst Bishop of Leicester, John Austin
prepared and presented by Canon R.A. Horton (Rector)
    Sidney Derek Cranage (adult)
    Philip John Cameron Wood (11)
    Henry James Gardner (11)
    Steven Leonard Shellard (12)
    Louisa Janet Wood (13)
    Kitty Alexandra Burrows (14)
2008, Nov 29, at Leicester Cathedral, by Lord Bishop of Leicester, Timothy Stevens
prepared and presented by Canon R.A. Horton (Rector)
    Paul David Worth (adult)
    Angela Natasha Keates (adult)
    Linzi Joanne McGunnigle (adult)
    Susan Jane Knight (adult)

St Leonard's Church, Swithland: Marriages

ABBOT: Mary m1702 Thomas Pollard; Mary m1734 John Kiddyer.
ABEL: Isaac m1786 Mary Clayton.
ADAMS: Thomas (24 son of John Adams) m1842 Martha Hodge (23); John (son of John Adams) m1860 Charlotte Handley (daughter of George Handley); John (widower, son of John Adams) m1870 Eliza Stanyed (daughter of Joseph Stanyed); Emily (23 daughter of John Adams) m1896 Charles Prinnell Sherman (29 son of George Sherman); Martha Ann (22 daughter of John Adams) m1897 Thomas Henry James (22 son of Thomas James); Sarah Jane (25 daughter of John Adams) m1897 John Henry Devereux (25 son of Charles Devereux); Florry (25 daughter of John Adams) m1904 William Edward Compton (26 son of William Edward Compton); Margaret Eliza (24 daughter of John Adams) m1907 George Leonard Pople (24 son of George Pople); John (widower, son of John Adams) m1910 Harriet Bayliss (widow, daughter of John Griffiths); Fay Marie (18 daughter of Brian Edward Adams) m1981 Andrew James Copson (23 son of David Leslie Copson).
ADCOCK: Sarah m1731 John Leverett; Anne m1761 Robert Broomfield; William m1815 Mary Rower.
ADLARD: Percy Scott (26 son of Harry Walter Scott Adlard) m1922 Muriel Minkley (22 daughter of Herbert Minkley).
ALDERSON: Paul Ronald (39 son of Frederick Alderson) m1997 Sarah Charis Hardy (p.m.d,44 daughter of Fergus Donald Cameron).
ALLEN: Harry (22 son of Henry Allen) m1917 Edith Emily Minkley (21 daughter of Herbert Minkley); Hilda (27 daughter of William Allen m1936 Frederick Charles William Parker (27 son of Charles Parker); Muriel Myra (37 daughter of William Allen) m1959 Arthur William Cockerill (46 son of Lewis Cockerill); Christopher Maclaren (25 son of Reginald Charles Shaw Allen) m 1964 Sally Elizabeth Copson (21 daughter of John Ambrose Copson); Rachel Elizabeth (24 daughter of Christopher Maclaren Allen) m1980 Nicholas Richard John Mullins (24 son of Colin Mullins); Charles Maclaren (30 son of Christopher Maclaren Allen) m1999 Joanne Elizabeth Cole (p.m.d, 28 daughter of Sydney Dennis Elson)28 daughter of Keith Henry Baker).
ALLUM: William m1799 Jane Johnson.
ALLWOOD: Frederick (son of William Allwood) m1866 Mary Matts (daughter of Joseph Matts).
ANDREWS: Ann m1707 William Barnet.
ARNOLD: William m1731 Elizabeth Baker.
ASHE: Mary m1740 William Preston.
ASHER: Albert Henry Gordon (26 son of Frederic Asher) m1916 Mabel Helen Underwood (25 daughter of Tom Underwood).
ASHTON: Thomas m1768 Elizabeth Bonsor.
ASTIN: Mary m1797 George Lovatt.
ATKINS: Thomas m1749 Sarah Smith.
AUSTIN: David Alexander (25 son of Alfred Gordon Austin) m1982 Juliet Anne Siddons (21 daughter of Alan John Siddons).
AVERY: Valentine (gent) m1732 Elizabeth Choyce.
AYRES: Michael David (26 son of David Anthony Ayres) m1990 Elizabeth Louise Holloway (22 daughter of Kenneth Frank Holloway).
AXON: Helen (18 daughter of Brian Axon) m1984 Andrew Michael Brook Lawson (28 son of Donald Michael Brook Lawson).
BACKWELL: Ernest Alfred (42 son of Alfred Price Backwell) m1933 Edith Lilian Wallace (37 daughter of Henry Alfred Wallace).
BAGGERLEY: Richard m1734 Sarah Browne.

BAILEY: Hugh Windle (25 son of Arthur Charles John Bailey) m1947 Rosemary Berridge (23 daughter of Isaac Lovell Berridge).
BAKER: Mary m1680 John Shaw; Elizabeth m1731 William Arnold; Guy Christopher Scott (24 son of George Henry Baker) m1969 Gillian Mary Briers (23 daughter of Samuel Eric Briers).
BAKEWELL: Robert m1702 Elizabeth Brown; John m1733 Mary Bostock.
BALL: Dorothy m1634 Adrian Chettle; Richard m1635 Elizabeth Wood; Ann m1770 John Clark; Hannah m1805 William Johnson; Margaret Winifred Mary (25 daughter of Walter Winter Ball) m1935 Herbert Henry Lambourne (27 son of Henry Lambourne).
BALLARD: Francis m1766 Mary Sarson.
BAMFORD: Valerie Ann Squire (23 daughter of Frank Ernest Bamford) m1963 David Paterson (23 son of Kenneth Robert Paterson).
BAMPTON: Ann (widow, 32 daughter of James Noon) m1872 Thomas Chapman (widower, 42 son of John Chapman).
BANBURY: Kathleen Hilda (24 daughter of George Charles Banbury) m1950 William Squires Bingham (25 son of William Edgar Bingham).
BANCROFT: Diane Anne (21 daughter of Harold James Bancroft) m1973 Charles Richard Rolls (24 son of Sidney Laurence Rolls).
BAPTON: Elizabeth m1781 William Broomfield.
BARBER: Roger William (24 son of Frank Gordon Barber) m1947 Brenda Carr (23 daughter of Robert Harold Carr).
BARKER: John (25 son of John Barker) m1851 Sarah Brookhouse (19 daughter of William Brookhouse); Eliza (25 daughter of James Barker m1854 Thomas Hodge (20 son of William Hodge).
BARNET: William m1707 Ann Andrews; Anne m1726 John Branston; Mary m1735 John Read.
BARRETT: Susan Margaret (22 daughter of Percy Charles Barrett) m1976 Mark Bradley Gripper (24 son of William Anthony Gripper).
BARSON: Thomas m1814 Ann Newby.
BATE: Valerie Edwards (24 daughter of Harold Bate) m1973 Paul Richardson (24 son of John Henry Richardson).
BATES: Anna m1731 William Walker; Daniel m1783 Jenny Clarke; Jane m1786 Stephen Clarke; Elizabeth m1804 John Bunney; Jane m1811 Thomas Palmer; Frances m1813 Richard Bayley; Sarah m1818 Edmund Rinals; Amy (25 daughter of William Bates) m1840 Thomas Langham (30); Daniel (22 son of Daniel Bates) m1847 Jane Cox (31 daughter of William Cox); Sarah (26 daughter of Daniel Bates) m1857 Thomas John Toone (28 son of William Toone); George (son of Daniel Bates) m1859 Jane Clark (daughter of Stephen Clark); Juliana Ann (daughter of Thomas Bates) m1878 James Schofield (son of Matthew Schofield); John Thomas (40 son of William James Bates) m1908 Amelia Stafford Evans (29 daughter of Thomas Evans); Fanny Gertrude (25 daughter of William James Bates) m1932 George Stanley Wakerling (24 son of George William Wakerling).
BATTERHAM: Tina Marie (22 daughter of Ivan Michael Batterham) m1989 Jonathan Mark Lawson (23 son of David Thomas Lawson).
BAUM: Elizabeth m1750 William Simson; Thomas m1757 Sarah Page; William m1763 Jane Brewin; Mary m1768 John Street; Jane m1797 John Berrington; Sarah m1815 Samuel Bunney; Ann m1817 Zachariah Raynor; Edward (20 son of John Baum) m1853 Ann Swinfer (22 daughter of Daniel Swinfor); Sarah Maria (daughter of John Baum) m1877 John Matthews).
BAXTER: Ann m1814 George Morris; George (21 son of William Baxter) m1842 Mary Ann Ruford (20); Charles Edward (24 son of Abraham Baxter) m1900 Edith Hodges (22 daughter of John Henry Hodges); Bryan Reginald (23 son of Charles Edward Baxter) m1929 Dorothy Vera Briers (24 daughter of Samuel Briers).

BAYLEY: Richard m1813 Frances Bates.
BAYLISS: Harriet (widow, daughter of John Griffiths) m1910 John Adams (widower, son of Thomas Adams).
BEACH: Jonathan Mark (22 son of Dennis Henry Beach) m1990 Sarah Frances Northam (21 daughter of John Malcolm Northam).
BEASLEY: John m1770 Mary Johnson; Joseph m1793 Jane Lovett; Mary m1794 Thomas Lander.
BEAUMONT: Alison (33 daughter of Ronald Beaumont) m1990 Nicholas Frank Holloway (26 son of Kenneth Frank Holloway).
BEEBY: Laura Kate (27 daughter of Brian Joseph Beeby) m2009 David John Monks (27 son of Arthur Monks); Jennie Mary (27 daughter of Brian Joseph Beeby) m2010 Jonathan David Garratt (29 son of Michael Steven Garratt).
BEEDELL: Timothy John (25 son of Victor Thomas Beedell) m1982 Pamela Mary Walters (24 daughter of Francis Raymond Walters).
BENNETT: John m1698 Mary Perkin; John m1723 Martha Hancock; Mary m1745 George Kirby.
BENSON: Jane m1823 John Weston; Sarah Jane (24 daughter of Roy Benson) m1988 Richard William Freer (25 son of William Richard Freer).
BENTLEY: John m1745 Ann Cook; Ann m1762 William Snow; Sarah Field (21 daughter of Walter Richard Bentley) m1981 Andrew John Brooks (25 son of John Rippon Brooks); Iain Ewart George (28 son of Walter Richard Bentley) m1991 Clare Elizabeth France (28 daughter of Anthony John France).
BERRIDGE: Peter Lovell (23 son of Isaac Lovell Berridge) m1945 Barbara Nora Mais (26 daughter of John Leslie Mais); Rosemary (23 daughter of Isaac Lovell Berridge) m1947 Hugh Windle Bailey (25 son of Arthur Charles John Bailey).
BERRINGTON: John m1797 Jane Baum.
BERRISON: Ann m1825 Benjamin Petts.
BESTON: Matthew m1788 Ann Cliff; Elizabeth m1790 William Brown.
BETTS: William (son of George Betts) m1841 Mary Brookhouse (19).
BINGHAM: William Squires (25 son of William Edgar Bingham) m1950 Kathleen Hilda Banbury (24 daughter of George Charles Banbury).
BIRD: Thomas m1704 Mary Mason; Sarah m1801 Samuel Brown; Ann m1809 William Greasley; Elizabeth m1832 Thomas Hill.
BISHOP: Jane (24 daughter of Ivan Raymond Bishop) m1989 David Miles William Hargrave (24 son of Peter John William Hargrave).
BLACKWELL: Mary m1722 Benjamin Palmer.
BLAISSE: Folkert Boudewifn (28 son of Pieter Alphons Blaisse) m1974 Rosalind Mary Garnett-Clarke (25 daughter of Peter Geoffrey Garnett-Clarke).
BLANKLEY: Hellen m1678 James Harris.
BLOCKLEY: Thomas (widower, 37 son of John Blockley) m1852 Jane Chapman (widow, 31 daughter of George Morris).
BLOOMFIELD: Mary m1751 John Burrow.
BLOW: David James (31 son of Bernard Stanhope Blow) m2010 Victoria Rachael Brooks (26 daughter of Stephen John Brooks)
BLUNFILL: Robert m1718 Mary Prior.
BOCOCK: Christopher George Frederick (23 son of George Frederick Charles Bocock) m1965 Gillian Rosemary North (22 daughter of Eric Frank North); Georgina Jane (19 daughter of Christopher George Frederick Bocock) m 1988 Paul James Dexter (24 son of Roy Dexter).
BODDY: Sheila Mary Vazeille (25 daughter of James Alexander Vazeille Boddy) m1952 Alan Brook Harker (22 son of John Thwaite Harker).
BODELL: Rebecca m1729 James Chaplin.
BODLE: Thomas m1698 Anne Jackson.
BOLTER: Catherine m1708 John Brown.
BONE: Barbara Wellington (22 daughter of Wellington Arthur Bone) m1928 George Thomas Taylor Wood (widower, 41 son of John Henry Wood).

BONIFACE: Roy (24 son of Lawrence Boniface) m1961 Norma Winifred Cassie [formerly known as Gwenda Florence Cassie](26 daughter of William Cock Cassie).

BONNEYWELL: David (20 son of Trevor Ingram Bonneywell) m1989 Mandy Jane Elson (19 daughter of Sydney Dennis Elson); Mandy Jane Bonneywell (p.m.d, 28 daughter of Sydney Dennis Elson) m1998 Alan Johnson (32, son of Peter Donald Johnson)

BONSELL: Joseph (son of William Bonsell) m1878 Eliza Gascoigne (daughter of Thomas Gascoigne).

BONSOR: Elizabeth m1768 Thomas Ashton.

BOSTOCK: Mary m1733 John Bakewell; Sarah m1776 John Laurence; Joseph m1815 Sarah Lakin.

BOTHERWAY: Mary (20 daughter of Timothy Botherway) m1857 George Hamson (25 son of John Hamson).

BOTT: Carl David (26 son of David Bott) m1990 Beverley Ruth Ellis (23 daughter of James Michael Ellis).

BOULTER: Neil David (pmd, 36, son of David Garside Boulter) m2004 Lisa Christianne Smith (32 daughter of Malcolm Keith Smith)

BOWING: Barbara m1794 William Peat.

BOWLER: John m1830 Diana Brown; Mary Louisa (20 daughter of John Bowler) m1891 William Brown (21 son of George Brown).

BOWLEY: Joseph Ernest (36 son of Ernest Bowley) m1952 Jean Gwendolyn Carpenter (23 daughter of James John Carpenter).

BOYER: Charles (widower, 68 son of William Boyer) m1894 Louisa Selby (widow, 43 daughter of John Brooks).

BRADLEY: Herbert Edgar (24 son of Ernest Bradley) m1931 Evelyn Mary Minkley (23 daughter of Herbert Minkley).

BRADSHAW: John (27 son of John Bradshaw) m1898 Mary Charlotte Raynor (26 daughter of Thomas Raynor).

BRAMBY: William m1805 Hannah Mee.

BRAMLEY: Thomas m1792 Alice Johnson; Thomas m1807 Ann Doughty.

BRAMWELL: David Nicholas (26 son of Dennis Bramwell) m1984 Elizabeth Anne Cross (spinster, 23 daughter of Thomas Reid Turnbull).

BRANDRIK: Anne (20 daughter of Reinert Andreas Brandrik) m1988 Anthony Manias (29 son of Nicholas Manias).

BRA(W)NSTON: Anne m1716 William Westley; William m1725 Jane Pollard; John m1726 Anne Barnet; Henry m1741 Mary Dexter; Ann m1743 Joseph Preston; Thomas m1751 Mary Wheat; Elizabeth m1751 Thomas Hardway; Mary m1752 John Hetterley; Mary m1760 Thomas Pollard; Ann m1772 William Wood.

BREWIN: Jane m1763 William Baum; Elizabeth m1766 William Clark.

BREWOOD: Mary m1732 Edward Heich; Sarah m1734 Charles Pole.

BRIERS: Dorothy Vera (24 daughter of Samuel Briers) m1929 Bryan Reginald Baxter (23 son of Charles Edward Baxter); Gillian Mary (23 daughter of Samuel Eric Briers) m1969 Guy Christopher Scott Baker (24 son of George Henry Baker); Helen Louise (20 daughter of Grahame Briers) m1990 Anthony Thomas Finn (25 son of William Finn).

BROADHURST: Ruth m1633 William Smith.

BROMLEY: Joseph m1822 Sarah Raynor.

BROOKE: Thomas Griffith (28 son of Robert Henry Brooke) m1934 Laurie Paterson (28 daughter of William Paterson).

BROOKHOUSE: William m1789 Elizabeth Brooksby; William m1822 Hannah Vesty; William (widower) m1833 Elizabeth Brown (widow); Mary (19 daughter of William Brookhouse) m1841 William Betts; Sarah (19 daughter of William Brookhouse) m1851 John Barker (25 son of Joseph Barker); Elizabeth (19 daughter of William Brookhouse) m1856 George Seal (22 son of John Seal); William (widower, son of William Brookhouse) m1860 Elizabeth Glover (daughter of William Glover).

BROOKS: John m1748 Hannah Dexter; Elizabeth m1776 Thomas Fukes; Andrew John (25 son of John Rippon Brooks) m1981 Sarah Field Bentley (21 daughter of Walter Richard Bentley); Victoria Rachael (26 daughter of Stephen John Brooks) m2010 David James Blow (31 son of Bernard Stanhope Blow)

BROOKSBY: Abel (clerk) m1701 Alice Palmer; Mary (daughter of Abel Brooksby) m1723 John Pochin; Elizabeth m1789 William Brookhouse; Thomas m1796 Dorothy Marson; Dorothea m1827 George Wesley; Elizabeth m1837 Thomas Lines; Sarah (19 daughter of Thomas Brooksby) m1838 William Hill.

BROOMFIELD: Robert m1761 Anne Adcock; Elizabeth m1773 Samuel Humber; William m1781 Elizabeth Bapton; Henry m1781 Ann Steaton; Anne m1828 Joseph Burton.

BROUGH: Austin James (29 son of Ian James Brough) m2002 Gail Patricia Lilley (26 daughter of Roy Lilley)

BROUGHTON: Margaret (24 daughter of Leonard Broughton) m1933 Harry George Powell (27 son of Mansell Powell).

BROWN(E): Robert m1624 Elizabeth Smith; Elizabeth m1702 Robert Bakewell; John m1708 Catherine Bolter; Robert m1716 Elizabeth Fielding; Sarah m1734 Richard Baggerley; Mary m1740 William Needham; Thomas m1778 Ann Brown; William m1790 Elizabeth Beston; John m1790 Mary Spencer; Sarah m1797 John Crag; Jane m1798 John Tansley; William m1801 Elizabeth James; Catherine m1801 William Cars; Samuel m1801 Sarah Bird; Elizabeth m1804 Samuel Priestley (widower); William m1808 Elizabeth Matthews; Samuel (widower) m1816 Elizabeth Jones; Diana m1830 John Bowler; James m1831 Sarah Pickering; Mary m1831 Edward Topley; Elizabeth (widow) m1833 William Brookhouse (widower); Henry (21 son of Henry Brown) m1882 Hannah Dable (19 daughter of William Dable); William (21 son of George Brown) m1891 Mary Louisa Bowler (20 daughter of John Bowler); Joanna (28 daughter of George Brown) m1905 Charles Henry Holt (24 son of John Holt); Emma (29 daughter of George Brown) m1911 Alfred Minkley (21 son of George Minkley); Valerie Ann Brown (daughter of James Ronald Brown) m1998 Michael John (36 son of Nicholas Kevin Tobin)

BRYSON: John Winks (53 son of David Bryson) m2004 Elizabeth Mary Chappell (pmd, 43 daughter of Jack Jabez Smith)

BUCHANAN: James Alexander (25 son of James Alexander Buchanan) m1982 Sally Angela Wale (24 daughter of Dennis Harry Wale).

BUNNEY: Alice m1731 Job Cramp; David m1794 Elizabeth Pitts; John m1804 Elizabeth Bates; Elizabeth m1805 William Dawson; Samuel m1815 Sarah Baum; Sarah (widow) m1834 John Thorpe (widower); William (son of Samuel Bunney) m1839 Ann Pearson (19); Ann (widow, 36 daughter of Edward Searton) m1846 William Emmerson (59); William (23 son of William Bunney) m1850 Elizabeth Stapleton (21 daughter of George Stapleton); Henry (22 son of William Bunney) m1854 Mary Carter (18 daughter of William Carter); James (23 son of William Bunney) m1856 Harriett Elliott (29 daughter of John Elliott); Sarah Jane (daughter of Charles Bunney) m1869 Thomas Ratcliffe (son of Thomas Ratcliffe); Walter (son of William Bunney) m1870 Mary Ann Hill (daughter of Thomas Hill); Edith Emily Sarah (23 daughter of Samuel Bunney) m1899 Albert Crampton (24 son of Thomas Crampton); Mary Ellen (24 daughter of Frederick Bunney) m1907 Charles Wainwright (26 son of Charles Wainwright); Joseph (43 son of Walter Bunney) m1913 Jane Vessey (widow, 44 daughter of John Mills); Gwendoline Polly (25) m1919 William George Sears (23 son of George Sears); Herbert Allan (29 son of John Bunney) m1923 Dorothy Ann Pratt (28 daughter of Charles Benjamin Pratt); Leslie Everard (24 son of Alwyne Everard Bunney) m1930 Vera Ivy Shipp (23 daughter of Harry Shipp); Kathleen Margaret May (26 daughter of Sidney Oswald Bunney) m1944 Thomas Donald Musgrove (23 son of Herbert Thomas Musgrove); Maurice Edwin Charles (25 son of Charles Benjamin Bunney) m1952 Margaret Beatrice Horsfield (26 daughter of Richard Bernard Horsfield); Barbara Ellen (23 daughter of Charles Benjamin Bunney) m1952 George Albert Lowes (28 son of John Lowes); Susan Melanie (27 daughter of Maurice Edwin Charles Bunney) m1980 Alan James Woodard (33 son of George Arthur Woodard).

BURCHNALL: Osborne Frederick Benjamin (25 son of Osborne R. Burchnall) m1960 Jennifer Mary McCurry (24 daughter of Arthur L. McCurry).

BURDELL: Robin George (28 son of John Ellis Burdell) m1986 Susan Mary Seary (27 daughter of Cyril Robert Seary).

BURGESS: Sarah m1717 Thomas Poole; Margaret m1745 Jacob Pollard.

BURGOYNE: Bessie (24 daughter of William Burgoyne) m1931 Ronald Taylor (26 son of Frederick William Taylor).

BURROW: John m1751 Mary Broomfield.

BURTON: John m1703 Mary Siston; Margaret m1767 Thomas Chambers; Henry m1772 Dorothy Johnson; Thomas m1774 Ann Kilbourn; Joseph m1794 Ann Creswell; Henry m1807 Elizabeth Sweeney; Joseph m1828 Anne Broomfield; Ann (widow) m1836 Samuel Lewin; Sarah (20 daughter of Joseph Burton) m1850 Henry Smith (24 son of John Smith); Mary (widow, 51 daughter of Ernest Elkington) m1967 Charles Walter Marston (55 son of Henry Marston); Mary Rachel (widow, daughter of Frank Bowler) m 2001 Peter Brian Hancock (widower, son of Leonard Hancock) .

BURY: Andrew Graham (27 son of Christopher John Bury) m1985 Jane Elizabeth Garton (27 daughter of Thomas Willoughby Garton).

BUSWELL: Jeanette Helen (23 daughter of Derek Alfred Buswell) m1991 Simon Roger Palmer (24 son of Roger Palmer).

BUTLER: Freda (35 daughter of Henry Cavendish Butler, Earl of Lanesborough) m1931 Francis Cyril Oliphant Valentine (33 son of William Roderick Harris Valentine); Raymond (24 son of Frederick Butler) m1955 Barbara Mary Flack (22 daughter of Edward John Flack); Michael John (25 son of Herbert Butler) m1983 Sandra Collis (daughter of Jeffrey Dennis Collis).

BUTT: Mary m1755 William Clark.

BUTTERY: Joseph William (21 son of Joseph Buttery) m1897 Martha Gazy (20 daughter of Samuel Gazy).

BYFORD: Margaret Elizabeth (25 daughter of Charles Barrie Byford) m1991 Peter Norman John Green (33 son of Norman Dennis Green)

CAIRNS: Ian Vance (26 son of Hugh Cairns) m1991 Karen Juliette Thomas (24 daughter of Brian Thomas).

CALLADINE: Elizabeth m1805 Richard Vesty.

CAMERON: Alison Elizabeth Meakin (21 daughter of Fergus Donald Cameron) m1972 Antoine Elias Khouri (25 son of Elias Khouri).

CARPENTER: Jean Gwendolyn (23 daughter of James John Carpenter) m1952 Joseph Ernest Bowley (36 son of Ernest Bowley).

CARR: Brenda (23 daughter of Robert Harold Carr) m1947 Roger William Barber (24 son of Frank Gordon Barber).

CARROLL: Lesley (, daughter of William Patrick Carroll) m1990 Nigel James Marston (27 son of David Marston).

CARS: William m1801 Catherine Brown.

CARTER: Frances m1827 William Morris; Sarah (20 daughter of William Carter) m1851 Joseph Ross (23 son of Joseph Ross); Mary (18 daughter of William Carter) m1854 Henry Bunney (22 son of William Bunney); Frank (31 son of William Henry Carter) m1938 Vera Gwendoline Lorraine Wright (23 daughter of Fred Wright); Jennifer Mary (22 daughter of Dick Carter) m1949 Noel Staughton Hutchinson (24 son of Leonard Staughton Hutchinson).

CASHMORE: Edwin Mark (son of Luke Cashmore) m1879 Elizabeth Bowley Underwood (daughter of Samuel Shaw Underwood).

CASSIE: Norma Winifred [formerly known as Gwenda Florence Cassie](26 daughter of William Cock Cassie) m1961 Roy Boniface (24 son of Lawrence Boniface).

CAULDWELL: Alice m1774 John Pollard.

CAVE: Joseph m1729 Emmatt Middleton.
CHALLONER: Julie Amanda (26 daughter of Maurice William Challoner) m1988 Charles David McDermott (27 son of Albert David McDermott).
CHAMBERLAIN: Sarah m1784 William Limbert.
CHAMBERS: Thomas m1767 Margaret Burton.
CHAPLIN: James m1729 Rebecca Bodell; Susanna m1732 Samuel Wright.
CHAPMAN: Henry m1768 Lydia Perkins; Jane (widow, 31 daughter of George Morris) m1852 Thomas Blockley (widower, 37 son of John Blockley); Thomas (widower, 42 son of John Chapman) m1872 Ann Bampton (widow, 32 daughter of James Noon); Heather (28 daugher of Lawrence Ervin Chapman) m 1999 Liam Doyle (34 son of Richard Patrick Doyle).
CHAPPELL: Elizabeth Mary (pmd, 43 daughter of Jack Jabez Smith) m2004 John Winks Bryson (53 son of David Bryson).
CHARLTON: George m1798 Mary James; Mary m1819 Jeffery Spence; Jane m1827 John Ward.
CHETTLE: Adrian m1634 Dorothy Ball.
CHILTON: Harold James (48 son of William Chilton) m1940 Barbara Helen Gandon (41 daughter of Herbert Gandon).
CHOICE: Elizabeth m1732 Valentine Avery.
CHURCH: Thomas m1791 Ann Phillips.
CLARK(E): Elizabeth m1638 Robert Shearsby; Elizabeth m1704 John Lewin; Elizabeth m1706 Thomas Dix; Samuel m1718 Anne Sydderns; Thomas m1731 Abigail Hurst; Thomas m1733 Elizabeth Stephenson; Jane m1744 William Westley; Stephen m1748 Elizabeth Clark; Elizabeth m1748 Stephen Clark; William m1755 Mary Butt; William m1766 Elizabeth Brewin; Elizabeth m1770 John Newbold; John m1770 Ann Ball; Elizabeth m1773 Joshua White; Stephen m1777 Jinny Fennelow; William m1782 Anne Clarke (widow); Jenny m1783 Daniel Bates; Stephen m1786 Jane Bates; Ann m1793 Thomas Wild; John m1794 Susannah Rodwell; Thomas Clarke m1815 Mary Newby (widow); Jane m1817 Henry Hind (widower); Stephen m1820 Sarah Lockwood; Ann m1820 John Simpson; James m1823 Elizabeth Thorpe; William m1825 Sarah Preston; Ann m1826 Samuel Vesty; Jane m1830 Daniel Preston; John m1834 Susan Norman; Elizabeth (19 daughter of John Clarke) m1840 William Wakerley; Stephen (27 son of Stephen Clarke) m1848 Jemima Lovatt (36 daughter of Daniel Lovatt); John (26 son of John Clark) m1849 Joanna Raynor (widow, 24 daughter of Joseph Garner); Jane (daughter of Stephen Clark) m1859 George Bates (son of Daniel Bates); Susannah (daughter of Samuel Clarke) m1860 Thomas Spencer (son of Edward Spencer); Herbert Ezra (26 son of Alfred Clarke) m1957 Gwendoline Margaret Rudkin (24 daughter of Walter Rudkin); Marcus John Nunneley (29 son of Robert Hamilton Clark) m1982 Lucy Clare Stobart (25 daughter of Peter Brian Halisenton Stobart); Robert Jonathan (30 son of Derek John Thomas Clarke) m1991 Melanie Tracey Shand (28 daughter of Alfred Charles Paul Shand).
CLAYTON: Mary m1786 Isaac Abel.
CLEAVER: George (34 son of John Cleaver) m1885 Mary Spencer (18 daughter of John Spencer).
CLIFF: Ann m1788 Matthew Beston.
COCKERILL: Ada Elizabeth (27 daughter of Lewis Cockerill) m1937 William Stanley Porch (23 son of Frank Porch); George Thomas (37 son of Lewis Cockerill) m1940 Vera Iris Treen (27 daughter of William Sydney Treen); Arthur William (46 son of Lewis Cockerill) m1959 Muriel Myra Allen (37 daughter of William Allen).
COLE: Richard Anthony (26 son of Anthony Victor Cole) m1996 Rebecca Jane Hodges (24 daughter of Graham Peter Hodges).
COLEBURNE: Anne m1733 David Jee.
COLE: Joanne Elizabethe (p.m.d,28 daughter of Keith Henry Baker) m1999 Charles Maclaren Allen (30 son of Christopher Maclaren Allen)

Appendix D: Parish Registers

COLEMAN: Richard (son of William Coleman) m 1858 Sarah Clarke (daughter of Stephen Clarke).

COLLIS: Sandra (daughter of Jeffrey Dennis Collis) m1983 Michael John Butler (25 son of Herbert Butler).

COMPTON: William Edward (26 son of William Edward Compton) m1904 Florry Adams (25 daughter of John Adams).

COOK(E): George m1723 Mary Hornbuckle; Ann m1745 John Bentley; Elizabeth m1788 Thomas Lovitt; Thomas Henry (32 son of William Cook) m1893 Mary Ann Stevens (31 daughter of William Stevens); Albert (42 son of William Cook) m1919 Phyllis Whatnall (23 daughter of Oliver Whatnall).

COOLEDGE Sarah Louise Cooledge (30 daughter of John Cooledge) m2005 Eric Barry Marshall (34 son of Barry Norton)

COOMBES: Gary Bayley (23 son of Stanley Betterson Coombes) m1964 Patricia Rosslyn McLeod (21 daughter of Colin McLeod).

COOPER: James m1706 Ann Dudly; Sarah (widow) m1805 Henry Thornton; Abraham (son of Charles Cooper) m1864 Elizabeth Jarratt (daughter of Charles Jarratt); Betty Mary (19 daughter of Edmund Cooper) m1945 Leslie Stanley Gray (son of Charles Stanley Gray).

COPSON: Nellie (20 daughter of Ambrose Copson) m1906 William Horace Hallam (25 son of William Hallam); Elsie Mary (21 daughter of Alfred Ernest Copson) m1939 Frederick Jarvis Glover (23 son of John William Glover); Jean (21 daughter of Harry Copson) m1939 Wilfred Ernest Radford (24 son of Ernest Henry Radford); Cynthia Mary (19 daughter of John Ambrose Copson) m1960 Donald Wilson (23 son of John Stanley Wilson); Rosemarie Bettyne Carole (24 daughter of John Ambrose Copson) m1964 Richard Charles Morris (29 son of Alfred Richard Morris); Sally Elizabeth (21 daughter of John Ambrose Copson) m1964 Christopher Maclaren Allen (25 son of Reginald Charles Shaw Allen); Leonard Harry (37 son of Charles Copson) m1969 Judith Leslie Toach (23 daughter of Thomas Richard Toach); Roger John Ambrose (23 son of John Ambrose Copson) m1972 Linda Carole Rusden (23); Sheila Mary (25 daughter of Alfred George Copson) m1977 Charles Stuart Hague (27 son of Frank Hague); Andrew James (23 son of David Leslie Copson) m1981 Fay Marie Adams (18 daughter of Brian Edward Adams); Lucy Clare (23 daughter of Leonard Harry Copson) m1993 Raffaele D'Orsi (25 son of Luigi D'Orsi).

COX: Jane (31 daughter of William Cox) m1847 Daniel Bates (22 son of Daniel Bates); Della Marie (20 daughter of Brian Joseph Cox) m1989 Martin Stuart Hall (29 son of Derek Hall).

CRAG: John m1797 Sarah Brown.

CRAMP: Thomas m1695 Hannah Newberry; Job m1731 Alice Bunney.

CRAMPTON: Albert (24 son of Thomas Crampton) m1989 Edith Emily Sarah Bunney (23 daughter of Samuel Bunney).

CRAWFORD: Martha (24 daughter of Richard John Crawford) m1900 John Fletcher (25 son of Joseph Fletcher).

CRESSWELL: Ann m1794 Joseph Burton; Susannah m1812 Benjamin Hill.

CROOKS: William m1813 Elizabeth Pagett.

CROSS: Susan Jane (spinster, 26 daughter of Thomas Reid Turnbull) m 1983 Russell Dart Scriville (29 son of Robert Arthur Scriville); Elizabeth Anne (spinster, 23 daughter of Thomas Reid Turnbull) m1984 David Nicholas Bramwell (26 son of Dennis Bramwell).

CURD: Gregory Nigel (40 son of Donald William Curd m 2010 Haley Billinder Tubby (28 daughter of Richard Morris Tubby)

CUFFLING: Elizabeth (25 daughter of William Cuffling) m1876 William Kerby (24 son of William Kerby); Emma (21 daughter of William Cuffling) m1885 Andrew Miles Meadows (21 son of Thomas Meadows); Mary Ann (23 daughter of William Cuffling) m1887 Henry Robert Milner (27 son of Charles Thomas Milner).

CUMBERLIDGE: Charlotte Lucy (22 daughter of John Cumberlidge) m1891 Thomas Henry Rose (25 son of Thomas Rose).

CUNNINGHAM: William (19 son of Edwin Cunningham) m1888 Fanny Marie Godbald (19 daughter of George Godbald).

DABLE: Hannah (19 daughter of William Dable) m1882 Henry Brown (21 son of Henry Brown).

DALY: Brian Vincent (33 son of Lucius Martin Daly) m1980 Patricia Elizabeth Fanshawe (26 daughter of Gordon Lennox Fanshawe).

DAN: John m1680 Mary Hessel.

DANCE: Stewart Harold (24 son of Harold Edmund Dance) m1959 Pamela Mary Lloyd (21 daughter of George Lewis Lloyd).

DAVIDSON: Alfred Roy (23 son of John Davidson) m1918 Emily Mary Lloyd (18 daughter of Percival George Lloyd).

DAVIES: John Charles (25 son of John Frederick Davies) m1993 Carol Anne Wood (25 daughter of Allan Charles Wood); Andrew Christopher (29 son of Keith Davies) m1995 Sarah Louise Dobson (daughter of Peter Dobson).

DAVIS: Russell Michael John (24 son of Michael Leonard Davies) m1995 Nicola Kate Morris (23 daughter of Francis Wynn Morris); Richard William (pmd 50 son of William Davis) m 2000 Helen Anne Syme (pmd 42 daughter of Peter Richard Harrison).

DAWKINS: James m1790 Sarah Toone.

DAWSON: Ann m1638 Bartholomew Webster; Ann m1714 Thomas Smith; William m1805 Elizabeth Bunney.

DAY: Ann m1775 John Skelton.

DEAKIN: Rachel Alison (34 daughter of John David Deakin) m2002 Stephen Alan Howarth Sykes (44 son of Alan Haworth Sykes)

DEAKINS: Mary m1705 Thomas Hews.

DEEMING: Jane (daughter of Thomas Deeming) m1859 Thomas Raynor (son of Zechariah Raynor).

DEVEREUX: John Henry (25 son of Charles Devereux) m1897 Sarah Jane Adams (25 daughter of John Adams).

DEXTER: William m1715 Mary Parker; Elizabeth m1737 Thomas Porter; Thomas (son of Edward Dexter) m1838 Elizabeth Oldershaw; Paul James (24 son of Roy Dexter) m1988 Georgina Jane Bocock (19 daughter of Christopher George Frederick Bocock).

DIX: Thomas m1706 Elizabeth Clark.

DIXON: Rosamund Mary Francis Trevelyan (daughter of James Murray Dixon) m1913 Hans Patrick Hamilton (son of Peter Fisher Percival Hamilton); Eleanor Margaret Trevelyan (daughter of James Murray-Dixon) m1923 Henry James Walsh (son of William Walsh); Eleanor Margaret Trevelyan Murray (daughter of James Murray Murray-Dixon) m1923 Henry James Walsh (son of William Walsh); Sarah Rachel (31 daughter of Hugh Frederick Dixon) m1995 Simon Francis Evans (31 son of Michael John Evans).

DOBSON: Sarah Louise (daughter of Peter Dobson) m1995 Andrew Christopher Davies (29 son of Keith Davies).

DOD: John m1733 Anne Marsden.

DODS: Dorothy m1806 John Stafford.

D'ORSI: Raffaele (25 son of Luigi D'Orsi) m1993 Lucy Clare Copson (23 daughter of Leonard Harry Copson).

DOUBLEDAY: Harold (27 son of Richard Dixon Doubleday) m1912 Katherine May Pepper (30 daughter of Edwin Pepper).

DOUGHTY: Ann m1807 Thomas Bramley; John (widower, 40 son of Richard Doughty) m1849 Sarah Doughty (39 daughter of Joseph Doughty; Sarah (39 daughter of Joseph Doughty) m1849 John Doughty (widower, 40 son of Richard Doughty); Martha (daughter of Joseph Doughty) m1865 John Warren (son of John Warren).

Appendix D: Parish Registers

DOWALL: Ebenezer m1786 Mary Squires.
DOYLE: Liam (34 son of Richard Patrick Doyle) m1999 Heather Chapman (28 daughter of Lawrence Ervin Chapman)
DRACKLEY: Frances (26 daughter of William Drackley) m1856 Edward Wildman (36 son of William Wildman).
DUDLEY: Ann m1706 James Cooper.
DUFFEN: Joseph m1807 Alice Pick.
DUNNE: Charles Thomas (22 son of Kenneth Robert Dunne) m 1970 Lynn Marion Haynes (20 daughter of John Henry Haynes).
DURBER: Heather Mary (26 daughter of John Macdonald Durber) m1985 John Rhys Howells (31 son of William Henry Howells).
DUTTON: Esther Lorraine (31 daughter of Robert James Dutton) m1998 Tony Ranjit Liddar (36 son of Gurbakhsh Singh Liddar);
DYKES: John m1765 Mary Featherstone.
EAGLEFIELD: Elizabeth m1754 Thomas Raynor.
EDENBROW: Heather Joy (22 daughter of Harold Edenbrow) m1966 William Robert Spencer (22 son of Arthur Spencer).
ELLIOTT: Harriett (29 daughter of John Elliott) m1856 James Bunney (23 son of William Bunney).
ELLIS: James m1785 Mary Ralphs; Jane Elizabeth (24 daughter of James Michael Ellis) m1989 Richard William Mee (31 son of Robert William Mee); Beverley Ruth (23 daughter of James Michael Ellis) m1990 Carl David Bott (26 son of David Bott).
ELLWAY: Gerald David (24 son of Edwin John Ellway) m1968 Susan Mary Hackett (25 daughter of William Gordon Hackett).
ELSON: Mandy Jane (19 daughter of Sydney Dennis Elson) m1989 David Bonneywell (20 son of Trevor Ingram Bonneywell); Phillipa Louise (29 daughter of Sydney Dennis Elson) m1997 Stephen Barry Godley (p.m.d, 35 son of Barry Frederick Godley).
EMBLEY: Elizabeth (widow) m1796 Thomas Thomas (widower).
EMMERSON: William (widower, 59) m1846 Ann Bunney (widow, daughter of Edward Searton).
ESTLIN: Thomas m1745 Elizabeth Prior.
EVANS: Amelia Stafford (29 daughter of Thomas Evans) m1908 John Thomas Bates (40 son of William James Bates); Geriant Reynolds (28 son of David Clifford Evans) m1982 Pamela Pope (33 daughter of Richard Arthur Pope); Simon Francis (31 son of Michael John Evans) m1995 Sarah Rachel Dixon (31 daughter of Hugh Frederick Dixon).
EVERSHED: Audrey Louise (spinster, 27 daughter of John Eric Jelly) m1990 Stuart Ian Riley (26 son of James Arthur Riley).
EYRE: Sarah m1786 Benjamin Glover; Elizabeth m1807 Jacob Nurse; Elizabeth m1812 Thomas Sutton.
EYTON: Bridget m1721 William Greasley.
FANSHAWE: Patricia Elizabeth (26 daughter of Gordon Lennox Fanshawe) m1980 Brian Vincent Daly (33 son of Lucius Martin Daly); Caroline Mary (29 daughter of Gordon Lennox Fanshawe) m1986 Paul Anthony Hamilton (29 son of Ian Michael Hamilton).
FARMER: Thomas m1829 Mary Vesty; Doreen Margaret (daughter of Stephen Farmer) m1951 Stuart Arthur Smith (son of James Arthur Smith); Ann Barbara Davis (23 daughter of John Aird Farmer) m1975 Andrew Ian Reid (26 son of Andrew Miller Reid).
FARRAR: John m1728 Mary Middleton.
FAULKS: William (widower, 48 son of Thomas Faulks) m1895 Eliza Hill (21 daughter of Thomas Hill).
FAVELL: Linda Anne (21 daughter of Colin Neville Favell) m1982 Kevin Paul Lynch (26 son of John Patrick Lynch).

FAVER: Rosemary Ann (28 daughter of Herbert Faver) m1987 Benjamin Michael Gidley Wright (24 son of John Michael Gidley Wright).

FEASEY: Ann Gillian (25 daughter of William Doncaster Feasey) m1968 John Malcolm Harmer (25 son of Stanley Gordon Harmer).

FEATHERSTONE: Mary m1765 John Dykes.

FENNELOW: Jinny m1777 Stephen Clarke.

FERNLEY: John m1751 Mary Goodman; Mary m1788 William Hutchinson.

FEWKES: Thomas m1776 Elizabeth Brooks; Thomas (widower) m1799 Mary Oadby.

FIELDING: Martha m1634 Samuel Huxley; Elizabeth m1716 Robert Browne; Amey m1724 John Wildman; Mary m1737 Thomas Ingram.

FINLAY: Donald Crawford (27 son of William Crawford Finlay) m1983 Diana Margaret Walters (21 daughter of Francis Raymond Walters).

FINN: Anthony Thomas (25 son of William Finn) m1990 Helen Louise Briers (20 daughter of Grahame Briers).

FISHER: Mary m1747 Samuel Tookey; Thomas m1787 Mary Sharp; David John (30 son of Sydney Fisher) m 1990 Jane Elizabeth Orton (39 daughter of Charles Victor Orton).

FISK: Stanley (27 son of Herbert William Fisk) m1948 Edna May Hastings (26 daughter of George Hastings).

FLACK: Barbara Mary (22 daughter of Edward John Flack) m1955 Raymond Butler (24 son of Frederick Butler).

FLETCHER: Mary m1718 John Lacy; Sarah m1776 George Symons; John (25 son of Joseph Fletcher) m1900 Martha Crawford (24 daughter of Richard John Crawford).

FLINT: William m1789 Ann Haddon; John Richard (25 son of Richard Joseph Flint) m1956 Edith Mary Sills (22 daughter of Sidney Sills).

FOLEY: Vincent David Patrick (28 son of Timothy John Foley) m1972 Elizabeth Ruth Lloyd Harris (24 daughter of Waldron Harris).

FOLWELL: Muriel (30 daughter of Arthur Ernest Folwell) m1932 Wilfred Edward Snow (30 son of H. Cyprian Snow); Hela (22 daughter of Arthur Ernest Folwell) m1936 Reginald Henry Hobbs (26 son of Henry James Hobbs).

FOULK: Nellie (daughter of Thomas Foulk) m1909 George Edward Tomlin (son of John Tomlin).

FOWLER: Philip m1835 Jemimah North.

FRANCE: Clare Elizabeth (, 28 daughter of Anthony John France) m1991 Iain Ewart George Bentley (28 son of Walter Richard Bentley).

FRANKS: Hannah m1801 Thomas Vesty.

FREEMAN: Mary m1726 Joseph Prior; Marc Christopher (26 son of Ronald Freeman) m2004 Elena Lazourenko (22, daughter of Irina Lazourenko – *father's name not given).*

FREER: Richard William (25 son of William Richard Freer) m1988 Sarah Jane Benson (24 daughter of Roy Benson); Julia (20 daughter of John Frederick Freer) m1989 Simon Nicholas Thorpe (22 son of Nicholas John Thorpe); Julia Caroline (21 daughter of Peter William Freer) m1996 Martin John Leake (23 son of John Michael Leake).

FROST: Colin Peter (21 son of Walter Frost) m1957 Margaret Adrienne Hulse (18 daughter of Arthur Harry Hulse); Joanne (29 daughter of Brian William Frost) m1991 Timothy John Wilkins (31 son of John Charles Wilkins).

GANDON: Barbara Helen (41 daughter of Herbert Gandon) m1940 Harold James Chilton (48 son of William Chilton).

GARDNER: Carl (31 son of Peter Gardner) m2004 Rachel Ovenden (28 daughter of Keith Ovenden)

GARAI: Bertrand Henry (32 son of Bernard Garai) m1952 Muriel Jean Walker (23 daughter of David Alexander Walker).

GARNER: Joseph m1797 Mary Swinfield.

GARNETT-CLARKE: Rosalind Mary (25 daughter of Peter Geoffrey Garnett-Clarke) m1974 Folkert Bondewifn Blaisse (28 son of Pieter Alphons Blaisse).
GARRATT: Jonathan David (29 son of Michael Steven Garratt) m2010 Jennie Mary Beeby (27 daughter of Brian Joseph Beeby)
GARTON: Jane Elizabeth (27 daughter of Thomas Willoughby Garton) m1985 Andrew Graham Bury (27 son of Christopher John Bury).
GASCOIGNE: Eliza (daughter of Thomas Gascoigne) m1878 Joseph Bonsell (son of William Bonsell).
GASKELL: Pauline Janet (22 daughter of Henry Brian Gaskell) m1962 David John Hunt (23 son of David Hunt).
GAUNT: William m1789 Elizabeth West.
GAZY: Frances Elen (22 daughter of Samuel Gazy) m1896 Reginald Edward Herbert Peacock (30 son of John Peacock); Martha (20 daughter of Samuel Gazy) m1897 Joseph William Buttery (21 son of Joseph Buttery).
GEARY: Helena m1775 Robert Preston.
GEORGE: Caroline Anne (19 daughter of Frederick Charles George) m1967 Michael Tilley (21 son of Henry Tilley).
GERMAN: Sarah m1798 William Simpson.
GIBSON: Thomas m1633 Mary Sutton.
GILBERT: Mary m1698 John Hall; Elizabeth m1700 Robert Hews; Elizabeth m1734 James Passand; William m1747 Martha Perkins.
GILES: William m1801 Elizabeth Whatnall.
GIMSON: Rosamund Leslie (21 daughter of Henry Hay Gimson) m1938 Orson Wright (30 son of Herbert Charles Wright); Benjamin Russell (son of Josiah Russell Gimson) m1947 Gweneth Mary Kilby (daughter of Walter Kilby).
GLENN: Francis m1633 Elizabeth Haycock; Mary m1702 Henry Guilford.
GLOVER: Anne m1734 Benjamin Pare; Benjamin m1738 Elizabeth Hews; Robert m1744 Elizabeth Johnson; Benjamin m1786 Sarah Eyre; Elizabeth (daughter of William Glover) m1860 William Brookhouse (son of William Brookhouse); John (38 son of James Glover m1907 Edith Mary Pepper (27 daughter of Edwin Pepper); Frederick Jarvis (23 son of John William Glover) m1939 Elsie Mary Copson (21 daughter of Alfred Ernest Copson).
GOADBY: Michael m1789 Ann Johnson.
GODBALD: George (son of Robert Godbald) m1862 Emma Waterfield (daughter of Joseph Waterfield); George (son of Robert Godbald) m1866 Mary Lovet (daughter of Joseph Lovet); Fanny Maria (19 daughter of George Godbald) m1888 William Cunningham (19 son of Edwin Cunningham).
GODFREY: Frederick Lindesay (29 son of Ernest Henry Godfrey) m1932 Lois Mary Gladys Turner (28 daughter of Archibald Turner).
GODKIN: John Richard Hayward (42 son of Jack Noel Godkin) m1964 Geraldine Sheila Gregory (37 daughter of William Victor Gregory).
GODLEY: Stephen Barry (p.m.d, 35 son of Barry Frederick Godley) m1997 Phillipa Louise Elson (29 daughter of Sydney Dennis Elson).
GOLDSMITH: Sheila Ann (20 daughter of Gordon Arthur Goldsmith) m1969 Brian Richard Rowlinson (26 son of Gilbert Charles Rowlinson).
GOODMAN: Mary m1751 John Fernley.
GOULD: Bruce (26 son of Job Gould) m1934 Millicent Hewitt (23 daughter of Leonard Hewitt).
GOW: Margaret (45 daughter of George Shaw) m1906 Charles Picker (widower, 47 son of Joseph Picker).
GOWER: Thomas m1766 Elizabeth Shenton.
GRANEEK: Helen Blathwayt (23 daughter of Maurice Graneek) m1975 Richard Anthony Humble (25 son of George Humble).
GRANGER: Grace m1638 George Shellington.
GRAY: Joseph m1767 Elizabeth Yates; John m1783 Ann Noon; Leslie Stanley (son of Charles Stanley Gray) m1945 Betty Mary Cooper (19 daughter of Edmund Cooper).

GREASLEY: William m1721 Bridget Eyton; William m1809 Ann Bird; George (widower, 37 son of William Greasley) m1846 Jane Norman (36 daughter of William Norman).

GREEN: Peter Norman John (33 son of Norman Dennis Green) m1991 Margaret Elizabeth Byford (25 daughter of Charles Barrie Byford).

GREENWOOD: Martin Robert (25 son of Ernest Robert Greenwood) m1971 Hannah Mary Whyte (24 daughter of David Connacher Whyte).

GREGG: Elizabeth m1783 Joseph Johnson.

GREGORY: Geraldine Sheila (37 daughter of William Victor Gregory) m1964 John Richard Hayward Godkin (42 son of Jack Noel Godkin); Olga Muriel Fay (daughter of William Victor Gregory) m1972 Waldron Harris (widower, son of Waldron Harris).

GRETTON: Elizabeth m1829 John Platts.

GRIPPER: Mark Bradley (24 son of William Anthony Gripper) m1976 Susan Margaret Barrett (22 daughter of Percy Charles Barrett).

GUILFORD: Henry m1702 Mary Glenn.

HACKET: John m1721 Catherine Smith.

HACKETT: Susan Mary (25 daughter of William Gordon Hackett) m1968 Gerald David Ellway (24 son of Edwin John Ellway).

HADDON: Ann m1789 William Flint.

HAGUE: Charles Stuart (27 son of Frank Hague) m1977 Sheila Mary Copson (25 daughter of Alfred George Copson).

HALE: Nathaniel (widower) m1773 Martha Waldrom; Mary (widow, 48 daughter of William Wilding) m1850 Joseph Lockwood (37 son of Thomas Lockwood); Philip Raymond (24 son of Raymond Hale) m1987 Jill Anne Isom (24 daughter of Thomas Owen Isom).

HALFORD: Sheila Marguerite (widow, 57 daughter of Samuel Daniel) m1987 Edward Victor Parker (divorced, 47 son of Edward James Parker).

HALL: John m1698 Mary Gilbert; Sabina m1729 Henry Watson; Hannah m1741 Thomas Wright; Henry m1764 Ann Sarson; Ann m1789 John Johnson; John Henry (illegitimate, 26) m1890 Sarah Ann Pratt (26 daughter of Joseph Pratt); Lesley Marjorie (24 daughter of James William Hall) m1966 Robert Charles Wilde (27 son of Charles Edwin Wilde); Martin Stuart (29 son of Derek Hall) m1989 Della Marie Cox (20 daughter of Brian Joseph Cox).

HALLAM: William Horace (25 son of William Hallam) m1906 Nellie Copson (20 daughter of Ambrose Copson).

HAMBLING: John Henry (20 son of Humphrey Matthew Hambling) m1877 Mary Ann Stanyard (daughter of Joseph Stanyard).

HAMILTON: Hans Patrick (son of Peter Fisher Percival Hamilton) m1913 Rosamund Mary Francis Trevelyan Dixon (daughter of James Murray Dixon); Paul Anthony (29 son of Ian Michael Hamilton) m1986 Caroline Mary Fanshawe (29 daughter of Gordon Lennox Fanshawe).

HAMSON: George (25 son of John Hamson) m1857 Mary Botherway (20 daughter of Timothy Botherway).

HANCOCK: Martha m1723 John Bennet; Peter Brian (widower, son of Leonard Hancock) m 2001 Mary Rachel Burton (widow, daughter of Frank Bowler).

HANDLEY: Charlotte (daughter of George Handley) m1860 John Adams (son of John Adams); George (son of George Handley) m1870 Elizabeth Wakley (daughter of Francis Wakley); Margaret (25 daughter of Joseph James Handley) m1966 Keith Cyril Waldram (24 son of Cyril Waldram).

HANFORD: Olive Agnes (23 daughter of Richard Frederick Handford) m1920 Horace Minkley (21 son of George Minkley).

HANNIBAL: Sally Christine (21 daughter of Leslie Ernest Hannibal) m1975 Christopher Howard Lawson (22 son of Howard Gordon Lawson).

HARDWAY: Thomas m1751 Elizabeth Brawnson.

HARDY: Sarah Charis (p.m.d, 44 daughter of Fergus Donald Cameron) m1997 Paul Ronald Alderson (39 son of Ronald Frederick Alderson).
HARGRAVE: David Miles William (24 son of Peter John William Hargrave) m1989 Jane Bishop (24 daughter of Ivan Raymond Bishop).
HARKER: Alan Brook (22 son of John Thwaite Harker) m1952 Sheila Mary Vazeille Boddy (25 daughter of James Alexander Vazeille Boddy).
HARLEY: Thomas m1825 Gertrude Simpson.
HARMER: John Malcolm (25 son of Stanley Gordon Harmer) m1968 Ann Gillian Feasey (25 daughter of William Doncaster Feasey).
HARRIMAN: Mary m1827 Francis Raynor; Thomas m1837 Mariah Vesty.
HARRINGTON: Jeremy Ian (29 son of Norman Donald Harrington) m1995 Joanne Louise Constance Simms (23 daughter of Anthony Andrew Simms).
HARRIS: James m1678 Hellen Blankley; Isaac m1777 Ann Johnson; Waldron (widower, son of Waldron Harris) m1972 Olga Muriel Fay Gregory (daughter of William Victor Gregory); Elizabeth Ruth Lloyd (24 daughter of Waldron Harris) m1972 Vincent David Patrick Foley (28 son of Timothy John Foley); Elinor Jane Waldron (24 daughter of Waldron Harris) m1976 Peter John Kinal (25 son of Dmytro Kinal); Neil Christopher (30 son of Thomas Henry Harris) m1982 Jane Louise Sturgess (23 daughter of Reginald Walter Sturgess).
HARRISON: Sarah m1786 John Stableford; Joan Lilian Moyra (19 daughter of Joseph Henry Harrison m1942 John Bartram Saunders (20 son of Bartram Ernest Saunders); Lucy Anne (23 daughter of Jeffrey Cecil Harrison) m1990 Richard Pavesi (26 son of Fiorenzo Pavesi); Laura Jane (27 daughter of Jeffrey Cecil Harrison) m1993 Edward Robert Charles Ross (25 son of Christopher George Ross).
HARROD: William (24 son of Peter James Harrod) m1988 Amanda Jane Taylor (23 daughter of Gordon Maurice Taylor).
HARWOOD: George William (40 son of George William Harwood) m1940 Nora Charlotte Jones (32 daughter of James Alfred Jones).
HASTINGS: Henry m1714 Jane Swane; Edna May (26 daughter of George Hastings) m1948 Stanley Fisk (27 son of Herbert William Fisk).
HATCHER: William m1779 Ann Hull.
HAWKES: Lucy Michelle Hawkes (31 daughter of Martyn Hawkes) m2009 Stefan Adam Stachou (31 son of Andrzej Stachou)
HAYCOCK: Elizabeth m1633 Francis Glenn.
HAYNES: John Henry (29 son of Henry Haynes) m1932 Gladys Mary Lloyd (21 daughter of Percival George Lloyd); Sheila Ann (20 daughter of John Henry Haynes) m1953 Raymond Paul Rose (20 son of Charles Frederick Rose); John Edward (27 son of John Henry Haynes) m1965 Janice Beatrice Ann Houghton (23 daughter of Alfred Thomas Houghton); Lynn Marion (20 daughter of Henry John Haynes) m1970 Charles Thomas Dunne (22 son of Kenneth Robert Dunne).
HEATH: William Frederick Gordon (25 son of Gerald Gordon Heath) m1981 Phillipa Clare Smith (22 daughter of David William Smith).
HEFFORD: Elizabeth m1825 Francis Wakerley; Elke (22 daughter of William Hefford) m 2000 Jason Wayne Morris (28 son of Derick John Morris).
HEICH: Richard m1708 Mary Siston; Edward m1731 Mary Brewood.
HEMSLEY: Benjamin m1800 Elizabeth Johnson; Benjamin m1809 Mary Hutchinson; Benjamin (29 son of Benjamin Hemsley) m1887 Eliza Hannah Raynor (21 daughter of Thomas Raynor).
HENSON: William m1717 Anne Prier.
HERBERT: Edna Minnie (29 daughter of Job Herbert) m1932 George Lewis Lloyd (26 son of Percival George Lloyd); Albert (widower, 68 son of Henry Herbert) m1944 Adeline Margaret Joscelyne (47 daughter of Frederick Hedley Joscelyne).
HESSEL: Mary m1680 John Dan.
HETTERLEY: John m1752 Mary Brawnson.

HEWITT: Millicent (23 daughter of Leonard Hewitt) m1934 Bruce Gould (26 son of Job Gould).

HEWS/HUGHES: Robert m1700 Elizabeth Gilbert; Thomas m1705 Mary Deakins; Elizabeth m1738 Benjamin Glover; Elizabeth m1742 Thomas Simpson; Thomas m1762 Rosamond Searson; Sarah (widow) m1765 John Pickard; Elizabeth Anne (24 daughter of Malcolm John Hughes) m1986 Stephen Monk Jones (26 son of Thomas Philip Jones).

HIBBIT: Michael Oliver Douglas Hibbitt (50 son of Douglas Cecil Hibbit) m1998 Clare Catherine Reynolds (36 daughter of Brian Francis Reynolds)

HICKLING: Edward m1809 Elizabeth Woodward.

HIGGS: Harriett (daughter of William Higgs) m1879 Henry Squires (son of Henry Squires).

HILL: Thomas m1783 Elizabeth Ward; Hannah m1804 John Hopkins; Elizabeth m1812 William Potter; Benjamin m1812 Susannah Cresswell; Thomas m1832 Elizabeth Bird; William (24 son of Benjamin Hill) m1838 Sarah Brooksby (19); Samuel (son of Samuel Hill) m1867 Cordelia Morris (daughter of George Morris); Mary Ann (daughter of Thomas Hill) m1870 Walter Bunney (son of William Bunney); Eliza (21 daughter of Thomas Hill) m1895 William Faulks (widower, 48 son of Thomas Faulks).

HIND: Stephen m1698 Hannah Moore; Rachel (widow) m1708 John Paget (widower); Robert m1721 Elizabeth Keatley; Henry (widower) m1817 Jane Clarke.

HOBBS: Reginald Henry (26 son of Henry James Hobbs) m1936 Hela Folwell (22 daughter of Arthur Ernest Folwell).

HODEN: Elizabeth m1804 Benjamin Pollard.

HODGE(S): Matthew m1816 Ann James; Martha (23 daughter of Matthew Hodge) m1842 Thomas Adams (24); Thomas (20 son of William Hodge) m1854 Eliza Barker (25 daughter of James Barker); Hannah (20 daughter of Thomas Hodges) m1880 Charles Lynes (widower, son of William Lynes); Harriet (26 daughter of Thomas Hodges) m1894 George Austin Talbot (25 son of Charles Talbot); Clara Helen Hodges (23 daughter of John Henry Hodges) m1896 John Watson (23 son of John Watson); Edith (22 daughter of John Henry Hodges) m1900 Charles Edward Baxter (24 son of Abraham Baxter); Rebecca Jane (24 daughter of Graham Peter Hodges) m1996 Richard Anthony Cole (26 son of Anthony Victor Cole).

HODGKINSON: Elizabeth m1807 William Johnson.

HOLIDAY: Ernest James (30 son of George Holiday) m1931 Sarah Winifred Snodin (36 daughter of John Snodin).

HOLLOWAY: Elizabeth Louise (22 daughter of Kenneth Frank Holloway) m1990 Michael David Ayres (26 son of David Anthony Ayres); Nicholas Frank (26 son of Kenneth Frank Holloway) m1990 Alison Beaumont (33 daughter of Ronald Beaumont); Nicholas Frank (pmd 40, son of Kenneth Frank Holloway) m2004 Clare Elizabeth Broughton (pmd 38 daughter of Albert William Thomas Broughton).

HOOD: George Thomas Taylor (widower, 41 son of John Henry Wood) m1928 Barbara Wellington Bone (22 daughter of Wellington Arthur Bone).

HOPKINS: John m1804 Hannah Hill.

HORNER: Elizabeth m1769 Thomas Smitham.

HORNSBY: Ivy Annie Elsie (34 daughter of John Hornsby) m1935 Arthur Ernest Stevenson (25 son of Ernest Stevenson).

HORSFIELD: Margaret Beatrice (26 daughter of Richard Bernard Horsfield) m1952 Maurice Edwin Charles Bunney (25 son of Charles Benjamin Bunney).

HOUGHTON: Janice Patricia Ann Houghton (23 daughter of Alfred Thomas Houghton) m1965 John Edward Haynes (27 son of John Henry Haynes).

HO(U)LT: Anne m1727 William Smith; Charles Henry (24 son of John Holt) m1905 Joanna Brown (28 daughter of George Brown); Kathleen Grace (24 daughter of Samuel Hoult) m1932 William Kilby (widower, 37 son of Thomas Kilby).

HOVEY: Thomas m1722 Jane Preston.
HOWDEN: Ellener m1687 John Parker.
HOWARD: Bruce Kenneth (44 son of Kenneth Howard) m2008 Sheila Marie Jownally (39 daughter of Sheik Fazil Jownally)
HOWELLS: John Rhys (31 son of William Henry Howells) m1985 Heather Mary Durber (26 daughter of John Macdonald Durber).
HOWLETT: David John Barfoot (33 son of William George Francis Howlett) m1991 Judith Mary Rodgers (32 daughter of Douglas Malcolm Rogers); Katharine Louise (29 daughter of William George Francis Howlett) m1992 Clayton William John Johnston (32 son of George Beverley Johnston).
HUBBARD: Annie Lizzie (21 daughter of John Hubbard) m1885 Edgar Norton (19 son of Charles Norton).
HUDSON: Elizabeth m1687 Thomas Mais; Elizabeth m1698 Benjamin Lewin; Sarah m1769 Benjamin Pollard; Ann m1837 John Thompson.
HUGHES: See Hews.
HULL: Ann m1779 William Hatcher; Mary m1785 William Snow.
HULSE: Margaret Adrienne (18 daughter of Arthur Harry Hulse) m1957 Colin Peter Frost (21 son of Walter Frost).
HUMBER: Thomas m1739 Sarah Walker; Samuel m1773 Elizabeth Broomfield.
HUMBLE: Richard Anthony (25 son of George Humble m1975 Helen Blathwayt Graneek (23 daughter of Maurice Graneek).
HUNT: Reginald Norman (19 son of Arthur George Hunt) m1948 Jean Margery McClintock (18 daughter of Patrick McClintock); David John (23 son of David Hunt) m1962 Pauline Janet Gaskell (22 daughter of Henry Brian Gaskell).
HURST: Abigail m1731 Thomas Clarke.
HUTCHINSON: William m1734 Alice Walker; William m1758 Jane Johnson; William m1788 Mary Ferneley; Mary m1809 Benjamin Hemsley; Noel Staughton (24, son of Leonard Staughton Hutchinson) m1949 Jenifer Mary Carter (22 daughter of Dick Carter).
HUXLEY: Samuel m1634 Martha Fielding.
HYMAN: Kenneth Stanley (31 son of Harry Cooper Hyman) m1966 Moraig Douglas Wallace (23 daughter of Douglas Ormsby Wallace).
INGRAM: Thomas m1737 Mary Fielding; Susan Graine (22 daughter of Ralph Herbert Ingram) m1963 David Christopher Wren (25 son of Joseph Stanley Wren).
IRISH: Joseph m1736 Mary Poultney.
ISOM: Jill Anne (24 daughter of Thomas Owen Isom) m1987 Philip Raymond Hale (24 son of Raymond Hale).
JACKSON: Anne m1698 Thomas Bodle.
JAMES: Mary m1798 George Charlton; Elizabeth m1801 William Brown; Ann m1816 Matthew Hodges; Thomas Henry (22 son of Thomas James) m1897 Martha Ann Adams (22 daughter of John Adams); Nicola Karen (37 daughter of Anthony John James) m2004 Timothy Hugh Clare May (27 son of Geoffrey John May).
JARRATT: Elizabeth (daughter of Charles Jarratt) m1864 Abraham Cooper (son of Charles Cooper).
JARVIS: Anne m1727 John Martin; Susannah m1833 Edward Willars.
JAYES: Judith Shipley (27 daughter of Herbert Shipley Jayes) m1980 Mark Jonathan Walton (27 son of Wilfred Walton).
JEE: David m1733 Anne Coleburne.
JELLEY: Gladys Marguerita (19 daughter of William Robert Jelley) m1934 Patrick Barry Poole Pippin (son of John Philip Pippin).
JENNINGS: Eleanor m1704 George Woolley.
JOSCELYNE: Adeline Margaret (47 daughter of Frederick Hedley Joscelyne) m1944 Albert Herbert (widower, 68 son of Henry Herbert).
JOHN: David Neil (25 son of David John) m1979 Fiona Mary Brook Lawson (21 daughter of Donald Michael Brook Lawson).

JOHNSON: Thomas m1730 Alice Mountney; Elizabeth m1738 John Kellum; Elizabeth m1744 Robert Glover; Jane m1758 William Hutchinson; Thomas m1760 Elizabeth Smallwood; John m1761 Elizabeth Turner; William m1763 Elizabeth Kemp; Mary m1770 John Beasley; Dorothy m1772 Henry Burton; Elizabeth m1773 Robert Taylor; Ann m1777 Isaac Harris; Jane m1778 James Smart; Joseph m1783 Elizabeth Gregg; Mary m1787 Richard Quinton; John m1789 Ann Hall; Ann m1789 Michael Goadby; Alice m1792 Thomas Bramley; Jane m1799 William Allum; Elizabeth m1800 Benjamin Hemsley; William m1806 Hannah Ball; William m1807 Elizabeth Hodgkinson; Maria m1808 Jacob Nurse; Frances (widow) m1833 Thomas Ward; Arthur (25 son of Thomas James Johnson) m1908 Frances Mills (26); Alan Johnson (32, son of Peter Donald Johnson) m1998 Mandy Jane Bonneywell (p.m.d, 28 daughter of Sydney Dennis Elson).

JOHNSTON: Clayton William John (32 son of George Beverley Johnston) m1992 Katherine Louise Howlett (29 daughter of William George Francis Howlett).

JONES: Elizabeth m1816 Samuel Brown (widower); Nora Charlotte (32 daughter of James Alfred Jones) m1940 George William Harwood (40 son of George William Harwood); David Gwynfor (27 son of Robert Evans Jones) m1958 Doreen Hazel Rudkin (22 daughter of Walter Rudkin); Carys Anne (22 daughter of Peter Melfin Jones) m1972 John Andrew Swanwick (24 son of Leonard Wright Swanwick); Simon John (batchelor, 24 son of Barry Martin) m1985 Gillian Denise Newton (21 daughter of Arthur Rowland Newton); Stephen Monk (26 son of Thomas Philip Jones) m1986 Elizabeth Anne Hughes (24 daughter of Malcolm John Hughes); Wendy Ann (26 daughter of Thomas Philip Jones) m1988 Christopher Michael Wreightt (29 son of Peter Hadfield Wreightt).

JOSCELYNE: Adeline Margaret (47 daughter of Frederick Hedley Joscelyne) m1944 Albert Herbert (widower, 68 son of Henry Herbert).

JOWNALLY: Sheila Marie (39 daughter of Sheik Fazil Jownally) m2008 Bruce Kenneth Howard (44 son of Kenneth Howard)

JUDD: Ann m1726 Joseph Sheppard.

KEATLEY: Elizabeth m1721 Robert Hind.

KELLUM: John m1738 Elizabeth Johnson.

KELM: John (widower) m1771 Ann Whatnall (widow).

KEMP: Elizabeth m1763 William Johnson.

KERBY: William (24 son of William Kerby) m1876 Elizabeth Cuffling (25 daughter of William Cuffling).

KERR: Peter (pmd, 39 son of Peter Kerr) m1996 Maxine Shipman (39 daughter of Terence William Shipman).

KHOURI: Antoine Elias (25 son of Elias Khouri) m1972 Alison Elizabeth Meakin Cameron (21 daughter of Fergus Donald Cameron).

KIDDYER: John m1734 Mary Abbot.

KILBOURN: Ann m1774 Thomas Burton.

KILBY: William (widower, 37 son of Thomas Kilby) m1932 Kathleen Grace Hoult (24 daughter of Samuel Hoult); Gweneth Mary (daughter of Walter Kilby) m1947 Benjamin Russell Gimson (son of Josiah Russell Gimson).

KIMBER: Robert Bryan (25 son of Bryan Kimber) m2003 Davinia Lucinda Leake (23 daughter of John Michael Leake)

KINAL: Peter John (25 son of Dmytro Kinal) m1976 Elinor Jane Waldron Harris (24 daughter of Waldron Harris).

KINGSTON: Robert John (29 son of Geoffrey Kingston) m 2000 Nicola Karen Reynolds (29 daughter of Leon Michael Reynolds)

KIRBY: George m1745 Ann Cook; Ann m1813 William Preston; Sarah m1814 Thomas Preston.

KIRKE: William m1719 Isabella Prior; Angela Marjorie (22 daughter of Edward Kirke) m1963 Alan David Raynor (24 son of Raymond Norton Raynor).

KNIGHT: Martin James (30 son of John Knight) m1991 Rebecca Zoë (26 daughter of Michael Roalfe)

KNOPP: Sonia Ingrid (daughter of Manfred Gunter Knopp) m1981 Alan Postlethwaite (23 son of Arnold Postlethwaite).
KOW: Mary m1811 Henry Burton.
KRARUP: William Nicholas Christian (29 son of Michael John Krarup) m1990 Jacqueline Anita Page (28 daughter of Leon Page).
LACY: John m1718 Mary Fletcher.
LAKIN: Elizabeth m1812 Barfoot Richardson; Sarah m1815 Joseph Bostock.
LAMBOURNE: Herbert Henry (27 son of Henry Lambourne) m1935 Margaret Winifred Mary Ball (25 daughter of Walter Winter Ball).
LANCASTER: Robert Alan (24 son of John Cargill Lancaster) m1971 Caroline Elizabeth Fairfax Scott (24 daughter of John William Fairfax Scott).
LANDER: Thomas m1794 Mary Beasley; William (30 son of James Lander) m1855 Sarah Renals (26 daughter of Edmund Renals).
LANE: Richard Elliott (26 son of Charles Frederick Lane) m1935 Elizabeth Joyce Viccars (26 daughter of William Arnold Viccars).
LANGFORD: Margaret Doreen (23 daughter of Edward Walter Langford) m1948 William Punshon (25 son of Ernest Punshon).
LANGHAM: Thomas (30 son of Thomas Langham) m1840 Amy Bates (25).
LAPHAM: Susan Ann (25 daughter of Nigel Frederick Lapham) m1978 Waldeman Marian Sroczynski (26 son of Leon Sroczynski).
LAURANCE: John m1776 Sarah Bostock.
LAWRENCE: Florence May (daughter of Ernest James Lawrence) m1949 George Raymond Nixon (son of George Nixon).
LAWSON: Christopher Howard (22 son of Howard Gordon Lawson) m1975 Sally Christine Hannibal (21 daughter of Leslie Ernest Hannibal); Fiona Mary Brook (21 daughter of Donald Michael Brook Lawson) m1979 David Neil John (25 son of David John); Andrew Michael Brook (28 son of Donald Michael Brook-Lawson) m1984 Helen Axon (18 daughter of Brian Axon); Helen Jane (24 daughter of David Thomas Lawson) m1988 Christopher Mark Tuckley (22 son of Graham Tuckley); Jonathan Mark (23 son of David Thomas Lawson) m1989 Tina Marie Batterham (22 daughter of Ivan Michael Batterham); Magnus Rogvauld Ninian (29) m1997 Barbara Dawn Wright (p.m.d, 27 daughter of David William Wright).
LAZOURENKO: Elena (22, daughter of Irina Lazourenko -*father's name not given*) m2004 March Christopher Freeman (26 son of Ronald Freeman)
LEAGO: Thomas m1719 Anne Prior.
LEAKE: Martin John (23 son of John Michael Leake) m1996 Julia Caroline Freer (21 daughter of Peter William Freer); Davinia Lucinda (23 daughter of John Michael Leake) m2003 Robert Bryan Kimber (25 son of Bryan Kimber).
LEE: William m1702 Elizabeth Whatnall; Samuel William (25 son of Thomas Lee) m1886 Sarah Jane Raynor (22 daughter of Thomas Raynor); Adeline Eliza Lee (24 daughter of Samuel William Lee) m1918 George Wilmore (39 son of William Wilmore); Winifred Lilian Bertha (25 daughter of Samuel William Lee) m1927 Reginald Luard Reeder (20 son of Arthur Reeder); Jennifer Elizabeth (21 daughter of Colin Alfred Lee) m1964 Frank Nicholas Tarratt (24 son of Frank Bernard Tarratt); Margaret Lilian (widow, 55 daughter of Horace Clark) m1965 Frank Bernard Tarratt (widower, 64 son of Frank Peake Tarratt).
LEES: Susan Phyllis (20 daughter of Douglas Robert Lees) m1972 Michael James Smith (27 son of Cyril James Smith).
LEVERETT: John m1731 Sarah Adcock.
LEWIN: Benjamin m1698 Elizabeth Hudson (widow); Elizabeth (widow) m1701 John Mee; John m1704 Elizabeth Clark; Mary m1760 John Pollard; Joseph m1762 Ann Pollard; Samuel m1836 Ann Burton (widow); Ann (widow, 40 daughter of William Morris) m1851 William Raynor (widower, 22 son of Zechariah Raynor).
LIDDAR: Tony Ranjit (36 son of Gurbakhsh Singh Liddar) m1998 Esther Lorraine Dutton (31 daughter of Robert James Dutton)

LILLEY: Gail Patricia (26 daughter of Roy Lilley) m2002 Austin James Brough (29 son of Ian James Brough)
LIMBERT: William m1784 Sarah Chamberlain; Sarah m1789 John Pollard.
LING: Christopher Mark (25 son of David Brian Ling) m1994 Joanna Jane Taylor (29 daughter of Gordon Maurice Taylor).
LLOYD: John m1772 Mary Major; Emily Mary (18 daughter of Percival George Lloyd) m1918 Alfred Roy Davidson (23 son of John Davidson); Violet Annie (24 daughter of Percival George Lloyd) m1922 George Spence (26 son of Thomas Spence); Percival William (22 son of Percival George Lloyd) m1930 Doris Annie Turner (22 daughter of James Turner); George Lewis (26 son of Percival George Lloyd) m1932 Edna Minnie Herbert (29 daughter of Job Herbert); Gladys Mary (21 daughter of Percival George Lloyd) m1932 John Henry Haynes (29 son of Henry Haynes); Dorothy Freda (26 daughter of Percival George Lloyd) m1938 William Harold Sharpe (32 son of William Sharpe); Sidney Edward (26 son of Percival George Lloyd) m1942 Phyllis Mary Yates (26 daughter of Horace Edward Yates); Herbert Roy (23 son of Percival George Lloyd) m1942 Mildred Doris Manley (23 daughter of James Manley); Peter William (23 son of Percival William Lloyd) m1954 Doreen Mary Newitt (21 daughter of Charles Edward Newitt); Pamela Mary (21 daughter of George Lewis Lloyd) m1959 Stewart Harold Dance (24 son of Harold Edmund Dance); Rodney Edward (26 son of Sidney Edward Lloyd) m1971 Sherin Allison Rutter (21 daughter of William Allison Rutter); Emma Sherin (32 daughter of Rodney Edward Lloyd) m2005 Matthew David Ray (30, son of Edmund Matthew Thomas Ray, NSW Australia)
LOCKWOOD: Sarah m1820 Stephen Clarke; Joseph (37 son of Thomas Lockwood) m1850 Mary Hale (widow, 48 daughter of William Wilding).
LOVETT: John m1684 Ann Stiff; John (widower) m1733 Mary Wylde (widow); Ann m1741 Squire Whatnall; Thomas m1788 Elizabeth Cooke; Jane m1793 Joseph Beasley; William m1793 Elizabeth Wilson; George m1797 Mary Astin; Mary m1801 Francis Morris; Jemima (36 daughter of Daniel Lovatt) m1848 Stephen Clarke; Mary (daughter of Joseph Lovet) m1866 George Godbald (son of Robert Godbald).
LOWES: George Albert (28 son of John Lowes) m1952 Barbara Ellen Bunney (23 daughter of Charles Benjamin Bunney).
LUMMAS: Sara m1637 Francis Patchet.
LYNCH: Kevin Paul (26 son of John Patrick Lynch) m1982 Linda Anne Favell (21 daughter of Colin Neville Favell).
LYNES: Richard m1801 Ruth Wooding; Sarah m1830 John Morris; Thomas (widower) m1837 Elizabeth Brooksby; Charles (widower, son of William Lynes) m1880 Hannah Hodges (20 Thomas Hodges); Hannah (widow, 21 daughter of Thomas Hodges) m1886 Thomas Walter Palmer (21 son of George Palmer).
LYON: Richard m1633 Joan Pickwell.
MAIS: Barbara Nora (26 daughter of John Leslie Mais) m1945 Peter Lovell Berridge (23 son of Isaac Lovell Berridge).
MAJOR: Mary m1772 John Lloyd.
MALTBY: Judith Margaret (23 daughter of Robert William Maltby) m1972 Leslie James McLintic (24 son of William James McLintic).
MANIAS: Anthony (29 son of Nicholas Manias) m1988 Anne Brandrik (20 daughter of Reinert Andreas Brandrik).
MANLEY: Mildred Doris (23 daughter of James Manley) m1942 Herbert Roy Lloyd (23 son of Percival George Lloyd).
MARLOW: Jill Veronica (20 daughter of George Donald Marlow) m1977 Anthony Richard Wright (22 son of Edwin Albert Wright).
MARSDEN: Anne m1733 John Dod.
MARSHALL: Ann (18 daughter of Alan William Marshall) m1978 Andrew Scott Mutch (18 son of Robert Mutch); Eric Barry (34 son of Barry Norton) m2005 Sarah Louise Cooledge (30 daughter of John Cooledge).
MARSON: Dorothy m1796 Thomas Brooksby.

MARSTON: Charles Walter (55 son of Henry Marston) m1967 Mary Burton (widow, 51 daughter of Ernest Elkington); Nigel James (27 son of David Marston) m1990 Lesley Carroll (28, daughter of William Patrick Carroll).
MARTIN: John m1727 Anne Jarvice.
MASON: Mary m1704 Thomas Bird.
MATTHEWS: Elizabeth m1808 William Brown; John (son of William Matthews) m1877 Sarah Maria Baum (daughter of John Baum).
MATTS: Harriet (daughter of Joseph Matts) m1862 Stephen Simpson (son of John Simpson); Mary (daughter of Joseph Matts) m1866 Frederick Allwood (son of William Allwood).
MAY: Timothy Hugh Clare (27 son of Geoffrey John May) m2004 Nicola Karen James (37 daughter of Anthony John James)
MAYS: Thomas m1687 Elizabeth Hudson.
McCLINTOCK: Jean Margery (18 daughter of Patrick McClintock) m1948 Reginald Norman Hunt (19 son of Arthur George Hunt); Patricia Anne (20 daughter of Patrick McClintock) m1954 Richard Edward Trevor Roper (25 son of Richard Teynham Trevor Roper).
McCURRY: Jennifer Mary (24 daughter of Arthur L. McCurry) m1960 Osborne Frederick Benjamin Burchnall (25 son of Osborne R. Burchnall).
McDERMOTT: Charles David (27 son of Albert David McDermott) m1988 Julie Amanda Challoner (26 daughter of Maurice William Challoner).
McLEOD: Patricia Rosslyn (21 daughter of Colin McLeod) m1964 Gary Bayley Coombes (23 son of Stanley Betterson Coombes).
McLINTIC: Leslie James (24 son of William James McLintic) m1972 Judith Margaret Maltby (23 daughter of Robert William Maltby).
MEADOWS: Andrew Miles (21 son of Thomas Meadows) m1885 Emma Cuffling (21 daughter of William Cuffling).
MEASURES: Margaret m1747 John Warner.
MEE: John m1701 Elizabeth Lewin (widow); Hannah m1805 William Bramby; Robert (22 son of Herbert Mee) m1939 Irene Elsie Minkley (24 daughter of Herbert Minkley); Richard William (31 son of Robert William Mee) m1989 Jane Elizabeth Ellis (24 daughter of James Michael Ellis).
MIDDLETON: Mary m1728 John Farrar; Emmatt m1729 Joseph Cave.
MILLER: John Henry (29 son of Henry Miller) m1893 Mary Price (29 daughter of Frederick Price).
MILLS: Frances (26) m1908 Arthur Johnson (25 son of Thomas James Johnson).
MILNER: Henry Robert (27 son of Charles Thomas Milner) m1887 Mary Ann Cuffling (23 daughter of William Cuffling).
MINKLEY: Alfred (21 son of George Minkley) m1911 Emma Brown (29 daughter of George Brown); Edith Emily (21 daughter of Herbert Minkley) m1917 Harry Allen (22 son of Henry Allen); Violet Lilian (23 daughter of George Minkley) m1919 Joseph Stafford (26 son of Pharoah Stafford); Horace (21 son of George Minkley) m1920 Olive Agnes Hansford (23 daughter of Richard Frederick Hansford); Muriel (22 daughter of Herbert Minkley) m1922 Percy Scott Adlard (26 son of Harry Walter Scott Adlard); Doris (24 daughter of Herbert Minkley) m1926 Albert Edward Vann (24 son of Alfred Vann); Evelyn Mary (23 daughter of Herbert Minkley) m1931 Herbert Edgar Bradley (24 son of Ernest Bradley); Kathleen (29 daughter of George Minkley) m1936 Charles Henry Willis (33 son of Harry Willis); Gladys Elizabeth (26 daughter of Herbert Minkley) m1938 William Norman Moore (29 son of Percy Victor Moore); Irene Elsie (24 daughter of Herbert Minkley) m1939 Robert Mee (22 son of Herbert Mee); Dorothy Kathleen May (19 daughter of Horace Minkley) m1942 Albert Carter Snow (29 son of Matthew Snow).
MONKS: David John (27 son of Arthur Monks) m2009 Laura Kate Beeby (27 daughter of Brian Joseph Beeby)
MOORE: Hannah m1698 Stephen Hind; Mary m1752 Benjamin Yeomans; Rebecca

m1788 William Plowright; Catherine (daughter of Charles Moore) m1866 George Morris (son of George Morris); William Norman (29 son of Percy Victor Moore) m1938 Gladys Elizabeth Minkley (26 daughter of Herbert Minkley).

MORRIS: Francis m1801 Mary Lovatt; George m1814 Ann Baxter; William m1827 Frances Carter; John n1830 Sarah Lines; George (son of Francis Morris) m1837 Mary Prince (widow, nee Flewin); Catherine (daughter of George Morris) m1860 Joseph Woods (son of William Woods); George (son of George Morris) m1866 Catherine Moore (daughter of Charles Moore); Cordelia (daughter of George Morris) m1867 Samuel Hill (son of Samuel Hill); Richard Charles (29 son of Alfred Richard Morris) m1964 Rosemarie Bettyne Carole Copson (24 daughter of John Ambrose Copson); Nicola Kate (23 daughter of Francis Wynn Morris) m1995 Russell Michael John Davies (24 son of Michael Leonard Davies); Jason Wayne (28 son of Derick John Morris) m 2000 Elke Hefford (22 daughter of William Hefford).

MOUNTNEY: Alice m1730 Thomas Johnson.

MUGFORD: Hilda Millicent (22 daughter of James Mugford) m1910 Arthur Williams (28 son of George Williams).

MULLINS: Nicholas Richard John (24 son of Colin Mullins) m1980 Rachel Elizabeth Allen (24 daughter of Christopher Maclaren Allen).

MUSGROVE: Thomas Donaldson (23 son of Herbert Thomas Musgrove) m1944 Kathleen Margaret May Bunney (26 daughter of Sidney Oswald Bunney).

MUTCH: Andrew Scott (18 son of Robert Mutch) m1978 Ann Marshall (18 daughter of Alan William Marshall).

NEEDHAM: William m1740 Mary Brown; Henry Holyoak (29 son of Henry Needham) m1917 Doris Olivia Bannister Pepper (25 daughter of Edwin Pepper).

NESBITT: Peter John (24 son of William John Nesbitt) m1977 Hazel Irene Walters (21 daughter of Francis Raymond Walters).

NEWBERRY: Hannah m1695 Thomas Cramp.

NEWBOLD: John m1770 Elizabeth Clarke.

NEWBY: Ann m1814 Thomas Barson; Mary (widow) m1815 Thomas Clarke.

NEWITT: Doreen Mary (21 daughter of Charles Edward Newitt) m1954 Peter William Lloyd (23 son of Percival William Lloyd).

NEWTON: John m1802 Ann Pitts; Gillian Denise (21 daughter of Arthur Rowland Newton) m1985 Simon John Jones (24 son of Barry Martin); Sarah Jane (22 daughter of Hayden Henry Newton) m2004 Jamie Stephen Reynolds (28 son of Stephen Paul Reynolds).

NIXON: George Raymond (son of George Nixon) m1949 Florence May Lawrence (daughter of Ernest James Lawrence).

NOON: Ann m1783 John Gray.

NORMAN: Susan m1834 John Clarke; Jane (36 daughter of William Norman) m1846 George Greasley (widower, 37 son of William Greasley).

NORTH: John m1802 Mary Nurse; Jemimah m1835 Philip Fowler; Gillian Rosemary (22 daughter of Eric Frank North) m1965 Christopher George Frederick Bocock (23 son of George Frederick Charles Bocock).

NORTHAM: Sarah Frances (21 daughter of John Malcolm Northam) m1990 Jonathan Mark Beach (22 son of Dennis Henry Beach); Nicholas John Edward (26 son of John Malcolm Northam) m1992 Susan Joyce Webb (24 daughter of John Adam Webb).

NORTON: Edgar (18 son of Charles Norton) m1885 Annie Lizzie Hubbard (21 daughter of John Hubbard).

NURSE: Mary m1802 John North; Jacob m1807 Elizabeth Eyre; Jacob m1808 Maria Johnson; Elizabeth (24 daughter of Jacob Nurse) m1890 Thomas George Raynor (26 son of Thomas Raynor).

OADBY: Mary m1799 Thomas Fewkes.

OLDERSHAW: Elizabeth (daughter of Thomas Oldershaw) m1838 Thomas Dexter; Henry (40 son of Thomas Oldershaw) m1847 Mary Oldershaw (30 daughter of

Henry Oldershaw); Mary (daughter of Henry Oldershaw) m1847 Henry Oldershaw (40 son of Thomas Oldershaw).

OLIVER: Mary m1734 William Palmer; Alfred (22 son of John Oliver) m1905 Elizabeth Jane Picker (21 daughter of Charles Picker); Sandra Elizabeth (21 daughter of James Stanley Oliver) m1967 Robert Alan Smith (22 son of Henry Smith).

ORERS: John m1718 Susanna Woodford.

ORTON: Jane Elizabeth (39 daughter of Charles Victor Orton) m1990 David John Fisher (30 son of Sydney Fisher).

OSENTON: Edith Helen (29 daughter of George Osenton) m1926 Leslie Taylor (24 son of Frederick William Taylor).

OVENDEN: Rachel Ovenden (28 daughter of Keith Ovenden) m2004 Carl Gardner (31 son of Peter Gardner)

PAGE: Sarah m1757 Thomas Baum; Thomas m1763 Mary Smith; Jacqueline Anita (28 daughter of Leon Page) m1990 William Nicholas Christian Krarup (29 son of Michael John Krarup); Jason Robert Stoddart Page (29 son of Adam Stoddart Page) m1998 Justine Rosalind Proctor (28 daughter of Julian Hickman Proctor)

PAGET: John (widower) m1708 Rachel Hind (widow); Elizabeth m1813 William Crooks.

PALMER: Alice m1701 Abel Brooksby; Benjamin m1722 Mary Blackwell; William m1734 Mary Oliver; Elizabeth m1752 John Westley; Hannah m1808 Samuel Preston; Thomas m1811 Jane Bates; Thomas Walter (21 son of George Palmer) m1886 Hannah Lynes (widow, 21 daughter of Thomas Hodges); Simon Roger (24 son of Roger Palmer) m1991 Jeanette Helen Buswell (23 daughter of Derek Alfred Buswell).

PARE: Benjamin m1734 Anne Glover.

PARKER: John m1687 Ellener Howden; Mary m1715 William Dexter; Frederick Charles William (27 son of Charles Parker) m1936 Hilda Allen (27 daughter of William Allen); Edward Victor (divorced, 47 son of Edward James Parker) m1987 Sheila Marguerite Halford (widow, 57 daughter of Samuel Daniel).

PARKINSON: Alan Parkinson (34, son of Alfred Herbert Parkinson) m 1998 Sally Griffin (31 daughter of Paschal Francis Griffin)

PARSONS: Anthony Leigh (29 son of Henry Lionel Parsons) m1972 Carol Kathleen Simmons (22 daughter of Charles Rupert Simmons).

PASSAND: James m1734 Elizabeth Gilbert.

PATCHET: Francis m1637 Sara Lummas.

PATERSON: Laurie (28 daughter of William Paterson) m1934 Thomas Griffith Brooke (28 son of Robert Henry Brooke); David (23 son of Kenneth Robert Patersons) m1963 Valerie Ann Squire Bamford (23 daughter of Harry Frank Ernest Bamford).

PAVESI: Richard (26 son of Fiorenzo Pavesi) m1990 Lucy Anne Harrison (23 daughter of Jeffrey Cecil Harrison).

PAWLEY: Samuel m1788 Sarah Randel.

PEACOCK: Reginald Edward Herbert (30 son of John Peacock) m1896 Frances Ellen Gazy (22 daughter of Samuel Gazy).

PEAKE: Elizabeth m1731 Thomas Pollard.

PEARS: John Simon (23 son of John Pears) m1870 Isabel Rogers (18 daughter of Richard Rogers).

PEARSON: Anne (19 daughter of Edward Pearson) m1839 William Bunney.

PEET: Thomas m1785 Rebecca Snow; Ann m1785 Joseph Sears; William m1794 Barbara Bowring.

PEPPER: Edith May (daughter of Edwin Pepper) m1907 John Glover (38 son of James Glover); Katherine May (30 daughter of Edwin Pepper) m1912 Harold Doubleday (27 son of Richard Dixon Doubleday); Doris Olivia Bannister (25 daughter of Edwin Pepper m1917 Henry Holyoak Needham (29 son of Henry Needham).

PERCIVAL: Laura Jayne Deana (30 daughter of Alan Percival) m2010 Sean David Wareing (29 son of Stephen John Wareing)
PERKIN: Mary m1698 John Bennet; Martha m1747 William Gilbert.
PERKINS: Lydia m1768 Henry Chapman.
PETCHER: Joseph m1734 Sarah Walker.
PETTS: Elizabeth m1794 David Bunney; Ann m1802 John Newton; Benjamin m1825 Ann Berreson; Benjamin (widower) m1829 Mary Ward; Sarah (23 daughter of Benjamin Petts) m1854 Joseph Pratt (27 son of Henry Pratt).
PHILLIPS: Ann m1791 Thomas Church.
PICK: Alice m1807 Joseph Duffen.
PICKARD: John (widower) m1765 Sarah Hughes (widow).
PICKER: Jane Elizabeth (21 daughter of Charles Picker) m1905 Alfred Oliver (22 son of John Oliver); Charles (widower, 47 son of Joseph Picker) m1906 Margaret Gow (45 daughter of George Gow).
PICKERING: Anne m1698 Benjamin Preston; Sarah m1831 James Brown.
PICKWELL: Joan m1633 Richard Lyon.
PILTON: Martin Frederick (30 son of Peter Frederck Pilton) m1988 Jacqueline Suzanne Wainwright (26 daughter of Marcus Beresford Wainwright).
PLATTS: John m1829 Elizabeth Gretton.
PLOWRIGHT: William m1788 Rebecca Moore.
POCHIN: John m1723 Mary Brokesby (daughter of Abel Brokesby).
POLE: Charles m1734 Sarah Brewood.
POLLARD: Thomas m1702 Mary Abbot; Jane m1725 William Branston; William m1729 Elizabeth Smith; Thomas m1731 Elizabeth Peake; Jacob m1745 Margaret Burges; Thomas m1760 Mary Braunston; John m1760 Mary Lewin; William m1761 Elizabeth Prior; Ann m1762 Joseph Lewin; Benjamin m1769 Sarah Hudson; John m1774 Alice Caudwell; Elizabeth m1775 Thomas Wootnall; Ann m1775 Robert Preston; Elizabeth m1787 Anthony Woodford; John m1789 Sarah Limbert; Ann m1792 Thomas Wood; Benjamin m1804 Elizabeth Hoden.
POOLE: Thomas m1717 Sarah Burgess.
POPE: Pamela (33 daughter of Richard Arthur Pope) m1982 Geriant Reynolds Evans (28 son of David Clifford Evans).
POPLE: George Leonard (24 son of George Pople) m1907 Margaret Eliza Adams (24 daughter of John Adams).
PORCH: William Stanley (23 son of Frank Porch) m1937 Ada Elizabeth Cockerill (27 daughter of Lewis Cockerill).
PORTE: David Timothy (25 son of Donald McKenzie Porte) m1980 Veronica Lois Wright (22 daughter of John Michael Gidley Wright).
PORTER: Thomas m1737 Elizabeth Dexter; Elizabeth m1741 William Soares; Alfred (24 son of Joseph Porter) m1927 Helen Mary Taylor (20 daughter of Frederick William Taylor).
POSTLETHWAITE: Alan (23 son of Arnold Postlethwaite) m1981 Sonia Sonia Ingrid Knopp (daughter of Manfred Gunter Knopp).
POTTER: William m1812 Elizabeth Hill; William Sharp m1834 Elizabeth Richardson.
POULTNEY: Mary m1736 Joseph Irish.
POWELL: Harry George (27 son of Mansell Powell) m1933 Margaret Broughton (24 daughter of Leonard Broughton).
PRATT: Joseph (27 son of Henry Pratt) m1854 Sarah Petts (23 daughter of Benjamin Petts); Joseph (20 son of Joseph Pratt) m1886 Annie Robbins (18 daughter of John Robbins); Sarah Ann (26 daughter of Joseph Pratt) m1890 John Henry Hall (26, illegitimate); Mary Elizabeth (21 daughter of Joseph Pratt) m1891 James Henry Woods (21 son of Joseph Woods); Dorothy Ann (28 daughter of Charles Benjamin Pratt) m1923 Herbert Allan Bunney (29 son of John Bunney).
PRESTON: Benjamin m1698 Anne Pickering; Jane m1722 Thomas Hovey; William m1740 Mary Ashe; Joseph m1743 Ann Branston; Robert m1775 Ann Pollard; Robert m1775 Helena Gery; Christian m1783 Thomas Raynor; Thomas m1792

Mary Vesty; John m1793 Elizabeth Squire; Martha m1795 William Wykes; Richard m1804 Jane Walton; Samuel m1808 Hannah Palmer; William m1813 Ann Kirby; Thomas m1814 Sarah Kirby; Sarah m1825 William Clarke; Joshua m1829 Mary Watson; Daniel m1830 Jane Clark; John m1832 Ann Worrall; Ann (widow, daughter of John Kirby) m1839 George Thorp; Mary (21 daughter of Joseph Preston) m1845 William Taylor (26); Simeon (24 son of William Preston) m1855 Elizabeth Thorpe (20 daughter of John Thorpe); Arthur (23 son of William Preston) m1856 Mary Thorpe (22 daughter of Samuel Thorpe).

PRICE: Mary (29 daughter of Frederick price) m1893 John Henry Miller (29 son of Henry Miller).

PRIESTLEY: Samuel (widower) m1804 Elizabeth Brown.

PRINCE: Mary (widow, daughter of Stephen Flewin) m1837 George Morris.

PRIOR: Anne m1717 William Henson; Mary m1718 Robert Blunfill; Anne m1719 Thomas Leago; Isabella m1719 William Kirke; Joseph m1726 Mary Freeman; Robert m1738 Elizabeth Thornton; Elizabeth m1745 Thomas Estlin; Elizabeth m1761 William Pollard.

PROCTOR: Justine Rosalind Proctor (28 daughter of Julian Hickman Proctor) m1998 Jason Robert Stoddart Page (29 son of Adam Stoddart Page)

PUNSHON: William (25 son of Ernest Punshon) m1848 Margaret Doreen Langford (23 daughter of Walter Ernest Langford).

PURDY: Charlie (33 son of Thomas Purdy) m1919 Peggy Elizabeth Selby (35 daughter of William Selby).

QUINTON: Richard m 1787 Mary Johnson.

RADFORD: Wilfred Ernest (24 son of Ernest Henry Radford) m1939 Jean Copson (21 daughter of Harry Copson).

RALPHS: Mary m1785 James Ellis.

RANDEL: Sarah m1788 Samuel Pawley.

RATCLIFFE: Thomas (son of Thomas Ratcliffe) m1869 Sarah Jane Bunney (daughter of Charles Bunney).

RAY: Matthew David (30, son of Edmund Matthew Thomas Ray, NSW Australia) m2005 Emma Sherin (32 daughter of Rodney Edward Lloyd)

RAYNOR: Thomas m1754 Elizabeth Eaglefield; Thomas m1783 Christian Preston; Ann m1798 John Wakerley; Zechariah m1817 Ann Baum; Sarah m1822 Joseph Bromley; Francis m1827 Mary Harryman; Elizabeth (22 daughter of Zachariah Raynor) m1848 Thomas Roe (35 son of William Roe); Joanna (widow, 24 daughter of Joseph Garner) m1849 John Clarke (26 son of John Clarke); William (widower, 22 son of Zachariah Raynor) m1851 Ann Lewin (widow, 40 daughter of William Morris); Thomas (son of Zachariah Raynor) m1859 Jane Deeming (daughter of Thomas Deeming); Sarah Jane (22 daughter of Thomas Raynor)m 1886 Samuel William Lee (25 son of Thomas Lee); Eliza Hannah (21 daughter of Thomas Raynor) m1887 Benjamin Hemsley (29 son of Benjamin Hemsley); Thomas George (26 son of Thomas Raynor) m1890 Elizabeth Nurse (24 daughter of Jacob Nurse); Mary Charlotte (26 daughter of Thomas Raynor) m1908 John Bradshaw (27 son of John Bradshaw); Alan David (24 son of Raymond Norton Raynor) m1963 Angela Marjorie Kirke (22 daughter of Edward Kirke).

READ: John m1735 Mary Barnet.

REED: Alison (22 daughter of Ernest John Watts Reed) m1966 Robert Harold Whowell (24 son of George Harold Whowell).

REEDER: Reginald Luard (20 son of Arthur Reeder) m1927 Winifred Lilian Bertha Lee (25 daughter of Samuel William Lee).

REID: Andrew Ian (26 son of Arthur Miller Reid) m1975 Ann Barbara Davis Farmer (23 daughter of John Aird Farmer).

RENALS: Sarah (26 daughter of Edmund Renals) m1855 William Lander (30 son of James Lander).

REYNOLDS: Nicola Karen (29 daughter of Leon Michael Reynolds) m 2000 Robert John Kingston (29 son of Geoffrey Kingston); Jamie Stephen Reynolds (28 son of

Stephen Paul Reynolds) m2004 Sarah Jane Newton (22 daughter of Hayden Henry Newton).

RICHARDSON: Barfoot m1812 Elizabeth Lakin; Elizabeth m1834 William Sharp Potter; Paul (24 son of John Henry Richardson) m1973 Valerie Edwards Bate (24 daughter of Harold Bate).

RILEY: Stuart Ian (26 son of James Arthur Riley) m1990 Audrey Louise Evershed (spinster, 27 daughter of John Eric Jelley).

RINALS: Edmund m1818 Sarah Bates.

RIPPIN: Patrick Barry Poole (26 son of John Phillip Rippin) m1934 Gladys Marguerita Jelley (19 daughter of William Robert Jelley).

ROALFE: Rebecca Zoë (26 daughter of Michael Roalfe) m1991 Martin James Knight (30 son of John Knight)

ROBBINS: Annie (18 daughter of John Robbins) m1886 Joseph Pratt (20 son of Joseph Pratt).

RODWELL: Susannah m1794 John Clarke.

ROE: Thomas (35 son of William Roe) m1848 Elizabeth Raynor (22 daughter of Zachariah Raynor).

ROGERS: Isabel (18 daughter of Richard Rogers) m1870 John Simon Pears (23 son of John Pears); Judith Mary (32 daughter of Douglas Malcolm Rogers) m1991 David John Barfoot Howlett (33 son of William George Francis Howlett).

ROLLS: Charles Richard (24 son of Sidney Laurance Rolls) m1973 Diane Anne Bancroft (21 daughter of Harold James Bancroft).

ROPER: Richard Eric Trevor (25 son of Richard Teynham Trevor Roper) m1954 Patricia Anne McClintock (20 daughter of Patrick McClintock).

ROSE: Thomas Henry (25 son of Thomas Rose) m1891 Charlotte Lucy Cumberlidge (22 daughter of John Cumberlidge); Raymond Paul (20 son of Charles Frederick Rose) m1953 Sheila Ann Haynes (20 daughter of John Henry Haynes).

ROSS: Joseph (23 son of Joseph Ross) m1851 Sarah Carter (20 daughter of William Carter); Edward Robert Charles (25 son of Robert Christopher George Ross) m1993 Laura Jane Harrison (27 daughter of Jeffrey Cecil Harrison).

ROTHWELL: John Kevin (27 son of William Hastings Rothwell) m1989 Victoria Angela Willson (30 daughter of George Herbert Willson).

ROWER: Mary m1815 William Adcock.

ROWLINSON: Brian Richard (26 son of Gilbert Charles Rowlinson) m1969 Sheila Ann Goldsmith (20 daughter of Gordon Arthur Goldsmith).

RUDKIN: Gwendoline Margaret (24 daughter of Walter Rudkin) m1957 Herbert Ezra Clarke (26 son of Alfred Clarke); Doreen Hazel (22 daughter of Walter Rudkin) m1958 David Gwynfor Jones (27 son of Robert Evans Jones); Dorothy Mary Elizabeth (27 daughter of Walter Rudkin) m1958 David Graham Walters (23 son of Henry William Walters).

RUFORD: Mary Ann (20 daughter of William Ruford) m1842 George Baxter (20).

RUSDEN: Linda Carole (23) m1972 Roger John Ambrose Copson (23 son of John Ambrose Copson).

RUTTER: Sherin Allison (21 daughter of William Allison Rutter) m1971 Rodney Edward Lloyd (26 son of Sidney Edward Lloyd).

SAUNDERS: John Bartram (20 son of Bartram Ernest Saunders) m1942 Joan Lilian Moyra Harrison (19 daughter of Joseph Henry Harrison).

SCHOFIELD: James (son of Matthew Schofield) m1878 Juliana Ann Bates (daughter of Thomas Bates).

SCIVILLE: Russell Dart (29 son of Robert Arthur Sciville) m1983 Susan Jane Cross (spinster, 26 daughter of Thomas Reid Turnbull).

SCOTT: Caroline Elizabeth Fairfax (24 daughter of John William Fairfax Scott) m1971 Robert Alan Lancaster (24 son of John Cargill Lancaster).

SEAL: George (22 son of John Seal) m1856 Elizabeth Brookhouse (19 daughter of William Brookhouse).

SEARS: William George (23 son of George Sears) m1919 Gwendoline Polly Bunney (25).

Appendix D: Parish Registers

SEARSON: Rosamond m1762 Thomas Hughes; Ann m1764 Henry Hall; Mary m1766 Francis Ballard.

SEARY: Susan Mary (27 daughter of Cyril Robert Seary) m1986 Robin George Burdell (28 son of John Ellis Burdell).

SELBY: Louisa (widow, 43 daughter of John Brooks) m1894 Charles Boyer (widower, 68 son of William Boyer); Peggy Elizabeth (35 daughter of William Selby) m1919 Charlie Purdy (33 son of Thomas Purdy).

SHAND: Melanie Tracey (28 daughter of Alfred Charles Paul Shand) m1991 Robert Jonathan Clarke (30 son of Derek John Thomas Clarke).

SHARMAN: Ann m1787 Edward Townsend.

SHARP: Mary m1787 Thomas Fisher.

SHARPE: William Harold (32 son of William Sharpe) m1938 Dorothy Freda Lloyd (26 daughter of Percival George Lloyd); William Paul (25 son of William Harold Sharpe) m1966 Lynne Mary Webster (19 daughter of Harold Webster).

SHARRARD: John Henry (son of William Craddock Sharrard) m1879 Mary Ann Margaret Underwood (daughter of Samuel Shaw Underwood).

SHAW: John m1680 Mary Baker.

SHEARSBY: Robert m1638 Elizabeth Clarke.

SHENTON: Elizabeth m1766 Thomas Gower; Samuel m1807 Ann Vesty.

SHEPPARD: Joseph m1726 Ann Judd.

SHERIDAN: Paul John (pmd 43 son of John Sheridan) m2005 Maxine Dawn Sheridan-Knowles (pmd 36 daughter of Stanley Arthur Knowles)

SHERIDAN-KNOWLES: Maxine Dawn (pmd 36 daughter of Stanley Arthur Knowles) m2005 Paul John (pmd 43 son of John Sheridan)

SHERMAN: Charles Pinnell (29 son of George Sherman) m1896 Emily Adams (23 daughter of John Adams).

SHIPMAN: Maxine (39 daughter of Terence William Shipman) m1996 Peter Kerr (p.m.d. 39 son of Peter Kerr).

SHIPP: Vera Ivy (23 daughter of Harry Shipp) m1930 Leslie Everard Bunney (24 son of Alwyne Everard Bunney).

SIDDONS: Juliet Anne (21 daughter of Alan John Siddons) m1982 David Alexander Austin (25 son of Alfred Gordon Austin).

SILLS: Edith Mary (22 daughter of Sidney Sills) m1956 John Richard Flint (25 son of Richard Joseph Flint).

SIMMONS: Carol Kathleen (22 daughter of Charles Rupert Simmons) m1972 Anthony Leigh Parsons (29 son of Henry Lionel Parsons); Elizabeth Mary (22 daughter of Charles Rupert Simmons) m1975 Eric Stephen Wright (26 son of Frederick William Wright).

SIMMS: Joanne Louise Constance (23 daughter of Anthony Andrew Simms) m1995 Jeremy Ian Harrington (29 son of Norman Donald Harrington).

SIMPSON: Thomas m1742 Elizabeth Hughs; William m1750 Elizabeth Baum; William m1798 Sarah German; John m1820 Ann Clarke; Gertrude m1825 Thomas Harley; Stephen (son of John Simpson) m1862 Harriet Matts (daughter of Joseph Matts); Margaret Christine (20 daughter of Charles Frederick Simpson) m1961 Barry Towell (22 son of Lawrence Towell).

SISTON: Mary m1703 John Burton; Mary m1704 Thomas Smith; Mary m1708 Richard Heich.

SKELLET: Jane m1742 Thomas Wean.

SKELLINGTON: George m1638 Grace Granger.

SKELTON: John m1775 Ann Day.

SMALLWOOD: Elizabeth m1760 Thomas Johnson.

SMART: James m1778 Jane Johnson.

SMITH: Elizabeth m1624 Robert Browne; William m1633 Ruth Broadhurst; Thomas m1704 Mary Siston; Mary m1707 William Ward; Thomas m1714 Ann Dawson; Catherine m1721 John Hacket; William m1727 Anne Holt; Thomas m1728

Catherine Spawton; William m1728 Elizabeth Ward; Elizabeth m1729 William Pollard; Thomas m1748 Ann Porter; Sarah m1749 Thomas Atkins; Thomas 1750 Elizabeth Widdowson; Mary m1763 Thomas Page; Henry (24 son of John Smith) m1850 Sarah Burton (20 daughter of Joseph Burton); Thomas Leslie (26 son of Thomas William Smith) m1933 Clarice Wainwright (28 daughter of Charles Wainwright); Stuart Arthur (son of James Arthur Smith) m1951 Doreen Margaret Farmer (daughter of Stephen Farmer); Gillian Ann (21 daughter of Thomas Percival Smith) m1965 William Robert Suckling (25 son of William Edward Suckling); Robert Alan (22 son of Henry Smith) m1967 Sandra Elizabeth Oliver (21 daughter of James Stanley Oliver); Michael James (27 son of Cyril James Smith) m1972 Susan Phyllis Lees (20 daughter of Douglas Robert Lees); Phillipa Clare (22 daughter of David William Smith) m1981 William Frederick Gordon Heath (25 son of Gerald Gordon Heath); Helen Mary Smith (21 daughter of David William Smith) m1983 Ronald William Smith (23 son of John Edward Smith); Ronald William (23 son of John Edward Smith) m1983 Helen Mary (21 daughter of David William Smith); Joanna Jane (21 daughter of David William Smith) m1989 Francis Joseph Zimmer (23 son of Ludwig Karl Zimmer): Michael (44 son of Donald Smith) m2003 Catherine Krynaric (32,daughter of Rita Tasiaux); Lisa Christianne (32 daughter of Malcolm Keith Smith) m2004 Neil David Boulter (pmd, 36, son of David Garside Boulter).

SMITHAM: Mary m1768 Samuel Soars; Thomas m1769 Elizabeth Horner.

SMITTEN: Louisa Jane (27 daughter of Frank Ronald Smitten) m2002 Stephen Paul Swann (29 son of Peter Stuart Swann)

SNODIN: Sarah Winifred (36 daughter of John Snodin) m1931 Ernest James Holiday (30 son of George Holiday).

SNOW: William m1762 Ann Bentley; William m1765 Mary Hull; Rebecca m1785 Thomas Peet; Wilfred Edward (30 son of H. Cyprian Snow) m1932 Muriel Folwell (30 daughter of Arthur Ernest Folwell); Albert Carter (29 son of Matthew Snow) m1942 Dorothy Kathleen May Minkley (19 daughter of Horace Minkley).

SOARES: William m1741 Elizabeth Porte.

SPAWTON: Catherine m1728 Thomas Smith.

SPENCE: Jeffery m1819 Mary Chalton; George (26 son of Thomas Spence) m1922 Violet Annie Lloyd (24 daughter of Percival George Lloyd).

SPENCER: Mary m1790 John Brown; Ann m1792 Richard Wilson; Thomas (son of Edward Spencer) m1860 Susannah Clarke (daughter of Samuel Clarke); Mary (18 daughter of John Spencer) m1885 George Cleaver (34 son of John Cleaver); William Robert (22 son of Srthur Spencer) m1966 Heather Joy Edenbrow (22 daughter of Harold Edenbrow).

SQUIRES: Mary m1786 Ebenezer Dowall; Elizabeth m1793 John Preston; Henry (son of Henry Squires) m1879 Harriet Higgs (daughter of William Higgs).

SROCZYNSKI: Waldeman Marian (26 son of Leon Sroczynski) m1978 Susan Ann Lapham (25 daughter of Nigel Frederick Lapham).

STABLEFORD: John m1786 Sarah Harrison.

STACHOU: Stefan Adam (31 son of Andrzej Stachou) m2009 Lucy Michelle Hawkes (31 daughter of Martyn Hawkes)

STAFFORD: John m1806 Dorothy Dods; Joseph (26 son of Pharaoh Stafford) m1919 Violet Lilian Minkley (23 daughter of George Minkley).

STANYARD: Eliza (daughter of Joseph Stanyed) m1870 John Adams (widower, son of Thomas Adams); Mary Ann (daughter of Joseph Stanyard) m1877 John Henry Hambling (20 son of Humphrey Matthew Hambling).

STANYON: Jean Phyllis (20 daughter of John William Stanyon) m1954 Ivor William Wright (24 son of Horace Victor Wright).

STAPLETON: Elizabeth (21 daughter of George Stapleton) m1850 William Bunney (23 son of William Bunney).

STEATON: Ann m1781 Henry Broomfield.

STENHOUSE: Robin Frank Thomas (23 son of Frank Hughes Stenhouse) m1960 Barbara Gillian Thornton (22 daughter of James Coward Thornton).
STEPHENSON: Elizabeth m1733 Thomas Clarke.
STEVENS: Mary Ann (31 daughter of William Stevens) m1893 Thomas Henry Cook (32 son of William Cook).
STEVENSON: Ann m1815 Benjamin Willford; Arthur Ernest (25 son of Ernest Stevenson) m1935 Ivy Annie Elsie Hornsby (34 daughter of John Hornsby).
STIFF: Ann m1684 John Lovett.
STOBART: Lucy Clare (25 daughter of Peter Brian Halisenton Stobart) m1982 Marcus John Nunneley Clark (29 son of Robert Hamilton Clark).
STREET: John m1768 Mary Baum.
STURGESS: Jane Louise (23 daughter of Reginald Walter Sturgess) m1982 Neil Christopher Harris (30 son of Thomas Henry Harris).
SUCKLING: William Robert (25 son of William Edward Frederick Suckling) m1965 Gillian Ann Smith (21 daughter of Thomas Percival Smith).
SUTTON: Mary m1633 Thomas Gibson; Thomas m1812 Elizabeth Eyre.
SWAIN: Jane m1714 Henry Hastings.
SWANN: Stephen Paul (29 son of Peter Stuart Swann) m2002 Louisa Jane Smitten (27 daughter of Frank Ronald Smitten)
SWANWICK: John Andrew (24 son of Leonard Wright Swanwick) m1872 Carys Anne Jones (22 daughter of Peter Melfin Jones).
SWEENEY: Elizabeth m1827 William Burton.
SWINFER: Ann (22 daughter of Daniel Swinfer) m1853 Edward Baum (20 son of John Baum).
SWINFIELD: Mary m1797 Joseph Garner.
SYDDERNS: Anne m1718 Samuel Clarke.
SYKES: Stephen Alan Howarth (44 son of Alan Howarth Sykes) m2002 Rachel Alison Deakin (34 daughter of John David Deakin)
SYME: Helen Anne (pmd 42 daughter of Peter Richard Harrison) m 2000 Richard William Davis (pmd 50 son of William Davis)
SYMONDS: George m1776 Sarah Fletcher.
SZYMANSKI: Mark Ryszard (29 son of Witold Janusz Wojciech Szymanski) m1984 Hilary Ann Walters (29 daughter of Francis Raymond Walters).
TALBOT: George Austin (25 son of Charles Talbot) m1894 Harriet Hodges (26 daughter of Thomas Hodges).
TANSLEY: John m1798 Jane Brown.
TARRATT: Frank Nicholas (24 son of Frank Bernard Tarratt) m1964 Jennifer Elizabeth Lee (21 daughter of Colin Alfred Lee); Frank Bernard (widower, 64 son of Frank Peake Tarratt) m1965 Margaret Lilian Lee (widow, 55 daughter of Horace Clark).
TAYLOR: Robert m1773 Elizabeth Johnson; William (26) m1845 Mary Preston (21 daughter of Joseph Preston); Leslie (24 son of Frederick William Taylor) m1926 Edith Helen Osenton (29 daughter of George Osenton); Helen Mary (20 daughter of Frederick William Taylor) m1927 Alfred Porter (24 son of Joseph Porter); Ronald (26 son of Frederick William Taylor) m1931 Bessie Burgoyne (24 daughter of William Burgoyne); Amanda Jane (23 daughter of Gordon Murice Taylor m1988 William Harrod (24 son of Peter James Harrod); Joanna Jane (29 daughter of Gordon Maurice Taylor) m1984 Christopher Mark Ling (25 son of David Brian Ling); Virginia May (26 daughter of Gordon Maurice Taylor) m1996 William Stuart Turnbull (26 son of Andrew Richard Turnbull).
THOMAS: Thomas (widower) m1796 Elizabeth Embley (widow); Karen Juliette (24 daughter of Brian Thomas) m1991 Ian Vance Cairns (26 son of Hugh Cairns).
THOMPSON: John m1826 Hannah Thorpe; John m1837 Ann Hudson.
THORNTON: Elizabeth m1738 Robert Pryor; Martha m1753 Thomas Walker; Henry m1805 Sarah Cooper; Barbara Gillian (22 daughter of James Coward Thornton) m1960 Robin Frank Thomas Stenhouse (23 son of Frank Hughes Stenhouse).

THORPE: Elizabeth m1823 James Clarke; Hannah m1826 John Thompson; Richard m1833 Elizabeth Ward; John (widower) m1834 Sarah Bunney (widow); George (son of William Thorp) m1839 Ann Preston (widow, nee Kirby); Elizabeth (20 daughter of John Thorpe) m1855 Simeon Preston (24 son of William Preston); Mary (22 daughter of Samuel Thorpe) m1856 Arthur Preston (23 son of William Preston); Simon Nicholas (22 son of Nicholas John Thorpe m1989 Julia Freer (20 daughter of John Frederick Freer).

TILLEY: Michael (21 son of Henry Tilley) m1967 Caroline Anne George (19 daughter of Frederick Charles George).

TOACH: Judith Leslie (23 daughter of Thomas Richard Toach) m1969 Leonard Harry Copson (27 son of Charles Copson).

TOBIN: Michael John (36 son of Nicholas Kevin Tobin) m1998 Valerie Ann Brown (daughter of James Ronald Brown)

TOMLIN: George Edward (son of John Tomlin) m1909 Nellie Foulk (daughter of Thomas Foulk).

TOOKEY: Samuel m1747 Mary Fisher.

TOONE: Sarah m1790 James Dawkins; Thomas John (28 son of William Toone) m1857 Sarah Bates (26 daughter of Daniel Bates).

TOPLEY: Edward m1831 Mary Brown.

TOWELL: Barry (22 son of Lawrence Towell) m1961 Margaret Christine Simpson (20 daughter of Charles Frederick Simpson).

TOWNSEND: Edward m1787 Ann Sharman.

TREEN: Vera Iris (27 daughter of William Sydney Treen) m1940 George Thomas Cockerill (37 son of Lewis Cockerill).

TUBBY: Haley Billinder Tubby (28 daughter of Richard Morris Tubby) m 2010 Gregory Nigel Curd (40 son of Donald William Curd)

TUCKLEY: Christopher Mark (22 son of Graham Tuckley) m1988 Helen Jane Lawson (24 daughter of David Thomas Lawson).

TURNBULL: William Stuart (26 son of Andrew Richard Turnbull) m1996 Virginia May Taylor (26 daughter of Gordon Maurice Taylor).

TURNER: Elizabeth m1761 John Johnson; Doris Annie (22 daughter of James Turner) m1930 Percival William Lloyd (22 son of Percival George Lloyd); Lois Mary Gladys (28 daughter of Archibald Turner) m1932 Frederick Lindesay Godfrey (29 son of Ernest Henry Godfrey); Gladys Marie (widow, daughter of Geoffrey Ellis) m1946 Albert Linwood Wright (widower, son of Sidney John Wright).

UNDERWOOD: Elizabeth Bowley (daughter of Samuel Shaw Underwood) m1879 Edwin Mark Cashmore (son of Luke Cashmore); Mary Ann Margaret (daughter of Samuel Shaw Underwood) m1879 John Henry Sharrard (son of William Craddock Sharrard); Mabel Helen (25 daughter of Tom Underwood) m1916 Albert Henry Gordon Asher (26 son of Frederic Asher).

VALENTINE: Francis Cyril Oliphant (33 son of William Roderick Harris Valentine) m1931 Freda Butler (35 daughter of Henry Cavendish Butler, Earl of Lanesborough).

VANN: Albert Edward (24 son of Alfred Vann) m1926 Doris Minkley (24 daughter of Herbert Minkley).

VESSEY: Jane (widow, 44 daughter of John Mills) m1913 Joseph Bunney (43 son of Walter Bunney).

VESTY: Mary m1792 Thomas Preston; Robert m1792 Jane Warren; Thomas m1801 Hannah Franks; Richard m1805 Elizabeth Calladine; Ann m1807 Samuel Shenton; Hannah m1822 William Brookhouse; Samuel m1826 Ann Clarke; Mary m1829 Thomas Farmer; Mariah m1837 Thomas Harriman.

VICCARS: Elizabeth Joyce (26 daughter of William Arnold Viccars) m1935 Richard Elliott Lane (26 daughter of Charles Frederick Lane).

VILLAGE: William Stanley (33 son of William Village) m1940 Gwynneth Enid Wallace (25 daughter of Henry Alfred Wallace).

Appendix D: Parish Registers 663

WAINWRIGHT: Charles (26 son of Charles Wainwright) m1907 Mary Ellen Bunney (24 daughter of Frederick Bunney); Clarice (28 daughter of Charles Wainwright) m1933 Thomas Leslie Smith (26 son of Thomas William Smith); Jacqueline Suzanne (26 daughter of Marcus Beresford Wainwright) m1988 Martin Frederick Pilton (30 son of Peter Frederick Pilton).

WAKELING: George Stanley (24 son of George William Wakeling) m1932 Fanny Gertrude Bates (25 daughter of William James Bates).

WAKERLEY: John m1798 Ann Raynor; Francis m1825 Elizabeth Hefford; Mary m1826 David Wilson; William (son of Thomas Wakerly) m1840 Elizabeth Clarke (19); Elizabeth (daughter of Francis Wakley) m1870 George Handley (son of George Handley).

WALDRON: Martha m1773 Nathaniel Hale.

WALDRAM: Keith Cyril (24 son of Cyril Waldram) m1966 Margaret Handley (25 daughter of Joseph James Handley).

WALE: Sally Angela (24 daughter of Dennis Harry Wale) m1982 James Alexander Buchanan (25 son of James Alexander Buchanan).

WALKER: William m1731 Anna Bates; Alice m1734 William Hutchinson; Sarah m1734 Joseph Petcher; Sarah m1739 Thomas Humber; Muriel Jean (23 daughter of David Alexander Walker) m1952 Bertrand Henry Garai (32 son of Bernard Garai).

WALLACE: Edith Lilian (37 daughter of Henry Alfred Wallace) m1933 Ernest Alfred Backwell (42 son of Alfred Price Backwell); Gwynneth Enid (25 daughter of Henry Alfred Wallace) m1940 William Stanley Village (33 son of William Village); Moraig Douglas (23 daughter of Douglas Ormsby Wallace) m1966 Kenneth Stanley Hyman (31 son of Harry Cooper Hyman).

WALSH: Henry James (son of William Walsh) m1923 Eleanor Margaret Trevelyan Murray Dixon (daughter of James Murray Dixon).

WALTERS: David Graham (23 son of Henry William Walters) m1958 Dorothy Mary Elizabeth Rudkin (27 daughter of Walter Rudkin); Hazel Irene (21 daughter of Francis Raymond Walters) m1977 Peter John Nesbitt (24 son of William John Nesbitt); Pamela Mary (24 daughter of Francis Raymond Walters) m1982 Timothy John Beedell (25 son of Victor Thomas Beedell); Diana Margaret (21 daughter of Francis Raymond Walters) m1983 Donald Crawford Finlay (27 son of William Crawford Finlay); Hilary Ann (29 daughter of Francis Raymond Walters) m1984 Mark Ryszard Szymanski (29 son of Witold Janusz Wojciech Szymanski).

WALTON: Jane m1804 Richard Preston; Mark Jonathan (27 son of Wilfred Walton) m1980 Judith Shipley Jayes (27 daughter of Herbert Shipley Jayes).

WALSH: Kerry Lorraine (31 daughter of Patrick Joseph Walsh) m2002 Nicholas Alan West (26 son of Theodore Alan West)

WARD: William m1707 Mary Smith; Elizabeth m1728 William Smith; Thomas m1753 Martha Thornton; Elizabeth m1783 Thomas Hill; John m1827 Jane Charlton; Mary m1829 Benjamin Petts; Elizabeth m1833 Richard Thorpe; Thomas m1833 Frances Johnson (widow).

WAREING: Sean David (29 son of Stephen John Wareing) m2010 Laura Jayne Deana Percival (30 daughter of Alan Percival)

WARNER: John m1747 Margaret Measures.

WARREN: Jane m1792 Robert Vestey; John (son of John Warren) m1865 Martha Doughty (daughter of Joseph Doughty).

WARRINGTON: Andrew John (28 son of Robert William Warrington) m1988 Susan Mary Wood (22 daughter of Allan Charles Wood).

WATERFIELD: Emma (daughter of Joseph Waterfield) m1862 George Godbald (son of Robert Godbald).

WATSON: Henry m1729 Sabina Hall; Mary m1829 Joshua Preston; John (23 son of John Watson) m1896 Clara Helen Hodges (23 daughter of John Henry Hodges).

WEAN: John m1702 Mary Weston; Thomas m1742 Jane Skellet.
WEBB: Susan Joyce (24 daughter of John Adam Webb) m1992 Nicholas John Edward Northam (26 son of John Malcolm Northam).
WEBSTER: Bartholemew m1638 Ann Dawson; Thomas m1830 Ann Whatoffe; Lynne Mary (19 daughter of Harold Webster) m1966 William Paul Sharpe (25 son of William Harold Sharpe).
WEST: Elizabeth m1789 William Gaunt; Nicholas Alan (26 son of Theodore Alan West) m 2002 Kerry Lorraine Walsh (31 daughter of Patrick Joseph Walsh)
WESTLEY: William m1716 Anne Branston; William m1744 Jane Clark; John m1752 Elizabeth Palmer.
WESTON: Mary m1702 John Wean; John m1823 Jane Benson; George William (29 son of Edwin Weston) m1949 Olive Winifred Louvain Wright (32 daughter of Fred Wright).
WHATMORE: Phyllis (38 daughter of Oliver Whatmore) m1919 Albert Cook (42 son of William Cook).
WHATNALL: Elizabeth m1702 William Lee; Squire m1741 Ann Lovett; Ann (widow) m1771 John Kelm (widower); Ann m1799 Benjamin Wilson; Elizabeth m1801 William Giles.
WHEAT: Mary m1751 Thomas Brawnson.
WHITE: Joshua m1773 Elizabeth Clarke.
WHATOFFE: Ann m1830 Thomas Webster.
WHOWELL: Robert Harold (24 son of George Harold Whowell) m1966 Alison Reed (22 daughter of Ernest John Watts Reed).
WHYTE: Hannah Mary (24 daughter of David Connacher Whyte) m1971 Martin Robert Greenwood (25 son of Ernest Robert Greenwood).
WIDDOWSON: Elizabeth m1750 Thomas Smith.
WILD: Thomas m1793 Ann Clark.
WILDE: Robert Charles (27 son of Charles Edwin Wilde) m1966 Lesley Marjorie Hall (24 daughter of James William Hall).
WILDMAN: John m1724 Amey Fielding; Edward (36 son of William Wildman) m1856 Frances Drackley (26 daughter of William Drackley).
WILKINS: Timothy John (31 son of John Charles Wilkins) m1991 Joanne Frost (29 daughter of Brian William Frost).
WILLARS: Edward m1833 Susannnah Jarvis.
WILLFORD: Benjamin m1815 Ann Stevenson.
WILLIAMS: Arthur (28 son of George Williams) m1910 Hilda Millicent Mugford (22 daughter of James Mugford).
WILLIS: Charles Henry (33 son of Harry Willis) m1936 Kathleen Minkley (29 daughter of George Minkley).
WILLSON: Victoria Angela (30 daughter of George Herbert Willson) m1989 John Kevin Rothwell (27 son of William Hastings Rothwell).
WILMORE: George (39 son of William Wilmore) m1918 Charlotte Adeline Eliza Lee (24 daughter of Samuel William Lee).
WILSON: Richard m1792 Ann Spencer; Elizabeth (widow) m1793 William Lovat; Benjamin m1799 Ann Whatnall; David m1826 Mary Wakerley; Donald (23 son of John Stanley Wilson) m1960 Cynthia Mary Copson (19 daughter of John Ambrose Copson).
WOOD: Elizabeth m1635 Richard Ball; William m1772 Ann Braunston; Thomas m1792 Ann Pollard; Susan Mary (22 daughter of Allan Charles Wood) m1988 Andrew John Warrington (28 son of Robert William Warrington); Carol Anne (25 daughter of Allan Charles Wood) m1993 John Charles Davies (25 son of John Frederick Davies).
WOODARD: Alan James (33 son of George Arthur Woodard) m1980 Susan Melanie Bunney (27 daughter of Maurice Edwin Charles Bunney).
WOODFORD: Susannah m1718 John Orers; Anthony m1787 Elizabeth Pollard.

Appendix D: Parish Registers

WOODING: Ruth m1801 Richard Lines.
WOODS: Joseph (son of William Woods) m1860 Catherine Morris (daughter of George Morris); James Henry (21 son of Joseph Woods) m1891 Mary Elizabeth Pratt (21 daughter of Joseph Pratt).
WOODWARD: Elizabeth m1809 Edward Hickling.
WOOLLEY: George m1704 Eleanor Jennings.
WOOTNALL: Thomas m1775 Elizabeth Pollard.
WORRALL: Ann m1832 John Preston.
WORTH: Sarah m1807 Henry Burton.
WREIGHITT: Christopher Michael (29 son of Peter Hadfield Wreighitt) m1988 Wendy Ann Jones (26 daughter of Thomas Philip Jones).
WREN: David Christopher (25 son of Joseph Stanley Wren) m1963 Susan Graine Ingram (22 daughter of Ralph Herbert Ingram).
WRIGHT: Samuel m1732 Susanna Chaplin; Thomas m1741 Hannah Hall; Orson (30 son of Herbert Charles Wright) m1938 Rosamund Leslie Gimson (21 daughter of Henry Hay Gimson); Vera Gwendoline Lorraine (23 daughter of Fred Wright) m1938 Frank Carter (31 son of William Henry Carter); Albert Linwood (widower, son of Sidney John Wright) m1946 Gladys Marie Turner (widow, daughter of Geoffrey Ellis); Olive Winifred Louvain (32 daughter of Fred Wright) m1949 George William Weston (29 son of Edwin Weston); Ivor William (24 son of Horace Victor Wright) m1954 Jean Phyllis Stanyon (20 daughter of John William Stanyon); Eric Stephen (26 son of Frederick William Wright) m1975 Elizabeth Mary Simmons (22 daughter of Charles Rupert Simmons); Anthony Richard (22 son of Edwin Albert Wright) m1977 Jill Victoria Marlow (20 daughter of George Donald Marlow); Veronica Lois (22 daughter of John Michael Gidley Wright) m1980 David Timothy Porte (25 son of Donald McKenzie Porte); Benjamin Michael Gidley (24 son of John Michael Gidley Wright) m1987 Rosemary Ann Faver (28 daughter of Herbert Faver); Barbara Dawn (p.m.d,27 daughter of David William Wright) m1997 Magnus Rogvauld Ninian Lawson (29).
WYKES: William m1795 Martha Preston.
WYLDE: Mary (widow) m1733 John Lovet (widower).
YATES: Elizabeth m1767 Joseph Gray; Phyllis Mary (26 daughter of Horace Edward Yates) m1942 Sidney Edward Lloyd (26 son of Percival George Lloyd).
YEOMANS: Benjamin m1752 Mary Moore.
YOUNG: Nathan Edward (26 son of Robert David Young) m1999 Zoë Sharp (25 daughter of Graham Kenneth Sharp)
ZIMMER: Francis Joseph (23 son of Ludwig Karl Zimmer) m1989 Joanna Jane Smith (21 daughter of David William Smith).

Marriages of Swithland Residents in Other Parishes

Source: Phillimore; Marriage Licences 1570–1729.

BAKER: Daniel (of Swithland) m1616 Joan Nicholson of Borton-on-the-Wolds, at Prestwold;
BALL: Elizabeth (of Swithland) m1787 William Clark of Swithland, at Frisby.
BARWELL: Joseph (of Swithland) m1831 Elizabeth Cresswell, at Quorn.
BAUM: Sarah (of Swithland) m1764 John Waldram of Cropston, at Thurcaston.
BLANKLEY: Francis (of Swithland) m1610 Mary Flower (of Anstey).
BLOOMFIELD: Henry (of Swithland) m1781 Ann Cleaton, at Sileby.
BOLTER: George (of Swithland) m1710 Sarah Gee (a servant at Thurcaston parsonage), at Thurcaston.

BRAMLEY: William (of Swithland) m1805 Hannah nee Johnson, at Quorn.
BREWIN: Barbara (of Swithland) m1794 William Peat of Cropston, at Thurcaston; Thomas (of Swithland) m1807 Ann Doughty, at Syston.
BROWN: Catharine (of Swithland) m1802 William Soar of Woodhouse, at Woodhouse.
BUNNEY: William (of Swithland) m1826 Martha Baum, at Quorn.
BURCHNELL: Richard (of Swithland) m1804 Betsy Sarson, at Quorn; Richard (of Swithland) m1809 Ann Hardy of Groby, at Ratby.
CHAPMAN: David (of Swithland) m1805 Ann Glover, at Belgrave.
CLARK: Jane (of Swithland) m1688 Thomas Kinnes (gent), at Belgrave; Thomas (of Swithland) m1714 Elizabeth Gimson of Swithland, at Woodhouse; Samuel (of Swithland) m1773 Elizabeth Derry, at Woodhouse; James (of Swithland) m1783 Rebecca Skillington, at Wymeswold; William (of Swithland) m1787 Elizabeth Ball of Swithland, at Frisby.
DANVERS: Francis (of Swithland) m1614 Bridgett Barfote (of Shakerston); Mrs Elizabeth (of Swithland) m1660 William Palmer (eldest son of Archdale Palmer Esq of Wanlip), at Thurcaston.
ELAT (?ELLIOTT): John (of Sweedland) m1746 Elizabeth Platts of Thurmaston, at Belgrave.
FENELEY: Charles (of Swithland) m1760 Isabell Leager, at Ratby.
FEWKES: Thomas (widower, of Swithland) m1819 Esther Lewin (widow), at Thurcaston.
GILBERT: Robert (of Swithland) m1706 Hannah Sharpe of Tilton, at Tilton.
GIMSON: Elizabeth (of Swithland) m1714 Thomas Clark of Swithland, at Woodhouse.
GODWIN: Thomas (of Swithland) m1733 Mary Bromet of Cropston, at Thurcaston.
HALL: Samuel (of Derby) m1808 Catherine Pollard of Quorn, at Quorn.
HEATHE: John (of Swithland, labourer) m1585 Margaret Rowe, at Walton-le-Wolds.
HILL: Thomas (of Swithland, labourer) m1784 Elizabeth Ward, at Quorn.
HIND: Elizabeth (of Swithland) m1749 Edward Johnson, at Glenfield; Henry (of Swithland) m1785 Mary Adcock, at Syston; Thomas (of Swithland) m1812 Sarah Thornton of Cropston, at Thurcaston.
HUGHES: Thomas (of Swithland) m1745 Elizabeth Lewin of Swithland, at Glenfield.
JACKSON: Elizabeth (of Swithland) m1689 George Allen of Cropston, at Evington.
JOHNSON: Edward (of Swithland) m1749 Elizabeth Hind of Swithland, at Glenfield; John (of Swithland) m1749 Sarah Tookey of Glenfield, at Glenfield; William (of Swithland) m1757 Ann Forman, at Ratby; Robert (of Swithland) m1759 Elizabeth Lawrence, at Thurcaston; William (of Swithland m1786 Mary Parkinson, at Quorn; William (of Swithland) m1798 Elizabeth Storer, at Woodhouse.
LEAKE: Thomas (of Swithland) m1836 Mary Isom, at Thurcaston.
LEWIN: Elizabeth (of Swithland) m1745 Thomas Hughes of Swithland, at Glenfield.
LOVITT: William (of Swithland) m1723 Ann Barber of Rotherby, at Rotherby.
MOOR: Sarah (of Swithland) m1743 John Braunson, at Glenfield.
NICHOLS: Ann (of Swithland) m1698 Richard Hytch of Thurcaston, at Thurcaston.
PAWLEY: Samuel (of Swithland) m1788 Sarah Randon, at Sileby.
PECK: Zacharias (of Swithland) m1634 Isabella Reonald of Cotes, at Prestwold.
PERKINS: Thomas (of Swithland) m1709 Elizabeth Andrew of Cropston, at Thurcaston.
POLLARD: Thomas (of Swithland) m1738 Hannah Wrencher of Wanlip, at Wanlip; William (of Swithland) m1762 Elizabeth Fernely, at Woodhouse; John (of Swithland) m1774 Elizabeth Miles of Burton-on-the Wolds, at Prestwold; Benjamin (of Swithland) m1784 Catherine Squire, at Quorn.
PORTE: John (of Swithland) m1725 Rebecca Judd of Barkby Thorpe, at Barkby.
PRESTON: John (of Swithland) m1793 Elizabeth Squire, at Woodhouse.

PRIDE: Samuel (of Seeland) m1694 Ann Hollin, at Quorn.
PRIOR: Joseph (of Swithland) m1713 Elizabeth Simpkin (of Blaby); Thomas (of Swithland) m1806 Elizabeth Bennet, at Quorn.
SCHRAEDER: John Phillips (of Swithland) m1775 Rebekah Sutton, at Quorn.
SMITH: John (of Swithland) m1614 Suzanna Hampson (of Quorn).
STABLEFORD: John (of Swithland) m1786 Sarah Harrison, at Woodhouse.
SMITH: William (of Swedeland) m1722 Elizabeth Foulds, at Woodhouse.
THORNTON: Elizabeth (of Swithland) m1829 Nathaniel Harriman of Woodhouse, at Woodhouse.
TOON: Sarah Copson (of Swithland) m1822 Thomas Spencer of Woodhouse, at Woodhouse.
VESTY: Thomas (of Swithland) m1802 Hannah Franks, at Syston.
WARD: John (of Swithland, widower) m Mary Cant, at Quorn.
WESTLEY: William (of Swedeland) m Grace Smith of Woodhouse, at Woodhouse.
WOLTON: Jane (of Swithland) m1804 Richard Preston of Woodhouse, at Woodhouse.
YEOMANS: John (of Swithland) m1820 Elizabeth Preston of Woodhouse, at Woodhouse.

St Leonard's Church, Swithland: Burials

——: Thomas 1617, — 1624, — 1625, — 1701, Ann 1741, Catherine 1745, William 1760, — 1763, Hannah 1763, John 1763, Elizabeth 1770, — 1771, Robert 1771, — 1773, — 1774, John 1776, Elizabeth 1782.
ADAMS: William 1854 (1), Harriett 1869 (18), Matthew 1873 (22), Joe 1883 (3), Matilda 1888 (Inf), Thomas 1895 (85), Martha 1901 (81), Eliza 1909 (63), John 1924 (78).
ADCOCK: Albert 1975 (75) Lilian Margaret 1975 (73).
ADNETT: George Voiles 1935 (53), Alice 1957 (70).
ALLAN: Matthew 2008 (41).
ALLCOAT: Gwendoline Mary 1982 (69), Winston Hollis 1984 (75).
ANDREWS: Richard 1711, Anne 1732.
ARMSON: Ann 1816 (Inf).
ASHBY: John 1633.
ASTILL: John 1809.
AVERY: Dorothy Marion 2002 (89).
BACON: Agrilla 1727 (51).
BAKER: John 1638.
BALL: Nicholas 1634, Walter Winter 1940 (74), Florence 1955 (77).
BANBURY: Kathleen Ada 1974 (73), Harry Andrew 1986 (83).
BARBER: Constance Flora 1960 (74), Frank Gordon 1984 (99), Brenda 2006 (82).
BARKER: Eliza 1854 (1).
BARLOW: Diana 1835 (26).
BARNES: Elizabeth 1952 (81).
BARNET: John 1711, William 1719, William 1748 (26), Ann 1755, William 1756 (77).
BARRATT: Edna Flo 1907 (Inf).
BARRETT: Ida Gwendolyn 1996 (77), Percy Charles 2000 (79).
BARTON: Maurice Holdsworth 1973 (83).
BATE: Harold 1989 (71).
BATES: Harold 1743, Catherine 1803 (Inf), Daniel 1812, James 1829 (Inf), Jenny 1837 (6), Daniel 1858 (70), Frances 1858 (66), Thomas 1870 (67), Juliana 1877 (74), John 1884 (52), William James 1896 (57), Catherine Ann 1907 (41), Ann 1931

(87), William James 1945 (75), Anthony Michael 1955 (24), Matthew Daykin 1956 (84), Mary Ann 1965 (89), Frank 1966 (64), Ida Olive 1983 (78), William James 1985 (82), Millicent Clara 1990 (82).

BAUM: Anne 1709, George 1709, Harold 1773, Ann 1776, Elizabeth 1782, Elizabeth 1787 (Inf), Jane 1795, Mary 1809 (43), William 1810, Thomas 1814 (Inf), Thomas 1819 (Inf), Thomas 1822 (Inf), Frederick 1844 (1), William 1851 (87), William 1855 (14), Edward 1857 (24), Phebe 1874 (65), Ethel 1881 (4), John 1881 (72), Archibald George Locton 1882 (2), Laura Fanny 1891 (48).

BAXTER: Charles Edward 1957 (81).

BEACHELL: Winifred Yvonne 1980 (66), John Alexander 1983 (74).

BEAKE: William 1712.

BEASLEY: William 1773, Lucy 1777, John 1793.

BENNET: Mary 1728, John 1729, Elizabeth 1730, Martha 1730, Elizabeth 1732, Elizabeth 1740, John 1740, Elizabeth 1742, John 1745, Martha 1748, Elizabeth 1758.

BENSON: Roy 1994 (65).

BENTLEY: Mary 1754, George 1757, Catharine 1759.

BERRINGTON: Mary 1809, Alice 1812 (Inf).

BERRISON: John 1817 (17), John 1836 (62), Jane 1851 (79).

BESSON: Ann 1799, Mary 1802.

BESTON: Mary 1790 (Inf).

BETTS: Mary 1703, William 1717.

BIDDLES: Elizabeth 1635.

BILSON: Sarah 1796.

BIRD: Mabel 1638, Elizabeth 1679, Mary 1696, Mary 1701, John 1702, Thomas 1717.

BLACKWELL: Richard 1688, Frank James 1994 (82).

BLANKLEY: Francis 1679.

BLOOMFIELD: Robert 1749, William 1749, Henry 1758, Sarah 1764, Elizabeth 1789, William 1790 (Inf), Mary 1793, Ann 1798 John 1799, William 1799, Robert 1820 (70), Sarah 1841 (88).

BODLE: Thomas 1700, Ann 1702(31).

BOLTER: Elizabeth 1711, George 1712, Mary 1717, Elizabeth 1720, George 1721, Sarah 1739.

BONSER: Constant 1819(70).

BORROWS: Mabel 1636.

BOSTOCK: Frances 1829 (Inf), Joseph 1833 (43), Johanah 1834 (8).

BOTT(S): John 1624, Catherine 1688, Catherine 1703, John 1727, William 1730.

BOULTON: Elizabeth 1761.

BOWLER: John 1867 (64), Thomas 1884 (86), Jim 1886 (26), Elizabeth 1893 (74), John 1906 (72), Mary 1906 (70).

BOWYER: James Edward 1975 (69).

BOYER: Charles 1917 (93).

BRAMLEY: Anne 1818 (23), Elizabeth 1829 (36), Thomas 1829 (57), Alice 1831 (63).

BRA(W)NSTON: — 1699, Henry 1708 (47), Jane 1733 (69), Jane 1734, Ann 1742, Henry 1749, Thomas 1749, Mary 1750, William 1753, Pleasant 1754, John 1756 (58), Harry 1756, Ann 1757, Anne 1761, William 1761, Ann 1769, Ann 1782 (73), Henry 1784, Mary 1795, John 1799.

BRIERLEY: Ann 1754, Jonathan 1754, Mary 1754.

BRIERS: Stephen Andrew 1970 (3).

BROOK(E): Elizabeth 1761, John Hector 1966 (64), Stanley Leonard Riley 1979 (72).

BROOK-LAWSON : Donald Michael 2006 (76).

BROOKHOUSE: Thomas 1827 (20), William 1829 (25), Hannah 1831 (22), Joseph 1838(1), Elizabeth 1840 (70), William 1842 (83), John 1846 (Inf), John 1849, Elizabeth 1858 (66), William 1872 (83).

BROOKSBY (BRUXBY): Anthony 1704, Alice 1709, Abel 1735 (60), Alice 1742 (70), Francis 1822 (88), Mary 1840 (30), Dorothy 1853 (74), Thomas 1853 (79).

BROOMFIELD: Mary 1760, Jane 1761, Sarah 1777 (53), Mary 1830 (95), Henry 1839 (81).

BROWN: Elizabeth 1681, John 1681, Thomas 1687, Thomas 1702, Catherine 1710, Dorothy 1713, Mary 1716, Anne 1719, Anne 1722, John 1730, Elizabeth 1735, Robert 1735, Jane 1766, Lucy 1776, Elizabeth 1801, William 1802, Elizabeth 1803 (Inf), Samuel 1803 (Inf), Daniel 1804 (Inf), Ann 1806 (Inf), Sarah 1806 (Inf), Daniel 1808 (Inf), Elizabeth 1808, Anne 1813 (1), Ann 1816 (86), Samuel 1816 (Inf), Mary 1819 (56), Sarah 1822 (15), Samuel 1826 (56), William 1830 (27), Eliza 1833 (49), Thomas 1839 (Inf), Mary 1840 (Inf), John 1846 (Inf), Elizabeth 1850 (Inf), Sarah 1857 (48), Mary Ann 1863 (1), Joseph 1873 (Inf), James 1875 (7), James Edward 1879 (Inf), Joseph Thomas 1888 (Inf), Elizabeth Ann 1896 (25), George 1907 (71), Sarah 1917 (80), George 1938 (73), Wilfred 1971 (60), Edith Noreen 1989 (75).

BRYAN: Thomas Leigh 1915 (47), Sheila Joy 1988 (53), John 1994 (72).

BRYSON: Josephine Mary 2003 (83) – *service only*.

BUNNEY: Michael 1808 (60), Mary 1816 (70), Elizabeth 1823 (53), Anne 1828 (17), Isaac 1832 (5), Mary 1832, Harriet 1841 (2), William 1841 (24), Walter 1845 (7), Mary 1847 (34), William Thompson 1848 (1), Edmund 1854 (6), Samuel 1861 (42), Sarah 1861 (Inf), Lewis 1862(2), Samuel George 1862 (1), William 1862 (64), Benjamin 1864 (2), Daniel 1866 (34), Samuel 1866 (4), Catherine 1868 (1), Charles Edmond 1868 (10), William George 1869 (2), Frederick 1870 (35), Martha Lucy 1871 (14), William 1880 (39), Elizabeth 1883 (59), Martha 1887 (85), Rosa rebecca 1883 (3), Elizabeth 1890 (25), George 1893 (64), William 1895 (40), Charles 1900 (78), Mary 1902 (66), James 1906 (73), George William 1907 (30), William 1907 (81), Jane 1908 (80), Henry 1911 (79), Elizabeth 1913 (84), Beatrice Alice 1917 (22), Samuel 1918 (66), Laurence 1920 (2 days), Johnson 1920 (46), Walter 1924 (78), Edith May 1925 (39), John 1927 (72), Frederick 1929 (70), Mary Ann 1929 (82), Catherine 1931 (68), Emma 1934 (80), Jane 1937 (74), Sarah Ann 1939 (75), Bertie Hemsley 1940 (57), Alfred Edwin 1951 (60), Samuel Arthur 1951 (52), Joseph 1961 (90), Annie Violetta 1976 (89), Annie Maria 1977 (84), Sidney Oswald 1978 (86), Edith Evelyn 1981 (82), Phyllis Mabel 1981 (73), Beatrice May 2007 (87).

BURBAGE: Barbara 1714.

BURNABY: Ann 1762, Ann1769, Ann 1781.

BURROWS: Kathlyn Mary 1931 (6), Alfred 1976 (75), Kathleen 1993 (91).

BURTON: Elizabeth 1680, Henry 1747, Hannah 1769, Henry 1793, Ann 1793 (Inf), Dorothy 1803, Frank 1815 (4), Francis 1825 (1), Edward 1827 (4), Joseph 1832 (29), Harriet 1833 (5), Henry 1836 (83), John 1836 (45), Margaret 1836 (3), Johnson 1837 (4), Thomas 1837 (40), Joseph 1839 (65), Anne 1840 (73), Henry 1843 (44), Mary 1844 (75), Mary Ann 1848 (1), Zilpah 1848 (1), Fanny 1852 (17), Walter Thomas 1852 (1), Elizabeth 1854 (2), Mary 1884 (67), Sarah Elizabeth 1893 (49), Henry 1895 (71).

BUSH: Maria 1866 (62).

BUTCHER : Joan Ethel 2006 (90), Susan Joan 2006 (58).

BUTLER: George John Danvers 1866 (72), Frederica Emma 1870 (62), John Vansittart Danvers 1905 (66), Anne Elizabeth 1909 (65), John Brinsley Danvers 1912 (19), Dorothea Gladys Ellen More 1920 (47), Charles John Brinsley 1929 (63) Georgina Ione 1947 (6), Henry Cavendish 1950 (82), Winifred 1970 (93), Grace Lilian 1983 (96), Denis Anthony Brian 1998 (80).

BUTTERFIELD: Stephen Archibald 1981(25).

CARNALL: Walter Francis Ian 1981 (81), Muriel 2001 (98).

CARTER: Thomas 1792 (Inf), James 1806, William 1806 (Inf), William 1817 (56), James 1829 (19), Nancy 1834 (70), William 1865 (57), Sarah 1880 (80).

CARPENTER: David Martin 2003 (71)

CHAMBERLAIN: William 1695.

CHAPMAN: Lydia 1793, Thomas 1807 (Inf), Mary 1815 (Inf),William 1847 (22), Emma 1867 (41), Anne 1870 (26), William 1870 (Inf), Thomas 1894 (65).
CHARLESWORTH: Sarah 1822 (73).
CLARIDGE: George 1880 (47).
CLARK: Isobel 1680, Jane 1711 (20), Elizabeth 1717 (70), Anne 1719, Stephen 1726 (81), Mary 1727 (47), Sarah 1729, Samuel 1733 (42), William 1733 (51), Stephen 1770, Elizabeth 1772, Ann 1774, John1774 (14), Jane 1776, John 1778, John 1780, Samuel 1781, Mary 1785, Samuel 1785, Ann 1786, James 1787 (Inf), Elizabeth 1788, William 1788, Stephen 1791 (13), Samuel 1793 (70), Ann 1794 (Inf), John 1795, Richard 1798 (Inf), Elizabeth 1804, William 1810, Stephen 1818 (61), Elizabeth 1829 (81), William 1832 (54), Jane 1833 (76), Stephen 1833 (84), Rupert 1836 (22), Jane 1837 (81), Sarah 1841 (1), Susannah 1847 (72), Fanny 1849 (19), John 1849 (76), Fanny 1861 (4), Stephen 1875 (82), Sarah 1880 (80), Jemima 1885 (70), Walter Thomas James 1885 (1), Elizabeth 1886 (48), Charlotte 1887 (84), Thomas 1900 (78).
CLARKSON: Walter 2002 (80).
COCKERILL: Lewis 1938 (57), Ada Mary 1965 (88), Arthur William 1983 (70).
COLLINS: Mary 1739.
COOK: Mary 1789 (Inf), William 1789 (Inf), Edwin 1875 (2), Jane 1903 (68), William Bowman 1905 (39), William 1916 (83), Annie Laura 1917 (46), Albert 1947 (70).
COOPER: Ruth 1981 (96).
COPSON: Mary 1932 (71), Ambrose 1943 (81), Jane Lesley 1954 (6), Harry 1962 (70), Charles 1963 (73), Vera Elizabeth 1969 (78), Annie Mary 1971 (77), Alfred George 1986 (67), Mary Joan 1986, Simon Charles 1993 (36), John Ambrose 1998 (82), David Leslie 2000 (80), Leonard Henry 2005 (74).
COULSON: Robert Bernard 1989 (39), Bernard 1997 (76), Ethel 1999 (?).
COY: John 1708.
CRAMP: Anne 1741, John 1923 (78), Lavinia 1931 (81).
CRAMPTON: Charles Samuel 1901 (1).
CRISP: Elizabeth 1637.
CROCKETT: Barbara 1995 (81).
CROSS: Sarah 1783, Jonathan Peter Mark 1995 (32).
CUFFLING: Lucy 1853 (1), William 1876 (53), David 1898 (41), Mary Ann 1900 (78).
DANCE: Mary Louisa Lucy 1874 (1).
DANN: Herbert James 1870 (Inf).
DAFT: Joseph 1718.
DAPH: Samuel 1730.
DANVERS: Elizabeth 1677, Henry 1708, Samuel 1708, Mary 1711, Elizabeth 1719, Frances 1724 (18Mo), Frances 1740 (9), Elizabeth 1743 (57), Joseph 1753, Joseph 1756, Frances 1759, Henry 1759, John Watson 1769 (13), John 1796.
DAWS: William 1762.
DAVINSON: Ruth 1816 (55).
DAYKIN: Ann 1875 (70), John 1875 (68).
DETHICK: Thomas 1797.
DEWICK : Frederick Neil Miles 2004 (89), Betty 2006 (87).
DIXON: Henry Edward Otto Murray 1917 (31), Etheldreda Murray 1943 (87), James Murray 1944 (92).
DO(A)RE: Edward 1680, Edward 1681, John 1685, Edward 1719, Mary 1720.
DOUGHTY: Anne 1833 (47), Elizabeth 1841 (24), Elizabeth Matilda 1843 (28), Mary Ann 1850 (37), Joseph 1872 (88).
DOWELL: Norman Charles 1989 (69), Mary Ruth 2005 (84).
DRAYTON: Henry 1739, Elizabeth 1750.
DUFLEY: Elizabeth 1782.
EDWARDS: Miriam 1967 (64).
EGGLESTONE : Wallace Henry 2004 (83).

ELSON : Sydney Dennis 2005 (79).
EYRE: Joseph 1777, Sarah 1777 (72), Matthew 1783 (43).
FANSHAWE: Gordon Lennox 1983 (65).
FARMER: Thomas 1758, Joseph 1759, Stephen 1976 (82), Ruth Elizabeth 1984 (89).
FENNELOW: Ann 1758, John 1771, Mary 1809 (82), Ellen 1757.
FERNELEY: Charles 1760.
FIELDING: John 1704, Alice 1730, Hester 1730.
FLETCHER: Elizabeth 1807.
FRANKS: John 1727, William 1728, Elizabeth 1729, Joseph 1729, Samuel 1736, Sarah 1758.
FRESHWATER : Donald Cole 2004 (80).
FROST: Robert Dashwood 1945 (20), Ella Hawkins 1960 (69), Cecil Dashwood 1976 (96).
GADD: Thomas 1854 (1), Sarah Ann 1855 (4).
GAMBLE: Ruth 1833 (2), Ruth 1836 (23), William Haywood 1891 (72), Sarah 1895 (82), Clara 1956 (95).
GARGARIN: Clara 1901 (47).
GAZY: Angelina 1926 (80), Samuel 1929 (84).
GEORGE: Sarah 1946 (84), Lilian Elsie 1978 (85).
GIBBS: Hannah 1900 (78).
GILBERT: Elizabeth 1634, Arthur 1683, John 1690, Robert 1698 (54), Robert 1707, Henry 1713, Hannah 1714, Robert 1716, Hannah 1722, Anne 1725, Anne 1727 (83), Samuel 1729 (9), Mary 1734 (11), Martha 1749 (29), Robert 1749 (70), Mary 1757, Hannah 1759 (77), Sophia 1762.
GIMSON: Harry Hay 1969 (89), Alice Webb 1974 (93), William Nicholas 1986 (43).
GLOVER: Abraham 1703, Anne 1712, Thomas 1746 (6), Elizabeth 1764.
GODBALD: Susannah 1871 (1), Emma 1877 (1), Sarah Helen 1879 (1), George 1889 (60).
GODDARD: Eleanor 1850 (58).
GODFREY: Louis Mary Gladys 1973 (69), Frederick Lindesay 1984 (82).
GODKIN: Geraldine Sheila 1994 (67), John Richard Hayward 2001 (79).
GOODE: John 1781.
GOODMAN: Ann 1737 (47), Stephen 1754.
GRACE: Mary Anne 1986 (86).
GREASLEY: Jane 1820 (22), Nancy 1839 (58), William 1839 (56), Elizabeth 1845 (30), George 1848 (39).
GREENWOOD: Margery 1994 (84), Ernest Robert 2000 (91).
GREGORY: William Victor 1965 (66), Ada 1988 (88).
GRUNDY: William 1723.
GUILFORD: Elizabeth 1706, Henry 1710, Elizabeth 1715.
HACKET(T): John 1718, Elizabeth 1722, Grizam 1729, Catherine 1769, William Gordon 1972 (67), Mary Noreen 2010 (98).
HADDON: John 1718, Anna Amelia 1934 (69).
HALES : Mary 1807.
HALIFAX: Philip Noel 1972 (69), Myra Maud 1976 (72).
HALL: Anne 1624, Dorothy 1673, Francis 1680, Anne 1692, Francis 1708, — 1719, Francis 1734, William 1738, Elizabeth 1747 (63), Elizabeth 1762 (51), Nathaniel 1770 (86), William 1790 (4), Nathaniel 1796.
HAMMOND: Herbert 1951 (64), Richard Keith Curtis 1940 (23), Florence Elizabeth 1978 (95).
HANDLEY: Thomas 1862 (Inf), George 1878 (69), Mary 1886 (73), Joseph James 1981 (74).
HARDY: Isaac 1810 (Inf), Sarah 1810 (26), Elizabeth 1811 (61), Samuel 1828 (81).
HARDY SMITH: John Arthur 1942 (58), Marie Adeline 1996 (75), John 2003 (89)
HARRIMAN: Hannah 1841 (4), Maria 1842 (Inf), Maria 1857 (41), Thomas 1861 (44).
HARRIS: Selina 1861 (55), George 1871 (56), Buddug 1970 (58), Waldron 1979 (66).

HARRISON: Agnes 1953 (51), Joseph Harry 1966 (71), Hilda May 1967 (78), Ralph Stone 1996 (73), Leslie 2001 (89), Lilian Rebecca 2010 (85).
HAWKINS: Martha 1819 (76).
HAYNES: John Henry 1963 (60), Gladys Mary 1997 (86).
HEMSLEY: Elizabeth 1809 (35), Joseph 1825 (26), Elizabeth 1827 (25), Harriet 1856 (1), Joseph 1897 (72), Jemima 1899 (73), Sophia 1935 (71), Jane Ann 1937 (65), William 1938 (73).
HERBERT: Dorothy Herbert 1938 (58), Albert 1964 (88), Richard 1970 (54), Samuel Frank 1976 (64), Adeline 1977 (81), Jean Leslie 2001 (82).
HERCOCK: Alexander Nicholas 1973 (11), William Barry 1997 (66).
HERMS: Thomas 1738.
HEWS/HUGHES: Elizabeth 1706, Mary 1706, Mary 1711, Mary 1716, George 1719, Thomas 1719, Jonathan 1720, John 1725, John 1727, Mary 1730, Elizabeth 1744 (73), Eleanor 1745, Robert 1747 (77), Ann 1757, Elizabeth 1757 (6), John 1758, Elizabeth 1760, Elizabeth 1765, Thomas 1765.
HEYGATE: Isabella 1859 (63).
HEITCH: Ann 1707, Mary 1733.
HICK: Rebecca 1677.
HILL: Elizabeth 1775, Thomas 1794, Thomas 1816 (60), Elizabeth 1830 (75), Mary Anne 1830 (Inf), Sarah 1846 (26), Sarah 1846 (Inf), Laura Fanny 1853 (13), Fanny 1854 (Inf), Fanny 1864 (7), Thomas 1871 (78), Elizabeth 1879 (65), Thomas 1923 (80), Charlotte 1929 (83).
HIND: Jane 1625, Henry 1681, Alice 1687, Jane 1692, Hannah 1700, Mary 1703, Robert 1703, Thomas 1748(84), James 1765, John 1772, Ann 1789, Elizabeth 1798 (Inf), Eliza 1801 (Inf), Henry 1801, Mary 1806, Mary Ann 1812 (16), Mary 1820 (67), Henry 1886 (73), Sarah 1893 (73), Henrietta Maria Louisa 1900 (40), Sarah Jane 1922 (75).
HIPWELL: Stanley 1969 (71), Mary 1996 (94).
HITCHCOCK: Mary 1783.
HOARE: Susannah 1754 (75).
HO(W)DEN: Eleanor 1681, George 1681, Samuel 1684, Mary 1687.
HODGE(S): John 1817 (Inf), Martha 1818 (Inf), Jane 1839 (17), John 1843 (17), Eliza 1853 (Inf), Matthew 1854 (64), Anne 1864 (67), Eliza Ann 1878 (15), Zoe 1885 (11), Thomas 1911 (77), Eliza 1918 (89), John Henry 1920 (68), Sarah Jane 1947 (93).
HOLLIN: Richard 1767, Thomas 1768.
HOLLIS: Jane 1720.
HOLLOWAY: Christopher William 1998 (32).
HOLMES: Eva 1987 (83), George Winton 1990 (91).
HOLT: Hannah 1890 (59), Mary Ann 1895 (71), James 1897 (73).
HOOD: Christian 1713.
HORNE: Christopher Thomas Nicol 1986 (22).
HORNER: William 1846 (51), Thomas 1854 (89).
HORNSBY: Jane Ann 1937 (65), John 1940 (82).
HOROUNEE: John 1788.
HOWKINS: Margaret 1682.
HUBBARD: Adela Mary 1880 (Inf), Elizabeth 1886 (43), Elizabeth 1956 (63), Albert Ernest 1965 (71).
HUDSON: James 1637, Ann 1688, Francis 1697, John 1698, Elizabeth 1706, Francis 1708, Eliza 1851 (18), Madeleine Thora 1954 (36).
HUGHES: see HEWS.
HULL: Sarah 1759, Mary 1766, Joseph 1780.
HULLHOUSE: Elizabeth 1757.
HUNT: Pamela 1951 (10 mo), David 1974 (72), David John 1997 (58).
HUTCHINSON: John 1792, Mary 1796, Thomas 1796, William 1803, Mary 1815 (63), William 1821 (Inf).

HYTCH: Robert 1700.
INGLESTON: John 1797.
INGRAM: Ralph Herbert 1996 (89), Gwendolen 1998 (83)
JACKMAN: Stanley Radcliffe 1985 (79), Beatrice 1987 (79).
JACKSON: Joanna 1700 (68), Thomas 1700 (63).
JAMES: Grace 1802, Hannah 1827 (51).
JARRAT: Lydia 1766, Thomas 1766.
JAYES: Joan 1982 (67), Herbert Shipley 1983 (71).
JELLIS: Esther 1876 (54).
JOHNSON: Edward 1715, Joyce 1719, Friza 1728, Mary1732, Robert 1735, David 1738, John 1753, Joseph 1760, Dorothy 1784, Charlotte 1786 (6), Frizzy 1791, Elizabeth 1797 (55), Francis 1806 (Inf), John 1807 (74), Elizabeth 1810 (75) William 1811 (72), Henry 1812 (12), William 1821 (38), Joseph 1823 (14), Mary Ann 1830 (20), Francis 1836 (27), Thomas 1849 (77), Frances 1850 (76), Charlotte 1874 (31), Arthur 1905 (62).
JONES: [Unnamed] 1954 (Stillborn child of Richard Talbot and Jane).
JORDAINE: John 1796.
KERSLAKE: Alan Herbert 1978 (70), Norah 2001 (94).
KILBY: Walter 1954 (73), Mary Elizabeth 1967 (90).
KINDALE: Mary 1742.
KING: John 1811.
KINGSTON: Betty Anna 1959 (33).
KIRBY: Mary 1791, George 1798, John 1812, Sarah 1837 (77).
KIRKMAN: Amy 1704.
LABROM: Brian Walter 1993 (70), Olive 2001 (79), Karen Mary 2006 (50).
LAKIN: John 1837 (77).
LAMBERT: Lucy 1929 (82).
LANCASHIRE: John Owen 1959 (94), Mabel Annie 1971 (95).
LANE: Christian 1727.
LERRAD: Charles 1848 (38).
LAWRENCE: John 1748.
LEA: Thomas 1702.
LEAKE: Mary Anne 1837 (2), Samuel 1927 (75), Mary Elizabeth 1934 (76), Hannah Elizabeth 1951 (67).
LEATHERLAND: John William 1967 (64), Ada Mary 1980 (78).
LEWIN: Anne 1699, Benjamin 1701, Elizabeth 1764, Joseph 1785, Ann 1787, Bertha Ellen 1840 (Inf), John 1843 (Inf), Jane 1848 (3), Jemima 1848 (Inf), Ann 1849 (1), Rebecca 1849 (12), Samuel 1849 (35), Thomas 1860 (18).
LEWIS: Lydia 1800 (Inf).
LIDDLE: Phyllis 1987 (80).
LIEGER: Mary 1749.
LIQUORISH: John 1741.
LLOYD: Mary 1805, John 1814 (77), Hannah Matilda King 1933 (57), Percival George 1945 (73), Frederick Percival 1978 (75), Percival William 1995 (86), Sidney Edward 1995 (80), Doris Anne 1999 (91), Phyllis May 2007 (91).
LOCKINGTON: Brenda Jean 2001 (61).
LOMAS: Alice Mary 1897 (43).
LOVETT: Elizabeth 1680, Ann 1700, John 1710, Henry 1718 (63), Anne 1723, Mary 1729, Elizabeth 1736, Henry 1737, Thomas 1743, Mary 1749, Elizabeth 1754, Isabella 1754, William 1762, Jane 1769, Thomas 1785, George 1801, Elizabeth 1802, John 1811, Ann 1902 (67), Henry 1902 (69).
LOWES: Arthur Peverall 1986 (73).
LUMLEY: Marjorie Ruth 2001 (88), John Alick 2005 (88).
LY(I)NES: Richard 1839 (73), Elizabeth 1843 (3), Ruth 1851 (77), Ann 1877 (45), Charles 1883 (49), Caroline Eliza 1944 (76), Louisa Alice 1947 (69).

McCLINTOCK: Doris Lilian May 1943 (9Mo).
McCURRY: Arthur Llwellyn 1974 (76).
MAGEE: Barbara Daisy 1994 (81), John Kidd 1997 (84).
MANTON: Cyril Frederick 1974 (57).
MARLOW : Kingsley Hamnett 2010 (79).
MATBOWS: — 1744.
MATTHEWS: Thomas 1691, Samuel 1695, Thomas 1696, Nathaniel 1700, Michael 1723, Hannah 1737.
MAYO: Elizabeth 1709.
MEADOWS: Hilda Newton 1980 (75), Sydney Robert 1984.
MEE: Robert 1993 (76), Irene Elsie 1999 (84).
MILLS: Joseph 1713, Sarah 1890 (75).
MINKLEY: Jane 1911 (70), Marjorie 1913 (Inf), Mary Sophia 1929 (61), Herbert 1938 (65), George 1944 (75), Mary Ann 1953 (76), Charles Edward 1982 (72).
MORRIS: Sarah 1815 (3), Anne 1820 (Inf), Hannah 1828 (Inf), Thomas 1829 (20), George 1843 (24), Francis 1845 (70), Caroline 1848 (1), Emma Sophia 1848 (6), Ann 1849 (63), Caroline 1851 (33), Caroline 1852 (1), Mary 1860 (98), George 1863 (76), Francis 1880 (30), Amelia 1883 (38), Mary 1884 (83), George 1897 (88), Margaret Ellen 2004 (84).
MUMMERY: Harold Walter 1961 (70), Susan Louise 1975 (83).
MURRAY: Sydney Brian Patrick 1974 (65).
MUSGROVE: Thomas Donaldson 1989 (66).
NAYLER : Leonard Stanley 2004 (88).
NETTLETON: Millicent 1961 (83).
NEWBOLD: Edward 1764, Sarah 1768 (29), Edward 1769 (30).
NEWB(Y)RY: Elizabeth 1701, Elizabeth 1788, Hannah 1788, Martha 1788, Mary 1788.
NICHOLLS: Robert 1684, Anne 1685, Thomas 1687 (16).
NICKELSON: William 1702 (59), Ann 1705.
NORTH: Olive 1994 (83), Eric Frank 2003 (90).
NOURSE: Jacob 1830 (82), Sarah 1836 (78).
OLIVER: Edith Norah 1995 (79), James Stanley 2000 (86).
ORTON: Charles Victor 1964 (58), Ruth Jessie 1999 (81).
OSBORNE: Robert Brian 1999 (54).
PAGE: Thomas 1785, Sheila 1998 (91), Henry William 1998 (88), John Robert Houfton 2002 (60).
PAGET: Frances 1677, Elizabeth Maria 1846 (Inf).
PALMER: Marion Hilda 1887 (Inf), Gertrude 1888 (Inf), Walter Thomas 1915 (57).
PARKER: — 1695, John 1696, John 1720 (81), Mary 1726.
PARKINSON: William 1724.
PATCHET: Rachel 1712.
PATERSON: Janet Una 1919 (15), William 1926 (55), William Ernest 1927 (25), Edmund Keith 1933 (21), Emily Elizabeth 1937 (67).
PAULEY: Samuel 1827 (60), Sarah 1832 (72).
PEAKE: Elizabeth 1727.
PEARSON: Faith 1838 (43).
PEBODY: John 1703, Hannah 1717.
PEPPER: Albert Edwin 1926 (51), Edwin 1935 (88), Emma 1943 (94).
PERKIN(S): Dorothy 1687, Thomas 1746 (71), Elizabeth 1761, John 1765 (49), William 1793 (82), Samuel 1798.
PERKINSON: Thomas 1732, Richard 1726, Elizabeth 1713.
PETTS: Samuel 1819 (80), Ann 1828 (25), Milley 1828 (Inf), Anne 1829 (1), Benjamin 1864 (64), Mary 1874 (72).
PHILLIPS: Gerald Aubrey Vincent 1984 (78).
PICK: Katherine 1706.
PICKER: Annie 1906 (47).

PICKERING: Hannah 1810 (Inf).
POALE: Mary 1684.
POLLARD: John 1729, Elizabeth 1738 (45), — 1750, Eizabeth 1756, William 1769, Mary 1773, Hannah 1776, John 1778, Thomas 1778, William 1802, Elizabeth 1809 (69), John 1817 (72).
POPPLE: Selina 1934 (66).
PORTER: Anne 1682, Catherine 1682, Henry 1678, Anne 1708, Thomas 1725, Mary 1727, Thomas 1739, Thomas 1740, Catharine 1741.
POTTER: William 1814 (1), John Lakin 1834 (Inf), William Sharpe 1834 (Inf), Richard 1857 (53), Susannah 1869 (27), Elizabeth Sharp 1877 (29), Susannah Sharpe 1889 (82), Hope Eleanor 1993 (83), William Herbert 1997 (89), Mabel 2005 (92), Richard Keith 2010 (93).
POWELL: Karen Jennifer 1998 (55).
PRATT: William 1882 (23), Sarah Hilda 1893 (1), Joseph 1902 (77), Sarah 1914 (82), Charles Benjamin 1946 (76), Ada 1969 (99), Donald Redvers 1978 (78), Bessie 1982 (83).
PRESTON: Jane 1740, Mary 1740, Ruth 1741, William 1778, Thomas 1798, Anne 1819 (83), Joseph 1825 (79), William 1825 (86), Martha 1828 (Inf), Joseph 1830 (Inf), Peter 1833 (1), Jane 1835 (19), Alex 1848 (Inf), William 1848 (26), Rosa 1849 (10), Mary 1862 (28), Elizabeth 1865 (2), Joseph 1867 (77), Joshua 1872 (67), Mary 1877 (69), William 1892 (70), Eliza 1909 (78), Alex 1915 (64), George 1919 (84), Laurence 1920 (Inf), Mary 1933 (76).
PRIESTLEY: Sarah Maria 1887.
PRIOR: John 1673, Isobel 1679, Joseph 1679, Elizabeth 1698, Samuel 1705, Joseph 1721, Elizabeth 1724, Robert 1724, Samuel 1725, Anne 1728, Dorothy 1732, Elizabeth 1737, Robert 1747, Henry 1748, Robert 1756, Joseph 1767 (80), John 1774, Sarah 1776, Sarah 1777, Stephen 1803, Sarah 1824 (75), John 1833 (19), Thomas 1833 (23), Sarah 1834 (26), Elizabeth 1846 (71), Thomas 1849 (75).
PUGH: David John 2002 (68).
RADCLIFFE Sydney 1990 (81), Lilian May 1999 (93).
RADFORD John Henry 2004 (86), Dorothy Mary 2007 (87).
RATCLIFFE: Sarah Jane 1874 (30).
RAWORTH: Sarah 1682, — 1696, Elizabeth 1704, Sarah 1707, Sarah 1722, John 1731, Robert 1731, William 1734 (46), — 1744.
RAYNOR: Mary 1736, John 1773, Thomas 1796, Elizabeth 1820 (90), John 1848 (1), Ann 1850 (31), Harry 1850 (Inf), Frederick 1853 (1), Samuel 1860 (Inf), Zachariah 1861 (69), William 1863 (43), Anne 1864 (67), Mahala 1878, Mary 1878 (62), Robert 1879 (65), Frank 1888 (83), Mary 1892 (94), Edith Annie 1904 (1), Thomas George 1904 (41), Jane 1912 (76), Thomas 1913 (78).
REED: Mary 1786, John 1813 (65).
RICHARDSON: Ann 1806 (Inf), Elizabeth 1822 (29), John Lakin 1818 (5), William 1821 (1).
RIGBY: Charlotte 1780, James 1784.
RILEY: Edward James 1941 (77).
RINGROSE: Alice Vera 1933 (6).
ROALFE : Kathleen Rita June 2004 (68).
ROGERS: Dinah 1895 (78), Richard 1895 (75), Henry 1913 (63).
ROPER: Richard 1808.
ROWNTREE CLIFFORD: Hugh 2005 (88).
RUDKIN: Elizabeth 1740, Elizabeth 1750, Sophia 1863 (Inf), Emma 1864 (1), Mary Emma 1965 (67), Walter 1980 (77).
SANDERS: Elizabeth 1735, Joseph 1750.
SHAKESBY: Harold 1976 (64).
SHARP: Elizabeth Ann 1881 (19).
SHAW: Elizabeth Victoria 1991 (89).

SHELTON: Sarah 1808 (Inf), Mary 1809, Mary 1816 (Inf).
SHRIVE: Evelyn Clara 1976 (86), Walter Edgar 1981 (92).
SIDEBOTTOM: Frances 1878 (Inf), Maurice 1884 (19).
SIMMON(D)S: John Henry 1932 (70), Martha Adeliza 1952 (86), Reginald Alfred 1975.
SIMPSON: Elizabeth 1748, John 1748, Mary 1795 (Inf), Garthren 1799 (Inf), Anne 1823 (69), Matthew 1827 (66), Hannah 1830 (49), Mary 1831 (34), John Matthew 1839 (18), Mary Ann 1848 (24), Matthew 1849 (60), John 1851 (56), William 1860 (65), Anne 1862 (70), Ann 1864 (65), Joseph 1866 (76), Elizabeth 1869 (83), Matthew 1895 (73), Mark Edward 1931 (28).
SISTON: Elizabeth 1634, Mary 1635, Ann 1681, Will 1681, Isobel 1695, John 1700 (69), Temperance 1714 (76).
SKEVINGTON: John 1851 (11), Jane 1855 (39), Mary Ann 1861 (44), Joseph 1867 (58).
SMEATON : Christine Leslie 2008 (72).
SMITH: Ann 1637, Ursula 1679, Hannah 1718, Elizabeth 1724 (13), Thomas 1736, Mary 1753 (81), Elizabeth 1757, Elizabeth 1765, Thomas 1778, Thomas 1793, John 1807, Mary 1852 (54), Susan 1924 (48), Maureen Hazel 1935 (14Mo), Thomas 1952 (82), Elizabeth 1961 (96), Stuart Arthur 1963 (58), Charles Eric 1992 (71), Roland George 1990 (61), Jean Margaret 1996 (64), Elisabeth 2009 (47).
SNOW: William 1763, Ann 1784, Mary 1785 (Inf), Mary 1810, William 1816 (78), Anne 1819 (Inf).
SPENCE: Jeffery 1827 (63), Mary 1839 (61), George 1937 (41).
SPENCER: Edward 1857 (Inf), Edwin 1859 (1), John 1889 (61), Violet Amelia 1943 (44).
SQUIRE: Elizabrth 1633, Henry 1685.
STANLEY: James 1950 (55).
STATHAM: Royston John 1983 (50), Hilda Marion 2000 (64).
STEEL: John 1783.
STEPHENS: John 1685.
STEVENSON: Ivy Annie Elsie 1971 (71), Arthur Ernest 1988 (78).
STOKES: Mark 1917 (51).
STONE: Enid Gladys 1951 (2), Herbert Henry 1988 (66).
SUMMAT: — 1637.
SUTTON: Mary 1636, Mary 1827 (76).
SWAIN: Alice 1714.
SWAYNE: Thomas 1706.
SYMINGTON, Reginald 1997 (91).
TARRATT: Margaret Lilian 1977 (67), Frank Bernard 1996 (95).
TAYLOR: Henry 1784, Elizabeth 1789, Mary 1789, William 1802, Leslie 1927 (Inf), George Henry 1979 (83), Dorothy May 1980 (84), Austin James 1990 (45).
THOMPSON: Robert 1698, Rihard 1833, Hannah 1834 (27).
THORNTON: Jane 1817 (Inf), Anne 1820 (38).
THORPE: Lydia 1677, Hannah 1767, Elizabeth 1795, John Clarke 1795, Joseph 1806, Elizabeth 1824 (1), William 1828 (57), Lydia 1832, Samuel 1835(3), George 1838 (Inf), Mary 1838 (70), John 1847 (Inf), Samuel 1858 (61), Ellen 1861 (3), John 1865 (73), George 1868 (67), Sarah 1868 (77), Mary 1875 (73), William 1881 (56), Edward 1886 (62).
TOMLIN: Sarah Annie Maria 1921 (71), John 1929 (81).
TOONE: Jane 1862 (73).
TOWNSEND: Sophia 1814 (Inf).
TURNBULL : Thomas Reid 2004 (84).
TURNER: Archibald 1928 (67).
TWIGGER: Joan Lilian Moira 1949 (27).
TYERS: Edward 1917 (78), Elizabeth 1929 (88).
UNDERWOOD: Elizabeth 1933 (75), Tom 1936 (77).
VARNHAM: — 1789.

VERNUM: John 1758.
VESTY: Mary 1772, John 1784, Sarah 1788, Elizabeth 1819 (Inf), Mary 1822 (84), William 1829 (25), Thomas 1833 (55), Samuel 1836 (29), Thomas 1850 (47), Hannah 1856 (72).
WAIN: Elizabeth 1743.
WAKEFIELD: Martha 1942 (64), Benjamin Howard 1957 (81).
WAKELIN: Letitia 1854 (13).
WAKERL(E)Y: Mary 1803 (Inf), Sarah 1813 (2), Anne 1835 (62), John 1837 (60).
WALKER: John 1746 (71), Sarah 1748 (76), John 1758, Margaret 1968 (70), David Alexander 1979 (95).
WALLACE: Mary 1633, Mary 1634, Henry Alfred 1934 (63), Sarah 1959 (86).
WALTON: Lucy 1804.
WARD: Elizabeth 1704, Samuel 1704, William 1706, Mary 1712, William 1753 (89), Jane 1762, Hannah 1772, Jane 1776, George 1830 (Inf), Jane 1830 (25), James 1835 (45), James 1842 (83), Thomas 1871 (76).
WARREN: John 1826 (72), Frances 1835 (83).
WATSON: Matthew 1723, Thomas 1727, Mary 1728, Mary 1728, Thomas 1729, James 1734, Michael 1746, Frances 1880 (53).
WELLS: William 1762, Percy 1971 (72), Florence Eveline Cooke 1983 (87).
WEST: Roy William 1993 (72).
WESTLEY: William 1717, Henry 1727, Jane 1729, Anne 1733 (41), John 1734, Mary 1734, William 1754 (62), William 1775, Grace 1778, Jane 1800.
WESTON: Mary 1847 (67), Sheila Ann Halton 1998 (72).
WHATMOUGH: Edith Jane 1937 (42).
WHATNALL: William 1707, Mary 1713, Daniel 1716, William 1717, Daniel 1718 (43), Mary 1737, William 1744, Mary 1745, Richard 1829 (2).
WHEATLEY: Thomas 1813 (1).
WHITE: John 1765.
WILDMAN: Anne 1725.
WILKINS: William 1880 (30), Alice 1881 (2).
WILKINSON: John William 1932 (77).
WILLSON: George Herbert 2001 (72), Zoë Sonia 2005 (75).
WILSON: Anne 1808, David 1837 (10), Ernest Franklin 1978 (71).
WOOLERTON: William 1783, Mary 1806, Sarah 1806 (Inf), Susannah 1819 (80).
WOOD: Kathleen Isobel Lindsey 1979 (79), John Lindsay 1986 (95), Nancy 1987.
WOODFORD: Elizabeth 1685, John 1707.
WOODGATE: Henry James 1965 (80), Hedwich Joanne Caroline 1968 (79).
WOODS: Catherine 1903 (79), Joseph 1909 (76), George Morris 1940 (76).
WOODSON: Septima 1752, Henry 1759.
WOODWARD: William 1799 (Inf), William 1800, William 1807.
WOOLHOUSE: Mary 1859 (72).
WOOTNALL: James 1776, Susannah 1787.
WORTNALL: Richard 1823 (42), William 1825 (81).
WRIGHT: Sarah 1741, Henry 1839 (Inf), Mary 1846 (Inf), John 1850 (37), Albert Linwood 1950 (75), Gladys Marie Linwood 1977 (94).

– APPENDIX E –

Family Trees

The following pages of this appendix contain the family trees of:

Danvers of Swithland
Butler of Belturbet, Co. Cavan; Earls of Lanesborough
Bunney family of Swithland

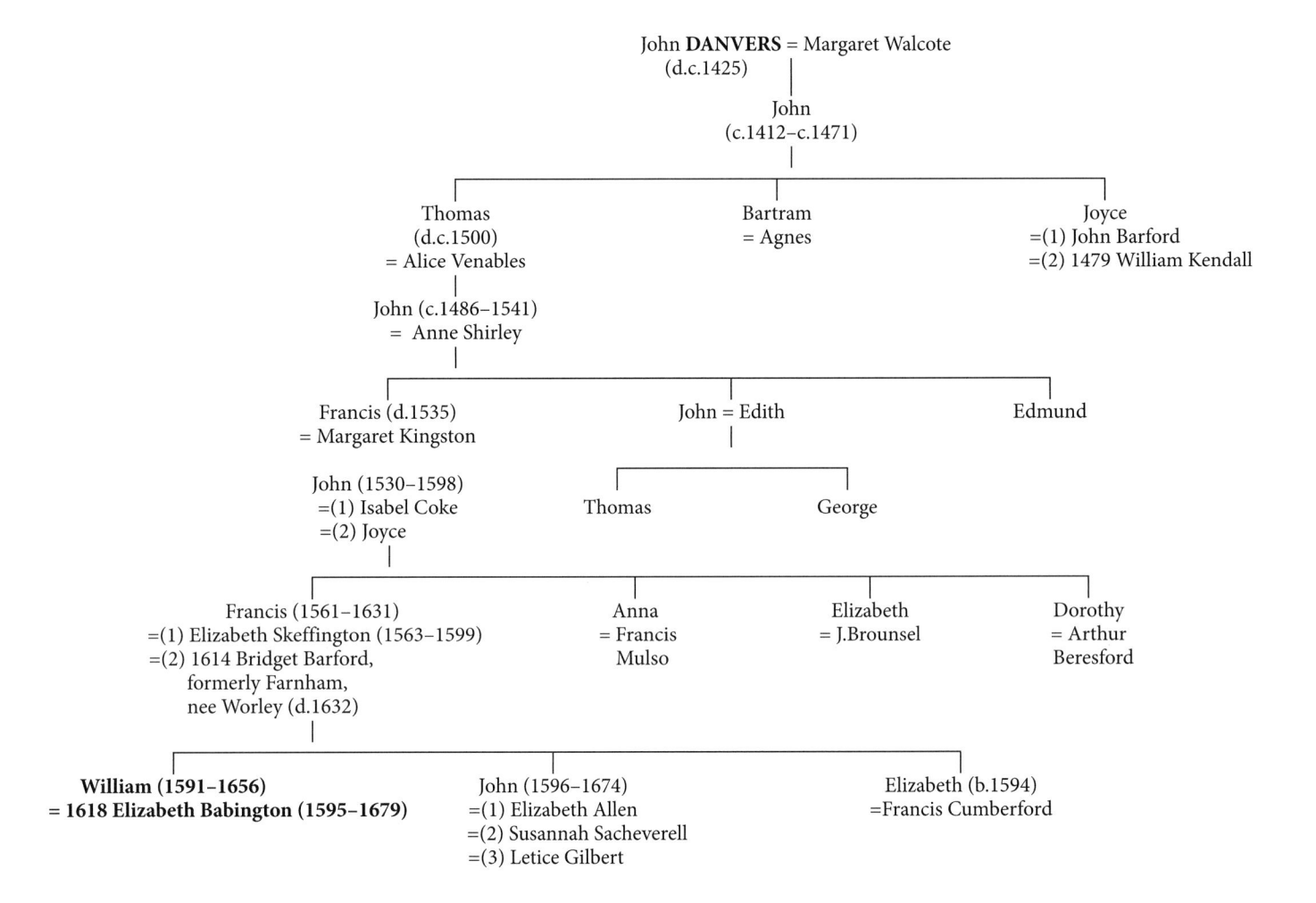

DANVERS of Swithland, Leicestershire

```
John DANVERS = Margaret Walcote
   (d.c.1425)
        │
        ├─────────────────────────────┬──────────────────┐
    Thomas                      John            Bartram        Joyce
   (d.c.1500)              (c.1412–c.1471)      = Agnes      =(1) John Barford
   = Alice Venables                                           =(2) 1479 William Kendall
        │
    John (c.1486–1541)
    = Anne Shirley
        │
        ├──────────────────────────┐
    Francis (d.1535)            Edmund
    = Margaret Kingston
        │
    John (1530–1598)
    =(1) Isabel Coke
    =(2) Joyce
        │
        ┌────────────┬──────────┬─────────┬──────────┬──────────┐
                John = Edith
                    │
        Thomas   George   Anna      Elizabeth   Dorothy
                         = Francis  = J.Brounsel = Arthur
                           Mulso                   Beresford
    Francis (1561–1631)
    =(1) Elizabeth Skeffington (1563–1599)
    =(2) 1614 Bridget Barford,
         formerly Farnham,
         nee Worley (d.1632)
        │
        ├──────────────────────────────────────┐
    John (1596–1674)                    Elizabeth (b.1594)
    =(1) Elizabeth Allen                =Francis Cumberford
    =(2) Susannah Sacheverell
    =(3) Letice Gilbert

**William (1591–1656)**
**= 1618 Elizabeth Babington (1595–1679)**
```

DANVERS of Swithland, Leicestershire, continued

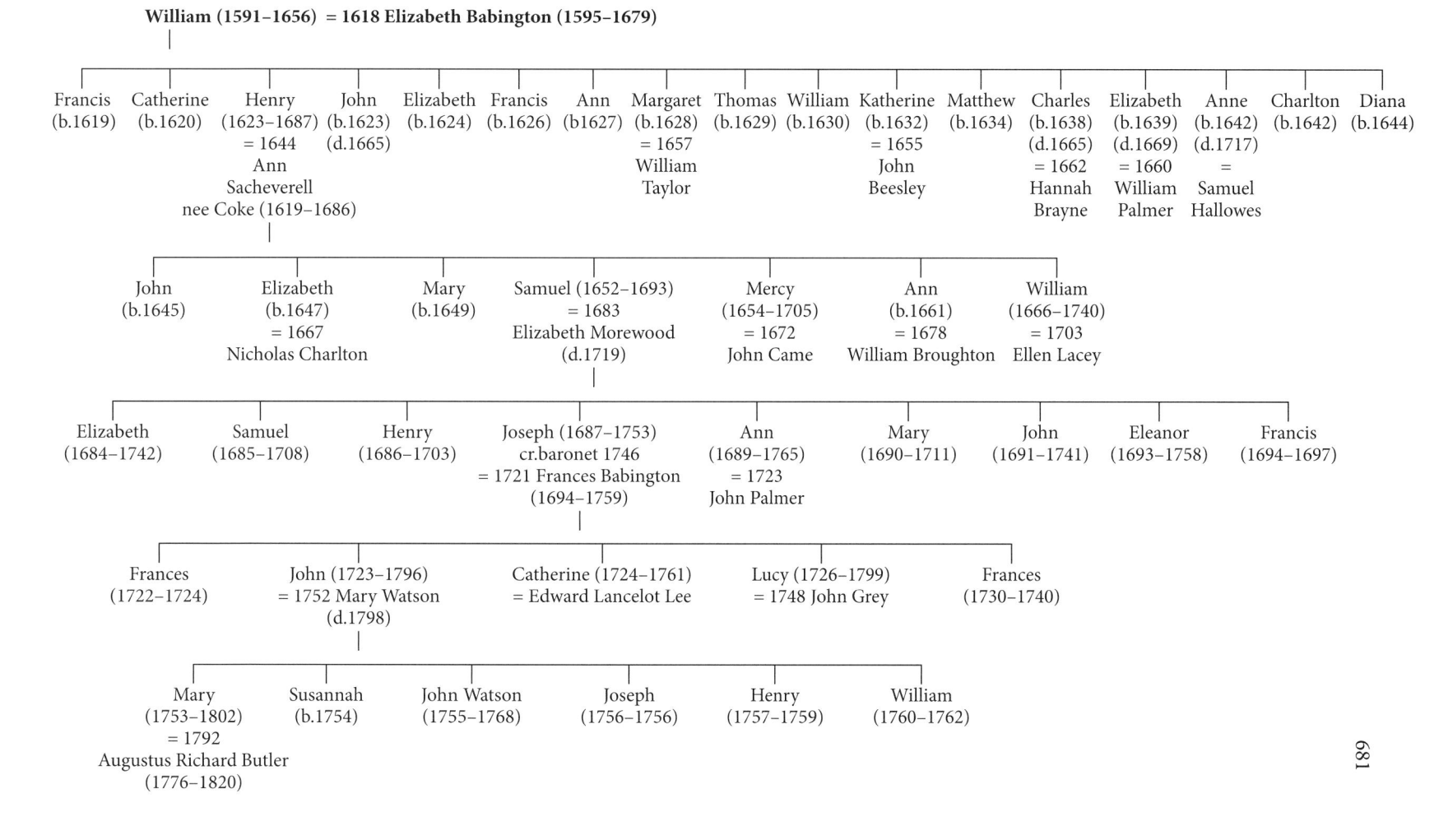

William (1591–1656) = 1618 Elizabeth Babington (1595–1679)

Children of William and Elizabeth:

- Francis (b.1619)
- Catherine (b.1620)
- Henry (1623–1687) =1644 Ann Sacheverell nee Coke (1619–1686)
- John (b.1623) (d.1665)
- Elizabeth (b.1624)
- Francis (b.1626)
- Ann (b.1627)
- Margaret (b.1628) =1657 William Taylor
- Thomas (b.1629)
- William (b.1630)
- Katherine (b.1632) =1655 John Beesley
- Matthew (b.1634)
- Charles (b.1638) (d.1665) =1662 Hannah Brayne
- Elizabeth (b.1639) (d.1669) =1660 William Palmer
- Anne (b.1642) (d.1717) = Samuel Hallowes
- Charlton (b.1642)
- Diana (b.1644)

Children of Henry and Ann:

- Elizabeth (b.1647) =1667 Nicholas Charlton
- Mary (b.1649)
- Samuel (1652–1693) =1683 Elizabeth Morewood (d.1719)
- Mercy (1654–1705) =1672 John Came
- Ann (b.1661) =1678 William Broughton
- William (1666–1740) =1703 Ellen Lacey

Children of Elizabeth and Nicholas Charlton:
- John (b.1645)

Children of Samuel and Elizabeth Morewood:
- Samuel (1685–1708)
- Henry (1686–1703)
- Joseph (1687–1753) cr. baronet 1746 =1721 Frances Babington (1694–1759)
- Ann (1689–1765) =1723 John Palmer
- Mary (1690–1711)
- John (1691–1741)
- Eleanor (1693–1758)
- Francis (1694–1697)

Children of Joseph and Frances:
- Elizabeth (1684–1742)
- John (1723–1796) =1752 Mary Watson (d.1798)
- Catherine (1724–1761) = Edward Lancelot Lee
- Lucy (1726–1799) =1748 John Grey
- Frances (1730–1740)

Children of John and Mary Watson:
- Frances (1722–1724)
- Mary (1753–1802) =1792 Augustus Richard Butler (1776–1820)
- Susannah (b.1754)
- John Watson (1755–1768)
- Joseph (1756–1756)
- Henry (1757–1759)
- William (1760–1762)

681

BUTLER of Belturbet, Co. Cavan; the Earls of Lanesborough

Humphrey **BUTLER** (1700–1768) = 1726 Mary Berry
2nd Viscount Lanesborough
cr.1756 1st Earl of Lanesborough

Brinsley (1728–1779) 2nd Earl of Lanesborough
= 1754 Jane Rochfort (1737–1828)

- Robert Herbert (1759–1806) 3rd Earl of Lanesborough = Elizabeth La Touche (d.1788)
- Augustus Richard (1776–1820) = (1) 1792 Mary Danvers (d.1802); = (2) 1802 Eliza Bizarre Sturt (d.1811)
- Mary = George Ponsonby
- Catherine (d.1823) = George Marlay
- Charlotte (d.1808) = 1806 Clement Debbeig
- Louisa (d.1820)
- Caroline
- Sophia (d.1840) = 1787 Luigi Berselli Marquis Marescoti

Children of Robert Herbert:
- Brinsley David (1783–1847) 4th Earl of Lanesborough
- George John Danvers (1794–1866) 5th Earl of Lanesborough = (1) 1815 Frances Arabella Fremantle (d.1850); = (2) 1851 Frederica Emma Hunter nee Bishop (d.1870)
- George Augustus (d.1798)

Children of Augustus Richard:
- Elizabeth Sophia (1801–1877) = 1828 Henry Dumaresque
- George William Augustus (1803–1838)
- Emily Jane (1806–1895) = 1836 George Somerville Digby
- Augustus Richard (1807–?1844)
- Charles Augustus (1809–1849) = 1838 Letitia Rudyerd Ross nee Freese (d.1884)
- Charles Augustus Ashley (b.1808)
- Henry Cavendish (1811–1891) = (1) 1842 Cecilia Agnes Taylor (d.1882); = (2) 1883 Sarah Emerson-Tennent nee Armstrong (d.1940)

Children of George John Danvers:
- John Vansittart Danvers (1839–1905) 6th Earl of Lanesborough = 1864 Anne Elizabeth Clarke (1844–1909)
- Charles Henry Danvers (1844–1879) = 1872 Alice Ward
- Frances Georgina Danvers (d.1907) = 1866 Loftus Fitzwigram
- Emily Rosa Danvers (d.1900) = 1869 William Vinicombe Davy
- Harriet Eliza Danvers (1848–1924) = (1) 1876 Francis Mount Barlow; = (2) 1886 Charles Harrison
- Harry Halpin Cavendish (1884–1966) = 1908 Lucie Sophia Blanche Hales

Children of John Vansittart Danvers:
- **Charles John Brinsley** (1865–1929)
- **Henry Cavendish** (1868–1950)
- **Francis Almeric** (1872–1925)
- **Brian Danvers** (1876–1916)
- **Winifred** (1879–1970)

Children of Harry Halpin Cavendish:
- **Henry** (b.1909)
- **Maureen Mary** (1913–1940)
- **Anthony** (1916–1943)

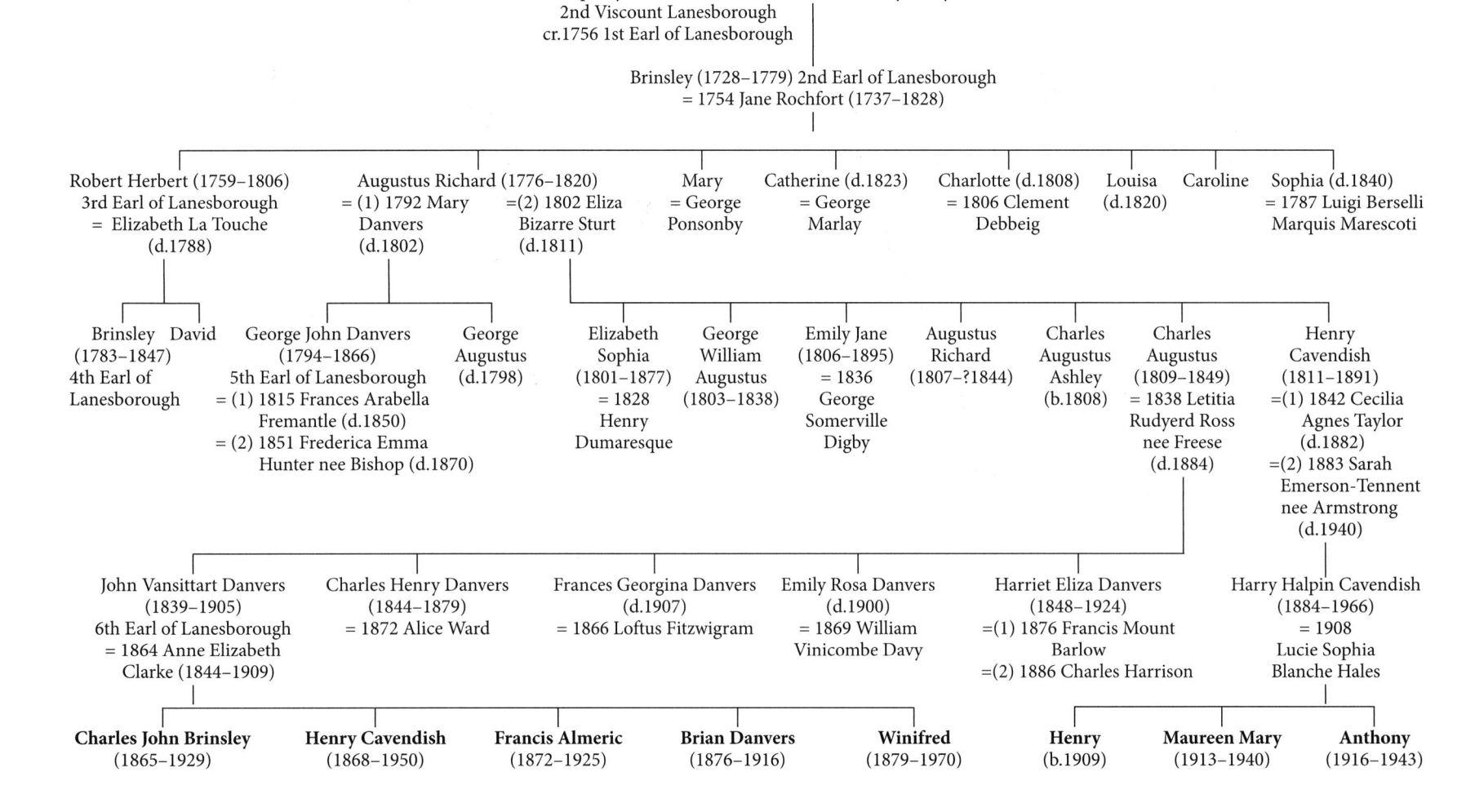

BUNNEY FAMILY of Swithland, Leicestershire

Handwritten genealogical family tree chart. Root couple: **David BUNNEY** (m.1794) = **Elizabeth Pitts** (1770-1823).

Their children include Ann (b.1819), Samuel (1795-1833) m.1815 Sarah Edwin (1794-1868), William (1798-1862) m.1826 Martha Bown (1803-1857), and Mary (b.1845).

Samuel (1795-1833) = Sarah Edwin (1794-1868) branch

Children: William (1816-1880) m.1839 Ann Rearson (b.1820); Samuel (1818-1861); Mary (1822-1877); Charles (1823-1900) = Elizabeth ? (1824-1883); Isaac (1827-1832); Daniel (1832-1866).

- **William (1816-1880) = Ann Rearson:** children include Charles William (1841-1930) m.1864 Sarah Ann Betts; Eliza Ann (1842); Betsy (1848); Fanny Sarah (1870); Joseph William (1872); Alice Annie (b.1877) m.1914 Ernest Pike; Swinton (b.1880) m. Jane ?; Lucy (b.1876) = Ernest Bennington; Evelyn Gwendolen (b.1907); Valorie (b.1896) m.1918 Charles Joshua Bray.

- **Charles (1823-1900) = Elizabeth ?:** children include Sarah Jane (1845-1874) m.1869 Thomas Ratcliffe; Joseph (b.1847); Edmund (1849-1854); Samuel (1851-1918) m.(2) Emma ? (1859-1934); William (1854-1895); John (1856-1927) m.1894 Catherine Hensley (1863-1931); Charles Edmund (1858-1862); Louis Benjamin (1860-1862); Elizabeth (1865-1880); Catherine Ann (1867-1868).
  - Edith Emily Sarah (b.1876) m.1899 Albert Crampton; Alwyn Everald (b.1876) m. Clara ?; Winifred Lilian Bertha (b.1886) m. Jack Lawndon; Hilda May (b.1885) m. Joseph Harrison; Leslie (b.1906); Eileen; Ellen Veva (b.1908); Ellen Polly (b.1894) m.1915 William George Sears.
  - Bertie Hensley (1883-1940); Annie Margaret (b.1885); Maurice Ronald (b.1888) m.(1) Frances Florence Newbold, m.(2) Walter ?; Laura (b.1889); Sidney Oswald (b.1891) m. Annie Maria Kilby; Dorothy (b.1892); Herbert (b.1894); Charles Benjamin (b.1896) m. Ellen Launer.
  - Frances Dorn (b.1912); Kathleen Margaret May (b.1917); Mary Ruth (b.1921).
  - Maurice Edwin Charles (b.1920) m.1952 Margaret Beatrice Horsfield; Barbara (b.1923) m.1953 George Lowe; Victor John (b.1924) m.1945 Vera Wilby; Attie (b.1925) m.1945 Ronald Scott; Maureen Anne (b.1927) m.1950 Peter William Elliott; Catherine Anne Ruddiphatt m.(1) William ? m.(2) Anthony Rose; Frances.
  - Susan Melanie (b.1950) m.1980 Alan Woodward; Judith Mary (b.1953); Mark William (b.1957); Sarah Louise (b.1959); Joanna (b.1961); Emma (b.1967).
  - Sophie (b.1984); Joshua Isabel (b.1989) (b.1994).

William (1798-1862) = Martha Bown (1803-1857) branch

Children: William (1826-1907) = Elizabeth Stapleton (1828-1913); George (1830-1893) m. Jane Thompson (1828-1908); Henry (1832-1911) m.1851 Mary Cartler (1834-1902); Samuel (b.1834); James (1834-1906) m.1856 Harriet Elliott (1836-1870); Frederick Henry (1838-1895) m.1870 Elizabeth ? (b.1843); Walter (1845-1924) m.1870 Mary Ann Hill (1847-1923); Fanny (b.1843).

- **William (1826-1907) = Elizabeth Stapleton:** children Eliza Ann (b.1854); George William (1856-1907); Fanny Elizabeth (b.1859); Frederick James Thompson (1859-1929) m.1882 Sarah Ann Spencer (1844-1932); William Elizabeth (1849-1848); Edward (b.1849) m. Ellen Hill; Henry Thompson (b.1852); Mary Jane (b.1849); Lucy Ellen (b.1876); Launnia (b.1863).
  - Thomas Thompson (b.1855); Samuel Walter (1861-1866); William George Donald (1867-1860); Mary Ellen (b.1882); Rosa Rebecca (1884-1968); Annie Violetta (1887-1976) m.1909 Charles Wainwright; Alfred Edwin (1891-1951) m.1915 Ethel May Bunney (1884-1934); Lilian Elsie (b.1893) m. Henry George; Beatrice Alice (1895-1917); Edith Evelyn (1898-1961).
  - Samuel Arthur (1903-1985) m. Hilda Boulton; David Victor (1937-1970) m. May Lawrence/Laura (b.1900); Phyllis Constance Wilhelmina (1913-1985); Frances; Betty; Ken m. Monica Neale; John (b.1932); Clarence (b.1914) m. Bernard Wainwright (d.1994); Beatrice May (b.1920).

- **Henry (1832-1911) = Mary Cartler:** children Maria (b.1857); William (b.1859); Letitia (b.1861); Sarah Elizabeth (1865-1929); Mary Ethel (b.1883); James Carter (b.1855).

- **James (1834-1906) = Harriet Elliott:** Martha Lucy (1857-1871); Samuel George (1860-1862).

- **Walter (1845-1924) = Mary Ann Hill:** Joseph (1890-1960) m.1913 Jane Lindsey McMills (1883-1937); Johnson (1893-1920).

CREATED BY BOB OSBORNE

Glossary

acre	principal unit of land area until 2007; originally amount of land that could be ploughed in a single day with oxen; area varied pre-14th century according to local usage, eg. Leics c. 2309 sq.yds; standardized by Edward I (1305) at 40 rods x 4 rods, 4840 sq. yards
advowson	right of presentation to an ecclesiastical benefice
allotment	allocation of lands parcelled out under an Enclosure Award
armiger	a person entitled to use a coat of arms
apparitor	official messenger of a civil or ecclesiastical court
assart	to enclose or clear forest or waste land
bailiff	agent of the lord of the manor, charged with collecting rents etc.
benefice	ecclesiastical living or preferment
carr	hollow place which is moist and boggy
Chancery	court of equity in England and Wales, which followed a set of loose rules to avoid the possible harshness (inequity) of common law
clerical titles	chaplain: unbeneficed priest of a chapel; curate: any minister who has the cure of souls; rector: one who has the parsonage and great tithes; vicar: does the 'duty' of the parish for the person who receives the tithes
close	hedged, fenced or walled piece of land – not a field
commissary	a representative or deputy; principal official of a manor court
Commissioners, Church	combined (1948) the assets and the work of **Queen Anne's Bounty** and the **Ecclesiastical Commissioners**
Commissioners, Ecclesiastical	a corporate body authorized by Parliament (1836) to determine the distribution of revenues of the Church of England
Commissioners, Enclosure	persons named in an Enclosure Act and appointed to carry out its provisions
conventicle	a religious meeting, especially a secret or illegal one, such as those held by dissenters in England and Scotland in the 16th and 17th centuries.
croft	piece of enclosed ground for tillage or pasture, usually arable area near a house
delinquent	also **malignant**, **scandalous**, terms applied generally to royalists after a declaration in Parliament in 1642
delapidations	the burden and charge of repairing a parsonage house
demesne	lands of or belonging to lord of the manor
dissenters	Protestant nonconformists, eg. Presbyterians, Congregationalists, Baptists, Quakers, Unitarians, Methodists

entail	law restricting inheritance of land to a particular heir or class of heirs (e.g. male); settle land on persons in succession, none of whom can dispose of it
fine	sum of money payable on admission to, or purchase of, a land holding
forfeiture	practice whereby those convicted of high treason forfeited immediately all possessions to the Crown
furlong	measure of length 220 yds; convenient length for oxen to plough before needing to rest
glebe	land assigned to incumbent of a parish as part of his benefice and the endowment of the church
hatchment	funerary escutcheon painted on a square panel and hung, in the style of a diamond, first outside the house of a deceased person and later in church
hearth tax	tax introduced in 1662 on hearths, more precisely chimneys, in order to relieve Charles II's financial difficulties
hereditaments	any kind of property that can be inherited, such as hereditary titles of honour or dignity, heritable titles of office, coats of arms, Prescriptive Barony, rights of way, tithes, advowsons, pensions, annuities, rents, franchises, etc
highways, surveyor of	or **waywarden**, parish officer appointed under the Highway Act (1555) to take charge of road repairs
homage	pledge or loyalty sworn by tenants to their lord of the manor
hundred	administrative division of a shire or county
husbandman	tenant farmer, as distinct from **yeoman**
indenture	form of contract between two parties
induction	introduction of a cleric into the possession of the temporalities of a benefice
institution	installation of a cleric into the possession of the spiritualities of a benefice (cure of souls)
Interregnum	the time when a throne is vacant between the death or abdication of a monarch and the accession of his/her successor, e.g. the period between the execution of Charles I (1649) and the restoration of Charles II (1660)
interregnum	period of vacancy in a church benefice, between the resignation of one incumbent and the induction of another
intruder	Puritan minister installed in a benefice after the expulsion of the 'lawful' incumbent during the **Interregnum**
inquisition post mortem	local enquiry into the lands held by people of some status, in order to discover what income and rights were due to the crown
jointure	property settled on a woman at marriage to be hers on death of her husband
lay subsidy	taxes assessed against the laity ('common' people)
leasehold	tenure held for a term of years, or for life, or for a given number of lives, or for a period designated by the landlord
manor	a territorial unit originally held, by feudal tenure, by a landlord, **lord of the manor**, himself a tenant of the Crown, who, by right could hold a **manor court** for his own tenants
mark	mediaeval unit of currency
messuage	dwelling house and its appurtenances, such as outbuildings, garden and sometimes land

moiety	half share
muster rolls	lists of local inhabitants liable for military service and the equipment they were required to have
ordinary	ecclesiastical superior of any kind: archbishop, bishop, archdeacon
overseer of the poor	principal parish officer concerned with the administration of the Poor Law, 1601-1834; overseers' duties given to the Guardians of the Poor 1834 -1928 when overseers became assessors and collectors; office abolished 1928
pannage	payment made by tenants to their lords for the right to pasture their pigs in the lord's waste or woods; the right itself
parish	civil: district for which separate rate was levied; ecclesiastical: area of ground committed to the charge of one minister, including a church
parish clerk	lay officer given minor duties connected with the parish church
parson	properly, a rector
patronage	right of appointment to an ecclesiastical living
peculiar	ecclesiastical district exempt from the jurisdiction of the bishop of the diocese
perch	or **pole**, measuring **rod** between 15 and 24 feet; statute perch = 16½ feet
pinfold	a pound for stray animals
pluralism	simultaneous holding of more than one ecclesiastical office or benefice
presentation	nomination of a clerk in holy orders by the patron to the ordinary (usually diocesan bishop)
purgatory	receptacle for ashes beneath or in front of a fire; a Swithland field name
Queen Anne's Bounty	fund established in 1704 by Queen Anne for the augmentation of the maintenance of poor clergy from her revenues from first fruits and tithes
recusants	Nonconformists, especially Roman Catholics, who declined to attend their parish church
registrar	keeper of records for the manor court
rolls	**coram rege** – records of proceedings in the court of King's Bench later than those in the curia regis rolls; **curia regis** – plea rolls (records) of the central (royal) courts of the English common law; **de banco** – plea rolls from the court of common pleas, which dealt with most of the civil cases; **assize** – records from local courts where justices were appointed by the monarch
rod	also known as a **pole** or **perch**
rood	1. one quarter of an acre, 40 square perches; 2. crucifix placed in a church over the entrance to the chancel or choir
roundhead	Parliamentarian or Puritan, so called because the hair was cut in a close circular fashion
seisin	lawful possession, the right to hold, e.g. seized of a messuage
sequestration	the act or process of legally confiscating somebody's property temporarily until a debt that person owes is paid, a dispute is settled, or a court order obeyed; in church, management of temporal responsibilities during a vacancy in a benefice

sheriff	chief officer of the Crown in each county, appointed annually, nominally entrusted with executing the laws and maintaining peace and order
sough	or **suf**, an underground channel for draining water out of a mine or quarry
surplice	loose-fitting white ecclesiastical vestment with wide sleeves
surplice fees	fees paid to Church of England clergy for occasional duties, baptisms, marriages etc.
surrogate	deputy for the commissary in the manor court
tenement	holding consisting of house and land
terrier	inventory of possessions, especially of landed property; church inventory
thirdborough	deputy constable
tithe	ancient obligation on all parishioners to maintain their parish priest from the fruits of the earth in his parish
vesica	a shape which is the intersection of two circles with the same radius, intersecting in such a way that the centre of each circle lies on the circumference of the other
virgate	measure of land, size varied from 15-60 acres depending on soil quality
warren, free	a type of warrant, franchise or privilege conveyed by the sovereign in mediaeval England to a subject, promising to hold them harmless for killing game of certain species, e.g. hare, coney, pheasant, partridge, within a stipulated area, usually a wood or small forest
waste	inferior land used commonally
yeoman	freeholder cultivating his own land

Heraldic Terms

annulet	a ring
azure	heraldic colour blue
bend	a diagonal band across the shield
bendlet	the diminutive of a **bend**
cockatrice	heraldic beast, two-legged dragon with rooster's head
engrailed	a dividing line indented along the edge with small curves
eradicated	uprooted (of plants)
gorged	encircled around neck or throat
griffin	heraldic beast with the body of a lion and the head and wings of an eagle
gueulles	heraldic colour red
masclets	lozenge or diamond
fourche	forked, usually of a lion's tail
queue	an animal's tail
lyon rampant	lion rearing up, with only one (rear) paw on the ground
fretty	interwoven design of six pieces
barres	horizontal strips
bizants	gold circles or roundels representing gold coins
chevron	inverted V, rafter shaped
molet, mullet	five pointed star
nowed	knotted, usually of a lion's tail
purpure	heraldic colour purple
sable	heraldic colour black
saltire	a diagonal or St Andrew's cross
torteau	a red roundel
label	a horizontal strip with short vertical descenders known as points, usually three, almost always occuring near the top of the shield.
vert	heraldic colour green
wyvern	heraldic beast, winged reptilian creature with dragon's head, hindquarters of a snake or lizard with two legs or none, and a barbed tail.

Bibliography

Published Sources
Acheson, Eric, *A Gentry Community: Leicestershire in the 15th Century*, Cambridge, 1992.
Ashton, Norman, *Leicestershire Water Mills*, Sycamore Press, 1977.
Aubrey, John, *The Natural History of Wiltshire*, printed by John Britton, 1847.
Anon., *Leicestershire: Historical, Biographical and Pictorial,* Alan North, London, 1909.
Bailey, Brian, *The Industrial Heritage of Britain*, Ebury Press, London, 1982.
Barber, Richard (ed.), *John Aubrey, Brief Lives*, Boydell Press, 1982.
Barnes, Alan and Renshaw, Martin, *The Life and Work of John Snetzler*, Scolar Press, 1994.
Barrett, D.W., *Life and Work among the Navvies*, London: Wells Gardner, Darton and Co., 1880.
Bateson, Mary (ed.), *Records of the Borough of Leicester, 1103–1603*, 3 vols. Cambridge, 1899–1905.
Beresford, Maurice, *The Lost Villages of England*, Lutterworth Press, 1963.
Betjeman, John, *In Praise of Churches*, John Murray, 1996.
Billson, Charles & others, *Vestiges of Paganism in Leicestershire*, Heart of Albion Press, 1994.
Boyd-Hope, G. and Sargent, A, *Railways and Rural Life – SWA Newton and the Great Central Railway,* English Heritage, 2007.
Bolam, Gordon, *Three Hundred Years 1662–1962*, Derry & Sons, Nottingham, 1962.
Boulton, James D. (ed.), *The Letters of D.H. Lawrence*, Vol. 1, 1901–13, CUP, 1979.
Burgess, Frederick, 'English Sepulchral Monuments: Swithland Slate Carvers', in *The Monumental Journal*, Vol. xxii, No.12, December 1955.
Burgess, Frederick, *English Churchyard Memorials*, Lutterworth Press, 1963.
Burgess, Walter H., *History of Loughborough Unitarian Congregation, being a chapter in the story of Loughborough nonconformity: With some account of the Old Mountsorrel Meeting House*, 1908.
Burton, William, *Description of Leicestershire*, 1622.
Capp, B.S., *The Fifth Monarchy Men*, Faber, 1972.
Chadwick, Owen, *Victorian Miniature*, Cambridge, 1991.
Chadwick, Owen *The Victorian Church,* Oxford, 1970.
Chapman, Colin R., *Ecclesiastical Courts, Their Officials and Their Records*, The King's England Press, 1992.
Clare, George E. & Ross, Walter G., *Ideal Homes for the People*, J.H. Clark & Co., Chelmsford, 1902.
Clarke, A.B., *Some Leicestershire Clandestine Marriages with index*, Leicestershire Archaeological Society, 1955.
Clarke, Benjamin, *1894, Glimpses of Ancient Hackney and Stoke Newington,* London Borough of Hackney, 1986.

Clinton, Douglas (ed.), *The Civil War in Leicestershire*, Leicestershire Museums, 1995.
Crippen, T.G. (ed.), *Transactions of the Congregational Historical Society,* Vol. 5.
Conybeare, Eliza, 'Rothley Temple in the Olden Time, 1874', Rothley History Society, *Chronicle,* 3.
Cox, J. Charles, *Notes on the churches of Derbyshire*, London, 1877.
Crosby, T., *English Baptists*, London, 1739.
Cross, Claire, *Church and People 1450–1660*, Fontana, 1976.
Curtis, J., *Topological History of the County of Leicester*, Ashby de la Zouche, 1831.
Danvers, Gary & Webster, Jane, *Memorials of the Danvers Family,* GD Press, New Zealand, 1995.
Danvers, June W. (ed), *Danvers Papers,* Leicestershire Records Office, 1984.
Danvers, Tony, *Memorials of the Swithland and Shepshed Danvers Families*, 2010.
Dare, M.P., *Charnwood Forest and its Environs*, Edgar Backus, Leicester, 1925.
Dickens, A.G., *The English Reformation*, Batsford, 1967.
Dictionary of National Biography, 1885–1900, Macmillan & Co., London.
Doran, Susan & Durston, Christopher, *Princes, Pastors and People*, Routledge, 1991.
Doubleday H.A. & de Walden H. (eds.), *The Complete Peerage*, London, 1929.
Dryden, Alice (ed.), *Memorials of Old Leicestershire*, George Allen & Sons, 1911.
Elliott, Bernard, *The History of Humphrey Perkins School*, Leicestershire, 1965.
Elliott, Bernard, *The History of Loughborough College School*, Leicestershire, 1971.
Ellis, Shirley, *A Mill on the Soar – a personal and company narrative*, privately printed and published, 1978.
Evans, George Eyre, *The Midland Churches*, Dudley, 1899.
Evans, George Eyre, *Vestiges of Protestant Dissent,* F & E Gibbons, 1897.
Evans, John, *List of Dissenting Congregations and Ministers in England and Wales 1715–29*, Dr. Williams Library, London, MS 38.4.
Evans, R.H., 'Non-conformists in Leicestershire 1669', *Leics Arch & Hist Society Transactions,* Vol. xxv.
Everard, J. Breedon, *Charnwood Forest*, Leicester, 1907.
Fairbairn, A.N. (ed.), *The Leicestershire Plan*, Heinemann, 1980.
Farnham, G.F., *Leicestershire Mediaeval Village Notes*, Leicester, 1925.
Farnham, G.F., *Charnwood Forest and its Historians,* Edgar Backus, Leicester, 1930.
Farnham, G.F., *Leicestershire Mediaeval Pedigrees*, Leicester, 1925.
Finberg, J., *Exploring Villages,* Sutton Publishing, 1958.
Firth, J., *Highways and Byways in Leicestershire*, Macmillan, 1926.
Fletcher G. Dimock, *Leicestershire Pedigrees and Royal Descents*, Clarke & Hodgson, Leicester, 1887.
Flower, John, *Views of Ancient Buildings in the Town and County of Leicester*, Leicester, 1826.
Ford, George H., *Double Measure: A study of the novels and stories of D.H. Lawrence*, Holt, Rinehart and Winston, New York, 1965.
Fox, L., *A Country Grammar School: a history of Ashby de la Zouch Grammar School through four centuries, 1567–1967,* Governors of the Foundation, 1967.
Fuggles, J.F., 'Parish Clergy in the Archdeaconry of Leicester', in *Transactions Leics. Historical Society,* Vol. 46, 1970–1.
Galsworthy, D.W & Dawber, E. Guy, *Old Cottages, Farm Houses and other Stone Buildings in the Cotswold District*, Batsford,1904.

Gardner, Ronald E., *A History of the Swithland Woods,* Leicestershire, 1998.
Gardiner, William, *Music and Friends*, Longman, London 1838.
Gilchrist R. & Olivia M., *Religious Women in Medieval East Anglia*, Centre of East Anglian Studies, University of East Anglia, 1993.
Gilchrist, R., *Gender and Material Culture: the Archaeology of Religious Women*, London, 1993.
Godfrey, J.R., *Historic Memorials of the Barton and Melbourne General Baptist Church*, London, 1891.
Gordon, Alexander (ed.), *Freedom after Ejection, A review (1690–1692) of Presbyterian and Congregational nonconformity in England and Wales*, Manchester, 1917.
Grant Uden, B.G. (ed.), *The Recipe Book 1659–1672 of Archdale Palmer, Gent. Lord of the Manor of Wanlip in the County of Leicestershire*, Sycamore Press, Wymondham, 1986.
Greaves, R.L., *Saints and Rebels*, Mercer University Press, 1985.
Greaves R.L. & Zaller R. (ed), *Biographical Dictionary of British Radicals in the 17th Century*, Vol. 1, Harvester Press, 1982.
Gwillim, Peter & Whatmore, Christopher, *Slate Engraving, Research and Design,* Leicester, 1964.
Hall, Christopher, *Society and Puritanism in Pre-Revolutionary England,* London, 1964.
Hadfield, C.N., *Charnwood Forest: A Survey*, Leicestershire County Council, 1952.
Hart, A. Tindal, The *Eighteenth Century Country Parson 1689–1830*, Wilding, 1955
Hartopp, H, *Roll of the Mayors of the Borough and Lord Mayors of the City of Leicester 1209–1935*, Leicester, 1935.
Hartopp H. (ed.), *Register of Freemen of Leicester*, Vol. 1, 1196–1770.
Harvie, C. & Matthew, H.C.G., *Nineteenth Century Britain*, OUP, 2000.
Hayward, John (ed.), *Complete Poetry and Selected Prose* [of John Donne], Bloomsbury, 1929.
Herbert, Albert, 'Swithland Slate Headstones', *Transactions*, vol. 22, Leicestershire Archaeological and Historial Society, 1943–44.
Herbert, George, *The Complete English Works*, Everyman's Library, A. Pasternak (ed.), new edition 1995.
Hollings, J.F., *The History of Leicester during the Great Civil War*, Leicester, 1840.
Horwood, A.R., 'Prehistoric Leicestershire', in *Memorials of Old Leicestershire*, Alice Dryden (ed.), George Allen & Sons, 1911.
Joseph, Ivimey, *History of the English Baptists*, London, 1814.
Jacob, W.M., *Lay People and Religion in the Early Eighteenth Century,* Cambridge. 1996.
Knight, Sheila J. & Schultka, Henrietta, *Countesthorpe: A Leicestershire Parish Before and After Enclosure*, Leicestershire Museums, 1991.
Lane, G.E., *Henry Danvers: Contender for Religious Liberty*, The Fauconberg Press, 1972.
Latham, R. & Matthews, W. (eds.), *Diary of Samuel Pepys*, Vol. 6, University of California, 1972.
Lee, Joyce & Dean, Jon, *Curiosities of Leicestershire & Rutland*, S.B. Publishing, 1995.
Leslie, Shane, *Letters of Mrs FitzHerbert*, Burns Oates, 1940.
Lloyd, P., 'The Coroners of Leicestershire in the early fourteenth century', *Transactions*, Vol. 56 Leicestershire Archaeological and Historical Society, 1980–1.

Luttrell, N., *A Brief Historical Relation of State Affairs from September 1678 to April 1714*, 6 vols., Oxford, 1857.
Macaulay, T., The *History of England*, Vol. 1, Penguin, first published 1848.
Macnamara, F.N., *Memorials of the Danvers Family*, Hardy & Page, London 1895.
Marshall, William, *The Rural Economy of the Midland Counties*, 2 vols, London, 1790.
Marshall, William, *Review and Abstract of the County Reports to the Board of Agriculture*, Great Britain, 1818.
Matthews, A.G., *Calamy Revised*, Oxford, 1934.
Matthews, A.G., *Congregational Churches of Staffordshire*, Oxford, 1924.
Matthews, A.G., *Walker Revised,* Oxford, 1948.
McFarlane, K.B., *John Wycliffe and the Beginnings of English Non-conformity*, Hodder Arnold, 1972.
McLachlan, H., *English Education under the Test Acts*, Manchester University Press, 1931.
Meadows, S.R., *Swithland*, 1965.
Mee, Wilfred E., *Quorn Baptists*, 1960, accessed at www.quornmuseum.com
Moore, A. Percival, *Leicestershire Livings in the Reign of James I*, Leicester, 1907.
Moorman, J.R.H., *Church Life in England in the Thirteenth Century*, Cambridge, 1946.
Mott, F.T., *Charnwood Forest*, W Kent and Co., 1868.
Nichols, John *The History and Antiquities of the County of Leicester*, 4 vols. in 8 parts, 1795–1812, London.
Paget, Guy, *Leicestershire*, Robert Hale, London, 1950.
Palmer, Roy, *The Folklore of Leicestershire & Rutland*, The History Press Ltd., 2002.
Patterson, A. Temple, *Radical Leicester – A History of Leicester 1780–1850*, Leicester, 1954.
Pearce, Edward, *The Great Man: Sir Robert Walpole – Scoundrel, Genius and Britain's First Prime Minister*, Jonathan Cape, 2007,
Phillimore, W.P.W. (ed.), The *Rolls of Hugh de Wells, Bishop of Lincoln, 1209–1235*, Vol. 3, Lincoln Records Society, 1912.
Potter, T.R., *The History and Antiquities of Charnwood Forest*, London, 1842.
Pounds, N.J.G., *A History of the English Parish*, Cambridge, 2000.
Pye, N. (ed.), *Leicester and its Region,* Leicester, 1972.
Ramsey, D.A., *The Leicestershire Slate Industry*, privately published, 2000.
Rose, Michael E., *The English Poor Law 1780–1930*, David & Charles, 1971.
Rouse, A.L., *The Regicides and the Puritan Revolution*, Duckworth, 1994.
Rowley, Trevor, *The High Middle Ages 1200–1550*, Routledge, Kegan & Paul, 1986.
Ruddy, Austin J., *To the Last Round: the Leics. and Rutland Home Guard 1940–45*, Breedon Books Publishing, 2007.
Sedgwick, Romney (ed.), *The House of Commons, 1715–1754*, 2 vols, HMSO, London, 1970.
Scaysbrook, P.A., *The Civil War in Leicestershire and Rutland,* Melon Publications, Oxon, 1977.
Shaw, William, *A History of The English Church 1640–1660*, Longmans, Green & Co., 1900.
Shirren, A.J., *The Chronicles of Fleetwood House*, London, 1951.
Simon, Brian (ed.), *Education in Leicestershire 1540–1940*, Humanities Press, New York, 1969.
Smeaton, Christine L., *Melon Soup and Tomato Juice*, Biograph, 2007
Snow, E.E., *A History of Leicestershire Cricket*, Edgar Backus, 1949.

Snow, E.E. (comp.), *Country House Cricket Grounds of Leicestershire and Rutland*, ACS publications, 1998.

Spanton, John, *Companion to Charnwood Forest*, Loughborough, 1858.

Spencer, J. & Spencer, T., *Leicestershire and Rutland Notes and Queries and Antiquarian Gleaner*, Vol. 3, 1895. Republished 2010 by BiblioBazaar, LLC.

Squires, Anthony & Jeeves, Michael, *Leicestershire & Rutland Woodlands*, Kairos Press, 1994.

Squires, A.E. & Humphrey, R.W., *The Medieval Parks of Charnwood Forest*, Sycamore Press, 1986

Stephen, Leslie (ed.), *Directory of National Biography*, London, 1888.

Taylor, A., *The History of the English General Baptists*, Vol. 2, London, 1818.

Temple Patterson, A., *Radical Leicester: A History of Leicester 1780–1850*, Leicester, 1954.

Thirsk, Joan (ed.), *The Agrarian History of England & Wales 1500–1640*, Cambridge, 1967.

Throsby, John, *The Memoirs of the Town and County of Leicester*, 1777.

Throsby, John, *Select Views in Leicestershire*, Leicester, 1790.

Throsby, John, *Supplementary Volume to the Leicestershire Views, containing a Series of Excursions to the Villages and Places of Note in that County*, Leicester, 1790.

Torbet, Robert G., *A History of the Baptists*, Judson Press, 1950.

Toulman, Joshua, *Protestant Dissenters*, London, 1814.

Trubshaw, Bob, *Standing Stones and Mark Stones of Leicestershire and Rutland*, Heart of Albion, 1991.

Vaisey, D. (ed), *The Diary of Thomas Turner 1754–1765*, CTR Publishing, 1994.

Victoria County History of Staffordshire.

Wallace, H. Frank, *A Highland Gathering: Being Some Leaves from a Stalker's Diary*, Eyre and Spottiswoode, London, 1932.

Walton, Izaak, *The Life of Dr John Donne*, first published 1640. Republished as *The Lives of John Donne and George Herbert*. Vol. XV, Part 2, The Harvard Classics, New York: P.F. Collier & Son, 1909–14.

Welding, J.D. (ed.), *Leicestershire in 1777: An Edition of Prior's Map of Leicestershire*, Leicestershire Museums, Arts & Record Service, 1984.

Who's Who in Leicestershire, 1935, Ebenezer Bayliss & Sons Ltd.

Wilson, Walter, *The History and Antiquities of Dissenting Churches and Meeting Houses*, 4 vols, London, from 1808.

Wix, Don & Keil, Ian, *Rawlins: The First 300 Years*, Rawlins Community College, 1992.

Woodforde, John, *The Truth about Cottages*, Routledge & Kegan Paul, 1969.

Woodward, Stephen F., *Swithland Wood: A Study of its History and Vegetation*, Leicestershire Museums, 1992.

Wykes, David L., 'Bardon Park Meeting House', in *Leics. Arch. and Hist. Soc. Transactions*, Vol. LXIV, 1990.

Index

Page numbers printed in bold type refer to illustrations.

A. H. Swain & Co. Ltd. (insurance brokers), 395
Abdy, Grace Lillian (second wife of Henry Cavendish Butler), 34, **35**, 525
Able, Edward, 186–7
About Prayer, (Godfrey F.L.), 500
Ackroyd, William (Quorn), 316
Ackworth, Reverend William (Vicar of Rothley), 386
Act of Uniformity 1662, 118, 161
Adams, Albert, 309, 429
Adams, Eliza, 309
Adams, Emily, 309, **309**
Adams, Florrie, 309
Adams, John, 64, 234, 290, 309, 317
Adams, Martha, 309
Adams, Mrs Stanley, 472
Adams, Stanley, 407, 461
Adams, Thomas, 317
Adcock, Mr, 506
Adcock, Mrs, 506
Adcock, Shelley, 501, 513, 514
Adcock, Tina, 501
Adderley, Bill, 322
Adderley, Jean, 322
Adderley, John, 197, 386
Adderley, Robert, 386
Adeliza (wife of Hugh de Grandmesnil), 2
Adkin, Elizabeth, **341**
Adkin, Ethel, 320
Adkin, James, 476
Adkin, John, **339**
Adkin, Margaret, **339**
Adnett, Alice, 309, 463, 467
Adnett, Dorothy, 336, **338**
Adnett, Eric, **338**
Adnett, Ernest, **338**
Adnett, George, 309, 463
Adnett, Thomas George, 467
Adnett, Tom, **338**
Ado Ekiti Hospital (Nigeria), 136
Agar, William (curate), 126, 587
Agnes Ferrers, Lady (of Groby Hall), 376
agricultural depression, 206–7
Ainsworth, Thomas, 67

air raid wardens, 52, 478
Aitken, George, 461
Albaster Hay, 15
Alefounder, Robert, 45
Alexander, G. E. L., 479
Alexander of Bowden (rector 1298), 113, 583
Allen, Charles Maclaren, 460
Allen, James Stanley, 341
Allen, Olive, **252**, **253**, **337**
Allen, Sally Elizabeth, 56, 63, 509, 514
Allen, William, 251, 265
allotments, 53, 485, 486
Alston, Philip (rector 1735), 57, 119, 370, 584
Alternative Service Book (1980), 520
Amicia (wife of Simon de Montfort), 3
Andrews, Keith, 512, 513, 523, 525, 538
Angel, John, 45
animal husbandry, 191, 201
Anstey Pastures, 125, 207
Appel, Fritz, 477, **477**
archaeological discoveries, 390, **391**, 544
Archdeaconry of Leicester, 42
archery, 440
Arnold, Edward (bell caster), 81
Ashby Castle, 144, 145
Ashton, Adrian, 501
Ashton, Helen, 501, 508
Ashton, John, 498
Ashton, Mrs, 506
Ashton, Simon, 501
Ashwell, George, 461
assarting, 1
assessors of taxes *see* rating assessors
Assheton, Thomas, 8
Astill, John, 386
Astills Dairy, Cropston, 287
Astills Farm, 287
Atkinson, Eric, 523, 538
Audley family, coat of arms, 76
Aylestone, 145, 149
Ayres, Joseph, 191

Babington, Elizabeth (wife of William Danvers), 12, 80
Babington, Frances (wife of Joseph Danvers), 14, 80
Babington, Matthew, 386
Babington, Thomas (1544–1610), 11
Babington, Thomas (1575–1645), 380–1
Babington, Thomas (1758–1837), 25, 47, 383–4, 385–6
Bacon, Agrilla (née Jackson), 77
Bacon, Richard, 77
Bailey, Mrs, 461
Baker, Arthur, 461
Baker, Daniel, 116, 190
Baker, G., 410
Baker, John, 190
Bakewell, Robert, 197
Ball, Nicholas, 190
Ball, William, 64
Ballards, 192
Banbury, Alfred, 491
Banbury, Faith, **339**, 491
Banbury, Harry, 52, **210**, 212, 213, 275, 418, 491, 505
Baptists, 150, 169–76
Barber, Francis (Greasley, Notts), 231
Barber, John, 8
Bardon Meeting House, 164, **164**
Bardon Park, 47, 163, 164, 167
Barebones Parliament, 13, 151
Barford, Robert, 11
Barford, Joyce, 11
Barker, John, 386
Barlow, Disney Charles, 294
Barlow, Pru (journalist), 487, 488
Barn Close, 196
Barnes, Florence, 489
Barnes, Robert, 489
Barnet, William, 286
Barnett, Geoffrey, 416
Barnett, Harold D. M., 416
Barnett, Isabel, 416, 502
Barnett, Joseph, 53, 429
Barnett, William, 196
Baron Buske Close, 190
Barons' War (1258–85), 5
Barrett, Emily, 313

Barrett, Joseph, 265
Barrett, Joseph (carter), 313, **314**
Barrett, Percy, 105, 523, 531, 532, **534**, 538, 540, 542, 546, 547
Barrow Poor Law Union, 67, 318, 326 n.62
Barrow Rural District Council, 37, 485, 486
Barrow-on-Soar, 12, 20, 26, 171, 217
Barrs, Walter, 386
Barry, Joseph (school teacher), 282, 331
Barton, Clement T., 417, 461
Barton, Maurice, 206, 304, 461, 475
Basford, Walter J., 417
Bassell Meadow, 263, 264, 265
Basset, Walter, 5
Bate, Graham Paul, 508
Bate, Harold, 499, 504, 513
Bate, L. Joy, 63
Bates, Ann, 205, 212, 313, 463
Bates, Beatrice Amy, 463
Bates, Catherine Anne, 205, 212, 265
Bates, Daniel, 56, 58, 66, 177, 201, 203, 206, 212, 292, 302, 303, 318, 428
Bates, Edith, 465
Bates, Frances, 302
Bates, John Thomas, 52, 53
Bates, Juliana, 205, 212, 265
Bates, Juliana Ann, 205, 212, 265
Bates, Mary Ann Lucy, 463
Bates, Mary Juliana, 212, 313, 463
Bates, Matthew Daykin, 63, 68, 205, 212, 313, 318, 463
Bates, Michael, 68
Bates, Miss, 467
Bates, Reverend A. N. (Humberstone), 249
Bates, Thomas, 55, 56, 58, 89–90, 203, 205, 212, 265, 386, 428
Bates, William (d. 1832), 177, 201, 202, 212, 265
Bates, William James (1840–96) 56, 58, 68, 205, 212, **312**, 312,313
Bates, William James jnr. (1870–1945) 68, 463
Battie, Richard (rector 1653), 118, 583
Baum, A. John, 292
Baum, George, 292
Baum, Harold, 310, 312
Baum family, 278, 292
family tree, 310
Baxter, Charles Edward, 213, 298
Baxter, Elizabeth, 320
Baxter, Richard (writer), 153, 163
Beachell, John, 56, 58, 298, 507, 511, 512, 525
Beachell, Mrs, 505
Beal, Mrs, 461
Beasley, John, 234
Beaton, Carolyn (head teacher), 345, 346

Beaumont, Mary, 193
Beaumont, Robert, Earl of Leicester, 3
family tree, 4
Bedingfield, Edward, 154
Beeby, Annie Elizabeth, 466
Beeby, Brian, 211, 271, 275
Beeby, Janet, 522, **534**, 547
Beeby, Laura, **534**, 547
Beeby, Norman, 275
Beeby, William, 466
Beers, Mary, 336
Beers, Thomas, 56, 98, 279
Bellamy, Peter, 230
bell-ringing, 459–60, 480, 487, 488, 494, 499, 500, 502, 511–12, 523, 532–4, **534**, 535–6, 540, 547
Belvoir Castle, 144, 145
Bennet, John, 191, 230, 231
Bennett, Arthur Henry, 393, 414
Bennett, John, 393
Bennion, Charles, 222, 404
Benson, Audrey, 105
Benson, Roy, 105
Bentley, Percival Arthur, 396
Bentley, William, 396
Bentley Manufacturing Company, 396
Beresford, 416
Berridge, Barbara, 287
Berridge, I. L, 52, 53, 213, 476, 482
Berridge, Peter, 287
Berry, William Henry, 53, 56
Beston, Elizabeth, 433
Beston, Thomas, 234
Bettoney, John (Oadby), 241
Biddle, Edward, 109
Biddle, Henry, 109
Biddle, Robert (Mountsorrel), 109, 382
Biddles, Elizabeth, 109
Biddles, Margaret, 109
Biddles, Robert, 109
Biddles, Thomas, 109, 386
Birchenall, Alan, 284
Birchy, Richard de (rector 1356), 113, 581
Bird Hill, 460
Birkhead, John, 45
Birstall, 118, 119
Bishop, Frederica Emma (wife of George John Butler Danvers), 29, **29**, 93
Bishop, William, 198
Black Annis' Bower (melodrama), 376
Black Spinney, 269
Blackbourn, Mr and Mrs, 306
Blackbrook Reservoir, 248
blacksmiths, 286
Blackwell, J. (headmistress), **334**, 335, 346
Blakwing, Jane, 193
will, 578
Blanchmains *see* Robert 'Blanchmains,' Earl of Leicester

Blankley, Francis, 147–8
Blankley, Joseph (Kimboulton), 193
Blankley, William, 148
Blinman, Richard (dissenter), 153
Bloomfield, Sarah, 67
Bloxham, Winnie, **338**, 339
Blue Bell Public House (Mountsorrel), 28
Bluebell Service, 223–4, **224**, 470–1, 494, 502, 529–30, 538
Bluebird Guild, 322, 449, 455, 457, 516
Bocock, Georgiana, 514
Bocock, Julie, 514
Boddy, Reverend Alexander, 410
Boddy, James Alexander Vazeille, 104, 410
Bodle, Anne, 78
Bodle, Thomas, 77, 78
Boley, Elizabeth (Mountsorrel), 193
Boley, Thomas (Mountsorrel), 193
Bolley, Henry, 190
Bolter, George, 56
Bone, Arthur, 461, 465, 466, 470
Bone, Barbara Wellington, 466
Bone, Minnie Laura, 466
bonfire night, 504, 522
Book of Common Prayer, 76, 143, 148, 160, 161, 518
Bosse, Michael, 192
Bossu *see* Robert 'le Bossu,' Earl of Leicester
Bostock, Joseph, 201
Bostock, Mary, 67
Botterill, George, **455**, 466
Botterill, John, **338**
Boughton, A., 491
Boulter, Arthur Everard Leigh, 474
Boulton, Mrs, 505
boundary stones, 220
Bowers, P. H. (Archdeacon of Loughborough), 208, 296
Bowes-Lyon, H. M., 287
Bowler, John, 282, 283, 298
Boyden, Tom, 206, 304, 512
Boyer, Charles, 181, 317, 318
Bradgate Lodge, 234
see also Hallgates
Bradgate Park, 3, 34, 144, 155, 219, 221–2, 229, 404
Bradgate Park Trust, 222
Bradgate Woods Ltd, 414
Braginton, Ellen (teacher), 405
Bramley, Ann, 109, 382
Bramley, Elizabeth, 178
Bramley, Thomas, 234
Bramley, William, 178, 234, 236
Brand, Edwards & Branson (architects), 404
Brand, Kate *see* Watkins, Dorothy Kate (second wife of Charles John Brinsley Butler)
Brand, The, 131, 229, 236, 239, 324, 435

Brand Hill, 230, 231, 234, 235, 443
Brand Road, 233–4
Branston, Jane, 193
Braunston, Henry, 193, 195, 196
Braunston, Jane, 193, 312
Braunston, John, 193, 196
Braunston, William, 193, 195, 196, 312
Braunston family tree, 311
Braunstone's Lane, 196
Bream, Mary, 342
Brewin, Reverend R., 180
Brex, Catherine, 67
Brex, Thomas, 67
brick making, 382–3, 387
Brickyard Farm, 208, 387, 410, 414, 418, 451, 475
Briers, Daphne, 306
Briers, Eric, 284
Briers, Gillian, 491
Briers, Grahame, 306
Briers, Mrs, 476
Briers, Samuel, 52, **210**, 284, **285**, 460, 476, 497
Brieryshaw, 461
Briesley, Thomas (Mountsorrel), 263
Brigman, Elizabeth, 187
Brinsley, John, Lord Newtown Butler, 336
British Hosiery Trust, 415–16
British Pentecostal Movement, 410
British Thread Mills, 415
British United Shoe Machinery Company, 404
Broad Hill quarry, 219, 387, 418
Broken Heart, The (drama), 376
Brook, Mr and Mrs, 298
Brook, Mrs, 513
Brook Farm, 203, 282–3, 300
Brook House, 127, 179
Brookby, Joseph, 317
Brooke-Hunt, Godfrey Leveson, 319
Brooke-Hunt, Olive, 324, 516
Brookfield Farm, 418
Brookhouse, Elizabeth, 67, 178
Brookhouse, Thomas, 17, 317
Brookhouse, William, 67, 178, 289, 317
Brookhouse, William Jnr., 67
Brook-Lawson, E. D. P. (Trish), 63, 308, **308**, 504, 505
Brook-Lawson, Michael, 504
Brooksby, Abel (rector 1700), 44, 45, 57, 78, 79, 119, 584
Brooksby, Alice, 78, 79, 119
Brooksby, Dorothy, 299
Brooksby, Thomas, 299
Broome Croft Close, 189
Brown, Ann, 433
Brown, Ann (b. 1805), 434
Brown, Anne (b. 1818), 434
Brown, Catherine, 67
Brown, Cedric, 312

Brown, Claude, 404
Brown, Daniel (b. 1804), 433
Brown, Daniel (b. 1808), 433
Brown, David, 494
Brown, Diana (b. 1809), 433
Brown, Dorothy, 290
Brown, Eleanor, 194
Brown, Eliza (b. 1811), 434
Brown, Elizabeth (b. 1803), 433
Brown, Elizabeth (b. 1815), 434
Brown, George, 317, 332, 434, 464
Brown, Gertrude, 404
Brown, Henry (b. 1823), 317, 434
Brown, Isaac (b.1827), 434
Brown, James, 434
Brown, Jane, 67
Brown, Jane (b. 1811), 433
Brown, Jane (b. 1826), 434
Brown, Joan, 312
Brown, John (b. 1795), 433
Brown, Mary (b. 1809), 434
Brown, Michael, 494
Brown, Paul (journalist), 486–7
Brown, Ray, 494, 502, 505
Brown, Samuel (b. 1773), 434
Brown, Samuel (b. 1798), 433
Brown, Samuel (b. 1806), 434
Brown, Sarah, 318, 434
Brown, Sarah (b. 1806), 433
Brown, Thomas, 67
Brown, Thomas (b. 1790), 433
Brown, William (.b.1769), 433–4
Brown, William (.b.1793), 433
Brown, William (d. 1802), 433
Browne, Richard, 45
Browne, Robert, 189–90
Browne Barsell Meadow, 190
Brownes Wharleys Close, 189
Brownhill Crescent (Rothley), 412, 417
No. 7, Anmer (Kenmare), 394
No. 11, 414
Browns Hey, 192
Bruxby, Francis (rector 1814), 57, 120, 584
Bruxby, Thomas, 178
Bryan, Debbie, 513
Bryan, Mrs, 477, 513
Bryan, Sheila (head mistress), 343, 344, **344**, 346, 487, 523, 538
Buckley, William, 272
Buddon Wood, 12, 15–16, 20, 147, 217–19, **218**, 360, 380
Bull, Rev C. R., 503
Bunney, A. E., 64
Bunney, Alwyn, 64, 68, 287, **289**, 464
Bunney, Ann, 67
Bunney, Annie (daughter of John), 464, 467
Bunney, Annie Violetta, 319, 463,
Bunney, Annie Maria (wife of Sid), 289, 466, 467, 487, 516, 518
Bunney, Barbara, **339**

Bunney, Beatrice M., **228**, **318**, 319, **338**, 435, 458, 491, 492, 493, **493**, 548
Bunney, Charles, 68, 130, 179, 180, 212, 287, 434, 435
Bunney, Charles Benjamin (Ben), 52, **210**, 212, 213, 292, 497
Bunney, Clara, 287
Bunney, David, 434
Bunney, Dorothy, 465
Bunney, Edith Evelyn, 320, 458, 463, 491
Bunney, Edward, 317, 434
Bunney, Elizabeth, 434
Bunney, Elizabeth (wife of Charles), 434
Bunney, Elizabeth (wife of William Jnr.), 434, 435
Bunney, Ellen (wife of Ben), 292, 435, 466, 476
Bunney, Emma (wife of Samuel), 287, 292, 429, 434, 435, 458, 463
Bunney, Ethel May, **318**
Bunney, Fred, 64, 289, 318, **431**, 434, 435, 463
Bunney, Fred Jnr., **431**
Bunney, George, 67, 234, 289, 317, 434, 435
Bunney, Gwendoline, 435
Bunney, Harriet, 299, 434, 435
Bunney, Henry, 289, 317, 332, 434
Bunney, Hilda May, 463
Bunney, James, 299, 317, 434, 435
Bunney, Jane (wife of George), 67, 289, 434, 435, 464
Bunney Jane (wife of Joe), 290, 464
Bunney, Jemima, 299
Bunney, John, 68, 212, 213, 435
Bunney, John (of Rothley Plain), 386
Bunney, Johnson, 463
Bunney, Joseph, 299,
Bunney, Joseph (son of Walter), 69, **298**, **431**, 435, 455, 460, 463
Bunney, Kathleen, 336
Bunney, Les, **453**, **455**
Bunney, Letitia, 289
Bunney, Louisa, 435
Bunney, Martha, 298, 434
Bunney, Mary (wife of Henry), 289, 434
Bunney, Mary (daughter of Sid), **338**, 458
Bunney, Mary Ann (wife of Walter), 435, 463
Bunney, Maurice, 339, 491
Bunney, May, **338**, 464
Bunney, Michael, 201
Bunney, Michael (architect), 402, 412
Bunney, Mrs C. B., 476
Bunney, Samuel, 53, 64, 68, 131, **288**, **289**, 292, 429, 434
Bunney, Samuel (son of Charles), 434, 435

Bunney, Samuel (son of Samuel), 67, 234, 240, 298
Bunney, Sarah (née Baum), 434
Bunney, Sarah Ann, 463
Bunney, Sarah Elizabeth, 289, 332
Bunney, Sarah (wife of Fred), 434, 435, 463
Bunney, Sid, 213, 289, 430, 435, 491, 499, 506, 526
Bunney, Walter, 53, 64, 234, 289, 298, 434, 435, 463
Bunney, William, 200, 201
Bunney, William (husband of Martha), 66, 67, 234, 298, 317, 434, 435
Bunney, William Jnr (husband of Elizabeth), 279, 429, 434, 435
Bunney, William (son of Henry), 289
Bunney family, 424, 434
Bunneys Closes, 292
Bunyan, John (writer), 145, 153
Burbage, Thomas, 386
Burbidge, Maria, 386
Burchnell, Richard, 202, 212, 265
Burford, Samuel Francis, 404
Burgess, Charles, 318
Burgoyne, Bessie, 466
burials, 77, 105–8, **106**
Burrage, Barbara, 476
Burrage, Robert, 476
Burrows, Alfred, 363, 365
Burrows, John, 45
Burrows, Kathleen, 363
Burrows, Kathlyn, 363
Burrows, Kitty, 224, 538
Burrows, Louie (Quorn), 347, 363–5, **365**
Burrows, Nicholas, 290
Burton, Elizabeth, 67
Burton, Frances Matilda, 308
Burton, Mrs G. M., 476
Burton, Henry, 67, 234, 292, 317, 321, 324
Burton, James, 67
Burton, John, 67, 178
Burton, Joseph, 67
Burton, Kezia, 67
Burton, Mary, 67, 321, 324
Burton, Rachel, 67
Burton, Sydney, 417
Burton, Victor, 396
Burton, William, 74, 76, 381
Bury, Judith Letitia, 15–16, 218
bus services, 432–3
Busby, William, 218
Buswell, Jeanette, 514
Buswell, Derek, 499
Buswell & Mawby (leather mercers), 414
Butchnell, Joseph (Leicester), 241
Butler, Brian Danvers, 132, 296, 438, 439, 445

Butler, Brinsley, 1st Viscount Lanesborough, 22
Butler, Brinsley, 2nd Earl of Lanesborough, 22–3
Butler, Charles John Brinsley, 7th Earl of Lanesborough, 31–4, **33**, **34**, 51, 52, 101–2, 107, 207, 208, 294, 295, **451**, 460, 465, 471
Butler, Denis Anthony Brian, 9th Earl of Lanesborough, 35–8, **36**, **37**, 51–2, 81, 108, 210–11, 255, 485, 486, 487, 513, 538–9
Butler, Eileen Gladys, 32
Butler, Frances Arabella *see* Fremantle, Frances Arabella (wife of George John Butler Danvers)
Butler, Francis, 21–2
Butler, Francis Almeric, **451**
Butler, Freda (daughter of Henry Cavendish Butler), **452**
Butler, Frederica Emma *see* Bishop, Frederica Emma (wife of George John Butler Danvers)
Butler, Georgina Ione, 108, 480, 480–1
Butler, Harriet Eliza Danvers, 125
Butler, Henry Cavendish, 8th Earl of Lanesborough, 34–5, **35**, 51, 52, 107, **452**, 480
Butler, Humphrey, 1st Earl of Lanesborough, 22
Butler, John Brinsley, 32
Butler, John Vansittart Danvers, 6th Earl of Lanesborough, 29–31, **30**, **31**, 97–8, 107, 125, 129, 207, 248–9, 313, 388, 437–8
Butler, Letitia Rudyerd Ross, 125
Butler, Moyra Elizabeth, 32
Butler, Robert Herbert, 3rd Earl of Lanesborough, 29
Butler, Sir Stephen, 21
Butler family, 21–3
Butler Danvers, Augustus Richard, 21, 23–6, 29, 66, 86, 108, 197, 199, 201, 212, 220, 267, 275, 385
Butler Danvers, George John, 5th Earl of Lanesborough, 24, 26–9, **27**, 86–7, 92–3, 94, 107, 123, 202, 203, 236, 267, 268, 316
landholdings on Rothley Plain, 386
village school, 282, 331
Butterley, Mrs, 505
Buxton, Derek (priest in charge, Woodhouse), 542
Bybrooke Farm, 207, 210, 211, 213, 287, 340, 434
list of occupiers, 212
Byford, Hazel, Baroness, 529, **533**
Byford, C. B., 54
Byfords (hosiery company), 416
Byspham, William, 8

Callis, Edward (Woodhouse), 230
Calmont, Robert de (rector 1360), 114
Campbell, Henry (rector 1841), 124, 584
camping, 225–6, **225**, **226**, 442–3, **443**, 459
canals, 229, 235, 239
Capewell, Edward, **533**
Capewell, Tom, **533**
Capewell, Val, **534**, 535, 547
Cardale, George (curate), 119, 370, 586
Carlile, Edward Wilson (rector 1973), 137–8, 286, 487, 514, 519, 526–7, 528, 538, 586
Carlo, Yvonne de (film star), 35–6, **36**, 41 n.116, 482
Carnall, Ian, 498, 501, 502, 505, 524
carol singing, 504
Carpenter, A., 491
Carpenter, Anne, 536
Carpenter, David, **280**, 491, 536
Carpenter, Jim, 64, 279, **280**, 478, 479, 498
Carr, Maurice, 487, 497, 498, 504
Carr, Mrs, 504
Carr, Mrs (Three Oaks) 477
Carr Close, 8
carriers, 432
Carroll, Lewis (author), 124
Carter (widow), 317
Carter, Peter, 8
Carter, William, 316, 318
Case, Elizabeth, 193
Case, Thomas, 45
Castledine, Thomas, 386
Cattail (Cattel) Piece, 193
Cedars, The (Cropston), 365
censuses, 31, 125, 178, 200, 423, 423–7
Chambers, Andrew, 461
Chambers, Arthur, 461
Chantrell, Fred, **210**, 212, 213
Chapman, David, 27–8, 66, 200, 201, 212, 273, 275
Chapman, Thomas, 284, 285
charities, 109–10
Charles, John, 429
Charles, William, 241
Charles I, 14, 143, 144, 146, 347, 349, 353
Charles II, 13, 155, 161, 353, **354**
Charley (priory), 112
Charley Knoll, 382
Charnia Grove, 258, 277, 536
Charnwood Archery and Lawn Tennis Club, 33, 35
Charnwood Children's Home, 513
Charnwood Forest, 25, 47–8, 112, 123, 186, 384
Charnwood Forest: a survey (Hadfield), 370

Charnwood Forest and its Environs (Dare), 370
Charnwood Forest Archery and Lawn Tennis Society, 440
Charnwood Forest Croquet Club, 438–9
Charnwood Forest (Everard), 369
Charnwood Forest Lawn Tennis Club, 440
Charnwood Preparatory School, 401, 405–6, **405**, **406**
Chaucer, Geoffrey (poet), 43
Chaveney, Henry, 218
Chell, Lisa, 514
Cheveney, Peter, 147, 218
Cheyne Walk, Chelsea, 14, **15**, 18
child labour, 429
Childers, Major, 439
Chippendale, John, 45
Chorlton, Mrs, 476
Christian Aid, 500, 529
Christmas, 456–8, 504
church courts, 42–3, 45
Church Green, 192
church memorials
  Boddy, James Alexander Vazeille, 104
  Brooksby, Abel (rector), 78–9
  Butler, Denis Anthony Brian, 9th Earl of Lanesborough, 38
  Butler Danvers, George John, 5th Earl of Lanesborough, 87
  Danvers, Francis (1561–1631), 76–7
  Danvers, John (1723–96), 85–6, 355–6
  Danvers family, 79–80, 82–4, 91, 100, 103
  Fremantle, Frances Arabella (wife of George John Butler Danvers), 87
  hatchments, 91–3
  Heygate family, 89
  Jackson family, 77–8
  Mackay, John (Rector), 104
  Murray-Dixon, James (rector 1884), 104, 135
  Osborne, Robert Brian, 105
  Pollard, Benjamin (at Quorn), 176
  Presbyterians, 77, 159–60
  Raworth family, 78
  Scot, Agnes, 74–5, **75**, 91, 103, 347–8, 374, 376–7
  Treweeke, George (rector), 90
  Turner, Archibald, 104, 322
Church Missionary Society, 136, 495–6, 513, 530
Church of England
  Diocesan Synod, 54, 516
  General Synod, 54, 515, 528
  ordination of women, 531
  proposed union with Methodist Church, 500

Church of England Assembly (Powers) Act, 462, 463, 467
Church of England Children's Society, 529
Church of England Men's Society, 137, 500, 503–4
church rates, 57, 58
churches, building of, 47–8
churchwardens, 55–60, 69
Civil War *see* English Civil War
Clarcke, Robert, 75
Clare, George E. (architect), 399, 402–3, 404, 405, 406–7, 408, 414
Clare & Ross, 402
Clare & Scott (architects), 403
Clarendon Code, 161
Clark, George Ronald, 56, 499, 504
Clark, Martha, 317
Clark, Mrs R., 502
Clark, Reuben, 45
Clark, Stephen (school teacher), 61, 282, 332
Clark, Thomas, 282, 283
Clarke, Ann, 171
Clarke, Ann Elizabeth Dixon (wife of John Vansittart Danvers Butler), 30
Clarke, Elizabeth, 193
Clarke, James, 317
Clarke, James (butcher), 317
Clarke, John, 193, 195, 196, 197, 315
Clarke, John (school teacher), 282, 331
Clarke, John Snr., 317
Clarke, Samuel, 282, 315, 316
Clarke, Stephen, 193, 300, 315, 317
Clarke, Stephen (head teacher), 346, 430
Clarke, William, 193, 200, 207, 233, 234, 284, 315, 388
Clarke, William (b.1756), 315, 316, 317
Clarke family, 107
  family tree, 316
Clifford, Hugh Rowntree, 63
Clifford, Sue Rowntree, 512
Clifford, Tony Rowntree, 512
Clore, Charles (financier), 396
Clore's Sear Holdings, 396
Close, Reverend William, M. A., 45
Clowes, Charles, 265
Clowes, George, 290, 318
Cock, Ward, 359
Cockerill, A. W., 212, 301
Cockerill, Mary Ann, 212, 213, 301
Coke, Isabel, 9
Coke, John (son of Sir John Coke), 146
Coke, Richard, 9
Coke, Sir John, 9, 13, 117, 146–7, 188
Coleman, Cecil R., 394
Coleman, John, 45

Coley, Nicola, 322
Coley, Roy, 322
Collected Poems (Lawrence), 364
Collins, Michael, 504, 506
Collins, Samuel, 45
Collis, Sidney Mark, 296, 445
Coltman, Anne (journalist), 487
Committee for Plundered Ministers 1642, 117
Common Worship, 521
Communist Manifesto, The, 397
Comyn, Alexander, Earl of Buchan, 4
Comyn, Elizabeth (wife of Alexander Comyn), 4
Comyn, Lord, of Whitwick, 376
convalescence, 443
Conventicle Act 1664, 161
Conybeare, Eliza (née Rose), 122
Cook, Albert, 56, 58, 98, 272, 464, 468
Cook, Annie, 272
Cook, Anthony, 491
Cook, Charles Herbert, 466, 489
Cook, Eliza, 466
Cook, Olive, 489
Cook, Robin, 342
Cook, Walter Reed, 404
Cook, William, 271, 272
Cook, William Bowman, 271–2
Cook family tree, 271
Cooke (Coke), Anne, 80
Cooke, Lewis Ganoys, 382
Cook's Plantation, 269
Cooledge, John, 284
Coote, Nina (croquet player), 438
Cope, Brigadier-General Sir Thomas, 478
Copley, Mrs, 513
Copson, A., 491, 499, 505
Copson, Alfred Ernest, 208, 213, 299, 417, 450, 466, 494, 523
Copson, Ambrose, 64, 68, 131, 208, 212, 273, 275, **275**, 294, 299, 360, 418, 450, 452, 464
Copson, Ben, 522
Copson, Charles, 208, 410, 414, 450, 450–1, **451**, 475
Copson, Cynthia, 491, **493**
Copson, Denis, **338**, 499
Copson, Dorothy, 339
Copson, Edith, 208, 299, 466
Copson, Elsie, **338**, 458
Copson, Fred, 64, **210**, 451, **451**, 454
Copson, Harry, 63, 208, **210**, 306, **431**, 450, 451, 452, 454, 464
Copson, Jane, **493**
Copson, Jean, 336, **338**
Copson, Joan, 306
Copson, John Ambrose (Jack), 306, **306**, 336, 337, **338**, 450, 451–2, 454, 455, 478, 491, 498, 503–4, 505, 513
Copson, John Charles, 336

Copson, L., 491
Copson, Leonard, **339**, 360
Copson, Leslie, **338**, 451, 458
Copson, Mrs M. J., 213
Copson, Mary, 452, 454, 464
Copson, May, 458
Copson, Michael, 494
Copson, Molly, **338**
Copson, Mrs A., 467
Copson, Mrs C., 505
Copson, Mrs F., 476
Copson, Mrs J., 476
Copson, Nigel, **341**, **493**, 498
Copson, Pat. D., 63, 451
Copson, Roger, 342, 491, **493**, 498
Copson, Rosemarie, **275**, 493, **493**
Copson, Sally, 481, 491, **493**, 494, 501
Copson, Sheila, **341**, 501, 504, 506
Copson, Simon, 501
Copson, Vera, 208, 306, 450, 458, 464
Copson family, 482 n.6
    family tree, 209
Copt Oak, 48, 380
Corahs (factory), 393, 394
Corbin, Mr and Mrs R. H., 505, 508
Corn Close, 263, 264, 265
Corporation Act 1661, 161
Cossington, 26
Cotes, 144–5
council housing, 489, **489**
County Questions Quiz, 535
Cox, Ann (Quorn), 357
Cox, Mrs, 476
Coy, Michael, 382
Coy, Peter, 382
Cradock, Norrice, 45
Cramp, John, 464
Cramp, Lavinia, 464
Cranage, Jayne, 54
Cranmer, Thomas (archbishop), 75
Cresswell, Joseph, 279
Creswell's Close, 283
cricket, 30, 33, 430–2, **431**, 437, 455
Crisps Close, 194
Crompton, Walter, 45
Cromwell, Oliver (Lord Protector), 13, 145, 150, 151, 155, 160
Crooks, Joseph, 301
Cropston, 197
Cropston Hall, 363
Cropston Leys Farm, 15
Cropston Reservoir, 240, 248, 273
Cropston Road, 476
croquet, 438–9
Croquet Association Gazette, 438
Cross Lane, 385
    Wantoma, 476
Crosseby, Roger (rector 1405), 114, 583
Crow Wood, 269
Cufflin, William, 386
Cuffling, David, 212, 275
Cuffling, Emma (daughter of Mary Ann), 204, 446

Cuffling, Fanny, **204**, 301, 332
Cuffling, John, 203, 212, 272, 301
Cuffling, Jonathan, 204
Cuffling, Joseph, 387
Cuffling, Mary Ann (née Dakin), 203, **203**, 212, 275, 446
Cuffling, William, 56, 58, 89–90, 130, 178–9, 203, 212, 273, 275, 332
Cuffling, William Henry, 52, 203–4, **204**, 212, 272, 275, 429
Cuffling family, 273, **274**
    family tree, 204
Cupit, Robert William, 464
curates, 124–5
Curd, Jean, 140, 509, 533, **534**, 544–5, 547
Curiosities of Leicestershire and Rutland (Lee and Dean), 368–9
Curzon, Colonel M., 438
Cutler, Norman, 509
Cutler, Pam, 509, 535

Daft, George, 230
Dale Walk, 269
Dalton, James (organist), 524
Dandridge, Bartholomew (artist), **17**
Daniell, Isabel (first wife of Henry Cavendish Butler), 34
Dann, Thomas, 272
Danvers, Ann (wife of Henry Danvers), 152–3
Danvers, Charles (of Dauntry 1568–1601), 349–50
Danvers, Charles William (of Shepshed), 99–100, 104
Danvers, Dame Frances (d. 1759), 92, 368
Danvers, Elizabeth (1639–69), 12, 84
Danvers, Elizabeth (wife of William Danvers), 83, 146, 155
Danvers, Elizabeth (wife of Samuel Danvers), 14, 80, 155, 191
Danvers, Frances (1722–24), 80
Danvers, Frances (1730–40), 80
Danvers, Francis (1561–1631), 11–12, 74, 76, 190, 218, 220, 369
    will, 554–5
Danvers, Francis (1683–97), 80
Danvers, Francis (c.1508–35), 9
Danvers, Francis (d. 1697), 77
Danvers, Henry, Earl of Danby (1573–1644), 350–1
Danvers, Henry (1622–87), 13, 17, 80, 150–5, 221
Danvers, Henry (d. 1759), 84
Danvers, John, 8
Danvers, John (of Rothley 1530–1598), 9, 186–7, 188
    will, 553–4
Danvers, John (of Chelsea and Oxford 1588–1655), 347, 351–5, **353**

Danvers, John (1723–96), 17, 18–21, 24, 80–2, 85–6, 232–3, 284, 355–6, 370, 459
    Land Tax assessments 1773, 197
    landholdings, 191, 193, 194, 195, 196, 212, 218, 220, 221, 275
    will, 574–5
Danvers, John, of Prescott (d. 1721), 91, 157, 355
    will, 556–68
Danvers, John (son of Thomas), 9
Danvers, John Watson (d. 1768), 84
Danvers, Joseph (1686–1753), 13, 14–17, **17**, 38, 77, 91–2, 119, 355
    alterations to church, 79–80, 369
    landholdings, 191, 193, 195–6, 218, 315
    school, 329–31
    tomb of, 107, 241–2, **242**, 368–70
    will, 330, 568–73
Danvers, Joseph (d.1756), 84
Danvers, Magdalen *see* Herbert, Magdalen
Danvers, Mary, 21–2, 23, 24–5, 27
    will, 575–6
Danvers, Patrick, 480, 484 n.52
Danvers, Samuel (d. 1693), 14, 77, 80, 148, 155
    will, 555–6
Danvers, Susannah, 84
Danvers, Thomas, 9
Danvers, Tony, **71**, 235 n.32
Danvers, William (1591–1656), 12–13, 63, 76, 79–80, 117, 146, 147, 149–50, 187, 188, 190, 191, 192, 218, 221
Danvers, William (of Shepshed 1666–1740), 27
Danvers, William (d.1762), 84
Danvers family, 349
    family tree, 9, 28, 350, 680, 681
    memorial, 82–4
Danvers' Woods, 220–1
Darby, Joseph, 45
Dare, M. Paul, 368–9, 370
Dauntsey, Elizabeth, 352
Davenport, Jean, 491
Davenport, Margery, 465
David Wilson Estates, 418–19
Davie, Peter, 476
Davies, Alfred, 395, 461
Davies, J., 498
Davies, Mrs, 504
Davies, Peter, 501
Davy, R., 501
Dawber, E. Guy (architect), 402, 404, **404**
Dawson, Alice, 187
Dawson, Elizabeth, 382–3
Dawson, John, 197, 382–3
Dawson, Lady Mary Harriet (wife of Henry David Erskine), 121, 122

Dawson, Mary, 383
Dawson-Damer, Minnie, 122
Deacon, Betty, 309
Deacon, Cyril, 309
Deacon, John, 67
Deakin, Christine, 514
Deakin, Rachel, 514
Delaforce, Stephen Robert (curate), 587
Dexter, Edward, 66, 201, 203, 272, 301, 428
Dexter, Evelyn (teacher), 342, 343
Dexter, Mary Ann, 301
Dickinson, John (curate), 119
Dicks, Mr, 408
Dimblebee, Richard, 284
Dimmock, Steve, 417
Dingley, Mr and Mrs, 497
Directory for the Worship of God in the Three Kingdoms, 148, 160
Dishley Grange, 197
Dixon, Henry Edward Otto Murray, 98, 286, 296, 347, 359–63, 360, 361, 362, 445
Dixon, James Murray (rector 1884) *see* Murray-Dixon, James (rector)
Dixon, Major, 63
Dixon, Margaret, **224**, 514
Dixon, Mr and Mrs, 491
Dixon, Sarah, 512
Dixon, Winifred (headmistress), 213, 340, **341**, 342, 346, 477
Dobson, Peter, **534**, 535, 547
Doddridge, Philip (hymn-writer), 167, 168
Dodsworth, John, 230
Dodworth, John, 381
Domesday Survey, 2, 141 n.1, 217, 380, 384
Donisthorpe, Frederick, 394
Donisthorpe, Joseph (Baptist minister), 170
Donisthorpe's (dyers), 394
Donne, John (poet), 347, 356
Dorrell, Stephen M. P., 542
Doughty, Joseph, 293, 428
Dransfield, Joseph, 52, 56, 58, 81, 137, 469, 472–3, 473–4, 490–1, 499, 502
Driver, Charles, 279
Du Pré, William (croquet player), 439
Dudley, John, 286
Dudley, Rev. John, 386
Dulson, Yvonne, 320
Dulwich, Bartholomew (rector 1446), 115
Dunelm Mill, 322
Dunham Linns, 221
Durham, Bernard, 56, **59**

Eagleston, E. J., 100

East Goscote court, 377, 380
Eastwood, Joseph, 461
Eatough, James, 407
Eatough's Ltd (shoe manufacturers), 407
Eayre, Joseph (bell caster), 81, 82
Ecclesiastical census 1851, 125
Eden, Anthony, 478
Eden, Michael (rector 1499), 115
Edenbrow, Elsie, 181, 489
Edenbrow, Harold, 489
education *see* schools
Edward II, 6–7, 381
Edward III, 113
Edward VI, 75, 115
Eggleston, Ann, 301
Eggleston, Elizabeth, 301
Egglestone, Wally, 501, 506
Elastic Mills, Leicester, 100, 108
electoral roll lists, 463–7
Elizabeth I, 350
Elizabeth II
  coronation, 482
  Silver Jubilee, 512
Elliott, Rev. John, 527–8
Ellis, Alfred, 125
Ellis, Herbert, 207
Ellis, Hilda, 494
Ellis, John, 239, 240
Ellis, Olive Margaret, 319–20
Ellis, Shirley, 394
Ellis, Vesty, **431**
Ellway, A., 499
Elson, Sydney, 105
Emerson, William, 282, 283
enclosures, 25, 47, 108, 119–20, 123, 187, 188–9, 191, 197–202, **199**, 264, 315
  Rothley Plain, 383–6, **384**
Engels, Friedrich (political theorist), 397
English Bible, 75–6
English Civil War, 12, 13, 117, 143–57, 190
En-Tout-Cas (sports tracks manufacturers), 404
Erdington, Thomas, 218
Erin Cortref, 475
Erskine, Anne, 124
Erskine, Henry David (rector 1817), 44, 45, 57, 121–4, **123**, 278, 584
Essex, Earl of, 350
evacuees, 339–40, 476–7
Evans, Amelia, 313
Everard, Bettyne Ione (wife of Denis Anthony Brian Butler), 35, 480–1
Everard, Breedon, 369
Everards (brewers), 285
Exlands Field, 185, 194
Exning Farm, 203, 210, 211, 213, 288, 292, 428, 435, 476, 497
  list of occupiers, 212

Eyre, Matthew, 169, 184 n.44, 243, 245
F. Hewitt & Son Ltd. (publishers of *Leicester Mercury*), 417
Fairey family, **226**
family trees
  Bates, 205
  Baum, 310
  Beaumont, 4
  Braunston, 311
  Butler, 22, 682, 683
  Clarke, 316
  Coke, 147, 152
  Cook, 271
  Copson, 209
  Cuffling, 204
  Danvers, 9, 28, 350, 680, 681
  Gilbert, 194
  Hemsley, 303
  Hind, 238
  Hodges, 62
  Hood, 164
  Kendall, 10
  Leatherland, 305
  Matthews, 164
  Morris, 299
  Pollard, 244
  Pratt, 300
  Prior, 357
  Quincy, de, 4
  Raynor, 290
  Shepey, 10
  Smalley, 264
  Wakerley, 297
  Walcote, 8
  Waleys, 5
  Ward, 282
Far Brick Kiln Close, 387
Farnham, Edward, 148
Farnham, Henry, 382
Farnham, Stephen, 8
Farnham, W. E. J. B., 248
Fawcett, Norman, 395
Fay, Sylvia, 476
Feasey, William, 284
Fenn, William, 476
Ferneley, Charles, 196
Ferrers, Elizabeth, 376
Ferrers, Henry, 7, 229
Ferrers, Margaret (wife of William Ferrers), 3, 4
Ferrers, Ralph, 7
Ferrers, William, Earl of Derby, 3, 5
Ferrers family, 74
  coat of arms, 76
feudal system, 2
Fewkes, Esther, 67
Fewkes, Miss, 505
Field, The, 361
field names, **189**
Fielding Johnson Hospital, 407
Fielding Johnson, Thomas, 407
Fielding Johnson, Thomas Paget, 407, 460

Fifth Monarchists, 150–1
First World War, 444–6
Firth, William, 234
Fisher, John (Cossington), 195, 263, 264
Fishers, Messrs (solicitors), 109
Fitzparnel, Robert, Earl of Leicester, 3, 110 n.5
Five Mile Act 1665, 161
5–10 Club, 535, 546
Fletcher, Henry, 194
Flower, John (artist), **27**, 41 n.97, 268
Folkingham, Nicholas, 45
football, 432
Forest End, 207
Forest End Cottages, 315–19
Forest End Farm, 58, 202, 203, 205, **205**, 210, 211, 213, 308, 312–13, 340, **427**, 428, 463, 465, 498
list of occupiers, 212
Forest Green, 192
Fosbrooke, Thomas Henry (architect), 391, 395, 403
Foster, George, 45
Foster, Mrs, 476
Foster, William, 45
Fowkes, Richard, 19, 26, 212, 265, 383, 386
Fox, William, 45
Fox Close, 192, 196
fox hunting, 34
Frank Newman & Son (land agents), 208, 210, **210**, 270
Frecknell, Charles, 318–19
Freestone, D., 63
Fremantle, Frances Arabella (wife of George John Butler Danvers), 26, 87, 92, 331
Freshwater, Don, 547
Friar's Tale, The (Chaucer), 43
Frisby, Adeline, 464
Frisby, Adeline Elizabeth, 464
Frisby, Geoffrey (curate), 133, 587
Frisby, John, 68
Frisby, Joseph, 284, 464, 467
Frisby, Miss, 467
Frisby, Mrs, 467
Frisby, William, 335
Frith, George, 64, 289
Frith, Hannah, 289
From the Cradle to the Grave (church pageant), 490–1, **490**, **492**
Frost, Charles, 408, 461
Frost, Robert Dashwood, 481

Gallops, The, 418–19
Galloway, John Bruce (land agent), 414
Gamble, Ernest, 491, 493
Gamble, Sarah, 308, 428
Gamble, William Haywood, 308, **309**, 428

gamekeepers, 279, 458–9
garden cities, 397–8
gardener's house, 210
Gardiner, William (of Leicester), 18, 82, 284
Garendon
 abbot, 114
 monastery, 186, 187
Garendon Park, 478
Garland, Fred, 477–8
Garner, Archibald Chamberlain, 395
Garton, Jo, 293, 513
Garton, Willoughby, 52, 293, 499, 512, 513, 522, 523, **534**, 535, 536, 538, 547
Gazy, Samuel, 318
Geary, Gordon, 540, 547
Gee, Captain R., 208, 295–6
Gee, Cecil George Gorham, 393, 407, 461, 473, 476
Gee, Harry Simpson, 393, 412
Gee, Percy, 393
Gentleman's Magazine, 359
George Oliver (Footwear), 405
ghosts, 371–74, 540
Gibbs, Edwin, 309
Gibbs, Hannah, 309
Gibs, William (rector 1525), 115
Gibson, Dr. T. Maitland, 417
Gibson, Norman E. V., 336
Gilbert, Arthur, 189, 192, 194
Gilbert, Edmonde, 380–1
Gilbert, Elizabeth, 189
Gilbert, Henry, 166
 will, 579
Gilbert, John, 196
Gilbert, Robert, 56, 163, 194, 196, 315
 will 1749, 262
Gilbert, William, 194
Gilbert family, 107
Gilberts Close, 189
Gill, Abraham, 239
Gillis, Georges (Belgian refugee), 340, 477
Gimson, Alice W., 467
Gimson, Ben, 272, 413, **413**, 469
Gimson, Benjamin, 412
Gimson, Ernest (architect), 412
Gimson, Fawcett and Kilby, 476
Gimson, Gweneth Mary, 35, 56, 58, **59**, **60**, 104, 110, 272, 459, 472, 491, 493, 502, 505, 505–6, 514, 527, 528, 529, 539
 see also Kilby, Gweneth
Gimson, Harry, 412
Gimson, Harry Hay, 412, 416, 461, 466, 467
Gimson, Josiah, 412
Gimson, Mrs H., 472
Gimson, Thomas, 196
Gimson, William, 222
Gipsy Lane, 385, 502
Girl Guides, 514

Gladwin, Peter, 476
glebe land, 120–1, 125, 130–1, 186, 191, 196, 202, 207, 208
Glover, Edwin, 336
Glover, John, **338**
Glover, Kathleen, **338**
Glover, Lewis, **338**
Godbald, George, 332
Godbald, Mary Ann, 332
Godbald, Mary J., 317
Goddard, Eleanor, 387
Goddard, G. H., 461
Goddard, Owen, 461
Goddard, Thomas Ward (curate), 126, 587
Godfrey, Frederick Lindesay, 136, 138, 312, **323**, 492, 498, 500, 507, 520, 525, 527, 528, 587
Godfrey, Lois, 54, 515, 529
 see also Turner, Lois Mary Gladys
Godfrey, Patrick, 476
Godley, S. B., 63
Golf Club, 460
Goodall, George, 317
Goodman, Henry, 272, 273
Goscote Hundred Court, 380
Gourlay, Carol, 501, 513
Grace, William (rector of Rearsby), 163
Grace Dieu Manor, 122
Grace Dieu Priory, 376
Granary, The, 498, 520
Grandmesnil, Hugh de, 2, 110 n.2, 112
Grandmesnil, Ivo de, 2, 3
Grandmesnil, Petronella de, 3, 4
Grantham, Lady Lucy, 117–18
gravestones, 106–7, **106**, 229, 240–1, **243**
Gray, Anne, 522
Greasley, Ann, 67
Greasley, William, 67
Great Central Railway, 31, 37, 207, 253–5, **254**, **255**, 257, 388, 432, 539
Great Linns North, 221
Great Linns South, 221
Great Meeting (Unitarian) Chapel, Leicester, 168, 182
Great Northern Railway, 254
Great Pit, 236, 239, 240
Great Slate Quarry, **223**
Green, Brian, **338**
Green, J. T., 476
Green, William, 52, 335, 337, 460
Gregory, Eleanor, 428
Gregory, Ernest, 476
Gregory, John, 320
Gregory, Mrs, 503
Gregory, Olga, 491, 495, 518
Gregory, Sheila, 491, 495
Grey, Edward, 376
Grey, Henry, 1st Earl of Stamford, 144

Grey, Henry, Marquis of Dorset, 187
Grey, Katherine Henrietta Venezia, 221, 222
Grey, Lord, of Groby, 380–1
Grieve, Peter, 277
Griffin, Paschal, 535, 540
Griffin, Pat, 535
Griffin Inn, 58, 203, 208, **210**, 283–5, **283**, 423, 428, 429, 432, 455, 460, 476, 487, 497, 498–9, 504, 513, 522
Grimley, John (Baptist minister), 170
Groby, 2, 3, 4
    manor, 186, 187, 191, 192, 220, 272, 380, 381
    quarry, 231, 236, 239, 240
    Swanimote Court, 380, 381, 419 n.4
Groby Hall, 376
Groby Peculiar Court, 42–8, 118, 119
Groves, Midge, 508
Grundy, Jonathan, 196
Grundy, Mrs Jonathan, 197
Grundy, Nicholas, 160, 182 n.1
Grundy, William, 160, 182 n.1
Guide Dogs for the Blind Association (Leicestershire), 37
Guildford, Henry (miller), 272
Gynsills House, 125, 130

Hackett, John, 230, 231
Hackett, Nicholas, 309
Hadfield, C. N., 370
Haggar, Henry (Baptist minister), 150
Hague, Stuart, 506
Haines, Freda, 491
Haines, John, 491
Hales, Thomas, 66, 200, 201
Hall, David, **341**
Hall, Dorathie, 106, 240
Hall, Dr., 498
Hall, Elizabeth, 382
Hall, James, 287
Hall, John, 197
Hall, Joseph, 382
Hall, Marjorie, 287
Hall, Nathaniel, 197
Hall, Rebecca, 382
Hall Farm, 8, 28, 41 n.97, 58, 130, 131, 179, 197, 200, 201, 202–4, 208, 210, 211, 213, 258, 273, 275, 360, 428, 450, 464
    barns, 276
    illustrations, **274**, **275**
    life on the farm, 452, 454
    list of occupiers, 212, 275
Hallam, Ralph, 275
Hallgate Farm, 222
Hallgate Wood, 220
Hallgates, 5, 15, 26, 235
Halstead Road, 418
Hames, Harry, 394
Hammond, Herbert, 461, 466, 505

Hammond, Ian, 491, 506
Hampson, John, 317
Hancock, Harry, 417
Hancock, Mary, **224**
Handley, George, 279, 297
Handley, Gladys, 300
Handley, Joseph, 300
Handley, Keith, 491
Handley, Margaret, 491
Hanford, Albert William, 395, 404, 461
Hanford, Freda Mary, 415
Hanford, Miss, 461
Hanford & Miller (hosiers), 404
Hannibal, L., 499
Hannibal, Sally Christine, 508
Hansford, Olive, 464
Harby, 58
Harcourt, Cecil Copp (rector 1956), 52, 137, 286, 474, 491, 493–4, 495, 585
Harding & Barnett (solicitors), 416
Harding & Williams (architects), 415
Hardwicke, Alan, 104–5
Hardwicke, Margaret, 522
Hardwicke, Timothy, 522
Hardy, Joseph (carrier), 432
Hardy, Samuel, 201, 272
Hardy, Thomas (novelist), 440–1
Hargreaves, Rev. F. C., 479
Harratt, Dinah, 319
Harrington, Barbara (teacher), **344**, 522–3, 538
Harrington, Simon, 509
Harris, George, 56, 203, 212, 284
Harris, John H., 461
Harris, Mrs Buddug, 505
Harris, Olga M. F., 63, 531
Harris, Dr. Waldron (Bill), 56, 58, 138, 505, 506, 508, 515–16, 518, 588
Harrison, B, 324
Harrison, Gordon, 491
Harrison, Hilda, 292, 465
Harrison, J. Stockdale (architect), 391, 396
Harrison, Jeff, 513, 527, 529, 547
Harrison, Joan, **338**, 340
Harrison, John E., 461
Harrison, Joseph, 292
Harrison, Lilian, 290, 292, 499
Harrison, Max, 63
Harrison, Mr (air raid warden), 52
Harrison, Mr and Mrs H. M., 213
Harrison, Mrs R., 491
Harrison, Ralph S., 213, 290, 292, **338**, 491
Harrison, Rosemary, 491
Harrison, William (rector 1458), 115
Harrop, Edna, 406
Harrop, Winifred, 406
Hartopp, Sir Edward, 145, 146–7, 152
Hartridge, James Stanley, 415

harvest suppers, 506–7
Harvey, Peter, 319
Harvey, Robert (solicitor), 391–2
Harwood, Benjamin, 387
Hastings, Henry, 144, 145
Hastings, William, Earl of Huntingdon, 218
Hawcliffe Hill (Mountsorrel), 387, 388
hawking, 116
Haynes, Lynn, **341**
Haynes, Sheila, **339**
Hays Close, 307
Hazelrig, Sir Arthur, 143
Heafford, William, 241
health, 333–4
health treatments, 13
Hearst, Ada, 291, 497
Hearst, Roger, 291, 497
hearth tax, 148, 152
    returns, 260–2, 278, 306
Heath, Frederick, 365
Heath, Mr, 460
Heatherill, James, 461
Heatherill, Margaret Scott, 466
Hebb, Arthur, 190
Hebb, William (rector 1516), 115, 583
Heighton, Gladys, 309
Heighton, Joseph, 309
Hemp Pit Hill, 123, 125
Hemsley, Alice, 458, 476
Hemsley, B., 410
Hemsley, Benjamin, 202, 203, 206, 212, 302–3, 303, 332
Hemsley, Benjamin Jnr., 64, **302**
Hemsley, Eliza, **302**
Hemsley, Jemima, 303
Hemsley, John, 64
Hemsley, Joseph (d. 1828), 239
Hemsley, Joseph, 302, 303, 317
Hemsley, William, 53, 64, 68, 206, 212, 302, 303, 332, 333
Hemsley family, **221**, 293, 302–3
    family tree, 303
Henry (priest c. 1371), 114
Henry, Colonel T., 438
Henry, Sir Edward Richard, 222
Henry I, 3
Henry III, 3, 5
Henry VIII, 75, 115, 187
Herbert, Adeline, 409, 410, 515
Herbert, Albert, 78, 98–9, 101, 102, 104, **108**, 409–10, 466, 470
Herbert, Dorothy, 410
Herbert, Edna Minnie, 466
Herbert, George (poet), 347, 351–2, 356–7
Herbert, Magdalen, 347, 351, 352, 356–7
Herbert, Mrs, 472
Herbert, Shirley, 513
Heron, William, 67

Herrick, John, 45
Herrick, John (poet), 374–6
Herrick, Sir William, 11
Herrick, Thomas Bainbrigge (Beaumanor), 236
Herrick, William, 236, 382
Herrick, William Perry, 387
Hewitt, Grace, 352, 353, **354**, 355
Hews, Alice, 382
Hews, George, 382
Hews, Robert, 191
Heygate, Captain W., 438, 440, 444
Heygate, Frederick William, 87, 89
Heygate, James, 26, 87
Heygate, Lady Isabella, 87, 89, 430
Heygate, William, 87, 89
Heyward, William, 45
Hickling, Alison, **341**
Hickling, William, 388
Hickling's Field, 417, 418
Highways and Byways in Leicestershire (Firth), 370
Hill, Ann, 67
Hill, John, 212, 265
Hill, Samuel, 286
Hill, Thomas, 67, 234, 317, 318, 456
Hillsborough, 461
Hilton, Joseph Arthur, 404
Hilton, Stephen, 404
Hinckley, priory of, 113
Hind, Henrietta Maria Louisa, 107, 237, **237**, 365–6
Hind, Henry, 176, 191, 306
Hind, Henry (d.1732), 230, 230–1, 234
Hind, Henry (1691–1773), 234
Hind, Henry (1726–1801), 191, 232–3, 234, 284, 307
Hind, Henry (1760–1820), 234, 235–6, 307
Hind, Henry (1786–1822), 236, 237
Hind, Henry (of Ibstock Manor 1814–66), 236
Hind, John (1802–80), 237
Hind, John (b. 1694), 241
Hind, Robert (husband of Alice), 192, 230, 306
Hind, Robert, 56
Hind, Robert (b. 1697) 241
Hind, Robert (1735–1812), 191
Hind, Sarah Jane, 107, 109–10, 237, **237**, 365–6
Hind, Sarah (of Ibstock Manor), 236
Hind, Stephen, 230, 231
Hind, Thomas, 192, 230
Hind, Thomas (b.1762), 191
Hind, William (b. 1788), 56, 57, 202, 236, 239, 307
Hind family, 107, 230–3, 236–7, **237**, 238, 239, 241, 260
Hind Leys High School, 343
Hind Sisters Homes, 109–10, 237, 347, 365–6

Hinde, Robert, 189
Hinde, Thomas (Houghton-on-the-Hill), 315
Hitch, William, 230
Hobey, John, 381
Hodge, Anne, 317
Hodges, Eliza, 62, 289
Hodges, Eliza Ann, 332
Hodges, Eliza (daughter of Thomas Hodges), 332
Hodges, Elizabeth, 56, 464, 467, 468
Hodges, John, 64, 297, 299, **431**
Hodges, John Henry, 297, 429
Hodges, Matthew, 61, 62, 178
Hodges, Sarah Jane, 297, **298**, 299, 429, 432, 464
Hodges, Thomas, 61, 62, 289–90, 298, 332
Hodgkiss, Mrs (teacher), 343
Hodkinson, Charles, 413
Hoggett, C. Francis, 461
Holden, Amy (teacher), 340, 342
Holliday, Leonard, **339**
Hollocks, Kenneth, 476
Hollocks, Vera, 476
Holloway, Louise, 523
Holly Croft, 213, 305–6, 476, 498
 see also Hollycroft Dairy
Hollycroft Dairy, 208, 451, 454, 481 n.7
Holton, Misses, 461
Holyoak, Edward John, 396
Holywell Haw, 376
Home Guard, 478–9
Hood, Christian, 159, 162–3
Hood, John (of Bardon Park), 167
Hood, Sarah (wife of Michael Matthews), 162
Hooley, Joseph, 43, 45
Hopkins, Herbert, 461
Horner, Ann, 67
Horner, Frederick William (curate), 126
Horner, Thomas, 67
Hornsby, Bernard, 296, 445
Hornsby, Ivy Annie Elsie, 445, 464, 467
Hornsby, Jane, 299–300, 464
Hornsby, John, 299–300
Hornsby, Mr and Mrs J., 290
Horsewood Leys Close, 189, 192
Horton, Anne (rector 2000), **59**, 139–40, **139**, **224**, **228**, 527, **533**, **534**, 535, 535–6, 547, **547**, 586
hosiery industry, 200–1, 396, 412
Hosking, Mr and Mrs, 298
Hoult, Ethel, 336
Hoult, Ethel Martha, 464
Hoult, Geoff, **338**
Hoult, Hannah, 308, 309
Hoult, James, 308, 309, 317
Hoult, Kathleen, 458, 464
Hoult, Mrs, 54, 467

Hoult, Pat, **338**
Hoult, S. W. T., 476
Hoult, Samuel, 52, 64, 68, **210**, 212, 301, 464, 467
Hoult, Thirlby, 336
House Close *see* Kinchley Hill Close
housing, 233–4, 262–3
housing development, 388–9, 391–6, 486
Houston, Catherine Alice, 404–5
Houston, Keyworth, 404–5
Howard, Alan, 476
Howard, Sir Ebenezer, 397
Howden, Mrs (Cropston), 476
Howes, Robert, 196
Howlett, Bill, 299
Howlett, Pam, 299, 529
Howson, Edith, 302
Howson, William, 206, 212, 302, 303
Huband, Richard, 8
Hubbard, Albert, 213, 289, 435
Hubbard, Cissy, 458
Hubbard, Elizabeth, 289, 465
Hubbard, Mr, (roadman), 69
Hubbard, Mr, 181
Hubbard, Mrs, 181
Hudson, Michael (rector 1567), 115, 583
Hull, Samuel (Loughborough), 245
Hulse, Mrs, 491
Humphrey Perkins Grammar School, 341
Hunt, Ada, 277, 499
Hunt, David, 208, 210, **210**, 213, 277, 476, 499
Hunt, David Jnr., 499, 538
Hunt, George, 404
Hunt, Janet, 499, 538
Hunt, William, 242–3, **243**
Hunt, William Robinson, 461
Huntingdon, Francis, Earl of, 357, 359
Huntley, Annie, 301
Huntley, Elizabeth (school teacher), 301, 346
Hutchinson, Lucy, 143
Hutchinson, William, 317
Hyman, Eric, 417
Hyman, Harry, 414, 417, 475
Hyman, J. L., 417
Hyman, Kenneth, 476
Hyman, Neville, **339**
Hyman, William, 388
Hynd, John (1540–95), 230
Hynde, John (1576–1641), 230

Ideal Homes for the People (Clare and Ross), 403
Illesley, Charles, 225, 279, 459
Illustrated Chronicle, 487
Illustrated Sporting and Dramatic News, 360–1
Ilminston, Peter de (rector 1278), 113

Imperial Typewriter Co. Ltd., 414
Ind, Elsie, 367 n.33, 464
Instruments of the Passion (church pageant), 492
Ironside, Alfred Allen, 393, 396, 404

J. Hardy Smith & Sons (leather suppliers), 415
Jackson, George, 387
Jackson, Johanna, 77
Jackson, Mary, 67
Jackson, Thomas (rector 1676), 77, 78, 118, 583
James, Elizabeth, 433
James, Vivienne A. (head teacher), 344, 346
James I, 350
James II, 22, 154, 155, 356
Jane Cox (box manufacturers), 417
Jarret, John (Mountsorrel), 189
Jebb, Sheilagh (missionary), 495–6
Jeffcoat, William, 279
Jefferat, Sarah, 428
Jefferson, Norman, 284
Jelley, Robert, 476
Jesson, Richard, 197
Jeyes, Mrs, 513
Joel, M. A., 127, 179
John (chaplain 1377), 114
John (King of England), 3
John, Les, 417
John Richardson & Co. Ltd. (pharmaceutical company), 394
Johnson, Ann, 171, 173–4
Johnson, Cecilia, 306
Johnson, Edward, 171, 191, 197
Johnson, Gerald Hugh Robert, 395, 461
Johnson, Harriet, 306
Johnson, John, 61
Johnson, John Jnr (Beaumanor), 212, 265
Johnson, John (slate cleaver), 234
Johnson, Joseph (Nottingham), 191
Johnson, Maria, 428
Johnson, Mary, 171
Johnson, Sarah, 67
Johnson, Thomas, 61, 234, 279, 290
Johnson, Trevor, 546
Johnson, William, 171, 173–4, 176, 235, 236, 315–16, 321
Johnson, William Jnr., 171, 173
Jones, G., 491
Jones, Gareth, 287
Jones, Harriet, 287
Jordan, Frances May, 467
Joscelyne, Frederic Henry, 408–9, 515
Joyce, Valerie, 140
Judd, Sir Andrew, 187
Julian of Norwich (anchoress), 74

Keates, Angela, 306
Keates, Duncan, 306
Keeper's Close, 258, 279
Keeper's Cottage, 279, **279**, **280**, 281, 325 n.2, **431**, 433, 435, 458, 497
Keepers Lodge, 210
Kelly's Directory, 429, 432
Kendall, Bartholomew, 10
Kendall, Henry (d. 1627), 11, 189–90, 194, 195, 230, 263
Kendall, Henry (son of Henry Kendall), 190, 218
Kendall, Katherine, 11
Kendall, Margaret, 10
Kendall, William, 11
Ketton, Reverend Howard, **224**
Kibart, Arthur, 461
Kilby, Cedric, 412, 430, 480, 481, **481**
Kilby, Frank, 413
Kilby, Gweneth, 135, 413, **413**, 469–70, **469**, 471, 479–80
  see also Gimson, Gweneth Mary
Kilby, Mary Elizabeth, 56, 59, 104, 110, 412–13, 466, 468–70, **469**, 491, 494, 499, 505
Kilby, Walter, 56, 58–9, 104, 110, 137, 223, 412–13, 461, 465, 466, 468–70, **469**, 472, 474, 495
Kimes, William (rector 1663), 118, 583
Kinchley Hill Close, 264, 265
Kinchley Hill Farm, 58, 195–6, 198, 202, 203, 205, 212, 249, 251, 263–6, **265**, 381, 428, 538
  list of occupiers, 265
Kinchley Hill Lane *see* Kinchley Lane
Kinchley House, 415, 418, 459, 461
Kinchley Lane, 385, 387
  Erin Cortref, 475
Kinder, Peter, 319
Kinder, Sandra, 319
Kingston, Edmund, 9, 188
Kingston, Margaret, 9
Kingston, Ralph, 9
Kinsley Hill Close, 190
Kinsley Hill Farm *see* Kinchley Hill Farm, 203
Kinsley Hill Road *see* Kinchley Lane
Kirby, Richard, 67
Kirby Muxloe castle, 229
Kirke, Richard, 190
Knight, Edward, 382
Knight, Richard, 382
Knox, William, 279

Labrom, Christine Anne, 508
Lady Land, 192, 230, 306
Lakin, John, 190, 201, 284
Lancaster, Duke of, 7
land leases, 191
Land Tax assessments 1773, 197, 215 n.79
Lane, Arthur, 225, 226

Lane, C. B., 476
Lane, Harold, 461
Lane, Mrs (headmistress), 335
Lane, Pamela, 476
Lane Hey wood, 192
Lanesborough, Earldom of, 26, 29, 38
  tombs, Swithland churchyard, **38**
Lanesborough Cricket Team, 437
Langley & Baines (architects, 402
Langstaffe, Nicholas (Burley, Rutland), 193
Langton, Joseph, 405, 461
Lantern Cross, **19**, **27**, 269, 270–1
Lapham, Susan, 501
Latham, Michael, M. P., 542
Latham, Wendy, 504, 506
Launde Abbey, 394, 498, 509
Lawrence, D. H. (novelist), 347, 363–5
Lawrence, Trish, 522
lay subsidy rolls, 259–60
Layne, Gertrude Conway (headmistress), 346
Le Fevre's shop, 460
Lead, David, **395**
Lead, Edith, 393, 396
Lead, William Henry, 393, 395–6, **395**, 414, 461
Lead William, **395**
Leake, H. Elizabeth, 466
Leake, Isaac, 203
Leake, William, 200, 201, 212
Learke Lane, 192
Leatherland, Ada, **303**, 476, 477
Leatherland, Ann, 501
Leatherland, Joan, 303, 304, **304**, 319, 491
Leatherland, John, 135, 206, **206**, 208, 212, 213, 303, **303**, **453**, **455**, 459, 460, 478, 494
Leatherland, John Jnr, **37**, 135, 206, **206**, 212, 295, 303, 304, **304**, 319, **339**, 460, 477, 478, 480, 491
Lee, Brenda (film star), 36
Lee, Elizabeth, 45–6
Lee, Gary, 140
Lee, William, 46
Leech, Mr, 407
Leeson, J. R., 479
Leeson, Mary, 412
Leicester, Siege of 1645, 145
Leicester Advertiser, 239–40, 487
Leicester and Leicestershire Historic Churches Preservation Trust, 530
  cycle ride, 532, **533**
Leicester and Leicestershire Proprietary School, 122
Leicester and Nottingham Journal, 233
Leicester Castle, 229, 374
Leicester Chronicle, 96, 374

Leicester Corporation, 207, 248, 273
Leicester Corporation Waterworks Act 1890, 249
Leicester Diocesan Board of Patronage, 109
Leicester Fever Hospital, 122
Leicester Footpaths Association, 130
Leicester Guildhall, 229, 391
Leicester Journal, 218–19, 221, 235, 387
Leicester Journal and Midland Counties Advertiser, 236
Leicester Mercury, 100–1, 102, 368, 369, 417
Leicester Museum, 360, 389
Leicester Navigation Canal, 235
Leicester Opera House, 403
Leicester Rotary Club, 222, 223, 240, 412
Leicester Royal Infirmary, 407
Leicester Unitarians, 407
Leicester Waterworks Company, 248
Leicestershire Caravan Mission to Village Children, 440, 443–4, **443**
Leicestershire County Council, 213, 219
Leicestershire County Cricket Club, 30, 33
Leicestershire Oral History Archive, 337, 450, 451, 451–2, 454
Leicestershire Scouts Council, 35
Leicestershire Yeomanry, 35, **36**
Leicestershire Yeomanry OCA (Old Comrades Association), 478
leisure activities, 429–32, 435–6, 455–6
Lethbridge, Christine (head teacher), 345, 346
Levet, Thomas, 45
library, Swithland village, 29, 429–30
Liddle, Phyllis, 320
Lidster, Canon Percy, 527
Life of George Herbert (Walton), 357
Lillingston, Captain, 438
Lines, Joe, **453**, **455**, 466
Lines, Thomas, 234
Link, The, 495, 496, 498, 500, 507–11, 515, 518, 521, 522–3, 524, 525–6, 527–8, 529, 531, 536, 537, 538, 539, 540, 544
Lint Close, 193
Lintern Ball, Andrew, 138, 537
Lintern Ball, Margaret, 524, 537
Lisle, Ambrose March Phillips de, 122
Little Barsell Meadow, 190
Little Close *see* Little Rough Close
Little Linns Wood *see* Little Lyns Spring Wood
Little Lyns Spring Wood, 192, 220
Little Moore Wood, 192
Little Rough Close, 263, 264, 265

Little Wharleys, 189
Liverpool, Lord, 120
Lloyd, Dorothy, **338**, 458
Lloyd, Emily May, 458
Lloyd, Emma, 459
Lloyd, Fred, **431**, **453**, 458, 465, 491
Lloyd, Fred (father of Percival George Lloyd), 458
Lloyd, George, **453**, 458–9, 465
Lloyd, Gladys, **338**, 458
Lloyd, Hannah (née King), 458, 464, 467
Lloyd, Herbert, 458
Lloyd, Mary, 459
Lloyd, Mr, 505
Lloyd, Mrs, 503
Lloyd, Patricia, **339**
Lloyd, Peggy, 287–8, 459, 460, 476
Lloyd, Percival George, 54, 56, 58, 137, 223, 279, **280**, 458, 464, 467
Lloyd, Percival William (Bill), 287–8, 440, **453**, 458, 459, 460, 466
Lloyd, Peter, **339**, 459
Lloyd, Phyllis, 459, 489, 491
Lloyd, Rodney, 430, 459, 491
Lloyd, Roy, **338**, **453**, 458, 459
Lloyd, Sherrin (née Rutter), 459
Lloyd, Ted, 337, **338**, **453**, 458, 459, 489, 491
Lloyd, Violet, 458, 460, 464, 467
Llwyd, John (rector 1761), 57, 86, 119–20, 196, 197, 200, 202, 584
Llwyd, Mary, 86
Local Defence Volunteers *see* Home Guard
Lockley, Harold, 528
Lockwood, Joseph, 387
Lodge Farm (Rothley), 388
Lollards, 114–15
London and North Western Railway, 254
Long, Henry (Wiltshire), 349–50
Long Cliff Hill, 388
Long Meadow *see* Wood Meadow
Longhurst, John (curate), 126, 278, 586
Longlands Farm, 58, 202, 203, 210, 211, 213, 284, 300–2, **301**, 432, 459
 list of occupiers, 212
Longmore, D. D., 287
Lord Chancellor, 108–9, 125
LOROS, 529, 530
Loseby, Thomas William, 52
Loughborough, 144
 Baptists, 170–1, 174, 175
 Methodist circuit, 178–80
Loughborough Dispensary, 122
Loughborough Echo, 371, 457–8
Loughborough Endowed Schools, 341
Loughborough Junior Technical School, 336–7

Loughborough Monitor and News, 437
Lovatt, George, 286
Lovett, Ann, 47
Lovett, Henry, 56, 230, 231, 284
Lovett, John, 56, 230, 231
Lowe, G., 523
Lowe, Jean, 476
Lowe, William, 52, 56, 58, 387, 388
Lower Green, 105, 108, 524
Lucas, Geoffry (architect), 402
Ludd, Ned, 201
Luddites, 201
Ludyard, William, 45
Lumley, John, 287, 513, 535
Lumley, Margery, 287
Luther, Martin (reformer), 75
Lutterworth, 10, 11, 114
Lynch, Mandy, 522
Lynes, Charles (head teacher), 61–2, 332, 346
Lynes, Charles W., 332
Lynes, Harriet A., 332
Lynes, Mary H., 332

Macaulay, Thomas (historian), 155
Mackay, Archdeacon John (rector 1931), 52, 53, 104, 136, 286, 430, 471, 472, 473, 495, 585
Magna Carta, 3
Main Street, Swithland cottages, 29
 No. 1, The Cottage, 99, 208, 236, 287, 321–4, **321**, 422, 449, 463, 464, 465, 476, 489
 No. 24 Wood Lane End Cottage, 319–20, **320**, 422
 No. 34–54, Forest End Cottages, **314**, 315–19, **319**, 433, 434
 No. 54, Pollard (Forest) House, 213, 313–14, **313**, **314**, 316, 429, 430, 442, 476
 No. 60, *see* Forest End Farm
 No. 62, 312
 No. 66, 498
 No. 67, Mole End Cottage, 478, 497
 No. 71, 497
 No. 75, 497
 No. 77, 497
 No. 78, The White House, 207, 234, 236, 260, 306–8, **307**, 331, 476, 504
 No. 81, Penny Cottage, 29, 308, 309, 310
 No. 82, 498
 No. 83, Cherry Tree Cottage, 29, 213, 308–10, **310**, 512
 No. 89, 512
 No. 91–101, 489
 No. 96, 498
 No. 99, 501
 No. 100, 498

No. 101, 459
No. 102, 498
No. 103, 512
No. 104, Holly Croft (Hollycroft), 210, 305–6, **305**, 451, 454, 476, 482 n.7, 498
No. 105, 512
No. 106, *see* Pit Close Farm
No. 107, 512
No. 109, 512
No. 110–12, *see* Longlands Farm
No. 111, 512
No. 113, 512
No. 118, Long Close, 213, 282, 283, 300
No. 120, Gladys Cottage, 299–300, **299**, 435, 445
No. 122, Corner Cottage, 213, 299, 482 n.7, 485
No. 123–125, Post Office Cottages, 29, 213, **296**, 297–8
No. 124 Pit Close Cottage, 292–3, **293**, 302, 435, 498, 513
No. 126, Troutbeck House, 498, 536
No. 127 Lanesborough Cottage, 213, **296**, 297–8, 434, 435
No. 128–130, *see* Exning Farm
No. 129, 497
No. 131, 497
No. 132, 29, 213, 292
No. 134, 29, 213, 292, 434, 435
No. 135, 497
No. 136, 210, 213, 289–90, 460, 485
No. 137, 290–1, **291**, 497
No. 138, 213, 290, 445, 485
No. 140–142, 29, 210, 213, 289, **291**, 434, 435
No. 141, 497
No. 143, 497
No. 144, Thatched Cottage, 29, 287–8, **288**, 434, 435, 476
No. 146, Langton House, 29, 287, **288**, 476
No. 152, 497
No. 153, Elmleah, 497, **497**, 522
No. 154, 497
No. 155, 536
No. 157, The Rectory (1993), 535, 536, **536**
No. 159, 536
No. 160, Rose Cottage, 213, 285–6, **285**
No. 173, Tower House, 494
No. 173–81, 486, 497
No. 178, 497
No. 180, 497
No. 188, The Woodyard, 536, **537**
No. 217, Hall Gardens, 210, 213, 277, **277**, 465, 499, 536
No. 250, North Lodge, 271–2, **271**
Mainline Steam Trust *see* Great Central Railway

Manchester, Sheffield and Lincolnshire Railway, 207, 253, 255, 388, 390
Maniac of Dane Hills, The (melodrama), 376
Mann, William (architect), 402, 405
Manners, Lord William, 16
Manners, Thomas, Earl of Rutland, 187
Manor House (Hall Farm), 522, 529
manorial courts, 5, 20, 42, 50, 380
manorial rights, 4–9
Mansfield, J. S., 386
Mapilton, John, 8
Maplehurst, 460, 479
Maplewell Road (Woodhouse Eaves), 479
Mapplewell, 231
March, Mrs, 505
Mareschal, John, 7
Marriages (Commonwealth), 149
Marriott, Pamela, **339**
Marsden, Miss (teacher), 405
Marshall, Audrey, **339**
Marshall, Christopher (rector 1506), 115
    will, 576–7
Marshall, Janet, **339**
Marshall, S., 410
Martin, Charles, 418, 461
Martin, Charles Hamilton, 478, 479
Martin, John, 387
Martin, Rev. Robert, 120
Martin, R. F., 131, 229, 240
Martin, Robert, 45
Martin, William, 235–6, 387
Martin, William Francis, 435–6
Martindale, Rosemary, **341**
Marx, Karl (political theorist), 397
Mary I, 115
Mason, Peter William Henry, 56
Mason, Thomas, 187
Mason Plan 1967, 343
Matthews, Anne, 167–8
Matthews, Elizabeth, 433
Matthews, Reverend Michael, 77, 103, 159–60, **160**, 161, 162–9, 328
    will, 579–80
Matthews, Sarah (wife of Michael Matthews), 163, 168
Matthews, Thomas, 163
Matts, John, 313
Matts, Joseph, 56, 58, 307, 313, **314**, 430, 434
Matts, William, 45
Mawby, Frederick, 414
Maxwell, Grace, 502
Maxwell, Harold Alexander (rector 1959), 137, 286, 495, 499, 500, 503–4, 507, 526, 585
May, Dan, **534**
May, Sarah Elizabeth, 52, **228**, 535, 536

McCrum, Maureen, 476
McCurry, Arthur, 395, 466
McCurry, Kathleen, 395
McLeod, Colin, 513
Meadows, Andrew Miles, 446
Meadows, Sydney, 372, 442, 472, 498, 499, 508, 509, 535
Meadows, Thomas, 204
Meadows, Thomas Miles, 446
Meakin, Hubert Percy, 445
Meakin, Mr and Mrs, 319
Mee, Irene, 309
Mee, John, 56
Mee, John Hindley (head teacher), 346
Mee, Robert, 56, 309, 528, 538
Melton Mowbray, 145, 149
Memorial Hall, 132, 136, 182, 208, 285, 293–6, **294**, 449, 455, 487, 512, 513, 522
Mense, N., 503
Merok, 461
Merston, William de (rector 1266), 113
Merttens, Frederick, 207, 388–90, 397, 398, 401, 410, 416, 442
Meston, Julia (second wife of Denis Anthony Brian Butler), 38
Methodists, 176–82, **180**, **181**, 500
Meynell, Margaret de, 5
Michael Bunney & Meakin (architects), 401–2
Michaelmas Annual Audit, 208, 210, **210**
Middle Field, 185, 194, 259
Middle Road, 385
Middleton, William, 316
Midland Railway, 239, 253, 254, 441
Miles, Samuel, 45
Mill Close, 196, 272, 315
Millais, John (artist), 360
millenarianism, 151–2
Millers Close, 194
mills, 272–3
Mills, Mary, 301
Milne Close, 189, 192, 230, 272–3
Milner, Frank, 204, 446
Milner, George, 204, 446
Milner, Henry Robert, 446
Milner, Mary Ann (née Cuffling), 204, **204**, 446
Minkley, A., 63, 467
Minkley, Albert Frederick, 464
Minkley, Alfred, 464
Minkley, Alice May, 464
Minkley, C., 491
Minkley, Charles Edward (Ted), 308–9, 466
Minkley, Colin, **339**
Minkley, Dorothy, **338**, 339
Minkley, E., 213
Minkley, Emma, 458, 464
Minkley, Evelyn, 466

Minkley, George, 64, 292, **338**, 464
Minkley, H., 64
Minkley, Herbert, 308, **453**, 464, 466
Minkley, Herbert Jnr, 308
Minkley, Horace, 308, 464, 466
Minkley, Horace George, 464
Minkley, Irene Elsie, 308, **338**
Minkley, John Thomas, 296, 445
Minkley, John William, 464
Minkley, Kathleen, 466
Minkley, Kitty, 458
Minkley, Mary Ann, 308, 464
Minkley, Mary Sophia, 334, 464
Minkley, Mr, 505
Minkley, Mrs, 476
Minkley, Mrs A., 467
Minkley, Mrs G., 467
Minkley, Mrs H., 467
Minkley, Muriel, 464
Minkley, Olive Agnes, 466
Minkley, Sally, 458
Missions to Seamen, 529
Mitchell, Arnold (architect), 402, 409
Mitford, Richard de (rector 1356), 114
Monke, Christopher, 115–16
Monmouth, Duke of, 154
Montfort, Simon de, 3, 5, 76
Moore, A., 324
Moore, Charlotte (headmistress), 346
Moore, Edward James, 464
Moore, Fielding (Glenfield), 239
Moore, Horace, 320, 467
Moore, Margery, 464
Moore, Thomas, 388
Moore, William, 461
More, Sir Thomas, 352
Morewood, Elizabeth (wife of Samuel Danvers), 14, 80, 91, 155, 191
Morewood, Joseph, 14, 80
Morgan, Frederick H., 461
Morris, Catherine, 299
Morris, Francis, 286
Morris, George, 212, 273, 275, 286, 299, 428
Morris, J. H., 63
Morris, John, 212, 234, 286, 317
Morris, William (designer), 178
Morris family tree, 299
Moss, R (builder), 407
Mothers' Union, 494, 499, 500, 502, 503, 514, 522, 525
Moughton, Sylvia, 476
Mount St Bernard's Abbey, 409
Mountney, Bartholomew, 196
Mountsorrel, 15–16, 17, 118
 Blue Bell Public House, 28
 burial ground, 19
 Butter Market, 19, **20**, 271
 Drill Hall, 479
 enclosures, 197
 English Civil War, 145

Presbyterians, 165–6
quarries, 19, 30, 40 n.57, 387
schools, 29, 329–30, 331, **337**
workhouse, 67
Mountsorrel Castle, 3
Mountsorrel Granite Company, 19, 40 n.57, 219, 253, 255, 331, 387, 388, 418, 435, 476, 478
Mountsorrel Hall, 264
Mowde Bush Hill, 380
Murcott, Harry (carrier), 432
murders, 8
Murray-Dixon, Charles Edward Trevelyan, 464
Murray-Dixon, Eleanor Margaret Trevelyan, 133, 464
Murray-Dixon, Etheldreda, 464
Murray-Dixon, Henry Edward Otto, *see* Dixon, Henry Edward Otto Murray
Murray-Dixon, James (rector 1884), **128**, **129**, **134**, 212, 286, 507, 585
 Armistice Day Service 1920, 448–9
 character, 129–30
 church restoration, 96–9, 131–3
 disapproval of Memorial Hall, 449
 early career, 128
 funeral, 135
 Hall Farm, 273, 275
 memorial, 104, 135
 Parish Meeting, 51, 52
 Parochial Church Council, 467
 resignation, 100–3, 133–4
 sale of the glebe and rectory, 130–1, 278
Murray-Dixon, Rosamund, 373
Musgrove, May, 228, **228**, 300, 319, 458, 460, 487, 491, 548
Musgrove, Stuart, 342
Musgrove, Tom, 300, 319
Mutch, Mr and Mrs, 319, 491
myths and legends
 Black Annis, 374–7
 Grey Lady, 371–4
 Lady Agnes, 376
 Mowde Bush Stone, 377
 Sir Joseph Danvers Tomb, 368–70

Naseby, Battle of 1645, 145
Nash, John (architect), 268
National Farm Survey, 475–6
navvies, 440–2, **441**
Naylor, Joan (acting headmistress), 340
Neale, Mrs (teacher), 342
Near Brick Kiln Close, 387
Needham, John Cleaver, 445
Nettleton, Millicent (headmistress), 133, 336, 337, 340, **340**, 346, 454, 463, 464, 465, 467
New English Bible, 515
New Park Field, 438

Newarke, Leicester, 229
Newbold, John, 197, 272
Newbold family, 107
Newell, George, 45, 46
Newman, Chris, 538
Newman, Frank *see* Frank Newman & Son (land agents)
News and Views, 543, 545
Newtown Linford, 15, 119, 139, 382, 385
Nicholles, William, 230
Nichols, John (historian), 44, **75**, 77, 78, **80**, 119, 231–2, 359, 369, 374, 382
non ecclesial vestry officers, 63
North, Allison, 491
North, David, 408, 491
North, Dominic, 408
North, Eric, **252**, 408, 476, 538
North, Gillian, 491
North, James, 236
North, Olive, 538
North Field *see* Middle Field
North Hey Close, 192, 220
Northam, Josephine H., 63, 509, 514
Norton family, coat of arms, 76
Nowell, Edward, 45
Nunckley Hill, 388, 418
Nunckley Hill Railway, 388
Nunckley Hill Spinney, 388

Oakleigh, (Cropston Road) 476
Oaks-in-Charnwood, 47–8
Oarton, Mary, 382
occupations, 423, 424, 425–6, 427–9, **427**
 see also child labour
Ogden, Clement (architect), 402
Old Coldstreamers' Association, 33
Old Dalby, 5–6, 7
Old Rectory, **127**, 131, 132, 210, 278–9, **278**
 Grey Lady, 371–4
Old Woodhouse, 137
Oldcastle's Rebellion (1414–15), 114–15
Oldershaw, John, 56, 58, 212, 300–1
Oldershaw, Thomas, 428
Oldershaw, Vincent, 301
Oliver, Arthur C., 405, 461
Oliver, Frederick James (rector 1925), 109–10, 135–6, 223, 286, **453**, 461, 466, 468, 470, 471, 585
Oliver, John (curate), 47, 119
Oliver, Marian, 466
open field system, 185–6, 187, 191
 Exlands Field, 185, 194, 198
 Middle Field, 185, 198, 259
 Over Field, 185, 198, 259
Oram, Thomas, 461
Orr, Frank William, 294
Orrell, Lawrence (rector 1480), 115

Orton, Charles, 489
Orton, Christine, 342
Orton, Jane, **341**, 498
Orton, Jessie, 489
Orton, Richard, 342, 491, 498
Osborne, Cyril, 415–16, **415**, 475
Osborne, Hazel, **415**
Osborne, Jill, **415**
Osborne, Lady, 302, **415**
Osborne, Peter, 540
Osborne, Robert (Bob), 54, 105, 111 n.57, 140, **224**, 245, **245**, **533**, 538, 539–40, **539**, 541, **546**
Outheby, Thomas de, 7
Over Field, 185, 198, 259
Overseers of the Poor, 64–8
Oxe Lersowe Close, 190
Oxford Movement, 97
Oxford Physic Garden, 350–1

Page, Mr and Mrs Adam, 38, 211, 270, 547
Page, Ruth, 54, 140
Paget, Edward James (rector 1841), 124, 125, 278, 430, 584
Paget, Mrs, 461
Paget, Rose Ellen, 403
Paget, Thomas, 403
Paget, Thomas Tertius, 403
Pagets Bank, 403
Pagett, Thomas, 383
Paine, John S., 404, 461
Palfreyman, Arthur, 462
Palmer, Archdale, 12–13, 231
Palmer, John, 231
Palmer, William (Wanlip), 12, 230
Pankhurst, Emmeline (suffragette), **285**
pannage, rights of, 380
Pares, Thomas, 45
Pares, William, 45
parish clerks, 60–2
parish constables, 63–4
Parish Matters, 509
Parish Meeting, 35, 49, 50, 51–2, 68, 130, 133, 251, 450, 512, 536
Park Close, 438
Park Farm, 418
Parker, Charles Theophilus, 313
Parker, Henry (Rothley), 189
Parker, John, 61
Parker, John (Rothley), 381
Parker, Rebecca, 192
Parochial Church Council, 53–4, 59–60, 99, 133, 462, 463, 467–8, 470–5, 496, 541–3
Parrs (bankers), 440
Parsons, William, 239
Pateman, Arthur, 414
Paterson, Andrew, 277
Paterson, Emily Elizabeth, 465, 467
Paterson, Keith, **338**
Paterson, Ken, **455**

Paterson, Laurie, 465
Paterson, M., 63
Paterson, Mac, **431**, **453**
Paterson, Malcolm, 466
Paterson, Lady Rowena, 460
Paterson, William, 56, 58, 98
Paton & Baldwin (Knitting yarn manufacturers), 410
Payne, Harry Alfred, 222
Payne, John, 272
Payne, Len Snr., **210**
Payne, Mrs, 505
Payne, Roland Jnr., **210**
Payne, Walter, 293
Peach, Harold, 287
Peak, William, 56
Pearson, Jane, 67
Pearson, Robert, 315
Peck, Dorothy, 521–2, 529
'peculiar' courts, 42–8
Pegg, Geoffrey, 407, 462
Pennethorne, James (architect), 268, 269, 271
Pentelow, Arthur, 277
Pentelow, Pearl, **339**, 495
Pentelow, Philip, **339**
Pepper, Albert, 56, 68, 465
Pepper, Alfred, 438
Pepper, Bill, **210**
Pepper, Bryan, **338**
Pepper, Charles, 429
Pepper, Edwin, 51, 53, 56, 58, 64, 68, 96, 98, 131, 212, 284, 301, 335, 465
Pepper, Emma, 465
Pepper, Kate, 465
Pepper, Mrs A., 54, 467
Pepper, Mrs E., 467
Pepper, Norman, **338**
Pepys, Samuel (diarist), 153, 352
Perkins, John, 191
Perkins, William, 195, 196, 230, 231
Perkyns, Thomas, 191
Pettipher, Walter, 462
Petts, Benjamin, 203, 234, 282, 283
Phases of English Life, 122
Phillips, John *see* Schraeder, John Phillips
Phoenix Barn, 53
Pickering, Sarah, 434
Pickhill Croft, 192
Pickthall, K., 410
Pingle, The, 307
Pit Close Farm, 58, 203, 206, 208, 211, 213, 302–5, **304**, 459, 476, 477, 478, 485
    list of occupiers, 212
Pit Close Field, 292
Pitts, Samuel, 315, 317
Plabys, William (rector 1465), 115
Place, Richard, 386
Place, William (Mountsorrel), 387
Plain Meadow *see* Red Meadow

Pluralities Act 1838, 124, 125
poaching, 455
Pochin, Major, 438
Pollard, Ann, 171
Pollard, Benjamin (Baptist minister and slate engraver 1754–1818), 169, 170–1, 172, 174–6, 245, 315
Pollard, Catherine, 171, 176
Pollard, John, 171, 173, 174, 236, 245, 313, 315, 316, 317, 321
Pollard, Joseph, 234, 245, 313, 428
Pollard, Kathryn, 514
Pollard, Malcolm, 342
Pollard, Sarah, 171, 173
Pollard, William, 193, 196
Pollard family, 243–5
    family tree, 244
Pollards, The (Strip), 292
Poor Laws, 64, 65–8
poor relief, 67, 68, 200
Porter, Joseph, 272
Porter, Major General, 145
Porter, William, 195
postal services, 432
Potter, Mrs, 462
Potter, Richard, 316
Potter, Susannah Sharpe, 316, 317, 428
Potter, William, 286
Pratt, Ada, 465
Pratt, Charles, 64, 181, **210**, 300, 460, 465, 476
Pratt, Dorothy, **300**, 465
Pratt, Joseph, 282, 283, 300, 332, 333
Pratt, Mrs, 181, 467, 476
Pratt, Mrs C. A., 213
Pratt, Sarah, 283
Pratt, Sarah Ann, 332
Pratt family tree, 300
Presbyterians, 77, 159–69
Prescott Manor, **156**, 157, 353, **354**, 355
Presgrave, Henry, 45
Presgrave, John, 45
Preston, A., 53
Preston, Alex, 68, 306
Preston, Ann, 67
Preston, Eliza, 306
Preston, Elizabeth, 67
Preston, Ellen, 67
Preston, Hannah, 67
Preston, Henry (carrier), 432
Preston, J. R., 318
Preston, Jane, 67
Preston, John, 67
Preston, John (child servant), 429
Preston, Joseph, 67, 289
Preston, Joshua, 428
Preston, Mary, 67, 306, 317, 465
Preston, May, 306
Preston, Richard, 67, 178, 236, 321
Preston, Robert, 171, 173
Preston, Thomas, 234, 317

Preston, William, 317
Prestwell's (bus company), 433
Price, Geoffrey, **341**
Price, Graham, 342
Price, Hilda, 487, 489
Price, Neville, 489
Price, William E., 462
Prier, John, **106**, 229, 240
Prier, Robert, 56
Prior, Emmeline, 322, 324, 449, 456, 465, 516
Prior, John, 328–9, 357–9
    1777 map of Leicestershire, **xx**, 272, 273, 358–9, **358**, **383**, 385
Prior, John (sequestrator), 56, 57
Prior, Joseph, 17, 20, 119, 193, 195–6, 312, 328–9, 357
Prior, Mary, 359
Prior, Robert, 191
Prior, Sarah, 201
Prior, Stephen, 197
Prior, Thomas, 201
Prior family, 107
    family tree, 357
Prychet, John, 8
Pryor, Stephen, 56
Pryor, Thomas, 66
public houses, 233, 283–5
    see also Griffin Inn
Pugh, David John, 56, 105, **224**, 528, 531, 532, **534**, 545, 547
Pugin, Augustus Charles (architect), 268
Pullhare, William (bailiff), 7
Puttocks, 186, 192
Pye, William J. W., 462
Pyehill, 186, 192
Pywell, Edward (Baptist minister), 176

quarries, 19, 30, 40 n.57, 219, **223**, 229, 255, 387, 388, 418
Quatremars, Godfrey de, 3
Quatremars, Lucy de (wife of Godfrey), 3
Quincy, Margaret de (wife of Saer de Quincy), 3
Quincy, Roger de, 3, 4
Quincy, Saer de, 3, 4, 39 n.11
Quorn, 20, 26, 118, 148
    Baptists, 169–73, 174–5, 245
    enclosures, 197
    schools, 336, 341, 364
Quorn Court, 307
Quorn Hunt, 34, 122
Quorn Mill, 26, 251, 273
Quorndon Road, 385

Rabbit Bridge, 478
Radcliffe, Sydney, 56, 513
Ragg, Abel, 167
railways, 31, 37, 207, 253–5, 257, 388, 390, 432

Rainbow, The (Lawrence), 364–5
Raiwet, Andrée (Belgian refugee), 340, 477
Ratcliffe, Edmund, 277
Rathbone Plot, 153
rating assessors, 52–3
Raven, Thomas, 316
Rawlins, Thomas, 163–4, 166–7, 328
Raworth, Anne, 78
Raworth, John, 78, 231
Raworth, Sarah, 78
Raworth, William, 78, 231
Raynor, Ann, 317
Raynor, Francis, 287, 290
Raynor, Jane, 289
Raynor, John, 234
Raynor, Mary, 287, 289
Raynor, Robert, 234, 317
Raynor, Sarah A., 332
Raynor, Thomas, 289, 290, 317, 332
Raynor, William, 317
Raynor, Zachariah, 67, 290, 316, 317
Raynor family tree, 290
Read, George, 313
Reader, Reg, **455**
Rearsby, 161, 163
Rectory, The (1898), 286–7, **286**, 461, 473–4, 541, 543
Rectory, The (1993), 535, 536, **536**, 543
Rectory Spinney, 33
Red Meadow, 263, 264, 265
Redland Aggregates Ltd., 219
Rees, M., 503
Reeve, Arthur (architect), 131
Reformation, 75–6, 115–16
Reginald of St Evroult (rector 1295), 113, 582
religious tolerance, 161, 163
Renshaw, Martin (organ restorer), 524
Reservoir House (Cropston), 476
Reservoir Recipe Book, 500, 529, 531
Reynolds, Joseph, 386
Reynolds, Norman, 290
Rich, Florence (teacher), 405
Richardson, Barfoot, 66
Richardson, Reginald Edensor Stanley, 394
Richardson, Stephen, 410, 414
Ridgeway, The, 390–1, **392**, 401, 414
    No. 19, Richmond, 414–15
    No. 23, Woodcote, 405
    No. 25, West Acre, 415–16, **415**, 459, 475
    No. 26, Fairfield, 404, 417
    No. 28, St Bernard's, 404–5
    No. 30, Herongate, 405
    No. 32, Red Walls, 395, 402, 404, **404**, 461
    No. 33, The Spinneys, 391, 393–5, **394**, 414, 462
    No. 36 Myamin (The Lawns) 403
    No. 38, Covertside, 414, 461

    No. 39, Three Oaks, 391, 395, 461, 466, 477
    No. 44, West Lawn, 393, 403–4
    No. 45, Uplands, 391–3, 407, 461, 476
    No. 54, Paigles, (The Cottage) 391, 396
    No. 60, Holly Lodge, 391, **392**, 393, 395–6, **396**, 414, 461
    No. 62, The Coppice, 391, 394–5, 404, 461, 479
Ridings, The, 138, 385, 401, 416–17
    No. 23, Bryngarth, 417
    No. 28, Aberfeldy, 395, 417, 476
    No. 75, Pax, 417
    No. 120, Linford Cottage, 388, 414, 417, 475, 476
Riley, Alfred, 462
Ringing Through the Year (hymn), 533–4
Ringrose, Alf, **339**
Ringrose, Margaret, **339**
Ritchie, Reverend Allan, 223
roads, 69
Robbins, C. H., 523
Robert 'Blanchmains,' Earl of Leicester, 3, 4
Robert 'le Bossu,' Earl of Leicester, 3, 4
Roberts, Christopher, **533**
Roberts, Janet, **224**, 522, 535
Roberts, John, **224**, 523, 532, **534**
Roberts, Matthew, **534**
Robinson, Rev. N., 503
Robson, Dennis (Methodist minister), 181
Rockley, George, 271
Rodgers, Richard, 277
Roe, John, 67
Roecliffe Manor, 26, 87, 123
Roecliffe Road, 236
Roger (chaplain 1206), 72, 112, 113, 582
Rogers, John, 45
Roman remains, 390, **391**, 399
Room, Susan, 514
Rose of Newarke, The (drama), 376
Ross, Edward, 459
Ross, Matthew, 459
Ross, Walter G. (architect), 403
Ross-shire Journal, 361, 363
Rothley, 17, 19, 25, 26, 119, 137, 138
    Baptists, 170, 171
    church, 144
    Golf Club, 33
    Hunt memorial stone, 242–3, **243**
    railway station, 390
    shoe factories, 393
Rothley Court Hotel, 389
Rothley Garden Suburb, 397, 398–403, **399**, **400**, 423, 442
    number of houses built, 417
Rothley Hall, 188

Rothley Park Estate Ltd, 414
Rothley Plain, 109, 123, 130, 186, 207, 249, 255, 379, 532
　brick making, 382–3, 387
　Domesday Survey, 380, 384
　enclosures, 383–6, **384**
　extent of, 381, **383**
　grazing rights, 380–1
　owners and tenants 1838, 386
　pannage, rights of, 380
　quarries, 387, 388
　rabbit warren disputes, 381–2
Rothley Plain Farm, 58, 207, 386–7, 388, 403, 410
Rothley Plain Football Club, 417
Rothley Plain Nursery, 476
Rothley Road, 385
Rothley Temple, 229
Rothley Temple Chapel, 121, 389, 414
Rothley Temple Estate, 11, 14, 34, 388–90, **389**
　future development, 419
　inter-war development, 414
　property sales, 413–14
　sale 1973, 418, 419
Rothley Temple Peculiar, 121–2
Roubir, Gilbert de (rector 1286), 113, 114, 582
Rough, The, 269
Rough Wall Leys, 263, 264, 265
Rouse, B. R., 476
Rowe, Rev. D., 491
Royce, Davis C., 462
Rubens, Ruth, 476
Rudkin, Dorothy, **339**, 493
Rudkin, Hazel, 491
Rudkin, Margaret, **339**, 491
Rudkin, Mr, 491
Rudkin, Thomas, 239
Rudkin, Walter, 491, 493, 505
Rupert, Prince, 144–5
Rushey Fields Farm, Woodhouse, 211
Rushey Lane, 385, 387
Ruskin, John (artist), 402
Russell, Richard (rector 1495), 115
Russell, Robert, 462
Ryall, Lesley, 494
Rye Close, 189, 192, 193
Rye House Plot, 154

S. & E. Langton (estate agents), 405
Sachaverell, Ann (née Coke), 13
Sadd, Clarence, 413, 462
Salisbury, James (engraver, London), 245, 247 n.52
Salvation Army, **224**
Sambrook, L. J. P., 63
Sanders, John Butler (curate), 124, 586
Sandfield Farm, 476
Sandhills Farm, Rothley, 210

Saunder, William, 8
Savage, Mr, 413
Saville, George, 45
scavenging, 478
School House, 281–2, **281**
schools, 17, 29, 72, 90, 122, 166, 213, 225, 328–9, 386, 444, 454, 522
　admission lists (1865–1980), 589–98
　attendance, 333, 335
　controlled status, 341–2
　early twentieth century, 334–8
　governors, 52
　head teachers, 346
　illustrations, **281**, **334**, **336**, **337**, **338**, **339**, **341**, **344**
　nineteenth century, 331–5
　Parents Association, 487
　primary school, 339–41
　punishments, 335, 337
　recent years, 345–6
　secondary education, 342, 343–4
　Sir Joseph Danvers, 329–31
Schraeder, John Phillips, 198–9, 284
Scoppie, Roger, 528
Scot, Agnes, 74–5, **75**, 91, 103, 347–50, 376–7
Scot, Hugh (bailiff), 7
Scott, Dorothy, 299
Scott, John, 299
Scott, Thomas (rector 1465), 115
Sculthorpe, Ann (Newark), 193
Second World War, 52, 475–81
Sellars, Betty, **338**
servants, 20, 428
sewerage, 33, 51, 251
sextons, 62
Sharman, W., 287
Sharp, Graham Kenneth, 56, 532, 534, **534**, 535, 547
Sharp, Jan, 535
Sharpe, Dorothy, **280**
Sharpe, George, 407
Sharpe, Harold, **280**
Sharpe, Mrs, 505
Sharpe, Paul, **280**
Shaw, Arthur, 234, 240
Shaw, Charles, 234, 240
Shaw, Joseph, 234, 239–40, 317
Shaw, William, 234, 240
Sheepy Parva, 11
Shefeud, Margaret de, 5
Shefeud, William de, 5
Shenton, Francis (Mountsorrel), 235, 236, 245, 321
Shepey, Alice de see Walcote, Alice
Shepey, Anne, 10
Shepey, Edmund, 10, 187
Shepey, Edward, 10, 220
Shepey, John, 9, 10
Shepey family, 220
Shepshed Secondary Modern School, 342

Sheridan, Rev. Peter, 140, 588
Sherrifhales academy (Shropshire), 161–2, **162**
Sherwood, Leslie, 442–3
Shipman, Len, 497
Shirley, Anne, 9
Shirley, Ralph, 9
shooting, **451**
shops, 292, 299, 308, 316, 428–9, 454
Shrive, Evelyn, 288, 505
Shrive, Walter, 288
Sibson, G. L., 213
Sibson, John Holmes, 387
Sidebottom, Kingsford Beauchamp (rector 1876), 95, 126, 278, 584–5
sidesmen, 62–3
Siege of Leicester 1645, 117
Sills, Edith, **339**, 491
Sills, Mr, 491
Simmons, C. R., 491
Simmons, Helen, **493**
Simmons, Miss W. A., 491, 504, 505
Simmons, Mr, 505
Simmons, Mr and Mrs, 466
Simmons, R., 491
Simpson, Albert, 462
Simpson, Charlotte, 212, 313
Simpson, Elizabeth, 58, 67
Simpson, Elizabeth (1786–1869), 67
Simpson, Harriet, 307
Simpson, Joseph, 67
Simpson, Margaret, 491
Simpson, Matthew, 56, 58, 66, 67, 201, 212, 312, 313
Simpson, Stephen, 307
Simpson, William, 56, 58, 203, 212, 313, 428
Skevington, Joseph, 386
Skevington, Joseph (1809–67), 386
Skyfington, Robert (rector 1400), 114
slate industry, 106, 169
　accidents, 239–40
　decline, 239–40, 248
　early history, 229
　engravers, 240–1
　Hind family, 230–3, 236–7, 239
　memorial, 547–8
　Millenium Commemoration Slate, 228, **228**
　nineteenth century development, 235–6
　production methods, 231–2
　quarries, **223**, 229
　seventeenth century, 230
Slate Pit Hay, 221
Slate Pit Hill, 231, 236
Slate Pit Hill Road, 225
Slate Pit Wood, 221
Slaters, Plasterers and Tallow Chandlers Guild, 241
Slatesplitters Arms (public house), 233

Small Meadow, 307
Smalley, Elizabeth, 196, 263
Smalley, Francis (Mountsorrel), 190, 195, 263, 265, 381
Smalley, John, 195
Smalley, Pentecoast, 195, 196
Smalley, Ralph, 192, 195, 263, 381
Smalley, Robert, 78, 196
Smalley family tree, 264
Smeaton, Angela, 514
Smeaton, Christine, 54, 70 n.8, 514
Smisby, 10, 39 n.28, 39 n.29
Smith, Anne, 501
Smith, Charles Edwin, 414–15, 462
Smith, Elizabeth, 62, 298, 465
Smith, Emmanuel, 192
Smith, Thomas Geoffrey Stuart (rector 1966), 137, 286, 495, 504, 507, 508, 514, 515, 516, 519, 524, 526, 585
Smith, Gillian, 491
Smith, Joanna, 514
Smith, Joseph (rector 1623), 116, 117–18, 148, 583
Smith, Mrs T., 213
Smith, R. G, 504
Smith, Roland, 292, 497
Smith, Susan, 465
Smith, Thomas, 298, 465
Smith, William (Lollard), 114
Smith Ayres Wood *see* Little Linns Wood
Smythe, Edmund (rector 1528), 115
Smythe, Gilbert (rector 1588), 44, 45, 115–16, 583
Snetzler, Johann (organ builder), 81–2
Snow, E. E., 430
Snow, Henry, 201
social change, 450, 486–7, 488–9
Society for the Propagation of Christian Knowledge (SPCK), 329
Solito Shoes, 393–4
Somery, Roger de, 218
Sough Mouth Spring, 319, **319**, 433
South Charnwood Central School, 339
South Field *see* Exlands
South Lodge, 271
Southam, Lynn, **341**
Southcott, Joanna (prophetess), 24
Southfields Farm, 418
Sparrow, James (Radcliffe), 241
speed limits, 53
Spence, Frank, **338**, 430, 459
Spence, George, 63, 290, 458, 460, 465
Spence, Lucy, 491
Spence, Violet, 290, 465
Spencer, Ann, 171
Spencer, James, 429
Spencer, John, 317, 332

Spencer, Sarah Ann, 332
Spencer, William, 234
sport, 430–2
Spurway, John, 395, 404, 417
Spurway, William John, 394–5
Spurways (carpet retailers), 395
Squire, Benjamin, 177
Squire, Henry, 192, 230
Squire, John, 196
Squires, Henry, 317
Squires, Linda, 501
St Ebrulph (convent), 5
St Evroult Abbey, 72–3, **73**, 108, 110 n.2, 112
St George's Church, Leicester, 245
St Leonard of Limousin, 72, **72**
St Leonard's Church, 12, 16–17, 18, 19, 410, 541–3, 543–4
   1863 Episcopal Visitation, 89
   1872 Episcopal Visitation, 126
   1905 Episcopal Visitation, 96, 131
   Altar Flower Ladies, 500, 504–5
   bells and bell-ringing, 81, 98, 104, 459–60, 480, 483 n.14, 494, 499, 500, 502, 511–12, 523, 532–4, **534**, 535–6, 540, 547
   Book of Remembrance, 104–5
   charities, 109–10
   choir, 493–4, 500, 501–2
   churchwardens, 55–60, 69
   churchyard, 105–8, 471, 506, 524, 526
   clock, 82, 98
   communion plate, 81
   covenants, 494
   Danvers chapel, 79–80, 86, 91, 100, 102–3, 104, 369, 539
   deanery representatives, 54
   disagreement with Leicester diocese, 541–3
   eighteenth century alterations, 79–80, **80**
   festivals, 521
   fifteenth century modifications, 74–5
   font, 80–1, **81**, 104
   Free-Will Offering Scheme, 469, 470, 471, 494–5
   glebe land, 120–1, 125, 130–1, 186, 191, 196, 202, 207, 208
   gravestones, 106–7, **106**, 229, 240
   Guild of Church Cleaners, 500, 504
   harvest suppers, 506–7
   illustrations of exterior, **71**, **80**, **96**, **97**, **107**
   illustrations of interior, **72**, **93**, **94**, **95**, **103**
   interregnum, 473–5, 527–8
   Lanesborough tombs, **38**
   lych gate, 108, **108**, 135, 322, 450, 470
   Millennium Extension, 105, 245, **245**, 531–2, 544–7, **547**

mission strategy, 543–4
missions, 495–6
nineteenth century interior, 86–95
non ecclesial vestry officers, 63
organ, 81–2, 91, 98, 103–4, 111 n.25, 132, 470, 524
pageants, 490–3, **490**, **492**, **493**
parish boundaries, 532
parish clerks, 60–2
parish magazine, 472, 489, 498, 499, 500, 505, 507–11, 515, 518, 521, 522–3, 524, 525–6, 527–8, 529, 531, 536, 537, 538, 539, 540, 543
parish registers, 89, 99, 119, 234
Parochial Church Council, 53–4, 59–60, 99, 133, 462, 467–8, 470–5, 496, 536–7, 541–3
patronage, 108–9
pews, 90, 91, 103, 104, 499
pulpit, 90, 94, 95
Reformation, 75–6
restoration, 96–104, 131–3, 468
School of Discipleship, 500
services, 90, 126, 494, 518–21
sextons, 62
sidesmen, 62–3
stipend, 473, 516
thirteenth century, 72–3
tithes, 198, 385
tower, 98, 131–2, 523
union of benefices, 137, 139–40, 536–7
value of living, 118–19, 126, 136, 142 n.45
welcome letters and leaflets, 499, 500
windows, 86, 87, **88**, 89, 98, 105, 111 n.34, 111 n.57, 348, 445–6, 539, **546**
see also church memorials; Sunday School
St Leonard's Football Team, 432
St Leonard's Guild, 494
St Mark's Church, Leicester, 136, 138
St Martin's Leicester, 122
Stableford, John, 171, 173
Stableford, Sarah, 171, 173
Stableford, William, 173
Stacey, Fred, 417
Staines & Smith, 415
Stamford and Warrington, Earl of, 120, 196, 197, 200, 207, 208, 220, 221, 235, 240, 307, 385
   dispute about Rothley Plain, 383–4
   landholdings on Rothley Plain, 386–7
Stamford's Woods, 221
Standage, Arthur, 466
Standing Stones and Mark Stones of Leicestershire and Rutland (Trubshaw), 377

Staples, Cliff, 417
Staynes, Josephine, **339**
Staynes, Patricia, 339, **339**
Staynes, Shirley, **339**
Stead and Simpson (shoe manufacturers), 393, 413
Stephen H. Hilton & Son (shoe retailers), 404
Stephens, Richard, 45
Stevens, Mrs, 476
Stevens, Rt. Rev. Timothy (Bishop of Leicester), 545–6, **547**
Stevenson, A. E., 213, 290
Stevenson, Arthur, 445
Stevenson, John, 272, 445
Stevenson, Mr, 513
Stevenson, V., 523
Stevenson, William, 382
Stibbe, Charles, 412, 462
Stibbe, Godfrey, 412
Stipendiary Curates Act 1813, 124–5
Stobart, Peter, 512
Stocking Close, 189, 196
Stocking Wood, 220, 222
Stockwell, Joe, 456
Stoke Newington, 13, 14, 152
Stokes, Edward, 45
Stone, Bert, 319
Stone, Frank F., 462
Stone, Jean, 319
Stone, John, 319, 342
Stone, Mrs, 491
Stone, Samuel, 407
Stonehurst Farm, Mountsorrel, 176–7
Storer, Thomas, 462
Stoughton, William, 45
street lights, 53
Sturt, Eliza, 24, 25
Sunday School, 95, 137, 331, 418, 492–3, **493**, 499, 500–1, 506, 513, 519, 522, 526, 531, 535
Surveyors of the Highways, 69
Sutton, Francis, 189, 190, 193, 286
Sutton, John de (rector 1275), 113
Sutton, Margery, 192, 193
Swain, Arthur Harry, 395, 416
Swain, Elizabeth, 67
Swain, James Christopher, 395
Swain, Jonathan, 67
Swann, Ann, 309
Swann, Peter, 309
Swinderby, William (Lollard), 114
Swithland
    Annual Church Meeting 1999, 49–50
    Baptists, 171–4, 176, 177
    best kept village competition, 506, 536
    census information, 423–7
    charitable support, 529–30
    Conservation Area, 53
    council housing, **489**
    earliest Royal Charter, **6**–**7**
    early history, 1–4
    electoral roll lists, 463–7
    enclosures, 25, 47, 108, 119–20, 123, 188–9, 197–202, **199**, 264, 315
    estate ownership dispute, 27–8
    field names, **189**
    film, 504, 535
    fruit flower and vegetable show, 513, 529
    housing, 262–3, 486
    library, 29, 429–30
    manorial rights, 4–9
    map 1777, **xx**
    medieval village, 258–60
    Memorial Hall, 132, 136, 182, 208, 285, 293–5, **294**, 449, 455, 482, 487, 512, 513, 522
    Men's Club, 137
    Methodist Chapel, **314**, 316, 442, 498
    Methodists, 176–82, **180**, **181**, 207
    Millennium celebrations, 547–8
    mills, 203, 251, 272–3, 428
    origin of name, 1
    Overseers of the Poor, 64–8
    parish constables, 63–4
    Parish Meeting, 35, 49, 50, 51–2, 68, 130, 133, 251, 450, 512, 536
    pavilion, 438, **439**
    population, 200, 258
    post office, 432, 454, **455**, 487
    Presbyterians, 159–69
    railway station, 255, **255**
    Revels, 517
    sale of estate 1954, 37
    savings society, 430
    social change, 450, 486–7, 488–9
    Tennis Club, 136
    town crier, 69, **298**, 435
    village lock-up, 276, **276**
    village stocks, 294
    village Wake, 432
    War Memorial, 208, 295–6, **295**, 444
    War Memorial Fund, 294
    water pump, **281**, 327 n.100, 433
Swithland (booklet), 499–500
    see also Meadows, Sydney
Swithland Church Men's Club, 487, 504, 511, 513, 524, 529
    see also Church of England Men's Society
Swithland Convalescent Home for Women, 443
Swithland Cricket Club, 430–2, **431**
Swithland Glebe Field, 388
Swithland Hall, 16, **18**, **19**, **27**, 38, 210, 365, 428, 461
    estate, 201, 208, 210–11, 213, 485–6
    estate workers, 450, 451–2, **453**
    gazebos, 276
    ice house, 269
    kitchen garden, 277
    Old Hall, 266–8, 370
    proposed road diversion, 267, **268**
    rebuilding of, 28, 29, 202, 268–9, **269**, **270**
    sale of, 37, 211, 270
    sale of contents 1978, 512
    social and leisure activities, 437–40
    see also Lantern Cross
Swithland Ladies Group, 521–2, 529
Swithland Lane, 379, 385, 387, 402, 403, 414
    Delafield, 477
    Glenmona, 461
    Harcla, 461
    Mill Hill Cottage, 461, 465
    No. 3, Fairview, 407, **407**, 462
    No. 5, Brentwood, 407, 461
    No. 7, Claremont, 407–8
    No. 9, The Woodlands, 407–8, 462
    No. 11, Stanswell, 408, 476
    No. 13, Glenarrif (Clairmarais), 461
    No. 15, Charnwood House, 408, 462
    No. 17, Churston, 408
    No. 19, Windycroft, 408, 461, 481
    No. 21, Berhampore (Flower Gate), 461
    No. 22–36, Railway Cottages, 390, **390**
    No. 25, Latharna, 461
    No. 27, Charnwood Preparatory School, 405–6, **405**, **406**
    No. 29, Sunnycroft, 461
    No. 31, Holmcroft, 461
    No. 34, 502
    No. 38, The Shrubbery (Greenfields), 408–9, **408**, 414
    No. 39, Sandbeck, 462
    No. 40, Redholm (The White House or Cottage), 408, 462
    No. 42, Coburn, 461
    No. 44, Clonmell (Holmwood), 408
    No. 46, The Laurels, 408, 418, 462
    No. 48, Crafers (Midrise), 408, 461
    No. 50, Sunnydene, 408, 413
    No. 52, The Chestnuts, 462
    No. 54, Woodside, 462
    No. 56, Billinge, 461
    No. 57–63, 403, 410, **411**
    No. 58, Northfield, 462
    No. 63, The Bungalow, 461, 466
    No. 65, The Homestead, 386, 387, 401, 403, 410, **411**, 412, 462
    see also Rothley Plain Farm
    No. 68, The Gables, 402, 409–10, **409**, 413, 414, 462, 466, 470, 502, 505

No. 70, Orchard House (Egerton), 410
No. 71, Westover (Freshfield), 412, 414
No. 72, Bracondale, 416, 514
No. 73, Brendon (Lexden), 412, 416, 462
No. 76, Daneway, 416, 461, 466
No. 77, Lynton, 412, 461
No. 79, Eastfield (Forest View), 412, 413, 461
No. 80, Grayrigg, 407, 462
No. 81, Maplecote, 412–13, **413**, 461, 466, 469
No. 82, The Oaks, 460, 461
No. 83, Nilgiris, 412, 461
No. 84, Rathnay (Little Tern), 461
No. 86, Ingledene, 407, 461
No. 88, Wayside, 407, 462
No. 90, Newlands, 406–7, **406**, 462
No. 130–34, Newtown Cottages, 387, 388
No. 135, The Byeways, 466
No. 140, Birkin, 462, 466
No. 146, Chaseside, 461, 466
No. 153, Budden View, 462
No. 155, Nithsdale (Beresford House), 462
No. 160, The Firs, 461
No. 207, 504
No. 223, 501
Swithland Mother and Toddlers Group, 522
Swithland Reservoir, 31, 33, 51, 205, 207, 219, 248–53, 263, 387–8, 478
   illustrations, **251**, **252**, **253**, **254**, **256**
   plan, **250**
   railway construction, 255
Swithland Spring Water, 275
Swithland Voluntary Aid Society, 444
Swithland Water Works, 251, **251**, 252, 265, 266, **266**, 538
Swithland Wood, 26, 130, **217**, 219, **220**, **221**, **222**
   Bluebell Service, 223–4, **224**, 470–1, 494, 502, 529–30, 538
   Danvers' Woods, 219, 220–1
   Stamford's Woods, 219, 221
   tourism, 442
Swithland Wood Farm, 123, 222, 459, 476, 532
   camp, 225–6, **225**, **226**, 442–3, **443**
Swithland Youth Club, 500, 514, 535
Swithland Youth Fellowship, 493–4, 499, 500, 501, 514, 529
Symes, Jane, 218
Symington, Mr, 505

T. G. Hunt & Son (shoe manufacturers), 404
Tapper, Theophilus, 45
Tarrutt, William (rector 1405), 114
Tarry, Alice, 465, 467
Taylor, A., 491
Taylor, Edith Helen, 466
Taylor, Frederick William, 64, 465
Taylor, G., 409, 414, 499
Taylor, H. G. Clough (agent), 30, 335, 432, 437
Taylor, Joseph (carrier), 432
Taylor, Leslie, 466
Taylor, Rev. A. W., 462
Taylor, Sarah, 465
Taylor, Stephen (Baptist minister), 176
Tea Pot Lane, 417–18
Tebbutt, Edward (Thurcaston), 333
Tebbutt, Jabez, 333
Tebbutt, Ralph (Frisby), 195, 200, 263–4
Tebbutt, Ralph Jnr., 212, 265
Tebbutt, Ralph Smalley, 264
Tebbutt, Robert, 263
telegraph office, 299
telephones, 460
   list of residents with telephones, 461–2
Templar, Sarah, 193
Temple Farm, 476
tennis, 438, 440
Theatre Royal, Leicester, 376
Theobald, John, 476
Thirlby, Thomas, 236
Thomas, Esther R., 324
Thomas, Lord Grey of Groby, 144, 145, 146, 155
Thomas, Thomas, 20
Thomas Rawlins School (Quorn), 336, 341
Thompson, Emily, 546
Thompson, Henry, 212
Thompson, Isabel, **533**, 546
Thompson, John, 67
Thompson, John (agricultural labourer), 317
Thompson, Joseph (agricultural labourer), 317
Thompson, Joseph, 317, **533**, 546
Thompson, Patrick, **533**
Thompson, Philip, **533**, **534**, 547
Thompson, William, 286
Thorburn, Alexander (artist), 360
Thornton's Farm (Cropston), 15
Thornton (widow), 317
Thornton, Ann, 386
Thornton, George (Mountsorrel), 190
Thornton, William, 386
Thornton Reservoir, 248
Thorpe (widow), 317
Thorpe, George, 67, 234, 317
Thorpe, John, 317, 434
Thorpe, Martha, 317
   see also Bunney, Martha
Thorpe, Mary, 317
Thorpe, Samuel, 67, 178, 234, 316, 317
Thorpe, Thomas, 67
Thorpe, William, 234
Three Crowns Inn, Leicester, 198
Throsby, John (antiquary), 18–19, **18**, 82, **164**, 218, **218**, 233, 266, 278, 369
Thurcaston, 15, 16, 17, 25, 123, 130, 139
   church, 240
   enclosures, 197
   parish registers, 149
Thurcaston Road, 385
Tickhill Croft, 186
Tilton, 149
tithes, 198, 385
Toleration Act 1689, 163, 164–5
Toll, Alexander, 300
Toll, Lorraine, 300
Tombs, Dorothea Gwladys (wife of Charles John Brinsley Butler), 32
Tomlin, John, 69, **69**, 465
Tomlin, Sarah Annie Maria (midwife), 69, 465
Tomlinson, John, 45
Tomorrow: a Peaceful Path for Real Reform (Howard), 397
Toneham, 461, 475
Tong Plot 1662, 152
tourism, 442–3, 459
Tovey, Nathaniel (rector of Aylestone), 149
Town and Country Planning Act (1962), 104
town crier, 69, **298**, 435
Town Street, 192
transport, 432–3, 456
   see also railways
transubstantiation, 114
Travers, Elias (rector of Thurcaston 1628–41), 240
Treatise on Baptism, 153, 157–8 n.26
Trevelyan, Etheldreda (wife of James Murray-Dixon), 128, 135
Treweeke, George (rector 1858), 90, 95, 124, 125–8, 278, 584
Trubshaw, Bob, 377
Truman, Thomas (Baptist minister), 174
Tucker, J., 499
Tuckers of Loughborough (architects), 403
Tuckett, Dr., 460
Tuckett, R. W., 438
Turkillestone, Roger de (rector 1224), 113
Turner, Archibald, 52, 54, 63, 99, 100, 104, **108**, 135, 138, 208, 295, 319, 321–2, 324, 335, 422–3, 450, 463, 465, 467, 467–8, 470, 516

Turner, Gladys Marie, 133, 134,
    135–6, 208, 321–2, **322**, 324,
    335, 449, 457–8, 465, 467
    see also Wright, Mrs Linwood
Turner, Lois Mary Gladys, 136, 138,
    323, 458, 465, 492
    see also Godfrey, Lois
Turner, Muriel, 320,
Turner, Thomas, 50–1
Turvey Leys Close, 192
Turvill, Richard, 187
Turville Leys, 187, 191
Tyers, C., 53
Tyers, Elizabeth, 289, 465
Tyers, Edward, 53, 64, 202, 212, 292
Tyldesley, Mr, 505
Tyldesley, Phyllis, 496, 500, 501, 503,
    505, 506, 513
Tyler, William, 272

Ulf (Saxon thegn), 1–2
Ulverscroft Priory, 186, 187
Underwood, Elizabeth, 291, 465
Underwood, Miss, 467
Underwood, Tom, 291, 465
Unitarians, 407
University College, Leicester, 407
Upper Close see Corn Close

Van Dyck, Anthony, 16, 21, 350, 351,
    366 n.7
Vann, Brian, 63, 105, 309, 445
Vann, Doris, 309
Vazeille, Mary, 410
VE Day fiftieth anniversary, 535
Venables, Alice, 9
Vestey, Thomas, 279
vestry meetings, 50–1, 53, 54
Vesty, Ann, 67
Vesty, Hannah, 67
Vesty, Thomas, 67
Viccars, William Arnold, 410, 412,
    462
Victoria Mills (hosiery
    manufacturers), 394
Vielage, Christopher, 491
Voce, Edward, 234
Vulcan Engineering Works, 412
Vynes, Robert de (rector 1472), 115

Wadland, Thomas, 45
Wagstaffe, Charlotte, 466, 470
Wagstaffe, Sidney H., 462, 466
Wainwright, Charles, 64, 313, 314,
    429, 465
Wainwright, J., 499
Wainwright, Jackie, 513
Wainwright, Marc, 512, **534**, 547
Wainwright, Mary Ellen, 213, 313,
    314, 465, 476
Wakeling, Mr, 505
Wakeling, Mrs, 505
Wakerley, Elizabeth, 297

Wakerley, Francis, 297
Wakerley family tree, 297
Wakerlin, Francis, 67
Walcote, Alice, 8–9
Walcote, John, 7–8, 186
Walcote, Margaret, 8
Walcote family, 218, 220
Wale, Richard, 386
Wale, William, 387
Wales, Richard,, 64
Waleys, Agnes, 7
Waleys, Beatrice le (wife of Oliver), 7
Waleys, Elizabeth, 7–8
Waleys, John le, 7
Waleys, Nicholas le, 5
Waleys, Oliver le, 6–7, 381
Waleys, Robert le, 4–5, 73, 186
Waleys, Robert le (son of Oliver), 7
Waleys, William, (rector 1340), 113
Waleys family, 220
    coat of arms, 76
Walker, David A., 462
Walker, E., 407
Walker, George, **210**, 212, 213, 312,
    313, 498
Walker, John, 56, 57, 119, 196, 286
Walker, Mr, 52
Walker, Richard, 286
Wallace, Henry A., 462
Waller, Eric George (head teacher),
    342, 343, 346
Waller, Lorna, 500, 501
Wallis, John (Thurcaston), **210**
Walpole, Horace (writer), 16
Walpole, Robert (prime minister), 16
Walsh, Elinor M. T. (née Murray
    Dixon), 465
Walsh, Henry James, 133
Walsh, Rachael, 514
Walters, Francis Raymond (priest-in-
    charge 1977), 138–9, **138**, 286,
    287, 373, 509, 513, 514–15, 518,
    519–20, 523, 527, 537, 538, 586
Walters, Gillian, 514, 531
Walters, Gillian (rector's wife), 531
Waltho, Kathleen, 105
Walton, Isaak (writer), 356, 357
Walton, Lesley, 509
Wane, John (Cropston), 230
Wanlip, 12, 119, 167
Wantoma, 476
Ward, Elizabeth (d.1727), 262
Ward, James, 66, 282
Ward, John, 45
Ward, Robert, 308
Ward, Thomas, 67
Ward family tree, 282
Wardale, Arthur, 477–8
Warden, Thomas, 189, 190
Warden, William, 189
Wardle, Jennifer, 491
Wardle, Mr, 491
Wardle, Mrs, 491

Wardle, Roger, 491
Ware, Abbey of, 112, 113–14, 141 n.15
Warner, Daniel, 387
Warner, E., 438
Warren, John, 206, 212, 302, 303
Warren, Martha, 302
Warren Hill, 382
Warwick, Geoffrey de (rector 1239),
    113
Water Gap Lane, 385
Waterfield, Richard (rector of
    Thurcaston), 124
Wathes, Mrs, 472
Watkin, Sir Edward, 253, 254
Watkins, Dorothy Kate (second wife
    of Charles John Brinsley
    Butler), 32, **451**
Watson, James, 167, 168
Watson, Michael, 168
Watson, Sarah, 167–8
Webb, Caroline (head teacher), 345,
    346
Weeks, Huw, 501
Welbeck Sixth Form Defence
    College, Woodhouse, 224
Wells, Esther, 67
Wells, Hugh de, Bishop of Lincoln, 113
Wells, James, 67
Wells, Percy, 494, 502, 511–12
Werge, Richard, 45
Wesley, Ann, 193
Wesley, Ben, 64
Wesley, Charles, 240
Wesley, Jane, 193
Wesley, John (Methodist), 176–7, 410
Wesley family, 107
Wessel, Harry, 393
Wessel, Robert L. (Bobby), 393
West Field, 194
Westfield Farm (Rothley), 388, 403,
    414, 417, 418
Westfield Lane, 401, 414, 417
Westley, William, 196
    will 1775, 262
Weston, Daniel, 317
Weston, John, 387
Weston, Trevor, 504
Whatnall, Daniel, 67
Whatnall, Mary, 46–7
Whatnall, Michael, 67
Whatnall, Richard (carrier), 432
Whatnall, Squire, 46–7
Whatnall, William (miller), 272
Whatoff, William, 212, 275
Wheeler, A. F. P., 479
Wheeler, Beryl (head teacher), 345,
    346
Wheeler, Nicholas, 542
Wheeler, Sir Arthur (stockbroker),
    415–16
Whetstone Pastures slate obelisk, 239
White, Peter (Master of Music,
    Leicester Cathedral), 524

White, William, 197, 272
White House (Cossington), 416
Whitehead, John, 381
White's Wood, 192, 220
Whitley, Elizabeth, 382
Whitley, Robert, 191, 192, 382
Whitley, Samuel, 381–2
Whitmore, Donald, 476
Whittle, E. H., 476
Whittle, L. F., 476
Whittle, William, 272, 382
Whyary Close *see* Rough Wall Leys
Whyman, Joseph (surveyor), 358
Whyte, Marjorie E., 63, 545
Whyte, Robert, 191
Whyte, Rowena Anne, 508
Whyte, Tom N., 63, 545–6
Wibbertoft, Robin de (rector 1398), 114
Wickham, Captain Nigel John Latham, 98, 445–6
Wifforn (public house), 233
   see also Griffin Inn
Wilde, Rev. W. Q., 386
Wildman, Edward, 212, 301
Wildt, Dr., 396
Wilford, Doris, 465
Wilkes, Bros & Co., 393
Wilkes, John Williams, 393–4
Wilkes, John, 462
Wilkinson, Richard, 535
William, H. J., 523
William I, 112
William II (Rufus), 2, 3
William III, 356
William IV, 122
William Moss and Sons (building contractors), 398
Williams, Harold, 512
Williamson, John, 428
Wills, Obadiah, 153
Willson, George, 498, 499–500
Willson, Zoë S., 63, 508, 509, 525
Wilson, John, 45

Wilson, Nathaniel, **453**, 466
Wilson, Richard, 315, 317
Wilson, T. M. (architect), 407
Winks, Jack Greville, 403
Winter, Colonel, 444
Wishart, Pat, 514
Wishart, Rosemary, 514
Wollaston, Richard, 320
Women in Love (Lawrence), 365
Wood, Betty (head teacher), 345, 346
Wood, Edward (Alderman), 249
Wood, G., 499
Wood, Joseph, 429
Wood, Thomas (Bingham), 241
Wood Farm, 476
Wood Lane, 385
Wood Meadow, 222, 265
Woodcock, Mr and Mrs, 319
Woodford, John, 315
Woodfords and Wormleighton (knitwear manufacturers), 394, 416
Woodgate (Rothley), 394
Woodhouse, charity school, 163, 164
Woodhouse, Reverend John, 161
Woodhouse, William, 165
Woodhouse and Swithland Rifle Club, 436
Woodhouse Eaves, 20, 26, 48, 108, 123, 125, 137, 139
   Baptists, 170, 171, 176
   Methodists, 177, 182
Woods, Catherine, 428
Woods, J., 53
Woods, James Henry, 332
Woods, Joseph, 299, 332, 428
Woods, Richard (rector 1491), 115
Woolley, Harry, **339**
Woolley, Jill, 105
Woolley, John, 387, 388, 418, 497
Woolley, Norah, 497, 503, 522
Woolley, William, 64, 308
Woolston, Frances, 298
Woolston, Thomas, 298

workhouse, 65–6, 67–8
Workhouse Close, 293
World War I *see* First World War
World War II *see* Second World War
Worley, Bridget, 11
Wormleighton, Clive, 389
Worshipful Company of Bakers, 539
Worshipful Company of Framework Knitters, 539
Worth, Samuel, 429
Wright, Alison, 309
Wright, Beth, 309
Wright, Edmund, 298
Wright, George, 15
Wright, Jeff, 309
Wright, John, 284
Wright, Julia (journalist), 487
Wright, Mrs Linwood, 137, 182, 287, 320, 322–3, 324, 474, 491, 492, 495, 516
   see also Turner, Gladys Marie
Wright, Suzannah, 284
Wright, Thomas (rector 1427), 115, 583
Wright, Tim, 513
Wright's Directory, 429
Wyatt, Robert Harvey (land surveyor), 199, 235–6
Wyclif, John, 114
Wyggeston Schools, 407
Wykes, Percy, 462
Wylde, William (rector 1362), 114
Wymeswold, 149

Yarburgh-Bateson, Hon. George Nicholas de, 222
Yew Tree and the Flowers (church pageant), 492, **493**
Young Wives, 500, 502, 503, 514

Zouche, Alan, Baron of Ashby, 3
Zouche, Elena (wife of Alan Zouche), 3